Writers' & Artists' YEARBOOK 2011

Writers' & Artists' YEARBOOK 2011

ONE HUNDRED AND FOURTH EDITION

A directory for writers, artists, playwrights, designers, illustrators and photographers

A&C Black · London

36 Soho Square, London W1D 3QY

This book is produced using paper that is made from wood grown in managed, sustainable forests. It is natural, renewable and recyclable. The logging and manufacturing processes conform to the environmental regulations of the country of origin.

A CIP catalogue record for this book is available from the British Library.

ISBN 10: 1-4081-24939
ISBN 13: 978-1-4081-2493-2

Typeset by QPM from David Lewis XML Associates Ltd

Printed in the UK by CPI William Clowes Ltd, Beccles NR34 7TL

About this *Yearbook*

The Editor welcomes readers to the *Writers' & Artists' Yearbook.*

Welcome to the *Writers' & Artists' Yearbook*, which has been published every year since 1906. It was, and still is, intended for writers and artists – both published and unpublished – to use as a source of advice, encouragement and practical information, as well as providing an up-to-date directory of contacts for the book industry.

Whether this is your first encounter with the *Yearbook* or you've been a loyal reader for years, you'll find all the information you need about getting published, from writing a proposal to getting to grips with copyright. It is divided into easy-to-use sections, the majority of which contain a mixture of articles and listings. Many of the articles are by famous authors who have been fans of the *Yearbook* throughout their career – some even cite it as their first stepping stone to getting published. For this reason, authors are glad to contribute to the *Yearbook* and pass on the benefit of their wisdom and success. Only between these pages can you find out why Joanna Trollope writes fiction, how J.K. Rowling found an agent *and* pick up writing tips from the likes of Terry Pratchett, Neil Gaiman and Bernard Cornwell.

New in the 2011 edition, Chimamanda Ngozi Adichie recounts her experiences of writing short stories, Kathy Lette ponders her career as a comic author and literary agent Simon Trewin gives invaluable advice to unpublished authors. We also have three new articles on the state of the publishing industry today, written by Nicholas Clee, Alexandra Pringle and Tom Tivnan, as well as a helpful piece by Alison Straw on how to cope if your manuscript is rejected.

To accommodate our increasing editorial content, we have moved some of our listings to the *Yearbook's* website (www.writersandartists.co.uk). These include *Editorial, literary and production services*, *Government offices and public offices* and *Picture agencies and libraries*. Also on the website you can find the Writers' & Artists' blog, exclusive interviews with authors, illustrators and other industry insiders, and even more expert advice on how best to get your manuscript accepted for publication.

We hope you enjoy reading this edition of the *Yearbook*.

Jo Herbert
Editor

Contents

Foreword – John Boyne ix

Newspapers and magazines

Getting started 1
Writing features for newspapers and magazines – Merope Mills 3
Writing for newspapers – Richard Keeble 6
Writing for magazines – Richard Keeble 28

Listings

National newspapers UK and Ireland 11
Regional newspapers UK and Ireland 19
Magazines UK and Ireland 33
Newspapers and magazines overseas 104
Syndicates, news and press agencies 118

Books

Getting started 123
Dos and don'ts of approaching a publisher – Michael Legat 126
Writing a synopsis – Rebecca Swift 131
Understanding the publishing process – Bill Swainson 230
Spotting a bestseller – Alexandra Pringle 235
One hundred years of fiction bestsellers – Alex Hamilton 237
Notes from a successful fiction author – Joanna Trollope 241
Notes from a successful short story author – Chimamanda Ngozie Adichie 243
Notes from a successful comic author – Kathy Lette 245
Notes from a successful fantasy author – Terry Pratchett 249
Notes from a successful crime author – Mark Billingham 251
Notes from a successful romantic novelist – Jane Green 253
Notes from a successful historical novelist – Bernard Cornwell 256
Notes from a successful biographer – Claire Tomalin 259
Notes from a successful travel author – William Dalrymple 262
The growth of travel guidebooks – Alex Hamilton 266
Notes from a successful non-fiction author – Simon Winchester 270
Notes from a successful MBS author – William Bloom 272
Ghostwriting – Andrew Crofts 276
Books published from blogs – Scott Pack 281
Notes from a literary editor – Claire Armitstead 284
Notes from a successful crossover author – Neil Gaiman 287
Notes from a successful children's author – J.K. Rowling 290
Writing and the children's book market – Chris Kloet 291
Is there a book in you? – Alison Baverstock 295
The state of commissioning – Nicholas Clee 299
Publishing agreements – Michael Legat 303
Notes from a successful self-publisher – G.P. Taylor 308
Doing it on your own – Peter Finch 310
FAQs about ISBNs 314
Marketing, publicising and selling books – Katie Bond 316
Helping to market your book – Alison Baverstock 320
How to publicise your book – Isabel Losada 324
A year in view of the publishing industry – Tom Tivnan 328
Print on demand – David Taylor 332
Who owns whom in publishing© 336
Public Lending Right 338
Vanity publishing – Johnathon Clifford 343

Listings

Book publishers UK and Ireland 136
Book publishers overseas 196
Audio publishers 221
Book packagers 224
Book clubs 346

Poetry

Notes from a passionate poet – Benjamin Zephaniah 349
Getting poetry published – Michael Schmidt 351
Approaching a poetry publisher – Roddy Lumsden 357

Listings

Poetry organisations – Paul McGrane 361

Television, film and radio

Notes from a successful television screenwriter – Andrew Davies 369
Adaptations from books – Kate Sinclair 372

Writing for television – Anji Loman Field 378
Notes from a successful soap scriptwriter – Mary Cutler 384
Writing drama for radio – Lee Hall 387
Stories on radio – Di Speirs 390
BBC broadcasting rights and terms 407

Listings

Inside the BBC – Emma Hurrell 395
Independent national television 410
Independent regional television 412
Digital, satellite and cable television 414
Television and film producers 419
Independent national radio 427
Digital audio broadcasting 428
Independent radio producers 430

Theatre

Writing for the theatre – Christopher William Hill 433

Listings

Theatre producers 438

Literary agents

The role of the literary agent – the late Giles Gordon 449
'I think I need an agent' – Mark Le Fanu 453
How literary agencies work – Catherine Clarke 455
How to get an agent – Philippa Milnes-Smith 458
Letter to an unsolicited author – Simon Trewin 461
How to attract the attention of a literary agent – Alison Baverstock 465
Notes from a literary scout – Suzy Lucas 469

Listings

Literary agents UK and Ireland 473
Literary agents overseas 496

Art and illustration

Freelancing for beginners – Fig Taylor 509
Illustrating for children's books – Maggie Mundy 516
How to get ahead in cartooning – Martin Rowson 523
Winning the greeting card game – Jakki Brown 527
The freelance photographer – Ian Thraves 535

Listings

Art agents and commercial art studios 519
Card and stationery publishers that accept illustrations and photographs 531

Societies, prizes and festivals

The Society of Authors 541
The Writers' Guild of Great Britain 544

Listings

Societies, associations and clubs 547
Prizes and awards 588
Literature festivals 615

Writers and artists online

Marketing yourself online – Mathew F. Riley and Simon Appleby 625
E-publishing – Jane Dorner 629
Ebooks – Stephen Cole 635
Setting up a website – Jane Dorner 641
Writing a blog – Isabella Pereira 647

Listings

Websites for writers – Jane Dorner 652
Websites for artists – Alison Baverstock 656

Resources for writers

Dealing with rejection – Alison Straw 659
The writer's ultimate workspace – Rib Davis 662
Writers' retreats – Maggie Gee 666
Indexing 669
Correcting proofs 671
Taking a writing course – Alison Baverstock 685

Listings

Libraries 678
Creative writing courses 688

Copyright and libel

Copyright questions – Michael Legat 697
UK copyright law – Amanda Michaels 700
The Copyright Licensing Agency Ltd 713
Authors' Licensing and Collecting Society 715
Design and Artists Copyright Society 717
Libel – Antony Whitaker 719

Finance for writers and artists

FAQs for writers 729
Income tax – Peter Vaines 731
Social security contributions – Peter Arrowsmith 741
Social security benefits – Peter Arrowsmith 749

Subject indexes 755
Index 785

'Never give up, never become discouraged, and set right to it, with the *Yearbook* your shining armour, your sword!' **Alexander McCall Smith**

'*Writers' & Artists' Yearbook* is like a magic carpet that would carry the writer anywhere' **Maeve Binchy**

'I know of no foolproof way of getting a first novel published. But there are ways of shortening the odds, and careful use of the *Writers' & Artists' Yearbook* is one of them' **Michael Ridpath**

Foreword

John Boyne has published six novels: *The Thief of Time* (2000), *The Congress of Rough Riders* (2001), *Crippen* (2004), *Next of Kin* (2006), *Mutiny on the Bounty* (2008) and *The House of Special Purpose* (2009). His two novels for younger readers are: *The Boy in the Striped Pyjamas* (2006) and *Noah Barleywater Runs Away* (2010). *The Boy in the Striped Pyjamas* was made into an award-winning film in 2006 and the novel won two Irish book awards, was voted the Bisto Book of the Year, and was shortlisted or won a host of international awards. It spent more than 80 weeks at No 1 in Ireland, topped the *New York Times* bestseller list, and has sold more than five million copies worldwide.

In 1994, I left Dublin for Norwich, where I had been accepted as a student on the MA in Creative Writing at the University of East Anglia. When I was packing I tried to fit as many books into my suitcase as possible, the books that I felt I couldn't live without. Franny came with me, as did her brother Zooey. Garp and Homer Wells. David Copperfield. Gatsby. Ten or so novels that I liked to dip in and out of whenever I felt in need of inspiration, stories that helped me remember why I wanted to be a writer. There was only one non-fiction book in the bag: the *Writers' & Artists' Yearbook*.

All the advice in the world for aspiring writers can be reduced to two simple tips: read as much as you possibly can and write every day. *Every day*. And that includes Christmas Day and your birthday. Never wait for the muse to arrive, she's not that accommodating; instead, sit down at your desk every morning, compose a sentence, examine it, change it slightly, then compose another. Repeat until nightfall.

It can be very helpful to join a writing group where your work is sometimes praised and often criticised. As a writer, you should have little interest in the former and be ready to listen to every word of the latter. Other people aren't always right, of course, but sometimes ... well, they just are. Remember that setting out on a novel is an exhilarating time, halfway through it's unbelievably hard work and towards the end there's a real excitement about finishing. I prefer never to rewrite when working on a first draft; power your way to the end, print out a few hundred pages of messy, uncoordinated prose, then be merciless at cutting and rewriting until you discover the story that you set out to tell. Think of a sculptor, chipping away at a block of stone, knowing instinctively that an object of great beauty lies at its heart. A writer is a sculptor, a pen is a chisel.

Of course, once the book exists we all need help in bringing it to readers. That's where this *Yearbook* comes in. When I completed my first novel in 1998 I opened the *Writers' & Artists' Yearbook* to the listings of literary agents, read through the summaries of each one and the type of material they represented, selected one at random and wrote a letter.

– *Hello*, I said. *I'm a new writer and I've written a book. Any chance you'd take a look at it?*
– *All right then*, came the reply. *Send it over.*

And I did. And 18 months later, in August 2000, my first novel, *The Thief of Time*, was published. And in the ten years since, having worked with a number of editors in different countries, I have learned one thing for certain: good writing will find its outlet, it will find a publisher, it will find readers. You absolutely have to believe this or there is no point in continuing.

I'm often asked to give talks to new writers about how to make the path to publication a little easier. The truth is that it can be very dispiriting at times, and it requires a huge amount of self-belief and determination to overcome every setback along the way. It can be unkind, even cruel. But this is the price we pay to bring our work to readers and frankly, it's cheap at half the price.

Writing is an art, publishing is a business. They exist alongside each other, sometimes in mutual harmony, sometimes with more hostile intent, but there's no changing the lie of the land: geographically, their borders touch, their rivers flow into each other. In today's publishing world, the writer must be a sort of goodwill ambassador between the two, always recognising the importance of the art while understanding that the business must be run properly for both countries to survive.

That is where this *Yearbook* proves so valuable. Hundreds of agents, publishers, writing courses, magazines and other useful bodies are here, with addresses and phone numbers attached. And while it's easy to get discouraged when a book that you have poured your heart and soul into does not find success first time out, a real writer knows when it's time to move on and start the next one. So keep going until your agent phones you and begins the conversation with the words you long to hear:

Are you sitting down? I've got some good news for you…

John Boyne

Newspapers and magazines
Getting started

Of the titles included in the newspapers and magazines section of this *Yearbook*, almost all offer opportunities to the writer. Many publications do not appear in our lists because the market they offer for the freelance writer is either too small or too specialised, or both. To help writers get started, we offer some guidelines to consider before submitting material.

Study the market

• The importance of studying the market cannot be overemphasised. It is an editor's job to know what readers want, and to see that they get it. Thus, freelance contributions must be tailored to fit a specific market; subject, theme, treatment, length, etc. must meet the editor's requirements. This is discussed further in *Writing features for newspapers and magazines* on page 3, *Writing for newspapers* on page 6 and *Writing for magazines* on page 28.

• Magazine editors frequently complain about the unsuitability of many submissions, so before sending an article or feature, always carefully study the editorial requirements of the magazine – not only for the subjects dealt with but for the approach, treatment, style and length. These comments will be obvious to the practised writer but the beginner can be spared much disappointment by buying copies of magazines and studying their target market in depth.

• For additional information on markets, see the UK volume of *Willings Press Guide*, which is usually available at local reference libraries.

Check with the editor first

• Before submitting material to any newspaper or magazine it is advisable to first contact the relevant editor. The listings beginning on page 11 give the names of editors for each section of the national newspapers. A quick telephone call or email to a magazine will establish the name of the relevant commissioning editor.

• Most newspapers and many magazines expect copy to be sent by email.

• Editors who accept postal submissions expect them to be well presented: neatly typed, double spaced, with good margins, on A4 paper is the standard to aim at. Always enclose an sae (stamped addressed envelope) for the return of unsuitable material.

• It is not advisable to send illustrations 'on spec'; check with the editor first. See *Picture agencies and libraries* on this *Yearbook's* website (www.writersandartists.co.uk) for listings. For a list of publications that accept cartoons see page 781.

Explore the overseas market

• The lists of overseas newspapers and magazines in the *Yearbook* contain only a selection of those journals which offer a market for the freelance writer. For fuller listings, refer to *Willings Press Guide* Volume 2 (Europe) and Volume 3 (World). The overseas market for stories and articles is small and editors often prefer their fiction to have a local setting. Some editors require their contributors to be residents of that country.

• Some overseas magazine titles have little space for freelance contributions but many of them will consider outstanding work.

• Proposals or finished articles mailed overseas from the UK (including the Republic of Ireland) should always be accompanied by return postage in the form of International Reply Coupons (IRCs). IRCs can be exchanged in any foreign country for stamps representing the minimum postage payable on a letter sent from one country to another. (The current version of the IRC has an expiry date of 31 December 2011; after this date, IRCs with this expiry date can no longer be exchanged for postage. See www.royalmail.com for details.)
• It is worth considering using an agent to syndicate material written for the overseas market. Most agents operate on an international basis and are more aware of current market requirements. Again, return postage should always be included. Listings for *Syndicates, news and press agencies* start on page 118.

Understand how newspapers and syndicates work

• The larger newspapers and magazines buy many of their stories, and the smaller papers buy general articles, through well-known syndicates. Another avenue for writers is to send printed copies of their stories published at home to an agent for syndication overseas.
• For the supply of news, most of the larger UK and overseas newspapers depend on their own staffs and press agencies. The most important overseas newspapers have permanent representatives in the UK who keep them supplied, not only with news of special interest to the country concerned, but also with regular summaries of British news and with articles on events of particular importance. While many overseas newspapers and magazines have a London office, it is usual for manuscripts from freelance contributors to be submitted to the headquarters' editorial office overseas. Listings of *National newspapers UK and Ireland* start on page 11.

Payment

• It has always been our aim to obtain and publish the rates of payment offered for contributions by newspapers and magazines. Many publications, however, are reluctant to state a standard rate, since the value of a contribution may be dependent not upon length but upon the standing of the writer or of the information given. Many other periodicals prefer to state 'by negotiation' or 'by arrangement', rather than giving precise payment information.
• A number of magazines will accept and pay for letters to the editor, brief fillers and gossip paragraphs, as well as puzzles and quizzes. *Magazines by subject area* starting on page 755 provides a rough guide to these markets.

See also...

- *Regional newspapers UK and Ireland*, page 19
- *Newspapers are listed together with magazines for Australia* (page 104), *Canada* (page 109), *New Zealand* (page 111), *South Africa* (page 113) and *USA* (page 116)

Writing features for newspapers and magazines

Merope Mills outlines a route to success for prospective feature writers to follow.

The news about the press this last year has been pretty disheartening. At newspapers and magazines across the country, budgets have been cut, staff numbers slashed and freelancers' contracts have been terminated. The mainstream press and news-stand magazines are all struggling to cope in the face of an advertising downturn and increased competition from the web (in some cases, from online versions of their own publications). Established magazine titles such as *Arena* have closed. It's a grim picture, but one that doesn't spell the end for writers. Ten national newspapers and their Sunday sister titles are still in print, as are 8,000-plus mainstream magazines, not to mention regional titles, and smaller, alternative publications. That's a lot of pages to fill – and somebody has to write them. Making the right approach, especially if you are unknown to an editor, is more essential than ever if you are to develop a relationship and have a long and rewarding career.

Starting out

If you're new to writing, the best thing you can do is play to your strengths. Do your friends tell you your emails make them fall off their chairs laughing? Then maybe a humorous column beckons. Do you have a specialist knowledge? A green-fingered writer might be able to spot a gap in the market in a gardening title, for example. When starting out in journalism, it is often best to stick to factual journalism that you can write about entertainingly. Most comment and analysis columnists these days are personalities who already carry authority – novelists, television personalities or journalists who have built up a reputation across many years. If you're just at the start of your career, then your opinion (though extremely valid) will count for very little unless it's backed up by something solid. The majority of newspaper and magazine freelancers are feature writers as news reporters tend to be on staff.

The internet

The web is both a threat and an opportunity for newspapers and magazines right now. Every title has an online presence and it's worth acquainting yourself with that. A newspaper or magazine has a limited number of pages and therefore a limited number of people that can write for it. Its online equivalent, on the other hand, can accommodate a much larger number of voices. Again, if you have a niche subject and a valid angle on a story then if the newspaper or magazine editor can't accommodate you in print, perhaps they might be able to online.

If you already have your own blog, then so much the better (see *Writing a blog* on page 647). In newspapers, it used to be traditional for writers to work their way up through local papers. Today, the talent seems increasingly to come from the web. Its advantages are plain for everyone: a writer with a blog has a stash of readily available, easily accessible cuttings that clearly establish their identity. Better still for an editor, if it's a good blog it may even have built up its own raft of followers who would keenly follow the blogger if they were to shift to print.

As editor of *Weekend* magazine at the *Guardian*, one of my most recent signings was of a make-up columnist named Lauren Luke. She made her name doing videos of herself putting on make-up in her bedroom at home. It sounds simple, but her authenticity and winning personality (not to mention her dog snoring on the bed in the background!) has attracted a raft of followers. By the time I discovered her, over 20 million people had watched her videos on YouTube. She currently writes a weekly column about make-up for us, and does videos for guardian.co.uk. Other writers who started out on the web but now write in print include: Ariana Huffington (of the *Huffington Post*), the Baghdad blogger Salam Pax, and Belle du Jour (whose blog became a magazine column, then a television series starring Billie Piper).

Ideas

Good ideas are the essence of a good journalist. But you must avoid the obvious. Don't write to a magazine or newspaper editor suggesting an interview with Madonna – it's likely they've already had that idea and probably aren't casting around for writers. If you're just starting out, think laterally. Look in the less obvious sections or supplements for columns that an editor might struggle to fill. In a travel magazine or newspaper travel section, for example, you probably won't be able to bag a 2,000-word commission on a Maldives beach holiday, but there may be a small regular section on B&Bs or budget holidays around the UK that grander, established writers probably won't be pitching for. Don't be shy of writing about yourself and your own experiences. Again the rise of the internet means that newspapers and magazines increasingly see the value of readers' stories and contributions. Look for those 'first person' slots and think if you've got a good personal story that would suit. From tiny acorns like that, whole careers can grow. Once you've established contact and written something, however small, bigger things may well flourish.

Contacting the publication

Whether you are published or unpublished, the most important thing is to write a convincing email or letter. Keep your idea succinct – no more than two paragraphs. (Think of it like the newspaper or magazine's standfirst. On publication, they have to sell the idea to the readers in a few brief sentences – so you should be able to do the same.) If you've written before, include a few links to your most relevant work. Lots of people tell me they write for the *Guardian*, but all too often I find myself searching the archive for their byline, never to find it. It's so much easier to point to your work within your pitch.

It sounds obvious, but make sure your idea is right for the publication you're contacting. Don't blanket-email every title you can think of with the same idea, hoping that somewhere it will stick. It's good for an editor to know that you're familiar with their product and that you're suggesting your idea for their section and readership. I get way too many ideas that are a completely wrong fit for the *Guardian*. It's a waste of everybody's time. Above all, the most important thing you can do is *read* the publication you're pitching to, before getting in contact.

Get the right person

It's a writer's instinct to send things to the editor of the publication, but there's often someone else who will get to your idea quicker and give you an answer. Perhaps it's the deputy editor, the commissioning editor or the features editor. If it's a more specific idea – to do with fashion, health or food, for example – find out who is in charge of that area and contact them. Make a call first to see who the best person to receive your pitch is, if you're not sure. Always address them by name. If you can't be bothered to write a personal email, it doesn't suggest you're likely to be a thorough journalist.

Style

Again, read the publication, and writers you particularly admire. They might be owned by the same company – Murdoch's News International – but there's a world of difference between writing for the *Sun* and *The Times*. They might both deal in celebrity and fashion, but *Grazia* and *Vogue* have completely different styles and sections. You must adapt to the publication, and think about whether the way you've written a piece is suitable.

There is no formula to writing features you can follow for every publication, but it is common to start a piece with some 'colour'. This means beginning a piece by focusing on one anecdote or one particular person's story or quote before broadening it out to explain why their tale matters and what it represents. By the third or fourth paragraph there should really be an explanation of what trend/event/issue your piece is about. The body of any feature should have enough case studies (usually at least three people) to back up the facts and opinions that make the thrust of the piece.

Money

You've had an idea accepted – now what? The first thing to do is agree a fee. Most commonly you will be offered the publication's lineage fee (a standard rate, paid by the word). This can vary widely, so make sure you're happy with this before you start. The National Union of Journalists (www.nuj.org.uk) offers a guide to freelance rates that is worth checking. Also make it clear if you will be submitting expenses receipts and try and give a rough estimate of what these might be, so your editor can budget for them. Establish who owns copyright beforehand, in case you want to sell second rights to another publication. Having said that, most titles have a syndication service and are more likely to be able to place it elsewhere for you, taking a cut if they do. This is worth investigation.

Deadlines and editing

Don't miss a deadline – even if you are sure that the piece won't be printed imminently. You probably aren't familiar with the title's production schedule and deadlines are usually there for a reason, so don't ignore them. It's also better to be open to your editor's thoughts and rewriting suggestions. Their job is to make the piece better, not worse, so it's better not to be a prima donna about your copy. If you're not sure of the reason for the changes, just ask!

Breaking into the industry isn't easy, but writing for newspapers and magazines can have many rewards – from meeting interesting people, to seeing your name in print for the first time, to receiving a cheque for your first published piece of work. All you need is a nice style, some good ideas and a little bit of luck!

Merope Mills writes for the *Guardian*.

See also...

- *Writing for newspapers*, page 6
- *Writing for magazines*, page 28

Writing for newspapers

As the global economic downturn threatens the very existence of newspapers, Richard Keeble explores the new challenges for freelance journalists.

Over the last year or so, the global economic downturn has appeared to threaten the very existence of newspapers in the UK. Sales of local and national newspapers are, in general, slumping as advertising revenue falls away and as media consumers migrate increasingly to the internet.

In February 2010, most of the ten mass selling national daily newspapers recorded year-on-year falls in circulation: the *Independent*, for instance, was down 10% to 183,000. Similarly, the circulations of all the Sundays dropped – with the 'quality' *Independent on Sunday* down 13% to 155,600 and the tabloid *Sunday Mirror* down 5% to 1,226,000. Even the country's biggest selling daily, the Rupert Murdoch-owned tabloid *Sun*, managed a rise of just 0.63% to 2,972,000. Circulations of Scotland's nationally audited newspapers also continued to slump. Massive job cuts were under way throughout the industry. And, as investigative reporter Nick Davies argues in his controversial, bestselling book on the state of Britain's journalism, *Flat Earth News*, over the last 20 years, the average time allowed for national newspaper journalists to find and check their stories has been cut to a third of its former level. Inevitably standards have dropped. Some doomsters are even predicting the death of the newspaper industry.

In this environment the position of the freelance becomes especially hazardous. Top investigative journalist Phillip Knightley, author of the seminal history of war correspondents, *The First Casualty*, even commented: 'My work as a freelance has dried up almost totally. What little remains is so poorly paid it is hardly worthwhile turning on the computer. My main outlets are now overseas: India, the Gulf, Australia. And the occasional book review.' Jon Grubb, editor of the *Lincolnshire Echo*, commented: 'Regional daily newspapers the size of the *Echo* have never had a large freelance budget. The budget we did have tended to be spent on regular columnists in specialist subjects like fishing or jazz. Only very occasionally did we offer freelance payments for specific jobs. A lot of that freelance work is continuing and we still pay for it but our budgets have been squeezed and we are looking to make savings wherever possible.'

Newspapers can then still offer opportunities to freelances – but only if you are prepared to work extremely hard. As Tessa Mayes, freelance investigative reporter and regular contributor to the *Spectator* and *Spiked Online*, stressed: 'Broadsheet newspapers began to cut general budgets for freelances about five years ago. However, a scoop is a scoop, and with the right story (although increasingly it has to be a major one), newspapers still find budgets to avoid the competition getting it. Freelance investigative journalists have always had to get funding for lengthy investigations from all sorts of places, not just one media source. These days, however, we'll sell the story to a British newspaper, put it online, put it in a book, try and sell it worldwide through syndication agencies, sell the TV/DVD/film rights if possible, and put it in another book. Job done!'

The freelance challenge

Launching into a freelance career never was easy: it's certainly now more difficult than ever. Many freelances are former full-time staffers who have developed a specialism, sent out linage (freelance copy paid by the line) to nationals and then, through either choice or redundancy, taken the plunge and gone solo or started a small agency. With newspapers increasingly laying off experienced full-time staffers, competition amongst freelances has intensified. And while freelances enjoy certain 'freedoms' not permitted to staff writers, they still cannot avoid the constraints and ethical dilemmas that all journalists face. For instance, you may be very critical of the political and ethical stances of the mainstream press. Thus you may decide to join the ranks of the 'citizen journalists' and launch your own blog or you may choose to contribute (largely unpaid) to an ethnic-minority, left-wing, religious, peace-movement or environmental newspaper, news magazine or website and gain your money from other employment. One of the greatest journalists of the last century, George Orwell, committed himself to small-scale, left-wing, literary journals and largely ignored the seductive appeal of Fleet Street. It was his deliberate political choice. Or you may be happy to sell your copy to a Rupert Murdoch-owned newspaper (such as *The Times* or *Sunday Times*). But always be fully aware there are political and ethical implications behind your journalistic decisions.

Why contacts are crucial

Very few freelances are generalists. They instead develop a specialism (or a discreet range of linked specialisms) and become valuable to editors because of their specialist knowledge, experience and contacts. Thus your major task in launching into a freelance career is to build up a contacts book containing sources' phone numbers, addresses, fax and pager numbers, email and website details. You may have to go to meetings, conferences and press launches, and/or ring up spokespersons of political parties, companies and campaigning bodies. All this takes a lot of time. But from your sources will come ideas for stories, details of events to attend, quotes, and specialist (and hopefully exclusive) information. Many freelances place contact details on a computer database as a back-up while those investigating sensitive issues (such as national security, spying, the arms and drugs trade, share dealings) tend to keep details of important exclusive sources in their heads. Police have been known to raid the homes and computers of journalists involved in sensitive areas and thus every step has to be taken to preserve the anonymity of such contacts.

The skills of interviewing are crucial to all freelances. You normally have to prepare in advance of the meeting and be confident enough in the subject to maintain a flowing interview – while recording accurately at the same time. It's far from easy. You may be tempted to use a tape recorder. But what if it breaks down at the crucial moment? For all interviews you need to make a written note. You may not have the time to learn a shorthand technique such as Teeline (in which 100 words a minute is the industry standard) but you do need to develop your own reliable rapid writing technique.

Get to know the market for your specialist area of interest. Study the different writing styles, the lengths of the sentences and articles in the differing publications. Try to establish, by examining byline patterns, the amount of freelance work accepted and in which particular areas. Analyse the advertising in the publications to get a feel for the intended target readership. Read recent issues (in either their print or online versions) carefully to get an idea of the stories covered and, more importantly, not covered. See who are the prominent sources used in stories and those who have been missed or marginalised. Get used to creating files of cuttings and printouts of web pages. Well-maintained filing cabinets can be invaluable research tools. And when you read documents, journal articles and books, file the notes from these too. But don't become over-reliant on cuttings and websites. Journalists often report inaccurately so checking is usually necessary. Significantly, the Press Complaints Commission (the watchdog promoting an ethical Code of Practice for print journalists) has advised: 'Cuttings are an essential part of newspaper research but too many journalists now seem to act in the belief that to copy from ten old stories is better than to write a new one with confirmation by proper fresh enquiry.'

The need for imaginative flair

As a freelance you will have to develop a special journalistic imagination. Ideas will be your lifeblood. A new report highlights a national survey showing students are increasingly going without sleep and as a result their academic work and health are suffering. Do a local follow-up: go to the colleges and universities in your area and interview students, counsellors, lecturers, etc. about the issues involved. Better still, take the opposite line and do a feature for the women's section of a Sunday newspaper highlighting career women who need only a few hours sleep a day – and yet still thrive. Or take a major international story such as the dispute between the two nuclear-armed neighbours India and Pakistan. Again think local. Many British cities have Indian and Pakistani communities but their views have been largely ignored. So why not interview people from these countries about the issues? Are they afraid? What do they see as the political factors behind the crisis and what are their solutions? Are there any human interest angles to help humanise the reports? In all these cases you have to move quickly while the issues are still newsworthy.

A lot of starting-up freelances imagine a life sitting at home bashing out on the computer words of wisdom on a range of topics to an admiring public. But it is rare for a freelance career to start in this way. Columnists tend to be experienced journalists, novelists, comedians or other media celebrities and their views are seen by editors to carry authority. As Andrew Marr, former editor of the *Independent* and the BBC's political editor, comments in *My Trade: A Short History of British Journalism* (Macmillan 2004), 'A very few top journalists are earning salaries that would be regarded as good in the City. One tabloid columnist is said by colleagues to be on £500,000. There is a broadsheet writer on £300,000.' But there are exceptions to this rule. A local newspaper may want to carry an opinionated column from a reader presenting a particular viewpoint – such as that of a youngster, a football fan or an asylum seeker. In this way the paper is striving to make its mark on the local community, with a column aimed at getting people talking – and possibly provoking letters (for or against).

To blog – or not to blog?

Is it worth a freelance blogging? Frankly, yes. A blog and a website help you establish your special identity in the ever-crowded media landscape. Strong, well-informed opinion in a niche subject area (such as media, intelligence, ethical tourism, farming, trade unions) is particularly needed in the new world of 'viewspapers'. And if you are seen to deliver this on a regular basis (your blogs sparking informed comments and controversy) you may well be noticed. Newspapers may come seeking help on a story: you may first provide quotes; next you may be commissioned to write a feature. Successful blogging freelances have even been asked to write books on their specialist area. But be realistic: all this requires a lot of hard work – and luck helps here, too.

The rewards of reviewing

Arts reviewing for local papers has its obvious attractions. Most journalists come from humanities backgrounds (resulting in the unfortunate marginalisation of science news in the press) and so there tends to be fierce competition for these posts. Most will be filled by staffers or experienced freelances. But if you have the necessary specialist knowledge, have built up contacts in the area and can write in a lively, original way, you may well find an opening. Reviews serve many functions. They provide basic information: for example, that a play has just opened and can be seen at the theatre indicated. For people who intend to see, read or hear a work (or in the case of broadcasting have already seen or heard it), the review gives an opinion carrying some authority to compare with their own. Yet usually the vast majority of readers will never experience directly the work under review. A concert may have been attended by no more than a hundred people. The review must then exist as a piece of writing in its own right. It must entice the reader through the colour and quality of its prose.

All newspapers have their own house style. This is outlined in a document called the stylebook (occasionally handbook or sheet), though it is increasingly carried onscreen and on the newspaper's website. For instance, you can check out the *Guardian's* stylebook on its website. Stylebooks tend to focus on such elements as spellings (gaol or jail?, Gaddafi or Khadaffi?), punctuation, abbreviations, the use of capitals, titles, Americanisms to avoid, the handling of quotations. Ethical issues, such as the handling of anonymous quotes or how to refer to people with disabilities, can also be covered. Take a close look at your target publications and study their styles. Freelances are not expected to present copy perfectly according to style: sub-editors are on hand to prepare copy for publication. But if your copy shows some awareness of the house style, then the editors will be impressed.

Some basic requirements

As a freelance you will need internet access on your computer. Most copy is now supplied via email and companies are increasingly supplying press releases through email. You will also need an accountant to advise on tax liabilities, and a pension plan. If you become particularly successful you will have to pay VAT. Most freelances keep in regular touch with their local tax inspector. Remember to log for tax purposes all relevant expenses, such as stationery, office equipment, book and travel expenses. If you are starting out as a freelance it might be worth negotiating an overdraft facility of at least £3,000–£4,000 with your bank manager after presenting them with a business plan drawn up by an accountant. Membership of the freelance branch of the National Union of Journalists (NUJ) is worth considering. The NUJ, along with local education centres, runs courses for starting-up freelances which can help develop skills and confidence (see www.nujtraining.org.uk).

Journalism remains a job carrying enormous personal rewards. It is difficult, challenging (politically, ethically, physically) and, even during the current economic crisis, it can still be fun. It requires a formidable range of knowledge and skills. And journalists need to be curious, persistent, imaginative and daring. In the words of Nicholas Tomalin, the *Sunday Times* foreign correspondent killed on the Golan Hights in 1973, journalists should cultivate 'rat-like cunning, a plausible manner and a little literary ability'. There is a glamorous side to the job, which Hollywood has helped to promote. No wonder the queues for entering the industry remain in credit-crunch Britain so long.

Richard Keeble is Professor of Journalism at Lincoln University. He has written or edited 15 books, including *The Newspapers Handbook* (Routledge, 4th edn 2005) and *Ethics for Journalists* (Routledge, 2nd edn 2009). He is also joint editor of *Ethical Space: The International Journal of Communication Ethics* (www.communication-ethics.net).

See also...

- *Writing features for newspapers and magazines*, page 3
- *Writing for magazines*, page 28

Further reading

Adams, Sally, *Interviewing for Journalists*, Routledge, 2nd edn, 2009

Davies, Nick, *Flat Earth News*, Chatto and Windus, 2008; pbk 2009

Evans, Harold, *Essential English for Journalists, Editors and Writers*, Pimlico, 2000

Franklin, Bob, *Packaging Politics: Political Communications in Britain's Media Democracy*, Arnold, 2nd edn, 2004

Frost, Chris, *Reporting for Journalists*, Routledge, 2nd edn, 2010

Gibson, Janine (ed.), *Media 08: The Essential Guide to the Changing Media Landscape*, Guardian Newspapers, 2007

Greenslade, Roy, *Press Gang*, Macmillan, 2003; pbk 2004

Harcup, Tony, *Journalism: Principles and Practice*, Sage, 2nd edn, 2009

Harcup, Tony, *The Ethical Journalist*, Sage, 2007

Hicks, Wynford, *English for Journalists*, Routledge, 3rd edn, 2006

Hicks, Wynford, with Harriett Gilbert and Sally Adams, *Writing for Journalists*, Routledge, 1999

Jones, Linda, *The Greatest Freelance Writing Tips in the World*, The Greatest in the World Ltd, 2007

Keeble, Richard (ed.), *Print Journalism: A Critical Introduction*, Routledge, 2005; pbk 2006

McKane, Anna, *Newswriting*, Sage, 2006

Pilger, John, *Hidden Agendas*, Vintage, 1998

Pilger, John, *Tell Me No Lies: Investigative Journalism and its Triumphs*, Cape, 2004; pbk 2005

Randall, David, *The Universal Journalist*, Pluto, 3rd edn, 2007

Sarikakis, Karen, *British Media in a Global Era*, Arnold, 2004

Websites

www.cpbf.org.uk – Campaign for Press and Broadcasting Freedom

http://ethicaljournalisminitiative.org – initiative of the International Federation of Journalists

www.freelanceuk.co.uk – a useful resource for freelances

www.holdthefrontpage.co.uk – covers local newspapers in the UK; gives training news and lists job vacancies

www.indymedia.org.uk – alternative news site promoting progressive politics

www.journalism.co.uk – excellent site with a special section devoted to freelancing

www.londonfreelance.org/fl/index.html – London Freelance Branch of the National Union of Journalists

www.medialens.org – radical media monitoring site: a necessary critique of the mainstream

www.nuj.org.uk – National Union of Journalists

www.pressgazette.co.uk – *Press Gazette*, trade magazine for UK journalists

www.thefword.org.uk – feminist site campaigning against sexist media

www.the-latest.co.uk – lively citizen journalism site

www.worldwidefreelance.com – site for freelances with an international focus

National newspapers UK and Ireland

Daily Express

Northern & Shell Building, 10 Lower Thames Street, London EC3R 6EN
tel 0208-612 7000
email news-desk@express.co.uk
website www.express.co.uk
Editor Peter Hill
Daily Mon–Fri 40p, Sat 70p
Supplements **Daily Express Saturday**

Exclusive news; striking photos. Leader page articles (600 words); facts preferred to opinions. Payment: according to value.

City Editor Peter Cunliffe
Deputy Editor Hugh Whittlow
Diary Editor Lizzie Catt
Environment Editor John Ingham
Features Editor Fergus Kelly
Literary Editor Caroline Jowitt
News Editor Geoff Maynard
Political Editor Macer Hall
Sports Editor Bill Bradshaw
Women's Editor Tina Moran

Daily Express Saturday Magazine

Editor Graham Bailey
Free with paper
Magazine.

Daily Mail

Northcliffe House, 2 Derry Street, London W8 5TT
tel 020-7938 6000 *fax* 020-7937 3251
email managingeditor@dailymail.co.uk
website www.dailymail.co.uk
Editor Paul Dacre
Daily Mon–Fri 50p, Sat 80p
Supplements **Weekend**

Founded 1896.

City Editor Alex Brummer
Diary Editor Richard Kay
Education Correspondent Laura Clark
Features Editor Leaf Kalfayan
Foreign Editor David Harding
Health Editor Justine Hancock
Business & Property Correspondent Becky Barrow
Literary Editor Sandra Parsons
Money Editor Tony Hazell
News Editor Keith Poole
Picture Editor Paul Silva
Political Editor James Chapman
Showbiz Editor Sara Nathan
Head of Sport Lee Clayton
Travel Editor Mark Palmer
Weekend Editor Lisa Collins

Daily Mirror

1 Canada Square, Canary Wharf, London E14 5AP
tel 020-7293 3000
email mirrornews@mirror.co.uk
website www.mirror.co.uk
Editor Richard Wallace
Daily Mon–Fri 45p, Sat 55p
Supplements **The Ticket, We Love Telly!, Your Life**

Top payment for exclusive news and news pictures. Freelance articles used, and ideas bought: send synopsis only. 'Unusual' pictures and those giving a new angle on the news are welcomed; also cartoons. Founded 1903.

Business Editor Clinton Manning
Features Editor Carole Watson
Health Editor Emily Cook
Letters Editor Fiona Parker
News Editor Barry Rabbetts
Picture Editor Ian Down
Political Editor Bob Roberts
Sports Editor Dean Morse

Daily Record

1 Central Quay, Glasgow G3 8DA
tel 0141-309 3000 *fax* 0141-309 3340
email reporters@dailyrecord.co.uk
London office 1 Canada Square, Canary Wharf, London E14 5AP
tel 020-7293 3000
website www.record-mail.co.uk
Editor Bruce Waddell
Daily Mon–Fri 35p, Sat 65p
Supplements **Saturday, Living, TV Record, Road Record, Recruitment Record**

Topical articles, from 300–700 words; exclusive stories of Scottish interest and exclusive colour photos.

Executive Editor Bob Caldwell
Features Editor Melanie Harvey
News Editor Andy Lines
Sports Editor Austin Barrett

Saturday

Editor Jayne Savva
Free with paper
Lifestyle magazine and entertainment guide. Reviews, travel features, shopping, personalities. Payment: by arrangement. Illustrations: colour.

Daily Sport

19 Great Ancoats Street, Manchester M60 4BT
tel 0161-236 4466 *fax* 0161-236 4535
website www.dailysport.co.uk
Editor Pam McVitie
Daily Mon–Fri 50p

Factual stories and series. Length: up to 1,000 words. Illustrations: b&w and colour photos, cartoons. Payment: £30–£5,000. Founded 1988.

Features & News Editor Neil Goodwin
Sports Editor Marc Smith
Deputy Editor Gary Doran
Sunday Sport Editor Nick Appleyard

Daily Star

Express Newspapers, Northern & Shell Building,
10 Lower Thames Street, London EC3R 6EN
tel 020-8612 7000 *fax* 020-8612 7401
email news@dailystar.co.uk
website www.dailystar.co.uk
Editor Dawn Neesom
Daily Mon–Fri 20p, Sat 30p
Supplements **Hot TV**

Hard news exclusives, commanding substantial payment. Major interviews with big-star personalities; short features; series based on people rather than things; picture features. Payment: by negotiation. Illustrations: line, half-tone. Founded 1978.

Music Editor Kim Dawson
Associate Editor Ian Trueman
Sports Editor Howard Wheatcroft
Deputy Editor (news) John McJannet

Daily Star Sunday

Express Newspapers,
The Northern and Shell Building,
10 Lower Thames Street, London EC3R 6EN
tel (0871) 520 7424 *fax* (0871) 434 7967
website www.dailystarsunday.co.uk
Editor Gareth Morgan
Sun 85p
Supplements **Take 5**

Opportunities for freelances.

The Daily Telegraph

111 Buckingham Palace Road, London SW1W 0DT
tel 020-7931 2000 *fax* 020-7931 2938
email dtnews@telegraph.co.uk
website www.telegraph.co.uk
Editor Tony Gallagher
Daily Mon–Fri £1, Sat £1.50
Supplements **Arts & Books, Business2 & Jobs, Gardening, Motoring, Property, Sport, Telegraph Magazine, Television & Radio, Travel, Weekend, Your Money**

Articles on a wide range of subjects of topical interest considered. Preliminary letter and synopsis required. Length: 700–1,000 words. Payment: by arrangement. Founded 1855.

Arts Editor Sarah Crompton
City Editor Richard Fletcher
Education Editor Graeme Paton
Environment Editor Charles Clover
Fashion Editor Hilary Alexander
Features Editor Genevieve Fox
Foreign Editor Will Kinnaird
Health Features Editor Genevieve Fox
News Editor Matthew Bayley
Picture Editor Lucy Verey
Political Editor Andrew Porter

Electronic Telegraph

email et@telegraph.co.uk
website www.telegraph.co.uk/
Editor Marcus Warren
Daily Free to internet subscribers
Based on *The Daily Telegraph*. Founded 1994.

Juiced

website www.juiced.com
Weekly Free to internet subscribers
Student magazine.

Planet

website www.the-planet.co.uk
Free to internet subscribers
Travel writing from *The Daily Telegraph* and *The Sunday Telegraph*.

Telegraph Magazine

Editor Michelle Lavery
Free with Sat paper
Short profiles (about 1,600 words); articles of topical interest. Preliminary study of the magazine essential. Illustrations: all types. Payment: by arrangement. Founded 1964.

Financial Times

1 Southwark Bridge, London SE1 9HL
tel 020-7873 3000 *fax* 020-7873 3076
email news.desk@ft.com
website www.ft.com
Editor Lionel Barber
Daily Mon–Fri £2, Sat £2.30
Supplements **Business Books, Companies & Markets, FT Digital Business, FTfm, FT Global Traveller, FT Reports, House and Home, How To Spend It, FT Weekend, Money**

Articles of financial, commercial, industrial and economic interest. Length: 800–1,000 words. Payment: by arrangement. Founded 1888.

Arts Editor Jan Dalley
Banking Editor Patrick Jenkins
Deputy Editor Martin Dickson
Travel Editor Rahul Jacob
International Affairs Editor David Gardner
Investment Correspondent Kate Burgess
Acting Lex Editor John Paul Rathbone
Political Editor George Parker
Special Reports Editor Michael Skapinker
US Managing Editor Chrystia Freeland
FT Weekend Editor Andrew Davis
World News Editor Alec Russell

The Guardian

King's Place, 90 York Way, London N1 9GU
tel 020-3353 2000
email national@guardian.co.uk
1 Scott Place, Manchester M3 3GG
tel 0161-908 3898 *fax* 0161-832 7200

website www.guardian.co.uk, commentisfree.com
Editor Alan Rusbridger
Daily Mon–Fri £1, Sat £1.90
Supplements **Education, Film & Music, G2, The Guide, Review, Media, Society, Weekend, Family, Work, Money**

Few articles are taken from outside contributors except on its feature and specialist pages. Illustrations: news and features photos. Payment: from £295.72 per 1,000 words; £125–£350 (depending on size) for illustrations. Founded 1821.

Arts Editor Melissa Denes
Business Editor Dan Roberts
commentisfree.com Editor Georgina Henry
Deputy Editor Ian Katz / Katherine Viner
Economics Editor Larry Elliott
Education Editor Claire Phipps
Fashion Editor Jess Cartner-Morley
Features Editor Emily Wilson / Clare Margetson
Film & Music Editor Michael Hann
Head of International News Harriet Sherwood
The Guide Editor Malik Meer
Head of National News Nick Hopkins
Literary Editor Claire Armitstead
Media Editor Jane Martinson
Head of Media and Technology Steve Busfield
Head of Politics Will Woodward
Head of Society, Health, Education Patrick Butler
Review Editor Lisa Allardice
Society Editor Alison Benjamin
Head of Sport Paul Johnson
Technology Editor Charles Arthur
Travel Editor Isabel Choat

Guardian Unlimited

website www.guardian.co.uk
Director of Digital Content Emily Bell

Weekend

Editor Merope Mills, *Commissioning Editor* Becky Barnicoat
Free with Sat paper

Features on world affairs, major profiles, food and drink, home life, the arts, travel, leisure, etc. Also good reportage on social and political subjects. Illustrations: b&w photos and line, cartoons. Payment: apply for rates.

The Herald

Herald & Times Group, 200 Renfield Street, Glasgow G2 3QB
tel 0141-302 7000 *fax* 0141-302 7007
email news@theherald.co.uk
London office 30 Cannon Street, London EC4M 6YJ
tel 020-7618 3421
website www.theherald.co.uk
Editor Jonathan Russell
Daily Mon–Fri 70p, Sat £1

Articles up to 1,000 words. Founded 1783.

Arts Editor Keith Bruce
Business Editor Ian McConnell
Deputy Editor Janette Harkess
Diary Editor Ken Smith
Features Editor Mark Smith
News Editor Callum MacDonald
Sports Editor Donald Cowey

The Independent

Northcliffe House, 2 Derry Street, London W8 5TT
tel 020-7005 2000 *fax* 020-7005 2999
email newseditor@independent.co.uk
website www.independent.co.uk
Editor-in-Chief Simon Kelner
Daily Mon–Fri £1, Sat £1.40
Supplements **Business Review, Education, The Information, Arts & Books Review, Property Supplement, Save & Spend, Traveller, Extra, Sport**

Occasional freelance contributions; preliminary letter advisable. Payment: by arrangement. Founded 1986.

Arts Editor David Lister
Business & City Editor Amy Frizell
Education Editor Richard Garner
Environment Editor Mike McCarthy
Features Editor Nicole Mowbray
Foreign Editor Katherine Butler
Health Editor Jeremy Laurance
Literary Editor Boyd Tonkin
Media Editor Ian Burrell
News Editor Oliver Wright
Picture Editor Lynn Cullen
Political Editor Andrew Grice
Sports Editor Christian Broughton

The Independent Magazine

email magazine@independent.co.uk
Editor Laurence Earle
Free with Sat paper

Profiles and illustrated articles of topical interest; all material commissioned. Preliminary study of the magazine essential. Length: 500–3,000 words. Illustrations: cartoons; commissioned colour and b&w photos. Payment: by arrangement. Founded 1988.

Independent on Sunday

Northcliffe House, 2 Derry Street, London W8 5TT
tel 020-7005 2000 *fax* 020-7005 2047
email sundaynews@independent.co.uk
website www.independent.co.uk
Executive Editor Lisa Markwell, *Editor-at-Large* Janet Street-Porter
Sun £1.80
Supplements **Business, The New Review**

News, features and articles. Illustrated, including cartoons. Payment: by negotiation. Founded 1990.

Arts Editor Mike Higgins
Assistant Editor David Randall
Business Editor Maggie Pagano
Deputy Editor James Hanning
Foreign Editor Ray Whitaker
Executive Editor (News) Peter Victor

Picture Editor Sophie Batterbury
Political Editor Jane Merrick
Sports Editor Marc Padgett
Executive Editor Lisa Markwell

The New Review
tel 020-7005 2000 *fax* 020-7005 2027
Editor Bill Tuckey
Free with paper
Original features of general interest with potential for photographic illustration. Material mostly commissioned. Length: 1,000–5,000 words. Illustrations: transparencies. Payment: £150 per 1,000 words.

Irish Daily Star
Independent Star Ltd, Star House,
62A Terenure Road North, Dublin 6w,
Republic of Ireland
tel (01) 4901228 *fax* (01) 4902193
email news@thestar.ie
website www.thestar.ie
Editor Gerard Colleran
Daily Mon–Sat €1.40

General articles relating to news and sport, and features. Length: 1,000 words. Illustrations: colour photos. Payment: by negotiation. Founded 1988.
Deputy Editor Danny Smyth
Deputy Editor (news) Michael O'Kane
Picture Editor Brian Dowling
Political Editor Catherine Halloran
Group Sports Editor Eoin Brannigan

Irish Examiner
City Quarter, Lapps Quay, Cork, Republic of Ireland
tel (021) 4272722 (newsroom) *fax* (021) 4275477
email (editor)@examiner.ie
website www.irishexaminer.ie
Editor Tim Vaughan
Daily Mon–Sat €1.80

Features. Material mostly commissioned. Length: 1,000 words. Payment: by arrangement. Founded 1841.
Executive Editor Dolan O'Hogan
Features Editor Vickie Maye
News Editor John O'Mahony
Picture Editor John O'Donovan
Sports Editor Tony Leen

Irish Independent
27–32 Talbot Street, Dublin 1, Republic of Ireland
tel (01) 7055333 *fax* (01) 8720304
email info@independent.ie
website www.independent.ie
Editor Gerard O'Regan
Daily Mon–Sat €1.80

Special articles on topical or general subjects. Length: 700–1,000 words. Payment: editor's estimate of value.
Business Editor Maeve Dineen
Education Editor John Walshe
Executive Editor Features Frank Coughlan
News Editor Shane Doram
Sports Editor Dave Courtney
Motoring Editor Eddie Cunningham
Health Correspondent Eilish O'Regan
News Editor Shane Doran
Political Editor Fionnan Sheehan
Security Editor Tom Brady

The Irish Times
The Irish Times Building, PO Box 74,
24–28 Tara Street, Dublin 2, Republic of Ireland
tel (01) 6758000 *fax* (01) 6758035
email editor@irishtimes.com
website www.irishtimes.com
Editor Geraldine Kennedy
Daily Mon–Fri €1.80, Sat, €2
Supplements **The Irish Times Magazine (Sat), Healthplus (Tue), Business This Week (Fri), Go Travel (Sat)**

Mainly staff-written. Specialist contributions (800–2,000 words) by commission on basis of ideas submitted. Payment: at editor's valuation. Illustrations: photos and line drawings.
Arts Editor Deirdre Falvey
Features Editor vacant
Finance Editor John McManus
Foreign Editor Denis Staunton
Literary Editor Caroline Walsh
News Editor Kevin O'Sullivan
Picture Editor David Sleator or Frank Miller
Sports Editor Malachy Logan

The Irish Times on the Web
website www.irishtimes.com
Online Editor Hugh Linehan

Mail on Sunday
Northcliffe House, 2 Derry Street, London W8 5TT
tel 020-7938 6000 *fax* 020-7937 3829
email editorial@mailonsunday.co.uk
website www.mailonsunday.co.uk
Editor Peter Wright
Sun £1.50
Supplements **The Mail on Sunday 2, Live, You**

Articles. Payment: by arrangement. Illustrations: line, half-tone; cartoons. Founded 1982.
Financial Mail Editor Lisa Buckingham
Features Editor Sian James
Literary Editor Susanna Gross
News Editor David Dillon
Picture Editor Sam Reilly
Political Editor Simon Walters
Sports Editor Malcolm Vallerius

Financial Mail on Sunday
tel 020-7938 6984
Editor Lisa Buckingham, *Personal Finance Editor* Jeff Prestridge
Part of main paper.

City, industry, business, and personal finance. News stories up to 1,500 words. Payment by arrangement. Full colour illustrations and photography commissioned.

Live Magazine
tel 020-7938 6033 *fax* 020-7937 7488
Editor Gerard Greaves
Free with paper
Interviews, entertainment-related features and TV listings. Length: 1,000–3,000 words. Illustrations: colour photos. Founded 1993.

Review
Editor George Thwaites
Investigative journalism, reportage, features, and film, TV, book and theatre reviews.

You
Editor Sue Peart, *Deputy Editor* Catherine Fenton
Free with paper
Women's interest features. Length: 500–2,500 words. Payment: by arrangement. Illustrations: full colour and b&w drawings commissioned; also colour photos.

Morning Star

(formerly Daily Worker)
People's Press Printing Society Ltd,
William Rust House, 52 Beachey Road,
London E3 2NS
tel 020-8510 0815 *fax* 020-8986 5694
email newsed@peoples-press.com
website www.morningstaronline.co.uk
Editor John Haylett
Daily Mon–Sat 60p

Newspaper for the labour movement. Articles of general interest. Illustrations: photos, cartoons, drawings. Founded 1930.
Arts & Media Editor Katie Gilmore
News Editor Daniel Coysh
Political Editor John Haylett
Sports Editor Greg Leedham
Features Editor Richard Bagley

News of the World

1 Virginia Street, London E98 1NW
tel 020-7782 4000 *fax* 020-7583 9504
email newsdesk@notw.co.uk
website www.newsoftheworld.co.uk, www.notw.co.uk
Editor Colin Myler
Sun £1
Supplements **Fabulous**

Uses freelance material. Payment: by negotiation. Founded 1843.
Associate Editor (Features) Jules Stenson
Associate Editor (News) Ian Edmondson
Executive Assistant Editor Neil Wallis
Political Editor Ian Kirby
PR Manager Hayley Barlow
Sports Editor Paul McCarthy

Fabulous
5th Floor, 1 Virginia Street, London E1 9SU
tel 020-7782 7900 *fax* 020-7782 7916
Editor Sally Eyden
Free with paper

The Observer

Kings Place, 90 York Way, London N1 9GU
tel 020-3353 2000 *fax* 020-3353 3189
website www.observer.co.uk
Editor John Mulholland
Sun £2
Supplements **Observer Magazine, Observer Food Monthly, The New Review, Sport**

Some articles and illustrations commissioned. Payment: by arrangement. Founded 1791.
Art Director Carolyn Roberts
Arts Editor Sarah Donaldson
Business Editor Ruth Sunderland
Cash Editor Lisa Bachelor
City Editor Richard Wachman
Comment Editor Ruaridh Nicoll
Fashion Editor Jo Jones
Assistant Editor (National & International News) Julian Coman
Home News Editor Lucy Rock
Literary Editor William Skidelsky
OFM Editor Allan Jenkins
Picture Editor Greg Whitmore
Political Editor Toby Helm
Readers' Editor Stephen Pritchard
The New Review Editor Jane Ferguson
Seven Days Editor Rob Yates
Sports Editor Brian Oliver
Travel Editor Joanne O'Connor

Observer Magazine
tel 020-3353 4175 *fax* 020-3353 3197
Editor Tim Lewis
Free with paper
Commissioned features. Length: 2,000–3,000 words. Illustrations: first-class colour and b&w photos. Payment: NUJ rates; see website for details.

The Observer Online
website www.observer.co.uk

The People

(formerly Sunday People)
1 Canada Square, Canary Wharf, London E14 5AP
tel 020-7293 3000 *fax* 020-7293 3517
email peoplenews@mgn.co.uk
website www.people.co.uk
Editor Lloyd Embley
Sun 90p
Supplements **The SP, Take it Easy**
Features Editor Caroline Waterston
News Editor Lee Harpin
Political Editor Nigel Nelson
Sports Editor James Brown

Exclusive news and feature stories needed.

Investigative and campaigning issues. Features and human interest stories as speciality. Strong sports following. Payment: rates high, even for tips that lead to published news stories.

Take it Easy
Editor Hanna Tavner
Free with paper

Scotland on Sunday

108 Holyrood Road, Edinburgh EH8 8AS
tel 0131-620 8620 *fax* 0131-620 8491
email newssos@scotlandonsunday.com
website www.scotlandonsunday.co.uk
Editor Ian Stewart
Sun £1.60

Features on all subjects, not necessarily Scottish. Payment: varies. Founded 1988.

News Editor Jeremy Watson
Political Editor Eddie Barnes

Spectrum Magazine
Editor Fiona Leith
Free with paper

The Scotsman

Barclay House, 108 Holyrood Road, Edinburgh EH8 8AS
tel 0131-620 8620 *fax* 0131-620 8616
email newsdeskts@scotsman.com
website www.scotsman.com
Editor John McLellan
Daily Mon–Fri 80p, Sat £1.10
Supplements **Saturday Magazine, Critique, Property, Motoring, Recruitment**

Considers articles on political, economic and general themes which add substantially to current information. Prepared to commission topical and controversial series from proved authorities. Length: 800–1,000 words. Illustrations: outstanding news pictures, cartoons. Payment: by arrangement. Founded 1817.

Arts Editor Andrew Eaton
Business Editor Terry Murden
Books Editor David Robinson
Education Correspondent Fiona MacLeod
Foreign Editor Rob Corbidge
Group News Editor Frank O'Donnell
Group Political Editor Eddie Barnes
Saturday Magazine Editor Alison Gray
Group Sports Editor Donald Walker

The Scottish Sun

News International Newspapers, Scotland, 6th Floor, Guildhall, 57 Queen Street, Glasgow G1 3EN
tel 0141-420 5200 *fax* 0141-420 5248
email scoop@thesun.co.uk
website www.thescottishsun.co.uk
Editor David Dinsmore
Daily Mon–Sat 30p

Scottish edition of *The Sun*. Illustrations: transparencies, colour and b&w prints, colour cartoons. Payment: by arrangement. Founded 1985.

Star Sunday

Independent Star Ltd, Star House, 62A Terenure Road North, Dublin 6w, Republic of Ireland
tel (01) 499 3400 *fax* (01) 4901538
email news.sunday@thestar.ie
Editor Des Gibson
Sun €2.10

Deputy Editor Paul Mallon
News Editor Fiona Hynes
Sports Editor Gavan Becton

The Sun

News Group Newspapers Ltd, 1 Virginia Street, London E1 9XP
tel 020-7782 4000 *fax* 020-7782 4095
email news@the-sun.co.uk
website www.the-sun.co.uk
Editor Dominic Mohan
Daily Mon–Fri 30p, Sat 55p
Supplements **Cashflow, The TV Mag**

Takes freelance material, including cartoons. Payment: by negotiation. Founded 1969.

Deputy Editors Geoff Webster, Simon Cosyns
Business Editor Steve Hawkes
Features Editor Derek Brown
Health Editor Emma Morton
Letters Editor Amanda Greenley
News Editor Chris Pharo
Picture Editor John Edwards
Political Editor Tom Newton Dunn
Showbiz Editor Gordon Smart
Sports Editor Mike Dunn
Travel Editor Lisa Minot
Women's Editor Sally Brook

The Sunday Business Post

80 Harcourt Street, Dublin 2, Republic of Ireland
tel (01) 6026000 *fax* (01) 6796496
email info@thepost.ie
website www.thepost.ie
Editor Cliff Taylor
Sun €2.40

Features on financial, economic and political topics; also lifestyle, media and science articles. Illustrations: colour and b&w photos, graphics, cartoons. Payment: by negotiation. Founded 1989.

Agenda Editor Gillian Nelis
Business Editor Nicola Cooke
Technology Editor Adrian Weckler
Marketing Editor Catherine O'Mahony
News Editor Gavin Daly
Political Correspondents Pat Leahy, Niamh Connolly
Property Editor Gillian Nelis

Sunday Express

Northern & Shell Building, 10 Lower Thames Street, London EC4R 6EN

tel 020-8612 7000 *fax* (0871) 434 7300
email news.desk@express.co.uk
website www.express.co.uk/Sunday
Editor Martin Townsend
Sun £1.30
Supplements **'S' Sunday Express, Property, Review, Sport, Travel, Financial**

Exclusive news stories, photos, personality profiles and features of controversial or lively interest. Length: 800–1,000 words. Payment: top rates. Founded 1918.

Features Editor Amy Packer
Comment Editor Graham Ball
News Editor Stephen Rigley
Deputy Political Editor Kirsty Buchanan
Sports Editor Scott Wilson

'S' Sunday Express

tel (0871) 520 7297 *fax* (0871) 520 7599
Editor Louise Robinson
Free with paper

Sunday Herald

200 Renfield Street, Glasgow G2 3QB
tel 0141-302 7800 *fax* 0141-302 7863
email news@sundayherald.com
website www.sundayherald.com
Editor Richard Walker
Sun £1.40
Supplements **Business, Sport, Sunday Herald Magazine, Scottish Review of Books, Fresh**

News and stories about Scotland, its characteristics and people. Opportunities for freelances with quality contacts. Founded 1999.

Business Editor Colin Donald
Digital Editor David Milne
Features Editor Allan Burnett
Magazine Editor Susan Flockhart
Assistant News Editor John Bynorth
Investigations Editor Paul Hutcheon
Sports Editors David Dick, Jonathan Jobson

Sunday Independent

27–32 Talbot Street, Dublin 1, Republic of Ireland
tel (01) 7055333 *fax* (01) 7055779
website www.independent.ie
Editor Aengus Fanning
Sun €2.50

Special articles. Length: according to subject. Illustrations: topical or general interest, cartoons. Payment: at editor's valuation.

Business Editor Shane Ross
Deputy Editors Anne Harris, Willie Kealy
Life Magazine Editor Brendan O'Connor
Sports Editor John Greene

Sunday Mail

1 Central Quay, Glasgow G3 8DA
tel 0141-309 3000 *fax* 0141-309 3587
email mailbox@sundaymail.co.uk
London office 1 Canada Square, Canary Wharf, London E14 5AP
website www.sundaymail.com
Editor Allan Rennie
Sun £1.30
Supplements **Entertainment, Fun on Sunday, Jobsplus!, 7-Days, Right at Home**

Exclusive stories and pictures of national and Scottish interest; also cartoons. Payment: above average.

Deputy Editor Jim Wilson
Health Editor Dr Gareth Smith
News Editor Brendan McGinty
Picture Editor Andrew Hosie
Supplements Editor Liz Cowan
Showbiz Editor Billy Sloan
Sports Editor George Cheyne

Sunday Mirror

1 Canada Square, Canary Wharf, London E14 5AP
tel 020-7293 3000 *fax* 020-7293 3939
email news@sundaymirror.co.uk
website www.sundaymirror.co.uk
Editor Tina Weaver
Sun Mirror £1
Supplements **Celebs On Sunday, Homes and Holidays**

Concentrates on human interest news features, social documentaries, dramatic news and feature photos. Ideas, as well as articles, bought. Payment: high, especially for exclusives. Founded 1963.

Assistant Editor (Features) Jill Main
Associate Editor Mike Small
Associate Editor (News) Nick Buckley
Deputy Editor James Scott
Picture Editor Mike Sharp
Sport Editor David Walker

Sunday Post

D.C. Thomson & Co. Ltd, 144 Port Dundas Road, Glasgow G4 0HZ
tel 0141-332 9933 *fax* 0141-331 1595
email mail@sundaypost.com
Albert Square, Dundee DD1 9QJ
tel (01382) 223131 *fax* (01382) 201064
website www.sundaypost.com
Editor Donald Martin
Sun £1
Supplements **Post Plus**

Human interest, topical, domestic and humorous articles, and exclusive news. Payment: on acceptance.

The Sunday Post Magazine

tel (01382) 223131 *fax* (01382) 201064
Editor Jan Gooderham
Monthly Free with paper
General interest articles. Length: 1000–2000 words. Illustrations: colour transparencies. Payment: varies. Founded 1988.

Sunday Telegraph

111 Buckingham Palace Road, London SW1W 0DT
tel 020-7931 2000

email stnews@telegraph.co.uk
website www.telegraph.co.uk
Editor Ian MacGregor
Sun £1.90
Supplements **Business, City, Home & Living, Money & Jobs Sport, Travel**

Occasional freelance material accepted.
City Editor Damian Reece
Comment Editor Chris Deerin
Deputy Editor Tim Jotischky
Diary Editor Tim Walker
Foreign Editor David Wastell
Literary Editor Michael Prodger
News Editor James P. Hall
Picture Editor Mike Spillard
Political Editor Patrick Hennessy
Seven Editor Ross Jones
Sports Editor Peter Mitchell
Travel Editor Maggie O'Sullivan

Stella

tel 020-7931 3649 *fax* 020-7931 3427
email stella@telegraph.co.uk
Editor Anna Murphy
Free with paper
All material is commissioned. Founded 1995.

The Sunday Times

1 Pennington Street, London E98 1ST
tel 020-7782 5000 *fax* 020-7782 5731
email newsdesk@sunday-times.co.uk
website www.sunday-times.co.uk
Editor John Witherow
Sun £2
Supplements **Appointments, Business, Culture, Ingear, Home, Money, News Review, Sport, Style, The Sunday Times Magazine, Travel**

Special articles by authoritative writers on politics, literature, art, drama, music, finance and science, and topical matters. Payment: top rate for exclusive features. Founded 1822.
Deputy Managing Editor Kathleen Herron
Culture Editor Helen Hawkins
Economics Editor David Smith
Literary Editor Andrew Holgate
News Editor Nick Hellen
Sports Editor Alex Butler
Travel Editor Christine Walker

The Sunday Times Magazine

tel 020-7782 7000
Editor Sarah Baxter
Free with paper
Articles and pictures. Illustrations: colour and b&w photos. Payment: by negotiation.

The Sunday Times Scotland

6th Floor, Guildhall, 57 Queen Street, Glasgow G1 3EN
tel 0141-420 5100 *fax* 0141-420 5262
website www.timesonline.co.uk
Sun £1.90
Founded 1988.
Editor Carlos Alba

The Times

1 Pennington Street, London E98 1TT
tel 020-7782 5000 *fax* 020-7782 5988
email home.news@thetimes.co.uk
website www.timesonline.co.uk
Editor James Harding
Daily Mon–Fri 90p, Sat £1.40
Supplements **Books, Body & Soul, Bricks & Mortar, Crème, Football Handbook, The Game, The Knowledge, Money, Times 2, Times Law, The Times Magazine, Times Sport, Travel**

Outside contributions considered from: experts in subjects of current interest and writers who can make first-hand experience or reflection come readably alive. Phone appropriate section editor. Length: up to 1200 words. Founded 1785.
Executive Editor Alex O'Connell
Deputy Editor Keith Blackmore
Education Editor Greg Hurst
Foreign Editor Richard Beeston
Health Editor Sam Lister
Home News Editor Robert Cole
Industrial Correspondent Angela Jameson
Literary Editor Erica Wagner
Media Editor Alexi Mostrous
Political Editor Roland Watson
Saturday Times Editor Louise France
Science Editor Mark Henderson
Sports Editor Tim Hallissey
Travel Editor Kathleen Wyatt
Times 2 Editor Emma Tucker

The Times Magazine

Editor Louise France
Free with Sat paper
Features. Illustrated.

Wales on Sunday

6 Park Street, Cardiff CF10 1XR
tel 029-2024 3600
email newsdesk@mediawales.co.uk
website www.icwales.co.uk
Editor Tim Gordon
Sun 85p
Supplements **Life on Sunday, Sport on Sunday**

National Sunday newspaper of Wales offering comprehensive news, features and entertainments coverage at the weekend, with a particular focus on events in Wales. Accepts general interest articles, preferably with a Welsh connection. Founded 1989.
News Editor Nick Rippington
Sports Editor Paul Abbandonato

Regional newspapers UK and Ireland

Regional newspapers are listed in alphabetical order under region. Some will accept and pay for letters to the editor, brief fillers, and gossip paragraphs, as well as puzzles and quizzes. See also *Writing for newspapers* on page 6.

BELFAST

Belfast Telegraph

124–144 Royal Avenue, Belfast BT1 1EB
tel 028-9026 4000 *fax* 028-9055 4506 (news only), 9055 4517 (features), 9055 4508 (sport)
email editor@belfasttelegraph.co.uk, newseditor@belfasttelegraph.co.uk
website www.belfasttelegraph.co.uk
Editor Mike Gilson
Daily Mon–Sat 65p

Any material relating to Northern Ireland. Payment: by negotiation. Founded 1870.

Irish News

113–117 Donegall Street, Belfast BT1 2GE
tel 028-9032 2226 *fax* 028-9033 7505
website www.irishnews.com
Editor Noel Doran
Daily Mon–Sat 70p

Articles of historical and topical interest. Payment: by arrangement. Founded 1855.

News Letter

2 Esky Drive, Portadown, Craigavon, Belfast BT63 5YY
tel 028-9089 7720 *fax* 028-3839 5599
email newsdesk@newsletter.co.uk
website www.newsletter.co.uk
Editor Darwin Templeton
Daily 62p

Pro-Union. Founded 1737.

Sunday Life

124–144 Royal Avenue, Belfast BT1 1EB
tel 028-9026 4000 *fax* 028-9055 4507
email slnews@belfasttelegraph.co.uk
website www.sundaylife.co.uk
Editor Martin Breen
Sun £1.10

Items of interest to Northern Ireland Sunday tabloid readers. Payment: by arrangement. Illustrations: colour and b&w pictures and graphics. Founded 1988.

CHANNEL ISLANDS

Guernsey Press and Star

PO Box 57, Braye Road, Vale, Guernsey GY1 3BW
tel (01481) 240240 *fax* (01481) 240235
website www.guernseypress.com
Editor Richard Digard
Daily Mon–Sat 45p

News and feature articles. Length: 500–700 words. Illustrations: colour and b&w photos. Payment: by negotiation. Founded 1897.

Jersey Evening Post

PO Box 582, Five Oaks, St Saviour, Jersey JE4 8XQ
tel (01534) 611611 *fax* (01534) 611622
email news@jerseyeveningpost.com
website www.thisisjersey.com
Editor Chris Bright
Daily Mon–Sat 45p

News and features with a Channel Islands angle. Length: 1,000 words (articles/features), 300 words (news). Illustrations: colour and b&w. Payment: £100 per 1,000 words. Founded 1890.

CORK

Evening Echo (Cork)

Evening Echo Publications Ltd, City Quarter, Lapps Quay, Cork, Republic of Ireland
tel (021) 4272722 *fax* (021) 4802135
email firstname.secondname@eecho.ie
website www.eveningecho.ie
Editor Maurice Gubbins
Daily Mon–Sat €1.30

Articles, features and news for the area. Illustrations: colour prints.

DUBLIN

Evening Herald

Independent House, 27–32 Talbot Street, Dublin 1, Republic of Ireland
tel (01) 7055722
email hnews@herald.ie
website www.herald.ie
Editor Stephen Rae
Daily Mon–Sat €1.10

Articles. Payment: by arrangement. Illustrations: line, half-tone, cartoons.

The Sunday Tribune

27–32 Talbot Street, Dublin 1, Republic of Ireland
tel (01) 631 4300 *fax* (01) 631 4390

email nhegarty@tribune.ie
website www.tribune.ie
Editor Noirin Hegarty
Sun €2.50
Supplements **People, Review**

Newspaper containing news (inc. foreign), articles, features and photo features. Length: 600–2,800 words. Illustrations: colour and b&w photos and cartoons. Payment: £100 per 1,000 words; £100 for illustrations. Founded 1980.

EAST ANGLIA

Cambridge Evening News

Winship Road, Milton, Cambs. CB24 6PP
tel (01223) 434437 *fax* (01223) 434415
email newsdesk@cambridge-news.co.uk
website www.cambridge-news.co.uk
Group Editor in Chief Colin Grant
Daily Mon–Sat 40p

The voice of Mid-Anglia – news, views and sport. Illustrations: colour prints, b&w and colour graphics. Payment: by negotiation. Founded 1888.

East Anglian Daily Times

30 Lower Brook Street, Ipswich, Suffolk IP4 1AN
tel (01473) 230023 *fax* (01473) 324871
website www.eadt.co.uk
Editor Terry Hunt
Daily Mon–Fri 50p, Sat 80p

Features of East Anglian interest, preferably with pictures. Length: 500 words. Illustrations: colour, b&w. Payment: negotiable; illustrations NUJ rates. Founded 1874.

Eastern Daily Press

Prospect House, Rouen Road, Norwich NR1 1RE
tel (01603) 628311 *fax* (01603) 623872
London office House of Commons Press Gallery, House of Commons, London SW1A 0AA
tel 020-7219 3384 *fax* 020-7222 3830
website www.edp24.co.uk
Editor Peter Waters
Daily Mon–Fri 50p, Sat 80p

Limited market for articles of East Anglian interest not exceeding 900 words. Founded 1870.

Evening Star

Archant Regional, Press House,
30 Lower Brook Street, Ipswich, Suffolk IP4 1AN
tel (01473) 230023 *fax* (01473) 324850
website www.eveningstar.co.uk
Editor Nigel Pickoner
Mon–Thu, and Sat 40p, Fri 80p

Norwich Evening News

Prospect House, Rouen Road, Norwich NR1 1RE
tel (01603) 628311 *fax* (01603) 623872
website www.eveningnews24.co.uk
Editor Tim Williams
Daily Mon–Sat 45p

Interested in local news-based features. Length: up to 500 words. Payment: NUJ or agreed rates. Founded 1882.

EAST MIDLANDS

Burton Mail

Burton Daily Mail Ltd, 65–68 High Street, Burton on Trent DE14 1LE
tel (01283) 524855 *fax* (01283) 515351
email editorial@burtonmail.co.uk
website www.burtonmail.co.uk
Editor Andy Parker
Daily Mon–Sat 38p

Features, news and articles of interest to Burton and south Derbyshire readers. Length: 400–500 words. Illustrations: colour and b&w. Payment: by negotiation. Founded 1898.

Chronicle & Echo, Northampton

Northamptonshire Newspapers Ltd, Upper Mounts, Northampton NN1 3HR
tel (01604) 467000 *fax* (01604) 467200
Editor David Summers
Daily Mon–Sat 43p

Articles, features and news – mostly commissioned – of interest to the Northampton area. Length: varies. Payment: by negotiation. Founded 1931.

Derby Evening Telegraph

Northcliffe House, Meadow Road, Derby DE1 2BH
tel (01332) 291111 *fax* (01322) 253027
website www.thisisderbyshire.co.uk
Editor Steve Hall
Daily Mon–Sat 35p

Articles and news of local interest. Payment: by negotiation.

The Leicester Mercury

St George Street, Leicester LE1 9FQ
tel 0116-251 2512 *fax* 0116-253 0645
website www.thisisleicestershire.co.uk
Editor Keith Perch
Daily Mon–Sat 36p

Occasional articles, features and news; submit ideas to editor first. Length/payment: by negotiation. Founded 1874.

Nottingham Evening Post

Castle Wharf House, Nottingham NG1 7EU
tel 0115-948 2000 *fax* 0115-964 4049
email newsdesk@nottinghameveningpost.co.uk
website www.thisisnottingham.co.uk
Editor Malcolm Pheby
Daily Mon–Sat 33p

Material on local issues considered. Founded 1878.

Peterborough Evening Telegraph
Telegraph House, 57 Priesgate,
Peterborough PE1 1JW
tel (01733) 555111 *fax* (01733) 313147
email news@peterboroughtoday.co.uk
website www.peterboroughtoday.co.uk
Editor Mark Edwards
Daily Mon–Sat 35p

LONDON

Evening Standard
Northcliffe House, 2 Derry Street, London W8 5EE
tel 020-3367 7000
website www.thisislondon.com
Editor Geordie Greig
Daily Mon–Fri Free

Articles of general interest considered, 1,500 words or shorter; also news, pictures and ideas. Founded 1827.

ES Magazine
Editor Sasha Slater
Weekly Free with paper on Fri

Feature ideas, exclusively about London. Payment: by negotiation. Illustrations: all types.

Homes and Property
Editor Janice Morley
Weekly Free with paper on Wed

UK property. Payment: by negotiation.

Metro
Northcliffe House, 2 Derry Street, London W8 5TT
tel 020-7651 5200 *fax* 020-7651 5202
email news.london@ukmetro.co.uk
website www.metro.co.uk
Editor Sarah Getty
Daily Mon–Fri Free

NORTH

Carlisle News and Star
CN Group, Newspaper House, Dalston Road,
Carlisle CA2 5UA
tel (01228) 612600 *fax* (01228) 612640
website www.newsandstar.co.uk
Editorial Director Neil Hodgkinson
Mon–Sat 45p

Evening Chronicle
ncjMedia Ltd, Groat Market,
Newcastle upon Tyne NE1 1ED
tel 0191-232 7500 *fax* 0191-232 2256
email ec.news@ncjmedia.co.uk
website www.chroniclelive.co.uk
Editor Paul Robertson
Daily Mon–Sat 42p

News, photos and features covering almost every subject of interest to readers in Tyne and Wear, Northumberland and Durham. Payment: by prior arrangement.

Evening Gazette
Gazette Media Company Ltd,
105–111 Borough Road, Middlesbrough TS1 3AZ
tel (01642) 245401 *fax* (01642) 234228
email news@eveninggazette.co.uk
website www.gazettelive.co.uk
Editor Darren Thwaites
Daily Mon–Sat 44p

News, and topical and lifestyle features. Length: 600–800 words. Illustrations: line, half-tone, colour, graphics, cartoons. Payment: £75 per 1,000 words; scale rate or by agreement for illustrations. Founded 1869.

Hartlepool Mail
Northeast Press Ltd, New Clarence House,
Wesley Square, Hartlepool TS24 8BX
tel (01429) 239333 *fax* (01429) 869024
email mail.news@northeast-press.co.uk
website www.hartlepoolmail.co.uk,
www.peterleemail.co.uk
Editor Joy Yates
Daily Mon–Sat 42p

Features of local interest. Length: 500 words. Illustrations: colour, b&w photos, line. Payment: by negotiation. Founded 1877.

The Journal
Groat Market, Newcastle upon Tyne NE1 1ED
tel 0191-232 7500 *fax* 0191-201 6044
email jnl.newsdesk@ncjmedia.co.uk
website www.journallive.co.uk
Editor Brian Aitken
Daily 50p

News, sport items and features of topical interest considered. Payment: by arrangement.

North-West Evening Mail
Newspaper House, Abbey Road, Barrow-in-Furness,
Cumbria LA14 5QS
tel (01229) 840150 *fax* (01229) 840164/832141
website www.nwemail.co.uk
Editor Jonathan Lee
Daily Mon–Sat 45p

Articles, features and news. Length: 500 words. Illustrations: b&w photos and occasional artwork. Covering the whole of South Cumbria. Founded 1898.

The Northern Echo
Priestgate, Darlington, Co. Durham DL1 1NF
tel (01325) 381313 *fax* (01325) 380539
website www.thenorthernecho.co.uk
Editor Peter Barron
Daily Mon–Sat 45p

Articles of interest to North-East and North Yorkshire; all material commissioned. Preliminary study of newspaper advisable. Length: 800–1,000 words. Illustrations: line, half-tone, colour – mostly commissioned. Payment: by negotiation. Founded 1870.

The Shields Gazette

Chapter Row, South Shields, Tyne & Wear NE33 1BL
tel 0191-427 4800 *fax* 0191-456 8270
website www.shieldsgazette.com
Editor John Szymanski
Daily Mon–Sat 43p

The Sunday Sun

Groat Market, Newcastle upon Tyne NE1 1ED
tel 0191-201 6201 *fax* 0191-201 6180
email scoop.sundaysun@ncjmedia.co.uk
website www.sundaysun.co.uk
Editor Colin Patterson
Sun 85p

Key requirements: immediate topicality and human sidelights on current problems. Particularly welcomed are special features of family appeal and news stories of special interest to the North of England. Length: 200–700 words. Payment: normal lineage rates, or by arrangement. Illustrations: photos. Founded 1919.

Sunderland Echo

Echo House, Pennywell, Sunderland, Tyne & Wear SR4 9ER
tel 0191-501 5800 *fax* 0191-534 5975
website www.sunderlandecho.com
Editor Rob Lawson
Daily Mon–Sat 43p

Local news, features and articles. Length: 500 words. Illustrations: colour and b&w photos, line, cartoons. Payment: negotiable. Founded 1875.

NORTH WEST

The Blackpool Gazette

Blackpool Gazette & Herald Ltd, Avroe House, Avroe Crescent, Blackpool Business Park, Squires Gate, Blackpool FY4 2DP
tel (01253) 400888 *fax* (01253) 361870
email editorial@blackpoolgazette.co.uk
website www.blackpoolgazette.co.uk
Editor David Helliwell
Daily Mon–Sat 40p

Local news and articles of general interest, with photos if appropriate. Length: varies. Payment: on merit. Founded 1929.

The Bolton News

Newspaper House, Churchgate, Bolton, Lancs. BL1 1DE
tel (01204) 537270 *fax* (01204) 537068
email newsdesk@theboltonnews.co.uk
website www.thisisbolton.co.uk
Editor-in-Chief Ian Savage
Daily Mon–Sat 40p

Founded 1867.

Lancashire Evening Post

Oliver's Place, Preston PR2 9ZA
tel (01772) 254841 *fax* (01772) 880173
email lep.newsdesk@lep.co.uk
website www.lep.co.uk
Editor Simon Reynolds
Daily Mon–Sat 32p

Topical articles on all subjects. Area of interest Wigan to Lake District, Lancs, and coast. Length: 600–900 words. Illustrations: colour and b&w photos, cartoons. Payment: by arrangement.

Lancashire Telegraph

Newspaper House, High Street, Blackburn, Lancs. BB1 1HT
tel (01254) 678678 *fax* (01254) 680429
website www.lancashiretelegraph.co.uk
Editor Kevin Young
Daily Mon–Sat 38p

Will consider general interest articles, such as property, motoring, finance, etc. Payment: by arrangement. Founded 1886.

Liverpool Daily Post

PO Box 48, Old Hall Street, Liverpool L69 3EB
tel 0151-227 2000 *fax* 0151-472 2506
website www.liverpooldailypost.co.uk
Editor Mark Thomas
Daily Mon–Sat 55p
Supplements **Box Office, Business Week, Day Six, Post Match, Style City**

Articles of general and topical interest to North West England. No verse or fiction. Payment: according to value. News and feature illustrations. Founded 1855.

Liverpool Echo

PO Box 48, Old Hall Street, Liverpool L69 3EB
tel 0151-227 2000 *fax* 0151-472 2474
website www.liverpoolecho.co.uk
Editor Alastair Machray
Daily Mon–Fri 45p, Sat 60p

Articles of up to 600–800 words of local or topical interest; also cartoons. Payment: according to merit; special rates for exceptional material. Connected with, but independent of, the *Liverpool Daily Post*. Articles not interchangeable.

Manchester Evening News

1 Scott Place, Hardman Street, Manchester M3 3RN
tel 0161-832 7200 *fax* 0161-211 2030 (editorial)
website www.manchestereveningnews.co.uk
Editor Paul Horrocks

Daily Mon–Sat 38p

Feature articles of up to 1,000 words, topical or general interest and illustrated where appropriate, should be addressed to the Features Editor. Payment: on acceptance.

Oldham Evening Chronicle

PO Box 47, Union Street, Oldham, Lancs. OL1 1EQ
tel 0161-633 2121 *fax* 0161-652 2111
email news@oldham-chronicle.co.uk
website www.oldham-chronicle.co.uk
Editor Jim Williams
Daily Mon–Fri 47p

News and features on current topics and local history. Length: 1,000 words. Illustrations: colour and b&w photos and line. Payment: £20–£25 per 1,000 words; £16.32–£21.90 for illustrations. Founded 1854.

SCOTLAND

The Courier and Advertiser

D.C. Thomson & Co. Ltd, 80 Kingsway East, Dundee DD4 8SL
tel (01382) 223131 *fax* (01382) 454590
London office 185 Fleet Street, London EC4A 2HS
tel 020-7400 1030 *fax* 020-7400 1089
website www.thecourier.co.uk
Editor Bill Hutcheon
Daily Mon–Sat 44p

Founded 1816 and 1801.

Dundee Evening Telegraph and Post

80 Kingsway East, Dundee DD4 8SL
tel (01382) 223131 *fax* (01382) 454590
email newsdesk@eveningtelegraph.co.uk
London office 185 Fleet Street, London EC4A 2HS
tel 020-7400 1030 *fax* 020-7400 1089
website www.eveningtelegraph.co.uk
Daily Mon–Fri 35p

Evening Express (Aberdeen)

Aberdeen Journals Ltd, PO Box 43, Lang Stracht, Mastrick, Aberdeen AB15 6DF
tel (01224) 690222 *fax* (01224) 699575
website www.eveningexpress.co.uk
Editor Damian Bates
Daily Mon–Sat 40p

Lively evening paper. Illustrations: colour and b&w. Payment: by arrangement.

Evening News (Edinburgh)

108 Holyrood Road, Edinburgh EH8 8AS
tel 0131-620 8620 *fax* 0131-620 8696
website www.edinburghnews.com
Editor Tom Little
Daily Mon–Sat 45p

Features on current affairs, preferably in relation to our circulation area. Women's talking points, local historical articles; subjects of general interest; health and beauty, fashion.

Glasgow Evening Times

200 Renfield Street, Glasgow G2 3QB
tel 0141-302 7000 *fax* 0141-302 6600
website www.eveningtimes.co.uk
Editor Tony Carlin
Daily Mon–Sat 45p

Founded 1876.

Inverness Courier

New Century House, Stadium Road, Inverness IV1 1FG
tel (01463) 233059 *fax* (01463) 238223
email editorial@inverness-courier.co.uk
website www.inverness-courier.co.uk
Editor Robert Taylor
2 p.w. Tue 55p, Fri 70p

Articles of Highland interest only. Unsolicited material accepted. Illustrations: colour and b&w photos. Payment: by arrangement. Founded 1817.

Paisley Daily Express

Scottish and Universal Newspapers Ltd, 14 New Street, Paisley, Renfrewshire PA1 1YA
tel 0141-887 7911 *fax* 0141-887 6254
website www.paisleydailyexpress.co.uk
Editor Anne Dalrymple
Daily Mon–Sat 42p

Articles of Paisley interest only. Considers unsolicited material.

The Press and Journal

Lang Stracht, Aberdeen AB15 6DF
tel (01224) 690222
email pj.editor@ajl.co.uk
website www.pressandjournal.co.uk
Editor Derek Tucker
Daily Mon–Fri 45p, Sat 60p

Contributions of Scottish interest. Payment: by arrangement. Illustrations: half-tone. Founded 1748.

SOUTH EAST

The Argus

Argus House, Crowhurst Road, Hollingbury, Brighton BN1 8AR
tel (01273) 544544 *fax* (01273) 505703
email news@theargus.co.uk
website www.theargus.co.uk
Group Editor Michael Beard
Daily Mon–Sat 38p

Established 1880.

Echo

Newspaper House, Chester Hall Lane, Basildon, Essex SS14 3BL

tel (01268) 522792 *fax* (01268) 469281
email echonews@nge.com
website www.echo-news.co.uk
Editor Martin McNeill
Daily Mon–Fri 38p

Mostly staff-written. Only interested in local material. Payment: by arrangement. Founded 1969.

Medway Messenger

Medway House, Ginsbury Close,
Sir Thomas Longley Road, Medway City Estate,
Strood, Kent ME2 4DU
tel (01634) 227800 *fax* (01634) 715256
website www.kentonline.co.uk
Editor Bob Bounds
Mon 50p, Fri 70p

Paper with emphasis on news and sport from the Medway Towns. Illustrations: line, half-tone.

The News, Portsmouth

The News Centre, London Road, Hilsea,
Portsmouth PO2 9SX
tel 023-9266 4488 *fax* 023-9267 3363
email newsdesk@thenews.co.uk
website www.portsmouth.co.uk
Editor Mark Waldron
Daily Mon–Sat 40p

Articles of relevance to southeast Hampshire and West Sussex. Payment by arrangement. Founded 1877.

Oxford Mail

Newspaper House, Osney Mead, Oxford OX2 0EJ
tel (01865) 425262 *fax* (01865) 425554
email news@nqo.com
website www.oxfordmail.co.uk
Editor Simon O'Neill
Daily 35p

Reading Evening Post

8 Tessa Road, Reading, Berks. RG1 8NS
tel 0118-918 3000 *fax* 0118-959 9363
email editorial@reading-epost.co.uk
website www.getreading.co.uk
Editor Andy Murrill
Daily Mon–Fri 40p

Topical articles based on current local news. Length: 800–1,200 words. Payment: based on lineage rates. Illustrations: half-tone. Founded 1965.

The Southern Daily Echo

Newspaper House, Test Lane, Redbridge,
Southampton SO16 9JX
tel 023-8042 4777 *fax* 023-8042 4545
email newsdesk@dailyecho.co.uk
website www.dailyecho.co.uk
Editor Ian Murray
Daily 38p

News, articles, features, sport. Length: varies. Illustrations: line, half-tone, colour, cartoons. Payment: NUJ rates. Founded 1888.

Swindon Advertiser

100 Victoria Road, Old Town, Swindon SN1 3BE
tel (01793) 528144 *fax* (01793) 542434
email newsdesk@swindonadvertiser.co.uk
website www.swindonadvertiser.co.uk
Editor Dave King
Daily Mon–Sat 40p

News and information relating to Swindon and Wiltshire only. Considers unsolicited material. Founded 1854.

SOUTH WEST

Bristol Evening Post

Temple Way, Old Market, Bristol BS99 7HD
tel 0117-934 3000 *fax* 0117-934 3570
website www.thisisbristol.co.uk
Editor-in-chief Mike Norton
Daily Mon–Sat 37p

Takes freelance news and articles. Payment: by arrangement. Founded 1932.

The Citizen

1 Clarence Parade, Cheltenham GL50 3NY
tel (01452) 420621 *fax* (01452) 420664
website www.thisisgloucestershire.co.uk
Editor Ian Mean
Daily Mon–Fri 37p, Sat 40p

Local news and features for Gloucester and its districts. Length: 1,000 words (articles/features), 300 words (news). Illustrations: colour. Payment: negotiable.

Daily Echo

Richmond Hill, Bournemouth BH2 6HH
tel (01202) 554601 *fax* (01202) 292115
email newsdesk@bournemouthecho.co.uk
website www.bournemouthecho.co.uk
Editor Neal Butterworth
Daily Mon–Fri 40p, Sat 60p

Established 1900.

Dorset Echo

Fleet House, Hampshire Road, Weymouth,
Dorset DT4 9XD
tel (01305) 830930 *fax* (01305) 830956
email newsdesk@dorsetecho.co.uk
website www.thisisweymouth.co.uk
Editor Toby Granville
Daily Mon–Fri 32p, Sat 40p

News and occasional features (1,000–2,000 words). Illustrations: b&w photos. Payment: by negotiation. Founded 1921.

Express & Echo

Express & Echo News & Media, Heron Road,
Sowton, Exeter EX2 7NF

tel (01392) 442211 *fax* (01392) 442287
website www.thisisexeter.co.uk
Editor Marc Astley
Daily Mon–Sat 35p

Features and news of local interest. Length: 500–800 words (features), up to 400 words (news). Illustrations: colour. Payment: lineage rates; illustrations negotiable. Founded 1904.

Gloucestershire Echo

1 Clarence Parade, Cheltenham, Glos. GL50 3NY
tel (01242) 271900 *fax* (01242) 271821
email echo.editor@glosmedia.co.uk
website www.thisisgloucestershire.co.uk
Editor Kevan Blackadder
Daily Mon–Fri 35p, Sat 45p

Specialist articles with Gloucestershire connections; no fiction. Founded 1873.

The Herald

17 Brest Road, Derriford Business Park, Plymouth PL6 5AA
tel (01752) 765500 *fax* (01752) 765527
email news@theplymouthherald.co.uk
website www.thisisplymouth.co.uk
Editor Bill Martin
Daily Mon–Sat 36p

Local news, articles and features. Will consider unsolicited material. Welcomes ideas for articles and features. Illustrations: colour and b&w prints.

Herald Express

Harmsworth House, Barton Hill Road, Torquay, Devon TQ2 8JN
tel (01803) 676000 *fax* (01803) 676228
website www.thisissouthdevon.co.uk
Editor Andy Phelan
Daily Mon–Sat 37p

Sunday Independent

The Sunday Independent Newspapers Ltd, Webbs House, Tindle Suite, Liskeard, Cornwall PL14 6AH
tel (01579) 342174 *fax* (01579) 341851
Editor John Noble
Sun 70p

News features on West Country topics; features/articles with a nostalgic theme; short quirky news briefs (must be original). Length: 600 words (features/articles), 300 words (news). Illustrations: colour, b&w. Payment: by arrangement. Founded 1808.

Western Daily Press

Bristol Evening Post and Press Ltd, Temple Way, Bristol BS99 7HD
tel 0117-934 3000 *fax* 0117-934 3574
email wdeditor@bepp.co.uk
website www.westerndailypress.co.uk
Editor Tim Dixon
Daily Mon–Fri 45p, Sat 65p

National, international or West Country topics for features or news items, from established journalists, with or without illustrations. Payment: by negotiation. Founded 1858.

The Western Morning News

17 Brest Road, Derriford, Plymouth PL6 5AA
tel (01752) 765500 *fax* (01752) 765535
website www.thisiswesternmorningnews.co.uk
Editor Alan Qualtrough
Daily Mon–Fri 45p, Sat 65p

Articles plus illustrations considered on West Country subjects. Founded 1860.

WALES

The Leader

NWN Media Ltd, Mold Business Park, Wrexham Road, Mold, Flintshire CH7 1XY
tel (01352) 707707 *fax* (01352) 700048
website www.leaderlive.co.uk
Editor Barrie Jones
Mon–Fri 45p

South Wales Argus

South Wales Argus, Cardiff Road, Maesglas, Newport, Gwent NP20 3QN
tel (01633) 810000 *fax* (01633) 777202
email newsdesk@gwent-wales.co.uk
website www.southwalesargus.co.uk
Editor Gerry Keighley
Daily Mon–Sat 38p

News and features of relevance to Gwent. Length: 500–600 words (features); 350 words (news). Illustrations: colour prints and transparencies. Payment: £30 (features), £20 (news) per item; £20–£25 (photos). Founded 1892.

South Wales Echo

6 Park Street, Cardiff CF10 1XR
tel (02920) 223333 *fax* (02920) 243640
email echo.newsdesk@walesonline.co.uk
website www.walesonline.co.uk
Editor Mike Hill
Daily Mon–Fri 49p, Sat 58p

Evening paper: news, sport, features, showbiz, news features, personality interviews. Length: up to 700 words. Illustrations: photos, cartoons. Payment: by negotiation. Founded 1884.

South Wales Evening Post

PO Box 14, Adelaide Street, Swansea SA1 1QT
tel (01792) 510000 *fax* (01792) 514697
email postbox@swwp.co.uk
website www.thisissouthwales.co.uk
Editor-in-Chief Spencer Feeney
Daily 40p

Western Mail

6 Park Street, Cardiff CF10 1XR
tel 029-2022 3333 *fax* 029-2058 3652
website www.walesonline.co.uk
Editor Alan Edmunds
Daily Mon–Fri 35p

Articles of political, industrial, literary or general and Welsh interest are considered. Illustrations: topical general news and feature pictures, cartoons. Payment: according to value; special fees for exclusive news. Founded 1869.

WEST MIDLANDS

Birmingham Mail

6th Floor, Fort Dunlop, Fort Parkway, Birmingham B24 9FF
tel 0121-236 3366 *fax* 0121-233 0271
London office 1 Canada Square, Canary Wharf, London E14 5AP
tel 020-7293 3000 *fax* 020-7293 3793
website www.birminghammail.net
Editor David Brookes
Daily Mon–Sat 40p

Features of topical Midland interest considered. Length: 400–800 words. Payment: by arrangement. Founded 1870.

The Birmingham Post

6th Floor, Fort Dunlop, Fort Parkway, Birmingham B24 9FF
tel 0121-234 5301 *fax* 0121-234 5667
London office 22nd Floor, 1 Canada Square, Canary Wharf, London E14 5AP
tel 020-7293 3455 *fax* 020-7293 3400
website www.birminghampost.net
Editor David Brookes
Daily Mon–Sat 70p

Authoritative and well-written articles of industrial, political or general interest are considered, especially if they have relevance to the Midlands. Length: up to 1,000 words. Payment: by arrangement.

Coventry Telegraph

Corporation Street, Coventry CV1 1FP
tel 024-7663 3633 *fax* 024-7655 0869
website www.coventrytelegraph.net
Editor Darren Parkin
Daily Mon–Sat 40p

Topical, illustrated articles with a Coventry or Warwickshire interest. Length: up to 600 words. Payment: by arrangement.

Express & Star

Queen Street, Wolverhampton WV1 1ES
tel (01902) 313131 *fax* (01902) 319721
email newsdesk@expressandstar.co.uk
London office Room 12, Press Gallery, House of Commons, London SW1A 0AA
website www.expressandstar.com
Editor Adrian Faber
Daily Mon–Sat 40p

Founded 1874.

The Sentinel

Staffordshire Sentinel News & Media Ltd, Sentinel House, Etruria, Stoke-on-Trent ST1 5SS
tel (01782) 602525 *fax* (01782) 602616
email editor@thesentinel.co.uk
website www.thisisthesentinel.co.uk
Editor Michael Sassi
Daily Mon–Sat 33p

Articles and features of topical interest to the north Staffordshire/south Cheshire area. Illustrations: colour and b&w. Payment: by arrangement. Founded 1873.

Shropshire Star

Waterloo Road, Ketley, Telford TF1 5HU
tel (01952) 242424 *fax* (01952) 254605
website www.shropshirestar.com
Editor Sarah Jane Smith
Daily Mon–Sat 40p

Evening paper: news and features. No unsolicited material; write to features editor with outline of ideas. Payment: by arrangement. Founded 1964.

Sunday Mercury

6th Floor, Fort Dunlop, Fort Parkway, Birmingham B24 9FF
tel 0121-236 3366 *fax* 0121-234 5877
website www.sundaymercury.net
Editor David Brookes
Sun 90p

News specials or features of Midland interest. Illustrations: colour, b&w, cartoons. Payment: special rates for special matter.

Worcester News

Berrows House, Hylton Road, Worcester WR2 5JX
tel (01905) 748200 *fax* (01905) 742277
email kw@worcesternews.co.uk
website www.worcesternews.co.uk
Editor Kevin Ward
Daily Mon–Sat 40p

Local and national news, sport and features. Will consider unsolicited material. Welcomes ideas for articles and features. Length: 800 words (features), 300 words (news). Payment: negotiable. Illustrations: colour jpg files.

YORKSHIRE/HUMBERSIDE

Evening Courier

PO Box 19, King Cross Street, Halifax HX1 2SF
tel (01422) 260200 *fax* (01422) 260341
email editor@halifaxcourier.co.uk
website www.halifaxcourier.co.uk

Editor John Furbisher
Daily Mon–Sat 42p

Evening News
17–23 Aberdeen Walk, Scarborough,
North Yorkshire YO11 1BB
tel (01723) 363636 *fax* (01723) 379033
website www.scarborougheveningnews.co.uk
Editor Ed Asquith
Mon–Sat 37p

Grimsby Telegraph
80 Cleethorpe Road, Grimsby,
North East Lincolnshire DN31 3EH
tel (01472) 360360 *fax* (01472) 372257
email newsdesk@grimsbytelegraph.co.uk
website www.thisisgrimsby.co.uk
Editor Michelle Lalor
Daily Mon–Sat 36p

Considers general interest articles. Illustrations: line, half-tone, colour, cartoons. Payment: by arrangement. Founded 1897.

The Huddersfield Daily Examiner
Trinity Mirror Huddersfield Ltd,
Queen Street South, Huddersfield HD1 3DU
tel (01484) 430000 *fax* (01484) 437789
email editor@examiner.co.uk
website www.examiner.co.uk
Editor Roy Wright
Daily Examiner 49p, Weekend Examiner 62p

No contributions required at present. Founded 1851.

Hull Daily Mail
Blundell's Corner, Beverley Road, Hull HU3 1XS
tel (01482) 327111 *fax* (01482) 315353
website www.thisishullandeastriding.co.uk
Editor John Meehan
Daily Mon–Sat 38p

Lincolnshire Echo
Brayford Wharf East, Lincoln LN5 7AT
tel (01522) 820000 *fax* (01522) 804493
website www.thisislincolnshire.co.uk
Editor Jon Grubb
Daily Mon–Sat 36p

The Press
Newsquest York, PO Box 29, 76–86 Walmgate,
York YO1 9YN
tel (01904) 653051 *fax* (01904) 612853
email newsdesk@thepress.co.uk
website www.yorkpress.co.uk
Managing Editor Steve Hughes
Daily Mon–Sat 45p

Articles of North and East Yorkshire interest. Length: 500–1,000 words. Payment: by arrangement. Illustrations: line, half-tone. Founded 1882.

Sheffield Star
York Street, Sheffield S1 1PU
tel 0114-276 7676 *fax* 0114-272 5978
website www.thestar.co.uk
Editor Alan Powell
Daily Mon–Sat 42p

Well-written articles of local character. Length: about 500 words. Payment: by negotiation. Illustrations: topical photos, line drawings, graphics, cartoons. Founded 1887.

Telegraph & Argus
Hall Ings, Bradford BD1 1JR
tel (01274) 729511 *fax* (01274) 723634
email bradford.editorial@bradford.newsquest.co.uk
website www.thetelegraphandargus.co.uk
Editor Perry Austin-Clarke
Daily Mon–Sat 40p

Daily paper: news, articles and features relevant to or about the people of West Yorkshire. Length: up to 1,000 words. Illustrations: line, half-tone, colour. Payment: features from £15; line from £5, b&w and colour photos by negotiation. Founded 1868.

Yorkshire Evening Post
PO Box 168, Wellington Street, Leeds LS1 1RF
tel 0113-2432701 ext. 1434, 8917 *fax* 0113-388536
website www.yorkshireeveningpost.co.uk
Editor Paul Napier
Daily Mon–Sat 37p

News stories and feature articles. Illustrations: colour and b&w, cartoons. Payment: by negotiation. Founded 1890.

Yorkshire Post
Wellington Street, Leeds LS1 1RF
tel 0113-243 2701 *fax* 0113-238 8537
London office Dolphyn Court, 10–11 Gt Turnstile Street, London WC1V 7JU
tel 020-7025 3640
website www.yorkshirepost.co.uk
Editor Peter Charlton
Daily Mon–Fri 53p, Sat 90p
Supplements **Yorkshire Post Magazine**

Authoritative and well-written articles on topical subjects of general, literary or industrial interests. Length: max. 1,200 words. Payment: by arrangement. Founded 1754.

Writing for magazines

Richard Keeble explains the different types of features that magazines run and offers advice to freelances on how to approach writing for them – as they face the fall-out from the credit crunch.

There are well over 8,000 mainstream magazines published in Britain – and many hundreds of alternative publications. Research suggests that weekly consumer magazines are read by 39% of adults and monthlies by 48%. Yet while there appears to be an enormous variety of publications, the sector is dominated by just two companies: IPC and EMAP. IPC was sold by Reed Elsevier to Cinven, an investment company, in January 1998 for £860 million and then to AOL Time Warner for £1.3 billion in August 2001. By 2007 it was valued at £1.5 billion. Magazine publishing is clearly big business! EMAP (with 90 consumer magazines) was valued in 2000 at £1.8 billion. But by January 2008 the company had broken up, with its consumer magazine and radio businesses being sold to German publisher H. Bauer for £1.14 billion while its Business to Business (B2B) portfolio was sold to the Guardian Media Group and private equity group Apax. And so the shuffling of seats amongst the top owners continued…

Inevitably, too, the magazine sector has not been able to avoid the fall-out from the mounting global economic crisis. For instance, sales of the men's magazine *FHM* plunged 15.2% in its year-on-year figures in February 2010 while the BBC's *Match of the Day* fell 20% to 63,980. In contrast, in the women's lifestyle section, both *Red* and *Vanity* achieved record circulations. Tessa Mayes, top freelance investigative reporter, commented: 'The freelance feature rates on women's magazines haven't changed for a decade. Today feature editors tend to spend a lot more time deliberating over whether to commission a piece. And they offer freelances one rather than several commissions at once. Why? Smaller budgets is one reason but another is that features are more likely to be done in-house these days, "borrowed" from sister titles or bought in from syndication agencies.'

The differing genres

Freelancing for magazines will normally involve writing features. So it's important from the outset to have a clear idea about the different journalistic genres. Each will have its own writing style, research strategy, tone, and place in the publication. Here is a selection of the genres you might expect to find in a representative range of magazines.

Hard news

Hard news has the highest status in newspapers and tends to be on the front pages, while magazines may have an opening section carrying hard news. Hard news features usually open with the most striking details and the information given subsequently is generally of lesser importance. Some background details may be needed to make the news intelligible but description, analysis, comment and the subjective 'I' of the reporter are either excluded or included only briefly.

Soft news

Here the news element is strong and prominent at or near the opening but is treated in a lighter way. Largely based on factual information and quotations, the writing is nonetheless more colourful, with an emphasis on description and comment. The tone, established in the intro (opening) section, may be witty or ironic. The separation of hard and soft news emerged in the second half of the 19th century: the first, linked to notions of accuracy, objectivity, neutrality, was used for transmitting information; the second was more an entertainment genre. Magazine opening sections usually adopt this softer approach to news.

News features

A news feature is usually longer than a straight news story. The news angle is prominent, though not necessarily in the opening section, and quotes again are important. It can contain analysis, comment, descriptions, historical background detail, eye-witness reporting and deeper coverage of the issues and the range of sources.

Timeless features

These have no specific news angle; the special interest is provided by the subject or sources. For example, such a feature could explore young people's experiences of dealing with sexually transmitted diseases or coming out in terms of sexual orientation.

Backgrounder/preview/curtain-raiser features

Here the emphasis is not so much on reporting the news as on explaining it, or setting the scene for an event about to happen. For instance, if a major anti-globalisation demonstration is planned for mid-July, that month's magazine (produced well in advance) might carry a feature highlighting the historical background, the arguments of the protestors, the range of voices expected on the march, the hopes of the organisers and the predicted turnout, and so on. A retrospective is a similar feature looking back on an event.

Colour features

These concentrate on descriptive, eye-witness reporting, quotations and the build-up of factual details. They need not have a strong news angle. You may visit Highgate cemetery and describe (for a travel or tourist magazine) your experience of walking through it and talking to people. What do they think of Karl Marx, who is buried there?

Eye-witness news features

These are based on your observations of a newsy event, incorporating such elements as description, conversations, interviews, analysis and comment. You may accompany a rock star for a week as they tour the country and describe the experience for a rock magazine.

Profiles (sometimes called interviews)

These are portraits in words, usually based on interviews with the subject and sometimes also with their friends, critics, relations, work colleagues, etc.

Reviews

Reviews include descriptions and assessments of works of art, television programmes, exhibitions, books, theatre shows, CDs, rock gigs and so on.

Lifestyle features

Lifestyle features include advice columns (such as on health or education matters, gardening or computer problems).

Comment pieces

If you have an original voice, confidence in your personal writing style and a wide range of interests, then you might well aim to become a columnist. Editorials, on the other hand, reflect the institutional voice of the publication and are rarely written by freelances.

Getting ideas

You must be immersed in your specialist area, regularly reading and building up cuttings files from the relevant publications, websites, press releases, newsletters of pressure groups, etc. You will need to generate a network of contacts at public events, informal social gatherings, conferences, press launches. And ideas will emerge from conversations with friends and family. Remember your best resources are your own experiences. You have a teenage son who is showing no interest in politics; you could then plan a feature looking at the broader picture, talking to teachers, the youngsters themselves, other parents and political commentators. After 20 years in the same rat-race job you (your family, four dogs and three cats) are quitting to live simply in a remote cottage in Northumbria; so why not write about it?

Developing magazine feature ideas from news reports needs a special imaginative flair. A report from a university media monitoring unit criticises the increasing intrusiveness of the paparazzi photographers. A daily or weekly newspaper (working to relatively short deadlines) will follow up the report, interviewing editors and photographers and placing the current controversy in its historical context. A magazine writer, on the other hand, will have the luxury of a slightly longer deadline – and this throws up opportunities. You could spend a week on the back of a paparazzi's motorbike zooming about the streets of London and describe the experience, the feelings of the photographer and the people they shoot. The feature could involve eye-witness descriptions, dialogue, factual details: as you describe your movements around London so your copy is given extra movement and colour.

The ethical/political challenge

Always be aware of the ethical/political dilemmas stories can throw up. You are planning a vox pop (a collection of snappy quotes usually accompanied by photographs) about the work of paparazzi photographers: think about the range of people to be shown, in terms of race, gender, age and authority. If someone will speak to you only 'off the record' what do you do? How important is it for your feature to present a balancing range of views? One of your sources is an outspoken racist or sexist: how do you deal with their quotes? And so on.

The feature package

It's often best to think in terms of producing not just one single article (of say 2,500 words) but a package of contrasting features. These will have different lengths and tones and will provide the sub-editor with material for a more interesting layout. Thus the paparazzi package might contain the main eye-witness, participatory feature (1,200 words), a background piece outlining the history of the paparazzi and taking in their alleged role in the death of Princess Diana and the ensuing controversy (700 words) and a profile of a prominent photographer who argues strongly for (or against) legislation to restrain intrusive photographers (600 words).

The structure of the feature

The opening section

Most features do not start with the traditional five Ws (who, what, where, when, why) and the H (how) of the hard news opening section. The writing can be more flexible – but there is still an urgency needed in the copy to attract the attention of the reader. One of the most popular devices for helping the reader understand a complex event or issue is to begin by focusing on the experience or views of an individual. You are writing a piece about poverty on a bleak housing estate in Manchester, so you focus on the plight of an elderly woman, shivering in her unheated semi and terrified of the yobs who have raided her home three times over the last year and thrown fireworks through her letterbox.

According to the convention in the UK, most news stories don't begin with direct quotations. But features – and in particular profiles – often do. Quotes are useful because they can be colourful, succinct, and convey a lot about the personality of the person quoted. Thus a feature about 'flexploitation' (as employers are increasingly using flexi-time working arrangements to extend their exploitation of white-collar staff) could begin: 'We all sit in rows now. You log in and log out – even for your 20-minute lunch break. It's more like clocking in at a factory.'

The 'I' of the reporter is only rarely prominent in news intros. But the tone of magazine features (and not just those by regular columnists) can be far more personal, idiosyncratic, even witty. A feature exploring an issue such as fox-hunting, or debt in the developing world, can open with your views; an intro section for a piece about hairdressing can focus on a recent bad experience; and so on. Similarly, while news reports hardly ever begin with a question, features often do. Thus a feature about the boom in ski-ing in the Alps in the New Year could start: 'Have you tried to secure your travel ticket for the Alps yet?'

The body of the text

While colour, description, opinion, analysis, narrative, quotes, dialogue and historical context may be important in features, they are all still built on the cement of factual or emotional accuracy and a clear sense of structure. Just as in news stories the most important information comes first, with the less important details thereafter, so the body of the feature text is usually intended to expand on an opening section. At the same time, the writing styles of magazine features can be far more colourful. Emotional tones (angry, witty, ironic, condemnatory, adulatory) can vary along with textual rhythms. Indeed, before launching into your writing, as well as planning the structure, it is crucial to identify the emotional core of the piece. Try always to be as authentic as possible (within the constraints of the editorial policy of your target publication).

The closing section

A hard news story carries information in the order of its news value. The last paragraph is the least important and can be cut without destroying the overall impact. Features can be different, with the final section carrying its own, crucial significance. One feature may explore a range of views or experiences and conclude by passing a comment on them; another may argue a case and come to a conclusion in the final section. The final paragraph may raise a pointed question, contain a striking direct quote, summarise an argument or look ahead to a possible future.

Pitching ideas

You can choose to write or phone in your idea to a commissioning editor. There is no hard rule here. But even after you have spoken to an editor, they may well want you to spell out the idea by fax, letter or email. Make sure the grammar, spelling, facts, and punctuation in your proposal (as in your copy) are spot on. And don't be tempted to spell out the idea at length. The essential idea should be summarised in one paragraph at most: 'With Martin Scorsese's *Gangs of New York* due to be released in two months, my

1,200-word feature will look critically at the way in which Hollywood has represented street gangs in the past.' Don't be vague. Don't say: 'I propose a feature about prostitution in inner cities.' Rather: 'A report published this week has highlighted the rise of prostitution in inner cities. To what extent are students (both male and female) funding their studies through prostitution?'

Dangers

Publications may steal your ideas and give them to someone else to follow up. And the freelance has absolutely no protection in law against this kind of theft. While written work can be copyrighted, ideas can occur to two people at the same time. One solution is to provide only a bare minimum of background details before the idea is accepted. Personal contact with the commissioning editor also helps create mutual trust and confidence. The best solution is to prove your abilities to the publication with a series of stories, sent on spec or to commission, so they will be concerned not to lose your work to other competitors. Make sure you have a copy of all submitted work. If it is rejected you may want to rework it with some new angles/quotes for a different publication. And be persistent: remember that *Gone with the Wind* was rejected 25 times before it was published.

Payment

How much should you expect to be paid? Well, the National Union of Journalists draws up a regularly updated list of minimum freelance rates which will give you some idea of what to expect. And remember that if you are a self-employed freelance you own the copyright to your work. This does not mean refusing further use of the material: you can license it, giving permission for a specific use for an agreed fee. Whatever freelancing you end up doing, enjoy the ethical, political, writing challenges. It's not easy but the personal rewards can be substantial. Good luck!

Richard Keeble is Professor of Journalism at Lincoln University. He has feelanced for a range of publications including *Tribune, Press Gazette, Peace News*, the *Journalist*, www.medialens.org and www.fifth-estate-online.co.uk.

See also...

- *Writing for newspapers,* page 6
- *Writing features for newspapers and magazines,* page 3

Further reading

Atton, Chris, *Alternative Media*, Sage, 2002

Atton, Chris and James F. Hamilton, *Alternative Journalism*, Sage, 2008

Glover, Stephen (ed.), *The Penguin Book of Journalism*, Penguin, 1999; pbk 2000

Hennessy, Brendan, *Writing Feature Articles*, Focal Press, 4th edn, 2006

Hicks, Wynford, with Harriett Gilbert and Sally Adams, *Writing for Journalists*, Routledge, 2nd edn, 2008

McKay, Jenny, *The Magazines Handbook*, Routledge, 2nd edn, 2005

Phillips, Angela, *Good Writing for Journalists*, Sage 2006

Willings Press Guide, Media Information Ltd, annual

Magazines UK and Ireland

Listings for regional newspapers start on page 19 and listings for national newspapers start on page 11. For quick reference, magazines are listed by subject area starting on page 755.

Accountancy

145 London Road, Kingston-upon-Thames, Surrey KT2 6SR
tel 020-8247 1389 *fax* 020-8247 1195
email accountancynews@cch.co.uk
website www.accountancymagazine.com
Editor Sally Percy
Monthly £84 p.a. Quarterly £21 (UK), £24.90 (overseas)

Articles on accounting, taxation, financial, legal and other subjects likely to be of professional interest to accountants in practice or industry, and to top management generally. Founded 1889.

Accountancy Age

Incisive Media, 32–34 Broadwick Street, London W1A 2HG
tel 020-7316 9000 *fax* 020-7316 9250
email news@accountancyage.com
website www.accountancyage.com
Editor Gavin Hinks
Weekly £2 (£100 p.a.)

Articles of accounting, financial and business interest. Illustrations: colour photos; freelance assignments commissioned. Payment: by arrangement. Founded 1969.

Accounting & Business

Association of Chartered Certified Accountants, 29 Lincolns Inn Fields, London WC2A 3EE
tel 020-7059 5000 *fax* 020-7059 5050
email info@accaglobal.com
website www.accaglobal.com
Editor Chris Quick
10 p.a. £10 £85 p.a.

Journal of the Association of Chartered Certified Accountants. Accountancy, finance and business topics of relevance to accountants and finance directors. Length: 1100 words. Illustrated. Founded 1998.

Acumen Literary Journal

6 The Mount, Higher Furzeham, Brixham, South Devon TQ5 8QY
tel (01803) 851098
email pwoxley@aol.com
website www.acumen-poetry.co.uk
Editor Patricia Oxley
3 p.a. (Jan/May/Sept). £4.50 or £12.50 p.a.

Poetry, literary and critical articles, reviews, literary memoirs, etc. Send sae with submissions. Payment: small. Founded 1985.

Aeroplane Monthly

IPC Media Ltd, The Blue Fin Building, 110 Southwark Street, London SE1 0SU
tel 020-3148 4100
email editoraero@ipcmedia.com
website www.aeroplanemonthly.com
Editor Michael Oakey
Monthly £3.99

Articles and photos relating to historical aviation. Length: up to 3000 words. Illustrations: line, half-tone, colour, cartoons. Payment: £60 per 1000 words, payable on publication; photos £10–£40; colour £80 per page. Founded 1973.

Aesthetica Magazine

PO Box 371, York YO23 1WL
tel (01904) 479168
email info@aestheticamagazine.com
website www.aestheticamagazine.com
Editor Cherie Federico
Bi-monthly £3.90

National arts and cultural magazine featuring visual arts, film, theatre, literature and music. News and articles. For freelance opportunities conact the editor. Founded 2002.

Africa-Asia Confidential

Asempa Ltd, 73 Farringdon Road, London EC1M 3JQ
tel 020-7831 3511 *fax* 020-7831 6778
website www.africa-asia-confidential.com
Editor Patrick Smith
Monthly £49 p.a. students, £271 p.a. institutions, £319 companies

News on the Africa–Asia axis. Unsolicited contributions welcome but must be exclusive and not published elsewhere. Length: 1200 words (features), 600 words (briefings). Payment: from £200 per 1000 words. No illustrations. Founded 2007.

Africa Confidential

Asempa Ltd, 73 Farringdon Road, London EC1M 3JQ
tel 020-7831 3511 *fax* 020-7831 6778
website www.africa-confidential.com
Editor Patrick Smith
Fortnightly £737 p.a.

News and analysis of political and economic developments in Africa. Unsolicited contributions welcomed, but must be exclusive and not published elsewhere. Length: 1200-word features, 200-word pointers. Payment: from £300 per 1000 words. No illustrations. Founded 1960.

Africa: St Patrick's Missions

St Patrick's, Kiltegan, Co. Wicklow,
Republic of Ireland
tel (059) 6473600 *fax* (059) 6473622
email africa@iol.ie
website www.spms.org
Editors Rev. Tom Kiggins, Rev. Martin Smith
9 p.a. £8 p.a. (€12)

Articles of missionary and topical religious interest. Length: up to 1000 words. Illustrations: line, half-tone, colour.

African Business

IC Publications Ltd, 7 Coldbath Square,
London EC1R 4LQ
tel 020-7841 3210 *fax* 020-7841 3211
email editorial@africasia.com
website www.africasia.com
Editor Anver Versi
Monthly £2.70, £40 p.a.

Articles on business, economic and financial topics of interest to businessmen, ministers, officials concerned with African affairs. Length: 1000–1400 words; shorter coverage 500 words. Illustrations: line, half-tone, cartoons. Payment: £90–£100 per 1000 words; £1 per column cm for illustrations. Founded 1978.

Agenda

The Wheelwrights, Fletching Street, Mayfield,
East Sussex TN20 6TL
tel/fax (01435) 873703
email editor@agendapoetry.co.uk
website www.agendapoetry.co.uk
Editor Patricia McCarthy
Quarterly. £28 p.a. (£35 libraries, institutions and overseas); £22 OAPs/students

Poetry and criticism. Study the journal before submitting MSS with an sae, or by email. Include email address and a brief biography. Young poets and artists aged 16–38 are invited to submit work for online Broadsheets.

AIR International

Key Publishing Ltd, PO Box 100, Stamford,
Lincs. PE9 1XQ
tel (01780) 755131 *fax* (01780) 751323
email airint@keypublishing.com
Editor Mark Ayton
Monthly £4.20 (£41 p.a.)

Technical articles on aircraft; features on topical aviation subjects – civil and military. Length: up to 3000 words. Illustrations: colour transparencies/prints, b&w prints/line drawings. Payment: £50 per 1000 words or by negotiation; £20 colour, £10 b&w. Founded 1971.

All Out Cricket

Unit 3–23 Kennington Court, 1–3 Brixton Road,
London SW9 6DE
tel 020-3176 0187
email att@alloutcricket.com
website www.alloutcricket.com
Editor Andy Afford
12 p.a. £3.95 (£45 p.a.)

Magazine of the Professional Cricketers' Association. Humour, insight, expert commentary interviews, photography and lifestyle. Email editor with ideas first. Payment by negotiation. Founded 2004.

Amateur Gardening

IPC Media Ltd, Westover House, West Quay Road,
Poole, Dorset BH15 1JG
tel (01202) 440840 *fax* (01202) 440860
website www.amateurgardening.com
Editor Tim Rumball
Weekly £1.90

No longer accept unsolicited material. Founded 1884.

Amateur Photographer

(incorporating Photo Technique)
IPC Media, The Blue Fin Building,
110 Southwark Street, London SE1 0SU
tel 020-3148 5000
email amateurphotographer@ipcmedia.com
website www.amateurphotographer.co.uk
Editor Damien Demolder
Weekly £2.40 (£122.40 p.a.)

Editorial submissions are not encouraged. Founded 1884.

Ambit

17 Priory Gardens, London N6 5QY
tel 020-8340 3566
website www.ambitmagazine.co.uk
Editor Martin Bax *Poetry Editors* Henry Graham, Carol-Ann Duffy *Prose Editor* Geoff Nicholson *Art Editor* Mike Foreman
Quarterly. £7 inc. p&p (£28 p.a. UK, £30/€44 Europe, £32/$64 rest of world; £40 p.a., £42/€62 p.a., £44/$88 p.a. institutions)

Poetry, short fiction, art, poetry reviews. New and established writers and artists. Payment: by arrangement. Illustrations: line, half-tone, colour. Founded 1959.

AN Magazine

AN: The Artists Information Company, 1st Floor,
7–15 Pink Lane, Newcastle upon Tyne NE1 5DW
tel 0191-241 8000 *fax* 0191-241 8001
email edit@a-n.co.uk
website www.a-n.co.uk
Editor Gillian Nicol
Monthly £8

Magazine for visual and applied artists and arts professionals, including a round-up of current shows and projects, in-depth reviews, art and cultural news, special features plus opportunities and art vacancies. There are 12-month subscription options for artists, arts individuals and organisations which include a password to the website plus free copies of a-n Collections, Research papers and other special titles as published. Illustrations: transparencies and digital images. Payment: £130 per 1000 words. Founded as *Artists Newsletter* in 1980.

Angler's Mail

IPC Media Ltd, The Blue Fin Building,
110 Southwark Street, London SE1 0SU
tel 020-3148 4159 *fax* 020-3148 8129
email anglersmail@ipcmedia.com
website www.anglersmail.com
Editor Tim Knight, *Features Editor* Richard Howard
Weekly £1.50

News items about coarse fishing. Payment: by agreement.

Angling Times

Bauer Consumer Media, Bushfield House,
Orton Centre, Peterborough PE2 5UW
tel (01733) 395106 *fax* (01733) 465844
email rich.lee@bauermedia.co.uk
website www.gofishing.co.uk/Angling-Times
Editor Richard Lee
Weekly £1.60, £60 p.a.

Articles, pictures, news stories, on all forms of angling. Illustrations: line, half-tone, colour. Payment: by arrangement. Founded 1953.

Apollo

22 Old Queen Street, London SW1H 9HP
tel 020-7961 015 0
email editorial@apollomag.com
website www.apollo-magazine.com
Editor Oscar Humphries
Monthly £5.95

Scholarly and topical articles of about 2000–3000 words on art, architecture, ceramics, photography, furniture, armour, glass, sculpture, and any subject connected with art and collecting. Interviews with collectors. Exhibition and book reviews, articles on current developments in museums and art galleries, regular columns on the art market and contemporary art. Payment: by arrangement. Illustrations: colour. Founded 1925.

Aquila

New Leaf Publishing Ltd, PO Box 2518, Eastbourne, East Sussex BN21 2BB
tel (01323) 431313 *fax* (01323) 731136
email info@aquila.co.uk
website www.aquila.co.uk
Editor Jackie Berry
Monthly £40 p.a.

Dedicated to encouraging children aged 8–13 to reason and create, and to develop a caring nature. Short stories and serials of up to 3 parts. Occasional features commissioned from writers with specialist knowledge. Approach in writing with ideas and sample of writing style, with sae. Length: 700–800 words (features), 1000–1100 words (stories or per episode of a serial). Payment: £75 (features); £90 (stories), £80 (per episode). Founded 1993.

The Architects' Journal

EMAP Construct, Greater London House,
Hampstead Road, London NW1 7EJ
tel 020-7728 5000
website www.architectsjournal.co.uk
Editor Kieran Long
Weekly £4 (£150 p.a.)

Articles (mainly technical) on architecture, planning and building accepted only with prior agreement of synopsis. Illustrations: photos and drawings. Payment: by arrangement. Founded 1895.

Architectural Design

John Wiley & Sons, 3rd Floor, International House,
7 High Street, London W5 5DB
tel 020-8326 3815 *fax* 020-8326 3801
Editor Helen Castle
6 double issues p.a., £22.99 single issue, £110 p.a.

International architectural publication comprising an extensively illustrated thematic profile and magazine back section, *AD Plus*. Uncommissioned articles not accepted. Illustrations: drawings and photos, line (colour preferred). Payment: by arrangement. Founded 1930.

The Architectural Review

EMAP Construct, Greater London House,
Hampstead Road, London NW1 7EJ
tel 020-7728 4591 *fax* 020-7728 4400
email kieran.long@emap.com
website www.arplus.com
Editor-in-Chief Kieran Long
£9 for 3 issues and then £52 p.a.

Articles on architecture and the allied arts. Writers must be thoroughly qualified. Length: up to 3000 words. Payment: by arrangement. Illustrations: photos, drawings, etc. Founded 1896.

Architecture Today

161 Rosebery Avenue, London EC1R 4QX
tel 020-7837 0143 *fax* 020-7837 0155
website www.architecturetoday.co.uk
Editor Chris Rogers
10 p.a. £4.50, £45 p.a.

Mostly commissioned articles and features on today's European architecture. Length: 200–800 words. Illustrations: colour. Payment: by negotiation. Founded 1989.

Art Business Today

The Fine Art Trade Guild, 16–18 Empress Place,
London SW6 1TT
tel 020-7381 6616 *fax* 020-7381 2596

email abt@fineart.co.uk
website www.artbusinesstoday.co.uk
5 p.a. £26 p.a.

Distributed to the fine art and framing industry. Covers essential information on new products and technology, market trends and business analysis. Length: 800–1600 words. Illustrations: colour photos, cartoons. Payment: by arrangement. Founded 1905.

Art Monthly

4th Floor, 28 Charing Cross Road,
London WC2H 0DB
tel 020-7240 0389 *fax* 020-7497 0726
email info@artmonthly.co.uk
website www.artmonthly.co.uk
Editor Patricia Bickers
10 p.a. £4.40 (£44 p.a.)

Features on modern and contemporary visual artists and art history, art theory and art-related issues; exhibition and book reviews. All material commissioned. Length: 750–1500 words. Illustrations: b&w photos. Payment: features £100–£200; none for photos. Founded 1976.

The Art Newspaper

70 South Lambeth Road, London SW8 1RL
tel 020-7735 3331 *fax* 020-7735 3332
email contact@theartnewspaper.com
website www.theartnewspaper.com
Editor Jane Morris
11 p.a. £6.95, £69 p.a.

International coverage of visual art, news, politics, law, exhibitions with some feature pages. Length: 200–1000 words. Illustrations: b&w photos. Payment: £120 per 1000 words. Founded 1990.

Art Quarterly

The Art Fund, Millais House, 7 Cromwell Place,
London SW7 2JN
tel 020-7225 4800 *fax* 020-7225 4848
email info@artfund.org
website www.artfund.org
Editor Caroline Bugler
Quarterly Free to members

Magazine of the Art Fund. Features on current events in the art world and extensive coverage of the Art Fund's campaigns and grant-giving activities.

Art Review

Art Review Ltd, 1 Sekforde Street, London EC1R 0BE
tel 020-7107 2760 *fax* 020-7107 2761
email editorial@artreview.com
website www.artreview.com
Editor Mark Rappolt
Monthly £5 (£29 p.a.)

Modern and contemporary art and style features and reviews. Proposals welcome. Payment: from £350 per 1000 words. Illustrations: colour. Founded 1949.

The Artist

The Artists' Publishing Co. Ltd, Caxton House,
63–65 High Street, Tenterden, Kent TN30 6BD
tel (01580) 763673
Editor Sally Bulgin
Monthly £3.50

Practical, instructional articles on painting for all amateur and professional artists. Payment: by arrangement. Illustrations: line, half-tone, colour. Founded 1931.

Artists & Illustrators

26–30 Old Church Street, London SW3 5BY
tel 020-7349 3150 *fax* 020-7349 3160
email info@artistsandillustrators.co.uk
website www.artistsandillustrators.co.uk
Editor Steve Pill
Monthly £3.75

Practical and inspirational articles for amateur and professional artists. Length: 500–1500 words. Illustrations: high resolution digital images, hand-drawn illustrations. Payment: variable. Founded 1986.

AS Magazine

Hampton House, 2 Weymouth Street,
London W1W 5BT
tel 020-7636 4343 *fax* 020-7636 2323
email editor@asmagazine.co.uk
website www.amateurstagemagazine.co.uk
Editor Charles Vance
Monthly £2.40

Articles on all aspects of the amateur theatre, preferably practical and factual. Length: 600–2000 words. Illustrations: photos, line drawings. Payment: none. Founded 1946.

Assent

Room E701, Kedleston Road, University of Derby,
Derby DE22 1GB
Poetry Editors Adrian Buckner, Jason Lee, *Reviews* Julia Gaze (5 Charlton Grove, Beeston, Notts. NG9 1GY)
3 p.a. £4 £12 p.a. (£20 overseas)

Poems, reviews, articles. Payment: complimentary copy. Founded 1946.

Astronomy Now

Pole Star Publications, PO Box 175, Tonbridge,
Kent TN10 4ZY
tel (01732) 446110 *fax* (01732) 300148
email editorial2010@astronomynow.com
website www.astronomynow.com
Editor Keith Cooper
Monthly £3.25

Specialises in translating exciting astronomy research into articles for the lay reader. Also covers amateur astronomy with equipment reviews and observing notes. Send sae for writers' guidelines. Length: 1000–2000 words. Payment: 15p per word; from £10 per photo. Founded 1987.

Athletics Weekly

Descartes Publishing Ltd, PO Box 1026,
Peterborough PE1 9GZ

tel (01733) 808550 *fax* (01733) 808530
email jason.henderson@athletics-weekly.com
website www.athleticsweekly.com
Editor Jason Henderson
Weekly £2.95

News and features on track and field athletics, road running, cross country, fell and race walking. Material mostly commissioned. Length: 300–1500 words. Illustrations: colour and b&w action and head/shoulder photos, line. Payment: varies. Founded 1945.

Attitude

Ground Floor, 211 Old Street, London EC1V 9NR
tel 020-7608 6446 *fax* 020-7608 6320
email attitude@attitude.co.uk
website www.attitude.co.uk
Editor Matthew Todd
Monthly £3 £26 for 13 issues subscription

Men's style magazine aimed primarily but not exclusively at gay men. Covers style/fashion, interviews, reviews, celebrities, humour. Illustrations: colour transparencies, b&w prints. Payment: £150 per 1000 words; £100 per full page illustration. Founded 1994.

The Author

84 Drayton Gardens, London SW10 9SB
tel 020-7373 6642
Editor Andrew Rosenheim
Quarterly £12

Organ of the Society of Authors. Commissioned articles from 1000–2000 words on any subject connected with the legal, commercial or technical side of authorship. Little scope for the freelance writer: preliminary letter advisable. Illustrations: line, occasional cartoons. Payment: by arrangement. Founded 1890.

Auto Express

Dennis Publishing Ltd, 30 Cleveland Street, London W1T 4JD
tel 020-7907 6000 *fax* 020-7907 6234
email editorial@autoexpress.co.uk
website www.autoexpress.co.uk
Editor David Johns
Weekly £2

News stories, and general interest features about drivers as well as cars. Illustrations: colour photos. Payment: features £350 per 1000 words; photos, varies. Founded 1988.

Autocar

Haymarket Publishing Ltd, Teddington Studios, Broom Road, Teddington, Middlesex TW11 9BE
tel 020-8267 5630 *fax* 020-8267 5759
email autocar@haymarket.com
website www.autocar.co.uk
Editor Chas Hallett
Weekly £2.80

Articles on all aspects of cars, motoring and the motor industry: general, practical, competition and technical. Illustrations: line (litho), colour and electronic (Illustrator). Press day news: Thursday. Payment: varies; mid-month following publication. Founded 1895.

Aviation News

Key Publishing, PO Box 100, Stamford PE9 1XQ
tel (01780) 751323
email editor@aviation-news.co.uk
website www.aviation-news.co.uk
Editor David Baker
Monthly £3.90

Covers all aspects of aviation. Many articles commissioned; will consider competent articles exploring fresh ground or presenting an individual point of view on technical matters. Illustrated, mainly with photos. Payment: by arrangement.

Back Street Heroes

19th Floor, 1 Canada Square, Canary Wharf, London E14 5AP
tel 020-7772 8300 *fax* 020-7772 8585
Editor Stu Garland
Monthly £3.99

Custom motorcycle features plus informed lifestyle pieces. Illustrations: colour, cartoons. Payment: by arrangement. Founded 1983.

Backtrack

Pendragon Publishing, PO Box 3, Easingwold, York YO61 3YS
tel/fax (01347) 824397
email pendragonpublishing@btinternet.com
website www.pendragonpublishing.co.uk
Editor Michael Blakemore
Monthly £3.70

British railway history from1820s to 1980s. Welcomes ideas from writers and photographers. Articles must be well researched, authoritative and accompanied by illustrations. Length: 3000–5000 words (main features), 500–3000 words (articles). Illustrations: colour and b&w. Payment: £30 per 1000 words, £18.50 colour, £10.00 b&w. Founded 1986.

Balance

Diabetes UK, 10 Parkway, London NW1 7AA
tel 020-7424 1000 *fax* 020-7424 1001
email info@diabetes.org.uk
website www.diabetes.org.uk
Editor Martin Cullen
Bi-monthly £3.95

Articles on diabetes and related health and lifestyle issues. Length: 1000–1500 words. Payment: by arrangement. Illustrations: colour. Founded 1935.

The Banker

FT Business, 1 Southwark Bridge, London SE1 9HL
tel 020-7775 6359

email stephen.timewell@ft.com
website www.thebanker.com
Editor-in-Chief Stephen Timewell
Monthly £245 p.a.

Articles on investment banking and finance, retail banking, banking technology, banking services and systems; bank analysis and top 1000 listings. Illustrations: half-tones and full colour of people, charts, tables, maps, etc. Founded 1926.

Baptist Times

PO Box 54, 129 Broadway, Didcot, Oxon OX11 8XB
tel (01235) 517670 *fax* (01235) 517678
website www.baptisttimes.co.uk
Editor Mark Woods
Weekly 80p (£53 p.a.)

Religious or social affairs, news, features and reviews. Payment: by arrangement. Founded 1855.

BBC magazines – see Inside the BBC, page 395

BBC Countryfile Magazine
website www.bbccountryfile.com

BBC Easy Cook
website www.bbcmagazines.com/ads/easycook

BBC Gardeners' World
website www.gardenersworld.com

BBC Good Food
website www.bbcgoodfood.com

BBC Good Homes
website www.bbcgoodhomes.com

BBC History Magazine
website www.bbchistorymagazine.com

BBC Music Magazine
website www.bbcmusicmagazine.com

BBC Top Gear
website www.topgear.com

BBC Wildlife
website www.wildlifemagazine.com

Focus
website www.focusmag.co.uk

Gardens Illustrated
website www.gardensillustrated.com

Homes & Antiques
website www.homesandantiques.com

Olive
website www.olivemagazine.co.uk

Sky at Night Magazine
website www.skyatnightmagazine.com

What to Wear
website www.bbcmagazines.com/whattowear

The Beano

D.C. Thomson & Co. Ltd, 80 Kingsway East, Dundee DD4 8SL
email adigby@dcthompson.co.uk
185 Fleet Street, London EC4A 2HS
tel 020-7400 1030 *fax* 020-7400 1089
Editor Alan Digby
Weekly £1.35

Comic strips for children aged 6–12. Series, 11–22 pictures. Artwork only. Payment: on acceptance.

Bella

H Bauer Publishing, Academic House, 24–28 Oval Road, London NW1 7DT
tel 020-7241 8000 *fax* 020-7241 8056
Editor Julia Davis
Weekly 85p

Women's magazine with celebrity interviews, exclusive photos, real life stories, high street fashion, diet advice, health, food and travel. Payment: by arrangement. Founded 1987.

Best

ACP–NatMag, 33 Broadwick Street, London W1F 0DQ
tel 020-7339 4500 *fax* 020-7339 4580
Editor Jackie Hatton, *Features Editor* Charlotte Seligman
Weekly 89p

Short stories. No other uncommissioned work accepted, but always willing to look at ideas/outlines. Length: 1000 words for short stories, variable for other work. Payment: by agreement. Founded 1987.

Best of British

Church Lane Publishing Ltd, The Clock Tower, 6 Market Gate, Market Deeping, Lincs PE6 8DL
tel (01778) 342814, 380906 *fax* (01778) 342814
email info@bestofbritishmag.co.uk
website www.bestofbritishmag.co.uk
Editor Linne Matthews
Editor-in-Chief Ian Beacham
Monthly £3.75

Nostalgic features about life in the 1940s, 1950s and 1960s together with stories celebrating interesting aspects of Britain today. Length: max. 1200 words. Illustrations: colour and b&w. Payment: at editor's discretion. Founded 1994.

The Big Issue

1–5 Wandsworth Road, London SW8 2LN
tel 020-7526 3200 *fax* 020-7526 3201
email info@thebigissue.com
website www.bigissue.com
Editor-in-Chief Charles Howgego
Weekly £1.50, £250 p.a.

Features, current affairs, reviews, interviews – of general interest and on social issues. Length: 1000 words (features). No short stories or poetry. Illustrations: colour and b&w photos and line. Payment: £160 per 1000 words. Founded 1991.

The Big Issue Cymru

55 Charles Street, Cardiff CF10 2GD
tel 029-2025 5670 *fax* 029-2025 5673
email editorial@bigissuecymru.co.uk
website www.bigissuecymru.co.uk
Editor Rachel Howells
Weekly £1.50

The Welsh edition of *The Big Issue*. Content is relevant to Wales: some articles are taken from the main London edition but news, features, arts and music coverage are locally sourced. Considers unsolicited material. Welcomes ideas for articles and features. No poetry or short stories. Length: 1000–1500 words (articles/features), 200–400 words (news). Illustrations: colour and b&w prints and artwork. Payment: by arrangement. Founded 1994.

The Big Issue in the North

The Big Issue in the North Ltd, The Big Life Group, 123 Moss Lane East, Manchester M15 5DD
tel 0161-831 5550
website www.bigissueinthenorth.com
Editor Kevin Gopal
Weekly £2

Articles of general interest and on social issues; arts features and news covering the north of England. No fiction or poetry, except by the homeless. Contact the editorial department to discuss ideas. Length: 1000 words (features/articles), 300–500 (news), 700 (arts features). Payment: £120 per 1000 words/12p per word. Colour transparencies, puzzles and quizzes. Founded 1992.

The Big Issue in Scotland

The Big Issue in Scotland Ltd, 2nd Floor, 43 Bath Street, Glasgow G2 1HW
tel 0141-352 7260 *fax* 0141-333 9049
email editorial@bigissuescotland.com
website www.bigissuescotland.com
Editor Paul McNamee
Weekly £1.50

Features on social issues, human rights, the environment, injustice, Scotland, medical, health and crime plus news and arts coverage. Also international features/news. Length: 1000–2000 words (articles); 300–400 words (news). Illustrations: colour and b&w. Payment: £120 per 1000 words; £60 per photo/illustration. Founded 1993.

The Big Issue South West

5 Brunswick Court, Brunswick Square, Bristol BS2 8PE
tel 0117-916 6593 *fax* 0117-916 6599
email admin@bigissuesouthwest.co.uk
website www.bigissuesouthwest.co.uk
Editor Charles Howgego
Weekly £1.50

Social news, general interest features and arts information for the South West. Considers unsolicited material. Length: 1200 words (articles/features), 100–1200 words (news). Payment: negotiable. Illustrations: colour, payment negotiable. Founded 1991.

Bike

Bauer Consumer Media, Media House, Lynchwood, Peterborough PE2 6EA
tel (01733) 468181 *fax* (01733) 468196
email bike@bauermedia.com
website www.bikemagazine.co.uk
Editor Tim Thompson
Monthly £4.10

Motorcycle magazine. Interested in articles, features, news. Length: articles/features 1000–3000 words. Illustrations: colour and b&w photos. Payment: £140 per 1000 words; photos per size/position. Founded 1971.

Bird Watching

Bauer Consumer Media, Media House, Lynchwood, Peterborough PE2 6EA
tel (01733) 468201
website www.birdwatching.co.uk
Editor Sheena Harvey
Monthly £3.95

Broad range of bird-related features and photography, particularly looking at bird behaviour, bird news, reviews and UK birdwatching sites. Limited amount of overseas features. Emphasis on providing accurate information in entertaining ways. Send synopsis first. Length: up to 1200 words. Illustrations: emailed jpgs and photo images on CD, bird identification artwork. Payment: by negotiation. Founded 1986.

Birding World

Sea Lawn, Coast Road, Cley next the Sea, Holt, Norfolk NR25 7RZ
tel (01263) 740913 *fax* (01263) 741014
email steve@birdingworld.co.uk
website www.birdingworld.co.uk
Editor Steve Gantlett
Monthly £47 p.a. (£54 p.a. Europe; £58 p.a. rest of the world, airmail)

Magazine for keen birdwatchers. Articles and news stories about mainly European ornithology, with the emphasis on ground-breaking new material and identification. Length: up to 3000 words (articles); up to 1500 words (news). Illustrations: good quality colour photos of birds. Founded 1987.

Birdwatch

Solo Publishing Ltd, The Chocolate Factory, 5 Clarendon Road, London N22 6XJ

tel 020-8881 0550 *fax* 020-8881 0990
website www.birdwatch.co.uk
Editor Dominic Mitchell
Monthly £3.95

Topical articles on all aspects of birds and birding, including conservation, identification, sites and habitats, equipment, overseas destinations. Length: 700–1500 words. Illustrations: high-res jpegs (300 dpi at 1500 pixels min. width) of wild British and European birds considered; submit on CD/DVD. Artwork by negotiation. Payment: from £50 per 1000 words; colour: photos £15–£40, cover £75, line by negotiation; b&w: photos £10, line £10–£40. Founded 1991.

Bizarre

Dennis Publishing, 30 Cleveland Street, London W1T 4JD
tel 020-7907 6000 *fax* 020-7907 6439
email bizarre@dennis.co.uk
website www.bizarremag.com
Editor David McComb
Monthly £3.50

Features on strange events, adventure, cults, weird people, celebrities, etc. Study the magazine for style before submitting ideas by post or fax. No fiction. Payment: 20p per word. Colour transparencies and prints: £200 per dps, £125 per page. Founded 1997.

Black Beauty & Hair

Hawker Publications, 2nd Floor, Culvert House, Culvert Road, London SW11 5DH
tel 020-7720 2108 *fax* 020-7498 3023
email info@blackbeautyandhair.com
website www.blackbeautyandhair.com
Editor Irene Shelley
Bi-monthly £3 (£15 p.a.)

Beauty and style articles relating specifically to the black woman; celebrity features. True-life stories and salon features. Length: approx. 1000 words. Illustrations: colour and b&w photos. Payment: £100 per 1000 words; photos £25–£75. Founded 1982.

Black Static

TTA Press, 5 Martins Lane, Witcham, Ely, Cambs. CB6 2LB
website www.ttapress.com
Editor Andy Cox
Bi-monthly £3.95 (£21 for 6 issues)

New horror and dark fantasy stories. Also interviews with, and profiles of, authors and film-makers. Send sae with all submissions. Considers unsolicited material and welcomes ideas for articles and features. Length: 3000–4000 words (articles and features), short stories unrestricted. Illustrations: send samples and portfolios. Payment: by arrangement. Founded 1994.

Bliss

Brockbourne House, 77 Mount Ephraim, Tunbridge Wells, Kent TN4 8BS
tel (01892) 500100 *fax* (01892) 545666
email bliss@panini.co.uk
website www.blissmag.co.uk
Editor Leslie Sinoway
Monthly £2.50

Glamorous young women's glossy magazine. Bright, intimate, American A5 format, with real life reports, celebrities, beauty, fashion, shopping, advice, quizzes. Payment: by arrangement. Founded 1995.

Blueprint

Progressive Media Markets, 6–14 Underwood Street, London N1 7JQ
tel 020-7549 2542
email vrichardson@blueprintmagazine.co.uk
website www.blueprintmagazine.co.uk
Acting Editor Peter Kelly, *Associate Editor* Tim Abrahams
12 p.a. £4.75 (£49 p.a.)

Magazine for architects and designers. Interested in articles, features and reviews. Length: up to 2,500 words. Illustrations: colour and b&w photos and line. Payment: negotiable. Founded 1983.

BMA News

British Medical Association, BMA House, Tavistock Square, London WC1H 9JP
tel 020-7383 6122 *fax* 020-7383 6566
Editors Caroline Winter-Jones, Carol Harris
49 p.a. £92 p.a.

News and features. Length: 700–2000 words (features), 100–300 words (news). Illustrations: any colour and b&w artwork. Payment: by negotiation. Founded 1966.

The Book Collector

(incorporating Bibliographical Notes and Queries)
The Collector Ltd, PO Box 12426, London W11 3GW
tel 020-7792 3492 *fax* 020-7792 3492
email editor@thebookcollector.co.uk
website www.thebookcollector.co.uk
Editorial Board Nicolas Barker (Editor), A. Edwards, J. Fergusson, T. Hofmann, D. McKitterick, Joan Winterkorn
Quarterly £50 p.a.; Europe (airmail) £60 (€76.50 by credit card only); rest of the world (airmail) £65 (US$105)

Articles, biographical and bibliographical, on the collection and study of printed books and MSS. Payment: for reviews only. Founded 1952.

Book and Magazine Collector

5th Floor, 31–32 Park Row, Leeds LS2 5JD
tel 0113-200 2929 *fax* 0113-200 2928
email editor@bookandmagazinecollector.com
Editor Christopher Peachment
13 p.a. £3.50

Articles about collectable authors/publications/ subjects. Articles must be bibliographical and include a full bibliography and price guide (no purely biographical features). Approach in writing or email with ideas. Length: 2000–4000 words. Illustrations: colour and b&w artwork. Payment: £200 per article. Founded 1984.

Books Ireland

11 Newgrove Avenue, Dublin 4, Republic of Ireland
tel (01) 2692185
email booksi@eircom.net
Editor Jeremy Addis, *Features Editor* Shirley Kelly
Monthly (exc. Jan, Jul, Aug) €3.50 (€35 p.a.)

Reviews of Irish-interest and Irish-author books, articles of interest to librarians, booksellers and readers. Length: 800–1400 words. Payment: €100 per 1000 words. Founded 1976.

The Bookseller

VNU Entertainment Media Ltd, 5th Floor, Endeavour House, 189 Shaftesbury Avenue, London WC2H 8TJ
tel 020-7420 6006 *fax* 020-7420 6103
email felicity.wood@thebookseller.co.uk
website www.thebookseller.com
Editor-in-Chief Neill Denny, *Features Editor* Tom Tivnan
Weekly £4.40, £170 p.a.

Journal of the UK publishing, bookselling trade and libraries. While outside contributions are welcomed, most of the journal's contents are commissioned. Length: about 1000–1500 words. Payment: by arrangement. Founded 1858.

Bookworld

Christchurch Publishers Ltd, 2 Caversham Street, London SW3 4AH
tel/fax 020-7351 4995
email leonard.holdsworth@btinternet.com
Editor Leonard Holdsworth
Monthly £5

Special features and reviews of interest to serious book collectors, booksellers and librarians. Articles and ideas for articles welcome. Illustrations: b&w and colour. Payment: by negotiation. Established 1980.

Bowls International

Key Publishing Ltd, PO Box 100, Stamford, Lincs. PE9 1XQ
tel (01780) 755131 *fax* (01780) 751323
Editor Melvyn Beck
Monthly £3.20

Sport and news items and features; occasional, bowls-oriented short stories. Illustrations: colour transparencies, b&w photos, occasional line, cartoons. Payment: sport/news approx. 25p per line, features approx. £50 per page; colour £25, b&w £10. Founded 1981.

Brass Band World Magazine

Impromptu Publishing Ltd, 2nd Floor, Century House, 11 St Peter's Square, Manchester M2 3DN
tel 0161-236 9526 *fax* 0161-247 7978
email info@brassbandworld.com
website www.brassbandworld.com
Editor Carol Jarvis
Monthly £3.85

Articles, features and news of brass bands internationally. Reviews of concerts and contests, personality profiles, tips, and news from colleges for students, players and audiences. Payment: negotiable. Founded 1981.

British Birds

4 Harlequin Gardens, St Leonards on Sea TN37 7PF
tel (01424) 755155
email editor@britishbirds.co.uk
website www.britishbirds.co.uk
Editor Dr Roger Riddington
Monthly £49 p.a. UK, £56 p.a. overseas

Publishes major papers on identification, behaviour, conservation, distribution, ecology, movements, status and taxonomy with official reports on: rare breeding birds, scarce migrants and rare birds in Britain. Payment: token. Founded 1907.

British Chess Magazine

44 Baker Street, London W1U 7RT
tel 020-7486 8222 *fax* 020-7486 3355
email bcmchess@compuserve.com
website www.bcmchess.co.uk
Editor John Saunders
Monthly £3.70, £38 p.a.

Authoritative reports and commentary on the UK and overseas chess world. Payment: by arrangement. Founded 1881.

British Deaf News

British Deaf Association, Bushell Street Mill, Bushell Street, Preston, Lancs PR1 2SP
tel (01772) 259725
fax (05603) 115657 Textphone (05603) 115295
email bdn@bda.org.uk
website www.bda.org.uk
Editor Alison Gudgeon
Monthly £2, £20 p.a. non-members (£15 p.a. BDA members)

Interviews, features, reviews, articles, news items, letters dealing with deafness. Payment: by arrangement. Illustrations: line, half-tone. Founded 1872.

The British Journal of Photography

32–34 Broadwick Street, London W1A 2HG
tel 020-7316 9000 *fax* 020-7316 9003
email bjp.editor@bjphoto.co.uk
website www.bjp-online.com
Editor Simon Bainbridge
Monthly £6.99

Focus on all aspects of professional photography: articles on fine art, commercial, fashion, social and press, alongside technical reviews of the latest software and equipment. Founded 1854.

British Journalism Review

Sage Publications, 1 Oliver's Yard, 55 City Road, London EC1Y 1SP
tel 020-7324 8500 *fax* 020-7324 8600
email editor@bjr.org.uk
website www.bjr.org.uk
Editor Bill Hagerty
Quarterly £36 p.a. (overseas rates on application)

Comment/criticism/review of matters published by, or of interest to, the media. Length: 1500–3000 words. Illustrations: b&w photos. Payment: by arrangement. Founded 1989.

British Medical Journal

BMJ Publishing Group, BMA House, Tavistock Square, London WC1H 9JR
tel 020-7387 4499 *fax* 020-7383 6418
email fgodlee@bmj.com
website www.bmj.com
Editor Dr Fiona Godlee
Weekly Free to members of BMA. For subscription details see website.

Medical and related articles. Payment: by arrangement. Founded 1840.

British Philatelic Bulletin

Royal Mail, 35–50 Rathbone Place, London W1T 1HQ
fax 020-7441 4744
email john.r.holman@royalmail.co.uk
website www.royalmail.com/stamps
Editor J.R. Holman
Monthly £1.20

Articles on any aspect of British philately – stamps, postmarks, postal history; also stamp collecting in general. Length: up to 1500 words (articles); 250 words (news). Payment: £75 per 1000 words. Illustrations: colour. Founded 1963.

British Woodworking

Freshwood Publishing, Ampney St Peter, Cirencester, Glos. GL7 5SH
tel (01285) 850481
email nick.gibbs@britishwoodworking.com
website www.britishwoodworking.com
Editor Nick Gibbs
Bi-monthly £3.50 (£18.50 p.a.)

Articles and features for woodworking hobbyists. Includes projects, news and wood-related articles. Length: 2500 words. Payment: by arrangement.

Broadcast

Greater London House, Hampstead Road, London NW1 7EJ
tel 020-7728 5512 *fax* 020-7728 5555
email lisa.campbell@emap.com
website www.broadcastnow.co.uk
Editor Lisa Campbell
Weekly £4.95

For people working or interested in the UK and international broadcast industry. News, features, analysis and opinions. Covers the latest developments in programming, commissioning, digital, technology and post-production. Illustrations: colour, b&w, line, cartoons.

Building

Building Magazine, UBM Information Ltd, 3rd Floor, 245 Blackfriars Road, London SE1 9UY
tel 020-7560 4000 *fax* 020-7560 4004
email building@cmpi.biz
website www.building.co.uk
Editor Denise Chevin
Weekly £2.90

Covers all aspects of the construction industry from architecture to development to social housing, industrial and manufacturing aspects of the building industry. Will consider articles on architecture at home and abroad; also news and photos. Payment: by arrangement. Founded 1842.

Building Design

UBM Information Ltd, Ludgate House, 245 Blackfriars Road, London SE1 9UY
tel 020-7921 5000 *fax* 020-7921 8244
email buildingdesign@ubm.com
website www.bdonline.co.uk
Editor Amanda Baillieu
Subscription only.

News and features on all aspects of building design. All material commissioned. Length: up to 1500 words. Illustrations: colour and b&w photos, line, cartoons. Payment: £150 per 1000 words; illustrations by negotiation. Founded 1970.

The Burlington Magazine

14–16 Duke's Road, London WC1H 9SZ
tel 020-7388 8157 *fax* 020-7388 1230
email editorial@burlington.org.uk
website www.burlington.org.uk
Editor Richard Shone
Monthly £15.50

Deals with the history and criticism of art; book and exhibition reviews; illustrated monthly Calendar section. Potential contributors must have special knowledge of the subjects treated; MSS compiled from works of reference are unacceptable. Length: 500–5000 words. Payment: up to £140. Illustrations: colour photos. Founded 1903.

Buses

Ian Allan Publishing Ltd, Riverdene Business Park, Molesey Road, Hersham, Surrey KT12 4RG
tel (01932) 266600 *fax* (01932) 266601
Editor Alan Millar, PO Box 14644, Leven KY9 1WX
tel (01333) 340637 *fax* (01333) 340608

email buseseditor@btconnect.com
website www.busesmag.com
Monthly £3.70

Articles of interest to both road passenger transport operators and bus enthusiasts. Preliminary enquiry essential. Illustrations: digital, colour transparencies, half-tone, line maps. Payment: on application. Founded 1949.

Business Life

85 Strand, London WC2R 0DW
tel 020-7550 8000 *fax* 020-7550 8250
email businesslife@cedarcom.co.uk
website www.cedarcom.co.uk
Editor Derek Harbinson
10 p.a. Free

Inflight magazine for British Airways passengers. Articles and features of interest to the European business traveller. All material commissioned; approach in writing with ideas. Length: 850–2500 words. Illustrations: colour photos and line. Payment: £250 per 1000 words; £100–£400 for illustrations. Founded 1986.

Business Traveller

Panacea Publishing, Cardinal House,
39–40 Albemarle Street, London W1S 4TE
tel 020-7647 6330
email editorial@businesstraveller.com
website www.businesstraveller.com
Editor Tom Otley
10 p.a. £3.95 (£42.95 p.a.)

Articles, features and news on consumer travel aimed at individual frequent international business travellers. Submit ideas with recent clippings and a CV. Length: varies. Illustrations: colour for destinations features; send lists to Deborah Miller, Picture Editor. Payment: on application. Founded 1976.

Cambridgeshire Journal

Cambridge Newspapers Ltd, Winship Road, Milton, Cambridge CB4 6PP
tel (01223) 434434 *fax* (01223) 434415
Content Editor Alice Ryan
Monthly £2.45

Articles, features and news of interest to Cambridgeshire: history, people, events, natural history and other issues. Also regional lifestyle, i.e. gardens, homes and fashion. Founded 1994.

Campaign

Haymarket Business Publications Ltd,
174 Hammersmith Road, London W6 7JP
tel 020-8943 5000
website www.brandrepublic.com
Editor Gordon MacMillan
Weekly £3.20

News and articles covering the whole of the mass communications field, particularly advertising in all its forms, marketing and the media. Features should not exceed 2000 words. News items also welcome. Press day, Wednesday. Payment: by arrangement.

Canals & Rivers

PO Box 618, Norwich NR7 0QT
tel (01603) 708930
email chris@themag.fsnet.co.uk
website www.canalsandrivers.co.uk
Editor Chris Cattrall
Monthly £3.30

News, views and articles on UK inland waterways and cruising features, DIY articles and historical features. Length: 1500 words (articles/features), 300 words (news). Payment: £100; £25 (news). Illustrations: colour, plus b&w cartoons. Founded 1978.

Candis

Newhall Publications Ltd, Newhall Lane, Hoylake, Wirral CH47 4BQ
tel 0151-632 3232
email fiction@candis.co.uk
website www.candis.co.uk
Editor Debbie Attewell
Monthly £3 Subscription only

Candis magazine including health news, celebrity interviews plus features. For fiction guidelines see www.candis.co.uk/guidelines.

Car

Bauer Consumer Media, 3rd Floor, Media House, Lynchwood, Peterborough PE2 6EA
tel (01733) 468379 *fax* (01733) 468660
email car@bauermedia.com
Editor Phil McNamara
Monthly £4.20

Top-grade journalistic features on car driving, car people and cars. Length: 1000–2500 words. Payment: minimum £350 per 1000 words. Illustrations: b&w and colour photos to professional standards. Founded 1962.

Car Mechanics

Broadway Court, Broadway, Peterborough PE1 1RP
tel (0173) 334 7559 *fax* (0173) 389 1342
email cm.ed@kelsey.co.uk
website www.carmechanicsmag.co.uk
Editor Martyn Knowles
Monthly £3.85

Practical articles on maintaining, repairing and uprating modern cars for DIY plus the motor trade. Always interested in finding new talent for our rather specialised market but study a recent copy before submitting ideas or features. Email outlining feature recommended. Payment: by arrangement. Illustrations: line drawings, colour prints, transparencies or digital images. Supply package of text and pictures.

Caravan Magazine

IPC Inspire, Leon House, 233 High Street, Croydon CR9 1HZ
tel 020-8726 8000 *fax* 020-8726 8290
email victoria_bentley@ipcmedia.com
website www.caravanmagazine.co.uk
Editor Victoria Bentley
Monthly £3.80

Lively articles based on real experience of touring caravanning, especially if well illustrated by photos. Payment: by arrangement. Founded 1933.

Caring Business

CMP Information, Ludgate House, 245 Blackfriars Road, London SE1 9UY
tel 020-7921 8502 *fax* 020-7560 4014
website www.caringbusiness.co.uk
Editor Olufunmi Majekodunmi
Monthly £64 p.a.

Specialist contributions relating to the commercial aspects of nursing and residential care, including hospitals. Payment: £50 per 1000 words. Illustrations: line, half-tone. Founded 1985.

Carousel – The Guide to Children's Books

Ephraim Phillips House, 54–76 Bissell Street, Birmingham B5 7HP
tel 0121-622 7458
email carousel.guide@virgin.net
website www.carouselguide.co.uk
Editor Jenny Blanch
3 p.a. £11.25 p.a. (£16 p.a. Europe; £19 p.a. rest of world)

Reviews of fiction, non-fiction and poetry books for children, plus in-depth articles; profiles of authors and illustrators. Length: 1200 words (articles); 150 words (reviews). Illustrations: colour and b&w. Payment: by arrangement. Founded 1995.

Cat World

Ancient Lights, 19 River Road, Arundel BN18 9EY
tel (01903) 884988 *fax* (01903) 885514
email laura@ashdown.co.uk
website www.catworld.co.uk
Editor Laura Quiggan
Monthly £2.95

Bright, lively articles on any aspect of cat ownership. Articles on breeds of cats and veterinary articles by acknowledged experts only. No unsolicited fiction. All submissions by email or on disk. Illustrations: colour prints, transparencies, TIFFs. Payment: by arrangement. Founded 1981.

Caterer & Hotelkeeper

Reed Business Information Ltd, Quadrant House, The Quadrant, Sutton, Surrey SM2 5AS
tel 020-8652 3500 *fax* 020-8652 8973
email caterernews@rbi.co.uk
Editor Mark Lewis
Weekly £3.10

Articles on all aspects of the hotel and catering industries. Length: up to 1500 words. Illustrations: line, half-tone, colour. Payment: by arrangement. Founded 1874.

The Catholic Herald

Herald House, Lambs Passage, Bunhill Row, London EC1Y 8TQ
tel 020-7448 3603 *fax* 020-7256 9728
email editorial@catholicherald.co.uk
website www.catholicherald.co.uk
Editor Luke Coppen
Weekly £1.20

Independent newspaper covering national and international affairs from a Catholic/Christian viewpoint as well as church news. Length: articles 800–1200 words. Illustrations: photos of Catholic and Christian interest. Payment: by arrangement.

Catholic Pictorial

36 Henry Street, Liverpool L1 5BS
tel 0151-522 1007 *fax* 0151-522 1008
email p.heneghan@rcaol.co.uk
Editor Peter Heneghan
Monthly £1

News and photo features (maximum 800 words plus illustration) of Merseyside, regional and national Catholic interest only; also cartoons. Has a strongly social editorial and is a trenchant tabloid. Payment: by arrangement. Founded 1961.

Catholic Times

Gabriel Communication, Landmark House, 4th Floor, Station Road, Cheadle, Hulme SK8 7JH
tel 0161-488 1700 *fax* 0161-488 1701
email kevin.flaherty@totalcatholic.com
website www.totalcatholic.com
Editor Kevin Flaherty
Weekly £1

News (400 words) and news features (800 words) of Catholic interest. Illustrations: colour and b&w photos. Payment: £30–£80; photos £50. Relaunched 1993.

Ceramic Review

25 Foubert's Place, London W1F 7QF
tel 020-7439 3377 *fax* 020-7287 9954
email emmanuelcooper@ceramicreview.com
website www.ceramicreview.com
Editor Emmanuel Cooper
6 p.a. £6.30 cover price (£36 p.a.)

Magazine containing practical and critical features on contemporary ceramic art and craft around the world. Welcomes articles: practical, technical or experiential; also looking at the role of ceramics within contemporary culture.

Chapman

4 Broughton Place, Edinburgh EH1 3RX
tel 0131-557 2207
email chapman-pub@blueyonder.co.uk
website www.chapman-pub.co.uk
Editor Dr Joy Hendry
3 p.a. £24 p.a.

Poetry, short stories, reviews, criticism, articles on Scottish culture. Illustrations: line, half-tone, cartoons. Payment: £8 per page; illustrations by negotiation. Founded 1970.

Chartered Secretary

ICSA Information & Training Ltd, 16 Park Crescent, London W1B 1AH
tel 020-7612 7045 *fax* 020-7612 7034
email chartsec@icsa.co.uk
website www.charteredsecretary.net
Editor Kevin Eddy, *Assistant Editor* Gareth Pearce
Monthly £90 p.a. (free to members)

Official magazine of The Institute of Chartered Secretaries and Administrators. Practical and topical articles (2000+ words) on law, governance, finance and management affecting company secretaries and other senior administrators in business, not-for-profit sector, local and central government and other institutions in Britain and overseas.

Chat

IPC Connect Ltd, The Blue Fin Building, 110 Southwark Street, London SE1 0SU
tel 020-3148 5000
website www.ipcmedia.com
Editor Gilly Sinclair
Weekly 80p

Tabloid weekly for women: Reader's letters; tips; true life features. Payment: by arrangement. Founded 1985.

Child Education PLUS

Book End, Range Road, Witney OX29 0YD
tel (01926) 887799 *fax* (01926) 883331
email childed@scholastic.co.uk
website www.scholastic.co.uk/childedplus
Editor Tim Major
Monthly £4.25

For teachers concerned with the education of children aged 4–7. Articles by specialists on practical teaching ideas and methods. Length: 600–1,200 words. Payment: by arrangement. Profusely illustrated with photos and artwork; also two A2 colour posters. Founded 1924.

Church of England Newspaper

Religious Intelligence Ltd, 14 Great College Street, London SW1P 3RX
tel 020-7878 1001 *fax* 020-7878 1031
email cen@churchnewspaper.com
website www.churchnewspaper.com
Editor Colin Blakely
Weekly £1

Anglican news and articles relating the Christian faith to everyday life. Evangelical basis; almost exclusively commissioned articles. Study of paper desirable. Length: up to 1000 words. Illustrations: photos, line drawings, cartoons. Payment: c. £40 per 1000 words; photos £22, line by arrangement. Founded 1828.

Church Times

13–17 Long Lane, London EC1A 9DJ
tel 020-7776 1060 *fax* 020-7776 1086
email news@churchtimes.co.uk
website www.churchtimes.co.uk
Editor Paul Handley
Weekly £1.10

Articles on religious topics are considered. No verse or fiction. Length: up to 1000 words. Illustrations: news photos, sent promptly. Payment: £100 per 1000 words; Periodical Publishers' Association negotiated rates for illustrations. Founded 1863.

CIRCA

The Priory, John Street West, Dublin 8, Republic of Ireland
tel/fax (1) 640 1585
email editor@recirca.com
website www.recirca.com
Editor Peter FitzGerald
Quarterly €25 p.a. (Rep. of Ireland, Northern Ireland), €34.50 outside RoI and NI

Covers contemporary visual arts in Ireland with news, reviews, previews, interviews and feature articles. The magazine is dedicated to reflecting visual culture as it unfolds throughout Ireland while also reporting on important developments further afield. Welcomes proposals for feature articles: email ideas or texts to the editor.

Classic Boat Magazine

IPC Media, Leon House, 233 High Street, Croydon CR9 1HZ
tel 020-8726 8000 *fax* 020-8726 8195
email cb@ipcmedia.com
website www.classicboat.co.uk
Editor Dan Houston
Monthly £4.40

Cruising and technical features, restorations, events, new boat reviews, practical, maritime history; news. Study of magazine essential: read 3–4 back issues and send for contributors' guidelines. Length: 500–2000 words. Illustrations: colour and b&w photos; line drawings of hulls. Payment: £75–£100 per published page. Founded 1987.

Classic Cars

Bauer Consumer Media, Media House, Lynchwood, Peterborough Business Park, Peterborough PE2 6EA
tel (01733) 468000 *fax* (01733) 468888

email classic.cars@bauermedia.com
website www.classiccarsmagazine.co.uk
Editor Phil Bell
Monthly £4.20

Specialist articles on older cars. Length: from 500–4000 words (subject to prior contract). Illustrations: half-tone, colour. Payment: by negotiation.

Classic Rock

Future Publishing Ltd, 30 Monmouth Street, Bath BA1 2BW
tel (01225) 442244 *fax* (01225) 446019
website www.classicrockmagazine.com
Editor in Chief Scott Rowley, *Editor* Siân Llewellyn
13 p.a. £4.99

'The definitive voice in rock journalism' focusing on hard rock, heavy metal and the older generation of 'Rockers'. Features the real stories behind rock legends with in-depth profiles, interviews, news overviews, tour dates, retrospective articles and reviews.

Classic Stitches

D.C. Thomson & Co. Ltd, 80 Kingsway East, Dundee DD4 8SL
tel (01382) 223131 *fax* (01382) 452491
email editorial@classicstitches.com
website www.classicstitches.com
Editor Mrs Bea Neilson
Bi-monthly £4.20

Creative needlework ideas and projects; needlework-based features on designers, collections, work-in-progress and exhibitions. Submissions also welcome for e-mag on website. Length: 1000–1500 words. Illustrations: digital colour photos. Payment: negotiable. Founded 1994.

Classical Music

Rhinegold Publishing Ltd, 241 Shaftesbury Avenue, London WC2H 8TF
tel 020-7333 1742 *fax* 020-7333 1769
email classical.music@rhinegold.co.uk
website www.rhinegold.co.uk
Editor Keith Clarke
Fortnightly £3.95

News, opinion, features on the classical music business. All material commissioned. Illustrations: colour photos and line; colour covers. Payment: minimum £100 per 1000 words; from £50 for illustrations. Founded 1976.

Classics Monthly

Future Excite, 30 Monmouth Street, Bath BA1 2BW
tel/fax (01225) 442244
Editor Gary Stretton
Monthly £3.99

News photos and stories of classic car interest and illustrated features on classic car history, repairs, maintenance and restoration. Study magazine before submitting material. Features must have high level of subject knowledge and technical accuracy. Length: up to 2000 words (features); 200 words (news). Illustrations: colour and b&w. Payment: £120 per 1000 words plus £100 per set of supporting photos (features); £120 per 1000 words plus photos based on £100 per page (news). Founded 1997.

Climb Magazine

PO Box 21, Buxton, Derbyshire SK17 9BR
tel (01298) 72801
email neilp@climbmagazine.com
website www.climbmagazine.com
Editor Neil Pearsons
12 p.a. £3.50

Climbing magazine covering mainly British rock climbing. Features all aspects of climbing worldwide from bouldering to mountaineering. Contact Editor to discuss requirements. Founded 1987.

Climber

The Maltings, West Street, Bourne, Lincs. PE10 9PH
tel (01778) 391000 *fax* (01778) 394748
email climbercomments@warnersgroup.co.uk
website www.climber.co.uk
Editor Andy McCue
Monthly £3.50

Articles on all aspects of rock climbing/ mountaineering in Great Britain and abroad, and on related subjects. Study of magazine essential. Length: 1500–2000 words. Illustrations: colour transparencies. Payment: according to merit. Founded 1962.

Closer

Bauer Consumer Media, Endeavour House, 189 Shaftsbury Avenue, London WC2H 8JG
tel 020-7437 9011
email closer@closermag.co.uk
website www.closeronline.co.uk
Editor Lisa Burrow
Weekly £1.30

Women's entertainment magazine with true-life stories and celebrity articles, letters, listings and reviews. Payment by negotiation.

Coin News

Token Publishing Ltd, Orchard House, Duchy Road, Heathpark, Honiton, Devon EX14 1YD
tel (01404) 46972 *fax* (01404) 44788
Editor John W. Mussell
Monthly £3.65

Articles of high standard on coins, tokens, paper money. Send text in digital form. Length: up to 2000 words. Payment: by arrangement. Founded 1964.

Commando

D.C. Thomson & Co. Ltd, Albert Square, Dundee DD1 9QJ

tel (01382) 223131 *fax* (01382) 322214
8 per month £1.35

Fictional stories set in time of war told in pictures. Scripts: about 135 pictures. Synopsis required as an opener. New writers encouraged; send for details. Payment: on acceptance.

Commercial Motor

Reed Business Information Ltd, Quadrant House, The Quadrant, Sutton, Surrey SM2 5AS
tel 020-8652 3500 *fax* 020-8652 8988
website www.roadtransport.com
Editor Justin Stanton
Weekly £1.80 (£110 p.a.)

Technical and road transport articles only. Length: up to 1500 words. Payment: varies. Illustrations: drawings and photos. Founded 1905.

Community Care

Reed Business Information Ltd, Quadrant House, The Quadrant, Sutton, Surrey SM2 5AS
tel 020-8652 3500 *fax* 020-8652 4739
email comcare.children@rbi.co.uk, comcare.adults@rbi.co.uk
website www.communitycare.co.uk
Editor Bronagh Miskelly
Weekly £2.45

Articles, features and news covering the Social Services sector.

Company

National Magazine House, 72 Broadwick Street, London W1V 2BP
tel 020-7439 5000 *fax* 020-7312 3797
website www.company.co.uk
Editor Victoria White
Monthly £2

Articles on a wide variety of subjects, relevant to young, independent women. Most articles are commissioned. Payment: usual magazine rate. Illustrated. Founded 1978.

Computer Arts

Future Publishing Ltd, Computer Arts, 30 Monmouth Street, Bath BA1 2BW
tel (01225) 442244
email ca.mail@futurenet.co.uk
website www.computerarts.co.uk
Editor Gillian Carson
Monthly £6

Magazine for digital artists and designers with in-depth tutorials together with tips for web design, typography, 3D, animation, motion graphics and multimedia. Also reviews the latest hardware and software releases and includes interviews with the leading figures in the global design world.

Computer Weekly

Reed Business Information Ltd, Quadrant House, The Quadrant, Sutton, Surrey SM2 5AS
tel 020-8652 3500 *fax* 020-8652 8979
email computer.weekly@rbi.co.uk
website www.computerweekly.com
Editor Brian McKenna
Weekly £3.35

Feature articles on IT-related topics for business/industry users. Length: 1200 words. Illustrations: b&w and colour photos, line, cartoons. Payment: £253 per 1000 words; negotiable for illustrations. Founded 1966.

Computeractive

Incisive Media, 32–34 Broadwick Street, London W1A 2HG
tel 020-7316 9000
website www.computeractive.co.uk
Editor Paul Allen
Fortnightly £1.79

Magazine offering 'simple clear advice' on computers with workshops, product reviews, internet news and group tests.

Condé Nast Traveller

Vogue House, Hanover Square, London W1S 1JU
tel 020-7499 9080 *fax* 020-7493 3758
email cntraveller@condenast.co.uk
website www.cntraveller.com
Editor Sarah Miller
Monthly £3.70

Lavishly photographed articles on all aspects of travel, featuring exotic destinations and those close to home. Specialist pieces include food and wine, motoring, health, foreign correspondents, travel news, hotels. Illustrations: colour. Payment: by arrangement. Founded 1997.

Contemporary

Studio 56, 4 Montpelier Street, London SW7 1EE
tel 020-7019 6205
email info@contemporary-magazine.com
website www.contemporary-magazine.com
Editor Brian Muller
Monthly £5.95

International magazine with extensive coverage of visual arts, architecture, fashion, film, photography, books, music, dance and sport. Also includes interviews, profiles and art news from around the world. Length: varies. Illustrations: colour transparencies, hi-res scans. Payment: £100 per 1000 words; none for photos. Founded 1997; relaunched 2002.

Contemporary Review

(incorporating the Fortnightly)
Contemporary Review Co. Ltd, PO Box 1242, Oxford OX1 4FJ
tel (01865) 201529 *fax* (01865) 201529
email editorial@contemporaryreview.co.uk
website www.contemporaryreview.co.uk

Editor Dr Richard Mullen
£39.20 p.a.

Independent review dealing with questions of the day, chiefly politics, international affairs, religion, literature, the arts. Mostly commissioned, but with limited scope for freelance authors with authoritative knowledge. TS returned only if sae enclosed. Intending contributors should study journal first. Length: 2000–3000 words. No illustrations. Payment: £5 per page (500 words), 2 complimentary copies. Founded 1866.

Cosmopolitan

National Magazine House, 72 Broadwick Street, London W1F 9EP
tel 020-7439 5000 *fax* 020-7439 5016
Editor-in-Chief Louise Court
Monthly £3.50

Articles. Commissioned material only. Payment: by arrangement. Illustrated. Founded 1972.

Cotswold Life

Archant Life South, Cumberland House, Oriel Road, Cheltenham, Glos. GL50 1BB
tel (01242) 216050 *fax* (01242) 255116
email editorial@cotswoldlife.co.uk
website www.cotswoldlife.co.uk
Editor Mike Lowe
Monthly £3.25

Articles on the Cotswolds, including places of interest, high-profile personalities, local events, arts, history and food. Unsolicited ideas welcome.

Country

CGA, Chalke House, Station Road, Codford, Warminster BA12 0JX
tel (01985) 850706 *fax* (01985) 850378
email enquiries@thecga.co.uk
website www.thecga.co.uk
Editor Simon Moss
8 p.a. Controlled circulation: members only

Magazine of the Country Gentlemen's Association. News and features covering rural events, countryside, leisure, heritage, homes and gardens. Some outside contributors used. Payment: by arrangement. Founded 1893.

Country Homes and Interiors

IPC Magazines Ltd, The Blue Fin Building, 110 Southwark Street, London SE1 0SU
tel 020-3148 5000
Editor Rhoda Parry
Monthly £3.60

Articles on country homes and gardens, interior designs, lifestyle. Payment: from £250 per 1000 words. Founded 1986.

Country Life

IPC Media Ltd, The Blue Fin Building, 110 Southwark Street, London SE1 0SU
tel 020-3148 5000 *fax* 020-3261 5139
website www.countrylife.co.uk
Editor Mark Hedges, *Deputy Editor* Rupert Uloth
Weekly £3

Illustrated journal chiefly concerned with British country life, social history, architecture and the fine arts, natural history, agriculture, gardening and sport. Length: about 1000 or 1300 words (articles). Illustrations: mainly colour photos. Payment: according to merit. Founded 1897.

Country Living

National Magazine House, 72 Broadwick Street, London W1F 9EP
tel 020-7439 5000 *fax* 020-7439 5093
website www.allaboutyou.com
Editor Susy Smith
Monthly £3.60

Up-market home-interest magazine with a country lifestyle theme, covering interiors, gardens, crafts, food, wildlife, rural and green issues. Do not send unsolicited material or valuable transparencies. Illustrations: line, half-tone, colour. Payment: by arrangement. Founded 1985.

Country Smallholding

Archant Regional Ltd, Fair Oak Close, Exeter Airport Business Park, Clyst Honiton, Exeter EX5 2UL
tel (01392) 888481 *fax* (01392) 888449
email editorial.csh@archant.co.uk
website www.countrysmallholding.com
Editor Simon McEwan
Monthly £3.50

The magazine for smallholders. Practical, how-to articles, and seasonal features, on organic gardening, small-scale poultry and livestock keeping, country crafts, cookery and general subjects of interest to smallholders and others. Approach the Editor in writing or by phone or email with ideas. Length: up to 1,400 words. Payment: on application. Founded 1975 as *Practical Self-Sufficiency*.

Country Walking

Bauer Consumer Media, Media House, Lynchwood, Peterborough Business Park, Peterborough PE2 6EA
tel (01733) 468205
website www.ifto.com
Editor Jonathan Manning
Monthly £3.90

Features. Length: 1000 words on average. Illustrations: digital images. Payment: by arrangement. Founded 1987.

The Countryman

Country Publications Ltd, The Water Mill, Broughton Hall, Skipton, North Yorks BD23 3AG
tel (01756) 701381 *fax* (01756) 701326
email editorial@thecountryman.co.uk
Editor Paul Jackson

Monthly £3.25

Every area of rural life. Copy must be trustworthy, well-written, brisk, cogent and light in hand. Articles up to 1200 words. Skilful sketches of life and character from personal knowledge and experience. Dependable natural history based on writer's own observation. Really good matter from old unpublished letters and MSS. Study magazine before submitting material. Illustrations: b&w and colour photos and drawings, but all must be exclusive and out of the ordinary. Payment: approx. £75 per 1000 words. Founded 1927.

Craftsman craft&design Magazine

PO Box 5, Driffield, East Yorkshire YO25 8JD
tel (01377) 255213
email info@craftanddesign.net
website www.craftanddesign.net
Editor Angie Boyer
Bi-monthly £5.95 (£35 p.a.)

Articles, features and news on craft makers and other areas of the craft industry. Aims to promote quality craftsmanship. Welcomes ideas for articles and features. Length: 1000 words (articles and features). Payment £100 per 1000 words. Illustrations: colour prints, transparencies or digital images on CD. All editorial copy dates etc. at www.craftanddesign.net/editorial. Founded 1983.

Criminal Law & Justice Weekly (incorporating Justice of the Peace)

LexisNexis, 35 Chancery Lane, London WC2A 1EL
tel 020-7400 2828
email diana.rose@lexisnexis.co.uk
Consulting Editor Adrian Turner, *Send material to* Diana Rose, Publishing Manager
Weekly £315 p.a.

Professional journal. Articles on criminal and local government law and associated subjects including family law, criminology, medico-legal matters, penology, police, probation. Information on articles and contributions sent on request. Email for author guidelines. Founded 1837.

Critical Quarterly

Newbury, Crediton, Devon EX17 5HA
tel (01359) 242375 *fax* (01359) 242880
website www.criticalquarterly.com
Editor Colin MacCabe
Quarterly £30 p.a.

Fiction, poems, literary criticism. Length: 2000–5000 words. Study magazine before submitting MSS. Payment: by arrangement. Founded 1959.

Cumbria Magazine

Country Publications Ltd, The Water Mill, Broughton Hall, Skipton, North Yorkshire BD23 3AG
tel (01756) 701381 *fax* (01756) 701326
email editorial@cumbriamagazine.co.uk
Features editor Kevin Hopkinson
Monthly £2.35

Articles of genuine rural interest concerning the Lake District and surrounding areas, and its people. Short length preferred. Illustrations: first-class photos. Payment: £70 per 1,000 words. Pictures extra. Founded 1951.

Custom Car

Kelsey Publishing Ltd, Cudham Tithe Barn, Berry's Hill, Cudham, Kent TN16 3AG
tel (01959) 541444 *fax* (01959) 541400
email cc.ed@kelsey.co.uk
website www.kelsey.co.uk
Editor David Biggadyke
Monthly £3.85

Hot rods, customs and drag racing. Length: by arrangement. Payment: by arrangement. Founded 1970.

Custom PC

Dennis Publishing Ltd, 30 Cleveland Street, London W1T 4JD
tel 020-7907 6000 *fax* 020-7907 6835
website www.custompc.co.uk
Editor Alex Watson
Monthly £3.75

Magazine covering performance PC hardware, technology and games with full-page and DPS single product reviews, group tests, and practical and technical features.

Cycle Sport

IPC Media, Leon House, 233 High Street, Croydon CR9 1HZ
tel 020-8726 8462 *fax* 020-8726 8499
email cyclesport@ipcmedia.com
website www.cyclesport.co.uk
Managing Editor Robert Garbutt, *Deputy Editor* Edward Pickering
Monthly £4

Articles and features on European professional racing. Specially commissions most material but will consider unsolicited material. Welcomes ideas for articles and features. Length: 1500–2500 words. Illustrations: transparencies, colour and b&w artwork and cartoons, digital images. Payment: £120 per 1000 words; £50–£150 illustrations. Founded 1991.

Cycling Weekly

IPC Media, Leon House, 233 High Street, Croydon CR9 1HZ
tel 020-8726 8462 *fax* 020-8726 8499
email cycling@ipcmedia.com
website www.cyclingweekly.co.uk
Editor Robert Garbutt
Weekly £2.60

Racing and technical articles. Illustrations: topical

photos with a cycling interest considered; cartoons. Length: not exceeding 2000 words. Payment: by arrangement. Founded 1891.

Cyphers

3 Selskar Terrace, Ranelagh, Dublin 6, Republic of Ireland
tel (01) 4978 866 *fax* (01) 4978 866
website www.cyphers.ie
€21/$36 for 3 issues

Poems, fiction, translations. Payment: €15 per page. Founded 1975.

Dairy Farmer

Riverbank House, Angel Lane, Tonbridge TN9 1SE
tel (01732) 377273
email peter.hollinshead@ubm.com
website www.farmersguardian.com
Editor Peter Hollinshead
14 p.a. £3.75

In-depth, technical articles on all aspects of dairy farm management and milk marketing. Length: normally 800–1400 words with colour photos. Payment: by arrangement.

Dalesman

Country Publications Limited, The Water Mill, Broughton Hall, Skipton, North Yorkshire BD23 3AG
tel (01756) 701381 *fax* (01756) 701326
email editorial@dalesman.co.uk
Editor Paul Jackson
Monthly £2.35

Articles and stories of genuine interest concerning Yorkshire (1000 words). Payment: £70 per 1000 words plus extra for useable photos/illustrations. Founded 1939.

Dance Today

The Dancing Times Ltd, 45–47 Clerkenwell Green, London EC1R 0EB
tel 020-7250 3006 *fax* 020-7253 6679
email dancetoday@dancing-times.co.uk
website www.dance-today.co.uk
Editor Katie Gregory
Monthly £1.75

Ballroom, popular and social dancing from every aspect, ranging from competition reports to dance holiday features, health and fitness articles, and musical reviews. Well-informed freelance articles are used, but only after preliminary arrangements. Payment: by arrangement. Illustrations: action photos preferred, colour only. Founded 1956.

Dancing Times

The Dancing Times Ltd, 45–47 Clerkenwell Green, London EC1R 0EB
tel 020-7250 3006 *fax* 020-7253 6679
email dt@dancing-times.co.uk
website www.dancing-times.co.uk
Editor Jonathan Gray
Monthly £2.95

Ballet, contemporary dance and all forms of stage dancing from general, historical, critical and technical angles. Well-informed freelance articles used occasionally, but only after preliminary arrangements. Payment: by arrangement. Illustrations: occasional line, action photos preferred; colour welcome. Founded 1910.

The Dandy

D.C. Thomson & Co. Ltd, Albert Square, Dundee DD1 9QJ
tel (01382) 223131 *fax* (01382) 322214
185 Fleet Street, London EC4A 2HS
tel 020-7400 1030 *fax* 020-7400 1089
email cgraham@dthompson.co.uk
Editor Craig Graham
Fortnightly £1.99

Comic strips and features for boys aged 7–10 years. Picture stories with 7–10 pictures per page, 1–4pp per story. Promising artists are encouraged. Payment: on acceptance.

Dare

River Publishing, Number One, Neal Street, London WC2H 9QL
tel 020-7306 0304 *fax* 020-7306 0303
Editor Nathalie Gibbins
Free

Women's magazine predominently featuring aspirational yet affordable beauty and fashion.

Darts World

MB Graphics, 25 Orlestone View, Ham Street, Ashford, Kent TN26 2LB
tel (01233) 733558
website www.dartsworld.com
Editor Michael Beeken
Monthly £2.95

Articles and stories with darts theme. Illustrations: half-tone, cartoons. Payment: £40–£50 per 1000 words; illustrations by arrangement. Founded 1972.

The Dawntreader

132 Hinckley Road, Stoney Stanton, Leics. LE9 7NE
email dawnidp@btinternet.com
website www.indigodreamsonline.com
Editors Ronnie Goodyer and Dawn Bauling
Quarterly £4, £15 p.a.

Poetry, short stories and articles encompassing themes of the mystic, myth, legend, landscape, nature and love. New writers welcome. No payment. Sae essential. Founded 2007.

Decanter

IPC Inspire, The Blue Fin Building, 110 Southwark Street, London SE1 0SU
tel 020-3148 5000

email editor@decanter.com
website www.decanter.com
Editor Guy Woodward
Monthly £3.95

Articles and features on wines, wine travel and food-related topics. Welcomes ideas for articles and features. Length: 1000–1800 words. Illustrations: colour. Payment: £250 per 1000 words. Founded 1975.

delicious.

Seven Publishing Group, Sea Container's House, 20 Upper Ground, London SE1 9PD
tel 020-7775 7775 *fax* 020-7775 7705
email info@deliciousmagazine.co.uk
website www.deliciousmagazine.co.uk
Editor Karen Barnes
Monthly £3.20

Articles on food, recipes, preparation, trends, chefs, wine and ingredients. Ideas welcome. Founded 2003.

Derbyshire Life and Countryside

Archant Life, 61 Friargate, Derby DE1 1DJ
tel (01332) 227850 *fax* (01332) 227860
email joy.hales@derbyshirelife.co.uk
website www.derbyshirelife.co.uk
Editor Joy Hales
Monthly £2.50

Articles, preferably illustrated, about Derbyshire life, people and history. Length: up to 800 words. Some short stories set in Derbyshire accepted; no verse. Payment: according to nature and quality of contribution. Illustrations: photos of Derbyshire subjects. Founded 1931.

Descent

Wild Places Publishing, PO Box 100, Abergavenny NP7 9WY
tel (01873) 737707
email descent@wildplaces.co.uk
website www.wildplaces.co.uk
Editor Chris Howes
Bi-monthly £4.50

Articles, features and news on all aspects of cave and mine sport exploration. Submissions must match magazine style. Length: up to 2000 words (articles/features), up to 1000 words (news). Illustrations: colour and b&w. Payment: on consideration of material based on area filled. Founded 1969.

Devon Life

Archant Life South, Archant House, Babbage Road, Totnes, Devon TQ9 5JA
tel (01803) 860910 *fax* (01803) 860926
email devonlife@archant.co.uk
website www.devon.greatbritishlife.co.uk
Editor Jane Fitzgerald
Monthly £3.45

Articles on all aspects of Devon, including places of interest, personalities, local events, arts, history and food. Unsolicited ideas welcome. Founded 1963.

The Dickensian

The Dickens Fellowship, Dickens House, 48 Doughty Street, London WC1N 2LX
fax (01227) 827001
email M.Y.Andrews@ukc.ac.uk
Editor Prof. Malcolm Andrews, School of English, Rutherford College, University of Kent, Canterbury, Kent CT2 7NX
3 p.a. £16 p.a. (£25 p.a. institutions; reduced rate for Dickens Fellowship members)

Welcomes articles on all aspects of Dickens's life, works and character. Payment: none. Send contributions (enclose sae if return required) and editorial correspondence to the Editor.

Digital Camera

Future Publishing Ltd, 30 Monmouth Street, Bath BA1 2BW
(01225) 442244 *fax* (01225) 446019
email editor.dcm@futurenet.com
website www.dcmag.co.uk
Editor Geoff Harris
Monthly £5.99

Practical guide to creating better photographs. Each issue contains inspirational images, expert techniques and essential tips for capturing great images and on how to perfect them on a computer. Also includes details on the latest cameras, accessories and software.

Digital Camera Buyer

Imagine Publishing Ltd, Richmond House, 33 Richmond Hill, Bournemouth BH2 6EZ
tel (01202) 586200
email DCBsite@imagine-publishing.co.uk
website www.digicambuyer.co.uk
Deputy Editor Matt Tuffin
Monthly £3.99

Comprehensive buyer's guide for all levels of camera with reviews, buying advice and shooting tips.

Director

116 Pall Mall, London SW1Y 5ED
tel 020-7766 8950 *fax* 020-7766 8840
email director-ed@iod.com
website www.director.co.uk
Editor Richard Cree
Monthly £3.50 (£42 p.a.)

Authoritative business-related articles. Send synopsis of proposed article and examples of printed work. Length: 500–2000 words. Payment: by arrangement. Illustrations: colour. Founded 1947.

Disability Now

(published by Scope)
6 Market Road, London N7 9PW
tel 020-7619 7323 *minicom* 020-7619 7332

fax 020-7619 7331
email editor@disabilitynow.org.uk
website www.disabilitynow.org.uk
Editor Ian Macrae
Monthly £1.80 (free to qualifying individuals); tape version free to people with visual impairment or severe disability

Newspaper for people with different types of disability, carers and professionals, and anyone interested in disability. News and comment on anything of interest in the disability field: benefits, services, equipment, jobs, politics, motoring, holidays, sport, relationships, the arts. All regular contributors have a disability (unless they are a parent of someone with a disability). Preliminary letter or email desirable. Founded 1984.

Diva

Millivres Prowler Ltd, Spectrum House, Unit M, 32-34 Gordon House Road, London NW5 1LP
tel 020-7424 7400 *fax* 020-7424 7401
email edit@divamag.co.uk
website www.divamag.co.uk
Editor Jane Czyzselska
Monthly £3.25

Lesbian life and culture: articles and features. Length: 200–2000 words. Illustrations: colour. Payment: £15 per 100 words; variable per photo; variable per illustration. Founded 1994.

Diver

55 High Street, Teddington, Middlesex TW11 8HA
tel 020-8943 4288 *fax* 020-8943 4312
email enquiries@divermag.co.uk
website www.divernet.com
Editor-in-Chief Nigel Eaton, *Editor* Steve Weinman
Monthly £3.99

Articles on sub aqua diving and related developments. Length: 1500–2000 words. Illustrations: colour. Payment: by arrangement. Founded 1953.

DIY Week

Faversham House Group Ltd, 232A Addington Road, South Croydon CR2 8LE
tel 020-8651 7100 *fax* 020-8651 7117
website www.diyweek.net
Editor Will Parsons
Fortnightly £102 p.a.

Product and city news, promotions and special features of recent developments in DIY houseware and garden retailing. Payment: by arrangement. Founded 1874.

Dogs Today

The Doghouse, 4 Bonseys Lane, Chobham, Surrey GU24 8JJ
tel (01276) 858880 *fax* (01276) 858860
email editorial@dogstodaymagazine.co.uk
website www.dogstodaymagazine.co.uk
Editor Beverley Cuddy
Monthly £3.75

Study of magazine essential before submitting ideas. Interested in human interest dog stories, celebrity interviews, holiday features and anything unusual – all must be entertaining and informative and accompanied by illustrations. Length: 800–1200 words. Illustrations: colour, preferably digital. Payment: negotiable. Founded 1990.

The Dolls' House Magazine

Guild of Master Craftsman Publications Ltd, 86 High Street, Lewes, East Sussex BN7 1XN
website www.thegmcgroup.com
Monthly £47.88 p.a. UK

Dorset Life – The Dorset Magazine

7 The Leanne, Sandford Lane, Wareham, Dorset BH20 4DY
tel (01929) 551264 *fax* (01929) 552099
email office@dorsetlife.co.uk
Editor John Newth
Monthly £2.40

Articles (about 1200 words), photos (colour) and line drawings with a specifically Dorset theme. Payment: by arrangement. Founded 1967.

Drapers

Emap Inform, Greater London House, Hampstead Road, London NW1 7EJ
tel 020-7728 5000 *fax* 020-7812 3760
email drapers@emap.com
website www.drapersonline.com
Editor Jessica Brown
Weekly £3.20

Business editorial aimed at fashion retailers, large and small. Payment: by negotiation. Illustrations: colour and b&w photos. Founded 1887.

The Dublin Review

PO Box 7948, Dublin 1, Republic of Ireland
tel/fax (01) 6788627
website www.thedublinreview.com
Editor Brendan Barrington
Quarterly €30 p.a. (€45 overseas)

Essays, criticism, reportage and fiction for the intelligent general reader. Payment: by arrangement. Founded 2000.

Early Music

c/o Faculty of Music, University of Cambridge, 11 West Road, Cambridge CB3 9DP
tel (01223) 335178
email earlymusic@oupjournals.org
website http://emoxfordjournals.org
Editor Francis Knights
Quarterly £62 p.a.

Lively, informative and scholarly articles on aspects of medieval, renaissance, baroque and classical music.

Payment: £20 per 1000 words. Illustrations: line, half-tone, colour. Founded 1973.

East Lothian Life

1 Beveridge Row, Belhaven, Dunbar,
East Lothian EH42 1TP
tel (01368) 863593 *fax* (01368) 863593
email info@eastlothianlife.co.uk
website www.eastlothianlife.co.uk
Editor Pauline Jaffray
Quarterly £2.50

Articles and features with an East Lothian slant. Length: up to 1000 words. Illustrations: b&w photos, line, cartoons. Payment: negotiable. Founded 1989.

Eastern Art Report

Eastern Art Publishing Group, PO Box 13666,
London SW14 8WF
tel 020-8392 1122 *fax* 020-8392 1422
email ear@eapgroup.com
website www.eapgroup.com
Publisher/Editor-in-Chief Sajid Rizvi, *Send material to* Shirley Rizvi, Executive Editor
Bi-monthly £6 (£30 p.a. individual, £60 p.a. institutions)

Original, well-researched articles on all aspects of the visual arts – Buddhist, Islamic, Judaic, Indian, Chinese and Japanese; reviews. Length of articles: min. 1500 words. Illustrations: colour transparencies, b&w photos; no responsibility accepted for unsolicited material. Payment: by arrangement. Founded 1989.

Easy Living

Condé Nast Publications UK Ltd,
68 Old Bond Street, London W1S 4PH
tel 020-7499 9080
email easylivingeditorial@condenast.co.uk
website www.easylivingmagazine.com
Editor Susie Forbes
Monthly £3.40

Women's magazine that 'optimises time without compromising on style', covering fashion, the home, beauty and health, recipes, and relationships. Founded 2005.

The Ecologist

Unit 102, Lana House Studios,
116–118 Commercial Street, London E1 6NF
tel 020-7422 8100 *fax* 020-7422 8101
email editorial@theecologist.org
website www.theecologist.org
Editor Mark Anslow
10 p.a. £3.50

Fully referenced articles on economic, social and environmental affairs from an ecological standpoint. Study magazine first for level and approach. Length: 1000–5000 words. Illustrations: line, half-tone. Payment: by arrangement.

Economica

STICERD, London School of Economics,
Houghton Street, London WC2A 2AE
tel 020-7955 7855 *fax* 020-7955 6951
Editors Prof. F. Caselli, Prof. F. Cowell,
Dr A. Michaelides, Prof. P.N. Sorensen
Quarterly £209 per volume (apply for subscription rates)

Learned journal covering the fields of economics, economic history and statistics. Payment: none. Founded 1921; New series 1934.

The Economist

25 St James's Street, London SW1A 1HG
tel 020-7830 7000 *fax* 020-7839 2968
website www.economist.com
Editor John Micklethwait
Weekly £3.90

Articles staff-written. Founded 1843.

The Edge

65 Guinness Buildings, London W6 8BD
tel (0845) 456 9337
website www.theedge2010.com
Editor David Clark
Quarterly £4

Reviews and features: film (indie, arts), books, popular culture. Fiction: see magazine or website for examples/tone. For guidelines send sae or see website. Payment: negotiable. For sample issue send cheque payable to 'The Edge'.

Edinburgh Review

22a Buccleugh Place, Edinburgh EH8 9LN
tel 0131-651 1415 *fax* 0131-651 1415
email edinburgh.review@ed.ac.uk
website www.edinburghreview.org.uk
Editor Brian McCabe
3 p.a. £17 p.a. (£34 institutions)

Fiction, poetry, clearly written articles on Scottish and international cultural and philosophical ideas. Payment: by arrangement. Founded 1969.

Education Journal

Devonia House, 4 Union Terrace, Crediton,
Exeter EX17 3DY
tel (01363) 774455 *fax* (01363) 776592
email info@educationpublishing.com
website www.educationpublishing.com
Editor Demitri Coryton
11 p.a. £3.65

Features on policy, management and professional development issues. Major documents and reports gutted down to a brief digest; documents and research listings. Research section combining original reports and updates on research projects. Coverage of parliamentary debates and answers to parliamentary questions, giving statistical data by LEA. Reference section that includes coverage of all circulars, conference reports and opinion column. Length: 1000 words. Illustrations: photos, cartoons. Payment: by arrangement. Founded 1903; relaunched 1996.

Electrical Review

6 Laurence Pountney Hill, London EC4R 0BL
tel 020-7933 8999 *fax* 020-7933 8998
email elinorem@electricalreview.co.uk
website www.electricalreview.co.uk
Editor Elinore MacKay
Monthly £3.50 (£160 p.a.)

Technical and business articles on electrical and control engineering; outside contributions considered. Electrical news welcomed. Illustrations: photos and drawings, cartoons. Payment: according to merit. Founded 1872.

ELLE (UK)

Hachette Filipacchi UK, 64 North Row, London W1K 7LL
tel 020-7150 7000 *fax* 020-7150 7670
website www.elleuk.com
Editor Lorraine Candy
Monthly £3.30

Commissioned material only. Payment: by arrangement. Illustrations: colour. Founded 1985.

Embroidery

The Embroiderers' Guild,
Apt 41 Hampton Court Palace, Surrey KT8 9AU
tel (01260) 273891
email jo.editor@btinternet.com
website www.embroiderersguild.com/embroidery
Editor Joanne Hall
6 p.a. £4.90 (£29.40 p.a.)

News and illustrated features on all aspects of embroidery in contemporary design, fashion, illustration, interiors, art, general textiles and world embroidery. Features on internationally renowned makers, artists and designers working with textiles, stitch and embroidery. News covering exhibitions, books, interiors and products, plus event listings, book and exhibition reviews, and opportunities.

Empire

Bauer Consumer Media, Mappin House,
4 Winsley Street, London W1W 8HF
tel 020-7182 8000 *fax* 020-7182 8703
website www.empireonline.com
Editor Mark Dinning
Monthly £3.70

Guide to film and video: articles, features, news. Length: various. Illustrations: colour and b&w photos. Payment: approx. £300 per 1000 words; varies for illustrations. Founded 1989.

Energy Engineering

Gillard Welch Ltd, 6A New Street,
Warwick CV34 4RX
tel (01926) 408242 *fax* (01926) 408206
email steve@energyengineering.co.uk
website www.energyengineering.net.co.uk
Editor Steve Welch
12 p.a. £9

'For innovators in technology, manufacturing and management': features and news. Contributions considered on all aspects of engineering. Illustrations: colour. Founded 1866.

The Engineer

Centaur Communications Ltd, St Giles House,
50 Poland Street, London W1F 7AX
tel 020-7970 4437 *fax* 020-7970 4189
email jon.excell@centaur.co.uk
website www.theengineer.com
Editor Jon Excell
Fortnightly £2.70

Features and news on innovation and technology, including profiles, analysis. Length: up to 800 words (news), 1000 words (features). Illustrations: colour transparencies or prints, artwork, line diagrams, graphs. Payment: by negotiation. Founded 1856.

Engineering in Miniature

TEE Publishing Ltd, The Fosse, Fosse Way,
Radford Semele, Leamington Spa, Warks. CV31 1XN
tel (01926) 614101 *fax* (01926) 614293
email info@engineeringinminiature.co.uk
website www.engineeringinminiature.co.uk
Managing Editor C.L. Deith
Monthly £2.95

Articles containing descriptions and information on all aspects of model engineering. Articles welcome but technical articles preferred. Payment dependent on pages published. Founded 1979.

The English Garden

Archant House, Oriel Road, Cheltenham,
Gloucestershire GL50 1BB
email theenglishgarden@archant.co.uk
Editor Tamsin Westhorpe
Monthly £3.75

Features and photography on gardens in the English style, plant genera and garden design. Length: 800 words. Illustrations: colour photos and artwork. Payment: variable. Founded 1997.

Envoi

Meirion House, Glan yr afon, Tanygrisiau,
Blaenau Ffestiniog, Gwynedd LL41 3SU
tel (01766) 832112
website www.envoipoetry.com
Editor Jan Fortune-Wood
3 p.a. £15 p.a.

New poetry, including sequences, collaborative works and translations; reviews; articles on modern poets and poetic style; poetry competitions; adjudicator's reports. Sample copy: £5. Payment: complimentary copy. Founded 1957.

The Erotic Review

31 Sinclair Road, London W14 0NS
tel 020-7371 1532
email jmaclean@eroticprints.org
website www.eroticreviewmagazine.com
Editor Jamie Maclean
10 p.a. inc. 2 double issues £3

Up-market literary magazine for sensualists and libertines. Length: 1000 words (articles and features), 1000–2000 (short stories). Illustrations: colour and b&w prints, artwork and cartoons. Payment: £50–£75 (articles and features), £50–£75 (short stories); £50 (prints and artwork), £40 (cartoons). Founded 1995.

Esquire

National Magazine House, 72 Broadwick Street, London W1F 9EP
tel 020-7439 5000 *fax* 020-7439 5675
website www.esquire.co.uk
Editor Jeremy Langmead
Monthly £3.99

Quality men's general interest magazine – articles, features. No unsolicited material or short stories. Length: various. Illustrations: colour and b&w photos, line. Payment: by arrangement. Founded 1991.

Essentials

IPC Media, The Blue Fin Building, 110 Southwark Street, London SE1 0SU
tel 020-3148 7211
Editor Jules Barton-Breck
Monthly £2.70

Features, fashion, health, beauty, cookery, travel, consumer. Illustrations: colour. Payment: by negotiation. Founded 1988.

Essex Life

427 High Road, Woodford Green, Essex IG8 0XE
tel (01903) 703730
email editorialenquiries@essexlife.net
website www.essexlifemag.co.uk
Editor Julian Read
Monthly £2.95

No unsolicited material. Founded 1952.

Eventing

IPC Inspire, The Blue Fin Building, 110 Southwark Street, London SE1 0SU
tel 020-3148 5000 *fax* 020-3148 8127
email julie_harding@ipcmedia.com
Editor Julie Harding
Monthly £3.80

News, articles, features, event reports and opinion pieces – all connected to the sport of horse trials. Mostly commissioned, but all ideas welcome. Length: up to 1500 words. Illustrations: colour and b&w, mostly commissioned. Payment: by arrangement. Founded 1984.

Evergreen

PO Box 52, Cheltenham, Glos. GL50 1YQ
tel (01242) 537900 *fax* (01242) 537901
Editor Stephen Garnett
Quarterly £4.25

Articles about Great Britain's heritage, culture, countryside, people and places. Length 250–2000 words. Illustrations: digital; colour transparencies only accepted when accompanying articles. Payment: £25 per 1000 words, £10 poems (12–24 lines). Founded 1985.

Everyday Practical Electronics

Wimborne Publishing Ltd, Sequoia House, 398A Ringwood Road, Ferndown, Dorset BH22 9AU
tel (01202) 873872 *fax* (01202) 874562
email editorial@epemag.wimborne.co.uk
website www.epemag.com
Editor Matt Pulzer
Monthly £3.95

Constructional and theoretical articles aimed at the student and hobbyist. Length: 1000–5500 words. Payment: £55–£90 per 1000 words. Illustrations: line, half-tone. Founded 1971.

Executive PA

15-17 Blackfrairs Lane, London EC4V 6ER
tel 020-7236 1118 *fax* 020-7489 5809
website www.executivepa.net
Editor Cora Lydon
Quarterly £21 p.a.

Business to business for working senior secretaries. Length: 700–1400 words. Illustrations: colour. Payment: £140 per 1000 words. Founded 1991.

Families First

(formerly Home & Family)
The Mothers' Union, Mary Sumner House, 24 Tufton Street, London SW1P 3RB
tel 020-7222 5533
email familiesfirst@themothersunion.org
Editor Catherine Butcher
Bi-monthly £2

Short articles on parenting, marriage, family life, Christian faith, fair trade and community life. Payment: from £80 per 1000 words. Illustrations: colour photos and occasionally illustrations. Few unsolicited articles are accepted. Enclose sae. Founded 1954.

Family History Monthly

Unit 101, 140 Wales Farm Road, London W3 6UG
tel (0208) 752 8181 *fax* (0208) 752 8185
email penny.law@metropolis.co.uk
Editor Penny Law
Monthly £3.75

Articles on all aspects of genealogy and British history plus listings, news and reviews. Ideas welcome.

Particularly interested in articles on social, military and economic history since 1750 and family history case studies in first person. Does not publish anything above 3000 words. Submit 100 word feature ideas via email. Contact editor for guidelines. Payment: £60 per published 1000 words, but pay more for particularly good material. Founded 1995.

Family Law Journal

Kensington Square House, 12–14 Ansdell Street, London W8 5BN
tel 020-7396 9292 *fax* 020-7396 9300
email geraldine.morris@legalease.co.uk
website www.legalease.co.uk
Family Law Journal Editor Geraldine Morris
Monthly £135 p.a.

Articles concerning developments and practical issues in family law, written for and by lawyers working in the field. Length from 1,500 words, no payment, no illustrations. Email for more details. Founded 1971.

Family Tree

61 Great Whyte, Ramsey, Huntingdon, Cambs PE26 1HJ
tel (01487) 814050 *fax* (01487) 711361
website www.family-tree.co.uk
Editor Helen Tovey
Every 4 weeks £3.99, £45 p.a.

Articles on any genealogically related topics. Payment: by arrangement. Founded 1984.

Farmers Weekly

Reed Business Information, Quadrant House, The Quadrant, Sutton, Surrey SM2 5AS
tel 020-8652 4911 *fax* 020-8652 4005
email farmers.weekly@rbi.co.uk
website www.fwi.co.uk
Editor Jane King
Weekly £2.25

Articles on agriculture from freelance contributors will be accepted subject to negotiation. Founded 1934.

The Feminist Review

Palgrave Macmillan Ltd, Brunel Road, Houndmills, Basingstoke, Hants RG21 6XS
tel (01256) 329242 *fax* (01256) 810526
website www.feminist-review.com
Edited by a Collective, supported by a group of corresponding editors
3 p.a. £42

Aims to unite research and theory with political practice and contribute to the development of both as well as the exploration and articulation of the socio-economic realities of women's lives. Welcomes contributions from the spectrum of contemporary feminist debate. Empirical work – both qualitative and quantitative – is particularly welcome. In addition, each issue contains some papers which are themed around a specific debate. Founded 1979.

FHM (For Him Magazine)

Bauer Consumer Media, Endeavour House, 189 Shaftesbury Avenue, London WC2H 8JG
tel 020-7182 8000 *fax* 020-7182 8021
email general@fhm.com
website www.fhm.com
Editor Anthony Noguera
Monthly £3.80

Features, fashion, grooming, travel (adventure) and men's interests. Length: 1200–2000 words. Illustrations: colour and b&w photos, line and colour artwork. Payment: by negotiation. Founded 1987.

The Field

IPC Inspire, The Blue Fin Building, 110 Southwark Street, London SE1 0SU
tel 020-3148 5000
website www.thefield.co.uk
Editor Jonathan Young
Monthly £4

Specific, topical and informed features on the British countryside and country pursuits, including natural history, field sports, gardening and rural conservation. Overseas subjects considered but opportunities for such articles are limited. No fiction or children's material. Articles, length 800–2000 words, by outside contributors considered; also topical 'shorts' of 200–300 words on all countryside matters. Illustrations: colour photos of a high standard. Payment: on merit. Founded 1853.

Film Ireland

Filmbase, Curved Street, Temple Bar, Dublin 2, Republic of Ireland
tel (353) 1 6796716 *fax* (353) 1 6796717
email editor@filmbase.ie
website www.filmireland.net
Editor Niamh Creely
Bi-monthly €6

Aims to be an open and pluralist forum for the exchange of ideas and news on filmmaking and cinema, both Irish and international. Special reports, interviews and reviews; acts as a unique archival mirror of film activity in Ireland. Founded 1987.

Film Review

Visual Imagination Ltd, 9–10 Blades Court, Deodar Road, London SW15 2NU
tel 020-8875 7417 *fax* 020-8875 1588
email filmreview@visimag.com
website www.visimag.com/filmreview, www.filmreviewonline.com
Editor Nikki Baughan
Every 4 weeks £3.99

Features and interviews on mainstream cinema; film and DVD reviews. No fiction. Length: 1000–3000 words (features), 350 words (reviews). Illustrations: colour and b&w. Payment: £80 per 1000 words; £20 for first image, £10 per additional image. Founded 1950.

Financial Adviser

Financial Times Business, 1 Southwark Bridge, London SE1 9HL
tel 020-7775 3000
email hal.austin@ft.com
website www.ftadviser.com
Editor Hal Austin
Weekly £99 p.a. Free to financial intermediaries working in financial services

Topical personal finance news and features. Length: variable. Payment: by arrangement. Founded 1987.

FIRE

PO Box 100, Chichester PO18 8HD
tel (01243) 576444 *fax* (01243) 576456
email Andrew.lynch@beywayspublishing.com
website www.fire-magazine.com
Editor Andrew Lynch
Monthly £10.30 (£76 p.a.)

Articles on firefighting and fire prevention from acknowledged experts only. Length: 600 words. No unsolicited contributions. Illustrations: dramatic firefighting or fire brigade rescue colour photos. Also *Fire International*. Payment: by arrangement. Founded 1908.

Fishing News

INTRAFISH, 6th Floor, Eldon House, 2 Eldon Street, London EC2M 7LS
tel 020-7650 1034 *fax* 020-7650 1050
email tim.oliver@fishingnews.co.uk
website www.fishingnews.co.uk
Editor Cormac Burke
Weekly £1.85

News and features on all aspects of the commercial fishing industry. Length: up to 1000 words (features), up to 500 words (news). Illustrations: colour and b&w photos. Payment: negotiable. Founded 1913.

Flight International

Reed Business Information Ltd, Quadrant House, The Quadrant, Sutton, Surrey SM2 5AS
tel 020-8652 3842 *fax* 020-8652 3840
website www.flightinternational.com
Editor Michael Targett
Weekly £2.85

Deals with all branches of aerospace: operational and technical articles, illustrated by photos, engineering cutaway drawings; also news, paragraphs, reports of lectures, etc. News press days: Thurs, Fri. Illustrations: tone, line, colour. Payment: by agreement. Founded 1909.

Flora International

The Fishing Lodge Studio, 77 Bulbridge Road, Wilton, Salisbury, Wilts. SP2 0LE
tel (01722) 743207 *fax* (01722) 743207
email floramag@aol.com
Editor Maureen Foster
Bi-monthly £3.95

Magazine for flower arrangers and florists. Also features flower-related articles, flower arrangers' gardens and flower-related crafts. Will consider unsolicited material. Welcomes ideas for articles and features. Length: approx. 1000 words (articles/features). Illustrations: transparencies, colour prints or high-res files on CD. Payment: £60 per 1000 words, £10–£20 illustrations. Founded 1974.

Fly-Fishing & Fly-Tying

Rolling River Publications, The Locus Centre, The Square, Aberfeldy, Perthshire PH15 2DD
tel (01887) 829868 *fax* (01887) 829856
email MarkB.ffft@btinternet.com
website www.flyfishing-and-flytying.co.uk
Editor Mark Bowler
12 p.a. £3.10

Fly-fishing and fly-tying articles, fishery features, limited short stories, fishing travel. Length: 800–2000 words. Illustrations: colour photos. Payment: by arrangement. Founded 1990.

Folio

2nd Floor, Bristol News and Media, Temple Way, Bristol BS99 7HD
tel 0117-942 8491 *fax* 0117-934 3566
email editor@foliomagazine.co.uk
website www.foliomagazine.co.uk
Editor Mike Gartside
Monthly Free

Articles, features, interviews and news on people, places and events with a local connection (Bristol and Bath area). No short stories or poems. Unsolicited material considered. Length: 600–2000 words (features), variable (news). Illustrations: colour and b&w. Payment: by negotiation. Founded 1994.

Fortean Times

Box 2409, London NW5 4NP
tel 020-7907 6235 *fax* 020-7907 6139
email david_sutton@dennis.co.uk
website www.forteantimes.com
Editor David Sutton
13 p.a. £4.25

Journal of strange phenomena, experiences, related subjects and philosophies. Articles, features, news, reviews. Length: 500–5000 words; longer by arrangement. Illustrations: colour photos, line and tone art, cartoons. Payment: by negotiation. Founded 1973.

Fortnight – An Independent Review of Politics and the Arts

11 University Road, Belfast BT7 1NA
tel 028-9023 2353 *fax* 028-9023 2650
email r.goldsmith@fortnight.org
website www.fortnight.org
Editor Rudie Goldsmith

Monthly. £2.50

Current affairs analysis, reportage, opinion pieces, cultural criticism, book reviews, poems. Illustrations: line, half-tone, cartoons. Payment: by arrangement. Founded 1970.

FourFourTwo

Haymarket, Teddington Studios, Broom Road, Teddington, Middlesex TW11 9BE
tel 020-8267 5848 *fax* 020-8267 5061
website www.fourfourtwo.magazine.co.uk
Editor David Hall
Monthly £3.60

Football magazine with 'adult' approach: interviews, in-depth features, issues pieces, odd and witty material. Length: 2000–3000 (features), 100–1500 words (Up Front pieces). Illustrations: colour transparencies and artwork, b&w prints. Payment: £200 per 1000 words. Founded 1994.

France

Archant House, Oriel Road, Cheltenham, Glos. GL50 1BB
tel (01242) 216050 *fax* (01242) 216094
email editorial@francemag.com
website www.francemag.com
Editor Carolyn Boyd
Monthly £3.99

Informed quality features and articles on the real France, ranging from cuisine to culture to holidays exploring hidden France. Length: 800–2000 words. Payment: £100 per 1000 words; £50 per page/pro rata for illustrations. Founded 1989.

Freelance Market News

Sevendale House, 7 Dale Street, Manchester M1 1JB
tel 0161-228 2362 *fax* 0161-236 9440
email fmn@writersbureau.com
website www.freelancemarketnews.com
Editor Angela Cox
11 p.a. £29 p.a.

Information on UK and overseas publications with editorial content, submission requirements and contact details. News of editorial requirements for writers. Features on the craft of writing, competitions, letters page. Founded 1968.

The Friend

173 Euston Road, London NW1 2BJ
tel 020-7663 1010 *fax* 020-7663 1182
email news@thefriend.org
website www.thefriend.org
Editor Judy Kirby
Weekly £1.70

Material of interest to Quakers and like-minded people; political, social, economic, environmental or devotional, considered from outside contributors. Length: up to 1200 words. Illustrations: b&w or colour prints, b&w line drawings and cartoons by email preferred. Payment: not usually but will negotiate a small fee with professional writers. Founded 1843.

Frieze

81 Rivington Street, London EC2A 3AY
tel 020-3372 6111 *fax* 020-3178 7042
email editors@frieze.com
website www.frieze.com
8 p.a. £5.95 (£33.50 p.a.)

Magazine of European contemporary art and culture including essays, reviews, columns and listings. Frieze Art Fair is held every October in Regent's Park, London featuring over 150 of the most exciting contemporary art galleries in the world. Founded 1991.

Full House

Hubert Burda Media UK, The Tower, Phoenix Square, Colchester, Essex CO4 9HU
tel (01206) 851117 *fax* (01206) 849079
website www.fullhousemagazine.co.uk
Editor Dave Claridge
Weekly 50p

Women's magazine with real-life features and puzzles. Founded 2005.

The Furrow

St Patrick's College, Maynooth, Co. Kildare, Republic of Ireland
tel (01) 7083741 *fax* (01) 7083908
email furrow.office@may.ie
website www.thefurrow.ie
Editor Rev. Ronan Drury
Monthly €2.75

Religious, pastoral, theological, social articles. Length: up to 3000 words. Payment: average €20 per page (450 words). Illustrations: line, half-tone. Founded 1950.

Galleries

Barrington Publications, 54 Uxbridge Road, London W12 8LP
tel 020-8740 7020
email features@galleries.co.uk
website www.galleries.co.uk
Editor Andrew Aitken
Monthly £1.88 (£24 p.a.)

Art listings and editorial magazine describing current exhibitions and stock of over 500 commercial and public art galleries, galleries for hire and art services.

GamesMaster

Future Publishing Ltd, 30 Monmouth Street, Bath BA1 2BW
tel (01225) 442244 *fax* (01225) 446019
email gamesmaster@futurenet.co.uk
Editor-in-Chief Robin Alway
Every 4 weeks £3.99

The UK's longest running video games magazine, covering the biggest and best games across all formats.

The Garden

4th Floor, Churchgate, New Road,
Peterborough PE1 1TT
tel (0845) 260 0909 *fax* (01733) 341633
email thegarden@rhs.org.uk
Editor Ian Hodgson
Monthly £4.25

Journal of The Royal Horticultural Society. Features of horticultural or botanical interest on a wide range of subjects. Commissioned material only. Length: 1200–2500 words. Illustrations: 35mm or medium format colour transparencies, occasional b&w prints, botanical line drawings; digital images are not accepted for features. Payment: varies. Founded 1866.

Garden Answers

Bauer Consumer Media Ltd, Media House,
Lynchwood, Peterborough Business Park,
Peterborough PE2 6EA
tel (01733) 468000 *fax* (01733) 468888
email gardenanswers@bauermedia.co.uk
Editor Geoff Stebbings
Monthly £3.10

Some commissioned features and articles on all aspects of gardening. Study of magazine essential. Approach by letter with examples of published work. Length: approx. 750 words. Illustrations: colour transparencies, digital images and artwork. Payment: by negotiation. Founded 1982.

Garden News

Bauer Consumer Media Ltd, Media House,
Lynchwood, Peterborough Business Park,
Peterborough PE2 6EA
tel (01733) 237111 *fax* (01733) 465779
email clare.foggett@bauerconsumer.com
website www.gardennews-mag.com
Editor Clare Foggett
Weekly £1.70

Up-to-date information on everything to do with plants, growing and gardening. Illustrations: line, colour, cartoons. Payment: by negotiation. Founded 1958.

Gay Times – GT

Spectrum House, 32–34 Gordon House Road,
London NW5 1LP
tel 020-7424 7400 *fax* 020-7424 7401
email edit@gaytimes.co.uk
website www.gaytimes.co.uk
Editor Joseph Galliano
Monthly £3.75

Current affairs, opinion, culture, art, style, grooming, features and interviews. Length: up to 2000 words. Payment: by arrangement. Founded 1984.

Geographical

Circle Publishing, 1 Victoria Villas, Richmond,
Surrey TW9 2GW
tel 020-8332 2713 *fax* 020-8332 9307
email magazine@geographical.co.uk
website www.geographical.co.uk
Editor Geordie Torr
Monthly Free

Magazine of the Royal Geographical Society. Covers culture, wildlife, environment, science and travel. Illustrations: top quality transparencies, vintage material. Payment: by negotiation. Founded 1935.

Geographical Journal

Royal Geographical Society (with the Institute of
British Geographers), 1 Kensington Gore,
London SW7 2AR
tel 020-7591 3026 *fax* 020-7591 3001
email journals@rgs.org
Editor Prof. Klaus Dodds
4 p.a. £192 (print and online), £174 (print only)

Papers range across the entire subject of geography, with particular reference to public debates, policy-oriented agendas and notions of 'relevance'. Illustrations: photos, maps, diagrams. Founded 1893.

Geological Magazine

Cambridge University Press,
The Edinburgh Building, Shaftesbury Road,
Cambridge CB2 8RU
email geolmag@aegis-prm.com
website www.journals.cambridge.org/geo
Editors Dr M.B. Allen, Dr G.E. Budd, Dr A.G. Whitham
Bi-monthly £515/$868 print and online, £426/$823 online only, £30/$45 single article

Original articles on all earth science topics containing the results of independent research by experts. Also reviews and notices of current geological literature, correspondence on geological subjects. Submit MSS at http://mc.manuscriptcentral.com/geo. Length: variable. Payment: none. Founded 1864.

Gibbons Stamp Monthly

Stanley Gibbons Ltd, 7 Parkside, Ringwood,
Hants BH24 3SH
tel (01425) 472363 *fax* (01425) 470247
email hjefferies@stanleygibbons.co.uk
website www.stanleygibbons.co.uk
Editor Hugh Jefferies
Monthly £3.40

Articles on philatelic topics. Contact the Editor first. Length: 500–2500 words. Payment: by arrangement, £45 or more per 1000 words. Illustrations: photos, line, stamps or covers.

Glamour

6–8 Old Bond Street, London W1S 4PH
tel 020-7499 9080 *fax* 020-7491 2551

email editor@glamourmagazine.co.uk
website www.glamourmagazine.com
Editor Jo Elvin
Monthly £2

Lifestyle magazine containing fashion, beauty, real-life features and celebrity news aimed at women aged 18–34. Feature ideas welcome; approach with brief outline. Length: 500–800 words. Payment: by arrangement. Founded 2001.

Go Girl Magazine

Egmont Magazines, 239 Kensington High Street, London W8 6SA
tel 020-7761 3500
website www.gogirlmag.co.uk
Editor Emma Prosser
Every 3 weeks £2.30

Magazine for 7–11-year-old girls including fashion, beauty, celebrity news and gossip. Payment: by arrangement. Founded 2003.

Golf Monthly

IPC Inspire, The Blue Fin Building, 110 Southwark Street, London SE1 0SU
tel 020-3148 5000
email golfmonthly@ipcmedia.com
website www.golf-monthly.co.uk
Editor Michael Harris
Monthly £3.70

Original articles on golf considered (not reports), golf clinics, handy hints. Illustrations: half-tone, colour, cartoons. Payment: by arrangement. Founded 1911.

Golf World

Bauer Media, Media House, Lynchwood, Peterborough Business Park, Peterborough PE2 6EA
tel (01733) 468000 *fax* (01733) 468843
email chris.jones@bauermedia.co.uk
website www.golf-world.co.uk
Editor Chris Jones, *Acting Managing Director* Steve Prentice
Monthly £4.10

Expert golf instructional articles, 500–3000 words; general interest articles, personality features 500–3000 words. No fiction. No unsolicited material. Payment: by negotiation. Illustrations: line, half-tone, colour, cartoons. Founded 1962.

The Good Book Guide

29–30 Monument Business Park, Chalgrove, Oxon OX44 7RW
tel (01865) 893434 *fax* (01865) 893430
email hfoakes@gbgdirect.com
website www.thegoodbookguide.com
Editorial Director Hilary Foakes
Monthly £2.85

Review magazine recommending and selling the best books published in Britain.

Good Housekeeping

National Magazine House, 72 Broadwick Street, London W1F 9EP
tel 020-7439 5000 *fax* 020-7439 5616
email goodh.mail@natmags.co.uk
website www.goodhousekeeping.co.uk
Editor Rosemary Ellis
Monthly £3.40

Articles on topics of interest to intelligent women. No unsolicited features or stories accepted; approach by letter only. Homes, fashion, beauty and food covered by staff writers. Payment: magazine standards. Illustrations: commissioned. Founded 1922.

GQ

Condé Nast Publications, Vogue House, Hanover Square, London W1S 1JU
tel 020-7499 9080 *fax* 020-7495 1679
website www.gq-magazine.co.uk
Editor Dylan Jones
Monthly £3.95

Style, fashion and general interest magazine for men. Illustrations: b&w and colour photos, line drawings, cartoons. Payment: by arrangement. Founded 1988.

Granta

12 Addison Avenue, London W11 4QR
tel 020-7605 1360 *fax* 020-7605 1361
website www.granta.com
Editor John Freeman
Quarterly £10.99 (£29.95 p.a.)

Original literary fiction, non-fiction, memoir, reportage and photography. Study magazine before submitting work. No academic essays or reviews. Length: determined by content. Illustrations: photos. Payment: by arrangement. Founded 1889; reconceived 1979.

Grazia

BauerConsumer Media, Endeavour House, 189 Shaftesbury Avenue, London WC2H 8JG
tel 020-7437 9011 *fax* 020-7520 6599
email graziadaily@graziamagazine.co.uk
website www.graziadaily.co.uk
Editor-in-Chief Jane Bruton
Weekly £1.90

Women's magazine with the latest trends, gossip, fashion and news in bite-size pieces.

Green Futures

Overseas House, 19–23 Ironmonger Row, London EC1V 3QN
email post@greenfutures.org.uk
website www.greenfutures.org.uk
Editor-in-Chief Martin Wright
Quarterly £24 p.a., personal £34 p.a., non-profit organisation £57 p.a., businesses (subscription only)

Articles and features on environmental solutions and sustainable futures for people in government, business and higher education. Specially commissions most material. Welcomes ideas for news stories and features. Illustrations: high-res digital photos. Send material to Katie Shaw, Editorial and Marketing Coordinator. Founded 1996.

Green Pebble

Roos Hall Studio, Bungay Road, Beccles,
Suffolk NR34 8HE
tel (01502) 710427
email editor@greenpebble.co.uk
website www.greenpebble.co.uk
Editor Ruby Ormerod
Bi-monthly

Magazine dedicated to contemporary visual arts in East Anglia. Founded 2007.

Greetings Today

(formerly Greetings Magazine)
Lema Publishing, 1 Churchgates Wilderness,
Berkhamstead, Herts. HP4 2AZ
tel (01442) 289930 *fax* (01442) 289950
website www.greetingstoday.co.uk
Editor Lewis Eckett
Monthly £45 p.a. (other rates on application)

Articles, features and news related to the greetings card industry; includes Artists Directory for aspiring artists wishing to attract the eye of publishers. Mainly written in-house; some material taken from outside. Length: varies. Illustrations: line, colour and b&w photos. Payment: by arrangement. Founded 1999; first published 1972.

The Grocer

William Reed Publishing Ltd, Broadfield Park,
Crawley, West Sussex RH11 9RT
tel (01293) 613400 *fax* (01293) 610333
website www.thegrocer.co.uk
Editor Adam Leyland
Weekly £1.95

Trade journal: articles or news or illustrations of general interest to the grocery and provision trades. Payment: by arrangement. Founded 1861.

Grow Your Own

25 Phoenix Court, Hawkins Road,
Colchester CO2 8JY
tel (01206) 505979 *fax* (01206) 505905
email lucy.halsall@aceville.co.uk
website www.growfruitandveg.co.uk
Editor Lucy Halsall
Monthly £3.45

Magazine for kitchen gardeners of all levels of expertise. Will consider unsolicited material. Welcomes ideas for articles and features. Length: 1000 words (articles), 1500 words (features) 200 words (news). Illustrations: transparencies, colour prints and digital images. Payment: varies.

Guiding Magazine

17–19 Buckingham Palace Road, London SW1W 0PT
tel 020-7834 6242 *fax* 020-7828 5791
email guiding@girlguiding.org.uk
website www.girlguiding.org.uk
Editor Wendy Kewley
Monthly £2

Official magazine of Girlguiding UK. Articles of interest to women of all ages, with special emphasis on youth work and the Guide Movement. Articles on simple crafts, games and the outdoors especially welcome. Length: up to 600 words. Illustrations: line, half-tone, colour. Payment: £300 per 1000 words. Please contact editor with proposal first.

Guitarist

Future Publishing UK, 30 Monmouth Street,
Bath BA1 2BW
tel (01225) 442244 *fax* (01225) 446019
website www.futurenet.co.uk
Editor Mick Taylor
13 p.a. £5.25

Aims to improve readers' knowledge of the instrument, help them make the right buying choices and assist them in becoming a better player. Ideas for articles welcome. Founded 1984.

H&E Naturist

New Freedom Publications Ltd, Burlington Court,
Carlisle Street, Goole, East Yorkshire DN14 5EG
tel (01405) 760298 *fax* (01405) 763815
email editor@henaturist.net
website http://henaturist.net/joomla
Editor Sam Hawcroft
Monthly £3.95

Articles on naturist travel, clubs, beaches and naturist lifestyle experiences from the UK, Europe and the world. Length: 800–1200 words. Illustrations: prints and digital images featuring naturists in natural settings; also cartoons, humorous fillers and features with naturist themes. Payment: by negotiation but guidelines for contributors and basic payment rates available on request.

Hairflair & Beauty

Freebournes House, Freebournes Road, Witham,
Essex CM8 3US
tel (01376) 534534 *fax* (01376) 534546
Editor Ruth Page
Bi-monthly £2.50

Hair, beauty and health for the 18–30 age group. Not currently accepting freelance submissions or illustrations. Founded 1985.

Hampshire – The County Magazine

A&D Media Ltd, Jesses Farm, Snow Hill, Dinton,
Wilts. SP3 5HN
tel (01722) 716996
Editor Mark Allen, *Deputy Editor* Geoffrey Williams
Monthly £2.99

Factual articles concerning all aspects of Hampshire, past and present. Length: 600–1500 words. Payment:

by arrangement. Illustrations: mainly colour photos. Founded 1960.

Harper's Bazaar

National Magazine House, 72 Broadwick Street, London W1F 9EP
tel 020-7439 5000 *fax* 020-7439 5506
website www.natmags.co.uk
Editor Lucy Yeomans
Monthly £3.99

Features, fashion, beauty, art, theatre, films, travel, interior decoration – some commissioned. Founded 1929.

Health Club Management

Leisure Media Company Ltd, Portmill House, Portmill Lane, Hitchin, Herts. SG5 1DJ
tel (01462) 431385 *fax* (01462) 433909
email healthclub@leisuremedia.com
website www.health-club.co.uk
Editor Liz Terry
£36 p.a.

Official publication of the Fitness Industry Association. Articles on the operation of health clubs, day spas, fitness and sports centres. Items on consumer issues and lifestyle trends as they affect club management are welcomed. Length: up to 1500 words. Illustrations: colour and b&w photos. Payment: by arrangement. Founded 1995.

Healthy

1 Neal Street, London WC2H 9QL
tel 020-7306 0304 *fax* 020-7306 0314
website www.healthy-magazine.co.uk
Editor Jane Druker
9 p.a. £1.75

Holland & Barrett magazine. Health and nutrition information, features, tips, news and recipes, all from a holistic health angle. Ideas from freelancers welcome, with a view to commissioning. It does not do product reviews, won't mention products not available in Holland & Barrett and cannot mention any brand names in the copy. Email ideas in first instance. Payment by negotiation. Founded 1996.

Heat

Bauer Consumer Media, Endeavour House, 189 Shaftesbury Avenue, London WC2H 8JG
tel 020-7437 9011 *fax* 020-7859 8670
email heat@bauerconsumer.com
website www.heatworld.com
Editor Sam Delaney
Weekly £1.65

Features and news on celebrities. Founded 1999.

Hello!

Wellington House, 69–71 Upper Ground, London SE1 9PQ
tel 020-7667 8700 *fax* 020-7667 8716
Editor-in-Chief Eduardo Sanchez Perez
Weekly £2

News-based features – showbusiness, celebrity, royalty; exclusive interviews. Payment: by arrangement. Illustrated. Founded 1988.

Hertfordshire Countryside

Beaumonde Publications Ltd, PO Box 5, Hitchin, Herts. SG5 1GJ
tel (01462) 422014 *fax* (01462) 422015
email martin_small@btconnect.com
Editor Sandra Small
Monthly £2.25

Articles of county interest. No poetry, puzzles or crosswords. Length: approx. 1000 words. Payment: negotiable. Founded 1946.

Hi-Fi News

IPC Inspire, Leon House, 233 High Street, Croydon CR9 1HZ
tel 020-8726 8311 *fax* 020-8726 8397
email hifinews@ipcmedia.co.uk
website www.hifinews.com
Editor Paul Miller
Monthly £4

Articles on all aspects of high-quality sound recording and reproduction; also extensive record review section and supporting musical feature articles. Audio matter is essentially technical, but should be presented in a manner suitable for music lovers interested in the nature of sound. Length: 2000–3000 words. Illustrations: line, half-tone. Payment: by arrangement. Founded 1956.

High Life

Cedar Communications Ltd, 85 Strand, London WC2R 0DW
tel 020-7550 8000 *fax* 020-7550 8250
email high.life@cedarcom.co.uk
website www.cedarcom.co.uk
Editor Kerry Smith
Monthly Free £37 p.a.

Inflight consumer magazine for British Airways passengers. Articles on entertainment, travel, fashion, business, sport and lifestyle. All material commissioned; approach in writing with ideas. Length: 850–2500 words. Illustrations: colour photos and line. Payment: £250 per 1000 words; £100–£400 for illustrations. Founded 1973.

History Today

20 Old Compton Street, London W1D 4TW
tel 020-7534 8000
email admin@historytoday.com
website www.historytoday.com
Editor Paul Lay
Monthly £4.95

History in the widest sense – political, economic, social, biography, relating past to present; world history as well as British. Length: 3500 words (articles); 600–1200 words (news/views). Illustrations: prints and original photos. Do not send original material until publication is agreed. Accepts freelance contributions dealing with genuinely new historical and archaelogical research. Payment: by arrangement. Send sae for return of MS. Founded 1951.

Home Words

77 Verulam Road, St Albans AL3 4DJ
tel (01727) 833400 *fax* 020-7776 1086
email terence@harrowweald.org
website www.churchtimes.co.uk
Editor Terence Handley-MacMath
Monthly 5p

Leading national insert for C of E parish magazines. Articles of interest to parishes; poems. Items should bear the author's name and address; include return postage or send by email. Length: up to 450 words, accompanied by photos/illustrations. Payment: by arrangement. Founded 1905.

Homes and Gardens

IPC Magazines Ltd, The Blue Fin Building, 110 Southwark Street, London SE1 0SU
tel 020-3148 5000
email homesandgardens@ipcmedia.com
website www.homesandgardens.com
Editor Deborah Barker
Monthly £3.30

Articles on home interest or design, particularly well-designed British interiors (snapshots should be submitted). Length: articles, 900–1000 words. Illustrations: all types. Payment: generous, but exceptional work required; varies. Founded 1919.

Horse & Hound

IPC Inspire, 9th Floor, The Blue Fin Building, 110 Southwark Street, London SE1 0SU
tel 020-3148 4562 *fax* 020-3148 8127
email jenny_sims@ipcmedia.com
website www.horseandhound.co.uk
Editor Lucy Higginson
Weekly £2.40

Special articles, news items, photos, on all matters appertaining to equestrian sports. Payment: by negotiation.

Horse & Pony Magazine

33 Broad Street, Stamford, Lincs. PE9 1RB
tel (01780) 754900
email s.whittington@bournepublishinggroup.co.uk
website www.horseandpony.com
Editor Sarah Whittington
Monthly £2.40

Equestrian magazine for girls aged 8–14 containing riding and horse-care know-how, games and competitions, top rider info and posters.

Horse and Rider

Headley House, Headley Road, Grayshott, Surrey GU26 6TU
tel (01428) 601020 *fax* (01428) 601030
email djm@djmurphy.co.uk
website www.horseandrideruk.com
Editor Nicky Moffatt
Monthly £3.70

Sophisticated magazine covering all forms of equestrian activity at home and abroad. Good writing and technical accuracy essential. Length: 1500–2000 words. Illustrations: photos and drawings, the latter usually commissioned. Payment: by arrangement. Founded 1959.

Hortus

Bryan's Ground, Stapleton, Nr Presteigne, Herefordshire LD8 2LP
tel (01544) 260001 *fax* (01544) 260015
email all@hortus.co.uk
website www.hortus.co.uk
Editor David Wheeler
Quarterly £38 p.a. (UK), £44 p.a. (Europe), £48 p.a. (Rest of World)

Articles on decorative horticulture: plants, gardens, history, design, literature, people; book reviews. Length: 1500–5000 words, longer by arrangement. Illustrations: line, half-tone and wood-engravings. Payment: by arrangement. Founded 1987.

Hot Press

13 Trinity Street, Dublin 2, Republic of Ireland
tel (01) 2411500 *fax* (01) 2411539
email info@hotpress.ie
website www.hotpress.com
Editor Niall Stokes
Fortnightly €3.50

High-quality, investigative stories, or punchily written offbeat pieces, of interest to 16–39 year-olds, including politics, music, sport, sex, religion – whatever's happening on the street. Length: varies. Illustrations: colour with some b&w. Payment: by negotiation. Founded 1977.

House & Garden

Vogue House, 1 Hanover Square, London W1S 1JU
tel 020-7499 9080 *fax* 020-7629 2907
Editor Susan Crewe
Monthly £3.70

Articles (always commissioned), on subjects relating to domestic architecture, interior decorating, furnishing, gardens and gardening, exhibitions, travel, food and wine.

House Beautiful

National Magazine House, 72 Broadwick Street, London W1F 9EP
tel 020-7439 5000 *fax* 020-7439 5141
email houseb.mail@natmags.co.uk
website www.allaboutyou.com/housebeautiful
Editor Bernadette Fallon
Monthly £3.20

Specialist features for the homes of today. We do not accept unsolicited manuscripts. Illustrated. Founded 1989.

Housebuilder

Byron House, 7–9 St James's Street,
London SW1A 1EE
tel 020-7960 1630 *fax* 020-7960 1631
website www.house-builder.co.uk
Editor Ben Roskrow
11 p.a. £7 (£77 p.a.)

Official Journal of the Home Builders Federation published in association with the National House-Building Council. Technical articles on design, construction and equipment of dwellings, estate planning and development, and technical aspects of house-building, aimed at those engaged in house and flat construction and the development of housing estates. Preliminary letter advisable. Length: articles from 500 words, preferably with illustrations. Payment: by arrangement. Illustrations: photos, plans, construction details, cartoons.

HQ Poetry Magazine

(The Haiku Quarterly)
39 Exmouth Street, Swindon SN1 3PU
tel (01793) 523927
Editor Kevin Bailey
3-4 p.a. £2.80 (4 issues £10 p.a., £13 non-UK)

International in scope, publishes both experimental and traditional work. About one third of the content is devoted to haikuesque and imagistic poetry. Also includes review section and articles. Payment: small. Founded 1990.

I'm Pregnant!

D.C. Thomson & Co Ltd, 80 Kingsway East,
Dundee DD4 8SL
tel (01382) 575130 *fax* (01382) 452491
185 Fleet Street, London EC4A 2HS
tel 020-7400 1030 *fax* 020-7400 1090
Quarterly £4.99

Features aimed at pregnant women and new mothers.

ICIS Chemical Business

Reed Business Information, Quadrant House,
The Quadrant, Sutton, Surrey SM2 5AS
tel 020-8652 3500 *fax* 020-8652 3375
email icbeditorial@icis.com
website www.icischemicalbusiness.com
Editor Joseph Chang
Weekly £293.30 p.a. (online subscription saving 30%)

Articles and features concerning business, markets and investments in the chemical industry. Length: 1000–2000 words; news items up to 400 words. Payment: £150–£200 per 1000 words.

Icon Magazine

Media 10, National House, High Street, Epping,
Essex CM16 4BD
tel (01992) 570030 *fax* (01992) 570031
email justin@icon-magazine.co.uk
website www.iconeye.com
Editor Justin McGuirk
Monthly £4.50

Articles on new buildings, interiors, innovative design and designers. Payment by negotiation. Founded 2003.

Ideal Home

IPC Media Ltd, The Blue Fin Building,
110 Southwark Street, London SE1 0SU
tel 020-3148 5000 *fax* 020-3148 8121
Editorial Director Isobel McKenzie-Price
Monthly £3.20

Lifestyle magazine, articles usually commissioned. Contributors advised to study editorial content before submitting material. Payment: according to material. Illustrations: usually commissioned. Founded 1920.

Improve Your Coarse Fishing

Bauer Media, Media House, Lynchwood,
Peterborough PE2 6EA
tel (01733) 468000 *fax* (01733) 468300
email kevin.green@bauermedia.co.uk
website www.gofishing.co.uk
Editor Kevin Green
Monthly £3.25

Articles on technique and equipment, the best venues, news and features. Ideas welcome by email. Founded 1991.

In Style

IPC Southbank, The Blue Fin Building,
110 Southwark Street, London SE1 0SU
tel 020-3148 5000 *fax* 020-3148 8166
Editor Eilidh MacAskill
Monthly £3.60

Fashion, beauty and celebrity lifestyle magazine for style-conscious women aged 25–44. Rarely accepts unsolicited material. Founded 2001.

Index on Censorship

60 Farringdon Road, London EC1R 3GA
tel 020-7324 2522
email jo@indexoncensorship.org
website www.indexonline.org
Editor Jo Glanville
Quarterly £9.50 (£32 p.a.)

Articles up to 3000 words dealing with all aspects of free speech and political censorship. Illustrations: b&w, cartoons. Payment: £75 per 1000 words. Founded 1972.

Inform

ISPAL, Abbey House, 1650 Arlington Business Park,
Theale, Berks RG7 4SA
tel (08444) 180077 *fax* (0118) 929 8001

email businessdevelopment@ispal.org.uk
website www.ispal.org.uk
Editor Jonathan Wilson
Monthly

Official journal of the Institute for Sport, Parks and Leisure (ISPAL). Articles on amenity, children's play, tourism, leisure, parks, entertainment, recreation and sports management, cultural services. Payment: by arrangement. Illustrations: line, half-tone. Founded 1985.

Inside Soap

Hachette Filipacchi (UK) Ltd, 64 North Row, London W1K 7LL
tel 020-7150 7000 *fax* 020-7150 7683
website www.insidesoap.co.uk
Editor Steven Murphy
Weekly £1.40

Gossip and celebrity interviews with soap and popular TV characters on terrestrial and satellite channels. Submit ideas by email in first instance. Payment by negotiation.

Inspire Magazine, CPO

Garcia Estate, Canterbury Road, Worthing, West Sussex BN13 1BW
tel (01903) 264556 *fax* (01903) 537321
email russbravo@cpo.org.uk
website www.inspiremagazine.org.uk
Editor Russ Bravo
Monthly free/donation; available in churches

Magazine with 'good news' stories of Christian faith in action and personal testimonies. Length: 400–700 words (features). Freelance articles used rarely. Payment: up to £85.

Insurance Age

Incisive Media, 32–34 Broadwick Street, London W1A 2HG
tel 020-7316 9115 *fax* 020-7316 9313
email martin.friel@incisivemedia.com
website www.insuranceage.com
Editor Martin Friel
Monthly £5

News and features on general insurance and the broker market, personal, commercial, health and Lloyd's of London. Payment: by negotiation. Founded 1979.

Insurance Brokers' Monthly

Insurance Publishing & Printing Co., 7 Stourbridge Road, Lye, Stourbridge, West Midlands DY9 7DG
tel (01384) 895228
website www.brokersmonthly.co.uk
Editor John Sadler
Monthly £88 p.a.

Articles of technical and non-technical interest to insurance brokers, intermediaries and others engaged in the general insurance industry. Length: 700–1500 words. Payment by arrangement. Founded 1950.

InterMedia

International Institute of Communications, 24–25 Nutford Place, London W1H 5YN
tel 020-7723 7210 *fax* 020-7723 6982
email s.mcclelland@iicom.org
Editor Stephen McClelland
Bi-monthly £95 p.a.

International journal concerned with policies, events, trends and research in the field of communications, broadcasting, telecommunications and associated issues, particularly cultural and social. Preliminary letter essential. Illustrations: b&w line. Payment: by arrangement. Founded 1970.

International Affairs

The Royal Institute of International Affairs, Chatham House, 10 St James's Square, London SW1Y 4LE
tel 020-7957 5728
email swolf@chathamhouse.org.uk
Editor Caroline Soper
6 p.a. (£70 p.a. individuals, £370 p.a. institutions)

Serious long-term articles on international affairs; approx. 50 books reviewed each issue. Preliminary letter advisable. Article length: average 7000 words. Illustrations: none. Payment: by arrangement. Founded 1922.

Interzone

TTA Press, 5 Martins Lane, Ely, Cambs. CB6 2LB
website www.ttapress.com
Editor Andy Cox
Bimonthly £3.95 (£21 for 6 issues)

Science fiction and fantasy short stories, articles, interviews and reviews. Read magazine before submitting. Length: 2,000–6,000 words. Illustrations: colour. Payment: by arrangement. Founded 1982.

Investors Chronicle

Number One, Southwark Bridge, London SE1 9HL
tel 020-7873 3000
website www.investorschronicle.co.uk
Editor Jonathan Eley
Weekly £3.75 (£115 p.a.)

Journal covering investment and personal finance. Occasional outside contributions for features are accepted. Payment: by negotiation.

Ireland's Own

Channing House, Upper Rowe Street, Wexford, Republic of Ireland
tel (053) 91 40140 *fax* (053) 91 40192
email irelands.own@peoplenews.ie
Editor Phil Murphy
€1.25p

Short stories: non-experimental, traditional with an

Irish orientation (1800–2000 words); articles of interest to Irish readers at home and abroad (750–900 words); general and literary articles (750–900 words). Monthly special bumper editions, each devoted to a particular seasonal topic. Suggestions for new features considered. Payment: varies according to quality and length. Founded 1902.

Irish Arts Review

State Apartments, Dublin Castle, Dublin 2, Republic of Ireland
tel (1) 679 3525 *fax* (1) 633 4417
website www.irishartsreview.com
Editor John Mulcahy
Quarterly €56, €75 (UK)

Magazine committed to promoting Irish art and heritage around the world with reviews of Irish painting, design, heritage, sculpture, architecture, photography and decorative arts.

Irish Farmers Journal

Irish Farm Centre, Bluebell, Dublin 12, Republic of Ireland
tel (01) 4199530 *fax* (01) 4520876
email edit@farmersjournal.ie
website www.farmersjournal.ie
Editor Matthew Dempsey
Weekly €2.40

Readable, technical articles on any aspect of farming. Length: 700–1000 words. Payment: £100–£150 per article. Illustrated. Founded 1948.

Irish Journal of Medical Science

Royal Academy of Medicine, Frederick House, 19 South Frederick Street, Dublin 2, Republic of Ireland
tel (01) 6334820 *fax* (01) 6334918
email journal@rami.ie
website www.ijms.ie
Send material to Prof. David Bouchier-Hayes
Quarterly €42 (Ireland and EU €156 p.a., non-EU €192 p.a.)

Official Organ of the Royal Academy of Medicine in Ireland. Original contributions in medicine, surgery, midwifery, public health, etc; reviews of professional books, reports of medical societies, etc. Illustrations: line, half-tone, colour.

Irish Medical Times

24–26 Upper Ormond Quay, Dublin 7, Republic of Ireland
tel (01) 8176300 *fax* (01) 8176335
email editor@imt.ie
website www.imt.ie
Editor Terence Cosgrave
Weekly €5.10 (€236 p.a.)

Medical articles. Length: 850–1000 words. Payment: £100 per 1000 words.

Irish Pages: A Journal of Contemporary Writing

The Linen Hall Library, 17 Donegall Square North, Belfast BT1 5GB
tel 028-9043 4800
email editor@irishpages.org
website www.irishpages.org
Editor Chris Agee
Biannual. £10/€14

Poetry, short fiction, essays, creative non-fiction, memoir, essay reviews, nature writing, translated work, literary journalism, and other autobiographical, historical and scientific writing of literary distinction. Publishes in equal measure writing from Ireland and abroad. Payment: only pays for certain commissions and occasional serial rights. Founded 2002.

The Irish Post

Irish Post Media Ltd, 1st Floor, West Wing, 26–28 Hammersmith Grove, London W6 7HA
tel 020-8741 0649 *fax* 020-8741 3382
website www.irishpost.co.uk
Weekly, Wed £1.30

Coverage of all political, social and sporting events relevant to the Irish community in Britain. Contains the best guide to Irish entertainment in Britain.

Irish Printer

Grattan House, Temple Road, Blackrock, Co. Dublin, Republic of Ireland
tel (01) 764 2700 *fax* (01) 764 2750
website www.irishprinter.ie
Editor Grainne Burns
Monthly €99.79 p.a.

Technical articles and news of interest to the printing industry. Length: 800–1000 words. Illustrations: colour and b&w photos. Payment: €140 per 1000 words; photos £30. Founded 1974.

Irish Tatler

Harmonia Ltd, Rosemount House, Dundrum Road, Dublin 14
tel (01) 2405300 *fax* (01) 6619757
email jcollins@harmonia.ie
website www.harmonia.ie
Editor Jessie Collins
Monthly €2.95 (€24 p.a.)

General interest women's magazine: beauty, interiors, fashion, cookery, current affairs, reportage and celebrity interviews. Length: 2000–4000 words. In association with ivenus.com. Payment: by arrangement.

Jane's Defence Weekly

Sentinel House, 163 Brighton Road, Coulsdon, Surrey CR5 2YH
tel 020-8700 3700 *fax* 020-8763 1007
website jdw.janes.com
Editor Peter Felstead
Weekly £280 p.a. online US $1795 p.a. (5-year archive on CD-Rom)

International defence news; military equipment; budget analysis, industry, military technology, business, political, defence market intelligence. Payment: minimum £200 per 1000 words used. Illustrations: colour. Founded 1984.

Jewish Chronicle

25 Furnival Street, London EC4A 1JT
tel 020-7415 1500 *fax* 020-7405 9040
email editorial@thejc.com
website www.thejc.com
Editor Stephen Pollard
Weekly 90p

Authentic and exclusive news stories and articles of Jewish interest from 500–1500 words are considered. Includes a lively arts and leisure section and regular travel pages. Payment: by arrangement. Illustrations: of Jewish interest, either topical or feature. Founded 1841.

The Jewish Quarterly

6 Park End, London NW3 2SE
tel 020-7443 5155 *fax* 020-7443 5159
email editor@jewishquarterly.org
website www.jewishquarterly.org
Editor Rachel Lasserson
Quarterly £4.95 (£25 p.a., £35 Europe, £45 overseas)

Articles of Jewish interest, literature, history, music, politics, poetry, book reviews, fiction. Illustrations: colour. Founded 1953.

Jewish Telegraph

Telegraph House, 11 Park Hill, Bury Old Road, Prestwich, Manchester M25 0HH
tel 0161-740 9321 *fax* 0161-740 9325
email manchester@jewishtelegraph.com
1 Shaftesbury Avenue, Leeds LS8 1DR
tel 0113-295 6000 *fax* 0113-295 6006
email leeds@jewishtelegraph.com
Harold House, Dunbabin Road, Liverpool L15 6XL
tel 0151-475 6666
email liverpool@jewishtelegraph.com
May Terrace, Giffnock, Glasgow G46 6LD
tel 0141-621 4422 *fax* 0141-621 4333
email [firstinitialsurname]@jewishtelegraph.com
website www.jewishtelegraph.com
Editor Mike Cohen
Weekly Manchester 60p, Leeds 55p, Liverpool 35p, Glasgow 60p

Non-fiction articles of Jewish interest, especially humour. Exclusive Jewish news stories and pictures, international, national and local. Length: 1000–1500 words. Payment: by arrangement. Illustrations: line, half-tone, cartoons. Founded 1950.

Journal of Alternative and Complementary Medicine

Fern Lodge, 5 Cotterill Street, Hereford HR4 0HH
tel (01432) 353656 *fax* (01432) 354010
Editor Dr K.A. Jobst
Monthly £200 p.a.

Feature articles on complementary and alternative medicine, paradigm, practise and policy (up to 3000 words) and news stories (up to 500 words). Unsolicited material welcome but not eligible for payment unless commissioned. Illustrations: line, half-tone, colour. Payment: by negotiation. Founded 1983.

Junior

Magicalia Publishing Ltd, 15–18 White Lion Street, London N1 9PG
tel 020-7843 8800
email editorial@juniormagazine.co.uk
website www.juniormagazine.co.uk
Editor Catherine O'Dolan
Monthly £3.50

Glossy up-market parenting magazine aimed at mothers of children aged 0–8 and reflects the shift in today's society towards older mothers and fathers who have established their careers and homes. Intelligent and insightful features and the best in fashion. Specially commissions most material. Welcomes ideas for articles and features. Payment: £150 per 1,000 words (articles/features/short fiction), £300 per feature (colour and b&w photos/artwork). Founded 1998.

Kent Life

28 Teville Road, Worthing, West Sussex BN11 1UG
tel (01622) 762818 *fax* (01622) 663294
email sarah.sturt@kent-life.co.uk, michael.palmer@kent-life.co.uk
website www.kent-life.co.uk
Editor Sarah Sturt, *Assistant Editor* Michael Palmer
Monthly £2.95

Local lifestyle magazine 'celebrating the best of county life'. Features local people, social events and entertainment and promotes local towns and villages, walks and heritage. Welcomes ideas for articles and features, length: 1000 words (articles/features). Illustrations: hi-res jpgs preferred, colour and b&w prints, colour artwork. Payment: negotiable.

Kerrang!

Bauer Consumer Media, Mappin House, 4 Winsley Street, London W1W 8HF
tel 020-7182 8406 *fax* 020-7312 8910
website www.kerrang.com
Editor Nichola Browne
Weekly £2.20

News, reviews and interviews; music with attitude. All material commissioned. Illustrations: colour. Payment: by arrangement. Founded 1981.

Kids Alive! (The Young Soldier)

The Salvation Army, 101 Newington Causeway, London SE1 6BN
tel 020-7367 4911 *fax* 020-7367 4710
email kidsalive@salvationarmy.org.uk
website www.salvationarmy.org.uk/kidsalive

Editor Justin Reeves
Weekly 50p (£25 p.a. including free membership of the Kids Alive! Club)

Children's magazine: pictures, scripts and artwork for cartoon strips, puzzles, etc; Christian-based with emphasis on education re addictive substances. Payment: by arrangement. Illustrations: half-tone, line and 4-colour line, cartoons. Founded 1881.

Kitchen Garden

Mortons Media Group Ltd, Media Centre, Morton Way, Horncastle, Lincs. LN9 6JR
tel (01507) 529396 *fax* (01507) 529495
email sott@mortons.co.uk
website www.kitchengarden.co.uk
Editor Steve Ott
Monthly £3.60

Magazine for people with a passion for growing their own vegetables, fruit and herbs. Includes practical tips and inspirational ideas. Specially commissions most material. Welcomes ideas for articles and features. Length: 700–2000 (articles/features). Illustrations: colour transparencies, prints and artwork; all commissioned. Payment: varies. Founded 1997.

Koi

Origin Publishing, Tower House, Fairfax Street, Bristol BS1 3BN
tel 0117-927 9009 *fax* 0117-934 9008
email beckierodgers@originpublishing.co.uk
website www.koimag.co.uk
Editor Beckie Rodgers
Every 4 weeks £3.95

A practical and informative guide to keeping Koi as a hobby, from pond construction to Koi health care. Also includes features on the hobby in Japan. Length 800–1700 words (articles), 2000–3000 words (features), 150 words (news). Payment: £80–£170 (articles), £200–£300 (features). Illustrations: colour.

The Lady

39–40 Bedford Street, London WC2E 9ER
tel 020-7379 4717 *fax* 020-7836 4620
email editor@lady.co.uk
website www.lady.co.uk
Editor Rachel Johnson
Weekly £1.80

British and foreign travel, fashion, beauty, interiors, food and cookery, exclusive cover images and interviews with women over 40, pets, holidays, health, cultural reviews, books section, general interest features, short stories and serials, comment, columns and diaries. Plus classified ads, holiday cottages, and pages of puzzles. Will consider unsolicited MSS of around 1000 words. Founded 1885.

Lancashire Magazine

Oyston Mill, Strand Road, Preston PR1 8UR
tel (01772) 761277 *fax* (01772) 739202
email info@lancashiremagazine.co.uk
website www.lancashiremagazine.co.uk
www.lancashiremagazine.tv
Editor Anthony Skinner
Monthly £1.95 (£10 p.a.)

Articles about people, life and places in all parts of Lancashire. Length: 700–1000 words. Payment: £70–£100. Illustrations: full colour. Founded 1977.

Lancet

32 Jamestown Road, London NW1 7BY
tel 020-7424 4910 *fax* 020-7424 4911
email editorial@lancet.com
website www.thelancet.com
Editor Dr Richard Horton
Weekly £126 p.a.

Research papers, review articles, editorials, correspondence and commentaries on international medicine, medical research and policy. Consult the Editor before submitting material. Founded 1823.

The Lawyer

Centaur Communications Group, St Giles House, 50 Poland Street, London W1F 7AX
tel 020-7970 4000 *fax* 020-7970 4640
email editorial@thelawyer.com
website www.thelawyer.com
Editor Catrin Griffiths
Weekly £2.65

News, articles, features and views relevant to the legal profession. Length: 600–900 words. Illustrations: as agreed. Payment: £125–£150 per 1000 words. Founded 1987.

Legal Week

32–34 Broadwick Street, London W1A 2HG
tel 020-7316 9000 *fax* 020-7316 9278
email alex.novarese@incisivemedia.com
website www.legalweek.com
Editor Alex Novarese
Weekly £4.40

News and features aimed at business lawyers. Length: 750–1000 words (features), 300 words (news). Payment: £200 upwards (features), £75–£100 (news). Considers unsolicited material and welcomes ideas for articles and features. Founded 1999.

Leisure Painter

Caxton House, 63–65 High Street, Tenterden, Kent TN30 6BD
tel (01580) 763315 *fax* (01580) 765411
email ingrid@tapc.co.uk
website www.painters-online.co.uk
Editor Ingrid Lyon
Monthly £3.50

Instructional articles on painting and fine art. Payment: £75 per 1000 words. Illustrations: line, half-tone, colour, original artwork. Founded 1967.

LGC (Local Government Chronicle)

Emap Public Sector, Greater London House, Hampstead Road, London NW1 7EJ

tel 020-7728 5000 *fax* 020-7728 3700
email lgcnews@emap.com
website www.lgcplus.com
Editor Emma Maier
Weekly £4.40

Aimed at senior managers in local government. Covers politics, management issues, social services, education, regeneration, industrial relations and personnel, plus public sector finance and Scottish and Welsh local government. Length: 1000 words (features). Illustrations: b&w and colour, cartoons. Payment: by arrangement. Founded 1855.

Life & Work: Editorially Independent Magazine of the Church of Scotland

121 George Street, Edinburgh EH2 4YN
tel 0131-225 5722 *fax* 0131-240 2207
email magazine@lifeandwork.org
Editor Lynne McNeil
Monthly £1.60

Articles not exceeding 1200 words and news; occasional stories. Study the magazine and contact the Editor first. Payment: by arrangement. Illustrations: photos and colour illustrations.

Lincolnshire Life

County House, 9 Checkpoint Court, Sadler Road, Lincoln LN6 3PW
tel (01522) 527127 *fax* (01522) 842000
email editorial@lincolnshirelife.co.uk
website www.lincolnshirelife.co.uk
Editor Josie Thurston
Monthly £2.60

Articles and news of county interest. Approach in writing. Length: up to 1500 words. Illustrations: colour photos and line drawings. Payment: varies. Founded 1961.

The Linguist

The Chartered Institute of Linguists, Saxon House, 48 Southwark Street, London SE1 1UN
tel 020-7940 3100 *fax* 020-7940 3125
email linguist.editor@googlemail.com
website www.iol.org.uk/linguistmagazine
Editor Miranda Moore
Bi-monthly £39 p.a.

Articles of interest to professional linguists in translating, interpreting and teaching fields. Articles usually contributed, but payment by arrangement. All contributors have special knowledge of the subjects with which they deal. Length: 1500–2000 words.

The List

14 High Street, Edinburgh EH1 1TE
tel 0131-550 3050 *fax* 0131-557 8500
email editor@list.co.uk
website www.list.co.uk
Editor Claire Sawyer
Fortnightly £2.20 (£45 p.a.)

Events guide for Glasgow and Edinburgh covering film, theatre, music, clubs, books, city life, art, and TV and video. Publishes special issues to support major arts events and festivals. Considers unsolicited material and welcomes ideas. Length: 200 words (articles), 800 words and above (features). Illustrations: transparencies and colour prints. Payment: £20 (articles), from £60 (features); £25–£50. Founded 1985.

The Literary Review

44 Lexington Street, London W1F 0LW
tel 020-7437 9392 *fax* 020-7734 1844
email editorial@literaryreview.co.uk
website www.literaryreview.co.uk
Editor Nancy Sladek
Monthly £3.50 (£35 p.a.)

Reviews, articles of cultural interest, interviews, profiles, monthly poetry competition. Material mostly commissioned. Length: articles and reviews 800–1500 words. Illustrations: line and b&w photos. Payment: £25 per article; none for illustrations. Founded 1979.

Living France Magazine

Archant Life, Archant House, Oriel Road, Cheltenham, Glos. GL50 1BB
tel (01242) 216050 *fax* (01242) 216094
email editorial@livingfrance.com
website www.livingfrance.com
Editor Eleanor O'Kane
13 p.a. £3.99

Articles on travel, property and aspects of living in France, from having a baby to setting up utilities. Interviews with expats also featured. Founded 1990.

Loaded

IPC Ignite, The Blue Fin Building, 110 Southwark Street, London SE1 0SU
tel 020-3148 5000 *fax* 020-3148 8107
email martin.daubney@ipcmedia.com
website www.loaded.co.uk
Editor Martin Daubney
Monthly £2.50

Magazine for men aged 18–30. Music, sport, sex, humour, travel, fashion, hard news and popular culture. Address longer features (2000 words) to Features Editor, and shorter items to Handbook Editor. Payment: by arrangement. Founded 1994.

LOGOS

5 Beechwood Drive, Marlow, Bucks. SL7 2DH
tel (01628) 483371 *fax* (01628) 477577
email logos-marlow@dial.pipex.com
website www.logos-journal.org
Editor Emeritus Gordon Graham
Editor Charles Levine (*email* logos-editor@att.net, *tel* (01718) 577 1175)
Quarterly £48 p.a. (£120 p.a. institutions)

In-depth articles on publishing, librarianship and

bookselling with international or interdisciplinary appeal. Length: 3500–7000 words. Payment: 10 offprints/copy of issue. Founded 1990.

The London Magazine: A Review of Literature and the Arts

Administration Flat 5, 11 Queen's Gate, London SW7 5EL
email admin@thelondonmagazine.net
website www.thelondonmagazine.net
Editor Steven O'Brien
Bi-monthly £6.95 (£33 p.a.)

Poems, stories (2000–5000 words), memoirs, critical articles, features on art, photography, theatre, music, architecture, etc. Sae essential (3 IRCs from abroad). Submissions by email accepted. Payment: by arrangement. First published in 1732.

London Review of Books

28 Little Russell Street, London WC1A 2HN
tel 020-7209 1101 *fax* 020-7209 1102
email edit@lrb.co.uk
Editor Mary-Kay Wilmers
Fortnightly £3.20

Features, essays, poems. Payment: by arrangement.

Lothian Life

Larick House, Whitehouse, Tarbert, Argyll PA29 6XR
tel (01880) 730360
email editor@lothianlife.co.uk
website www.lothianlife.co.uk
Editor Susan Coon
Online publication only

Articles, profiles etc with a Lothians angle. Length: 500–2000 words. Founded 1995.

MacUser

Dennis Publishing Ltd, 30 Cleveland Street, London W1T 4JD
tel 020-7907 6000
email mailbox@macuser.co.uk
website www.macuser.co.uk
Editor Nik Rawlinson
Fortnightly £3.99

News, reviews, tutorials and features on Apple computer products and topics of interest to their users. Commissioned reviews of products compatible with Mac computers required. Occasional requirement for features relating to Mac-based design and publishing and general computing and internet issues. Ideas welcome. Length: 2000–5000 words (features), approx. 500 words (news), 300–2500 words (reviews). Illustrations: commissioned from Mac-based designers. Payment: £190 per 1000 words; competitive (artwork). Founded 1985.

Macworld

101 Euston Road, London NW1 2RA
tel 020-7756 2877
email karen_haslam@macworld.co.uk
website www.macworld.co.uk
Editor Karen Haslam
14 p.a. £5.99

All aspects of Apple Macintosh computing, primarily for professional users: industry news, product testing, tips and how-to features. Specially commissions most material. Welcomes ideas for articles and features. Digital pictures only. Founded 1989.

Management Today

174 Hammersmith Road, London W6 7JP
tel 020-8267 4610 *fax* 020-7267 4976
Editor Matthew Gwyther
Monthly £3.90

Company profiles and analysis – columns from 1000 words, features up to 3000 words. Payment: £350 per 1000 words. Illustrations: colour transparencies, always commissioned. Founded 1966.

Marie Claire

European Magazines Ltd, 7th Floor, The Blue Fin Building, 110 Southwark Street, London SE1 0SU
tel 020-3148 7513
email marieclaire@ipcmedia.com
website www.marieclaire.co.uk
Editor Trish Halpin
Monthly £3.40

Feature articles of interest to today's woman; plus fashion, beauty, health, food, drink and travel. Commissioned material only. Payment: by negotiation. Illustrated in colour. Founded 1988.

Market Newsletter

Bureau of Freelance Photographers, Focus House, 497 Green Lanes, London N13 4BP
tel 020-8882 3315
email info@thebfp.com
website www.thebfp.com
Editor John Tracy
Monthly £54 p.a. UK (£70 overseas); free to members of BFP

Current information on markets and editorial requirements of interest to writers and photographers. Founded 1965.

Marketing Week

Centaur Communications, 50 Poland Street, London W1F 7AX
tel 020-7970 4000 *fax* 020-7970 6722
website www.marketingweek.co.uk
Editor Mark Choueke
Weekly £2.95

Aimed at marketing management. Accepts occasional features and analysis. Length: 1000–2000 words. Payment: £250 per 1000 words. Founded 1978.

Maxim

Dennis Publishing Ltd, 30 Cleveland Street, London W1T 4JD

tel 020-7907 6000 *fax* 020-7907 6020
email ben-raworth@dennis.co.uk
website www.maxim.co.uk
Editorial Director Ben Raworth
Monthly £3.70

Glossy men's lifestyle magazine with news, features and articles. All material is commissioned. Length: 1,500–2,500 words (features), 150–500 words (news). Illustrations: transparencies. Payment: by negotiation. Founded 1995.

Mayfair

Paul Raymond Publications, 3rd Floor,
207 Old Street, London EC1V 9NR
tel 020-7608 6300 *fax* 020 7608 6380
email mayfair@paulraymond.com
website www.paulraymond.com
Editor Matt Berry
Monthly £3.80

Classic British adult magazine containing features ranging from those on motorbikes and celebrities to those of a more explicit nature, as well as several photo sets. Short stories. Welcomes ideas for articles and features. Length: 1200–1500 words. Illustrations: colour, cartoons. Payment: negotiable. Founded 1965.

MBUK (Mountain Biking UK)

Future Publishing Ltd, 30 Monmouth Street,
Bath BA1 2BW
tel (01225) 442244 *fax* (01225) 446019
email mbukmail@futurenet.co.uk
website www.bikeradar.com
Editor Danny Walter
Every 4 weeks £4.20

Magazine for mountain bike enthusiasts with features, reviews, news and world and domestic racing coverage.

Medal News

Token Publishing Ltd, Orchard House, Duchy Road,
Heathpark, Honiton, Devon EX14 1YD
tel (01404) 46972 *fax* (01404) 44788
email info@tokenpublishing.com
website www.tokenpublishing.com
Editor John Mussell
10 p.a. £3.65

Well-researched articles on military history with a bias towards medals. Send text in digital form. Length: up to 2000 words. Illustrations: if possible. Payment: by arrangement; none for illustrations. Founded 1989.

Media Week

Haymarket Publishing Ltd, 174 Hammersmith Road,
London W6 7JP
tel 020-8267 5000
email steve.barrett@haymarket.com
Editor Steve Barrett
Weekly £3.30

News and analysis of the UK media industry. Illustrations: full colour and b&w. Founded 1985.

Men Only

Paul Raymond Publications, 3rd Floor,
207 Old Street, London EC1V 9NR
tel 020-7608 6300 *fax* 020-7608 6380
email menonly@paulraymond.com
Editor Matt Berry
Monthly £3.80

High-quality glamour photography; explicit sex stories (no erotic fiction); male interest features – sport, humour, entertainment, hedonism. Proposals welcome. Payment: by arrangement. Founded 1971.

Men's Health

Natmag Rodale Ltd, 33 Broadwick Street,
London W1F 0DQ
tel 020-7339 4400 *fax* 020-7339 4444
website www.menshealth.co.uk
Editor Morgan Rees
10 p.a. £3.80

Active pursuits, grooming, fitness, fashion, sex, career and general men's interest issues. Length 1000–4000 words. Ideas welcome. No unsolicited MSS. Payment: by arrangement. Founded 1994.

Methodist Recorder

122 Golden Lane, London EC1Y 0TL
tel 020-7251 8414
email editorial@methodistrecorder.co.uk
website www.methodistrecorder.co.uk
Managing Editor Moira Sleight
Weekly £1.60

Methodist newspaper; ecumenically involved. Limited opportunities for freelance contributors. Preliminary letter advised. Founded 1861.

Military Modelling

PO Box 6017, Leighton Buzzard LU7 2FA
tel/fax (01525) 370389
email ken.jones@myhobbystore.com
website www.militarymodelling.com
Editor Ken Jones
Monthly £3.95

Articles on military modelling. Length: up to 2000 words. Payment: by arrangement. Illustrations: line, half-tone, colour.

Minor Monthly

Poundbury Publishing Ltd, Middle Farm,
Middle Farm Way, Poundbury, Dorchester DT1 3RS
tel (01202) 469199
email russ@poundbury.co.uk
website www.minormonthly.com
Editor Russ Harvey
Monthly £2.40

Magazine for the Morris Minor owner and

enthusiast: news, features, profiles and workshops. Specially commissions most material but will consider unsolicited material. Length: 1000 words (articles/features). Illustrations: colour prints. Payment: negotiable. Founded 1995.

Mixmag

Development Hell Ltd, 90–92 Pentonville Road, London N1 9HS
tel 020-7078-8417 *fax* 020-7833-9900
email mixmag@mixmag.net
website www.mixmag.net
Editor Nick DeCosemo
Monthly £3.95

Dance music and clubbing magazine. No unsolicited material. Payment: £200 per 1000 words. Illustrations: colour and b&w. Founded 1984.

Mizz

Panini UK, Brockbourne House, 77 Mount Ephraim, Tunbridge Wells TN4 8AR
tel (01892) 500100 *fax* (01892) 545666
email mizz@panini.co.uk
website www.mizz.com
Editor Karen O'Brien
Fortnightly £2.30

Articles on any subject of interest to girls aged 10–14. Approach in writing. Payment: by arrangement. Illustrated. Founded 1985.

Model Boats

MyHobbyStore Ltd, PO Box 718, Orpington, Kent BR6 1AP
tel (0844) 412 2262 *fax* (01689) 899266
website www.modelboats.co.uk
Editor Paul Freshney
Monthly £3.85

Founded 1964.

Model Engineer

MyHobbyStore Ltd, PO Box 718, Orpington, Kent BR6 1AP
tel (01847) 821136
Editor David Clark
Fortnightly £2.95

Detailed description of the construction of models, small workshop equipment, machine tools and small electrical and mechanical devices; articles on small power engineering, mechanics, electricity, workshop methods, clocks and experiments. Payment: £50 per page. Illustrations: line, half-tone, colour. Founded 1898.

Modern Language Review

Modern Humanities Research Association, c/o 1 Carlton House Terrace, London SW1Y 5AF
email mail@mhra.org.uk
website www.mhra.org.uk
Quarterly £22 p.a. (individual), £126 (institutions)

Articles and reviews of a scholarly or specialist character on English, Romance, Germanic and Slavonic languages and literatures. Payment: none, but offprints are given. Founded 1905.

Mojo

Bauer Consumer Media, Mappin House, 4 Winsley Street, London W1W 8HF
tel 020-7182 8616 *fax* 020-7182 8596
email mojo@bauermedia.co.uk
website www.mojo4music.com
Editor Phil Alexander
Monthly £4.50

Serious rock music magazine: interviews, news and reviews of books, live shows and albums. Length: up to 10,000 words. Illustrations: colour and b&w photos, colour caricatures. Payment: £250 per 1000 words; £200–£400 illustrations. Founded 1993.

Moneywise

Standon House, 21 Mansell Street, London E1 8AA
tel 020-7680 3600
website www.moneywise.co.uk
Editor Johanna Gornitzki
Monthly £4.25

Financial and consumer interest features, articles and news stories. No unsolicited MSS. Length: 1500–2000 words. Illustrations: willing to see designers, illustrators and photographers for fresh new ideas. Payment: by arrangement. Founded 1990.

More!

Bauer Consumer Media, Endeavour House, 189 Shaftesbury Avenue, London WC2H 8JG
tel 020-7208 3165 *fax* 020-7208 3595
website www.moremagazine.co.uk
Editor Chantelle Horton
Weekly £1.50

Celebrities, fun, gossip and sexy features, how-to articles aimed at young women. Study of magazine essential. Length: 900–1100 words. Illustrated. Founded 1988.

Mother & Baby

Endeavour House, 189 Shaftsbury Avenue, London WC2H 8JG
tel 020-7347 1869
website www.motherandbabymagazine.com
Editor Miranda Levy
Monthly £2.70

Features and practical information including pregnancy and birth and babycare advice. Expert attribution plus real-life stories. Length: 1000–1500 words (commissioned work only). Payment: by negotiation. Illustrated. Founded 1956.

Motor Boat and Yachting

IPC Media Ltd, The Blue Fin Building, 110 Southwark Street, London SE1 0SU

tel 020-3148 4651 *fax* 020-3148 8127
email mby@ipcmedia.com
website www.mby.com
Editor Hugo Andreae
Monthly £4.50

General interest as well as specialist motor boating material welcomed. Features up to 2000 words considered on all sea-going aspects. Payment: varies. Illustrations: high-resolution photos. Founded 1904.

Motor Boats Monthly

IPC Magazines Ltd, 9th Floor,
The Blue Fin Building, 110 Southwark Street,
London SE1 0SU
tel 020-3148 4664
email mbm@ipcmedia.com
website www.mbmclub.com
Editor Carl Richardson
Monthly £4.20

News on motorboating in the UK and Europe, cruising features practical guides and anecdotal stories. Mostly commissioned – send synopsis to the Editor. Length: news up to 200 words, features up to 4000 words. Illustrations: digital colour. Payment: by arrangement. Founded 1987.

Motor Caravan Magazine

IPC Inspire, Leon House, 233 High Street,
Croydon CR9 1HZ
tel 020-8726 8248 *fax* 020-8726 8299
email victoria.bentley@ipcmedia.com
website www.motorcaravanmagazine.co.uk
Editor Victoria Bentley
Monthly £3.50

Touring, products, motorhome tests, practical features. Length: up to 2000 words. Payment: £60 per page. Founded 1985.

Motor Cycle News

Bauer Consumer Media Media House,
Peterborough Business Park, Lynchwood,
Peterborough PE2 6EA
tel (01733) 468000 *fax* (01733) 468028
email mcn@motorcyclenews.com
website www.motorcyclenews.com
Editor Marc Potter
Weekly £1.99

Features (up to 1000 words), photos and news stories of interest to motorcyclists. Founded 1955.

Motorcaravan Motorhome Monthly (MMM)

PO Box 88, Tiverton, EX16 7ZN
tel (01778) 392439
email mmmeditor@warnersgroup.co.uk
website www.outandaboutlive.co.uk
Editor Mike Jago
Monthly £3.40

Articles including motorcaravan travel, owner reports and DIY. Length: up to 2500 words. Payment: by arrangement. Illustrations: line, half-tone, colour prints and transparencies, high quality digital. Founded 1966 as *Motor Caravan and Camping*.

Mslexia

PO Box 656, Newcastle upon Tyne NE99 1PZ
tel 0191-233 3860 *fax* 0191-233 3882
email postbag@mslexia.co.uk
website www.mslexia.co.uk
Editor Daneet Steffens
Quarterly from £18.75 p.a.

Magazine for women writers which combines features and advice about writing, with new fiction and poetry by women. Considers unsolicited material. Length: up to 2200 words (short stories), up to 4 poems of no more than 40 lines each in any style which must relate to current themes (or adhere to poetry competition rules). Articles/features by negotiation. Illustrations: mono art, photos, colour transparencies. Payment: by negotiation. Founded 1998.

Muscle & Fitness

Weider Publishing, 10 Windsor Court,
Clarence Drive, Harrogate,
North Yorkshire HG1 2PE
tel (01423) 504516 *fax* (01423) 561494
website www.muscle-fitness-europe.com
Editor Chris Lund
Monthly £3.60

A guide to muscle development and general health and fitness. Founded 1988.

Music Teacher

Rhinegold Publishing Ltd,
239–241 Shaftesbury Avenue, London WC2H 8TF
tel 020-7333 1747 *fax* 020-7333 1765
email music.teacher@rhinegold.co.uk
website www.rhinegold.co.uk
Editor Clare Stevens
Monthly £4.95

Information and articles for both school and private instrumental teachers, including reviews of books, music, CD-Roms and other music-education resources. Articles and illustrations must both have a teaching, as well as a musical, interest. Length: articles 1000–2000 words. Payment: £120 per 1000 words. Founded 1908.

Music Week

CMPi, 1st Floor, Ludgate House,
245 Blackfriars Road, London SE1 9UY
email paul@musicweek.com
website www.musicweek.com
Editor Paul Williams
Weekly £3.80 (£160 p.a.)

News and features on all aspects of producing, manufacturing, marketing and retailing music. Payment: by negotiation. Founded 1959.

Musical Opinion

1 Exford Road, London SE12 9HD
tel 020-8857 1582
email musicalopinion@hotmail.co.uk
website www.musicalopinion.com
Editor Robert Matthew-Walker
Bi-monthly £4.50 (£28 p.a.)

Suggestions for contributions of musical interest, scholastic, educational, anniversaries and ethnic. Dance, DVD, CD, opera, festival, book, music reviews. All editorial matter must be commissioned. Payment: on publication. Illustrations: colour photos. Founded 1877.

Musical Times

7 Brunswick Mews, Hove, East Sussex BN3 1HD
Editor Antony Bye
4 p.a. £9.50 (£38 p.a.)

Musical articles, reviews, 500–6000 words. All material commissioned; no unsolicited material. Illustrations: music. Founded 1844.

My Weekly

D.C. Thomson & Co. Ltd, 80 Kingsway East, Dundee DD4 8SL
tel (01382) 223131 *fax* (01382) 452491
email myweekly@dcthomson.co.uk
185 Fleet Street, London EC4A 2HS
tel 020-7400 1030 *fax* 020-7400 1089
Weekly 82p

Modern women's magazine aimed at 50+ age group. No unsolicited MSS considered. Send ideas or pitches to relevant department editor. Payment by negotiation. Illustrations: colour. Founded 1910.

My Weekly Pocket Novel

D.C. Thomson & Co. Ltd, 80 Kingsway East, Dundee DD4 8SL
tel (0800) 318846
email myweekly@dcthomson.co.uk
Editor Maggie Seed
4 p.m. £1.50

25,000–30,000-word romantic stories for women. Payment: on acceptance; competitive for the market. No illustrations.

The National Trust Magazine

The National Trust, Heelis, Kemble Drive, Swindon SN2 2NA
tel (01793) 817716
email sue.herdman@nationaltrust.org.uk
website www.nationaltrust.org.uk
Editor Sue Herdman
3 p.a. £3.95 Free to members

Lifestyle title with focus on the National Trust, encompassing interiors, gardens, food, UK travel, wildlife, environment, topical features and celebrity content. No unsolicited articles. Length: 1000 words (features), 200 words (news). Illustrations: colour transparencies and artwork. Payment: by arrangement; picture library rates. Founded 1932.

Natural World

Think Publishing Ltd, The Pall Mall Deposit, 124–128 Barlby Road, London W10 6BL
tel 020-8962 3020 *fax* 020-8962 8689
Editor Rupert Paul, *Publisher* Ian McAuliffe
3 p.a. Free to members

National magazine of the Wildlife Trusts. Short articles on the work of the UK's 47 wildlife trusts. Unsolicited MSS not accepted. Length: up to 1200 words. Payment: by arrangement. Illustrations: line, colour. Founded 1981.

Naturalist

The University, Bradford BD7 1DP
tel (01274) 234212 *fax* (01274) 234231
email m.r.d.seaward@bradford.ac.uk
Editor Prof M.R.D. Seaward MSc, PhD, DSc
Quarterly £20 p.a.

Original papers on all kinds of British natural history subjects, including various aspects of geology, archaeology and environmental science. Length: immaterial. Illustrations: photos and line drawings. Payment: none. Founded 1875.

Nature

Macmillan Magazines Ltd, The Macmillan Building, 4 Crinan Street, London N1 9XW
tel 020-7833 4000 *fax* 020-7843 4596
email nature@nature.com
website www.nature.com/nature
Editor Philip Campbell
Weekly £10 (£130 p.a.)

Devoted to scientific matters and to their bearing upon public affairs. All contributors of articles have specialised knowledge of the subjects with which they deal. Illustrations: line, half-tone. Founded 1869.

Nautical Magazine

Brown, Son & Ferguson Ltd, 4–10 Darnley Street, Glasgow G41 2SD
tel 0141-429 1234 *fax* 0141-420 1694
email info@skipper.co.uk
website www.skipper.co.uk
Editor R.B.P. Brown
Monthly £34.20 p.a. (£39.60 p.a. overseas)

Articles relating to nautical and shipping profession, from 1500–2000 words; also translations. Payment: by arrangement. No illustrations. Founded 1832.

NB Magazine

RNIB, 105 Judd Street, London WC1H 9NE
tel 020-7391 2070
email nbmagazine@rnib.org.uk
Editor Ann Lee
Monthly £3 (£32.40 p.a.)

Articles on eye health and sight loss for professionals. Published in clear print, braille, audio CD and email editions. Length: from 500 words. Payment: by arrangement. Illustrations: high-res jpg files on disk only. Founded 1930; as *Beacon* 1917, then *New Beacon*.

.net

Future Publishing Ltd, Beaufort Court,
30 Monmouth Street, Bath BA1 2BW
tel (01225) 442244 *fax* (01225) 732291
email netmag@futurenet.co.uk
website www.netmag.co.uk
Editor Dan Oliver
Monthly CD edition £5.99

Articles, features and news on the internet. Length: 1000–3000 words. Payment: negotiable. Illustrations: colour. Founded 1994.

New Humanist

1 Gower Street, London WC1E 6HD
tel 020-7436 1171 *fax* 020-7079 3588
email info@newhumanist.org.uk
website www.newhumanist.org.uk
Editor Caspar Melville
Bi-monthly £3.90

Articles on current affairs, philosophy, science, literature, religion and humanism. Length: 500–1500 words. Illustrations: colour photos. Payment: nominal. Founded 1885.

New Internationalist

55 Rectory Road, Oxford OX4 1BW
tel (01865) 811400 *fax* (01865) 793152
email ni@newint.org
website www.newint.org
Editors Vanessa Baird, Chris Bozier, Jess Worth, Hadari Ditmars, Dinyar Godrej
Monthly £3.25 (£32.85 p.a.)

World issues, ranging from food to feminism to peace – examines one subject each month. Length: up to 2000 words. Illustrations: line, half-tone, colour, cartoons. Payment: £230 per 1000 words. Founded 1973.

New Law Journal

Lexis Nexis Butterworths, Halsbury House,
35 Chancery Lane, London WC2A 1EL
tel 020-7400 2580 *fax* 020-7400 2583
email newlaw.journal@lexisnexis.co.uk
website www.newlawjournal.co.uk
Editor Jan Miller
48 p.a. £7 (£230 p.a.)

Articles and news on all aspects of the legal profession. Length: up to 2000 words. Payment: by arrangement.

New Media Age

Centaur Media plc, St Giles House, 50 Poland Street, London W1F 7AX
020-7970 4000 *fax* 020-7970 4863
website www.nma.co.uk
Editor Justin Pearse
Weekly £99 p.a.

Magazine devoted to interactive media, marketing and advertising. Founded 1996.

New Musical Express (NME)

(incorporating Melody Maker)
IPC Ignite, The Blue Fin Building,
110 Southwark Street, London SE1 0SU
tel 020-3148 5000 *fax* 020-3148 8107
Editor Krissi Murison
Weekly £2.20

Authoritative articles and news stories on the world's rock and movie personalities. Length: by arrangement. Preliminary letter or phone call desirable. Payment: by arrangement. Illustrations: action photos with strong news angle of recording personalities, cartoons.

New Scientist

Lacon House, 84 Theobalds Road,
London WC1X 8NS
tel 020-7611 1200 *fax* 020-7611 1250
email news@newscientist.com
website www.newscientist.com
Editor Jeremy Webb
Weekly £3.40

Authoritative articles of topical importance on all aspects of science and technology. Intending contributors should study recent copies of the magazine and initially send only a 200-word synopsis of their idea. NB: Does not publish non-peer reviewed theories, poems or crosswords. Payment: varies but average £300 per 1000 words. Illustrations: all styles, cartoons; contact art dept.

New Statesman

(formerly New Statesman & Society)
7th Floor, John Carpenter House,
John Carpenter Street, London EC4Y 0AN
tel 020-7730 3444 *fax* 020-7336 5203
email info@newstatesman.co.uk
website www.newstatesman.co.uk
Editor Jason Cowley
Weekly £2.95

Interested in news, reportage and analysis of current political and social issues at home and overseas, plus book reviews, general articles and coverage of the arts, environment and science seen from the perspective of the British Left but written in a stylish, witty and unpredictable way. Length: strictly according to the value of the piece. Illustrations: commissioned for specific articles, though artists' samples considered for future reference; occasional cartoons. Payment: by agreement. Founded 1913.

New Theatre Quarterly

Oldstairs, Kingsdown, Deal, Kent CT14 8ES
email simontrussler@btinternet.com
Editors Simon Trussler, Maria Shevtsova

Quarterly £30 (£65 p.a.)

Articles, interviews, documentation, reference material covering all aspects of live theatre. An informed, factual and serious approach essential. Preliminary discussion and synopsis desirable. Payment: by arrangement. Illustrations: line, half-tone. Founded 1985; as *Theatre Quarterly* 1971.

New Welsh Review

PO Box 170, Aberystwyth, Ceredigion SY23 1WZ
tel (01970) 628410
email editor@newwelshreview.com
website www.newwelshreview.com
Editor Kathryn Gray
Quarterly £5.99, £23.96 p.a.

Literary – critical articles, short stories, poems, book reviews, interviews and profiles. Especially, but not exclusively, concerned with Welsh writing in English. Length: up to 3000 words (articles). Send by email or hard copy with an sae for return of material. Decisions within 3 months of submission. Illustrations: colour. Payment: £50 per 1000 words (articles); £25 per poem, £75 per short story, £40 per review. Founded 1988.

The New Writer

PO Box 60, Cranbrook, Kent TN17 2ZR
tel (01580) 212626
email admin@thenewwriter.com
website www.thenewwriter.com
Editor Suzanne Ruthven *Publisher* Merric Davidson
6 p.a. £4.50 plus monthly e-news bulletin

Features, short stories from guest writers and from subscribers, poems, news and reviews. Seeks forward-looking articles on all aspects of the written word that demonstrate the writer's grasp of contemporary writing and current editorial/publishing policies. Length: approx. 1000 words (articles), longer pieces considered; 1000–2000 words (features). Payment: £20 per 1000 words (articles), £10 (stories), £3 (poems). Founded 1996.

newbooks magazine

4 Froxfield Close, Winchester SO22 6JW
tel (01962) 620320
email guy@newbooksmag.com
website www.newbooksmag.com
Publisher Guy Pringle

Bi-monthly £22.20 p.a.

The magazine for readers and reading groups. Includes extracts from new books, articles and features about and by authors, how the book trade works and how books reach publication and find a readership. Check out our website or email for a free introductory copy.

The Newspaper

Young Media Holdings Ltd, PO Box 400, Bridgwater TA6 9DT
tel 0845-094 0646
email editor@thenewspaper.org.uk
website www.thenewspaper.org.uk
Managing Editor Phil Wood
6 p.a. Subscription only

Newspaper aimed at 8–14-year-old schoolchildren for use as part of the National Curriculum. Contains similar columns as in any national daily newspaper. Not currently looking for new writers/articles. Founded 2000.

Now

IPC Connect, The Blue Fin Building, 110 Southwark Street, London SE1 0SU
tel 020-3148 5000 *fax* 020-3148 8110
website www.nowmagazine.co.uk
Editor Abigail Blackburn
Weekly £1.10

Showbiz magazine of celebrity gossip, news, fashion, beauty and lifestyle. Most articles are commissioned or are written by in-house writers. Founded 1996.

Nursery Education Plus

Scholastic Ltd, Book End, Range Road, Witney, Oxon IX29 0YD
tel (01993) 893456 *fax* (01993) 893222
email earlyyears@scholastic.co.uk
website www.scholastic.co.uk/nurseryedplus
Editor Tracey Brand
Monthly £38.25 p.a.

News, features, professional development and practical theme-based activities for professionals working with 0–5 year-olds. Activity ideas based on the Early Learning Goals. Material mostly commissioned. Length: 500–1000 words. Illustrations: colour and b&w; colour posters. Payment: by arrangement. Founded 1997.

Nursery World

22 Bute Gardens, London W6 7HN
tel 020-8267 8409
website www.nurseryworld.co.uk
Editor Liz Roberts
Weekly £99 p.a.

For all grades of primary school, nursery and child care staff, nannies, foster parents and all concerned with the care of expectant mothers, babies and young children. Authoritative and informative articles, 800 or 1300 words, and photos, on all aspects of child welfare and early education, from 0–8 years, in the UK. Practical ideas, policy news and career advice. No short stories. Payment: by arrangement. Illustrations: line, half-tone, colour.

Nursing Times

EMAP Public Sector, Greater London House, Hampstead Road, London NW1 7EJ
tel 020-7728 5000
website www.nursingtimes.net
Editor Alastair McLellan

Weekly £1.60

Articles of clinical interest, nursing education and nursing policy. Illustrated articles not longer than 2000 words. Press day: Friday. Illustrations: photos, line. Payment: NUJ rates; by arrangement for illustrations. Founded 1906.

Nuts

Blue Fin Building, 110 Southwark Street, London SE1 0SU
tel 020-3148 5000
email nutsmagazine@ipcmedia.com
website www.nuts.co.uk
Editor Dominic Smith
Weekly £1.40

Lads' magazine featuring sport, news, TV, women and true stories.

Official UK Playstation 2 Magazine

Future Publishing UK, 30 Monmouth Street, Bath BA1 2BW
tel (01225) 442244 *fax* (01225) 732285
website www.playstation.co.uk
Editor Nick Ellis
13 p.a. £5.99

Non-technical magazine for the Playstation owner. Payment: by arrangement. Founded 1995.

OK!

Northern & Shell Building, 10 Lower Thames Street, London EC3R 6EN
tel (0871) 434 1010 *fax* (0871) 434 7305
website www.ok-magazine.com
Editor Lisa Byrne
Weekly £2.50

Exclusive celebrity interviews and photographs. Submit ideas in writing. Length: 1000 words. Illustrations: colour. Payment: £150–£250,000 per feature. Founded 1993.

Old Tractor

Kelsey Publishing Ltd, Cudham Tithe Barn, Berry's Hill, Cudham, Kent TN16 3AG
tel (01959) 541444 *fax* (01959) 541400
email ot.mag@kelsey.co.uk
website www.oldtractor.co.uk
Editor Stuart Gibbard
Monthly £39.60 p.a.

Articles and features on tractors and agricultural engineering for the enthusiast, the collector and the serious historian. Ideas welcome but an in-depth knowledge of the subject is essential. Payment by negotiation. Founded 2003.

The Oldie

65 Newman Street, London W1T 3EG
tel 020-7436 8801 *fax* 020-7436 8804
email editorial@theoldie.co.uk
website www.theoldie.co.uk
Editor Richard Ingrams
Monthly £3.50

General interest magazine reflecting attitudes of older people but aimed at a wider audience. Features (600–1000 words) on all subjects, as well as articles for specific sections. Be familiar with the magazine prior to submitting work. See website for further guidelines. Enclose sae for reply/return of MSS. No poetry. Illustrations: welcomes b&w and colour cartoons. Payment: approx. £80–£100 per 1000 words; minimum £50 for cartoons. Founded 1992.

Opera

36 Black Lion Lane, London W6 9BE
tel 020-8563 8893 *fax* 020-8563 8635
email editor@opera.co.uk
website www.opera.co.uk
Editor John Allison
13 p.a. £4.60

Articles on general subjects appertaining to opera; reviews; criticisms. Length: up to 2000 words. Payment: by arrangement. Illustrations: photos.

Opera Now

241 Shaftesbury Avenue, London WC2H 8TF
tel 020-7333 1740 *fax* 020-7333 1769
email opera.now@rhinegold.co.uk
website www.rhinegold.co.uk
Editor Ashutosh Khandekar
Bi-monthly £5.95

Articles, news, reviews on opera. All material commissioned only. Length: 150–1500 words. Illustrations: colour and b&w photos, line, cartoons. Payment: £120 per 1000 words. Founded 1989.

Orbis

17 Greenhow Avenue, West Kirby, Wirral CH48 5EL
tel 0151-625 1446
email carolebaldock@hotmail.com
website www.kudoswritingwordpress.com
Editor Carole Baldock
Quarterly £5 (£5/€10/$11 overseas) £17 p.a. (£20/€30/$36 overseas)

Poetry, prose (1000 words), news, reviews, views, letters. Up to 4 poems by post; via email, overseas only, up to 2 in body (no attachments). Enclose sae/2 IRCs with all correspondence. Payment: £50 for featured writer. £50 Readers' Award: for piece(s) receiving the most votes (4 winners submitted to Forward Poetry Prize, Single Poem Category); £50 split between 4 (or more) runners-up. Founded 1968.

OS Magazine

Peebles Media Group, Bergius House, Clifton Street, Glasgow G3 7LA
tel 0141-567 6000 *fax* 0141-331 1365
email km.mcallister@peeblesmedia.com
website www.osmagazine.co.uk
Editor Mike Travers

Bi-monthly £31 p.a.

Serious features on anything of interest to senior secretaries and executive PAs. No unsolicited MSS; ideas only. Illustrations: colour transparencies and prints. Payment: by negotiation. Founded 1986.

Other Poetry

Fourlawshill Top, Bellingham, Hexham, Northumberland NE48 2EY
website www.otherpoetry.com
Editors Peter Armstrong, Peter Bennet, James Roderick Burns, Jo Colley
2 or 3 p.a. £4.50 or £13/$30 for three issues

Poetry. Submit up to 4 poems with sae. Payment by free subscription. Founded in 1979.

Our Dogs

1 Lund Street, Trafford Park, Manchester M16 9EJ
tel (0870) 731 6500 *fax* (0870) 731 6501
email editorial@ourdogs.co.uk
website www.ourdogs.co.uk
Editor Alison Smith
Weekly £2

Articles and news on the breeding and showing of pedigree dogs. Illustrations: b&w photos. Payment: by negotiation; £10 per photo. Founded 1895.

Park Home & Holiday Caravan

IPC Media Ltd, Leon House, 233 High Street, Croydon CR9 1HZ
tel 020-8726 8253 *fax* 020-8726 8299
email phhc@ipcmedia.com
Editor Alex Melvin
Every 4th Friday (13 p.a.) £2.90

Informative articles on residential mobile homes (park homes) and holiday static caravans – personal experience articles, site features, news items. No preliminary letter. Payment: by arrangement. Illustrations: line, half-tone, colour transparencies, digital images, cartoons. Founded 1960.

PC Advisor

IDG Communications Ltd, 101 Euston Road, London NW1 2RA
tel 020-7756 2800
email paul_trotter@idg.co.uk
website www.pcadvisor.co.uk
Editor Paul Trotter
Monthly CD edition £3.99, DVD edition £4.99

Aimed at PC-proficient individuals who are looking for IT solutions that will enhance their productivity at work and at home. Includes information on the latest hardware and software and advice on how to use PCs to maximum effect. Features are commissioned; unsolicited material may be considered. Length: 1500–3000 words (features). Illustrations: colour artwork. Payment: dependent on feature type. Founded 1995.

PC Answers

Future Publishing Ltd, 30 Monmouth Street, Bath BA1 2BW
tel (01225) 442244 *fax* (01225) 732295
email christian.hall@futurenet.co.uk
website www.futurenet.co.uk
Editor Christian Hall
13 p.a. £5.99

Reviews, news and practical/how-to features for home PC users, excluding games. Length: 2500 words (features). Illustrations: colour. Payment: by negotiation. Founded 1991.

PC Plus

Future Publishing Ltd, 30 Monmouth Street, Bath BA1 2BW
tel (01225) 442244 *fax* (01225) 446019
email martin.cooper@futurenet.co.uk
website www.pcplus.co.uk
Editor Martin Cooper
Every 4 weeks £6.49 inc. DVD

For the discerning, dedicated computing enthusiast who loves technology, the magazine includes tutorials and features, and the DVD carries full software products, essential utilities and bonus video material. Each issue is made up of opinion, analysis, and hardware and software labs verdicts.

PC Pro

Dennis Publishing Ltd, 30 Cleveland Street, London W1T 4JD
tel 020-7907 6000 *fax* 020-7907 6304
email features@pcpro.co.uk
website www.pcpro.co.uk
Editor Tim Danton
Monthly £3.99

IT in-depth industry comment and news, reviews and tests, aimed at IT professionals and enthusiasts. Email feature ideas; read magaine first.

Peace News

5 Caledonian Road, London N1 9DY
tel 020-7278 3344 *fax* 020-7278 0444
email editorial@peacenews.info
website www.peacenews.info
Editors Milan Rai, Emily Johns
10 p.a. £12 p.a.

Political articles based on nonviolence in every aspect of human life. Illustrations: line, half-tone. No payment. Founded 1936.

Pensions World

LexisNexis Butterworths, Tolley House, 2 Addiscombe Road, Croydon CR9 5AF
tel 0845-370 1234 *fax* 020-8212 1920
email stephanie.hawthorne@lexisnexis.co.uk
website www.pensionsworld.co.uk
Editor Stephanie Hawthorne
Monthly £129 p.a.

Specialist articles on pensions, investment and law. No unsolicited articles; all material is commissioned. Length: 1500 words. Payment: by negotiation. Founded 1972.

People Management

Personnel Publications Ltd, 17 Britton Street,
London EC1M 5TP
tel 020-7324 2729 *fax* 020-7324 2791
email editorial@peoplemanagement.co.uk
website www.peoplemanagement.co.uk
Editor Rob MacLachlan
Fortnightly £5 (£95 p.a.)

Magazine of the Chartered Institute of Personnel and Development. News items and feature articles on recruitment and selection, training and development; pay and performance management; industrial psychology; employee relations; employment law; working practices and new practical ideas in personnel management in industry and commerce. Length: up to 2500 words. Payment: by arrangement. Illustrations: contact art editor.

People's Friend

D.C. Thomson & Co. Ltd, 80 Kingsway East,
Dundee DD4 8SL
tel (01382) 223131 *fax* (01382) 452491
Send material to The Editor, Angela Gilchrist
Weekly 82p

Fiction magazine for women of all ages. Serials (60,000–70,000 words) and complete stories (1500–3000 words) of strong romantic and emotional appeal. Considers stories for children. Includes knitting and cookery. No preliminary letter required. Illustrations: colour. Payment: on acceptance. Founded 1869.

People's Friend Pocket Novel

D.C. Thomson & Co. Ltd, 80 Kingsway East,
Dundee DD4 8SL
tel (01382) 223131 *fax* (01382) 452491
email tsteel@dcthomson.co.uk
Editor Tracey Steel
2 p.m. £1.80

50,000–55,000-word family and romantic stories aimed at 30+ age group. Payment: by arrangement. No illustrations.

Period Living

Centaur Media, St Giles House, 50 Poland Street,
London W1F 7AX
tel 020-7970 4433 *fax* 020-7970 4438
email period.living@centaur.co.uk
website www.periodliving.co.uk
Editor Sarah Whelan
Monthly £3.40

Articles and features on decoration, furnishings, renovation of period homes; gardens, crafts, decorating in a period style. Illustrated. Payment: varies, according to work required. Founded 1990.

Personal Computer World

Incisive Media, Haymarket House,
28–29 Haymarket, London SW1Y 4RX
tel 020-7316 9000 *fax* 020-7316 9313
website www.pcw.co.uk
Editor Kelvyn Taylor
Monthly £3.99 (CD edition) £4.99 (DVD edition)

Articles about computers, reviews, features and how-to advice. Length: 800–5000 words. Payment: from £150 per 1000 words. Illustrations: line, half-tone, colour. Founded 1978.

The Photographer

PO Box 9337, Witham, Essex CM8 2UT
tel (01279) 503871
email editor@bipp.com
website www.bipp.com
Editor Jonathan Briggs
Monthly £4.25

Journal of the BIPP covering conventional and digital imaging and images. Authoritative reviews, news, views and high-quality photographs.

Pick Me Up

IPC Connect Ltd, The Blue Fin Building,
110 Southwark Street, London SE1 0SU
tel 020-3148 5000 *fax* 020-3148 8112
email pickmeup@ipcmedia.com
website www.pickmeupmagazine.co.uk
Editor June Smith-Sheppard
Weekly 68p

Upbeat women's magazine containing real-life stories and puzzles.

Picture Postcard Monthly

15 Debdale Lane, Keyworth, Nottingham NG12 5HT
tel 0115-937 4079 *fax* 0115-937 6197
email reflections@postcardcollecting.co.uk
website www.postcardcollecting.co.uk
Editor Brian Lund
Monthly £2.60 (£33 p.a.)

Articles, news and features for collectors of old or modern picture postcards. Length: 500–2000 words. Illustrations: colour and b&w. Payment: £27 per 1000 words; 50p per print. Founded 1978.

The Pink Paper

Millivres Prowler Group, Spectrum House,
32–34 Gordon House Road, London NW5 1LP
tel 020-7424 7400 *fax* 020 7424 7401
email editorial @pinkpaper.com
website www.pinkpaper.com
Editor Tris Reid-Smith
Fortnightly Free

National newspaper for lesbians and gay men. Features (500–1000 words) and news (100–500 words) plus lifestyle section (features 350–1000 words) on any gay-related subject. Founded 1987.

Planet

PO Box 44, Aberystwyth, Ceredigion SY23 3ZZ
tel (01970) 611255 *fax* (01970) 611197

email planet.enquiries@planetmagazine.org.uk
website www.planetmagazine.org.uk
Editor Helle Michelsen
4 p.a. £5.75 (£22 p.a.)

Short stories, poems, topical articles on Welsh current affairs, politics, the environment and society. New literature in English. Length of articles: 2000–3500 words. Payment: £50 per 1000 words for prose; £30 minimum per poem. Illustrations: line, half-tone, cartoons. Founded 1970–9; relaunched 1985.

PN Review

(formerly Poetry Nation)
Dept of English, University of Glasgow, 5 University Gardens, Glasgow G12 8QH; Carcanet Press Ltd, 4th Floor, Alliance House, 30 Cross Street, Manchester M2 7AQ
tel 0161-834 8730 *fax* 0161-832 0084
email info@carcanet.co.uk
website www.pnreview.co.uk
Editor Michael Schmidt
6 p.a. £6.99 £36 p.a.

Poems, essays, reviews, translations. Submissions by post only. Payment: by arrangement. Founded 1973.

Poetry Ireland Review/Éigse Éireann

2 Prouds Lane, off St Stephens Green, Dublin 2, Republic of Ireland
tel (01) 478 9974 *fax* (01) 478 0205
email publications@poetryireland.ie
website www.poetryireland.ie
Editor Caitriona O'Reilly
Quarterly €7.99, €30.50 p.a.

Poetry. Features and articles by arrangement. Payment: €40 per contribution or 1 year's subscription; €75 reviews. Founded 1981.

Poetry London

81 Lambeth Walk, London SE11 6DX
tel/fax 020-7735 8880
email admin@poetrylondon.co.uk
website www.poetrylondon.co.uk
Editors Colette Bryce, Scott Verner, Martha Kapos, Tim Dooley
The International poetry magazine 3 p.a. £16 p.a.

Poems of the highest standard, articles/reviews on any aspect of modern poetry. Comprehensive listings of poetry events and resources. Contributors must be knowledgeable about contemporary poetry. Payment: £20 minimum. Founded 1988.

Poetry Review

22 Betterton Street, London WC2H 9BX
tel 020-7420 9883 *fax* 020-7240 4818
email poetryreview@poetrysociety.org.uk
website www.poetrysociety.org.uk
Editor Fiona Sampson
Quarterly £30 p.a., £50 (institutions, schools and libraries)

Poems, features and reviews. Send no more than 6 poems with sae. Preliminary study of magazine essential. Payment: £50+ per poem.

Poetry Wales

57 Nolton Street, Bridgend CF31 3AE
tel (01656) 663018
email poetrywales@seren-books.com
website www.seren-books.com, www.poetrywales.co.uk
Quarterly £5 £20 p.a.; 2-year private subscription £36; annual institutional subscription £30 (rates for abroad available on request)

Poetry, criticism and commentary from Wales and around the world. Payment: by arrangement. Founded 1965.

Police Journal

Vathek Publishing, Bridge House, Dalby, Isle of Man IM5 3BP
tel (01624) 844056 *fax* (01624) 845043
website www.vathek.com
Quarterly £131 p.a. (print only) £158 (print and online) £117 (online only)

Articles of technical or professional interest to the Police Service throughout the world. Payment: none. Illustrations: line drawings. Founded 1928.

Police Review

Jane's Information Group, 133 Houndsditch, London EC3A 7AH
tel 020-3159 3579 *fax* 020-3159 3276
email ppr@janes.com
website www.policereview.com
Editor Chris Herbert
Weekly £1.95 (£92 p.a.)

News and features of interest to the police and legal professions. Length: 200–1500 words. Illustrations: colour photos, line, cartoons. Payment: NUJ rates. Founded 1893.

The Political Quarterly

Wiley-Blackwell, 9600 Garsington Road, Oxford OX4 2DQ
tel (01865) 776868 *fax* (01865) 714591
website www.wiley.com
Editors Andrew Gamble, Tony Wright MP
4 p.a. (£288 p.a. premium print and online rate institutions, £27 p.a. individuals)

Topical aspects of national and international politics and public administration; takes a progressive, but not a party, point of view. Send articles to Assistant Editor. Length: average 5000 words. Payment: about £125 per article. Founded 1930.

PONY Magazine

Headley House, Headley Road, Grayshott, Surrey GU26 6TU
tel (01428) 601020 *fax* (01428) 601030

Editor Janet Rising
13 issues p.a. £2.99

Lively articles and short stories with a horsy theme aimed at readers aged 8–16. Technical accuracy and young, fresh writing essential. Length: up to 800 words. Payment: by arrangement. Illustrations: drawings (commissioned), photos, cartoons. Founded 1949.

Post Magazine & Insurance Week

32–34 Broadwick Street, London W1A 2HG
tel 020-7316 9000
email postmag@incisivemedia.com
website www.postonline.co.uk
Editor Jonathan Swift
Weekly £6.70

Commissioned specialist articles on topics of interest to insurance professionals; news. Illustrations: colour photos and illustrations, colour and b&w cartoons and line drawings. Payment: £200 per 1000 words; photos £30–£120, cartoons/line by negotiation. Founded 1840.

Poultry World

Reed Business Information, Quadrant House, The Quadrant, Sutton, Surrey SM2 5AS
tel 020-8652 4020 *fax* 020-8652 4006
email poultry.world@rbi.co.uk
website www.fwi.co.uk
Editor Philip Clarke
Monthly £3

Articles on poultry breeding, production, marketing and packaging. News of international poultry interest. Payment: by arrangement. Illustrations: photos, line.

PR Week

22 Bute Gardens, London W6 7HN
tel 020-8267 4370
email danny.rogers@haymarket.com
website www.prweek.com
Editor Danny Rogers
Weekly £3.70

News and features on public relations. Length: approx. 800–3000 words. Payment: £250 per 1000 words. Illustrations: colour and b&w. Founded 1984.

Practical Boat Owner

Westover House, West Quay Road, Poole, Dorset BH15 1JG
tel (01202) 440820
email pbo@ipcmedia.com
website www.pbo.co.uk
Editor Sarah Norbury
Monthly £4.10

Yachting magazine. Hints, tips and practical articles for cruising skippers. Send synopsis first. Payment: by negotiation. Illustrations: photos or drawings. Founded 1967.

Practical Caravan

Haymarket Magazines, Teddington Studios, Teddington Lock, Broom Road, Teddington TW11 9BE
tel 020-8267 5629 *fax* 020-8267 5725
email practical.caravan@haymarket.com
website www.practicalcaravan.com
Editor Nigel Donnelly
Monthly £3.80

Caravan-related travelogues, caravan site reviews; travel writing for existing regular series; technical and DIY matters. Illustrations: colour. Payment negotiable. Founded 1967.

Practical Fishkeeping

Media House, Lynchwood, Peterborough Business Park, Peterborough PE2 6EA
tel (01733) 468000
website www.practicalfishkeeping.co.uk
Editor Matt Clarke
13 p.a. £3.50

Practical fishkeeping in tropical and coldwater aquaria and ponds. Heavy emphasis on inspiration and involvement. Good colour photography always needed, and used. No verse or humour, no personal biographical accounts of fishkeeping unless practical. Payment: by worth. Founded 1966.

Practical Parenting

Magicalia Limited, 15–18 White Lion Street, Islington, London N1 9PD
tel 020-7843 8800
website www.practicalparenting.co.uk
Editor Daniella Delaney
Monthly £2.80

Articles on parenting, baby and childcare, health, psychology, education, children's activities, personal birth/parenting experiences. Send article by email to jenny.stallard@magicalia.com. Illustrations: colour photos, line; commissioned only. Payment: by agreement. Founded 1987.

Practical Photography

Bauer, Media House, Lynchwood, Peterborough PE2 6EA
tel (01733) 468000 *fax* (01733) 468387
website www.practicalphotography.co.uk
Editor-in-Chief Andrew James
Monthly £3.90

Aimed at anyone who seeks to take excellent quality pictures. Excellent potential for freelance pictures: must be first rate – technically and pictorially – and have some relevance to photographic technique. Freelance ideas for words welcome (the more unusual ideas stand the greatest chance of success). Send synopsis of feature ideas in the first instance. Payment: negotiable but typically £80 per page pro rata for images and £120–£140 per 1000 words. Founded 1959.

Practical Wireless

PW Publishing Ltd, Arrowsmith Court, Station Approach, Broadstone, Dorset BH18 8PW

tel (0845) 803 1979 *fax* (01202) 659950
email rob@pwpublishing.ltd.uk
website www.pwpublishingltd.uk
Editor Rob Mannion
Monthly £3.50, £38 p.a.

Articles on the practical and theoretical aspects of amateur radio and communications. Constructional projects. Telephone or email for advice and essential PW author's guide. Illustrations: in b&w and colour; photos, line drawings and wash half-tone for offset litho. Payment: by arrangement. Founded 1932.

Practical Woodworking

MyHobbyStore Ltd, Berwick House, 8–10 Knoll Rise, Orpington, Kent BR6 0EL
tel (0168) 9899200 *fax* (0168) 9899266
Editor Neil Mead
Bi-Monthly £4.99

Articles of a practical nature covering any aspect of woodworking, including woodworking projects, tools, joints or timber technology. Illustrated.

The Practising Midwife

54 Siward Road, Bromley BR2 9JZ
tel 020-8464 0304 *fax* (0871) 224 7390
website www.thepractisingmidwife.com
Editor Jennifer Hall
Monthly £60 p.a. (£57 direct debit), (£36 p.a. students, £34.20 direct debit), Newly qualified midwives £50 (or £47.50 direct debit)

Disseminates research-based material to a wide professional audience. Research and review papers, viewpoints and news items pertaining to midwifery, maternity care, women's health and neonatal health with both a national and an international perspective. All articles submitted are anonymously reviewed by external acknowledged experts. Length: 1000–2000 words (articles); 150–400 words (news); up to 1000 words (viewpoints). Illustrations: colour transparencies and artwork. Payment: by arrangement. Founded 1991.

The Practitioner

Practitioner Medical Publishing Ltd, 10 Fernthorpe Road, London SW16 6DR
tel 020-8677 3508 *fax* 020-8664 7429
email editor@thepractitioner.co.uk
website www.thepractitioner.co.uk
Editor Corinne Short
Monthly (£85 p.a. UK, £138 p.a. overseas)

Articles on advances in medicine of interest to GPs and vocational registrars, and others in the medical profession. Founded 1868.

Prediction

IPC Inspire, Leon House, 233 High Street, Croydon CR9 1HZ
tel 020-8726 8000 *fax* 020-8726 8299
email prediction@ipcmedia.com
website www.predictionmagazine.co.uk
Editor Marion Williamson
Monthly £2.95

Articles on astrology and all esoteric subjects. Length: up to 3000 words. Payment: by arrangement. Illustrations: large-format colour transparencies or photos. Founded 1936.

Press Gazette

John Carpenter House, John Carpenter Street, London EC4Y 0AN
tel 020-7936 6432
website www.pressgazette.co.uk
Editor Dominic Ponsford
Weekly £3 (£115 p.a.)

News and features of interest to journalists and others working in the media. Length: 1200 words (features), 300 words (news). Payment: approx. £230 (features), news stories negotiable. Founded 1965.

Pride

Pride House, 55 Battersea Bridge Road, London SW11 3AX
tel 020-7228 3110 *fax* 020-7228 3121
email info@pridemagazine.com
website www.pridemagazine.com
Publisher C. Cushnie
Monthly £2.80

Lifestyle magazine incorporating fashion and beauty, travel, food and entertaining articles for the woman of colour. Length: 1000–3000 words. Illustrations: colour photos and drawings. Payment: £100 per 1000 words. Founded 1991; relaunched 1997.

Prima

National Magazine Company, 72 Broadwick Street, London W1F 9EP
tel 020-7439 5000 *fax* 020-7312 4100
Editor Maire Fahey
Monthly £2.70

Articles on fashion, home, crafts, health and beauty, cookery; features. Founded 1986.

Prima Baby

National Magazine Co Ltd, 72 Broadwick Street, London W1F 9EP
tel 020-7312 3852 *fax* 020-7312 3744
website www.babyexpert.com
Editor Elaine Griffiths
Monthly £2.50

Magazine for women covering all aspects of pregnancy and childbirth and life with children aged up to 3 years; plus health, fashion. Length: up to 1500 words. Illustrations: colour transparencies. Payment: by arrangement. Founded 1994.

Private Eye

6 Carlisle Street, London W1D 3BN
tel 020-7437 4017 *fax* 020-7437 0705
email strobes@private-eye.co.uk
website www.private-eye.co.uk

Editor Ian Hislop
Fortnightly £1.50 (£28 p.a.)

Satire. Payment: by arrangement. Illustrations: b&w, line, cartoons. Founded 1961.

Professional Photographer

Archant Specialist Ltd, The Mill,
Bearwalden Business Park, Wendens Ambo,
Saffron Walden, Essex CB11 4GB
tel (01799) 544200 *fax* (01799) 544201
Editor Grant Scott
Monthly £3.60

Articles on professional photography, including technical articles, photographer profiles and coverage of issues affecting the industry. Length: 1000–2000 words. Illustrations: colour and b&w prints and transparencies, or digital files; diagrams if appropriate. Payment: from £200. Founded 1961.

Prospect Magazine

Prospect Publishing Ltd, 2 Bloomsbury Place,
London WC1A 2QA
tel 020-7255 1281 *fax* 020-7255 1279
email editorial@prospect-magazine.co.uk
website www.prospect-magazine.co.uk
Editor David Goodhart
Monthly £4.50

Political and cultural monthly magazine. Essays, features, special reports, reviews, short stories, opinions/analysis. Length: 3000–6000 words (essays, special reports, short stories), 1000 words (opinions). Illustrations: colour and b&w. Payment: by negotiation. Founded 1995.

Psychologies

Hachette Filipacchi UK Ltd, 64 North Row,
London W1K 7LL
tel 020-7150 7000
email psychologies@hf-uk.com
website www.psychologies.co.uk
Editor Louise Chunn *Deputy Editor* Clare Longrigg, *Features Editors* Rebecca Alexander, Catherine Jones
Monthly £3.40

Women's magazine with a focus on 'what we're like, not just what we look like' with features covering relationships, family and parenting, personality, behaviour, health, wellbeing, beauty, society and social trends, travel, spirituality and sex. Welcomes new ideas by email which fit into one of these areas, and suggestions should offer a combination of psychological insight and practical advice.

Pulse

CMP Medica Ltd, Ludgate House,
245 Blackfriars Road, London SE1 9UY
tel 020-7921 8102 *fax* 020-7921 8132
email feedback@pulsetoday.co.uk
website www.pulsetoday.co.uk
Editor Jo Haynes
Weekly Free on request

Articles and photos of direct interest to GPs. Purely clinical material can only be accepted from medically qualified authors. Length: 600–1200 words. Payment: £150 average. Illustrations: b&w and colour photos. Founded 1959.

Q Magazine

Bauer Consumer Media, Mappin House,
4 Winsley Street, London W1W 8HF
tel 020-7436 1515 *fax* 020-7182 5457
email q@ecm.bauerconsumer.com
website www.q4music.com
Editor Paul Rees
Monthly £3.90

Glossy music guide. All material commissioned. Length: 1200–2500 words. Illustrations: colour and b&w photos. Payment: £350 per 1000 words; illustrations by arrangement. Founded 1986.

RA Magazine

Royal Academy of Arts, Burlington House,
Piccadilly, London W1J 0BD
tel 020-7300 5820 *fax* 020-7300 8032
website www.ramagazine.org.uk
Acting Editor Nigel Billen
Quarterly £4.95 (£20 p.a.)

Visual arts and culture articles relating to the Royal Academy of Arts and the wider British and international arts scene. Length:150–1800 words. Illustrations: consult the Editor. Payment: average £250 per 1000 words; illustrations by negotiation. Founded 1983.

Racing Post

Floor 23, 1 Canada Square, Canary Wharf,
London E14 5AP
tel 020-7293 3000 *fax* 020-7293 3758
email editor@racingpost.co.uk
website www.racingpost.com
Editor Bruce Millington
Mon–Fri £1.70, Sat £1.90, Sun £1.80

News on horseracing, greyhound racing and sports betting. Founded 1986.

Radio Control Models and Electronics

Magicalia Publishing, Berwick House,
8–10 Knoll Rise, Orpington, Kent BR6 0EL
tel (01689) 899200 *fax* (01689) 899266
Editor Graham Ashby
Monthly £3.80

Well-illustrated articles on topics related to radio control. Payment: £45 per published page. Illustrations: line, half-tone. Founded 1960.

Radio Times

BBC Worldwide Ltd, 201 Wood Lane,
London W12 7TQ

tel 020-8433 3400 *fax* 020-8433 3160
email radio.times@bbc.co.uk
website www.radiotimes.com
Editor Ben Preston
Weekly £1.10

Articles that preview the week's programmes on British TV and radio. All articles are specially commissioned – ideas and synopses are welcomed but not unsolicited MSS. Length: 600–2500 words. Payment: by arrangement. Illustrations: mostly in colour; photos, graphic designs or drawings.

Rail

Bauer Media Ltd, Lynchwood,
Peterborough Business Park, Peterborough PE2 6EA
tel (01733) 468000
email rail@bauermedia.co.uk
website www.rail-magazine.com
Managing Editor Nigel Harris
Fortnightly £3.30

News and in-depth features on current UK railway operations. Length: 2000–3000 words (features), 250–400 words (news). Illustrations: colour and b&w photos and artwork. Payment: £75 per 1000 words; £20 per photo except cover (£70). Founded 1981.

Railway Gazette International

DVV Media UK Ltd, NINE, Sutton Court Road,
Sutton, Surrey SM1 4SZ
tel 020-8652 5200 *fax* 020-8652 5210
email editor@railwaygazette.com
website www.railwaygazette.com
Editor Chris Jackson
Monthly £80 p.a.

Deals with management, engineering, operation and finance of railways worldwide. Articles of practical interest on these subjects are considered and paid for if accepted. No 'enthusiast'-oriented articles. Phone or email to discuss proposals. Illustrated articles, of 1000–2000 words, are preferred. A preliminary letter is required.

Railway Magazine

IPC Inspire, The Blue Fin Building,
110 Southwark Street, London SE1 0SU
tel 020-3148 5000 *fax* 020-3148 8122
website www.railwaymagazine.co.uk
Editor Nick Pigott
Monthly £3.35

Illustrated magazine dealing with all railway subjects; no fiction or verse. Articles from 1500–2000 words accompanied by photos. Preliminary letter desirable. Payment: by arrangement. Illustrations: colour transparencies, half-tone and line. Founded 1897.

Reach Poetry

132 Hinckley Road, Stoney Stanton, Leics. LE9 7NE
email indigodreamspress@rocketmail.com
website www.indigodreamsonline.com
Editor Ronnie Goodyer
Monthly £4, £45 p.a.

Unpublished and original poetry. Submit up to 3 poems for consideration by post (include sae for reply) or email. New poets encouraged. No payment; £50 prize money each issue. Founded 1998.

Reader's Digest

The Reader's Digest Association Ltd,
11 Westferry Circus, Canary Wharf,
London E14 4HE
tel 020-7715 8000 *fax* 020-7715 8716
email theeditor@readersdigest.co.uk
website www.readersdigest.co.uk
Editor-in-Chief Gill Hudson
Monthly £3.49 (£42 p.a.)

Original anecdotes – £100 for up to 150 words – are required for humorous anecdotes.

Real People

The National Magazine Company Ltd,
33 Broadwick Street, London W1F 0DQ
020-7439 5000
email samm.taylor@natmags.co.uk
website www.realpeoplemagazine.co.uk
Editor Samm Taylor
Weekly

Magazine for women with real-life tales of ordinary people coping with extraordinary events plus puzzles section.

Reality

Redemptorist Communications, 75 Orwell Road,
Rathgar, Dublin 6, Republic of Ireland
tel (01) 4922488 *fax* (01) 4922654
email info@redemptoristpublications.com
website www.redemptoristpublications.com
Editor Rev. Gerry Moloney CSSR
Monthly €1.70

Illustrated magazine for Christian living. Illustrated articles on all aspects of modern life, including family, youth, religion, leisure. Length: 1000–1500 words. Payment: by arrangement; average £50 per 1000 words. Founded 1936.

Record Collector

Diamond Publishing, 140 Wales Farm Road,
London W3 6UG
tel 020-8752 8172 *fax* 020- 8752 8186
email alan.lewis@metropolis.co.uk
website www.recordcollectormag.com
Editor-in-Chief Alan Lewis
Monthly £3.90

Covers all areas of music, with the focus on collectable releases and the reissues market. Specially commissions most material but will consider unsolicited material. Welcomes ideas for articles and features. Length: 2,000 (articles/features), 200 (news). Illustrations: transparencies, colour and b&w prints, scans of rare records; all commissioned. Payment: negotiable. Founded 1980.

Red

Hachette Filipacchi UK Ltd, 64 North Row, London W1K 7LL
tel 020-7150 7600 *fax* 020-7150 7684
website www.redmagazine.co.uk
Editor-in-chief Sam Baker, *Send material to* Lindsay Frankel, Features Director
Monthly £3.50

High-quality articles on topics of interest to women aged 25–45: humour, memoirs, interviews and well-researched investigative features. Approach with ideas in writing in first instance. Length: 900 words upwards. Illustrations: transparencies. Payment: NUJ rates minimum. Founded 1998.

Red Pepper

Socialist Newspaper (Publications) Ltd, 1B Waterlow Road, London N19 5NJ
email office@redpepper.org.uk
website www.redpepper.org.uk
Co-editors Hilary Wainwright, Michael Calderbank, James O'Nions
Bi-Monthly £3.95

Independent radical magazine: news and features on politics, culture and everyday life of interest to the left and greens. Material mostly commissioned. Length: news/news features 200–800 words, other features 800–2000 words. Illustrations: photos, graphics. Payment: for investigations, otherwise only exceptionally. Founded 1994.

Reform

(published by United Reformed Church)
86 Tavistock Place, London WC1H 9RT
tel 020-7916 8630 *fax* 020-7916 2021 (FAO 'Reform')
email reform@urc.org.uk
Contact Kay Parris
11 issues p.a. £1.80 (£19.80 p.a.)

Articles of religious or social comment. Illustrations: graphic artists/illustrators. Payment: by arrangement. Founded 1972.

Report

ATL, 7 Northumberland Street, London WC2N 5RD
tel 020-7930 6441 *fax* 020-7930 1359
email report@atl.org.uk
website www.atl.org.uk
Editor Alex Tomlin
9 p.a. £2.50 (£15.50 p.a. UK; £27 p.a. overseas) Free to members

The magazine from the Association of Teachers and Lecturers (ATL). Features, articles, comment, news about nursery, primary, secondary and further education. Payment: minimum £120 per 1000 words.

Restaurant Magazine

Broadfield Park, Crawley RH11 9RT
tel (01293) 613400
email editorial@restaurantmagazine.co.uk
website www.bighospitality.co.uk
Editor Paul Wootton
Bi-weekly £1.95

Articles, features and news on the restaurant trade. Specially commissions most material. Welcomes ideas for articles and features. Illustrations: colour transparencies, prints and artwork. Payment: variable. Founded 2001.

Retail Week

EMAP Retail, Greater London House, Hampstead Road, London NW1 7EJ
tel 020-7728 5000
website www.retail-week.com
Editor Tim Danaher
Weekly £2.75 (£137.50 p.a.)

Features and news stories on all aspects of retail management. Length: up to 1400 words. Illustrations: colour photos. Payment: by arrangement. Founded 1988.

The Rialto

PO Box 309, Aylsham, Norwich NR11 6LN
website www.therialto.co.uk
Editor Michael Mackmin
3 p.a. £5.50 (£19 p.a., £16 low income)

For poets and poetry. Submit up to 6 poems; sae essential. Payment: by arrangement. Founded 1984.

Right Start

Ten Alps Publishing, 9 Savoy Street, London WC2E 7HR
tel 020-7878 2338 *fax* 020-7379 6261
Editor Lynette Lowthian
Bi-monthly £2.50 (£10.90 p.a.)

Features on all aspects of preschool and infant education, child health and behaviour. No unsolicited MSS. Length: 800–1500 words. Illustrations: colour photos, line. Payment: varies. Founded 1989.

Royal National Institute of Blind People (RNIB)

105 Judd Street, London WC1H 9NE
tel 020-7388 1266 *fax* 020-7388 2034
textphone (0845) 7585691
email shop@rnib.org.uk
website www.rnib.org.uk

Published by the Royal National Institute of Blind People, the following titles are available via email and in braille, unless otherwise stated. *3FM*, *Access IT*, *Aphra*, *Big Print newspaper* (large print only), *Blast Off!* (children's magazine), *Braille at Bedtime* (7–11 year-olds; braille), *Broadcast Times* (email only), *Channels of Blessing*, *Chess Magazine* (braille), *Compute IT*, *Contention*, *Conundrum* (disk and braille), *Cricket Fixtures*, *Daily Bread* (disk and braille), *Daisy TV Listings* (Daisy format), *Daisy*

Radio Listing (Daisy format), *Football Fixtures* (email, Daisy and braille), *Good Vibrations*, *Insight* (clear print, audio CD, braille, email), *The Max* (boys aged 16–19), *Missy* (girls aged 12–15), *Money Matters*, *Music Magazine* (disk and braille), *NB* (print, email, Daisy, audio CD, braille), *New Product Guide* (braille, large print, email, Daisy), *Journal of Physiotherapy*, *Physiotherapy* (disk, cassette tape, braille), *Physiotherapy Frontline* (cassette tape), *Piano Tuners' Quarterly* (email, tape, braille), *Progress*, *Proms Guide*, *Pure* (girls aged 16–19), *Radio Guide*, *Ready, Steady, Read* (for new readers of braille in braille only), *Rhetoric*, *Scientific Enquiry* (disk and braille), *Shaping Up*, *Shop Window*, *Shop Window Christmas Guide*, *Short Stories*, *SP*, *Television Guide*, *Theological Times* (disk, cassette tape, braille), *Upbeat*, *Vibe* (boys aged 12–15), *You & Your Child*, *Vision* (clear print, email, braille, Daisy format).

Rugby World

IPC Media Ltd, 9th Floor, The Blue Fin Building, 110 Southwark Street, London SE1 0SU
tel 020-3148 5000
email Paul_Morgan@ipcmedia.com
Editor Paul Morgan
Monthly £3.90

Features and exclusive news stories on rugby. Length: approx. 1200 words. Illustrations: colour photos, cartoons. Payment: £120. Founded 1960.

Runner's World

Natmag Rodale Ltd, 33 Broadwick Street, London W1F 0DG
tel 020-7339 4400 *fax* 020-7339 4420
email rwedit@natmag-rodale.co.uk
website www.runnersworld.co.uk
Editor Andy Dixon
Monthly £4.30

Articles on running, health and fitness, and nutrition. Payment: by arrangement. Illustrations: line, half-tone, colour. Founded 1979.

Running Fitness

14 Priestgate, Peterborough PE1 1JA
(01733) 353356 *fax* (01733) 891342
email rf.ed@kelsey.co.uk
website www.runningfitnessmag.co.uk
Editor David Castle
Monthly £4, £36.30 p.a.

Practical articles on all aspects of running lifestyle, especially road running training and events, and advice on health, fitness and injury. Illustrations: colour photos, cartoons. Payment: by negotiation. Founded 1985.

RUSI Journal

Whitehall, London SW1A 2ET
tel 020-7747 2600
email journal@rusi.org
website www.rusi.org
Editor Dr Ian Kerns
Bi-monthly £141 p.a.

Journal of the Royal United Services Institute for Defence and Security Studies. Articles on international security, military sciences, defence technology and procurement, and military history; also book reviews and correspondence. Length: 3000–3500 words. Illustrations: b&w photos, colour transparencies, maps and diagrams.

Safety Education Journal

Royal Society for the Prevention of Accidents, Edgbaston Park, 353 Bristol Road, Birmingham B5 7ST
tel 0121-248 2000 *fax* 0121-248 2001
website www.rospa.org.uk
Editor Janice Cave
3 p.a. £12.50 p.a. for members of Safety Education Department (£15 p.a. non-members)

Articles on every aspect of good practice in safety education including safety of teachers and pupils in school, and the teaching of road, home, water, leisure and personal safety by means of established subjects on the school curriculum. All ages. Founded as *Child Safety* 1937; became *Safety Training* 1940; *Safety Education* 1966.

Saga Magazine

Saga Publishing Ltd, The Saga Building, Enbrook Park, Sandgate, Folkestone, Kent CT20 3SE
tel (01303) 771523 *fax* (01303) 776699
Editor Katy Bravery
Monthly £24.95 p.a. Subscription only

General interest magazine aimed at the intelligent, literate 50+ reader. Wide range of articles from human interest, 'real life' stories, intriguing overseas interest (not travel), some natural history, celebrity interviews, photographic book extracts – all relevant to 50+ audience. Articles mostly commissioned or written in-house, but genuine exclusives welcome. Illustrations: colour, digital media; mainly commissioned but top-quality photo feature suggestions sometimes accepted. Payment: competitive rate, by negotiation. Founded 1984.

Sainsbury's Magazine

Seven Publishing Group Ltd, 20 Upper Ground, London SE1 9PD
tel 020-7633 0266 *fax* 020-7401 9423
website www.sainsburysmagazine.co.uk
Editor Helena Lang
Monthly £1.40

Features: general, food and drink, health, beauty, homes; all material commissioned. Length: up to 1500 words. Illustrations: colour and b&w photos and line illustrations. Payment: varies; £400 per full page for illustrations. Founded 1993.

Sarasvati

132 Hinckley Road, Stoney Stanton, Leics. LE9 7NE
email dawnidp@btinternet.com
website www.indigodreamsonline.com

Editors Ronnie Goodyer and Dawn Bauling
Bi-monthly £4, £22 for 6 issues

International poetry and short story magazine. New writers/poets encouraged. No payment. Sae essential; email submissions welcome. Founded 2008.

The School Librarian

The School Library Association, Unit 2, Lotmead Business Village, Lotmead Farm, Wanborough, Swindon SN4 0UY
tel (01793) 791787 *fax* (01793) 791786
email info@sla.org.uk
website www.sla.org.uk
Editor Steve Hird
Quarterly £45 p.a.

Official journal of the School Library Association. Articles on school library management, use and skills, and on authors and illustrators, literacy, publishing. Reviews of books, CD-Roms, websites and other library resources from preschool to adult. Length: 1800–3000 words (articles). Payment: by arrangement. Founded 1937.

Scientific Computing World

Europa Science Ltd, The Spectrum Building, The Michael Young Centre, Purbeck Road, Cambridge CB2 8PD
tel (01223) 211147 *fax* (01223) 211107
website www.scientific-computing.com
Editor Warren Clark
6 p.a. £11 (£95 p.a.) Free to qualifying subscribers

Features on hardware and software developments for the scientific community, plus news articles and reviews. Length: 800–2000 words. Illustrations: colour transparencies, photos, electronic graphics. Payment: by negotiation. Founded 1994.

The Scots Magazine

D.C. Thomson & Co. Ltd, 80 Kingsway East, Dundee DD4 8SL
tel (01382) 223131
email mail@scotsmagazine.com
website www.scotsmagazine.com
Monthly £1.90

Articles on all subjects of Scottish interest and poetry, but must also be Scottish. Illustrations: colour and b&w photos. Articles paid on acceptance: unsolicited material considered. Preliminary enquiries advised. Founded 1739.

The Scottish Farmer

Newsquest, 200 Renfield Street, Glasgow G2 3QB
tel 0141-302 7732 *fax* 0141-302 7799
email alasdair.fletcher@thescottishfarmer.co.uk
Editor Alasdair Fletcher
Weekly £2

Articles on agricultural subjects. Length: 1000–1500 words. Payment: £80 per 1000 words. Illustrations: line, half-tone, colour. Founded 1893.

Scottish Field

Special Publications, Craigcrook Castle, Craigcrook Road, Edinburgh EH4 3PE
tel 0131-312 4550 *fax* 0131-312 4551
email editor@scottishfield.co.uk
Editor Richard Bath
Monthly £3.40

Lifestyle magazine: interiors, food, travel, wildlife, heritage, general lifestyle. Founded 1903.

Scottish Home and Country

42 Heriot Row, Edinburgh EH3 6ES
tel 0131-225 1724 *fax* 0131-225 8129
email magazine@swri.demon.co.uk
website www.swri.org.uk
Editor Liz Ferguson
Monthly £1.10

Articles on crafts, cookery, travel, personal experience, rural interest, women's interest, health, books. Length: up to 1000 words, preferably illustrated. Illustrations: colour prints/transparencies, b&w, hi-res jpg files, cartoons. Payment: by arrangement. Founded 1924.

Scottish Memories

Strathclyde Business Centre, 120 Carstairs Street, Glasgow G40 4JD
tel 0141-554 9944 *fax* 0141-554 9955
email info@scottish-memories.co.uk
website www.scottish-memories.co.uk
Editor George Forbes
Monthly £2.95

Features on any aspect of Scottish nostalgia or history, from primeval times to the 1990s. Contact the Editor with an outline in the first instance. Length: 1000 words. Illustrations: colour and b&w. Payment: £70 per 1000 words; £20 per photo. Founded 1993.

Screen International

EMAP Media, Greater London House, 1 Hampstead Road, London NW1 7EJ
tel 020-7728 5000
email screeninternational@hotmail.com
website www.screendaily.com
Editor Conor Dignam
Weekly £3.60 (£160 p.a.)

International news and features on the international film business. No unsolicited material. Length: variable. Payment: by arrangement.

Sea Angler

Bauer Media, Media House, Lynchwood, Peterborough Business Park, Peterborough PE2 6EA
tel (01733) 395147 *fax* (01733) 468843
Editor Mel Russ
Monthly £3.25

Topical articles on all aspects of sea-fishing around

the British Isles. Payment: by arrangement. Illustrations: colour. Founded 1973.

Sea Breezes

Media House, Cronkbourne, Tromode, Douglas, Isle of Man IM4 4SB
tel (01624) 696573 *fax* (01624) 661655
website www.seabreezes.co.im
Editor A.C. Douglas
Monthly £3.25

Factual articles on ships and the sea past and present, preferably illustrated. Length: up to 4000 words. Illustrations: line, half-tone, colour. Payment: by arrangement. Founded 1919.

SelfBuild & Design

151 Station Street, Burton on Trent, Staffs. DE14 1BG
tel (01283) 742950 *fax* (01283) 742957
email ross.stokes@sbdonline.co.uk
website www.sbdonline.co.uk
Editor Ross Stokes
Monthly £3.99

Articles on house construction for individual builders. Welcomes ideas for articles. Payment: £100–£200 per 1000 words. Illustrations: colour prints, transparencies and digital.

Sewing World

Traplet Publications Ltd, Traplet House, Pendragon Close, Malvern WR14 1GA
tel (01684) 588500 *fax* (01684) 594888
email sw@traplet.co.uk
Editor Wendy Gardiner
Monthly £3.95

'Sewing magazine for sewing machine enthusiasts.' Articles and step-by-step projects. Length: 1000–1500 words (articles). Illustrations: colour. Payment: £100 per article including illustrations. Founded 1995.

SFX Magazine

Future Publishing Ltd, 30 Monmouth Street, Bath BA1 2BW
tel (01225) 442244
email sfx@futurenet.co.uk
website www.sfx.co.uk
Editor Dave Bradley, *Features Editor* Nick Setchfield
Every 4 weeks £3.99

Sci-fi and fantasy magazine covering TV, films, DVDs, books, comics, games and collectables. Founded 1995.

She

National Magazine House, 72 Broadwick Street, London W1F 9EP
tel 020-7439 5000 *fax* 020-7312 3940
email editor@shemagazine.co.uk
Send material to Marie Campbell, PA to Editor (*tel* 020-7312 3757)
Monthly £3.30, £15 p.a.

No unsolicited MSS. Ideas with synopses welcome on subjects ranging from health and relationships to child care. Payment: NUJ freelance rates. Illustrations: photos. Founded 1955.

Ships Monthly

IPC Country & Leisure (Marine), 222 Branston Road, Burton-on-Trent, Staffs. DE14 3BT
tel (01283) 542721 *fax* (01283) 546436
Editor Iain Wakefield
Monthly £3.95

Illustrated articles of shipping interest – both mercantile and naval, preferably of 20th and 21st century ships. Well-researched, factual material only. No short stories or poetry. 'Notes for Contributors' available. Mainly commissioned material; preliminary letter essential, with sae. Payment: by arrangement. Illustrations: half-tone and line, colour transparencies, prints and digital images on CD with thumbprint contact sheet. Founded 1966.

Shooting Times and Country Magazine

IPC Inspire, The Blue Fin Building, 110 Southwark Street, London SE1 0SU
tel 020-3148 4741 *fax* 020-3148 8175
email steditorial@ipcmedia.com
website www.shootingtimes.co.uk
Editor Camilla Clark
Weekly £2.10

Articles on fieldsports, especially shooting, and on related natural history and countryside topics. Unsolicited MSS not encouraged. Length: up to 2000 words. Payment: by arrangement. Illustrations: photos, drawings, colour transparencies. Founded 1882.

The Shop: A Magazine of Poetry

Skeagh, Schull, Co Cork, Republic of Ireland
email theshop@theshop-poetry-magazine.ie
website www.theshop-poetry-magazine.ie
Editor John Wakeman, Hilary Wakeman
3 p.a. Annual subscription: Ireland €25/£16.50, rest of world £20/€30/US$40

Poems on any subject in any form and occasional essays on poetry, especially Irish poetry. No submissions by email. Illustrations welcome. Length: 2000–3000 words (essays); any (poems). Payment: by arrangement. Founded 1999.

Shout

2 Albert Square, Dundee DD1 9QJ
tel (01382) 223131 *fax* (01382) 200880
email shout@dcthomson.co.uk
185 Fleet Street, London EC4A 2HS
tel 020-7400 1030 *fax* 020-7400 1089
website www.shoutmag.co.uk
Editor Maria Welch
Fortnightly £2.20

Colour gravure magazine for 11–14 year-old girls.

Pop, film and 'soap' features and pin-ups; general features of teen interest; emotional features, fashion and beauty advice. Payment: on acceptance. Founded 1993.

The Shropshire Magazine

Shropshire Newspapers, Ketley, Telford TF1 5HU
tel (01952) 242424 *fax* (01952) 254605
website www.shropshiremagazine.com
Editor Neil Thomas
Monthly £2.50

Articles on topics related to Shropshire, including countryside, history, characters, legends, education, food; also home and garden features. Length: up to 1500 words. Illustrations: colour. Founded 1950.

Sight and Sound

BFI, 21 Stephen Street, London W1T 1LN
tel 020-7255 1444 *fax* 020-7436 2327
website www.bfi.org.uk/sightandsound
Editor Nick James
Monthly £3.95

Topical and critical articles on world cinema; reviews of every film theatrically released in the UK; book reviews; DVD reviews; festival reports. Length: 1000–5000 words. Payment: by arrangement. Illustrations: relevant photos, cartoons. Founded 1932.

The Sign

c/o 77 Verulam Road, St Albans AL3 4DJ
tel (01727) 833400
website www.churchtimes.co.uk
Editor Terence Handley MacMath
Monthly 5p

Leading national insert for C of E parish magazines. Articles of interest to parishes; poems. Items should bear the author's name and address; return postage essential or send by email. Length: up to 450 words, accompanied by photos/illustrations. Payment: by arrangement. Founded 1905.

Ski and Board

The Ski Club of Great Britain, The White House, 57–63 Church Road, London SW19 5SB
tel 020-8410 2000 *fax* (0845) 4580781
email editor@skiclub.co.uk
website www.skiclub.co.uk
Editor Arnie Wilson
Monthly in winter (Oct–Jan) £3.75

Articles, features, news, true life stories, ski tips, equipment reviews, resort reports – all in connection with skiing and snowboarding. Currently not seeking new commissions. Payment: up to £250 per 1000 words; £50–£200 per photo/illustration. Founded as *Ski Survey* 1972.

The Skier and Snowboarder Magazine

Mountain Marketing Ltd, PO Box 386, Sevenoaks, Kent TN13 1AQ
tel (0845) 3108303
email skierandsnowboarder@hotmail.com
Editor Frank Baldwin
5 p.a. (July-May) £2

Ski features, based around a good story. Length: 800–1000 words. Illustrations: colour action ski photos. Payment: by negotiation. Founded 1984.

Slightly Foxed

Slightly Foxed Ltd, 67 Dickinson Court, 15 Brewhouse Yard, London EC1V 4JX
020-7549 2121/2111 0870 1991245
email all@foxedquarterly.com, gailpirkis@foxedquarterly.com
website www.foxedquarterly.com
Publisher/Co-editor Gail Pirkis
Quarterly UK £9, overseas £11

Informal and independent-minded magazine of book reviews. Each issue contains 96pp of recommendations for books of lasting interest, old and new, both fiction and non-fiction – books that have inspired, amused, and sometimes even changed the lives of the people who write about them.

Slim at Home

Aceville Publications Ltd, 25 Phoenix Court, Hawkins Road, Colchester CO2 8JY
tel (01206) 505972
email naomi@aceville.co.uk
Editor Naomi Abeykoon
10 p.a. £2.60

Features on health and emotional weight-loss issues. Length: 800 or 1400 words. No unsolicited MSS at this time. Send feature summary by email in first instance. Freelance entries occasionally accepted. Payment: by arrangement. Founded 1972.

Slimming World magazine

Clover Nook Road, Alfreton, Derbyshire DE55 4RF
tel (01773) 546071
email editorial@slimmingworld.com
website www.slimmingworldmagazine.com
Editor Elise Wells
7 p.a. £2.65 (£1.50 members)

Magazine about healthy eating, fitness and feeling good with real-life stories of how Slimming World members have changed their lives, recipes and menu plans, health advice, beauty and fitness tips, features, competitions and fashion.

Smallholder

Hook House, Wimblington March, Cambs. PE15 0QL
tel (01354) 741538 *fax* (01354) 741182
email liz.wright1@btconnect.com
website www.smallholder.co.uk
Editor Liz Wright
Monthly £3.25

Articles of relevance to small farmers about livestock

and crops, organics, conservation, poultry, equipment. Items relating to the countryside considered. Email for guidelines. Send for specimen copy. Length: single-page article 700 words; DPS 1200–1400 words with pictures. Payment: by negotiation; more for commissions and technical livestock articles.

Smartphone Essentials

Imagine Publishing Ltd, Richmond House,
33 Richmond Hill, Bournemouth, Dorset, BH2 6EZ
website www.smartphonedaily.co.uk
Editor Andy Betts
Monthly £5.99

Magazine focused on mobile computing, with an emphasis on cutting edge smartphones, including iPhone and Blackberry devices, as well as satnav and other areas of consumer technology.Unsolicited material rarely accepted; contact the Editor in advance.

Snooker Scene

Hayley Green Court, 130 Hagley Road, Halesowen, West Midlands B63 1DY
tel 0121-585 9188 *fax* 0121-585 7117
email clive.everton@talk21.com
website www.snookerscene.com
Editor Clive Everton
Monthly £3 (£30 p.a.)

News and articles about the snooker and billiards scene for readers with more than a casual interest in the games. Payment: by arrangement. Illustrations: photos. Founded 1971.

Solicitors' Journal

Waterlow Professional Publishing,
6–14 Underwood Street, London N1 7JQ
tel 020-7490 0049 *fax* 020-7324 2366
email editorial@solicitorsjournal.co.uk
website www.solicitorsjournal.com
Editor Jean-Yves Gilg
Weekly £219 p.a.

Articles, by practising lawyers or specialist journalists, on subjects of practical interest to solicitors. Articles on spec should be sent on disk or by email. Length: up to 1800 words. Payment: by negotiation. Founded 1856.

The Songwriter

International Songwriters Association, PO Box 46, Limerick City, Republic of Ireland
tel (061) 228837
Editor James D. Liddane
Quarterly

Articles on songwriting and interviews with music publishers and recording company executives. Length: 400–5000 words. Payment: by arrangement. Illustrations: photos. Founded 1967.

Songwriting and Composing

Sovereign House, 12 Trewartha Road, Praa Sands, Penzance, Cornwall TR20 9ST
tel (01736) 762826 *fax* (01736) 763328
email songmag@aol.com
website www.songwriters-guild.co.uk
General Secretary Carole Jones
Quarterly Free to members

Magazine of the Guild of International Songwriters and Composers. Short stories, articles, letters relating to songwriting, publishing, recording and the music industry. Payment: negotiable upon content £25–£60. Illustrations: line, half-tone. Founded 1986.

The Spark Magazine

Blue Sax Publishing Ltd, 86 Colston Street, Bristol BS1 5BB
tel 0117-914 3434 *fax* 0117-914 3444
email editor@thespark.co.uk
website www.thespark.co.uk
Commissioning Editor Vicki West
Quarterly free

'A free thinking magazine about positive change for the West Country.' Features on health, fitness, the environment, social and community issues. Welcomes ideas for features and articles with a regional angle. See website for guidelines. Length: varies. Illustrations: colour cover. Payment: £10 per 100 words. Founded 1993.

Spear's Wealth Management Survey (WMS)

5 Jubilee Place, London SW3 3TD
tel 020-7591 2900
email info@spearmedia.co.uk
website www.spearmedia.co.uk, www.spearwms.com
Editor William Cash
Quarterly £25 per issue

Provides an informative, entertaining, objective guide to all aspects of wealth management and the high-net-worth (HNW) lifestyle. Readership mostly comprises individuals who hold over £5 million in financial assets. Length: 700–2000 words (articles and features). Colour and b&w cartoons. Payment: 40p per word; £150 for cartoons. Founded 2003.

The Spectator

22 Old Queen Street, London SW1H 9HP
tel 020-7961 0200
email editor@spectator.co.uk
website www.spectator.co.uk
Editor Fraser Nelson
Weekly £3.20

Articles on current affairs, politics, the arts; book reviews. Illustrations: colour and b&w, cartoons. Payment: on merit. Founded 1828.

Spectator Business

22 Old Queen Street, London SW1H 9HP
tel 020-7961 0200 *fax* 020-7961 0058
email editor@spectator.co.uk
website www.spectator.co.uk/business

Editor Martin Vander Weyer
Quarterly £4.50

News, features, analysis and comment on global business and finance. Brings a prescient overview of business trends and market conditions every week, providing information on managing investments and wider geo-political issues, as well as detailed background information on companies, markets, people and opportunities. Founded 2007.

Spirit & Destiny

H. Bauer Publishing, Academic House, 24–28 Oval Road, London NW1 7DT
tel 020-7241 8000 *fax* 020-7241 8056
Editor Rhiannon Powell
Monthly £2.90

'For women who want the best possible future.' Entertaining and informative women's interest magazine with additional features on astrology and psychic matters, holistic therapies and alternative lifestyles. Founded 2002.

Springboard

Corrimbla, Ballina, County Mayo, Republic of Ireland
email bobgroom@eircom.net
Editor Robert Groom
Quarterly £15/€20 p.a.

A non-profit making magazine with short stories, poetry, articles and competition news. Aims to bring together writers from all countries and has 4 competitions that are free to subscribers: short story, poetry, article and children's short story. The winner and runner up in each category is published in the following issue and receives a certificate and cash prize. No unsolicited material. Founded 1990.

The Squash Player

460 Bath Road, Longford, Middlesex UB7 0EB
tel (01753) 775511 *fax* (01753) 775512
email editor@squashplayer.co.uk
website www.squashplayer.co.uk
Editor Ian McKenzie
Bi-monthly £24 p.a.

Covers all aspects of playing squash. All features are commissioned – discuss ideas with the Editor. Length: 1000–1500 words. Illustrations: unusual photos (e.g. celebrities), cartoons. Payment: £75 per 1000 words; £25–£40 for illustrations. Founded 1971.

Staffordshire Life Magazine

Staffordshire Newspapers Ltd, The Publishing Centre, Derby Street, Stafford ST16 2DT
tel (01785) 257700 *fax* (01785) 253287
email editor@staffordshirelife.co.uk
website www.staffordshirelife.co.uk
Editor Louise Elliott
12 p.a. £2

County magazine for Staffordshire. Historical articles; features on county personalities. No short stories. Contact the Editor in the first instance. Length: 500–800 words. Illustrations: colour transparencies and prints. Founded 1948; relaunched 1980.

The Stage

Stage House, 47 Bermondsey Street, London SE1 3XT
tel 020-7403 1818 *fax* 020-7357 9287
email editor@thestage.co.uk
website www.thestage.co.uk
Editor Brian Attwood
Weekly £1.20

Original and interesting articles on professional stage and broadcasting topics may be sent for the Editor's consideration. Length: 500–900 words. Payment: £100 per 1000 words. Founded 1880.

Stamp Magazine

IPC Inspire, Leon House, 233 High Street, Croydon CR9 1HZ
tel 020-8726 8000 *fax* 020-8726 8299
Editor Guy Thomas
Monthly £3.45

Informative articles and exclusive news items on stamp collecting and postal history. Preliminary letter. Payment: by arrangement. Illustrations: line, half-tone, colour. Founded 1934.

Stand Magazine

School of English, University of Leeds, Leeds LS2 9JT
tel 0113-233 4794
email stand@leeds.ac.uk
website www.standmagazine.org
Managing Editor Jon Glover
Quarterly £6.50 plus p&p £25 p.a.

Poetry, short stories, translations, literary criticism. Send sae/IRCs for return. Payment: £20 per 1000 words (prose); £20 per poem. Founded 1952.

Staple

114–116 St Stephen's Road, Nottingham NG2 4JS
Editor Wayne Burrows
3 p.a. £25 p.a. (£35 overseas)

Poetry, fiction, articles and reviews. Payment: £10–25 fiction/articles. Founded 1982.

Star Trek Magazine

Titan Magazines, Titan House, 144 Southwark Street, London SE1 0UP
tel 020-7620 0200 *fax* 020-7803 1803
Editor Paul Simpson
13 p.a. £27.99

Up-to-date news about every aspect of *Star Trek*, including all TV series and films, cast interviews, behind-the-scenes features and product reviews. Payment: by arrangement. Founded 1995.

The Strad

Newsquest Magazines, 2nd Floor, 30 Cannon Street, London EC4M 6YJ

tel 020-7618 3456 *fax* 020-7618 3483
email thestrad@orpheuspublications.com
website www.thestrad.com
Editor Ariane Todes
12 p.a. £3.75 (£40.95 p.a.)

Features, news and reviews for string instrument players, teachers, makers and enthusiasts – both professional and amateur. Specially commissions most material but will consider unsolicited material. Welcomes ideas for articles and features. Length: 1000–2000 (articles/features), 100–150 (news). Payment: £150–£300 (articles/features), varies for news. Illustrations: transparencies, colour and b&w prints and artwork, colour cartoons; some commissioned. Founded 1890.

Studies, An Irish quarterly review

35 Lower Leeson Street, Dublin 2, Republic of Ireland
tel (01) 6766785 *fax* (01) 6767493
email studies@jesuit.ie
website www.studiesirishreview.com
Editor Rev. Fergus O'Donoghue SJ
Quarterly €10

General review of social comment, literature, history, the arts. Published by the Irish Jesuits. Articles written by specialists for the general reader. Critical book reviews. Preliminary letter. Length: 4000 words. Founded 1912.

Stuff

Haymarket Ltd, Teddington Studios, Broom Road, Teddington, Middlesex TW11 9BE
tel 020-8267 5036 *fax* 020-8267 5019
email stuff@haymarket.com
website www.stuff.tv
Editor Fraser Macdonald
Monthly £3.99, £32.40 p.a.

Articles on gadgets, gear, technology, lifestyle, news and reviews. Payment by negotiation. Founded 1996.

Suffolk Norfolk Life

Today Magazines Ltd, The Publishing House, Station Road, Framlingham, Suffolk IP13 9EE
tel (01728) 622030 *fax* (01728) 622031
email todaymagazines@btopenworld.com
website www.suffolknorfolklife.com
Editor William Locks
Monthly £2.20

Articles relevant to Suffolk and Norfolk – current topics plus historical items, art, leisure, etc. Considers unsolicited material and welcomes ideas for articles and features. Send via email. Length: 900–1500 words. Illustrations: transparencies, digital colour and b&w prints, b&w artwork and cartoons. Payment: £40–£80 per article. Founded 1989.

Sugar

Hachette Filipacchi, 64 North Row, London W1K 7LL
tel 020-7150 7000 *fax* 020-7150 7001
Editor Annabel Brog
Monthly £2.45

Magazine for young women aged 13–19. Fashion, beauty, entertainment, features. Send synopsis first. Will consider unsolicited material. Interested in real-life stories (1200 words), quizzes. Payment: negotiable. Founded 1994.

Surrey Life

Holmesdale House, 46 Croydon Road, Reigate, Surrey RH2 0NH
tel (01737) 240419
email editor@surreylife.co.uk
website www.surreylife.co.uk
Editors Katharine Elton, Caroline Harrap
Monthly £2.95

Articles on Surrey, including places of interest, high-profile personalities, local events, arts, history and food. Founded 1970.

Swimming Times Magazine

Swimming Times Ltd, 41 Granby Street, Loughborough, Leics. LE11 3DU
tel (01509) 632230 *fax* (01509) 618701
email swimmingtimes@swimming.org
website www.britishswimming.org
Editor Peter Hassall
Monthly £2.80 plus p&p

Official journal of the Amateur Swimming Association and the Institute of Swimming. Reports of major events and championships; news and features on all aspects of swimming including synchronised swimming, diving and water polo, etc; accompanying photos where appropriate; short fiction with a swimming theme. Unsolicited material welcome. Length: 800–1500 words. Payment: by arrangement. Founded 1923.

The Tablet

1 King Street Cloisters, Clifton Walk, London W6 0GY
tel 020-8748 8484 *fax* 020-8748 1550
email thetablet@thetablet.co.uk
website www.thetablet.co.uk
Editor Catherine Pepinster
Weekly £2.40

Catholic weekly: religion, philosophy, politics, society, books and arts. International coverage. Freelance work commissioned: do not send unsolicited material. Length: various. Illustrations: cartoons and photos. Payment: by arrangement. Founded 1840.

Take a Break

H. Bauer Publishing Ltd, Academic House, 24–28 Oval Road, London NW1 7DT
tel 020-7241 8000 *fax* 020-7241 8056
website www.bauer.com
Editor John Dale

Weekly 80p

Lively, tabloid women's weekly. True life features, health and beauty, family, short stories (up to 1500 words); lots of puzzles. Payment: by arrangement. Illustrated. Founded 1990.

Take a Break's Take a Puzzle

H. Bauer Publishing, Academic House, 24–28 Oval Road, London NW1 7DT
tel 020-7241 8000 *fax* 020-7241 8056
email take.puzzle@bauer.co.uk
website www.bauer.com
Editor Guy Haslam
Monthly £1.95

Puzzles. Fresh ideas always welcome. Illustrations: colour transparencies and b&w prints and artwork. Work supplied on Mac-compatible disk preferred. Payment: from £25 per puzzle, £30–£90 for picture puzzles and for illustrations not an integral part of a puzzle. Founded 1991.

TATE ETC

20 John Islip Street, London SW1P 4RG
tel 020-7887 8724 *fax* 020-7887 3940
email tateetc@tate.org.uk
website www.tate.org.uk/tateetc
Editor Simon Grant
3 p.a. £5

Independent visual arts magazine: features, interviews, previews and opinion pieces. Length: up to 3000 words but always commissioned. Illustrations: colour and b&w photos. Payment: negotiable.

Tatler

Vogue House, Hanover Square, London W1S 1JU
tel 020-7499 9080 *fax* 020-7409 0451
website www.tatler.co.uk
Editor Catherine Ostler
Monthly £3.70

Smart society magazine favouring sharp articles, profiles, fashion and the arts. Illustrations: colour, b&w, but all commissioned. Founded 1709.

Taxation

2 Addiscombe Road, Croydon CR9 5AF
tel 020-8686 9141
email taxation@lexisnexis.co.uk
website www.taxation.co.uk
Editor Mike Truman
Weekly £7

Updating and advice concerning UK tax law and practice for accountants and tax experts. All articles written by professionals. Length: 2000 words (articles). Payment £150 per 1000 words. Founded 1927.

The Teacher

National Union of Teachers, Hamilton House, Mabledon Place, London WC1H 9BD
tel 020-7380 4708 *fax* 020-7387 8458
Editor Elyssa Campbell-Barr
8 p.a. Free to NUT members

Articles, features and news of interest to all those involved in the teaching profession. Length: 650 words (single page), 1200–1300 (double page). Payment: NUJ rates to NUJ members. Founded 1872.

Technology Ireland

Enterprise Ireland, The Plaza, East Point Business Park, Dublin 3
tel (01) 727 2954 *fax* (01) 727 2086
email technology.ireland@enterprise-ireland.com
website www.technologyireland.ie
Editor Kathy Burke
6 p.a. €54 plus VAT p.a.

Articles, features, reviews, news on current business, innovation and technology. Length: 1500–2000 words. Illustrations: line, half-tone, colour. Payment: varies. Founded 1969.

Television

Kildare House, 3 Dorsett Rise, London EC4Y 8EH
tel 020-7822 2810
email publications@rts.org.uk
website www.rts.org.uk
Editor Steve Clarke
Monthly £8 (£82 p.a.)

Articles on the technical aspects of domestic TV and video equipment, especially servicing, long-distance TV, constructional projects, satellite TV, video recording, teletext and viewdata, test equipment, monitors. Payment: by arrangement. Illustrations: photos and line drawings for litho. Founded 1950.

Tempo

Cambridge University Press, The Edinburgh Building, Shaftesbury Road, Cambridge CB2 8RU
Editorial address PO Box 171, Herne Bay, Kent CT6 6WD
email macval@compuserve.com
Editor Calum MacDonald
Quarterly; (institutions) £63/$107 online only, £73/$123 print and online

Authoritative articles on contemporary music. Length: 2000–4000 words. Payment: by arrangement. Illustrations: music type, occasional photographic or musical supplements.

The TES

26 Red Lion Square, Holborn WC1R 4HQ
tel 020-3194 3000
fax 020-3194 3202 (news), 020-3194 3200 (features)
email newsdesk@tes.co.uk, features@tes.co.uk
website www.tes.co.uk
Editor Gerard Kelly
Weekly £1.40

Education newspaper. Articles on education written

with special knowledge or experience; news items; books, arts and equipment reviews. Check with the news or picture editor before submitting material. Outlines of feature ideas should be emailed. Illustrations: suitable photos and drawings of educational interest, cartoons. Payment: standard rates, or by arrangement.

TES Magazine
Weekly Free with TES
Magazine for teachers focusing on their lives, inside and outside the classroom, investigating the key issues of the day and highlighting good practice. Length: 800 words max.

The TES Cymru

Sophia House, 28 Cathedral Road, Cardiff CF11 9LJ
tel 029-2066 0201 *fax* 029-2066 0207
email cymru@tes.co.uk
website www.tes.co.uk/cymru
Editor Gerard Kelly
Weekly £1.40

Education newspaper. Articles on education, teachers, teaching and learning, and education policy in Wales. Length: up to 800 words (articles). Illustrations: line, half-tone. Payment: by arrangement. Founded 2004.

The TESS

Thistle House, 21–23 Thistle Street,
Edinburgh EH2 1DF
tel 0131-624 8333 *fax* 0131-467 8019
website www.tes.co.uk/scotland
Editor Neil Munro
Weekly £1.50

Education newspaper. Articles on education, preferably 800–1000 words, written with special knowledge or experience. News items about Scottish educational affairs. Illustrations: line, half-tone. Payment: by arrangement. Founded 1965.

TGO (The Great Outdoors) Magazine

Newsquest, 200 Renfield Street, Glasgow G2 3QB
tel 0141-302 7700 *fax* 0141-302 7799
email cameron.mcneish@tgomagazine.co.uk
website www.tgomagazine.co.uk
Editor Cameron McNeish
Monthly £3.40 (£36 p.a.)

Articles on walking or lightweight camping in specific areas, mainly in the UK, preferably illustrated. Length: 700–2000 words. Payment: by arrangement. Illustrations: colour. Apply for guidelines. Founded 1978.

that's life!

H. Bauer Publishing Ltd, Academic House,
24–28 Oval Road, London NW1 7DT
tel 020-7241 8000 *fax* 020-7241 8008
Editor Sophie Hearsey
Weekly 68p

Dramatic true life stories about women. Length: average 1000 words. Illustrations: colour photos and cartoons. Payment: up to £500. Founded 1995.

Third Way

13–17 Long Lane, London EC1A 9PN
tel 020-7776 1071 *fax* 020-7776 1087
email editor@thirdway.org.uk
website www.thirdway.org.uk
Editor Simon Jones
10 p.a. £2.90 (£29 p.a.)

Aims to present biblical perspectives on the political, social and cultural issues of the day. Payment: by arrangement on publication. Email submissions preferred. Founded 1977.

This England

PO Box 52, Cheltenham, Glos. GL50 1YQ
tel (01242) 537900 *fax* (01242) 537901
Editor Stephen Garnett
Quarterly £3.75

Articles about Great Britain's traditions, customs and places of interest. Regular features on nostalgic entertainment including songs, films, radio and TV. Length 250–2000 words. Illustrations: digital; colour transparencies only accepted when accompanying articles. Payment: £15 per 1000 words, £4 poems (12–24 lines). Founded 1985.

Time Out

Time Out Group Ltd, Universal House,
251 Tottenham Court Road, London W1T 7AB
tel 020-7813 3000 *fax* 020-7813 6001
email timeout@cisubs.co.uk
website www.timeout.com
Acting Editor Mark Frith
Weekly £2.99

Listings magazine for London covering all areas of the arts, plus articles of consumer and news interest. Illustrations: colour and b&w. Payment by negotiation. Founded 1968.

The Times Educational Supplement – see The TES

The Times Educational Supplement Scotland – see The TESS

Times Higher Education

26 Red Lion Square, London WC1R 4HQ
tel 020-3194 3000 *fax* 020-3194 3300
website www.timeshighereducation.co.uk
Editor Ann Mroz
Weekly £1.95
Articles on higher education written with special knowledge or experience, or articles dealing with academic topics. Also news items. Illustrations: suitable photos and drawings of educational interest. Payment: by arrangement. Founded 1971.

TLS (The Times Literary Supplement)

Times House, 1 Pennington Street, London E98 1BS
tel 020-7782 5000 *fax* 020-7782 4966
website www.the-tls.co.uk
Editor Peter Stothard
Weekly. £2.70

Will consider poems for publication, literary discoveries and articles on literary and cultural affairs. Payment: by arrangement.

Today's Golfer

Bauer Media, Media House, Lynchwood, Peterborough Business Park, Peterborough PE2 6EA
tel (01733) 468000 *fax* (01733) 468843
email andy.calton@bauermedia.co.uk
website www.todaysgolfer.co.uk
Editor-in-Chief Andy Calton
Monthly £4.10

Specialist features and articles on golf instruction, equipment and courses. Founded 1988.

Today's Pilot

Key Publishing Ltd, PO Box 100, Stamford, Lincs. PE9 1XQ
tel (01780) 755131 *fax* (01780) 757261
email dave.unwin@keypublishing.com
website www.todayspilot.co.uk
Editor Dave Unwin
Monthly £3.95

General aviation magazine providing information and inspiration for the recreational aviator. Considers unsolicited material. Submit suggestions or an outline in the first instance. Length: 3000 words (articles/features), 1000 words (news). Illustrations: colour. Payment: negotiable (words); £20 per image. Founded 2000.

Top Santé Health & Beauty

Bauer Consumer Media, Endeavour House, 189 Shaftesbury Avenue, London WC2H 8JG
tel 020-7520 6592
Editor Sharon Parsons
Monthly £2.90

Articles, features and news on all aspects of health and beauty. Ideas welcome. No unsolicited features. Payment: illustrations by arrangement. Founded 1993.

Total Film

2 Balcombe Street, London NW1 6NW
tel 020-7042 4000 *fax* 020-7042 4839
email totalfilm@futurenet.co.uk
website www.totalfilm.com
Editor Aubrey Day
Monthly £3.90

Movie magazine covering all aspects of film. Email ideas before submitting material. Not seeking interviews or reviews. Length: 400 words (news items); 1000 words (funny features). Payment: £150 per 1000 words; up to £1500 per picture. Founded 1996.

Total Off-Road

151 Station Street, Burton on Trent, Staffs. DE14 1BG
tel (01283) 742950 *fax* (01283) 742957
email editorial@toronline.co.uk
Editor Alan Kidd
Monthly £3.75

Features on off-roading: competitions, modified vehicles, overseas events. Length 1200–3000 words. Payment: £100 per 1000 words. Illustrations: colour and b&w prints, transparencies and digital images. keen to hear from photographers attending UK/overseas off-road events. Preliminary email strongly advised.

Trail

Bauer, Media House, Lynchwood, Peterborough PE2 6EA
tel (01733) 468363
email trail@bauermedia.co.uk
website www.trailroutes.com
Editor Matt Swaine
Monthly £3.40

Outdoor activity magazine focusing mainly on high level walking with some scrambling and climbing. Some opportunities for freelances. Good ideas welcome.

Traveller

Traveller & Publishing, 4th Floor, 45-49 Brompton Road, London SW3 1DE
tel 020-7581 6156
email traveller@and-publishing.co.uk
website www.traveller.org.uk
Editor Amy Sohanpaul
Quarterly Free to members of WEXAS, the traveller's club; back issues £4.95

Adventurous and authentic travel writing. Narrative features describe personal journeys to remarkable places. Unsolicited material considered if prose and pictures are excellent. See website for guidelines. Length: 1000 words. Illustrations: transparencies, b&w prints plus high resolution digital images. Payment: £200 per 1000 words; colour £50 (£150 cover). Founded 1970.

Tribune

9 Arkwright Road, London NW3 6AN
tel 020-7433 6410 *fax* 020-7433 6419
email mail@tribunemagazine.co.uk
Editor Chris McLaughlin, *Deputy Editor* Keith Richmond, *Arts Editor* George Osgerby
Weekly £2

Political, literary, with Socialist outlook. Informative articles (about 900 words), news stories (250–300 words). No unsolicited reviews or fiction. Payment: by arrangement. Illustrations: cartoons, photos.

Trout and Salmon

Bauer Media, Media House, Lynchwood, Peterborough PE2 6EA
tel (01733) 468000 *fax* (01733) 468843
email troutandsalmon@bauermedia.co.uk
Editor Andrew Flitcroft
Monthly £3.20

Articles of good quality with strong trout or salmon angling interest. Length: 400–2000 words, accompanied if possible by good quality colour prints. Payment: by arrangement. Illustrations: line, colour transparencies and prints, cartoons. Founded 1955.

Truck & Driver

Reed Business Information, Quadrant House, The Quadrant, Sutton, Surrey SM2 5AS
tel 020-8652 3721
Editor Will Shiers
Monthly £2.85

News, articles on trucks, personalities and features of interest to truck drivers. Words (on disk or electronically) and picture packages preferred. Length: approx. 1500 words. Illustrations: colour transparencies, digital and artwork, cartoons. Payment: negotiable. Founded 1984.

Trucking

Future Publishing Ltd, 30 Monmouth Street, Bath BA1 2BW
tel (01225) 442244
email steev.hayes@futurenet.co.uk
website www.truckingmag.co.uk
Editor Steev Hayes
Monthly £2.60

For truck drivers, owner–drivers and operators: news, articles, features and technical advice. Length: 750–2500 words. Illustrations: mostly 35mm digital. Payment: by negotiation. Founded 1983.

The Trumpet

44A Selby Road, London E11 3LT
tel 020-8522 6600 *fax* 020-8522 6699
email info@the-trumpet.com
website www.the-trumpet.com
Editor-in-Chief Femi Okutubo
Fortnightly Free (£30 p.a.)

Newspaper for the UK's African population. Founded 1995.

TV Quick

H. Bauer Publishing Ltd, Academic House, 24–28 Oval Road, London NW1 7DT
tel 020-7241 8000 *fax* 020-7241 8020
website www.tvquick.co.uk
Editor-in-Chief Jon Peake
Weekly 80p

TV listings magazine featuring TV-related material. Payment: by arrangement. Founded 1991.

TV Choice

Editor-in-Chief Jon Peake
Weekly 38p
Founded 1999.

Total TV Guide

Editor-in-Chief Jon Peake
Weekly £1
Founded 2003.

TVTimes Magazine

IPC Media Ltd, The Blue Fin Building, 110 Southwark Street, London SE1 0SU
tel 020-3148 5615 *fax* 020-3148 8115
website www.tvtimes.co.uk
Editor Ian Abbott
Weekly £1.05

Features with an affinity to ITV, BBC1, BBC2, Channels 4 and 5, satellite and radio personalities and TV generally. Length: by arrangement. Photographs: commissioned only. Payment: by arrangement.

TwelvePoint.com

2 Elliott Square, London NW3 3SU
website www.scriptwritermagazine.com
Weekly

Previously *ScriptWriter Magazine*. Web-based portal about scriptwriting for everyone who works with scripts – from writers and script editors to producers and broadcasters.

U magazine

Rosemount House, Dundrum Road, Dublin 14, Republic of Ireland
tel (01) 240 5300
website www.harmonia.ie
Editor Jennifer Stevens
Fortnightly €1.50

Fashion and beauty magazine for 18–25 year-old Irish women, with celebrity interviews, talent profiles, real-life stories, sex and relationship features, plus regular pages on the club scene, movies, music and film. Also travel, interiors, health, food, horoscopes. Material mostly commissioned. Payment: varies. Founded 1978.

Ulster Business

Greer Publications, 5B Edgewater Business Park, Edgewater Road, Belfast Harbour Estate, Belfast BT3 9JQ
tel 028-9078 3200 *fax* 028-9078 3210
email davidcullen@greerpublications.com
website www.ulsterbusiness.com
Editor David Elliott
Monthly £27.50 p.a.

Feature-based magazine with general business-related editorial for management level and above. Specially commissions most material but will consider unsolicited material. Welcomes ideas for articles and features. Length: 800 words (articles), 1500 words (features). Payment: £60–£80 (articles), £120 (features). No illustrations required. Founded 1987.

Ulster Grocer

Greer Publications, 5B Edgewater Business Park, Belfast Harbour Estate, Belfast BT3 9JQ
tel 028-9078 3200 *fax* 028-9078 3210
email kathyj@writenow.prestel.co.uk
Editor Kathy Jensen
Monthly Controlled circulation

Topical features (1000–1500 words) on food/grocery retailing and exhibitions; news (200 words) with a Northern Ireland basis. All features commissioned; no speculative articles accepted. Illustrations: colour photos. Payment: features £275, product news £160. Founded 1972.

Under 5

Pre-school Learning Alliance,
The Fitzpatrick Building, 188 York Way,
London N7 9AD
tel 020-7697 2500 *fax* 020-7697 8607
website www.pre-school.org.uk
Editor Mandy Murphy
10 p.a. £30 p.a.

Articles on the role of adults, especially parents/preschool workers, in young children's learning and development, including children from all cultures and those with special needs. Length: 600–1200 words. Founded 1962.

The Universe

4th Floor, Landmark House, Station Road, Cheadle, Hulme SK8 7JH
tel 0161-488 1700 *fax* 0161-488 1701
website www.totalcatholic.com
Editor Joe Kelly
Weekly £1 (£57 p.a.)

Catholic Sunday newspaper. News stories, features and photos on all aspects of Catholic life required; also cartoons. Send sae with MSS. Payment: by arrangement. Founded 1860.

Vanity Fair

The Condé Nast Publications Ltd, Vogue House, Hanover Square, London W1S 1JU
tel 020-7499 9080 *fax* 020-7409 0783
website www.vanityfair.co.uk
Editor-in-Chief Graydon Carter
Monthly £3.90

Media, glamour and politics for grown-up readers. No unsolicited material. Payment: by arrangement. Illustrated.

The Vegan

The Vegan Society, Donald Watson House,
21 Hylton Street, Birmingham B18 6HJ
tel 0121-523 1730 *fax* 0121-523 1749
email editor@vegansociety.com
website www.vegansociety.com
Editor Rosamund Raha
Quarterly £2.50 (£10 p.a.)

Articles on health, nutrition, cookery, vegan lifestyle, land use, animal rights. Length: approx. 1000 words. Payment: by arrangement. Illustrations: photos, cartoons, line drawings – foods, animals, livestock systems, crops, people, events; colour for cover. Founded 1944.

Venue

Venue Publishing, Bristol News & Media,
Temple Way, Bristol BS99 7HD
tel 0117-942 8491 *fax* 0117-942 0369
email editor@venue.co.uk
website www.venue.co.uk
Editor Joe Spurgeon
Weekly £1.50

Listings magazine for Bristol and Bath combining comprehensive entertainment information with local features, profiles and interviews. Length: by agreement. Illustrations: colour. Payment: £9.90 per 100 words. Founded 1982.

Vintage Tractor & Countryside Heritage

Church Lane Publishing Ltd, The Clock Tower,
6 Market Gate, Market Deeping, Lincs. PE6 8DL
tel/fax (01778) 342814
email stuart@gibbardtractors.co.uk
website www.vtmag.co.uk
Editor Stuart Gibbard *tel* (01406) 380740
Monthly £3.80

Features on the golden age of tractors and nostalgic countryside matters from the days when life was simpler and farming was at the heart of every village. Unrivalled historical content, nostalgic photographs and fascinating interviews with people who were there at the time. Length: max. 2000 words. Illustrations: colour and b&w. Payment: at editor's discretion. Founded 1981.

Viz

Dennis Publishing, 30 Cleveland Street,
London W1T 4JD
tel 020-7907 6000 *fax* 020-7907 6020
email viz@viz.co.uk
website www.viz.co.uk
Editor Joel Enos
10 p.a. £3

Cartoons, spoof tabloid articles, spoof advertisements. Illustrations: half-tone, line, cartoons. Payment: £300 per page (cartoons). Founded 1979.

Vogue

Vogue House, 1 Hanover Square, London W1S 1JU
tel 020-7499 9080 *fax* 020-7408 0559
website www.vogue.co.uk
Editor Alexandra Shulman

Monthly £4.00

Fashion, beauty, health, decorating, art, theatre, films, literature, music, travel, food and wine. Length: articles from 1000 words. Illustrated.

The Voice

6th Floor, Northern & Shell Tower, 4 Selsdon Way, London E14 9GL
tel 020-7510 0340 *fax* 020-7510 0341
email newsdesk@the-voice.co.uk
website www.voice-online.co.uk
Editor Steve Pope
Weekly 85p

Weekly newspaper for black Britons. Includes news, features, arts, sport and a comprehensive jobs and business section. Illustrations: colour and b&w photos. Open to ideas for news and features on sports, business, community events and the arts. Founded 1982.

Young Voices

website www.young-voices.co.uk
Editor Dionne Grant
Monthly, 2nd Tues of each month £2.40

News, features, reviews, showbiz highlights and current affairs for 11–19 year-olds. Founded 2003.

walk

The Ramblers' Association, 2nd Floor, Camelford House, 87–90 Albert Embankment, London SE1 7TW
tel 020-7339 8540 *fax* 020-7339 8501
email dominic.bates@ramblers.org.uk
website www.walkmag.co.uk
Editor Dominic Bates
Quarterly £3.50 Free to members

Magazine of the Ramblers' Association. Articles on walking, access to countryside and related issues. Material mostly commissioned. Length: up to 1500 words. Illustrations: colour photos, preferably high quality, digitally supplied. Payment: by agreement. Founded 1935.

Wallpaper

IPC Media, The Blue Fin Building, 110 Southwark Street, London SE1 0SU
tel 020-3148 5000 *fax* 020-3148 8119
email contact@wallpaper.com
website www.wallpaper.com
Editor-in-Chief Tony Chambers
12 p.a. £4

Interiors, architecture, fashion, entertainment and travel. Payment: by arrangement. Founded 1996.

Wanderlust

PO Box 1832, Windsor SL4 1YT
tel (01753) 620426
website www.wanderlust.co.uk
Editor Dan Linstead, *Publisher* Lyn Hughes
8 p.a. £3.99

Features on independent, adventure and special-interest travel. Visit website www.wanderlust.co.uk/about for 'Guidelines for contributors'. Length: up to 2500 words. Illustrations: high-quality colour slides or digital. Payment: by arrangement. Founded 1993.

The War Cry

The Salvation Army, 101 Newington Causeway, London SE1 6BN
tel 020-7367 4900 *fax* 020-7367 4710
email warcry@salvationarmy.org.uk
website www.salvationarmy.org/warcry
Editor Major Nigel Bovey
Weekly 20p (£26 p.a.)

Voluntary contributions: Human interest stories of personal Christian faith. Founded 1879.

Waterstone's Books Quarterly

Seven Squared, Sea Containers House, 20 Upper Ground, London SE1 9PD
tel 020-7775 5777 *fax* 020-7775 5711
email ed.wood@squareonegroup.co.uk
website www.subscribeonline.com/wbq
Editor Ed Wood
Quarterly £2.50

Customer magazine for Waterstone's bookshop. Covers new books and literary markets with book reviews, interviews and articles about the latest developments in the book trade. Founded 2001.

Waterways World

Waterways World Ltd, 151 Station Street, Burton-on-Trent DE14 1BG
tel (01283) 742950 *fax* (01283) 742957
website www.waterwaysworld.com
Editor Richard Fairhurst
Monthly £3.50

Feature articles on all aspects of inland waterways in Britain and abroad, including historical material; factual and technical articles preferred. No short stories or poetry. See website for 'Notes for WW Contributors'. Payment: £70 per page (including illustrations). Illustrations: digital, colour transparencies or prints, line. Founded 1972.

Wedding Magazine

IPC Southbank, 7th Floor, The Blue Fin Building, 110 Southwark Street, London SE1 0SU
tel 020-3148 7790 *fax* 020-3148 8117
email wedding@ipcmedia.com
Editor Catherine Westwood
Bi-monthly £4.90

Ideas and inspiration for modern brides. Fashion and beauty, information for grooms, real life weddings, planning advice, gift list ideas and honeymoon features. Unsolicited features not accepted. Founded 1985.

The Week

The Week Ltd, 6th Floor, Compass House, 22 Redan Place, London W2 4SA

tel 020-7907 6180 *fax* 020-7034 0478
email editorialadmin@theweek.co.uk
website www.theweek.co.uk
Editor Caroline Law, *Editor-in-chief* Jeremy O'Grady
Weekly £19.99 per 13 issues

Magazine that distils the best from the British and foreign press into 44pp, including news, art, science, business, property and leisure. Founded 1995.

The Weekly News

D.C. Thomson & Co. Ltd, Albert Square, Dundee DD1 9QJ
tel (01382) 223131
email weeklynews@dcthomson.co.uk
137 Chapel Street, Manchester M3 6AA
tel 0161-834 5122
144 Port Dundas Road, Glasgow G4 0HZ
tel 0141-332 9933
185 Fleet Street, London EC4A 2HS
tel 020-7400 1030
Weekly 80p

Real-life dramas of around 1000 words told in the first person. General interest fiction. Payment: on acceptance.

Weight Watchers Magazine

River Publishing Ltd, 1 Neal Street, London WC2H 9QL
tel 020-7306 0304 *fax* 020-7836 6646
email wwmagazine@riverltd.co.uk
Editor Mary Frances
12 p.a. £2.60

Features: health, beauty, news; food-orientated articles; success stories: weight-loss, motivation, wellbeing. All material commissioned. Length: up to 3 pages. Illustrations: colour photos and cartoons. Payment: by arrangement.

What Car?

Haymarket Motoring Magazines Ltd, Teddington Studios, Broom Road, Teddington, Middlesex TW11 9BE
tel 020-8267 5688 *fax* 020-8267 5750
email editorial@whatcar.com
website www.whatcar.com
Group Editor Steve Fowler
Monthly £4.35

Road tests, buying guide, consumer stories and used car features. No unsolicited material. Illustrations: colour and b&w photos, line drawings. Payment: by negotiation. Founded 1973.

What Laptop

2 Balcombe Street, London NW1 6NW
tel 020-7042 4000
website www.whatlaptop.co.uk
Editor Alex Bentley
Monthly £3.99

News, reviews and help for anyone who wants to buy or has bought a laptop or handheld computer. Discuss ideas for features with the Editor in the first instance; welcomes ideas for features. Length: up to 1600 words. Payment: by arrangement. Founded 1999.

What's on TV

IPC Media Ltd, 6th Floor, The Blue Fin Building, 110 Southwark Street, London SE1 0SU
tel 020-3148 5000 *fax* 020-3148 8116
Editor Colin Tough
Weekly 47p

Features on TV programmes and personalities. All material commissioned. Length: up to 250 words. Illustrations: colour and b&w photos. Payment: by agreement. Founded 1991.

WI Life

(formerly WI Home & Country)
104 New King's Road, London SW6 4LY
tel 020-7731 5777 *fax* 020-7736 4061
Editor Neal Maidment
8 p.a. as part of the WI subscription

Journal of the National Federation of Women's Institutes for England and Wales. Publishes material related to the Federation's and members' activities with articles of interest to members, mainly written in-house and by WI members. Illustrations: colour photos and artwork. Payment: by arrangement.

Windows Vista: The Official Magazine

Future Publishing Ltd, 30 Monmouth Street, Bath BA1 2BW
tel (01225) 442244 *fax* (01225) 446019
email www.windowsvistamagazine.com
Every 4 weeks £4.99

Magazine about Microsoft's operating system with guides for the beginner and articles on how to get the most from your PC. Also reviews and advice for buying the best and most appropriate hardware and software.

The Wisden Cricketer

2nd Floor, 123 Buckingham Palace Road, London SW1W 9SL
tel 020-7705 4911
email twc@wisdencricketer.com
website www.wisdencricketer.com
Editor John Stern
Monthly £3.75

Cricket articles of exceptional interest (unsolicited pieces seldom used). Length: up to 3000 words. Payment: by arrangement. Illustrations: half-tone, colour.

Woman

IPC Connect, The Blue Fin Building, 110 Southwark Street, London SE1 0SU
tel 020-3148 5000 *fax* 020-3148 8113

Editor Karen Livermore
Weekly 90p

News, celebrity and real life features, of no more than 1000 words. Particular interest in celebrity and diet exclusives. Payment: by negotiation. Digital images only. Underwent major relaunch in 2006/2007, advised to read magazine prior to submission. Fiction not published. Founded 1937.

Woman Alive

(formerly Christian Woman)
Christian Publishing and Outreach, Garcia Estate, Canterbury Road, Worthing, West Sussex BN13 1BW
tel (01903) 264556
email womanalive@cpo.org.uk
website www.womanalive.co.uk
Editor Jackie Stead
Monthly £2.40

Aimed at women aged 25 upwards. Celebrity interviews, topical features, Christian issues, profiles of women in interesting occupations, Christian testimonies and real life stories, fashion, beauty, travel, health, crafts. All feature articles should be illustrated. Length: 750–1600 words. Payment £70–£125. Founded 1982.

Woman and Home

IPC Southbank Ltd, The Blue Fin Building, 110 Southwark Street, London SE1 0SU
tel 020-3148 5000
Editor Sue James
Monthly £3.40

Centres on the personal and home interests of the lively minded mature, modern woman. Articles dealing with fashion, beauty, leisure pursuits, gardening, home style; features on topical issues, people and places. Fiction: complete stories from 3000–4500 words in length. Illustrations: commissioned colour photos and sketches. Non-commissioned work is not accepted and cannot be returned. Founded 1926.

Woman's Own

IPC Connect Ltd, The Blue Fin Building, 110 Southwark Street, London SE1 0SU
tel 020-3148 5000 *fax* 020-3148 8127
Acting Editor Jayne Marsden
Weekly 92p

Modern women's magazine aimed at the 35–50 age group. No unsolicited features or fiction. Illustrations: colour and b&w: interior decorating and furnishing, fashion. Address work to relevant department editor. Payment: by arrangement.

Woman's Way

Harmonia Ltd, Rosemount House, Dundrum Road, Dublin 14, Republic of Ireland
tel (01) 240 5300 *fax* (01) 661 9757
email atoner@harmonia.ie
website www.harmonia.ie
Editor Áine Toner
Weekly €1.39/£1.39

Human interest, personality interviews, features on fashion, beauty, celebrities and investigations. Founded 1963.

Woman's Weekly

IPC Connect, The Blue Fin Building, 110 Southwark Street, London SE1 0SU
tel 020-3148 5000 *fax* 020-3148 8113
Editor Diane Kenwood
Weekly 82p

Lively, family-interest magazine. One 3-part fiction serial, averaging 4000 words each instalment, of general emotional interest, and several short stories of 1000–2000 words of general emotional interest. Stories up to 6000 considered for Fiction Special. Celebrity and strong human interest features, health, finance and consumer features, plus beauty, diet and travel; also inspirational and entertaining personal stories. Payment: by arrangement. Illustrations: full colour fiction illustrations, small sketches and photos. Founded 1911.

Woman's Weekly Fiction Special

IPC Connect, The Blue Fin Building, 110 Southwark Street, London SE1 0SU
tel 020-3148 5000
Editor Gaynor Davies
10 issues p.a. £1.85

Minimum 20 stories each issue of 1000–5000 words of varied emotional interest, including romance, humour and mystery. Payment: by arrangement. Illustrations: full colour. Founded 1998.

The Woodworker

MyHobbyStore Ltd, Hadlow House, 9 High Street, Green Street Green, Orpington, Kent BR6 6BG
tel (01689) 869876
Editor Ralph Laughton
Monthly £3.60

For the craft and professional woodworker. Practical illustrated articles on cabinet work, carpentry, wood polishing, wood turning, wood carving, rural crafts, craft history, antique and period furniture; also wooden toys and models, musical instruments; timber procurement, conditioning, seasoning; tool, machinery and equipment reviews. Payment: by arrangement. Illustrations: line drawings and digital photos.

The Word

Development Hell Ltd, 90–92 Pentonville Road, London N1 9HS
tel 020-7520 8625 *fax* 020-7833 9900
email mail@wordmagazine.co.uk
website www.wordmagazine.co.uk
Editor Mark Ellen
Monthly £4.50

Music magazine focusing on music legends and their lives. Founded 2003.

Workbox

Ebony Media Ltd, PO Box 25, Liskeard, Cornwall PL14 6XX
tel (01579) 340100 *fax* (01579) 340400
email workbox@ebony.co.uk
website www.ebony.co.uk/workbox
Editor Carole D'Silva
Bi-monthly £3.25

Features, of any length, on all aspects of needlecrafts. No 'how-to' articles. Send sae with enquiries and submissions. Illustrations: good colour transparencies. Payment: by agreement. Founded 1984.

World Fishing

The Old Mill, Lower Quay, Fareham PO16 0RA
tel (01329) 825335 *fax* (01329) 825330
email thills@worldfishing.net
website www.worldfishing.net
Editor Carly Wills
Monthly £95 p.a.

International journal of commercial fishing. Technical and management emphasis on catching, processing and marketing of fish and related products; fishery operations and vessels covered worldwide. Length: 500–1500 words. Payment: by arrangement. Illustrations: photos and diagrams for litho reproduction. Founded 1952.

The World of Interiors

The Condé Nast Publications Ltd, Vogue House, 1 Hanover Square, London W1S 1JU
tel 020-7499 9080 *fax* 020-7493 4013
website www.worldofinteriors.co.uk
Editor Rupert Thomas
Monthly £4.10

All material commissioned: send synopsis/visual reference for article ideas. Length: 1000–1500 words. Illustrations: colour photos. Payment: £500 per 1000 words; photos £125 per page. Founded 1981.

World Soccer

IPC Inspire, The Blue Fin Building, 110 Southwark Street, London SE1 0SU
tel 020-3148 5000 *fax* 020-3148 8128
website www.worldsoccer.com
Editor Gavin Hamilton
Monthly £3.60

Articles, features, news concerning football, its personalities and worldwide development. Length: 600–2000 words. Payment: by arrangement. Founded 1960.

The World Today

Chatham House, 10 St James's Square, London SW1Y 4LE
tel 020-7957 5712 *fax* 020-7957 5710
email wt@chathamhouse.org.uk
website www.theworldtoday.org
Editor Graham Walker, *Assistant Editor* Alison Coulridge
Monthly £2.50 (£35 p.a. individual, £104 p.a. institutional, £28 p.a. student)

Analysis of international issues and current events by journalists, diplomats, politicians and academics. Length: 1000–1800 words. Payment: nominal. Founded 1945.

Writers' News

5th Floor, 31–32 Park Row, Leeds LS1 5JD
tel 0113-200 2929 *fax* 0113-200 2928
website www.writersnews.co.uk
Editor Jonathan Telfer
Monthly £44.90 p.a. (£39.90 p.a. CC/DD), inc. subscription to *Writing Magazine*

News, competitions, markets. Length: up to 350 words. Illustrations: colour, line, half-tone. Payment: by arrangement. Founded 1989.

Writing Magazine

5th Floor, 31–32 Park Row, Leeds LS1 5JD
tel 0113-200 2929 *fax* 0113-200 2928
website www.writersnews.co.uk
Editor Jonathan Telfer
Monthly £3.70 £25 p.a.

Articles on all aspects of writing. Length: 400–1500 words. Illustrations: full colour, line, half-tone. Payment: by arrangement. Founded 1992.

Yachting Monthly

IPC Media, The Blue Fin Building, 110 Southwark Street, London SE1 0SU
tel 020-3148 5000 *fax* 020-3148 8128
email yachting_monthly@ipcmedia.com
website www.yachtingmonthly.com
Editor Paul Gelder
Monthly £3.90

Articles on all aspects of seamanship, navigation, the handling of sailing craft, and their design, construction and equipment. Well-written narrative accounts of cruises in yachts. Length: up to 1800 words (articles), up to 1800 words (narratives). Illustrations: colour transparencies and prints, cartoons. Payment: quoted on acceptance. Founded 1906.

Yachting World

IPC Inspire, The Blue Fin Building, 110 Southwark Street, London SE1 0SU
tel 020-3148 5000 *fax* 020-3148 8127
email yachting_world@ipc.media.com
website www.yachtingworld.com
Editor Andrew Bray
Monthly £4.20

Practical articles of an original nature, dealing with

sailing and boats. Length: 1500–2000 words. Payment: varies. Illustrations: digital files, drawings, cartoons. Founded 1894.

Yachts and Yachting

196 Eastern Esplanade, Southend-on-Sea, Essex SS1 3AB
tel (01702) 582245 *fax* (01702) 588434
email editorial@yachtsandyachting.com
website www.yachtsandyachting.com
Editor Gael Pawson
Fortnightly £3.99

Technical sailing and related lifestyle articles. Payment: by arrangement. Illustrations: line, halftone, colour. Founded 1947.

Yoga & Health

PO Box 16969, London E1W 1FY
tel 020-7480 5456 *fax* 020-7480 5456
email janesill@aol.com
website www.yogaandhealthmag.co.uk
Editor Jane Sill
Monthly £3

Payment: by arrangement. Founded 1983.

Yorkshire Life

1200 Century Way, Thorpe Park, Leeds LS15 8ZA
tel 0113-251 5027 *fax* 0113-251 5100
website www.yorkshirelife.co.uk
Editor Esther Leach
Monthly £2.75

Articles on Yorkshire, including places of interest, high-profile personalities, local events, arts, history and food. Unsolicited ideas welcome. Founded 1946.

Yorkshire Ridings Magazine

Oyston Mill, Strand Road, Preston PR1 8UR
tel (01772) 761277 *fax* (01772) 761277
Editor Anthony Skinner
Bi-monthly £1.40

Articles exclusively about people, life and character of the 3 Ridings of Yorkshire. Length: up to 1000 words. Payment: £70-£100. Illustrations: colour, b&w photos; prints preferred. Founded 1964.

You & Your Wedding

NatMag at Hearst UK, National Magazine House, 72 Broadwick Street, London W1F 9EP
tel 020-7439 5000 *fax* 020-7439 2985
email yywinfo@natmags.co.uk
website www.youandyourwedding.co.uk
Editor Miranda Eason
Bi-monthly £4.60

Articles, features and news covering all aspects of planning a wedding. Submit ideas by email. Illustrations: colour. Payment: negotiable.

Young Writer Magazine

5th Floor, 31–32 Park Row, Leeds LS1 5JD
tel (0113) 200 2929 *fax* (0113) 200 2928
email youngwriter@writersnews.co.uk
website www.youngwriter.org
Editor Matthew Hill
3 p.a. £3.75 (£10 p.a.)

Specialist magazine for young writers under 18 years old: ideas for them and writing by them. Includes interviews by children with famous writers, fiction and non-fiction pieces, poetry; also explores words and grammar, issues related to writing (e.g. dyslexia), plus competitions with prizes. Length: 750 or 1500 words (features), up to 400 words (news), 600 words (short stories – unless specified otherwise in a competition), poetry of any length. Illustrations: colour – drawings by children, snapshots to accompany features. Payment: most children's material is published without payment. Free inspection copy. Founded 1995.

Your Cat Magazine

BPG (Stamford) Ltd, Roebuck House, 33 Broad Street, Stamford, Lincs. PE9 1RB
tel (01780) 766199 *fax* (01780) 766416
email s.parslow@bournepublishinggroup.co.uk
website www.yourcat.co.uk
Editor Sue Parslow
Monthly £3.10

Practical advice on the care of cats and kittens, general interest items and news on cats, and true life tales and fiction. Length: 800–1500 words (articles), 200–300 (news), up to 1000 (short stories). Illustrations: colour transparencies and prints. Payment: £80 per 1000 words. Founded 1994.

Your Dog Magazine

BPG (Stamford) Ltd, Roebuck House, 33 Broad Street, Stamford, Lincs. PE9 1RB
tel (01780) 766199 *fax* (01780) 754774
website www.yourdog.co.uk
Editor Sarah Wright
Monthly £3.40

Articles and information of interest to dog lovers; features on all aspects of pet dogs. Length: approx. 1500 words. Illustrations: mainly digital images but colour transparencies, prints and line drawings also accepted. Payment: £100 per 1000 words. Founded 1994.

Your Horse

Bauer Media, Media House, Lynchwood, Peterborough PE2 6EA
tel (01733) 395056
email julie.brown@bauermedia.com
Editor Julie Brown
Every 4 weeks £3.60

Practical horse care, riding advice and inspiration for riders and owners. Send feature ideas with examples of previous published writing. Specially commissions most material. Welcomes ideas for articles and features. Length: 1500 words. Payment: £140 per 1000 words. Founded 1983.

Yours

Bauer Publishing, Media House,
Peterborough Business Park, Peterborough PE2 6EA
tel (01733) 468000
Editor Valery McConnell
Fortnightly £1.40

Features and news about and/or of interest to the over-50s age group, including nostalgia and short stories. Study of magazine essential; approach in writing in the first instance. Length: articles up to 1000 words, short stories up to 1000 words. Payment: at the Editor's discretion or by agreement. Founded 1973.

Zest

National Magazine House, 72 Broadwick Street, London W1F 9EP
tel 020-7439 5000 *fax* 020-7312 3750
email zest.mail@natmags.co.uk
Editor Mandie Gower, *Send material to* zest.mail@natmags.co.uk
Monthly £3.40

Health and beauty magazine. Commissioned material only: health, fitness and beauty, features, news and shorts. Length: 50–2000 words. Illustrations: colour and b&w photos and line. Payment: by arrangement. Founded 1994.

Zoo

Bauer Consumer Media, Mappin House,
4 Winsley Street, London W1W 8HF
tel 020-7182 8000 *fax* 020-7182 8300
email info@zooweekly.co.uk
website www.zootoday.co.uk
Editor Tom Etherington
Weekly £1.50

Entertainment magazine for young men with news, sport, photos, stories, jokes, listings and reviews. Founded 2004.

Newspapers and magazines overseas

Listings are given for newspapers and magazines in Australia (below), Canada (page 109), New Zealand (page 111) and South Africa (page 113). For information on submitting material to the USA see page 116. Newspapers are listed under the towns in which they are published.

AUSTRALIA

(Adelaide) Advertiser

31 Waymouth Street, Adelaide, SA 5000
tel (08) 8206 2000 *fax* (08) 8206 3669
website www.news.com.au/adelaidenow
Editor Mel Mansell
Daily Mon–Fri $1.10, Sat $1.80

Descriptive and news background material, 400–800 words, preferably with pictures; also cartoons. Founded 1858.

(Adelaide) Sunday Mail

31 Waymouth Street, Adelaide, SA 5000
postal address GPO Box 339, Adelaide, SA 5001
tel (08) 1300 130370 *fax* (08) 8206 3669
website www.news.com.au/adelaidenow
Editor Phillip Gardner
Sun $1.80

Founded 1912.

AQ – Australian Quarterly

Australian Institute of Policy and Science, PO Box M145, Missenden Road NSW 2050
tel (02) 9810 5642 *fax* (02) 9810 2406
website www.aips.net.au
Editor James Morris
6 p.a. $72 p.a. individuals/schools, $120 p.a. organisations ($145 Asia/Oceania; $165 elsewhere)

Peer-reviewed articles for the informed non-specialist on politics, law, economics, social issues, etc. Length: 3500 words preferred. Payment: none. Founded 1929.

Art & Australia

Art & Australia Pty Ltd, 11 Cecil Street, Paddington NSW 2021
email editorial@artandaustralia.com.au
website www.artandaustralia.com
Managing Editor Michael Fitzgerald
$80 p.a.

Articles with a contemporary perspective on Australia's traditional and current art, and on international art of Australian relevance, plus exhibition and book reviews. Length: 2000–3000 words (articles), 600–1200 words (reviews). Payment: $500 per 1000 words. Illustrations: colour transparencies or tiff files. Founded 1916 as *Art in Australia*.

Art Monthly Australia

LPO Box 8321, ANU Acton, ACT 0200
tel (02) 6125 3988 *fax* (02) 6125 9794
email art.monthly@anu.edu.au
website www.artmonthly.org.au
Editor Maurice O'Riordan
10 p.a. March–Dec $9.95

Contemporary visual arts: reviews, commentary, news and book reviews. Specially commissions most material but will consider unsolicited material. Welcomes ideas for articles and features. Length: negotiable. Payment: $300 (AUD) per 1000 words. Founded 1987.

Artlink

PO Box 8141, Station Arcade, Adelaide, South Australia 5000
tel (61) 8212 8711 *fax* (61) 8212 8911
email info@artlink.com.au
website www.artlink.com.au
Quarterly

Thematic art magazine linking art and society. Relevant articles and ideas welcome. Payment: $300 per 1000 words. Email CV and examples of work.

The Australian Financial Review

Fairfax Business Media, GPO Box 55, Melbourne, Victoria 3001
tel 1800-887969
website www.afr.com
Editor Kathy Bail
London office 1 Bath Street, London EC1V 9LB
tel 020-7688 2777 *fax* 020-7688 3499
Daily Mon–Sat $3

Investment business and economic news and reviews; government and politics, production, banking, commercial, and Stock Exchange statistics; company analysis. General features in Friday *Weekend Review* supplement.

Australian Flying

Yaffa Publishing Group, GPO Box, Sydney, NSW 2001
tel (02) 9281 2333 *fax* (02) 9281 2750
email info@yaffa.com.au
website www.yaffa.com/au, www.australianflying.com.au
Editor Justin Grey
6 p.a. $7.25

Covers the Australian light aircraft industry. Payment: by arrangement.

Australian Geographic

54 Park Street, Sydney, NSW 2000
tel (02) 9263 9813 *fax* (02) 9263 9810

website www.australiangeographic.com.au
Editor Ian Connellan
Quarterly $59.95 p.a.

Articles and features about Australia, particularly life, technology and wildlife in remote parts of the country. Material mostly commissioned. Length: articles, 300–800 words, features, 2000–3000 words. Illustrations: all commissioned. Payment: from $500 per 1000 words; illustrations by negotiation. Founded 1986.

Australian Heritage

Hallmark Editions, PO Box 84, Hampton, Victoria 3188
email editor@halledit.com.au
website www.heritageaustralia.com.au
Quarterly $65 p.a. outside Australia

Non-fiction articles on Australia's history and cultural and natural heritage. Length: 1500–3000 words. Payment: $500–$1500 by arrangement. Illustrations: photos, artwork. Founded 2005.

Australian Home Beautiful

Pacific Magazines, 35–51 Mitchell Street, McMahons Point, NSW 2060
tel (02) 9464 3218 *fax* (02) 9464 3263
website www.housebeautiful.com.au
Editor Wendy Moore
Monthly $59 p.a.

Interior decoration, furnishing, gardening, cookery, etc. Unsolicited MSS not accepted. Founded 1925.

Australian House and Garden

Level 10, 54 Park Street, Sydney, NSW 2000
tel (02) 9282 8456 *fax* (02) 9267 4912
email h&g@acpmagazines.com.au
website www.acp.com.au
Editor Lisa Green
Monthly $6.95

Factual articles dealing with interior decorating, home design, gardening, wine, food. Preliminary letter essential. Payment: by arrangement. Illustrations: line, half-tone, colour. Founded 1948.

Australian Journal of Politics and History

School of Political Science and International Studies, University of Queensland, St Lucia, Queensland 4072
tel (07) 3365 3163 *fax* (07) 3365 1388
website www.blackwellpublishing.com, www.polsis.uq.edu.au
Editor Ian Ward and Andrew Bonnell
4 p.a. $101/£59 p.a. individuals; $231/£225 institutions

Australian, European, Asian, Pacific and international articles. Special feature: regular surveys of Australian Foreign Policy and State and Commonwealth politics. Length: 8000 words max. Illustrations: line, only when necessary. Payment: none.

Australian Photography

Yaffa Publishing Group, 17–21 Bellevue Street, Surry Hills, NSW 2010
tel (02) 9281 2333 *fax* (03) 9690 8636
email robertkeeley@yaffa.com.au
Editor Robert Keeley
London office 2 Milford Road, London W13 9HZ
tel 020-8579 4836
Contact Robert Logan
Monthly $6.75

Illustrated articles: picture-taking techniques, technical. Length: 1200–2500 words with colour and/or b&w prints or slides. Payment: $80 per page. Founded 1950.

Australian Powerboat

Yaffa Publishing Group, 17–21 Bellevue Street, Surry Hills, NSW 2010
tel (02) 9281 2833 *fax* (02) 9281 2750
Editor Mick Fletoridis
6 p.a. $75 p.a.

Articles and news on boats and boating, racing, water skiing and products. Length: 1500 words (articles), 200 words (news). Illustrations: colour (transparencies preferred). Payment: $100 per 1000 words; from $30. Founded 1976.

The Australian Women's Weekly

ACP Magazines Ltd, 54 Park Street, Sydney, NSW 2000
tel (02) 9282 8000 *fax* (02) 9267 4361
postal address GPO Box 4178, Sydney, NSW 2000
Editor-in-Chief Helen McCabe
Monthly $6.60

Fiction and features. Length: fiction 1000–5000 words; features 1000–4000 words plus colour or b&w photos. Payment: according to length and merit. Fiction illustrations: sketches by own artists and freelances.

Aviation Business

17–21 Bellevue Street, Surry Hills, NSW 2010
tel (02) 9281 2333 *fax* (02) 9281 2750
email dougnancarrow@aviationbusiness.com.au
website www.aviationbusiness.com.au
Editor Doug Nancarrow
6 p.a.

Aviation business magazine for industry professionals focusing on Asia Pacific. Welcomes ideas for features. Length: 800–2000 words (features). Payment: on application. Illustrations: digital images only. Founded 1918.

The Big Issue Australia

148 Londsdale Street, Melbourne, Victoria 3001
tel (03) 9663 4533 *fax* (03) 9663 4252
email editorial@bigissue.org.au
website www.bigissue.org.au
Editor Alan Attwood

6 p.a. $78

Profiles and features of general interest and on social issues and entertainment, arts reviews. No fiction. Length: 1000–2500 words (features), up to 900 words (news), 200 words (reviews). Payment: 15c per word (features), $30 (reviews). Founded 1996.

Bookseller & Publisher

Level One, 607 St Kilda Road, Melbourne, Victoria 3004
tel (03) 8517 8399 *fax* (03) 8517 8399
email bookseller.publisher@thorpe.com.au
website www.booksellerandpublisher.com.au
Editor Matthia Dempsey
9 p.a.

Founded 1921.

(Brisbane) The Courier-Mail

Queensland Newspapers Pty Ltd, Campbell Street, Bowen Hills, Brisbane, Queensland 4006
tel 1300-304020 *fax* (07) 3666 6696
email cos@couriermail.com.au
website www.news.com.au
Editor David Fagan
Daily $1

(Brisbane) The Sunday Mail

Queensland Newspapers Pty Ltd, PO Box 130, Campbell Street, Bowen Hills, Brisbane, Queensland 4001
tel 1300 304 020 *fax* (07) 3666 6696
email deegan@qnp.newsltd.com.au
Editor Elizabeth Deegan
Sun $2 GST inc.

Anything of general interest. Length: up to 1500 words. Illustrations: line, photos, b&w and colour, cartoons. Rejected MSS returned if postage enclosed.

Camera

Nextmedia, 55 Chandos Street, St Leonards, NSW 2065
tel (02) 9901 6100 *fax* (02) 9901 6198
website www.next.com.au, www.avhub.com.au
Editor Paul Burrows
Bi-monthly $6.50

Magazine for amateur photographers and digital imaging enthusiasts covering techniques, test reports, new products. Considers unsolicited material. Welcomes ideas for articles and features. Length: 750–1500 words (features/articles). Illustrations: colour prints and transparencies. Payment: $300–$500. Founded 1979.

Cordite Poetry Review

PO Box 393, Carlton South, Victoria 3053
email cordite@cordite.org.au
website www.cordite.org.au
Editor David Prater
3 p.a. Free

Publishes on the internet poetry by new and emerging Australian authors, alongside feature articles, reviews, news and gossip items, audio poetry and special competitions. Welcomes material from overseas writers (no payment). Length: 100–3000 words (articles and features). Payment: $50–$100; $50 per poem. Illustrations: colour and b&w. Submissions by email only. Founded 1997.

Dance Australia

Yaffa Publishing Group, 17–21 Bellevue Street, Surry Hills, NSW 2010
tel (02) 9281 2333 *fax* (02) 9281 2750
email dance@yaffa.com.au
website www.yaffa.com.au
Editor Karen van Ulzen
Bi-monthly $7.25

Articles and features on all aspects of dance in Australia. Material mostly commissioned, but will consider unsolicited contributions. Illustrations: b&w and colour photos, line drawings, cartoons. Payment: $200 per 1000 words; illustrations by negotiation. Founded 1980.

Dolly

54–58 Park Street, Sydney, NSW 2000
tel (02) 9282 8000 *fax* (02) 9267 4361
website www.ninemsn.com.au/dolly
Editor Tiffany Dunk
Monthly $5.95

Features on teen fashion, health and beauty, personalities, music, social issues and how to cope with growing up, etc. Length: not less than 1000 words. Illustrations: colour, b&w, line, cartoons. Payment: by arrangement. Founded 1970.

Harper's Bazaar

ACP Publishing Pty Ltd, 54 Park Street, Sydney, NSW 2000
tel (02) 9282 8000 *fax* (02) 9267 4361
email bazaar@acpmagazines.com.au
website www.harpersbazaar.com.au
10 p.a. $7.95

Fashion, health and beauty, celebrity news, plus features. Length: 3000 words. Illustrations: colour and b&w photos. Founded 1998.

Island

PO Box 210, Sandy Bay, Tasmania 7006
tel (03) 6226 2325
email island.magazine@utas.edu.au
website www.islandmag.com
Editor Gina Mercer

Short stories, poetry and essays of social, environmental and cultural significance. Payment: $100 per poem, $150 for short stories, $150 per 1000 words for articles.

(Launceston) Examiner

Box 99, PO Launceston, Tasmania 7250
tel (03) 633 67111 *fax* (03) 633 47328

website www.examiner.com.au
Editor Fiona Reynolds
Daily $1.20

Accepts freelance material. Payment: by arrangement.

Meanjin
Melbourne University Publishing,
187 Gratton Street, Carlton, Victoria 3053
tel (03) 9342 0300 *fax* (03) 9342 0399
email meanjin@unimelb.edu.au
website www.meanjin.com.au
Editor Sophie Cunningham
Quarterly $105 (overseas)

Cultural commentary, fiction, poetry, essays and discussion of contemporary issues, e.g. biography, drugs, travel. See website for submission guidelines. Payment: $50 per poetry item, min. $100 prose. Founded 1941.

(Melbourne) The Age
The Age Company Ltd, 655 Collins Street, Docklands, Melbourne, Victoria 3008
tel (03) 8667 2000 *fax* (03) 8667 2332
Editor-in-Chief Paul Ramadge, *Senior Deputy Editor* Mark Baker, *Deputy Editor* Steve Foley
Daily Mon–Fri $1.50, Sat $2.50, Sun $2

Independent liberal morning daily; room occasionally for outside matter. *Good Weekend* and *Sunday Life* (illustrated weekend magazines); *Insight*; *A2* (includes literary reviews). Accepts occasional freelance material.

(Melbourne) Herald Sun
HWT Tower, 40 City Road, Southbank, Melbourne 3006
tel (03) 9292 2000 *fax* (03) 9292 2112
website www.news.com.au/heraldsun
Editor Bruce Guthrie
Send material to Peter Helme, Syndications Manager
Daily Mon–Fri $1.10, Sat $1.50, Sun $1.70

Accepts freelance articles, preferably with illustrations. Length: up to 750 words. Illustrations: half-tone, line, cartoons. Payment: on merit.

(Melbourne) Sunday Herald Sun
HWT Tower, 40 City Road, Southbank, Melbourne 3006
tel (03) 9292 2963 *fax* (03) 9292 2080
website www.heraldsun.com
Editor Damon Johnston
Weekly $1.80

Accepts freelance articles, preferably with illustrations. Length: up to 2000 words. Illustrations: colour. Payment: on merit.

Natural Health and Vegetarian Life
Skiptons Arcade, Suite 28, 541 High Street, Penrith, NSW 2750
email info@health.org.au
website www.health.org.au, www.veg-soc.org
Editors Roger French, Mark Berriman

Magazine of the Natural Health Society of Australia and the Australian Vegetarian Society. Welcomes contributions. Length: 700–2500 words.

NW Magazine
54 Park Street, Sydney, NSW 2000
tel (02) 9282 8285 *fax* (02) 9264 6005
Editor Nicole Byers
Weekly $4.95

News and features on celebrities, food, new products, fashion and astrology. Illustrated. Payment: by negotiation. Founded 1993.

OK! Magazine
Northern and Shell, PO Box 4088, Sydney, NSW 2001
tel (02) 8622 9222
Weekly

Exclusive celebrity interviews and photographs. Founded 2004.

Overland
PO Box 14428, Melbourne, Victoria 8001, Australia
tel +61 (3) 9919 4163 *fax* +61 (3) 9687 7614
email overland@vu.edu.au
website www.overland.org.au
Editor Jeff Sparrow
Quarterly AU$54 p.a. (AU$96 overseas)

Literary and cultural. Australian material preferred. Payment: by arrangement. Illustrations: line, half-tone, cartoons.

People Magazine
Civic Tower, Level 18, 66–68 Goulburn Street, Sydney, NSW 2000
tel (02) 9288 9648 *fax* (02) 9283 7923
Editor Michael Pickering
Weekly $4.40

National weekly news-pictorial. Mainly celebrity stories. Photos depicting glamour, show business, unusual occupations, rites, customs. Payment: $300 per page, text and photos.

(Perth) The Sunday Times
34 Stirling Street, Perth, Western Australia 6000
tel (08) 9326 8212 *fax* (08) 9221 1121
website www.sundaytimes.news.com.au
Editor Sam Weir
Sun $2.20

Topical articles to 800 words. Payment: on acceptance. Founded 1897.

(Perth) The West Australian
50 Hasler Road, Osborne Park, Western Australia 6017
tel (08) 9482 3111 *fax* (08) 9482 3177
website www.thewest.com.au
Editor Brett McCarthy
Daily Mon–Fri $1.30, Sat $2.30

Articles and sketches about people and events in Australia and abroad. Length: 300–700 words. Payment: Award rates or better. Illustrations: line, half-tone. Founded 1833.

Positive Words

PO Box 798, Heathcote 3523, Victoria, Australia
email positivewordsmagazine@live.com.au
Editor Sandra Lynn James
Monthly

Creative writing. Email for submission details or send 3x1RL for sample copy. Length: short stories up to 1000 words; poetry (one page). Payment: complementary copy.

Quadrant

Suite 2/5 Rosebery Place, Balmain, NSW 2041
postal address PO Box 82, Balmain, NSW 2041
tel (02) 9818 1155 *fax* (02) 8580 4664
website www.quadrant.org.au
Editor Keith Windschuttle
Literary Editor Les Murray
Monthly $6.50

Articles, short stories, verse, etc. Prose length: 2000–5000 words. Payment: min. $90 articles/stories, $60 reviews, $40 poems; illustrations by arrangement.

Reader's Digest (Australia)

GPO Box 3548, Sydney, NSW 1149
tel (02) 9018 6227 *fax* (02) 9018 7250
Editor-in-Chief Thomas Moore
Monthly $5.99 (inc. GST)

Articles on Australian subjects by commission only. No unsolicited MSS accepted. Length: 2000–3000 words. Payment: up to $4000 per article; $500 for 'My Story'; brief filler paragraphs, $50–$250. Illustrations: half-tone, colour.

Rock

Prime Creative Media, 11–15 Buckhurst Street, South Melbourne, Victoria 3205
tel (03) 9682 0148 *fax* (03) 9682 0044
email management@wild.com.au
website www.rock.com.au
Editor Ross Taylor
Quarterly $8.99

Australian rockclimbing and mountaineering articles, features and news. See website for guidelines to contibutions. Length: 2000 words (articles/features), 200 words (news). Payment: $100 per page (words and pictures). Founded 1978.

The Sun-Herald

Level 4, 1 Darling Island Road, Pyrmont, NSW 2009
tel (02) 9282 2833 *fax* (02) 9282 2151
website www.sunherald.com.au
Editor Simon Dulhunty
Weekly $2

Topical articles to 1000 words; news plus sections on current affairs, entertainment, finance, sport and travel. Payment: by arrangement.

(Sydney) The Daily Telegraph

News Ltd, 2 Holt Street, Surry Hills, NSW 2010
tel (02) 9288 3000 *fax* (02) 9288 2608
website dailytelegraph.com.au
Editor Garry Linnell
Daily Mon–Fri $1, Sat $1.60

Modern feature articles and series of Australian or world interest. Length: 1000–2000 words. Payment: according to merit/length.

The Sydney Morning Herald

1 Darling Island Road, Pyrmont, NSW 2009
tel (02) 9282 2822
London office 1 Bath Street, London EC1V 9LB
tel 020-7688 2777
website www.smh.com.au
Editor Allan Oakley
Daily $1.20

Saturday edition has pages of literary criticism and also magazine articles, plus glossy colour magazine. Topical articles 600–4000 words. Payment: varies, but minimum $100 per 1000 words. Illustrations: all types. Founded 1831.

(Sydney) The Sunday Telegraph

News Ltd, 2 Holt Street, Surry Hills, Sydney, NSW 2010
tel (02) 9288 3000 *fax* (02) 9288 3311
website www.sundaytelegraph.com.au
Editor Neil Breen
Weekly $1.80

News and features. Illustrations: transparencies. Payment: varies. Founded 1935.

Traveltalk

PO Box 329, North Beach, Western Australia 6920
tel 618 9240 3888 *fax* 618 9240 2796
email editorial@traveltalk.biz
website www.traveltalknow.com
Editor Craig Sinclair
Quarterly $4.95

Travel news and features focusing on popular travel destinations, in Australia and international. Prefers to receive a list of ideas and sample of material initially. Length: 600 words (articles), 1200–1800 words (features), 150–450 words (news). Payment: 40 cents per published word. Founded 2002.

Vogue Australia

180 Bourke Road, Alexandria, NSW 2015
postal address Locked Bag 5030, Alexandria, NSW 2015
tel (02) 9353 6666 *fax* (02) 9353 6600
website www.vogue.com.au
Editor-in-Chief Kirstie Clements
Monthly $8.50

Articles and features on fashion, beauty, health, business, people and the arts of interest to the modern woman of style and high spending power. Ideas welcome. Length: from 1000 words. Illustrations: colour and b&w. Founded 1959.

Wild

Prime Creative Media, 11–15 Buckhurst Street, South Melbourne, Victoria 3205
tel (03) 9690 8766 *fax* (03) 9682 0044
website www.wild.com.au
Editor Ross Taylor
6 p.a. $8.99

'Australia's wilderness adventure magazine.' Illustrated articles of first-hand experiences of the Australian wilderness, plus book and track reviews, product tests. See website for guidelines for contributors. Length: 2500 words (articles), 200 words (news). Payment: $150 per published page. Founded 1981.

Woman's Day

54–58 Park Street, Sydney, NSW 2000
tel (02) 9282 8508 *fax* (02) 9267 4360
Editor Fiona Connoley
Weekly $4

National women's magazine; news, show business, fiction, fashion, general articles, cookery, home economy, health, beauty.

CANADA

The Beaver: Canada's History Magazine

Bryce Hall, Main Floor, University of Winnipeg, 515 Portage Avenue, Winnipeg, Manitoba R3B 2E9
tel 204-988-9300 *fax* 204-988-9309
email editors@historysociety.ca
website www.thebeaver.ca
Editor Mark Reid
Bi-monthly $41.70 p.a. (taxes incl.)

Articles on Canadian history. Length: 1500–3000 words, with illustrations. Payment: on acceptance. Illustrations: b&w and colour archival photos or drawings. Founded 1920.

Canadian Bookseller

1255 Bay Street, Suite 902, Toronto, Ontario M5R 2A9
tel 416-467-7883 *fax* 416-467 7886
email editor@cbabook.org
website www.cbabook.org
Editor Emily Sinkins
Quarterly $37.80 (Canadian non-members)

Publishing industry news and contacts.

Canadian Literature

University of British Columbia, Buchanan E158, 1866 Main Mall, Vancouver, BC V6T 1Z1
tel 604-822-2780 *fax* 604-822-5504
email can.lit@ubc.ca
website www.canlit.ca
Editor Margery Fee
4 p.a. $52.50 p.a. ($105 p.a. institutions; outside Canada $130)

Articles on Canadian writers and writing in English and French. No fiction. Length: up to 6500 words. Payment: none. Founded 1959.

Canadian Screenwriter

366 Adelaide Street West, 401 Toronto, ON MSV 1R9
tel 416-979-7907 *fax* 416-979-9273
website www.wgc.ca/magazine
Editor David Kinahan
3 p.a. $20

Industry news, and advice and writing help for TV, radio, film and new media.

Canadian Writer's Journal

PO Box 1178, New Liskeard, Ontario P0J 1P0
tel 705-647-5424 *fax* 705-647-8366
email cwj@cwj.ca
website www.cwj.ca
Editor Deborah Ranchuk
Bi-monthly $35 p.a.

News on markets and articles on writers' aspirations for dedicated apprentice and professional Canadian writers. Considers unsolicited material. Founded 1984.

Chatelaine

One Mount Pleasant Road, Toronto, Ontario M4Y 2Y5
tel 416-764-2424 *fax* 416-764-2431
website www.chatelaine.com
Editor Maryam Sanati
Monthly $20 p.a.

Women's interest articles; Canadian angle preferred. Payment: on acceptance.

The Dalhousie Review

Dalhousie University, Halifax, Nova Scotia B3H 4R2
tel 902-494-2541 *fax* 902-494-3561
email Dalhousie.Review@dal.ca
website www.dalhousiereview.dal.ca
Editor Anthony Stewart
3 p.a. ($22.50 p.a., $28 outside Canada)

Articles on history, literature, political science, philosophy, sociology, popular culture, fine arts; short fiction; verse; book reviews. Usually not more than 3 stories and 10–12 poems in any one issue. Length: prose, up to 5000 words; verse, less than 40 words. Contributors receive 2 copies of issue and 10 offprints of their work.

Descant

50 Baldwin Street, Toronto, Ontario M5T 1L4
tel 416-593-2557 *fax* 416-593-9362

email info@descant.ca
website www.descant.ca
Editor Karen Mulhallen
Quarterly $28 p.a.

Literary magazine: short fiction, poetry and essays, previously unpublished. Payment: $100 (articles and fiction) on publication. Illustrations: b&w. Founded 1970.

The Fiddlehead

Campus House, 11 Garland Court,
UNB PO Box 4400, Frederiction, NB E3B 5A3
tel 506-453-3501
email fiddlehd@unb.ca
website www.thefiddlehead.ca
Editor Ross Leckie
Quarterly Can.$10 $30 p.a. Canada ($36 US/international)

Reviews, poetry, short stories. Payment: approx. $40 per printed page. Founded 1945.

(Hamilton) The Spectator

44 Frid Street, Hamilton, Ontario L8N 3G3
tel 905-526-3333
website www.hamiltonspectator.com
Publisher Dana Robbins
Daily Mon–Fri $1, Sat $1.85

Articles of general interest, political analysis and background; interviews, stories of Canadians abroad. Length: 800 words maximum. Payment: rate varies. Founded 1846.

International Journal of Canadian Studies

250 City Centre, Suite 303, Ottawa, Ontario K1R 6K7
tel 613-789-7834 *fax* 613-789-7830
email guy.leclair@iccs-ciec.ca
website www.iccs-ciec.ca
Managing Editor Guy Leclair
6 p.a. US$40 p.a. (US$65 p.a. institutions)

Major academic review of Canadian studies. Articles of general as well as scholarly interest on history, politics, literature, society, arts. Length: 7000–10,000 words.

Inuit Art Quarterly

2081 Merivale Road, Ottawa, Ontario K2G 1G9
tel 613-224-8189 *fax* 613-224-2907
email iaq@inuitart.org
website www.inuitart.org
Editor Marybelle Mitchell
Quarterly $7.95

Features, original research, artists' profiles, news. Contributors are expected to have a thorough knowledge of the arts. Length: varies. Illustrations: colour and b&w photos and line. Payment: by arrangement. Founded 1985.

The Malahat Review

University of Victoria, PO Box 1700 STN CSC, Victoria, BC V8W 2Y2
tel 250-721-8524 *fax* 250-472-5051
email malahat@uvic.ca (queries only)
website www.malahatreview.ca
Editor John Barton
Quarterly $35 p.a. ($40 p.a. USA, $45 p.a. elsewhere)

Short stories, poetry, creative non-fiction, reviews. Payment: $40CAD per magazine page. Founded 1967.

Neo-opsis Science Fiction Magazine

4129 Carey Road, Victoria, BC V8Z 4G5
tel 250-881-8893
email neoopsis@shaw.ca
website www.neo-opsis.ca
Editor Karl Johanson
3 p.a. CA$7.95 (CA$8.95 to US, CA$11.50 to UK)

Science fiction short stories, articles, opinion columns and reviews. Considers unsolicited material. Length: up to 4000 words (articles), up to 6000 words (short stories). Illustrations: b&w cartoons. Payment: 2.5c per word with max. of $125 for short stories; $30 per illustration. Founded 2003.

Outdoor Canada

54 Patrick Street, Toronto, Ontario M5T 1V1
tel 416-599-2000
email editorial@outdoorcanada.ca
website www.outdoorcanada.ca
Editor Patrick Walsh
6 p.a. $23.70

Articles on Canada's best fishing and hunting adventures and destinations, conservation issues related to angling and hunting, plus news on gear and techniques. Send idea first. Length: 2000–4000 words for articles, 100–600 words for shorter features. Average payment .50 cent per word.

Photo Life

185 Rue St Paul, Quebec, QC G1K 3W2
tel 1-800 905 7468 1-800 664 2739
email info@photolife.com
website www.photolife.com
Publisher Guy Poirier
6 p.a. $27 p.a.

Covers all aspects of photography of interest to amateur and professional photographers. Length: 800–1500 words. Illustrations: colour and b&w photos. Payment: by arrangement. Founded 1976.

Queen's Quarterly

Queen's University, Kingston, Ontario K7L 3N6
tel 613-533-2667 *fax* 613-533-6822
email queens.quarterly@queensu.ca
website www.queensu.ca/quarterly
Editor Dr Boris Castel
Quarterly $6.50 ($20 p.a.; $40 p.a. institutions)

A multidisciplinary scholarly journal aimed at the general educated reader – articles, short stories and poems. Length: 2500–3500 words (articles), 2000 (stories). Payment: by negotiation. Founded 1893.

Quill & Quire

PO Box 819, Markham, Ontario L3P 8A2
tel 416-364-3333 *fax* 416-595-5415
email info@quillandquire.com
website www.quillandquire.com
Editor Stuart Woods
12 p.a. $59.95 p.a. (outside Canada $95 p.a.)

Articles of interest about the Canadian book trade. Payment: from $100. Illustrations: line, half-tone. Subscription includes Canadian Publishers Directory (2 p.a.). Founded 1935.

Reader's Digest (Canada)

1125 Stanley Street, Montreal, QC H3B 5H5
tel 514-940-0751 *fax* 514-940-3637
email editor@readersdigest.ca
website www.readersdigest.ca
Monthly 24.97 p.a.

Original articles on all subjects of broad general appeal, thoroughly researched and professionally written. Outline or query only. Length: 3000 words approx. Payment: from $2700. Also previously published material. Illustrations: line, half-tone, colour.

(Toronto) The Globe and Mail

444 Front Street West, Toronto, Ontario M5V 2S9
website www.theglobeandmail.com
Editor John Stockhouse
Daily 70c

Unsolicited material considered. Payment: by arrangement. Founded 1844.

Toronto Life

111 Queen Street East, Suite 320, Toronto, Ontario M5C 1S2
tel 416-364-3333 *fax* 416-861-1169
email editorial@torontolife.com
website www.torontolife.com
Editor Sarah Fulford
Monthly $24 p.a.

Articles, profiles on Toronto and Torontonians. Illustrations: line, half-tone, colour. Founded 1966.

Toronto Star

1 Yonge Street, Toronto, Ontario M5E 1E6
tel 416-367-2000 *fax* 416-869-4328
London office Level 4A, PO Box 495, Virginia Street, London E1 9XY
tel 020-7833 0791
website www.thestar.com
Editor Michael Cooke
Daily Mon–Fri 30c, Sat $1, Sun 75c ($123 p.a.)

Features, life, world/national politics. Payment: by arrangement. Founded 1892.

(Vancouver) The Province

200 Granville Street, Suite 1, Vancouver, BC V6C 3N3
tel 604-605-2000 *fax* 604-605-2759
website www.theprovince.com
Editor-in-Chief Wayne Moriarty
Daily Mon–Fri $1, Sun $2

Founded 1898.

Vancouver Sun

200 Granville Street, Vancouver, BC V6C 3N3
tel 604-605-2000 *fax* 604-605-2308
London office Canwest News, 8 Heath Mansions, Hampstead Grove, London NW3 6SL
tel 020-7435 5103
website www.canada.com/vancouversun
website www.vancouversun.com
Editor Patricia Graham
Daily Mon–Thu 80c; Fri, Sat $1.50 ($205 p.a.)

Mix arts magazine. Travel, Op-Ed pieces considered. Payment: by arrangement.

Winnipeg Free Press

1355 Mountain Avenue, Winnipeg, MB R2X 3B6
tel 204-697-7000 *fax* 204-697-7412
email city-desk@freepress.mb.ca
website www.winnipegfreepress.com
Publisher Bob Cox, *Editor* Margo Goodhand
Daily Sun–Thurs 80c, Fri $1, Sat $1.50

Some freelance articles. Founded 1872.

NEW ZEALAND

(Auckland) New Zealand Herald

PO Box 32, Auckland
tel (09) 379 5050 *fax* (09) 373 6421
email newsdesk@herald.co.nz
website www.nzherald.co.nz
Editor Tim Murphy
Daily Mon–Fri $1.80, weekend $3

Topical and informative articles 800–1100 words. Payment: minimum $150–$300. Illustrations: colour negatives or prints. Founded 1863.

(Auckland) Sunday News

PO Box 1327, Auckland
tel (09) 925 9700
email editor@sunday-news.co.nz
website www.stuff.co.nz/sunday-times
Editor Mitchell Murphy
Sun $1.80

News, sport and showbiz, especially with NZ interest. Illustrations: colour and b&w photos. Founded 1963.

(Christchurch) The Press

Private Bag 4722, Christchurch
tel (03) 379 0940
email editorial@press.co.nz
website www.stuff.co.nz/the-press
Editor Andrew Holden
Daily Mon–Fri $1.20, Sat $2.50

Articles of general interest not more than 800 words. Illustrations: photos and line drawings, cartoons. Payment: by arrangement.

(Dunedin) Otago Daily Times

52 Stuart Street, PO Box 517 Dunedin, New Zealand
tel (03) 477 4760 *fax* (03) 474 7421
website www.odt.co.nz
Editor Murray Kirkness
Daily $1, Sat/Sun $1.50

Any articles of general interest up to 1000 words, but preference is given to NZ writers. Topical illustrations and personalities. Payment: current NZ rates. Founded 1861.

Freelance

PO Box 1426, Palmerston North 4440
email alysoncm@clear.net.nz
Editor Alyson B. Cresswell
Quarterly $30

Magazine of the NZ Freelance Writers' Association. Welcomes ideas for articles on all genres of writing. Payment: $10 (490–900 words). Payment on acceptance.

Hawke's Bay Today

PO Box 180, Karamu Road North, Hastings 4156
tel (06) 873 0800 *fax* (06) 873 0812
email editor@hbtoday.co.nz
website www.hbtoday.co.nz
Editor Antony Phillips
Daily $1

Limited requirements. Payment: $30 upwards for articles, $30 upwards for photos.

(Invercargill) The Southland Times

PO Box 805, Invercargill
tel (03) 211 1130 *fax* (03) 211 1098
email news@stl.co.nz
website www.stuff.co.nz/southlandtimes
Editor F.L. Tulett
Daily Mon–Fri $1, Sat $1.40

Articles of up to 800 words on topics of Southland and Otago interest. Payment: by arrangement. Illustrations: colour, cartoons. Founded 1862.

Management Magazine

Mediaweb Ltd, PO Box 5544, Wellesley Street, Auckland
tel (09) 845 5114 *fax* (09) 845 5116
email editor@management.co.nz
website www.management.co.nz
Monthly $6.95

Articles on the practice of management skills and techniques, individual and company profiles, coverage of organisational leadership and management trends and topics. A NZ/Australian angle or application preferred. Length: 2,000 words. Payment: by arrangement; minimum 30c per word. Illustrations: photos, line drawings.

The Nelson Mail

PO Box 244, 15 Bridge Street, Nelson 7040
tel (03) 546 2881 *fax* (03) 546 2802
email thereporter@nelsonmail.co.nz
website www.stuff.co.nz/nelson-mail
Editor Paul McIntyre

(New Zealand) Sunday Star-Times

PO Box 1327, Auckland 1140
tel (09) 302 1300 *fax* (09) 309 0258
email news@star-times.co.nz
website www.stuff.co.nz/sunday-star-times
Editor David Kerneys
Sun $2.50

New Zealand Woman's Day

100 Beaumont Street, Westhaven, Auckland 1010
tel (09) 308 2700 *fax* (0800) 277412
email ask@ndc.co.nz
Editor Sarah Henry
Weekly $4.10

Celebrity interviews, exclusive news stories, short stories, gossip. Length: 1000 words. Illustrations: colour transparencies; payment according to use. Payment: by arrangement. Founded 1989.

NZ House & Garden

PO Box 6341, Wellesley Street, Auckland 1036
tel (09) 909 6913
website www.nzhouseandgarden.co.nz
Editor Kate Coughlan, *Associate Editor* Sally Duggan
Monthly $8.90

Glossy magazine that celebrates New Zealand's most interesting houses and beautiful gardens. Inspiration for food and entertaining, and a resource for decor and travel. Considers unsolicited material. Welcomes ideas for articles and features. Length: 500–1000 words. Payment: $400–$600. Illustrations: colour transparencies. Founded 1994.

Takahe

Takahe Collective Trust, PO Box 13335, Christchurch 8141
email admin@takahe.org.nz
website www.takahe.org.nz
3 p.a. $30 p.a. ($40 international)

Quality short fiction 3000 words maximum, poetry reviews and artwork. Founded 1989.

Taranaki Daily News

49–65 Currie Street, New Plymouth
tel (06) 759 0800 *fax* (06) 758 6849
email editor@tnl.co.nz
website www.taranakidailynews.co.nz
Editor Jonathan MacKenzie
Daily $1.10, Sat $1.40

Articles preferably with a Taranaki connection. Payment: by negotiation. Illustrations: half-tone, cartoons. Founded 1857.

The Timaru Herald
PO Box 46, Bank Street, Timaru 7940
tel (03) 684 4129
email editor@timaruherald.co.nz
website www.stuff.co.nz/timaru-herald
Editor David King
Daily 75c

Topical articles. Payment: by arrangement. Illustrations: colour or b&w prints.

(Wellington) The Dominion Post
PO Box 3740, 40 Boulcott Street, Wellington 6140
tel (04) 474 0000
fax (04) 474 0350, (04) 474 0185 (editor)
email editor@dompost.co.nz
website www.dompost.co.nz
Editor Bernadette Courtney
Daily Mon–Fri $1.50, Sat $2.50

General topical articles, 600 words. Payment: NZ current rates or by arrangement. News illustrations, cartoons. Founded 2002 with the merger of *The Dominion* and *The Evening Post*.

Your Home and Garden
Australian Consolidated Press (New Zealand) Ltd, PO Box 92512, Wellesley Street, Auckland 1036
tel (09) 308 2700 *fax* (09) 308 2878
Editor Leanne Moore
Monthly $7.40

Advice, ideas and projects for homeowners – interiors and gardens. Length: 1000 words. Illustrations: digital images. Payment: 35c per word/$75 per transparency. Founded 1991.

SOUTH AFRICA

Africa Wild
Africa Wild Publishing (Pty) Ltd, PO Box 13333, Dowerglen, Ext. 7, 1612
tel (11) 454-0535 *fax* (11) 454-0538
email editor@africawildgroup.co.za
website www.africawildgroup.co.za
Editor-in-Chief Cheri-Ann Potgieter
11 p.a. R29,95

Travel magazine covering Southern Africa with articles on wildlife, conversation, nature and tourism.

Bona
Caxton Magazines, PO Box 1610, 2121 Parklands, KwaZulu-Natal
tel (11) 88 90600
website www.bona.co.za
Monthly R8,50

Articles on human drama, sport, music, health, social and consumer issues of interest to black people. Length: up to 1000 words. Payment: on publication. Illustrations: colour jpegs or prints.

(Cape Town) Cape Times
Newspaper House, 4th Floor, 122 St George's Mall, Cape Town 8001
postal address PO Box 11, Cape Town 8000
tel (021) 488-4911 *fax* (021) 488 4744
website www.capetimes.co.za
Editor Tyrone August
Daily R5

Contributions must be suitable for a daily newspaper and must not exceed 800 words. Illustrations: photos of outstanding South African interest. Founded 1876.

Car
PO Box 180, Howard Place 7450
tel (021) 530-3100 *fax* (021) 531-2212
email car@ramsaymedia.co.za
website www.cartoday.com
Editor John Bentley
Monthly R28,95

New car announcements with photos and full colour features of motoring interest. Payment: by arrangement. Illustrations: colour, cartoons. Founded 1957.

Daily Dispatch
Dispatch Media (Pty) Ltd, 35 Caxton Street, East London 5201
tel (043) 702-2000 *fax* (043) 743-5155
email letters@dispatch.co.za
postal address PO Box 131, East London 5200
website www.dispatch.co.za
Editor Andrew Trench
Daily Mon–Sat R2,70

Newspaper for the Eastern Cape region. Features of general interest, especially successful development projects in developing countries. Contributions welcome. Illustrations: colour and b&w photographs, artwork, cartoons; provides research facility for a fee to authors and publications. Length: approx. 1000 words (features). Payment: R500; R100 photographs. Founded 1872.

Destiny
Ndalo Media (Pty) Ltd, Bryanston Corner, 1st Floor, Building B, 18 Ealing Crescent (off Culross Road), CNR Main Road & Bryanston Drive, Bryanston 2191
PO Box 2077, Lonehill 2062
tel (11) 300-6700 *fax* (11) 300-6767
email destiny.editor@ndalo-media.com
website www.destinyconnect.com
Editor Khany Dhlomo
Monthly R26,95

Business and lifestyle for women. Aims to provide business and financial information that connects, supports and inspires women who are professionals, entrepreneurs, businesswomen and general business enthusiasts. Founded 2007.

Drum
PO Box 1802, Cape Town 8000
tel (021) 406-2682 (021) 406-2592

website pmdluli@media24.com
Editor Esmaré Weideman
Weekly R8,75

TV listings magazine with articles and gossip on celebrities, lifestyle features and puzzles.

(Durban) The Mercury

Independent Newspapers KwaZulu-Natal Ltd, PO Box 47549, Durban 4023
tel (031) 308-2911
website www.themercury.co.za
Editor Angela Quintal
Daily Mon–Fri R4,80

Serious background news and inside details of world events. Length: 700–900 words. Illustrations: photos of general interest. Founded 1852.

Fairlady

Box 1802, Cape Town 8000
tel (021) 446-5131 *fax* (021) 446-5058
email flmag@fairlady.com
website www.fairlady.com
Editor Suzy Brokensha
Monthly R22,95

Magazine for women in their 30s covering beauty, fashion, food and interior design. Includes 8 features per issue for which it seeks topical stories written to style. Considers unsolicited material. Length: about 1800 words. Illustrations: colour and b&w prints, colour artwork. Payment: R1.50 per word; R250 per photo, approx. R500 per illustration. Founded 1965.

Farmer's Weekly

368 Jan Smuts Avenue, Craighall 2196, PO Box 1797, Pinegowrie 2123
tel (11) 889-0836 *fax* (11) 889-0862
email farmersweekly@caxton.co.za
website www.farmersweekly.co.za
Editor Chris Burgess
Weekly R12,55

Articles, generally illustrated, up to 1000 words, on all aspects of practical farming and research with particular reference to conditions in Southern Africa. Includes women's section which accepts suitable, illustrated articles. Illustrations: line, half-tone, colour, cartoons. Payment: according to merit. Founded 1911.

Femina Magazine

Media24 Magazine Division, 7th Floor, Media City, 1 Heerengracht, Foreshore, Cape Town
tel (021) 446-5180
email gohara@media24.com
Editor Glynis O'Hara
Monthly R20,95

Magazine for women aged 40 and over with articles on culture, celebrities, parenting, relationships, real-life drama, popular science and human interest.

Garden and Home

Caxton House, 368 Jan Smuts Avenue, Craighall Park 2196
tel (11) 449-1010
email gardenhome@caxton.co.za
website www.gardenandhome.co.za
Editor Mary Jane Harris
Monthly R21,95

Well-illustrated articles on gardening suitable for southern hemisphere. Articles for home section on furnishings, decor ideas, food. Payment: by arrangement. Illustrations: half-tone, colour, cartoons.

Go!

8th Floor, Media City, 1 Heerengracht, Cape Town 8001
PO Box 1802, Cape Town 8000
tel (021) 446-1287
email editor@gomag.co.za
website www.gomag.co.za
Editor-in-Chief Bun Booyens
Monthly R20

Travel magazine covering Southern African with articles on places, food, photographing and equipment.

Ideas

PO Box 1802, Cape Town 8000
tel (021) 406-3185 *fax* (021) 406-2929
email ideased@media24.com
website www.ideasmag.co.za
Editor Terena Le Roux
Monthly R24,95

Features on beauty and fashion, food, knitting, needlecraft, crafts, home and garden, health and parenting. Length: up to 1400 words (features/ stories). Payment: R1,50 per word. Colour transparencies. Founded 1980.

Independent Newspapers Gauteng

PO Box 1014, Johannesburg 2000
tel (011) 633-9111 *fax* (011) 836-8398
website www.iol.co.za, www.star.co.za, www.pretorianews.co.za

Johannesburg **The Star** Daily R3,50
Saturday Star R4,20
Sunday Independent R9
Pretoria **Pretoria News** Daily R3,20

Accepts articles of general and South African interest; also cartoons. Payment: in accordance with an editor's assessment.

Independent Newspapers Kwa-Zulu Natal Ltd

18 Osborne Street, Greyville, Durban 4023
tel (031) 308-2400 *fax* (031) 308-2427
website www.iol.co.za, www.themercury.co.za, www.thepost.co.za

Durban **Daily News** Daily
The Mercury Daily
The Post Weekly R16,60 p.m.

Independent on Saturday

Accepts articles of general and South African interest; also cartoons. Payment: in accordance with an editor's assessment.

Independent Newspapers (South Africa) Ltd

PO Box 1014, Johannesburg 2000
tel (11) 633-2994 *fax* (11) 834-6059
website www.iol.co.za, www.capeargus.co.za
Cape Town **Argus** Daily R3,50
Saturday Argus R4
Sunday Argus R4,50
Cape Times Daily R3,80

Accepts articles of general and South African interest; also cartoons. Payment: in accordance with an editor's assessment.

(Johannesburg) Sunday Times

4 Biermann Avenue, Rosebank, Johannesburg 2196
tel (011) 280-5155
email tellus@sundaytimes.co.za
website www.timeslive.co.za
Editor Mondli Makhavya
Sun R8

Articles of political or human interest, from a South African angle if possible. Maximum 1000 words long and 2–3 photos. Shorter essays, stories and articles of a light nature from 500–750 words. Payment: average rate £100 a column. Illustrations: colour and b&w photos, line drawings.

Living and Loving

CTP Caxton Magazines, 4th Floor, Caxton House, 368 Jan Smuts Avenue, Craighall Park, Johannesburg
tel (011) 293-6117
postal address PO Box 218 Parklands 2121
website www.living-loving.co.za
Editor Carlien Wessels
Monthly R21,95

Parenting magazine: from pregnancy to preschool. Articles about behaviour and development in the first 5 years of life. First-person parenting experiences – pregnancy and the growing child. Medical news/breakthroughs of interest to parents worldwide. Payment: by merit, on acceptance and publication. Founded 1970.

Men's Health

Touchline Media, PO Box 16368, Vlaeberg 8018
tel (021) 408-3800 *fax* (021) 408-1200
email bestlife@touchline.co.za
website www.mh.co.za
Editorial Director Jason Brown
Monthly R35

Magazine for men with articles on health, relationships, food, culture and finance.

Move!

Media24, PO Box 785266, Sandton 2146
tel (11) 263 4795
email mzwane@media24.com
website www.movemag.co.za
Editor Makhosazana Zwane-Siguqa
Weekly R7

Magazine for women with articles on celebrities, fashion and beauty, food and home, and advice, together with puzzles and TV listings. Include sae with all submissions.

O: The Oprah Magazine

21 St John's Street, Cape Town 8001
tel (021) 464-6200 *fax* (021) 465-8190
email info@assocmags.co.za
Editor in Chief Jane Raphaely
Monthly R26.95

Women's magazine with articles on Mind, Body & Spirit, health, food and style, all aimed to inspire.

People

CTP Ltd, Caxton House, 2nd Floor, 368 Jan Smuts Avenue, Craighall Park
Private Bag X005, Roosevelt Park 2129
tel (011) 889-0600 *fax* (011) 889-0794
email andrea@caxton.co.za
website www.peoplemagazine.co.za
Editor Andrea Caknis
Weekly R12,95

Celebrity articles and gossip, real-life stories and TV listings.

Sailing

(incorporating SA Yachting)
PO Box 1849, Westville 3630
tel (031) 709-6087 *fax* (031) 709-6143
email sailing@iafrica.com
website www. sailing.co.za
Editor Richard Crockett
Monthly

Articles and features for the safety of dinghy, cruising, keelboat and racing sailors. Welcomes ideas for articles and features. Will consider unsolicited material. Illustrations: colour.

Soul

PO Box 2930, Vanderbijlpark 1900
email venessa@finessemag.co.za
Editor-in-Chief Venessa Shueman
11 p.a. 13,95

Women's magazine with the focus on Mind, Body & Spirit themes.

Southern Cross

PO Box 2372, Cape Town 8000
tel (021) 465-5007 *fax* (021) 465-3850
email editor@scross.co.za
website www.scross.co.za
Editor Gunther Simmermacher
Weekly R4,50

National English-language Catholic weekly. Catholic

news reports, world and South African. Length: 550 words (articles). Illustrations: photos of Catholic interest from freelance contributors. Payment: 17c per word; illustrations R30.

True Love

PO Box 784696, Sandton 2146
tel (11) 322-0880 *fax* (11) 322-0709
website www.truelove.co.za
monthly R18,95

Magazine for women with articles on health, Mind, Body & Spirit, careers and business, parenting, lifestyle, and fashion and beauty. Founded 1972.

The Witness

45 Willowton Road, Pietermaritzburg 3200
tel (033) 355-1111 *fax* (033) 355-1122
email fikile.moya@witness.co.za
Editor Fikile Moya
Daily R4.40

Accepts topical articles. All material should be submitted direct to the Editor in Pietermaritzburg. Length: 500–1000 words. Payment: average of R600 per 1000 words. Founded 1846.

World Airnews

PO Box 35082, Northway, Durban 4065
tel (31) 564-1319 *fax* (31) 563-7115
email tom@airnews.co.za
website www.airnews.co.za
Editor Tom Chalmers
Monthly £36 p.a.

Aviation news and features with an African angle. Payment: by negotiation.

Your Family

PO Box 473016, Parklands 2121, Gauteng
tel (011) 889-0600
website www.yourfamily.co.za
Editor Patti Garlick
Monthly R19,95

Cookery, knitting, crochet and homecrafts. Family drama, happy ending. Payment: by arrangement. Illustrations: continuous tone, colour and line, cartoons.

USA

The *Yearbook* does not contain a detailed list of US magazines and journals. Volume 3 of *Willings Press Guide* is the most useful general reference guide to US publications, available in most reference libraries. For readers with a particular interest in the US market, the publications listed here will be helpful (payments to the US should be made in US funds).

In many cases it is best to send a preliminary enquiry by email giving a rough outline of your article or story. Most magazines will supply guidelines to authors. Make it clear what rights are being offered for sale as some editors like to purchase material outright, thus securing world copyright, i.e. the traditional British market as well as the US market. Send the material direct to the US office of the journal and not to any London office.

If you submit material to US journals by post, include a covering letter, together with return postage in the form of International Reply Coupons (IRCs). IRCs can be exchanged in any foreign country for stamps representing the minimum postage payable on a letter sent from one country to another.

American Markets Newsletter

1974 46th Avenue, San Francisco, CA 94116
email sheila.oconnor@juno.com
Editor Sheila O'Connor
6 p.a. £34 p.a. (£63 for 2 years)

Editorial guidelines for US, Canadian and other overseas markets, plus information on press trips, non-fiction/fiction markets and writers' tips. Free syndication for all subscribers. Sample issue £5.95 (payable to S. O'Connor).

Willings Press Guide

Cision UK Ltd, Chess House, 34 Germain Street, Chesham, Bucks. HP5 1SJ
tel (0870) 7360010 (UK), (1494) 797225 (international)
fax (0870) 7360011 (UK), (1494) 797224
email enquiries@willingspress.com
website www.willingspress.com
£420 3-volume set; £365 2 volumes; £255 1 volume

Three volumes contain details of over 50,000 newspapers, broadcasters, periodicals and special interest titles in the UK and internationally. Usually available at local reference libraries or direct from the publisher. Also available as an online product.

The Writer

Kalmbach Publishing Co., 21027 Crossroads Circle, PO Box 1612, Waukesha, WI 53187
tel 262-796-8776 *fax* 262-796-1615
email editor@writermag.com
website www.writermag.com
Monthly $29 p.a.

Contains articles of instruction on most writing genres, lists of markets for MSS, and special features of interest to fiction writers and freelance writers everywhere.

Writer's Digest

Writer's Digest, 4700 East Galbraith Road, Cincinnati, OH 45236
tel 513-531-2690 *fax* 513-891-7153
email writersdigest@fwmedia.com
website www.writersdigest.com
Monthly $19.96 p.a.

Magazine for writers who want to write better and sell more; aims to inform, instruct and inspire the freelance and fiction writer.

Writer's Digest Books

4700 East Galbraith Road, Cincinannati, OH 45236
tel 513-531-2690 *fax* 513-531-2902
website www.writersdigest.com

Publishes annually *Novel & Short Story Writer's Market, Children's Writer's & Illustrator's Market, Poet's Market, Photographer's Market, Artist's & Graphic Designer's Market, Guide to Literary Agents* and many other books on creating and selling writing and illustrations. Also *Writer's Digest* magazine (see above).

Syndicates, news and press agencies

Before submitting material, you are strongly advised to make preliminary enquiries and to ascertain terms of work. Strictly speaking, syndication is the selling and reselling of previously published work although some news and press agencies handle original material.

Academic File Information Services

Eastern Art Publishing Group, PO Box 13666, London SW14 8WF
tel 020-8392 1122 *fax* 020-8392 1422
email afis@eapgroup.com
website www.eapgroup.com
Managing Editor Sajid Rizvi, *Executive Editor* Shirley Rizvi

Feature and photo syndication with special reference to the developing world and immigrant communities in the West. Founded 1985.

Advance Features

Stubbs Wood Cottage, Hammerwood, East Grinstead, West Sussex RH19 3QE
tel (01342) 850480
email advancefeatures@aol.com
website www.advancefeatures.uk.com
Managing Editor Peter Norman

Crosswords: daily, weekly and theme; general puzzles. Daily and weekly cartoons for the regional, national and overseas press (not single cartoons).

AFP (Agence France-Presse)

Centre Point, 25th Floor, 101–103 New Oxford Street, London WC1A 1DD
tel 020-7010 8750 *fax* 020-7010 8751
email london.economics@afp.com
website www.afp.com

Major news agency with journalists in 165 countries and 5 regional headquarters.

Australian Associated Press

111 Buckingham Palace Road, London SW1W 0DT
tel 020-3262 0058 *fax* 020-7821 0851
email news.london@aap.com.au
website www.aap.com.au

News service to the Australian, New Zealand and Pacific Island press, radio and TV. Founded 1935.

Neil Bradley Puzzles

Linden House, 73 Upper Marehay, Ripley, Derbyshire DE5 8JF
tel (01773) 741500 *fax* (01773) 741555
email bradcart@aol.com
Director Neil Bradley

Supplies visual puzzles to national and regional press; emphasis placed on variety and topicality with work based on current media listings. Daily single frame and strip cartoons. Founded 1981.

Brainwarp

PO Box 198, Birchwood, Warrington WA3 9AZ
tel (01925) 765878
email sarah@brainwarp.com
website www.brainwarp.com
Company Trixie Roberts, Tony Roberts, Sarah Simmons

Writes and supplies original crosswords, brainteasers, wordsearches, quizzes and word games to editors for the printed page. Does not accept work from external sources. Standard fees for syndicated puzzles. Customised work negotiable. Founded 1987.

Bulls Presstjänst AB

Fabrikörvägen 8, Box 1228, 13128 Nacka Strand, Sweden
tel (08) 55520600 *fax* (08) 55520665
website www.bullspress.com

Bulls Pressedienst GmbH
Eysseneckstrasse 50, D-60322 Frankfurt am Main, Germany
tel (069) 959 270 *fax* (069) 959 27222
email sales@bullspress.de

Bulls Pressetjeneste A/S
Hammersborg torg 3, N-0179 Oslo, Norway
tel 22 98 26 60 *fax* 22 20 49 78
email info@bulls.se

Bulls Pressetjeneste
Ostbanegade 9, DK–2100 Copenhagen, Denmark
tel 35 38 90 99 *fax* 35 38 25 16
email kjartan@bulls.dk

Oy Fennopress Ab – a Bulls Company
Arabianranta 6, FIN–00560, Helsinki, Finland
tel (09) 612 96 50 *fax* (09) 656 092
email info@bullspress.fi

Bulls Press SP. z o.o.
17 Rejtana str. 24, 02–516 Warsaw, Poland
tel (22) 845 90 10 *fax* (22) 845 90 11
email office@bulls.com.pl

Bulls Press
Tornimäe 7–091, EE–10145 Tallinn, Estonia
tel (372) 66 96 737 *fax* (372) 660 13 13
email pilt@bulls.ee

Market newspapers, magazines, weeklies and advertising agencies in Sweden, Denmark, Norway, Finland, Iceland, Poland, The Baltic States, Germany, Austria and German-speaking Switzerland.

Syndicates human interest picture stories; topical and well-illustrated background articles and series; photographic features dealing with science, people, personalities, glamour; genre pictures for advertising;

condensations and serialisations of bestselling fiction and non-fiction; cartoons, comic strips, film and TV rights, merchandising and newspaper graphics online.

Cartoons & Wordgames

341 Stockport Road, Mossley,
Ashton-under-Lyne OL5 0RS
tel (01457) 834883 *fax* (01457) 838783
email email@wordgames.co.uk
website www.wordgames.co.uk
Managing Editor Tom Williams

Crosswords, puzzles, cartoons. Founded 1980.

Celebritext

56 Sidney Road, London SW9 0TS
tel 020-7733 4777
email info@celebritext.com
website www.celebritext.com
Contact Lee Howard

Specialises in music, film and TV celebrity interviews. Commission: 50%. Founded 2000.

Copyline Scotland

Room 2, 28 Church Street, Inverness IV3 1EH
tel (01463) 710695 *fax* (01463) 713695
email copylinescotland@aol.com
Directors David Love, Maureen Love

Copywriting, writing press releases, covering news events for national and local media. Founded 1988.

The Daily & Sunday Telegraph Syndication

Telegraph Media Group,
111 Buckingham Palace Road, London SW1W 0DT
tel 020-7931 1010 *fax* 020-7931 2867
email syndication@telegraph.co.uk
website www.telegraph.co.uk/syndication

News, features, photography; worldwide distribution and representation.

Europa-Press

Fabrikkörvägen 8, Box 1228, 13128 Nacka Strand, Sweden
tel 85 2210300 210300 *fax* 885 2210300
email richard@europapress.se
website www.europapress.se
Director Richard Steinsvik

Market: newspapers, magazines, weeklies and websites in Sweden, Denmark, Norway, Finland, and the Baltic states. Syndicates high-quality features of international appeal such as topical articles, photo features – b&w and colour, women's features, short stories, serial novels, non-fiction stories and serials with strong human interest, comic strips.

Europress Features (UK)

18 St Chads Road, Didsbury,
Nr Manchester M20 4WH
tel 0161-445 2945
email lauenbergandpartners@yahoo.com

Representation of newspapers and magazines in Europe, Australia, United States. Syndication of top-flight features with exclusive illustrations – human interest stories – showbusiness personalities. 30–35% commission on sales of material successfully accepted; 40% on exclusive illustrations.

FAMOUS*

13 Harwood Road, London SW6 4QP
tel 020-7731 9333 *fax* 020-7731 9330
email info@famous.uk.com
website www.famous.uk.com

Celebrity picture and feature agency. Supplies showbiz content to newspapers, magazines, websites, TV stations, mobile phone companies, books and advertisers worldwide. Represents celebrity journalists and photographers from LA, New York, Europe and Australia, syndicating their copy around the globe. Open to new material. Terms: 50%. Founded 1990.

ForesightNews

The Profile Group (UK) Ltd, Johnson Building,
77 Hatton Garden, London EC1N 8JS
tel 020-7190 7830 *fax* 020-7190 7858
email hotline@foresightnews.co.uk,
international@foresightnews.co.uk,
eu@foresightnews.co.uk, law@foresightnews.co.uk,
health@foresightnews.co.uk,
scienceandtech@foresightnews.co.uk,
education@foresightnews.co.uk,
media@foresightnews.co.uk,
business@foresightnews.co.uk,
sport@foresightnews.co.uk,
transport@foresightnews.co.uk,
environment@foresightnews.co.uk
website www.foresightnews.co.uk
Contact Chris Woods, Editor, *Deputy Editor* Ben Brill

Offers a vast fully searchable database of forthcoming news and events spanning 15 broad category areas and hundreds sub-categories including UK and EU politics, international news, business, crime, environment, defence and security, health, entertainment, royals and sport, delivering information to subscribers before it is reported.

Government News Network (GNN)

Room HR332, Hercules House, Hercules Road,
London SE1 7DU
tel 020-7261 8527 *fax* 020-7928 5696
website www.nds.coi.gov.uk

Government press office making national issues relevant to local audiences.

Graphic Syndication

4 Reyntiens View, Odiham, Hants RG29 1AF
tel (01256) 703004
email flantoons@btinternet.com
Manager M. Flanagan

Cartoon strips and single frames supplied to newspapers and magazines in Britain and overseas. Terms: 50%. Founded 1981.

Guardian/Observer Syndication

Kings Place, 90 York Way, London N1 9GU
tel 020-3353 2539 *fax* 020-3353 3167
email permissions.syndication@guardian.co.uk
website www.syndication.guardian.co.uk
Contact May Chiem

International syndication services of news and features from *The Guardian* and *The Observer*. Unable to syndicate content which hasn't been published in its own titles.

Hayters Teamwork

Image House, Station Road, London N17 9LR
tel 020-8808 3300 *fax* 020-8808 1122
email sport@hayters.com
website www.hayters.com
Managing Directors Nick Callow, Gerry Cox

Sports news, features and data supplied to all branches of the media. Commission: negotiable according to merit. Part of Info Strada. Founded 1955.

Headliners

Rich Mix, 35–47 Bethnal Green Road, London E1 6LA
tel 020-7749 9360 *fax* 020-7729 5948
email enquiries@headliners.org
website www.headliners.org
Director Fiona Wyton

Offers young people aged 8–18 the opportunity to write on issues of importance to them, for newspapers, radio and TV. Founded 1995.

Independent Radio News (IRN)

6th Floor, 200 Grant Way, Isleworth, London TW7 5QD
tel 020-7585 4525 *fax* 020-7430 4092
email radio@bskyb.com
website www.irn.co.uk
Managing Director John Perkins

National and international news.

INS (International News Service) and Irish News Service

UK office 7 King's Avenue, Minnis Bay, Birchington-on-Sea, East Kent CT7 9QL
tel (01843) 845022
Editor & Managing Director Barry J. Hardy PC, *Photo Editor* Jan Vanek, *Secretary* K.T. Byrne

News, sport, book and magazine reviews (please forward copies), TV, radio, photographic department; also equipment for TV films, etc. Offices in Dublin and Switzerland. Trading over 50 years.

International Fashion Press Agency

Penrose House, Birtles Road, Whirley, Cheshire SK10 3JQ
tel (01625) 615323 *fax* (01625) 432284
email ifpressagy@aol.com
Managing Director P. Bentham

Monitors and photographs international fashion collections and developments in textile and fashion industry. Specialist writers on health, fitness, beauty and personalities. Undertakes individual commissioned features. Supplies syndicated columns/pages to press, radio and TV (NUJ staff writers and photographers).

International Press Agency (Pty) Ltd

Sunrise House, 56 Morningside, Ndabeni 7405, South Africa
tel (021) 531-1926 *fax* (021) 531-8789
email inpra@iafrica.com
UK office 5 Cloister House, 53 Griffiths Road, London SW19 1SS
tel 020-8767 4828
email uabarnett@inpra.co.uk
website www.inpa.co.za
Manager Mrs T. Temple
Managing Editor Mrs U.A. Barnett PhD

South African agents for many leading British, American and continental press firms for the syndication of press photos and features for the South African market. Founded 1934.

Joker Feature Service (JFS)

PO Box 253, 6040 AG, Roermond, The Netherlands
tel (0475) 337338 *fax* (0475) 315663
email info@jfs.nl
Managing Director Ruud Kerstens

Feature articles, serial rights, tests, cartoons, comic strips and illustrations, puzzles. Handles TV features, books, internet sites; also production for merchandising.

Knight Features

20 Crescent Grove, London SW4 7AH
tel 020-7622 1467 *fax* 020-7622 1522
website www.knightfeatures.com
Director Peter Knight, *Associates* Gaby Martin, Andrew Knight, Samantha Ferris

Worldwide selling of strip cartoons, puzzles, crosswords, horoscopes and serialisations. Exclusive agent in UK and Republic of Ireland for United Media Inc. of New York, and for Garfield. Founded 1985.

London at Large Ltd

Zenith House, 155 Curtain Road, London EC2A 3QY
tel 020-7613 2299 *fax* 020-7613 3822
email info@londonatlarge.com
website www.londonatlarge.com
Editor Kerri Darn

Forward planner serving the media: lists press contacts for parties, celebrities, launches, premieres, music, film, video and book releases. Founded 1985.

London Press Service

23 Theydon Avenue, Woburn Sands,
Milton Keynes MK17 8PN
tel (0190) 858 7559
email londonpress@btconnect.com
Editor Dick Meredith

Newsfeatures about innovation, achievement, etc in the UK's business, scientific and technological sectors to help promote UK trade and attract inward investment. Part of BERR (Department for Business, Enterprise and Regulatory Reform). Commission: by arrangement. Founded 1950s.

Maharaja Features Pvt. Ltd (1969)

5/226 Sion Road East, Sion, Bombay 400 022, India
tel 91-22-24097951
email mahafeat@gmail.com
Editor Mrs R. Ravi, *Managing Editor* K.R.N. Swamy

Syndicates feature and pictorial material of interest to Asian readers to newspapers and magazines in India, UK and elsewhere. Specialises in well-researched articles on India by eminent authorities for publication in prestigious journals throughout the world. Also topical features. Length: 1000–1500 words. Illustrations: b&w prints, colour transparencies, digital photographs.

Market News International

1 Canada Square, 42nd Floor, Canary Wharf,
London E14 5DR
tel 020-7862 7404 *fax* 020-7862 7425
website www.marketnews.com

Provides news, data and analysis on financial markets from around the world.

National Association of Press Agencies (NAPA)

c/o Mercury Press Agency, Unit 218,
Century Buildings, Tower Street, Liverpool L3 4BJ
tel (0870) 609 1935
email enquiries@napa.org.uk
website www.napa.org.uk
Directors Denis Cassidy, Chris Johnson, Matt Bell, Mark Solomons
Membership £250 p.a.

A network of independent, established and experienced press agencies serving newspapers, magazines, TV and radio networks. Founded 1983.

New Blitz Literary & TV Agency

Via di Panico 67, 00186 Rome, Italy
postal address CP 30047–00193, Rome 47, Italy
tel (06) 686 4859 *fax* (06) 686 4859
email blitzgacs@inwind.it
Manager Giovanni A.S. Congiu

Syndicates worldwide: cartoons, comic strips, humorous books with drawings, feature and pictorial material, topical, environment, travel. Average rates of commission 60/40%, monthly report of sales, payment 60 days after the date of monthly report.

PA Puzzles – see The Press Association

Photoshot

29–31 Saffron Hill, London EC1N 8SW
tel 020-7421 6000 *fax* 020-7421 6006
email info@photoshot.com
website www.photoshot.com
Managing Director Charles Taylor

Quality imagery. Collections include: UPPA – daily national and international business, political and establishment news; Starstock – live images of celebrity and entertainment personalities; Stay Still – celebrity portraiture; Talking Sport – live and archival sporting images; NHPA – nature; Photoshot Assignment – creative photographic commissions. Founded 1929.

Pixfeatures

5 Latimer Road, Barnet, Herts. EN5 5NU
tel 020-8449 9946 *fax* 020-8449 9946
Contact Peter Wickman

News agency and picture library. Specialises in selling pictures and features to British and European press.

The Press Association

292 Vauxhall Bridge Road, London SW1V 1AE
tel 0870-120 3200 *fax* 0870-120 3201
website www.pressassociation.co.uk
Chief Executive Clive Marshall, *Managing Director* Steven Brown

PA Entertainment Entertainment content including showbiz, lifestyle, food, fashion, health, property, travel, horoscopes, crosswords and cartoons

PA News Fast and accurate news, photography and information to print, broadcast and electronic media in the UK and Ireland.

PA Sport In-depth coverage of national and regional sports, transmitting a huge range of stories, results, pictures and updates every day.

PA Listings Page- and screen-ready information from daily guides to 7-day supplements on sports results, TV and radio listings, arts and entertainment, financial and weather listings tailored to suit requirements.

PA Digital Top quality content including news and sport for a wide range of multimedia customers.

PA WeatherCentre Continuously updated information on present and future weather conditions; consultancy services for media and industry. Founded 1868.

The Puzzle House

Ivy Cottage, Battlesea Green, Stradbroke,
Suffolk IP21 5NE
tel (01379) 384656 *fax* (01379) 384656
email puzzlehouse@btinternet.com
website www.thepuzzlehouse.co.uk
Partners Roy Preston and Sue Preston

Supply original crosswords, quizzes and puzzles of all types. Commissions taken on any topic, with all age ranges catered for. Wide selection of puzzles available for one-off usage. Founded 1988.

Rann Communication

Level 1, 18–20 Grenfell Street, Adelaide, SA 5000, Australia
postal address GPO Box 958, Adelaide, SA 5000, Australia
tel (08) 8211 7771 *fax* (08) 8212 2272
email reception@rann.com.au
website www.rann.com.au
Managing Director Chris Rann

Full range of professional PR, press releases, special newsletters, commercial and political intelligence, media monitoring. Welcomes approaches from organisations requiring PR representation or press release distribution. Founded 1982.

Reuters News

The Quadrangle, 180 Wardour Street, London W1A 4YG
tel 020-7437 9787
email general.info@thomsonreuters.com
website www.thomsonreuters.com

The largest international news agency – provides global information and news services to the world's newspapers, websites, TV networks, radio stations, as well as direct to business professionals in the financial, legal, tax and accounting, scientific, healthcare and media markets. Merged with Thomson Financial News in 2008.

Sirius Media Services

Suite 3, Stowmarket Business Centre, Needham Road, Stowmarket, Suffolk IP14 2AH
tel (01449) 678878 *fax* (0870) 912 8041
website www.siriusmedia.co.uk

Crosswords, puzzles and quizzes.

Solo Syndication Ltd

17–18 Haywards Place, London EC1R 0EQ
tel 020-7566 0360 *fax* 020-7566 0388
Contact William Gardiner

Worldwide syndication of newspaper features, photos, cartoons, strips and book serialisations. Represents the international syndication of Associated Newspapers (*Daily Mail, Mail on Sunday, Evening Standard*) and Universal Press Syndicate, Creators Syndicate and the Christian Science Monitor Service in Africa and the Middle East.

Southern News Service

Exchange House, Hindhead, Surrey GU26 6AA
tel (01428) 607330 *fax* (01428) 606351
email denis@cassidyandleigh.com
Partners Denis Cassidy and Donald Leigh

News stories, features and court coverage. Full picture service, digital and ISDN. Public relations words and pictures. Founded 1960.

Thomson Financial News – see Reuters News

Visual Humour

5 Greymouth Close, Stockton-on-Tees TS18 5LF
tel (01642) 581847
email peterdodsworth@btclick.com
website www.businesscartoons.co.uk/shop
Contact Peter Dodsworth

Daily and weekly humorous cartoon strips; also single panel cartoon features (not gag cartoons) for possible syndication in the UK and abroad. Picture puzzles also considered. Submit photocopy samples only initially, with sae. Founded 1984.

Wessex News, Features and Photos Agency

Quill House, Charnham Lane, Hungerford, Berks. RG17 0EY
tel (01488) 686810 *fax* (01488) 683548
email news@britishnews.co.uk
website www.britishnews.co.uk
Contact Jim Hardy, Editor

Freelance press agency with a network of writers and photographers across the UK. Offices in Berkshire and Manchester. only considers stories of interest to the UK media. Founded 1981.

World Entertainment News Network (WENN)

35 Kings Exchange, Tileyard Road, London N7 9AH
tel 020-7607 2757 *fax* 020-7700 4649
email lloyd@wenn.com
website www.wenn.com

Provides the world's media with up-to-the-minute entertainment news and photos. Offices in Los Angeles, New York and Las Vegas.

Books

Getting started

To help authors get started with writing we offer some guidelines to consider before submitting material to a publisher. Notes from successful authors in fiction (Joanna Trollope), short stories (Chimamanda Ngozie Adichie), comedy (Kathy Lette), fantasy (Terry Pratchett), crime (Mark Billingham), romantic fiction (Jane Green), historical fiction (Bernard Cornwell), biography (Claire Tomalin), travel (William Dalrymple), non-fiction (Simon Winchester), MBS (William Bloom), ghostwriting (Andrew Crofts), crossover writing (Neil Gaiman), children's writing (J.K. Rowling) and self-publishing (G.P. Taylor) start on page 241. For notes from a passionate poet (Benjamin Zephaniah) see page 349 and for notes from a successful television screenwriter (Andrew Davies) see page 369.

There is more competition to get published than ever before. Hundreds of manuscripts (also referred to as typescripts) of would-be books land on the desks of publishers and literary agents every day. Both publishers and literary agents acknowledge that potential authors have to be really dedicated (or perhaps very lucky) in order to get their work published. So how can you give yourself the best chance of success? The following seven pointers will give you a head start to get your material noticed by a publisher.

1. Agent or publisher?

• First decide whether to approach an agent or to go it alone and submit your material direct to a publisher. Many publishers, particularly of fiction, will only consider material submitted through a literary agent. See *The role of the literary agent* on page 449, *'I think I need an agent'* on page 453, *How literary agencies work* on page 455, *How to get an agent* on page 458 and *Publishing agreements* on page 303 for some of the pros and cons of each approach.

• Whether you choose to approach an agent or a publisher, your work will be subjected to rigorous commercial assessment.

2. Choose the right publisher or agent

• Study the entries in this *Yearbook*, examine publishers' lists and their websites, and look in the relevant sections in libraries and bookshops for the names of publishers which might be interested in seeing your material.

• A list of literary agents starts on page 473. See *Letter to an unsolicited author* on page 461.

• Listings of publishers' names and addresses start on page 136.

• A list of *Publishers of fiction*, by fiction genre, is on page 762 and a list of *Publishers of non-fiction* starts on page 765.

• The market for children's books is considered in *Writing and the children's book market* on page 291. The list of *Children's book publishers and packagers* on page 776 includes publishers of poetry for children and teenage fiction. A list of *Literary agents for children's books* is on page 780. See also *Children's Writers' & Artists' Yearbook 2011* (A&C Black, 2010).

• Publishers which consider poetry for adults are listed on page 779. See also *Getting poetry published* on page 351 and *Poetry organisations* on page 361.

• The electronic book market is in its infancy and has no set standards or provision but holds potential for some authors. See *E-publishing* on page 629 and *Ebooks* on page 635.
• Authors are strongly advised not to pay for the publication of their work. A reputable publishing house will undertake publication at its own expense, except possibly for works of an academic nature. See *Doing it on your own* on page 310 and *Notes from a successful self-publisher* on page 308 for an introduction to self publishing, and *Vanity publishing* on page 343.

3. Prepare your material well

• Presentation is important. For example, no editor will read a handwritten manuscript. If your material is submitted in the most appropriate format a publisher will be more inclined to give attention to it. See *Dos and don'ts of approaching a publisher* on page 126.
• Many publishers' websites give guidance for new writers.
• It is understandable that writers, in their eagerness to show their work to others in the hope of getting it published as soon as possible, will send their manuscript in a raw state. Do not send your manuscript to a publisher until it is *ready* to be seen as it could ruin your chances. Be confident that your work is as good as it can be.

4. Approach the publisher or literary agent in the way they prefer

• Submit your work to the right person within the publishing company or literary agency. Ring or email first to find out who is the best person to receive your work. If the listing in this *Yearbook* does not specify, also ask whether they want a synopsis (see *Writing a synopsis* on page 131) and sample chapters or the complete manuscript. Many publishers' and literary agents' and websites give guidance on how to submit material.
• Never send your only copy of the manuscript. Whilst every reasonable care will be taken of material in a publisher's possession, responsibility cannot be accepted if material is lost or damaged.
• Always include an sae with enough postage for the return of your material. Send International Reply Coupons (IRCs) if you are writing from outside the country or if you are submitting material from the UK to the Republic of Ireland. (The current version of the IRC has an expiry date of 31 December 2011; after this date, IRCs with this expiry date can no longer be exchanged for postage. See www.royalmail.com for details.)

5. Write a convincing letter

• Compose your preliminary letter with care. Writers have been known to send out such letters in duplicated form, an approach unlikely to stimulate a publisher's interest. See *Dos and don'ts of approaching a publisher* on page 126.

Publishers' contracts

Following a publishing company's firm interest in a MS, a publisher's contract is drawn up between the author and the publisher (see *Publishing agreements* on page 303). If the author is not entirely happy with the contract presented to them or wishes to take advice, he/she could ask their literary agent, the Society of Authors or the Writers' Guild of Great Britain to check the contract on their behalf – providing the author has an agent and/or is a member of those organisations. Otherwise, the author can either check it for himself (for guidance, see *An Author's Guide to Publishing* and *Understanding Publishers' Contracts*, both books by Michael Legat; see page 303), or seek advice from a solicitor. Before consulting a solicitor, make sure that they are familiar with publishing agreements and can give informed advice. Many local firms have little or no experience of such work and their opinion can often be of limited value and the cost may outweigh any possible gains.

Books

• When submitting a manuscript to a publisher, it is a good idea to let them know that you know (and admire!) what they already publish. You can then make your case about where your submission will fit in their list. Let them know that you mean business and have researched the marketplace. See *Understanding the publishing process* on page 230.
• What is the unique selling point of the material you are submitting for publication? You may have an original authorial 'voice', or you may have come up with an amazingly brilliant idea for a series. If, after checking out the marketplace, you think you have something truly original to offer, then believe in yourself and be convincing when you offer it around.

6. Get out and network

• Writing can be a lonely business – don't work in a vacuum. Talk to others of your discipline at literature festivals, conferences and book groups; find out if there are any writer groups in your area. Consider doing a course – see *Taking a writing course* on page 685 and *Creative writing courses* on page 688.
• Go to a festival and be inspired! There are many literature festivals held throughout the year (see *Literature festivals* on page 615) which new and well-known authors appear at. You may be able to hear a talk or lecture given by an author you admire, and even meet them afterwards.

7. Don't give up!

• Editors receive hundreds of manuscripts every day. For a publisher, there are many factors that have to be taken into consideration when evaluating these submissions, the most important of which is 'Will it sell?' See *The state of commissioning* on page 299 and *Spotting a bestseller* on page 235.
• Be prepared to wait for a decision on your work. Editors and agents are both very busy people so be patient when waiting for a response. Don't pester them too soon.
• Publishing is a big business and it is ever more competitive. Even after an editor has read your work, there are many other people involved before a manuscript is acquired for publication. People from the sales, marketing, publicity, rights and other departments all have to be convinced that the book is right for their list and will sell.
• The harsh reality of submitting a manuscript to a publisher or literary agent is that you have to be prepared for rejection (see *Dealing with rejection* on page 659). But practically all successful authors have received such rejections from a publisher at some time so you are in good company.
• Have patience, persevere. Good luck!

See also ...

- *Dealing with rejection*, page 659
- *Book publishers in Australia* (page 196); in *Canada* (page 199); in *New Zealand* (page 202); in *South Africa* (page 204); and in the *USA* (page 206)
- *Ghostwriting*, page 276
- *Is there a book in you?*, page 295
- *Book packagers*, page 224

Dos and don'ts of approaching a publisher

You want the book you've written to be published. So how do you set about it? Where will you send the typescript? Probably to a publisher, but to which one? Michael Legat offers guidelines on how to proceed.

Finding a publisher

Do your market research in public libraries and bookshops, and especially in *Writers'& Artists' Yearbook*, to find out which publishers bring out the kind of book you have written. While looking at the *Yearbook* entries, note which publishers are willing to consider books submitted to them directly, rather than through an agent, and which require a letter of enquiry first. Incidentally, if you are hoping to interest an agent, they almost all want an enquiry letter first.

10 Any Street, Any Town,
Any County

Messrs Dickens and Thackray,
83 Demy Street,
London WC45 9BM 12th March

Dear Sirs,

May I please send for your consideration the novel I have written.

Yours sincerely,

L. Hopeful

This letter is far too brief. It gives no information about the kind of novel the author wishes to submit, nor of its length, it doesn't include a sae, and it doesn't even reveal the writer's sex. And since the writer doesn't use a question mark and has misspelt 'Thackeray', it's a good bet that the book will need meticulous and time-consuming copy-editing.

Enquiry letters

An enquiry letter should be businesslike. Don't grovel ('it would be an honour to be published by so distinguished a firm'), don't make jokes ('my Mum says it's smashing, but maybe you'll think she's prejudiced'), don't be aggressive ('I have chosen you to publish my book, kindly send me your terms by return'). It is a good idea to write to whichever editor in the publishing house is responsible for books of the kind you have written (a phone call will provide this information – but take care to get the right title and spelling of the editor's name). Enclose a stamped addressed envelope. Look at the examples of the two poor enquiry letters followed by a good one on page 129.

You may have noticed that none of the letters refers to sending a disk or email. Such submissions may well become standard in a few years' time, but that stage has not yet been reached. However, once a book has been accepted, the publisher will certainly want a copy of the book on disk if it is available.

Presentation

Assuming that a publishing firm agrees to look at your book, the editor will expect to see a well-presented typescript (sometimes called a manuscript, abbreviated to MS). Here are some dos and don'ts about its appearance.

Use a typewriter or a computer, or get a secretarial service to translate your handwriting on to a disk. Don't expect a publisher to read a handwritten script, even if you have a fine Italian hand.

Choose a good quality white A4 paper (preferably not continuous listing paper, or if you must use it, at least separate the pages and remove the perforated edges). Whatever paper you use don't type on both sides, and don't use single spacing (which publishers abhor, and usually refuse to read) – one side of the paper only and double spacing is the rule. And do leave a good margin, at least 3cm, all around the text, using the same margins throughout, so as to have the same number of lines on each page (except at the beginning and end of chapters). Double spacing and good margins allow space for your last-minute corrections to the typescript, for any copy-editor's amendments, and for instructions to the printer. And, not least in importance, a typescript in that style is much easier to read.

Always begin chapters on a new page. Justify on the left hand side only. Don't use blank lines between paragraphs (in the style of most typed letters nowadays), but indent the first line of each paragraph a few spaces. Blank lines should be used only to indicate a change of subject, or time, or scene, or viewpoint.

Be consistent in your choice of variant spellings, capitalisation, use of subheadings, etc. Make up your mind whether you are going to use -ise or -ize suffixes, for example, and whether, if 'village hall' appears in your text, you will type 'village hall' or Village Hall'.

For plays, use capitals for character names and underline stage directions or print them in italics. Use single spacing for dialogue, but leave a blank line between one character's speech and that of the next character to speak.

Poetry should be typed in exactly the way that the poem would appear in a printed version, using single or double spacing and various indentations as the poet wishes.

Organising the pages

Number the pages (or 'folios', as publishers like to call them) straight through from beginning to end. Don't start each chapter at folio 1. If you need to include an extra folio after, say, folio 27, call it folio 27a and write at the foot of folio 27: 'Folio 27a follows'. Then write at the foot of 27a: 'Folio 28 follows'. Obviously, if you want to insert more than one page, you would use '27a', '27b', '27c', and so on. Some writers like to use part of the book's title as well as the folio number: 'Harry 27', for example, but this is not essential.

Create a title page for the book, showing the title and your name or pseudonym. Add your name and address in the bottom right hand corner, and also type it on the last folio of the typescript, in case the first folio becomes detached. You can also add a word count, if you wish (if using the word-counting facility on your computer, round the figure up or down to the nearest thousand or five thousand). If you want to include a list of your previously published books, a dedication, a quotation, a list of contents or of illustrations, an assertion of your moral rights, or any similar material, use a separate page for each item. Leave these pages unnumbered or use small roman figures – i, ii, iii, etc – so that the first folio to have an Arabic number will be the first page of your text.

When fastening the typescript together, don't use pins (which scratch), paperclips (which pick up other papers from a busy editor's desk), or staples (which make it difficult to read). Don't ever fasten the pages together in one solid lump, and it's best to avoid ring binders too. Don't use plastic folders – they are slippery and can very easily cascade off a pile on the editor's desk (which won't please the editor). Almost all publishers prefer to handle each folio separately, so put the typescript into a wallet-type folder, or more than one if necessary. Put the title of the book and your name and address on the outside of the folder.

If illustrations form a large part of your book and you expect to provide them yourself they should be included with the typescript, and equally a selection should accompany a synopsis and specimen chapters. Send copies rather than originals. If your book is for children don't complete all the illustrations until the publisher has decided on the size of the book and the number of illustrations. If you have a friend who wants to supply illustrations for your book, do make sure that they will be up to publishing standard before you accept the offer. You may put off a children's publisher by suggesting an illustrator – they like to choose.

Waiting for a decision

Many publishers take what seems to be an unconscionable time to give a verdict on typescripts submitted to them. However, a decision whether or not to publish may not be easy, and several readings and consultations with other departments in the publishing house often have to take place before the editor can be sure of the answer. If you have heard nothing after two months, send a polite letter of enquiry; if you get no response, ask for your typescript back, and try another publisher.

Don't expect to be given reasons for rejection. Publishers do not have time to spend on books and authors which they are not going to publish. However, if the rejection letter

12 Any Street, Any Town,
Any County

Messrs Dickens and Thackeray,
83 Demy Street,
London WC45 9BM

14th March

Dear Sirs,

May I please send you the novel I have written, which I want to get published? It's called Wendy Chiltern. That's the name of the heroine. I am a 76-year-old grandmother, but all my friends say that I am very young for my age and I can certainly claim to be 'with it'. I belong to the Townswomen's Guild, and I do a lot of work at the local Church, and I play Bridge regularly, so you can tell my mind's still as sharp as ever.

I have been writing ever since I was a little girl, without trying to get anything published, but my friends have persuaded me to try my luck with this book. One of them said it was better than anything by Jackie Collins. Any publisher would jump at it, she said. They are all so enthusiastic, that I just had to 'have a go'…

The book is 57 pages long. It is properly typed, and all the spelling mistakes have been corrected. I should tell you that I am aware that the novel has some faults. It is just a little slow to get started, but once you're into it I am sure you won't be able to put it down.

If your reply is favourable, I shall bring the typescript to your office and perhaps you could spare me a few minutes to talk about it.

Yours sincerely,

Louise Hopeless (Mrs)

This letter is far too long, and includes masses of irrelevant information about the author. The fact that the lady's friends said they liked the book is no recommendation – what else are they going to say to their friend? And no editor is going to be tempted by a slow beginning, however honest it may be for the author to point it out. The book is almost certainly typed in single spacing with minuscule margins, and even so will be a long way short of book-length. And publishers do not spend time interviewing would-be authors – the lady should leave the typescript at reception, and let it speak for itself.

contains any compliments on your work, you can take them at face value – publishers tend not to encourage authors unless they mean it.

Copyright material

Copyright exists as soon as you (or anyone else) records anything original to you on paper or film or disk. If you want to quote or otherwise use any material which is someone else's copyright, even if it is a short extract, you will have to get permission to do so, and possibly pay a fee. This applies not only to the text of a book, but also to letters and photographs, the copyright of which belongs to the letter-writer and photographer respectively. You must always give full acknowledgement to the source of the material. Use copyright material without such clearance and acknowledgement, and you are guilty of plagiarism – and another name for plagiarism is stealing. There are some circumstances in which you may use small amounts of text under a rule called 'Fair Dealing'. If your book has been accepted for publication, the publisher will be able to give you advice on the matter. (See also articles on copyright starting on page 697.)

Proofs

When your book is accepted by a publisher you may be asked to do further work on it, and a copy-editor may check the typescript line by line and word by word. As the author you should see the final copy before it goes to the printer, and this is almost your last

14 Any Street, Any Town,
Any County

Ms Ann Clarke,
Messrs Dickens and Thackeray,
83 Demy Street,
London WC45 9BM

16th March

Dear Ms Clarke,

May I please send you my novel, My Son, my Son, for your kind consideration? It is approximately 87,000 words in length and is a contemporary story, telling of the devastating effect on the marriage of the central characters when their 17-year-old son announces that he is gay. It is aimed at the same market as that of Joanna Trollope, although my characters might be described as a little further down the class scale.

I have written a number of articles which have been published not only in my local newspaper, but in a couple of cases in 'The Lady', and once in 'The Observer'. This is my first work of fiction, but I have two other novels with similar backgrounds in mind.

I enclose a sae and look forward to hearing from you. Perhaps you will let me know whether you would prefer to see a synopsis and specimen chapters, or the entire book. And may I submit the material on disk or by email, or would you prefer hard copy?

Yours sincerely,

Lucilla Possible

A good enquiry letter. The writer has (we can presume) found out to whom to address the letter, and how the lady spells her name. The letter is brief, but gives a clear picture of what the novel is about, and suggests its possible market, telling the publisher all that is necessary at this stage. It makes the two points that the writer has had some success with her work (do always include such details, provided that they are for professional publications), and that she intends to write other books. It also asks about the possibility of sending a synopsis and specimen chapters rather than the complete book, and that is in fact the way in which most publishers nowadays like to see new material (especially for non-fiction books, but also for novels). Of course, no enquiry letter, however satisfactory, can guarantee a favourable response, but at least with this one no editorial hackles should rise.

chance to make any changes, whether they are simply the correction of literals or are more extensive than that. You should be aware that many publishers nowadays do not use copy-editors and rely on the author to provide an error-free typescript.

At a later stage you will be sent proofs from the printer, which you will have to read with great care. Any errors which the printer has made are corrected without charge, but if you alter anything else, the publisher will have to pay for the changes and will be entitled to pass on to you any costs which exceed 10–15% of the cost of composition (i.e. the setting of the book in type). That sounds as though it gives you a lot of leeway, but alterations at proof stage are hugely expensive, so avoid them if you possibly can.

Michael Legat became a full-time writer after a long and successful publishing career. He is the author of a number of highly regarded books on publishing and writing.

See also...

- *Getting started*, page 123
- *Writing a synopsis*, page 131
- *Dealing with rejection*, page 659
- *Correcting proofs*, page 671
- *Notes from a successful fiction author*, page 241
- *Notes from a successful short story author*, page 243
- *Notes from a successful non-fiction author*, page 270
- *Notes from a successful children's author*, page 290
- *Writing and the children's book market*, page 291
- *Understanding the publishing process*, page 230
- *Publishing agreements*, page 303
- *The role of a literary agent*, page 449
- *How literary agencies work*, page 455
- *How to get an agent*, page 458
- *Letter to an unsolicited author*, page 461
- *Copyright questions*, page 697
- *UK copyright law*, page 700

Writing a synopsis

When publishers and literary agents ask for a synopsis to be submitted, writers often misunderstand what is required. Rebecca Swift provides clarification.

The dictionary definition of 'synopsis' (derived from the Ancient Greek meaning) is 'a brief description of the contents of something'. The purpose of a synopsis is to inform a literary agent or publisher of the type of book you are writing/have written in a concise, appealing fashion, conveying that you are in command of your subject matter. If you want your manuscript to be given serious consideration, a good synopsis is a crucial part of your submission.

This *Writers' & Artists' Yearbook* will inform you that most publishing houses no longer accept direct submissions but those that do (usually the smaller houses) will most often ask for a cover letter, synopsis and sample chapters rather than a whole work in the first instance. The same applies to literary agents. To put it simply, the sample chapters are to show how you write, and the synopsis is to tell the reader what happens when they have finished reading them. This will help inform the publisher/literary agent whether they think it is worth their while to read more. Then, if they want to read more, they will ask you. (For guidance on preparing your manuscript and writing a cover letter, see *Dos and don'ts of approaching a publisher* on page 126.)

So, the bottom line is this – if you want to have your manuscript read in its entirety you must invest time in getting your cover letter and book synopsis right. I know from my experiences at The Literary Consultancy (TLC) that many writers can get disconcerted and nervous by having to produce a synopsis and there are usually two reasons why.

First, a writer might have an unwieldy story that they themselves are not 100% convinced by, or a non-fiction project that they do not really know enough about. If this is so, summarising can be difficult because the thinking through and planning of the project has not been thorough the first place.

In this instance, I would urge the writer to question why this process is so difficult. If it is because the story is insufficiently clear, persuasive or gripping, then more work needs to be done to get the manuscript into the kind of shape that would persuade an agent or editor to consider it further.

Second, a writer might genuinely be able to write a good book but not be experienced in the art of summarising a work in an effective manner. A few might even consider the act of doing so demeaning. If this is the case, I would urge you to think not of yourself, but of the reader, and treat the project as a literary exercise which you should try to enjoy: a challenge and opportunity to show your work off in its essential form. It might help to refer to book blurbs, or plot summaries in reference books such as *The Oxford Companion to Literature*, or online, for example in Wikipedia.

In addition to letting a professional reader know what happens in your manuscript, the synopsis will also let them know at a glance if you have thought about how your work fits into the market. This is critical in non-fiction, less so with fiction, although with fiction awareness of what genre you have written in is vital. Also, if what you are writing coincides with any major anniversaries for example, or might have a marketing 'hook' of any other kind, this is important to mention if not within the synopsis itself, then within a cover letter (see below).

Fiction synopses

A fiction synopsis should comprise of a brief summary followed by a more detailed synopsis. But before writing either of these, you must clarify which genre your work fits into.

The most important thing to realise about fiction in respect of how you present it to representatives of the publishing industry is that it breaks down into different types, or genres. For those who think that the obsession with genres is a modern phenomenon, the lines from Polonius' famous speech in *Hamlet* might serve to prove the opposite. He describes the actors who have come to court as 'The best actors in the world … for tragedy, comedy, history, pastoral, pastoral-comical, historical-pastoral, scene individable, or poem unlimited'. Some of these dramatic forms are familiar and others not. There are always more genres being invented or cross-fertilised. It can be difficult to keep up!

The most popular genres today are, broadly speaking: crime, thriller, psychological thriller, detective, sci-fi, horror, comic, chic-lit, lad's lit, historical, saga, literary, experimental, graphic, erotic, fantasy, romantic, women's commercial fiction and literary–commercial crossover – or, as it's becoming more widely coined, 'Lit Lite'.

Classifying your novel within a genre can be a challenge. This is largely because when most people start to write a novel they do so without having studied the genre they are writing for. Although when you start to write, you feel free to explore, practise and experiment without thinking in terms of the defining limits of a genre, by the time you come to submitting your work to be published, it is very important to know which genre your work fits into. In all art forms there are rule breakers, but almost inevitably – as in the cases of Picasso, Virginia Woolf and, more recently, the US writer Michael Cunningham – even the greatest 'artists' have studied the traditional forms/genres before taking any risks.

A good starting point is to read books you consider similar to the one you are writing that are already published, and note how they are classified on the back cover. By reading, and sometimes studying literature and writing through other routes, you will also learn the possibilities and limits offered by your chosen genre. The bad news is if you don't clarify what kind of book you have written, the chances are it will reflect in the text. If you don't clearly inform the agent or editor what your book is about and which category it falls into, it may all too quickly be labelled as a work which 'falls between stools', is impossible to market and so doesn't get considered any further.

Writing a brief summary

Having made it your top priority to identify what type of novel you have written, you can make a start on your all-important synopsis. All good synopses should begin with a brief summary of 30–75 words, the sort of thing which appears on a book's back cover. For example, had you written *Pride and Prejudice* today:

> *Pride and Prejudice* is a contemporary, literary romance about a woman who falls in love with a man she thinks she hates.

Or,

> *Pride and Prejudice*, a contemporary, literary novel, tells the story of Elizabeth Bennett, a proud, intelligent woman, one of five sisters, whose mother is committed to marrying her children off as a matter of urgency. Elizabeth meets Darcy, owner of a grand estate, but considers him overly proud, arrogant and undesirable. In time, she learns that he is not all that he appears to be, and revises her prejudice, before they fall deeply in love.

Both these examples, one short, one longer, serve to whet the appetite for more detail to follow.

An example of an ostensibly weak synopsis, which rambles and fails to emphasise the most important points quickly enough, might be:

> Set at some point in the nineteenth century, five sisters are looking for husbands. Or is Mary, really? Anyway, their mother is a real fuss pot and annoys everybody. Outside their house there are lots of fields and it is sometimes raining. The girls' father is gentle and kind, with grey hair but not good at standing up to his wife always. Mr Bingley is an important character who is very handsome, but is he as handsome as Mr Darcy? It is hard to tell! ...

Hopefully you can see the clear differences between the two.

Writing a detailed synopsis

Following the brief summary should be a more detailed synopsis of 350–450 words. Literary agents do not want a detailed chapter-by-chapter breakdown (if they do, they'll ask for one) as reading them can be tiresome and difficult to follow. The main aim of the longer synopsis is to give a detailed overview which clearly and concisely conveys how the story flows and unfolds, and (very importantly) what is interesting about it. The longer synopsis should also reconfirm when the story is set (i.e. is it contemporary or historical?); the setting or background (e.g. is Thatcher's government in its last throes or are we in a quiet Devonshire village where nothing ever happens, but there is a sense of impending doom?); inform the reader about the central character (i.e. what is interesting about them and what happens on their journey), as well as giving brief reference to other characters that are directly pivotal to the plot. The longer synopsis should also highlight the dramatic turning points and tell the reader of any other salient information which will help convey what kind of work it is, how well imagined are the characters involved and how well thought through and alluring is the plot.

Cover letter

Alongside the synopsis should also be an excellent, economically written and confident sounding cover letter. This should simply address a well-researched literary agent by name (never put a generic 'Dear Sir/Madam').

In this you should say that you are enclosing a novel called 'X', which is a thriller/literary/coming-of-age/horror novel (identify genre). It does not matter if this is repeated on the synopsis page. You may also wish to refer to writers you feel you are similar too, although do be careful not to have misplaced arrogance in this. You might say, 'I write in the genre of John Grisham because he is a writer I read and hugely admire' or you might say, 'This is a novel in which *To Kill a Mocking Bird* meets *Crash*' or 'Harper Lee meets J.G. Ballard' – but do be careful that you know you have the talent to claims like these. Otherwise, let the agent decide and they will help market you to the publisher, and the publisher will then help market you to the public. If you admire an agent for a particular reason, such as they publish a hero or heroine of yours, let them know.

Biographical note

If you have something interesting to say about yourself, such as that you have won a writing competition or published before in relevant publications, do include this briefly in the cover letter. It is for you to judge what is of particular interest about you, and how much to say, but you should also provide a fuller biographical note which sits well at the bottom of the synopsis page. This should be between 50 and 200 words as a guide. If you have been published, provide a summarised list of publications here. If you have not, or are trying to hide a career you think has gone off track and want to appear fresh, keep it brief and mention what you do, your age and anything that makes you sound interesting. If your career is related to your subject matter, then do say this. For example, 'I worked as a miner for 20 years' if your book is set in a mining community. Do avoid listing technical publications as evidence of writing ability if you are submitting fiction. There is an enormous difference between writing technically and writing fiction, and if you don't seem to know this it is not impressive. This is different for non-fiction. As a rule, err on the side of brevity if necessary. If the reader loves your work they will be in touch to find out more about you. For help with learning how to self-market read *Marketing Your Book: An Author's Guide* by Alison Baverstock.

It should be noted that if the work is literary, there may be less emphasis on plot and more on the quality of the prose. Due to current climates and publishing trends, this is a difficult time to publish literary fiction without strong plots, although things undoubtedly will change.

Non-fiction synopses

A synopsis for a work of non-fiction performs a different function. The consideration of whether a non-fiction book has a potential market is generally more straightforward than for new fiction. In the case of non-fiction you should certainly have carefully researched your market before submission and ideally list the competitors in the field, outlining why your project is different and why you are the writer best positioned to write the book you have. Also, you should be able to list any marketing opportunities you believe your book may have, such as identifiable, or even guaranteed readers such as students if you teach a course, anniversary tie-ins and so on.

A literary agent is often prepared to sell a non-fiction work on synopsis and chapters only. This is an extreme rarity in the case of fiction. This is because it is easier for people to see if there is a market gap that can be filled by the project, before the work is finished.

You may not need an agent for particular, more niche types of non-fiction book. In these cases publishers may well be prepared to take direct submissions from you. Again, this is because in the area of self-help or business books for example, the publisher of a list will know clearly what its gaps are. It may have a standard format it is looking to sell books in. You should certainly research these formats and contact editors of specialised lists to find out if they have space for your idea, and so that they can let you know exactly how they like work to be presented before forming the project in your mind.

I think it best in general for the non-fiction writer to prepare two different types of proposal. The first would form an initial pitch and the second the follow-up proposal if the editor or literary agent asks to see more. Both documents need to be thoroughly persuasive as these may go directly towards securing a book deal.

The initial pitch for non-fiction

This should be no more than one to two pages. Include a brief summary (e.g. '*Flying High* is a book about the history of aeronautics' or '*My Name was Glory* is the biography of

Amanda Flemming, maid to Queen Gertrude and unknown holder of the Secret Chalice') and a description of the contents of the book, with an argument for why it should be published now and why you are qualified to write it. Ideally, you should also include an overview of other work in the field, and argue why yours fills an important gap. In addition, you should include a chapter breakdown, giving a provisional title for each chapter with a brief summary (30–75 words, as a guide only) of the contents of each chapter to show how the book is structured throughout. Here also, spell out any ideas you have about how the book might be marketed. As non-fiction markets are more specific than fiction markets, it is useful for the author to let the agent or editor know what hooks there might be to help sell copies. As I have said, if you are lucky enough to have any guaranteed markets, such as students on a course you teach, do of course inform the industry of this.

If you can, estimate a word count for the work. For some pre-formatted non-fiction titles, there will be a word-length you will be expected to hit anyway. You will discover this as you research.

The second pitch

The more in-depth synopsis with sample chapter should include the initial pitch, but with any added material you can muster in terms of defending your position as author or the book's market chances. Most importantly in the longer pitch you need to show that you can write the book. Provide more in-depth chapter breakdowns (100–150 words each) and 5,000–10,000 words of polished, irresistibly clear and well-written text to show that you are capable of executing your intentions in a winning manner. Write the introduction and the opening chapter if possible to really show you mean business. Those two together would usually take you to between 5,000 and 10,000 words.

Conclusion

Whilst it is worth spending time ensuring you have a good, short, confident cover letter and synopsis, it is important to stress that there is nothing as important to an editor than the quality of your writing and your ability to sustain the interest of a reader in the main body of the text. A synopsis is not a magic wand that will influence the real standard of a work. I have seen perfectly polished synopses followed by poor writing. The net result of this is that one feels excited, only to be let down, which is off-putting in itself. If you have the skill to write a gripping synopsis, ensure that you have used your energies wisely in advance of submitting and make sure that the book itself is as good as it can be. Focus, particularly, on the fine-tuning of the opening 50 pages. Unless your synopsis and summary are actively off-putting, they should generally serve as a flag to indicate to the reader where they are beginning and then as a guide to the story beyond the extract submission. If the agent or publisher likes what they see well enough to ask for more … well done! Oh and good luck.

Rebecca Swift worked as an editor at Virago Press and writer, before co-founding The Literary Consultancy (www.literaryconsultancy.co.uk) with Hannah Griffiths in 1996. She has edited two books for Chatto & Windus and published poetry in *Staple*, *Vintage New Writing* and *Virago New Poets.*

Book publishers UK and Ireland

*Member of the Publishers Association or Publishing Scotland
†Member of the Irish Book Publishers' Association

AA Publishing
Automobile Association and Business Services, Contact Centre, Lambert House, Stockport Road, Cheadle SK8 2DY
tel (01256) 491524 *fax* 0161-488 7544
email customersupport@theaa.com
website www.theAA.com
Directors Rupert Miles (Ceo), David Watchus (editorial), Richard Firth (production), Steve Wing (mapping services), Terry Lee (sales & marketing)

Travel, atlases, maps, leisure interests, including *Essential Guides*, *Spiral Guides*, *City Packs* and *Explorer Travel Guides* and *Key Guides*. Founded 1979.

Abacus – see Little, Brown Book Group

Absolute Classics – see Oberon Books

Absolute Press
Scarborough House, 29 James Street West, Bath BA1 2BT
tel (01225) 316013 *fax* (01225) 445836
email office@absolutepress.co.uk
website www.absolutepress.co.uk
Publisher and Managing Director Jon Croft, *Directors* Meg Avent (editorial), Matt Inwood (art)

General list: cookery, food-related topics, wine, lifestyle. No unsolicited MSS. Founded 1979.

Academic Press – see Elsevier Ltd

Acorn Editions – see James Clarke & Co. Ltd

Addison-Wesley – see Pearson UK

Adlard Coles Nautical – see A&C Black Publishers Ltd

Age UK
(formerly Age Concern Books)
Freepost (SWB 30375), Ashburton, Devon TQ13 7ZZ
tel 020-8765 7200 *fax* 020-8765 7211
website www.ageuk.org.uk
Commissioning Editor Peter Hooper

Age UK works with and for older people. Books on health and care, finance, leisure, policy, retirement, housing, computing, training, rights. Founded 1973.

Airlife Publishing – see The Crowood Press

Philip Allan – see Hodder Education Group

Ian Allan Publishing Ltd
Riverdene Business Park, Molesey Road, Hersham, Surrey KT12 4RG
tel (01932) 266600 *fax* (01932) 266601
email info@ianallanpublishing.co.uk
website www.ianallanpublishing.com
Publishing Manager Nick Grant

Transport: railways, aircraft, shipping, road; naval, military and social history; reference books and magazines; sport and cycling guides; popular culture.

Classic Publications (imprint)
Military aviation.

Lewis Masonic (imprint)
Freemasonry.

Midland Publishing (imprint)
Transport: civil and military aviation.

Oxford Publishing Company (imprint)
Transport: railways, road.

J.A. Allen
Clerkenwell House, 45–47 Clerkenwell Green, London EC1R 0HT
tel 020-7251 2661 *fax* 020-7490 4958
email allen@halebooks.com
website www.allenbooks.co.uk
Publisher Lesley Gowers

Horse care and equestrianism including breeding, racing, polo, jumping, eventing, dressage, management, carriage driving, breeds, horse industry training, veterinary and farriery. Books usually commissioned but willing to consider any serious, specialist TSS on the horse and related subjects. Imprint of Robert Hale Ltd (page 158). Founded 1926.

George Allen & Unwin Publishers – acquired by HarperCollins Publishers

Allen Lane – see Penguin Group (UK)

Alligator Books Ltd
(Pinwheel Division)
Gadd House, Arcadia Avenue, London N3 2JU
tel 020-8371 6622 *fax* 020-8371 6633
email sales@pinwheel.co.uk
website www.alligatorbooks.co.uk

Children's licensed character titles, fiction, non-fiction, colouring and activity books. Subsidiary of International Greetings Plc. For submissions, see Pinwheel.

Pinwheel Children's Books (imprint)
website www.alligatorbooks.co.uk
Children's fiction, non-fiction, novelty and interactive titles and picture books. Ages 0–10 years. Unsolicited novelty book concepts, picture book MSS and illustration samples welcome – in writing only. No telephone submissions. Do not reply or return unsuccessful submissions. Address submissions to 'C. Swift – Bath' at the above address.

Allison & Busby Ltd
13 Charlotte Mews, London W1T 4EJ
tel 020-7580 1080 *fax* 020-7580 1180
email susie@allisonandbusby.com
website www.allisonandbusby.com
Publishing Director Susie Dunlop, *Sales manager* Lesley-Anne Crooks
Fiction, genre fiction, general non-fiction, true crime. No unsolicited MSS accepted.

Allyn & Bacon – see Pearson UK

Alma Books
London House, 243–253 Lower Mortlake Road, Richmond, Surrey TW9 2LL
tel 020-8948 9550 *fax* 020-8948 5599
website www.almabooks.co.uk
Directors Alessandro Gallenzi, Elisabetta Minervini
Contemporary literary fiction (60% English-language originals, 40% translations) and non-fiction. No unsolicited MSS by email. Founded 2005.

The Alpha Press – see Sussex Academic Press

Amberley Publishing
Cirencester Road, Chalford, Stroud, Glos. GL6 8PE
tel (01285) 760030
website www.amberleybooks.com
Chief Executive Alan Sutton, *Chief Operating Officer* Alan Marley, *Sales Manager* Stephen Lambe
Local and specialist history publishing. Founded 2008.

Amgueddfa Cymru – National Museum Wales
Cathays Park, Cardiff CF10 3NP
tel 029-2057 3155 *fax* 029-2057 3321
email books@museumwales.ac.uk
website www.museumwales.ac.uk
Head of Publishing Mari Gordon
Books based on the collections and research of Amgueddfa Cymru for adults, schools and children, in both Welsh and English.

a-n The Artists Information Company
Head office: 1st Floor, 7–15 Pink Lane, Newcastle upon Tyne NE1 5DW
tel 0191-241 8000 *fax* 0191-241 8001
email edit@a-n.co.uk
website www.a-n.co.uk
Information, research and publications for the visual arts sector including www.a-n.co.uk with online expert publications, professional development resources including toolkits, *a-n Magazine* 10 issues annually, and portfolio of user-generated specialist websites including Interface, Artists Talking, Jobs and opps and Degrees unedited. Editor Gillian Nicol. Founded 1980.

Andersen Press Ltd
20 Vauxhall Bridge Road, London SW1V 2SA
tel 020-7840 8703 (editorial) 020-7840 8701 (general)
fax 020-7233 6263
email andersenpress@randomhouse.co.uk
website www.andersenpress.co.uk
Managing Director/Publisher Klaus Flugge, *Directors* Philip Durrance, Joëlle Flugge, Rona Selby (editorial), Sarah Pakenham (rights), Mark Hendle (finance)
Children's books: picture books, junior and teenage fiction (send synopsis and first 3 chapters with sae); no short stories or poetry. International co-productions. Founded 1976.

The Angels' Share – see Neil Wilson Publishing Ltd

Angry Robot – see HarperCollins Publishers

Anness Publishing
88–89 Blackfriars Road, London SE1 8HA
tel 020-7401 2077 *fax* 020-7775 4441
email info@anness.com
website www.annesspublishing.com, www.lorenzbooks.com, www.southwaterbooks.com, www.aquamarine.co.uk
Managing Director Paul Anness, *Publisher* Joanna Lorenz
Practical illustrated books on lifestyle, cookery, crafts, reference, gardening, health and children's non-fiction. Founded 1988.

Anness Publishing
website www.annesspublishing.com
High-quality illustrated non-fiction: lifestyle, cookery, crafts, gardening.

Lorenz Books (hardback imprint)
website www.lorenzbooks.com
High-quality illustrated non-fiction: lifestyle, cookery, crafts, gardening.

Southwater (paperback imprint)
website www.southwaterbooks.com
Illustrated promotional books on practical subjects.

Hermes House (promotional imprint)
website www.hermeshouse.com
Photolibrary of over 400,000 images generated in the process of developing 3000 titles in the past 15 years.

Practical Pictures (image licensing)
website www.practicalpictures.com

Anova Books
The Old Magistrate's Court, 10 Southcombe Street, London W14 0RA
tel 020-7605 1400 *fax* 020-7605 1401
email customerservices@anovabooks.com
website www.anovabooks.com
Chairman Robin Wood, *Chief Executive* Polly Powell, *Operations & Production Director* David Proffit

Founded 2005; formerly Chrysalis Books Group.

Batsford (imprint)
Publisher Tina Persaud
Chess and bridge, art techniques, film, fashion and costume, practical craft, gardening, embroidery, lace, woodwork.

Collins & Brown (imprint)
Publisher Katie Cowan
Lifestyle and interiors, cookery, gardening, photography, practical arts, health and beauty, hobbies and crafts, natural history, history, ancient civilisation and general interest, including Good Housekeeping branded books.

Conway (inc. Brasseys Military, Putnam Aeronautical)
Publisher John Lee
History and highly illustrated reference books on naval and maritime, aviation and military subjects.

National Trust (imprint)
Heritage, gardens, cookery.

Paper Tiger (imprint)
Science fiction and fantasy art.

Pavilion (imprint)
Associate Publisher Anna Chiefetz
Cookery, gardening, travel, sport, photography, art, popular culture, gift.

Portico (imprint)
Narrative non-fiction, humour, popular culture, quirky reference, sport.

Robson Books (imprint)
General non-fiction, biography, music, humour, sport.

Salamander (imprint)
Packager of made-to-order books on cookery, crafts, military, natural history, music, gardening, hobbies, transport, sports, popular reference.

Anova Children's Books – see Pavilion Children's Books

Antique Collectors' Club Ltd
Sandy Lane, Old Martlesham, Woodbridge, Suffolk IP12 4SD
tel (01394) 389950 *fax* (01394) 389999
email info@antique-acc.com
website www.antiquecollectorsclub.com
Managing Director Diana Steel

Fine art, antiques, fashion, design, gardening and garden history, architecture. Founded 1966.

Anvil Books/The Children's Press†
45 Palmerston Road, Dublin 6, Republic of Ireland
tel (01) 4973628 *fax* (01) 496 8263
Directors Rena Dardis (managing), Margaret Dardis (editorial)

Anvil: Irish history and biography. Children's Press: adventure fiction for ages 9–14. Unsolicited MSS not accepted. Founded 1964.

Anvil Press Poetry
Neptune House, 70 Royal Hill, London SE10 8RF
tel 020-8469 3033 *fax* 020-8469 3363
email anvil@anvilpresspoetry.com
website www.anvilpresspoetry.com
Director Peter Jay

Poetry. Submissions only by post with sae. Founded 1968.

Appletree Press Ltd†
tel 028-9024 3074 *fax* 028-9024 6756
email reception@appletree.ie
website www.appletree.ie
Director John Murphy

Gift books, guidebooks, history, Irish interest, Scottish interest, photography, sport, travel. Founded 1974.

Aquamarine – see Anness Publishing

Arabia Books – see Haus Publishing Ltd

Arc Publications
Nanholme Mill, Shaw Wood Road, Todmorden, Lancs. OL14 6DA
tel (01706) 812338 *fax* (01706) 818948
email info@arcpublications.co.uk
website www.arcpublications.co.uk
Directors Tony Ward, Angela Jarman, *Editors* John Kinsella (international), Jean Boase-Beier (translation), Philip Wilson (translation – 'classic series'), John W. Clarke (UK & Ireland), Angela Jarman (music)

Specialises in contemporary poetry and neglected work from the past: poetry from the UK and Ireland; world poetry in English; and bilingual translations (individual poets and anthologies). Refer to website for current publication list/catalogue and submissions policy. No unsolicited MSS.

Arcadia Books Ltd
15–16 Nassau Street, London W1W 7AB
tel 020-7436 9898
email info@arcadiabooks.co.uk
website www.arcadiabooks.co.uk
Publisher Gary Pulsifer, *Associate Publisher* Daniela de Groote, *Managing Editor* Angeline Rothermundt

Original fiction, fiction in translation, autobiography, biography, travel, gender studies, gay books. Publishers of José Eduardo Agualusa's *The Book of Chameleons*, winner of the Independent Foreign Fiction Prize 2007 and Dominique Manotti's *Lorraine Connection*, winner of the International Dagger 2008. Submissions via literary agents only. Founded 1996.

BlackAmber (imprint)
Black and Asian writing.

Bliss Books (imprint)
Popular fiction and non-fiction.

Euro Crime (imprint)
Quality crime from Europe.

The Maia Press (imprint)
Début fiction both in English and in translation.

Architectural Press – see Elsevier Ltd

Arcturus – see W. Foulsham & Co. Ltd

Arden Shakespeare – see A&C Black Publishers Ltd

Arris Publishing Ltd

12 Main Street, Adlestrop, Moreton-in-Marsh, Glos. GL56 0UN
tel (01608) 658758
email victoriama.huxley@btinternet.com
website www.arrisbooks.com
Managing Director Geoffrey Smith, *Publishing Director* Victoria Huxley

History, politics, *The Traveller's History* series, *The Travellers' Wildlife Guides*. Imprint: Chastleton Travel. Founded 2003.

Arrow Books Ltd – see The Random House Group Ltd

Ashgate Publishing Ltd

Wey Court East, Union Road, Farnham GU9 9PT
tel (01252) 736600 *fax* (01252) 736736
email info@ashgatepub.co.uk
website www.ashgate.com
Chairman Nigel Farrow, *Managing Director and Humanities Publishing Director* Rachel Lynch, *Social Sciences Publishing Director* Adrian Shanks, *President Ashgate US* Barbara Church
Humanities Ann Donahue (Literary Studies, 19th–20th centuries), Erika Gaffney (Literary Studies to 18th century; Visual Studies), Heidi May (Music), Sarah Lloyd (Theology & Religious Studies), Thomas Gray (History), John Smedley (Publishing Director, Variorum imprint; History)
Social Sciences Alison Kirk (Law), Guy Loft (Aviation), Kirstin Howgate (International Relations; Politics), Val Rose (Human Geography; Planning & Design), Neil Jordan (Sociology), Dymphna Evans (Publisher, Reference and LIM)

Publishes a wide range of academic research in the social sciences and humanities, professional practice publications in the management of business and public services, and illustrated books on art, architecture and design. Founded 1967.

Gower (imprint)
website www.gowerpub.com
Publishing Director & Commissioning Editor Jonathan Norman
Business, management and training.

Lund Humphries (imprint)
website www.lundhumphries.com
Managing Director Lucy Myers
Art and architectural history.

Variorum (imprint)
Publishing Director John Smedley
History.

Ashmolean Museum Publications

Beaumont Street, Oxford OX1 2PH
tel (01865) 278010 *fax* (01865) 278108
website www.ashmolean.org
Contact Declan McCarthy

Fine and applied art of Europe and Asia, archaeology, history, numismatics. No unsolicited MSS. Photographic archive. Museum founded 1683.

Aslib (The Association for Information Management)

207 Davina House, 137–149 Goswell Road, London EC1V 7ET
tel 020-7253 3349 *fax* 020-7490 0577
email furtherinformation@aslib.com
website www.aslib.com

For books and journals contact Emerald *tel* (01206) 796351; for *Managing Information* magazine contact Graham Coult (editor), gcoult@aslib.com.

Atlantic Books

Ormond House, 26–27 Boswell Street, London WC1N 3JZ
tel 020-7269 1610 *fax* 020-7430 0916
email enquiries@groveatlantic.co.uk
Ceo & Publisher Toby Mundy, *Editor-in-Chief* Ravi Mirchandani

Literary fiction, thrillers; history, current affairs, politics, reference, biography, memoir. Strictly no unsolicited submissions or proposals. Subsidiary of Grove/Atlantic Inc., New York. Founded 2000.

Atlantic Europe Publishing Co. Ltd

Greys Court Farm, Greys Court, Henley-on-Thames, Oxon RG9 4PG
tel (01491) 628188 *fax* (01491) 628189
email info@atlanticeurope.com
website www.atlanticeurope.com, www.curriculumvisions.com

Director Dr B.J. Knapp

Children's primary school class books: science, geography, technology, mathematics, history, religious education. No MSS accepted by post; submit by email only with no attachments. Founded 1990.

Atom – see Little, Brown Book Group

Atrium – see Cork University Press

Attic Press – see Cork University Press

Aureus Publishing Ltd

Castle Court, Castle-upon-Alun, St Bride's Major, Vale of Glamorgan CF32 0TN
tel (01656) 880033 *fax* (01656) 880033
email info@aureus.co.uk
website www.aureus.co.uk
Director Meuryn Hughes

Rock and pop, autobiography, biography, sport; also music. Founded 1993.

Aurora Metro

67 Grove Avenue, Twickenham TW1 4HX
tel 020-3261 0000 *fax* 020-8898 0735
email info@aurorametro.com
website www.aurorametro.com
Director Cheryl Robson

Drama (including plays for young people), fiction, non-fiction and translation.

Aurum Press Ltd

7 Greenland Street, London NW1 0ND
tel 020-7284 7160 020-7485 4902
email firstname.surname@aurumpress.co.uk
website www.aurumpress.co.uk
Directors Bill McCreadie (managing), Laurence Orbach (non-executive), Mick Mousley (non-executive)

General, illustrated and non-illustrated adult non-fiction: biography and memoirs, military, visual arts, film, sport, travel, fashion, home interest. Imprints: Argentum (photography), Jacqui Small (lifestyle). Founded 1977.

Authentic Media Ltd

c/o 500 Avebury Boulevard, Milton Keynes MK9 2BE
tel (0190) 8 54 7872
email info@authenticmedia.co.uk
website www.authenticmedia.co.uk
Publisher Mark Finnie

Biblical studies, Christian theology, ethics, history, mission, commentaries. Imprints: Paternoster, Authentic, Spring Harvest, Keswick, Youthwork, Evangelical Alliance, Regnum, Rutherford House, Paternoster Periodicals.

Avon – see HarperCollins Publishers

Award Publications Ltd

The Old Riding School, The Welbeck Estate, Worksop, Notts. S80 3LR
tel (01909) 478170 *fax* (01909) 484632
email info@awardpublications.co.uk

Children's books: full colour picture story books; early learning, information and activity books. No unsolicited material. Founded 1954.

Bernard Babani (publishing) Ltd

The Grampians, Shepherds Bush Road, London W6 7NF
tel 020-7603 2581/7296 *fax* 020-7603 8203
Director M.H. Babani

Practical handbooks on radio, electronics and computing.

Bailliere Tindall – see Elsevier Ltd (Health Sciences)

Duncan Baird Publishers

6th Floor, Castle House, 75–76 Wells Street, London W1T 3QH
tel 020-7323 2229 *fax* 020-7580 5692
website www.dbp.co.uk
Directors Duncan Baird (managing), Bob Saxton (editorial), Roger Walton (art), Alex Mitchell (international sales), Ryan Tring (financial), Adela Cory (production)

Health and wellbeing, cookery, Mind, Body & Spirit, cultural reference. Founded 1992.

Bantam – see Transworld Publishers

Bantam Press – see Transworld Publishers

Bantam Press (children's) – see The Random House Group Ltd

Barefoot Books Ltd

124 Walcot Street, Bath BA1 5BG
tel (01225) 322400 *fax* (01225) 322499
email info@barefootbooks.co.uk
website www.barefootbooks.com
Editor-in-Chief Tessa Strickland, *Executive Editor* Emma Parlin

Children's picture books and audiobooks: myth, legend, fairytale, cross-cultural stories. No MSS currently being commissioned. Founded 1993.

Barrington Stoke

18 Walker Street, Edinburgh EH3 7LP
tel 0131-225 4113 *fax* 0131-225 4140
email info@barringtonstoke.co.uk
website www.barringtonstoke.co.uk
Chairman Ben Thomson, *Managing Director* Sonia Raphael, *Editorial Manager* Kate Paice

Short fiction and non-fiction, specially adapted and presented for reluctant, struggling and dyslexic readers, aged 9–12 and 13+, with reading ages of 6–8. Short fiction (15,000 words) for adults with a reading age of 8. No picture books, no unsolicited submissions. Founded 1998.

Batsford – see Anova Books

BBC Audiobooks Ltd
St James House, The Square, Lower Bristol Road, Bath BA2 3BH
tel (01225) 878000
website www.bbcaudiobooks.com, www.audiobookcollection.com
Directors Paul Dempsey (managing), Jan Paterson (publishing)

Large print books and complete and unabridged audiobooks: general fiction, crime, romance, mystery/thrillers, westerns, non-fiction. Does not publish original books. Imprints: Chivers Large Print, Chivers Audio Books, Black Dagger Crime, Windsor Large Print, Galaxy Children's Large Print. Formed in 2002 from the amalgamation of Chivers Press, Cover To Cover and BBC Radio Collection.

BBC Books – see The Random House Group Ltd

BBC Children's Books – see Penguin Group (UK)

BBC Worldwide Ltd – see page 395

Beautiful Books
36–38 Glasshouse Street, London W1B 5DL
tel 020-7734 4448 *fax* 020-3070 0764
email office@beautiful-books.co.uk
website www.beautiful-books.co.uk
Managing Director Simon Petherick

Adult fiction and non-fiction.

Submission details Send a 2pp synopsis, the first 30pp of text, plus a short biography about yourself with sae for return of material. Founded 2004.

Belair – see Folens Publishers

Bell & Hyman Ltd – acquired by HarperCollins Publishers

Berg Publishers
1st Floor, Angel Court, 81 St Clements Street, Oxford OX4 1AW
tel (01865) 245104 *fax* (01865) 791165
website www.bergpublishers.com
Managing Director Kathryn Earle

Fashion studies, design studies, food studies, cultural studies, visual culture, social anthropology, film studies. Founded 1983.

Berlin Verlag – see Bloomsbury Publishing Plc

Berlitz Publishing – see Insight Guides/Berlitz Publishing

BFI Publishing
Palgrave Macmillan, The Macmillan Building, 4 Crinan Street, London N1 9XW
tel 020-7833 4000 *fax* 020-7843 4640
website www.palgrave.com/bfi
Head of Publishing Rebecca Barden

Film, TV and media studies; general, academic and educational resources on moving image culture. Founded 1982.

Clive Bingley Ltd – see Facet Publishing

BIOS Scientific Publishers – see Taylor and Francis Group

Birlinn Ltd
West Newington House, 10 Newington Road, Edinburgh EH9 1QS
tel 0131-668 4371 *fax* 0131-668 4466
email info@birlinn.co.uk
website www.birlinn.co.uk
Directors Hugh Andrew, Neville Moir, William MacRobert, Jan Rutherford, Maria White

Scottish history, local interest/history, Scottish humour, guides, military, adventure, history, archaeology, sport, general non-fiction. Imprints: John Donald, Polygon. Founded 1992.

Polygon (imprint)
New international and Scottish fiction, poetry, short stories, popular Scottish and international general interest. No unsolicited poetry accepted.

John Donald (imprint)
Scottish academic titles.

Mercat Press (imprint)
Walking guides.

Birnbaum – see HarperCollins Publishers

A&C Black Publishers Ltd*
36 Soho Square, London W1D 3QY
tel 020-7758 0200 *fax* 020-7758 0222
email enquiries@acblack.com
website www.acblack.com
Chairman Nigel Newton, *Managing Director* Jill Coleman, *Deputy Managing Director* Jonathan Glasspool, *Directors* Oscar Heini (production), Janet Murphy (Adlard Coles Nautical), Jayne Parsons (children's and music), David Wightman (sales), Chris Facey (finance)

Children's and educational books (including music) for 3–15 year-olds, ceramics, art and craft, drama, ornithology, reference (*Who's Who, Whitaker's Almanack*), sport, theatre, books for writers, dictionaries. Subsidiary of Bloomsbury Publishing Plc. Founded 1807.

Adlard Coles Nautical (imprint)
Nautical.

Andrew Brodie (imprint)
Children's, educational.

Featherstone Education (imprint)
Children's, educational.

Christopher Helm (imprint)
Ornithology.

The Herbert Press (imprint)
Visual arts.

Methuen Drama (imprint)
Drama.

Pica Press (imprint)
Ornithology.

T & AD Poyser (imprint)
Ornithology, natural history.

Thomas Reed (imprint)
Nautical.

Reeds Nautical Almanac (imprint)
Navigation and port information.

Arden Shakespeare (imprint)
Drama/English.

John Wisden and Co. Ltd (imprint)
Sports.

Black Ace Books

PO Box 7547, Perth PH2 1AU
tel (01821) 642822 *fax* (01821) 642101
website www.blackacebooks.com
Publisher Hunter Steele, *Art, Publicity & Sales Director* Boo Wood

Fiction, Scottish and general; new editions of outstanding recent fiction. Some biography, history, psychology and philosophy. No submissions without first visiting website for latest list details and requirements. Imprints: Black Ace Books, Black Ace Paperbacks. Founded 1991.

Black & White Publishing Ltd*

29 Ocean Drive, Edinburgh EH6 6JL
tel 0131-625 4500 *fax* 0131-625 4501
email mail@blackandwhitepublishing.com
website www.blackandwhitepublishing.com
Directors Campbell Brown (managing), Alison McBride

Non-fiction: humour, biography, crime, sport, cookery, general. Fiction: classic Scottish, contemporary, crime. Founded 1999.

Black Dagger Crime – see BBC Audiobooks Ltd

Black Dog Publishing London UK

10A Acton Street, London WC1X 9NG
tel 020-7713 5097 *fax* 020-7713 8682
email editorial@blackdogonline.com
website www.blackdogonline.com

Contemporary art, architecture, design, photography.

Black Lace – see Virgin Books, page 182

Black Swan – see Transworld Publishers

BlackAmber – see Arcadia Books Ltd

Blackstaff Press Ltd†

4C Heron Wharf, Sydenham Business Park, Belfast BT3 9LE
tel 028-9045 5006 *fax* 028-9046 6237
email info@blackstaffpress.com
website www.blackstaffpress.com
Managing Editor Patsy Horton

Adult fiction, biography, history, sport, politics, cookery, natural history, humour and travel. See website for submission guidelines before sending material. Founded 1971.

Blackstone Press Ltd – acquired by Oxford University Press

Blackwater Press – see Folens Publishers

John Blake Publishing Ltd

(incorporating Metro Books and Smith Gryphon Ltd)
3 Bramber Court, 2 Bramber Road, London W14 9PB
tel 020-7381 0666 *fax* 020-7381 6868
email words@blake.co.uk
website www.johnblakepublishing.co.uk

Popular non-fiction, including biographies, true crime, food and drink, health. No unsolicited fiction. Founded 1991.

Bliss Books – see Arcadia Books Ltd

Bloodaxe Books Ltd

Highgreen, Tarset, Northumberland NE48 1RP
tel (01434) 240500 *fax* (01434) 240505
email editor@bloodaxebooks.com
website www.bloodaxebooks.com
Directors Neil Astley, Simon Thirsk

Poetry. Send sample of up to a dozen poems with sae. No email submissions or correspondence. No disks. Founded 1978.

Bloomsbury Publishing Plc*

36 Soho Square, London W1D 3QY
tel 020-7494 2111 *fax* 020-7434 0151
website www.bloomsbury.com
Non-executive Chairman Jeremy Wilson, *Founder and Chief Executive* Nigel Newton, *Executive Director* Richard Charkin, *Group Finance Director* Colin Adams, *Non-executive Directors* Charles Black, Mike Mayer

Bloomsbury Publishing UK (imprint)
Directors Alexandra Pringle (adult publishing), Sarah Odedina (children's publishing), Kathleen Farrar

(marketing – sales & publicity), David Ward (UK sales), Kathleen Farrar (international marketing & sales), Penny Edwards (production), Stephanie Duncan (digital), Michael Fishwick (publishing), Ruth Logan (rights), Katie Bond (publicity), Nelka Bell (finance)
Fiction, biography, illustrated, travel, children's, trade paperbacks and mass market paperbacks. No unsolicited MSS. Founded 1986.

Bloomsbury Academic (imprint of A&C Black)
Managing Director Jonathan Glasspool, *Publisher* Dr Frances Pinter, *Editors* Caroline Wintersgill, Emily Salz
Monographs and textbooks in the humanities and social sciences.

A&C Black Publishers Ltd (subsidiary)
Managing Director Jill Coleman
See page 141.

Berg (imprint of Bloomsbury Academic)
Managing Director Kathryn Earle
See page 141.

Bloomsbury Information (imprint)
Managing Director Kathy Rooney
Reference.

Blue Door – see HarperCollins Publishers

Blue Guides Ltd
27 John Street, London WC1N 2BX
email editorial@blueguides.com
website www.blueguides.com
Blue Guides (cultural travel guide books), *Visible Cities* and *art/shop/eat* series.

BMJ Books – see Wiley-Blackwell

Boatswain Press Ltd – now Nautical Data Ltd

Bodleian Library Publishing
Osney One, Osney Mead, Oxford OX2 0EW
tel (01865) 283850 *fax* (01865) 277620
email publishing@bodleian.ox.ac.uk
website www.bodleianbookshop.co.uk
Head of Publishing Samuel Fanous
History, literature, arts, history of the book, botanical, cartographic and facsimiles and editions. All titles are related to the Bodleian Library's collections. Founded 1604.

The Bodley Head – see The Random House Group Ltd

Bodley Head Children's Books – see The Random House Group Ltd

Booth-Clibborn Editions
Studio 83, 235 Earls Court Road, London SW5 9FE
tel 020-7565 0688 *fax* 020-7244 1018
email info@booth-clibborn.com
website www.booth-clibborn.com
Illustrated books on art, popular culture, graphic design, photography. Founded 1974.

Bounty – see Octopus Publishing Group

Bowker
18–20 St Andrew's House, St Andrew Street, London EC4A 3AG
tel 020-7832 1770 *fax* 020-7832 1710
email sales@bowker.co.uk
website www.bowker.com
Managing Director Doug McMillan
Publishes bibliographic information for the library, business and publishing communities in print and online formats. Flagship products include *Books in Print, Global Books in Print* and *Syndetic Solutions.*

Boxtree – see Macmillan Publishers Ltd

Marion Boyars Publishers Ltd
24 Lacy Road, London SW15 1NL
tel 020-8788 9522 *fax* 020-8789 8122
email catheryn@marionboyars.com
website www.marionboyars.co.uk
Directors Catheryn Kilgarriff, Rebecca Gillieron (Editorial)
Literary fiction, film, memoirs, travel, cultural studies, jazz, music, cookery. Will only consider fiction submitted through an agent. Founded 1975.

Boydell & Brewer Ltd
Whitwell House, St Audrey's Park Road, Melton, Woodbridge, Suffolk IP12 1SY
tel (01394) 610600 *fax* (01394) 610316
email editorial@boydell.co.uk
website www.boydellandbrewer.com
Medieval studies, early modern and modern history, maritime history, literature, archaeology, art history, music, Hispanic studies. No unsolicited MSS. See website for submission guidelines. Founded 1969.

James Currey (imprint)
website www.jamescurrey.com
Academic studies of Africa and developing economies.

Bradt Travel Guides Ltd
23 High Street, Chalfont St Peter, Bucks. SL9 9QE
tel (01753) 893444 *fax* (01753) 892333
email info@bradtguides.com
website www.bradtguides.com
Managing Director Donald Greig
Travel and wildlife guides with emphasis on unusual destinations and ethical/positive travel.

Brandon/Mount Eagle Publications†
(incorporating Brandon Book Publishers Ltd, 1982)
Cooleen, Dingle, Co. Kerry, Republic of Ireland

tel (353) 66 9151463 *fax* (353) 66 9151234
Publisher Steve MacDonogh

Fiction, biography and current affairs. No unsolicited MSS.

Brasseys Military – see Anova Books

Nicholas Brealey Publishing
3–5 Spafield Street, London EC1R 4QB
tel 020-7239 0360 *fax* 020-7239 0370
email rights@nicholasbrealey.com
website www.nicholasbrealey.com
Managing Director Nicholas Brealey

Business and economics, popular psychology, cross-cultural studies, travel writing. Founded 1992 in London; also has offices in Boston. Imprints include Davies-Black business books and Intercultural Press.

Breedon Books Publishing Co. Ltd – see The Derby Books Publishing Company Ltd

Brilliant Publications
Unit 10, Sparrow Hall Farm, Edlesborough, Dunstable LU6 2ES
tel (01525) 222292 *fax* (01525) 222720
email info@brilliantpublications.co.uk
website www.brilliantpublications.co.uk
Managing Director Priscilla Hannaford

Practical resource books for teachers and others concerned with the education of 0–13 year-olds. All areas of the curriculum published, but specialises in modern foreign languages, art and design, developing thinking skills and PSHE. Some series of books for reluctant readers, aimed at 7–11 year-olds. No children's picture books, non-fiction books or one-off fiction books. See 'Manuscripts guidelines' on website before sending proposal. Founded 1993.

The British Library (Publications)*
Publishing Office, The British Library, 96 Euston Road, London NW1 2DB
tel 020-7412 7535 *fax* 020-7412 7768
email publishing_editorial@bl.uk
website www.bl.uk
Managers David Way (publishing), Catherine Britton (editorial)

Book arts, bibliography, music, maps, oriental, manuscript studies, history, literature, facsimiles, audio and multimedia. Founded 1979.

British Museum Company Ltd*
38 Russell Square, London WC1B 3QQ
tel 020-7323 1234 *fax* 020-7436 7315
email publicity@britishmuseum.co.uk
website www.britishmuseum.co.uk
Managing Director Brian Oldman, *Director of Publishing* Rosemary Bradley

General and specialist adult and children's books on art history, archaeology, history, and world cultures. Division of The British Museum Company Ltd. Founded 1973.

Brockhampton Press – see Caxton Publishing Group

Andrew Brodie – see A&C Black Publishers Ltd

Brown, Son & Ferguson, Ltd*
4–10 Darnley Street, Glasgow G41 2SD
tel 0141-429 1234 (24 hours) *fax* 0141-420 1694
email info@skipper.co.uk
website www.skipper.co.uk
Editorial Director Richard B.P. Brown

Nautical books, plays. Founded 1860.

Bryntirion Press
(formerly Evangelical Press of Wales)
Bryntirion, Bridgend CF31 4DX
tel (01656) 655886 *fax* (01656) 665919
email office@emw.org.uk
website www.emw.org.uk
Publications Officer Gethin Rhys

Theology and religion (in English and Welsh). Founded 1955.

Burns & Oates – see The Continuum International Publishing Group Ltd

Business Plus – see Headline Publishing Group

Buster Books – see Michael O'Mara Books Ltd

Butterworth-Heinemann – see Elsevier Ltd

Butterworths – see LexisNexis

Cadogan Guides – see New Holland Publishers (UK) Ltd

Calmann & King Ltd – see Laurence King Publishing Ltd

Cambridge University Press*
The Edinburgh Building, Shaftesbury Road, Cambridge CB2 8RU
tel (01223) 312393 *fax* (01223) 315052
email information@cambridge.org
website www.cambridge.org
Chief Executive of the Press Stephen R.R. Bourne, *Managing Director, Europe, Middle East & Africa* Andrew Gilfillan, *Managing Director, Academic Publishing* Andrew Brown, *Managing Director, Cambridge Learning (English Language Teaching and Education)* Hanri Pieterse

Anthropology and archaeology, art history, astronomy, biological sciences, classical studies, computer science, dictionaries, earth sciences, economics, educational (primary, secondary, tertiary), e-learning products, engineering, English language teaching, history, language and literature, law, mathematics, medical sciences, music, philosophy, physical sciences, politics, psychology, reference, technology, social sciences, theology, religion. Journals (humanities, social sciences, science, technical and medical). The Bible and Prayer Book. Founded 1534.

Campbell Books – see Macmillan Publishers Ltd

Canongate Books Ltd*

14 High Street, Edinburgh EH1 1TE
tel 0131-557 5111 *fax* 0131-557 5211
email info@canongate.co.uk
website www.canongate.net
Publisher Jamie Byng, *Directors* Kathleen Anderson (financial), Caroline Gorham (production), Jenny Todd (sales & marketing), Polly Collingridge (rights), Anya Serota (publishing), Nick Davies (non-fiction), *Senior Editor* Francis Bickmore (fiction)

Adult general non-fiction and fiction: literary fiction, translated fiction, memoir, pop science, humour, travel, popular culture, history and biography. No unsolicited MSS. Founded 1973.

Canopus Publishing Ltd

15 Nelson Parade, Bedminster, Bristol BS3 4HY
tel 0117-963 3366
email robin@canopusbooks.com
website www.canopusbooks.com
Directors Robin Rees, Tom Spicer, *Commissioning Editor* Jim Revill

Popular science and astronomy. Founded 1999.

Canterbury Press – see SCM Canterbury Press Ltd

Jonathan Cape Children's Books – see The Random House Group Ltd

Carcanet Press Ltd

4th Floor, Alliance House, 30 Cross Street, Manchester M2 7AQ
tel 0161-834 8730 *fax* 0161-832 0084
email info@carcanet.co.uk
website www.carcanet.co.uk
Director Michael Schmidt

Poetry, *Fyfield* series, Oxford Poets, translations. Founded 1969.

Carlton Publishing Group

20 Mortimer Street, London W1T 3JW
tel 020-7612 0400 *fax* 020-7612 0401
email enquiries@carltonbooks.co.uk
website www.carltonbooks.co.uk
Chairman Jonathan Goodman, *Editorial Director* Piers Murray Hill

No unsolicited MSS; synopses and ideas welcome, but no fiction or poetry. Imprints: Carlton Books, André Deutsch, Goodman, Prion Books. Founded 1992.

Carlton Books (division)

Sport, music, history, military history, puzzles, lifestyle, popular culture, crime, children's interactive.

André Deutsch (division)

Autobiography, biography, history, current affairs.

Goodman (imprint)

Art and design.

Prion Books (division)

Humour, nostalgia, drink.

Cassell Illustrated – see Octopus Publishing Group

Cassell Reference – see Weidenfeld & Nicolson

Caterpillar Books – see Magi Publications

Kyle Cathie Ltd

23 Howland Street, London W1T 4AY
tel 020-7692 7215 *fax* 020-7692 7260
email general.enquiries@kyle-cathie.com
website www.kylecathie.com
Publisher & Managing Director Kyle Cathie

Health, beauty, food and drink, gardening, reference, style, design, Mind, Body & Spirit. Founded 1990.

Catholic Truth Society

40–46 Harleyford Road, London SE11 5AY
tel 020-7640 0042 *fax* 020-7640 0046
email editorial@cts-online.org.uk
website www.cts-online.org.uk
Chairman Rt Rev. Paul Hendricks, *General Secretary* Fergal Martin LLB, LLM

General books of Roman Catholic and Christian interest, bibles, prayer books, RE, and booklets of doctrinal, historical, devotional or social interest. MSS of 11,000–15,000 words with up to 6 illustrations considered for publication as booklets. Founded 1868.

Caxton Publishing Group

20 Bloomsbury Street, London WC1B 3JH
tel 020-7636 7171 *fax* 020-7636 1922
website www.caxtonpublishing.com
Director Finbarr McCabe

Reprints, promotional books, remainders. Imprints: Caxton Editions, Brockhampton Press, Knight Paperbacks.

CBD Research Ltd

15 Wickham Road, Beckenham, Kent BR3 5JS
tel 020-8650 7745 *fax* 020-8650 0768

email cbd@cbdresearch.com
website www.cbdresearch.com
Directors S.P.A. Henderson, A.J.W. Henderson

Directories, reference books, bibliographies, guides to business and statistical information. Founded 1961.

Chancery House Press (imprint)

Unusual non-fiction/reference works. Preliminary letter and synopsis with return postage essential.

Cengage Learning

Cheriton House, Andover SP10 5BE
tel (01264) 332424 *fax* (01264) 342745
email emea.editorial@cengage.com
website www. cengage.co.uk
Contact Publishing Director

Actively commissioning texts for further education and higher education courses in the following disciplines: IT, computer science and computer applications; accounting, finance and economics; marketing; international business; human resource management; operations management; strategic management; organisational behaviour; business information systems; quantitative methods; psychology; hairdressing and beauty therapy; childcare; catering and hospitality; motor vehicle maintenance. Submit proposal either by email or by post.

Century – see The Random House Group Ltd

The Chalford Press – see The History Press Ltd

Chambers Harrap Publishers Ltd – see Hodder Education Group

Chancery House Press – see CBD Research Ltd

Channel 4 Books – see Transworld Publishers

Chapman Publishing

4 Broughton Place, Edinburgh EH1 3RX
tel 0131-557 2207
email chapman-pub@blueyonder.co.uk
website www.chapman-pub.co.uk
Editor Joy Hendry

Poetry and drama: *Chapman New Writing Series*. Also the *Chapman Wild Women Series*. Founded 1970.

Paul Chapman Publishing – see SAGE Publications Ltd

Chartered Institute of Personnel and Development

CIPD Publishing, 151 The Broadway, London SW19 1JQ
tel 020-8612 6200 *fax* 020-8612 6201
email publish@cipd.co.uk
website www.cipd.co.uk/bookstore
Publishing Manager Ruth Lake

Personnel management, training and development.

Cherrytree Books – see Zero to Ten Ltd

The Chicken House

2 Palmer Street, Frome, Somerset BA11 1DS
tel (01373) 454488 *fax* (01373) 454499
email chickenhouse@doublecluck.com
website www.doublecluck.com
Managing Director & Publisher Barry Cunningham, *Deputy Managing Director* Rachel Hickman

Fiction for age 7+, picture books and teenage. No unsolicited MSS. See website for competition details. Part of Scholastic Inc.

Child's Play (International) Ltd

Ashworth Road, Bridgemead, Swindon, Wilts. SN5 7YD
tel (01793) 616286 *fax* (01793) 512795
email office@childs-play.com
website www.childs-play.com
Chairman Adriana Twinn, *Publisher* Neil Burden

Children's educational books: board, picture, activity and play books; fiction and non-fiction. Founded 1972.

Chivers Press – see BBC Audiobooks Ltd

Christian Education*

(incorporating RE Today Services and International Bible Reading Association)
1020 Bristol Road, Selly Oak, Birmingham B29 6LB
tel 0121-472 4242 *fax* 0121-472 7575
email enquiries@christianeducation.org.uk
website www.christianeducation.org.uk

Publications and services for teachers of RE including *REtoday* magazine, curriculum booklets, training material for children and youth workers in the Church. Worship resources for use in primary schools. Activity Club material and Bible reading resources.

Chrysalis Books Group – now Anova Books

Churchill Livingstone – see Elsevier Ltd (Health Sciences)

Churchwarden Publications Ltd

PO Box 420, Warminster, Wilts. BA12 9XB
tel (01985) 840189 *fax* (01985) 840243
email enquiries@churchwardenbooks.co.uk
Directors J.N.G. Stidolph, S.A. Stidolph

Church administration. Ideas and MSS welcome.

Cicerone Press

2 Police Square, Milnthorpe, Cumbria LA7 7PY
tel (01539) 562069 *fax* (01539) 563417

email info@cicerone.co.uk
website www.cicerone.co.uk
Managing Director Jonathan Williams

Guidebooks: walking, trekking, mountaineering, climbing, cycling, etc in Britain, Europe, and worldwide.

Cima Books – now Cico Books (imprint)

Cisco Press – see Pearson UK

T&T Clark International – see The Continuum International Publishing Group Ltd

James Clarke & Co. Ltd

PO Box 60, Cambridge CB1 2NT
tel (01223) 350865 *fax* (01223) 366951
email publishing@jamesclarke.co.uk
website www.jamesclarke.co.uk

Theology, philosophy, history and biography, biblical studies, literary criticism; academic and reference books. Founded 1859.

Lutterworth Press (subsidiary)

History and biography, arts, literature and criticism, educational titles, biblical studies, theology, mission, religious reference. Imprints: Acorn Editions, Patrick Hardy Books.

Classical Comics

PO Box 7280, Litchborough, Towcester NN12 9AR
tel (0845) 812 3000
email info@classicalcomics.co.uk
website www.classicalcomics.com
Managing Director Clive Bryant

Graphic novel adaptations of classical literature.

Cló Iar-Chonnachta Teo.†

Indreabhán, Conamara, Co. Galway, Republic of Ireland
tel (091) 593307 *fax* (091) 593362
email cic@iol.ie
website www.cic.ie
Director Micheál Ó Conghaile, *General Manager* Deirdre O'Toole

Irish-language – novels, short stories, plays, poetry, songs, history; CDs (writers reading from their works in Irish and English). Promotes the translation of contemporary Irish fiction and poetry into other languages. Founded 1985.

Co & Bear Productions

63 Edith Grove, London SW10 0LB
tel 020-7351 5545 *fax* 020-7351 5547
email info@cobear.co.uk
website www.scriptumeditions.co.uk
Publisher Beatrice Vincenzini

High-quality illustrated books on lifestyle, photography, art. Imprints: Scriptum Editions, Cartago. Founded 1996.

Collins & Brown – see Anova Books

Collins Languages/COBUILD – see HarperCollins Publishers

Collins Gem – see HarperCollins Publishers

Collins Geo – see HarperCollins Publishers

Colourpoint Books

Colourpoint House, Jubilee Business Park, Jubilee Road, Newtownards, Co. Down, Northern Ireland BT23 4YH
tel (028) 9182 6339 *fax* (028) 9182 1900
email info@colourpoint.co.uk
website www.colourpoint.co.uk
Publishers Malcolm Johnston, Wesley Johnston, *Marketing* Denise Martin

Irish and general interest including local history; transport (covering the whole of the British Isles), buses, road and railways; educational textbooks and resources; fiction. Short queries by email. Full submission in writing including details of proposal, sample chapter/section, your qualification/experience in the topic, full contact details and return postage. Imprints: Colourpoint Educational, Plover Fiction. Founded 1993.

The Columba Press†

55A Spruce Avenue, Stillorgan Industrial Park, Blackrock, Co. Dublin, Republic of Ireland
tel (1) 2942556 *fax* (1) 2942564
email info@columba.ie
website www.columba.ie
Publisher & Managing Director Seán O'Boyle

Religion (Roman Catholic and Anglican) including pastoral handbooks, spirituality, theology, liturgy and prayer; counselling and self-help. Founded 1985.

Connections Book Publishing Ltd

St Chad's House, 148 King's Cross Road, London WC1X 9DH
tel 020-7837 1968 *fax* 020-7837 2025
email info@connections-publishing.com
website www.connections-publishing.com
Directors Nick Eddison, Ian Jackson, David Owen

Illustrated non-fiction books, kits and gift titles: broad, popular list including MBS, health, self-help and relationships. Imprint: Bookinabox (gifts). Founded 1993.

Conran Octopus – see Octopus Publishing Group

Constable & Robinson Ltd*

3 The Lanchesters, 162 Fulham Palace Road, London W6 9ER
tel 020-8741 3663 *fax* 020-8748 7562
email enquiries@constablerobinson.com
website www.constablerobinson.com

Chairman & Publisher Nick Robinson, *Joint Managing Directors* Pete Duncan and Nova Jayne Heath, *Finance Director* Adrian Andrews, *Rights* Eryl Humphrey Jones

Unsolicited sample chapters, synopses and ideas welcome with return postage. Do not send MSS; no email submissions. Founded 1795 (Constable); 1983 (Robinson).

Constable (imprint)

Biography, current affairs, general and military history, travel and endurance, landscape photography.

Robinson (imprint: paperbacks)

Crime fiction, the *Mammoth* series, the *Brief History* series, psychology (including the *Overcoming* series).

Right Way (imprint)

Practical, 'how to' paperbacks and websites, including food and drink, gardening, self-help and pastimes.

Consumers' Association – see Which? Ltd

The Continuum International Publishing Group Ltd

The Tower Building, 11 York Road, London SE1 7NX
tel 020-7922 0880 *fax* 020-7922 0881
email info@continuumbooks.com
website www.continuumbooks.com
Ceo Oliver Gadsby, *Directors* Robin Baird-Smith (publishing), Bob Marsh (finance), Ken Rhodes (sales & marketing), Louise Cameron (production), *Publishers* Sarah Campbell, Anna Fleming

Serious non-fiction, academic and professional, including scholarly monographs and educational texts and reference works in education, film, history, linguistics, literary studies, media studies, music, philosophy, politics; and in biblical studies, religious studies and theology. Imprints: Burns & Oates, Continuum, Network Continuum, T&T Clark International, Thoemmes Press, Mowbray.

Conway – see Anova Books

Thomas Cook Publishing

Unit 9, Coningsby Road, Peterborough PE3 8SB
tel (01733) 416477 *fax* (01733) 416688
email publishing-sales@thomascook.com
website www.thomascookpublishing.com
Head of Travel Books Lisa Bass

Travel guides, rail maps and timetables. Founded 1873.

Corgi – see Transworld Publishers

Corgi Children's Books – see The Random House Group Ltd

Cork University Press†

Youngline Industrial Estate, Pouladuff Road, Togher, Cork, Republic of Ireland
tel (021) 4902980 *fax* (021) 4315329
website www.corkuniversitypress.com
Publications Director Mike Collins

Irish literature, history, cultural studies, landscape studies, medieval studies, English literature, musicology, poetry, translations. Founded 1925.

Attic Press and Atrium (imprints)

email corkuniversitypress@ucc.ie

Books by and about women in the areas of social and political comment, women's studies. Cookery, biography and Irish cultural studies (trade).

Council for British Archaeology

St Mary's House, 66 Bootham, York YO30 7BZ
tel (01904) 671417 *fax* (01904) 671384
email info@britarch.ac.uk
website www.britarch.ac.uk
Director Mike Heyworth, *Publications Officer* Catrina Appleby

British archaeology – academic; practical handbooks; general interest archaeology. *British Archaeology* magazine. Founded 1946.

Country Books

(incorporating Ashridge Press)
Courtyard Cottage, Little Longstone, Bakewell, Derbyshire DE45 1NN
tel (01629) 640670
email dickrichardson@country-books.co.uk

Local history (new and facsimile reprints), walking books and the Senior Citizens' Good Food Guides. Books for the National Trust, Chatsworth House, Peak District NPA, Derbyshire County Council. Established 1995.

Countryside Books

2 Highfield Avenue, Newbury, Berks. RG14 5DS
tel (01635) 43816 *fax* (01635) 551004
website www.countrysidebooks.co.uk
Partners Nicholas Battle, Suzanne Battle

Books of local or regional interest, usually on a county basis: walking, outdoor activities, local history; also heritage, genealogy, aviation. Accepts proposals; submit outline and one chapter only to the Managing Director. Founded 1976.

Cover to Cover – see BBC Audiobooks Ltd

CRC Press – see Taylor and Francis Group

Creme de la Crime

PO Box 523, Chesterfield S40 9AT
tel (01246) 520835
email info@cremedelacrime.com
website www.cremedelacrime.com
Managing Editor Lynne Patrick

Crime fiction. Detailed guidelines available on website. Founded 2003.

Crescent Moon Publishing
PO Box 393, Maidstone, Kent ME14 5XU
tel (01622) 729593
email cresmopub@yahoo.co.uk
website www.crescentmoon.org.uk
Director Jeremy Robinson *Editors* C. Hughes, B.D. Barnacle

Literature, poetry, arts, cultural studies, media, cinema, feminism. Submit sample chapters or 6 poems plus sae, not complete MSS. Founded 1988.

Cressrelles Publishing Co. Ltd
10 Station Road Industrial Estate, Colwall, Malvern, Herefordshire WR13 6RN
tel (01684) 540154 *fax* (01684) 540154
email simon@cressrelles.co.uk
website www.cressrelles.co.uk
Directors Leslie Smith, Simon Smith

General publishing. Founded 1973.

J. Garnet Miller (imprint)
Plays and theatre textbooks.

Kenyon-Deane (imprint)
Plays and drama textbooks for amateur dramatic societies. Plays for women.

Crombie Jardine Publishing Ltd
Office 2, 3 Edgar Buildings, George Street, Bath BA1 2FJ
email admin@crombiejardine.com
website www.crombiejardine.com

Specialises in impulse-buy humour and gift books for the adult market. Founded 2004.

Crown House Publishing Ltd
Crown Buildings, Bancyfelin, Carmarthen SA33 5ND
tel (01267) 211345 *fax* (01267) 211882
email books@crownhouse.co.uk
website www.crownhouse.co.uk
Chairman Martin Roberts, *Directors* David Bowman (managing director), Glenys Roberts, David Bowman, Karen Bowman, Caroline Lenton

Publisher of Neuro-Linguistic Programming (NLP), hypnosis. counselling and psychotherapy, personal, business and life coaching, education, accelerated learning, thinking skills and personalising learning. Founded 1998.

The Crowood Press
The Stable Block, Ramsbury, Marlborough, Wilts. SN8 2HR
tel (01672) 520320 *fax* (01672) 520280
email enquiries@crowood.com
website www.crowood.com
Directors John Dennis (chairman), Ken Hathaway (managing)

Sport, motoring, aviation, military, martial arts, walking, fishing, country sports, farming, natural history, gardening, DIY, crafts, dogs, equestrian, theatre. Founded 1982.

Airlife Publishing (imprint)
Aviation, technical and general, military, military history.

Benjamin Cummings – see Pearson UK

James Currey – see Boydell & Brewer Ltd

Curzon Press Ltd – now RoutledgeCurzon – see Taylor and Francis Group

Terence Dalton Ltd
Water Street, Lavenham, Sudbury, Suffolk CO10 9RN
tel (01787) 249290 *fax* (01787) 248267
website www.terencedalton.com
Director T.A.J. Dalton

Non-fiction.

Darton, Longman & Todd Ltd
1 Spencer Court, 140–142 Wandsworth High Street, London SW18 4JJ
tel 020-8875 0155 *fax* 020-8875 0133
email editorial@darton-longman-todd.co.uk
website www.darton-longman-todd.co.uk
Editorial Director Brendan Walsh

Spirituality, prayer and meditation; theology and religious studies; personal growth, pastoral care and bereavement; political, environmental and social issues. Founded 1959.

David & Charles Ltd
Brunel House, Newton Abbot, Devon TQ12 4PU
tel (01626) 323200 *fax* (01626) 323319
email postmaster@davidandcharles.co.uk
website www.davidandcharles.co.uk
Managing Director James Woollam

High-quality illustrated non-fiction specialising in crafts, hobbies, art techniques, writing books, gardening, natural history, equestrian, DIY, military history, photography. Founded 1960.

Giles de la Mare Publishers Ltd
PO Box 25351, London NW5 1ZT
tel 020-7485 2533 *fax* 020-7485 2534
email gilesdelamare@dial.pipex.com
website www.gilesdelamare.co.uk
Chairman Giles de la Mare

Non-fiction: art, architecture, biography, history, music, travel. Telephone before submitting MSS. Founded 1995.

Dean – see Egmont Books

Dedalus Ltd
24 St Judith's Lane, Sawtry, Cambs. PE28 5XE
tel (01487) 832382

email info@dedalusbooks.com
website www.dedalusbooks.com
Chairman Juri Gabriel, *Directors* Eric Lane (managing), Robert Irwin (editorial), Mike Mitchell (translations)

Original fiction in English and in translation; Dedalus European Classics, Dedalus concept books. Founded 1983.

Richard Dennis Publications

The Old Chapel, Shepton Beauchamp, Ilminster, Somerset TA19 0LE
tel (01460) 240044 *fax* (01460) 242009
email books@richarddennispublications.com
website www.richarddennispublications.com

Books for collectors specialising in ceramics, glass, illustration, sculpture and facsimile editions of early catalogues.

The Derby Books Publishing Company Ltd

(formerly Breedon Books Publishing Co. Ltd)
3 The Parker Centre, Mansfield Road, Derby DE21 4SZ
tel (01332) 384235 *fax* (01332) 292755
email submissions@dbpublishing.co.uk
website www.dbpublishing.co.uk
Directors Steve Caron (managing), Jane Caron (finance)

Football, sport, local history, heritage. No fiction. Unsolicited MSS welcome. Preliminary letter essential. Founded 2009.

André Deutsch – see Carlton Publishing Group

diehard

91–93 Main Street, Callander FK17 8BQ
tel (01877) 339449
website www.poetryscotland.co.uk
Director Sally Evans (editorial)

Scottish poetry. Founded 1993.

Digital Press – see Elsevier Ltd

Discovery Walking Guides Ltd

21 Upper Priory Street, Northampton NN1 2PT
tel (01604) 244869 *fax* (01604) 752576
email ask.discovery@ntlworld.com
website www.walking.demon.co.uk
Chairman Rosamund C. Brawn

'Walk!' walking guidebooks to UK and European destinations. 'Tour & Trail Super-Durable' large-scale maps for outdoor adventures. 'Drive' touring maps. GPS The Easy Way. Digital 'Personal Navigator Files' for GPS users. Welcomes project proposals from technologically proficient walking writers. Founded 1994.

John Donald – see Birlinn Ltd

Dorling Kindersley – see Penguin Group (UK)

Doubleday Children's Books – see The Random House Group Ltd

Doubleday (UK) – see Transworld Publishers

The Dovecote Press Ltd

Stanbridge, Wimborne Minster, Dorset BH21 4JD
tel (01258) 840549 *fax* (01258) 840958
email online@dovecotepress.com
website www.dovecotepress.com
Editorial Director David Burnett

Books of local interest: *County in Colour* series, natural history, architecture, history. Founded 1974.

Little Toller Books (imprint)
Republishes classics of nature writing and rural life.

Dref Wen

28 Church Road, Whitchurch, Cardiff CF14 2EA
tel 029-2061 7860 *fax* 029-2061 0507
website www.drefwen.com
Directors Roger Boore, Anne Boore, Gwilym Boore, Alun Boore

Welsh language publisher. Original Welsh language novels for children and adult learners. Original, adaptations and translations of foreign and English language full-colour picture story books for children. Educational material for primary/secondary school children in Wales and England. Founded 1970.

University College Dublin Press†

Newman House, 86 St Stephen's Green, Dublin 2, Republic of Ireland
tel (01) 477 9813/9812 *fax* (01) 477 9821
email ucdpress@ucd.ie
website www.ucdpress.ie
Executive Editor Barbara Mennell

Irish studies, history and politics, literary studies, sociology. Founded 1995.

Gerald Duckworth & Co. Ltd

First Floor, 90–93 Cowcross Street, London EC1M 6BF
tel 020-7490 7300 *fax* 020-7490 0080
email info@duckworth-publishers.co.uk
website www.ducknet.co.uk
Director Peter Mayer (publisher)

General trade publishers with a strong academic division. Imprints: Duckworth, Bristol Classical Press, Duckworth Overlook, Nonesuch Press. No unsolicited fiction submissions. Founded 1898.

Dunedin Academic Press

Hudson House, 8 Albany Street, Edinburgh EH1 3QB
tel 0131-473 2397 *fax* (01250) 870920

email mail@dunedinacademicpress.co.uk
website www.dunedinacademicpress.co.uk
Director Anthony Kinahan

Earth science, social sciences, music, humanities. See website for submission guidelines. Founded 2000.

Earthscan

Dunston House, 14A St Cross Street,
London EC1N 8XA
tel 020-7841 1930 *fax* 020-7242 1474
email earthinfo@earthscan.co.uk
website www.earthscan.co.uk
Managing Director Jonathan Sinclair Wilson

Academic and professional: sustainable development, climate and energy, natural resource management, cities and built environment, business and economics, design and technology. Imprint of Earthscan Ltd.

Ebury Press – see The Random House Group Ltd

Eden – see Transworld Publishers

Edinburgh University Press*

22 George Square, Edinburgh EH8 9LF
tel 0131-650 4218 *fax* 0131-650 3286
email editorial@eup.ac.uk
website www.euppublishing.com
Chairman Ivon Asquith, *Chief Executive* Timothy Wright, *Head of Book Publishing* Ms Jackie Jones, *Head of Sales and Marketing* Catriona Murray

Academic publishers of scholarly books and journals: African studies, media and cultural studies, Islamic studies, geography, history, law, linguistics, literary studies, philosophy, politics, Scottish studies, American studies, religious studies, sociology, classical and ancient history. Trade: Scottish language, literature and culture, Scottish history and politics.

Éditions Aubrey Walter/Gay Men's Press

99A Wallis Road, London E9 5LN
tel 020-8986 4854 *fax* 020-8533 5821
website www.gmppubs.co.uk
Publisher Aubrey Walter

Visual work by gay artists and photographers, usually in the form of a monograph showcasing one artist's work. Work may be submitted on disk, email, transparency, photocopy or photograph.

The Educational Company of Ireland†

Ballymount Road, Walkinstown, Dublin 12,
Republic of Ireland
tel (01) 4500611 *fax* (01) 4500993
email info@edco.ie
website www.edco.ie
Executive Directors Martina Harford (Chief Executive), Robert McLoughlin, *Commissioning Editors* Robert Healy, Michele Staunton

Educational MSS on all subjects in English or Irish language. Trading unit of Smurfit Kappa Group – Ireland. Founded 1910.

Educational Explorers (Publishers)

Unit 5, Feidr Castell Business Park,
Fishguard SA65 9BB
tel/fax (08456) 123912
email enquiries@cuisenaire.co.uk
website www.cuisenaire.co.uk
Directors M.J. Hollyfield, D.M. Gattegno

Educational. Recent successes include: mathematics – *Numbers in colour with Cuisenaire Rods*; languages – *The Silent Way*; literacy, reading – *Words in Colour*; educational films. No unsolicited material. Founded 1962.

Egmont Books*

103 Westerhill Road, Bishopbriggs,
Glasgow G64 2QT
tel (08445) 768113 *fax* (08445) 768114
email service@egmont.co.uk
website www.egmont.co.uk
Directors Robert McMenemy (Managing), Cally Poplak (Egmont Press)

Children's books: picture books, fiction (ages 4–16). Authors include Michael Morpurgo, Jenny Nimmo, William Nicholson, Helen Oxenbury, Enid Blyton, Andy Stanton, Julia Golding, Jan Fearnley and Lydia Monks. Will consider submissions sent by email to: childrensreader@euk.egmont.com. No submissions by post. Send a short synopsis and the first 2–3 chapters. Will not respond to individual submissions unless successful. Founded 1878.

Egmont Publishing (imprint)

239 Kensington High Street, London W8 6SA
tel 020-7761 3500 *fax* 020-7761 3510
Director David Riley

Annuals, activity books, novelty books, film/TV tie-ins, licensed character list. Characters include Thomas the Tank Engine, Barbie, Mr Men, Miffy, Postman Pat, Action Man.

Eland Publishing Ltd

61 Exmouth Market, London EC1R 4QL
tel 020-7833 0762 *fax* 020-7833 4434
email info@travelbooks.co.uk
website www.travelbooks.co.uk
Directors Rose Baring, John Hatt, Barnaby Rogerson, Stephanie Allen

Reprints of classic travel literature. No unsolicited typescripts. Email in first instance. Founded 1982.

Element – see HarperCollins Publishers

11:9 – see Neil Wilson Publishing Ltd

Edward Elgar Publishing Ltd

The Lypiatts, 15 Lansdown Road, Cheltenham,
Glos. GL50 2JA

tel (01242) 226934 *fax* (01242) 262111
email info@e-elgar.co.uk
website www.e-elgar.com
Managing Director Tim Williams

Economics, business, law, public and social policy. Founded 1986.

Elliot Right Way Books – see Constable & Robinson Ltd

Elliott & Thompson
27 John Street, London WC1N 2BX
tel 020-7831 5013 *fax* 020-7831 5011
email mark@eandtbooks.com
website www.eandtbooks.com
Chairman Lorne Forsyth

Lifestyle, food and drink, sport, music, history and adult fiction. Founded 2001.

ELM Publications and Training
Seaton House, Kings Ripton, Huntingdon, Cambs. PE28 2NJ
tel (01487) 773254 *fax* (01487) 773359
email elm@elm-training.co.uk
website www.elm-training.co.uk
Managing Director Sheila Ritchie

Business and management development books, packs and resources; training materials and training courses; some e-learning materials. Founded 1977.

Elsevier Ltd*
The Boulevard, Langford Lane, Kidlington, Oxford OX5 1GB
tel (01865) 843434 *fax* (01865) 843970
website www.elsevier.com
Ceo Health Sciences Division (Books & Journals) Michael Hansen, *Ceo Science & Technology (Books & Journals)* Herman van Campenhout

Academic and professional reference books; scientific, technical and medical books, journals, CD-Roms and magazines. No unsolicited MSS, but synopses and project proposals welcome. Imprints: Academic Press, Architectural Press, Bailliere Tindall, Butterworth-Heinemann, Churchill Livingstone, Digital Press, Elsevier, Elsevier Advanced Technology, Focal Press, Gulf Professional Press, JAI, Made Simple Books, Morgan Kauffman, Mosby, Newnes, North-Holland, Pergamon, Saunders. Division of Reed Elsevier, Amsterdam.

Elsevier Ltd (Butterworth Heinemann)*
The Boulevard, Langford Lane, Kidlington, Oxford OX5 1GB
tel (01865) 474010
website www.elsevierdirect.com
Managing Director Jim Donohue (Science & Technology Books)

Books and electronic products across business, technical, for students and professionals.

Elsevier Ltd (Health Sciences)*
The Boulevard, Langford Lane, Kidlington, Oxford OX5 1GB
tel (01865) 843434 *fax* (01865) 843970
website www.elsevier.com, www.elsevierhealth.com
Ceo Michael Hansen

Medical books and journals. No unsolicited MSS but synopses and project proposals welcome. Imprints: Bailliere Tindall, Churchill Livingstone, Elsevier, Mosby, Pergamon, Saunders.

Encyclopaedia Britannica (UK) Ltd
2nd Floor, Unity Wharf, 13 Mill Street, London SE1 2BH
tel 020-7500 7800 *fax* 020-7500 7878
email enquiries@britannica.co.uk
website www.britannica.co.uk
Managing Director Ian Grant, *VP of Operations* Jane Helps

Enitharmon Press/Enitharmon Editions
26B Caversham Road, London NW5 2DU
tel 020-7482 5967 *fax* 020-7284 1787
email info@enitharmon.co.uk
website www.enitharmon.co.uk
Director Stephen Stuart-Smith

Poetry, literary criticism, fiction, translations, artists' books. No unsolicited MSS. No freelance editors or proofreaders required. Founded 1967.

Lawrence Erlbaum Associates – see Taylor and Francis Group

Euro Crime – see Arcadia Books Ltd

Euromonitor International plc
60–61 Britton Street, London EC1M 5UX
tel 020-7251 8024 *fax* 020-7608 3149
email info@euromonitor.com
website www.euromonitor.com
Directors T.J. Fenwick (managing), R.N. Senior (chairman)

Business and commercial reference, marketing information, European and International Surveys, directories. Founded 1972.

Europa Publications Ltd – see Taylor and Francis Group

Evangelical Press of Wales – see Bryntirion Press

Evans Publishing Group*
2A Portman Mansions, Chiltern Street, London W1U 6NR
tel 020-7487 0920 *fax* 020-7487 0921
email sales@evansbooks.co.uk
website www.evansbooks.co.uk
Directors Brian Jones (managing), A.O. Ojora

(Nigeria), Alex Evans (Sales), Danny Daly (Finance), *UK Publisher* Su Swallow

Educational books, particularly preschool, school library and teachers' books for the UK, primary and secondary for Africa, the Caribbean. Submissions welcome but do not respond if unsuccessful. Part of the Evans Publishing Group. Founded 1908.

Everyman – see The Orion Publishing Group Ltd

Everyman's Library

Northburgh House, 10 Northburgh Street, London EC1V 0AT
tel 020-7566 6350 *fax* 020-7490 3708
website www.randomhouse.com/knopf/classics
Publisher David Campbell

Everyman's Library (clothbound reprints of the classics); *Everyman's Library Children's Classics*; *Everyman's Library Pocket Poets*; *Everyman Guides*; *Everyman City Map Guides*. No unsolicited submissions. Imprint of Alfred A. Knopf.

University of Exeter Press

Reed Hall, Streatham Drive, Exeter EX4 4QR
tel (01392) 263066 *fax* (01392) 263064
email uep@exeter.ac.uk
website www.exeterpress.co.uk
Publisher Simon Baker

Academic and scholarly books on history, local history (Exeter and the South West), archaeology, classical studies, English literature, film history, performance studies, medieval studies, maritime studies. Imprints include: University of Exeter Press, Bristol Phoenix Press, The Exeter Press. Founded 1958.

Helen Exley®

16 Chalk Hill, Watford, Herts. WD19 4BG
tel (01923) 474480 *fax* (01923) 818733/249795
website www.helenexleygiftbooks.com
Directors Dalton Exley, Helen Exley (editorial), Lincoln Exley, Richard Exley

Popular colour gift books for an international market. No unsolicited MSS. Founded 1976.

Expert Books – see Transworld Publishers

Faber and Faber Ltd*

Bloomsbury House, 74–77 Great Russell Street, London WC1B 3DA
tel 020-7927 3800 *fax* 020-7927 3801
website www.faber.co.uk
Chief Executive & Publisher Stephen Page, *Commercial Director* David Tebbutt, *Editorial Directors* Lee Brackstone, Walter Donohue, Julian Loose, Belinda Matthews, *Sales Director* Will Atkinson, *Publicity Director & Associate Publisher, Original Arts* Rachel Alexander, *Marketing Director* Jo Ellis, *Production Director* Nigel Marsh, *Rights Director* Jason Cooper, *Publishing Director Children's Books* Julia Heydon-Wells

High-quality general fiction and non-fiction, children's fiction and non-fiction, drama, film, music, poetry. Unsolicited submissions accepted for poetry only. For information on poetry submission procedures, ring 020-7465 0189, or consult the website. No unsolicited MSS.

Fabian Society

11 Dartmouth Street, London SW1H 9BN
tel 020-7227 4900 *fax* 020-7976 7153
email info@fabians.org.uk
website www.fabians.org.uk
General Secretary Sunder Katwala

Current affairs, political thought, economics, education, environment, foreign affairs, social policy. Also controls NCLC Publishing Society Ltd. Founded 1884.

Facet Publishing*

7 Ridgmount Street, London WC1E 7AE
tel 020-7255 0590 *fax* 020-7255 0591
email info@facetpublishing.co.uk
website www.facetpublishing.co.uk
Managing Director CILIP Enterprises John Woolley

Library and information science, information technology, reference works, directories, bibliographies.

Clive Bingley Ltd (imprint)

Library and information science, reference works.

Library Association Publishing (imprint)

Library and information science, information technology, reference works, directories, bibliographies.

CJ Fallon

Ground Floor, Block B, Liffey Valley Office Campus, Dublin 22, Republic of Ireland
tel (01) 6166400 *fax* (01) 6166499
email editorial@cjfallon.ie
website www.cjfallon.ie
Executive Directors Brian Gilsenan (managing), John Bodley (financial)

Educational textbooks. Founded 1927.

Falmer Press – now RoutledgeFalmer, see Taylor and Francis Group

David Fickling Books – see The Random House Group Ltd

Fig Tree – see Penguin Group (UK)

Findhorn Press Ltd

Delft Cottage, Dyke, Forres, Scotland IV36 2TF
tel (01309) 690582 *fax* (01317) 772711

email info@findhornpress.com
website www.findhornpress.com

Mind, Body & Spirit and healing. Founded 1971.

Fineleaf Publishing

Moss Cottage, Pontshill, Ross-on-Wye HR9 5TB
tel (01989) 750369 *fax* (01989) 750369
website www.fineleaf.co.uk
Editor Philip Gray

Landscape, local history, arts. Founded 2006.

First and Best in Education

Earlstrees Court, Earlstrees Road, Corby, Northants. NN17 4HH
tel (01536) 399011 *fax* (01536) 399012
email sales@firstandbest.co.uk
website www.shop.firstandbest.co.uk
Contact Anne Cockburn (editor)

Education-related books (no fiction). Currently actively recruiting new writers for schools; ideas welcome. Send sae with submissions. Founded 1992.

Fitzrovia Press Ltd

10 Grafton Mews, London W1T 5JG
tel 020-7380 0749
email info@fitzroviapress.co.uk, pratima@fitzroviapress.co.uk
website www.fitzroviapress.co.uk
Publisher Richard Prime, *Marketing Director* Pratima Patel

Fiction and non-fiction: Hinduism and creative writing grounded in Eastern philosophy that explores spirituality in the West. Submit outline plus sample chapter; no complete MSS. Founded 2008.

Five Star – see Serpent's Tail (imprint)

Flambard Press

Holy Jesus Hospital, City Road, Newcastle upon Tyne NE1 2AS
tel (0191) 233 3865 *fax* (01434) 674178
email editor@flambardpress.co.uk
website www.flambardpress.co.uk
Editors Peter Lewis, Margaret Lewis, Will Mackie

Poetry and literary fiction. Founded 1990.

Flame Tree Publishing

Crabtree Hall, Crabtree Lane, London SW6 6TY
tel 020-7386 4700 *fax* 020-7386 4701
email info@flametreepublishing.com
website www.flametreepublishing.com
Managing Director Frances Bodiam, *Publisher/ Creative Director* Nick Wells

Music, reference, art, cookery, education; children's. Part of The Foundry Creative Media Company Ltd. Founded 1992.

Floris Books*

15 Harrison Gardens, Edinburgh EH11 1SH
tel 0131-337 2372 *fax* 0131-347 9919
email floris@florisbooks.co.uk
website www.florisbooks.co.uk
Commissioning Editor Sally Martin

Religion, science, philosophy, holistic health, organics, Mind, Body & Spirit, Celtic studies, crafts; children's books: board, picture books, activity books. Founded 1978.

Kelpies (imprint)

Contemporary Scottish fiction from picture books to novels for 8–12 year-olds. Annual Kelpies Prize, see website.

Flyleaf Press†

4 Spencer Villas, Glenageary, Co. Dublin, Republic of Ireland
tel (1) 284 5906
email books@flyleaf.ie
website www.flyleaf.ie
Managing Editor James Ryan

Irish family history. Founded 1988.

Focal Press – see Elsevier Ltd

Folens Publishers*

Waterslade House, Thame Road, Haddenham, Bucks. HP17 8NT
tel (01 844) 576 8115 *fax* (01844) 296 666
email folens@folens.com
website www.folens.com
Managing Director Adrian Cockell, *Director of Publishing* Peter Burton, *Primary Publisher* Zoe Nichols, *Secondary Publisher* Abigail Woodman

Primary and secondary educational books. Imprints: Folens, Belair. Founded 1987.

Folens Publishers

Hibernian Industrial Estate, off Greenhills Road, Tallaght, Dublin 24, Republic of Ireland
tel (01) 4137200 *fax* (01) 4137282
email info@folens.ie
website www.folens.ie
Chairman Dirk Folens, *Managing Director* John O'Connor

Educational (primary, secondary, comprehensive, technical, in English and Irish). Founded 1956.

Blackwater Press (imprint)

General non-fiction, Irish interest. Founded 1993.

Footprint Handbooks

6 Riverside Court, Lower Bristol Road, Bath BA2 3DZ
tel (01225) 469141 *fax* (01225) 469461
email contactus@footprintbooks.com
website www.footprintbooks.com
Directors Andy Riddle (managing), Patrick Dawson (editorial), *Commissioning Editor* Alan Murphy

Travel guides.

W. Foulsham & Co. Ltd

The Oriel, Thames Valley Court,
183–187 Bath Road, Slough, Berks. SL1 4AA
tel (01753) 526769 *fax* (01753) 535003
Managing Director B.A.R. Belasco, *Editorial Director* W. Hobson

Life issues. General know-how, cookery, health and alternative therapies, hobbies and games, gardening, sport, travel guides, DIY, collectibles, popular new age. Imprints: Foulsham, Quantum. Founded c. 1800.

Quantum (imprint)

Mind, Body & Spirit, popular philosophy and practical psychology.

Four Courts Press†

7 Malpas Street, Dublin 8, Republic of Ireland
tel (01) 4534668 *fax* (01) 4534672
email info@fourcourtspress.ie
website www.fourcourtspress.ie
Managing Director Martin Healy

Academic books in the humanities, especially history, Celtic and medieval studies, art, theology. Founded 1970.

Fourth Estate – see HarperCollins Publishers

Free Association Books

1 Angel Cottages, Milespit Hill, London NW7 1RD
tel 020-8906 0396
email info@fabooks.com
website www.fabooks.com
Publisher & Managing Director T.E. Brown

Social sciences, psychoanalysis, psychotherapy, counselling, cultural studies, social welfare, addiction studies, child and adolescent studies. No poetry, science fiction or fantasy. Founded 1984.

Free Press – see Simon & Schuster UK Ltd

W.H. Freeman – see Macmillan Publishers Ltd

Samuel French Ltd*

52 Fitzroy Street, London W1T 5JR
tel 020-7387 9373, 020-7255 4300 *fax* 020-7387 2161
email theatre@samuelfrench-london.co.uk
website www.samuelfrench-london.co.uk
Directors Leon F. Embry (chairman, USA), Vivien Goodwin (managing), Amanda Smith, Paul Taylor

Publishers of plays and agents for the collection of royalties. Will consider full-length plays only if been performed professionally. One-act scripts, if received a production of some kind, should be submitted in full. Scripts not returned without an sae. Founded 1830.

The Friday Project – see HarperCollins Publishers

Frontline – see Pen & Sword Books Ltd

FT Prentice Hall – see Pearson UK

David Fulton – see Taylor and Francis Group

Gaia Books – see Octopus Publishing Group

Galaxy Children's Large Print – see BBC Audiobooks Ltd

The Gallery Press†

Loughcrew, Oldcastle, Co Meath, Republic of Ireland
tel 049-854 1779 *fax* 049-854 1779
email gallery@indigo.ie
website www.gallerypress.com
Editor/Publisher Peter Fallon

Poetry, drama, and occasionally fiction – by Irish authors only at this time. Founded 1970.

Gallic Books

Worlds End Studios, 134 Lots Road,
London SW10 0RJ
tel 020-7349 7112 *fax* 020-7351 5044
email info@gallicbooks.com
website www. gallicbooks.com
Managing Director Jane Aitken, *Editorial Director* Pilar Webb

French writing in translation. Only accepts submissions from French publishers or from agents representing French authors. Founded 2007.

Garland Science – see Taylor and Francis Group

J. Garnet Miller – see Cressrelles Publishing Co. Ltd

Garnet Publishing Ltd

8 Southern Court, South Street, Reading RG1 4QS
tel (01189) 597847 *fax* (01189) 597356
email dan@garnetpublishing.co.uk
website www.garnetpublishing.co.uk
Editorial Manager Dan Nunn

Art, architecture, photography, fiction, religious studies, travel and general, mainly on the Middle East and Islam. Accepts unsolicited material only if relevant to Islam and the Middle East. Founded 1991.

Ithaca Press (imprint)

Post-graduate academic works, especially on the Middle East.

South Street Press (imprint)

Non-fiction, including *Behind the Headlines* series.

Geddes & Grosset

144 Port Dundas Road, Glasgow G4 0HZ
tel 0141-567 2830 *fax* 0141-567 2831

email info@gandg.sol.co.uk
Publishers Ron Grosset, Mike Miller

Popular reference and children's non-fiction. Founded 1988.

Gibson Square

tel 020-7096 1100 *fax* 020-7993 2214
email info@gibsonsquare.com
website www.gibsonsquare.com
Publisher Martin Rynja

Non-fiction: biography, current affairs, philosophy, politics, cultural criticism, psychology, history, travel, art history. Submissions must have a high potential to provoke debate; see website for guidelines.

Gill & Macmillan Ltd†

Hume Avenue, Park West, Dublin 12, Republic of Ireland
tel (01) 500 9500 *fax* (01) 500 9596
website www.gillmacmillan.ie

Biography or memoirs, educational (secondary, university), history, literature, cookery, current affairs, guidebooks, Irish-interest non-fiction. Founded 1968.

Ginn – see Pearson UK

GL Assessment

The Chiswick Centre, 414 Chiswick High Road, London W4 5TF
tel 020-8996 8445 *fax* 020-8996 3660
email information@gl-assessment.co.uk
website www.gl-assessment.co.uk
Group Education Director Andrew Thraves

Testing and assessment services for education and health care, including literacy, numeracy, thinking skills, ability, learning support and online testing. Founded 1981.

Godsfield Press – see Octopus Publishing Group

The Goldsmith Press Ltd

Newbridge, Co. Kildare, Republic of Ireland
tel (045) 433613 *fax* (045) 434648
email viv1@iol.ie
website www.gerardmanleyhopkins.org
Directors V. Abbott, D. Egan, *Secretary* B. Ennis

Literature, art, Irish interest, poetry. Unsolicited MSS not returned. Founded 1972.

Gollancz – see The Orion Publishing Group Ltd

Gomer Press

Llandysul, Ceredigion SA44 4JL
tel (01559) 362371 *fax* (01559) 363758
email gwasg@gomer.co.uk
website www.gomer.co.uk, www.pontbooks.co.uk
Managing Director Jonathan Lewis, *Publishing Director* Mairwen Prys Jones, *Editors* to be appointed (Adult, Welsh), Ceri Wyn Jones (Adult, English), Sioned Lleinau, Rhiannon Davies (Children's, Welsh), Viv Sayer (Children's, English)

History, travel, photography, biography, art, poetry and fiction of relevance to Welsh culture, in English and in Welsh. Picture books, novels, stories, poetry and teaching resources for children. No unsolicited MSS; prelimary enquiry essential. Imprint: Pont Books (English books for children). Founded 1892.

Goss & Crested China Club

62 Murray Road, Horndean, Waterlooville PO8 9JL
tel (023) 9259 7440 *fax* (023) 9259 1975
email info@gosschinaclub.co.uk
website www.gosschinaclub.co.uk
Managing Director Lynda J. Pine

Goss & Crested heraldic china, antique porcelain. Publishing and bookselling division of Goss & Crested China Club. Founded 1967.

Government Supplies Agency†

Publications Division, Office of Public Works, 51 St Stephen's Green, Dublin 2, Republic of Ireland
tel (01) 6476000 *fax* (01) 661 0747

Irish government publications.

Gower – see Ashgate Publishing Ltd

Granta Publications

12 Addison Avenue, London W11 4QR
tel 020-7605 1360 *fax* 020-7605 1361
website www.granta.com
Magazine Editor John Freeman, *Publishing Director* Sara Holloway

Literary fiction, memoir, political non-fiction, travel, history, etc. Founded 1982. (Magazine founded in 1979.)

Green Books

Foxhole, Dartington, Totnes, Devon TQ9 6EB
tel (01803) 863260 *fax* (01803) 863843
email edit@greenbooks.co.uk
website www.greenbooks.co.uk
Publisher John Elford

Environment (practical and philosophical). No fiction or children's books. No MSS; submit synopsis with covering letter, preferably by email. Founded 1987.

Green Print – see Merlin Press Ltd

Gresham Books Ltd

19/21 Sayers Lane, Tenterden, Kent TN30 6BW
tel (01580) 767596 *fax* (01580) 764142
email info@gresham-books.co.uk
website www.gresham-books.co.uk
Managing Director Nicholas Oulton

Books

Hymn books, Prayer books, Service books, school histories and Companions.

Grub Street Publishing

4 Rainham Close, London SW11 6SS
tel 020-7924 3966/738 1008 *fax* 020-7738 1009
email post@grubstreet.co.uk
website www.grubstreet.co.uk
Principals John B. Davies, Anne Dolamore

Adult non-fiction: military, aviation history, cookery. Founded 1992.

Guild of Master Craftsman Publications Ltd

166 High Street, Lewes, East Sussex BN7 1XU
tel (01273) 477374 *fax* (01273) 478606
website www.thegmcgroup.com, www.ammonitepress.com
Joint Managing Directors Jennifer Phillips, Jonathan Phillips

Leisure and hobby subjects; practical, illustrated crafts, including photography, needlecrafts, dolls' houses and woodworking. Founded 1979.

Guinness World Records

3rd Floor, 184–192 Drummond Street, London NW1 3HP
tel 020-7891 4567 *fax* 020-7891 4501
website www.guinnessworldrecords.com

Guinness World Records, *GWR Gamer's Edition*, TV and brand licensing, records processing. No unsolicited MSS. A Jim Pattison Group company. Founded 1954.

Gulf Professional Press – see Elsevier Ltd

Gullane Children's Books

185 Fleet Street, London EC4A 2HS
tel 020-7400 1084 *fax* 020-7400 1037
email stories@gullanebooks.com
website www.gullanebooks.com
Publisher Simon Rosenheim

Picture and novelty books for children aged 0–8 years.

Hachette Children's Books*

338 Euston Road, London NW1 3BH
tel 020-7873 6000 *fax* 020-7873 6024
website www.hachettechildrens.co.uk
Managing Director Marlene Johnson

Children's non-fiction, reference, information, gift, fiction, picture, novelty and audiobooks. Unsolicited material is not considered other than by referral or recommendation. Formed by combining Watts Publishing with Hodder Children's Books in 2005. Part of Hachette UK (see page 157).

Hodder Children's Books (imprint)
Publishing Director Anne McNeil
Fiction, picture books, novelty, general non-fiction and audiobooks.

Orchard Books (imprint)
Executive Director Penny Morris
Fiction, picture and novelty books.

Franklin Watts (imprint)
Publishing Director Rachel Cooke
Non-fiction and information books.

Wayland (imprint)
Publishing Director Joyce Bentley
Non-fiction and information books.

Hachette UK*

338 Euston Road, London NW1 3BH
tel 020-7873 6000 *fax* 020-7873 6024
website www.hachette.co.uk
Chief Executive Tim Hely Hutchinson, *Directors* Martin Neild (managing, Headline and Ceo H&S and John Murray), Jamie Hodder-Williams (managing, H&S General), Philip Walters (Ceo, Hodder Education), Chris Evans (Coo), Kate Wilson (Ceo Headline), Marlene Johnson (managing, Hachette Children's), Peter Roche (deputy Ceo/Ceo Orion), Malcolm Edwards (managing, Orion), Alison Goff (Ceo Octopus), Ursula Mackenzie (Ceo Little, Brown Book Group), Pierre de Cacqueray (finance), Richard Kitson (commercial), Susan Taylor (group hr), Malcolm Edwards (managing, Hachette Livre Australia), David Young (Ceo Hachette Book Group USA), Clare Harington (Group Communications)

Part of Hachette Livre SA since 2004. Hachette UK group companies: Hachette Children's Books (page 157), Headline Publishing Group (page 160), Hodder Education Group (page 161), Hodder & Stoughton (page 161), Hodder Faith (page 161), John Murray (page 170), Little, Brown Book Group (page 165), Octopus Publishing Group (page 172), Orion Publishing Group (page 174), Hachette Ireland, Hachette Australia (page 197), Hachette New Zealand (page 203), Hachette Book Publishing India Private Ltd.

Halban Publishers

22 Golden Square, London W1F 9JW
tel 020-7437 9300 *fax* 020-7437 9512
email books@halbanpublishers.com
website www.halbanpublishers.com
Directors Martine Halban, Peter Halban

General fiction and non-fiction; history and biography; Jewish subjects and Middle East. No unsolicited MSS considered; preliminary letter or email essential. Founded 1986.

Haldane Mason Ltd

PO Box 34196, London NW10 3YB
tel 020-8459 2131 *fax* 020-8728 1216
email info@haldanemason.com
website www.haldanemason.com
Directors Sydney Francis, Ron Samuel

Illustrated non-fiction books and box sets, mainly for children. No unsolicited material. Imprints: Haldane

Mason (adult), Red Kite Books (children's). Founded 1995.

Robert Hale Ltd

Clerkenwell House, 45–47 Clerkenwell Green, London EC1R 0HT
tel 020-7251 2661 *fax* 020-7490 4958
email enquire@halebooks.com
website www.halebooks.com
Directors John Hale (managing & editorial), Robert Kynaston (financial)

Adult general non-fiction and fiction. Founded 1936.

Halsgrove Publishing

Halsgrove House, Ryelands Industrial Estate, Bagley Road, Wellington, Somerset TA21 9PZ
tel (01823) 653777 *fax* (01823) 216796
email sales@halsgrove.com
website www.halsgrove.com
Managing Director Julian Davidson, *Publisher* Simon Butler

Regional books for local-interest readers in the UK. Also illustrated books on individual artists. Founded 1986.

Hamish Hamilton – see Penguin Group (UK)

Hamlyn – see Octopus Publishing Group

Patrick Hardy Books – see James Clarke & Co. Ltd

Harlequin Mills & Boon Ltd*

Eton House, 18–24 Paradise Road, Richmond, Surrey TW9 1SR
tel 020-8288 2800 *fax* 020-8388 2899
website www.millsandboon.co.uk
Directors Mandy Ferguson (managing), Stuart Barber (financial & IS), Angela Meredith (production & operations), Karin Stoecker (editorial), Tim Cooper (direct marketing), Jackie McGee (human resources), Clare Somerville (retail marketing and sales director), Ian Roberts (sales director).

Founded 1908.

Historical™ (imprint)
Senior Editor L. Fildew
Historical romance fiction.

Medical™ (imprint)
Senior Editor S. Hodgson
Contemporary romance fiction.

Mills & Boon Romance™ (imprint)
Senior Editor Kimberley Young
Contemporary romance fiction.

Mira Books® (imprint)
Women's fiction.

Modern Extra™ (imprint)
Senior Editor Bryony Green
Contemporary romance fiction.

Modern Romance™ (imprint)
Executive Editor Tessa Shapcott
Contemporary romance fiction.

Silhouette® (imprint)
Senior Editor Lesley Stonehouse
Popular romantic women's fiction.

HarperCollins Entertainment – see HarperCollins Publishers

HarperCollins Publishers*

77–85 Fulham Palace Road, London W6 8JB
tel 020-8741 7070 *fax* 020-8307 4440
also at Westerhill Road, Bishopbriggs, Glasgow G64 2QT
tel 0141-772 3200 *fax* 0141-306 3119
website www.harpercollins.co.uk
Ceo/Publisher Victoria Barnsley, *Publisher* Belinda Budge

All fiction and trade non-fiction must be submitted through an agent, or unsolicited MSS may be submitted through the online writing community at www.authonomy.com. Owned by News Corporation. Founded 1819.

Angry Robot (imprint)
Publisher Marc Gascoigne
Science fiction and fantasy (print and digital). Established 2008.

Avon
website www.avon-books.co.uk
Associate Publisher Caroline Ridding
Women's commercial fiction.

HarperFiction
Publisher Lynne Drew
General, historical fiction, crime and thrillers, women's fiction.

Blue Door (imprint)
Publisher Patrick Janson-Smith
Commercial fiction. Established 2008.

Voyager (imprint)
Publishing Director Jane Johnson
Fantasy/science fiction.

Harper NonFiction
Publisher Carole Tonkinson

HarperCollins (imprint)
Publishing Director David Brawn (Agatha Christie, J.R.R. Tolkien, C.S. Lewis),

HarperTrue (imprint)
Publisher Carole Tonkinson
True life stories. Established 2008.

HarperSport (imprint)
Publishing Director Jonathan Taylor
Sporting biographies, guides and histories.

Books

HarperCollins Audio (imprint)
Head of Audio Jo Forshaw
See page 222.

Harper Thorsons/Element (imprint)
Publisher Carole Tonkinson

HarperCollins Children's Books
website www.harpercollinschildrensbooks.co.uk
Managing Director Mario Santos

Quality picture books for under 7s; fiction for age 6 up to young adult; graphic novels; TV and film tie-ins; properties.

PRESS BOOKS
Managing Director John Bond

Fourth Estate (imprint)
Publishing Director/Publisher Nick Pearson

Fiction, literary fiction, current affairs, popular science, biography, humour, travel.

The Friday Project
email info@thefridayproject.co.uk
website www.thefridayproject.co.uk
Publisher Scott Pack

Books developed from popular websites with publishing initiatives that embrace new digital technology. Imprints: Friday Books, Friday Fiction, Friday Food, Friday Children's, Friday Instants.

HarperPress (imprint)
Publishing Directors Arabella Pike (non-fiction), Clare Smith (fiction)

Blue Door (imprint)
Publisher Patrick Janson-Smith

Commercial fiction. Established 2008.

Harper Perennial (imprint)
Publishing Director tba

Paperback fiction and non-fiction.

Collins Reference (division and imprint)
Managing Director Katie Fulford, *Publishing Directors* Denise Bates (illustrated reference), *Associate Publisher* Myles Archibald (natural history)

Guides and handbooks, Times World Atlases, phrase books and manuals on popular reference, art instruction, illustrated, cookery and wine, crafts, DIY, gardening, military, natural history, pet care, pastimes. Imprints: Collins, Collins Gem, Jane's, Times Books.

Collins Language (division and imprint)
Managing Director Robert Scriven, *Publishing Directors* Graeme Harvey (digital development), Elaine Higgleton (editorial)

Bilingual and English dictionaries, English dictionaries for foreign learners.

Collins Education (division)
Managing Director Nigel Ward

Books, CD-Roms and online material for UK primary and secondary schools and colleges.

Collins Geo (division and imprint)
Managing Director Sheena Barclay

Illustrated non-fiction: natural history, DIY, house and home, maps, atlases, street plans and leisure guides.

HarperTrue – see HarperCollins Publishers

Harvill Secker – see The Random House Group Ltd

Haus Publishing Ltd

70 Cadogan Place, London SW1X 9AH
tel 020-7838 9055 *fax* 020-7235 1999
email haus@hauspublishing.com
website www.hauspublishing.co.uk
Publisher Barbara Schwepcke, *Editorial Director* Robert Pritchard

The *Life & Times* series of illustrated biographies. Imprints: Armchair Traveller (literary travel writing), HausBooks (biography, general non-fiction). Founded 2002.

Arabia Books (imprint)
70 Cadogan Place, London SW1X 9AH
tel 020-7838 9055 *fax* 020-7235 1999
email barbara@hauspublishing.com
website www.arabia-books.co.uk
Directors Barbara Schwepke, Harry Hall

Arabic fiction (contemporary and modern) in English translation.

Hawthorn Press

1 Lansdown Lane, Stroud, Glos. GL5 1BJ
tel (01453) 757040 *fax* (01453) 751138
email info@hawthornpress.com
website www. hawthornpress.com

'Books for a creative, peaceful and sustainable world' for adults and children. Founded 1981.

Hay House Publishers

292B Kensal Road, London W10 5BE
tel 020-8962 1230 *fax* 020-8962 1239
email info@hayhouse.co.uk
website www.hayhouse.co.uk
Managing Director and Publisher Michelle Pilley, *Sales Director* Diane Hill

Mind, Body & Spirit, self-help, health. Head office in San Diego, California. Founded 1984; in UK 2003.

Haynes Publishing

Sparkford, Yeovil, Somerset BA22 7JJ
tel (01963) 440635 *fax* (01963) 440001
website www.haynes.co.uk
Directors J.H. Haynes (chairman), J. Haynes (vice-chairman and managing), J. Yates-Round, M. Minter, M.J. Hughes, G.R. Cook, J. Bunkum

Car and motorcycle service and repair manuals, car handbooks/servicing guides; DIY books for the home; car, motorcycle, motorsport and leisure activities.

Haynes Book Division (imprint)
email mhughes@haynes.co.uk
Editorial Director Mark Hughes
Cars, motorcycles and motorsport (including related biographies), plus other transport; practical books on home DIY and computing.

Haynes Motor Trade Division (imprint)
email mminter@haynes.co.uk
Editorial Director Matthew Minter
Car and motorcycle service and repair manuals and technical data books.

Headland Publications
Editorial office Tŷ Coch, Galltegfa, Llanfwrog, Ruthin, Denbighshire LL15 2AR
and 38 York Avenue, West Kirby, Wirral CH48 3JF
tel (0151) 625 9128
email headlandpublications@hotmail.co.uk
website www.headlandpublications.co.uk
Editor Gladys Mary Coles
Poetry, anthologies of poetry and prose. No unsolicited MSS. Founded 1970.

Headline Publishing Group*
338 Euston Road, London NW1 3BH
tel 020-7873 6000 *fax* 020-7873 6024
email info@headline.co.uk
website www.headline.co.uk, www.hachettelivreukco.uk
Managing Director Jane Morpeth, *Director of Publishing* Marion Donaldson, *Publishing Director* Imogen Taylor
Commercial and literary fiction (hardback and paperback), and popular non-fiction including autobiography, biography, food and wine, gardening, history, popular science, sport, TV tie-ins. Publishes under Headline, Headline Review, Little Black Dress, Business Plus. Part of Hachette UK (see page 157).

William Heinemann – see The Random House Group Ltd

Heinemann – see Pearson UK

Christopher Helm – see A&C Black Publishers Ltd

The Herbert Press – see A&C Black Publishers Ltd

Hermes House – see Anness Publishing

Nick Hern Books Ltd
The Glasshouse, 49A Goldhawk Road, London W12 8QP
tel 020-8749 4953 *fax* 020-8735 0250
email info@nickhernbooks.demon.co.uk
website www.nickhernbooks.co.uk
Publisher Nick Hern, *Commissioning Editor* Matt Applewhite
Theatre and performing arts books, professionally produced plays, screenplays. Initial letter required. Founded 1988.

Hesperus Press Ltd
4 Rickett Street, London SW6 1RU
tel 020-7610 3331 *fax* 0 20-7610 3337
email info@hesperuspress.com
website www.hesperuspress.com
Fiction and poetry by Classical authors in English and in translation. Classic and modern classic fiction, non-fiction, poetry and biography in English and translation. Founded 2001.

Hilmarton Manor Press
Calne, Wilts. SN11 8SB
tel (01249) 760208 *fax* (01249) 760379
email mailorder@hilmartonpress.co.uk
website www.hilmartonpress.co.uk
Editorial Director Charles Baile de Laperriere
Fine art, antiques, visual arts, wine. Founded 1969.

Hippo – see Scholastic Ltd

Hippopotamus Press
22 Whitewell Road, Frome, Somerset BA11 4EL
tel (01373) 466653 *fax* (01373) 466653
email rjhippopress@aol.com
Editors Roland John, Anna Martin
Poetry, essays, criticism. Submissions from new writers welcome. Founded 1974.

Historical™ – see Harlequin Mills & Boon Ltd

The History Press Ltd
The Mill, Briscombe Port, Stroud, Glos. GL5 2QG
tel (01453) 883300 *fax* (01453) 883233
website www.thehistorypress.co.uk
Directors Stuart Biles (Ceo), Gareth Swain (finance)

The History Press (imprint)
Head of Publishing Laura Perehinec
Local, specialist and general history: military, aviation, maritime, transport, biography, archaeology, sport.

Nonsuch (imprint)†
Classic literature, travel, exploration, military, biography, letters and diaries. Founded 2003.

Phillimore (imprint)
British local history and genealogy.

Pitkin (imprint)
History, heritage, leisure, travel.

Spellmount (imprint)
Military history.

Sutton Publishing (imprint)
General academic and specialist illustrated history books.

Tempus (imprint)
History and local history.

Hobsons Publishing plc
IDT House, 44 Featherstone Street,
London EC1Y 8RN
tel 020-7250 6600 *fax* 020-7250 6601
email enquiries@hobsons.co.uk
website www.hobsons.uk.com
Group Managing Director Len Metheny

Database publisher of educational and careers information under licence to CRAC (Careers Research and Advisory Centre). Founded 1974.

Hodder & Stoughton*
338 Euston Road, London NW1 3BH
tel 020-7873 6000 *fax* 020-7873 6024
website www.hodder.co.uk,
www.hachettelivreukco.uk
Managing Director Jamie Hodder-Williams, *Deputy Managing Director* Lisa Highton, *Non-fiction* Rowena Webb, *Sceptre* Carole Welch, *Fiction* Carolyn Mays, *Audio* Rupert Lancaster

Commercial and literary fiction; biography, autobiography, history, humour, Mind, Body & Spirit, travel, lifestyle and cookery and other general interest non-fiction; audio. No unsolicited MSS or synopses. Publishes under Hodder & Stoughton, Sceptre, Mobius. Part of Hachette UK (see page 157).

Hodder Children's Books – see Hachette Children's Books

Hodder Education Group*
338 Euston Road, London NW1 3BH
tel 020-7873 6000 *fax* 020-7873 6325
website www.hoddereducation.co.uk,
www.hachettelivreukco.uk
Chief Executive Thomas Webster, *Finance Director* Alex Jones, *Managing Directors* David Swarbrick (consumer learning), C P Shaw (tertiary), Lis Tribe (schools), *Editorial Directors* Vivian Marr (consumer languages), Robert Sulley (science and international), Steve Connolly (digital publishing), Jim Belben (humanities and modern languages), *Business Operations Director* Alyssum Ross, *Sales and Marketing Directors* Janice Tolan (schools and FE), Tim Mahar (trade, HE and health sciences), *Directors* Paul Cherry (Philip Allan), John Mitchell (Hodder Gibson)

Medical (Hodder Arnold), consumer education and self-improvement (Hodder Education and Teach Yourself), school (Hodder Education, Hodder Gibson and Philip Allan), dictionaries, reference and language publishing (Chambers). Part of Hachette Ltd (see page 157).

Hodder Faith*
338 Euston Road, London NW1 3BH
tel 020-7873 6000 *fax* 020-7873 6024
email faitheditorialenquiries@hodder.co.uk
website www.hodderfaith.com
Managing Director Jamie Hodder-Williams

Bibles, Christian books, biography/memoir. Publishes New International Version (NIV) of the Bible, Today's New International Version (TNIV) of the Bible, New International Reader's Version (NIrV) of the Bible. Part of Hachette UK (see page 157).

Hodder Gibson*
2A Christie Street, Paisley PA1 1NB
tel 0141-848 1609 *fax* 0141-889 6315
email hoddergibson@hodder.co.uk
website www.hoddergibson.co.uk,
www.hoddereducation.co.uk,
www.hachettelivre.co.uk
Managing Director John Mitchell

Educational books specifically for Scotland. No unsolicited MSS. Part of Hachette UK (see page 157).

Hodder Headline Ltd – see Hachette UK

Hodder Wayland – see Hachette UK

Honno Ltd (Welsh Women's Press)
Honno, Unit 14, Creative Units,
Aberystwyth Arts Centre, Penglais Campus,
Aberystwyth, Ceredigion SY23 3GL
tel (01970) 623150 *fax* (01970) 623150
email post@honno.co.uk
website www.honno.co.uk
Editor Caroline Oakley

Literature written by women in Wales or with a Welsh connection. All subjects considered – fiction, non-fiction, autobiographies. No poetry or works for children considered. Honno is a community co-operative. Founded 1986.

Hopscotch Educational Publishing Ltd
St Jude's Church, Dulwich Road, London SE24 0PB
tel 020-7501 6736 *fax* 020-7978 8316
email sales@hopscotchbooks.com
website www.hopscotchbooks.com
Publishing Manager Angela Morano-Shaw

National Curriculum teaching resources for primary school teachers. Founded 1997.

Step Forward Publishing Ltd
Early years teacher resources.

Quay Books
tel 020-7501 6705 *fax* 020-7978 8316
Editorial Manager Maria Anguita
Nursing, midwifery and medical.

House of Lochar
Isle of Colonsay, Argyll PA61 7YR
tel (01951) 200323
email lochar@colonsay.org.uk
website www.houseoflochar.com

Managing Director Georgina Hobhouse, *Editorial Director* Kevin Byrne

Scottish history, transport, Scottish literature. Founded 1995.

How To Books Ltd

Spring Hill House, Spring Hill Road, Begbroke, Oxford OX5 1RX
tel (01865) 375794 *fax* (01865) 379162
email info@howtobooks.co.uk
website www.howtobooks.co.uk
Publisher & Managing Director Giles Lewis, *Editorial Director* Nikki Read

Self-help reference. Practical books that inspire. Subjects covered include starting a small business, business and management, career development, living and working abroad, property, lifestyle, personal transformation, study skills and student guides, creative writing and others. Book proposals welcome. Founded 1991.

Hutchinson – see The Random House Group Ltd.

Hutchinson Children's Books – see The Random House Group Ltd

Icon Books Ltd

The Omnibus Business Centre, 39–41 North Road, London N7 9DP
tel 020-7697 9695 *fax* (01763) 208080
email info@iconbooks.co.uk
website www.iconbooks.co.uk, www.introducingbooks.com
Directors Peter Pugh (chairman), Simon Flynn (managing), Duncan Heath (editorial), Andrew Furlow (sales & marketing), Najma Finlay (publicity)

Popular, intelligent non-fiction: *Introducing* series, literature, history, philosophy, politics, psychology, sociology, cultural studies, religion, science, current affairs, computers, women, anthropology, humour, music, cinema, linguistics, economics. Imprint: Wizard Books (children's, *Fighting Fantasy* gamebook series). Submission details: will consider unsolicited MSS (adult non-fiction only). Founded 1991.

ICSA Information & Training Ltd

16 Park Crescent, London W1B 1AH
tel 020-7612 7020 *fax* 020-7612 7034
email publishing@icsa.co.uk
website www.icsabookshop.co.uk
Joint Managing Directors Clare Grist Taylor, Susan Richards

Publishing company of the Institute of Chartered Secretaries and Administrators, specialising in information solutions for legal and regulatory compliance. Founded 1981.

Igloo Books Ltd

Cottage Farm, Mears Ashby Road, Sywell, Northants NN6 0BJ
tel (01604) 741116 *fax* (01604) 670495
email publishing@igloo-books.com
website www.igloo-books.com

Adult and children's: cookery, lifestyle, gift, trivia/crosswords, fiction (UK only); novelty, board, picture, activity books, education. Founded 2005.

The Ilex Press Ltd

210 High Street, Lewes, East Sussex BN7 2NS
tel (01273) 403124 *fax* (01273) 487441
website www.ilex-press.com

Highly illustrated technical books on digital photography, digital art and imaging, video and audio, web design, 3D art and design. See website before submitting MS.

Imperial War Museum

Lambeth Road, London SE1 6HZ
tel 020-7416 5438/1 *fax* 020-7416 5374
email mail@iwm.org.uk
website www.iwm.org.uk

In-house art and gift titles; also works in association with larger publishing houses on subjects such as military and social history, photography, children's books, gift, art and cookery.

Imprint Academic

PO Box 200, Exeter EX5 5HY
tel (01392) 851550 *fax* (01392) 851178
email anthony@imprint.co.uk
website www.imprint-academic.com
Publisher Keith Sutherland, *Managing Editor* Anthony Freeman

Books and journals in politics, philosophy and psychology for both academic and general readers. Book series include *St Andrews Studies in Philosophy and Public Affairs*. Unsolicited MSS, synopses and ideas welcome with return postage only. Founded 1980.

In Pinn – see Neil Wilson Publishing Ltd

Independent Music Press

PO Box 69, Church Stretton, Shrops. SY6 6WZ
tel/fax (01694) 720049
email info@impbooks.com
website www.impbooks.com
Music Editor Martin Roach

Music: biography, youth culture/street style/subcultures. No unsoliticed MSS; submissions via literary agents only. Founded 1992.

Indepenpress Publishing Ltd*

25 Eastern Place, Brighton BN2 1GJ
tel (01273) 272758 *fax* (01273) 261434
email info@penpress.co.uk
website www.indepenpress.co.uk
Directors Lynn Ashman (managing), Grace Rafael (production), Caroline Walsh (rights)

Literary fiction, general fiction, children's fiction, selected non-fiction. Founded 1996.

Pen Press (imprint)
Self-publishing.

Pulp Press (imprint)
Pulp fiction.

Pink Press (imprint)
Gay and lesbian fiction.

Infinite Ideas

36 St Giles, Oxford OX1 3LD
tel (01865) 514888 *fax* (01865) 514777
email info@infideas.com
website www.infideas.com
Joint Managing Directors David Grant, Richard Burton

Lifestyle, *52 Brilliant Ideas* series (health, fitness, relationships; leisure and lifestyle; sports, hobbies and games; careers, finance and personal development), business books. *Infinite Success* series (re-interpreted personal development and business classics); *Feelgood Factory* series (lifestyle). Submit business book proposals directly to richard@infideas.com. Founded 2003.

Insight Guides/Berlitz Publishing

58 Borough High Street, London SE1 1XF
tel 020-7403 0284 *fax* 020-7403 0290
website www.insightguides.com, www.berlitzpublishing.com
Managing Director Katharine Leck

Travel, language and related multimedia. Founded 1970.

Institute of Public Administration†

Vergemount Hall, Clonskeagh, Dublin 6, Republic of Ireland
tel (01) 2403600 *fax* (01) 2698644
email rboyle@ipa.ie
website www.ipa.ie
Publisher Richard Boyle

Government, economics, politics, law, public management, health, education, social policy and administrative history. Founded 1957.

Inter-Varsity Press

Norton Street, Nottingham NG7 3HR
tel 0115-978 1054 *fax* 0115-942 2694
email sales@ivpbooks.com
website www.ivpbooks.com
Senior Commissioning Editor E. Trotter

Theology and religion.

Irish Academic Press Ltd†

2 Brookside, Dundrum Road, Dublin 14, Ireland
tel (20) 89 52 9526 *fax* (20) 89 52 9242
email info@iap.ie
website www.iap.ie

Scholarly books especially in 19th and 20th century history, literature, heritage and culture. Imprints: Irish University Press, Irish Academic Press. Founded 1974.

Ithaca Press – see Garnet Publishing Ltd

JAI – see Elsevier Ltd

Jane's – see HarperCollins Publishers

Jane's Information Group

163 Brighton Road, Coulsdon, Surrey CR5 2YH
tel 020-8700 3700 *fax* 020-8700 3751
website www.janes.com
Managing Director Scott Key

Professional business-to-business publishers in hardcopy and electronic multimedia of military, aviation, naval, defence, reference, police, geopolitical. Consumer books in association with HarperCollins Publishers.

Jarrold Publishing – see The History Press Ltd

Jordan Publishing Ltd

21 St Thomas Street, Bristol BS1 6JS
tel 0117-923 0600 *fax* 0117-925 0486
website www.jordanpublishing.co.uk
Managing Director Caroline Vandridge-Ames

Law and business administration. Also specialist Family Law imprint (including the *Family Law Journal*). Books, looseleaf services, serials, CD-Roms and online.

Michael Joseph – see Penguin Group (UK)

Kenilworth Press – see Quiller Publishing Ltd

Kenyon-Deane – see Cressrelles Publishing Co. Ltd

Laurence King Publishing Ltd*

(formerly Calmann & King Ltd)
361–373 City Road, London EC1V 1LR
tel 020-7841 6900 *fax* 020-7841 6910
email enquiries@laurenceking.co.uk
website www.laurenceking.co.uk
Directors Laurence King (managing), Nicholas Perren (chairman), Simon Gwynn (marketing), Philip Cooper (editorial), John Stoddart (financial)

Illustrated books on design, contemporary architecture, art, interiors and fashion for the professional, student and general market. Founded 1976.

Kingfisher – see Macmillan Publishers Ltd

Kingscourt – see McGraw-Hill Education

Jessica Kingsley Publishers*

116 Pentonville Road, London N1 9JB
tel 020-7833 2307 *fax* 020-7837 2917

email post@jkp.com
website www.jkp.com
Managing Director Jessica Kingsley

Psychology, psychiatry, arts therapies, social work, special needs (especially autism and Asperger Syndrome), education, law, practical theology and a small children's list focusing on books for children with special needs. Founded 1987.

Singing Dragon (imprint)

Focuses on oriental and complementary medicine, health, and Chinese martial arts.

Kluwer Law International

250 Waterloo Road, London SE1 8RD
tel 020-7981 0600
email sales@kluwerlaw.com
website www.kluwerlaw.com
Publisher Simon Bellamy

International law.

Charles Knight – see LexisNexis

Knight Paperbacks – see Caxton Publishing Group

Kogan Page Ltd*

120 Pentonville Road, London N1 9JN
tel 020-7278 0433 *fax* 020-7837 6348
website www.koganpage.com
Chairman Phillip Kogan, *Directors* Helen Kogan (managing), Louis Cameron (production), Mark Briars (financial), Ben Glover (sales), Jon Finch (editorial)

Education, training, business and management, human resource management, transport and distribution, marketing, sales, advertising and PR, finance and accounting, directories, small business, careers and vocational, personal finance, international business. Founded 1967.

Kube Publishing Ltd

(formerly the Islamic Foundation)
Markfield Conference Centre, Ratby Lane, Markfield, Leics. LE67 9SY
tel (01530) 249230 *fax* (01530) 249656
email info@kubepublishing.com
website www.kubepublishing.com
Managing Director Haris Ahmad

Books on Islam for adults and children.

Kudos Books – see Top That! Publishing plc

Ladybird – see Penguin Group (UK)

Peter Lang Ltd

Evenlode Court, Main Road, Long Hanborough, Witney OX29 8SZ
tel (01993) 880088 *fax* (01993) 882040
email oxford@peterlang.com
website www.peterlang.com
Directors Tony Albala (managing), Fritz Schmutz (finance), Dr Graham Speake (publishing), *Commissioning Editors* Nick Reynolds, Hannah Godfrey

Academic: humanities and social sciences. Founded 2006.

Lawrence & Wishart Ltd

99A Wallis Road, London E9 5LN
tel 020-8533 2506 *fax* 020-8533 7369
email lw@lwbooks.co.uk
website www.lwbooks.co.uk
Directors Sally Davison (editorial), J. Rutherford, A. Greenaway, B. Kirsch

Cultural studies, current affairs, history, socialism and Marxism, political philosophy, politics, popular culture.

Letts and Lonsdale

PO Box 113, Holme, Carnforth, Lancs. LA6 1WL
tel (01539) 564911 *fax* (01539) 564167
email enquiries@lettsandlonsdale.co.uk
website www.lettsandlonsdale.com
Directors Andrew Ware (managing), Helen Jacobs (publishing)

Study and revision guides for children of all ages, from preschool to A Level. Subsidiary of HarperCollins Publishers.

Lewis Mason – see Ian Allan Publishing Ltd

LexisNexis

(formerly LexisNexis Butterworths)
Halsbury House, 35 Chancery Lane, London WC2A 1EL
tel 020-7400 2500 *fax* 020-7400 2842
email customer.services@lexisnexis.co.uk
website www.lexisnexis.co.uk

Division of Reed Elsevier (UK) Ltd. Founded 1974.

Butterworths (imprint)

Legal and tax and accountancy books, journals, looseleaf and electronic services.

Charles Knight (imprint)

Looseleaf legal works and periodicals on local government law, construction law and technical subjects.

Tolley (imprint)

Law, taxation, accountancy, business.

Library Association Publishing – see Facet Publishing

The Lilliput Press Ltd†

62–63 Sitric Road, Arbour Hill, Dublin 7, Republic of Ireland

tel (01) 6711647 *fax* (01) 6711233
email info@lilliputpress.ie
website www.lilliputpress.ie
Managing Director Antony T. Farrell

General and Irish literature: essays, memoir, biography/autobiography, fiction, criticism; Irish history; philosophy; Joycean contemporary culture; nature and environment. Founded 1984.

Frances Lincoln Ltd

4 Torriano Mews, Torriano Avenue,
London NW5 2RZ
tel 020-7284 4009 *fax* 020-7485 0490
email reception@frances-lincoln.com
website www.frances-lincoln.com
Directors John Nicoll (managing), Maurice Lyon (editorial, children's books), Jon Rippon (finance), Gail Lynch (sales), Andrew Dunn (editorial, adult books), Helen Fraser, David Kewley, Sarah Roberts (non-executive)

Illustrated, international co-editions: gardening, architecture, environment, interiors, art, walking and climbing, gift, children's books. Founded 1977.

Lion Hudson plc*

Wilkinson House, Jordan Hill Road,
Oxford OX2 8DR
tel (01865) 302750 *fax* (01865) 302757
email info@lionhudson.com
website www.lionhudson.com
Managing Director Paul Clifford

Books for children and adults. Subject areas include Christian Spirituality, reference, biography, history, contemporary issues and inspiration. Also specialises in children's Bibles and prayer collections, as well as picture stories and illustrated non-fiction. Founded 1971 as Lion Publishing; merged with Angus Hudson Ltd in 2003.

Lion (imprint)

email katek@lionhudson.com
Commissioning Editor Kate Kirkpatrick

Christian books for general readers: information and reference, history, spirituality and prayer, issues, self-help.

Monarch Books

email tonyc@lionhudson.com
Editorial Director Tony Collins

Christian books: biography, issues of faith and society, humour, church resources. Submit synopsis and 2 chapters with return postage.

Little, Brown Book Group*

100 Victoria Embankment, London EC4Y 0DY
tel 020-7911 8000 *fax* 020-7911 8100
email info@littlebrown.co.uk
website www.littlebrown.co.uk
Ceo & Publisher Ursula Mackenzie, *Deputy Publisher* David Shelley, *Coo* David Kent, *Directors* Julian Shaw (Finance), Richard Beswick (editorial), Antonia Hodgson (editorial), Robert Manser (group sales, publicity and marketing), Ben Groves-Raines (commercial), Diane Spivey (rights)

Hardback and paperback fiction and general non-fiction. No unsolicited MSS. Part of Hachette UK (see page 157). Founded 1988.

Abacus (division)

Managing Director Richard Beswick

Trade paperbacks.

Atom (division)

website www.atombooks.co.uk
Publishing Director Tim Holman, *Editorial Director* Samantha Smith

Teen fiction with a fantastical edge.

Hachette Digital (division)

Editorial Director Sarah Shrubb

CDs and ebooks. See page 222.

Little, Brown (division)

Managing Director Richard Beswick, *Publishing Director* Tim Whiting

General books: politics, biography, crime fiction, general fiction.

Orbit (division)

website www.orbitbooks.com
Publishing Director Tim Holman, *Editorial Director* Darren Nash

Science fiction and fantasy.

Piatkus (division)

website www.piatkus.co.uk
Publishing Director, Non-fiction Tim Whiting, *Senior Commissioning Editor* Ann Lawrence, *Senior Editor, Fiction* Emma Beswetherick

Fiction and general non-fiction.

Sphere (division)

website www.twbookjuice.co.uk
Publishing Director Antonia Hodgson, *Editorial Directors* Hilary Hale, Joanne Dickinson, David Shelley

Hardbacks and paperbacks: original fiction and non-fiction.

Virago (division)

website www.virago.co.uk
Publisher Lennie Goodings

Women's literary fiction and non-fiction.

Little Black Dress – see Headline Publishing Group

Little Tiger Press – see Magi Publications

Liverpool University Press

4 Cambridge Street, Liverpool L69 7ZU
tel 0151-794 2233 *fax* 0151-794 2235

email lup@liv.ac.uk
website www.liverpool-unipress.co.uk

French and Francophone studies, Hispanic and Lusophone studies, Liverpool interest titles, science fiction studies, art history, slavery studies and postcolonial studies. Founded 1899.

Livewire – see The Women's Press

Logaston Press

Little Logaston, Logaston, Woonton, Almeley, Herefordshire HR3 6QH
tel (01544) 327344
email logastonpress@btinternet.com
website www.logastonpress.co.uk
Proprietors Andy Johnson, Karen Johnson

History, social history, archaeology and guides to rural west Midlands and central and south Wales. Welcomes submission of ideas: send synopsis first. Founded 1985.

Lonely Planet

2nd Floor, 186 City Road, London EC1V 2NT
tel 020-7106 2100 *fax* 020-7106 2101
website www.lonelyplanet.com
Founders Tony Wheeler, Maureen Wheeler, *Managing Director* Douglas Schatz, *Regional Publisher* Imogen Hall

Country and regional guidebooks, city guides, *Encounter* citybreak guides, *Discover* country guides, phrasebooks, walking guides, cycling guides, diving and snorkelling guides, pictorial books, healthy travel guides, wildlife guides, travel photography. Also a digital image library (Lonely Planet Images) and a TV company. London office established 1991.

Longman – see Pearson UK

Lorenz Books – see Anness Publishing

Luath Press Ltd

543/2 Castlehill, The Royal Mile, Edinburgh EH1 2ND
tel 0131-225 4326 *fax* 0131-225 4324
email gavin.macdougall@luath.co.uk
website www.luath.co.uk
Director Gavin MacDougall

Modern fiction, history, travel guides, poetry. Founded 1981.

Lund Humphries – see Ashgate Publishing Ltd

Lutterworth Press – see James Clarke & Co. Ltd

McGraw-Hill Education*

McGraw-Hill House, Shoppenhangers Road, Maidenhead, Berks. SL6 2QL
tel (01628) 502500
email emea_queries@mcgraw-hill.com
website www.mcgraw-hill.co.uk
Managing Director, UK/Northern & Central Europe John Donovan, *Director Operations/Finance EMEA* Alan Martin, *Managing Director MEA* Thanos Blintzios, *Sales & Marketing Director MEA* Lefteris Souris, *General Manager Content & Digital Development EMEA* Shona Mullen, *Marketing Director Europe/South Africa* Alice Duijser, *General Manager UK Schools* Rob Ince, *Director Professional/Medical Division UK/NE* Emma Gibson

Higher education: business, economics, computing, maths, humanities, social sciences, world languages. Professional: business, computing, science, technical, medical, general reference.

Kingscourt (imprint)

website www.kingscourt.co.uk

Primary and secondary education.

Open University Press (imprint)

email enquiries@openup.co.uk
website www.openup.co.uk

Social sciences.

Osborne (imprint)

Science, engineering, maths, computer science.

Macmillan Children's Books Ltd – see Macmillan Publishers Ltd

Macmillan Heinemann English Language Teaching – see Macmillan Publishers Ltd

Macmillan Publishers Ltd*

The Macmillan Building, 4 Crinan Street, London N1 9XW
tel 020-7833 4000 *fax* 020-7843 4640
website www.macmillan.com
Chief Executive Annette Thomas, *Directors* Julian Drinkall, S.C. Inchcoombe, D.J.G. Knight, Dr A. Thomas, J. Wheeldon, A. Forbes Watson, W.H. Farries, R. Gibb (Australia)

Pan Macmillan (division)

20 New Wharf Road, London N1 9RR
tel 020-7014 6000 *fax* 020-7014 6001
website www.panmacmillan.com
Managing Director Anthony Forbes-Watson, *Publishers* Jon Butler (Macmillan non-fiction, Sidgwick & Jackson, Boxtree), Jeremy Trevathan (Macmillan fiction & Macmillan New Writing), Paul Baggaley (Picador)

Novels, literary, crime, thrillers, romance, science fiction, fantasy and horror. Autobiography, biography, business, gift books, health and beauty, history, humour, natural history, travel, philosophy, politics, world affairs, theatre, film, gardening, cookery, popular reference. Publishes under

Macmillan, Tor, Pan, Picador, Sidgwick & Jackson, Boxtree, Macmillan Audio, Macmillan New Writing. No unsolicited MSS except through Macmillan New Writing. Founded 1843.

Macmillan (imprint)
Picador Publisher Paul Baggaley, *Non-Fiction Publisher* Jon Butler, *Fiction Publisher* Jeremy Trevathan, *Editorial Directors* Georgina Morley, Kate Harvey
Hardback commercial fiction including genre fiction, romantic, crime and thrillers. Hardback serious and general non-fiction including autobiography, biography, economics, history, military history, philosophy, politics and world affairs, popular reference titles.

Tor (imprint)
Science fiction, fantasy and thrillers published in hardback and paperback.

Pan (imprint)
Paperback imprint for Macmillan and Sidgwick & Jackson imprints. Founded 1947.

Picador (imprint)
Publisher Paul Baggaley, *Editorial Director* Kate Harvey
Literary international fiction, non-fiction and poetry published in hardback and paperback. Founded 1972.

Sidgwick & Jackson (imprint)
Publisher Jon Butler, *Editorial Director* Ingrid Connell
Hardback popular non-fiction including celebrity and show business to music and sport. Founded 1908.

Macmillan New Writing (imprint)
website www.macmillannewwriting.com
Editorial Director Will Atkins
Founded as a way of finding talented new writers who might otherwise go undiscovered. Publishes full-length novels by authors who have not previously published a novel. All genres considered and all submissions are assessed but MSS must be complete. No advance but the author pays nothing and receives a royalty of 20% on net sales. Send the complete novel by email via the website. Founded 2006.

Boxtree (imprint)
Publisher Jon Butler
Brand and media tie-in titles, including TV, film, music and internet, plus entertainment licences, pop culture, humour in hardback and paperback.

Macmillan Digital Audio (imprint)
Digital Director Sara Lloyd
Audio imprint for the entire Pan Macmillan list. See page 222.

Campbell Books (imprint)
Editorial Director Suzanne Carnell
Early learning, pop-up, novelty, board books for the preschool market.

Kingfisher (imprint)
tel 020-7014 6000 *fax* 020-7014 6001
Director Emma Hopkin, *Publishing Director* Martina Challis
Children's books. Non-fiction: activity books, encyclopedias, general history, religion, art, music, philosophy, folklore, language, mathematics, nature, science and technology.

Young Picador (imprint)
Editorial Director Sarah Dudman
Literary fiction in paperback and hardback for the young adult market.

Palgrave Macmillan (division)*
Publishers Association or Publishing ScotlandBrunel Road, Houndmills, Basingstoke, Hants RG21 6XS
tel (01256) 329242 *fax* (01256) 479476
website www.palgrave.com
Managing Director Dominic Knight, *Publishing Directors* Margaret Hewinson (college), Sam Burridge (scholarly & reference), David Bull (journals)
Textbooks, monographs and journals in academic and professional subjects. Publishes in both hard copy and electronic formats.

W.H. Freeman (imprint)
tel (01256) 332807 *fax* (01256) 330688
Science, medicine, economics, psychology, sociology.

Macmillan Education Ltd (division)
Macmillan Oxford, 4 Between Towns Road, Oxford OX4 3PP
tel (01865) 405700 *fax* (01865) 405701
email info@macmillan.com
website www.macmillaneducation.com
Chief Executive Julian Drinkall, *Publishing Directors* Alison Hubert (Africa, Caribbean, Middle East, Asia), Kate Melliss (Spain), Sharon Jervis (Latin America), Sue Bale (Dictionaries), Angela Lilley (International ELT)
ELT titles and school and college textbooks and materials in all subjects for the international education market in both book and electronic formats.

Made Simple Books – see Elsevier Ltd

Magi Publications
1 The Coda Centre, 189 Munster Road, London SW6 6AW
tel 020-7385 6333 *fax* 020-7385 7333
website www.littletigerpress.com
Publishers Monty Bhatia, Jude Evans, Jane Harris, Jamie Asher
Children's picture books, novelty books, board books, pop-up books and activity books for preschool age to 7 years, and fiction for 6–12 year-olds. Will consider new material from authors and illustrators; see imprint websites for guidelines. Imprints: Caterpillar Books, Little Tiger Press, Stripes (fiction), Roar Publishing. Founded 1987.

The Maia Press Ltd
15–16 Nassau Street, London W1W 7AB
tel 020-7436 9898
website www.maiapress.com

Original fiction by new and established authors. No unsolicited MSS. Part of Arcadia Books. Founded 2003.

Mainstream Publishing Co. (Edinburgh) Ltd*
7 Albany Street, Edinburgh EH1 3UG
tel 0131-557 2959 *fax* 0131-556 8720
email enquiries@mainstreampublishing.com
website www.mainstreampublishing.com
Directors Bill Campbell, Peter MacKenzie, Fiona Brownlee (marketing, publicity & rights), Ailsa Bathgate (editorial), Neil Graham (production), Douglas Nicoll (finance)

Biography, autobiography, art, sport, health, guidebooks, humour, current affairs, history, politics, true crime. Founded 1978.

Management Books 2000 Ltd
Forge House, Limes Road, Kemble, Cirencester, Glos. GL7 6AD
tel (01285) 771441 *fax* (01285) 771055
email info@mb2000.com
website www.mb2000.com
Directors N. Dale-Harris, R. Hartman

Practical books for working managers and business professionals: management, business and lifeskills, and sponsored titles. Unsolicited MSS, synopses and ideas for books welcome.

Manchester University Press
Oxford Road, Manchester M13 9NR
tel 0161-275 2310 *fax* 0161-274 3346
email mup@manchester.ac.uk
website www.manchesteruniversitypress.co.uk
Chief Executive David Rodgers *Head of Sales & Marketing* Simon Bell *Head of Editorial* Matthew Frost

Works of academic scholarship: literary criticism, cultural studies, media studies, art history, design, architecture, history, politics, economics, international law, modern-language texts. Textbooks and monographs. Founded 1904.

Mandrake of Oxford
PO Box 250, Oxford OX1 1AP
tel (01865) 243671
email mandrake@mandrake.uk.net
website www.mandrake.uk.net
Directors Mogg Morgan, Kim Morgan

Art, biography, classic crime studies, fiction, Indology, magic, witchcraft, philosophy, religion. Query letters only. Founded 1986.

Mango Publishing
PO Box 13378, London SE27 OZN
tel 020-8480 7771 *fax* 020-8480 7771
email info@mangoprint.com
website www.mangoprint.com

Poetry, fiction and non-fiction from the wider Caribbean region, the UK, the USA and Canada. Also translations of works not originally written in English. Founded 1995.

Manson Publishing Ltd*
73 Corringham Road, London NW11 7DL
tel 020-8905 5150 *fax* 020-8201 9233
email manson@mansonpublishing.com
website www.mansonpublishing.com
Managing Director Michael Manson

Medical, scientific, veterinary. Founded 1992.

Mantra Lingua
Global House, 303 Ballards Lane, London N12 8NP
tel 020-8445 5123 *fax* 020-8446 7745
email info@mantralingua.com
website www.mantralingua.com
Managing Director M. Chatterji

Innovative resources and technologies to support language learning and literacy. Dual language books narrated in multiple languages by the TalkingPEN. Considers picture book MSS under 1000 words, artwork submission, and non-fiction proposals. Founded 1984.

Marino Books – see The Mercier Press

Marshall Cavendish
5th Floor, 32–38 Saffron Hill, London EC1N 8FH
tel 020-7421 8120 *fax* 020-7421 8121
email info@marshallcavendish.co.uk
website www.marshallcavendish.co.uk
Managing Editor Susan McGing

English language teaching. Founded 1969.

Kenneth Mason Publications Ltd
The Book Barn, Westbourne, Hants PO10 8RS
tel (01243) 377977 *fax* (01243) 379136
email bookshop@kennethmason.co.uk
website www.kennethmason.co.uk
Directors Kenneth Mason (chairman), Piers Mason (managing), Michael Mason, Anthea Mason

Nautical, slimming, health, fitness; technical journals. Founded 1958.

Kevin Mayhew Ltd
Buxhall, Stowmarket, Suffolk IP14 3BW
tel (01449) 737978 *fax* (01449) 737834
email info@kevinmayhew.com
website www.kevinmayhew.com
Directors Kevin Mayhew (chairman), Tim Messinger (sales and marketing), Barbara Mayhew

Christianity: prayer and spirituality, pastoral care, preaching, liturgy worship, children's, youth work, drama, instant art. Music: hymns, organ and choral, contemporary worship, piano and instrumental. Contact Manuscript Submissions Dept before sending MSS/synopses. Founded 1976.

Meadowside Children's Books

185 Fleet Street, London EC4A 2HS
tel 020-7400 1084 *fax* 020-7400 1037
email info@meadowsidebooks.com
website www.meadowsidebooks.com
Publisher Simon Rosenheim

Picture books, junior fiction and young adult fiction. Founded 2003.

Medical™ – see Harlequin Mills & Boon Ltd

Mentor Books†

43 Furze Road, Sandyford Industrial Estate, Dublin 18, Republic of Ireland
tel (353) 1 295 2112 *fax* (353) 1 295 2114
email admin@mentorbooks.ie
website www.mentorbooks.ie
Managing Director Daniel McCarthy, *Editor* Treasa O'Mahony

General: non-fiction, humour, biographies, politics, crime, history, guidebooks. Educational (secondary): languages, history, geography, business, maths, sciences. No unsolicited MSS. Founded 1980.

Mercat Press – see Birlinn Ltd

The Mercier Press†

Unit 3, Oak House, Riverview Business Park, Blackrock, Cork, Republic of Ireland
tel 021-461 4700 *fax* 021-461 4802
email pr@mercierpress.ie
website www.mercierpress.ie
Directors J.F. Spillane (chairman), C. Feehan (managing), M.P. Feehan

Irish literature, folklore, history, politics, humour, academic, current affairs, health, mind and spirit, general non-fiction, children's. Founded 1944.

Merlin Press Ltd

99B Wallis Road, London E9 5LN
tel 020-8533 5800
email info@merlinpress.co.uk
website www.merlinpress.co.uk
Managing Director Anthony Zurbrugg

Radical history and social studies. Letters/synopses only.

Green Print (imprint)

Green politics and the environment.

Merrell Publishers Ltd

81 Southwark Street, London SE1 0HX
tel 020-7928 8880 *fax* 020-7928 1199
email mail@merrellpublishers.com
website www.merrellpublishers.com
Publisher Hugh Merrell, *Managing Editor* Claire Chandler, *Sales Manager* Lulu Cane

High-quality illustrated books on all aspects of visual culture, including art, architecture, photography and design. Unsolicited proposals welcomed but must be accompanied by return postage.

Methodist Publishing House

17 Tresham Road, Orton, Southgate, Peterborough PE3 6SG
tel (01733) 235962 *fax* (01733) 390325
email customer.services@mph.org.uk

Hymn and service books, general religious titles, church supplies. Imprints: Epworth, Methodist Publishing House. Founded 1773.

Methuen Drama – see A&C Black Publishers Ltd

Methuen Publishing Ltd

8 Artillery Row, London SW1P 1RZ
tel 020-7802 0018 *fax* 020-7828 1244
website www.methuen.co.uk
Managing Director Peter Tummons, Editor Naomi Tummons

Literary fiction and non-fiction: biography, autobiography, travel, history, sport, humour, film, performing arts. No unsolicited MSS.

Politico's Publishing (imprint)

Politics, current affairs, political biography and autobiography.

Metro Books – see John Blake Publishing Ltd

Michelin Maps and Guides

Hannay House, 39 Clarendon Road, Watford, Herts. WD17 1JA
tel (01923) 205240 *fax* (01923) 205241
email travelpubsales@uk.michelin.com
website www.michelin.co.uk/travel
Commercial Director Ian Murray

Tourist guides, maps and atlases, hotel and restaurant guides.

Midland Publishing – see Ian Allan Publishing Ltd

Miller's – see Octopus Publishing Group

Mills & Boon Romance™ – see Harlequin Mills & Boon Ltd

Milo Books Ltd

The Old Weighbridge, Station Road, Wrea Green, Preston PR4 2PH
tel (01772) 672900 *fax* (01772) 687727
email info@milobooks.com
website www.milobooks.co.uk
Publisher Peter Walsh

True crime, sport, autobiography/biography, current affairs. Founded 1997.

Mira Books® – see Harlequin Mills & Boon Ltd

Mitchell Beazley – see Octopus Publishing Group

Mobius – see Hodder & Stoughton

Modern Extra™ – see Harlequin Mills & Boon Ltd

Modern Romance™ – see Harlequin Mills & Boon Ltd

Monarch Books – see Lion Hudson plc

Morgan Kauffman – see Elsevier Ltd

Morrigan Book Company

Killala, Co. Mayo, Republic of Ireland
tel (096) 32555
email morriganbooks@gmail.com
Publishers Gerry Kennedy, Hilary Kennedy

Non-fiction: general Irish interest, biography, history, local history, folklore and mythology. Founded 1979.

Mosby – see Elsevier Ltd (Health Sciences)

Mount Eagle Publications Ltd – see Brandon/Mount Eagle Publications

Murdoch Books UK Ltd

Erico House, 6th Floor North,
93–99 Upper Richmond Road, London SW15 2TG
tel 020-8785 5995 *fax* 020-8785 5985
email info@murdochbooks.co.uk
website www.murdochbooks.co.uk
Publisher Kay Scarlett (Australia)

Non-fiction: homes and interiors, gardening, cookery, craft, DIY, narrative non-fiction, history, travel. Owned by Australian publisher Murdoch Books Pty Ltd.

John Murray (Publishers)*

338 Euston Road, London NW1 3BH
tel 020-7873 6000 *fax* 020-7873 6446
website www.johnmurray.co.uk, www.hachettelivre.co.uk
Managing Director Roland Philipps, *Non-fiction* Eleanor Birne, *Fiction* Kate Parkin

Quality commercial fiction and non-fiction: travel, history, entertainment, reference, biography and memoir, real-life stories. No unsolicited MSS without preliminary letter. Part of Hachette UK (see page 157).

Myriad Editions

59 Lansdowne Place, Brighton BN3 1FL
tel (01273) 720000
email info@myriadeditions.com
website www.myriadeditions.com
Directors Candida Lacey (managing), Bob Benewick, Judith Mackay

State of the World atlases, original fiction, innovative non-fiction and documentary comic books. Founded 1993.

National Maritime Museum Publishing

NMM Publishing, National Maritime Museum, Park Row, Greenwich, London SE10 9NF
tel 020-8312 8615
email publishing@nmm.ac.uk
website www.nmm.ac.uk/publishing
Head of Publishing Rachel Giles, *Project Managers* Eliza Marciniak, Emily Winter

Books supporting the museum's mission to illustrate to everyone the importance of the sea, ships, time and the stars.

National Trust – see Anova Books

Natural History Museum Publishing

Cromwell Road, London SW7 5BD
tel 020-7942 5336 *fax* 020-7942 5010
email publishing@nhm.ac.uk
website www.nhm.ac.uk/publishing
Head of Publishing Colin Ziegler

Natural sciences, entomology, botany, geology, mineralogy, palaeontology, zoology, history of natural history. Founded 1881.

Nautical Data Ltd

The Book Barn, White Chimney Row, Westbourne, Hants PO10 8RS
tel (01243) 389352 *fax* (01243) 379136
email enquiries@nauticaldata.com
website www.nauticaldata.com
Directors Piers Mason, Michael Benson-Colpi

Yachting titles.

NCVO Publications

(incorporating Bedford Square Press)
Regent's Wharf, 8 All Saints Street, London N1 9RL
tel 020-7713 6161 *fax* 020-7713 6300
email ncvo@ncvo-vol.org.uk
website www.ncvo-vol.org.uk
Head of Publications Emma Moore

Imprint of the National Council for Voluntary Organisations. Practical guides, reference books, directories and policy studies on voluntary sector concerns including management, employment, trustee development and finance. No unsolicited MSS accepted.

Neate Publishing

33 Downside Road, Winchester, Hants SO22 5LT
tel (01962) 841479 *fax* (01962) 841743
email sales@neatepublishing.co.uk
website www.neatepublishing.co.uk

Directors Bobbie Neate (managing), Ann Langran, Maggie Threadingham

Non-fiction books, educational packs, CDs and posters for primary school children. Founded 1999.

Nelson Thornes Ltd*

Delta Place, 27 Bath Road, Cheltenham, Glos. GL53 7TH
tel (01242) 267287 *fax* (01242) 253695
email cservices@nelsonthornes.com
website www.nelsonthornes.com
Managing Director Mary O'Connor

Print and electronic publishers for the educational market: primary, secondary, further education, professional. Part of the Infinitas Learning group.

New Beacon Books

76 Stroud Green Road, London N4 3EN
tel 020-7272 4889 *fax* 020-7281 4662
email newbeaconbooks@btconnect.com
website www.newbeaconbooks.co.uk
Directors Sarah White, Michael La Rose, Janice Durham

Small specialist publishers: general non-fiction, fiction, poetry, critical writings, concerning the Caribbean, Africa, African–America and Black Britain. No unsolicited MSS. Founded 1966.

New Cavendish Books

3 Denbigh Road, London W11 2SJ
tel 020-7229 6765 *fax* 020-7792 0027
email sales@newcavendishbooks.co.uk
website www.newcavendishbooks.co.uk

Specialist books for the collector; art reference, Thai guidebooks. Founded 1973.

River Books (associate imprint)

The art and architecture of Southeast Asia.

New Holland Publishers (UK) Ltd

Garfield House, 86–88 Edgware Road, London W2 2EA
tel 020-7724 7773 *fax* 020-7258 1293
email postmaster@nhpub.co.uk
website www.newhollandpublishers.com
Managing Director Steve Connolly

Illustrated non-fiction books on natural history, sports and hobbies, animals and pets, travel pictorial, travel maps and guides, reference, gardening, health and fitness, practical art, DIY, food and drink, outdoor pursuits, craft, humour, gift books. New proposals accepted (send CV and synopsis and sample chapters in first instance; sae essential).

Cadogan Guides (imprint)

email cadogan@nhpub.co.uk
Travel guides and travel literature.

New Island Books†

2 Brookside, Dundrum Road, Dundrum, Dublin 14, Republic of Ireland
tel (01) 2989937 *fax* (01) 2982783
email editor@newisland.ie, sales@newisland.ie
website www.newisland.ie
Publisher Edwin Higel

Fiction, poetry, drama, humour, biography, current affairs. Submissions by hard copy only. No emails. Send first 3 chapters, synopsis, an essay and sae for return. Founded 1992.

New Playwrights' Network

10 Station Road Industrial Estate, Colwall, Nr Malvern, Herefordshire WR13 6RN
tel (01684) 540154 *fax* (01684) 540154
email simon@cressrelles.co.uk
website www.cressrelles.co.uk
Publishing Director Leslie Smith

General plays for the amateur, one-act and full length.

New Rider – see Pearson UK

New Theatre Publications/The Playwrights' Co-operative

2 Hereford Close, Woolston, Warrington, Cheshire WA1 4HR
tel 0845-331 3516, (01925) 485605 *fax* 0845-331 3518
email info@plays4theatre.com
website www.plays4theatre.com
Directors Ian Hornby, Alison Hornby

Plays for the professional and amateur stage. Submissions encouraged. Founded 1987.

Newnes – see Elsevier Ltd

Nexus – see Virgin Books, page 182

Nia – see The X Press

Nightingale Press

6 The Old Dairy, Melcombe Road, Bath BA2 3LR
tel (01225) 478444 *fax* (01225) 478440
email sales@manning-partnership.co.uk
website www.manning-partnership.co.uk
Directors Garry Manning (managing), Roger Hibbert (sales)

Humour, gift, health, language and learning, lifestyle and relationships. Owned by the Manning Partnership Ltd. Founded 1997.

Nonsuch Publishing Ltd – see The History Press Ltd

North-Holland – see Elsevier Ltd

Northcote House Publishers Ltd

Horndon House, Horndon, Tavistock, Devon PL19 9NQ
tel (01822) 810066 *fax* (01822) 810034
email northcote.house@virgin.net
website www.northcotehouse.co.uk
Directors B.R.W. Hulme, A.V. Hulme (secretary)

Education and education management, educational dance and drama, literary criticism (*Writers and their Work*). Founded 1985.

W.W. Norton & Company

Castle House, 75–76 Wells Street, London W1T 3QT
tel 020-7323 1579 *fax* 020-7436 4553
website www.wwnorton.co.uk
Managing Director Alan Cameron

English and American literature, economics, music, psychology, science. Founded 1980.

NWP – see Neil Wilson Publishing Ltd

Oak Tree Press†

19 Rutland Street, Cork, Republic of Ireland
tel (021) 431 3855 *fax* (021) 431 3496
email info@oaktreepress.com
website www.oaktreepress.com
Directors Brian O'Kane, Rita O'Kane

Business management, enterprise, accountancy and finance, law. Special emphasis on titles for small business owner/managers. Founded 1991.

Oberon Books

521 Caledonian Road, London N7 9RH
tel 020-7607 3637 *fax* 020-7607 3629
email info@oberonbooks.com
website www.oberonbooks.com
Managing Director Charles Glanville *Publisher* James Hogan *Editor* Stephen Watson

New and classic play texts, programme texts and general theatre and performing arts books. Founded 1986.

O-Books Publishing Ltd

The Bothy, Deershot Lodge, Park Lane, Ropley, Hants SO24 0BE
email office1@o-books.net
website www.o-books.net
Director John Hunt

Global spirituality and Mind, Body & Spirit, history, religion and philosophy. See website for submission procedure. Imprints: O-Books, Zero Books, Circle Books. Founded 1989.

The O'Brien Press Ltd†

12 Terenure Road East, Rathgar, Dublin 6, Republic of Ireland
tel (01) 492 3333 *fax* (01) 492 2777
email books@obrien.ie
website www.obrien.ie
Directors Michael O'Brien, Ide ní Laoghaire, Ivan O'Brien

Adult: biography, politics, history, true crime, sport, humour, reference. Children's: fiction for all ages; illustrated fiction series – *Panda Cubs* (age 3+), *Pandas* (age 5+), *Flyers* (age 6+) and *Red Flag* (8+); novels (10+) – contemporary, historical, fantasy. No poetry, adult fiction or academic. Unsolicited MSS (sample chapters only), synopses and ideas for books welcome – submissions will not be returned. Founded 1974.

The Octagon Press Ltd

78 York Street, London W1H 1DP
tel 020-7193 6456 *fax* 020-7117 3955
email admin@octagonpress.com
website www.octagonpress.com
Director Anna Murphy

Travel, biography, literature, folklore, psychology, philosophy, with the focus on East–West studies. Welcomes single page book proposals via email. Unsolicited MSS not accepted. Founded 1960.

Octopus Publishing Group*

Endeavour House, 189 Shaftesbury Avenue, London WC2 8JY
tel 020-7632 5400
email info@octopus-publishing.co.uk
website www.octopus-publishing.co.uk
Chief Executive Alison Goff, *Deputy Ceo* Andrew Welham

Part of Hachette UK (see page 157).

Bounty (imprint)

tel 020-7531 8601 *fax* 020-7531 8607
email bountybooksinfo-bp@bountybooks.co.uk
Publishing & International Sales Director Polly Manguel

Promotional publishing, adult books.

Cassell Illustrated (imprint)

tel 020-7531 8400 *fax* 020-7531 8650
email info-ci@cassell-illustrated.co.uk
website www.cassell-illustrated.co.uk

Illustrated books for the international market specialising in gardening, history and heritage, health and humour.

Conran Octopus (imprint)

tel 020-7531 8628 *fax* 020-7531 8627
email info-co@conran-octopus.co.uk
website www.conran-octopus.co.uk
Publishing Director Lorraine Dickey

Quality illustrated books, particularly lifestyle, cookery, gardening.

Gaia Books (imprint)

email enquiries@gaiabooks.com
website www.gaiabooks.com
Publisher Jo Hemmings

Illustrated reference books on ecology, natural living, health and the mind.

Godsfield Press (imprint)

email enquiries@godsfieldpress.com
website www.godsfieldpress.com
Publisher Jo Hemmings

Highly illustrated books for adults in the area of

Mind, Body & Spirit with an emphasis on practical application and personal spiritual awareness.

Hamlyn (imprint)
tel 020-7531 8573 *fax* 020-7537 0514
email info-ho@hamlyn.co.uk
website www.hamlyn.co.uk
Publisher Jo Hemmings

Popular illustrated non-fiction, particularly cookery, health and parenting, home and garden, sport and reference.

Miller's (imprint)
email firstname.lastname@millers.uk.com
Publisher David Lamb

Quality illustrated books on antiques and collectables.

Mitchell Beazley (imprint)
tel 020-7531 8400 *fax* 020-7531 8650
email info-mb@mitchell-beazley.co.uk
website www.mitchell-beazley.co.uk
Publisher David Lamb

Quality illustrated books, particularly antiques, gardening, craft and interiors, wine.

Philip's (imprint)
tel 020-7531 8459 *fax* 020-7531 8460
email george.philip@philips-maps.co.uk
website www.philips-maps.co.uk
Mapping Director David Gaylard

Atlases, maps, astronomy, encyclopedias, globes.

The Oleander Press

16 Orchard Street, Cambridge CB1 1JT
tel (01638) 500784
website www.oleanderpress.com
Managing Director Dr Jane Doyle

Travel, language, Libya, Arabia and Middle East, Cambridgeshire, history, reference, classics. MSS welcome with sae for reply. Founded 1960.

Michael O'Mara Books Ltd

9 Lion Yard, Tremadoc Road, London SW4 7NQ
tel 020-7720 8643 *fax* 020-7627 8953
email enquiries@mombooks.com
website www.mombooks.com
Chairman Michael O'Mara, *Managing Director* Lesley O'Mara, *Commissioning Editorial Director* Lindsay Davies, *Commissioning Editorial Director* Louise Dixon, *Editorial Director* Toby Buchan

General non-fiction: biography, humour, history. See website for submission guidelines. Imprint: Buster Books (non-fiction for children and novelty). Founded 1985.

Omnibus Press/Music Sales Ltd

14–15 Berners Street, London W1T 3LJ
tel 020-7612 7400 *fax* 020-7612 7545
email music@musicsales.co.uk
website www.omnibuspress.com
Chief Editor Chris Charlesworth

Rock music biographies, books about music. Founded 1976.

On Stream Publications Ltd†

Currabaha, Cloghroe, Blarney, Co. Cork, Republic of Ireland
tel (353) 21 438 5798
email info@onstream.ie
website www.onstream.ie
Owner Rosalind Crowley

Cookery, wine, travel, human interest non-fiction, local history, academic and practical books. Founded 1986.

Oneworld Classics/Calder Publications

243–253 Lower Mortlake Road, Richmond, Surrey TW9 2LL
tel 020-8948 9550 *fax* 020-8948 5599
email info@oneworldclassics.com
website www.oneworldclassics.com
Managing Director Alessandro Gallenzi

European, international and British fiction and plays, art, literary, music and social criticism, biography and autobiography, essays, humanities and social sciences, European classics. No unsolicited MSS. Inquiry letters must include an sae. Series include: *English National Opera Guides, New Writing and Writers*. Founded 2007.

Oneworld Publications

185 Banbury Road, Oxford OX2 7AR
tel (01865) 310597 *fax* (01865) 310598
email info@oneworld-publications.com
website www.oneworld-publications.com
Director Juliet Mabey (publisher)

Fiction and general non-fiction: current affairs, politics, history, popular science, philosophy, psychology, green issues, world religions and Islamic studies; literary fiction with a global perspective. No unsolicited MSS; email or send proposal via website. Founded 1986.

Onlywomen Press Ltd

40d St Lawrence Terrace, London W10 5ST
tel 020-8354 0796
email onlywomenpress@btconnect.com
website www.onlywomenpress.com
Managing Director Lilian Mohin

Lesbian feminist fiction, non-fiction and books for children. Founded 1974.

Open Gate Press*

(incorporating Centaur Press, founded 1954)
51 Achilles Road, London NW6 1DZ
tel 020-7431 4391 *fax* 020-7431 5129
email books@opengatepress.co.uk
website www.opengatepress.co.uk
Directors Jeannie Cohen, Elisabeth Petersdorff, Sandra Lovell

Psychoanalysis, philosophy, social sciences, religion, animal welfare, the environment. Founded 1988.

Open University Press – see McGraw-Hill Education

Orbit – see Little, Brown Book Group

Orchard Books – see Hachette Children's Books

The Orion Publishing Group Ltd*

Orion House, 5 Upper St Martin's Lane, London WC2H 9EA
tel 020-7240 3444 *fax* 020-7240 4822
website www.orionbooks.co.uk
Directors Arnaud Nourry (chairman), Peter Roche (chief executive), Malcolm Edwards (deputy chief executive)

No unsolicited MSS; approach in writing in first instance. Part of Hachette UK (see page 157). Founded 1992.

Orion Paperbacks (division)

Managing Director Susan Lamb

Mass market fiction and non-fiction under Everyman, Orion and Phoenix imprints.

Orion Trade (division)

Directors Lisa Milton (managing), John Wood (fiction publishing)

Hardcover fiction (popular fiction in all categories), non-fiction and audio.

Gollancz (imprint)

Contact Simon Spanton

Science fiction and fantasy.

Orion Children's Books (division)

Publisher Fiona Kennedy

Fiction for younger and older readers, picture books.

Weidenfeld & Nicolson

See page 193.

Osborne – see McGraw-Hill Education

Oshun – see Random House Struik (Pty) Ltd

Osprey Publishing Ltd

Midland House, West Way, Botley, Oxford OX2 0PH
tel (01865) 727022 *fax* (01865) 727017
email info@ospreypublishing.com
website www.ospreypublishing.com
Directors Rebecca Smart (managing), Chris Tinsley (finance), Kate Moore (editorial), Richard Sullivan (marketing), Sarah Broadway (sales), Joanna Sharland (rights)

Illustrated history of war and warfare, and military aviation. Founded 1968.

Oversteps Books Ltd

6 Halwell House, South Pool, Nr Kingsbridge, Devon TQ7 2RX
tel (01548) 531969
email alwynmarriage@overstepsbooks.com
website www.overstepsbooks.com
Director/Managing Editor Dr Alwyn Marriage

Poetry. Send or email 3 poems that have been published, giving details of the magazines in which they appeared, the dates or issue numbers and the email addresses of the Editors. Founded 1992.

Peter Owen Publishers

73 Kenway Road, London SW5 0RE
tel 020-7373 5628/370 6093 *fax* 020-7373 6760
email antonia@peterowen.com
website www.peterowen.com
Directors Peter L. Owen (managing), Antonia Owen (editorial), Simon Smith (rights)

Art, belles lettres, biography and memoir, literary fiction, general non-fiction, history, theatre and entertainment. No highly illustrated books. Do not send fiction without first speaking to the Editorial Dept unless it is by an established novelist. No mass-market genre fiction, short stories or poetry; first novels only rarely published.

Oxford Publishing Company – see Ian Allan Publishing Ltd

Oxford University Press*

Great Clarendon Street, Oxford OX2 6DP
tel (01865) 556767 *fax* (01865) 556646
email enquiry@oup.com
website www.oup.com
Ceo Nigel Portwood, *Group Finance Director* David Gillard, *Academic Journals & OUP USA Managing Director* Tim Barton, *UK Children's & Educational Division Managing Director* Kate Harris, *ELT Division Managing Director* Peter Marshall, *UK Human Resources Director* Caroline James-Nock, *Academic Sales Director* Alastair Lewis

Archaeology, architecture, art, belles-lettres, bibles, bibliography, children's books (fiction, non-fiction, picture), commerce, current affairs, dictionaries, drama, economics, educational (infants, primary, secondary, technical, university), encyclopedias, English language teaching, electronic publishing, essays, foreign language learning, general history, hymn and service books, journals, law, medical, music, oriental, philosophy, political economy, prayer books, reference, science, sociology, theology and religion; educational software; *Grove Dictionaries of Music & Art*. Trade paperbacks published under the imprint of Oxford Paperbacks. Founded 1478.

Palgrave Macmillan – see Macmillan Publishers Ltd

Pan – see Macmillan Publishers Ltd

Pan Macmillan – see Macmillan Publishers Ltd

Pandora Press – see Rivers Oram Press

Paper Tiger – see Anova Books

Paperbooks Publishing Ltd

2 London Wall Buildings, London EC2M 5UU
tel 020-7448 5137
email info@legend-paperbooks.co.uk
website www.legendpress.co.uk
Managing Director Tom Chalmers

Contemporary fiction (not overly genre-specific).

Particular Books – see Penguin Group (UK)

Pavilion – see Anova Books

Pavilion Children's Books

10 Southcombe Street, London W14 0RA
tel 020-7605 1400 *fax* 020-7605 1401
website www.anovabooks.com
Publisher Ben Cameron

Children's books: from baby and picture books to illustrated classics and interactive books. Part of the Anova Books Group. Submissions via an agent only.

Pavilion Publishing (Brighton) Ltd

(Part of OLM Group)
Richmond House, Richmond Road, Brighton BN2 3RL
tel (01273) 623222 *fax* (0844) 880 5062
email info@pavpub.com
website www.pavpub.com
Ceo, OLM Group Peter O'Hara

Health and social care training resources in a variety of fields including learning disability, mental health, vulnerable adults, housing, drugs and alcohol, staff development, children, young and older adults. Founded 1987.

Payne-Gallway – see Pearson UK

Peachpit Press – see Pearson UK

Pearson UK*

Edinburgh Gate, Harlow, Essex CM20 2JE
tel (0845) 313 6666 *fax* (0845) 313 7777
website www.pearsoned.co.uk
President Rod Bristow

Allyn & Bacon (imprint)

Higher education, humanities, social sciences.

BBC Active (imprint)

Learning resources for children and adults.

Cisco Press (imprint)

Cisco-systems authorised publisher. Material for networking students and professionals.

Benjamin Cummings (imprint)

Higher education, science.

FT Prentice Hall (imprint)

Business for higher education and professional.

Harcourt (imprint)

Educational resources for teachers and learners at Primary, Secondary and Vocational level. Provides a range of published resources, teachers' support, and pupil and student material in all core subjects for all ages. Imprints: Ginn, Heinemann, Payne-Gallway, Raintree, Rigby.

Longman (imprint)

Education for higher education, schools, ELT.

New Rider (imprint)

Graphics and design.

Peachpit Press (imprint)

Internet and general computing.

Penguin Longman (imprint)

ELT.

Prentice Hall (imprint)

Academic and reference textbooks.

QUE Publishing (imprint)

Computing.

SAMS Publishing (imprint)

Professional computing.

Wharton (imprint)

Business.

York Notes (imprint)

Literature guides for students.

Pen & Sword Books Ltd

47 Church Street, Barnsley, South Yorkshire S70 2AS
tel (01226) 734555 *fax* (01226) 734438
email editorialoffice@pen-and-sword.co.uk
website www.pen-and-sword.co.uk
Managing Director Charles Hewitt, *Publishing Manager* Henry Wilson, *Commissioning Editors* Peter Coles, Rupert Harding, *Publishing Director* Michael Leventhal

Military history, aviation history, naval and maritime, general history, local history. Imprints: Leo Cooper, Frontline Books, Pen & Sword Military Classics, Pen & Sword Aviation, Pen & Sword Naval & Maritime, Remember When, Seaforth.

Frontline (imprint)

Military history.

Wharncliffe (imprint)
Local history.

Pen Press – see Indepenpress Publishing Ltd

Penguin Group (UK)*

80 Strand, London WC2R 0RL
tel 020-7010 3000 *fax* 020-7010 6060
website www.penguin.co.uk
Chairman & Gobal Ceo John Makinson, *Penguin UK & DK Ceo* Peter Field, *Deputy Ceo* Tom Wheldon

Owned by Pearson plc.

Penguin General Books (literary division)
Managing Director Joanna Prior
No unsolicited MSS or synopses.

Viking (imprint)
Publishing Director Venetia Butterfield, *Editorial Directors* Tony Lacey, Eleo Gordon, Mary Mount, Joel Rickett, Will Hammond
Fiction and general non-fiction for adults. Founded 1925.

Portfolio (imprint)
Publishing Director Joel Rickett
Business. Launched September 2010.

Hamish Hamilton (imprint)
Publishing Director Simon Prosser, *Editorial Directors* Juliette Mitchell, Anna Kelly
Fiction, belles-lettres, biography and memoirs, current affairs, history, literature, politics, travel. No unsolicited MSS or synopses.

Fig Tree (imprint)
Publishing Director Juliet Annan, *Editorial Director* Jenny Lord
Fiction and general non-fiction. No unsolicited MSS or synopses.

Penguin Ireland (imprint)
Irish Book Publishers' Association, 25 St Stephen's Green, Dublin 2, Republic of Ireland
tel (01) 661 7695 *fax* (01) 661 7696
email info@penguin.ie
website www.penguin.ie
Managing Director Michael McLoughlin, *Publishing Director* Patricia Deevy, *Editor* Brendan Barrington
Fiction and non-fiction, mainly of Irish origin, but published to travel beyond the Irish market. Unsolicited MSS accepted.

Michael Joseph (commercial division)
Managing Director Louise Moore, *Editors* Louise Moore (commercial women's fiction, celebrity non-fiction), Stefanie Bierwerth (crime fiction), Alex Clarke (commercial male fiction), Mari Evans (commercial historical fiction & women's fiction), Kate Burke (commercial women's fiction & crime), Lydia Newhouse (commercial women's fiction), Daniel Bunyard (commercial non-fiction, popular culture & military), Lindsey Evans (cookery), Katy Follain (commercial non-fiction & popular culture)

Penguin Press (division)
Managing Director Stefan McGrath, *Publishing Directors* Stuart Proffitt (Allen Lane), Simon Winder (Allen Lane), Adam Freudenheim (Penguin Classics), Georgina Laycock, Alexis Kirschbaum, Will Goodlad, Helen Conford (Particular Books)
Serious adult non-fiction, reference, specialist and classics. Imprint: Allen Lane. Series: *Penguin Classics, Penguin Modern Classics*. No unsolicited MSS or synopses.

Particular Books (imprint)
Publishing Director Helen Conford, *Editorial Director* Georgina Laycock
Non-fiction. Founded 2009.

Penguin Digital
Managing Director Anna Rafferty, *Head of Online Development* Jeanette Turmaine, *Online Content Manager* Ashley Wilks, *Online Design Manager* Tom Johnson, *Digital Publisher* Jeremy Ettinghausen

Children's Division
Managing Director Stephanie Barton, *Managing Director Puffin, Ladybird Core, Warne Editorial* Francesca Dow, *Puffin Publishing Director (fiction)* Sarah Hughes, *Puffin Editorial Director (picture books)* Louise Bologaro, *Puffin Editorial (Characters)* Kate Hayler, *Editorial Director, Puffin Classics* Elv Moody, *Publisher, Razorbill* Amanda Punter
Children's paperback and hardback books: wide range of picture books, board books and novelties; fiction; non-fiction and popular culture. No unsolicited MSS or synopses.

Razorbill (imprint)
Publisher Amanda Punter
Commercial teen fiction. Launched 2010.

BBC, Ladybird, Warne
Ladybird and Warne Editorial Nicole Pearson, *BBC Editorial Director* Juliet Matthews, *BBC/Ladybird Design* Kirsty Billingham, *Ladybird Licensing* Eric Huang, *Warne Design* Ronnie Fairweather
Specialises in preschool illustrated developmental books for ages 0–6, non-fiction 0–8; licensed brands; children's classic publishing and merchandising properties. No unsolicited MSS.

Dorling Kindersley (division)
website www.dk.com
Deptuy Ceos Andrew Philips, John Duhigg, *Global Publisher* Miriam Farbey
Illustrated non-fiction for adults and children: gardening, health, medical, travel, food and drink, history, natural history, photography, reference, pregnancy and childcare, film and TV.

Brady (division)
Publisher David Waybright, *Business Development Manager* Brian Saliba

Computer games strategy guides and collectors' editions.

Travel (division)
website www.traveldk.com, www.roughguides.com
Managing Director John Duhigg, *Publishing Directors* Douglas Amrine (Dorling Kindersley), Clare Currie, Andrew Lockett (Rough Guide Reference), *Digital Publisher* Peter Buckley

Travel guides, illustrated travel books, phrasebooks and digital products; popular culture and lifestyle guides. Includes *Rough Guides* and *DK Eyewitness Travel*.

Penguin Longman – see Pearson UK

Pergamon – see Elsevier Ltd (Health Sciences)

Persephone Books
59 Lamb's Conduit Street, London WC1N 3NB
tel 020-7242 9292 *fax* 020 7242 9272
email info@persephonebooks.co.uk
website www.persephonebooks.co.uk
Managing Director Nicola Beauman

Reprints of forgotten classics by 20th century women writers with prefaces by contemporary writers. Founded 1999.

Phaidon Press Ltd
Regent's Wharf, All Saints Street, London N1 9PA
tel 020-7843 1000 *fax* 020-7843 1010
email enquiries@phaidon.com
website www.phaidon.com
Publisher Richard Schlagman, *Chairman* Andrew Price, *Directors* Amanda Renshaw (deputy publisher), James Booth-Clibborn

Visual arts, lifestyle and culture.

Philip's – see Octopus Publishing Group

Phillimore & Co. Ltd – see The History Press Ltd

Phoenix – see The Orion Publishing Group Ltd

Phoenix Yard Books
Phoenix Yard, 65 Kings Cross Road, London WC1X 9LW
tel 020-7239 4968
email info@phoenixyardbooks.com, submissions@phoenixyardbooks.com
website www.phoenixyardbooks.com
Commissioning Editor Emma Langley

Picture books, poetry and fiction for ages 3–13. Specialism in character publishing. Particularly seeking character-based young fiction (ages 6–9) and comics/graphic novel material. Founded 2009.

Piatkus – see Little, Brown Book Group

Pica Press – see A&C Black Publishers Ltd

Picador – see Macmillan Publishers Ltd

Piccadilly Press
5 Castle Road, London NW1 8PR
tel 020-7267 4492 *fax* 020-7267 4493
email books@piccadillypress.co.uk
website www.piccadillypress.co.uk
Managing Director & Publisher Brenda Gardner

Early picture books, parental advice trade paperbacks, trade paperback teenage non-fiction and teenage fiction. Founded 1983.

Pimlico – see The Random House Group Ltd

Pink Press – see Indepenpress Publishing Ltd

Pinwheel Children's Books – see Alligator Books Ltd

Pipers' Ash Ltd
Pipers' Ash, Church Road, Christian Malford, Chippenham, Wilts. SN15 4BW
tel (01249) 720563 *fax* (0870) 0568916
email pipersash@supamasu.com
website www.supamasu.com
Editorial Director Alfred Tyson

Poetry, short stories, local histories; historical novels, biographies, plays, philosophy, translations, children's, general non-fiction. New authors with talent and potential encouraged. Founded 1976.

Pitkin Publishing Ltd – see The History Press Ltd

The Playwrights Publishing Company
70 Nottingham Road, Burton Joyce, Notts. NG14 5AL
tel 0115-931 3356
email playwrightspublishingco@yahoo.com
website www.playwrightspublishing.co.uk
Proprietor Liz Breeze, *Consultant* Tony Breeze

One-act and full-length drama published on the internet. Serious work and comedies, for mixed cast, all women or schools. Reading fee unless professionally produced or unwaged; sae required. Founded 1990.

Plexus Publishing Ltd
25 Mallinson Road, London SW11 1BW
tel 020-7924 4662 *fax* 020-7924 5096
email plexus@plexusuk.demon.co.uk
website www.plexusbooks.com
Directors Terence Porter (managing), Sandra Wake (editorial)

Film, music, biography, popular culture, fashion. Imprint: Eel Pie. Founded 1973.

Pluto Press

345 Archway Road, London N6 5AA
tel 020-8348 2724 *fax* 020-8348 9133
email pluto@plutobooks.com
website www.plutobooks.com
Chairman Roger van Zwanenberg, *Managing Director* Anne Beech, *Sales Director* Simon Liebesny, *Head of Marketing* Alec Gregory, *Publicity Manager* Jon Wheatley

Politics, anthropology, development, media, cultural, economics, history, Irish studies, Black studies, Islamic studies, Middle East, international relations.

Pocket Books – see Simon & Schuster UK Ltd

Point – see Scholastic Ltd

The Policy Press

University of Bristol, 4th Floor, Beacon House, Queen's Road, Bristol BS8 1QU
tel 0117-331 4054 *fax* 0117-331 4093
email tpp-info@bristol.ac.uk
website www.policypress.org.uk
Director Alison Shaw, *Deputy Director* Julia Mortimer

Social science, specialising in social and public policy, criminology, social work and social welfare. Founded 1996.

Policy Studies Institute (PSI)

50 Hanson Street, London W1W 6UP
tel 020-7911 7500 *fax* 020-7911 7501
email psi-admin@psi.org.uk

Economic, cultural, social and environmental policy, political institutions, social sciences.

Politico's Publishing – see Methuen Publishing Ltd

Polity Press

65 Bridge Street, Cambridge CB2 1UR
tel (01223) 324315 *fax* (01223) 461385
website www.politybooks.com

Social and political theory, politics, sociology, history, media and cultural studies, philosophy, literary theory, feminism, human geography, anthropology. Founded 1983.

Polygon – see Birlinn Ltd

Pomona Books

PO Box 50, Hebden Bridge, West Yorkshire HX7 8WA
tel (01422) 846900
email admin@pomonauk.co.uk
website www.pomonauk.co.uk
Publishing Director Mark Hodkinson

Fiction, biography, memoir. Not currently accepting manuscripts.

Pont Books – see Gomer Press

Poolbeg Press Ltd

123 Grange Hill, Baldoyle Industrial Estate, Dublin 13, Republic of Ireland
tel (01) 8321477 *fax* (01) 8321430
email info@poolbeg.com
website www.poolbeg.com
Directors Kieran Devlin (managing), Paula Campbell (publisher), Brian Langan (non-fiction editor)

Popular fiction, non-fiction, current affairs. Imprint: Poolbeg. Founded 1976.

Portfolio Books – see Penguin Group (UK)

Portico – see Anova Books

Portland Press Ltd

Charles Darwin House, 12 Roger Street, London WC1N 2JL
tel 020-7685 2410 *fax* 020-7685 2469
email editorial@portlandpress.com
website www.portlandpress.com
Directors Rhonda C. Oliver (managing), John Misselbrook (finance), John Day (IT), Adam Marshall (marketing)

Biochemistry and molecular life science books for graduate, postgraduate and research students. Illustrated science books for children: *Making Sense of Science* series. Founded 1990.

Portobello Books Ltd

12 Addison Avenue, London W11 4QR
tel 020-7605 1380
email mail@portobellobooks.com
website www.portobellobooks.com
Sales Director Brigid MacLeod, *Rights Director* Angela Rose, *Publisher* Philip Gwyn Jones, *Editorial Director* Laura Barber

Internationalist literature; activist non-fiction. Unsolicited submissions accepted except from residents of North America: address to Submissions Editor. Founded 2005.

T & AD Poyser – see A&C Black Publishers Ltd

Preface Publishing – see The Random House Group Ltd

Prestel Publishing Ltd

4 Bloomsbury Place, London WC1A 2QA
tel 020-7323 5004 *fax* 020-7636-8004
email sales@prestel-uk.co.uk
website www.prestel.com
Managing Director Andrew Hansen, *Commissioning Editor* Philippa Hurd

Art, architecture, photography, design, travel, cultural history and ethnography. Headquarters in Munich with offices in New York and London. Founded 1924.

Princeton University Press – Europe

6 Oxford Street, Woodstock, Oxon OX20 1TW
tel (01993) 814500 *fax* (01993) 814504
email admin@pupress.co.uk
website http://press.princeton.edu
Publishing Director – Europe Richard Baggaley

Economics, finance, political theory and the humanities. Part of Princeton University Press, USA. European office founded 1999.

Prion Books – see Carlton Publishing Group

Profile Books Ltd*

3A Exmouth House, Pine Street, London EC1R 0JH
tel 020-7841 6300 *fax* 020-7833 3969
email info@profilebooks.com
website www.profilebooks.com
Publisher & Managing Director Andrew Franklin, *Associate Publisher* Daniel Crewe

General non-fiction: history, biography, current affairs, popular science, politics, business, management, humour. Also publishers of *The Economist* books. No unsolicited MSS; phone or send preliminary letter. Founded 1996.

Serpent's Tail (imprint)
email info@serpentstail.com
website www.serpentstail.com
Publisher Peter Ayrton

Fiction and non-fiction; literary and non-mainstream work, and work in translation. No unsolicited MSS. Founded 1986.

Psychology Press*

27 Church Road, Hove, East Sussex BN3 2FA
tel 020-7017 6000 *fax* 020-7017 6717
website www.psypress.com

Psychology textbooks and monographs. Imprint of Taylor and Francis Group.

Routledge (imprint)
website www.routledgementalhealth.com

Clinical psychology and psychiatry.

Puffin – see Penguin Group (UK)

Pulp Press – see Indepenpress Publishing Ltd

Pushkin Press

12 Chester Terrace, London NW1 4ND
tel 020-7730 0750 *fax* 020-7730 1341
email books@pushkinpress.com
website www.pushkinpress.com
Publisher Melissa Ulfane

Continental European literature in translation. Founded 1997.

Putnam Aeronautical – see Anova Books

Quadrille Publishing

5th Floor, Alhambra House,
27–31 Charing Cross Road, London WC2H 0LS
tel 020-7839 7117 *fax* 020-7839 7118
email enquiries@quadrille.co.uk
website www.quadrille.co.uk
Directors Alison Cathie (managing), Jane O'Shea (editorial), Helen Lewis (art), Vincent Smith (production)

Illustrated non-fiction: cookery, food and drink, gift and humour, craft, health and beauty, gardening, interiors, Mind, Body & Spirit. Founded 1994.

Quantum – see W. Foulsham & Co. Ltd

The Quarto Group, Inc.

226 City Road, London, EC1V 2TT
tel 020-7700 9000 *fax* 020-7253 4437
email info@quarto.com
website www.quarto.com
Chairman & Ceo Laurence Orbach, *Chief Financial Officer* Mick Mousley, *Creative Director* Bob Morley, *Director of Publishing* Piers Spence

Independent publishing group encompassing traditional and co-edition publishing. Co-edition books are licensed to third parties all over the world, with bestselling titles often available in 20+ languages. UK-based operations include the following autonomously run business units, or imprints. See separate entries for Aurum Press Ltd and Jacqui Small on page 140 and RotoVision on page 183.

Marshall Editions
email linda.cole@quarto.com
Publisher Linda Cole

QED Publishing Ltd
email zetad@quarto.com
Associate Publisher Zeta Davies

Quantum Publishing Ltd
email helen.nally@quarto.com
Publisher Helen Nally

Quarto Children's Books Ltd
email quartokids@quarto.com, sueg@quarto.com
Publisher Sue Grabham, *Art Director* Jonathan Gilbert

Co-edition publisher of innovative Books-Plus for children. Highly illustrated paper-engineered, novelty and component-based titles for all ages, but primarily preschool (3+), 5–8 and 8+ years. Mainly non-fiction, early concepts and curriculum-based topics for the trade in all international markets. Opportunities for freelance paper engineers, artists, authors, editors and designers. Unsolicited MSS not accepted.

Quarto Publishing plc
email paulc@quarto.com
Publisher Paul Carslake

qu:id
email nigelb@quidpublishing.com
Publisher Nigel Browning

Quintessence
email tristandl@quarto.com
Publisher Tristan de Lancey

Quintet Publishing Ltd
email JamesT@quarto.com
Publisher James Tavendale

QUE Publishing – see Pearson UK

Quercus Publishing Plc

21 Bloomsbury Square, London WC1A 2NS
tel 020-7291 7200 *fax* 020-7291 7201
email jenny.ellis@quercusbooks.co.uk
website www.quercusbooks.co.uk
Directors Mark Smith (managing/Ceo), Mike McGrath (Coo), Wayne Davies (contract publishing), David North (trade publishing), Jon Riley (editor-in-chief), Roisin Heycock (children's publishing), Caroline Proud (sales director), Ron Beard (paperbacks), David Murphy (key accounts), Lucy Ramsey (publicity), Emma Ward (rights and co-editions).

Fiction and non-fiction. Founded 2005.

Maclehose Press (imprint)
Publisher Christopher Maclehose

Quest – see Top That! Publishing plc

Quiller Publishing Ltd

Wykey House, Wykey, Shrewsbury, Shrops. SY4 1JA
tel (01939) 261616 *fax* (01939) 261606
email info@quillerbooks.com
website www.countrybooksdirect.com
Managing Director Andrew Johnston

Kenilworth Press (imprint)
Equestrian (riding, training, dressage, eventing, show jumping, driving, polo). Publisher of BHS official publications.

Quiller Press (imprint)
Specialises in all country and country sports subjects, including fishing, shooting, cookery, humour, and all field sports.

The Sportsman's Press (imprint)
All country subjects and general sports including fishing, fencing, shooting, equestrian and gunmaking; wildlife art.

Swan Hill Press (imprint)
Country and field sports activities, including fishing, cookery, shooting, falconry, equestrian, gundog training, natural history, humour.

Radcliffe Publishing Ltd

18 Marcham Road, Abingdon, Oxon OX14 1AA
tel (01235) 528820 *fax* (01235) 528830
email contact.us@radcliffemed.com
website www.radcliffe-oxford.com
Directors Gregory Moxon (managing), Gill Nineham (editorial), Margaret McKeown (financial)

Primary care, child health, palliative care, nursing, pharmacy, dentistry, counselling, healthcare organisation and management examination revision aids. Founded 1987.

Ragged Bears Publishing Ltd

Unit 14A, Bennett's Field Trading Estate, Southgate Road, Wincanton, Somerset BA9 9DT
tel (01963) 34300
email info@raggedbears.co.uk
website www.raggedbears.co.uk
Managing Director Henrietta Stickland

Independent publishing house publishing preschool picture and novelty books, first chapter books to young teen fiction. Emailed submissions preferred but if posted send sae. Do not send original artwork. Imprint: Ragged Bears. Founded 1994.

Raintree – see Pearson UK

The Random House Group Ltd*

20 Vauxhall Bridge Road, London SW1V 2SA
tel 020-7840 8400
website www.randomhouse.co.uk
Chairman/Ceo Gail Rebuck, *Deputy Ceo* Ian Hudson, *Directors* Larry Finlay (RHCB and Managing Director, Transworld), Mark Gardiner (finance), Brian Davies (Ebury Publishing and Managing Director, overseas operations), Richard Cable (CCV and Managing Director Random House Enterprises), Garry Prior (sales), Mark Williams (Managing Director Distribution)

Subsidiary of Bertelsmann AG.
Group consists of 6 publishing companies comprising 40 imprints.

Random House Audio Books
tel 020-7840 8519 *fax* 020-7233 6127
Commissioning Editor Zoe Howes
See page 223.

Random House Digital
tel 020-7840 8400
Director of Digital Fionnuala Duggan

Cornerstone (company)
Managing Director Susan Sandon, *Publicity Director* Charlotte Bush, *Marketing Director* Claire Round
No unsolicited MSS accepted.

Arrow Books Ltd (imprint)
tel 020-7840 8414 *fax* 020-7840 6127
Publishing Director Kate Elton
Paperback fiction and non-fiction.

Century (imprint)
tel 020-7840 8569 *fax* 020-7233 6127
Publishing Director Ben Dunn, *Editorial Director* Jack Fogg

Fiction, biography, autobiography, general non-fiction, true crime, humour.

Hutchinson (imprint)
tel 020-7840 8400 *fax* 020-7233 6127
Publishing Director Caroline Gascoigne, *Editorial Director* Paul Sidey
Fiction: literary and women's fiction, adventure, crime, thrillers. Non-fiction: biography, memoirs, general history, politics, travel, current affairs.

Preface Publishing (imprint)
tel 020-7840 8424
email prefacesubmissions@randomhouse.co.uk
Publisher Trevor Dolby, *Publishing Director* Rosie de Courcy
Commercial fiction and non-fiction. Unsolicited MSS accepted by email.

Random House Books (imprint)
tel 020-7840 8451 *fax* 020-7840 6127
Publishing Director Nigel Wilcockson
Non-fiction: social and cultural history, current affairs, popular culture, reference, business and economics.

William Heinemann (imprint)
tel 020-7840 8400 *fax* 020-7233 6127
Publishing Director Jason Arthur
Fiction and general non-fiction: crime, thrillers, literary fiction, translations, history, biography, science.

Windmill Books (imprint)
tel 020-7840 8414 *fax* 020-7840 6127
website www.windmill-books.co.uk
Editorial Director Stephanie Sweeney
B-format paperback fiction and non-fiction.

CCV (company)
Managing Director Richard Cable, *Deputy Managing Director* Faye Brewster, *Publisher* Dan Franklin, *Deputy Publishing Director* Rachel Cugnoni, *Publicity Director* Christian Lewis, *Marketing Director* Roger Bratchell

The Bodley Head (imprint)
tel 020-7840 8784 *fax* 020-7233 6117
Publishing Director Will Sulkin
Non-fiction: history, current affairs, politics, science, biography, economics.

Jonathan Cape (imprint)
tel 020-7840 8608 *fax* 020-7233 6117
Publishing Director Dan Franklin, *Deputy Publishing Director* Robin Robertson
Biography and memoirs, current affairs, drama, fiction, history, poetry, travel, politics, graphic novels, photography.

Chatto & Windus (imprint)
tel 020-7840 8745 *fax* 020-7233 6117
Publishing Director Clara Farmer, *Editorial Directors* Becky Hardie, Jenny Uglow
Belles-lettres, biography and memoirs, current affairs, fiction, history, poetry, politics, philosophy, translations, travel. No unsolicited MSS.

Harvill Secker (imprint)
tel 020-7840 8893 *fax* 020-7233 6117
Publishing Director Liz Foley, *Editorial Director* Stuart Williams
English literature and world literature in translation. Non-fiction (history, current affairs, literary essays, music). No unsolicited MSS.

Pimlico (imprint)
tel 020-7840 8836 *fax* 020-7233 6117
Publishing Director Rachel Cugnoni
History, biography, literature. Exclusively in paperback. No unsolicited MSS.

Square Peg (imprint)
tel 020-7840 8608 *fax* 7233 6117
Editorial Director Rosemary Davidson
Eclectic, idiosyncratic and commercial non-fiction including humour, illustrated and gift books, food, nature, memoir, travel, parenting. Unsolicited MSS with sae.

Vintage (imprint)
tel 020-7840 8836 *fax* 020-7233 6117
Publishing Director Rachel Cugnoni, *Editorial Director Vintage Classics* Laura Hassan
Quality fiction and non-fiction. Predominantly in paperback. No unsolicited MSS.

Yellow Jersey Press (imprint)
tel 020-7840 8621 *fax* 020-7233 6117
Editorial Director Matthew Phillips
Sport and leisure activities. Unsolicited MSS (first 3 chapters only) accepted with sae.

Ebury Publishing (company)
website www.eburypublishing.co.uk
Managing Director Fiona MacIntyre, *Publisher* Jake Lingwood, *Publicity Director* Sarah Bennie, *Marketing Director* Diana Riley

BBC Books (imprint)
tel 020-7840 8400 *fax* 020-7840 8406
Senior Publishing Director Shirley Patton
TV and radio tie-ins and books linked to BBC brands and personalities.

Ebury Press (imprint)
tel 020-7840 8400 *fax* 020-7840 8406
Senior Publishing Director Non-Illustrated Andrew Goodfellow, *Publishing Director Illustrated* Cary Smith, *Editorial Director Fiction* Gillian Green
General commercial non-fiction, autobiography, memoir, popular history, sport, travel writing, popular science, humour, film and TV tie-ins, music, popular reference, cookery, lifestyle.

Rider (imprint)
tel 020-7840 8400 *fax* 020-7840 8406
Editorial Director Judith Kendra
Inspirational titles across the spectrum of psychology,

philosophy, international affairs, biography, current affairs, history, psychology, travel and spirituality.

Time Out (imprint, in partnership with Time Out Group)
tel 020-7840 8798 *fax* 020-7840 8406
Publishing Brand Manager Luthfa Begum
Travel, film, reference and lifestyle published in a unique partnership with *Time Out Guides*.

Vermilion (imprint)
tel 020-7840 8400 *fax* 020-7840 8406
Senior Commissioning Editor Miranda West, *Commissioning Editor* Julia Kellaway
Personal development, health, diet, relationships, parenting.

Virgin Books (imprint, in partnership with Virgin Group)
tel 020-7840 8400
email editorial@virgin-books.co.uk
Marketing Director Vickie Boff, *Publicity Director* Jessica Axe, *Editorial Directors* Ed Faulkner, Louisa Joyner
Health and popular culture: entertainment, showbiz, arts, film and TV, music, humour, biography and autobiography, popular reference, true crime, sport, travel, memoir, environment.

Random House Children's Books (company)
61–63 Uxbridge Road, London W5 5SA
tel 020-8579 2652 *fax* 020-8579 5479
website www.kidsatrandomhouse.co.uk
Annie Eaton (Publisher, fiction), Fiona MacMillan (Publisher, colour and licensing and RHCSE), Becky Stradwick (Editorial Director, fiction), Kelly Hurst (Editorial Director, fiction), Helen Mackenzie Smith (Editorial Director, picture books), Natascha Biebow (Senior Commissioning Editor, picture and novelty/ preschool books), Alice Corrie (Commissioning Editor, colour and custom books), Margaret Hope (Art Director)
Picture books, novelty and gift books, preschool and pop-ups, fiction, non-fiction and audio CDs.
Imprints: Bantam Press, Bodley Head Children's Books, Jonathan Cape Children's Books, Corgi Children's Books, Doubleday Children's Books, David Fickling Books, Hutchinson Children's Books, Red Fox Children's Books, Tamarind. No unsolicited MSS or original artwork or text.

Tamarind Books (imprint)
61–63 Uxbridge Road, London W5 5SA
tel 020-8231 6800 *fax* 020-8231 6737
email info@tamarindbooks.co.uk
website www.tamarindbooks.co.uk
Commissioning Editor Patsy Isles
Multicultural children's picture books and posters. All books give a high positive profile to black children. Unsolicited material welcome with return postage. Founded 1987.

David Fickling Books (imprint)
31 Beaumont Street, Oxford OX1 2NP
tel (01865) 339000 *fax* (01865) 339009
email dfickling@randomhouse.co.uk
website www.davidficklingbooks.co.uk
Publisher David Fickling, *Editor* Bella Pearson
Picture books, fiction for 5–8 and 9–12 year-olds, teenage fiction and poetry. Will consider unsolicited MSS (first 3 chapters only); include covering letter and sae and allow 3 months for response. If possible, find an agent first. Founded 2000.

Transworld Publishers
See page 191.

Ransom Publishing Ltd

51 Southgate Street, Winchester SO23 9EH
tel (01962) 862307 *fax* (05601) 148881
email ransom@ransom.co.uk
website www.ransom.co.uk
Directors Jenny Ertle (managing), Steve Rickard (creative)

Books for reluctant and struggling readers covering high interest age/low reading age titles, quick reads, reading schemes. Range of accompanying workbooks and teacher's guides. Series include *Goal!*, *Boffin Boy*, *Dark Man*, *Trailblazers*, *Siti's Sisters*, *321 Go!* and *Cutting Edge*. Will consider unsolicited MSS. Email in first instance. Founded 1995.

RBI Search

(formerly Reed Business Information)
Windsor Court, East Grinstead House, Wood Street, East Grinstead, West Sussex RH19 1XA
tel (01342) 326972 *fax* (01342) 335860
email info@rbi.co.uk
website www.reedbusiness.com
Managing Director Dominic Feltham

Online information specialists including leading search engines such as kellysearch.com and bankersalmanac.com covering industrial, financial, travel and media sectors, including gazetteers.com, hotelsearch and Kemps. Part of Reed Elsevier plc. Founded 1983.

The Reader's Digest Association Ltd

11 Westferry Circus, Canary Wharf, London E14 4HE
tel 020-7715 8000 *fax* 020-7715 8600
website www.readersdigest.co.uk
Managing Director C.J. Spratling, *Editor-in-Chief* Gill Hudson

Monthly magazine, condensed and series books; also DIY, computers, puzzles, gardening, medical, handicrafts, law, touring guides, encyclopedias, dictionaries, nature, folklore, atlases, cookery, music.

Reaktion Books

33 Great Sutton Street, London EC1V 0DX
tel 020-7253 1071 *fax* 020-7253 1208
email info@reaktionbooks.co.uk
website www.reaktionbooks.co.uk
Publisher Michael R. Leaman

Art history, design, architecture, history, cultural studies, film studies, food history, animal studies, Asian studies, travel writing, photography. Founded 1985.

Red Dress Ink™ – see Harlequin Mills & Boon Ltd

Red Fox Children's Books – see The Random House Group Ltd

Thomas Reed – see A&C Black Publishers Ltd

Reed Books – now Octopus Publishing Group

William Reed Directories

Broadfield Park, Crawley, West Sussex RH11 9RT
tel (01293) 613400 *fax* (01293) 610310
email directories@william-reed.co.uk
website www.william-reed.co.uk
Director Mark de Lange, *Content Manager* Daniel Verrells

Publishers of leading business-to-business directories and reports, including *The Retail and Shopping Centre Directory* and *The Grocer Directory of Manufacturers and Suppliers.*

Reed Educational and Professional Publishing Ltd – see Harcourt (imprint)

Reeds Nautical Almanac – see A&C Black Publishers Ltd

Religious and Moral Education Press (RMEP)*

13–17 Long Lane, London EC1A 9PN
tel 020-7776 7540 *fax* 020-7776 7556
email order@norwichbooksandmusic.co.uk
website www.rmep.co.uk

Books for infant, primary and secondary school pupils and teachers on religious, moral, personal and social education, and citizenship. An imprint of Hymns Ancient & Modern Ltd. Founded 1980.

Reynolds & Hearn Ltd

61A Priory Road, Kew, Richmond, Surrey TW9 3DH
tel 020-8940 5198 *fax* 020-8940 7679
email enquiries@rhbooks.com
website www.rhbooks.com
Directors Richard Reynolds (managing), Marcus Hearn (editorial), David Pratt, Geoffrey Wolfson

Film, TV, photography, music, media. Established 1999.

Rider – see The Random House Group Ltd

Rigby – see Pearson UK

Rising Stars*

PO Box 105, Rochester, Kent ME2 4BE
(0800) 091 1602 *fax* (0800) 091 1603
email info@risingstars-uk.com
website www.risingstars-uk.com

Educational publisher of books and software for primary school age children. Titles are linked to the National Curriculum Key Stages, QCA Schemes of Work, National Numeracy Framework or National Literacy Strategy. Approach by email with ideas for publishing.

River Books – see New Cavendish Books

Rivers Oram Press

144 Hemingford Road, London N1 1DE
tel 020-7607 0823 *fax* 020-7609 2776
email ro@riversoram.com
website www.riversoram.com
Directors Elizabeth Rivers Fidlon (managing), Anthony Harris

Non-ficton: social and political science, current affairs, social history, gender studies, sexual politics, cultural studies. Founded 1991.

Pandora Press (imprint)

Feminist press. General non-fiction: biography, arts, media, health, current affairs, reference and sexual politics.

Roar Publishing – see Magi Publications

Robinson – see Constable & Robinson Ltd

Robson Books – see Anova Books

George Ronald

3 Rosecroft Lane, Oaklands, Welwyn, Herts. AL6 0UB
tel (01438) 716062 *fax* (0870) 762 6242
email sales@grbooks.com
website www.grbooks.com
Managers E. Leith, M. Hofman

Religion, specialising in the Bahá'í Faith. Founded 1939.

RotoVision

Sheridan House, 112–116A Western Road, Hove, East Sussex BN3 1DD
tel (01273) 727268 *fax* (01273) 727269
email sales@rotovision.com
website www.rotovision.com

Illustrated books on design, photography and the performing arts. Part of the Quarto Group.

Rough Guides – see Penguin Group (UK)

Roundhouse Group

Maritime House, Basin Road North, Hove BN41 1WR
tel (01273) 704962 *fax* (01273) 704963
email sales@roundhousegroup.co.uk
website www.roundhousegroup.co.uk
Publisher Alan T. Goodworth

Film, cinema, and performing arts; reference books. No unsolicited MSS. Founded 1991.

Route

PO Box 167, Pontefract, West Yorkshire WF8 4WW
tel (01977) 797695
email info@route-online.com
website www.route-online.com
Contact Ian Daley, Isabel Galan

Contemporary fiction (novels and short stories) and performance poetry. Unsolicited MSS discouraged. See website for current guidelines.

Routledge-Cavendish – see Taylor and Francis Group

Routledge – see Psychology Press

Royal Collection Publications

Stable Yard House, St James's Palace, London SW1A 1JR
tel 020-7024 5584 *fax* 020-7839 8168
website www.royalcollection.org.uk
Publisher Jacky Colliss Harvey, *Commissioning Editor* Kate Owen, *Publishing Assistants* Debbie Bogard, Nina Chang

Subjects from within the Royal Collection. Founded 1993.

Royal National Institute of Blind People (RNIB)

PO Box 173, Peterborough, Cambs. PE2 6WS
tel (0303) 1239999 *fax* (01733) 375001
email shop@rnib.org.uk
website www.rnib.org.uk

Magazines, catalogues and books for blind and partially sighted people, to support daily living, leisure, learning and employment reading needs. Produced in braille, audio, large/legible print and email. For complete list of magazines see page 85. Founded 1868.

Ryland Peters & Small

20–21 Jockey's Fields, London WC1R 4BW
tel 020-7025 2200 *fax* 020-7025 2201
email info@rps.co.uk
website www.rylandpeters.com
Directors David Peters (managing), Alison Starling (publishing), Leslie Harrington (art), Denise Lie (rights), Danny Parnes (UK & export sales)

High-quality illustrated books on food and drink, home and garden, babies and children, gift books. Founded 1995.

Cico Books (imprint)

tel 020-7025 2280 *fax* 020-7025 2281
email mail@cicobooks.co.uk
website www.cicobooks.co.uk
Publisher Cindy Richards

Lifestyle and interiors, crafts and Mind, Body & Spirit. Founded 1999.

SAGE Publications Ltd*

1 Oliver's Yard, 55 City Road, London EC1Y 1SP
tel 020-7324 8500 *fax* 020-7324 8600
email info@sagepub.co.uk
website www.sagepub.co.uk
Directors Stephen Barr (managing), Katharine Jackson, Ziyad Marar, Richard Fidczuk, Phil Denvir, Clive Parry, Carol Irwin, Blaise Simqu (USA), Sara Miller McCune (USA), Paul R. Chapman

Social sciences, behavioural sciences, humanities, science, technology and medicine. Journals, books and electronic media for academic, educational and professional markets. Founded 1971.

Paul Chapman Publishing (imprint)

website www.paulchapmanpublishing.co.uk
Publisher Marianne Lagrange

Education: academic and professional books for students, practitioners and school leaders.

St Pauls

St Pauls Publishing, 187 Battersea Bridge Road, London SW11 3AS
tel/fax 020- 7978 4300
email editorial@stpaulspublishing.com
website www.stpaulspublishing.com

Theology, ethics, spirituality, biography, education, general books of Roman Catholic and Christian interest. Founded 1948.

Salamander – see Anova Books

Salariya Book Company Ltd

Book House, 25 Marlborough Place, Brighton BN1 1UB
tel (01273) 603306 *fax* (01273) 693857
email salariya@salariya.com
website www.salariya.com
Director David Salariya

Children's non-fiction. Imprints: Book House, Scribblers, Scribo. Founded 1989.

Salt Publishing

14A High Street, Fulbourn, Cambridge CB21 5DH
tel (01223) 882220 *fax* (01223) 882260
email sarah-jayne@saltpublishing.com
website www.saltpublishing.com
Publishing Director Christopher Hamilton-Emery

Poetry, literary criticism, essays and biography for an international market.

SAMS Publishing – see Pearson UK

Saunders – see Elsevier Ltd (Health Sciences)

Alastair Sawday Publishing Ltd

The Old Farmyard, Yanley Lane, Long Ashton, Bristol BS41 9LR

tel (01275) 395430 *fax* (01275) 393388
email info@sawdays.co.uk
website www.sawdays.co.uk,
www.special-escapes.co.uk

Special Places to Stay series of guidebooks and *Fragile Earth Books* on global green issues. Founded 1994.

S.B. Publications

14 Bishopstone Road, Seaford, East Sussex BN25 2UB
tel (01323) 893498 *fax* (01323) 893860
email sbpublications@tiscali.co.uk
website www.sbpublications.co.uk
Proprietor Lindsay Woods

Local history, local themes (e.g. walking books, guides), specific themes. Founded 1987.

Scala Publishers

Northburgh House, 10 Northburgh Street,
London EC1V 0AT
tel 020-7490 9900 *fax* 020-7336 6870
email sales@scalapublishers.com
website www.scalapublishers.com
Chairman David Campbell, *Directors* Henry Channon, Jan Baily, Antony White, *Director of Museum Publications US* Jennifer Wright, *Commissioning Editor UK* Jenny McKinley

Art, architecture, guides to museums and art galleries, antiques. Founded 1992.

Sceptre – see Hodder & Stoughton

Schofield & Sims Ltd

Dogley Mill, Fenay Bridge, Huddersfield HD8 0NQ
tel (01484) 607080 *fax* (01484) 606815
email post@schofieldandsims.co.uk
website www.schofieldandsims.co.uk
Chairman C.N. Platts

Educational: nursery, infants, primary; posters. Founded 1901.

Scholastic Ltd*

Euston House, 24 Eversholt Street,
London NW1 1DB
tel 020-7756 7761 *fax* 020-7756 7795
website www.scholastic.co.uk
Chairman M.R. Robinson

Children's fiction and non-fiction and education resources for primary schools. Owned by Scholastic Inc. Founded 1964.

Scholastic Children's Books (division)

Euston House, 24 Eversholt Street, London
NW1 1DB
tel 020-7756 7756 *fax* 020-7756 7795
email publicity@scholastic.co.uk
Managing Director Elaine McQuade, *Editorial Director, Non-fiction* Lisa Edwards, *Editorial Director, Fiction* Polly Nolan, *Editorial Director, Preschool* Katherine Halligan, *Rights Director* Antonia Pelari, *Sales & Marketing Director* Hilary Murray Hill

Activity books, novelty books, picture books, fiction for 5–12 year-olds, teenage fiction, series fiction and film/TV tie-ins. Imprints include Hippo, Point, Scholastic Fiction, Scholastic Non-fiction, Scholastic Press. Will consider unsolicited submissions: send synopsis and sample chapter only.

The Chicken House

See page 146.

Scholastic Educational Resources (division)

Villiers House, Clarendon Avenue, Leamington Spa
CV32 5PR
tel (01926) 887799 *fax* (01926) 883881
Managing Director Denise Cripps
Professional books and classroom materials for primary teachers and magazines (*Nursery Education Plus, Child Education Plus, Junior Education Plus, Literacy Time Plus*).

Scholastic Book Clubs (division)

See page 346.

Scholastic Book Fairs (division)

See page 347.

Science Museum

Exhibition Road, London SW7 2DD
tel 0870-870 4771 *fax* 020-7942 4362
website www.nmsi.ac.uk, www.sciencemuseum.org.uk

History of science and technology, museum guides.

Science Navigation Group

34–42 Cleveland Street, London W1T 4LB
tel 020-7323 0323 *fax* 020-7580 1938
email info@sciencenavigation.com
website www.sciencenavigation.com
Chairman Vitek Tracz

Biological sciences, medicine, pharmaceutical science, internet communities, electronic publishing.

SCM Canterbury Press Ltd*

13–17 Long Lane, London EC1A 9PN
tel 020-7776 7540 *fax* 020-7776 7556
website www.scm-canterburypress.co.uk
Publishing Director Christine Smith

Theological books with special emphasis on text and reference books and contemporary theology for both students and clergy. Founded 1929.

Canterbury Press (imprint)

St Mary's Works, St Mary's Plain, Norwich NR3 3BH
tel (01603) 612914 *fax* (01603) 624483
Religious books for the general market, church resources and liturgy.

SCM Press (imprint)

Academic theology.

SCM Press – see SCM Canterbury Press Ltd

SCP Publishers Ltd

(trading as Scottish Cultural Press)
Unit 6, Newbattle Abbey Business Park,
Newbattle Road, Dalkeith EH22 3LJ

tel 0131-660 6366 fax (0870) 285 4846
email info@scottishbooks.com
website www.scottishbooks.com
Directors Brian Pugh, Avril Gray

Scottish non-fiction and Scots language, children's writing. Unsolicited MSS not accepted; send letter, telephone or email in first instance. Founded 1992.

Scottish Children's Press
'Scottish books for anyone interested in Scotland.' Literature, history, archaeology, biography and environmental history.

Scripture Union

207–209 Queensway, Bletchley, Milton Keynes, Bucks. MK2 2EB
tel (01908) 856000 *fax* (01908) 856111
email info@scriptureunion.org.uk
website www.scriptureunion.org.uk
Director of Ministry Delivery Terry Clutterham

Christian books and Bible reading materials for people of all ages; educational and worship resources for churches; children's fiction and non-fiction; adult non-fiction. Founded 1867.

Seafarer Books Ltd

102 Redwald Road, Rendlesham, Woodbridge, Suffolk IP12 2TE
tel (01394) 420789
email info@seafarerbooks.com
website www.seafarerbooks.com
Commissioning Editor Patricia Eve

Books on traditional sailing and stories of the sea, mainly narrative.

Search Press Ltd

Wellwood, North Farm Road, Tunbridge Wells, Kent TN2 3DR
tel (01892) 510850 *fax* (01892) 515903
email searchpress@searchpress.com
website www.searchpress.com
Directors Martin de la Bédoyère (managing), Caroline de la Bédoyère (rights), Rosalind Dace (editorial)

Arts, crafts, leisure. Founded 1970.

Seren

57 Nolton Street, Bridgend CF31 3AE
tel (01656) 663018
email general@serenbooks.com
website www.serenbooks.com
Publisher Mick Felton

Poetry, fiction, drama, history, film, literary criticism, biography, art – mostly with relevance to Wales. Founded 1981.

Severn House Publishers

9–15 High Street, Sutton, Surrey SM1 1DF
tel 020-8770 3930 *fax* 020-8770 3850
email sales@severnhouse.com
website www.severnhouse.com
Chairman Edwin Buckhalter, *Publishing Director* Amanda Stewart

Hardcover and paperback adult fiction for the library market: romances, crime, thrillers, detective, adventure, war, science fiction, some large print. No unsolicited MSS; submissions via literary agents or send query letter first.

Shearsman Books

58 Velwell Road, Exeter EX4 4LD
tel (01392) 434511
email editor@shearsman.com
website www.shearsman.com
Contact Tony Frazer

Contemporary poetry in English and in translation.

Sheldon Press – see Society for Promoting Christian Knowledge

Sheldrake Press

188 Cavendish Road, London SW12 0DA
tel 020-8675 1767 *fax* 020-8675 7736
email enquiries@sheldrakepress.co.uk
website www.sheldrakepress.co.uk
Publisher J.S. Rigge

History, travel, architecture, cookery, music; stationery. Founded 1979.

Shepheard-Walwyn (Publishers) Ltd

107 Parkway House, Sheen Lane, London SW14 8LS
tel 020-8241 5927
email books@shepheard-walwyn.co.uk
website www.shepheard-walwyn.co.uk
Director A.R.A. Werner

History, biography, political economy, perennial philosophy; illustrated gift books; Scottish interest. Founded 1971.

Shire Publications

Midland House, West Way, Botley, Oxford OX2 0PH
tel (01865) 811332 *fax* (01865) 242009
email shire@shirebooks.co.uk
website www.shirebooks.co.uk
Managing Director Rebecca Smart, *Publisher* Nick Wright

Discovering paperbacks, Shire Libraries, Shire Archaeology, Shire History and Shire Collections. Founded 1962.

Short Books Ltd

3A Exmouth House, Pine Street, London EC1R 0JH
tel 020-7833 9429 *fax* 020-7833 9500
email melanie@shortbooks.co.uk
website www.shortbooks.co.uk
Editorial Directors Rebecca Nicolson, Aurea Carpenter

Non-fiction and fiction. No unsolicited MSS. Founded 2000.

Sidgwick & Jackson – see Macmillan Publishers Ltd

Sigma Press
Stobart House, Pontyclerc, Penybanc Road, Ammanford, Carmarthenshire SA18 3HP
tel (01269) 593100 *fax* (01269) 596116
email info@sigmapress.co.uk
website www.sigmapress.co.uk
Directors Nigel Evans, Jane Evans

Leisure: country walking, cycling, regional heritage, ecology, folklore; biographies. Founded 1979.

Silhouette® – see Harlequin Mills & Boon Ltd

Simon & Schuster UK Ltd*
222 Gray's Inn Road, London WC1X 8HB
tel 020-7316 1900 *fax* 020-7316 0331/2
website www.simonandschuster.co.uk
Directors Ian Chapman (managing), Suzanne Baboneau (publishing), Ingrid Selberg (children's publishing)

Commercial and literary fiction; general and serious non-fiction; children's. No unsolicited MSS. Founded 1986.

Free Press (imprint)
Publisher Mike Jones

Serious adult non-fiction: history, biography, current affairs, science.

Simon & Schuster (imprint)
Illustrated non-fiction and bespoke publishing.

Pocket Books (imprint)
Publisher Julie Wright

Mass-market fiction, media tie-in and non-fiction paperbacks.

Simon & Schuster Audioworks
Fiction, non-fiction and business.

Simon & Schuster Children's Publishing
Picture books, pop-up, novelty, fiction and non-fiction.

Smith Gryphon Ltd – see John Blake Publishing Ltd

Colin Smythe Ltd*
PO Box 6, Gerrards Cross, Bucks. SL9 8XA
tel (01753) 886000 *fax* (01753) 886469
website www.colinsmythe.co.uk
Directors Colin Smythe (managing & editorial), Leslie Hayward, Ann Saddlemyer

Irish biography, phaleristics, heraldry, Irish literature and literary criticism, Irish history. Founded 1966.

Snowbooks Ltd*
120 Pentonville Road, London N1 9JN
tel 0790 406 2414
email info@snowbooks.com
website www.snowbooks.com
Directors Emma Barnes (managing), Rob Jones, *Publisher* Anna Torborg

Genre fiction: fantasy, sci-fi and horror. General non-fiction. See website for submission guidelines. Founded 2004.

Society for Promoting Christian Knowledge*
36 Causton Street, London SW1P 4ST
tel 020-7592 3900 *fax* 020-7592 3939
email publishing@spck.org.uk
website www.spck.org.uk
Director of Publishing Joanna Moriarty

Founded 1698.

Sheldon Press (imprint)
Popular medicine, health, self-help, psychology.

SPCK (imprint)
Theology and academic, liturgy, prayer, spirituality, biblical studies, educational resources, mission, gospel and culture.

Society of Genealogists Enterprises Ltd
14 Charterhouse Buildings, Goswell Road, London EC1M 7BA
tel 020-7251 8799 *fax* 020-7250 1800
email sales@sog.org.uk
website www.sog.org.uk
Chief Executive June Perrin

Local and family history books, fiche, disks, CDs, software and magazines plus extensive library facilities.

South Street Press – see Garnet Publishing Ltd

Southwater – see Anness Publishing

Souvenir Press Ltd
43 Great Russell Street, London WC1B 3PD
tel 020-7580 9307/8
email sp.trade@ukonline.co.uk
Managing Director Ernest Hecht

Archaeology, biography and memoirs, educational (secondary, technical), general, humour, practical handbooks, psychiatry, psychology, sociology, sports, games and hobbies, travel, supernatural, parapsychology, illustrated books. No unsolicited fiction or children's books; initial enquiry by letter essential for non-fiction.

SPCK – see Society for Promoting Christian Knowledge

Spellmount Ltd – see The History Press Ltd

Sphere – see Little, Brown Book Group

Spon – see Taylor and Francis Group

Sportsbooks Ltd*
PO Box 422, Cheltenham, Glos. GL50 2YN
tel (01242) 256755 *fax* (0560) 310 8126

email info@sportsbooks.ltd.uk
website www.sportsbooks.ltd.uk
Directors Randall Northam, Veronica Northam

Sport.

The Sportsman's Press – see Quiller Publishing Ltd

Springer-Verlag London Ltd*

Ashbourne House, The Guildway,
Old Portsmouth Road, Guildford GU3 1LP
tel (01483) 734666 *fax* (01483) 734411
website www.springer.com
General Manager Beverley Ford

Medicine, computing, engineering, mathematics, chemistry, biosciences. Founded 1972.

Stacey International

128 Kensington Church Street, London W8 4BH
tel 020-7221 7166 *fax* 020-7792 9288
email info@stacey-international.co.uk
website www.stacey-international.co.uk
Chairman Tom Stacey, *Managing Director* Max Scott

Illustrated non-fiction, encyclopedic books on regions and countries, Islamic and Arab subjects, world affairs, children's books, art, travel, belles-lettres. Imprints: Capuchin Classics (19th and 20th century fiction classics), Gorilla Guides. Founded 1973.

Stainer & Bell Ltd

PO Box 110, Victoria House, 23 Gruneisen Road, London N3 1DZ
tel 020-8343 3303 *fax* 020-8343 3024
email post@stainer.co.uk
website www.stainer.co.uk
Directors Keith Wakefield (joint managing), Carol Wakefield (joint managing & secretary), Amanda Aknai, Antony Kearns, Andrew Pratt, Nicholas Williams

Books on music, religious communication. Founded 1907.

Stenlake Publishing Ltd

54–58 Mill Square, Catrine Ayrshire KA5 6RD
tel (01290) 552233
email sales@stenlake.co.uk
website www.stenlake.co.uk
Managing Director Richard Stenlake

Local history, railways, transport, aviation, canals and mining covering Wales, Scotland, England, Northern Ireland, Isle of Man and Republic of Ireland. Founded 1997.

Stripes – see Magi Publications

Summersdale Publishers Ltd

46 West Street, Chichester, West Sussex PO19 1RP
tel (01243) 771107 *fax* (01243) 786300
email submissions@summersdale.com
website www.summersdale.com
Managing Director Alastair Williams *Editorial Director* Jennifer Barclay, *Sales Director* Nicky Douglas

Popular non-fiction, particularly travel writing, humour and gift books. Also publishes eBooks and audiobooks. See website for guidelines. Founded 1990.

Sunflower Books

PO Box 36160, London SW7 3WS
tel/fax 020-7589 2377
email mail@sunflowerbooks.co.uk
website www.sunflowerbooks.co.uk
Directors P.A. Underwood (editorial), S.J. Seccombe

Travel guidebooks.

Sussex Academic Press

PO Box 139, Eastbourne, East Sussex BN24 9BP
tel (01323) 479220
email edit@sussex-academic.co.uk
website www.sussex-academic.co.uk
Editorial Director Anthony Grahame

Theology and religion, British history and Middle East studies. Founded 1994.

The Alpha Press (imprint)
Religion, history, sport.

Sutton Publishing – see The History Press Ltd

Swan Hill Press – see Quiller Publishing Ltd

Sweet & Maxwell*

100 Avenue Road, London NW3 3PF
tel 020-7393 7000 *fax* 020-7393 7010
website www.sweetandmaxwell.co.uk
Directors Peter Lake (Managing), Ashley Doody (Technology), Chris Elvin (Customer Operations), John Galvin (Finance), Dick Greener (Legal Affairs), Hilary Lambert (Commercial), Terri Hawksworth (Sales & Marketing), Giles Grant (Strategy & Business Development), Mark Potter (Human Resources), Mark Seaman (Editorial & Production)

Law. Part of Thomson Reuters Ltd. Founded 1799; incorporated 1889.

Tamarind Books – see The Random House Group Ltd

Tango Books Ltd

PO Box 32595, London W4 5YD
tel 020-8996 9970 *fax* 020-8996 9977
email sales@tangobooks.co.uk
website www.tangobooks.co.uk
Directors Sheri Safran, David Fielder

Children's fiction and non-fiction novelty books, including pop-up, touch-and-feel and cloth books. Maximum 500 words. No poetry. Submissions with sae or by email.

Tarquin Publications

99 Hatfield Road, St Albans AL1 4ET
tel (01727) 833866 *fax* (0845) 4566385
email info@tarquinbooks.com
website www.tarquinbooks.com
Director Andrew Griffin

Mathematics and mathematical models, puzzles, codes and logic; paper cutting, paper engineering and pop-up books for intelligent children. No unsolicited MSS; send suggestion or synopsis in first instance. Founded 1970.

Taschen UK Ltd

5th Floor, 1 Heathcock Court, 415 Strand, London WC2R 0NS
tel 020-7845 8585 *fax* 020-7836 3696
email contact-uk@taschen.com
website www.taschen.com

Art, architecture, design, film, lifestyle, photography, popular culture, sex. Founded 1980.

Tate Publishing

The Lodge, Millbank, London SW1P 4RG
tel 020-7887 8869/70 *fax* 020-7887 8878
email tgpl@tate.org.uk
website www.tate.org.uk
Publishing Director Roger Thorp, *Operations Director* Robert Read, *Production Manager* Sarah Tucker, *Head of Licensing* Jo Matthews, *Head of Merchandise* Helena Lawrence

Publishers for Tate in London, Liverpool and St Ives. Exhibition catalogues, art books, children's books and diaries, posters, etc. Also product development, picture library and licensing. Division of Tate Enterprises Ltd. Founded 1995.

I.B.Tauris & Co. Ltd

6 Salem Road, London W2 4BU
tel 020-7243 1225 *fax* 020-7243 1226
email mail@ibtauris.com
website www.ibtauris.com
Chairman/Publisher Iradj Bagherzade, *Managing Director* Jonathan McDonnell

History, biography, politics, international relations, current affairs, Middle East, religion, cultural and media studies, film, art, archaeology, travel guides. Founded 1983.

Tauris Academic Studies (imprint)

Academic monographs on history, political science and social sciences.

Tauris Parke Books (imprint)

Illustrated books on architecture, design, photography, cultural history and travel.

Tauris Parke Paperbacks (imprint)

Non-fiction trade paperbacks: biography, history, travel, cinema, art, cultural history.

Taylor and Francis Group*

2 and 4 Park Square, Milton Park, Abingdon, Oxon OX14 4RN
tel 020-7017 6000 *fax* 020-7017 6699
email info@tandf.co.uk
website www.tandf.co.uk, www.informa.com
Managing Director, Taylor & Francis Books Jeremy North

Academic and reference books.

Routledge (imprint)

website www.routledge.com
Addiction, anthropology, archaeology, Asian studies, business, classical studies, counselling, criminology, development and environment, dictionaries, economics, education, geography, health, history, Japanese studies, library science, language, linguistics, literary criticism, media and culture, nursing, performance studies, philosophy, politics, psychiatry, psychology, reference, social administration, social studies/sociology, women's studies, law. Directories, international relations, reference, yearbooks.

Garland Science (imprint)

website www.garlandscience.com
Bioscience textbooks and scholarly works.

Psychology Press

See page 179.

Spon (imprint)

website www.sponpress.com
Architecture, civil engineering, construction, leisure and recreation management, sports science.

CRC Press (imprint)

website www.crcpress.com
Science: physics, mathematics, chemistry, electronics, natural history, pharmacology and drug metabolism, toxicology, technology, history of science, ergonomics, production engineering, remote sensing, geographic information systems, engineering.

Teach Yourself – see Hodder Education Group

Telegraph Books

Telegraph Media Group Ltd,
111 Buckingham Palace Road, London SW1W 0DT
tel 020-7931 2887 *fax* 020-7931 2929
email support@books.telegraph.co.uk
website www.books.telegraph.co.uk
Publisher Morven Knowles

Personal finance, crosswords, sport, humour, cookery, health, general, gardening, history – usually by *Telegraph* journalists and contributors, and co-published with major publishing houses. Founded 1920.

The Templar Company Ltd

The Granary, North Street, Dorking, Surrey RH4 1DN

tel (01306) 876361 *fax* (01306) 889097
email info@templarco.co.uk
website www.templarco.co.uk
Managing & Creative Director Amanda Wood, *Sales & Marketing Director* Ruth Huddleston, *Submissions* Deborah Simmons

Publisher and packager of high-quality illustrated children's books, including novelty books, picture books, pop-up books, board books, fiction, non-fiction and gift titles.

Tempus – see The History Press Ltd

Thames & Hudson Ltd*

181A High Holborn, London WC1V 7QX
tel 020-7845 5000 *fax* 020-7845 5050
email sales@thameshudson.co.uk
website www.thamesandhudson.com
Directors T. Neurath (chair), C. Kaine (deputy chair), J. Camplin (managing), L. Dietrich, T. Evans, C. Ferguson, C. Frederking, P. Hughes, P. Meades, B. Meek, J. Neurath, N. Palfreyman, C. Ridler

Illustrated non-fiction for an international audience, especially art, architecture, graphic design, garden and landscape design, archaeology, cultural history, historical reference, fashion, photography, ethnic arts, mythology, religion.

Think Books

Think Publishing Ltd, The Pall Mall Deposit, 124–128 Barlby Road, London W10 6BL
tel 020-8962 3020 *fax* 020-8962 8689
email watchdog@thinkpublishing.co.uk
website www.thinkpublishing.co.uk
Chairman Ian McAuliffe, *Chief Executive* Tilly Boulter

Specialises in books on the outdoors, gardening and wildlife. Publishes with the Wildlife Trusts, the Royal Horticultural Society and the Campaign to Protect Rural England, and others. Founded 2005.

Thoemmes Press – see The Continuum International Publishing Group Ltd

D.C. Thomson & Co. Ltd – Publications

2 Albert Square, Dundee DD1 9QJ
tel (0138) 222 3131
website www.dcthompson.co.uk
London office 185 Fleet Street, London EC4A 2HS

Publishers of newspapers and periodicals. Children's books (annuals), based on weekly magazine characters; fiction. For fiction guidelines, send a large sae to Central Fiction Dept.

Thomson Round Hall

43 Fitzwilliam Place, Dublin 2, Republic of Ireland
tel (01) 6625301 *fax* (01) 6625302
email info@roundhall.ie
website www.roundhall.thomson.com
Director & General Manager Julie Clarke

Law. Part of Thomson Legal & Regulatory (Europe) Ltd.

Stanley Thornes (Publishers) Ltd – see Nelson Thornes Ltd

Tide Mill Press – see Top That! Publishing plc

Time Out – see The Random House Group Ltd

Time Warner – see Little, Brown Book Group

Times Books – see HarperCollins Publishers

Titan Books

144 Southwark Street, London SE1 0UP
tel 020-7620 0200 *fax* 020-7620 0032
email editorial@titanemail.com
website www.titanbooks.com
Publisher & Managing Director Nick Landau, *Editorial Director* Katy Wild

Graphic novels, including *Simpsons* and *Batman*, featuring comic-strip material; film and TV tie-ins and cinema reference books. No fiction or children's proposals, no email submissions and no unsolicited material without preliminary letter. Email or send large sae for current author guidelines. Division of Titan Publishing Group Ltd. Founded 1981.

Tolley – see LexisNexis

Top That! Publishing plc

Marine House, Tide Mill Way, Woodbridge, Suffolk IP12 1AP
tel (01394) 386651 *fax* (01394) 386011
email info@topthatpublishing.com
website www.topthatpublishing.com
Directors Barrie Henderson (managing), Simon Couchman (creative), Stuart Buck (production), Douglas Eadie (financial), Daniel Graham (editorial), Dave Greggor (sales)

Top That! Kids (imprint)

Children's activity, picture, reference and gift books. Founded 1998.

Kudos Books (imprint)

Adult books, humour, lifestyle and gift sets. Founded 2003.

Imagine That! (imprint)

Children's and adult book packaging for publishers and retailers worldwide. Founded 2004.

Tide Mill Press (imprint)
Preschool novelty, picture and early learning books. Founded 2007.

Quest (imprint)
Children's internet-linked fiction and activity books. Founded 2008.

Tor – see Macmillan Publishers Ltd

Torque – see The History Press Ltd

Transworld Publishers*
61–63 Uxbridge Road, London W5 5SA
tel 020-8579 2652 *fax* 020-8579 5479
email info@transworld-publishers.co.uk
website www.booksattransworld.co.uk
Managing Director Larry Finlay, *Publisher* Bill Scott-Kerr

Company of the Random House Group Ltd; subsidiary of Bertelsmann AG. No unsolicited MSS accepted.

Bantam (imprint)

Bantam Press (imprint)
Publishing Director Sally Gaminara

Fiction and general non-fiction: cookery, business, crime, health and diet, history, humour, military, music, paranormal, self-help, science, travel and adventure, biography, autobiography.

Black Swan (imprint)
Publisher Bill Scott-Kerr

Paperback quality fiction and non-fiction.

Transworld Sport & Entertainment (imprint)
Publishing Director Doug Young

Channel 4 books and cookery. TV tie-ins.

Corgi (imprint)
Senior Editorial Director Linda Evans

Paperback general fiction and non-fiction.

Doubleday (UK) (imprint)
Publishing Director Marianne Velmans

Literary fiction and non-fiction.

Eden (imprint)
Publishing Director Susanna Wadeson

Environmental: the Eden Project.

Expert Books (imprint)
Expert Brand Manager Gareth Pottle

Gardening and DIY.

Transworld Ireland (imprint)
Publisher Eoin McHugh, *Publishing Director* (crime and thrillers) Selina Walker

Trentham Books Ltd
Westview House, 734 London Road, Oakhill, Stoke-on-Trent, Staffs. ST4 5NP
tel (01782) 745567 *fax* (01782) 745553
email tb@trentham.books.co.uk
Editorial office 28 Hillside Gardens, London N6 5ST
tel 020-8348 2174
website www.trentham-books.co.uk
Directors Dr Gillian Klein (editorial), Barbara Wiggins (executive)

Education (including specialist fields – multi-ethnic issues, equal opportunities, bullying, design and technology, early years), social policy, sociology of education, European education, women's studies. Does not publish books for use by parents or children, or fiction, biography, reminiscences and poetry. Founded 1978.

Troubador Publishing Ltd
5 Weir Road, Kibworth Beauchamp, Leicester LE8 0LQ
tel 0116-279 2299 *fax* 0116-279 2277
email enquiries@troubador.co.uk
website www.troubador.co.uk
Directors Jeremy Thompson (managing), Jane Rowland (editorial), Julia Fuller (marketing)

Fiction and non-fiction with specialist lists in Italian studies and communication ethics. Self-publishing imprint: Matador. Founded 1996.

TSO (The Stationery Office)
Head office St Crispins, Duke Street, Norwich NR3 1PD
tel (0160) 362 2211 *fax* (0870) 6005533
website www.tso.co.uk
Chairman Miles Toulson-Clarke

Publishing and information management services: business, current affairs, directories, general, pharmaceutical, professional, reference, *Learning to Drive*.

Ulric Publishing
PO Box 55, Church Stretton, Shrops. SY6 6WR
tel (01694) 781354 *fax* (01694) 781372
website www.ulricpublishing.com
Directors Ulric Woodhams, Elizabeth Oakes

Non-fiction: military and motoring history. No unsolicited MSS.

Ulverscroft Group Ltd*
The Green, Bradgate Road, Anstey, Leicester LE7 7FU
tel 0116-236 4325 *fax* 0116-234 0205
email m.merrill@ulverscroft.co.uk
website www.ulverscroft.com

Large print books: fiction and non-fiction, Classics. Unabridged and abridged audio books: fiction and non-fiction.

Unicorn Press

47 Earlham Road, Norwich NR2 3RD
tel (01603) 886151
website www.unicornpress.org
Publisher Hugh Tempest-Radford, *Sales & Editorial Director* Lucy Hulme

Art reference: art history, architecture, artists' monographs, gallery and museum catalogues. Founded 1994.

Merlin Unwin Books Ltd

Palmers House, 7 Corve Street, Ludlow, Shrops. SY8 1DB
tel (01584) 877456 *fax* (01584) 877457
email books@merlinunwin.co.uk
website www.merlinunwin.co.uk
Chairman Merlin Unwin, *Managing Director* Karen McCall

Countryside books. Founded 1990.

Usborne Publishing Ltd

Usborne House, 83–85 Saffron Hill, London EC1N 8RT
tel 020-7430 2800 *fax* 020-7430 1562
email mail@usbornebooksathome.co.uk
website www.usborne.com
Directors Peter Usborne, Jenny Tyler (editorial), Robert Jones, Keith Ball, David Harte, Lorna Hunt

Children's books: reference, practical, craft, natural history, science, languages, history, geography, preschool, fiction. Founded 1973.

V&A Publishing

Victoria and Albert Museum, South Kensington, London SW7 2RL
tel 020-7942 2696 *fax* 020-7942 2967
email vapubs@vam.ac.uk
website www.vandashop.com
Head of Publishing Mark Eastment

Popular and scholarly books on fine and decorative arts, architecture, contemporary design, fashion and photography. Founded 1980.

Vallentine Mitchell

5th Floor, Middlesex House, 29/45 High Street, Edgware, Middlesex HA8 7UU
tel 020-8952 9526 *fax* 020-8952 9242
email info@vmbooks.com
website www.vmbooks.com
Directors Stewart Cass (managing), A.E. Cass, H.J. Osen, Hon. C.V. Callman

Jewish history, Judaism, Holocaust studies, Jewish culture, Jewish biography.

Variorum – see Ashgate Publishing Ltd

Veritas Publications†

Veritas House, 7–8 Lower Abbey Street, Dublin 1, Republic of Ireland
tel (01) 8788177 *fax* (01) 8786507
email publications@veritas.ie
website www.veritas.ie

Liturgical and Church resources, religious school books for primary and post-primary levels, biographies, academic studies, and general books on religious, moral and social issues.

Vermilion – see The Random House Group Ltd

Verso Ltd

6 Meard Street, London W1V 3HR
tel 020-7437 3546 *fax* 020-7734 0059
email enquiries@verso.co.uk
website www.verso.com
Directors Giles O'Bryen (Managing Director), Rowan Wilson (sales & marketing), Robin Blackburn, Tariq Ali

Current affairs, politics, sociology, economics, history, philosophy, cultural studies. Founded 1970.

Viking – see Penguin Group (UK)

Vintage – see The Random House Group Ltd

Virago – see Little, Brown Book Group

Virgin Books – see The Random House Group Ltd

Virtue Books Ltd

Edward House, Tenter Street, Rotherham S60 1LB
tel (01709) 365005 *fax* (01709) 829982
email info@virtue.co.uk
website www.virtue.co.uk
Directors Peter E. Russum, Margaret H. Russum

Books for the professional chef: catering and drink.

The Vital Spark – see Neil Wilson Publishing Ltd

Voyager – see HarperCollins Publishers

University of Wales Press

10 Columbus Walk, Brigantine Place, Cardiff CF10 4UP
tel 029-2049 6899 *fax* 029-2049 6108
email press@wales.ac.uk
website www.uwp.co.uk

Academic and educational (Welsh and English). Specialises in Welsh and Celtic studies, selected fields within humanities and social sciences: European studies, political philosophy, literature. Founded 1922.

Walker Books Ltd

87 Vauxhall Walk, London SE11 5HJ
tel 020-7793 0909 *fax* 020-7587 1123
website www.walker.co.uk
Directors David Heatherwick, Helen McAleer, Karen

Lotz, Roger Alexander (non-executive), Sarah Foster, Harold G. Gould OBE (non-executive), Jane Harris, Jane Winterbotham, Alan Lee

Children's: picture books, non-fiction and novelty titles; junior and teenage fiction. Founded 1980.

Wallflower Press

97 Sclater Street, London E1 6HR
tel 020-7729 9533
email info@wallflowerpress.co.uk
website www.wallflowerpress.co.uk
Editorial Director Yoram Allon

Cinema and the moving image, including TV, animation, documentary and artists' film and video – both academic and popular. Contact by email in first instance. Founded 1999.

Warburg Institute

University of London, Woburn Square, London WC1H 0AB
tel 020-7862 8949 *fax* 020-7862 8955
email warburg@sas.ac.uk
website http://warburg.sas.ac.uk

Cultural and intellectual history, with special reference to the history of the classical tradition.

Ward Lock Educational Co. Ltd

BIC Ling Kee House, 1 Christopher Road, East Grinstead, West Sussex RH19 3BT
tel (01342) 318980 *fax* (01342) 410980
email wle@lingkee.com
website www.wardlockeducational.com
Directors Au Bak Ling (chairman, Hong Kong), Au King Kwok (Hong Kong), Au Wai Kwok (Hong Kong), Albert Kw Au (Hong Kong), *Company Secretary* Eileen Parsons

Primary and secondary pupil materials, Kent Mathematics Project: *KMP BASIC* and *KMP Main* series covering Reception to GCSE, *Reading Workshops*, *Take Part* series and *Take Part* starters, teachers' books, music books, *Target* series for the National Curriculum: *Target Science* and *Target Geography*, religious education. Founded 1952.

Warne – see Penguin Group (UK)

Warner/Chappell Plays Ltd – see Josef Weinberger Plays Ltd

Franklin Watts – see Hachette Children's Books

The Watts Publishing Group Ltd – see Hachette Children's Books

Wayland – see Hachette Children's Books

Weidenfeld & Nicolson

(part of the Orion Publishing Group Ltd)
Orion House, 5 Upper St Martin's Lane, London WC2H 9EA
tel 020-7240 3444 *fax* 020-7240 4822
Managing Director Lisa Wilton, *Publisher* Alan Samson, *Publishing Director, Fiction* Kirsty Dunseath

Biography and autobiography, current affairs, history, travel, fiction, literary fiction, military history and militaria.

Weidenfeld & Nicolson Illustrated

Editor-in-Chief Michael Dover

Quality illustrated non-fiction: gardening, cookery, wine, art and design, health and lifestyle, history, popular culture, archaeology, British heritage, literature, fashion, architecture, natural history, sport and adventure.

Josef Weinberger Plays Ltd

12–14 Mortimer Street, London W1T 3JJ
tel 020-7580 2827 *fax* 020-7436 9016
email general.info@jwmail.co.uk
website www.josef-weinberger.com

Stage plays only, in both acting and trade editions. Preliminary letter essential.

Welsh Academic Press

PO Box 733, Cardiff CF14 7ZY
tel (029) 2021 8187
email post@welsh-academic-press.com
website www.welsh-academic-press.com

History, politics, biography, Celtic studies, Scandinavian and Baltic studies, education. Founded 1994.

Wharncliffe – see Pen & Sword Books Ltd

Which? Ltd

2 Marylebone Road, London NW1 4DF
tel 020-7770 7000
email books@which.co.uk
Head of Which? Books Angela Newton

Part of Consumers' Association. Founded 1957.

Which? Books (imprint)

Restaurant guide (*The Good Food Guide*), law, personal finance, property and key life events.

Whittet Books Ltd

BSP House, Station Road, Linton CB21 4NW
tel (01223) 894870 *fax* (01223) 894871
email mail@whittetbooks.com
website www.whittetbooks.com
Director George J. Papa

Natural history, countryside, horticulture, poultry, livestock, pets, horses. Founded 1976.

John Wiley & Sons Ltd*

The Atrium, Southern Gate, Chichester, West Sussex PO19 8SQ
tel (01243) 779777 *fax* (01243) 775878
email customer@wiley.co.uk
Senior Vice President Europe and International Development Steve Smith

Print and electronic products, specialising in scientific, technical and medical books and journals; professional and consumer books and subscription services; and textbooks and other educational materials for undergraduate and graduate students as well as lifelong learners. Global headquarters in Hoboken, New Jersey, with operations in the USA, Europe, Asia, Canada and Australia.

Wiley-Blackwell*

9600 Garsington Road, Oxford OX4 2DQ
tel (01865) 776868 *fax* (01865) 714591
website www.wiley.com
Senior Vice President Eric Swanson

Books and journals in medicine, veterinary medicine, dentistry, nursing and allied health, science (particularly biology, chemistry and geology), social sciences, business and humanities. Journals are delivered online through Wiley Interscience. Wiley-Blackwell was created in 2007 when Blackwell Publishing merged with Wiley's Global Scientific, Technical and Medical business.

BMJ Books (imprint)
Medicine, self-help, alternative medicine.

Neil Wilson Publishing Ltd*

G/2, 19 Netherton Avenue, Glasgow G13 1BQ
tel 0141-954 8007 *fax* 0560-150 4806
email info@nwp.co.uk
website www.nwp.co.uk
Managing Director Neil Wilson

Submissions by email only. Include covering letter, author CV, synopsis and sample chapter.

The Angels' Share (imprint)
website www.angelshare.co.uk
Whisky-related matters (leisure, reference, history, memoir); other food and drink categories.

11:9 (imprint)
website www.11-9.co.uk
Scottish Arts Council/National Lottery-funded project to bring new Scottish fiction writing to the marketplace. Not commissioning at present.

In Pinn (imprint)
website www.theinpinn.co.uk
The outdoors: travel, hillwalking, climbing.

NWP (imprint)
Scottish interest subjects including history, biography, true crime, culture and reference.

The Vital Spark (imprint)
website www.vitalspark.co.uk
Scottish humour.

Philip Wilson Publishers Ltd

109 Drysdale Street, London N1 6ND
tel 020-7033 9900 *fax* 020-7033 9922
email pwilson@philip-wilson.co.uk
website www.philip-wilson.co.uk
Chairman P. Wilson, *Director* S. Prohaska

Fine and applied art, collecting, museums. Founded 1975.

Windmill Books – see The Random House Group Ltd

Windsor Large Print – see BBC Audiobooks Ltd

John Wisden and Co. Ltd – see A&C Black Publishers Ltd

Wizard – see Icon Books Ltd

WLR Media & Entertainment

6–14 Underwood Street, London N1 7JQ
website www.wilmington.com
Managing Director Polly Augherinos

Publications: *Hollis PR Annual*, *Hollis Sponsorship Newsletter*, *Hollis Europe* and *The Knowledge*.

Wolters Kluwer (UK) Ltd*

(fomerly Croner.CCH Group Ltd)
145 London Road, Kingston-upon-Thames, Surrey KT2 6SR
tel 020-8547 3333 *fax* 020-8547 2638
email info@croner.co.uk
website www.croner.co.uk, www.cch.co.uk, www.wolterskluwer.co.uk

Human resources, health and safety, tax and accountancy, education and healthcare, manufacturing and construction. Looseleaf, consultancy and online information services. Founded 1948.

The Women's Press

27 Goodge Street, London W1T 2LD
tel 020-7636 3992 *fax* 020-7637 1866
email david@the-womens-press.com
website www.the-womens-press.com
Acting Managing Director David Elliott

Books by women in the areas of literary and crime fiction, biography and autobiography, health, culture, politics, handbooks, literary criticism, psychology and self-help, the arts. Founded 1978.

Livewire (imprint)
Books for teenagers and young women.

Wooden Books

Signature, 20 Castlegate,
York YO1 9RP *or* Central Books, 99 Wallis Road, London E9 5LN
email info@woodenbooks.com
website www.woodenbooks.com
Directors John Martineau (managing), Anthony Brandt (secretary), Michael Glickman (overseas)

Books

Magic, mathematics, ancient sciences, esoteric. Quality b&w illustrators may submit samples. Founded 1996.

Woodhead Publishing Ltd

Abington Hall, Granta Park, Great Abington, Cambridge CB21 6AH
tel (01223) 891358 *fax* (01223) 893694
email wp@woodheadpublishing.com
website www.woodheadpublishing.com
Managing Director Martin Woodhead

Engineering, materials, welding, textiles, commodities, food science and technology, environmental science, mathematics, information and knowledge management (Chandos Publishing imprint). Founded 1989.

Wordsworth Editions Ltd

8B East Street, Ware, Herts. SG12 9HJ
tel (01920) 465167 *fax* (01920) 462267
email enquiries@wordsworth-editions.com
website www.wordsworth-editions.com
Managing Director Helen Trayler

Reprints of classic books: literary, children's; poetry; reference; Special Editions; mystery and supernatural. Founded 1987.

The X Press

PO Box 25694, London N17 6FP
tel 020-8801 2100 *fax* 020 8885 1322
email vibes@xpress.co.uk
website www.xpress.co.uk
Editorial Director Dotun Adebayo, *Marketing Director* Steve Pope

Black interest popular novels, particularly reflecting contemporary ethnic experiences. *Black Classics* series: reprints of classic novels by black writers. Founded 1992.

Nia (imprint)

Literary black fiction.

Y Lolfa Cyf.

Talybont, Ceredigion SY24 5HE
tel (01970) 832304 *fax* (01970) 832782
email ylolfa@ylolfa.com
website www.ylolfa.com
Director Garmon Gruffudd, *Editor* Lefi Gruffudd

Welsh-language popular fiction and non-fiction, music, children's books; Welsh-language tutors; Welsh interest books in English. Founded 1967.

Yale University Press London*

47 Bedford Square, London WC1B 3DP
tel 020-7079 4900 *fax* 020-7079 4901
email firstname.lastname@yaleup.co.uk
website www.yalebooks.co.uk
Managing Director Robert Baldock, *Marketing Director* Kate Pocock, *Publishers* Gillian Malpass (art history), Sally Salvesen (architecture and decorative arts), Heather McCallum (trade books), *Head of Rights* Anne Bihan

Art, architecture, history, economics, political science, religion, history of science, biography, current affairs and music. Founded 1961.

Yellow Jersey Press – see The Random House Group Ltd

York Notes – see Pearson UK

Young Picador – see Macmillan Publishers Ltd

Zambezi Publishing Ltd

PO Box 221, Plymouth PL2 2YJ
tel (01752) 367300 *fax* (01752) 350453
email info@zampub.com
website www.zampub.com
Contact Sasha Fenton, Jan Budkowski

Mind, Body & Spirit. Founded 1999.

Zed Books Ltd

7 Cynthia Street, London N1 9JF
tel 020-7837 4014 (general) *fax* 020-7833 3960
email zed@zedbooks.net
website www.zedbooks.co.uk
Editors Ken Barlow, Tamsine O'Riordan

Social sciences on international issues; women's studies, politics, development and environmental studies; area studies (Africa, Asia, Caribbean, Latin America, Middle East and the Pacific). Founded 1976.

Zero to Ten Ltd

327 High Street, Slough, Berks. SL1 1TX
tel (0175) 357 8499 *fax* (0175) 357 8488
email sales@evansbrothers.co.uk
Publishing Director Su Swallow

Non-fiction for children aged 0–10: board books, toddler books, first story books, etc. Part of the Evans Publishing Group. Submissions welcome but don't respond to unsuccessful submissions. Founded 1997.

Cherrytree Books (imprint)

UK Publisher Su Swallow

Children's non-fiction illustrated books mainly for schools and libraries.

ZigZag Education

Unit 3, Greenway Business Centre, Doncaster Road, Bristol BS10 5PY
tel 0117-950 3199 *fax* 0117-959 1695
email (author) submissions@PublishMeNow.co.uk
website (customer) www.zigzageduation.co.uk, (author) www.PublishMeNow.co.uk
Development Director John-Lloyd Hagger, *Strategy Director* Mike Stephens

Teaching resources for UK secondary schools: English, maths, ICT, geography, history, science, business studies, politics. Founded 1998.

Book publishers overseas

Listings are given for book publishers in Australia (below), Canada (page 199), New Zealand (page 202), South Africa (page 204) and the USA (page 206).

AUSTRALIA

**Member of the Australian Publishers Association*

Access Press
PO Box 398, Carnarvon, West Australia 6701
tel (08) 9941 2265 *fax* (08) 9941 2298
Managing Editor Jenny Walsh

Australiana, biography, non-fiction. Commissioned works and privately financed books published and distributed. Founded 1974.

ACER Press
19 Prospect Hill Road, Private Bag 55, Camberwell, Victoria 3124
tel (03) 9277 5555 *fax* (03) 9277 5500
email info@acer.edu.au
website www.acer.edu.au
Publishing Manager Andrew Wattson

Publisher of the Australian Council for Educational Research. Produces a range of books and kits.

Allen & Unwin Pty Ltd*
83 Alexander Street, Crows Nest, NSW 2065
postal address PO Box 8500, St Leonards, NSW 1590
tel (02) 8425 0100 *fax* (02) 9906 2218
email info@allenandunwin.com
website www.allenandunwin.com
Directors Patrick Gallagher (Chairman), Paul Donovan (Executive Director), Robert Gorman (CEO), David Martin (finance), Sue Hines (trade publishing)

General trade, including fiction and children's books, academic, especially social science and history. Founded 1990.

Michelle Anderson Publishing Pty Ltd*
PO Box 6032, Chapel Street North, South Yarra 3141
tel (03) 9826 9028 *fax* (03) 9826 8552
email mapubl@bigpond.net.au
website www.michelleandersonpublishing.com
Director Michelle Anderson

General health and mind/body. Founded 2004.

Books & Writers Network Pty Ltd
(incorporating Wild & Woolley and Fast Books)
17 Military Road, Watsons Bay, NSW 2030
tel (02) 9337 6844
email books@fastbooks.com.au
website www.wildandwoolley.com.au
Director Pat Woolley

Offers short and long run printing, design, editing, layout, promotion, and a new on-line bookshop for self published books. Founded 1974.

Cambridge University Press Australian Branch*
477 Williamstown Road, Private Bag 31, Port Melbourne, Victoria 3207
tel (03) 8671 1400 *fax* (03) 9676 9966
email customerservices@cambridge.edu.au
website www.cambridge.edu.au
Chief Executive Stephen Bourne

Academic, educational, reference, English as a second language.

Cengage Learning Australia*
Level 7, 80 Dorcas Street, South Melbourne, Victoria 3205
tel (03) 9685 4111 *fax* (03) 9685 4199
website www.cengage.com.au

Educational books.

Dominie Pty Ltd
Drama (Plays & Musicals), 8 Cross Street, Brookvale, NSW 2100
tel (02) 9938 8686 *fax* (02) 9938 8690
email dominie@dominie.com.au
website www.dominie.com.au/drama

Australian representatives of publishers of plays and agents for the collection of royalties for Samuel French Ltd, Hanbury Plays, Samuel French Inc., The Society of Authors, Bakers Plays, Nick Hern Books, Pioneer Drama and Dominie Musicals.

EA Books
Engineers Media, PO Box 588, Crows Nest, NSW 2065
tel (02) 9438 5355 *fax* (02) 8823 6526
email eabooks@engineersmedia.com.au
website www.eabooks.com.au
Managing Editor Dietrich Georg

Publishing company of the Institution of Engineers Australia.

Elsevier Australia*
Tower 1, Level 12, 475 Victoria Avenue, Chatswood NSW 2067
tel (02) 9422 8500 *fax* (02) 9422 8501
email customerserviceau@elsevier.com
website www.elsevier.com.au
Managing Director Rob Kolkman

Science, medical and technical books. Imprints: Academic Press, Butterworth-Heinemann, Churchill Livingstone, Endeavour, Excerpta Medica, Focal Press, The Lancet, MacLennan and Petty, MD

Books

Consult, Morgan Kauffman, Mosby, Saunders, Science Direct, Syngress. Established 1972.

Hachette Australia Pty Ltd*

Level 17, 207 Kent Street, Sydney, NSW 2000
tel (02) 8248 0800 *fax* (02) 2848 0810
email auspub@hachette.com.au
website www.hachette.com.au
Directors Malcolm Edwards (Managing Director), Chris Raine, David Cocking, Louise Sherwin-Stark, Matt Richell, Fiona Hazard, Jodie Mann, Matt Hoy

General, children's. No unsolicited MSS.

HarperCollins Publishers (Australia) Pty Ltd Group*

postal address PO Box 321, 25 Ryde Road, Pymble, NSW 2073
tel (02) 9952 5000 *fax* (02) 9952 5555
website www.harpercollins.com.au
Publishing Director Shona Martyn

Literary fiction and non-fiction, popular fiction, children's, reference, biography, autobiography, current affairs, sport, lifestyle, health/self-help, humour, true crime, travel, Australiana, history, business, gift, religion.

Kangaroo Press – see Simon & Schuster (Australia) Pty Ltd

Lantern – see Penguin Group (Australia)

Lawbook Co.

Level 5, 100 Harris Street, Pyrmont, NSW 2009
tel (02) 8587 7980 *fax* (02) 8587 7981
website www.thomsonreuters.com.au
Ceo Tony Kinnear

Law. Part of Thomson Legal.

LexisNexis Butterworths Australia*

Tower 2, 475–495 Victoria Avenue, Chatswood, NSW 2067
tel (02) 9422 2174 *fax* (02) 9422 2405
postal address Level 9, Locked Bag 2222, Chatswood Delivery Centre, Chatswood, NSW 2067
website www.lexisnexis.com.au
Publishing Director James Broadfoot

Accounting, business, legal, tax and commercial.

Lonely Planet*

90 Maribyrnong Street, Footscray, Victoria 3011
postal address Locked Bag 1, Footscray, Victoria 3011
tel (03) 8379 8000 *fax* (03) 8379 8111
website www.lonelyplanet.com
Ceo Matt Goldberg, *Directors* Tony Wheeler, Maureen Wheeler, *Publishing Director* Geoff Stringer

Country and regional guidebooks, city guides, *Encounter* citybreak guides, *Discover* country guides, phrasebooks, walking guides, diving and snorkelling guides, pictorial books, healthy travel guides, wildlife guides, travel photography. Also a digital image library (Lonely Planet Images) and a TV company. Offices in London and Oakland, USA. Founded 1973.

McGraw-Hill Education*

Level 2, The Everglade Building, 82 Waterloo Road, North Ryde NSW 2113
postal address Private Bag 2233, Business Centre, North Ryde, NSW 1670
tel (02) 9900 1800 *fax* (02) 9900 1980
website www.macgraw-hill.com.au
Publishing Director Nicole Meehan, *Managing Director* Murray St Leger

Educational publisher: higher education, primary and secondary education (grades K–12) and professional (including medical, general and reference). Division of the McGraw-Hill Companies. Founded 1964.

Macmillan Education Australia Pty Ltd*

Melbourne office Level 1, 15–19 Claremont Street, South Yarra, Victoria 3141
tel (03) 9825 1000 *fax* (03) 9825 1015
email mea@macmillan.com.au
Sydney office Level 25, BT Tower, 1 Market Street, Sydney, NSW 2000
tel (02) 9285 9177 *fax* (02) 9285 9190
website www.macmillan.com.au
Managing Director Stewart Gill, *Primary Literacy Publisher* Col Gillespie, *Primary Teacher Resource and Text Publisher* Sharon Dalgleish, *Primary Library Publisher* Carmel Heron, *General Manager Secondary* Peter Saffin

Educational books.

Melbourne University Publishing*

187 Grattan Street, Carlton, Victoria 3053
tel (03) 9342 0300 *fax* (03) 9342 0399
email mup-info@unimelb.edu.au
website www.mup.com.au
Ceo/Publisher Louise Adler

Academic, scholastic and cultural; educational textbooks and books of reference. Imprints: Miegunyah Press, Victory Books. Founded 1922.

National Archives of Australia*

PO Box 7425, Canberra Business Centre, ACT 2610
tel (02) 6212-3603 *fax* (02) 6213-3914
email angela.mcadam@naa.gov.au
website www.naa.gov.au
Publications Angela McAdam

Australia history (post Federation) and politics, genealogy, reference. Founded 1944; publishing books since 1989.

Pan Macmillan Australia Pty Ltd*

Level 25, 1 Market Street, Sydney, NSW 2000
tel (02) 9285 9100 *fax* (02) 9285 9190
email pan@macmillan.com.au
website www.macmillan.com.au

Directors James Fraser (publishing), Peter Phillips (sales), Andrew Farrell (publicity & marketing)

Commercial and literary fiction; children's fiction, non-fiction and character products; non-fiction; sport.

Penguin Group (Australia)*

250 Camberwell Road, Camberwell, Victoria 3124
tel (03) 9811 2400 *fax* (03) 9811 2620
postal address PO Box 701, Hawthorn, Victoria 3122
website www.penguin.com.au
Ceo Gabrielle Coyne, *Publishing Director* Robert Sessions

Fiction, general non-fiction, current affairs, sociology, economics, environmental, travel guides, anthropology, politics, children's, health, cookery, gardening, pictorial and general books relating to Australia. Imprints: Penguin Books, Lantern, Viking. Founded 1946.

University of Queensland Press*

PO Box 6042, St Lucia, Queensland 4067
tel (07) 3365 7244 *fax* (07) 3365 7579
email uqp@uqp.uq.edu.au
website www.uqp.com.au
General Manager Greg Bain

Non-fiction and academic in the fields of Australian history, Australian biography, Australian politics and current affairs, Australian social and cultural issues, and Australian indigenous issues. Australian fiction (adult, young adult and children's). Via agents only. Founded 1948.

Random House Australia Pty Ltd*

Level 3, Pacific Highway, North Sydney, NSW 2060
tel (02) 9954 9966 *fax* (02) 9954 4562
email random@randomhouse.com.au
website www.randomhouse.com.au
Managing Director Margaret Seale, *Head of Publishing, Random House* Jane Palfreyman, *Head of Publishing, Bantam Doubleday* Fiona Henderson, *Children's Publisher* Lindsay Knight, *Illustrated Publisher* Jude McGee, *Sales & Marketing Director* Carol Davidson, *Publicity Director* Karen Reid

General fiction and non-fiction; children's, illustrated. MSS submissions – for Random House and Transworld Publishing, unsolicited non-fiction accepted, unbound in hard copy addressed to Submissions Editor. Fiction submissions are only accepted from previously published authors, or authors represented by an agent or accompanied by a report from an accredited assessment service. Imprints: Arrow, Avon, Ballantine, Bantam, Black Swan, Broadway, Century, Chatto & Windus, Corgi, Crown, Dell, Doubleday, Ebury, Fodor, Heinemann, Hutchinson, Jonathan Cape, Knopf, Mammoth UK, Minerva, Pantheon, Pavilion, Pimlico, Random House, Red Fox, Rider, Vermilion, Vintage, Virgin. Subsidiary of Bertelsmann AG.

Scholastic Australia Pty Ltd*

76–80 Railway Crescent, Lisarow, Gostord, NSW 2250
tel (02) 4328 3555 *fax* (02) 4323 3827
website www.scholastic.com.au
Publisher Andrew Berkhut

Children's fiction and non-fiction. Founded 1968.

Simon & Schuster (Australia) Pty Ltd*

Suite 2, Lower Ground Floor, 14–16 Suakin Street, Pymble, NSW 2073
tel (02) 9983 6600 *fax* (02) 9988 4293 (editorial)
postal address PO Box 33, Pymble NSW 2073
website www.simonandschuster.com.au

Spinifex Press*

504 Queensberry Street, North Melbourne, Victoria 3051
postal address PO Box 212, North Melbourne, Victoria 3051
tel (03) 9329 6088 *fax* (03) 9329 9238
website www.spinifexpress.com.au
Managing Director Susan Hawthorne

Feminism and women's studies, art, astronomy, occult, education, gay and lesbian, health and nutrition, technology, travel, eBooks. No unsolicited MSS. Founded 1991.

UNSW Press*

University of New South Wales, UNSW Sydney, NSW 2052
tel (02) 9664 0900 *fax* (02) 9664 5420
email publishing@unsw.edu.au
website www.unswpress.com.au
Managing Director Kathy Bail, *Publisher* Phillipa McGuinness

Academic and general non-fiction. Politics, history, society and culture, popular science, environmental studies, Aboriginal studies. Includes imprints UNSW Press, New South and Choice. Founded 1962.

UWA Publishing*

UWA Publishing, University of Western Australia, M419, 35 Stirling Highway, Crawley 6009, Western Australia
tel (618) 6488 3670 *fax* (618) 6488 1027
email admin@uwap.uwa.edu.au
website www.uwap.uwa.edu.au
Director Terri-ann White

Fiction, general non-fiction, natural history, contemporary issues. Founded 1935.

Viking – see Penguin Group (Australia)

John Wiley & Sons Australia, Ltd*

42 McDougall Street, Milton, Queensland 4064
tel (07) 3859 9755 *fax* (07) 3859 9715
email aushighered@wiley.com
website www.wiley.com.au
Managing Director Heather Linaker

Books

Educational, technical, atlases, professional, reference, trade journals. Imprints: John Wiley & Sons, Jacaranda, Wrightbooks, Wiley-Blackwell, Frommer's, Jossey-Bass. Founded 1954.

Wiley-Blackwell Publishing*
Level 2, 155 Cremorne Street, Cremorne, Victoria 3121
tel (03) 9274 3100 *fax* (03) 9274 3101
email melbourne@wiley.com
website www.blackwellpublishing.com
Publishing Director Mark Robertson

Medical, healthcare, life, physical, earth sciences, professional.

CANADA

**Member of the Canadian Publishers' Council*

†Member of the Association of Canadian Publishers

Annick Press Ltd†
15 Patricia Avenue, Toronto, Ontario M2M 1H9
tel 416-221-4802 *fax* 416-221-8400
email annickpress@annickpress.com
website www.annickpress.com
Co-editors Rick Wilks, Colleen MacMillan, *Creative Director* Sheryl Shapiro

Preschool to young adult fiction and non-fiction. Founded 1975.

Boardwalk Books – see Dundurn Press

Butterworths Canada Ltd – see LexisNexis Canada Inc.

Castle Street Mysteries – see Dundurn Press

The Charlton Press
PO Box 820, Station Willowdale B, North York, Ontario M2K 2R1
tel 416-488-1418 *fax* 416-488-4656
email chpress@charltonpress.com
website www.charltonpress.com
President W.K. Cross

Collectibles, Numismatics, Sportscard price catalogues. Founded 1952.

Doubleday Canada
5900 Finch Avenue East, Scarborough, Ontario M1B 0A2
tel 416-977-7891 *fax* 416-977-8707
website www.doubledaycanada.ca
Chairman John Neale, *Publisher* Maya Mavjee

General trade non-fiction; fiction; young adults. Division of Random House of Canada Ltd. Founded 1942.

Douglas & McIntyre Ltd†
2323 Quebec Street, Suite 201, Vancouver, BC V5T 4S7
tel 604-254-7191 *fax* 604-254-9099
email dm@dmpibooks.com
website www.dmpibooks.com
President Mark Scott

General list, including Greystone Books imprint: Canadian biography, art and architecture, natural history, history, native studies, Canadian fiction. Unsolicited MSS accepted. Founded 1971.

Dundurn Press†
3 Church Street, Suite 500, Toronto, Ontario M5E 1M2
tel 416-214-5544
email info@dundurn.com
website www.dundurn.com
President J. Kirk Howard

Popular non-fiction, fiction, scholarship, history, biography, young adult, art. Part of the Dundurn Group. Founded 1973.

Boardwalk Books; Sandcastle Books (imprints)
Young adult fiction.

Castle Street Mysteries (imprint)
Mystery fiction.

Hounslow Press (imprint)
Popular non-fiction.

Simon & Pierre Publishing (imprint)
Theatre, drama, fiction, translations.

ECW Press Ltd†
2120 Queen Street E, Suite 200, Toronto, Ontario M4E 1E2
tel 416-694-3348 *fax* 416-698-9906
email info@ecwpress.com
website www.ecwpress.com
Publisher Jack David

Popular culture, TV and film, sports, humour, general trade books, biographies, guidebooks. Founded 1979.

Fitzhenry & Whiteside Ltd
195 Allstate Parkway, Markham, Ontario L3R 4T8
tel 800-387-9776 *fax* 800-260-9777
email godwit@fitzhenry.ca
website www.fitzhenry.ca
Publisher Sharon Fitzhenry

Trade, educational, children's books. Founded 1966.

Gold Eagle Books – see Harlequin Enterprises Ltd

Harlequin Enterprises Ltd*
PO Box 615, Fort Erie, Ontario L2A 5X3
tel 1888-432-4879
email customer_ecare@harlequin.ca
website www.eharlequin.com
Publisher/Ceo Donna Hayes

Books

Fiction for women, romance, inspirational fiction, African–American fiction, action adventure, mystery. Non-fiction for women, launching autumn 2008. Founded 1949.

Harlequin Books (imprint)
Contemporary and historical romance fiction in series.

Silhouette Books (imprint)
Contemporary romance fiction in series.

Steeple Hill (imprint)
Director, Global Single Titles Editorial Margaret O'Neill Marbury
Contemporary inspirational romantic fiction in series.

Luna Books (imprint)
Romantic fantasy.

HQN Books (imprint)
Romantic single title fiction, contemporary and historical.

Mira Books (imprint)
Fiction for women, contemporary and historical dramas, family sagas, romantic suspense and relationship novels.

Gold Eagle Books (imprint)
Series action adventure fiction.

Worldwide Mystery (imprint)
General Manager, Kimani Press Glenda Howard
Contemporary mystery fiction. Reprints only.

Kimani Press (imprint)
Contemporary romance fiction in series.

Spice (imprint)
Executive Editor, Non-fiction Deborah Brody
Women's erotic fiction.

HarperCollins Publishers Ltd*

2 Bloor Street East, 20th Floor, Toronto, Ontario M4W 1A8
tel 416-975-9334
email hccanada@harpercollins.com
website www.harpercollins.ca
President David Kent

Publishers of literary fiction and non-fiction, history, politics, biography, spiritual and children's books. Founded 1989.

Hounslow Press – see Dundurn Press

HQN Books – see Harlequin Enterprises Ltd

Key Porter Books Ltd

6 Adelaide Street East, 10th Floor, Toronto, Ontario M5C 1H6
tel 416-862-7777 *fax* 416-862-2304
email info@keyporter.com
website www.keyporter.com
Publisher Jordan Fenn

Fiction, nature, history, Canadian politics, conservation, humour, biography, autobiography, health, current events, personal finance, food and drink, cooking, self help, parenting, young adult fiction, children's books, hockey. Founded 1981.

Kids Can Press Ltd†

29 Birch Avenue, Toronto, Ontario M4V 1E2
tel 416-925-5437 *fax* 416-960-5437
email customerservice@kidscan.com
website www.kidscanpress.com/canada/
Publisher Karen Boersma

Juvenile/young adult books. Founded 1973.

Kimani Press – see Harlequin Enterprises Ltd

Knopf Canada – see Random House of Canada Ltd

LexisNexis Canada Inc.*

123 Commerce Valley Drive East, Suite 700, Markham, Ontario L3T 7W8
tel 905-479-2665
email info@lexisnexis.ca
website www.lexisnexis.ca

Law and accountancy. Division of Reed Elsevier plc.

Lone Pine Publishing

10145–81 Avenue, Edmonton, Alberta T6E 1W9
tel 7403-433-9333 *fax* 7403-433-9646
email info@lonepinepublishing.com
website www.lonepinepublishing.com
President Grant Kennedy, *General Manager* Shane Kennedy

Natural history, outdoor recreation and wildlife guidebooks, self-help, gardening, popular history. Founded 1980.

Luna Books – see Harlequin Enterprises Ltd

McClelland & Stewart Ltd†

75 Sherbourne Street, 5th Floor, Toronto, Ontario M5A 2P9
tel 416-598-1114 *fax* 416-598-7764
email editorial@mcclelland.com
website www.mcclelland.com
President & Publisher Douglas Pepper

General. Founded 1906.

McGill-Queen's University Press†

3430 McTavish Street, Montreal, Quebec H3A 1X9
tel 514-398-3750 *fax* 514-398-4333
email mqup@mcgill.ca
Queen's University, Kingston, Ontario K7L 3N6
tel 613-533-2155 *fax* 613-533-6822

email kingstonmqup@queensu.ca
website www.mqup.mcgill.ca

Academic, non-fiction, poetry. Founded 1969.

McGraw-Hill Ryerson Ltd*

300 Water Street, Whitby, Ontario L1N 9B6
tel 905-430-5000 *fax* 905-430-5020
website www.mcgrawhill.ca
President & Ceo David Swail

Educational and trade books.

Mira Books – see Harlequin Enterprises Ltd

Napoleon & Company†

235–1173 Dundas Street E, Toronto,
Ontario M4M 3P1
tel 416-465-9961 *fax* 416-465-3241
email napoleon@napoleonandcompany.com
website www.napoleonandcompany.com
Publisher Sylvia McConnell, *Editor* Allister Thompson

Children's books and adult fiction. Founded 1990.

Nelson Education*

1120 Birchmount Road, Scarborough,
Ontario M1K 5G4
tel 416-752-9448 *fax* 416-752-8101
website www.nelson.com
President Greg Pilon, *Vice President, Market Development* Chris Besse, *Senior Vice President, Media Services* Susan Cline, *Vice President, Higher Education* James Reeve

Educational publishing: school (K–12), college and university, career education, measurement and guidance, professional and reference, ESL titles. Division of Thomson Canada Ltd. Founded 1914.

NeWest Press†

201 8540, 109 Street, Edmonton, AB T6G 1E6
tel 780-432-9427 *fax* 780-433-3179
email info@newestpress.com
website www.newestpress.com
Directors Doug Barbour (President), Don Kerr (Vice-President)

Fiction, drama, poetry and non-fiction. Founded 1977.

Oberon Press

205–145 Spruce Street, Ottawa, Ontario K1R 6P1
tel 613-238-3275 *fax* 613-238-3275
email oberon@sympatico.ca
website www.oberonpress.ca

General fiction, short stories, poetry, some biographies, art and children's. Only publishes Canadian writers.

Oxford University Press, Canada*

8 Sampson Mews, Suite 204, Don Mills,
Ontario M3C 0H5
tel 416-441-2941 *fax* 416-444-0427
website www.oupcanad.com
President David Stover

Educational and academic.

Pearson Canada*

(formerly Prentice Hall Canada and Addison-Wesley Canada)
26 Prince Andrew Place, Toronto, Ontario M3C 2T8
tel 416-447-5101 *fax* 416-443-0948
website www.pearsoned.ca
President Allan Reynolds

Academic, technical, educational, children's and adult, trade.

Penguin Group (Canada)*

90 Eglinton Avenue East, Suite 700, Toronto,
Ontario M4P 2Y3
tel 416-925-2249 *fax* 416-925-0068
email online@ca.penguingroup.com
website www.penguin.ca
President and Publisher David Davidar

Literary fiction, memoir, non-fiction (history, business, current events). No unsolicited MSS; submissions via an agent only. Imprints: Penguin Canada, Viking Canada, Puffin Canada. Founded 1974.

Pippin Publishing Corporation

PO Box 242, Don Mills, Ontario M3C 2S2
tel 416-510-2918 *fax* 416-510-3359
email cynthia@pippinpub.com
website www.pippinpub.com
President/Editorial Director Jonathan Lovat Dickson

ESL/EFL, teacher reference, adult basic education, school texts (all subjects), general trade (non-fiction).

Random House of Canada Ltd*

1 Toronto Street, Suite 300, Toronto,
Ontario M5C 2V6
tel 416-364 4449 *fax* 416-364-6863
website www.randomhouse.ca
Chairman John Neale

Adult and children's. Imprints: Canada, Doubleday Canada (page 199), Knopf Canada, Random House Canada, Seal Books, Vintage Canada. Subsidiary of Bertelsmann AG. Founded 1944.

Red Dress Ink – see Harlequin Enterprises Ltd

Ronsdale Press†

3350 West 21st Avenue, Vancouver, BC V6S 1G7
tel 604-738-4688 *fax* 604-731-4548
email ronsdale@shaw.ca
website www.rondalepress.com
Director Ronald B. Hatch

Canadian literature: fiction, poetry, biography, books of ideas, children's young adult novels. Founded 1988.

Books

Sandcastle Books – see Dundurn Press

Silhouette Books – see Harlequin Enterprises Ltd

Simon & Pierre Publishing – see Dundurn Press

Spice – see Harlequin Enterprises Ltd

Steeple Hill – see Harlequin Enterprises Ltd

Thompson Educational Publishing†

20 Ripley Avenue, Toronto, Ontario M6S 3N9
tel 416-766-2763 *fax* 416-766-0398
email info@thompsonbooks.com
website www.thompsonbooks.com
President Keith Thompson, *Vice-President* Faye Thompson

Social sciences. Founded 1989.

University of Toronto Press Inc.†

10 St Mary Street, Suite 700, Toronto, Ontario M4Y 2W8
tel 416-978-2239 *fax* 416-978-4738
email publishing@utpress.utoronto.ca
website www.utpress.utoronto.ca
President/Publisher John Yates

Founded 1901.

Tundra Books Inc.†

75 Sherbourne Street, 5th Floor, Toronto, Ontario M5A 2P9
tel 416-598-4786
email tundra@mccelland.com
website www.tundrabooks.com
Publisher Kathy Lowinger

High-quality children's picture books.

Women's Press

180 Bloor Street West, Suite 801, Toronto, Ontario M5S 2V6
tel 416-929-2774 *fax* 416-929-1926
email info@cspi.org
website www.womenspress.ca
Editor James MacNevin

The ideas and experiences of women: fiction, creative non-fiction, children's books, plays, biography, autobiography, memoirs, poetry. Owned by Canadian Scholars' Press. Founded 1987.

Worldwide Mystery – see Harlequin Enterprises Ltd

NEW ZEALAND

**Member of the Publishers Association of New Zealand (PANZ)*

Auckland University Press*

University of Auckland, Private Bag 92019, Auckland
tel (09) 373-7528 *fax* (09) 373-7465
email aup@auckland.ac.nz
website www.auckland.ac.nz/aup
Director Sam Elworthy

NZ history, NZ poetry, Maori and Pacific studies, politics, art, biography, science and natural history, health, business. Founded 1966.

David Bateman Ltd*

30 Tarndale Grove, Albany Business Park, Bush Road, Auckland
tel (09) 415-7664 *fax* (09) 415-8892
email bateman@bateman.co.nz
website www.bateman.co.nz
Chairman/Publisher David L. Bateman, *Directors* Janet Bateman, Paul Bateman (joint managing), Paul Parkinson (joint managing)

Natural history, gardening, encyclopedias, sport, art, cookery, historical, juvenile, travel, motoring, maritime history, business, art, lifestyle. Founded 1979.

Bush Press Communications Ltd

postal address PO Box 33029, Takapuna 0740, Auckland, New Zealand
41 Hauraki Road, Takapuna 0622
tel (09) 486-2667
email bush.press@clear.net.nz
Governing Director/Publisher Gordon Ell ONZM

NZ non-fiction, particularly outdoor, nature, travel, architecture, crafts, Maori, popular history. Founded 1979.

The Caxton Press*

PO Box 25088, 113 Victoria Street, Christchurch
tel (03) 366-8516 *fax* (03) 365-7840
email peter@caxton.co.nz
website www.caxton.co.nz
Director Peter Watson

Local history, tourist pictorial, Celtic spirituality, parent guide, book designers and printers. Founded 1935.

Cengage Learning New Zealand*

Unit 4B, Rosedale Office Park, 331 Rosedale Road, Albany, North Shore 0632
postal address PO Box 33376, Takapuna, North Shore 0740
tel (09) 415 6850 *fax* (09) 415 6853

Educational books.

Dunmore Press Ltd*

PO Box 25080, Wellington 6146
tel (04) 472-2705 *fax* (04) 471-0604
email books@dunmore.co.nz
website www.dunmore.co.nz
Director Sharmian Firth

Education, history, sociology, business studies, general non-fiction. Founded 1970.

Hachette New Zealand Ltd*

PO Box 100–749, North Shore Mail Centre, Auckland 0745
tel (09) 478-1000 *fax* (09) 478-1010
email admin@hachette.co.nz
Managing Director Kevin Chapman, *Editorial Director* Warren Adler

Sport, cooking, travel, general.

Halcyon Publishing Ltd

PO Box 360, Auckland 1140
tel (09) 489 5337 *fax* (09) 489 5218
email info@halcyonpublishing.co.nz
Managing Director/Publisher Graham Gurr

Hunting, shooting, fishing, outdoor interests. Founded 1982.

HarperCollins Publishers (New Zealand) Ltd*

31 View Road, Glenfield, Auckland 0627
tel (09) 443-9400 *fax* (09) 443-9403
email editors@harpercollins.co.nz
postal address PO Box 1, Shortland Street, Auckland
website www.harpercollins.co.nz
Managing Director Tony Fisk, *Commissioning Editor* Tracey Wogan

General literature, non-fiction, reference, children's.

Learning Media Ltd*

Level 4, Willeston House, 22–28 Willeston Street, PO Box 3293, Wellington 6001
tel (4) 472-5522 *fax* (4) 472 6444
email info@learningmedia.co.nz

Educational books, websites and CD-Roms for New Zealand and international markets. Texts in English, Maori and 5 Pacific languages. Founded 1993.

LexisNexis NZ Ltd

181 Wakefield Street, Wellington 6011
tel (04) 385-1479 *fax* (04) 385-1598
email customer.service@lexisnexis.co.nz
postal address PO Box 472, Wellington 6140
website www.lexisnexis.co.nz
Publisher John Henton

Law, business, academic.

McGraw-Hill Book Company New Zealand Ltd*

Level 8, 56–60 Cowley Street, Ellerslie, Auckland
postal address Private Bag 11904, Ellerslie, Auckland 1005
tel (09) 526-6200
website www.mcgraw-hill.com

Educational publisher: higher education, primary and secondary education (grades K–12) and professional (including medical, general and reference). Division of the McGraw-Hill Companies. Founded 1974.

New Zealand Council for Educational Research

Box 3237, Education House, 178–182 Willis Street, Wellington 6011
tel (04) 384-7939 *fax* (04) 384-7933
email info@nzcer.org.nz
website www.nzcer.org.nz
Director Robyn Baker, *Publisher* Bev Webber

Education, including educational policy and institutions, early childhood education, educational achievement tests, Maori education, curriculum and assessment, etc. Founded 1934.

Otago University Press*

University of Otago, PO Box 56, Dunedin 9054
tel (03) 479-8807 *fax* (03) 479-8385
email university.press@otago.ac.nz
website www.otago.ac.nz/press
Publisher Wendy Harrex

New Zealand and Pacific history, social and cultural studies, as well as a wide range of scholarly to general books. Also publishes New Zealand's longest-running literary journal, *Landfall*. Founded 1958.

Pearson Education New Zealand Ltd*

Private Bag 102902, Rosedale, North Shore 0745, Auckland
tel (09) 442-7400 *fax* (09) 442-7401
email customer.service@pearsonnz.co.nz
website www.pearsoned.co.nz
General Manager Adrian Keane

New Zealand educational books.

Penguin Group (NZ)*

Private Bag 102902, Rosedale, North Shore 0745, Auckland
tel (09) 442-7400 *fax* (09) 442-7401
website www.penguin.co.nz
Managing Director Margaret Thompson, *Publishing Director* Geoff Walker

Adult and children's fiction and non-fiction. Imprints: Penguin, Viking, Puffin Books. Founded 1973.

Random House New Zealand Ltd*

Private Bag 102950, North Shore Mail Centre, Auckland 0725
tel (09) 444-7197 *fax* (09) 444-7524
email admin@randomhouse.co.nz
website www.randomhouse.co.nz
Managing Director Karen Ferns

Fiction, general non-fiction, gardening, cooking, art, business, health, children's. Subsidiary of Bertelsmann AG. Founded 1977.

RSVP Publishing Company*

PO Box 47166, Ponsonby, Auckland 1144
tel/fax (09) 372-8480

email rsvppub@iconz.co.nz
website www.rsvp-publishing.co.nz
Managing Director/Publisher Stephen Ron Picard

Fiction, metaphysical, children's. Founded 1990.

Scholastic New Zealand Ltd*

21 Lady Ruby Drive, East Tamaki, Auckland
tel (09) 274-8112 *fax* (09) 274-8114
email publishing@scholastic.co.nz
postal address Private Bag 94407, Botany, Manukau 2163
website www.scholastic.co.nz
Senior Editor Penny Scown

Children's books. Founded 1962.

Victoria University Press*

Victoria University of Wellington, PO Box 600, Wellington
tel (04) 463-6580 *fax* (04) 463-6581
email victoria-press@vuw.ac.nz
website www.victoria.ac.nz/vup
Publisher Fergus Barrowman, *Editor* Kyleigh Hodgson

Academic, scholarly books on NZ history, sociology, law; Maori language; fiction, plays, poetry. Founded 1974.

Viking Sevenseas NZ Ltd*

201A Rosetta Road, Raumati
tel (04) 902-8240 *fax* (04) 902-8240
email vikings@paradise.net.nz
website www.booksofnewzealand.co.nz
Managing Director M.B. Riley

Natural history books on New Zealand only.

SOUTH AFRICA

**Member of the Publishers' Association of South Africa*

Ad Donker – see Jonathan Ball Publishers (Pty) Ltd

Jonathan Ball Publishers (Pty) Ltd*

PO Box 33977, Jeppestown 2043
tel (011) 601 8000 *fax* (011) 601 8183
email enquiries@inetimagery.co.za
website www.jonathanball.co.za
postal address PO Box 33977, Jeppestown 2043
Publishing Director Jeremy Boraine

Founded 1977.

Ad Donker (imprint)
Africana, literature, history, academic.

Jonathan Ball (imprint)
General publications, current affairs, politics, business history, business, reference.

Delta Books (imprint)
General South African trade non-fiction.

Sunbird Publishers (imprint)
Illustrated wildlife, tourism, maps, travel.

Cambridge University Press*

(African Branch)
Lower Ground Floor, Nautica Building,
The Water Club, Beach Road, Granger Bay,
Cape Town 8005
tel (021) 412-7800 *fax* (021) 419-8418
email capetown@cambridge.org
website www.cambridge.org/africa
Director Colleen McCallum

African Branch of CUP, responsible for sub-Saharan Africa. Publishes distance learning materials and textbooks for various African countries, as well as primary reading materials in 28 local African languages.

Clever Books Pty Ltd*

2nd Floor, Melrose Arch Piazza, 34 Whiteley Road, Melrose North 2196
tel (011) 731 3300 *fax* (011) 731 3500
email info@cleverbooks.co.za

Managing Director J. Steenhuisen

Educational titles for the RSA market. Owned by Macmillan South Africa. Founded 1981.

Delta Books – see Jonathan Ball Publishers (Pty) Ltd

Fernwood Press CC

PO Box 481, Simon's Town, 7995 Cape
tel (21) 786 2460 *fax* (21) 786 2478
email ferpress@iafrica.com
website www.fernwoodpress.co.za
Directors Pieter Struik, Pam Struik

Illustrated non-fiction reference works on southern Africa's cultural and natural history. Founded 1991.

Galago Publishing (Pty) Ltd

PO Box 1645, Alberton 1450
tel (11) 907-2029 *fax* (11) 869-0890
email lemur@mweb.co.za
website www.galago.co.za
Managing Director Fran Stiff, *Publisher* Peter Stiff

Southern African interest: military, political, hunting. Founded 1981.

Jacklin Enterprises (Pty) Ltd

PO Box 521, Parklands 2121
tel (011) 265-4200 *fax* (011) 314-2984
email service@jacklin.co.za
Managing Director M.A.C. Jacklin

Children's fiction and non-fiction; Afrikaans large print books. Subjects include aviation, natural history, romance, general science, technology and transportation. Imprints: Mike Jacklin, Kennis Onbeperk, Daan Retief.

Juta & Company Ltd*

1st Floor, Sunclare Building, 21 Dreyer Street, Claremont 7708
tel (021) 659 2300 *fax* (021) 659 2360
email cserv@juta.co.za
website www.juta.co.za
Ceo Lynne du Toit

Academic, learning, health, law and electronic. Founded 1853.

University of KwaZulu-Natal Press*

Private Bag X01, Scottsville, 3209 KwaZulu-Natal
tel (033) 260-5226 *fax* (033) 260-5801
email books@ukzn.ac.za
website www.ukznpress.co.za
Publisher Glenn Cowley

Southern African social, political, economic and military history, gender, natural sciences, African poetry and literature, genealogy, education, biography. Founded 1948.

Maskew Miller Longman (Pty) Ltd*

PO Box 396, Howard Drive, Pinelands 7405, Cape Town 8000
tel (021) 532-6000 *fax* (021) 531-8103
email customerservices@mml.co.za
website www.mml.co.za
Publishing Director Dorette Louw

Educational and general publishers.

NB Publishers (Pty) Ltd*

PO Box 879, Cape Town 8000
tel (021) 406-3033 *fax* (021) 406-3812
email nb@nb.co.za
website www.nb.co.za
Managing Director Eloise Wessels

General: Afrikaans fiction, politics, children's and youth literature in all the country's languages, non-fiction. Imprints include Tafelberg, Human & Rousseau, Pharos and Kwela. Founded 1950.

New Africa Books (Pty) Ltd*

99 Garfield Road, Claremont, Cape Town 7700
tel (21) 674-4136 *fax* (21) 674-3358
email info@newafricabooks.co.za
postal address PO Box 46962, Glosderry 7702
website www.newafricabooks.co.za
Publisher Jeanne Homnid

General books, textbooks, literary works, contemporary issues, children and young adult. Formed as a result of the merger of David Philip Publishers (founded 1971), Spearhead Press (founded 2000) and New Africa Educational Publishing.

David Philip (imprint)

Academic, history, social sciences, politics, biography, reference, education.

Spearhead (imprint)

Current affairs, also business, self-improvement, health, natural history, travel.

Oxford University Press Southern Africa*

Vasco Boulevard, N1 City, Goodwood, Cape Town 7460
tel (021) 596-2300 *fax* (021) 596-1234
email oxford.za@oup.com
postal address PO Box 12119, N1 City, Cape Town 7463
website www.oxford.co.za
Managing Director E. Kotze

Pan Macmillan South Africa*

Private Bag X19, Northlands, Johannesburg 2116
tel (011) 731 3440 *fax* (011) 684 2728
website www.panmacmillan.co.za
Managing Director Mrs Terry Morris

Imprints: Ravan Press, Picador Africa, Giraffe Books

Random House Struik (Pty) Ltd

80 McKenzie Street Gardens, Cape Town 8001
PO Box 1144, Cape Town 8000, South Africa
tel (021) 462-4360
email info@struik.co.za
website www.struik.co.za
Managing Director Stephen Johnson

General illustrated non-fiction: SA politics, sport, business and contemporary fiction. Founded 1962.

Oshun (imprint)

Life guides, memoirs and lighthearted entertainment for women.

Zebra Press (imprint)

Life guides, memoirs and lighthearted entertainment for women.

Shuter and Shooter Publishers (Pty) Ltd*

110 CB, Downes Road, Pietermaritzburg 3201, KwaZulu-Natal
tel (033) 846-8700 *fax* (033) 846-8701
email sales@shuters.com
postal address PO Box 13016, Cascades 3202, KwaZulu-Natal
website www.shuters.com
Managing Director Mrs P. B. Chetty

Core curriculum-based textbooks for use at foundation, intermediate, senior and further education phases. Supplementary readers in various languages; dictionaries; reading development kits, charts. Literature titles in English, isiXhosa, Sesotho, Sepedi, Setswana, Tshivenda, Xitsonga, Ndebele and Siswati. Founded 1925.

Sunbird Publishers – see Jonathan Ball Publishers (Pty) Ltd

Unisa Press*

University of South Africa, PO Box 392, Unisa, Muckleneuk, Pretoria 0003

tel (012) 429-3316 *fax* (012) 429-3449
email unisa-press@unisa.ac.za
website www.unisa.ac.za/press/
Director Elizabeth le Roux

Theology and all academic disciplines. Publishers of University of South Africa. Imprint: UNISA. Founded 1957.

Van Schaik Publishers*

PO Box 12681, Hatfield, Pretoria 0028
tel (012) 342-2765 *fax* (012) 430-3563
email vanschaik@vanschaiknet.com
website www.vanschaiknet.com
CEO Leanne Martini

Texts for the tertiary and private FET markets in South Africa. Founded 1915.

Wits University Press*

3 Jubilee Street, Parktown, Aletta Sutton Building, Johannesburg 2193
tel (011) 484-5974 *fax* (011) 643 5769
email witspress@wup.wits.ac.za
postal address PO Wits, Johannesburg 2050
website www.witspress.wits.ac.za
Publisher Veronica Klipp

Zebra Press – see Random House Struik (Pty) Ltd

USA

**Member of the Association of American Publishers Inc.*

Abbeville Press, Inc.

137 Varick Street, New York, NY 10013
tel 212-366-5585 *fax* 212-366-6966
email abbeville@abeville.com
website www.abbeville.com
Publisher/President Robert Abrams

Fine art and illustrated books. Founded 1977.

ABC-Clio

130 Cremona Drive, Santa Barbara, CA 93117
tel 805-968-1911 *fax* 866-270-3856
website www.abc-clio.com

Academic resources for secondary and middle schools, colleges and universities, libraries and professionals (librarians, media specialists, teachers). Founded 1971.

Abingdon Press

201 Eighth Avenue, PO Box 801, Nashville, TN 37202–0801
tel 615-749-6290 *fax* 615-749-6372
website www.abingdonpress.com
President Neil Alexander, *Vice President* Tammy Gaines

General interest, professional, academic and reference – primarily directed to the religious market; children's non-fiction. Imprint of United Methodist Publishing House.

Harry N. Abrams Inc.

115 West 18th Street, New York, NY 10011
tel 212-206-7715 *fax* 212-519 1210
email abrams@abramsbooks.com
website www.abramsbooks.com
Ceo/President Michael Jacobs

Art and architecture, photography, natural sciences, performing arts, children's books. No fiction. Founded 1949.

Ace – see Penguin Group (USA), Inc.

The University of Alabama Press

Box 870380, Tuscaloosa, AL 35487-0380
tel 205-348-5180 *fax* 205-348-9201
website www.uapress.ua.edu
Director Daniel J.J. Ross

American and Southern history, African–American studies, religion, rhetoric and communication, Judaic studies, literary criticism, anthropology and archaeology. Founded 1945.

Alpha – see Penguin Group (USA), Inc.

Amistad – see HarperCollins Publishers

Applause Theatre and Cinema Book Publishers

19 West 21st Street, Suite 201, New York, NY 10010
tel 212-575-9265 *fax* 212-575-9270
email info@applausepub.com
website www.applausepub.com
Publisher Michael Messina

Performing arts. Founded 1980.

Arcade Publishing

116 John Street, Suite 2810, New York, NY 10038
tel 212-475-2633 *fax* 212-353-8148
email arcadeinfo@arcadepub.com
website www.arcadepub.com
President/Editor-in-Chief Richard Seaver, *Publisher* Jeannette Seaver

General trade, including adult hard cover and paperbacks. No unsolicited MSS. Founded 1988.

ArcheBooks Publishing Inc.

6081 Silver King Boulevard, Suite 903, Cape Coral, FL 33914
tel 239-542-7595 (toll free) *fax* 239-542-0080
email info@archebooks.com
website www.archebooks.com
Publisher Robert E. Gelinas

Fiction and non-fiction (history and true crime). Send submissions via a literary agent. Founded 2003.

The University of Arkansas Press

McIlroy House, McIlroy Avenue, Fayetteville, AR 72701

tel 800-626-0090 *fax* 479-575-6044
email uapress@uark.edu
website www.uapress.com
Director Lawrence J. Malley

History, humanities, literary criticism, Middle East studies, African–American studies, poetry. Founded 1980.

Atlantic Monthly Press – see Grove/Atlantic Inc.

Avery – see Penguin Group (USA), Inc.

Avon – see HarperCollins Publishers

Back Bay Books – see Little, Brown & Company

Baker's Plays

7611 Sunset Boulevard, Hollywood, CA 90046
tel 323-876-0579 *fax* 323-876-5482
email info@bakersplays.com
website www.bakersplays.com
President Leon Embry, *UK Agent* Samuel French Ltd

Plays and books on the theatre. Also agents for plays. Division of Samuel French Inc. Founded 1845.

Ballantine Books – see Random House Inc.

Bantam Books – see Random House Inc.

Barron's Educational Series Inc.

250 Wireless Boulevard, Hauppauge, NY 11788
tel 800-645-3476 *fax* 631-434-3723
email barrons@barronseduc.com
website www.barronseduc.com
Chairman/Ceo Manuel H. Barron, *President/Publisher* Ellen Sibley

Test preparation, juvenile, cookbooks, Mind, Body & Spirit, crafts, business, pets, gardening, family and health, art, study guides, school guides. Founded 1941.

Beacon Press

25 Beacon Street, Boston, MA 02108
tel 617-742-2110 *fax* 617-723-3097
website www.beacon.org
Director Helene Atwan

General non-fiction in fields of religion, ethics, philosophy, current affairs, gender studies, environmental concerns, African–American studies, anthropology and women's studies, nature. Founded 1854.

Bella Books

PO Box 10543, Tallahessee, FL 32302
tel 800-729-4992 *fax* 850-576-3498
website www.bellabooks.com

Lesbian fiction: mystery, romance, science fiction. Founded 1973.

Berkley Books – see Penguin Group (USA), Inc.

Bloomsbury USA

Suite 315, 175 Fifth Avenue, New York, NY 10010
tel 212-674-5151 *fax* 212-982-2837
website www.bloomsburyusa.com
Publisher George Gibson, *Executive Editors* Anton Mueller, Kathy Belden, *Associate Publisher* Sabrina Farber, *Director Publicity* Peter Miller, *Publisher, Bloomsbury Press* Peter Ginna, *Publisher, Walker Books* George Gibson

Publishers of literary fiction, general non-fiction and children's (picture books, early chapter books, middle grade fiction, teen fiction). Adult division does not accept unsolicited MSS; children's division will consider unsolicited MSS. No material will be returned, and only accepted MSS will receive a reply. Wholly owned subsidiary of Bloomsbury Plc. Founded 1998.

R.R. Bowker*

630 Central Avenue, New Providence, NJ 07974
tel 908-286-1090
email info@bowker.com
website www.bowker.com
President & Ceo Annie M. Callanan

Bibliographies and reference tools for the book trade and literary and library worlds, available in hardcopy, on microfiche, online and CD-Rom. Reference books for music, art, business, computer industry, cable industry and information industry. Division of Cambridge Information Group.

Boyds Mills Press

815 Church Street, Honesdale, PA 18431
website www.boydsmillspress.com

Fiction, non-fiction, and poetry trade books for children and young adults. Founded 1991.

Burford Books

32 Morris Avenue, Springfield, NJ 07081
tel 888-672-5247 *fax* 973-258-0113
email info@burfordbooks.com
website www.burfordbooks.com
President Peter Burford

Outdoor activities: golf, sports, fitness, nature, travel. Founded 1997.

Cambridge University Press*

32 Avenue of the Americas, New York, NY 10013
tel 212-924-3900 *fax* 212-691-3239
email newyork@cambridge.org
website www.cambridge.org/us

Academic and professional; Cambridge Learning (ELT, primary and secondary education).

Candlewick Press

99 Dover Street, Somerville, MA 02144
tel 617-661-3330 *fax* 617-661-0565

email bigbear@candlewick.com
website www.candlewick.com
President/Publisher Karen Lotz, *Editorial Director/ Associate Publisher* Liz Bicknell

Books for babies through teens: board books, picture books, novels, non-fiction, novelty books. Submit material through a literary agent. Subsidiary of Walker Books Ltd, UK. Founded 1991.

Cannongate US – see Grove/Atlantic Inc.

Center Street

Hachette Book Group USA, 237 Park Avenue, New York, NY 10017
email centerstreetpub@hbgusa.com
website www.hachettebookgroup.com

Books with traditional values for readers in the US heartland. Division of Hachette Book Group. Founded 2005.

University of Chicago Press*

1427 East 60th Street, Chicago, IL 60637
tel 773-702-7700 *fax* 773-702-2705
website www.press.uchicago.edu

Scholarly books and monographs (humanities, social sciences and sciences) general trade books, reference books, and 43 scholarly journals.

Chronicle Books

680 Second Street, San Francisco, CA 94107
tel 415-537-4200 *fax* 415-537-4460
email frontdesk@chroniclebooks.com
website www.chroniclebooks.com, www.chroniclekids.com
Chairman & Ceo Nion McEvoy, *Publisher* Christine Carswell

Cooking, art, fiction, general, children's, gift, new media, gardening, regional, nature. Founded 1967.

Coffee House Press

79 13th Avenue NE, Suite 110, Minneapolis, MN 55413
tel 612-338-0125 *fax* 612-338-4004
website www.coffeehousepress.org
Publisher Allan Kornblum

Literary fiction and poetry; collectors' editions. Founded 1984.

Collins – see HarperCollins Publishers

Columbia University Press

61 West 62nd Street, New York, NY 10023
tel 212-459-0600 *fax* 212-459-3677
email cup_publicity@columbia.edu
website http://cup.columbia.edu
Associate Director Jennifer Crewe

Scholarly, general interest, and professional books and upper-level textbooks in the humanities, social sciences, and earth and life sciences; reference works in print and electronic formats. Subjects include animal studies, Asian studies, conservation and environmental science, criminology, ecology, evolutionary studies, film, finance and economics, gender studies, history, international relations, journalism, literary and cultural studies, media studies, Middle East studies, neuroscience, paleontology, philosophy, political philosophy, political science, religion, social work. Publishes poetry, fiction and drama in translation only. Founded 1893.

Concordia Publishing House

3558 South Jefferson Avenue, St Louis, MO 63118
tel 314-268-1000
website www.cph.org
Publisher & Executive Director of Editorial Paul T. McCain

Religious books, Lutheran perspective. Few freelance MSS accepted; query first. Founded 1869.

Contemporary Books

130 East Randolph Street, Suite 400, Chicago, IL 60601
tel 800-621-1918
website www.mhcontemporary.com

Non-fiction. Imprints: Contemporary Books, Lowell House, Passport Books, VGM Career Books. Division of the McGraw-Hill Companies.

The Continuum International Publishing Group Inc.

80 Maiden Lane, Suite 704, New York, NY 10038
tel 212-953-5858 *fax* 212-953-5944
email info@continuumbooks.com
website www.continuumbooks.com
Vice-President/Senior Editor Frank Oveis

General non-fiction, education, popular culture, philosophy, politics, linguistics, history, literary criticism, religious studies. Founded 1999.

Cooper Square Publishing

4501 Forbes Boulevard, Suite 200, Lanham, Maryland 20706
tel 301-459-3366
website www.northlandpub.com

Part of the Rowman & Littlefield Publishing Group, founded 1949.

Northland Publishing (imprint)

website www.northlandbooks.com

American Southwest themes including home design, cooking, and travel. Founded 1958.

Luna Rising (imprint)

website www.northlandbooks.com

Northland Publishing's bilingual (Spanish–English) imprint.

NorthWord Books for Young Readers (imprint)
11571 K–Tel Drive, Minnetonka, MN 55343
tel 952-933-7537 *fax* 952-933-3630
email mbohr@nbnbooks.com
website www.nbnbooks.com

Picture books and non-fiction nature and wildlife books in interactive and fun-to-read formats. Not accepting MSS at present. Founded 1989.

Rising Moon (imprint)
email editorial@northlandbooks.com
website www.northlandbooks.com

Illustrated, entertaining, and thought-provoking picture books for children, including Spanish–English bilingual titles. Not accepting MSS at present.

Two-Can Publishing (imprint)
website www.northlandbooks.com

Non-fiction books and multimedia products to entertain and educate 2–12 year-olds. Not accepting MSS at present.

Cornell University Press*
(including ILR Press and Comstock Publishing Associates)
Sage House, 512 East State Street, Ithaca, NY 14850
tel 607-277-2338 *fax* 607-277-2374
email cupressinfo@cornell.edu
website www.cornellpress.cornell.edu
Director John G. Ackerman

Scholarly books. Founded 1869.

The Countryman Press
PO Box 748, Woodstock, VT 05091
tel 802-457-4826
email countrymanpress@wwnorton.com
website www.countrymanpress.com
Editorial Director Kermit Hummel

Outdoor recreation guides for anglers, hikers, cyclists, canoeists and kayakers, US travel guides, New England non-fiction, how-to books, country living books, books on nature and the environment, classic reprints and general non-fiction. No unsolicited MSS. Division of W.W. Norton & Co. Inc. Founded 1973.

Crown Publishing Group – see Random House Inc.

DAW Books Inc.
375 Hudson Street, 3rd Floor, New York, NY 10014
tel 212-366-2000 *fax* 212-366-2090
email daw@us.penguingroup.com
website www.dawbooks.com
Publishers Elizabeth R. Wollheim, Sheila E. Gilbert

Science fiction, fantasy, horror, and paranormal: originals and reprints. Imprints: DAW/Fantasy, DAW/Fiction, DAW/Science Fiction. Affiliate of Penguin Group (USA), Inc. Founded 1971.

Delacorte – see Random House Inc.

Dial Books for Young Readers – see Penguin Group (USA), Inc.

DNA Press
242 King Street, Pottstown, PA 19464
email editors@dnapress.com
website www.dnapress.com

Non-fiction books for adults and children on real estate, investing, business.

Tom Doherty Associates, LLC
175 5th Avenue, New York, NY 10010
tel 212-388-0100 *fax* 212-388-0191
email enquiries@tor.com
website www.us.macmillan.com/torforge.aspx, www.torforge.com

Fiction: general, historical, western, suspense, mystery, horror, science fiction, fantasy, humour, juvenile, classics (English language); non-fiction: adult and juvenile. Imprints: Tor, Forge, Orb, Starscope, Tor Teen. Founded 1980.

Dover Publications Inc.
31 East 2nd Street, Mineola, NY 11501
tel 516-294-7000 *fax* 516-742-6953
website www.doverpublications.com

Art, architecture, antiques, crafts, juvenile, food, history, folklore, literary classics, mystery, language, music, math and science, nature, design and ready-to-use art. Founded 1941.

Dutton – see Penguin Group (USA), Inc.

Dutton Children's Books – see Penguin Group (USA), Inc.

Faber and Faber, Inc. – see Farrar, Straus and Giroux, LLC

Facts On File Inc.
Infobase Publishing, 132 West 31st Street, New York, NY 10001
tel 800-322-8755 *fax* 800-678-3633
website www.factsonfile.com
Editorial Director Laurie E. Likoff

General reference books and services for colleges, libraries, schools and general public. Founded 1940.

Family Tree – see Writer's Digest Books

Farrar, Straus and Giroux, LLC
18 West 18th Street, New York, NY 10011
tel 212-741-6900 *fax* 212-633-9385 (adult division), 212-741-6973 (children's division)
website www.fsgbooks.com, www.fsgkidsbooks.com
President/Publisher Jonathan Galassi

Hill and Wang (imprint)
Publisher Thomas LeBien

General non-fiction, history, public affairs, graphic novels. Founded 1956.

North Point Press (imprint)
Literary non-fiction, with an emphasis on natural history, ecology, music, food writing and cultural criticism.

Faber and Faber, Inc.
18 West 18th Street, New York, NY 10011
tel 212-741-6900 *fax* 212-633-9385
website www.fsgbooks.com
Publisher Mitzi Angel
Fiction, general non-fiction, drama, poetry, film, music.

Firebird – see Penguin Group (USA), Inc.

Fodor's Travel Publications – see Random House Inc.

Samuel French Inc
45 West 25th Street, New York, NY 10010
tel 212 206 8990 *fax* 212 206 1429
email info@samuelfrench.com
website www.samuelfrench.com

Play publishers and authors' representatives (dramatic).

Getty Publications
1200 Getty Center Drive, Suite 500, Los Angeles, CA 90049
tel 310-440-7300 *fax* 310-440-7758
email communications@getty.edu
website www.getty.edu

Art, art history, architecture, classical art and archaeology, conservation. Founded 1958.

David R. Godine, Publisher Inc.
9 Hamilton Place, Boston, MA 02108
tel 617-451-9600 *fax* 617-350-0250
email info@godine.com
website www.godine.com
President David R. Godine

Fiction, photography, poetry, art, biography, children's, essays, history, typography, architecture, nature and gardening, music, cooking, words and writing, and mysteries. No unsolicited MSS. Founded 1970.

Gotham – see Penguin Group (USA), Inc.

Grand Central Publishing
(previously Warner Books Inc.)
237 Park Avenue, New York, NY 10017
tel 212-364-0600 *fax* 212-364-0928
email grandcentralpublishing@hbgusa.com
website www.hachettebookgroupusa.com

Fiction and non-fiction. Imprints: Aspect, Business Plus (business), Forever (romance), Vision (blockbuster fiction), Wellness Central (health and wellbeing), 5 Spot (women's fiction and non-fiction), Twelve, Springboard Press. Division of Hachette Book Group USA. Founded 1970.

Grosset & Dunlap – see Penguin Group (USA), Inc.

Grove/Atlantic Inc.*
841 Broadway, New York, NY 10003
tel 212-614-7850 *fax* 212-614-7886
website www.groveatlantic.com
Publisher Morgan Entrekin

Fiction, biography, autobiography, history, current affairs, social science, belles-lettres, natural history. No unsolicited MSS. Imprints: Atlantic Monthly Press, Cannongate US, Grove Press. Founded 1952.

Hachette Book Group USA
237 Park Avenue, 16th Floor, New York, NY10017
website www.hachettebookgroup.com

Divisions: Center Street (see page 208), Grand Central Publishing (see page 210), Hachette Audio, Little, Brown and Company, Little, Brown and Company Books for Young Readers, Yen Press (see page 220). Imprints: Faith Words, Orbit, Windblown Media.

Orbit (imprint)
website www.orbitbooks.net
Science fiction and fantasy.

Harcourt Trade Publishers*
215 Park Avenue South, New York, NY 10003
tel 212-592-1034 *fax* 212-420-5850
website www.hmhbooks.com
President/Publisher Dan Farley, *Editorial Director* Liz Van Doren

Fiction and non-fiction (history, biography, etc) for readers of all ages. Part of the Harcourt Houghton Mifflin Book Group.

HarperCollins Publishers*
10 East 53rd Street, New York, NY 10022
tel 212-207-7000
website www.harpercollins.com
President/Ceo Brian Murray

Fiction, history, biography, poetry, science, travel, cookbooks, juvenile, educational, business, technical and religious. No unsolicited material; all submissions must come through a literary agent. Founded 1817.

HarperCollins General Books Group (division)
President/Publisher Michael Morrison
Imprints: Amistad, Avon, Avon A, Avon Inspire, Avon Red, Caedmon, Collins, Collins Business, Collins Design, Collins Living, Ecco, Eos, Harper Mass Market, Harper Paperbacks, Harper Perennial, Harper Perennial Modern Classics, HarperAudio, HarperCollins, HarperCollins e-Books,

HarperEntertainment, HarperLuxe, HarperOne, William Morrow, Morrow Cookbooks, Rayo.

HarperInformation (division)
Imprints: Access, HarperBusiness, HarperResource, William Morrow Cookbooks.

HarperSanFrancisco (division)
Imprint: HarperSanFrancisco.

HarperCollins Children's Books (division)
1350 Avenue of the Americas, New York, NY 10019
tel 212-261-6500
website www.harperchildrens.com
President/Publisher Susan Katz

Children's classic literature. Imprints: Amistad Press, Julie Andrews Collection, Joanna Cotler Books, Eos, Laura Geringer Books, Greenwillow Books, HarperChildren's Audio, HarperCollins Children's Books, HarperEntertainment, HarperTeen, HarperTrophy, Rayo, Katherine Tegen Books.

Harvard University Press*
79 Garden Street, Cambridge, MA 02138
tel 401-531-2800 *fax* 401-531-2801
email hup@harvard.edu
website www.hup.harvard.edu
Director William P. Sisler, *Editor-in-Chief* Michael G. Fisher

History, philosophy, literary criticism, politics, economics, sociology, music, science, classics, social sciences, behavioural sciences, law.

Hastings House/Daytrips Publishers
PO Box 908, Winter Park, FL 32790-0908
tel 407-339-3600
email hastingsdaytrips@embarqmail.com
website www.hastingshousebooks.com
Publisher Peter Leers

Travel.

Hill and Wang – see Farrar, Straus and Giroux, LLC

Hippocrene Books Inc.
171 Madison Avenue, New York, NY 10016
tel 718-454-2366 *fax* 718-228-6355
email info@hippocrenebooks.com
website www.hippocrenebooks.com
President/Editorial Director George Blagowidow

International cookbooks, foreign language dictionaries, travel, military history, Polonia, general trade. Founded 1971.

Holiday House Inc.
425 Madison Avenue, New York, NY 10017
tel 212-688-0085 *fax* 212-421-6134
email info@holidayhouse.com
website www.holidayhouse.com
Vice President/Editor-in-Chief Mary Cash

General children's books. Send query letter before submitting MSS. Always include sase. No multiple submissions. Founded 1935.

Henry Holt and Company LLC*
175 Fifth Avenue, New York, NY 10010
tel 646-307-5095 *fax* 212-633-0748
website www.henryholt.com, www.henryholtkids.com
President/Publisher Dan Farley

History, biography, nature, science, novels, mysteries; books for young readers; trade paperback line. Imprints: Henry Holt, Metropolitan Books, Times Books, Holt Paperbacks. Founded 1866.

The Johns Hopkins University Press*
2715 North Charles Street, Baltimore, MD 21218–4319
tel 410-516-6900 *fax* 410-516-6968
email tcl@press.jhu.edu
website www.press.jhu.edu

History, literary criticism, classics, politics, environmental studies, biology, medical genetics, consumer health, religion, physics, astronomy, mathematics, education. Founded 1878.

Houghton Mifflin*
International Division, 1900 South Batavia Avenue, Geneva, IL 60134
tel 630-232-2550
website www.hmhco.com

Textbooks, instructional technology assessments, and other educational materials for teachers and students of all ages; also reference, and fiction and non-fiction for adults and young readers. Founded 1832.

HP Books – see Penguin Group (USA), Inc.

Hudson Street Press – see Penguin Group (USA), Inc.

Hyperion*
114 Fifth Avenue, New York, NY 10011
tel 800-242-7737
website www.hyperionbooks.com
President Robert Miller, *Vice-President/Publisher* Ellen Archer

General fiction and non-fiction, children's books. Division of Buena Vista Publishing, formerly Disney Book Publishing Inc. Founded 1990.

University of Illinois Press*
1325 South Oak Street, Champaign, IL 61820
tel 217-333-0950 *fax* 217-244-8082
email uipress@uillinois.edu
website www.press.illinois.edu
Director Willis G. Regier

American studies (history, music, literature, religion), working-class and ethnic studies, communications, regional studies, architecture, philosophy, women's studies, film, Classics. Founded 1918.

Indiana University Press

601 North Morton Street, Bloomington, IN 47404–3797
tel 812-855-8817 *fax* 812-855-8507
email iupress@indiana.edu
website www.indiana.edu/~iupress
Director Janet Rabinowitch

Specialises in the humanities and social sciences: African, African–American, Asian, cultural, Jewish and Holocaust, Middle East, Russian and East European, and women's and gender studies; anthropology, film, history, bioethics, music, paleontology, philanthropy, philosophy, and religion. Imprint: Quarry Books (regional publishing). Founded 1950.

International Marine Publishing

PO Box 235, Thomaston, ME 04861
tel 207-354-4014
website www.internationalmarine.com
www.raggedmountainpress.com
Editorial Director Jonathan F. Eaton

Imprints: International Marine (boats, boating and sailing); Ragged Mountain Press (sport, adventure/travel, natural history). A McGraw-Hill company.

Jove – see Penguin Group (USA), Inc.

University Press of Kansas

2502 Westbrooke Circle, Lawrence, KS 66045–4444
tel 785-864-4154 *fax* 785-864-4586
email upress@ku.edu
website www.kansaspress.ku.edu
Director Fred Woodward, *Editor-in-Chief* Michael Briggs, *Assistant Director/Marketing Manager* Susan K. Schott

American history (political, social, cultural, environmental), military history, American political thought, American presidency studies, law and constitutional history, political science. Founded 1946.

Knopf Doubleday Publishing Group – see Random House Inc.

Krause Publications

700 East State Street, Iola, WI 54990–0001
tel 800-258-0929
email info@krausebooks.com
website www.krausebooks.com
Publisher Dianne Wheeler

Antiques and collectibles: coins, stamps, automobiles, toys, trains, firearms, comics, records; sewing, ceramics, outdoors, hunting. Imprint of F&W Publications Inc.

Little, Brown & Company

1271 Avenue of the Americas, New York, NY 10020
tel 212-522-8700 *fax* 212-522-2067
email publicity@littlebrown.com
website www.hachettebookgroup.com

General literature, fiction, non-fiction, biography, history, trade paperbacks, children's. Founded 1837.

Back Bay Books (imprint)

Fiction and non-fiction. Founded 1993.

Little, Brown Books for Young Readers

website www.lb-kids.com, www.lb-teens.com
Publisher Megan Tingley, *Creative Director* Gail Doobinin

Picture books, board books, chapter books, novelty books and general non-fiction and novels for middle-grade and young adult readers.

Llewellyn Worldwide

2143 Wooddale Drive, Woodbury, MN 55125
tel 651-291-1970 *fax* 651-291-1908
email billk@llewellyn.com
website www.llewellyn.com
Publisher Bill Krause

New Age: alternative health and healing, astrology, earth-based religions, shamanism, Gnostic Christianity and Kabbalah; mystery novels and young adult novels. Founded 1901.

The Lyons Press

246 Goose Lane, Guilford, CT 06437
tel 203-458-4500
website www.lyonspress.com, www.globepequot.com
Associate Publisher Gene Brissie

Fishing, hunting, sports, health and fitness, outdoor skills, animals/pets, horses, games, history/current affairs, military history, nature, games, reference and non-fiction. An imprint of Globe Pequot Press. Founded 1978.

McGraw-Hill Professional*

2 Penn Plaza, 12th Floor, New York, NY 10121
tel 212-904-2000
website www.mhprofessional.com, www.mgeducation.com

McGraw-Hill Business

Management, investing, leadership, personal finance.

McGraw-Hill Consumer

Non-fiction: from health, self-help and parenting, to sports, outdoor and boating books. Publishing partnerships include Harvard Medical School and Standard & Poor's.

McGraw-Hill Education

Test-prep, study guides, language instruction, dictionaries.

McGraw-Hill Medical

Harrison's and reference for practitioners and medical students.

McGraw-Hill Technical
Science, engineering, computing, construction references.

Macmillan

175 Fifth Avenue, New York, NY 10010
tel 646-307-5151
email press.inquiries@macmillanusa.com
website http://us.macmillan.com

Imprints: Bedford/St Martins, Farrar, Straus & Giroux, Farrar, Straus & Giroux BYR, Feiwel & Friends, :01 First Second, Henry Holt and Company, Henry Holt BYR, Macmillan Audio, Palgrave Macmillan, Picador, Scientific American Inc., Square Fish, St Martin's Press (see page 217), Tor/Forge (see Tom Doherty Associates, LLC on page 209), W.H. Freeman and Worth.

McPherson & Company*

PO Box 1126, Kingston, NY 12402
tel 845-331-5807 *fax* 845-331-5807
email bmcpher@verizon.net
website www.mcphersonco.com
Publisher Bruce R. McPherson

Literary fiction; non-fiction: art criticism, writings by artists, film-making, etc; occasional general titles (e.g. anthropology). No poetry. No unsolicited MSS; query first. Distributed in UK by Central Books, London. Founded 1974.

The University of Massachusetts Press

PO Box 429, Amherst, MA 01004
tel 413-545-2217 *fax* 413-545-1226
email info@umpress.umass.edu
website www.umass.edu/umpress
Director Bruce Wilcox, *Senior Editor* Clark Dougan

Scholarly books and works of general interest: American studies and history, black and ethnic studies, women's studies, cultural criticism, architecture and environmental design, literary criticism, poetry, fiction, philosophy, political science, sociology, books of regional interest. Founded 1964.

The University of Michigan Press

839 Greene Street, Ann Arbor, MI 48104–3209
tel 734-764-4388 *fax* 734-615-1540
email um.press@umich.edu
website www.press.umich.edu/
Director Philip Pochoda

Scholarly and general interest works in literary and cultural theory, classics, history, theatre, women's studies, political science, law, American history, American studies, anthropology, economics, jazz; textbooks in English as a second language; regional trade titles. Founded 1930.

Microsoft Press*

One Microsoft Way, Redmond, WA 98052–6399
tel 425-882-8080 *fax* 425-936-7329
email 4bkideas@microsoft.com
website www.microsoft.com/learning/books/
Editorial Director Kim Fields

Computer books. Division of Microsoft Corp. Founded 1983.

Milkweed Editions

1011 Washington Avenue South, Suite 300, Minneapolis, MN 55415
tel 612-332-3192 *fax* 612-215-2550
email editor@milkweed.org
website www.milkweed.org
Publisher Daniel Slager

Fiction, poetry, essays, the natural world, children's novels (ages 8–14). Founded 1979.

University of Missouri Press

2910 LeMone Boulevard, Columbia, MO 65201
tel 573-882-7641 *fax* 573-884-4498
email upress@umsystem.edu
website www.umsystem.edu/upress
Director/Editor-in-Chief Beverly Jarrett

American and European history, African American studies, American, British and Latin American literary criticism, journalism, political philosophy, regional studies; short fiction. Founded 1958.

The MIT Press*

55 Hayward Street, Cambridge, MA 02142–1493
tel 617-253-5646 *fax* 617-258-6779
website mitpress.mit.edu
Director Ellen Faran

Architecture, art and design, cognitive sciences, neuroscience, linguistics, computer science and artificial intelligence, economics and finance, philosophy, environment and ecology, natural history. Founded 1961.

The Monacelli Press – see Random House Inc.

Morehouse Publishing Co.

PO Box 1321, Harrisburg, PA 17105
tel 717-541-8130 *fax* 717-541-8136
email morehouse@morehousegroup.com
website www.morehousepublishing.org
Executive Editor Nancy Fitzgerald

Religious books, spirituality. Imprint of Church Publishing Inc.

William Morrow – see HarperCollins Publishers

NAL – see Penguin Group (USA), Inc.

Thomas Nelson Publisher

PO Box 141000, Nashville, TN 37214
tel 800-251-4000
email publicity@thomasnelson.com
website www.thomasnelson.com
President and Ceo Michael Hyatt

Bibles, religious, non-fiction and fiction general trade books for adults and children. Founded 1798.

University of New Mexico Press

1312 Basehart Road SE, Albuquerque, NM 87106
tel 505-277-2346 *fax* 505-272-7141
email unmpress@unm.edu
website www.unmpress.com
Director Luther Wilson, *Managing Editor* Maya Allen-Gallegos

Western history, anthropology and archaeology, Latin American studies, photography, multicultural literature, poetry. Founded 1929.

The University of North Carolina Press*

116 South Boundary Street, Chapel Hill, NC 27514
tel 919-966-3561 *fax* 919-966-3829
email uncpress@unc.edu
website www.uncpress.unc.edu
Editor-in-Chief David Perry

American history, American studies, Southern studies, European history, women's studies, Latin American studies, political science, anthropology and folklore, classics, regional trade. Founded 1922.

North Light Books – see Writer's Digest Books

North Point Press – see Farrar, Straus and Giroux, LLC

Northland Publishing – see Cooper Square Publishing

NorthWord Books for Young Readers – see Cooper Square Publishing

W.W. Norton & Company Inc.*

500 Fifth Avenue, New York, NY 10110
tel 212-354-5500 *fax* 212-869-0856
website www.wwnorton.com
Editor-in-Chief Starling Lawrence

General fiction and non-fiction, music, boating, psychiatry, economics, family therapy, social work, reprints, college texts, science.

University of Oklahoma Press

2800 Venture Drive, Norman, OK 73069–8216
tel 405-325-2000 *fax* 405-325-4000
email cerakin@ou.edu
website www.oupress.com
Director B. Byron Price, *Editor-in-chief* Charles E. Rankin

American West, American Indians, classics, political science. Founded 1928.

Orbit – see Hachette Book Group USA

The Overlook Press*

141 Wooster Street, New York, New York 10012
tel 212-673-2210 *fax* 212-673-2296
website www.overlookpress.com
President & Publisher Peter Mayer

Non-fiction, fiction, children's books (*Freddy the Pig* series). Imprints: Ardis Publishing, Duckworth, Rookery Press. Founded 1971.

Oxford University Press*

198 Madison Avenue, New York, NY 10016
tel 212-726-6000 *fax* 919-677-1303
website www.oup.com/us
President Tim Barton

Academic and professional, Bibles, English language learning, English as a second language, higher education, law, medical, Oxford American Medical Publishing, music, reference, school and young adult.

Paragon House Publishers

1925 Oakcrest Avenue, Suite 7, St Paul, MN 55113–2619
tel 651-644-3087 *fax* 651-644-0997
email paragon@paragonhouse.com
website www.paragonhouse.com
Executive Director Gordon L. Anderson

Textbooks and general interest in philosophy, religion and non-fiction.

Peachtree Publishers

1700 Chattahoochee Avenue, Atlanta, GA 30318–2112
tel 404-876-8761 *fax* 404-875-2578
email hello@peachtree-online.com
website www.peachtree-online.com
President & Publisher Margaret Quinlin, *Submissions Editor* Helen Harriss

Children's picture books, novels and non-fiction. Adult non-fiction subjects include self-help, parenting, health, the South. No adult fiction.

Pelican Publishing Company*

1000 Burmaster Street, Gretna, LA 70053
tel 504-368-1175 *fax* 504-368-1195
email editorial@pelicanpub.com
website www.pelicanpub.com
Publisher/President Milburn Calhoun

Art and architecture, cookbooks, biography, travel, history, business, children's, motivational. Founded 1926.

Penguin Group (USA), Inc.*

375 Hudson Street, New York, NY10014
tel 212-366-2000
email online@penguingroup.com
website www.us.penguingroup.com
President Susan Petersen Kennedy, *Ceo* David Shanks

Consumer books in both hardcover and paperback for adults and children; also maps, calendars, audiobooks and mass merchandise products. Adult imprints: Ace Books, Alpha Books, Avery, Berkley

Books, Dutton, Amy Einhorn Books/Putnam, Gotham Books, HP Books, Hudson Street Press, Jove, New American Library, Penguin, Penguin Classics, The Penguin Press, Perigee Books, Plume, Portfolio, Prentice Hall Press, G.P. Putnam's Sons, Riverhead, Sentinel, Signet Classics, Jeremy P. Tarcher, Viking.

Ace
Editor-in-chief Ginjer Buchanan
Science fiction. Founded 1953.

Alpha
Vice-President & Publisher Marie Butler-Knight
Non-fiction and how-to guides, including the *Complete Idiot's Guides*. Founded 1991.

Avery
Publisher Megan Newman
Health, wellness, fitness, psychology, popular science.

Berkley Books
President, Publisher & Editor-in-chief Leslie Gelbman
Fiction and general non-fiction for adults. Imprints: Ace, Berkley, Jove. Founded 1955.

Dutton
President & Publisher Brian Tart
Fiction and non-fiction. Founded 1852.

Gotham
President & Publisher William Shinker
Business, current affairs, consumer reference, food writing, golf, health and fitness, memoirs, personal finance, popular culture, self-help, spirituality, sports, travel narrative, and narrative non-fiction. Founded 2003.

HP Books
Publisher, Vice-President & Senior Editor John Duff, *Associate Publisher & Editorial Director* Michael Lutfy
Self-help and how-to books: cooking, automotive, craft.

Hudson Street Press
Editor-in-chief Luke Dempsey
High-profile hardcover non-fiction. Founded 2003.

Jove
President, Publisher & Editor-in-chief Leslie Gelbman
Fiction.

NAL
Vice President/Publisher Kara Welsh
Fiction and general non-fiction. Imprints: DAW, NALAccent, NAL Caliber, NAL Jam, Onyx, Roc, Signet, Signet Eclipse.

Penguin
President & Publisher Kathryn Court
Fiction and non-ficiton including literature, biography, memoir, history, science, business, psychology, popular reference and self-help. Founded 1935.

Penguin Press
President & Publisher Ann Godoff
Literary non-fiction and select fiction. Founded 2003.

Perigee
Publisher, Vice-President & Senior Editor John Duff
Fiction and non-fiction.

Plume
President Clare Ferraro
Non-fiction and fiction, including multicultural, gay and lesbian, literary. Founded 1970.

Portfolio
Editorial Director Jeffrey Krames
Business: management, leadership, marketing, business narrative, investing, personal finance, economics, career advice. Founded 2001.

Prentice Hall Press
Publisher, Vice-President & Senior Editor John Duff
Business, health, and self-help/popular reference.

G.P. Putnam's Sons
Senior Vice-President, Publisher & Editor-in-chief Neil S. Nyren
Fiction and non-fiction.

Riverhead Books
Vice President & Executive Editor Sean McDonald and Sarah McGrath, *Executive Editor* Jake Morrissey
Literary fiction and quality non-fiction. Founded 1994.

Sentinel
Publisher Adrian Zackheim
Politics, history, public policy, culture, religion and international relations with a right-of-centre bias. Founded 2003.

Jeremy P. Tarcher
Vice-President & Publisher Joel Fotinos
Non-fiction, including health, psychology and philosophy.

Viking Press
President Clare Ferraro
Quality fiction and non-fiction. Founded 1925.

Penguin Books for Young Readers (division)
Children's picture books, board and novelty books, young adult novels, mass merchandise products. Imprints: Dial Books for Young Readers, Dutton Children's Books, Firebird, Grosset & Dunlap, Philomel, Price Stern Sloan, Puffin Books, G.P. Putnam's Sons Books for Young Readers, Razorbill, Speak, Viking Children's Books, Frederick Warne. Founded 1996.

University of Pennsylvania Press

3905 Spruce Street, Philadelphia, PA 19104–4112
tel 215-898-6261 *fax* 215-898-0404

email custserv@pobox.upenn.edu
website www.pennpress.org
Director Eric Halpern

American and European history, anthropology, art, architecture, business and economics, cultural studies, ancient studies, human rights, international relations, literature, Pennsylvania regional studies. Founded 1890.

Pennsylvania State University Press*

820 North University Drive, USB1, Suite C, University Park, PA 16802
tel 814-865-1329 *fax* 814-863-1408
email info@psupress.org
website www.psupress.org
Director Patrick Alexander

Art history, literary criticism, religious studies, philosophy, political science, sociology, history, Latin American studies and medieval studies. Founded 1956.

Perigee – see Penguin Group (USA), Inc.

The Permanent Press

4170 Noyac Road, Sag Harbor, NY 11963
tel 631-725-1101 *fax* 631-725-8215
website www.thepermanentpress.com
Directors Martin Shepard, Judith Shepard

Literary fiction and biographies, and autobiographies. Imprint: Second Chance Press. Founded 1978.

Philomel – see Penguin Group (USA), Inc.

Plume – see Penguin Group (USA), Inc.

Popular Woodworking – see Writer's Digest Books

Portfolio – see Penguin Group (USA), Inc.

Potomac Books Inc.

22841 Quicksilver Drive, Dulles, VA 20166
tel 703-661-1548 *fax* 703-661-1547
email pbimail@presswarehouse.com
website www.potomacbooksinc.com
Publisher Samuel R. Dorrance

National and international affairs, history (military and diplomatic); reference, biography. Founded 1984.

Prentice Hall Press – see Penguin Group (USA), Inc.

Mathew Price Ltd

12300 Ford Street, Suite 455, Dallas, TX 75234
tel 972-484-0500
email info@mathewprice.com
UK Office Albury Court, Albury, Thame, Oxon OX9 2LP
tel (01844) 337000 *fax* (01844) 339938
email mathewp@mathewprice.com
website www.mathewprice.com
Chairman Mathew Price

Illustrated fiction and non-fiction children's books for all ages for the UK and international market. Specialist in flap, pop-up, paper-engineered titles as well as conventional books. Unsolicited MSS accepted only by email. Founded 1983.

Price Stern Sloan – see Penguin Group (USA), Inc.

Princeton University Press*

Princeton, NJ 08540
tel 609-258-4900 *fax* 609-258-6305
postal address 41 William Street, Princeton, NJ 08540
website www.press.princeton.edu
Director Peter J. Dougherty, *Editor-in-Chief* Brigitta van Rheinberg

Scholarly and scientific books on all subjects. Founded 1905.

Puffin Books – see Penguin Group (USA), Inc.

G.P. Putnam's Sons – see Penguin Group (USA), Inc.

Rand McNally

PO Box 7600, Chicago, IL 60680
tel 847-329-8100
website www.randmcnally.com
President/Ceo Rob Apatoff

Maps, guides, atlases, educational publications, globes and children's geographical titles and atlases in print and electronic formats.

Random House Inc.*

1745 Broadway, 10th Floor, New York, NY 10019
tel 212-782-9000 *fax* 212-302-7985
website www.randomhouse.com
Chairman/Ceo Markus Dohle

General fiction and non-fiction, children's books. Subsidiary of Bertelsmann AG.

Random House Publishing Group (division)

Imprints: Ballantine Books, Bantam Books, Delacorte, Dell, Del Rey, Del Rey/Lucas Books, The Dial Press, The Modern Library, One World, Presido Press, Random House Trade Group, Random House Trade Paperbacks, Spectra, Spiegel & Grau, Villard Books.

The Monacelli Press (division)

Architecture, fine art, interior design, landscape architecture, fashion, photography, graphic design. Founded 1994.

Crown Publishing Group (division)

General fiction, non-fiction, illustrated books. Imprints: Amphoto Books, Back Stage Books,

Billboard Books, Broadway, Broadway Business, Crown, Crown Business, Crown Forum, Clarkson Potter, Broadway Business, Doubleday Religion, Harmony Books, Potter Craft, Potter Style, Ten Speed Press, Three Rivers Press, Tricycle Press, Shaye Areheart Books, Waterbrook Multnomah, Watson-Guptill.

Knopf Doubleday Publishing Group (division)
General fiction and non-fiction. Alfred A. Knopf, Anchor Books, Doubleday, Everyman's Library, Nan A. Talese, Pantheon Books, Schocken Books, Vintage.

Random House Audio Publishing Group (division)
For adults and children. Listening Library, Random House Audible, Random House Audio Assets, Random House Audio Dimensions, Random House Audio Roads, Random House Audio Voices, Random House Audio Price-less.

Random House Children's Books (division)
website www.randomhouse.com/kids, www.randomhouse.com/teens
Board books, activity books, picture books, novels for preschool children through to young adult. Divisions: Kids@Random (RH Children's Books), Golden Books.

Random House International (division)

The Random House Information Group (division)
Imprints: Fodor's Travel, Living Language, Prima Games, Princeton Review, Random House Puzzles and Games, Random House Reference, Sylvan Learning.

Random House Large Print (division)
Fiction and non-fiction in large print.

Rayo – see HarperCollins Publishers

Razorbill – see Penguin Group (USA), Inc.

Rising Moon – see Cooper Square Publishing

Riverhead Books – see Penguin Group (USA), Inc.

Rizzoli International Publications Inc.
300 Park Avenue South, New York, NY 10010
tel 212-387-3400 *fax* 212-387-3535
email publicity@rizzoliusa.com
website www.rizzoliusa.com
Publisher Charles Mires

Art, architecture, photography, fashion, gardening, design, gift books, cookbooks. Founded 1976.

Rodale Book Group*
733 Third Avenue, New York, NY 10017
tel 212-573-0300
website www.rodale.com

General health, women's health, men's health, senior health, alternative health, fitness, healthy cooking, gardening, pets, spirituality/inspiration, trade health, biography, memoir, current affairs, science, parenting, organics, lifestyle, self-help, how-to, home arts. Founded 1932.

Routledge
270 Madison Avenue, New York, NY 10016
tel 212-216-7800 *fax* 212-563-7854
website www.routledge.com
Vice President Sam Costanzo

Music, history, psychology and psychiatry, politics, business studies, philosophy, education, sociology, urban studies, religion, film, media, literary and cultural studies, reference, English language, linguistics, communication studies, journalism. Editorial office in the UK. Subsidiary of Taylor & Francis, LLC.

Running Press Book Publishers
125 S 22nd Street, Philadelphia, PA 19103-4399
tel 215-567-5080
email perseus.promos@perseusbooks.com
website www.perseusbooksgroup.com/runningpress
Publisher Chris Navratil, *Directors* Bill Jones (design), Greg Jones (editorial), Joanne Cassetti (production), Craig Herman (marketing)

General non-fiction, science, history, children's fiction and non-fiction, food and wine, pop culture, lifestyle, photo-essay, illustrated gift books. Imprints: Running Press, Running Press Miniature Editions, Running Press Kids, Courage Books. Member of the Perseus Books Group. Founded 1972.

Rutgers University Press
PO Box 8895, Chapel Hill, NC 27515-8895
tel 800-848-6224 *fax* 800-272-6817
website www.rutgerspress.rutgers.edu
Directors Marlie Wasserman, *Editor-in-Chief* Leslie Mitchner

Women's studies, anthropology, film and media studies, sociology, public health, popular science, cultural studies, literature, religion, history of medicine, Asian–American studies, African–American studies, American history, American studies, art history, regional titles. Founded 1936.

St Martin's Press Inc.*
175 Fifth Avenue, New York, NY 10010
tel 212-677-7456 *fax* 212-674-6132
website www.stmartins.com

Trade, reference, college. No unsolicited MSS. Imprints: St. Martin's Press, Griffin, Minotaur, Thomas Dunne Books, and Truman Talley Books. Founded 1952.

Scholastic Inc.*
557 Broadway, New York, NY 10012
tel 212-343-6100

website www.scholastic.com
Editorial Director Elizabeth Szabla

Innovative textbooks, magazines, technology and teacher materials for use in both school and the home. Scholastic is a global children's publishing and media company with a corporate mission to instill the love of reading and learning for lifelong pleasure in all children. Founded 1920.

Sentinel – see Penguin Group (USA), Inc.

Sheridan House Inc.*

145 Palisade Street, Dobbs Ferry, NY 10522
tel 914-693-2410 *fax* 914-693-0776
email info@sheridanhouse.com
website www.sheridanhouse.com
President Lothar Simon

Sailing, nautical, travel. Founded 1940.

Simon & Schuster Adult Publishing Group*

1230 Avenue of the Americas, New York, NY 10020
tel 212-698-7000 *fax* 212-698-7007
website www.simonandschuster.com
President & Ceo, Simon & Schuster Carolyn K. Reidy

General fiction and non-fiction. No unsolicited MSS. Imprints: Atria, Downtown Press, Fireside, Free Press, Howard Books, MTV®, Pocket Books, Scribner, Scribner Paperback Fiction, S&S Libros en Espanol, Simon & Schuster, Star Trek®, Strebor Books, Threshold Editions, Touchstone, Washington Square Press VHI®. Division of Simon & Schuster Inc. Founded 1924.

Simon & Schuster Children's Publishing Division*

1230 Avenue of the Americas, New York, NY 10020
tel 212-698-7200 *fax* 212-698-2793
website www.simonsayskids.com
Executive Publisher Jon Anderson, *Vice-President & Publisher* Valerie Garfield

Preschool to young adult, fiction and non-fiction, trade, library and mass market. Imprints: Aladdin Paperbacks, Atheneum Books for Young Readers, Libros para niños, Little Simon, Little Simon Inspirations, Margaret K. McElderry Books, Simon & Schuster Books for Young Readers, Simon Scribbles, Simon Pulse, Simon Spotlight. Division of Simon & Schuster, Inc. Founded 1924.

Soho Press Inc.

853 Broadway, New York, NY 10003
tel 212-260-1900 *fax* 212-260-1902
email soho@sohopress.com
website www.sohopress.com
Publisher Bronwen Hruska

Literary fiction, commercial fiction, mystery, memoir. Founded 1986.

Speak – see Penguin Group (USA), Inc.

Stackpole Books

5067 Ritter Road, Mechanicsburg, PA 17055
tel 717-796-0411 *fax* 717-796-0412
email sales@stackpolebooks.com
website www.stackpolebooks.com
Publisher Judith Schnell

Nature, outdoor sports, crafts and hobbies, history, military history, regional and travel. Founded 1935.

Stanford University Press*

1450 Page Mill Road, Palo Alto, CA 94304–1124
tel 650-723-9434 *fax* 650-725-3457
email info@www.sup.org
website www.sup.org

Scholarly (humanities and social sciences), professional (business, economics and management science), high-level textbooks. Founded 1925.

Ten Speed Press

1745 Broadway, 10th Floor, New York, NY 10019
tel 510-559-1600 *fax* 510-524-1052
email order@tenspeed.com
website www.randomhouse.com/crown/tenspeed
President Phil Wood, *Publisher* Lorena Jones

Career/business, cooking, practical non-fiction, health, women's interest, self-help, children's. Imprints: Celestial Arts, Crossing Press, Tricycle Press. Founded 1971.

University of Tennessee Press*

110 Conference Center Building, Knoxville, TN 37996
tel 865-974-3321 *fax* 865-974-3724
website www.utpress.org
Director Jennifer Siler

American studies: African–American studies, Appalachian studies, history, religion, literature, historical archaeology, folklore, vernacular architecture, material culture. Founded 1940.

University of Texas Press*

PO Box 7819, Austin, TX 78713–7819
tel 512-471-7233 *fax* 512-232-7178
email utpress@uts.cc.utexas.edu
website www.utexaspress.com
Director Joanna Hitchcock, *Assistant Director & Editor-in-Chief* Theresa May

Scholarly non-fiction: anthropology, classics and the Ancient World, conservation and the environment, film and media studies, geography, Latin American and Latino studies, Middle Eastern studies, natural history, ornithology, Texas and Western studies. Founded 1950.

Tor Books – see Tom Doherty Associates, LLC

Tuttle Publishing/Periplus Editions

Airport Business Park, 364 Innovation Drive, North Clarendon, VT 05759

tel 802-773-8930 *fax* 802-773-6993
email info@tuttlepublishing.com
website www.periplus publishinggroup.com
Ceo Eric Oey, *Publishing Director* Ed Walters

Asian art, culture, cooking, gardening, Eastern philosophy, martial arts, health. Founded 1948.

Two-Can – see Cooper Square Publishing

Viking Children's Books – see Penguin Group (USA), Inc.

Viking Press – see Penguin Group (USA), Inc.

Walker & Co.

175 Fifth Avenue, New York, NY 10010
tel 212-727-8300 *fax* 212-727-0984
website www.walkerbooks.com, www.walkeryoungreaders.com
Publisher Emily Easton (children's), George Gibson (adult)

General: biography, popular science, health, business, mystery, history, fiction; juvenile fiction and non-fiction, picture books. Division of Bloomsbury Publishing. Founded 1960.

University of Washington Press

4333 Brooklyn Avenue NE, Seattle, WA 98195–9570
postal address PO Box 50096, Seattle, WA 98145–5096
tel 206-543-4050 *fax* 206-543-3932
website www.washington.edu/uwpress
Director Patrick Soden

Anthropology, Asian–American studies, Asian studies, art and art history, aviation history, environmental studies, forest history, Jewish studies, literary criticism, marine sciences, Middle East studies, music, regional studies, including history and culture of the Pacific Northwest and Alaska, Native American studies, resource management and public policy, Russian and East European studies, Scandinavian studies. Founded 1909.

WaterBrook Press

12265 Oracle Blvd, Suite 200, Colorado Springs, CO 80921
tel 719-590-4999 *fax* 719-590-8977
email info@waterbrookpress.com
website www.randomhouse.com/waterbrook
President Stephen Cobb

Fiction and non-fiction with a Christian perspective. Subsidiary of Random House Inc. Founded 1996.

Watson-Guptill Publications

c/o Random House, 1745 Broadway, 3rd Floor, New York, NY 10019
tel 212-782-9000 212-572-6066
email info@watsonguptill.com
website www.watsonguptill.com, www.randomhouse.com/crown/watsonguptill

Art, crafts, how-to, comic/cartooning, photography, performing arts, architecture and interior design, graphic design, music, entertainment, writing, reference, children's. Imprints: Amphoto Books, Back Stage Books, Billboard Books, Watson-Guptill, Whitney Library of Design. Founded 1937.

Westminster John Knox Press

100 Witherspoon Street, Louisville, KY 40202–1396
tel 502-569-8400 *fax* 502-569-5113
email wjk@presbypub.com
website www.wjkbooks.com

Scholarly reference and general books with a religious/spiritual angle. Division of Presbyterian Publishing Corp.

John Wiley & Sons Inc.*

111 River Street, Hoboken, NJ 07030
tel 201-748-6000 *fax* 201-748-6088
email info@wiley.com
website www.wiley.com
President/Ceo William J. Pesce

Specialises in scientific, technical, medical, and scholarly journals, encyclopedias, books, and online products and services; professional/trade books, subscription products, training materials, and online applications and websites; and educational materials for undergraduate and graduate students and lifelong learners. Founded 1807.

Workman Publishing Company*

225 Varick Street, New York, NY 10014
tel 212-254-5900 *fax* 212-254-8098
email info@workman.com
website www.workman.com
Editor-in-chief Susan Bolotin

Popular non-fiction: business, cooking, gardening, gift books, health, how-to, humour, parenting, sport, travel. Founded 1968.

Writer's Digest Books

4700 East Galbraith Road, Cincinnati, OH 45236
tel 513-531-2690 *fax* 513-891-7185
email kelly.nickell@fwpubs.com
website www.writersdigest.com
Executive Editor Kelly Nickell

Market directories, books for writers, photographers and songwriters. Imprint of F&W Publications Inc. Founded 1920.

Family Tree (imprint)

Genealogy.

North Light Books (imprint)

Fine art, decorative art, crafts, graphic arts instruction books.

Popular Woodworking (imprint)

How-to in home building, remodelling, woodworking, home organisation.

Yale University Press*

PO Box 209040, New Haven, CT 06520-9040
tel 203-432-0960 *fax* 203-432-0948
website www.yale.edu/yup
Editorial Director Jonathan Brent

Scholarly books and art books.

Yen Press

Hachette Book Group USA, 237 Park Avenue, New York, NY 10017
email yenpress@hbgusa.com
website www.yenpress.us

Graphic novels and manga in all formats for all ages. Division of Hachette Book Group USA. Founded 2006.

Audio publishers

Many of the audio publishers listed below are also publishers of books.

Abbey Home Media plc

435–437 Edgware Road, London W2 1TH
tel 020-7563 3910 *fax* 020-7563 3911
email emma.evans@abbeyhomemedia.com
Managing Director Anne Miles

Specialises in the acquisition, production and distribution of quality audio/visual entertainment for children. Bestselling children's spoken word and music titles are available on CD and cassette in the Tempo range including *Postman Pat, Watership Down, Michael Rosen, Baby Bright, Wide Eye, SuperTed* and *Golden Nursery Rhymes*.

Barefoot Books Ltd

124 Walcot Street, Bath BA1 5BG
tel (01225) 322400 *fax* (01225) 322499
email info@barefootbooks.co.uk
website www.barefootbooks.co.uk
Publisher Tessa Stickland, *Group Executive Editor* Emma Parkin

Narrative unabridged audiobooks, spoken and sung. Established 1993.

Barrington Stoke

18 Walker Street, Edinburgh EH3 7LP
tel 0131-225 4113 *fax* 0131-225 4140
email info@barringtonstoke.co.uk
website www.barringtonstoke.co.uk
Chairman Ben Thomson, *Managing Director* Sonia Raphael, *Editorial Manager* Kate Paice

Short fiction and non-fiction, specially adapted and presented for reluctant, struggling and dyslexic readers, aged 9–12 and 13+, with reading ages of 6–8. Short fiction (15,000 words) for adults with a reading age of 8. No picture books, no unsolicited submissions. Founded 1998.

BBC Audiobooks Ltd

St James House, The Square, Lower Bristol Road, Bath BA2 3BH
tel (01225) 878000 *fax* (01225) 310771
email bbcaudiobooks@bbc.co.uk
website www.bbcaudiobooks.com
Managing Director Mike Bowen, *Publishing Director* Jan Paterson

Spoken word entertainment that can be enjoyed at convenience. Imprints include BBC Radio Collection, Cover to Cover Classics, BBC Cover to Cover, BBC Word for Word, Chivers Audiobooks, Chivers Children's Audiobooks. Formed in 2003 from the amalgamation of Chivers Press, Cover To Cover and BBC Radio Collection.

Beautiful Sounds

36–38 Glasshouse Street, London W1B 5DL
email info@beautifulsounds.co.uk
website www.beautifulsounds.co.uk

Produces audio digital downloads of books plus drama, interviews, live performance and debates. Division of The Beautiful Group. Founded 2008.

Bloomsbury Publishing Plc

36 Soho Square, London W1D 3QY
tel 020-7494 2111 *fax* 020-7734 8656
website www.bloomsbury.com
Contact Tram-Anh Doan

A broad selection of literary fiction and non-fiction.

Chrome Dreams

PO Box 230, New Malden, Surrey KT3 6YY
tel 020-8715 9781 *fax* 020-8241 1426
email contactus@chromedreams.co.uk
website www.chromedreams.co.uk
Owner Rob Johnstone

Cló Iar-Chonnachta Teo.

Indreabhán, Conamara, Co. Galway, Republic of Ireland
tel (091) 593307 *fax* (091) 593362
email cic@iol.ie
website www.cic.ie
Ceo Micheál Ó Conghaile, *General Manager* Deirdre O'Toole

Irish-language – novels, short stories, plays, poetry, songs; CDs (writers reading from their works), bilingual books. Promotes the translation of contemporary Irish poetry and fiction into other languages. Founded 1985.

Creative Content Ltd

Roxburghe House, 273–287 Regent Street, London W1B 2HA
tel (07771) 766838
email ali@creativecontentdigital.com
website www.creativecontentdigital.com
Publisher Ali Muirden, *Editorial Director* Lorelei King

Publishes audio digital downloads, on-demand CDs and ebooks in the business, language improvement, self-improvement and lifestyle genres. Founded 2008.

CSA Word

6A Archway Mews, London SW15 2PE
tel 020-8871 0220 *fax* 020-8877 0712
email info@csaword.co.uk
website www.csaword.co.uk
Managing Director Clive Stanhope, *Audio Director* Victoria Williams

CDs of classic literature such as Jane Austen, Charles Dickens, D.H. Lawrence and P.G. Wodehouse; also current literary authors. Publishes 25 titles a year and has 150 titles available, including many short stories. Founded 1991.

57 Productions

57 Effingham Road, London SE12 8NT
tel/fax 020-8463 0866
email info@57productions.com
website www.57productions.com
Director Paul Beasley

An agency and production company specialising in contemporary poetry. Represents a wide range of writers and performers, including Jean 'Binta' Breeze, Adrian Mitchell and Patience Agbabi. Publishes CDs by John Hegley and Benjamin Zephaniah. Runs an online programme: www.iPoems.org, www.poetryjukebox.com and poetryvideojukebox.com. Established 1992.

Hachette Digital

100 Victoria Embankment, London EC4Y 0DY
tel 020-7911 8056 *fax* 020-7911 8100 (publicity)
email hannah.torjussen@littlebrown.co.uk
tel 020-7911 8044 *fax* 020-7911 8100 (editorial)
email sarah.shrubb@littlebrown.co.uk (editorial)
Editorial Director Sarah Shrubb

The audiobook list includes both abridged and unabridged titles from Little, Brown, Headline and John Murray's bestselling authors such as Alexander McCall Smith, Patricia Cornwell and Martina Cole, as well as classics such as Joseph Heller's *Catch 22*, and titles from outside the lists such as Kate Grenville's Booker-shortlisted *The Secret River*. Has over 400 titles and publishes around 50 audiobooks a year. Launched in 2003.

Harper NonFiction

77–85 Fulham Palace Road, London W6 8JB
tel 020-8307 4706 *fax* 020-8307-4788 (editorial)
website www.harpercollins.co.uk

The commercial nonfiction list from celebrity autobiography to cookery, tv tie-in, humour and more at HarperCollins (see *Book publishers UK and Ireland*). The list includes Frankie Boyle, Chris Evans, Russell Brand, Stephen Fry, Gordon Ramsay, Sophie Dahl, Gok Wan and others.

HarperCollins Audio Books

77–85 Fulham Palace Road, London W6 8JB
tel 020-8741 7070 *fax* 020-8307 4818
website www.harpercollins.co.uk
Director David Roth-Ey, *Editorial* Jo Forshaw

Publishers of a wide range of genres including fiction, non-fiction, poetry, Classics, Shakespeare, comedy, personal development and children's. All works are read by famous actors. Established 1990.

Hodder & Stoughton Audiobooks

338 Euston Road, London NW1 3BH
tel 020-7873 6000 *fax* 020-7873 6024
website www.hodder.co.uk
Publisher Rupert Lancaster

Publishes authors from within the Hodder group as well as commissioning independent titles. List includes fiction and non-fiction. Authors include Stephen King, John le Carré, Alan Titchmarsh, Elizabeth George, Al Murray, Jeffery Deaver, Jodi Picoult, Pam Ayres, John Humphrys, Michael Parkinson, Peter Robinson and Clarissa Dickson Wright.

Isis/Soundings

Isis Publishing Ltd, 7 Centremead, Osney Mead, Oxford OX2 0ES
tel (01865) 250333 *fax* (01865) 790358
website www.isis-publishing.co.uk
Chief Executive Robert Thirlby

Complete and unabridged audiobooks: fiction, non-fiction, autobiography, biography, crime, thrillers, family sagas, mysteries, health, poetry, humour; large print books.

Library Magna Books Ltd

Magna House, Long Preston, Skipton, North Yorkshire BD23 4ND
tel (01729) 840225 *fax* (01729) 840683
website www.ulverscroft.co.uk
Managing Director Diane Allen

Audiobooks and large print books. Founded 1973.

Macmillan Digital Audio

20 New Wharf Road, London N1 9RR
tel 020-7014 6000 *fax* 020-7014 6001
email audiobooks@macmillan.co.uk
website www.panmacmillan.com
Digital Director Sara Lloyd

Adult fiction, non-fiction and autobiography, and children's. Established 1995.

Naxos AudioBooks

40A High Street, Welwyn, Herts. AL6 9EQ
tel (01438) 717808 *fax* (01438) 717809
email info@naxosaudiobooks.com
website www.naxosaudiobooks.com
Managing Director Nicolas Soames

Classic literature, modern fiction, non-fiction, drama and poetry on CD. Also junior classics and classical music. Founded 1994.

The Orion Publishing Group Ltd

5 Upper St Martin's Lane, London WC2H 9EA
tel 020-7240 3444 *fax* 020-7379 6158
email pandora.white@orionbooks.co.uk
Audio Manager Pandora White

Adult and children's fiction and non-fiction. Established 1998.

Penguin Audiobooks

80 Strand, London WC2R 0RL
tel 020-7010 3000

email audiobooks@penguin.co.uk
website www.penguin.co.uk/audio
Audio Publisher Jeremy Ettinghausen

The audiobooks list reflects the diversity of the Penguin book range, including classic and contemporary fiction and non-fiction, autobiography, poetry, drama and, in Puffin Audiobooks, the best of contemporary and classic literature for younger listeners. Authors include Nick Hornby, Claire Tomalin, Zadie Smith, Gervase Phinn, Dick Francis and Nicci French. Readings are by talented and recognisable actors. Over 300 titles are now available. Founded 1993.

Random House Audio Books

The Random House Group Ltd,
20 Vauxhall Bridge Road, London SW1V 2SA
tel 020-7840 8400
email audioeditorial@randomhouse.co.uk
website www.rbooks.co.uk/audio
Editorial Editor Zoe Howes

Authors include John Grisham, Kathy Reichs, Andy McNab, Robert Harris, Jack Dee, Dawn French, James Patterson, Ruth Rendell, Karin Slaughter, Peter Ackroyd, Ian McEwan, Sebastian Faulks. Established 1991.

Red Audio

7–14 Green Park, Sutton on the Forest,
York YO61 1ET
tel (01347) 810055 *fax* (01347) 812705
email customer.service@theredgroup.co.uk
website www.red-audio.co.uk
Ceo & Editor Steve Parks

CDs and MP3 downloads of business topics such as marketing, start-ups, management and motivation. Publishes approx. 8 titles a year and has over 30 titles available. Part of Red Studios UK Ltd. Founded 2001.

Simon & Schuster Audio

Simon & Schuster UK, 1st Floor,
222 Gray's Inn Road, London WC1X 8HB
tel 020-7316 1900 *fax* 020-7316 0332
email enquiries@simonandschuster.co.uk
website www.simonandschuster.co.uk
Digital and Audio Publisher Kirsty McNeil

Fiction and non-fiction audiobooks. Fiction authors include Jackie Collins, Lynda La Plante and Tom Rob Smith. Non-fiction authors include Stephen Covey, Rhonda Byrne, Anthony Robbins and Spencer Johnson. Established 1997.

SmartPass Ltd

15 Park Road, Rottingdean, Brighton BN2 7HL
tel (01273) 300742
email info@smartpass.co.uk
website www.smartpass.co.uk, www.spaudiobooks.com, www.shakespeareappreciated.com
Managing Director Phil Viner, *Creative Director* Jools Viner

SmartPass audio education resources present unabridged plays, poetry and dramatisations of novels as guided full-cast dramas for individual study and classroom use. Shakespeare Appreciated: full-cast unabridged plays with an explanatory commentary. SPAudiobooks: full-cast unabridged dramas of classic and cult texts.

Ulverscroft Group Ltd*

The Green, Bradgate Road, Anstey, Leicester LE7 7FU
tel 0116-236 4325 *fax* 0116-234 0205
email m.merrill@ulverscroft.co.uk
website www.ulverscroft.com

Large print books: fiction and non-fiction, Classics. Unabridged and abridged audio books: fiction and non-fiction.

Walker Books Ltd

87 Vauxhall Walk, London SE11 5HJ
tel 020-7793 0909 *fax* 020-7587 1123
website www.walker.co.uk
Senior Editor Hannah Whitaker

Includes the bestselling fiction series *Alex Rider* and *The Power of Five* by Anthony Horowitz and titles by award-winning authors Michael Morpurgo, Mal Peet and Vivian French. Audio series for young children include *Listen and Join In!* – based on twelve classic picture books and featuring story readings, songs and activities; and the non-fiction picture book and CD series *Nature Storybooks*.

Book packagers

Many modern illustrated books are created by book packagers, whose particular skills are in the areas of book design and graphic content. In-house desk editors and art editors match up the expertise of specialist writers, artists and photographers who usually work on a freelance basis.

act-two ltd – now John Brown Group – Children's Division

Aladdin Books Ltd

2–3 Fitzroy Mews, London W1T 6DF
tel 020-7383 2084 *fax* 020-7388 6391
email alexandra.mew@aladdinbooks.co.uk
website www.aladdinbooks.co.uk
Directors Charles Nicholas, Bibby Whittaker

Full design and book packaging facility specialising in children's non-fiction and reference. Founded 1980.

The Albion Press Ltd

Spring Hill, Idbury, Oxon OX7 6RU
tel (01993) 831094
Directors Emma Bradford (managing), Neil Philip (editorial)

Produces quality integrated illustrated titles from the initial idea to the printed copy. Specialises in children's books. Publishers' commissions undertaken. No unsolicited MSS. Founded 1984.

Amber Books Ltd

Bradley's Close, 74–77 White Lion Street, London N1 9PF
tel 020-7520 7600 *fax* 020-7520 7606/7607
email enquiries@amberbooks.co.uk
website www.amberbooks.co.uk
Managing Director Stasz Gnych, *Deputy Managing Director* Sara Ballard, *Publishing Manager* Charles Catton, *Head of Production* Peter Thompson, *Design Manager* Mark Batley, *Picture Manager* Terry Forshaw

Book packager creating illustrated non-fiction books for adults and children. Works include multi-volume sets for schools and libraries, highly illustrated reference series on dinosaurs, animals and birds, and a military list. Children's titles created under Tiptoe Books imprint. Opportunities for freelances. Founded 1989.

Nicola Baxter Ltd

PO Box 215, Framingham Earl, Yelverton, Norwich NR14 7UR
tel (01508) 491111
email nb@nicolabaxter.co.uk
website www.nicolabaxter.co.uk
Director Nicola Baxter

Full packaging service for children's books, from concept to disk or any part of the process in between. Produces both fiction and non-fiction titles in a wide range of formats, from board books to encyclopedias. Experienced in novelty books and licensed publishing. Opportunities for freelances. Founded 1990.

BCS Publishing Ltd

2nd Floor, Temple Court, 109 Oxford Road, Cowley, Oxford OX4 2ER
tel (01865) 770099 *fax* (01865) 770050
Managing & Art Director Steve McCurdy

Specialises in the preparation of illustrated non-fiction; provides a full creative, design, editorial and production service. Opportunities for freelances. Commissioned work undertaken.

Bender Richardson White

PO Box 266, Uxbridge, Middlesex UB9 5NX
tel (01895) 832444 *fax* (01895) 835213
email brw@brw.co.uk
website www.brw.co.uk
Directors Lionel Bender (editorial), Kim Richardson (sales & production), Ben White (design)

Specialises in children's and young people's natural history, science and family information. Opportunities for freelances. Founded 1990.

BLA Publishing Ltd

BIC Ling Kee House, 1 Christopher Road, East Grinstead, West Sussex RH19 3BT
tel (01342) 318980 *fax* (01342) 410980
Directors Au Bak Ling (chairman, Hong Kong), Albert Kw Au (Hong Kong)

High-quality illustrated reference books, particularly science dictionaries and encyclopedias, for the international market. Founded 1981.

The Book Guild Ltd

Pavilion View, 19 New Road, Brighton BN1 1UF
tel (01273) 720900 *fax* (01273) 723122
email info@bookguild.co.uk
website www.bookguild.co.uk
Directors Carol Biss (managing), Janet Wrench (production)

Offers a range of publishing options: a comprehensive package for authors incorporating editorial, design, production, marketing, publicity, distribution and sales; editorial and production only for authors requiring private editions; or a complete service for companies and organisations requiring books for internal or promotional purposes – from brief to finished book. Write for submission details. Founded 1982.

Bound Originals

Tithe Barn, Clouts Farm, Ide Hill Road, Bough Beech, Kent TN8 7PH
tel (07980) 621098
email lucy@boundoriginals.co.uk
website www.boundoriginals.co.uk
Managing Director Lucy Hulme

Packages small gift books mainly for non-publishing companies, often corporate giveaways for branding purposes. Specialises in gift books, animals, lifestyle, art. Founded 2004.

Breslich & Foss Ltd

2A Union Court, 20–22 Union Road, London SW4 6JP
tel 020-7819 3990 *fax* 020-7819 3998
email sales@breslichfoss.co.uk
website www.breslichfoss.co.uk
Directors Paula G. Breslich, K.B. Dunning

Books produced from MS to bound copy stage from in-house ideas. Specialising in crafts, lifestyle and children's non-fiction. Founded 1978.

John Brown Group – Children's Division

136–142 Bramley Road, London W10 6SR
tel 020-7565 3000 *fax* 020-7565 3060
email andrew.hirsch@johnbrownmedia.com
website www.johnbrownmedia.com
Ceo Andrew Hirsch (operations), Sara Lynn (creative)

Creative development and packaging of children's products including books, magazines, teachers' resource packs, partworks, CD-ROMs and websites.

The Brown Reference Group Ltd

1st Floor, 9–17 St Albans Place, London N1 0NX
tel 020-7424 5640 *fax* 020-7424 5641
email info@brownreference.com
website www.brownreference.com
Managing Director Sharon Hutton, *Children's Publisher* Anne O'Daly

Book, partwork and continuity set packaging services for trade, promotional and international publishers. Opportunities for freelances. Founded 1989.

Brown Wells & Jacobs Ltd

Foresters Hall, 25–27 Westow Street, London SE19 3RY
tel 020-8771 5115 *fax* 020-8771 9994
email graham@bwj-ltd.com
website www.bwj.org
Director Graham Brown

Design, editorial, illustration and production of high-quality non-fiction illustrated children's books. Specialities include pop-up and novelty books. Opportunities for freelances. Founded 1979.

Cambridge Publishing Management Ltd

Burr Elm Court, Main Street, Caldecote, Cambs. CB23 7NU
tel (01954) 214000 *fax* (01954) 214002
email initial.surname@cambridgepm.co.uk
website www.cambridgepm.co.uk
Managing Director Jackie Dobbyne, *Managing Editors* Karen Beaulah, Catherine Burch, Diane Teillol

Creative and highly skilled editorial and book production company specialising in complete project management of business, education, ELT, travel and illustrated non-fiction titles, from commissioning authors to delivery of final files to printer. Freelancers should send their CVs to Karen Beaulah. Founded 1999.

Canopus Publishing Ltd

15 Nelson Parade, Bedminster, Bristol BS3 4HY
tel 0117-963 3366
email tom@canopusbooks.com
website www.canopusbooks.com
Directors Tom Spicer, Robin Rees

Highly illustrated popular science and astronomy titles for international markets. Academic physics monographs and reference works. Founded 1999.

Carroll & Brown Ltd

20 Lonsdale Road, London NW6 6RD
tel 020-7372 0900 *fax* 020-7372 0460
email mail@carrollandbrown.co.uk
website www.carrollandbrown.co.uk
Managing Director Amy Carroll

Publishers and packagers of health, parenting, pregnancy and lifestyle titles. Opportunities for freelances. Founded 1989.

Cowley Robinson Publishing Ltd

(incorporating David Hawcock Books)
8 Belmont, Bath BA1 5DZ
tel (01225) 339999 *fax* (01225) 339995
email sales: anna.sainaghi@cowleyrobinson.com
Directors Stewart Cowley (publishing), David Hawcock, Phil Fleming (finance)

Specialises in children's novelty and paper-engineered formats for international co-editions. Licence and character publishing developments. Information and early learning. Founded 1998.

Creative Plus Publishing Ltd

2nd Floor, 151 High Street, Billericay, Essex CM12 9AB
tel (01277) 633005 *fax* (01277) 633003
email enquiries@creative-plus.co.uk
website www.creative-plus.co.uk
Managing Director Beth Johnson

Provides all editorial and design from concept to finished pages for books, partworks and magazines. Specialises in female interest, children's, gardening, illustrated non-fiction. Opportunities for freelances. Founded 1989.

Design Eye Ltd

226 City Road, London EC1V 2TT
tel 020-7812 8601 *fax* 020-7253 4370
email info@designeye.co.uk
website www.quarto.com/co_ed_designeye_uk.htm
Publisher Sue Grabham

Co-edition publisher of innovative Books-Plus for children. Highly illustrated, paper-engineered, novelty and component-based titles for all ages, but primarily children's preschool (3+), 5–8 and 8+ years. Mainly non-fiction, early concepts and curriculum-based topics for the trade in all international markets. Opportunities for freelance paper engineers, artists, authors, editors and designers. Unsolicited MSS not accepted. Founded 1988.

Diagram Visual Information Ltd

34 Elaine Grove, London NW5 4QH
tel 020-7485 5941 *fax* 020-7485 5941
email info@diagramgroup.com
website www.diagramgroup.com
Directors Bruce Robertson, Patricia Robertson

Research, writing, design and illustration of reference books, supplied as disks. Founded 1967.

Eddison Sadd Editions Ltd

St Chad's House, 148 King's Cross Road, London WC1X 9DH
tel 020-7837 1968 *fax* 020-7837 2025
email info@eddisonsadd.com
website www.eddisonsadd.com
Directors Nick Eddison, Ian Jackson, David Owen, Susan Cole, Sarah Rooney

Illustrated non-fiction books, kits and gift titles for the international co-edition market. Broad, popular list including MBS, health, self-help and relationships. Incorporates BOOKINABOX Ltd. Founded 1982.

Edition

PO Box 1, Moffat, Dumfriesshire DG10 9SU
tel (01683) 220808 *fax* (01683) 220012
email cameronhollis@cameronbooks.co.uk
Directors Ian A. Cameron, Jill Hollis

Illustrated non-fiction. Design, editing, typesetting and production from concept to finished book for galleries, museums, institutions and other publishers. Founded 1976.

Elm Grove Books Ltd

Elm Grove, Marsh Lane, Templecombe, Somerset BA8 0TQ
tel (01963) 362498
email hugh@elmgrovebooks.com, susie@elmgrovebooks.com
Directors Hugh Elwes, Susie Elwes

Packager of children's books. Founded 1993.

Focus Publishing

Focus Publishing (Sevenoaks) Ltd, 11A St Botolph's Road, Sevenoaks, Kent TN13 3AJ
tel (01732) 742456 *fax* (01732) 743381
email info@focus-publishing.co.uk
website www.focus-publishing.co.uk
Director Guy Croton

Illustrated non-fiction: gardening, wine and food, sport, aviation, DIY and crafts, transport, photography. Opportunities for freelances. Founded 1997.

Graham-Cameron Publishing & Illustration

The Studio, 23 Holt Road, Sheringham, Norfolk NR26 8NB
tel (01263) 821333 *fax* (01263) 821334
email enquiry@graham-cameron-illustration.com
and Duncan Graham-Cameron, 59 Hertford Road, Brighton BN1 7GG
tel (01273) 385890
website www.gciforillustration.com
Partners Mike Graham-Cameron, Helen Graham-Cameron, Duncan Graham-Cameron

Educational and children's books; information publications; sponsored publications. Illustration agency with 37 artists. Do not send unsolicited MSS. Founded 1985.

Hart McLeod Ltd

14 Greenside, Waterbeach, Cambridge CB25 9HP
tel (01223) 861495 *fax* (01223) 862902
email inhouse@hartmcleod.co.uk
website www.hartmcleod.co.uk
Directors Graham Hart, Joanne Barker

Primarily educational and general non-fiction with particular expertise in illustrated books, school texts, ELT and electronic and audio content. Opportunities for freelances and work experience. Founded 1985.

HL Studios Ltd

17 Fenlock Court, Blenheim Office Park, Long Hanborough, Oxford OX29 8LN
tel (01993) 881010 *fax* (01993) 882713
email info@hlstudios.eu.com
website www.hlstudios.eu.com

Primary, secondary academic education (geography, science, modern languages) and co-editions (travel guides, gardening, cookery). Multimedia (CD-Rom programming and animations). Opportunities for freelances. Founded 1985.

Hothouse Fiction Ltd

The Old Truman brewery, 91 Brick Lane, London E1 6QL

tel 020-3384 2609
email ben.horslen@hothousefiction.com
website www.hothousefiction.com
Directors Reg Wright, Richard Maskell, James Arnold-Baker, *Managing Editor* Ben Horslen

Complete fiction creation and packaging service producing new fiction for children and adults.

Ivy Contract

210 High Street, Lewes, East Sussex BN7 2NS
tel (01273) 403120 *fax* (01273) 487441
email (surname)@ivy-group.co.uk
website www.ivy-group.co.uk
Creative Director Peter Bridgewater, *Managing Director* Stephen Paul

Provides full editorial, design (and where required, production) service to develop ideas owned by its publishing clients. Specialises in building entire lists of illustrated books in all subject areas; developing individual titles; designing jackets/covers; producing sales material; rebranding. Opportunities for freelancers. Part of the Ivy Group.

The Ivy Press Ltd

210 High Street, Lewes, East Sussex BN7 2NS
tel (01273) 487440 *fax* (01273) 487441
email surname@ivy-group.co.uk
website www.ivy-group.co.uk
Creative Director Peter Bridgewater, *Managing Director* Stephen Paul

Packagers of illustrated trade books on art, lifestyle, popular culture, design, health and Mind, Body & Spirit. Opportunities for authors and freelances. Founded 1996.

Lexus Ltd

60 Brook Street, Glasgow G40 2AB
tel 0141-556 0440 *fax* 0141-556 2202
email peterterrell@lexusforlanguages.co.uk
website www.lexusforlanguages.co.uk
Director P.M. Terrell

Language books, especially bilingual dictionaries, phrasebooks and schoolbooks, as publisher and packager. *Lexus Travelmate* and *Chinese Classroom* series. Founded 1980.

Little People Books

The Home of BookBod, Knighton, Radnorshire LD7 1UP
tel (01547) 520925
email littlepeoplebooks@thehobb.tv
website www.thehobb.tv/lpb
Directors Grant Jessé (production & managing), Helen Wallis (rights & finance)

Packager of audio, children's educational and textbooks, digital publications. Parent company: Grant Jessé UK.

Market House Books Ltd

Suite B, Elsinore House, 43 Buckingham Street, Aylesbury, Bucks. HP20 2NQ
tel (01296) 484911
email books@mhbref.com
website www.markethousebooks.com
Directors Jonathan Law, Anne Kerr

Compilation of dictionaries, encyclopedias, and reference books. Founded 1970.

Marshall Editions Ltd

The Old Brewery, 6 Blundell Street, London N7 9BH
tel 020-7700 6764 *fax* 020-7700 4191
email jennij@marshalleditions.com
website www.marshalleditions.com
Publisher Jenni Johns

Highly illustrated non-fiction for adults and children, including history, health, gardening, home design, pets, natural history, popular science.

Monkey Puzzle Media Ltd

Gissing's Farm, Fressingfield, Eye, Suffolk IP21 5SH
tel (01379) 588044 *fax* (01379) 588055
email info@monkeypuzzlemedia.com
Director Roger Goddard-Coote

High-quality illustrated children's and adult non-fiction for trade, institutional and mass markets worldwide. Publishers' commissions undertaken. Founded 1998.

Orpheus Books Ltd

6 Church Green, Witney, Oxon OX28 4AW
tel (01993) 774949 *fax* (01993) 700330
email info@orpheusbooks.com
website www.orpheusbooks.com
Executive Directors Nicholas Harris (editorial, design & marketing), Sarah Hartley (production & design)

Children's illustrated non-fiction/reference. Opportunities for freelance artists. Founded 1993.

Paragon Publishing

4 North Street, Rothersthorpe, Northants NN7 3JB
tel (01604) 832149
email mark.webb@tesco.net
website www.intoprint.net
Proprietor Mark Webb

Packagers of non-fiction books: architecture and design, educational and textbooks, electronic (academic and professional), languages and linguistics, sports and games. All editorial and design services to complete PDFs.

Playne Books Ltd

Park Court Barn, Trefin, Haverfordwest, Pembrokeshire SA62 5AU
tel (01348) 837073
email playne.books@virgin.net
Design & Production Director David Playne, *Editor* Gill Davies

Specialises in highly illustrated adult non-fiction and books for very young children. All stages of production undertaken from initial concept (editorial, design and manufacture) to delivery of completed books. Currently not considering new projects. Founded 1987.

Tony Potter Publishing Ltd

1 Stairbridge Court, Bolney Grange Business Park, Stairbridge Lane, Bolney, West Sussex RH17 5PA
tel (01444) 232889 *fax* (01444) 232142
email info@tonypotter.com
website www.tonypotter.com
Directors Tony Potter (managing), Christine Potter

Creates high-quality children's titles as a packager and occasionally publishes under its own imprints: Tony Potter Books and Over the Moon. Opportunities for freelance editors, designers and illustrators. Also creates custom-designed books and innovative paper-based products for children and adults, particularly for own-brand. Founded 1997.

Quantum Publishing

6 Blundell Street, London N7 8BH
tel 020-7700 6700 *fax* 020-7700 4191
email helen.nally@quarto.com
website www.quarto.com
Publisher Helen Nally

Packager of a wide range of non-fiction titles. Part of the Quarto Group. Founded 1995.

The Quarto Group, Inc.

226 City Road, London, EC1V 2TT
tel 020-7700 9000 *fax* 020-7253 4437
email info@quarto.com
website www.quarto.com
Chairman & Ceo Laurence Orbach, *Chief Financial Officer* Mick Mousley, *Creative Director* Bob Morley, *Director of Publishing* Piers Spence

Independent publishing group encompassing traditional and co-edition publishing. Co-edition books are licensed to third parties all over the world, with bestselling titles often available in 20+ languages. UK-based operations include the following autonomously run business units, or imprints. See separate entries for Aurum Press Ltd and Jacqui Small on page 140 and RotoVision on page 183.

Marshall Editions

email linda.cole@quarto.com
Publisher Linda Cole

QED Publishing Ltd

email zetad@quarto.com
Associate Publisher Zeta Davies

Quantum Publishing Ltd

email helen.nally@quarto.com
Publisher Helen Nally

Quarto Children's Books Ltd

email quartokids@quarto.com, sueg@quarto.com
Publisher Sue Grabham, *Art Director* Jonathan Gilbert

Co-edition publisher of innovative Books-Plus for children. Highly illustrated paper-engineered, novelty and component-based titles for all ages, but primarily preschool (3+), 5–8 and 8+ years. Mainly non-fiction, early concepts and curriculum-based topics for the trade in all international markets. Opportunities for freelance paper engineers, artists, authors, editors and designers. Unsolicited MSS not accepted.

Quarto Publishing plc

email paulc@quarto.com
Publisher Paul Carslake

qu:id

email nigelb@quidpublishing.com
Publisher Nigel Browning

Quintessence

email tristandl@quarto.com
Publisher Tristan de Lancey

Quintet Publishing Ltd

email JamesT@quarto.com
Publisher James Tavendale

Salamander – see Anova Books

Savitri Books Ltd

4 Nutholt Lane, Ely, Cambs. CB7 4PL
tel (01353) 654327
email munni.srivastava@virginmedia.com
Director Mrinalini S. Srivastava

Packaging, publishing, design, production. Founded 1983.

Studio Cactus Ltd

Northgate Farm, Northgate Lane, Ellisfield, Basingstoke, Hants RG25 2QT
tel (01256) 409029
email mail@studiocactus.co.uk
website www.studiocactus.co.uk
Editorial Director Damien Moore, *Art Director* Amanda Lunn

High-quality illustrated non-fiction books for the international market. Undertakes book packaging/production services, from initial concept to delivery of final disk or printed books. Founded 1998.

Tangerine Designs Ltd

1 Limpley Mill, Lower Stoke, Limpley Stoke, Bath BA2 7FJ
tel (01225) 720001
website www.tangerinedesigns.co.uk
Managing Director Christine Swift

Packagers and co-edition publishers of children's books including novelty books and licensed titles. Concepts and cooperation proposals considered. Submissions only accepted via mail from UK, with sae. See website for submissions information. Member of the Publishers Association. Founded 2000.

The Templar Company Ltd

The Granary, North Street, Dorking, Surrey RH4 1DN
tel (01306) 876361 *fax* (01306) 889097
email info@templarco.co.uk
website www.templarco.co.uk
Managing & Creative Director Amanda Wood, *Sales & Marketing Director* Ruth Huddleston, *Submissions* Deborah Simmons

Publisher and packager of high-quality illustrated children's books, including novelty books, picture books, pop-up books, board books, fiction, non-fiction and gift titles.

Toucan Books Ltd

3rd Floor, 89 Charterhouse Street, London EC1M 6HR
tel 020-7250 3388 *fax* 020-7250 3123
website www.toucanbooks.co.uk
Directors Robert Sackville West, Ellen Dupont

International co-editions; editorial, design and production services. Founded 1985.

Emma Treehouse Ltd

The Studio, Church Street, Nunney, Frome, Somerset BA11 4LW
tel (01373) 836233 *fax* (01373) 836299
email sales@emmatreehouse.com
website www.emmatreehouse.com
Directors David Bailey, Richard Powell (creative & editorial)

Specialist creator of novelty books for children aged 0–7: bath books, books with a sound concept, cloth books, novelty books, flap books, touch-and-feel books. Packager and co-edition publisher with international recognition for its innovative and often unique concepts. The company has produced over 30 million books, translated into 33 different languages. Opportunities for freelance artists. Founded 1992

Tucker Slingsby Ltd

5th Floor, Regal House, 70 London Road, Twickenham TW1 3QS
tel 020-8744 1007 *fax* 020-8744 0041
email firstname@tuckerslingsby.co.uk
Directors Janet Slingsby, Del Tucker

Packager specialising in highly illustrated books. Creation, editorial and design to disk, digital files or finished copy of children's books and general interest adult titles. Opportunities for freelances and picture book artists. Founded 1992.

Working Partners Ltd

Stanley House, St Chad's Place, London WC1X 9HH
tel 020-7841 3939 *fax* 020-7841 3940
email enquiries@workingpartnersltd.co.uk
website www.workingpartnersltd.co.uk
Chairman Ben Baglio, *Managing Director* Chris Snowdon, *Creative Director* Rod Ritchie, *Operations Director* Charles Nettleton

Children's and young adult fiction series. Genres include: animal fiction, fantasy, horror, historical fiction, detective, magical, adventure. Unable to accept any MS or illustration submissions. Pays advance and royalty; retains copyright on all work created. Selects writers from unpaid writing samples based on specific brief provided. Always looking to add writers to database; to register details contact writers@workingpartnersltd.co.uk. Founded 1995.

Working Partners Two (division)

Managing Director Charles Nettleton

Adult fiction. Aims to create novels across most adult genres for publication in the UK, US and international houses. See above for submission guidelines. Founded 2006.

Understanding the publishing process

To someone who has never worked in publishing the way in which a manuscript is turned into a book can seem like magic but in reality, the process is fairly straightforward. However, no two publishing houses (big or small) do things quite alike and the real magic comes in the way that the different departments work together to give every book the best possible chance of success. Bill Swainson explains the process.

For the purposes of this article I have assumed a medium-sized publishing house, big enough to have a fairly clear division of roles – in smaller houses these roles frequently overlap – and I talk mainly about original (rather than paperback reprint) publishing.

To begin at the beginning. Communication is everything in publishing and while more and more business is done by email, publishers still receive a number of their submissions and send out packages and correspondence by post. So, the post-room staff, the computer wizards, the office management team, the receptionist who answers the telephone or welcomes visitors, all play a vital part in the process of making books. But it is the managing director or CEO of a company who draws all the threads together and gives the company its direction and drive.

Editorial

Every editorial department has a similar staff structure: commissioning editors (sometimes called acquiring editors) who take on a book and become its champion in the company, copy-editors (sometimes called desk editors) who do the close work on the manuscript, and editorial assistants who support them.

Every publishing company acquires its books from similar sources: literary agents and scouts, other publishers throughout the world, a direct commission from editor to author and, very rarely, by unsolicited proposal. The in-house process goes something like this: the commissioning editor will make a case for taking on a book at an 'acquisitions meeting' which is attended by all the other departments directly involved in publishing the book, including sales, marketing, publicity and rights. Lively discussions follow and final decisions are determined from a mixture of commercial good sense (estimated sales figures, likely production costs and author's track record) and taste – and every company's and every editor's taste is different.

Shortly after acquisition, an 'advance information' sheet is drafted by the commissioning editor. This is the earliest attempt to harness the excitement that led to the book being signed, and it contains all the basic information needed by the rest of the company, including the title, ISBN, format, likely extent (number of pages), price, rights holder, sales points, short blurb and biographical note. It is the first of many pieces of 'copy' that will be written about the book, and will be used as the template for all others, such as a catalogue entry, jacket blurb or press release.

It is now that the journey of the book really begins, with the finishing line some 10–12 months away. As soon as it arrives in the editorial department the manuscript will receive a 'structural edit'. This involves looking at the book as a whole, i.e. everything from its structure and narrative pacing to characterisation and general style, and in the case of non-fiction, looking at illustrations, appendices, bibliography, notes and index. The actual copy-editing usually only takes place when all of the main structural editorial decisions have been made. While commissioning editors may see certain titles through from beginning to end, it is more likely that they'll pass them to their editorial team to manage once the 'structure edit' has been completed, while still keeping a watching brief on every aspect of publication. It is at this stage that the more detailed work begins.

The copy-edit is another filtering process done with a very fine mesh net, designed to catch all the errors and inconsistencies in the text, from spelling and punctuation to facts, figures and tics of style. In some publishing houses this work is done onscreen, but surprisingly many editors still prefer to work direct on the typescript because it is easier to spot changes and see where decisions have been made along the way. Once the copy-edit has been completed, the author will be asked to answer any queries that may have arisen. When the commissioning editor, copy-editor and author are happy that the marked-up typescript is in the best possible shape, it is sent to the production department for design and typesetting.

From now on the book will shuttle between the editorial and production departments in the form of proofs, usually in three separate stages. First proofs are read by the author and a proofreader. This is the author's last chance to make any cuts or additions as amendments after this stage become tricky and expensive to implement. Both sets of amendments are then collated and sent to the production department to be made into second proofs. Second proofs, or 'revises', are checked against the collated first proofs and any last-minute queries are attended to. (An index, if needed, will be compiled at this stage.) The checked 'revised' proofs are then returned to the production department to be made into 'final' proofs. Final proofs are, in a perfect publishing world, what the name implies. They are checked against the second proofs, the index (if there is one) is proofread, the prelim pages double-checked and when all is present and correct – the text is ready for press.

Design

The design department's work on a new book begins usually 10–12 months in advance of the publication date. Hardback jackets and paperback covers are publishing's main selling tool. People say you can't judge a book by its cover, but because most (if not all) buying decisions are made by the trade's buyers before the book is printed – up until that time the cover *is* the book. It's what makes the buyer believe in a book's potential enough to order it, and it's one of the most important things that makes a browsing customer pick up a book in the bookshop and pay for it at the till.

Design also produces all other sales material that the marketing department decides it needs in order to make a good job of the 'sell in', including catalogues, order forms, 'blads' (lit. book layout and design, i.e. illustrated sales material), 'samplers' (booklets containing tantalising extracts), posters, book proofs (bound reading proofs) and advertisements. Much of this work is now done online on the company's website, or in the form of e-marketing campaigns.

Most companies try to develop a distinctive look for their books and it's the design department that creates it.

Production

The production department handles all aspects of book production including text design, although some of the very big companies have a separate department for this. The production department style (or format) the copy-edited typescript by drafting a brief known as a 'type specification' or 'spec'. The spec may be designed specifically for a unique book, or if the book is part of a series, the series spec will be used to give the books the same look and feel. The typescript is then usually despatched to an out-of-house typesetter, although some companies do their typesetting in-house, to be made to page proofs. Meanwhile, the production manager (working with the commissioning editor and the designer) will choose the binding materials and any embellishments, such as headband, coloured or printed endpapers, or marker ribbon. The print run is also decided (based on advance sales and track record) and an order is placed with the printer.

Most publishing companies use only a few printers, negotiating the best possible rate per book depending on the volume of work they agree to place with the printer. A key role of the production department is to buy print at a rate that allows each tightly budgeted book to make money, and equally important (especially when a book takes off) to manage the supply of reprints so that the publisher's warehouse is never short of stock.

Sales

'Selling in' in the home market (Britain and Ireland) is done increasingly by key account managers working with the chain buyers, as well as by a team of sales representatives. The reps visit bookshops in their designated area and try to achieve the sales targets set for each book. The number of copies sold pre-publication is known as the subscription sale, or 'sub'.

Selling books effectively to bookshops, both chains and independents and nowadays to supermarkets and internet and other retailers, takes time and careful planning. The British and Irish book trade has developed in such a way that the sales cycle has extended to cover the best part of a year. Even though the actual business of selling may not begin in earnest until eight or nine months prior to publication, the work of preparing sales material begins up to a year ahead. It can, however, be achieved in a shorter time frame and this allows a degree of flexibility for the publisher in case of a crisis or to take advantage of prime opportunities, such as issuing instant books on a burning topic of the day.

Many sales are also made in-house by phone, email and fax and, nowadays, the internet. Most publishers have their own websites and provide customers with the opportunity to buy their books either directly or by a link to another bookselling website. Book clubs are another market for publishers that used to be much more important, but today they are having a tough time of it in the face of stiff competition from the internet and the supermarkets.

Export sales are achieved using teams of international agents and reps run from in-house by the export sales department. While the bigger companies tend to have their own teams and the smaller companies use freelance agencies and reps, all face a different range of challenges to the home sales team. Here format, discount, royalty rates, shipping, and exchange rates are the key components. The margins are much tighter and it requires a lot of skill and *chutzpah* to generate significant sales and then to maintain a successful international presence.

Marketing

It could be said that the marketing department is the engine room of the sales department. It's responsible for originating all the sales material (catalogues, blads, samplers, etc) used by the sales team to persuade the buyers in the book trade to buy the company's books.

Marketing also works alongside the sales department in dealing directly with the big bookshops on special promotions ('Book of the Month', 'Debut', '3 for 2', etc) that are now such a common feature of the larger chains.

This department also prepares the advertising for the trade, such as the post-publication press advertising that, along with reviews and other publicity, persuades customers into the shops to buy a particular book. It also organises the company sales conferences at which each new season's publishing is presented to the sales reps and overseas agents for the first time. The run-up to the sales conference and the event itself is an exciting time and stimulates many of the best ideas on how to sell the new books.

Publicity

As the marketing department works to sell books with the emphasis on the 'sell in', the publicity department works with the author and the media on 'free' publicity with the emphasis on the 'sell through'. This covers reviews, features, author interviews, bookshop readings and signings, festival appearances, book tours and radio and television interviews and so on.

For each author and his or her book, the publicity department devises a campaign that will play to the book's or the author's strengths. For instance, best use will be made of written features or radio interviews for authors who are shy in public, just as full advantage will be made of public appearances for those authors who thrive on the thrill of showmanship. In short, the publicist's careful work (which like much of publishing is a mixture of inspiration and enthusiasm on the one hand and efficient planning and flexibility on the other) is designed to get the best results for each individual author and book.

Rights

It is the aim of the rights department to make the best use of all the rights that were acquired when the contract was first negotiated between publisher and author or the author's agent.

While literary agents are understandably keen to handle foreign and serial rights, many publishing houses have well-developed rights departments with good contacts and are also well placed to sell the rights of a book. Selling rights is very varied and includes anything from dealing with requests for film or television rights, the sale of translation rights to other countries, or serial rights to a newspaper, to smaller requests for permission to reprint a poem or an extract. All are opportunities to promote the book and earn additional income for author and publisher, and at the time of first publication the rights, sales, marketing and publicity departments all work closely together.

Book fairs are key venues for the sale of foreign rights. At the Frankfurt Book Fair in October and at the London Book Fair in April, publishers and agents from all participating countries meet to form a rights bazaar. Here, editors have the opportunity to hear about and buy new books from publishing houses all over the world. Occasionally rights are sold on the spot, but more commonly acquisition is completed later.

Paperbacks

Paperbacks are published approximately a year after the original publication. Paperback publishing is a key part of publishing today but is a quite different skill to hardback publishing, and in many respects is all about marketing. Efforts are made to identify and broaden the likely market (readership) for a book, making sure that the cover and presentation will appeal to a wide audience, and being ingenious about positioning an author's books in the marketplace where they can be best seen, bought and read. The means used vary from in-store promotions and advertising campaigns to author-led publicity and renewed press coverage in the 'paperback round-ups'. But the energy that drives this inspired and careful work of reinvention comes from the paperback publisher's vision and passion for the book and the author and the list as a whole.

Ebooks

Many publishing houses have already begun to respond to the challenge and opportunities of e-publishing. The launch of the Sony Reader and the Kindle have already created a market by providing the means of distribution, but the launch of the iPad in April 2010 will, it is widely believed, transform what is currently only a market in embryo. Whether ebooks will increase the overall market for books and reading or simply lead to a transfer of a proportion of sales from the printed word to the e-word remains to be seen. What is certain is that not least because they have invested in the editing and typesetting, publishers will want to exploit this new medium as another means by which to broadcast a writer's work to the world.

Accounts

Finally, every successful business needs a good finance department. Most publishing houses split the work into two areas – purchase ledger and royalties. Purchase ledger deals with all incoming invoices associated with the company's business. The royalties department deals exclusively with author advances (payable on acquisition, and on delivery or publication of a book) and with keeping account of the different royalty percentages payable on book sales, serial deals, film rights, permissions, etc. This is done so that both author and agent can see that an accurate record has been kept against the day when the book earns back its advance (the point at which the royalties earned equal the advance paid) and the author starts earning additional income.

A special business

This has been a potted breakdown of the inner workings of a medium-sized company. Publishing is a business, and commercial considerations will be apparent in every department, but it is a very special kind of business, one which frequently breaks many of the accepted business rules and often seems to make no sense at all – just think of the hundreds of different lines, formats, price points and discounts. At times it shouldn't work – but somehow, miraculously, it does.

Bill Swainson has worked for small, medium and large publishers since 1976 and is currently a Senior Commissioning Editor at Bloomsbury Publishing Plc. He is the editor of *The Encarta Book of Quotations* (Bloomsbury 2000).

See also...

- *Dealing with rejection*, page 659
- *A year in view of the publishing industry*, page 328
- *Helping to market your book*, page 320
- *Who owns whom in publishing*, page 336
- *The role of the literary agent*, page 449
- *How literary agencies work*, page 455
- *Notes from a successful fiction author*, page 241
- *Notes from a successful non-fiction author*, page 270

Books

Spotting a bestseller

Alexandra Pringle addresses the million dollar question of what makes a bestselling book.

Publishing, at least in the literary sector, is a strange combination of judgement, confidence, experience, instinct and sheer luck. It would be a wonderful and much simpler world if we could predict what people will want to read, or if we could separate our own taste from the publishing process. But if there is one thing that is true about publishing it is that it is infinitely complicated.

It is probably the case that statistically there are some editors who have a higher hit rate in choosing bestsellers than others; just as there are some people that go through life without bad things happening to them, who never slip over in the street or have a nasty divorce or have children who fail exams. But publishing, like life, is a messy business and one that is inevitably teeming with failure. For every book that sells over 100,000 copies there are dozens and dozens that sell fewer than 10,000.

Editors need to be optimists – they need to believe that every book they take on, which will entail hours and hours of work and thought and waking up in the middle of the night, has the chance to do something wonderful, to create the alchemy that will mean the book will do well, and could, just could, become that rare and wonderful thing, a bestseller.

Of course nowadays editors do not buy books in isolation. First they have to love a book, at best to distraction. Then they have to sell the book to colleagues, to people in sales and marketing, publicity and rights. If there aren't enough people who respond to the book, its chances of making it out there are slim. And then the editor has to be a robust engine that will drag the book up hill and down dale, through every bit of its process, from the text to the cover blurb to the bound proof to the finished creature and then out into the world. Without that stubborn effort, that sheer will, a book, like a neglected plant, will weaken and wither.

There are roughly two sorts of bestsellers (other than those that are simply the next book by an already bestselling author): those that are 'created' and those that find their way slowly and surely.

The first sort happens when a book is acquired and every single person in the company feels they have a bestseller on their hands from the outset. This is often after a hard-fought, adrenalin-fuelled auction where different departments have had to pitch in with marketing and publicity plans, with jacket designs and editorial comments and blandishments to the author. This can give the book a terrific start because the machine is up and running: there is a vision of what the book is and how it can be published. On the other hand it can create a high platform from which a book can crash and burn: the press can dislike a book because they feel it has been hyped – an unrealistic expectation may have been created in the excitement of the auction.

The second kind of bestseller is often the sweetest. These can be books by unknown authors that find their way into the outside world through stealth, that can be ignored by bookshops and by the press when first published, but that are passed, like a secret, from person to person, that can become bestsellers two, three or four years after first publication. We call these word-of-mouth bestsellers. We love them very much indeed.

Or they are by authors who you stay with and who stay with you over the process of a strange old marriage, and who after many years of publishing (often small, exquisite books that receive wonderful reviews and no sales to speak of), and years of the editor believing and hoping, suddenly produce a book that sets the publishing company alight, that gives them something to go out and shout about, that in turn sets the world alight. These are pretty lovely, too, and a source of especial joy and satisfaction to the editor.

One thing is clear: you can throw a fortune at a book in marketing and advertising and touring the author and while it will ensure the book is noticed, it does not of necessity make it a bestseller. In the end people will only read what they want to read. It is vital never to underestimate the intelligence and the wilfulness of the reading public.

People talk of 'the market' but I have never understood what that means, nor how anyone can begin to judge what people will want by studying buying trends and graphs and types of books that sell. For there may be one book about a Victorian murder that sells hundreds of thousands of copies, or a book about mathematics that captures the imagination of the public, but those that slavishly follow that model, hoping to capture some of that particular stardust, are usually bitterly disappointed.

What I do understand is that people cannot publish well and publish cynically. Whether you publish romance novels or high literature, or thrillers or books on animals, or food books or novels from far-flung countries, or books on cars or fridges or knitting, you have to believe in them.

After all, in the end, and in the absence of clairvoyance, all an editor really has is their own taste, their own belief. It is from this that all else springs.

Rather like J.M. Barrie's *Peter Pan*, Peter, of course, being the editor and Tinkerbell the author:

'If you believe,' he shouted to them, 'clap your hands; don't let Tink die.'

Many clapped.

Some didn't.

A few beasts hissed.

Tink was saved. First her voice grew strong, then she popped out of bed, then she was flashing through the room more merry and impudent than ever. She never thought of thanking those who believed, but she would have liked to get at the ones who had hissed.

Alexandra Pringle is Editor-in-Chief at Bloomsbury Publishing Plc.

See also...

- *The state of commissioning*, page 299
- *Understanding the publishing process*, page 230
- *A year in view of the publishing industry*, page 328
- *Who owns whom in publishing*, page 336

One hundred years of fiction bestsellers

Alex Hamilton pulls out some plums from 20th century fiction bestsellers.

Among bestsellers published before the Great War half a dozen authors' names still echo faintly, though the bulk of their work is little read. Gene Stratton Porter's *Freckles*, based on her life in a cabin by a swamp, sold two million copies, but is valued today only as a collectors' first edition. Among them also was Winston Churchill – not the statesman, but the author of *Richard Carvel*, the story of a naval officer under Paul Jones, selling more than a million copies, and with *The Crisis* and *The Crossing* he proved himself to be what publishers always look for – a career novelist with a following.

Frank Norris likewise promised well, when his fifth book, *The Pit*, scaled the heights, but almost simultaneously he died of appendicitis at the age of 32. Meanwhile Conan Doyle, the stayer of this bunch, peaked with his most admired Sherlock Holmes tale, *The Hound of the Baskervilles*, and when tired of him launched a second serial character, Professor Challenger, in *The Lost World*. Even their huge popularity could not quite match the exotica of Elinor Glyn who, with five million sales of her novel of passion, *Three Weeks*, set a marker for all candidates for the Number One spot.

If unable to write a book selling five million, try writing five that sell one million. This was more or less a habit of prolific producers of Westerns, whose pioneers were Owen Wister with *The Virginians*, and the daddy of them all, Zane Grey, with *Riders of the Purple Range*. These were authors of a genre that celebrated adventure and individual heroics in a way of life that was virtually obsolete. Though not a Western writer, Jack London in this sense belongs with them: his *The Call of the Wild*, whose heroics were actually those of a dog, sold a million and a half, and *The Sea Wolf* and *White Fang* almost as many. He was reputed to be the best-paid writer in America. Zane Grey, the Englishman J.T. Edson and Louis L'Amour each wrote more than 100 titles and for the latter the publishers claim a world sale of 270 million copies. The Western went great guns, so to speak, until about 1970, when relentless film and television exploitation had exhausted it.

Women and crime

The circumstances of long wars, when authors and readers are in the trenches and publishers' paper supplies are cut back, are a drag on bestselling books. All the same, there were women's names to conjure with in the Great War: Eleanor Porter, who passed the million mark with *Pollyanna*, the girl whose policy it was to be glad regardless; Ethel M. Dell of *The Way of an Eagle* and *Bars of Iron*, whose villains were hardly worse than her sadistic heroes; Mary Roberts Rinehart, first bestselling woman writer of detective fiction and, with *The Circular Staircase* and *K*, setting a rough-and-ready example for a later generation.

Their 'Golden Age' came in the Thirties and Forties. With a 350 million sales total Agatha Christie was top cat, marketed as 'A Christie for Christmas'. For some 50 years she always offered a puzzle, with her Belgian detective Hercule Poirot on hand to solve it until, like Conan Doyle, she took against her odd hero and switched to a second series character,

Miss Marple – with 66 detective stories published altogether. Most in demand were *The Murder of Roger Ackroyd* and *Murder on the Orient Express.* Belgium was not so much proud of Poirot as of the hundreds of brilliant atmospheric crime stories featuring Inspector Maigret by their author Georges Simenon, whose wife was rightly a martinet to scores of foreign translators (recording a thousand translations).

Other women crime writers climbing the ladder behind Christie included Margery Allingham and the New Zealander Ngaio Marsh; Dorothy L. Sayers, who fanned out the subdivisions of the genre editing her jumbo mystery anthologies, intrigued fans with *The Unpleasantness at the Bellona Club* and *Nine Tailors,* with their mandarin style and affected hero, Lord Peter Wimsey. All these and their equally popular male contemporaries, such as Erle Stanley Gardner (not far behind Christie), John Dickson Carr, S.S. Van Dine and Ellery Queen (who named his detective after himself), produced a relatively mild climate of crime compared with later developments, when the ethos (as with the Western in its declining years) turned nasty. Because of its capacity for change, the dexterity of its authors and the sheer bloody-mindedness of its personnel, the crime story has been the dominant genre of the century, even ahead of the romance in its many guises.

Between the wars

Between the wars the entertainers whom today we'd call 'brand names' were: P.G. Wodehouse, creator of *Jeeves* and frothy social comedies whose bubbles have not yet burst; E. Phillips Oppenheim, who lived luxury and deployed it in his high-life fiction, writing 100 books, mostly with a relay of mistresses on his yacht on the Riviera known as 'the floating double bed'; Rafael Sabatini, boisterous historical romantic, best known for *Captain Blood* and *The Sea Hawk*; Jeffrey Farnol, fey and sentimental, as in *The Chronicles of the Imp*; and Sapper, pseudonym for an ex-army officer who was the progenitor of a crude racist type of spy story, with *Bulldog Drummond* selling six million copies. The series was continued nine times after Sapper's death by another ex-army officer (much as Kingsley Amis and John Gardner kept James Bond going after the death of his creator, Ian Fleming). And who could resist the publisher's banner that declared, 'It is impossible not to be thrilled by Edgar Wallace'? He was a journalist able to turn his Dictaphone to any form in his 'factory of fiction', piling up 170 novels in three decades: African adventure with *Sanders of the River*, much melodrama – some, like *The Crimson Circle,* with a brilliant premise – and umpteen thrillers. On his death in 1931, when a packet of cigarettes cost 3d, a trade paperback 2s and a cottage £100, his royalties were running at £75,000 a year.

Beside the genre favourites, there were some *sui generis* storytellers with powerful appeal. Edna Ferber won a Pulitzer Prize in 1925 with *So Big*, followed it with *Show Boat,* and 25 years later when approaching 70, she came up with *Giant.* Pearl S. Buck also won a Pulitzer Prize (in 1932) with *The Good Earth*, which later won the Nobel Prize and led to five million sales. The Southern writer Erskine Caldwell won a $1,000 prize from the *Yale Review* for a short story, but his real money-spinners were *God's Little Acre* with eight million sales, and *Tobacco Road* with four million sales plus, as a play, the then longest stage run in American theatre history.

Two other big books, physically and commercially, were historical romances. At several hundred thousand words they seemed to be trying to reinstate the Victorian three-decker in one volume. Margaret Mitchell's *Gone with the Wind* sold eight million copies before the war, took her ten years to write and was her only book. Hervey Allen's *Anthony Adverse*, the baby-on-the-doorstep who grows up an adventurer, took him five years to write, but he was tougher than Mitchell and produced more hefty novels, even a trilogy, though never with the same *éclat*. By contrast James Hilton took only four days over *Goodbye Mr Chips*, a slight book to add to his other slight book, *Lost Horizon*, about a remote mountain paradise called Shangri-La, but both were commercial heavyweights.

The Second World War and after

The rising flow of big sellers was partly stalled by shortages in the Second World War. The force in fiction lay increasingly with Americans: John Steinbeck's *The Grapes of Wrath*, Ernest Hemingway's *For Whom the Bell Tolls* and the Lutheran minister Lloyd C. Douglas's novel deriving from the Crucifixion, *The Robe*, which accumulated four million sales. Near the end Kathleen Winsor added a saucy three million seller set in the time of Charles II, *Forever Amber*. The two British authors with similar results were Daphne du Maurier, whose *Rebecca* was brilliantly served by the Hitchcock movie (and *Frenchman's Creek* less well) and Somerset Maugham, a lifelong bestseller since 1915, with *The Razor's Edge*. Every one of the last dozen books mentioned was filmed, which of course prompted a second wave of sales.

In the immediate aftermath of the war there was no sudden eruption of blockbusters, despite the launch of new publishing houses and a growth in the number of titles that seems to have continued exponentially to the present day. However, two books carrying blatant messages had the rare distinction among bestsellers of being politically motivated: George Orwell's *Animal Farm*, followed by *1984*, which in 20 years each sold eight million copies. Between them appeared Norman Mailer's emotional response to the war, *The Naked and the Dead*, with a relatively modest three million sales.

The Fifties

In the Fifties the trade geared itself to a clutch of uncouth authors. The notable example is Mickey Spillane, who at one time had seven of his brutal thrillers in the Top 10, led by *I, the Jury*, all selling more than five million copies. Harold Robbins first showed at this time with *Never Love a Stranger* and *The Dream Merchants*, opening shots in a bombardment that for his total *oeuvre* eventually topped 150 million. Charts of two decades were overwhelmed by the glamour and snobbery of Ian Fleming's James Bond stories, starting with *Casino Royale*, and selling unbridled millions (40 plus) to this day. The archetypal blockbusters of the period were novels such as *Airport* and *Wheels* by Arthur Hailey, exploring the works of large organisations; *Peyton Place* by Grace Metalious, in tandem with its long-running television series, and slightly more serious, the vast doorstoppers by James Michener, *South Pacific* and *Hawaii*.

More lasting successes include *To Kill a Mockingbird* by Harper Lee, a classic of racist conflict in the American South, helped on beyond 10 million sales by its prescription for educational courses (William Golding's *Lord of the Flies* benefits in the same way); Joseph Heller's satire on military bureaucracy *Catch-22*, and the reclusive J.D. Salinger's *Catcher in the Rye*, a percentage of whose six million copies are said to have been urged by teenage girls on their boyfriends. Vladimir Nabokov's story of a middle-aged man's obsession with and seduction by a sub-teen girl, *Lolita*, seems to presage the imminent conflicts over censorship in the Sixties. The major test was the trial of Penguin Books in 1960, which ironically made a six million seller of perhaps the least of D.H. Lawrence's novels, *Lady Chatterley's Lover*, banned on its first publication 32 years earlier.

The Sixties

In the Sixties several books were boosted into orbit not so much by their actual sexual content as by the fuss that was made over it: *Candy* by Terry Southern, *Tropic of Cancer* by Henry Miller, *The Exhibitionist* by Henry Sutton, *Couples* by John Updike, *Portnoy's Complaint* by Philip Roth and *Myra Breckinridge* by Gore Vidal. Apart from Vidal, these writers' sales rarely returned to the highest level, despite their range and brilliance. The newcomers who appeared in the Top 10 and retained their position, as it were by right, were Irving Stone with his biographical novels, such as *The Agony and the Ecstasy* (about Michelangelo), Jacqueline Susann with the showbiz misery of *Valley of the Dolls* (10 million sales over 20 years), Mario Puzo with *The Godfather* (12 million), and two who changed the character of the thriller with their grasp of the intricacies of the Cold War: John le Carré opened with *The Spy Who Came in from the Cold*, while Len Deighton challenged Ian Fleming's picture of espionage with his first, *The Ipcress File*. For nearly 40 years there was always a new Deighton book high on the charts, until he called a halt on himself.

The Seventies and after

Other tireless British regulars over the last quarter of a century included the gothic romances of Victoria Holt, the adventures set in Africa by Wilbur Smith and the northern sagas of Catherine Cookson, whose paperback sales at her death had reached 55 million. Beginning with *The Day of the Jackal*, there was usually a million-selling thriller by Frederick Forsyth, and an automatic sale to half a million fans ready for the annual racecourse mystery from Dick Francis. Ahead of them all were the novels that Jeffrey Archer contrived from the extraordinary 'snakes and ladders' pattern of his own life, starting with *Not a Penny More, Not a Penny Less*. Across the eighties some would rack up close on five million copies, though slightly shaded by the actual top seller of the decade, the humorous *Secret Diary of Adrian Mole Aged 13¾* by Sue Townsend.

Science fiction 'greats', cheered on by countless Sci-cons and Hugo and Nebula Awards, appreciate club support but also duck out, like Kurt Vonnegut with *Slaughterhouse Five* and J.G. Ballard with *Empire of the Sun*. Bestsellers include Isaac Asimov's *Foundation Trilogy*, John Wyndham's *The Day of the Triffids*, and Arthur C. Clarke's *2001*. Short stories are key to science fiction and the key anthologist is Brian Aldiss, prolific author of the *Helliconia Trilogy*. Fantasy's leaders are J.R.R. Tolkien's *Lord of the Rings* (12 million) and Terry Pratchett's *Discworld* novels, begun in 1983 with *The Colour of Magic*. (Pratchett's sales, all genres, surpass 22 million.)

Almost as many American as British authors figured every year in the 100 fastsellers from British publishers between 1980 and 2000. One phenomenon was Stephen King, the most read horror writer after William Blatty's 10 million for *The Exorcist*, always among the leaders with massive frighteners such as *IT* and *Pet Sematary*. The other who never missed was Danielle Steel, who would prefer that her novels were not called romances, and who, like King and Cookson, sometimes had two or three titles in the same list. In the nineties John Grisham virtually took over the Number One spot with his thrillers about corporation lawyers and their illegal habits. As the millennium approached, however, he had to give way to J.K. Rowling. She with her *Harry Potter* series, and Dan Brown with his conspiracy thrillers, set an undreamt of pace for the 21st century.

Inevitably many unputdownable titles and storytellers are omitted from this fiction survey. Everyone will have a favourite that's been missed. Apologies from **Alex Hamilton**, who kept the *Guardian* Fastseller Chart for the last 25 years.

Books

Notes from a successful fiction author

Joanna Trollope shares her experiences of writing success.

I once said to a journalist – rather crossly – that it had only taken me 20 years to be an overnight success. This was in 1993, with my first number one (the paperback of *The Rector's Wife*) and the accompanying media assumption that I had come from nowhere to somewhere at meteoric speed.

People do, of course. Rare, rare people do, but most of us are trudging for years across the creative plateau, honing our skills and cajoling our sinking hearts and *hoping*. I wrote my first published book when my younger daughter was three. When *The Rector's Wife* appeared, she was almost 23, and there'd been ten books in the interim. Hardly *Bridget Jones*. Scarcely *White Teeth*.

But, on reflection, the long haul suited me. I learned about structure and dialogue and pace and characterisation at my own pace. I might have started with a readership so small it was almost invisible to the naked eye, but it grew, and it grew steadily in a manner that made it feel reliable, as is the case with long-term friendships. It also meant that when success came, it was absolutely lovely, no doubt about that, but there was no question of it turning my middle-aged head.

When I wrote my first published book – a historical novel called *Eliza Stanhope* set around the battle of Waterloo – the publishing climate was very different to how it is now. Many of the great publishing individuals were still alive, agents were a scarcer breed and writing was not seen as a way to becoming instantly, absurdly rich (and, in my view, never should be). I sent my manuscript – poorly typed on thin paper – off to Hamish Hamilton in a brown paper parcel. It was politely returned. I sent it – heart definitely in sink – to Hutchinson. They wrote back – a letter I still have – and invited me, like a job interview, to 'come and discuss my future'.

Even if the rest is history, it is not easy or simple history. There weren't any great dramas, to be sure, no cupboards stuffed with rejection slips, no pulped copies (that came later), but what there was instead was a simply enormous amount of perseverance. I don't want to sound too austere, but I find I rather believe in perseverance when it comes to writing. As V.S. Pritchett once said, most people write better if they *practise*.

And I have to say that I am still practising. I think it very unlikely that I will ever feel I have got it right, and I would be uneasy if that feeling went away. After all, only a very few geniuses – Sophocles, Shakespeare – could claim to be prophets or inventors. Most writers are translators or interpreters of the human condition, but no more. A hefty dose of humility in writing seems to me both seemly and healthy.

Readers, after all, are no fools. Readers may not have a writer's gift of the arrangement of events and people and language, but they know about life and humanity all right. They may even know much more about both than the writer. So not only must they never be forgotten, but they must never be underestimated or patronised either.

Which is one of the reasons, in my case, why I research my novels. For the readers' sake, as well as my own, I have to be as accurate as possible about, say, being the child of a broken home, or the widow of a suicide, or a mistress or an adopted man in his thirties. So, once I've decided upon the theme of a novel (and those can have brewed in my brain for years or be triggered by a chance remark overheard on a bus) I go and talk to people who are in the situation that I am exploring. And I have to say that in all the years of working this way, no one has ever turned me down, and everyone has exceeded my expectations.

This habit has had an unlooked-for advantage. During all the years I've been writing, the business of promotion has grown and grown, and fiction is notoriously difficult to talk about in any medium. But the research gives me – and journalists – subject matter which is, to my relief, honourably relevant but, at the same time, miles away from the inexplicable private, frequently uncomfortable place where writing actually goes on. 'Tell me,' people say, not actually understanding what they are asking, 'Tell me how you write'. Pass.

Joanna Trollope is the author of 14 contemporary novels, as well as a number of historical novels published under the name of Caroline Harvey, and a study of women in the British Empire called *Britannia's Daughters*. She lives in London.

Notes from a successful short story author

Chimamanda Ngozi Adichie shares her experiences of being a short story writer.

I have been writing since I was old enough to spell. It is difficult to say where it comes from, this urge to tell stories, and so I have convinced myself that it was simply meant to be. I like to think that I was born with a group of literary spirits hovering overhead and that they visit me from time to time to whisper in my ears. Writing has always been much more important to me than publishing and I think this is an important distinction to make, especially for beginning writers. When I start to write a story, I am not thinking of where it will be published, I am instead thinking of making it the best story it can be. Of course this sounds a bit simplistic, if not cliched, but I think writing stories is something that has to matter in a deep and metaphysical sense. You have to care about it, really care about it, and if that is the starting point of a good story, that story will definitely find a home.

I wrote a lot of poetry when I was younger – I even had a book of awful poems published in Nigeria when I was 15 – but I became drawn to the short story form after I moved to the United States to go to university. I am not entirely sure why but it was probably because I began to read more short stories. Most of my reading in Nigeria had been novels, although I first read and fell in love with Katherine Mansfield's stories when I was a teenager. So I began to write short stories. I joined an online writers' group where I read and critiqued the short stories of other writers – I found that very useful because it began to crystallise for me what I admired and did not admire in the form. I learned that I like realist fiction and that I am unwaveringly old-fashioned in my taste: I love fiction that has character and narrative at its heart. Postmodernism leaves me cold.

After I had written a few short stories, I then made the conscious decision that I wanted to be published. So I spent days at the library looking up information in books like the *Writers Market*, as well as magazines about writing. I needed to know how the whole thing worked. I didn't know, for example, that literary editors wanted stories to be double-spaced and it took me a while to figure out that the acronym 'sase' meant that one was required to include a self-addressed, stamped envelope. I bought a packet of envelopes. I double-spaced my stories. I copied out the names and addresses of a dozen literary journals and I sent off my stories. I remember the first sase that came back in the mail. I took it out of the mailbox, my hand slightly shaky because I thought that I was about to discover where my first published story would appear. It was, of course, a rejection. And the worst kind – a form rejection, which is a pre-typed letter that an assistant in a journal's paper-strewn office picks up from a ready pile on her desk, folds and slips into a sase. I was devastated. Other rejections came in slow succession, and with each form letter I read, I felt a little bit of my smug certainty melt away.

Why were those early stories rejected? Because some of them were just not good enough, and also because I had not targeted my stories properly. I had sent them to the best-known journals – always a good thing to do – but I had sent them only to the best-known journals. I had not considered the small, independent journals publishing wonderful fiction, edited by committed people but often unheard of. I decided to start over again. I revised some stories – and I find that reading the kind of fiction I love often helps me to see my own work in new ways. I read a lot of short stories while revising mine. The Ghanaian writer Ama Ata Aidoo is one of my favourite short story writers. Then I went back to the library, looked up the lesser-known journals in the writing reference books, and then read some of their back issues. I was often stunned by the quality of the work published. I knew I would be in good company if my story was published in any of them.

It took almost a year before my first acceptance letter came. Before that, though, the rejections became nicer; yes, it is in fact possible to get a nice rejection. A well-known editor wrote me a note – hand-written! – to say he liked my story, did not think it was right for his publication, but wanted me to send him something else. That was the kind of encouragement that made me perk up since writing is, sadly, in some ways an exercise in seeking validation. My first acceptance was for an online journal, called *Zoetrope Extra*, the online supplement of Francis Ford Coppola's print journal, *Zoetrope All-Story*. And then there was an acceptance from the *Iowa Review*. And then one from a journal in Canada.

I am still writing short stories and still find the process both frustrating and exhilarating. It has not become easier to write, if anything I find myself grumbling more and more about how the literary spirits are stingy about visiting. What is easier now is having access to publishing because I have an agent who sends my stories out. I still get rejections, of course, but I also now have editors contacting me to specifically ask for stories.

Because I write both novels and short stories, I am often asked about the differences between the two forms. I find short stories to be completely different from novels, obviously, but I don't think that short stories are the younger and less accomplished siblings of novels – which seems to be how some people look at them. They're equals, but different. To write a short story is to have very little space, to compress emotion, and because of that, I think that the form requires a kind of sustained focus that the novel doesn't necessarily require. And it also means that short stories have the potential to be powerful and affecting in ways that novels are not.

Chimamanda Ngozi Adichie was born in Nigeria in 1977. She is the author of a collection of short stories titled *The Thing Around Your Neck* (Fourth Estate 2009). Her novels include *Purple Hibiscus* (Harper Perennial 2003), for which she won the Orange Broadband Prize for Fiction in 2007 and *Half of a Yellow Sun* (Harper Perennial 2006). Her website is www.l3.ulg.ac.be/adichie.

Notes from a successful comic author

Kathy Lette ponders the serious business of being a comic writer.

To be a comic author, there are many technical terms you first need to master. For example did you know that 'brontosaurus' is an anthology of works by 19th century English sister authors? Then there's grammatical precision. A double negative is a complete no-no. Another top tip is that it's a good idea to name your child 'Pulitzer', so you can then say that you have one. Oh, and get an agent to deal with the financial side of things. Satirists are notoriously hopeless at handling money. We tend to spend half the time worrying about addition, half the time worrying about division and half the time worrying about subtraction.

But for any budding comic author it would be easier if you could be strapped into a publishing simulator to experience the terrors and exhilaration, to see if you have what it takes. Because the list of requirements is gruelling. The honing of cheerfulness to chat show perfection. The haemorrhaging of charisma at book signings. The psychotic episodes which accompany concluding your comic masterpiece after you have stopped finding it funny. (Satires are like sausages – you really don't want to know what goes into making them. But creating one can sometimes prove as much fun as removing your own IUD with barbecue tongs.) Then there's the loneliness. I occasionally get so sick of my own company that even my imaginary friend gets bored and runs off to play with someone more interesting. Worst of all is the dreaded book tour which involves flying hundreds of miles from Dipstick, Ohio, to Buffalo Fart, Wyoming, for a one-minute appearance on breakfast radio with a member of the 'Illiterati' whose reading material is limited to his bank balance and tarot cards.

Then there's the inane questions at book festivals. (1) Where do you get your ideas? And (2) Would you like to read my manuscript? And (3) What inspired you to write this comic novel? (Answer: The Inland Revenue. I thought I'd laugh my way to the bank.)

On the up side, writing a funny book is so much cheaper than therapy. Otherwise I'd be a permanent member of Couch Canyon. 'Poetic justice' is the only justice in the world – and I say that being married to a lawyer. A comic writer can always impale enemies on the end of your pen.

I first realised the wounding power of the pen as a teenager. The Aussie surfie males I grew up with disproved the theory of evolution – they were evolving into apes. These were the type of guys who thought 'sex drive' meant doing it in the car. (Most probably because of that little sign on the rear vision mirror that reads 'objects in this mirror may appear larger than they are'!)

Well, I could either have spent the rest of my life as a lesbian recluse doing calligraphy and working on my whittling, or I could exorcise my angst in a novel. So, I shish-kebabed those boys on my Bic biro in a book called *Puberty Blues.* It was published when I was 19 and became a bestseller. It was furious, yes, but also bleakly funny. The success of the novel taught me how much more effective it is to comically kneecap the opposition.

In the ten novels I've written since, I've lampooned many subjects. In *Girls Night Out* I set my satirical sights on married men who think monogamy is something you make dining room tables out of. In *The Llama Parlour*, I took aim at Hollywood – a place where they say 'have a nice day' and then shoot you. In *Foetal Attraction*, I blew a literary raspberry at natural childbirth – a case of stiff upper labia. In *Mad Cows*, I wanted to barbecue the sacred cow that claims that motherhood is the ultimate fulfilment for a female. Yes, I love my children with a primal passion but, like all mums, am occasionally tempted to shove them back into the condom vending machine for a refund!

Altar Ego was the antidote to Bridget Jones, because I don't believe a woman should wait around to be rescued by a Knight in Shining Armani. It seems to me that a perfect marriage is like an orgasm – many of them are faked.

Nip'n'tuck was a fast and furious attack on the facial prejudice older women endure and the cosmetic cowboys who want to disfigure us. (My mother told me never to pick my nose – especially from a catalogue!)

As it's 100 years since Emily Pankhurst tied herself to the railings and women still don't have equal pay, I then penned *Dead Sexy* – a satire on the sex war. (Why do men like intelligent women? Because opposites attract.)

How To Kill Your Husband – and other handy household hints was a cry for help for the generation of women who thought we were going to Have It All, but just ended up Doing It All. Even though women make up 50% of the workforce, we're still doing 99% of all the housework and childcare. The Dunkirk evacuation would have been easier to organise than a working mum getting her kids up and out of the house in the morning. Men always say they'd like to help more around the house, only they can't multi-task. This is just a biological cop out. Would any man have trouble multi-tasking at say, an orgy? (Men, take note, it is scientifically proven that no woman ever shot her husband while he was doing the vacuuming.)

My latest novel, *To Love , Honour and Betray*, poses the theory that teenagers are God's punishment for having sex in the first place. Living with a teenage daughter is a lot like living with the Taliban. A mum is not allowed to laugh, dance, sing or wear short skirts. My top tip for mums of teens is that when they're hitting you and kicking you and saying 'I wish you'd just die' – take a big drag on a cigarette and a big gulp of wine and say 'I'm doing my best darling'.

As you can see, I have a lot to get off my Wonderbra-ed chest. So, why use humour? Because if you can disarm with charm, you're more likely to get your message across. The author and critic Amanda Craig puts it more eloquently: 'Critics refuse to accept that literature can be profound, but also pleasurable; an experience which lifts the spirits while engaging the mind.' A thought backed up by no less than Dr Johnson, who observed, 'The true end of literature is to enable the reader better to enjoy life or better to endure it'.

Scientists tell us that laughter is innate; it originates in the oldest part of the brain, the hypothalamus. Biologists maintain that laughter increases our biological fitness. Anthropologists have revealed that the Eskimos hold laughing competitions and that women, in all cultures, laugh more often than men, *especially* in all-female groups. Why?

Well, living with the male of the species, we have so much to laugh about. Firstly, there's the fact that hypochondria is Greek for man. (If any man says he's not a hypochondriac, well, that's the only disease he *doesn't* have.) Then there's the fact that many marriages break up for religious reasons – he thinks he's a God and well, she just doesn't. Not to forget the fact that women are still getting concussion from hitting our heads on the glass ceiling – and we're expected to clean it whilst we're up there. The female of the species is also the butt of God's biological joke, beginning with periods (when a girl gets taken hostage by her hormones) followed by pregnancy and childbirth (which requires you to stretch your birth canal the customary five kilometres) – then ending with the menopause. Then just when everything goes quiet, what happens? *You grow a beard*. Is that fair I ask you? Yes, for the female of the species it's probably a case of laugh or ... your mascara runs.

Men always say that women can't tell jokes. Of course, this might be because we marry them. But perhaps one of the reasons men don't want to admit that women might be funny, is because they're terrified to think what it is we might be being funny about. Boys, to put you at your ease, let me just say that on our all-girl gatherings, we don't just talk about the length of your appendages.... We also talk about the *width*, which, after childbirth is much, much more important.

So, as you can see, basically I just write down the way women talk when there are no men around.

But the trouble with writing humorously is that it's so subjective. What one person finds funny, another finds fatuous, which can lead to some reviewer Rottweilering. And when it comes to criticism, if there were an Olympic Games for Hypocrisy, comic writers would win Gold. A glowing review, and we're sycophantic with praise – 'Critics! So perspicacious! Such literary taste and discernment!' Feelings explode in you like champagne. I once had a glowing review printed on a t-shirt and wore it for weeks. Hell, I had to be restrained from getting it tattooed onto my forehead.

But when we get a *bad* review critics become no better than pond scum. 'Critics! Ugh! Cyborgs that eat human flesh are less alien than book reviewers!'

There's no need for a printed t-shirt now as you're running away to Goa to live naked in a hollowed-out tree with Lord Lucan and Bin Laden. You begin to understand that there is a very fine line between book reviewing and homicide. Thoughts of murder cross your mind. The only thing which stops you is the hideously unflattering prison uniform. Although, you find yourself thinking, after a drink or two, at least the stripes are vertical, which would be vaguely slimming....

When you bump into a critic who has savaged your work, a few responses occur to you simultaneously: (1) Why can't you see her lobotomy scar? (2) How the hell does she fit her cloven hooves into those Prada shoes? But I suggest you simply shake his or her hand then say something like: 'It's really courageous of you to risk coming into contact with me *after the diagnosis*'.

That said, all writers need some constructive criticism – especially if you're writing comedy. How do you know if it's funny? My very scientific and high-tech test is to make an observation at the dinner table. If my female friends laugh, I write it down. But, it's pointless being precious about your material. I learnt this when writing a sitcom for Columbia Pictures in Hollywood. Lines, jokes and whole scenes were rejected on a daily basis. All those hugely successful television sitcoms such as *Seinfeld*, *Frasier* and *Friends*, etc are all actually written by about ten people. They lock you in a windowless room, which I use to call the 'gag gulag', where you make jokes all day. It's like being a stand-up comedian, except sitting down. The hilarious writing staff I worked with were all Jewish. I became so Jewish when I worked there – big hair, high shoes, talking with my hands – that I feel guilty that I'm not. But that hothouse atmosphere taught me that there is always a better and funnier line.

The best thing about being a comic writer is that people expect you to be immature and disorganised. This means you get to work in your PJs all day, drink heavily on the job and have affairs and call it research. But I principally became a satirist as it involves no heavy lifting. Except for those writers who lift whole sections of other people's work and then call it their own. But hey, you can't have all work and no plagiarism, right?

But if you really want to be a comic writer, your most important assignment is to think of a witty epithet. Spike Milligan's was: 'I told you I was sick.' I think mine will be: 'Finally – a good plot.'

Kathy Lette has written ten novels and two non-fiction books, the latest of which is *Men – A User's Guide* (Bantam Press 2010).

Notes from a successful fantasy author

Terry Pratchett gives pointers on how to write successfully in the fantasy genre.

Since a lot of fiction is in some way fantasy, can we narrow it down to 'fiction that transcends the rules of the known world'? And it might help to add 'and includes elements commonly classed as magical'. There are said to be about five fantasy sub-genres, from contemporary to mythic, but they mix and merge and if the result is good, who cares?

If you want to write it, you've probably read a lot of it – in which case, stop (see below). If you haven't read any, go and read lots. Genres are harsh on those who don't know the history, don't know the *rules*. Once you know them, you'll know where they can be broken.

Genres are also – fantasy perhaps most of all – a big bulging pantry of plots, conceits, races, character types, myths, devices and directions, most of them hallowed by history. You're allowed to borrow, as many will have done before you; if this were not the case there would only ever have been one book about a time machine. To stay with the cookery metaphor, they're all just ingredients. What matters is how you bake the cake: every decent author should have their own recipe and the best find new things to add to the mix.

Word building is an integral part of a lot of fantasy, and this applies even in a world that is superficially our own – apart, say, from the fact that Nelson's fleet at Trafalgar consisted of hydrogen-filled airships. It is said that, during the fantasy boom in the late Eighties, publishers would maybe get a box containing two or three three-runic alphabets, four maps of the major areas covered by the sweep of the narrative, a pronunciation guide to the names of the main characters and, at the bottom of the box, the manuscript. Please ... there is no need to go that far.

There is a term that readers have been known to apply to fantasy that is sometimes an unquestioning echo of better work gone before, with a static society, conveniently ugly 'bad' races, magic that works like electricity and horses that work like cars. It's EFP, or Extruded Fantasy Product. It can be recognised by the fact that you can't tell it apart from all the other EFP.

Do not write it, and try not to read it. Read widely outside the genre. Read about the Old West (a fantasy in itself) or Georgian London or how Nelson's navy was victualled or the history of alchemy or clock-making or the mail coach system. Read with the mindset of a carpenter looking at trees.

Apply logic in places where it wasn't intended to exist. If assured that the Queen of the Fairies has a necklace made of broken promises, ask yourself what it looks like. If there is magic, where does it come from? Why isn't everyone using it? What rules will you have to give it to allow some tension in your story? How does society operate? Where does the food come from? You need to know how your world *works*.

I can't stress that last point enough. Fantasy works best when you take it seriously (it can also become a lot funnier, but that's another story). Taking it seriously means that there must be rules. If *anything* can happen, then there is no real suspense. You are allowed to make pigs fly, but you must take into account the depredations on the local bird life and the need for people in heavily over-flown areas to carry stout umbrellas at all times. Joking aside, that sort of thinking is the motor that has kept the *Discworld* series moving for 22 years.

Somehow, we're trained in childhood not to ask questions of fantasy, like: how come only one foot *in an entire kingdom* fits the glass slipper? But look at the world with a questioning eye and inspiration will come. A vampire is repulsed by a crucifix? Then surely it can't dare open its eyes because everywhere it looks, in a world full of chairs, window frames, railings and fences, it will see something holy. If werewolves as Hollywood presents them were real, how would they make certain that when they turned back into human shape they had a pair of pants to wear? And in *Elidor*, Alan Garner, a master at running a fantasy world alongside and entwined with our own, memorably asked the right questions and reminded us that a unicorn, whatever else it may be, is also a big and very dangerous horse. From simple questions, innocently asked, new characters arise and new twists are put on an old tale.

G.K. Chesterton summed up fantasy as the art of taking that which is humdrum and everyday (and therefore unseen) and picking it up and showing it to us from an unfamiliar direction, so that we see it anew, with fresh eyes. The eyes could be the eyes of a tiny race of humans, to whom a flight of stairs is the Himalayas, or creatures so slow that they don't see fast-moving humanity at all. The eyes could even be the nose of our werewolf, building up an inner picture of a room by an acute sense of smell, seeing not just who is there now but who was there yesterday.

What else? Oh yes. Steer clear of 'thee' and 'thou' and 'waxing wroth' unless you are a genius, and use adjectives as if they cost you a toenail. For some reason adjectives cluster around some works of fantasy. Be ruthless.

And finally: the fact that it is a fantasy does not absolve you from all the basic responsibilities. It doesn't mean that characters needn't be rounded, the dialogue believable, the background properly established and the plots properly tuned. The genre offers all the palettes of the other genres, and new colours besides. They should be used with care. It only takes a tweak to make the whole world new.

Terry Pratchett OBE has written 37 novels in the *Discworld* series, the last 33 of which have all reached No 1 in the bestseller lists, the latest being *Unseen Academicals* (Doubleday 2009). He has written 50 books and co-authored about 50 more. His novel, *Nation*, for young adult readers, was adapted for the Royal National Theatre and staged over the 2009 Christmas season. The fourth *Tiffany Aching/Discworld* young adult novel, *I Shall Wear Midnight*, is due to be published in autumn 2010. He was knighted in the 2009 New Year's Honours List 'for services to literature'.

Notes from a successful crime author

Mark Billingham shares his experiences of writing success.

I am a writer because I'm a reader. That I'm a *crime* writer, however, is probably down to a desire to get free books… I'd always written stuff of one sort or another: silly stories at school, terrible poetry at university, so-so plays for community theatre companies. I'd drifted into a career in stand-up and writing comedy for television but my passion as a reader was for crime fiction, primarily of the darker and more disturbing kind.

Devouring the work of my favourite writers from both sides of the Atlantic was firing my imagination, feeding my head and heart, but as I had also developed an obsession for collecting the first editions of these authors, it was doing very little for my bank balance. My wife made the choice quite a simple one: get the books for free or get a divorce.

I'm still amazed at how easy it was – how little time and effort was involved. A couple of phone calls to the publicity departments of several big publishers, a bit of blather about how I was reviewing for my local paper, and suddenly the books came tumbling through the letterbox: package after package carried manfully to the door by my less-than-delighted postman. I did indeed start to review for my local paper and soon I was writing longer pieces, then articles for national magazines, and it wasn't very long before I was asked if I'd like to interview a couple of crime writers – this was major!

I can vividly remember the enormous and terrifying thrill of interviewing such crime-writing giants as Michael Connelly and Ian Rankin, and I still get a secret buzz from the fact that I can now count them among my friends. (This, for me, remains one of the greatest pleasures in becoming a published writer; that if you're lucky, those whose work you've admired for many years can end up propping up bars with you in exotic countries at ungodly hours…) So, I was a reader who adored crime fiction, who was lucky enough to be writing *about* it and who, occasionally, talked to those who actually *wrote* it.

Writing it myself, however, at the time seemed completely out of the question. Talking now to unpublished writers, I discover that such terror at the thought of sitting down and writing a novel is hugely common. Some of them are like housebricks for heaven's sake! Now, I tell those as daunted as I was then, that if you write 1000 words a day for a month, you're more or less a third of the way through a novel. It all sounds terribly straightforward of course, but it certainly didn't feel like that as I began trying to write my own crime novel.

One of the most common pieces of advice given to aspiring writers is to read, and it was at the point of starting what would become my first book, that I saw just how important this was. I was writing in an already overcrowded genre, and having read a great deal within it (or should that be *around* it?) I had a pretty good idea what not to write – that is, I knew those areas to which claims had already been successfully staked by others. Having decided therefore that my detective would not be a deerstalker-wearing cocaine fiend, or an Edinburgh-based Rolling Stones fan, I tried quite simply to write the sort of crime novel I enjoyed reading. I always imagine that such a stunningly basic notion would be obvious to all those who want to write. However, I'm constantly amazed to meet those claiming to have studied the industry carefully and to have spotted a sizeable gap on the bookshelves. Those who announce confidently that the world is finally ready for the crime-fighting antique-dealer/amateur veterinarian who, while not cooking and listening to opera, cracks tough cases with the help of a cat, in the mid-18th century Somerset countryside. If this is really what you're driven to write, then all power to you, but if you simply try and fill what you perceive to be a gap in the market, you're on a hiding to nothing.

I fully believed myself to be on a hiding to somewhat less than this, when I picked half a dozen agents from the *Writers' & Artists' Yearbook* and sent off the first 30,000 words of my novel. From this point on in the career path of almost any published writer, luck will play a part, and I must confess that I had more than my fair share of the very good sort.

Being taken on by an agent is wonderful, and if you're very fortunate, you will be taken on by a good one. Getting published is one thing but it helps if that publisher has enough faith in the book to spend a decent amount on marketing it – an amount so much more important than your advance. My still incomplete manuscript landed on all the right desks, and it was while in the incredible position of having to choose between agents, that I received the single best piece of advice I was given, or am able to pass on. Don't imagine that things are going well. Imagine that they are going badly. Imagine that *nobody* wants to publish your book, that the rejection letters come back in such numbers that the Royal Mail lays on special deliveries. When that happens, who will be the agent who will give you up as a bad lot, and who will be the one willing to fight? Which one will say 'well, if *they* don't want it I'm going to try X'? This is the agent to choose. In the course of any writer's life, a good agent, not to mention a good editor, will probably need to show more than once that they aren't afraid of a good scrap.

As far as further advice goes – beyond the encouragement to read and to write something every day – it is important to remember that lies (white or whoppers) and luck (of both kinds) may play a disproportionately large part in the way things turn out. Oh, and if you could avoid writing crime novels about a north London copper with a weakness for Tottenham Hotspur and Hank Williams, I'd be very grateful.

However, one small drawback to getting published and finding yourself trying to produce a book a year, is that you suddenly have far less time to read. This is hugely upsetting, and in my case doubly ironic considering that, with requests for reviews and endorsements, I now get more free books than ever. In fact, the only person unhappy about the way things turned out is my postman.

Mark Billingham is the author of an award-winning series of novels featuring London-based Detective Inspector Tom Thorne, the latest of which is *From the Dead* (Little, Brown), due to be published in 2010. He has also worked for many years as a stand-up comedian but now prefers to concentrate on crime writing, as those that read the books are not usually drunk and can't throw things at him.

Notes from a successful romantic novelist

Jane Green offers guidance on how to write successfully in the romance genre.

I never thought I wanted to be a romantic novelist. Quite apart from the fact it always makes me think of that sketch from *Little Britain* with a Barbara Cartlandesque pink-clad grande dame lying on a chaise longue eating chocolates, if I wanted to write anything I wanted it to be something more, well, *serious*. I wanted to write the great novel of our times, be feted by reviewers in *The Times*, rub shoulders with Ian McEwan and Kate Atkinson at parties, as we all bemoaned our sales whilst secretly delighting in our being shortlisted for the Orange prize.

I was an avid reader, always happiest as a child with my head buried in a book, and luckily, surprisingly for me, I found my voice very early on. It was the same voice I had used for years writing features for a national newspaper and it emerged again in my first novel, *Straight Talking*.

I didn't think about how to write, I wrote the only way I could, and it wasn't the great literary novel of our times, wasn't a book that could do anything other than sniff the Orange prize in passing, but it was enough to get me straight onto the bestseller lists.

That first novel came out shortly after *Bridget Jones's Diary*, giving birth to a new, explosive genre, a sub-genre of the romantic novel: 'chick lit'.

Romantic novels, and chick lit specifically, bring to mind many things, not all of them good. When I ask people what they expect of chick lit, they tell me a light tale of a single twenty-something living in a city and looking for Mr Right. They tell me they can always recognise chick lit because the covers are invariably pink and feature a pair of legs and designer shoes. Sometimes that's true, but more often than not it's very, very wrong. Today's romantic novel is a well-written and accurate reflection of the modern woman, with all her strengths and insecurities. It isn't always funny, but it always has an emotional honesty that resonates with real women, any age, anywhere.

Romantic novels deal with love. But not always, and certainly not in the way they used to – the days of Mills & Boon muscled heroes sweeping damsels in distress off their feet as the waves crash over their tanned and gorgeous bodies are long gone. The romantic novel of today reflects real life. It deals with relationships. Marriages. Friendship. Adultery. Mothers-in-law. Stepchildren. Loss. We've been told that chick lit is dying for over ten years, yet nobody's saying the same thing about our film equivalent, the romantic comedy, and chick lit doesn't seem to be going anywhere, just perhaps growing and changing as our readers grow and change.

Mostly, the romantic novel deals with life, funny, sad, difficult, poignant, and for us romantic novelists, inspiration is never far away.

I wrote my first book when I was in my late twenties, single, and fed up with all the awful relationships I'd had. Oddly enough, my first book dealt with a girl who was single, in her early thirties (I had to use *some* artistic licence) and fed up with all the awful relationships she'd had.

Ten years on I have moved continents, been married, had four children, divorced, remarried, and run the gamut of life in between, all of which has been reflected in the stories I tell and the books that I write. None of them are my story, but all of them are a piece of me, and all my books deal with issues that are affecting me, or the friends who surround me.

Which would be my first piece of advice for writing a romantic novel? Write what you know, not what you think will sell, and not a story that deals with an emotion with which you are entirely unfamiliar. I once read a novel about loss that was one of the most beautiful and real books I had ever read. I scoured the internet for interviews with the author, convinced she must have suffered the same fate as her heroine, and although she hadn't lost her husband, she had experienced grief: she knew what she was writing about.

There are certain skills you need to be an author and certain more specific skills required for a romantic author. Discipline is first and foremost for any author, any genre. Even now, after ten novels, I still find it far easier to procrastinate than to sit down and write. I have a routine of writing in the mornings while the children are in school. I used to work from home, thinking my writing each day took around eight hours, but it wasn't until I started writing at my local library that I realised it took, in fact, closer to three. The rest of the time was spent surfing the internet, compulsively buying things from strange websites that I neither wanted nor needed, welcoming phone calls from friends, and gardening.

Discipline is needed when you reach the point in your novel, or perhaps the several points, when you sit back and sigh, thinking, 'I just can't do this anymore'. Twelve books in, it still happens to me with every book. It would be so much easier to stop and give in to writer's block, but I plough through and write even when I don't feel like it, force myself to sit and finish my page, even when I have no idea what to write.

You need resilience to deal with initial rejections. The first agent I sent my book to wrote back to say she thought the characters were immature, the plot unrealistic, and the work 'frankly, unpublishable'. I sank into such a deep depression I almost stopped writing entirely. I'm glad I didn't. When I finally sent it out to other agents, they all phoned to say they loved it.

Enlarge your life. The more people you meet, the more things you do, the more inspiration will strike. Towards the end of my first marriage, just after I had written *Life Swap*, I felt my world had got very small and I truly worried that I didn't know what else to write about. My unhappiness was such that I had closeted myself away, living the solitary, isolated life you might expect a writer to lead, but not a life that serves a romantic novelist well. We need people. We need to be out there. We need to watch, listen, observe. We need to keep an open mind and have the humility to understand, to see things that other people might not see, to look at situations from every angle, to try and keep the big picture in mind.

Humility is a huge part of the creative process. My agent swears that every time an author rings him up and announces that the latest novel is the best one they've ever written, his heart sinks and he knows it's rubbish.

Luckily I don't have that problem. I think every book I write is ghastly until it's been read and validated by my publishers. Apparently this is a much healthier way to write. Nerve-wracking though, I'll admit.

Speaking of agents – you need one. I feel enormously lucky to have an agent who is so much more than the person who runs my business life. He is my mentor, my friend, the person I trust perhaps more than any other. He has my best interests at heart, and doesn't hesitate to jump in if anything in the publishing process is not as it should be.

Publishers are too inundated to take notice of an unsolicited manuscript these days. You need an agent, and you need a good one, one that the publishers will know, one that will get behind your book. Look for an agent who has a reputation, who represents authors you like, authors you know. An agent tapping away on a computer in a bedsit in Brighton with no authors to her name is as good as no agent at all.

Don't bother sending anything until your book is finished. Anyone can come up with a great idea, anyone can start a book, but few actually finish. Although you only need to send three chapters and a synopsis to an agent, it is so much better to have the finished manuscript on hand should they want to see more. It proves you can close a deal, and makes you more marketable in the eyes of the publishers, most of whom prefer to sign a two-book deal, to invest in someone with whom they have a future.

Another don't: as tempting as it may be to have everyone you know and love tell you what a genius you are, don't give it out to all your friends and family to read, nor take on a freelance editor. Everyone will have a different opinion, and too many cooks do indeed spoil the broth. Sadly Aunt Maisie loving your story does not a bestseller make.

Writing has been my life-saver many a time. It has been not just my job, but my passion, my catharsis, and my joy. It has lifted me up when life has not gone as planned, and helped me escape into another world, a world where you can be anyone you want, where happy endings are always possible, where anything can happen. And just as art so often imitates life, particularly in the genre of romantic fiction, sometimes life will imitate art, and the fairytales you write about may just end up coming true for you too.

Jane Green Warburg, who writes as **Jane Green**, is the author of many bestselling novels including: *Jemima J*, *Life Swap*, *The Beach House* and, most recently, *Girl Friday*. She lives in the USA with her husband and children.

Notes from a successful historical novelist

Bernard Cornwell shares his experience of writing successful historical novels.

You are going to get things wrong. None of us mean to, but we do. There were no rabbits in King Arthur's Britain, which I knew, but a helpful reader (there's always a helpful reader) wrote to tell me there were no snowdrops either. Got that wrong.

So, how to write an historical novel? The real question is how to write a successful novel and I know only one answer. Story, story, story. You are *not* an historian, your job is to be a storyteller. If you set out to educate folk then you will probably bore them. Your job is to entertain them, and the way to do that is by telling a story. If your ambition is to inform readers of the intricacies of the Elizabethan religious settlement then be honest about that ambition and write a non-fiction history. But if you want a bestseller then devise a story with Jesuits in the shrubbery, secret chambers behind the linenfold panelling and the flames of Tyburn waiting for the tale's climax. Then, having written that book, write another with the same main characters. Write a series.

Why a series? Because the sales of the tenth book, or the twentieth, will encourage the sales of the first and the second and the rest. Series do not go out of print like standalone novels. I began to write because I had fallen in love with an American woman who could not come to live in Britain, which meant I had to emigrate to the United States. The fly in that romantic ointment was that the American government refused me a work permit, so I airily told my bride-to-be that I would make a living by writing novels. That was 27 years ago and we're still married and I'm still writing, so it was not so desperate an idea as it seemed at the time. Yet it was desperate and, before emigrating, I sought advice. Peter Wolfe, a friend and the owner of his own publishing company, took me to lunch and told me never, never, to attempt fiction. He would not publish fiction. 'The market's too crowded,' he told me. So what do I do?, I asked him. You write a book, he said, called *My Friend the Cocker Spaniel*, a book full of good advice on how to raise, feed and exercise a Cocker Spaniel, and wherever puppies are sold and wherever dog food is sold and, indeed, wherever books are sold, *My Friend the Cocker Spaniel* will be on sale. He saw an objection coming and raised a hand to stop it. Once you've written *My Friend the Cocker Spaniel*, he continued, you go through the manuscript and you cross out the words Cocker and Spaniel and replace them with Dachshund. You have now written a second book called *My Friend the Dachshund*. Then you cross out Dachshund and put in Scottish Terrier. You get the idea. You write a series. I took that piece of Peter's advice even if I ignored his well meant injunction to avoid fiction.

I wrote historical fiction because I wanted to, because I liked it and because I was not capable of writing non-fiction. But I still needed help, so I did something which, in retrospect, seems obvious, but which very few aspiring writers actually do. I set out to learn how successful historical novelists wrote their books. I used three books: two of them were *Hornblower* novels by C.S. Forester and the third was *Imperial Governor* by George Shipway (an excellent and undervalued writer). I then disassembled those books. If you wanted the world to beat a path to your door by making a better mousetrap then the first thing you would do is discover how existing mousetraps work. You would take them apart, learn their secrets, and set out to do better. I am not saying I did better, but I did take those three books apart. I made huge charts which showed, paragraph by paragraph, where there was dialogue, where there was action, where there was flashback, where there was romance and so on. The charts revealed a structure. I did not slavishly copy the structure – indeed one reason to make the charts was a determination to use less of the things I disliked (flashback) and more of the things I liked, but when I found myself in difficulties with my first two or three books the charts were there to show me how successful writers had tackled the same problems. The answers to a lot of aspiring writers' problems are as close as the bookshelf. Use it.

Kurt Vonnegut once offered a splendid piece of advice. Every book starts with a question – a question the reader probably didn't know they wanted answered but the search for that answer is what will pull the reader through the book. That's the story. But too many historical novels begin by establishing a world. I have just finished the third in my series of novels around Alfred the Great and his successors, and once the book was done I discovered I could tear 9,000 words out of a 10,000-word first chapter. Those words were delivering information I thought the reader needed but they slowed the story to a crawl, so they had to go. I don't know if pacing a story can be taught, or whether it is an intuitive thing, but I do know that pacing needs work and, even after 43 novels, I still have to do that work.

Can writing be taught? I have a thoroughly old-fashioned view of this, which is probably founded on prejudice rather than on informed opinion, but I do know writing is a solitary vice and believe that it is best practised in solitude. Writing can be encouraged, perhaps, but taught? To teach something implies there is something to be taught and that suggests that the activity can be reduced to, if not rules, maxims. But there are no rules except to tell a story. I have met dozens of folk who belong to writers' groups or pay for writing courses but the chief activity of both seems to be criticism and I am not sure criticism helps aspiring writers whose confidence is frail. Only three opinions matter. The first is your own. You write for yourself. You write the books you want to read. The second opinion which matters is that of the professional gatekeeper, whether agent or publisher, and their views on writing differ hugely from the folk who teach it. The third vital opinion is the reader, and on that your success depends. I accept that I probably do not understand creative writing courses. None was available when I was an aspiring author so I managed without. Writers I admire tell me such courses can be helpful, so I shall merely say that the majority of successful writers never submit to them. Draw your own conclusion.

The most frequent questions I get are about research: how do I do it? How much time do I spend on it? The questions are virtually unanswerable. I assume no one writes historical fiction unless they first love history, and so virtually all your reading is research. I still read more history for pleasure than any other kind of book. Of course research has to be focused, but the real danger is doing too much research. If you are writing a novel about Jesuits in the Elizabethan shrubbery then you need to know a lot about the religious settlement, about social life and probably clothes, but do you need to know about Tudor farming practices? Maybe you do, but you will discover that need as you write the book – and a great deal of research is done while the book is being written. To believe that you must equip yourself with an encyclopaedic knowledge of the Tudor world before you begin writing is to guarantee you won't begin. Get on with it! Tell the story! The gaps in your knowledge will show up soon enough and there will be time to fill them. On the other hand, doing too little research has obvious dangers and can also deprive you of good story ideas. I'm currently writing a new *Sharpe* novel which is set in Cadiz in 1811 and I discovered, in an extremely dry and academic history of the diplomatic relations between Britain and Spain, a reference to the fire-rafts with which the French had hoped to burn the British fleet in Cadiz Harbour. That single unexpected reference has already supplied 10,000 words of the new book. The whole plot for *Gallow's Thief* came from a single footnote in an academic history of crime and punishment. In the end you will have to decide how much research to do, but beware the danger of doing too much and so never starting the novel.

Then, having done the research, you must reject a great deal of it. There is a terrible impulse to put in everything, just to prove how much you know, but nothing kills an historical novel like long passages written straight from your notebooks. And sometimes you must reject the true history to make the story work. When I wrote *Sharpe's Company*, which was about the ghastly siege of Badajoz in 1812, I knew that no British soldiers had succeeded in penetrating any of the three breaches on the night of the assault. The feint attack worked instead and the major attacks were all failures. But the drama of the story was in those three breaches and, if Sharpe was involved, Sharpe would get through, so I changed the history. You have to confess such inventions in a note at the book's end because many readers rely on an historical novelist to teach them something about history. It is always a pleasure, of course, when history serves up a plot and a timeline that does not need changing, but history is rarely so generous.

Above all, have fun. You write because you want to, not because you're forced to. If you enjoy the story then your excitement and enjoyment will show in the novel. You are an entertainer, not an historian, so entertain. And remember the one immutable rule in a business without any rules – tell a story!

Bernard Cornwell is the author of more than 40 novels, most of them historical, of which the best known are the *Sharpe* series of books. He lives in Cape Cod, Massachusetts, with his wife.

Notes from a successful biographer

Claire Tomalin shares her thoughts about what writing a successful biography entails.

A good biography is driven by the curiosity of the writer, a passion to get as close as possible to understanding what is going on in another life. Anyone can write a biography, provided they are prepared to put in a lot of work: research, reading, travel and, more than anything else, thought. As much as I dare to, I write for my own pleasure. I am fired by curiosity, by following a thread here, a filament there. I want to explore the past as one might explore a foreign country. In the process, I want to educate myself, and there is no better way to do this than to research, and then attempt to write a book.

Researching a biography can be even more fascinating than reading a story someone else has imagined, because of the detective element. You follow a trail that may lead to a series of closed doors or dead ends or, if you are lucky, to discoveries that change a part or the whole of the perspective on a person or a period. The central figure of a biography may become a prism through which you view a whole society, a whole period.

I am not sure about rules for biography, but I believe you must like your subject. Better still if you fall in love with her, or him, because there has to be an element of obsession. Devoting several years or decades of your own life to thinking and writing about someone else's life is like being married. There are ups and downs, days when you are irritated or disappointed, others when you are delighted and surprised. And you have to keep at it. This is alongside your real life, which tends to get sidelined while the notional, biographical marriage takes up increasing energy and space. Biographers do occasionally choose to write about someone they loathe and produce a hymn of hate, and that must be obsessive too. It is not something I would attempt. Serious dispassionate studies of monsters such as Stalin and Hitler are something different again, and make up a special category, requiring particular historical skills and iron nerves.

In both historical and literary biography it is important to create the world around your subject, both the physical and the intellectual. Context matters as much as character, and a biography that skimps on it is thin and unsatisfying. You need to let your reader see the houses, landscapes and cities, hear the noises in the streets, know what was being joked and argued about, how children were reared at the time, how people took their pleasures, how they wore their clothes and hair, what they disapproved of, what excited them, what they were ready to fight for, how the social classes interacted – and so on.

So you need a jackdaw mind, ready to search and pick about in many subjects – politics, painting and sculpture, topography, psychology, sociology, the theatre, fashion, military and naval history, medicine. For most of my books I have found myself in the Wellcome Library of Medical History, finding out about the illnesses of my subjects – from Katherine Mansfield's gonorrhoea to Pepys's kidney and bladder stones – and I have corresponded with physicians and surgeons, all wonderfully instructive and entertaining. You have to be a bit cautious too, because retired doctors enjoy making posthumous diagnoses and may get carried away (like the one who recently became convinced that Thomas Hardy and his wife had syphilis).

You must master the handwriting of your subject and other members of her/his circle. Carry a magnifying glass with you to help you with the tricky bits, and try copying, which

I find helps me to learn a hand. It gets easier as you go on. You must also find your way about archives, county records, libraries and museums, parish records and the public record office – plus websites and Google. Sadly, many archives are now on microfiche, fiddly to use and cruelly hard on the eyes. When I was working on Pepys [*Samuel Pepys: The Unequalled Self*] I thought I was going blind myself – luckily I was wrong.

You should do your own picture research. You should also suggest the order of the illustrations and caption them yourself, so interestingly that they will make a hesitant browser in a bookshop into a buyer. The advice came to me from my first editor, the late Tony Godwin, and I have followed it strictly. This is the journalistic side of your work, not to be despised.

You need academic skills too. You must write down all your sources carefully and legibly – book, volume, page, manuscript reference number, etc. – as you go along, and keep them in a safe place. When I wrote my first book I was innocent of this, and it took me a long time to check my sources after I thought I had finished, returning to the British Library and other archives to do the work again. There was one reference I could not find, and naturally this was the one readers kept asking me about. Now I always put sources on my computer next to the quotation or fact as soon as I get back from a research trip – if you use a laptop you can do it at once. And never fail to back up! Another piece of advice from a scholarly friend: always read through and check quotations in your text at proof stage, to make sure you have copied them exactly, and indicated cuts. Sometimes there is no correct answer to a question. Hardy called his novel *Tess of the D'Urbervilles* in some editions and *Tess of the d'Urbervilles* in others, and reference books continue to give both: whichever you use, somebody will write pointing out your mistake.

If possible, visit the places where your subject lived, and walk where he or she walked. The historian Richard Cobb advised me to go on horseback, or at least on a bicycle, when researching subjects who lived before modern transport arrived, so as to see the landscape as they experienced it. He also told me I should make sure to search archives where there might just possibly be something of interest, however unlikely it seemed. Following his advice, I wrote to the town archives in Le Havre, which had been bombed flat in the Second World War, to ask if they had a record of the birth of Mary Wollstonecraft's daughter Fanny in 1794. Two weeks later an official envelope from the archivist arrived with a photocopy of Fanny's birth certificate (for '*le vingt cinquième jour Floréal l'an second de la république française*') which no one, it seemed, had looked at for nearly 200 years. It also certified that her parents were married, which they were not. I nearly cried with joy and tenderness for that little *Françoise*, who certainly never saw her own birth certificate.

Researching Mrs Jordan, I searched for material by writing to as many of her descendants as I could track down – she had 13 children – and found letters written by her sons in the first decade of the 19th century. The first batch were in a fairly remote country house, and their owner kindly brought them out in a dusty box in which they were crumbling away – I had arrived just in time. In a still more distant location there were other letters, and superb portraits of her I had never seen or heard of. More material surfaced after the hardback was published, with letters and portraits appearing as I went round giving talks about it, and successive editions of the paperback crammed in these extra discoveries. Biographies don't die, they become your life companions.

They also bring you friends. While researching Katherine Mansfield I was able to visit her friend Ida Baker, then in her nineties, living alone in a cottage in the New Forest, almost blind and very deaf, for a precious conversation about her memories. The discovery of an unknown short story by Mary Shelley in Italy took me to a 100-room house in San Marcello Pistoiese in the Apennines, still lived in by the great-granddaughter of the little girl for whom Mary Shelley had written her story. They were an enchanting family and greatly generous to me.

Not all research is so adventurous or such fun as this of course. There are long hours of tedious work, disappointments and moments of horror when you find that someone else is working on the same subject and is due to publish their book six months before yours. Since there is nothing you can do about this, you have to take it as calmly as you can. But do everything possible to avoid the double review, a dreadful thing which compares and contrasts your two efforts and is usually dull and likely to kill both books stone dead.

You will never write a definitive biography, because such a thing does not exist. New material appears, attitudes change. The best you can hope to do is approach your subject in good faith. There will always be things you don't know and can't find out. For me, the constraints of biography are part of the attraction, the tug between the known and the unknown, the fact that you have to accept that there are multitudinous gaps in what you know and which your narrative must deal with. One absolute rule must be that, when you speculate, declare that you are doing so, and give the grounds for your speculation – otherwise you are writing romantic fiction, not biography.

You may make money from a biography if you are lucky, but I doubt if that is the usual first reason for writing one. It occurs to me that we embark on the study of other people's lives for the same reason we read fiction, go to plays or watch films: to get the feeling of being inside another skin. As Katherine Mansfield wrote, 'one life is not enough'. And there is much more to it than that. It is a journey on which you explore another century, enlarge your understanding, perhaps do justice to a forgotten figure, and with any luck cast light on the variety of human activity and achievement. An Oxford academic complained recently that a biography was 'nosy', but I would say it is a condition of intelligent human beings to be curious about other lives – to be just that, nosy.

Claire Tomalin worked in publishing and then journalism for many years, becoming literary editor first of the *New Statesman* and then of the *Sunday Times*, which she left in 1986 in order to write full time. She is also the author of *The Life and Death of Mary Wollstonecraft*, which won the Whitbread First Book Prize for 1974; *Shelley and His World* (1992); *Katherine Mansfield: A Secret Life* (1988), *The Invisible Woman: The Story of Nelly Ternan and Charles Dickens* (1991), which won the NCR Book Award for 1991, as well as the Hawthornden Prize and the 1990 James Tait Black Memorial Prize for Biography; *Mrs Jordan's Profession* (1995); *Jane Austen: A Life* (1997); and *Several Strangers* (1999), a collection of reviews and personal memoirs. *Samuel Pepys: The Unequalled Self* (2002) won the the Samuel Pepys Award and the 2002 Whitbread Book of the Year award. Her most recent book is *Thomas Hardy: The Time-Torn Man* (2006). She has edited selected *Poems of Thomas Hardy* (2006), *Poems of John Milton* (2008) and *Poems of John Keats* (2009) for Penguin Classics. She is currently working on a life of Charles Dickens.

Notes from a successful travel author

Bestselling travel writer William Dalrymple explains the rise of the travel genre and gives guidance on how to write a travel book.

In the summer of 1973 a minor American novelist named Paul Theroux asked his publishers if they would be interested in a book about trains.

Trains mean travel – a travel book: it was a novel idea (at least in 1973) and the publishers liked it. In fact they liked it so much they gave Theroux an advance, his first, of £250. *The Great Railway Bazaar*, an account of a journey from London Victoria to Tokyo Central, was published in 1975. None of Theroux's novels had ever sold in any quantity. But the *Great Railway Bazaar* swiftly sold over 1.5 million copies in 20 different languages.

The book did more than revive Theroux's flagging literary career: it kick-started what was to be the most important publishing phenomenon of the 1980s. The success of *The Great Railway Bazaar* inspired Bruce Chatwin to give up his job on the *Sunday Times Magazine* and to head off to South America. The result – *In Patagonia* – was published in 1977, the same year Patrick Leigh Fermor produced his great masterpiece, *A Time of Gifts*. By the early 1980s Eland Books were busy reprinting the great 19th century travellers and Thomas Cook had announced its Travel Writing Award. Soon the travel sections in bookshops were expanding from a single shelf at the rear of the shop to a wall at the shop front, flanking fiction.

Two decades later, however, after several hundred sub-Therouxs have penned rambling accounts of every conceivable rail, road or river journey between Kamchatka and Patagonia, the climate has changed from enthusiasm to one of undisguised boredom. Travel writers have found, to their alarm, that Theroux's feelings have increasingly been shared by the critics. The reaction has yet to filter down from the book pages to the bookshops: the likes of Bill Bryson, Tony Hawks and Dave Gorman continue to dominate the bestseller lists. But what is certain is that travel writing has lost some of its chic.

This backlash is not the end of the line. But now that everyone travels, writing travel books is a much more difficult business than it used to be, and while it's still fairly easy to write a travel book, to write a *good* travel book now takes real ingenuity. However fluent or witty your prose, it is simply no longer enough just to jump on a train: writers have had to dress up their journeys in some pretty fancy packaging if they want to be taken seriously. Certainly your proposal must be that much more spectacular than it used to have to be.

The travel book is potentially a vessel into which a wonderfully varied cocktail of ingredients can be poured: politics, archaeology, history, philosophy, art, magic – whatever. You can cross-fertilise the genre with other literary forms: biography, or anthropological writing; or, perhaps more interesting still, following in Bruce Chatwin's footsteps and muddying the boundaries of fiction and non-fiction by crossing the travel book with some of the wilder forms of the novel. The result of this tendency has been a crop of one or two rather wonderful books by younger writers: Katie Hickman's travels with a Mexican circus (wonderful idea), William Fiennes's quest for the snow goose or Jeremy Seal searching Turkey for the anthropology of the fez. Perhaps the best hybrid travel book is John Berendt's immensely successful *Midnight in the Garden of Good and* Evil – the book is half travel writing and half murder mystery, but wholly enjoyable. Below are some hints on how you can get into print.

The concept

These days you need some pretty fancy packaging – it's simply not enough to go off and write a book about travelling through France or Russia or Bolivia; it's certainly not the time to start putting in proposals about taking a dustbin cart to Borneo or a pogo stick to the Antarctic: the killing off of the Gimmicks School of Travel Writing is one of the more happy results of the recession (although Tony Hawks's hilarious parody of that sort of book, *Round Ireland with a Fridge*, is of course one of the bestselling travel books of the last few years).

To write about a country in a very general and unfocused way you have to be very good: Thubron can do it. But you have to be very good indeed to write a getting-into- the-soul-of-a-country travel book. An easier, less ambitious and more commercial option is the Relocation Book – about setting off from London or New York and building a new life for yourself in Tuscany, Spain or Provence. Peter Mayle's *A Year in Provence* kicked off a fashion for travel books of this sort and was followed by ex-Genesis drummer Chris Stewart's Andalucian memoir, *Driving Over Lemons* (and its sequel *A Parrot in the Pepper Tree*) and Frances Mayes's *Under the Tuscan Sun*, all of which got little critical attention but nevertheless turned into major bestsellers.

There is also a more serious strand of travel writing that aims to delve into the soul of a city: my own book on Delhi, *City of Djinns*, was written in the tradition of studies of remarkable cities such as Jan Morris's classic, *The World of Venice* and Geoffrey Moorhouse's wonderfully apocalyptic *Calcutta*.

If falling in love with a small fragment of the globe is as good a starting point for a travel book as any, then other passions can also provide a good take-off point. I think it's fair to say that to be a really interesting travel writer you've got to have some small obsession: Ryszard Kapuscinski loves revolutions and watching dictators fall; Redmond O'Hanlon likes birds, beasts and exotic diseases; Bruce Chatwin was on the lookout for ideas and for nomads. I don't think it really matters what your interest is – stamp collecting, train-spotting or whatever – as long as it's genuine and you can convey your enthusiasm for it, you've probably got the seed of a travel book in there.

The research

If your book is to have any sort of authority, a card index is a very useful tool for keeping track of your research. For my last two travel books, I kept two card indexes: one with anecdotes and references listed under places and one listed under themes. So for *From the Holy Mountain* one index contained a list of places I expected to pass through on and around my projected route (Istanbul, Aleppo, Damascus, etc.) and the other a list of potential themes, which grew as I read (magic, monks, ghost stories, miracle stories, etc.). So, when I came to write about a place or a theme, I had to hand a long list of the best stories I knew associated with each place.

Travel book shortlist

There is no better way to learn how to write travel books than simply to read other travel books. My own personal shortlist of the great travel books would include:

The Road to Oxiana by Robert Byron

Behind the Wall by Colin Thubron

Into the Heart of Borneo by Redmond O'Hanlon

Midnight in the Garden of Good and Evil by John Berendt

In Patagonia by Bruce Chatwin

The journey

Everyone goes about writing a travel book in a different way. I can only speak for myself when I talk of technique: for me the biggest mistake was to try to keep a logbook when I was exhausted at the end of the day. I think it is absolutely vital to have a notebook in your hands, always, and to scribble constantly: not so much full sentences, so much as lists of significant detail: the colour of a hillside, the shape of a tulip, the way a particular tree haunts a skyline. Creating fine prose comes later – back at home in front of the computer. On the road – even in a rickety bus or a bumpy jeep – the key is to get the raw material down before it is lost to memory.

Noting down dialogue is especially important – it's the key to any half-decent travel book and you simply can't remember the exact words even half an hour later, never mind at the end of an exhausting day. The travel writers I really admire all keep exceptionally detailed notes: Theroux, Thubron, Chatwin. So the first golden rule is: get it down. If you can't write down dialogue immediately, or openly, find some stratagem to get around the problem. I know one travel writer who, when in customs posts and police stations, pretends to have a bad stomach in order to keep disappearing to the lavatory to note dialogue, as doing it openly would be inadvisable.

Dialogue is the heart and soul of modern travel writing, for if 19th century travel writing was principally about place – about filling in the blanks of the map and describing remote places that few people had seen – 21st century travel writing is all about people: exploring the extraordinary diversity that still exists in the world beneath the veneer of globalisation. As Jonathan Raban once remarked: 'Old travellers grumpily complain that travel is now dead and that the world is a suburb. They are quite wrong. Lulled by familiar resemblances between all the unimportant things, they meet the brute differences in everything of importance.'

The second golden rule is to be open to the unexpected. Often one can set oneself a task – perhaps to go and search out some aspect of a particular place – and not notice good material if it's not what one is looking for at that moment. For example, in 1990 I went to Simla to interview two 'Stayers On' who had lived in Delhi in the 1930s and would, I hoped, be able to recreate the lost world of the Raj for me. In the event, however, I arrived ten years too late: both the ladies had gone badly senile and now imagined that they were being persecuted by prostitutes who popped up from beneath the floorboards and put dope in their food. I failed to get anything at all usable about 1930's Delhi, and left the old ladies feeling disappointed that I had wasted an afternoon. It was only later when I told my wife Olivia about the meeting that she pointed out that the bizarre afternoon would in fact make an excellent sequence in itself. It duly became one of the very best – and much the strangest – sections in *City of Djinns.* If the art of travel writing is at least partly about spotting the significant moment and discarding the irrelevant, then you have to be constantly alert.

In the same way, you often come across the best stories when you least expect them: when you've ticked off your interviews and visits for the day and settle down to have a drink in a bar or eat dinner. So often its exactly when you close your notebook and settle down to relax that you stumble across the most intriguing characters and funniest anecdotes.

A final rule: when you are taking notes, make sure you try to capture all the senses. When you write about a place, don't just give a physical description of somewhere: try to capture significant sounds and smells and the physical feel of a place. Also how your body responds to a particular location: in a hot climate, the roll of perspiration down the forehead, the grit of sand in your shoes, the grind of cicadas or the smell of frying chillies can recreate a sense of place much more immediately than a long physical description.

The same is true of building up a character: the way someone smells, or the timbre of their voice can help visualise a person much better than a lengthy physical description. Most important of all is dialogue: a well-chosen snatch of conversation can bring a person to life in a single sentence.

The writing

Everyone has their own rhythm. When I'm steaming away actually writing a book – a process that takes me anything between six months and a year – I tend to be unusually disciplined: getting up early, finishing email and chores by 8.30am and at my desk writing by no later than 9.30am. I break for lunch, go for a walk and then come back and go through a printout of the morning's work at teatime, and continue correcting and planning the next day until 7ish. My wife Olivia is incredibly good at telling me when what I have written is boring. If your partner is no good at this, find a friend who is. Going over and over and over a piece of prose until it is as perfect as you can make it is as important as anything else in the formation of a book.

Evocative travel writing

Here are some of my favourite examples of exceptionally good evocations of place or people:

- For a short and perfect evocation of a city look at Bruce Chatwin's description of Buenos Aires at the beginning of *In Patagonia* (p7)
- For a totally different approach – as wonderfully purple as Chatwin is sparse – see Patrick Leigh Fermor's description of walking through a German winter in *A Time of Gifts* (pp117–8)
- For bringing a character to life in a single page, take a look at John Berendt's description of the Lady Chablis in *Midnight in the Garden of Good and Evil* (pp96–8), or two passages by Bruce Chatwin in *In Patagonia:* the hippy miner (p54) and the Scottish farmer (pp66–7)
- See also Eric Newby's famous description of the explorer Wilfred Thesiger on pp246–8 of *A Short Walk in the Hindu Kush.*

The selling

Find an agent for this: never try to do it for yourself. If you know any writers, however distantly, ask them for an introduction to their agent. Otherwise, look in the literary agents section (page 473) of this *Yearbook*. Send the agent a well-written covering letter asking whether they would like to look at the finished manuscript, plus a four- or five-page synopsis of the plot together with a short biographical paragraph about yourself. During the 1980s it was possible to get book contracts and advance payments before you had actually written your travel book but these days that is less and less likely to happen, and the writing of a book is by its nature a big financial gamble. Only go ahead with the project if you are really passionate about it. But if you have something to say, don't despair and don't let early rebuffs from agents or publishers put you off: if you can make it work, travel writing is one of the most enjoyable and stimulating ways of life imaginable – especially when you're young and single and able to leave home for great chunks of the year. Go for it!

William Dalrymple was born in Scotland and brought up on the shores of the Firth of Forth. He has written many award-winning and bestselling books including *In Xanadu*, *City of Djinns* and *The Age of Kali*. He has also written and presented documentary series for television and radio. In 2002, William was awarded the Mungo Park Medal by the Royal Scottish Geographical Society for his 'outstanding contribution to travel literature'. His latest book, *Nine Lives: In Search of the Sacred in Modern India*, was published by Bloomsbury in September 2009.

The growth of travel guidebooks

Alex Hamilton holds up a mirror to the many faces of travel guides.

Aside from weddings abroad, any romance in guidebooks is largely incidental and has little to do with the final text, but 25 years ago Martin O'Brien left his job as travel editor of *Vogue*, went round the world and studied romance on the other side of the mirror (in a word, prostitution) in 21 cities, and published a book called *All The Girls* (Macmillan). That would be too many for anybody except perhaps Simenon, but O'Brien stuck to it, from Leningrad to Las Vegas, Caracas to Sydney, Hawaii to Budapest, and all stations to Reno. It was written rather as a sequence of adventures, a *bildungsroman*, than a guide for tourists, but if anyone plans a series to corner the guidebook market to international harlotry, O'Brien's is the marker.

The kind of guidebook to destinations we most commonly use was pioneered in the second century AD by Pausanias with his two-volume *Guide to Greece*, which took him 14 years of travel and detailed research to complete. In Peter Levi's modern translation, with his copious footnotes, 'this ancient Baedeker' (as Penguin call it) is still a wonderful companion to classical Greece – direct in its description of places and buildings, and irrigated with a thousand background stories, mythical and historical.

It's not known whether Karl Baedeker of Koblenz knew his Pausanias, but he did have German thoroughness. Beginning in 1827 as a small-scale tour operator leading short Rhine cruises, he produced his first guidebook for Rhine customers in 1832, and thereby almost accidentally came across the foundation of his company's fortunes. The profitability of guidebooks that matched the exponential increase of tourism during the 19th century outweighed tour earnings for Karl and his son.

The name Baedeker became synonymous with guidebook, even though some fakes such as *Argentina* (a marvellous copy of the style) pretended to be Baedekers. Londoner Bernard Shapero, at 25 the youngest member of the Antiquarian Booksellers Association, made a corner in Baedekers in the 1990s, estimating 5,000 collectors worldwide, a score of them fanatics willing to pay £2,500 and more for rare first editions such as *Athens* (1909). One of these, a German dentist, was closing in on the complete set of 1,100 Baedekers in all editions. Shapero had 1,500 Baedeker books on sale. 'Stick to Baedekers in English' he advised me, 'and the average pocket can cope'. The rarest are those of the 1840s and 1850s – if the plain paper cover survives, the price inflates. As with Pausanias, it's a special taste to travel with an obsolete guidebook.

Baedeker's contemporaries

Baedeker's British rival was publisher John Murray, who had Lord Byron as one, sort of, travel writer (see his exhilarating letters, and *Childe Harold* for travel in verse) and Byron's companion Hobhouse (*Journey Through Albania*) as another. The start of Murray's guidebooks, hugely successful with Victorian wayfarers, came in 1820 (when the first cross-Channel service began) with Mariana Starke's *Guide for Travellers on the Continent.* The series did so well that John Murray the Third combined business with pleasure and wrote several of the 165 titles himself. The winning streak lasted over a century, but today the publisher confines its travel to authors admired for their prose, such as Trevor Fishlock and Patrick Leigh Fermor.

The other key figure was Thomas Cook, who began in 1840 in a small way like Baedeker with cheap temperance excursions, but whose son John Mason Cook had such grand ideas that he did not flinch from conveying 18,000 British and Egyptian soldiers, 800 whalers and 130,000 tons of stores in a campaign designed to rescue General Gordon at Khartoum. (The expedition arrived late and failed to save Gordon, but that was the army's fault, not Cook's.) The history of the company is sprinkled with curious adventures, from one-off jollies to royal occasions and spellbinding scenes with film crews on exotic locations. Publications were a relatively slight part of the business, though for their own customers Cook's regularly created 'handbooks' – predecessors of modern brochures – which were demanding exercises, but occasionally a lifesaver for freelances willing to intoxicate themselves on gallons of marketing cliché.

Thomas Cook today has a separate branch for standard guidebooks (325 titles in print) and has expanded in the last four years with online support for new series: *City Spots*, *Hot Spots* and *Driving Around*. These are bundles of new and updated titles in fashionable small formats and are currently being rebranded as *Pocket Guides*. Recent successes include *Egypt and the Red Sea* and, unexpectedly, *Sarajevo*, because when British Airways revived the route it put a copy on every seat. However, the grand old durable among Cook guides is the annual *European Rail Timetable*, first issued in 1873.

The modern outlook

A modern guidebook begins to die as it goes to the printer and, as publishers realise, needs updating every two or three years. So, authors of 30 or more titles can find themselves endlessly renewing them, a regular income for the author but not as stimulating as the first voyage of discovery. (The pay for an update will be around a quarter of the initial advance – £17,000 then £5,000 is high – and generally on a flat fee rather than a royalty base.) Some professionals fix on a few destinations or themes as their life's work and make each book in consecutive editions their own. Others become part of a publishing team, with the individual fractions of their experience or research cobbled together by their firm's editors. Worldwide guidebook specialist Lonely Planet, founded postwar with a single title by a married couple of backpackers, developed a culture of young enthusiasts eager to doss in the cheapest places in the remotest spots, and now has more than 200 would-be contributors on its files. In 2010, out of 500 guides in print, its bestselling title in the UK was (as usual) their evergreen *Australia*: the 15th edition took Lonely Planet's total sales past 100 million.

The other significant initiative for people who liked to be independent of tour operators was the foundation in 1982 of Rough Guides, by Mark Ellingham. The writers were not afraid to express the down side of some places they visited and their tone made a fresh breeze through the stilted medium. Some of the early group of editors and authors were experienced in agency work, which gave them a no-nonsense approach well suited to the new younger generation of travellers. Published originally by Routledge & Kegan Paul, and later by Harrap Columbus, they are now in the Penguin group. To celebrate 25 years in business they have 25 new titles, each focusing on 25 varieties of 'Ultimate Experience' – neat and glamorous in style – *Journeys, Islands, Wonders, Ethical Travel*, as well as destinations – and a contrast with the black-and-white densely packed pages of their early series.

The modern eagerness to spend very little on travel may well have its origin even earlier than the Lonely Planet initiative. In 1945, at the end of his shooting war, an American army sergeant called Arthur Frommer found the chance to explore his surroundings, and put his notes together to write and publish *Europe on 5 Dollars a Day*. The invitation appealed to so many cash-strapped people in the postwar years that it led to further books, so many that today at 80 he is a consultant for Frommer Books, owned by Wiley, an American firm with more than 260 employees. The guidebooks haven't the verve of that first work, but they encompass a very broad perspective, including places where $5 wouldn't buy you a glass of water.

Cadogan Guides and the American MPC Guides are generally well written and local-culture conscious, and printed on heavy gloss paper that makes them easier to read than carry. Some of the Insight Guides are heavier still, due partly to their fondness for lovely pictures. Legend explains this strength/weakness as due to the ambition of its founder: Hans Hoffer, a German photographer who was frustrated by the lack of outlets for his pictures and in 1970 created his first guidebook to compensate. The firm now has a reduced list of 120 main titles, but because of the increasing preference of tourists for pocket books, they are backed by 200 editions on a lesser scale. *Dubai* is currently much in vogue, a challenge to guides. Less likely was their overall bestseller *Hawaii*, as common a title in America as *Paris* is in Europe. This was partly due to an Hawaiian hotelier who, like British Airways, gave a copy to every guest. *Australia*, *New Zealand*, *Puerto Rico* and *China* are also riding high. Normally a book earns its living within three years, selling 15,000–18,000 copies. In 2002, Insight acquired Berlitz's phrase books business, a trusted brand with 150 titles that average 40,000 copies a year.

The AA began publishing in 1990 and has 900 titles in print, half travel guides and half maps and atlases. (However, nothing on the scale of Millennium's huge world book of atlases, shown at the 2007 London Book Fair, priced £1,998.) By contrast, the AA sells more pocket guides (27% of the market) than any other firm. In a presently inauspicious outlook for all travel publishers, the Euro zone suffers while North Africa (Morocco, Egypt, Tunisia) looks up. At home the AA is developing 'Points of Interest' downloadable onto the Satnav – closest hotels, restaurants and pubs – and 'Days Out' for museums, pets, etc., such that bookings can be made from the car.

Grand ideas

The most ambitious guidebook project, a heavyweight literally and culturally, was created in 1993 by the late Pierre Marchand for the Gallimard Presse. It had an investment of £52 million, planning 200 titles, half of them on France, and to date has produced 150. In its first year they sold 17 million copies in 30 countries – five million in five years of *New York*. Marchand, who left school at 14, was a passionate autodidact, and organised a team at the publishing HQ to collate the work, often written in a crabby hand and musty style, of scores of local specialists and librarians and retired profs devoted to their own neighbourhood. Encyclopedic and massively illustrated, the books reflected Marchand's idea that his guides' first public should be educational, with tourists the second phalanx, but he did acknowledge that guides need tourists as much as tourists need guides. At the outset there was a chance that in the UK Dorling Kindersley would collaborate with their own Eyewitness Guides, but DK felt that tourists came first and eventually produced a similarly handsome series, filling the tourist's need to 'hit the ground flying' with an immediate set of options. These now come from Everyman, another Penguin imprint.

For addicts, however, the title 'daddy of them all' should go to *The South American Handbook*. Actually, it's a mere 87 years old (though founded on *The Anglo-South American*

Handbook, ed. W.H. Koebel, 1921). It was designed in 1923 as an annual to help in particular those 'commercial travellers' who took steamships to the neglected continent to work in communications, meat production, coffee, wood and domestic items like Panama hats. Its foreword ran through the attractions of ports of call *en route* (warm clothing for five days, tennis gear thereafter) via Le Havre, Oporto (passengers conveyed ashore by rowing boat), Lisbon, Madeira (landing by launch), St Vincent (vital to the cable company), the Azores, Bermuda, the Bahamas, Hispaniola (prospects of a large increase in Haitian agriculture), Barbados, Puerto Rico and Trinidad.

It canvassed major items of the economy, listed government ministers, advised on sport (limited to hunting, shooting and fishing) and a few hotels. In general it read like a sixth-form geography book. Its importance was shown by carrying about 500 advertisements, a custom long since lost to guidebooks. In 1930 it changed the company name to Trade and Travel Publications, until in the 1990s it blossomed out into scores of handbooks, with the colophon Footprint. The company calculates selling 8,000 copies of a handbook 'washes its face'. A unique feature of *The South American Handbook* (now 1,560 pages of 'bible paper') was that users saw it as their own and their tips along the decades gave it formidable breadth and strength. The tradition is kept up: hundreds of people who volunteer useful advice are credited (and buy a copy).

Starting out

Many guidebooks from the 25 leading outfits (out of more than 400 that include travel) are written by multiple hands. Their commissioning editors observe that the contributors' reward has to be the exotic experience rather than money. This is the common view among most firms, large or small (such as the independent Bradt Guides, delighted to sell 15,000 of *Ghana*, latest leader *Uganda*, but content if a new book does 4,000). Many professional travel writers supplement slim earnings from guidebooks by contributing to newspapers and magazines. Travellers are natural optimists – as professionals they must be. They bear in mind not only the problems of competition with staff journalists, pressure from travel advertising, and increasingly sophisticated free material on the internet, but what seem like threats to the business itself in the anxiety over climate change and airport security. Travel writers should reckon the effects on tourism and how to be part of a healthy solution. 'Literary' travel, incidentally, makes up a bare 11% of the total travel book turnover, with an average return of some £3,000 per title, and is a market dominated by half a dozen well-established bestsellers that in a year or two pass 100,000 copies, and go on.

Writers starting out on travel might think the world is now their parish, but veterans would dissuade them. Don't specialise in the world, they'd say, but in subjects you can get your head round, like cycling, spas, haunted hotels, film sites, writers' houses, travel painting, unexplained phenomena, hobby jazz, boutique cruise liners, cargo ship travel, crazy holiday ideas ... Move on later to more competitive areas: consumer protection, food and wine, climbing, cruising, shopping, travel with children, travel with mature people, cheap flights, best beaches... and now, ecotourism. All these and more are offered by members of the Guild of British Travel Writers (an average of 250 who, to belong, must earn more than half their income from travel writing). And don't neglect the updates.

Alex Hamilton is an award-winning travel writer and was for 15 years travel editor of the *Guardian*. He reckons a 'Guide to guidebooks' would be a Herculean task.

Notes from a successful non-fiction author

Simon Winchester shares his experiences of writing success.

The research is all done, the reading is complete. Files have been pored over, archives have been plundered. Those Who Know have been consulted. That Which Was Unknown has been explained and one fondly prays, made clear. I am, in consequence, or so I hope, now fully steeped in facts and awash with understanding. The book I have been planning for so very long is at last all in the forefront of my mind – structure, content, tone, pace and rhythm are all there. What now remains is simply – would that it were *simply* – to write it: 100,000 words, says the contract, due in just 100 days.

I live on a farm in the Berkshire Hills of western Massachusetts, and I have a small and ancient wooden barn, 100 yards or so from the main house. I have furnished it with books and a long desk on which are a variety of computers and two typewriters, one manual, the other electric. The farm is where I live. The barn is where I work. Each morning, well before the sun is up, I leave the comforts of the farm and enter this spartan, bookish little universe, and shut the allurements of domesticity behind me for the day. For a 100 days, in fact: for a 100 identical days of a solitary, writerly routine that, for me at least, is the only way I know to get a book properly and fully written.

Inside the barn I tend to follow an unvarying routine. First, as the dawn breaks, I spend two hours looking back over what I wrote the day before: I examine it with what I hope is a sharp and critical eye, checking it for infelicities of language, impropriety of grammar, expanding the inexact, refining the imprecise, making as certain as I can the minutiae of fact and detail. Only when I feel satisfied (never smug) that what I have on the screen represents as good a first draft as I can offer do I press the *print* button on the keyboard, and a few pages of A4 slither into the out-tray. Once that task is done I leave the barn and walk through the early sunlight back to the house for breakfast. I read the papers, drink enough coffee to kick-start both mind and body, and, at nine exactly, I head back again, this time to write for real.

I have a word counter at the top left of my computer screen. Purists may object, but my newspaper days have left me with deadline commitment, and this is the way that I like to work. Whenever I begin a book I set the counter with the start date, the number of words I have to write, the contract date and a very simple calculation – the number of words needed each day to meet the deadline. One hundred days, 100,000 words: 1,000 words each day is the initial goal. But things change: the writing life is imperfect, however noble the intentions. Some days are good and maybe I'll write 1,500 words, while others are much less satisfactory and, for a variety of reasons, I may write virtually nothing. So the following day's necessary word total will rise and fall depending on the achievement of the day before. It is that figure my system obliges me to set the night before that I'll see on my screen when I arrive in the cold dark before dawn: 1,245 words needed today, with 68 more days before the deadline? So be it.

I sit down, arrange my thoughts and hammer away without stopping for the next six hours – each day from nine in the morning until three in the afternoon. This is the solitary pleasure of writing – total concentration, pure lexical heaven. I write on, oblivious to everything around me. Except that I do know when I have done my six hours – because by the time the mid-afternoon is upon me, the sun will have shifted to the window in front of my desk, and in wintertime I have to suffer an uncomfortable hour or so of the sunset's glare. This gives me a perfect excuse to end this second stage of the day and to go off to do something quite different: a run along my country road, usually, followed by tea. By then it is six or so, the sun has fully set and the glare has been replaced by twilight glow. Then I return, for the day's third and final phase: planning for the next day.

I go back to my desk and arrange the papers, books and thoughts that I think I need for the next day's writing. Then I close down the computers – having been sure, of course, to have made the necessary calculations and set the counter to tell me how many words are due on the morrow – and walk back to the house. For a while I try to forget about the book (though I never can). I have dinner, go to a movie, have friends round – and am in bed, invariably, by midnight.

The next day it begins all over again. As before, I spend the first two hours of the morning looking back over what I have written in those six sunlit hours of the day before. As soon as I have tinkered and tweaked, I press *print*. I stack the A4 sheets neatly on the pile from the preceding day. Millimetre by millimetre, day by day, the pile grows taller and thicker, looking ever more substantial. In the first week it has the look and feel of a newspaper essay; after ten days or so, a magazine article; by a month, it's an outline, then chapter, a monograph, a dissertation – until finally, on one heaven-sent morning, I pick up the pile of paper and it has heft, weight and substance. And then it all changes.

The dream has been made solid. The former featherweight piece of ephemera has been transformed by time into a work-in-progress, a book-in-the-making. After a precisely calculated number of sunrises and sunsets, after yet more walks between barn and farmhouse, after setting and resetting the counter a score of times, and after hours spent reviewing and re-doing and printing and piling and collating and collecting – there, suddenly, is a finished product.

The pile of printed paper and digital confection of finished text will now be placed in the hands of the publishers, who by mysterious dint of designing, printing, binding and jacketing, will in due course turn it into a full-fledged book. *My* new book. After 100 days it is ready to be offered to the world. As for its fate – well, there lies ahead of it what will seem a lifetime of hoping – hoping that it will be lucky, do well and be loved by all. The wish and the prayer of any new parent, who has taken time and care to bring a newborn into the world. But that, of course, is another story. This is just the writing. What follows next is the reading, and that is much less exact of a science.

Simon Winchester OBE worked as a foreign correspondent for the *Guardian* and the *Sunday Times* for 30 years before turning to full-time writing. He is the author of some 20 books, including *The Surgeon of Crowthorne*, *The Map that Changed the World*, *Krakatoa*, *A Crack in the Edge of the World* and *The Man Who Loved China*. His most recent book, *Atlantic: The Biography of an Ocean*, is due to be published by HarperPress in September 2010. He divides his time between his small farm in the Berkshire Hills of western Massachusetts and New York.

Notes from a successful MBS author

William Bloom reveals the trials of writing for the Mind, Body & Spirit market.

What's it all about? What's the meaning of life? What's my purpose? How am I meant to live? These Big Questions are at the heart of the Mind, Body & Spirit (MBS) movement and its books. Not surprisingly, the quality of answers ranges across a wide spectrum, from self-centred banality to wisdom. It was ever so with philosophy and religion.

Free of the pulpit and the university chair, yet attempting to wrestle with these core issues, the MBS movement – also known as New Age and holistic – is an easy target for critics who question its authority. As a popular movement it does not appear to have gravitas or roots or a secure intellectual method. It is also a very recent phenomenon. Just as each generation tends to decry the next generation's music, so philosophers and religionists do not like the look of this new creature in their territory. The glitterati, the media intellectuals, are also suspicious.

So, first things first, as an MBS author in the UK, expect no respect! Almost without exception, the book pages of the national media will not give you any space except perhaps to make some snobbish wisecracks. The media likes to make fun of New Age ideas. But far from being a small niche fashion, MBS is now a nationwide lifestyle approach, which the glitterati themselves may adopt when its design elements (e.g. feng shui) are attractive or its healthcare strategies (e.g. stress control using visualisation) are pragmatically useful. Reflecting this, most newspapers carry MBS sections where the focus is mainly on health and beauty, and with only the occasional foray into anything actually to do with the soul or spirit.

But why is there this scepticism in the media? After years of watching and receiving their gibes – I can think of several times when BBC radio producers have reassured me that it was going to be a friendly interview, only to be met by the usual sarcasm (even once for an obituary piece on the *Sunday* programme!). I interpret the cynicism as the anxious outrage of people whose own worldview and lifestyle are threatened. It is a clash of paradigms and cultures. The quick-witted, speeding, red meat-eating, boozing, smoking hacks do not want to examine how they themselves live or their fixed ideas about the nature of reality and consciousness.

The cynicism of Grub Street is not helped by the number of authors in the MBS field whose work is indeed flaky, opinionated and harmful. One example of these flakes, sometimes called New Age fascists, is the brigade that chants the 'you create your own reality' mantra and has the cruelty to tone it towards people with life-threatening illness or, even worse, children caught up in war and famine. These fatalists who suggest that dying children in sub-Saharan Africa 'chose their destiny' are often the same people who then go gooey-eyed at angels, fairies and spooks. Not surprisingly the cynics are outraged by these attitudes. But, if you are a would-be MBS author or publisher, you cannot help but notice that books on angels, spooks and creating your own reality are perennial sellers.

On the positive side, however, MBS material often initiates and supports the very best in holistic and integrative healthcare. For example, the increasing awareness of the relationship between emotions, diet, social tensions and health has been pioneered by MBS bestsellers such as Deepak Chopra and Louise Hay. The notion of self-managed healthcare is deeply embedded in the holistic approach. The philosophical connection between the concepts of sub-atomic physics and mysticism, the alliance of feminism and eco-spirituality, the inclusive recognition that all religious traditions share important core features – these valuable elements in today's culture have all been initiated and nurtured by MBS authors.

As a body of knowledge and cultural movement, MBS presents a general worldview that opposes, to one degree or another, mainstream traditional culture. From an MBS perspective, mainstream culture might be provocatively caricatured as patriarchal, uncomfortable with emotional literacy, devoted to a crude billiard ball model of the universe in which only the solid is real, and peculiarly narrow-minded when presented with any concepts that include altered states of consciousness, metaphysics or the notion of energy/vitality as an important force in human affairs. MBS presents a more fluid model of an interconnected, interdependent universe in which matter, energy and consciousness are aspects of the same spectrum and interchangeable.

No wonder that mainstream commentators may be suspicious. Their worldview is under attack. The ongoing paradigm war in healthcare between scientific fundamentalists and holistic practitioners exemplifies this.

To better understand the MBS field it is useful to place it in its historical context and see it as part of the democratisation of information. It is a cliché now to notice that a few hundred years ago enquirers into the meaning of life would have been severely restricted in their research. Predominantly illiterate and with travel so difficult, their enquiry would have been limited to local authorities. Priests and 'wise women' would have been sources of information and we can only guess at the quality of their answers. We can surmise that their responses would have been clothed mainly in their particular culture. There was no interfaith movement, nor much multiculturalism. To enquire fully into the big questions would have required literacy and travel, both scarce resources. Even if you possessed both, there was no centre of education that housed information on *all* the world's religious traditions and their techniques; nor for example was there a body of study which we now call psychology.

The mushrooming of literacy and communications since the 19th century has transformed that situation. Answers to the great questions can be found now in thousands of different sources. Over the last decades, for the first time in human history, the spiritualities, beliefs and philosophies of *all* cultures are now accessible. The sacred books of all traditions are available and there is at least one website that claims to provide the texts of all of them.

Teachings that were previously passed on one to one, teacher to student – such as tribal shamanic secrets or yoga techniques – are also now part of the public domain. The esoteric strategies of traditional faiths – for example meditation, visualisation, body posture and prayer – historically restricted to the mystics of those traditions, are also on public view.

This is no shallow revolution. Freedom of information has dismantled the dominating hierarchies of restricted information – in religion more than in any other domain of knowledge. Historically the power of religious organisations, of all faiths, was maintained by the claim that only an ordained few had access to the truth. At one level, in terms of literacy, this was indeed a horribly accurate statement. In terms of social status it was also violent and repressive.

MBS can, in my opinion, be seen as the cultural movement that is exploring and expressing this new-found freedom. All the old secrets are now on display. The dominance based on a monopoly of claimed truth or a monopoly of information is dismantled. The holistic movement is young and in its developmental stages. It is so young that it hardly even recognises itself, let alone takes itself seriously, which would be a good first step for a movement that wants others to take it seriously.

In this historical context of cultural upheaval, it is no wonder that traditional religionists survey this scene and decry the smorgasbord, the spiritual supermarket. The books and the general media offerings seem to offer no grounding in a stable community, a trustworthy tradition or a set of ethics.

Domains of MBS

- New Science
- Psychology
- Gaia – The Living Earth
- Holistic Health and Healing
- Feminism and the Goddess
- Shamanic and Magical Traditions
- Mystic and Esoteric Religion
- Modern Prophesy

To a degree these protests are justified. The inevitable forces of commercialisation and popularisation have indeed appropriated some precious spiritual jewels and bowdlerised them, sometimes beyond recognition. The dumbing down and smorgasbord aspects of MBS are easy targets. But that vulgarisation has always existed in the field of belief, from saints' bones and lascivious monks through to shrouds and cure-all snake oil.

The impression of being a spiritual supermarket is, when looked at more closely, a strength. One of the most positive features of MBS is its willing integration of many domains that participate in the enquiry for meaning. When I edited *The Penguin Book of New Age and Holistic Writing* in 2000, I organised these domains in a way that is still relevant (see box). In one form or another you will find similar sections, located close to each other, in most bookshops. What these books have in common is that they are all accessible to a popular audience and are not academic. Within each of the categories there are substantial bestsellers. Publishers, of course, are looking to repeat them. At the time of writing this article, authors such as Deepak Chopra, Neil Donald Walsh, Caroline Myss and Eckhart Tolle are performing strongly. In fact, one set of statistics suggests that Tolle has now sold more books than the Dalai Lama or the Pope. In the past, writers such as John Grey, M. Scott Peck and Louise Hay have topped the bestseller lists. As I mentioned above, there is currently a fashion for books on angels, spiritualist mediums, positive psychology and how to use the energy of thought for personal success. Previous flavours of the month have included subjects such as relationships, creativity, quantum physics, detoxing, past lives and energy medicine.

But in writing directly for the national media, authors need to pitch their pieces carefully inside the limits of what editors feel they can reasonably accept. The sarcasm of their colleagues and 'bad science' jibes can have a powerful censoring effect.

Is there a secret to success in this field? I once heard a cynical commissioning editor saying that the recipe for an MBS bestseller is to: (a) Tell people what they already know; (b) Wrap it up so that they think they are reading it for the first time; (c) Write it so that the reader feels intelligent for understanding the material and is therefore part of a cutting edge or spiritual elite. This means that pioneering authors, the originators of concepts, may be overshadowed by the more populist authors who transform original and unique material into a more accessible form. So another piece of advice for MBS authors seeking success is to not be original, but to develop the original material of others. (I am of course waiting philosophically for other authors to make a mint out of my work.) This, of course, is not always the case. Fritjof Capra's *Tao of Physics* and Daniel Goleman's *Emotional Intelligence* are good examples of bestselling and pioneering books.

So – as an MBS author, as in most literary fields, you have a wide range of options. You can offer your work as a flaky mishmash of half-baked truisms laid out on the supermarket smorgasbord of commercialised religion, psychology and philosophy. Or you can be part of an important cultural liberation movement in which adults, free of traditional prejudices and with an open heart and mind, are supported in exploring the most profound questions about life and its meaning.

William Bloom is one of the UK's most experienced teachers, healers and authors in the field of holistic development. His books include *The Endorphin Effect* (2001), *Feeling Safe* (2002) and *Psychic Protection* (1996), all published by Piatkus, and *Soulution: The Holistic Manifesto* (Hay House 2004). *Three Golden Keys* is due to be published by Piatkus in 2011. See more at www.williambloom.com.

Ghostwriting

It is possible for an unknown writer to make a living as a full-time ghostwriter. Andrew Crofts shares some of his secrets on how to do it.

Why do it?

The greatest problem facing any professional writer is finding a steady supply of ideas and subjects so dazzlingly certain to appeal to the book-buying public that publishers are eager to buy. Not only are saleable ideas in short supply, it also takes an inordinate amount of time to research a new subject deeply enough to be able to sell it successfully. You might spend months researching a subject from a number of different sources and still be unable to find a buyer.

One answer is to collaborate with other people who lack writing skills and experience but have good stories to tell, either as fiction or non-fiction, or possess all the necessary information to create a book.

These people can be found in a number of places. They might be celebrities, who would impress publishers because of their notoriety, or ordinary people who have undergone extraordinary experiences. Alternatively, they might be experts in subjects that the public want to know more about.

It's much easier for publishers to market books by celebrities or established experts than those by unknown writers. Apart from a handful of literary stars, few people buy books because of the authors' names, and the media have a limited amount of space in which to write about them. But if you write the autobiography of a soap star, controversial politician or sporting hero, the resulting book will be widely written and talked about in the media. While the author is spending several weeks being whistled around all day from breakfast television to late night television, the ghost can stay comfortably at home and get on with their next project.

The speed with which you can gather the information for a ghosted book means that you can produce far more publishable material in the course of a year than if you were researching each book in order to write them under your own name. Publishers are also willing to pay higher advances because they can see how they will market the book once it is written. Ghosting makes it quite possible for an unknown writer to make a good full-time living as an author. It also provides you with broad writing experience and helps you to build contacts in the publishing industry to whom you can then sell other projects of your own.

Of all the advantages that ghosting offers, however, the greatest must be the opportunities that ghosts get to meet people of interest. It's a licence to ask the sort of impertinent questions that you truly want to know the answers to, and to be allowed inside some of the most extraordinary stories.

Ghosting a book for someone is like being paid to be educated by the best teachers in the world. Imagine, for instance, being asked to ghost *The Origin of the Species* for Darwin, or *The Decline and Fall of the Roman Empire* for Gibbon; being paid to learn everything that is in their heads and then turning their thoughts, words and notes into book form. Could there be a better form of education?

How to start

The first step could be to approach people you would like to ghost for and offer your services. That might mean your favourite celebrities, who you could write to care of their agents or television companies. It might be people you have read about in the press and who you think have stories that could be developed into books. It's usually possible to find some way of getting a letter or email to them.

A more practical first step, however, might be to approach people who you come across in everyday life and who have an expertise that you think would be popular with a wider audience. If you've been on a course, for instance, find out if the trainer has thought of turning their message into book form. Would a garage mechanic who's good at explaining why your car isn't working be able to supply the material for a book on car maintenance? What about your doctor doing a book on healthcare for a specialist sector of the market? The options are endless.

Anyone who has access to a captive marketplace, like training companies or public speakers, has a ready-made market for books. There are companies who might want to produce books by their chief executives for distribution to employees as well as to the outside world and public relations departments who would relish the idea of getting their clients' messages to wider audiences.

If you're already a writer in another field, approach your existing contacts. A show business journalist, for instance, has access to actors and singers. A sports writer can approach sportspeople they've interviewed in the past. People will nearly always prefer to work with a ghost they already know and trust and feel they have a rapport with, than with a stranger.

At the same time as approaching potential authors, you should also be letting the publishing world know that you're available to work as a ghost. Write to the literary agents and publishers listed in this *Yearbook* to let them know what your experience is and how they can contact you. They will often have clients who they know are not capable of doing their own writing.

How to sell projects

It's unusual for any publisher to buy a book idea without seeing a synopsis and some sample material. Once you're experienced you will sometimes be able to charge for writing synopses, but at the beginning it's probably wise to offer to do it for free in order to get projects off the ground.

A synopsis must be a hard-selling document that gives the publisher all the reasons why they should commission the book. It might be worth preparing a one- or two-page version first in order to catch their attention and then a longer document (between 5,000 and 10,000 words usually suffices) in order to get the message across. It must give the publishers confidence that the book will be written to a high standard and delivered on time. It must be something that their sales teams can immediately see how to sell. Give a brief biography of the author and demonstrate how promotable they will be.

Involve a literary agent, firstly because most publishers don't like dealing directly with authors and secondly because the agent can handle all the money side of the relationship, removing potential conflicts between the author and ghost.

Whenever possible, have one good agent representing both parties in the arrangement. The agent's prime interest will then be in getting the book well published, not in encouraging the ghost and the author to fight one another for larger shares of the resulting royalties. The agent can also act as a conciliatory go-between should the relationship between author and ghost break down.

Who pays the ghost?

How the ghost gets paid will depend largely on how speculative the project is and on the wishes of the author. It might be that the author is sufficiently confident of the book's success to suggest paying the ghost a fee. How much that fee will be depends on what the author can afford, what they are willing to pay and what the ghost is willing to do the job for. In other words, it's open for negotiation.

If the project already has a publisher and there is no speculative work involved, then it may be that the publisher will suggest a fee. Then there will be little or no room for negotiation. Any writer starting out should accept any book that is offered, even if the money is low, simply in order to build up a track record.

Where there is no publisher involved at the outset, and the author has no money, then suggest splitting all the proceeds 50/50, which includes advances, royalties and foreign rights sales, serialisation fees and payments for film and television rights.

If the author is a celebrity and it's obvious the book will make a large amount of money the ghost might have to accept a lower percentage, or a percentage that will become lower once he or she has received a pre-agreed amount; for example the proceeds might be split 50/50 until the ghost has received £50,000, at which stage his or her share might then drop to 40%, and might then drop again at £100,000.

It would be unwise to write an entire book unless some money has been forthcoming, either from a publisher or from the author, but there are cases where even this risk is worth taking. With fiction it is nearly always necessary to write the whole book before any publisher will make an offer, making it a highly risky business. Go into it with your eyes open, knowing that it is closer to buying a lottery ticket than earning a living.

What skills does a ghost need?

Ghosts must suppress their own egos completely when working on an autobiography – a good discipline for any writer. You're fulfilling a similar function to a barrister in court, using your skills to plead the case of your client. Authors need ghosts who will not challenge them, but will simply listen to what they have to say and understand why they did what they did. If the ghost wishes to be critical of the subject then they must step back and create an objective biography, not an autobiography.

It is essential for the ghost to make the subject feel completely comfortable in his or her company. If they think the ghost is going to criticise them, judge them or argue with them they will not relax, open up or talk honestly. It's not the ghost's job to try to make them change their opinions about anything or anyone, but rather to encourage them to tell their story in the most interesting and coherent way possible. The ghost must be able to coax them off their hobbyhorses and persuade them to answer all the questions that the eventual readers are likely to ask. The author must not sound bitter. Part of the ghost's job is to ensure that the author remains attractive and interesting to the reader.

Once the voice is on tape the ghost then has to create what amounts to an 80,000-word monologue, just as a playwright might do, staying completely in the author's character at all times, using the sort of vocabulary the author would use and expressing the same views, ideas and prejudices.

It's important that a ghost is interested in the subject; otherwise the project will become unbearable. Imagine spending that much time talking to someone who bores you, and then having to go away and write it out all over again.

A ghost must also be able to see the structure of a book from early on in the process. He or she then needs to be able to guide the subject into providing the right material, keeping them on track and clearing up any inconsistencies in the telling of the tale.

The ghosting process

Sometimes the author has already produced some written material that can provide the bulk of the background. More often the ghost will have a clean slate to work from.

How many hours of taping will be required depends on how succinct the author can be persuaded to be and how quickly the ghost can master the subject. I find that 10–20 hours of useful taping is generally enough to produce a strong first draft. For autobiographies it's important to get them to tell you the story chronologically, so that you know what they have and have not experienced at each stage of the tale. The sequence can always be changed for dramatic effect once the actual writing commences.

It is usually preferable to interview them on their own home ground, where they will be at their most relaxed and least guarded. You will also get a better idea of what their lives are like.

The first draft should be shown to no one until the author has okayed it. They have final veto on what should and shouldn't be in the final draft. Only if they're confident that they have the final say will they be completely open and honest with you. The ghost can advise and warn, but the author has the last word. (Once given the power to make changes they nearly always decide they can't actually think of a better way of putting things and leave the manuscript virtually untouched). If there is arguing to be done, let it be done by the agent and the publisher.

A ghost must expect no glory. Enjoy the experience of the researching and the writing and of being paid to do pleasant work. Sometimes your name will get mentioned on the cover of a book and sometimes it will appear only on the flyleaf. Sometimes you will get a mention in the acknowledgements and sometimes you will not appear at all. You may get billed as 'co-author', but it is more likely to say 'By Big Shot with Joe Bloggs' or 'as told to Joe Bloggs'. It's always useful to have your name there but it can never be allowed to become a problem if it disappears.

Why publishers use ghosts

Publishers like to use ghostwriters because they know they will be able to rely on them as professionals. They want to know that the book will arrive on time in a publishable form, conforming as nearly as possible to the synopsis or the brief.

Frequently the authors of the books are busy people and hard to get hold of. Sometimes they are temperamental. The publishers consequently rely on the ghosts to act as go-betweens and to make the process of publication as smooth as possible.

The ghost is also the subject's best friend in the publishing business. During the long months when the agent is trying to sell the project and the phone doesn't ring, he or she will assure them that this is perfectly normal and doesn't mean they will never find a publisher. When the publisher wants to change the title or favours a cover in the subject's least favourite colour, the ghost will again have to be there to assure them that it will all be okay on the night. Then, when the book comes out and the subject can't find it on the front table in any of their local book shops, the ghost will have to explain the economics of the business to them and try to dissuade them from ringing the publisher and ranting and raving.

Ghosting is an endlessly varied, interesting and rewarding job – relish every opportunity you are given to practice it.

Andrew Crofts was described in the *Independent* as 'the king of modern ghosts'. He has published over 80 ghosted books, a dozen of which have been No 1 on the *Sunday Times* bestseller list. He is also the author of *The Freelance Writer's Handbook – How to make money and enjoy life* (Piatkus 2002) and *Ghostwriting* (A&C Black 2004). His website is www.andrewcrofts.com.

Books published from blogs

Scott Pack explains the reality of how blogs become successful books.

'Washington sex blogger signs $300,000 book deal'. 'I blog, therefore I am £70,000 richer'. 'Blogger wins six-figure book contract'. 'Blogger's book turned into major TV series'.

Those are the headlines. Here is the reality. Brace yourself.

Most blogs are rubbish. They aren't read by anyone and are poorly written. They stand as much chance of being turned into books as the authors do of becoming the Pope. The internet is full of mindless drivel and finding something that would make a bestseller is like searching for a needle in a whole field of haystacks.

I didn't say it was impossible though.

The world of blogging has exploded in recent years and many in publishing see it as the potential next great breeding ground for writing talent. Because of this, unpublished writers are increasingly putting their work online in the form of blogs in the hope of a book deal. Like any other route to print, a chosen few will find success; most will remain ignored. So is it worth bothering in the first place and, if so, what are your chances of being spotted?

The traditional publishing model, at least as it currently stands, has authors sending work in to agents. Agents sign up the manuscripts they think they can sell and then proceed to tout them round publishing houses in search of a tasty advance. Simple really. Of course, there is more to it than that and there are several variations on the theme but the bulk of new books published in the UK have taken that route.

And the truth is that most of the bloggers who have secured massive book deals have taken precisely that route as well. Blogging may be adding a new element to the world of contemporary literature, but it hasn't changed the face of publishing. At least, it hasn't yet.

You'd like to think in this day and age that editors spend loads of time scouring the web for the hottest new talent, one hand on the mouse, the other on the chequebook. In fact, most of them are far too busy publishing books to waste hours browsing the internet. They rely on others to do the browsing, filtering and touching up for them. And that is increasingly the role of the agent.

Agents are proving quite proactive when it comes to bloggers. Some of the more savvy ones are identifying blogs with a buzz behind them and approaching the authors with the lure of a possible book deal. But here's the thing. They aren't plucking these sites out of thin air, they are targeting blogs and bloggers that already have a big audience. Most of the successful bloggers with book deals put in a lot of time and hard work into their websites before they were signed up.

So don't expect to simply chuck up a couple of chapters of your first novel and then be inundated with offers from Penguin, Random House and HarperCollins. It ain't gonna happen. That doesn't mean you shouldn't do it. Getting your work online can be a great way to spread the word, find an audience and generate feedback. The simple discipline of writing every day, or a couple of times a week, can improve your skill as a writer. There is a lot to be said for blogging just for the sake of it. It is fun, it can be rewarding, and it might just be the start of something. But do make sure you go into it with realistic expectations.

And when it comes to expectations, it is probably best to ignore thoughts of a book deal altogether. Embrace the blogging form for what it is. Become the best blogger you can be. Offer your readers something different, entertaining and interesting. If you can please your audience then you have succeeded; anything else that happens is a bonus.

But what makes one blog stand out from another? How is it that some bloggers end up making a fortune and seeing their book top the bestseller charts while others languish on page 267 of a Google search? The answer is both simple and impossibly vague and is precisely the same when it comes to bestselling books – because people want to read them.

When you look at the more successful blooks (blogs turned into books) they aren't just versions of the blog cut and pasted into book form. In converting a blog to a book, authors and editors usually revert to a more traditional style of writing. Whereas blog posts tend to be episodic, and sometimes quite random in terms of content and running order, the best blooks have a narrative arc, they tell a story.

The experience of browsing a blog online is very different from reading a physical printed book and that is reflected in how they are put together. When an agent or a publisher identifies that a blog has book potential they are usually looking beyond the individual posts and focusing more on the quality of writing and the standard of storytelling, and they will have one eye on the size of the potential audience.

And the audience for the book is different to that of the online version. *The Intimate Adventures of a London Call Girl* by Belle de Jour is perhaps the most famous of recent blog-to-book success stories. The book has sold over 250,000 copies, the television series starring Billie Piper was watched by millions and it is a pretty good bet that the vast majority of those readers and viewers have never seen the blog upon which it is based at all. Publishers may be interested in your visitor stats and the fact that you have 1000 page views a day but they cannot create a bestseller by simply selling copies of your book to your blog readers. They need to take your concept and sell it to the masses. The concept is the key.

Which is why a piece of fiction posted online, no matter how great a work of genius it may be, is probably not going to appeal to a publisher as much as *One Red Paperclip*, the story of an American guy who, starting with a red paperclip, kept swapping objects until he ended up with a house. Blogs about sex and the intimate goings on of their authors, have been some of the most popular and successful blooks of late. That bubble may well be about to burst but, when it does, it will be replaced with some other titillating subject, not a sudden surge of million-selling poetry books or works of philosophy.

If you are serious about starting a blog then you can probably have something online in a matter of minutes, but it would pay to do a bit of research first. Check out other bloggers who write on a similar subject. What can you do that is different? Are there any design features that you like and would like to emulate? What do you think others are doing right or wrong? Create the sort of site that you would want to visit.

It also makes sense to participate in other blogs. Read as much stuff as you can online and leave comments when you feel moved to do so. Most comments you leave will link back to your own site and a witty and incisive note on someone else's blog may have dozens of people visiting yours. The internet is a community and can be, by and large, a friendly one. People who like your writing will mention it on their sites and the more active you are the quicker word will spread.

For most people blogging is not the way to the Nobel Prize for Literature, neither is it a route to fame and fortune. It is simply what it is – a way of getting your words online. If you have something worthwhile to say then people will probably read it. If you are a wonderful writer then readers will spread the word and your audience will grow. If you have an unusual, original or intriguing and exciting concept that someone in a position of influence thinks they can make some money out of then, and probably only then, will you hear from an agent or publisher.

Having said that, if you venture into blogging with the intention of getting a book deal then you will probably fail. If you start a blog because you want to write and share your work with an online audience then you can only succeed.

Happy blogging.

Scott Pack is Publisher at The Friday Project, an imprint of HarperCollins. His own blog can be found at http://meandmybigmouth.typepad.com/scottpack.

See also...

- *Writing a blog*, page 647
- *Marketing yourself online*, page 625

Notes from a literary editor

Claire Armitstead gives an insight into the role of a literary editor.

The morning greets me with a grey mail bag containing 20–30 books which jut out at angles, waiting to be shucked from their cardboard pods and stuck on to the shelves. This first daily arrival used to excite me but, though I still love the smell of new books, their relentlessness can be dispiriting. The sad truth is that, of the 400 or so books that are delivered to the office every week, fewer than 40 will make it into the review pages. As an Eeyorish colleague once mourned, 'Newspaper literary desks are where books go to die'.

The central part of any literary editor's job is working out which of these hundreds of hopefuls to despatch and which to spare for the next round. Some decisions are easy, but they are usually the outright rejections. The *Guardian's* Review is a high-end literary section, so we don't review many celebrity biographies. Nor do we do self-help books or the sort of potboiler fiction that tops the library charts year after year. Though we all have our quirks, there is quite a big crossover between the various newspaper review sections which means that thousands of the books published each year will never be reviewed in them. Perhaps surprisingly, none of us tend to review the books that sell the most, and even when we do – as the chief executive of a major publisher remarked recently – we make no impact on their sales (though in certain arenas, for example history, I would argue that good reviews can make all the difference).

But to quibble about the impact of reviews on sales is to miss the whole point of book reviewing, which is a complicated negotiation between the culture of writing and reading. The role of the newspaper books pages is not to sell books: it is to entertain, inform and stimulate readers, some of whom spend so much of their time keeping up with the newspapers that they have little time in their lives to actually read books at all. Review pages are part of the intellectual and imaginative life of the UK and – with the extra scope granted by Guardian Unlimited and other websites – increasingly beyond it.

The most obvious function of the review is to tell people whether a book is good or bad. But there is a whole spectrum between those two extremes, and this is often where the character and colour of the books pages lie. A book may be well written but essentially dull or, conversely, badly written but packed with fascinating facts. Reviewers can offer a digest of the stuff people want to know about. They can mediate and simplify, bringing an academic thesis into the language of journalism and placing it within the available reading time of an ordinary person's working day. This is particularly true of non-fiction reviews, part of the purpose of which is to give a potted version of the book. After all, a reader can be very interested in advances in quantum physics and very unlikely to get through *A Brief History of Time* by Stephen Hawkings.

Commissioning the reviews

Once the obvious books have been discarded, the literary editor needs to whittle down the dozens of more or less worthy contenders for the limited space available. At this stage, only hard discipline will do. The books are separated into original fiction and non-fiction, with a separate bookcase for paperback re-issues. There are three commissioning editors on my desk and we work on a 'buck-stops' basis: the buck for fiction commissioning stops with one editor, and for paperbacks with another. This is essential if the fantasy commissions of our brainstorming sessions are to translate into actual reviews. It does not mean that we are huddled away in our own little corners – on the contrary, the indefinable spark of a books desk depends on the hours that every editor is prepared to spend reading that marginal proof by an unknown writer on the bus home. The commissions I am proudest of are reviews of those completely unexpected gems that only emerge from the most conscientious scouting.

But there are logistical limits to this sort of eureka commission. There are only so many hours in a day to look for them; there is only so much money in the budget to pay people to do so. When I started this job eight years ago, the *Guardian* books pages were over-commissioned by 50%, which meant that for every review that was used, another one was 'spiked'. This unfortunate state of affairs reflected a particular moment in publishing history when the rate at which books were produced had sped up beyond the capacity of any one set of books pages to give a comprehensive account of them. The margins are much tighter now, which means that we are less wasteful but the criteria for selection have to be very clear.

We have space for eleven 200-word paperback reviews a week, so paperbacks are sent out to a regular roster of reviewers on a weekly basis. Big reviews of first editions are more tricky – I may know that we will carry an average of nine original fiction reviews and 10–11 non-fiction reviews, but until the review is actually in my hand, I can never be absolutely sure what it will be like – ecstatic, condemning, indifferent; even long or short.

This is where the job of a literary editor is closer to that of a news, rather than a features, editor. A features editor can set the agenda, simply by deciding how many words to commission on a subject and instructing a writer to write them. The job of review pages, in contrast, is to report on books – though the way in which this is done depends on a series of choices by the literary editors.

Placing the reviews

Once we have selected which books to send out, chosen a reviewer and taken delivery of their review, the next step is deciding where to place it and, just as importantly, what to place it with. For instance, nobody would want to read page after page of bad-tempered reviews (yet there are weeks when every piece that comes in seems to be disparaging). On the other hand, no one would trust pages in which every review was a rave. The challenge is to respect the opinion of the critic, while creating pages that have life and variety and which – in journalistic terms – 'talk to' each other. Occasionally, if I feel the reviews coming up are in danger of being too dour, I will commission a 'turn' review, with the specific intent of bringing a bit of showbiz to the pages (though the good turn review can have its own crunchy wisdom, as when Professor Terry Eagleton wrote of Beckham's memoirs: 'One suspects that David Beckham wrote this book rather in the sense that the Pharaohs built the pyramids').

This sort of playful commissioning cannot be done lightly – it relies on an advance intelligence that enables the editor to see opportunities that a single critic might not spot. The same is true of spotting patterns and trends in publishing. In the last few years, for instance, there has been a rush of books about happiness, the perspectives of which have ranged from historical to scientific and philosophical. Something more interesting is clearly happening than a dozen books with the same word in the title. More mundane, perhaps, is the fashion for calling everything a biography: in the past 12 months we've had biographies of food, of cities, of an ocean and even of the ordnance survey map.

Intelligence-gathering ranges from the diligent (the twice-yearly hack through all the publishing catalogues to compile a list of every upcoming book in the next season) to what might pass as mere partying (yes, publishers do still hold book launches, but no, they are not all about getting drunk and behaving badly). It is often at parties that the connections are made, and the hidden enthusiasms revealed so that, for instance, Paul Theroux ends up reviewing a book about bees. If I don't go out a couple of times a week, I don't feel I'm doing my job properly.

In the end, however, it all comes back to the solitary relationship between the critic and the book, and to the difficult negotiations between inside knowledge and independence, expertise and humility, seriousness and the willingness to entertain.

For a variety of social, historical and economic reasons, literary critics are regarded as more compromised than those in any other art form. There is some truth in this, if only because writers are always reviewed by other writers. There is none of the separation of crafts and industries that exists between, say, reviewer and actor or reviewer and concert pianist. Connected to this is the fact that there is no tradition in the UK of giving jobs to literary critics, as there is for other art forms, so most reviewers have 'day jobs' – usually their own writing, or some sort of teaching, both of which bring with them dependencies and compromises.

The most difficult part of the literary editor's job is steering a path between these conflicts of interest to that ideal reviewer, who will be knowledgeable but not compromised, and wise, reasonable and witty. But if it is the most difficult part, it is also the most important, because however much people love to hate critics – and however alienated the critic is from the culture of hype in which we now live – they are an essential part of the cultural ecology: the carrion birds, pecking away at mediocrity, dishonesty and rot and clearing a space for works of real quality.

Above every grey mailbag of books that arrives in the office sits a flock of invisible critics just waiting for the signal to plunge in their beaks. For that, we must all be profoundly grateful.

Claire Armitstead is the *Guardian's* literary editor.

Notes from a successful crossover author

Neil Gaiman explains how he 'learned to stop worrying and became a crossover author'.

I didn't set out to be a crossover author, it just never occurred to me not to be. To put it another way, what I wanted to be was the kind of writer who told whatever stories he wanted in whatever medium he wanted, and I seem, more or less, to have got to that place. So, I can tell you how I did it. I'm just not sure I could tell you how you could do it too.

My first book was a children's book. I was about 22 when I wrote it, and I sent it to one publisher, and it came back with a nice note from the editor saying that it wasn't quite right for them, and I put it away for ever. I was a journalist for a while (it would be accurate to say that all I knew of being a journalist when I began was what I had gleaned from the 1983 edition of the *Writers' & Artists' Yearbook*). Then I wrote comics – mostly for grown-ups – and once I'd learned to write comics to my own satisfaction and thought it might be good fun to go and explore prose fiction, I was spoiled. The joy of writing comics is that it's a medium that people mistake for a genre: nobody seemed to mind whether I lurched from historical to fantasy to spy stories to autobiography to children's fiction, because it was all comics – a freedom that I treasured.

I started writing my first real children's book in 1991, a scary story for my daughter, Holly, called *Coraline*. I showed the first few chapters to my editor at Gollancz, Richard Evans. Now, Richard was a good editor and a smart man, and had just midwifed a book by Terry Pratchett and me, *Good Omens*, into existence. The next time I was in the Gollancz offices he took me to one side and said, 'Neil. I read the *Coraline* chapters, and I loved it. I think it's the best thing you've ever written. But I have to warn you, it's unpublishable'. I was puzzled: 'Why?' 'Well, it's a horror novel aimed at children and adults,' he told me, 'and I don't think we could publish a horror novel for children, and I really don't know how anyone could publish anything for adults and children at the same time.'

So I put the book away. I planned to keep writing it, in my own time, but there wasn't a lot of my own time about, and I managed about a thousand words in the next few years. I knew that unless someone was waiting for it, unless it had a chance of being read, I wasn't going to write it.

By now I had published a couple of books with Avon, and I sent it to my editor, Jennifer Hershey. 'It's great,' she said. 'What happens next?' I told her I wasn't really sure, but if she sent me a contract we would both find out! She did. The contract was for about 5% of what I'd got as an advance for my last novel, but it was a contract, and Jennifer said she would worry about how it was published when I handed it in.

Two years passed. I didn't have any more time, so I kept a notebook beside my bed and finished the book and handed it in. But I still had an adult novel, *American Gods*, to finish before *Coraline* would be published. Avon was taken over by HarperCollins, a publisher with a healthy children's publishing division, and somewhere in there it was decided that *Coraline* would be published by HarperCollins Children's. In the UK, the book was sold to Bloomsbury.

It was still a horror novel, still aimed at both adults and children, but the publishing landscape had changed in the previous handful of years. The success of the few books that had crossed over from children's fiction to the adult world – the *Harry Potter* books, Philip Pullman's *His Dark Materials*, the Lemony Snicket books – made it at least a feasible goal.

Coraline was published in the summer of 2002, which was, coincidentally, the first summer without a new *Harry Potter* book. Journalists had column inches to fill, and they wrote about *Coraline*, imagining a movement of adult novelists now writing children's books. In both the USA and the UK, it's fair to say, adults bought the book at first, not children. That came later, as teachers enjoyed it and began teaching it in schools, as word of mouth spread.

That was followed by *The Wolves in the Walls*, written by me and illustrated by artist Dave McKean. A children's picture book, again, it was initially bought by adults who liked what I wrote and what Dave painted – essentially the graphic novel audience who had come with us from comics. But it was read to children, and became popular with them, and now most of the copies I sign at signings are for younger readers.

I don't think you can plan for something to be a crossover book. But you can do things to make it easier. In my case, it was useful that I already had a large readership, one that had followed me from comics into prose, and who didn't seem to mind that none of my prose books resembled each other very much, except in having been written by me. It was also wonderful that I had supportive publishers in the USA and the UK, who were willing to take different approaches to the material.

I've just finished writing my next novel for children, *The Graveyard Book*, a book that began with me wondering what would happen if you took Kipling's *The Jungle Book* and relocated it to a graveyard. I wasn't really sure who I was writing it for. I just wanted it to be good. Dave McKean did a book cover for the US edition while I was still writing it, but once the book was done it was obvious that the cover was wrong. It looked like a book for ten year-olds, and only for ten year-olds. While the book I'd written would work for children, it worked just as well for adults, and we didn't want to exclude them. With tremendous good humour, Dave went back to the drawing board and produced a dozen new sketches. One of them seemed perfect – it showed a gravestone, which became the outline of a boy's face in profile. It could as easily have been a children's book cover or the cover of a Stephen King book; no one picking it up would feel excluded. (Another of Dave's sketches, of a baby walking on a bloody knife-edge in which a graveyard could be seen, would have been perfect for a book aimed at adults, but was thought a bit too edgy for children.)

In the UK, Bloomsbury had come up with their own strategy: two editions of *The Graveyard Book*, one aimed at children, one at adults. The children's edition would be illustrated by Paul Riddell, the adult edition by Dave McKean – and Dave's baby-on-a-knife-edge cover was ideal for what they wanted, something that was unashamedly aimed at adults.

And with all that – two versions of the book in the UK, one for children and one for adults, and one version in the USA aimed at both audiences – I have no idea if it will work for both sets of readers, or how well it will work if it does, or indeed, which approach will be more effective.

You can do your best to write a book for children that adults will like (or the other way around – in the USA there's the Young Adult Library Services awards that celebrate the books for adults that young readers latch on to); you can try not to mess up the publishing end of things (that first cover for the US version of *The Graveyard Book*, which looked like a book that only 'middle grade readers' might have enjoyed would have been a mis-step); you can try to bring an existing audience with you, if you have one, and a way of letting them know what you've done. But I'm not sure that any of this will guarantee anything. Publishers are less intimidated by crossover books now that a handful of them – a large handful, but a handful nonetheless – have worked, but the mechanics of bookselling, the fact that books have to go somewhere in a bookshop, and that somewhere may be in a place that adults or children don't go, that the adult and children's divisions of publishers are staffed by different people in different groups who don't always talk to each other or have the same objectives (or even the same catalogues) – all of these things serve to make it harder to be a crossover author and encourage you to stay put, to write something people will know where to shelve, to write the same sort of thing you wrote before.

I suppose you become a crossover author by taking risks, but they had better be the kind of risks that you enjoy taking. Don't set out to be a crossover author. Write the books you have to write, and if you write one that crosses boundaries, that finds readers in a variety of ages and types, then do your best to get it published in a way that lets all of them know it's out there.

Good luck.

Neil Gaiman has won three Hugo Awards, two Nebulas, four Bram Stokers, nine Locus Awards, four Geffen Awards, two Mythopoeia Awards, two British Science Fiction Association Awards, a World Fantasy Award, a British Fantasy Award and an International Horror Guild Award, among countless others! In 2007, films of *Beowulf* (which he co-wrote with Roger Avary) and *Stardust* (based on his novel) were released and in 2009 his children's fairytale nightmare classic *Coraline* (first published in 2002) was made into a full-length animated feature film. His most recent and very successful crossover novel *The Graveyard Book* (illustrated by Dave McKean) won the Newbury Medal and is soon to be made into a film (directed by Neil Jordan). He is listed in the *Dictionary of Literary Biography* as one of the top ten living post-modern writers and he says he owes it all to reading the *Writers' & Artists' Yearbook* as a young man.

Notes from a successful children's author

J.K. Rowling shares her experiences of writing success.

I can remember writing *Harry Potter and the Philosopher's Stone* in a café in Oporto. I was employed as a teacher at the language institute three doors along the road at the time, and this café was a kind of unofficial staffroom. My friend and colleague joined me at my table. When I realised I was no longer alone I hastily shuffled worksheets over my notebook, but not before Paul had seen exactly what I was doing. 'Writing a novel, eh?' he asked wearily, as though he had seen this sort of behaviour in foolish young teachers only too often before. '*Writers' & Artists' Yearbook*, that's what you need,' he said. 'Lists all the publishers and … stuff' he advised before ordering a lager and starting to talk about the previous night's episode of *The Simpsons*.

I had almost no knowledge of the practical aspects of getting published; I knew nobody in the publishing world, I didn't even know anybody who knew anybody. It had never occurred to me that assistance might be available in book form.

Nearly three years later and a long way from Oporto, I had almost finished *Harry Potter and the Philosopher's Stone*. I felt oddly as though I was setting out on a blind date as I took a copy of the *Writers' & Artists' Yearbook* from the shelf in Edinburgh's Central Library. Paul had been right and the *Yearbook* answered my every question, and after I had read and re-read the invaluable advice on preparing a manuscript, and noted the time-lapse between sending said manuscript and trying to get information back from the publisher, I made two lists: one of publishers, the other of agents.

The first agent on my list sent my sample three chapters and synopsis back by return of post. The first two publishers took slightly longer to return them, but the 'no' was just as firm. Oddly, these rejections didn't upset me much. I was braced to be turned down by the entire list, and in any case, these were real rejection letters – even real writers had got them. And then the second agent, who was high on the list purely because I like his name, wrote back with the most magical words I have ever read: 'We would be pleased to read the balance of your manuscript on an exclusive basis…'

J.K. Rowling is the bestselling author of the *Harry Potter* series (Bloomsbury). The first in the series, *Harry Potter and the Philosopher's Stone*, was the winner of the 1997 Nestlé Smarties Gold Prize and *Harry Potter and the Goblet of Fire* (2000) broke all records for the number of books sold on the first day of publication. The seventh book in the series, *Harry Potter and the Deathly Hallows*, was published in 2007, and *The Tales of Beedle the Bard* was published in 2008.

Writing and the children's book market

Thousands of new children's titles are published in the UK every year. Chris Kloet suggests how a potential author can best ensure that their work is published.

Despite the fragile economy, the profile of children's books has never been higher, with the value of children's books sold in the UK in 2009 worth over £400 million. Yet it can be difficult for the first-time writer to get published. It is a diverse, overcrowded market, with many thousands of titles currently in print, available both in the UK and from elsewhere via the internet. Children's publishers tend to fill their lists with commissioned books by writers they publish regularly, so they may have little space for the untried writer, even though they seek exceptional new talent. This is a selective, highly competitive, market-led business. Your work will be vying for attention alongside that of tried and tested children's writers, as well as titles from celebrities such as sports personalities and pop stars, and the offerings for children from established writers for adults, who seize the opportunity to widen their audience. Since every new book is expected to meet its projected sales target, your writing must demonstrate solid sales potential, as well as strength and originality, if it is to stand a chance of being published.

Is your work right for today's market? Literary tastes and fashions change. Publishers cater to children whose reading is now almost certainly different from that of your own childhood. In the present digital age, few want cosy tales about fairies and bunnies, jolly talking cars or magic teapots. Nor anything remotely imitative. Editors choose *original*, lively material – something witty, innovative and pacey. They look for polished writing with a fresh, contemporary voice that speaks directly and engages today's critical, tech-savvy young readers. These 'I want it and I want it now' children are used to multi-tasking via different platforms. Time poor, they are often easily bored.

Develop a sense of the market so that you can judge the potential for your work. Read widely and critically across the children's book spectrum for an overview, especially noting recent titles. Talk to children's librarians, who are expert in current tastes, and visit children's bookshops, both in the high street and online, and websites, such as Lovereading4kids, Writeaway and Achuka. As you read, pay attention to the different categories, series, genres and publishers' imprints. This will help you to pinpoint likely publishers. Before submitting your typescript, ensure that your targeted publisher currently publishes in your particular form or genre. Request catalogues from their marketing department; check out their website. Consult the publisher's entry under *Book publishers UK and Ireland* (see page 136). Many publishing houses now stipulate 'No unsolicited MSS or synopses'. Don't spend your time and postage sending work to them; choose instead a publisher who accepts unsolicited work.

You might consider approaching a literary agent who knows market trends, publishers' lists and the faces behind them. Most editors regard agents as filters and may prefer submissions from them, knowing that a preliminary critical eye has been cast over them.

Picture books

Books for babies and toddlers are often board books and novelties. Unless you are also a professional illustrator (see *Illustrating for children's books*, page 516) they present few opportunities for a writer. Picture books are aimed at children aged between two and five or six, and are usually 32 pages long, giving 12–14 double-page spreads, and illustrated in colour.

Although a story written for this format should be simple, it must be structured, with a compelling beginning, middle and end. The theme should interest and be appropriate for the age and experience of its audience. As the text is likely to be reread, it should possess a satisfying rhythm (but beware of rhymes). Ideally, it should be fewer than 1,000 words (and could be much shorter), must offer scope for illustration and, finally, it needs strong international appeal. Reproducing full-colour artwork is costly and the originating publisher must be confident of achieving co-productions with publishers overseas, to keep unit costs down. It has to be said: it is a tough field.

Submit a picture book text typed either on single-sided A4 sheets, showing page breaks, or as a series of numbered pages, each with its own text. Do not go into details about illustrations, but simply note anything that is not obvious from the text that needs to be included in the pictures.

Younger fiction

This area of publishing may present opportunities for the new writer. It covers stories written for the post-picture book stage, when children are reading their first whole novels. Texts vary in length and complexity, depending on the age and fluency of the reader, but tend to be between 1,000 and 6,000 words long.

Some publishers continue to bring out titles under the umbrella of various series, each targeted at a particular level of reading experience and competency, although these are now often replaced by individual author series. Categories are: beginning or first readers, developing or newly confident, confident, and fluent readers. Note that these are not the same as reading schemes published for the schools market and do not require such a restricted vocabulary. Stories for the bottom end of the age range are usually short, straight-through narratives illustrated throughout in colour, whereas those for older children are broken down into chapters and may be illustrated in black and white. The table on page 293 lists publishers' requirements for some currently published series. Check that your material is correct in terms of length and interest level when approaching a publisher with a submission for a series.

General fiction

Many novels for children aged 9–12+ are published, not in series, but as 'standalone' titles, each judged on its own merits. The scope for different types of stories is wide – adventure stories, fantasies, historical novels, science fiction, ghost and horror stories, humour, and stories of everyday life. Generally, their length is 20,000–40,000 words. This is a rough guide and is by no means fixed. For example, J.K. Rowling's *Harry Potter* novels weigh in at between 600–750+ closely printed pages, and publishers now seem more willing to publish longer texts. Stories for this age group are enjoying more popularity, as publishers seek to adjust the balance of their lists following a recent emphasis on the teenage novel.

Perhaps more than in other areas of juvenile fiction, the individual editor's tastes will play a significant part in the publishing decision, i.e they want authors' work which *they* like. They, and their sales and marketing departments, also need to feel confident of a new writer's ability to go on to write further books for their lists – nobody is keen to invest in an author who is just a one-book wonder.

Publisher	Series name	Length	Age group	Comments
A&C Black	Chameleons	1,200 words; 48 pages	5–7	Colour illustrations throughout
	Black Cats	14,000–17,000 words; 96–128 pages	8–12	B&w illustrations throughout
Egmont Books	Green Bananas	500 words; 48 pages	4+	Colour illustrations
	Blue Bananas	1,000 words; 48 pages	5+	Colour illustrations
	Red Bananas	2,000 words; 48 pages	6+	Colour illustrations
Franklin Watts	Tiddlers	50 words; 24 pages	3–5	Colour illustrations throughout
	Tadpoles	70 words; 24 pages	4–6	Colour illustrations throughout
	Leapfrog	180 words; 32 pages	5–7	Colour illustrations throughout
	Hopscotch	350–400 words; 32 pages	5–8	Colour illustrations throughout
Hodder Children's Books	Bite	35,000+ words	12+	Contemporary fiction
Orchard Books	Colour Crunchies	300–1,000 words	5–8	Colour illustrations
	Crunchies	1,000–2,500 words	5–7	B&w line illustrations
Usborne Publishing	First Reading	400–1,000 words; 32–48 pages	5–6	Colour illustrations throughout
	Young Reading	1,000–5,000 words; 48–64 pages	6–9	Colour illustrations throughout
Walker Books	Walker Stories	1,800 words; 64 pages	5+	B&w illustrations throughout
	Racing Reads	8,000 words; 80–96 pages	7–9	B&w illustrations throughout

When submitting your work it is probably best to send the entire typescript (see *Dos and don'ts of approaching a publisher*, page 126). Although some people advise sending in a synopsis with the first three chapters, a prospective publisher will need to see whether you can sustain a reader's interest to the end of the book.

Teenage fiction

Some of the published output for teenaged readers is published in series but increasingly, publishers are targeting this area of the market with edgy, hard-hitting novels about contemporary teenagers, which they publish as standalone titles. Note also the rise in popularity of graphic novels for this age group, although the first-time writer is unlikely to find many opportunities here. There is a current vogue for 'young adult' novels that have a crossover appeal to an adult audience and vice versa, for example Neil Gaiman's *The Graveyard Book* and Yann Martel's *The Life of Pi* are published in both juvenile and adult editions. Stephenie Meyer's teenage vampire romances, the bestselling *Twilight* saga, also appeal across a wide age range, with global sales of over 85 million copies to date.

Non-fiction

There is a wide variety in the type of information books published for the young. Hitherto the province of specialist publishers catering for the educational market, the field now encompasses an astonishing range of presentations and formats, including electronic, which are attractive to the young reader. Increasingly, children who use the internet to furnish their information needs are wooed into learning about many topics via entertaining and accessible paperback series such as the *Horrible Histories* and *Murderous Maths* published by Scholastic, and highly illustrated titles by publishers such as Usborne and Dorling Kindersley. In writing for this market, it goes without saying that you must research your subject thoroughly and be able to put it across clearly, with an engaging style. Familiarise yourself with the relevant parts of the National Curriculum. Check out the various series and ask the publishers for any guidelines. You will be well advised to check that there is a market for your book before you actually write it, as researching a subject can be both time consuming and costly. Submit a proposal to your targeted publisher, outlining the subject matter and the level of treatment, and your ideas about the audience for your book.

Chris Kloet is Editor-at-Large at Walker Books. She has written and reviewed children's books and has lectured widely on the subject.

Further reading

Children's Writers' & Artists' Yearbook 2011, A&C Black, 2010

See also...

- *Notes from a successful children's author*, page 290
- *Illustrating for children's books*, page 516

Is there a book in you?

Alison Baverstock examines what resources a writer needs to be a successfully published author.

One of the most disappointing things about finally getting a book published is the reaction of other people. You might have imagined they would be dead impressed by your achievement. Think again. The reality is that most will use your success as a spur to their own aspirations, and rather than even *pausing* to admire what you have done, they will most likely come straight out with one of the following comments:

- 'That's something I have always planned to do';
- 'I've always felt there was a book in me too'; or even more frustratingly,
- 'Lucky you to have the time.'

The desire to have a book with one's name on the front cover is seemingly universal: so many people daydream that one day, somehow, this will appear. For some, the desire is for the object with their name on it; others anticipate that this will be the springboard to greater things: fame, riches and a celebrity lifestyle. And there really are lots of people wanting this. The competition organised by the Channel 4 *Richard & Judy* daytime television show at the end of 2004 attracted over 45,000 entries, or 20 Royal Mail van loads.

Quite why it is such a common ambition is not hard to fathom. A book with your name on the cover is a solid achievement; it makes you feel both valid and validated (because others are investing in your talent). It offers significance and permanence amidst the 'changes and chances of this fleeting world'.

But given the vast disparity in numbers between those who want to try to get into print, and those who actually make it, how can you influence the process? Is it really true, as many suspect, that it is only the famous and well connected who get publishing deals, or will writing talent always win through?

Given that I have been a publisher, still work freelance within the industry (mainly running training courses on how to market books) and am also a writer (with 17 books and lots of articles to my name), I decided to try to theorise about *why* some people get into print and others do not; to define what are the resources would-be writers need. Some necessary talents are obvious (can you write?) and some less so, but it's not necessarily true that having all the obvious qualifications for writing will guarantee you a publication deal. Those running creative writing courses often say that it's often not the best writers who get published; more likely it's those with the most self-belief or determination – or those who make pragmatic choices about the publishing house most likely to take them on.

I have always liked lists, so here is my list of ten resources needed by would-be writers:

1. Real determination

If you lack this core attribute, you are missing the one key requirement for getting published. Writing for publication demands an intense determination because so many things are stacked against you. There is huge competition – publishers and agents have vast numbers of would-be writers to choose between; writing is hard and takes a long time; most writers earn little; there are bands of others helpfully telling you not to bother trying, as well as endless bothersome circumstances that present themselves, from manuscripts lost in the post to the editor who was about to commission your work changing job and moving to a house that has no interest in the kind of book you want to write. Those who make it into print will be sustained by the knowledge that nothing matters to them more, and just keep going.

2. An ability to write what other people want to read

Canny observers might start by asking whether would-be writers can write sufficiently well for publication. I am risking annoyance by dealing with this issue from the other side of the fence: placing emphasis on the consumer's judgement rather than just a quota of literary merit.

In any case, there is *no* particular style of writing or mastery of literary structure that will guarantee an audience; writing that one person finds banal or staid may find a wider audience amongst those who relate to the story told or the characters described. So rather than displaying your ease with syntax to your potential publisher and feeling aggrieved that those who are less 'literary' than you get published, concentrate your energies on trying to prove that other people want to read what you are able to write.

Assemble proof. Find parallels. If your work compares in subject matter or style to a popular writer, name them. Many books these days are announced as having parents ('Jilly Cooper and Joanna Trollope'). If your area of writing relates to a popular television programme or magazine, state how many people subscribe/watch and when. Tell the publisher how others respond to your work. For example, if you are writing for children, give readings in a local school and obtain feedback. If you are writing popular fiction, find out if your local paper would like to reproduce an extract and monitor the response. If you have just finished a novel, get friends to give you honest feedback on what they think, and if it is positive, pass it on with your manuscript to the publisher or agent you choose to approach.

3. Creativity

It is simply not possible for all writers to have imaginations that rival Shakespeare, but creativity is vital for the would-be writer, whatever the field you choose to publish in.

Whatever you are writing about, in whatever format, your decision on how to present your ideas is a creative one; there are many possibilities and part of the writer's job is to choose the style and format that you consider both most appropriate and interesting. Even if you are writing academic papers, the logic of presentation and the examples chosen to illustrate the points you want to make will come across best if they are selected with a creative sense of what will help to develop the reader's understanding, rather than just being the first ten that occur to you.

4. Support mechanisms for your writing

Some writers work best at times of personal turmoil; they find the spirit of 'this will show 'em' helps them produce their best work. Others need tea, toast and sympathy at regular intervals. The most valuable support mechanism is money; writing is, most usually, badly paid and someone needs to be able to pay the rent/mortgage and provide enough money for food whilst you are busy crafting your masterpiece. The second most valuable support mechanism is appreciation: being shown that you are taken seriously is immensely helpful to a writer.

5. A writing habit

It is surprising how many people long to write but can never quite get down to it. Getting published demands self-discipline and self-knowledge; an understanding of when are your best times for writing and a determination to stick to the schedules you establish. Having a 'writing habit' means you prioritise your writing, where you do it, what time you get started, how long you stick at it, under what circumstances you can be disturbed – and, of course, how everyone else in your life is conditioned to respond to these things. If you are not willing to alter your priorities and put the writing first – not all the time, but when you have promised yourself you will – it will be very difficult to get published.

6. Something to write about

Few books arrive in the writer's imagination fully formed. Writers I talk to often mention the importance of the random in sparking ideas: an overheard conversation, a curious coincidence, an unexpected gift, and there was general agreement on the importance of novels developing best when characters you believe in start to shape events – rather than relying on plot alone for narrative development. Find someone who interests you and write about them, rather than dreaming up an exciting series of events and then deciding to whom they should happen. In your search for interesting ideas, try to lead an interesting life. Keep fit and healthy, eat well, listen to as wide a variety of people as possible, whether in print or socially. It's surprising how often the spark occurs when you least expect it!

7. An ability to present yourself as a writer

Years ago someone commented to me that 'other people take you at your own estimation'. It is true, but it's an area of real difficulty for many writers: we want our writing to be taken seriously, yet, exposing our hopes of publication for general inspection feels as if we are tempting fate; will it compromise our ability to achieve anything? The ability to 'play the writer' on occasion demands self-confidence and the suspension of self-doubt – but will probably be well received by publishers and agents who are looking for not only someone who can write what others want to read, but who interviews well (for publicising the books) and is 'promoteable'. Don't forget that a publisher who decides to back your book is making an *investment* decision, on the grounds that you will, in the long or short term, make a profit for the house that sponsored you.

8. The ability to deal positively with rejection

All writers get rejected – whether it is their initial ideas ('we can see no market for that'), their initial outline ('this does not fit our list at the present time') or their final draft ('editorial policy has changed and your book no longer fits our list as we are seeking to develop it. Please feel free to approach another house'). Even once accepted, having your precious manuscript edited can feel close to rejection – especially if it comes back covered with red ink and 'suggestions for change/development'.

What matters here is how you *deal* with rejection. A publisher's rejection is not a rejection of you or your ability to write, or indeed you as a person – although it may feel like all those things. Rather, it is a specific reader's response to what you sent at that particular time. Absorb all the advice you get given and try to do nothing in a hurry (certainly not a rude email back) but if you want to get published, don't let rejections grind you down. The publishing industry abounds with stories of the much-turned-down manuscript that went on to make a fortune (*Harry Potter*, *Day of the Jackal*, Mary Wesley, etc).

9. A wide knowledge of other people's books

Good writers are almost invariably well read: because why would you seek to contribute to the canon of published work if you do not respect the output of those who are already part of it? Some writers find that whilst writing a particular type of book, they read other things (maybe works in translation or non-fiction if they're writing fiction); others withdraw from reading while they're writing as it puts them off – then they are further motivated to get writing so they can get back to reading once they've finished their manuscript. Others have favourite writers who inspire them – one described reading Jane Austen as 'like having a blood transfusion'. And don't think that writing a particular type of book (children's titles or romantic fiction are commonly cited here) excludes you from being well read; such a view reveals a very patronising attitude towards just how hard it is to write any kind of book. Whatever you want to write, you do best if you understand how *other* writers develop ideas. Trying to write without the inspiration of reading yourself is like leaving the house without breakfast, the car without petrol, the hand-held console without batteries (you quickly run out of juice).

10. An understanding of how publishing works

Publishing is not a charity. Publishers and agents are not in business to help you achieve personal satisfaction by writing a book; rather they exist to make products available to the reading public who will pay for access. Different houses commission different kinds of books in different formats according to their experience of the market, their customer base and their future plans. The more you know about this market the more specific you can make your pitch – and the more you are likely to be successful!

Conclusion

Most would-be writers are pessimistic optimists. They are doubtful whether their writing will find its true appreciative audience – but they keep going just the same. Each of you can probably point to a published writer whose work got into print without the resources I have outlined: the celebrity whose book was written by someone else; the chicklit novel that for some reason caught popular imagination and having got loads of press coverage achieved huge sales – even though you personally thought it was rubbish.

It's true, chance is a great thing, but please don't assume that all celebrity books are instant hits or that press coverage is routinely unplanned. And so many of today's bestselling writers spent years of hard graft before they achieved the celebrity status that we now assume came overnight. For the vast majority of would-be writers, it is the persistence of their slog, their self-belief and their determination that ultimately keeps them going and achieves the publishing deal. Faint heart never won fair lady. Good luck!

Alison Baverstock is a former publisher who has written 18 books. *Marketing Your Book: An Author's Guide* (A&C Black, 2nd edn 2008) gives writers guidance on how to present their work to agents, publishers and readers. *Is There a Book in You?* (A&C Black 2006) outlines the resources needed by writers and offers advice on how to achieve publication. She teaches marketing – to authors, publishers and others – at Kingston University. Her website is www.alisonbaverstock.com.

The state of commissioning

Nicholas Clee spoke to six editors at different mainstream publishing houses to find out their thoughts on commissioning books for the current market.

It has never been so easy to get your books published, and possibly never so difficult to pursue a career as an author. The two phenomena are related. The proliferation of small publishers and self-publishing operations, all potential outlets for authors who cannot find homes at the leading firms, is in part the result of the same trends that have brought about consolidation at the heart of the book industry. There is a polarisation, between niche markets and the mass market for which the publishing giants largely cater. Authors operating in the niches are seeing their incomes dwindle, while those lucky and talented enough to hit the bestseller lists are the industry's equivalents of Premier League footballers.

Those of us still entertaining ambitions to place books with mainstream houses have been watching these trends with alarm. We sense that publishers are commissioning more cautiously; that they are committing huge advances to prestige properties, but otherwise paying less generously; and that they are increasingly liable to drop authors rather than try patiently to nurture their careers.

To get a picture of the established publishers' commissioning policies, I asked six editors to talk about how they approached their jobs: Ingrid Connell of Macmillan, Daniel Crewe of Profile, Kate Mills of Orion, Alexandra Pringle of Bloomsbury, Simon Prosser of Hamish Hamilton, and my own editor, Selina Walker of Bantam Press at Transworld. Connell and Crewe are non-fiction editors, while Mills specialises in fiction; the others do both. Their thoughts, grouped under key questions, are below. First, a bit of preamble about how we got here.

The consolidation of book publishing gathered pace in the 1980s. It coincided with a similar trend in book retailing, with the growth of chains such as Waterstone's and Ottakar's eventually producing mergers and acquisitions, leaving us with one national specialist bookseller (Waterstone's), one national mixed-multiple bookseller (WHSmith), and one dominant online bookseller (Amazon). But this consolidated industry was until the mid-1990s operating with a pricing regime – the Net Book Agreement (NBA), under which prices on books could not be discounted – devised to support diversity. When the NBA went, supermarkets saw an opportunity to sell books as loss leaders, and Amazon was able to build its business by offering all books, and bestsellers particularly, at dramatically reduced prices. Bestselling titles – ranging from celebrity memoirs (Peter Kay, Dawn French), to. J.K. Rowling's Harry Potter novels, to books selected for the Richard & Judy television book club (*The Kite Runner*, *The Interpretation of Murder*) – sold in quantities that the industry had never previously achieved. But the overall market did not grow by much. Below the top rank, the sales figures were lower than before.

This new market changed the economic model underlying book contracts. Retailers were more powerful, and demanded bigger discounts, along with contributions to marketing costs. Base discounts rose to 50% or higher, and publishers often conceded more than 60% in order to get books in prominent displays and in three-for-two promotions. These concessions ate into royalties: authors started receiving four-fifths, three-fifths or even less of the standard rates. Authors whose books broke sales records thought it a fair exchange, but the rest felt the pinch. Now it seems that aggressive marketing of ebooks may depress prices still further.

What, in these circumstances, can authors expect of publishers? I asked the following questions.

Are you commissioning less?

Some time ago, publishers decided that they could sell more copies of fewer titles. They seem to have taken that policy as far as it will go. 'Our numbers are staying exactly the same,' Alexandra Pringle says. 'Four new fiction titles a month is the maximum we can do, because otherwise they wouldn't get enough oxygen. There'll be a lead, a subsidiary lead, a "wild horse" [an unconventional title, which just might capture people's imaginations], and perhaps a genre title.'

Ingrid Connell says of Macmillan: 'We're not commissioning less – we've never had an overstuffed list', and Simon Prosser confirms: 'The Hamish Hamilton list has always been small and selective, and that hasn't changed.' Kate Mills says of Orion: 'We do 60 new [fiction] titles, in hardback or trade paperback, a year.'

Are you commissioning more conservatively?

'We're certainly commissioning more cautiously, and possibly more conservatively,' Selina Walker says. 'And we're pulling back from paying large advances when there's a substantial risk of not earning out.' Simon Prosser says: 'It's harder to persuade yourself to take a risk on something you know is very left-field.'

As Daniel Crewe points out, publishers look at proposals in the knowledge that the number of large retailers that might back the subsequent books has diminished. Ingrid Connell gives an example: Borders was an enthusiastic supporter of books on music and popular culture; since the collapse of the chain, only a percentage of those sales has migrated elsewhere. Also, the decline in subscription figures, as booksellers cut their initial orders and reorder if necessary, has forced publishers to lower their print runs, to levels at which certain books become unviable. A paperback with a print run of only 2,000 copies is not, for a large publishing house, an attractive undertaking.

'I've taken on three new authors in the past six months – more than I've ever taken on in a similar period,' Kate Mills says. But it can be easier to sign up new authors, who do not have compromising sales records and who may have stories that will attract publicity, than established ones. 'I had to turn down a book by a brilliant writer, because the BookScan numbers [the sales record of previous books] were too low,' Ingrid Connell says. 'You can't overcome that.'

What factors convince you to take on a book?

The potential support of booksellers has already been mentioned. While editors are aware of the risks of second-guessing booksellers' responses, they say that, more than ever before, they have to form a clear picture of how they can make a book appealing to readers. 'People who think they understand what the market will want are mad,' Alexandra Pringle says. 'You can't publish for the market. For us at Bloomsbury, it's whether a range of people are excited about a book – in editorial, in sales, in marketing, in publicity, and in rights. With novels, it helps if they're easy to talk about in a paragraph. How you're going to publish has to be a kind of three-dimensional picture in your head.'

'It's very interesting that Alexandra, from a more literary list, looks on it in the same way as I do,' says Selina Walker at Bantam Press. 'We all have to be, to use a horrible word, market-facing.'

What influence does this market-led approach exert on what gets published?

All the editors insist that there is still room on their lists for quirky books, and even for apparently uncommercial ones. Alexandra Pringle says: 'Georgina Harding [*The Solitude of Thomas Cave*, *The Spy Game*] is an exceptional writer, but she's also a quiet writer – you don't have an obvious hook to help get her into the trade. But we continue to publish her. We continued to publish Kamila Shamsie, selling about 5,000 copies of each title, and then we brought out *Burnt Shadows*, which has sold 95,000 copies to date.'

Selina Walker says: 'I'm a great believer that a really good book will break out and find a market, especially if you're passionate about it right from the start – as Stieg Larsson's novels did for Quercus, and as *American Wife* [Curtis Sittenfeld] and *The Book Thief* [Marcus Zusak] did for us.'

Daniel Crewe says: 'I believe that you can create markets for a book. We had one recently that started with a very low sub [initial order from booksellers] but that went on to sell very well. If the publicity and marketing are good, you can get booksellers to respond to a market you've created. It sounds very idealistic, but if a book is good enough you ought to be able to make it work.'

Simon Prosser has taken on for Hamish Hamilton *The Collected Stories of Lydia Davis.* A 700-page volume of short stories by a little-known American writer is not the most obviously commercial venture. But the stories have influential fans; and Prosser loves them too. 'You have to have complete passion for a book, take a deep breath, and hope that there is something you can do to help it find a way to readers.'

A book that attempts to exploit a formula will not necessarily charm editors. 'It's a mistake to see a bandwagon and jump on it,' Kate Mills says. 'A few years ago, when chick lit sales were declining, a few of those authors decided to try writing blockbusters instead. I don't think the books fared very well. The books that are most successful are the genre-busters and genre-creators, such as Kate Mosse's *Labyrinth* – her passion for that story seeped off the page. A few authors have tried to follow her, but they haven't succeeded.'

Readers seem to yearn for empathy, Ingrid Connell says. So they like books by people who have been on television, and who have become part of their everyday lives – a television star is more likely to sell books than a Hollywood star. Heartwarming or heartbreaking stories, involving people or pets, are also in vogue.

What are the qualities of a successful author?

Authors have to be 'market-facing' too, editors agree. Tweeting, blogging, Facebooking, giving talks, thinking of angles for media coverage: these are all activities that are likely to win publishers' thanks.

One of Kate Mills' authors, Veronica Henry, wrote a piece for the *Daily Mail* about the 'nasty surprises' she encountered on moving to Exmoor. The piece attracted more than 200 comments, many of them angry, on the *Mail* website. 'But Veronica is realistic that this is all part of what an author has to do.'

How precarious are authors' careers?

The editors concede that it is difficult to persist with authors whose books fail to sell strongly. 'We published three books by Alessandro Baricco and couldn't make them work,' Simon Prosser says. 'Now Jamie [Byng, at Canongate] has taken him on – and that's good.

I hope he's successful.' Alexandra Pringle says: 'We drop very few authors, but just occasionally you come to the conclusion that you'll have to let another publisher have a go.'

However, the editors say that they make efforts to manage their authors' careers. 'I find that I spend less of my time acquiring and more with authors who are already on the list,' Selina Walker says. 'For example, we published five books by Stephen Clarke [*A Year in the Merde*, etc], with diminishing sales, so we came up with the idea for a bigger book, *1000 Years of Annoying the French*. It has been in *The Sunday Times* top ten for the past six weeks.'

At Orion, Kate Mills says: 'We have always prided ourselves on being a publisher of authors, not books – Ian Rankin is always held up as the great example. [Rankin published several novels with Orion before making his breakthrough.] If an author hasn't been selling well, we sit down and look at what we can do to improve things.'

The death of the midlist – occupied by authors whose books do not make the bestseller charts – has been a subject of debate for years. 'Midlist' has become almost a taboo word, a synonym for failure. But Kate Mills embraces it. 'To be midlist, solidly consistent, is no bad thing in this climate – although of course you hope that every author's career will have an upward trajectory. I can think of authors who might be classified as midlist but who are much loved, and we're delighted to have them.'

Are you optimistic?

Alexandra Pringle: 'I'm very optimistic. We're doing well. This is an exciting time for Bloomsbury.'

Simon Prosser: 'You couldn't stay in the business if you weren't an incorrigible optimist. I believe that people will carry on reading books and wanting stories, whether in print or on a Kindle or iPad – that's only a matter of format.'

There is every reason to be optimistic about books and reading. But, in spite of these editors' best hopes, the survival of the economic model of the industry that has sustained authors is less certain; and what will succeed it, no one knows.

Nicholas Clee is Joint Editor of the book industry information service BookBrunch (www.bookbrunch.co.uk).

See also...

- *A year in view of the publishing industry*, page 328
- *Who owns whom in publishing*, page 336
- *Spotting a bestseller*, page 235

Publishing agreements

Publisher's agreements are not a standard form and authors must take nothing for granted. Michael Legat navigates the reader through this complex document.

Any author, presented with so complex a document as a publisher's agreement, should read it carefully before signing, making sure that every clause is understood, and not taking anything for granted. Bear in mind that there is no such thing as a standard form. A given publisher's 'standard' contract may not only differ substantially from those of other publishers, but will often vary from author to author and from book to book. Don't be fooled into believing that it is a standard form because it appears to have been printed – most agreements are individually produced on a computer to give exactly that effect.

A fair and reasonable agreement

You should be able to rely on your agent, if you have one, to check the agreement for you, or – if you are a member – you can get it vetted by the Society of Authors or theWriters' Guild of Great Britain. But if you are on your own, you must either go to one of the solicitors who specialise in publishing business (probably expensive) or Do It Yourself. In the latter case it will help to compare the contract you have been offered, clause by clause, with a typical Minimum Terms Agreement such as those printed in my own books, *An Author's Guide to Publishing* and *Understanding Publishers' Contracts*.

Minimum Terms Agreement

The Minimum Terms Agreement (MTA), developed jointly by the Society of Authors and the Writers' Guild, is signed by a publisher on the one hand and the Society and the Guild on the other. It is not an agreement between a publisher and an individual author. It commits the publisher to offering his or her authors terms which are at least as good as those in the MTA. The intention is that only members of the Society and the Guild should be eligible for this special treatment, but in practice publishers who sign the agreement tend to offer its terms to all their authors. There is no standard MTA, and most signatory publishers have insisted on certain variations in the agreement; nevertheless, the more important basic principles have always been accepted. It must be pointed out that the MTA does not usually apply to:

- books in which illustrations take up 40% or more of the space;
- specialist works on the visual arts in which illustrations fill 25% or more of the space;
- books involving three or more participants in royalties; or
- technical books, manuals and reference books.

Since its origins in 1980, comparatively few publishers have signed a Minimum Terms Agreement, although the signatories include several major publishing houses. Some publishers have refused, claiming to treat their authors quite well enough already, while others say that each author and each book is so different that standard terms cannot be laid down. Nonetheless, the MTA has been a resounding success. Almost all non-signatory publishers have adopted some or all of its provisions, and even in the case of the excluded books mentioned above, the terms have tended to improve. All authors can now argue, from a position of some strength, that their own agreements should meet the MTA's standards.

The provisions of the MTA

The MTA is a royalty agreement (usually the most satisfactory form for an author), and it lays down the minimum acceptable royalties on sales, and the levels at which the rate should rise. These royalties are expressed as percentages of the book's retail price but can easily be adjusted to apply to royalties based on price received, a system to which a number of publishers are changing, increasing the percentages so that the author's earnings are not adversely affected. The MTA also covers the size of the advance (calculated in accordance with the expected initial print quantity and retail price), and recommended splits between publisher and author of moneys from the sale of subsidiary rights (including US and translation rights).

However, the MTA is not by any means concerned solely with money, but with fairness to the author in all clauses of a publishing agreement, special attention being paid to provisions designed to make the author/publisher relationship more of a partnership than it has often been in the past. While recognising the publisher's right to take final decisions on such matters as print quantity, publication date, retail price, jacket or cover design, wording of the blurb, promotion and publicity, and remaindering, the MTA insists that the author has a right to consultation (which should not be an empty formality but should mean that serious consideration is given to his or her views), in all such cases. Also the author's approval must be sought for the sale of any subsidiary rights.

Some essential clauses

Any publisher's agreement you sign should contain, in addition to acceptable financial terms, clauses covering:

• **Rights licensed.** A clear definition of whichrights you are licensing to the publisher. The publisher will normally require volume rights but the agreement must specify whether such rights will apply in all languages (or perhaps only in English) and throughout the world (or only in an agreed list of territories). If when selling a book to a British publisher you are not granting world rights, try to ensure that Canada (and preferably also Europe) is included in the territories granted exclusively to the British publisher. The duration of the publisher's licence should be spelt out; commonly this is for the period of copyright (currently the author's lifetime plus 70 years), although some publishers now accept a shorter term. A list of those subsidiary rights of which control is granted to the publisher must be included (make sure that the splits of moneys earned from these rights are in accordance with, or approximate reasonably to, those in the MTA, especially in the currently growing area of merchandising).

• **Publication date**. Commitment by the publisher to publication of the book by a specific date (usually within a year or 18 months from the delivery of the typescript). Avoid signing an agreement which is vague on this point, saying, for instance, only that the book will be published 'within a reasonable period'.

• **Copyright**. Confirmation that in all copies of the book the publisher will print a copyright notice in the author's name and a statement that the author has asserted his or her 'Right of Paternity' (the right to be identified as the author in future exploitation of the material in any form), and that a similar commitment will be required from any subsidiary licensee.

• **Fees and permissions**. Clarification, if the book is to include a professionally prepared index or material the copyright of which does not belong to the author, of whether the author or the publisher will be responsible for the fees (or if costs are to be shared, in what proportions) and the clearance of permissions.

• **Acceptable accounting procedures**. Most publishers divide the year into two six-month periods, accounting to the author, and paying any sums due, three months after the end of each period. Look askance at any less frequent accounting or longer delay after the royalty period. The publisher should also agree to pay the author the due share of any subsidiary moneys promptly on receipt, provided that the advance on the book has been earned.

- **Termination**. A clear definition of the various conditions under which the agreement shall be terminated, with reversion of rights to the author.

Clauses to question

You can question anything in a publisher's agreement before you sign it. Provided that you do so politely and are not just being difficult, the publisher should be prepared to answer every query, to explain, and where possible to meet your objections. Most publishing contracts are not designed to exploit the author unfairly, but you should watch out for:

- **Rights assigned elsewhere**. It is unwise to accept a clause which allows the publisher to assign the rights in your book to another firm or person without your approval.
- **Non-publication**.The contract for a commissioned book often includes wording which alludes to the publisher's acceptance of the work, implying that there is no obligation to publish it if he or she deems it unacceptable. It may be understandable that the publisher wants an escape route in case the author turns in an inferior work, but he or she should be obliged to justify the rejection, and to give the author an opportunity to revise the work to bring it up to standard. If, having accepted the book, the publisher then wishes to cancel the contract prior to publication, the author can usually expect to receive financial compensation, which should be non-returnable even if the book is subsequently placed with another publisher. However, this point is not normally covered in a publishing agreement.
- **Sole publisher**. Some agreements prohibit the author from writing similar material for any other publisher. This may clearly affect the author's earning ability.
- **Editing consultation**. Don't agree to the publisher's right to edit your work without any requirement for him or her to obtain your approval of any changes made.
- **Royalty rate.** While it is normal practice for an agreement to allow the publisher to pay a lower royalty on books which are sold at high trade discounts, such sales are more frequently made nowadays than in the past, and it is essential to make sure the royalty rate on high discount sales is not unfairly low.
- **Future books**. TheSociety of Authors and the Writers' Guild are both generally opposed to clauses giving the publisher the right to publish the author's next work, feeling that this privilege should be earned by the publisher's handling of the earlier book. If you accept an option clause, at least make sure that it leaves all terms for a future book to be agreed.

Electronic and other multimedia rights

The importance of electronic, digital and other multimedia rights, which already require a carefully worded clause in a contract, is likely to increase in years to come, when the only form of publication for a book may be on the internet or whatever may replace it as technology develops. In the meantime publishers, on the one hand, and literary agents and authors' organisations on the other, are in dispute about these rights, including other rights as yet unknown.

The two main issues are concerned with control of the rights and with royalties. Should these rights remain in the direct control of the author (possibly negotiating through an agent) or, as publishers maintain, be regarded as a part of volume rights, and therefore licensed to the publisher? If the publisher controls the rights, should the author receive a royalty of 15% or thereabouts on the publisher's receipts from sales of these rights, or at least 50% of the income, as the Society of Authors and the Association of Authors' Agents insist is fair? Until some agreement has been reached on these and other matters, it is advisable for authors to seek advice on suitable wording of the relevant clause from a literary agent or the Society of Authors or any other established body representing writers.

Joint and multiple authorship

In the case of joint authorship (a work so written that the individual contributions of the authors cannot be readily separated), the first written agreement should be between the authors themselves, setting out the proportions in which any moneys earned by the book will be split, specifying how the authors' responsibilities are to be shared, and especially laying down the procedure to be adopted should the authors ever find themselves in dispute. The terms of any publishing agreement which they sign (each author having an identical copy) should reflect their joint understanding. The total earnings should not be less than would be paid were the book by a single author, and the authors should have normal rights of consultation.

In the case of multiple authorship (when the work of each contributor can be clearly separated), each author is likely to have an individual contract, and may not be aware of what terms are offered to the others involved. Because of the possibility of disagreement between the authors, the publisher will probably offer little in the way of consultation. All the individual author can do is to ensure that the agreement appears to be fair in relation to the amount of work contributed, and that the author's responsibilities indicated by the contract refer only to his or her work.

Outright sale

As a general rule no author should agree to surrender his or her copyright to the publisher, although this may be unavoidable in the case of a book with many contributors, such as an encyclopedia. Even then, give up your copyright with great reluctance and only after an adequate explanation from the publisher of why you should (and probably a substantial financial inducement, including, if possible, provision for the payment of a further fee each time the book is reprinted). The agreement itself will probably be no more than a brief and unequivocal letter.

Subsidies and vanity publishing

Few commercial publishers will be interested in publishing your book on a subsidy basis (i.e. with a contribution from you towards costs), unless perhaps it is of a serious, highly specialised nature, such as an academic monograph, when a publisher who is well established within that particular field will certainly behave with probity and offer a fair contract. Vanity publishers, on the other hand, will accept your book with enthusiasm, ask for 'a small contribution to production costs' (which turns out to be a very substantial sum, not a penny of which you are likely to see again), and will fail to achieve any sales for your book apart from the copies which you yourself buy. If you want to put your own money into the publication of your book, try self-publishing (see page 310) – you will be far better off than going to a vanity house. How do you tell which are the vanity publishers? That's easy – they're the ones who put advertisements in the papers saying things like, 'Authors Wanted!'. Regular publishers don't need to do that.

Michael Legat became a full-time writer after a long and successful publishing career. He is the author of a number of highly regarded books on publishing and writing.

Further reading

Flint, Michael; Fitzpatrick, Nicholas and Thorne, Clive, *A User's Guide to Copyright*, Tottel Publishing, 6th edn, 2006

Legat, Michael, *An Author's Guide to Publishing*, Robert Hale, 3rd edn revised, 1998

Legat, Michael, *Understanding Publishers' Contracts*, Robert Hale, 2nd edn revised, 2002

Owen, Lynette (ed.) *Clark's Publishing Agreements: A Book of Precedents*, Tottel Publishing, 7th edn, 2007

Unwin, Sir Stanley, *The Truth About Publishing*, HarperCollins, 8th edn, 1976, o.p.

Notes from a successful self-publisher

G.P. Taylor shares his experiences of writing and self-publishing success.

Lying in bed and hearing that horrendous thud on the doormat is the unpublished author's worst nightmare. It is the thud of a returned manuscript – the tell-tale sound of rejection. Nevertheless, you get out of bed and grimly hold on to *faux* hope that this time the letter will read differently and that you've been accepted and will be published. But no, nothing is further from the truth. Instead, you're faced with a note, hastily typed by a spotty faced 16 year-old who says she enjoyed your manuscript but it doesn't 'fit in' with the list and the niche in the market for romantic-fantasy-gothic literature isn't as big as it once was.

The trouble is, there are just too many people writing these days. Since a certain young lady put pen to paper, fiction (especially children's fiction) has become a *perceived* means of gathering fame and fortune. Even the prestigious Faber and Faber have now closed its doors to the unsolicited manuscript. So why bother? Only a few titles get produced each year from new authors but I don't feel all is lost. The writer has now, thanks to the advent of the internet and email, a publishing house at their fingertips.

Once self-publishing was known as the 'vanity press' – for those failed authors who didn't feel their pride would allow them to die without first seeing a book in print. For a monumental fee, you would receive five copies of your book along with the promise that your book would appear in their magazine for the entire world to see and that copies would be sent to reviewers so that they could herald your arrival to a greater world. Sadly, editors and reviewers knew the names of all the vanity press imprints and, once spotted, would be heaped at the back of the office and sent to the local charity shop once a year.

It was when I found out this information that I decided to avoid the usual route to publication and go it *alone*. In a nutshell, Mount Publishing Ltd was born – established via Companies House and a credit card. I became the director, editor and tea boy of the newest and most prestigious name in publishing! However, I knew nothing and it showed. A PDF what? Typeset? Margins? All these were very new concepts, but thankfully there is help out there.

The first problem I faced was the printing. Very quickly I realised that the prices varied immensely. One company wanted to charge me £6 per paperback, which would have meant pricing my book at £12 – who would buy it at that price? This is the area where you have to be very careful. If you are self-publishing you have to keep the costs of your book down and there are many hidden overheads to look out for (don't forget postage!).

So, once again, reach out for help that's available. My blessing came in the shape of Mr David Sowter, who I found courtesy of the Society of Authors. David was the UK rep for W.S. Bookwell of Finland and quickly became the fount of all knowledge and good advice at the end of a phone. He knew what I wanted and where I should go, and was a guiding hand through the difficulties of file preparation and submission.

Within two weeks of sending off the manuscript to the printer I was greeted with 2,000 copies of my first book *Shadowmancer*. They filled my house – they were under the bed, in the toilet, I couldn't even enter my small office. All these books with nowhere to go. Now I faced my biggest problem so far: how to sell them.

Thankfully for us self-publishers, there is a ready supply of independent bookshops all too willing to help the new author on a 'sale or return' basis. The Whitby Bookshop quickly set me off on the right foot. A book signing and press call were all arranged for a rainy October morning, and as my wife tramped through the wet streets with a pram full of books, she turned to me and said 'I bet J.K. Rowling didn't have to do this'. Too true – but the excitement and hope I was feeling at this point more than made up for it.

Very quickly I came across another hurdle – the national bookshop chains (known to self-publishers as the Mafia). No one would deal with me, no one would talk to me. 'Graham who?' Was all they asked. 'Self-publisher? No thank you.' The kindly manager of my local Waterstone's suggested I contact a book distributor but when I did they turned me down flat. I then went to Bertram Books, another wholesaler which supplies Waterstone's, and thankfully they opted to give me a chance. Bingo! I was now selling my book to the shops.

Luck was well and truly on my side. Somewhere around this time, the story of *Shadowmancer* was spreading by word of mouth. From nowhere, people from all over the country were ringing my home wanting copies of the book. I couldn't believe it! Suddenly, hundreds of people wanted to read *Shadowmancer* and my house started to empty of books. I knew I was doing well when copies were selling on Ebay for large sums of money – I was outbidding J.K. Rowling!

Within a matter of weeks of the start of my self-publishing venture, I was signed to Faber and Faber. It was good timing because everyday was a constant stream of wrapping and posting books, an operation so large that my local Post Office could no longer accommodate me and I was forced to find alternative arrangements. Self-publishing is definitely not for the faint hearted!

From then on, the path to notoriety has been a fast one. *Shadowmancer* spent many weeks at the number one spot on the bestseller lists in both the USA and UK. The film rights were quickly bought by Universal Pictures and a multi-book deal was in the bag. I had sold out and gone the way of the establishment!

Would I recommend others to self-publish? Definitely. In fact, I receive several emails a day asking me what to do and how to do it. Ultimately, my advice is simple – research the area and check prices, get quotes and be as wary as a fox. Be prepared for disappointment as self-publishing is certainly not a get-rich-quick scheme. It cost me all I had in time, money and resources – and more! Finally, it is always best to set up a limited company just in case all goes wrong, oh and *never* remortgage your house – sell your vintage motorbike instead.

G.P. Taylor self-published his debut novel *Shadowmancer* in 2002. He was soon signed to Faber and Faber and G.P. Putnam & Son in the USA, and the book became an international bestseller, translated into 42 languages. His subsequent books *Wormwood, Tersias the Oracle* and *The Shadowmancer Returns: The Curse of Salamander Street* have also been bestsellers. His most recent books are *Mariah Mundi and the Midas Box* (2007) and *Mariah Mundi and the Ghost Diamonds* (2008). He used to be an Anglican Vicar but now writes full-time.

Doing it on your own

Reasons for self-publishing are varied. Many highly respected comtemporary and past authors have published their own works. Peter Finch introduces the concept and outlines the implications of such an undertaking.

Why bother?

You've tried all the usual channels and been turned down; your work is uncommercial, specialised, technical, out of fashion; you are concerned with art while everyone else is obsessed with cash; you need a book out quickly; you want to take up small publishing as a hobby; you've heard that publishers make a lot of money out of their authors and you'd like a slice – all reason enough. But be sure you understand what you are doing before you begin.

But isn't this cheating? It can't be real publishing – where is the critical judgement? Publishing is a respectable activity carried out by firms of specialists. Writers of any ability never get involved.

But they do. Start self-publishing and you'll be in good historical company: Horace Walpole, Balzac, Walt Whitman, Virginia Woolf, Gertrude Stein, John Galsworthy, Rudyard Kipling, Beatrix Potter, Lord Byron, Thomas Paine, Mark Twain, Upton Sinclair, W.H. Davies, Zane Grey, Ezra Pound, D.H. Lawrence, William Carlos Williams, Alexander Pope, Robbie Burns, James Joyce, Anaïs Nin and Lawrence Stern. All these at some time in their careers dabbled in doing it themselves. William Blake did nothing else. He even made his own ink, handprinted his pages and got Mrs Blake to sew on the covers.

But today it's different?

Not necessarily. This is not vanity publishing we're talking about although if all you want to do is produce a pamphlet of poems to give away to friends then self-publishing will be the cheapest way. Doing it yourself today can be a valid form of business enterprise. Being twice shortlisted for major literary prizes sharpened Timothy Mo's acumen. Turning his back on mass-market paperbacks, he published *Brownout on Breadfruit Boulevard* on his own. Billy Hopkin's Headline bestseller of Lancashire life, *High Hopes*, began as a self-published title. Susan Hill self-produced her short stories, *Listening to the Orchestra*, and as an example to us all Jill Paton Walsh's self-published *Knowledge of Angels* was shortlisted for the Booker Prize.

Can anyone do it?

Certainly. If you are a writer then a fair number of the required qualities will already be in hand. The more able and practical you are then the cheaper the process will be. The utterly inept will need to pay others to help them, but it will still be self-publishing in the end.

Where do I start?

With research. Read up on the subject. Make sure you know what the parts of a book are. You will not need to become an expert but you will need a certain familiarity. Don't rush. Learn.

What about ISBN numbers?

International Standard Book Numbers – a standard bibliographic code, individual to each book published, are used by booksellers and librarians alike. They are issued by the Nielsen

UK ISBN Agency at a cost of £111.86 including VAT for ten. Self-publishers may balk at this apparently inordinate expense but the ISBN is the device used by the trade to track titles and if you are serious about your book should be regarded as essential. There are full details of the Agency's services on its website (www.isbn.nielsenbook.co.uk); see *FAQs about ISBNs* on page 314.

Next?

Put your book together – be it the printed-out pages of your novel, your selected poems or your story of how it was sailing round the world – and see how large a volume it will make. If you have no real idea of what your book should look like, go to your local bookshop and hunt out a few contemporary examples of volumes produced in a style you would like to emulate. Take your typescript and your examples round to a number of local printers and ask for a quote.

How much?

It depends. How long is a piece of string? Unit cost is important: the larger the number of copies you have printed the less each will cost. Print too many and the total bill will be enormous. Printing has gone through a revolution in recent years. The arrival of POD (Printing on Demand) and other digital technologies have reduced costs and made short runs much more economic. But books are still not cheap.

Can I make it cost less?

Yes. Do some of the work yourself. If you want to publish poems and you are prepared to use a text set on your computer, you will make a considerable saving. Many word processing programs have publishing facilities which will enhance the look of your text. Could you accept home production, run the pages off on an office photocopier, then staple the sheets? Editions made this way can be very presentable.

For longer texts savings can be made by supplying the work as a digital file directly to a printer. But be prepared to shop around.

Who decides how it looks?

You do. No one should ever ask a printer simply to produce a book. You should plan the design of your publication with as much care as you would a house extension. Spend as much time and money as you can on the cover. It is the part of the book your buyer will see first. If you're stuck, employ a book designer.

How many copies should I produce?

Poetry books can sell about 200 copies, new novels sometimes manage 1,000, literary paperbacks 10,000, mass-market blockbusters half a million. But that is generally where there is a sales team and whole distribution organisation behind the book. Do not, on the one hand, end up with a prohibitively high unit cost by ordering too few copies. Fifty of anything is usually a waste of time. On the other hand, can you really sell 3,000? Will shops buy in dozens? They will probably only want twos and threes. Take care. Research your market first.

How do I sell it?

With all your might. This is perhaps the hardest part of publishing. It is certainly as time consuming as both the writing of the work and the printing of it put together. To succeed here you need a certain flair and you should definitely not be of a retiring nature. If you intend selling through the trade your costing must be correct and worked out in advance. Shops will want at least 35% (with national chains asking for even more) of the selling price as discount. You'll need about the same again to cover your distribution, promotion and other overheads, leaving the final third to cover production costs and any profit you may wish to make. Multiply your unit production cost by at least four. Commerical publishers often multiply by as much as nine.

Do not expect the trade to pay your carriage costs. Your terms should be at least 35% post free on everything bar single copy orders. Penalise these by reducing your discount to 25%. Some shops will suggest that you sell copies to them on sale or return. This means that they only pay you for what they sell and then only after they've sold it. This is a common practice with certain categories of publications and often the only way to get independent books into certain shops; but from the self-publisher's point of view it should be avoided if at all possible. Cash in hand is best but expect to have your invoices paid by cheque at a later date. Phone the shops you have decided should take your book or turn up in person and ask to see the buyer. Letters and sample copies sent by post will get ignored. Get a freelance distributor to handle all of this for you if you can. But expect to be disappointed. Independent book representatives willing to take on a one-off title are as rare as hen's teeth. Expect to have to go it alone.

What about promotion?

A vital aspect often overlooked by beginners. Send out as many review copies as you can, all accompanied by slips quoting selling price and name and address of the publisher. Never admit to being that person yourself. Invent a name: it will give your operation a professional feel. Ring up newspapers and local radio stations ostensibly to check that your copy has arrived but really to see if they are prepared to give your book space. Buying advertising space rarely pays for itself but good local promotion with 100% effort will generate dividends.

What about depositing copies at the British Library?

Under the Copyright Acts the British Library, the Bodleian Library, Oxford, the University Library, Cambridge, the National Library of Scotland, the Library of Trinity College Dublin and the National Library of Wales are all entitled to a free copy of your book which must be sent to them within one month of publication. One copy should go direct to the Legal Deposit Office at the British Library, Boston Spa, Wetherby, West Yorkshire LS23 7BY. The other libraries use the Agency for the Legal Deposit Libraries, 161 Causewayside, Edinburgh EH9 1PH (www.legaldeposit.org.uk). Contact them directly to find out how many copies they require.

And what if it goes wrong?

Put all the unsolds under the bed or give them away. It has happened to lots of us. Even the big companies who are experienced at these things have their regular flops. It was an adventure and you did get your book published. On the other hand you may be so successful that you'll be at the London Book Fair selling the film rights and wondering if you've reprinted enough.

Can the internet help?

The web has yet to quite take the place of traditional print but things could change soon. A good number of authors are setting up their own websites. From these they advertise themselves and their works, and offer downloadable samples and, in some cases, their complete books. No one has yet made a fortune here and the number of visits some sites claim to get are questionable. Nonetheless, this method of self-promotion comes highly recommended. Self-publishers should get on board now. See *Setting up a website* on page 641.

The power of blogging and social networking should also not be ignored. Self publishers will benefit enormously from setting up a Facebook page devoted to their titles, from sending out tweets pushing the works and from writing a blog about the whole process. None of this will cost anything more than time. Do it now.

The internet is also thick with operators offering to promote or publish work electronically. These range from companies which post sample chapters and then charge readers a fee for the complete work to professional ebook developers who offer books fully formatted for use on hand-held and other devices (see *E-publishing* on page 629 and *Ebooks* on page 635).

Peter Finch runs Academi, the Welsh National Literature Promotion Agency and Society of Writers. He is a poet, former bookseller and small publisher and author of the *How to Publish Yourself*. His website contains further advice for self-publishers (www.peterfinch.co.uk).

See also...

- *Print on demand*, page 332
- *Notes from a successful self-publisher*, page 308
- *Vanity publishing*, page 343

Further reading

Baverstock, Alison, *Marketing Your Book: An Author's Guide*, A&C Black, 2nd edn, 2006

Crosbie, Anna, *How to Publish Your Own Book*, How To Books, 2006

Dorsey, Jennifer, *Start Your Own Self-Publishing Business: Your Step-by-Step Guide to Success*, Entrepreneur Press, 2007

Finch, Peter, *How to Publish Yourself*, Allison & Busby, 4th edn, 2000

Lupton, Ellen, *Indie Publishing: How to Design and Produce Your Own Book*, Princeton University Press, 2008

Penn, Joanna, *From Idea to Book: Writing, Self-publishing and Print-on-demand… for Your Book*, Lulu, 2009

Poynter, Dan, *The Self-Publishing Manual: How to Write, Print and Sell Your Own Book*, Para Publishing, 2007

Rich, Jason R., *Self-Publishing for Dummies*, John Wiley, 2006

Robinson, Jeremy, *POD People – Beating the Print-on-Demand Stigma*, Breakneck Books, 2006

Rosenthal, Morris, *Print on Demand Book Publishing: A New Approach to Printing and Marketing Books for Publishers and Authors*, Foner Books, 2004

Ross, Marilyn and Collier, Sue, *The Complete Guide to Self-Publishing*, Writer's Digest Books, 5th edn, 2010

Shepard, Aaron, *Aiming at Amazon – The New Business of Self-Publishing, or How to Publish Your Books with Print on Demand and Online Book Marketing on Amazon.com*, Shepard Publications, 2007

The Self Publishing Magazine, www.selfpublishingmagazine.co.uk

FAQs about ISBNs

The ISBN Agency receives a large number of enquiries about the ISBN system. The most frequently asked questions are answered here.

What is an ISBN?

An ISBN (International Standard Book Number) is a product identifier used by publishers, booksellers and libraries for ordering, listing and stock control purposes. It enables them to identify a specific edition of a specific title in a specific format from a particular publisher. The digits are always divided into six parts, separated by spaces or hyphens. The six parts can be of varying length and are as follows:

- Prefix element – Distinguishes the ISBN from other types of product identifier which are used for non-book trade products; three-digit number that is made available by GS1. Prefixes that have already been made available by GS1 are 978 and 979, but there may be a further prefix allocation made in the future as required to ensure the continued capacity of the ISBN system.
- Group Identifier – Identifies a national, geographic or language grouping of publishers. It tells you which of these groupings the publisher belongs to (not the language of the book).
- Publisher Identifier – Identifies a specific publisher or imprint.
- Title Number – Identifies a specific edition of a specific title in a specific format.
- Check Digit – This is always and only the final digit which mathematically validates the rest of the number.

Since January 2007 all ISBNs are 13 digits long. The older ten-digit format can be converted to the 13-digit format by adding the 978 EAN prefix and recalculating the check digit.

Contact details

ISBN Agency for UK and Ireland
3rd Floor, Midas House, 62 Goldsworth Road, Woking GU21 6LQ
tel (0870) 777 8712 *fax* (0870) 777 8714
email isbn.agency@nielsen.com
website www.isbn.nielsenbook.co.uk

Do all books need to have an ISBN?

There is no legal requirement for an ISBN in the UK and Ireland and it conveys no form of legal or copyright protection. It is a product identifier.

What can be gained from using an ISBN?

If you wish to sell your publication through major bookselling chains, or internet booksellers, they will require you to have an ISBN to assist their internal processing and ordering systems. The ISBN also provides access to bibliographic databases such as Nielsen Book's database and information services, which are organised using ISBNs as references. These databases are used by the book trade – publishers, booksellers and libraries – for internal purposes, to provide information for customers and to source and order titles. ISBNs are also used by Nielsen Book's order routing and sales analysis services to monitor book sales. The ISBN therefore provides access to additional marketing opportunities which assist the sales and measurement of books and other published media.

Where can we get an ISBN?

ISBN prefixes are assigned to publishers in the country in which the publisher is based by the national agency for that country. The UK and Republic of Ireland Agency is run by Nielsen Book. The Agency introduces new publishers to the system, assigns prefixes to new and existing publishers and deals with any queries or problems in using the system. The UK ISBN Agency was the first ISBN agency in the world and has been instrumental in the set up and maintenance of the ISBN. Publishers based elsewhere will not be able to get numbers from the UK Agency but may contact them for details of the relevant agency in their market.

Who is eligible for ISBNs?

Any organisation or individual who is publishing a qualifying product for general sale or distribution to the market is eligible (see 'Which products do not qualify for ISBNs?').

What is a publisher?

It is sometimes difficult to decide who the publisher is and who their agent may be, but the publisher is generally the person or body which takes the financial risk in making a product available. For example, if a product went on sale and sold no copies at all, the publisher is usually the person or body which loses money. If you get paid anyway, you are likely to be a designer, printer, author or consultant of some kind.

How long does it take to get an ISBN?

In the UK and Ireland the 'Standard' service time is ten working days. There is also a 'Fast Track' service, which is a three-working day processing period.

How much does it cost to get an ISBN?

In the UK and Ireland there is a registration fee which is payable by all new publishers. The fees during 2010 are £111.86 including VAT for the Standard service and £170.61 including VAT for the Fast Track service. A publisher prefix unique to you will be provided and allows for ten ISBNs. Larger allocations are available where appropriate.

ISBNs are only available in blocks. The smallest block is ten numbers. It is not possible to obtain a single ISBN.

Which products do not qualify for ISBNs?

Calendars and diaries (unless they contain additional text or images such that they are not purely for time-management purposes); greetings cards, videos for entertainment; documentaries on video/CD-Rom; computer games; computer application programs; items which are available to a restricted group of people, e.g. a history of a golf club which is only for sale to members, or an educational course book only available to those registered as students on the course.

Can I turn my ISBN into a barcode?

Prior to 2007, ISBNs were only ten digits long, whereas the appropriate barcode was 13 digits long and was derived from the ISBN by adding a prefix and recalculating the check digit. From 1 January 2007, the appropriate barcode number will be the same as the 13-digit ISBN. Further information about barcoding for books is available on the Book Industry Communication website (www.bic.org.uk).

What is an ISSN?

An International Standard Serial Number is the numbering system for journals, magazines, periodicals, newspapers and newsletters. It is administered by the British Library, *tel* (01937) 546959.

Marketing, publicising and selling books

Publishers have their own staff to market, publicise and sell their books but authors can also contribute to this process. Katie Bond outlines how to be a publisher's 'dream author'.

Newspapers are full of discouraging stories about how publishers only want to take on novels by glamorous young things or misery memoirs or celebrity autobiographies. Let's quash that immediately: publishers want to publish the best books they can find in a wide variety of genres and sell the socks off them. In the selling process, a 'promotable author' can make a major difference and my aim here is to take you through the run-up to your publication and suggest how even the most 'normal' author can give their book a push.

Word-of-mouth sales

When a publisher signs up an author, it is said that every book must be sold three times: by the editor to the rest of the company, by the sales/marketing/publicity departments to the bookseller and by the bookseller to the consumer. The most powerful sales tool in publishing is word-of-mouth and this begins in-house. A commissioning editor can entice everyone in the company to read a book so that a hundred people are talking about it – every mention is a potential sale. A recent example is *The Kite Runner* by Khaled Hosseini. This was one of those slow-burn books that took two years to become an international bestseller and reading group favourite. Such was the passion of its editor, Arzu Tahsin, for this novel that everyone at Bloomsbury read it and was 100% behind the book. Everyone played a part in its success by recommending the book to friends – personal recommendation being the number one factor in influencing a purchase according to all book-buying surveys. If an author is aware of this, every person you meet – at your publishing house (whether they're in the accounts department, on reception or the Sales Director), in bookshops and libraries, or indeed anywhere in your professional capacity as 'an author' – becomes a VIP. I will never forget William Boyd – the first author I spoke to in my first job as a publicity assistant – asking and remembering my name and chatting to me when he called to speak to my boss. Having read and loved his books at university, I would have walked over hot coals to make sure that *The Blue Afternoon* was a success and any request of his was instantly top of my list. Geographical distance from your publisher may mean that you don't get the chance to visit them often but do try to meet as many people in different departments as possible, go to book launches and readings, keep an eye on your publisher's website so you're up to date with what they're doing, and find out if your local sales rep would like to meet up for coffee when they're next on your patch. The only caveat here is that publishers can become flustered by over-keen authors – one used to lurk outside our offices with with 'surprise' cappucinos!

Marketing and publicity

Marketing is an umbrella term that includes all the work a publisher does to promote or sell a book. Traditionally 'marketing' is categorised as anything paid for (catalogues, advertising, posters and bookshop promotions) and 'publicity' (media coverage, bookshop events and festivals) is free. There will be a person in both marketing and publicity departments assigned to your book and creating good relationships with both of them – particularly the publicist (although obviously I'm biased here) is crucial. Ask your editor to let you know who they are and contact them as early as possible to meet up and decide on a marketing and publicity plan.

The sell-in

The sales process begins 6–9 months prior to publication when the sales team use the marketing and publicity plans to begin selling books to the head offices of the major book chains – from Waterstone's to Tesco, Amazon and the wholesalers who supply independent bookshops. Closer to publication local sales reps also sell books to individual bookshops in their areas although the front-of-store promotions (3 for 2, Read of the Week, Book of the Month) will be decided at head office level. The 'sell-in' is this process of persuading the bookshops to stock a particular book. The marketing department produces sell-in materials including six-monthly catalogues promoting the publisher's spring and autumn lists, and AIs (advance information sheets), bound proofs and glossy brochures on individual books. The initial print run for a book is based on the sell-in figures of advance orders placed for it. The speed at which a book can be reprinted (except highly illustrated and special format books) minimises the clash between publisher caution and author optimism and prevents lost sales if the initial print run sells out quickly.

The sell-out

This is the magic moment when a customer decides to buy a book. Marketing and publicity are geared towards boosting the sell-out in a myriad of ways from advertising and media coverage to book jacket design and bookseller recommendation. A recent survey reported in the *Bookseller* revealed that 'The consumer needs at least five positive mentions of a product as well as easy availability before he will buy'. With over 120,000 new titles being published in the UK every year, it's a crowded marketplace and clear signposting is essential to enable the book to reach its target readership.

The book jacket and author photograph

'Never judge a book by its cover' is an outdated maxim. This is the most important marketing tool of all and can make or break a publication. Even if your novel was inspired by an old family portrait, don't insist on having it on the cover if it isn't an eye-catching image. Conversely, do ransack old photograph albums, magazines and art galleries for images that you love and that you think are right for your book. Candida Crewe's recent memoir *Eating Myself* has an utterly arresting black and white close-up photograph of her doleful childhood face on the jacket – the photograph was provided by her and taken by her mother. For the author photograph, definitely allow yourself a little vanity– a really good black and white portrait is a must for publicity purposes and you want to look your absolute best.

Publicity

Book publicity is incredibly varied and widespread from reviews to features, discussions to news stories, public appearances at bookshops, libraries and literary festivals to local stock signings and books for competition prizes. As a rough guide, a publicist starts work on book tours and magazine advertising as much as six months ahead of publication. Finished copies of a book are printed approximately 6–8 weeks prior to publication and this period is the key time for confirming the media coverage to run on publication. The publication date is the peg for the media, so coverage becomes increasingly unlikely months or even weeks after the publication date unless the book has taken off in a major way and its success becomes the story.

How authors can help

There is a limited amount that an author can do to help sales and marketing directly beyond being very nice to booksellers and librarians, providing details of any specialist sales outlets prior to publication and (gently, not forcefully) offering to sign copies of your book in bookshops after publication (having first checked anonymously that the bookshop does have copies in stock). If a bookshop doesn't have your book in stock, let your publisher know rather than complaining to the bookshop directly. Also avoid the temptation – however tantalising – of moving your book to a more prominent position on the shelves. One author was repeatedly caught doing this until WHSmith's head office threatened to send all copies of the book back to the publisher and refuse to stock it anymore.

Authors can best focus their energies on publicity where their input is vital. A publicist will be working on anything from 2–10 books in any one month so their time is limited. You need to give your publicist as much information as possible on your book, yourself and any potential publicity angles (see below). Together you can then agree the timescale of the publicity campaign, achievable and optimistic goals, how publicity will best sell your book and discuss any potential pitfalls. Be honest with your publicist and tell them the full story even if you decide not to talk about it to the media. Your publicist can advise you on how much of your private life to mine for publicity and how to maximise your control over the coverage. First-time novelist Clare Allan chose to write newspaper articles about how her ten years as a patient in mental hospitals had informed her novel *Poppy Shakespeare,* rather than be interviewed. Trust your instincts and don't let journalists pressurise you. Jon McGregor was longlisted for the Man Booker Prize for his first novel *If Nobody Speaks of Remarkable Things.* A *Guardian* journalist and photographer went to interview him in Nottingham and on discovering that he'd washed up dishes in a local restaurant to support himself whilst writing the book, tried to persuade him to be photographed at the kitchen sink. Jon declined. It was a wise decision as otherwise this picture would have haunted him for years.

Pre-publication checklist for the 'dream author'

Your publicist is your primary contact for sales/marketing/publicity so the information below should be given to them to help plan the campaign.

- Make contact with the marketer, publicist and local sales rep at your publisher.
- Fill in the publisher's author questionnaire and write a 500–1,000-word piece about how you came to write your book and what's new and different about it (for examples look at the 'I am the author of' section on Amazon.co.uk).
- Make contact with your local bookshop, library, writers' groups, reading groups and literary festival and let them know that your book is being published.
- Research specialist sales outlets (e.g. wool shops for a book about knitting or football club fanzines or maritime museums for a novel about Nelson).
- Give the sales team any relevant information to drive sales regionally (e.g. if you're Welsh/Scottish/Irish or you lived in Cornwall for 20 years and have a huge network of family and friends there though you've recently moved to Derby).

- Make a list of any possible media angles relating either to yourself or the book.
- Make a list of any media contacts, both local and national.
- Research any anniversaries, exhibitions, television series or films that tie in with your book or the themes of your book and could create media hooks.
- If you're writing non-fiction, list what's new and newsworthy in your book (e.g. new source material or new angle). Differentiate your book from others on the same subject and list the other books in the same field.
- As you know your book best, suggest 1,000–3,000-word extracts that might work as standalone newspaper pieces.
- Write a description of your book in approximately 100–300 words (think book jacket copy style).
- If you think you could write newspaper articles, write paragraph pitches of ideas with potential word lengths. (Think of specific newspapers when you're doing this and be ruthless. Ask yourself if the feature is *really* right for the *Daily Mail's* Femail pages/*The Times*' Comment pages/*The Observer's* Food Monthly.)
- Write a list of the contemporary authors you admire and particularly any authors whose work is similar to yours as their readers might enjoy your book.
- Look at your publisher's website and see if there is additional material you can provide – on your book or a review of another book or article/feature.
- If the idea of standing up in front of people and talking about your book makes you feel queasy, ask your publisher for media and presentation training (budget permitting of course). Alternatively, go to other author events to see what works and what doesn't. (Remember that shorter is *always* better and enlist the help of an honest friend for feedback.)
- Plan, prepare and practice your author event (from choosing the right passage for a reading from the book – one that is dramatic, self-contained, character-introducing, with the all-important want-to-read-on factor – to interacting with the audience). If you are nervous, write out your talk and say it aloud again and again in front of the mirror at home.
- Listen or watch every television or radio programme before you go on it and always know the presenter's name!

Above all, charm, good manners and hard-working professionalism are the staple of the 'dream author' and will open promotional doors time and time again. Joanna Trollope, *doyenne* of the book tour, says: 'I think the advice I'd give to a first time author is that *all* publicity (with some reservations, obviously, about the tabloids…!), however seemingly small, is worth doing because the whole process is really joining up the dots in a dot-to-dot picture (which *might* even turn out to be a little golden goose…) and that whatever you do, do it with the best grace possible because no-one in your professional life will ever forget that you were a treat to deal with.' Finally, when your close friends and family tell you how much they love your book, do ask them for a small favour: a rave review on Amazon never goes amiss.

Katie Bond has been Publicity Director at Bloomsbury since 1999 and has handled PR for many bestsellers including Sheila Hancock's *The Two of Us*, Margaret Atwood's *The Blind Assassin*, Donna Tartt's *The Little Friend* and J.K. Rowling's *Harry Potter* books, as well as winning the first British Book Award's Publicity Nibbie in 2005 for Susanna Clarke's *Jonathan Strange and Mr Norrell.*

Helping to market your book

Alison Baverstock offers guidance on how authors can help to enhance their publisher's efforts to sell their book. The information in this article is also relevant to self-publishers.

Having a book accepted for publication is immensely satisfying – all the more so if in the process you have amassed a thick pile of rejection letters spanning several years. At this stage, some authors decide that, having committed themselves to work with a professional publishing house, this is the end of their involvement in the process. They will move on thankfully to the writing of their next book.

Once you have delivered your manuscript, and it has been accepted for publication, a publisher should handle all aspects of your book's subsequent development, from copy-editing and production to promotion and distribution. But there is a sound pragmatism in remaining vigilant. When it comes to the marketing of your book, there is a huge amount that you can do to help it sell.

The challenging marketplace

Each year in Britain alone, over 130,000 books get published or come out in new editions. All compete for the attention of the same review editors, the same stock buyers in bookshops, and the largely static number of regular book-buying members of the general public. It follows that anything an author can do to help 'position' the book, to make it sound different, or just more interesting than those it competes with, will be a huge advantage.

The marketing of books is not usually an area of high spending and there are many reasons why. Books are cheap (a novel costs about the same as a cinema ticket, and much less than a round of drinks), the publishers' profit margins are low, booksellers claim a percentage of the purchase price as discount (35–50%) and supermarkets claim more, and books sell in relatively small quantities (a mass market novel selling 15,000 copies may be considered a 'bestseller' – compare that with the sales figures for DVDs or computer games). Your publisher will probably try to make maximum use of (free) publicity to stimulate demand using low-cost marketing techniques. They are far more likely to arrange for the insertion of a simple leaflet as a loose insert in a relevant publication, or organise a specific mailing to members of a relevant society, than book television or billboard advertising. Your assistance in helping them reach the market could be most important.

Examine your resources

Think in detail about what resources you have at your disposal that would help your book to sell, and then tell your publisher. Most houses send out an Authors' Publicity Form about six months before publication, asking you for details of your book and how you feel it can best be marketed. Whilst the house will probably not be able to fulfil all your ambitions (mass market advertising is not possible for every book), they will be particularly interested in your contacts. For example, were you at school with someone who is now a features writer on *The Times*? Even if you have not spoken since, they may still remember your name. Do your children attend the same school as a contact on your local paper? Do you belong to a society or professional organisation that produces a newsletter for members, organises a conference or regular dining club? All these communication channels provide opportunities for publishers to send information on your book to potential purchasers.

Even greater things may be achieved if you set up the arrangements yourself. Can you arrange for an editorial mention of your book in a society journal (which will carry more weight than an advertisement) or organise for your publisher to take advertising space at a reduced rate? Remember that the less it costs your publishing house to reach each potential customer, the more of the market they will be able to cover out of their planned budgetary spend.

Offer a peg to your publisher

In trying to stimulate demand for a book, publishers try to achieve publicity (or coverage in the media) at the time of publication. The most usual way of getting this is for the in-house publicist to write a press release about you and your book and send this out to journalists in the hope that they will be sufficiently interested to write about you, or even better decide to interview you.

Your publishing house will need 'pegs' on which to hang stories about you and your book, and it is helpful if you volunteer these rather than waiting to be asked. So, think back over your career and life in general. What is interesting about you? Are there any stories that arise out of the research for the book; incidents that give a flavour of the book and you as a writer?

Try to look at your life as others might see it; events or capabilities you take for granted might greatly interest other people. For example, novelist Catherine Jones (Kate Lace) is married to a former soldier, and moved house 15 times in 20 years. In that time she has produced three children and has had appointments with over 40 different classroom teachers. She speaks about her life in a very matter of fact way, but when she wrote her first novel, *Army Wives* (Piatkus), the media were quite fascinated by a world they clearly knew nothing about. They found military jargon particularly compelling, and this proved a wonderful (and headline-producing) peg on which to promote her book.

Make yourself available

For a mass market title, any publicity that can be achieved will need to be orchestrated at the time of publication. By this time the publisher will hopefully have persuaded booksellers to take stock and the books will be in the shops. If the publicity is successful, but peaks before the books are available to buy, you have entirely missed the boat. If there is no publicity on publication, and no consequent demand, the bookseller has the right to return the books to the publisher and receive a credit note. And in these circumstances it will be *extremely* difficult to persuade them to restock the title having been let down once.

Timing is therefore absolutely crucial, so make yourself available at the time of publication (this is not the time to take your well-earned break). Remember too that, unless you are a very big star, each different newspaper or programme approached will consider its own requirements exclusively, and will not be interested in your own personal scheduling. Not all journalists work every day, and even if they do they like to decide on their own priorities. If you ask for an interview to be rescheduled, it may be dropped completely.

Don't assume that only coverage in the national media is worth having and turn your nose up at local radio and newspapers; they can reach a very wide audience and be particularly effective in prompting sales. You may be able to extend the amount of time and space you get by suggesting a competition or reader/listener offer. Local journalists usually have a much friendlier approach than those who work on the nationals, so if you are a novice to the publicity process this can be a much easier start, and an opportunity to build your confidence.

Contributing text for marketing

At several stages in the production process your publisher may request your input. You may be asked to provide text for the book jacket or for an author profile, to check information that will be included in the publisher's annual catalogue, or to provide biographical information for their website.

Think in detail about the words you have been asked for, who will read them and in what circumstances, and then craft what you write accordingly. For example, the text on a fiction book jacket (or 'blurb') should not retell the story or give away the plot; rather it should send signals that convey atmosphere, whet the appetite of the reader and show what kind of book they can expect. The potential customer is likely to be reading the blurb in a hurry, perhaps whilst standing in a bookshop being jostled by other shoppers, so it is best to keep it brief.

A non-fiction blurb should establish what the book will do for the reader and what your qualifications are for writing it. Again, keep the details short. The key factor is relevance – what have you done, and what are you qualified to do, that is relevant to the publication in hand?

For both categories of book a third party recommendation will help enormously as this provides objective proof of what a book is like and how useful it is. When books have come out as hardbacks, then extracts from review coverage can be useful on the paperback edition. (Every author should keep a rigorous record of their review coverage, copies of which your publisher should send you. Things do sometimes go missing or get lost, and you are far more likely to remember the good ones, given that you are looking after a much smaller number of books than your publisher.) For previously unpublished authors, a relevant quotation is very helpful instead. Do you know anyone established in the appropriate field who could provide an endorsement for what you have written? Can you contact them and ask them to help? The endorsement does not have to be from someone famous, just someone relevant. For example, a children's book endorsed as a gripping read by a 10-year-old child, or an educational text endorsed by a student who had just passed her exams could both be effective.

You may be asked to check your details in a publisher's catalogue. Bear in mind that your entry will sit alongside everything else they publish, so it must be factual and clear, and not 'knock' other titles on their list.

If you are asked to write website copy, be sure to look at the relevant site before you draft something. Think about the context in which your material will be seen and read (by whom, how often and for how long) and use this information as the basis for writing.

Marketing after publication

Although most of the effort in marketing your book will inevitably occur at the time of publication (because next month's schedule will bring forward further titles that need the marketing department's attention), there is a great deal of opportunity to carry on selling your book afterwards.

So, if you are asked to speak at a conference or run a training course, ask if your book can be included in the package available to delegates, either as part of the overall price or at a reduced rate. Ask the publishing house for simple flyers (leaflets) on your book which you can hand out on suitable occasions. Then ask the organisers to put a copy inside the delegate pack, on every seat, or in a pile at the back of the hall (or preferably all three!).

Give your publishing house the details of speaking engagements or conferences at which they could usefully mount a display of all their titles (your own included). Even though they published your book, you cannot reasonably expect them to be specialists in every specific field you know intimately, so give them *all* the details they need. For a conference this would include the full title (not just the initials you refer to it by), the organiser's address and contact numbers (not the chairperson's address to which you should send associated papers), the precise dates and times, and any associated deadlines (e.g. stand bookings placed before a certain date may be cheaper). Finally, try to plan ahead rather than passing on key details at the last minute (this is one of publishers' most common complaints about authors!).

When authors get together they will moan about their publishers. But if that energy is channelled into helping promote the books, everyone benefits!

After ten years working in publishing **Alison Baverstock** set up her own marketing consultancy, specialising in running campaigns for the book trade and training publishers and authors to market more effectively. She is a well-established speaker on the book business and is Course Leader of the MA in Publishing at Kingston University. She is the author of *Marketing Your Book: An Author's Guide* (A&C Black, 2nd edn 2008) and *Is There a Book in You?* (A&C Black 2006), which offers would-be writers a checklist of resources they must have if they want to get published. Her website is www.alisonbaverstock.com.

See also...

- *Marketing, publicising and selling books,* page 316
- *How to publicise your book,* page 324
- *Marketing yourself online,* page 625

How to publicise your book

There are numerous ways that authors can help to promote their books. Isabel Losada created her own interactive website to be in touch with her readers and the book world in general. Here she talks about her website and shares other ideas for author self publicity.

There is a very annoying thing about publishing houses. They are publishing houses. Authors don't like this at all. We want them to be PR houses, promotional entrepreneurs and marketing experts. In an ideal world we would like entire publicity departments dedicated to promoting our books. Alas, this is not how it is.

Publicity departments

In one of my foreign publishing companies, my editor publishes 85 books a year. For every one published she looks at 10–15 books a week and reads at least five of them. The other two editors in this company each publish 75 and 60 books. This company has ONE publicity person who has responsibility for the promotion of 220 titles a year. So how many calls do you reckon he can make to try and sell an interview to the press? And imagine that your book is not about sport or sex... well it's a bleak picture ain't it?

Now, you may be lucky and your book may be published by one of the major UK publishing houses, there may be two people who work in the publicity department. And maybe even a work experience assistant too. But then they will have more books as well. Are you beginning to grasp the reality here?

The person most committed to getting your book out there is you. So don't moan about your publishing company, as many authors do – they have published your book after all. Get proactive and have fun with publicising your book. It's the only way to learn.

Be nice at all times to everyone as people who work in PR, publishing and marketing are under pressure and work very hard. What you need is cooperation – so, when you have a meeting with those who are working to promote your book, try to find out exactly what they are doing so that you can cover what they won't have time to do. Get as much information as you can, so you can help. For example, if you are going to visit a town as part of a promotional tour, it is relatively easy to fix up local radio interviews which can be done either in the town or 'down the line' from wherever you work or even from your home. Your publicity person won't have time to phone local newspapers but if you contact them with information about your event they will often be delighted. The best way to get people along to an event is to have someone you know who lives in the town rally their friends and for you to deal with local press and radio. It's hard work.

And that's the truth – you have to commit yourself to self promotion both with time and with money. I know one author who spends five years writing a book but will not give ten minutes to promoting it. Where is the logic in that? Your tax allows for expenses in the column 'Advertising and Promotion', so surely it's worth producing postcards, for example, that show the front cover of your book, at your own expense. You can give them to those people at parties who insist on asking 'What do you write?' – sometimes they'll ask you to sign the card and then go out and buy the book. And you can find 100 other uses for the postcards too. So decide whether to spend your money on promotional tools or to give it to the tax man.

Never walk past a bookshop without going in to sign copies of your books. Be very friendly to the booksellers. I once asked a bookseller where my books were and he said they had 75 copies in the basement. I asked if he'd like them signed and he looked at me wearily – he evidently didn't want to go down to the basement and find them. It was a hot day. 'Are you open to bribery?' I asked… 'If you will go and get them I will go out and buy you an ice-cream.' 'Magnum please,' he replied and went off to get the books. While I signed books – he ate his ice-cream. Having fun helps.

Websites

Then there is your website. Gotta have a website. And what is worse is that it's no good getting someone else to do it for you so that you aren't able to use it. You must be able to maintain it yourself and not have to ring someone (who's bound to be on holiday when you want them) every time you want to change or update something. Study other authors' websites. Some of them are truly dull – dead sites that just contain lots of downloadable pictures of the author and are evidently not designed for readers of the books. At the other end of the scale is www.neilgaiman.com, the genius of which few of us can even aspire to. Neil Gaiman's website obviously takes up a lot of his time every day but for his fans the contact must be a continual source of pleasure and satisfaction. My own website (www.isabellosada.com) is basically an amateur site that I built with a couple of flashy touches which I was given help with. But it gives me huge pleasure and I reply to every email, and accept all invitations to attend reading groups (as long as they pay my fares.) Friendly emails from readers about how much a reader has enjoyed a book is a great way to start or end the day. So you gotta have a website.

The Amazon websites (www.amazon.com and www.amazon.co.uk) are important too. Thousands of people look at them and read the reader reviews. If a reader sends you a glowing email (to your website of course) about your book it's perfectly acceptable to ask them if they would mind repeating their accolade in the form of a reader review on Amazon. It's funny when authors write their own reviews because regular users at Amazon can tell the difference immediately. A review that says it's by 'a reader' and doesn't give the name is usually an author that hasn't done their homework and is writing their own reviews. And why do it? Genuine reviews from fans are much more interesting. But be warned – watching the rating on Amazon can drive authors crazy. One minute your book is at number 12 and the next it's at 5,756 and you think – how did that happen? It's obviously a deliberate plan to baffle us. As to Facebook – don't be a dinosaur – join up. You'll soon understand why.

Publicity events

Keep all your press cuttings and put together your own list of reviews that are complimentary of your work. (Comments from any bad reviews can also be helpful – see 'Rejection letters' on my website!) This 'press pack' can then be sent to people when you want to introduce yourself and your work, for instance for interviews or literary festivals. Keep the details of all the people that you speak to and the conversations that you have with them. Who interviewed you and when? Don't assume that others will remember – they won't. I recently did a radio interview with a regional radio station with a presenter and I only realised at the last minute that he'd interviewed me twice before and I had no notes on this. I remembered just in time before inadvertently insulting him and humiliating myself. So keep notes.

When you do events, plan and prepare them like a professional entertainer would. Reading from your work is a skill that you may or may not have naturally. If you hate reading, don't do it. You'll be far more interesting and the audience will have a better time if you are happy. Have someone interview you about the book and your work instead. Check out the relevance to your audience. Ask them why they have come along. They may all secretly want to hear about your book before last. If you are promoting a book that is not your first – check that bookshops have copies of your backlist titles in stock too as there will always be people in the audience who will want those.

Go to other authors' events. My local Waterstone's in Clapham has a fantastic range of author events. By turning up for some of these free evenings out you'll soon have a feel of what makes a good evening and you may find other ways to support your fellow authors when you meet them.

Bookshops

Check the stock levels of your books (in the most gentle, kind and supportive way of course). I recently checked in a bookshop and found that orders for six copies of a title had been placed seven months previously. Somewhere between the chain, distributor and warehouse the order had been lost – but a couple of phone calls soon corrected this.

If you have written a book about horses and there isn't a copy in a riding shop you visit – don't be surprised. Small shops don't necessarily have accounts with all the publishing companies. If your book on Buddhism isn't in the Buddhist monastery bookshop that you'd expect to find it in, you could offer the bookshop manager a copy, explain why you think his customers would enjoy the book and ask if he or she would consider it. Sometimes just asking gently works wonders.

Do not turn books that are spine side out face side out in shops. It will simply annoy the booksellers who will turn it back when you are gone. And do not move your books around the shop without first speaking to the manager of the shop. If you think your book is shelved in the wrong place this is a serious problem but needs to be dealt with from the top, i.e. by your publishing company. Getting cross with bookshops won't help as books are shelved according to the category printed on the back cover. So don't annoy booksellers, find out what supports them – they are your friends.

Self-promotion

Be prepared to support other authors. You can use your website for this, for example by linking to other authors' pages if you are recommending their work. I have persuaded people to write articles about books I admire and even once persuaded a charity to promote a book to their 16,000 members. Look out for opportunities to support the work of authors that you admire. If you can benefit charities or causes that you support at the same time you are really making sense.

Always, always have a copy of your latest book about your person that you are happy to sell if someone asks. Sorry – but sometimes people (especially at parties) are thrilled that they can have a signed copy direct from the author. I know you are cringing – but it can be done gracefully and with a smile.

You may like to consider offering to visit book clubs that are reading your books. On my site I offer to go and talk at any club that will pay my fares, and the last offer that came in was from Switzerland. I also sign books and will post them to anyone who asks me to (in return for a cheque, of course) and I often give away foreign edition copies from my website. (What else can I do with six copies in Greek?) So basically be reader friendly. And bookshop friendly. And publishing company friendly and editor and agent friendly.

Lastly, you have to believe passionately in your work and genuinely want everyone to read it. Don't write just because you have been asked to – wait until you have something to say. Enough trees have been destroyed for our trade as it is. If you are passionate about what you write and your work makes a genuine and positive contribution your readers will sell your books for you. And it's true – with a lot of help from you – that ultimately it's still word of mouth that will sell your books.

Isabel Losada is the author of *New Habits: Why Today's Women Become Nuns, The Battersea Park Road to Enlightenment* (which has been translated into 14 languages), *A Beginner's Guide to Changing the World: For Tibet, With Love* (Bloombury), *One Hundred Reasons to be Glad* (Summersdale), *Men!* (Virgin) and *The Battersea Park Road to Paradise* (Watkins). She is also an actress and broadcaster and can be contacted through her website, www.isabellosada.com.

See also...

- *Marketing, publicising and selling books*, page 316
- *Helping to market your book*, page 320
- *Marketing yourself online*, page 625

A year in view of the publishing industry

Tom Tivnan presents a round-up of book industry news and trends for 2009.

When Will There Be Good News? The title of Kate Atkinson's 2008 novel, the ninth bestselling book of 2009, was just as likely to be the main question on the collective mind of the book trade after another 12 rocky months of recession-fuelled administrations, redundancies and a further decline in the market. For doom and gloom, the high street is the obvious starting point. Going into last year, publishers said the key to recovery was that all 'routes to market' (places to buy books from, to you and me) must remain open. Yet, in the run-up to Christmas, the chain Borders went into administration, with a loss of 1,150 jobs and about £35 million in annual sales. Irish booksellers Hughes & Hughes, which owned 24 stores in the UK and Ireland and had 225 employees, went into liquidation in April. Christian booksellers Wesley Owen also went to the wall, though a combination of buy-outs from some of the stores' staff and competitors meant that 23 of its 40 shops were spared.

Things were slightly better, but not by much, for publishers. Eight of the top ten had slumps in sales, including three of the 'Big Four' publishing groups that collectively make up around half of the trade: Random House was down by £24.4 million; Penguin £7.5 million and HarperCollins £15.2 million. Only top dog Hachette UK had growth, up 2% to £287.9 million. Redundancies overall slowed, but did not stop. Penguin slashed 100 jobs, 10% of its UK workforce. A radical restructure had lifestyle publisher David & Charles slashing staff numbers in half, from 140 to 70. Academic giant John Wiley dumped 30 jobs. On and on it went with tiny cuts here and there from the big boys to the small indies. And it continues: at press time, Octopus, the art and cookery imprint of Hachette, is in consultation with staff to shed a third of its workforce. Painful all, but perhaps the saddest cut may have been the closure after 190 years of the Edinburgh offices of Chambers, with the loss of 27 jobs. The dictionary and reference publisher, which was merged into parent Hachette's London and Paris offices, had operated in the Scottish capital since brothers William and Robert Chambers printed their first book, *The Songs of Robert Burns*, in 1819.

Adapt or die

The overall picture has left the trade jittery. The UK books market sold £1.752 billion (down 1.2% from the previous year) worth of books last year, shifting 235.7 million copies (down 0.5%). After a decade of solid, sometimes spectacular, growth that is the second year in a row of decline. Compared with the rest of the economy, though, those numbers don't look that bad – the retail sector as a whole declined 6% last year. So why is the trade suffering? The answer may be that it is becoming cheaper than ever for customers to buy books. For the past decade, discounting has deepened, driven by the supermarkets and online retailers like Amazon cutting prices. Last year, the difference between the recommended retail price and the average selling price (what punters actually paid for the books) topped over half a billion pounds, £573.5 million, the highest level of discounting in book trade history. In short, booksellers lopped an average of about 25% off the price of books.

The bulk of this is weighted towards massive discounts for new titles and the biggest bestsellers – somewhat perversely, the books that readers want to buy most. In its first week of release in April 2010, for example, Jamie Oliver's number one bestseller *Jamie Does…* was selling at almost 60% off its £25 list price. Competing with the deep discounting outlets has been an issue for over ten years for traditional bricks and mortar bookshops but has become particularly acute because of the pincer movement of economic woes and increased digitisation. High street chain booksellers, as they are currently configured, are an endangered species. They must adapt or die.

Yet fear not, dear reader, some cannier bookshops are going back to basics to survive. The nation's biggest dedicated books chain, Waterstone's, had a bruising year: sales over Christmas were down 8.5% and an at first disastrous move to a new centralised warehouse called 'The Hub' left many shops without key books. New head honcho Dominic Myers has called for sweeping changes, moving away from the previous regime's one-size-fits-all centralised buying programmes and giving more autonomy to the shops. Essentially making its staff into proper booksellers again. Meanwhile independent bookshop numbers fell again last year: 62 more closed than opened in 2009, the worst dip since 2004. Yet somewhat encouragingly, independent booksellers' overall market share remained level on 2008. In a declining market, then, indie shops effectively *gained* share. Indies that did prosper are the ones that did not try to play against Amazon or the supermarkets at the discount game, emphasising local service and their specialist knowledge.

Symbols and vampires

Despite the gloom there were some stunning successes. The most outstanding publishing event by far was the return in September 2009 of Dan Brown, the author of the biggest selling book of all time, *The Da Vinci Code*. Brown had not published a book since 2004, and his new conspiracy thriller *The Lost Symbol* was certain to be a bestseller, but the question was how big would it be, as it was his first UK hardback. It did pretty well, thanks: 551,000 copies sold in its first five days, the biggest and fastest selling adult hardback in publishing history (only J.K. Rowling's Harry Potter books have sold more copies in hardback). In fact *The Lost Symbol* smashed the total adult hardback sales record in just *two days* – the previous best being Thomas Harris' *Hannibal* (229,000). By mid-May 2010 it has sold 1.4 million copies.

If *The Lost Symbol* was the event of the year, Stephenie Meyer was the author. The Mormon mum of three responsible for the *Twilight* teen vampire romance series shifted an incredible £30 million worth of books last year, the highest single year total ever by any author not named Rowling. She held the top spot in the children's bestseller lists for an unparalleled 46 out of the last 52 weeks. Her influence extended far beyond her own books. She almost single-handedly reinvigorated the sluggish Young Adult market (books aimed at teenagers), sparking a wave of copycat 'paranormal romance' or 'dark fantasy' authors. The 'mini-me Meyers' – such as Charlaine Harris, L.J. Smith and the mother/daughter team P.C. and Kirsten Cast – still have not sated the public's demand for the genre.

It was a decent year for literature and 'lit-lite', middlebrow novels and upmarket thrillers favoured by reading groups. Hilary Mantel's *Wolf Hall* became the biggest selling Man Booker winner in the prize's 41 years, while Sebastian Barry's Costa Award Winner *The Secret Scripture* shifted over £2 million worth of books. One star author, sadly, could not enjoy his success. The Swedish crime writer Stieg Larsson died in 2004 before seeing any of his *Millennium* trilogy published. The books started slowly here when first published three years ago, but word-of-mouth and a film tie-in has propelled Larsson's *The Girl with the Dragon Tattoo*, *The Girl Who Played with Fire* and *The Girl Who Kicked the Hornets' Nest* from mere bestsellerdom to phenomenon. This past year, Larsson became the first ever author in translation to hit the overall number one on the UK bestseller list, and his sales are approaching Dan Brown level – £12 million in the 12 months to May 2010.

The big books of the year were almost exclusively fiction. In fact, the overall adult fiction market improved by 1.2%, while trade (non-textbooks) non-fiction tumbled dramatically: down 5.1%. This is partly due to publishers' caution in a recession, with lists cut back, risks avoided, and a reliance on big name genre writers (crime, thriller, science fiction and chick lit, mainly): James Patterson, Jodi Picoult, Terry Pratchett, Martina Cole and Sophie Kinsella all had stonking years. It is more difficult to build a 'brand' non-fiction author. Plus, the usual publishing cash cow, the celebrity memoir, failed to pull in the numbers. Is the celebrity memoir dead? Not exactly. Last year was simply decidedly B-list. Outside of Ant & Dec's *Ooh! What A Lovely Pair*, it was difficult to see any memoir catching fire with the public. When publishers were banking on the likes of Jack Dee, Chris Evans and Justin Lee Collins for their Christmas bonuses you know they were in trouble. This year, however, already looks far more A-list with rock legend Keith Richards, national treasures Judi Dench and Michael Caine, television star Gok Wan and Tony Blair (which does stretch the definition of 'celebrity', but it will be a monster book).

Tectonic shifts

For years, publishing has been harping on about an ebook and digitalisation tipping point. It appears to have finally come. Not necessarily in pure sales terms but in how publishers have changed focus and have become 'format agnostic'. It is not about books *per se*, but providing 'content' in a variety of ways, from print to digital. The past year has seen a succession of ebook devices enter or about to enter the UK market, with Amazon's Kindle and Apple's iPad causing almost febrile excitement among the trade and gadget geeks alike. The iPhone and other smartphones like Blackberry and those using Google's Android platform are touted by some as the key e-reading devices for the future. Google Editions – the internet giant's 'buy anywhere, read anywhere' mobile ebook platform will launch in late summer 2010. It's not only about *reading* ebooks anymore. The iPhone and iPad meant that enhanced apps entered the market for the first time. These ebooks allow users to read, listen and watch video, or do all three. The app for *Wolf Hall*, for example, included an audiobook along with the text, a specially commissioned new essay by Mantel, and a video of an interview between the author and historian David Starkey.

Publishers are bullish, with many predicting about 50% of books being read digitally by the end of this decade. They freely admit the problem is that they don't know exactly how they will be read: on dedicated e-readers, on mobile phones, on tablets like the iPad, on computers – or even on some new device. A further worry is whether publishers can adapt quickly enough. The stately pace of publishing has essentially been the same for about 100 years. Yet in the digital world, what was fresh and hip today may be old school tomorrow. The Sony e-reading device was brought out just three years ago in the UK and already feels like it should be in the antiquities room of the British Museum. Publishers must be far more nimble and, crucially, must attract more tech-savvy staff, with many in the trade this past year lamenting the industry's 'digital skills gap'.

It is difficult to overstate the tectonic shifts publishing is undergoing. There are grand, wide-ranging issues such as the government's Digital Economy Bill, which spells out piracy and copyright in this brave new world. The Google Books Settlement – ongoing complex legal wrangling in the USA between Google and publishers – will have deep implications on how books are sold digitally here. Publishers are now increasingly competing with technology companies and other creative industries to be the gatekeepers of content. Jamie Oliver, for example, recently released a very successful iPhone app, *20 Minute Meals.* Yet it wasn't his usual publisher (Penguin) that brought it to market but the television chef's own production company. Worryingly, the people who will be most influential in the UK book trade in the next decade may all reside on the west coast of America: Apple founder Steve Jobs, Amazon head honcho Jeff Bezos and Google's Larry Page and Sergey Brin. Digital completely upends the traditional way of selling books including pricing, how to distribute to customers, and copyright protection. It is a multi-channel world that publishers need to be ready for. As Victoria Barnsley, Chief Executive Officer of HarperCollins noted: 'The business model will become much more complicated. The days when we sold only hardbacks and paperbacks will be looked back on in wonder.'

Tom Tivnan is features editor of the *Bookseller*. Previously a freelance writer, his work has appeared in the *List*, the *Glasgow Herald*, the *Scotsman* and the *Independent*. He has also worked as a bookseller for Blackwell in Edinburgh and Barnes & Noble in the USA.

See also...

- *The state of commissioning*, page 299
- *Spotting a bestseller*, page 235
- *Print on demand*, page 332
- *Who owns whom in publishing*, page 336
- *E-publishing*, page 629
- *Ebooks*, page 635

Print on demand

David Taylor explains how print on demand is keeping books alive.

What is 'print on demand'?

Ever since mankind first started committing words to a physical form of delivery, whether on wood, stone, papyrus, illuminated text or moveable type, the method of supplying these for sale has largely followed a similar pattern: produce first and then sell. Of course, the risk in this is that the publisher can overproduce or underproduce. Overproduction means that the publisher has tied up cash in books that are waiting to be sold. Underproduction means that the publisher has run out and sales are being missed because the book is not available to buy.

If you walk around any publisher's distribution centre you will see huge quantities of books that have been printed and are awaiting sale, representing large amounts of cash tied up in physical inventory. One of the hardest decisions that a publisher has to make is how many copies of a title to print upon publication; equally hard is how many to reprint if the initial print run is sold. Get these wrong and it can cost the publisher dearly and, in some extreme cases, prove mortal to the business.

For others in the supply chain, this model is also deeply flawed. The author whose title sells well can fall into the limbo of 'out of stock' pending a reprint decision by the publisher. The bookseller, who has orders for a title but cannot supply them, also loses sales and disappoints customers. In some cases, those orders are of the moment and when that moment passes, so does the sale. Last but by no means least, the book buyer is frustrated as they are unable to buy the book that they wish to read.

The supply model is also famously inefficient characterised as it is by large amounts of speculative stock being printed, transported, stored in warehouses, transported again, returned from the bookseller if it does not sell and, in many cases, being pulped. Not only is this commercially inefficient, it is also environmentally costly involving large amounts of energy being used to print and transport books that may end their life in a landfill.

In the mid 1990s, developments in the then emerging field of digital printing started to hold out the possibility that this traditional 'print first then sell' model might be changed to a more commercially attractive 'sell first and then print' model. Such a supply model was premised upon a number of things coming together.

- Firstly, the technology of digital printing advanced to the stage where simple text-based books could be produced to a standard that was acceptable to publishers in terms of quality.
- Secondly, the speed of digital presses advanced so that a book could be produced upon the receipt of an order and supplied back to the customer within an acceptable timeframe.
- Thirdly, models started to emerge which married these digital printing capabilities to wholesaling and book distribution networks such that books could be stored digitally, offered for sale to the market with orders being fulfilled on a 'print-on-demand' (POD) basis from a virtual warehouse rather than a physical warehouse full of speculative inventory. This hybrid model requires a highly sophisticated IT infrastructure to allow the swift routing and batching of orders to digital print engines so that genuine single copy orders can be produced 'on demand'.

The first mover in developing this model was the US book wholesaler Ingram Book Group which, in 1997, installed a digital print line in their giant book wholesaling warehouse in Tennessee and started to offer a service to US publishers called Lightning Print. The service offered publishers the option of allowing Ingram to hold their titles in a digital format, offer them for sale via Ingram's vast network of bookselling customers and then print the title when it was ordered. In addition, the publisher signing up to the service could order copies for their own purposes.

Twelve years on, Lightning Source, as the company became known, has operations in both the USA and UK and is printing around 1.5 million books a month from a digital warehouse containing two million titles from over 11,000 publishers. The average print run per order is around 1.8 copies.

POD publishers

Digital printing technology has developed at a staggering pace since the mid 1990s and the quality of digitally printed titles is now almost indistinguishable from titles printed using offset machines. Speed of production has also improved at amazing rates; for example, Lightning Source now produces books on demand for Ingram customers within four hours of receiving the order, thereby allowing orders to be shipped within 24 hours back to the bookseller.

Whilst Lightning Source is the clear global leader, other players have entered the market. In the UK, Antony Rowe established a POD operation in partnership with the UK's biggest book wholesaler, Gardners, in early 2000. Antony Rowe's POD facility supplies orders on demand for Gardner's bookselling customers in a very similar model to that of Ingram and Lightning Source in the USA.

In Germany, the book wholesaler Libri has a POD operation, Books on Demand, which not only offers POD services to publishers, it also offers a self-publishing service to authors (see *Doing it on your own* on page 310). Lightning Source and Antony Rowe deal only with publishers.

One of the most significant moves in this area was the purchase in 2005 by Amazon of a small US POD business called Booksurge. Like Libri's Books on Demand model, Amazon also offers a self-publishing service to authors and is actively leveraging its dominance of the internet bookselling market to develop innovative packages for authors via this model and their Create Space brand. The consensus within the book trade appears to be that Amazon sees POD as a very important part of the way in which they manage their supply chain and as a key opportunity to improve service levels to their customers.

As digital print technology has improved, many traditional book printers have tried to enter this market and offer POD. However, without significant investment in the IT infrastructure needed to deliver single copy production at scale and speed and without allying that capability to an established book distribution or wholesaling network, many of these offers are effectively ultra short-run printing offers and cannot replicate the genuine POD supply model of a single copy printed when an order is received.

What POD means for authors

POD is impacting aspiring and published authors in different ways. One of the by-products of the emergence of POD has been the birth of a whole set of new publishing models. Removing the need to carry speculative inventory has reduced the barriers to entry for organisations which want to enter the publishing space. For example, in the US market, Lightning Source's supply model has allowed a large number of self-publishing companies to flourish and to offer aspiring authors a wide range of services to allow them to get their work into print. These companies will typically use a POD service like Lightning Source to do the physical printing and distribution of a title; in addition, they may use Lightning to have these titles listed for sale via book wholesalers like Amazon and Gardners, internet booksellers like Amazon, and physical bookshop chains such as Barnes & Noble and Waterstone's. Authors may also have the opportunity to order copies of their own titles. These companies will typically offer the aspiring author a set of support services covering editorial, marketing, design, etc.

The aspiring author

No longer does an author wanting to self-publish have to commit a large sum of money upfront to buy thousands of copies of his title and then have to sell them himself. The previously mentioned self-publishing organisations are large, sophisticated and have many tens of thousands of authors whose books are available for sale in mainstream book reselling outlets. In addition, there is a growing trend for what we might term traditional publishers to trawl self-published titles for potential; there have been several well-publicised cases of authors who started out by self-publishing before being picked up by one of the established publishing houses. There are also some signs that traditional publishers are starting to look at how they might build a self-publishing model into their traditional business.

The published author

The POD picture for the published author is a little more mixed. There is no doubt that traditional publishers are engaging more than ever before with the benefits that POD brings. The ability to reduce speculative inventory or get out of it completely, to ensure that sales are not missed, to reduce the risk of getting a reprint decision wrong, and even to bring titles back to life from the out-of-print graveyard, are all very attractive financial propositions. For the author who has a book already published, POD means sales are not missed and therefore royalties are forthcoming. Many books can languish in the 'reprint under consideration' limbo for years: POD removes that category and ensures that books are available for sale. Probably the thorniest issue is around the decision to put a book out of print and here most author contracts have simply not caught up with the new technologies. Some contracts still require that the publisher has to keep physical inventory of a title to show that it is in print, yet many tens of thousands of books are in print and there is no physical inventory held anywhere. An author may therefore find their title being put out of print because of such a clause even though the publisher is willing to keep it in print but does not want to keep speculative inventory printed before an order is received.

The flip side of this, of course, is that a publisher might use POD to retain the rights to the title by printing a small amount of inventory when really the best thing for the author might be to allow the title to go out of print and get the rights back. There have been many cases where rights have reverted to the author who has then either set himself up as an independent publishing company or utilised the services of one of the self-publishing companies mentioned earlier.

In conclusion, the advice for both aspiring authors and published authors is to do your homework. For an aspiring author, look carefully at the various self-publishing organisations out there and do your sums. Are you better off using them or do you want to set up your own publishing company? For published authors, take a long hard look at how your contract defines 'out of print'. The old definition was typically based on 'no physical copies in existence': POD has made that irrelevant and your contract should reflect these new realities if you are to take full advantage of them.

And finally, here is one of the most delicious ironies of this whole model. The death of the physical book has been predicted many times now we live in a digital age. POD has digital technology at its core and yet it is giving life to one of the oldest products on the planet: the paper book. POD is set to be at the heart of the way in which paper books are published, printed and distributed for many years to come. Without this new model, there would be far fewer books available to buy and read and I, for one, think that the world would be a duller place for that.

David Taylor has spent most of his 25 years in the book trade in bookselling and is currently Senior Vice President, Content Acquisition International, Ingram Content Group and Group Managing Director, Lightning Source UK Ltd.

See also...

- *Notes from a successful self-publisher*, page 308
- *Doing it on your own*, page 310
- *Vanity publishing*, page 343
- *E-publishing*, page 629
- *Ebooks*, page 635

Who owns whom in publishing

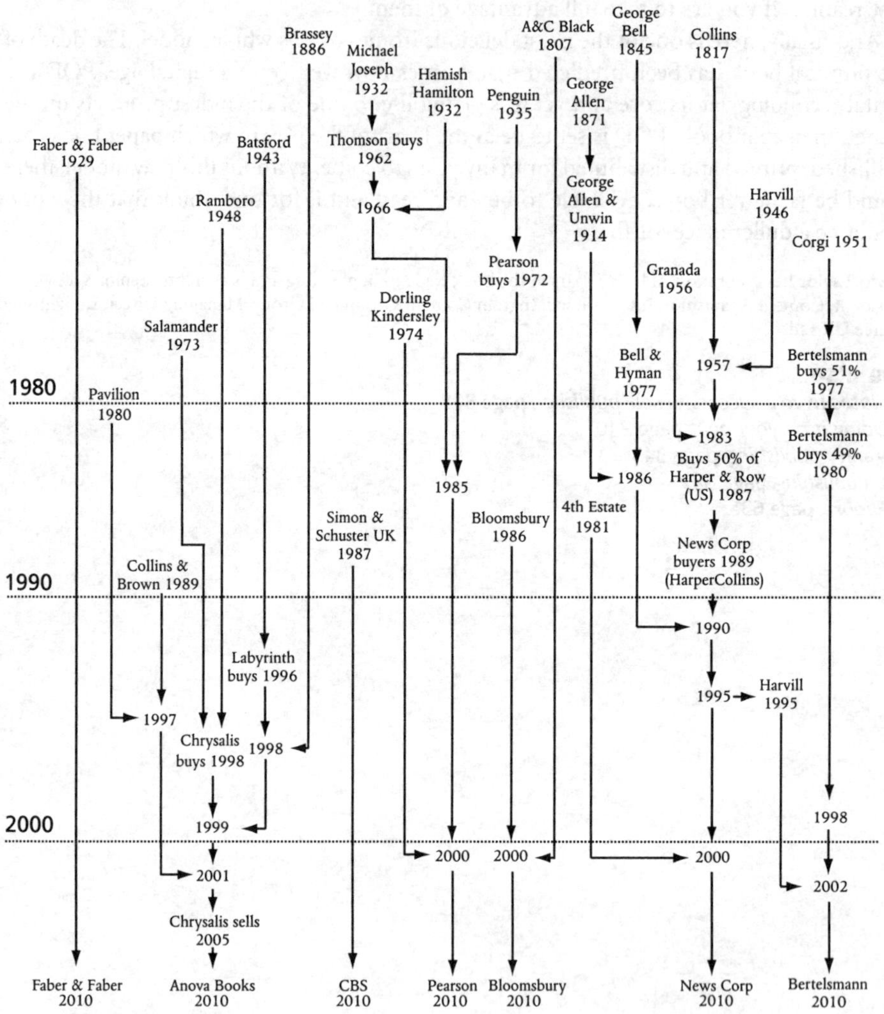

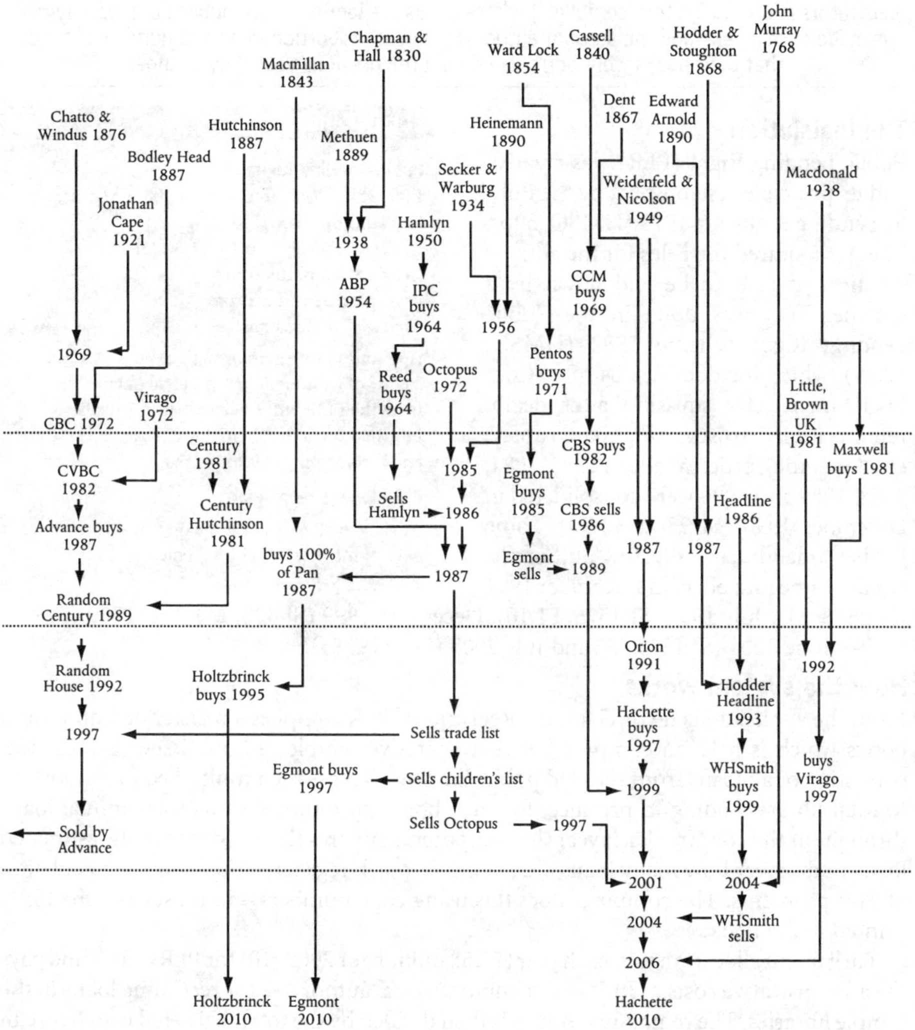
John Murray 1768
Chapman & Hall 1830
Cassell 1840
Hodder & Stoughton 1868
Ward Lock 1854
Macmillan 1843
Dent 1867
Edward Arnold 1890
Chatto & Windus 1876
Hutchinson 1887
Heinemann 1890
Methuen 1889
Bodley Head 1887
Secker & Warburg 1934
Weidenfeld & Nicolson 1949
Macdonald 1938
Jonathan Cape 1921
Hamlyn 1950
1938
ABP 1954
IPC buys 1964
CCM buys 1969
1956
1969
Pentos buys 1971
Reed buys 1964
Octopus 1972
Little, Brown UK 1981
Virago 1972
CBC 1972
Century 1981
CBS buys 1982
Maxwell buys 1981
CVBC 1982
1985
Egmont buys 1985
Century Hutchinson 1981
Sells Hamlyn
1986
CBS sells 1986
Headline 1986
Advance buys 1987
1987
1987
buys 100% of Pan 1987
Egmont sells
1989
1987
Random Century 1989
Orion 1991
Random House 1992
Holtzbrinck buys 1995
1992
Hodder Headline 1993
Hachette buys 1997
1997
Sells trade list
buys Virago 1997
Egmont buys 1997
Sells children's list
WHSmith buys 1999
1999
Sells Octopus
1997
Sold by Advance
2001
2004
2004
WHSmith sells
2006
Holtzbrinck 2010
Egmont 2010
Hachette 2010
Books

Public Lending Right

Under the PLR system, payment is made from public funds to authors (writers, translators, illustrators and some editors/compilers) whose books are lent out from public libraries. Payment is made once a year, and the amount authors receive is proportionate to the number of times that their books were borrowed during the previous year (July to June).

The legislation

Public Lending Right (PLR) was created, and its principles established, by the Public Lending Right Act 1979 (HMSO, 30p). The Act required the rules for the administration of PLR to be laid down by a scheme. That was done in the Public Lending Right Scheme 1982 (HMSO, £2.95), which includes details of transfer (assignment), transmission after death, renunciation, trusteeship, bankruptcy, etc. Amending orders made in 1983, 1984, 1988, 1989 and 1990 were consolidated in December 1990 (SI 2360, £3.90). Some further amendments affecting author eligibility came into effect in December 1991 (SI 2618, £1), July 1997 (SI 1576, £1.10), December 1999 (SI 420, £1), July 2000 (SI 933, £1.50), June 2004 (SI 1258 £3) and July 2005 (SI 1519, £3).

Further information

Public Lending Right
PLR Office, Richard House, Sorbonne Close, Stockton-on-Tees TS17 6DA
tel (01642) 604699 *fax* (01642) 615641
website www.plr.uk.com, www.plrinternational.com
Contact The Registrar

Application forms, information, publications and a copy of its *Annual Report* are all obtainable from the PLR Office. See website for further information on eligibility for PLR, loans statistics and forthcoming developments.

PLR Management Board

Advises the Registrar on the operation and future development of the PLR scheme.

How the system works

From the applications he receives, the Registrar of PLR compiles a register of authors and books which is held on computer. A representative sample of book issues is recorded, consisting of all loans from selected public libraries. This is then multiplied in proportion to total library lending to produce, for each book, an estimate of its total annual loans throughout the country. Each year the computer compares the register with the estimated loans to discover how many loans are credited to each registered book for the calculation of PLR payments. The computer does this using code numbers – in most cases the ISBN printed in the book.

Parliament allocates a sum each year (£7.58 million for 2009–10) for PLR. This Fund pays the administrative costs of PLR and reimburses local authorities for recording loans in the sample libraries. The remaining money is then divided by the total registered loan figure in order to work out how much can be paid for each estimated loan of a registered book.

Limits on payments

Bottom limit. If all the registered interests in an author's books score so few loans that they would earn less than £1 in a year, no payment is due.

Top limit. If the books of one registered author score so high that the author's PLR earnings for the year would exceed £6,600, then only £6,600 is paid. No author can earn more than £6,600 in PLR in any one year.

Money that is not paid out because of these limits belongs to the Fund and increases the amounts paid that year to other authors.

The sample

The basic sample represents only public libraries (no academic, school, private or commercial libraries are included) and only loans made over the counter (not consultations of books on library premises). It follows that only those books which are loaned from public libraries can earn PLR and make an application worthwhile.

The sample consists of the entire loans records for a year from libraries in more than 30 public library authorities spread through England, Scotland, Wales and Northern Ireland. Sample loans represent around 20% of the national total. All the computerised sampling points in an authority contribute loans data ('multi-site' sampling). The aim has been to increase the sample without any significant increase in costs. In order to counteract sampling error, libraries in the sample change every two to three years. Loans are totalled every 12 months for the period 1 July–30 June.

An author's entitlement to PLR depends, under the 1979 Act, on the loans accrued by his or her books in the sample. This figure is averaged up to produce first regional and then finally national estimated loans.

ISBNs

PLR depends on the use of code numbers to identify books lent and to correlate loans with entries on the register so that payment can be made. The system uses the International Standard Book Number (ISBN), which is required for all new registrations. Different editions (e.g. 1st, 2nd, hardcover, paperback, large print) of the same book have different ISBNs.

Authorship

In the PLR system the author of a book is the writer, illustrator, translator, compiler, editor or reviser. Authors must be named on the book's title page, or be able to prove authorship by some other means (e.g. receipt of royalties). The ownership of copyright has no bearing on PLR eligibility.

Summary of the 27th year's results

Registration: authors. When registration closed for the 27th year (30 June 2009) there were 37,429 authors and assignees.

Eligible loans. Of the 308 million estimated loans from UK libraries, 132 million belong to books on the PLR register. The loans credited to registered books – 42% of all library borrowings – qualify for payment. The remaining 58% of loans relate to books that are ineligible for various reasons, to books written by dead or foreign authors, and to books that have simply not been applied for.

Money and payments. PLR's administrative costs are deducted from the fund allocated to the Registrar annually by Parliament. Operating the Scheme this year cost £779,000, representing some 10% of the PLR fund. The Rate per Loan for 2009–10 was 6.29 pence and was calculated to distribute all the £6,760,000 available. The total of PLR distribution and costs is therefore the full £7.58 million which the Government provided in 2009–10.

The numbers of authors in various payment categories are as follows:

*362	payments at	£5,000–6,600
364	payments between	£2,500–4,999.99
850	payments between	£1,000–2,499.99
962	payments between	£500–999.99
3,423	payments between	£100–499.99
17,280	payments between	£1–99.99
23,241	TOTAL	

* Includes 250 authors whose book loans reached the maximum threshold

Books

Co-authorship/illustrators. In the PLR system the authors of a book are those writers, translators, editors, compilers andillustrators as defined above. Authors must apply for registration before their books can earn PLR. This can now be done online through the PLR website. There is no restriction on the number of authors who can register shares in any one book as long as they satisfy the eligibility criteria.

Writers and/or illustrators. At least one must be eligible and they must jointly agree what share of PLR each will take. This agreement is necessary even if one or two are ineligible or do not wish to register for PLR. Share sizes should be based on contribution. The eligible authors will receive the share(s) specified in the application. PLR can be any whole percentage. Detailed advice is available from the PLR office.

Translators. Translators may apply, without reference to other authors, for a 30% fixed share (to be divided equally between joint translators).

Editors and compilers. An editor or compiler may apply, either with others or without reference to them, to register a 20% share. Unless in receipt of royalties an editor must have written at least 10% of the book's content or more than ten pages of text in addition to normal editorial work. The share of joint editors/compilers is 20% in total to be divided equally. An application from an editor or compiler to register a greater percentage share must be accompanied by supporting documentary evidence of actual contribution.

Dead or missing co-authors. Where it is impossible to agree shares with a co-author because that person is dead or untraceable, then the surviving co-author or co-authors may submit an application without the dead or missing co-author but must name the co-

Most borrowed authors

Children's authors

1	Daisy Meadows
2	Jacqueline Wilson
3	Francesca Simon
4	Mick Inkpen
5	Julia Donaldson
6	Lauren Child
7	Lucy Cousins
8	Ian Whybrow
9	Enid Blyton
10	Janet & Allan Ahlberg
11	Roald Dahl
12	Fiona Watt
13	Tony Ross
14	Vivian French
15	Terry Deary
16	Eric Hill
17	Jeremy Strong
18	Jeanne Willis
19	Michael Morpurgo
20	Rose Impey

Authors of adult fiction

1	James Patterson
2	Nora Roberts
3	Danielle Steel
4	Josephine Cox
5	Ian Rankin
6	Alexander McCall Smith
7	Anna Jacobs
8	Clive Cussler
9	Jodi Picoult
10	Agatha Christie
11	Katie Flynn
12	Patricia Cornwell
13	M.C. Beaton
14	Jack Higgins
15	Michael Connelly
16	John Grisham
17	Tess Gerritsen
18	Rosie Harris
19	Maeve Binchy
20	Harlan Coben

These two lists are of the most borrowed authors in UK public libraries. They are based on PLR sample loans in the period July 2008–June 2009. They include all writers, both registered and unregistered, but not illustrators where the book has a separate writer. Writing names are used; pseudonyms have not been combined.

author and provide supporting evidence as to why that co-author has not agreed shares. The living co-author(s) will then be able to register a share in the book which will be 20% for the illustrator (or illustrators) and the residual percentage for the writer (or writers). If this percentage is to be divided between more than one writer or illustrator, then this will be in equal shares unless some other apportionment is requested and agreed by the Registrar.

The PLR Office can help to put co-authors (including illustrators) in touch with each other. Help is also available from publishers, the writers' organisations, and the Association of Illustrators.

Life and death. Authors can only be registered for PLR during their lifetime. However, for authors so registered, books can later be registered if first published within one year before their death or ten years afterwards. New versions of titles registered by the author can be registered posthumously.

Residential qualifications. With effect from 1 July 2000, PLR is open to authors living in the European Economic Area (i.e. EU member states plus Norway, Liechtenstein and Iceland). A resident in these countries (for PLR purposes) has his or her only or principal home there.

Eligible books

In the PLR system each separate edition of a book is registered and treated as a separate book. A book is eligible for PLR registration provided that:

- it has an eligible author (or co-author);
- it is printed and bound (paperbacks counting as bound);
- copies of it have been put on sale (i.e. it is not a free handout and it has already been published);
- it is not a newspaper, magazine, journal or periodical;
- the authorship is personal (i.e. not a company or association) and the book is not crown copyright;
- it is not wholly or mainly a musical score;
- it has an ISBN.

Notification and payment

Every registered author receives from the Registrar an annual statement of estimated loans for each book and the PLR due.

Sampling arrangements

To help minimise the unfairnesses that arise inevitably from a sampling system, the Scheme specifies the eight regions within which authorities and sampling points have to be designated and includes libraries of varying size. Part of the sample drops out by rotation each year to allow fresh libraries to be included. The following library authorities have been designated for the year beginning 1 July 2010 (all are multi-site authorities). This list is based on the nine government regions for England plus Northern Ireland, Scotland and Wales.

- East – Suffolk
- London – City of London, Islington, London Libraries Consortium (Enfield, Barking & Dagenham, Brent, Ealing, Hackney, Havering, Newham, Redbridge, Richmond Upon Thames, Tower Hamlets, Waltham Forest, Wandsworth)

- North East – Stockton-on-Tees, Sunderland
- North West & Merseyside – Blackburn with Darwen, Lancashire, Sefton
- South East – Brighton & Hove, Surrey
- South West – Cornwall
- West Midlands – Staffordshire, Warwickshire
- Yorkshire & The Humber – Rotherham, Sheffield
- Northern Ireland – All authorities
- Scotland – East Ayrshire, Glasgow, Scottish Borders
- Wales – Cardiff, Denbighshire & Flintshire, Monmouthshire.

Participating local authorities are reimbursed on an actual cost basis for additional expenditure incurred in providing loans data to the PLR Office. The extra PLR work mostly consists of modifications to computer programs to accumulate loans data in the local authority computer and to transmit the data to the PLR Office at Stockton-on-Tees.

Reciprocal arrangements

Reciprocal PLR arrangements now exist with the German, Dutch, Austrian and other European PLR schemes. Authors can apply for overseas PLR through the Authors' Licensing and Collecting Society. Authors resident in the European Economic Area can also now register for Irish PLR (www.plr.ie). Further information on PLR schemes internationally and recent developments within the EC towards wider recognition of PLR is available from the PLR Office or on the international PLR website.

Vanity publishing

Mainstream publishers invest their own money in the publishing process. In contrast, vanity publishers require an up-front payment from the author to produce a book. Johnathon Clifford highlights the perils of vanity publishing.

My research into vanity publishing began in 1990 when a 12-year-old girl wrote to me in my position as founder and Senior Trustee of the National Poetry Foundation, saying she had found a publisher willing to publish her work. I telephoned the 'publisher' under the guise of an aspiring author, and this call was all it took for them to agree to publish my work. Their offer was 100 copies of a 38-page book for a fee of £1900, with no need for them to see my poetry first.

Definition of vanity publishing

'Vanity publishing, also self-styled (often inaccurately) as 'subsidy', 'joint-venture', 'shared-responsibility' or even 'self' publishing, is a service whereby authors are charged to have their work published. Vanity publishers generally offer to publish a book for a specific fee, or offer to include short stories, poems or other literary or artistic material in an anthology, which the authors are then invited to buy.'

– Advertising Standards Authority definition of vanity publishing, 1997

Since then, I have written *Vanity Press & The Proper Poetry Publishers*, a book based on my extensive feedback from vanity companies, assisted the Advertising Standards Authority and collaborated in the making of television and radio programmes. In 1999, I was invited to the House of Lords to talk about the problem of vanity publishing and the need for a change in the law to stop 'rogue traders' in the publishing world. However, it was not until 2008 that the law was suitably changed to enable the authorities to better curb the excesses of rogue vanity publishers, should they wish. I provide a free advice pack in an effort to protect aspiring authors. The pack, apart from highlighting the business practices of vanity publishers, gives guidance on finding a mainstream publisher, internet publishing, the market for short stories and self-publishing.

The perils of vanity publishing

'Vanity publisher' is a phrase I coined in the early 1960s when two American companies were advertising widely in the British press offering to publish poems for £9 and £12 per poem, respectively. Since then the term has also come to mean 'any company that charges a client to publish a book'.

Mainstream publishers invest in the marketing and promotion of a book and make their profit from the sale of copies of the book. Vanity publishers make their money from up-front charges. One of the main drawbacks of being published by a vanity publisher is its lack of credibility within the industry. The majority of booksellers and library suppliers are loath to handle vanity books and few reviewers are willing to consider a book published in this way. The Business Unit Director of one of the UK's biggest booksellers wrote: 'We do not buy from vanity publishers except in exceptional circumstances. Their books are, with one or two exceptions, badly produced, over-priced, have poor, uncompetitive jackets and usually have no marketing support.'

I have amassed an extensive collection of documentation from authors who have approached one or other of the 100 plus vanity publishers operating in the UK. It consists of vanity publishers' initial promotional letters, subsequent written promises, the contracts and letters of complaint from the author, and the vanity publishers' response to those complaints. In recent years, court judgements have found that some vanity publishers are guilty of 'gross misrepresentation of the services they offer' and, as a result, some have been successfully sued and some forced into 'voluntary' liquidation – often only to swiftly reappear under different names.

How vanity publishers operate

Mainstream publishers never advertise for authors and almost never charge a client, whether known or unknown. Vanity publishers place advertisements wherever they possibly can inviting authors to submit manuscripts. Almost without exception, when authors submit work the vanity publisher will reply that they would like to publish the book but that, as an unknown, the author will have to pay towards the cost. Vanity publishers may tell the author they are very selective in the authors they accept and praise the work, but this is false flattery. I have not been able to find one person during the last 14 years, anywhere in the world, who has been turned down by a vanity publisher – however poorly written their book is. The vanity publisher may state that this is the way many famous authors in the past set out. This is untrue: not one of the quoted 'famous authors' started their writing career by paying a vanity publisher. The BBC programme *Southern Eye* reported that many authors had been sent exactly the same 'glowing report', whatever the subject or quality of their book.

Vanity publishers have charged aspiring authors anything from £1,800 up to (in one recorded instance) £20,000 for publishing their book. Many authors have borrowed thousands of pounds on the strength of promised 'returning royalties', as authors are often led to believe that the vanity publisher's marketing department will sell their book for them and that they will recoup their outlay via this service. In December 1997, *Private Eye* ran an article about three authors, one of whom had paid £2,400 and the other two £1,800 each to a vanity publisher, on the basis that their books would command a 'high level of royalties'. These royalties amounted to £16.35, £21.28 and £47.30 respectively. When the authors complained they each received a threatening letter from the vanity publisher's solicitor. The same company's business practices were featured on the BBC programme *Watchdog* in November 2002.

Some vanity publishers ask their clients to pay a 'subvention'. The standard dictionary definition of the word subvention is 'a grant, aid or subsidy paid by a government to an educational institution', so the term is meaningless when used in the context of vanity publishing. However the request for payment is worded, is the author who will bear the full cost of publishing their book. Not a share of, or a subsidy towards, but the whole cost and a healthy profit margin on top.

Few vanity publishers quote for a fixed number of copies, leaving the author with little idea what they have paid for. Vanity publishers may simply keep manuscripts 'on file' and only print-on-demand, making it difficult to deliver copies quickly enough to the outlets who *do* order them. There are also companies who propose that once book sales have reached a certain 'target' figure, the client's outlay will be refunded. The number of copies required to be sold is always well in excess of a realistic target.

Some companies claim that part of the service they offer is to send copies of your book to Whitakers, the Copyright Receipt Office and the British Library. In fact, this is a legal requirement for all UK publishers. Other companies claim a 'special' relationship which enables them to supply information on your book to particular outlets on the internet. But Amazon.co.uk, the biggest internet bookseller, does not support this and writes: 'Books are listed on Amazon.co.uk's website in a number of ways – we take feeds from BookData and Whitakers (who automatically update these details on our website) as well as from several wholesalers'.

Authors choosing to vanity publish should be aware that as soon as their last instalment has been paid, the vanity publisher has made maximum profit and does not need to sell a single copy of the author's book.

Self-publishing

Another way for an author to see their book in print is to self-publish (see my website). However, since self-publishing has become more acceptable some vanity publishers have tried to pass themselves off as self-publishers. For a book to be genuinely self-published, a name designated by the author as his or her publishing house must appear on the copyright page of the book as 'publisher' and the book's ISBN number must be registered by the ISBN Agency to that author as publisher.

All the copies of a self-published book are the property of the author. If an author does not wish to be involved with the sale and distribution of their book, this can be indicated in the 'Distributor (if different from Publisher)' section on the form sent to the ISBN Agency before publication.

On the title page of every book there is a paragraph which, in essence, states that 'All rights are reserved. No part of this book can be stored on a retrieval system or transmitted in any form or by whatever means without the prior permission in writing from the publisher'. I repeat, without the prior permission of the *publisher*. Not 'the author' who is supposed to have '*self*-published'.

Any company which publishes books under its own name or imprint cannot, by definition, claim to help authors to self-publish. The honest exception is where although the publisher's address appears on the title page, the paragraph above states 'without prior permission of the copyright holder', and the author appears as copyright holder on the same page. True self-publishing gives authors much greater control over the production and dissemination of their books.

Aspiring authors should be careful not to be taken in by the promises of some vanity publishers which have so often proved false. The legal phrase 'Caveat Emptor' (Buyer Beware) here becomes 'Caveat Scriptor' – 'Author Beware!'

Recommended companies

Amolibros
Loundshay Manor Cottage, Preston Bowyer, Milverston, Taunton TA4 1QF
tel (01823) 401527
website www.amolibros.co.uk
Contact Jane Tatam

Authors On Line
19 The Cinques, Gamlingay, Sandy, Beds. SG19 3NU
tel (01767) 652005
website www.authorsonline.co.uk
Contact Richard Fitt

Matador Troubador Publishing Ltd
5 Weir Road, Kibworth, Leicester LE8 0LQ
tel 0116-279 2299
website www.troubador.co.uk
Contact Jeremy Thompson

York Publishing Services Ltd
64 Hallfield Road, Layerthorpe, York YO31 7ZQ
tel (01904) 431213
website www.yps-publishing.co.uk
Contact Duncan Beal

Johnathon Clifford may be contacted via his website, www.vanitypublishing.info.

Book clubs

Artists' Choice
Artists' Choice Ltd, PO Box 3, Huntingdon, Cambs. PE28 0QX
tel (01832) 710201 *fax* (01832) 710488
website www.artists-choice.co.uk, www.acaward.com

Quarterly.

Baker Books
Manfield Park, Cranleigh, Surrey GU6 8NU
tel (01483) 267888 *fax* (01483) 267409
email enquiries@bakerbooks.co.uk
website www.bakerbooks.co.uk

School book club for children aged 3–16. Operates in the UK and in English medium schools overseas.

BCA
Hargreaves Road, Groundwell Ind. Estate, Swindon SN25 5BG
tel (01793) 723547 *fax* (01793) 747113
website www.member.booksdirect.co.uk

Books for Children, Fantasy & SF Book Club, The History Guild, Military and Aviation Book Society, The Railway Book Club, Books Direct, Omnibus.

Bibliophile
5 Datapoint, South Crescent, London E16 4TL
tel 020-7474 2474 *fax* 020-7474 8589
email orders@bibliophilebooks.com
website www.bibliophilebooks.com
Secretary Annie Quigley

To promote value-for-money reading. Upmarket literature and classical music on CD available from mail order catalogue (10 p.a.). Over 3000 titles covering art and fiction to travel, history and children's books. Founded 1978.

The Book People Ltd
Park Menai, Bangor LL57 4FB
tel (0845) 6024040 *fax* (0845) 6064242
email sales@thebookpeople.co.uk
website www.thebookpeople.co.uk

Popular general fiction and non-fiction, including children's and travel. Monthly.

Cygnus Book Club
PO Box 15, Llandeilo, Carmarthenshire SA19 6YX
tel (01558) 825500, (0845) 456 1577
fax (01558) 825517
email enquiries@cygnus-books.co.uk
website www.cygnus-books.co.uk

Includes psychology and self-help, diet, health and exercise, world religions, new economics and education, green issues, mythology, spirituality. Monthly. No unsolicited MSS.

The Folio Society
44 Eagle Street, London WC1R 4FS
tel 020-7400 4222 *fax* 020-7400 4242
website www.foliosociety.com

Fine editions of classic literature.

Letterbox Library
71–73 Allen Road, London N16 8RY
tel 020-7503 4801 *fax* 020-7503 4800
email info@letterboxlibrary.com
website www.letterboxlibrary.com

Specialises in children's books that celebrate equality and diversity.

The Poetry Book Society
4th Floor, 2 Tavistock Place, London WC1H 9RA
tel 020-8870 8403 *fax* 020-8870 0865
email info@poetrybooks.co.uk
website www.poetrybooks.co.uk, www.poetrybookshoponline.com, www.childrenspoetrybookshelf.co.uk

Runs a quarterly poetry book club, with poet selectors choosing the best new collection of the quarter, and the Children's Poetry Bookshelf, a 3 times yearly book club offering children's poetry to teachers, parents and grandparents. Also runs online poetry bookshop and distributes and sells CDs for the Poetry Archive. Awards the TS Eliot Prize for Poetry and, in partnership with the British Library, the Michael Marks Awards for Poetry Pamphlets. See also page 361.

Red House
PO Box 142, Bangor LL57 4ZP
tel 0845 606 4280 *fax* (0845) 606 4242
email enquiries@redhouse.co.uk
website www.redhouse.co.uk

Helps parents to select the right books for their children at affordable prices. A free monthly magazine features the best of the latest titles on offer, young reader reviews and fascinating insight into the minds of popular children's writers. Sponsors the Red House Children's Book Award (page 606). Founded 1979.

Scholastic Book Clubs and Fairs
Euston House, 24 Eversholt Street, London NW1 1DB
tel 020-7756 7756 *fax* 020-7756 7799
email scbenquiries@scholastic.co.uk
website www.scholastic.co.uk, http://clubs.scholastic.co.uk

Leading schools book clubs and fairs. Offers primary and secondary clubs and fairs.

Scholastic Book Fairs

Dolomite Avenue, Coventry Business Park, Coventry CV5 6UE
tel 0800 212281 (freephone)
website www.scholastic.co.uk/bookfairs
Managing Director Miles Stevens-Hoare

Sells directly to children, parents and teachers in schools through 25,000 week-long events held in schools throughout the UK.

Writers' Bookshelf

Writers' News, 5th Floor, 31–32 Park Row, Leeds LS1 5JD
tel 0113-200 2929 *fax* 0113-200 2928
email janet.davison@writersnews.co.uk

Books and magazines for writers.

Poetry
Notes from a passionate poet

Benjamin Zephaniah describes his route to being published.

'How did you first get published?' and 'can you give me any advice on getting published?' must be the two questions I am most regularly asked as I go poeting around this planet. And what really gets me is that for most of my poetic life I have found them so hard to answer without doing a long talk on race and culture, and giving a lesson on the oral traditions of the Caribbean and Africa. I'm trying hard not to do that now but I have to acknowledge that I do come out of the oral tradition and to some extent I am still very much part of the Jamaican branch of that tradition, which has now established itself in Britain. In reality, getting published wasn't that hard for me: I came to the page from the stage. I didn't wake up one day and decide to join the oral tradition, I simply started performing in churches and community centres, on street corners and on political rallies, and I really didn't care about being published in books – I used to say I just want to be published in people's hearts. Now I don't want to sound like a royal seeking sympathy or a surgeon evaluating her or his work, I just feel there's something very special about hearing people recite a poem of yours back to you when you know that it has never been written down: it means that they must have heard me recite the poem and it had such an impact on them that it left an impression on their minds – but I say hearts because it sounds more sensitive.

Someone with a PhD once told me that the most important thing I could do was to get published, so for what seemed like an eternity (in fact it was just a couple of months) I became the most depressed kid on the block as the rejections flooded in, and I took each rejection very personally. I soon stopped punishing myself and went back to performing. Within the black and Asian communities there was a large network of venues to perform in and I was happy there, performing for 'my people'. But it wasn't long before I started to make a bit of a name for myself in what we now call the mainstream, and then the publishers came running back to me, many of them apologising and saying that the person who sent the rejection letter to me had now moved on and they weren't very good anyway. I didn't blame the publishers; I wasn't angry with them. It was a time when the British publishing industry simply didn't understand Reggae and Dub poetry, and the performance scene as we know it today had hardly taken root. It's not practical to advise all budding poets to go down the route that I chose. Some poets simply don't want to perform whilst others want something published before they take to the stage – they literally want something to cling to as they recite – but I have to say there is nothing like looking your audience in the face and delivering your work to them in person.

I used to be able to give a run down of the poetry publishing and performance scene in Britain in about 30 minutes, but not any longer, with the internet and all that, the universe has changed. Not only are there hundreds of ways to get your poetry published, you can now publish your performance and have a worldwide hit without ever actually having a book or leaving your bedroom. You don't even have to tread the boards to become a performance poet. The choice is now yours: you can be a Dub poet, a pub poet, a cyber poet, a graffiti poet, a Rap poet, a naked poet, a space poet, a MySpace poet, a street poet, a geek poet, an underground poet, or a sound poet. You can go any way you want, but you must never forget to be a poet. You must never forget why you started writing (or performing) and you must love your art. The love I had for words as a baby has never left me, and when I was getting all those rejection letters and feeling so unwanted, my love for poetry never waned.

And another thing: read poetry. Many people tell me that they love poetry but after a minute or so of investigation I find that they only love their own poetry, and in many cases they only understand their own poetry. You can get a lot of help from teachers or in workshops, but reading other peoples' poetry is the best way of understanding poetry, it is the best way of getting into the minds of other poets. This great book that you now have in your hands and learned people who understand the industry are able to give you much better advice on getting published than I can, and if you do get published your publisher or agent should be offering you all the practical help you need. But you have to have the passion, you have to have the inspiration, you have to be a poet. Stay true.

Benjamin Zephaniah has been performing poetry since he was 11 years old. He has also written 11 books of poetry, four novels, and recorded five music CD albums. He spends much of his time encouraging young people to write poetry and has received 15 honorary doctorates in recognition of his work. His latest novel is *Teacher's Dead* (Bloomsbury Publishing 2007) and his most recent music CD is called *Naked*. His website is www.benjaminzephaniah.com.

Getting poetry published

Michael Schmidt examines the challenges for poets who wish to see their work published.

Start with this axiom: you have not come here to make money.

I write as a publisher who has spent over 30 years not making money out of poetry, and as a quondam poet whose rewards were never material, either. Money may be a consequence, but only in a few cases, usually obtained in the form of grants and bursaries, when a career is well beyond the point at which an article such as this is of interest.

In the old days, right up through the 1950s, there was a popular tradition of verse writing: people kept commonplace books for friends to write lines in when visiting. Or folk composed ballads, Christmas poems, dialect eclogues, limericks. Verse was part of social engagement. It took itself seriously in formal terms but made no pretence of being 'art'. There was a level of competence in making conventional verses, sometimes beyond English, in Latin or Greek, and most people could tell a good piece of verse from a bad one. Jane Austen's family was given to playful versing. In second-hand bookshops you find tomes with verse inscriptions. Like weekend painters, verse writers expressed themselves clearly and skilfully, bringing direct, strictly occasional pleasure to another person or a group. The ambition to Get Published At All Costs had not set in. Now it has; it has been endemic for three decades. The social space for verse has almost vanished, and with it the popular versifying skills. Such a loss has consequences. Dr Johnson in *The Life of Savage* reflects that 'negligence and irregularity, long continued, will make knowledge useless, wit ridiculous, and genius contemptible'. The creative writing culture of reception nowadays seems to be defined less as readership or audience, more as 'market'. Is this change regrettable? Yes. Has it brought any benefits? To the art of poetry, to poetry readership, very few.

Even today, weekend painters know their work will never hang in the Tate; amateur musicians (singers, instrumentalists, composers) content themselves with making music as an end in itself. But the occasional versifier is a dying breed, like the red squirrel, replaced by the interloping grey who, a year into writing, submits work to a dozen editors at once, declaring it to be original, relevant, topical. In the twinkling of an eye these strident creatures absorb, without troubling to learn names, the art of Chaucer, Spenser, Milton, Cowper, Dickinson, Walcott, Rich. Their opinion of modern poetry is low. But then they do not base their opinion on a very large sample. They will have heard of the market leaders and remember some of the poetry read at school.

As an editor at a small publishing house I receive over 2,000 full manuscripts a year (and many more submissions for *PN Review*). Telephone calls, letters and emails ask what kind of poetry we publish, whether we publish poetry at all, or how much it will cost to have poems printed. Few poets submitting are aware of the editorial contents of a poetry publisher's list, despite websites and other resources offering this information. Many have read, perhaps in this volume, which publishers have a poetry list and try, without doing a smidgen of research. Without reading. Few seem aware of how large a shoal of wannabe poets surrounds the little flotilla of publishers, editors and other validators. Poetry becomes a means to an end, not an end in itself: to be a poet, go for prizes, give readings and all the peripheral rewards which in the end poison and parch the individual spring, assuming it has more than illusory water in it.

Publishing in book form

An article of this kind usually proffers advice: how to present a manuscript, how to address an editor, what to expect from a contract, etc. I'd rather try to give writers who believe they have a body of publishable work a realistic sense of the chance of publication, and a realistic preparation for its aftermath, assuming the first goal is achieved. Better to counsel realism than foster illusion.

First, the chances of book publication. More than 1,500 new books of verse are published each year, but few are marketed or sold and fewer still reviewed. A list like the one I edit, with 30 poetry titles a year, accommodates at most two or three first collections. Other substantial poetry publishers go for a year or five without adding new names to their lists. Few first collections sell over 1,000 copies. Indeed, some may sell fewer than 300. The book trade has become resistant to all but the market leaders in poetry; few independent presses get their poets even into some of the leading chains. One publisher who has set out to change the equation is Salt, with its short run and print-on-demand approach, and its website and Podcasts. Others have followed, notably Shearsman; and Arc is active in all sorts of ways.

The ecology of poetry publishing, as distinct from that of standard trade publishing, is based more and more narrowly on events. A poet can publish his or her own work, paying a printer to do the job and selling at readings. But then, who is going to invite a self-published poet to read? A poet can go to one of the vanity presses and pay a more substantial sum for the promise of exposure. Again, such publication capitalises on illusion and, as the title proclaims, vanity (see *Vanity publishing*, page 343).

There *are* new opportunities which can be valuable. Any poet is free to post work on the web, in both text and voice form, inviting response. It's quite cheap to do so and response is almost immediate. There are electronic magazines as well. In a sense, the withering away of the poetry book trade is a harbinger of the wider impact of the web. Unfortunately, the web is not discriminating and it is hard to know how a critical take on work self-published on the web will develop. At every stage, it seems to me, poets are tempted to succumb, in their eagerness for publication, to acts of desperation. Publish and be damned! Luck would be a fine thing. There is not even a sufficient audience to damn new work on the web. The question must be, how to publish and be sufficiently visible to *be* damned, or welcomed, as the case may be. But we are getting ahead of ourselves: the first question must be the quality of the work and the motive of the writer.

Before looking for a publisher, writers of verse (as of anything else) should interrogate themselves. *Why* do I want to be published in book form? Is it mere whim or is my work genuinely original? The only way you can answer these questions is by wide reading, not only of contemporaries but also of poets from the past. To be able to judge your art, you must understand it, as you would any other. What makes my work original? In a few instances subject matter in itself can be sufficiently interesting to justify a book, but this is rare: it has more to do with the accidents of birth and upbringing than with any choices a poet might make. Originality is expressed in diction, prosody and form. It need not be dazzling. Edward Thomas recognised Robert Frost's originality, reviewing *North of Boston* in 1914: 'This is one of the most revolutionary books of modern times, but one of the quietest and least aggressive. It speaks, and it is poetry.'

A poet who sets out to get published without understanding in depth the art practised, and the nature of the work intended for publication, is on a hiding to very little. Chances are that such a poet will make decisions that ensure the poetry remains unread.

Ask, before you solicit editorial judgment, to whom your poetry is likely to appeal: To friends and family? The local community (is it in dialect, locally relevant in some way)? To a religious group? Is your work sufficiently distinctive to appeal beyond those groups from which your identity is derived?

Seeking critical appraisal

If a spouse, relation, teacher or friend, commends your verse, it will be gratifying, but how informed are they, and is their response to you as writer or to the writing? Is it courtesy or real validation? Kind Sir John Betjeman used to write a note to anyone who sent him poems saying 'you show potential' or 'talent'. Thousands of poets thus commended would take his endorsement and include it for the next 20 years with each magazine and volume submission. The commendation of a kind writer is, alas, not worth the paper it is written on. If an established writer believes in your work, he or she will make it a mission to send your work to an editor.

It is important to get a critical purchase on your work, not to overestimate it. Some poets accept that their level is, say, among small magazines; they are content to exist there in a community of similarly committed writers. They do not try for the 'better' magazines, knowing they haven't a chance of getting in. They may blame those magazines as elitist and cliquish and no doubt some of them are, but elites and cliques that are permeable to quality. Finding one's level is an early stage in establishing peace of mind: always to aim too high and so to invite rebuff finally undermines self-respect.

Never ask an editor for comments and criticisms unless you are willing to take them. I am often asked for 'a serious appraisal'. When work seems genuinely interesting I offer detailed advice, and often receive back angry letters or defences of work I have risked commenting upon. A poem works or fails to work; no amount of argufying can convert an experienced reader. I may come to understand more clearly what the intention of a poem *was*, and therefore better to understand how far short it has fallen.

Magazines, the internet and broadcasting

Most editors advise new writers to seek publication in magazines first. This is mixed advice. It assumes the poet writes 'filler' poems, the fast food that can be served up in a weekly journal. If you are published in magazines the editor does not respect, it may diminish his or her respect for your work. It is crucial, especially if you are not prolific, to try for publication in places where (a) the work will be widely read and (b) publication will increase your visibility. The *Times Literary Supplement* and *London Review of Books* have a curious and unpredictable taste; several specialised journals are worth trying, *Poetry Review*, *Stand*, *Poetry London*, *The North*, *The Dark Horse*, *The Anglo-Welsh Review* and *PN Review* among them. It is crucial to subscribe to journals you find congenial, read them regularly and get a sense of the wider world of contemporary publication. Among foreign magazines worth close attention are *Poetry*, *Raritan* and *Threepenny Review*.

Publication in web magazines can be satisfying; it can also be dangerous for your copyright (the work slips out of your control), and few editors of my acquaintance credit the web as a place to look for poems. Remember that a poem first published on the web is unlikely to be published in a reputable magazine.

Broadcasting is as unpredictable a medium of dissemination as the web. There are slots for various kinds of poetry on radio: dramatic, lyric, etc. Look at the broadcasting schedules, familiarise yourself with the poetry programmes and producers, locally and nationally. On many networks a broadcast poem is heard by quite a large, if not a discriminating or informed, audience. Editors have been known to track down poems heard in broadcast, especially in the poet's own voice if that poet is a good performer.

The importance of market research

You can do your market research for a book publisher in your personal library of modern poetry books (you ought to have one, with books by favourite authors from a variety of

Poetry magazines

Ambit
website www.ambitmagazine.co.uk

Quarterly magazine that prints original poetry, short fiction, art and reviews. Founded 1959.

Mslexia
website www.mslexia.co.uk

New writing by women.

The North
website www.poetrybusiness.co.uk

A poetry journal published by Smith-Doorstop and The Poetry Business in Huddersfield.

PN Review
website www.pnreview.co.uk

After 30-odd years, it is widely regarded as among the best publications for poetry, with a broad geographical and generic reach.

Poetry Review
website www.poetryreview.org.uk

The journal of the Poetry Society.

Poets & Writers
website www.pw.org

A magazine on the craft and business of writing.

The Reader
website www.thereader.co.uk

A quarterly literary magazine.

USA

Raritan Literary Magazine
Rutgers – The State University of New Jersey, 31 Mine Street, New Brunswick, NJ 08903, USA
tel 732-932-7887 *fax* 732-932-7855

The Threepenny Review
PO Box 9131, Berkeley, CA 94709, USA

Submissions should be sent with an sae.

Details for the other magazines mentioned in the article may be found in either *Magazines UK and Ireland* starting on page 33 or *Poetry organisations* on page 361.

Online

A Public Space
http://apublicspace.org

The Barcelona Review
www.barcelonareview.com

Contemporary Poetry Review
www.cprw.com

Jacket
www.jacketmagazine.com

Poetry Daily
www.poems.com

Publishers

Anvil Books
See page 138.

Arc Publications
See page 138.

Bloodaxe Books Ltd
See page 142.

Dedalus Ltd
See page 149.

Enitharmon Press
See page 152.

Flambard Press
See page 154.

The Poetry Business
See page 361.

Salt Publishing
See page 184.

Seren
See page 186.

Shearsman Books
See page 186.

imprints). Most have editorial priorities which are more or less coherent, expressed in anthologies or in the general choice offered. The chief imprints are Faber, Picador, Penguin, Cape and Chatto among larger players, and Arc, Anvil, Bloodaxe, Carcanet, Enitharmon, Salt and Seren among the independents. Many other valuable outlets exist. The Poetry Book Society makes a convenient selection and has useful catalogues, but trusting a book club's choices is no safer for the poetry than for the fiction lover. Always read *beyond*.

In approaching journal editors or publishers it is important to indicate that you know who they are, and why you have chosen them over others. A brief letter is sufficient. If you practise multiple submissions, warn the editors to whom you write. Some editors follow a geological time-scale in replying. If you have not had a reply in six weeks, feel free to send your work elsewhere, but should the first editor accept it in the end, you must immediately withdraw it from other editors.

Success is slow: a hundred rejections may precede an acceptance. Or acceptance may never quite come. If it doesn't, how do you deal with failure? Many wannabe poets who cannot get visibly published develop a strategy of blame. It is not, they insist, the quality of the work that deprives them of readership, it is the cabals that control the avenues of transmission. Jonathan Swift knew this:

If on Parnassus' top you sit,
You rarely bite, are always bit:
Each poet of inferior size
On you shall rail and criticise ...

Other poets study 'the market' and try to follow the latest fashion. Runt-Raines, runt-Muldoons and Motions, have given way to runt-Duffys and Armitages. Aping success can seem to work: in my late 'teens, when the *New Statesman* had rejected me several times, I wrote a poem in what I took to be the style of Ted Walker, a poet popular with the magazine's poetry editor. Sure enough, my verse was accepted. I had the same experience with *Poetry Now* on radio. The editor loved what he called 'the macabre' and I delivered precisely that. Such poems, cynically composed, had a short half-life. Imitation is part of any serious apprenticeship, but publishing unacknowledged imitations, especially if they are written not to develop skills but to achieve publication, is a form of failure.

Dealing with success

Assuming the Muses of publication smile, how do you deal with success? Success can be failure postponed. A book is edited, designed, published, and then falls into a black hole of neglect. A book is published and receives negative reviews. A book is published, receives good reviews, but fails to sell. A book is published, receives good reviews, sells, but the next book does less well and there is a future of diminishing returns. The judge at the pearly gates will declare, 'It is the sort of verse which was modern in its time'.

Real success is rare and has little to do with the strategies outlined here. No poet living in the UK at this time makes a living solely from writing poems. Most write and teach, or write and perform, or have a day job, or write in other genres (novels, radio and television plays, journalism) as well as poetry. Assuming the poetry is good and/or well received, there will be invitations to perform. Fees vary from about £100 to £1,000, depending on the occasion and the venue. A poet who is a good performer will read once or twice a week for a period of time and sell more books than a poet who cannot perform convincingly, even if the latter's poems are better. Indeed some apparently substantial reputations are based on performance skills rather than on the quality of the poetry.

Real success is judged less by the marketplace, more by a culture of reception which gradually grows alert to new work and explores it. It may be, if the work you are writing is original and challenging, that you will have to develop your own means of transmission on paper (a magazine, a pamphlet or book publishing house) or on the web. As long as the vehicles you create exist to serve not only your own work, but poetry more widely, whether the writing of fellow radicals or neglected texts from the past that helped shape your perspectives and formal approaches. The creation of such vehicles means that you retain control of production and dissemination; eventually the endeavour, particular and general, is acknowledged, the work read. You are in dialogue with readers.

The endorsement of an Establishment consisting of the larger publishers, specialist lists, journals and the academy, is not a guarantee of quality. What is a guarantee is a readership which will go out of its way to get hold of your work – a poem in a magazine, a pamphlet, an e-poem, a book – and will invest time and creative energy in reading you and taking bearings from what you propose.

It would be churlish of me not to mention that many poets spend their time and resources on entering competitions, and competitions are a way (the three or four major ones at least) of making yourself briefly visible. A competition-winning poem is not 'news that stays news', as Pound said poetry ought to be, but mere news. Mere news with money attached: not to be sneezed at. There is also the matter of fees and advances. For a 24-line poem published in a journal, payment will vary from £30 to £500, depending on the outlet. The advance for a book of poems, especially a first collection, will vary from £300 to £3,000, with the occasional mad exception.

In negotiating a publishing contract, it is worth remembering that the greatest value your poems will have in the long term for you, as for your publisher, is unlikely to be the book sales. What will matter in the end, assuming your work becomes established, is the subsidiary rights: anthology, quotation, broadcasting, electronic, translation. Several poetic estates live handsomely on subsidiary rights income. For three decades I have been publishing William Carlos Williams' poetry.

So much depends
upon
a red wheel
barrow...

Eight simple lines have earned Williams' estate, and his publisher, between £27 and £35 per week over that period.

Michael Schmidt OBE is editor of *PN Review* and director of Carcanet Press. He is Professor of Poetry at the University of Glasgow.

Approaching a poetry publisher

Roddy Lumsden outlines the route to getting a volume of poetry published and advises poets on when and how to approach a publisher.

If you follow the perils and pleasures of British poetry via the newspapers, you are excused for thinking things are in a bad way. The media rarely misses a chance to tell us how little we are selling or to report incidences of cronyism and infighting. Their interest is mainly in the peripheral areas of prizes and 'poetry celebrities'. In past editions of this *Yearbook*, this article noted optimistically that sales were better than reported and were thriving. However, there is no doubt that the economic situation has been having an effect on sales: books that might have sold 1,000 or more copies ten years ago are struggling to reach the break-even point, so publishers are tightening their belts.

Commercial publishers with poetry lists are currently more likely to drop poets than take them on – most have scaled down to a handful of books a year. Independent poetry presses are also being cautious. They still take on a small number of poets most years but, at a time when even well-known poets are not making them money, they are looking for poets who, via popular or specialist appeal, can market their work and sell hundreds of copies.

Large bookshops are stocking less poetry, alas, but other sales opportunities exist: smaller chains, specialist outlets, academic, library, overseas and online sales, and sales through poetry readings and courses. Although few poets can make a living from royalties and readings alone, there are certainly a few hundred British poets who make a comfortable, if far from lavish, living from poetry – universities, schoolwork, reviewing, residencies, editing, etc – or who combine this with other part-time employment. Given the unexpected rise in creative writing courses (there are now more than 600 full-time degree courses in creative writing in the UK, see page 688) which require experienced writers to pass on knowledge and techniques, there is now little need for poets to scrape by in an attic on a diet of lentils and divine inspiration.

Yet poetry publishing is a tricky business. Time was when a young chap had his mother type up his sheaf of poems – 20 or so would do – and sent them to the publisher, along with his note of recommendation from a mutual acquaintance at Cambridge and a list of a hundred friends and relatives who had vowed to purchase the slim volume. Things have changed. Until recent decades, few working-class or women writers would have considered attempting to publish. In recent years, at last, poetry books by women outnumber those by men, reflecting the fact that far more women write.

The postwar decades saw shifts in the ethos of British poets but changes affecting them in the century's latter decades were about 'infrastructure' – the rise of independent publishers, the creation of a circuit of poetry venues and literary festivals, government-backed subsidy and promotions, the stiffening of poetic factionalism, the confidence (and sheer numbers) of small magazines, the liberty/tyranny of the internet (with its bookselling and blogging, communities and catfights), the demise of 'broadsheet' interest, the desire for voices from outside the white middle class, the spread of residencies, commissions, fellowships and teaching opportunities.

In his 2004 T.S. Eliot lecture, Picador editor Don Paterson commented on the abundance of writers who, wanting a slice of these opportunities, push for publication before they are ready. Many writers, with hindsight, feel their first books lack cohesion. Another editor told me that many small press poets would have had a strong chance with bigger publishers had they been less impatient.

How much unpublished poetry is there? Let's look at some rough numbers. A late 1990s survey suggested 8% of the UK adult population had recently written a poem of some sort (of which two-thirds were women). Discounting the many who scribble in a diary or pen a quick verse in a card, we're still left with over a million writers who harbour some hope of publication. A few hundred poetry collections by individual writers are published most years. Most – admirable though they may be – are small-scale, from local presses, in pamphlet form, in small print runs. The better-known independent poetry presses (Anvil, Bloodaxe, Carcanet, Salt, Seren and others) publish over 150 books between them, while the few commercial presses (Cape, Chatto, Picador, Faber) venture only around 30 between them. However, these mainly comprise books by established poets from here or abroad (and new editions of work by deceased writers).

First books are few and far between, especially from bigger publishers. Having spoken to most poetry editors, and having done freelance editorial work too, I sympathise with publishers. Space for a debut sometimes comes at the expense of an older poet not selling well. It is difficult to promote a new poet – bookshops want anthologies, promoters want 'names'; despite all the opportunities listed above, poets have to work hard even after publication to make themselves known. Most first-timers are disappointed to find their collection is not met with a raft of reviews, shortlists and reading invitations. It is not unusual now for a poetry book to go unreviewed.

What publishers are looking for

So how do poets get published these days? Well, rarely from what is perceived to be the standard approach of simply submitting a manuscript to a publisher. My advice (and all editors and established poets will concur) is this: you *must* go through the hoops and tasks of learning your craft and proving yourself before considering an approach to a publisher. And no, you're not the exception, even if you are a brilliant young thing, or a late starter expecting short cuts. A first collection will contain 40–70 poems, and most poets will have written a few discarded efforts for each one that makes the cut.

Publishers will expect you to tell them where you have been published in magazine form. Broadly, your work should have appeared in several places. This should include well-established publications: vital though the little magazines are, you are frankly unlikely to be published in book form if the better-known periodicals are consistently turning down your poems. Publishers want you to have a substantial publication in good magazines and journals and the primary reason for this is that a track record of magazine publications shows commitment to a developing manuscript and an effort to develop a readership for your work.

A few years ago, I went through several boxes of manuscripts for an independent press. These scripts had already been deemed worth a third look: most submissions are returned quickly since editors become adept at identifying substandard work. They don't often make mistakes, and would make fewer if the process wasn't clogged by those who send too soon. The work I read was generally impressive, carefully assembled by capable writers and much of it as good as work I'd recently seen in book form. But this publisher only has room for one or two debuts each year. My task was to look for exceptional, original manuscripts and after a while, I found myself growing impatient with poems which were well written but overfamiliar in style and subject matter.

If you do feel you are ready to approach a publisher, you must find out their current submissions policy (see the listings in this *Yearbook* and look at publishers' websites). Some of the bigger lists go through periods where they will not look at any unsolicited work. Some prefer sample submissions of a dozen poems only. Don't make common mistakes: email submissions are rarely allowed; full return postage must be supplied; never ask for an email response, or a detailed critique; keep your covering letter short and pertinent; never drop the name of someone who has praised your work unless you have the express permission to do so.

For younger poets, the Eric Gregory Awards (see page 597) have been an important step up for decades now, though far from a guarantee of publication. The annual awards, run by the Society of Authors, offer grants to the most promising poets (published or not) under 30. Competition success can be another way to attract notice to your work, especially the Arvon Foundation (see page 589) and National Poetry (page 604) competitions. Every poet with serious ambitions should seek opportunities to recite their work and should make the effort to learn to read well, which does not require performance skills, just confidence and conviction.

How poets get published

Many people will whisper that it's 'who you know' that really counts. Well, certainly. This is not about nepotism and 'couch casting', rather, if you are keen to progress, you will seek out peers and mentors where you can. Find a writing group run by a worthy tutor (preferably one with books out from a press you have heard of). You may not live in an area where good writing classes or writers-in-residence are available, but residential courses such as those run by the excellent Arvon Foundation (see page 688) have been a step towards many a successful publication (and grants are available for those with more promise than funds). Above all else, read lots of poetry which is contemporary and engaging, for that's what you will have to be – there is no market for the retro or pastiche. And read widely – many feel, with some validity, that larger British poetry presses can favour the anodyne and the commercial.

For myself, a few years of feverish reading, writing and showing work to university writers-in-residence and to other young poets lead to an Eric Gregory Award which was followed by interest from a major publisher (Faber, whose editor had been on the award panel). I spent five years carefully building up a manuscript. Faber then featured my work in an anthology of eight promising poets but turned down the manuscript. I worked hard to improve it and sent a pamphlet (which I cheaply self-published) to a few other publishers. I was quickly approached by Bloodaxe, who were familiar with my work via the Award and publication in magazines. Here are some examples of how other poets got published:

Poet 'A' was a late starter and wrote in various ways. At a group, he found that poems in a certain style (which he had felt came too easy) were well received. He gladly went with this direction, and put effort into reading his poems aloud when he had the opportunity. A poetry editor saw him reading and asked to see his work.

Poet 'B' had a reputation as a performance poet but had begun writing more formally. He read widely and joined a weekly group with a tutor whose poetry he admired and worked hard on developing a new style of writing. He then did an Arvon Foundation course with a tutor he had encountered before, who was so impressed with his new work, she recommended him to a publisher she was working with.

Poet 'C' had placed poems in several magazines and had some commendations and prizes in a few competitions. She sent a dozen poems to a well-known publisher who asked to see more. She sent more for consideration, took some time off work to develop her manuscript and, in time, the book was accepted.

Most poets would prefer to be published by the bigger publishers with their distribution capabilities and the kudos which leads to their books being more widely read and reviewed. But regional presses can offer opportunities too: a poet I know is one of the 'best-known' poets in her region, does well from teaching and readings and sells up to a thousand copies of her small press books, considerably more than some nationally known poets. And just as certain publishers have a geographical bent, some tend towards poetry in certain genres. A few small presses go for work with a 'performance' edge, while others make available the work of innovative and experimental poets.

One step at a time

To summarise, until you are ready to publish – in fact, until those whose judgement you trust recommend you try – you should concentrate on magazines and journals (and, if you wish, entering competitions). Joining the Poetry Society and the Poetry Book Society (see page 574) are helpful steps. Find out which journals you appreciate and subscribe to them. Magazines constantly change (e.g. *Poetry London* was a low-level newsletter back in the 1990s and is now an impressive journal full of internationally known poets); they appear and disappear overnight; they often have strong styles – you know not to send your quatrains on otters to a hard-boiled 'zine, yet this sort of thing happens frequently.

So take your time, find a mentor, or someone who'll be honest and astute about your poetry, build up a manuscript slowly, with lots of revision, read and read more, find opportunities for reading in public, go to a writing group if you can, do an Arvon Foundation course. And keep in mind that there is far more pleasure in writing than in seeing your name on the spine of a book.

Roddy Lumsden's volume of selected poems, *Mischief Night*, his fifth poetry collection, *Third Wish Wasted*, and *Identity Parade* (an anthology of recent British and Irish poetry) are all published by Bloodaxe Books (2004, 2009 and 2010, respectively).

See also...

- *Publishers of poetry*, page 779
- *Getting poetry published*, page 351
- *Poetry organisations*, page 361
- *Notes from a passionate poet*, page 349

Poetry organisations

Poetry is one of the easiest writing art forms to begin with, though the hardest to excel at or earn any money from. Paul McGrane, Membership Manager at the Poetry Society, lists below the organisations which can help poets take their poetry further.

WHERE TO GET INVOLVED

Academi

3rd Floor, Mount Stuart House,
Mount Stuart Square, Cardiff Bay, Cardiff CF10 5FQ
tel 029-204 72266
email post@academi.org
website www.academi.org

The Welsh National Literature Promotion Agency which has a huge resource available for poets and poetry. It organises events and tours, promotes poets and poetry, offers poetry advice, locates poetry publishers, offers financial help to poets and to organisers wishing to book poets, and much more. To take advantage of their services you have to live or be in Wales, which has the largest number of poets per 1,000 population anywhere in the Western World.

The British Haiku Society

Flat 4, 2 Clifton Lawns, Ramsgate, Kent G11 9PB
website www.britishhaikusociety.org

The Society runs the prestigious annual James W. Hackett International Haiku Award, the Nobuyuki Yuasa Annual International Award for Haibun and the bienniel Sasakawa Prize worth £2,500 for original contributions in the field of haikai. It is active in promoting the teaching of haiku in schools and colleges, and is able to provide readers, course/workshop leaders and speakers for poetry groups, etc. Write for membership details. Founded 1990.

Commonword

6 Mount Street, Manchester M2 5NS
tel 0161-832 3777
email admin@cultureword.org.uk
website www.cultureword.org.uk

Commonword is a valuable resource for poets and writers in the North West. It provides support, training and publishing opportunities for new writers. It has helped to launch the careers of many of the region's leading poets and strives to seek out new talent in unexpected places.

Creative Arts East

Griffin Court, Market Street, Wymondham,
Norfolk NR18 0GU
tel (01953) 713390
email enquiries@creativeartseast.co.uk
website www.creativeartseast.co.uk

Creative Arts East is a fast-growing arts development agency which provides practical support to the arts community in Norfolk; directly promotes tours, exhibitions, and one-off performances and readings by professional artists and companies; and develops community-based arts projects which address social issues around isolation and disadvantage.

The agency was formally launched in 2002, and was set up to combine the collective expertise and energy of 4 smaller arts organisations: Rural Arts East, Norfolk Arts Marketing, Norfolk Literature Development and Create! Members receive the Norfolk Literature Network newsletter containing information, news, events listings and competitions.

The Poetry Book Society

4th Floor, 2 Tavistock Place, London WC1H 9RA
tel 020-7833 9247 *fax* 020-7833 5990
email info@poetrybooks.co.uk
website www.poetrybooks.co.uk, www.poetrybookshoponline.com, www.childrenspoetrybookshelf.co.uk

This unique book club for readers of poetry was founded in 1953 by T.S. Eliot, and is funded by Arts Council England. Every quarter, selectors choose one outstanding publication (the PBS Choice), and recommend 4 other titles, which are sent to members, who are also offered substantial discounts on other poetry books. The PBS also administers the T.S. Eliot Prize (see page 595), produces the quarterly membership magazine, the *Bulletin*, and provides teaching materials for primary and secondary schools. In addition, the PBS runs the Children's Poetry Bookshelf, offering children's poetry for 7–11 year-olds, with parent, school and library memberships and a new child-friendly website. Write for details.

The Poetry Business

Bank Street Arts, 32–40 Bank Street, Sheffield S1 2DS
email edit@poetrybusiness.co.uk
website www.poetrybusiness.co.uk

Dedicated to helping writers reach their full potential by running supportive workshops.

The Poetry Can

12 Great George Street, Bristol BS1 5RH
tel 0117-933 0900
email admin@poetrycan.co.uk
website www.poetrycan.co.uk

The Poetry Can is one of the few literature organisations in the UK specialising in poetry. It organises events such as the Bristol Poetry Festival; runs a lifelong learning programme; offers information and advice in all aspects of poetry.

Poetry Ireland

2 Prouds Lane, Off St Stephen's Green, Dublin 2, Republic of Ireland
tel 353 (01) 478 9974 *fax* 353 (0) 478 0205
email info@poetryireland.ie
website www.poetryireland.ie

Poetry Ireland is the national organisation dedicated to developing, supporting and promoting poetry throughout Ireland. It is a resource and information point for any member of the public with an interest in poetry and works towards creating opportunities for poets working or living in Ireland. It is grant-aided by both the Northern and Southern Arts Councils of Ireland and is a resource centre with the Austin Clarke Library of over 10,000 titles. It publishes the quarterly magazine *Poetry Ireland Review* and the bi-monthly newsletter *Poetry Ireland News*. Poetry Ireland organises readings in Dublin and nationally, and runs a Writers-in-Schools Scheme.

Poetry on Loan

Unit 116, The Custard Factory, Gibb Street, Birmingham B9 4AA
tel 0121-246 2770
email jonathan@bookcommunications.co.uk
website www.poetryonloan.org.uk
Coordinator Jonathan Davidson

Poetry on Loan is a scheme to promote contemporary poetry through libraries in the West Midlands. There are 30 participating libraries and the scheme supports events, displays, stock collections and commissions. It also runs poetry projects for young people.

The Poetry Society

22 Betterton Street, London WC2H 9BX
tel 020-7420 9880 *fax* 020-7240 4818
email info@poetrysociety.org.uk
website www.poetrysociety.org.uk

The Poetry Society was set up to help poetry and poets thrive in Britain and is a registered charity funded by the Arts Council England. The Society offers advice and information to all, with a more comprehensive level of information available to members. Members receive copies of the UK's most prominent poetry magazine, *Poetry Review*, and the Society's newsletter, *Poetry News*, each quarter. The Society's website provides information, news, poetry links and a useful FAQ page, as well as an interactive regional guide to poetry organisations, venues, publishers, magazines and bookshops around the UK through its Poetry Landmarks of Britain section.

The Society also publishes education resources (see later); promotes National Poetry Day; runs Poetry Prescription, a critical appraisal service available to members and non-members (20% discount to members); provides an education advisory and training service, school membership, youth membership and a website. A diverse range of events and readings frequently take place at the Poetry Café and the Poetry Studio at the Society's headquarters in London. The Society also programmes events and readings in other regions of the UK.

Competitions run by the Society include the annual National Poetry Competition, which is one of the largest open poetry competitions in the UK with a first prize of £5000, the biannual Corneliu M. Popescu Prize for European Poetry in Translation and the Foyle Young Poets of the Year Award. Founded 1909.

The Seamus Heaney Centre for Poetry

c/o School of English, Queen's University Belfast, Belfast BT7 1NN
tel 028-9097 1070
email shc@qub.ac.uk
website www.qub.ac.uk/schools/SeamusHeaneyCentreforPoetry Facebook: Seamus Heaney Centre for Poetry

The new Seamus Heaney Centre for Poetry (SHC) is designed to celebrate and promote poetry and artistic endeavour by poets from Northern Ireland. The Centre houses an extensive library of contemporary poetry volumes. It hosts regular creative writing workshops, a poetry reading group, and an ongoing series of readings and lectures by visiting poets and critics from all over the world. The SHC is chaired by the eminent poet, Ciaran Carson, and other resident poets include Medbh McGuckian.

Survivors Poetry

Studio 11, Bickerton House, 25–27 Bickerton Road, London N19 5JT
tel 020-7281 4654 *fax* 020-7281 7894
website www.survivorspoetry.com

A national charity which promotes the writing of survivors of mental distress. A Survivor may be a person with a current or past experience of psychiatric hospitals, ECT, tranquillisers or other medication, or a user of counselling services, a survivor of sexual abuse and any other person who has empathy with the experiences of survivors.

WHERE TO GET INFORMATION

The first place to start is your local library. They usually have information about the local poetry scene. Many libraries are actively involved in promoting poetry as well as having modern poetry available for loan. Local librarians promote writing activities with, for example, projects like Poetry on Loan and Poetry Places information points in West Midlands Libraries.

Arts Council England

website www.artscouncil.org.uk

Arts Council England has 9 regional offices and local literature officers can provide information on local poetry groups, workshops and societies (see page 547). Some give grant aid to local publishers and magazines and help fund festivals, literature projects and readings, and some run critical services.

The Northern Poetry Library

tel (01670) 534514 (poetry enquiries), 534524 (poetry dept)
email npl@northumberland.gov.uk
Membership Free to anyone living in Northumberland, Tyne and Wear, Durham, Cleveland and Cumbria.

The Northern Poetry Library has over 15,000 titles and magazines covering poetry published since 1945. For information about epic through to classic poetry, a full text database is available of all poetry from 600–1900. The library has free public internet access. Founded 1968.

The Poetry Library

Level 5, Royal Festival Hall, London SE1 8XX
tel 020-7921 0943/0664 *fax* 020-7921 0939
email poetrylibrary@rfh.org.uk
website www.poetrylibrary.org.uk
Membership Free with proof of identity and current address

The principal roles of the Poetry Library are to collect and preserve all poetry published in the UK since about 1912 and to act as a public lending library. It also keeps a wide range of international poetry. It has 2 copies of each title available and a collection of about 40,000 titles in English and English translation. The Library also provides an education service (see under 'Help for young poets and teachers', below).

The Library runs an active information service, which includes a unique noticeboard for lost quotations, and tracing authors and publishers from extracts of poems. Current awareness lists are available for magazines, publishers, competitions, bookshops, groups and workshops, evening classes and festivals on receipt of a large sae. The Library also stocks a full range of British poetry magazines as well as a selection from abroad. When visiting the Library, look out for the Voice Box, a performance space for literature; a programme is available from 020-7921 0906. Open 11am–8pm Tuesday to Sunday. Founded in 1953 by the Arts Council.

The Scottish Poetry Library

5 Crichton's Close, Canongate, Edinburgh EH8 8DT
tel 0131-557 2876
email reception@spl.org.uk
website www.spl.org.uk

The Scottish Poetry Library is the place for poetry in Scotland for the regular reader, the serious student or the casual browser. It has a remarkable collection of written works, as well as tapes and videos. The emphasis is on contemporary poetry written in Scotland, in Scots, Gaelic and English, but historic Scottish poetry – and contemporary works from almost every part of the world – feature too. They also have collections for the visually impaired. All resources, advice and information are readily accessible, free of charge. It holds regular poetry events, details of which are available on the library website. Founded 1984.

ONLINE RESOURCES

You can obtain a wealth of information at the click of a mouse these days. In addition to those listed above, good starting points are:

The Poetry Archive

website www.poetryarchive.org

The Poetry Kit

website www.poetrykit.org

The Poetry Society of America

website www.poetrysociety.org

WHERE TO GET POETRY BOOKS

See the Poetry Book Society, above. The Poetry Library provides a list of bookshops which stock poetry. For second-hand mail order poetry books try:

Baggins Book Bazaar

19 High Street, Rochester, Kent ME1 1PY
tel (01634) 811651 *fax* (01634) 840591
email godfreygeorge@btconnect.com
website www.bagginsbooks.co.uk

Secondhand bookshop with over half a million books in stock.

The Poetry Bookshop

The Ice House, Brook Street, Hay-on-Wye HR3 5BQ
tel (01497) 821812
website www.poetrybookshop.co.uk

Peter Riley

27 Sturton Street, Cambridge CB1 2QG
tel (01223) 576422
email priley@dircon.co.uk

Sweetens of Bolton

86 Deansgate, Bolton, Lancs. BL1 1BD
tel (01204) 528457

WHERE TO CELEBRATE POETRY

Festival information should be available from Arts Council England offices (see page 548). See also *Literature festivals* on page 615.

The British Council

10 Spring Gardens, London SW1A 2BN
tel 020-7389 3194 *fax* 020-7389 3199
website www.britishcouncil.org/arts-literature.htm

Send a large sae or visit the website for a list of forthcoming festivals.

WHERE TO PERFORM

In London, Express Excess, Short Fuse and Aromapoetry are 3 of the liveliest venues for poetry performances and they regularly feature the best performers. Poetry Unplugged at the Poetry Café is famous for its open mic nights (Tuesdays 7.30pm). Poetry evenings are held all over the UK and those listed below are worth checking out. Others can be found by visiting your local library or your Arts Council office, or by visiting the Landmarks of Britain section of the Poetry Society website (www.poetrysociety.org.uk/content/landmarks).

Apples & Snakes Performance Poetry

The Albany, Douglas Way, London SE8 4AG
tel 0845 5213460
email info@applesandsnakes.org
website www.applesandsnakes.org

Carlton Poets

The Carlton Centre, Carlton Road, Weston-Super-Mare
email marilynedbrooke@hotmail.com

CB1 Poetry

32 Mill Road, Cambridge CB1 2AD
tel (01223) 363271 ext. 2725
email cb1poetry@fastmail.fm
website www.cb1poetry.org.uk

Clitheroe Books Open Floor Readings

29 Moor Lane, Clithence BB7 1BE
tel (01200) 444242
email joharbooks@aol.com

Coffee House Poetry

PO Box 16210, London W4 1ZP
tel 020-7370 1434
email coffpoetry@aol.com
website www.coffeehousepoetry.org

Dead Good Poets Society

96 Bould Street, Liverpool L1 4HY
tel 07903 563327
email sarah@deadgoodpoetssociety.org.uk
website www.deadgoodpoetssociety.org.uk

Express Excess

The Enterprise, 2 Haverstock Hill, London NW3
tel 020-7485 2659

Hammer and Tongue

Hammer and Tongue HQ, The Old Music Hall, Oxford OX4 1JE
tel (01865) 403357
email events@hammerandtongue.co.uk
website www.hammerandtongue.co.uk

Poetry Café

22 Betterton Street, London WC2 9BX
tel 020-7420 9887
email poetrycafe@poetrysociety.org.uk

Shortfuse

The Camden Head, Camden Walk, Islington, London N1
website http://shortfuse.20six.co.uk

Tongues and Grooves

The Florence Arms, Florence Road, Southsea, Hants PO5 2NE
tel (02392) 734180
email enquiries@tongues-and-grooves.org.uk
website www.tongues-and-grooves.org.uk

COMPETITIONS

There are now hundreds of competitions to enter and as the prizes increase, the highest being £5,000 (first prize in the National Poetry Competition and the Arvon Foundation International Poetry Competition), so does the prestige associated with winning such competitions.

To decide which competitions are worth entering, make sure you know who the judges are and think twice before paying large sums for an anthology of 'winning' poems which will only be read by entrants wanting to see their own work in print. The Poetry Library publishes a list of competitions each month (available free on receipt of a large sae). See also *Getting poetry published* on page 351 and *Prizes and awards* on page 588.

Literary prizes are given annually to published poets and as such are non-competitive. An A–Z guide to literary prizes can be found on the Booktrust website (www.booktrust.org.uk). A current list of competitions can be found at www.poetrylibrary.org.uk/competitions

WHERE TO WRITE POETRY

Apples & Snakes

The Albany, Douglas Way, London SE8 4AG
tel 0845 5213460

A vital performance poetry agency dedicated to giving 'voice to challenging, diverse and dynamic poets…' Presents fortnightly shows at the Albany and holds occasional workshops. Founded 1982.

The Arvon Foundation

Lumb Bank – The Ted Hughes Arvon Centre, Heptonstall, Hebden Bridge, West Yorkshire HX7 6DF

tel (01422) 843714 *fax* (01422) 843714
email lumbbank@arvonfoundation.org
The Arvon Foundation at Totleigh Barton, Sheepwash, Beaworthy, Devon EX21 5NS
tel (01409) 231338 *fax* (01409) 231144
email totleighbarton@arvonfoundation.org
The Arvon Foundation at Moniack Mhor, Teavarren, Kiltarlity, Beauly, Inverness-shire IV4 7HT
tel (01463) 741675 *fax* (01463) 741733
email moniackmhor@arvonfoundation.org
The Hurst – The John Osborne Arvon Centre, Clunton, Craven Arms, Shrops. SY7 0JA
tel (01588) 640658 *fax* (01588) 640509
email thehurst@arvonfoundation.org
website www.arvonfoundation.org

The Arvon Foundation's 4 centres run 5-day residential courses throughout the year to anyone over the age of 16, providing the opportunity to live and work with professional writers. Writing genres explored include poetry, narrative, drama, writing for children, song writing and the performing arts. Bursaries are available to those receiving benefits. Founded in 1968.

Camden Poetry Group

Contact Hannah Kelly, 64 Lilyville Road, London SW6

Meets in Hampstead one Saturday per month from 6.30pm. Examples of work should be sent with a covering letter before coming to the first meeting.

Centerprise Literature Development Project

136 Kingsland High Street, London E8 2NS
tel 020-7254 9632 ext. 211, 214 *fax* 020-7923 1951
website www.centerpriseliterature.com
Contact Eva Lewin, Catherine Johnson

Offers a range of creative writing courses, events, surgeries, advice and information resources plus links with other writers' organisations. Groups include the Women's Poetry Group and the Black Writers' Group. The project is committed to developing new writing from all community and ethnic groups.

City Lit

Keeley Street, London WC2B 4BA
tel 020-7492 2652
email humanities@citylit.ac.uk
website www.citylit.ac.uk

City University Creative Writing and Poetry Courses

Northampton Square, London EC1V OHB
website www.city.ac.uk

Epsom Writers' Workshop

Epsom Centre, 1 Church Street, Epsom
Contact Stella Stocker *tel* 020-8668 3816

Kent & Sussex Poetry Society

Camden Centre, Market Square, Tunbridge Wells, Kent TN1 2SW
email info@kentandsussexpoetrysociety.org
website www.kentandsussexpoetrysociety.org

Lancaster University

Department of Continuing Education, Lancaster University, Ash House, Lancaster LA1 4YT
tel (01524) 592623/4
website www.lancs.ac.uk/

A range of part-time creative writing courses in various genres and at levels to suit both beginners and those with some experience.

London Writers' Circle

The Abbey Centre, 34 Great Smith Street, London SW1P 3BU
Contact Colleen McMath *tel* 020-8504 2506

Meets on fourth Monday in the month at 6.30pm.

Poetry Round

The Barkston Gardens Hotel, 34–44 Barkston Gardens, London SW5 0EW
tel 020-7373 7851

Meets on Mondays, 7.30–9.30pm, £2/£1 per session.

The Poetry School

81–83 Lambeth Walk, London SE11 6DX
tel (0845) 223 5274
website www.poetryschool.com

Offers courses and workshops in London, Manchester, York and the North East, Exeter and the South West, exploring key elements of poetic practice, complemented by lectures, discussions and seminars with some of the most renowned poets working today. Also international and online courses, and a postal tutorial service with Judy Gahagan and Myra Schneider.

The website has extensive links to poetry information and resources on the internet. The Poetry School was founded in 1997 by 3 poets – Mimi Khalvati, Jane Duran and Pascale Petit.

Poets Anonymous

Dog and Bull, Surrey Street, Croydon CR0 1RG
Also at The Primary Room, United Reformed Church, Addiscombe
email poets@poetsanon.org.uk
website www.poetsanon.org.uk

Meets at the Dog and Bull on the first Friday of each month at 8.15pm, £2/£1, and at the URC on the second Saturday of the month, 2.30–4pm, £1.50.

The Poet's House/Teach na hÉigse

Clonbarra, Falcarragh, County Donegal, Republic of Ireland
tel (074) 65470 *fax* (074) 65471
email phouse@iol.ie

The Poet's House runs 3 ten-day poetry courses in July and August. An MA degree in creative writing is validated by Lancaster University, and the Irish Language Faculty includes Cathal O'Searcaigh. The poetry faculty comprises 30 writers, including Paul Durcan and John Montagu.

Shortlands Poetry Circle

Ripley Arts Centre, 24 Sundridge Avenue, Bromley
email shortlands@poetrypf.co.uk
website www.poetrypf.co.uk/shortlands.html

South Norwood Writers' Workshop

South Norwood Centre, Sandown Road,
London SE24 4XC
Contact Stella Stocker *tel* 020-8668 3816

Meets on Wednesdays, 7.30–9.30pm.

Spread the Word

77 Lambeth Walk, London SE11 6DX
tel 020-7735 3111 *fax* 020-7735 2666
email info@spreadtheword.org.uk
website www.spreadtheword.org.uk

Surrey Poetry Circle

Guildford Institute of the University of Surrey,
Ward Street, Guildford GU1 4LH
Contact Pat Earnshaw *tel* (01483) 274389

Meets on first and third Thursday of the month, 7.30–10pm.

Ty Newydd

Taliesin Trust, Ty Newydd, Llanystumdwy,
Criccieth, Gwynedd LL52 0LW
tel (01766) 522811 *fax* (01766) 523095
email post@tynewydd.org
website www.tynewydd.org

Ty Newydd runs week-long writing courses encompassing a wide variety of genres, including poetry, and caters for all levels, from beginners to published poets. All the courses are tutored by published writers. Writing retreats are also available.

Wimbledon and Merton Poetry Group

Contact Russell Thompson *tel* (07969) 597967
email zzush@yahoo.co.uk

Meets on first Tuesday evening of each month.

GROUPS ON THE INTERNET

It is worth searching for discussion groups and chat rooms on the internet.

British–Irish Poets

website www.jiscmail.ac.uk/archives/british-irish-poets.html
Discussion list (innovative poetry).

The Poem

website http://thepoem.co.uk/discussion.htm
Discussion forum.

Poetry Free-for-all

website www.everypoet.org/pffa
Post your poems and comment on others.

The Poetry Kit

website www.poetrykit.org/wkshops2.htm
List of online workshop/discussion sites.

Local groups

Local groups vary enormously so it is worth shopping around to find one that suits your poetry. Up-to-date information can be obtained from Arts Council England regional offices (see page 548).

The Poetry Library publishes a list of groups for the Greater London area which will be sent out on receipt of a large sae.

The Poetry Society organises local groups for its members – visit www.poetrysociety.org.uk/content/membership/stanzas/ for details.

HELP FOR YOUNG POETS AND TEACHERS

National Association of Writers in Education (NAWE)

PO Box 1, Sheriff Hutton, York YO60 7YU
tel/fax (01653) 618429
email paul@nawe.co.uk
website www.nawe.co.uk

NAWE is a national organisation, which aims to widen the scope of writing in education, and coordinate activities between writers, teachers and funding bodies. It publishes the magazine *Writing in Education* and is author of a writers' database which can identify writers who fit the given criteria (e.g. speaks several languages, works well with special needs, etc) for schools, colleges and the community. Publishes *Reading the Applause: Reflections on Performance Poetry by Various Artists*. Write for membership details.

The Poetry Library

Children's Section, Royal Festival Hall,
London SE1 8XX
tel 020-7921 0664
website www.poetrylibrary.org.uk

For young poets, the Poetry Library has about 4000 books incorporating the SIGNAL Collection of Children's Poetry. It also has a multimedia children's section, from which cassettes and videos are available to engage children's interest in poetry.

The Poetry Library has an education service for teachers and writing groups. Its information file covers all aspects of poetry in education. There is a separate collection of books and materials for teachers and poets who work with children in schools, and teachers may join a special membership scheme to borrow books for the classroom.

Poetry Society Education

The Poetry Society, 22 Betterton Street,
London WC2H 9BX
tel 020-7420 9894 *fax* 020-7240 4818
email education@poetrysociety.org.uk
website www.poetrysociety.org.uk

The Poetry Society has an outstanding reputation for its exciting and innovative education work. For over 30 years it has been introducing poets into classrooms, providing comprehensive teachers' resources and producing colourful, accessible publications for pupils. It develops projects and schemes to keep poetry flourishing in schools, libraries and workplaces. Schemes like Poets in Schools, Poet in the City and Poetry Places (a 2-year programme of residencies and placements, funded by the Arts Council's 'Arts for Everyone' lottery budget) have enabled the Poetry Society to give work to hundreds of poets and allowed thousands of children and adults to experience poetry for themselves.

Through projects such as the Respect Slam and The Foyle Young Poets of the Year Award the Poetry Society gives valuable encouragement and exposure to young writers and performers.

Schools membership offers publications, training opportunities for teachers and poets, a free subscription to *Poems on the Underground* and a consultancy service giving advice on working with poets in the classroom. *Poetryclass*, an INSET training project, employs poets to train teachers at primary and secondary level. Youth membership is available to 11–18 year-olds and provides advice on developing writing skills, access to publication on the Poetry Society website, quarterly issues of *Poetry News*, and poetry books and posters.

YOUNG POETRY COMPETITIONS

Children's competitions are included in the competition list provided by the Poetry Library (free on receipt of a large sae).

Foyle Young Poets of the Year Award

The Poetry Society, 22 Betterton Street,
London WC2H 9BX
tel 020-7420 9894 *fax* 020-7240 4818
email education@poetrysociety.org.uk
website www.poetrysociety.org.uk

Free entry for 11–17 year-olds with unique prizes.

Christopher Tower Poetry Prize

Christ Church, Oxford OX1 1DP
tel/fax (01865) 286591
email info@towerpoetry.org.uk
website www.towerpoetry.org.uk/prize/index.html

An annual poetry competition from Christ Church, Oxford, open to 16–18 year-olds in UK schools and colleges. The poems should be no longer than 48 lines, on a different chosen theme each year. Prizes: £3000 (1st), £1000 (2nd), £500 (3rd). Every winner also receives a prize for their school.

FURTHER READING

Baldwin, Michael, *The Way to Write Poetry*, Hamish Hamilton, 1982, o.p.
Chisholm, Alison, *The Craft of Writing Poetry*, Allison & Busby, 1997, repr. 2001
Chisholm, Alison, *A Practical Poetry Course*, Allison & Busby, 1997
Corti, Doris, *Writing Poetry*, Writers News Library of Writing/Thomas & Lochar, 1994
Fairfax, John, and John Moat, *The Way to Write*, Elm Tree Books, 2nd edn revised, 1998
Finch, Peter, *How to Publish Your Poetry*, Allison & Busby, 3rd edn, 2000
Forbes, Peter, *Scanning the Century*, Penguin Books, 2000
Hamilton, Ian, *The Oxford Companion to Twentieth Century Poetry in English*, OUP, 1996
Hyland, Paul, *Getting into Poetry*, Bloodaxe, 2nd edn, 1997
Livingstone, Dinah, *Poetry Handbook for Readers and Writers*, Macmillan, 1992
O'Brien, Sean, *The Firebox*, Picador, 1998, o.p.
Padel, Ruth, *52 Ways of Looking at a Poem*, Vintage, 2004
Padel, Ruth, *The Poem and the Journey*, Vintage, 2008
Reading the Applause: Reflections on Performance Poetry by Various Artists, NAWE, 1999
Riggs, Thomas (ed.), *Contemporary Poets*, St James Press, 7th edn, 2001
Roberts, Philip Davies, *How Poetry Works*, Penguin Books, 2nd edn, 2000
Sampson, Fiona, *Writing Poetry*, Robert Hale, 2009
Sansom, Peter, *Writing Poems*, Bloodaxe, 1994, reprinted 1997
Sweeney, Matthew and John Williams, *Teach Yourself Writing Poetry*, Hodder and Stoughton, 3rd edn, 2008
Whitworth, John, *Writing Poetry*, A&C Black, 2006

USA

Breen, Nancy, *Poet's Market 2009*, Writer's Digest Books, USA, 2008

Fulton, Len, *Directory of Poetry Publishers 2007–2008*, Dustbooks, USA, 2008

Fulton, Len, *The International Directory of Little Magazines and Small Presses 2007–2008*, Dustbooks, USA, 2008

Preminger, Alex, *New Princeton Encyclopedia of Poetry and Poetics*, Princeton University Press, 3rd edn, 1993

See also...

- *Publishers of poetry*, page 779
- *Getting poetry published*, page 351
- *Approaching a poetry publisher*, page 357

Television, film and radio

Notes from a successful television screenwriter

Andrew Davies tells how he became a 'proper' writer.

I didn't begin as a screenwriter. I began as a poet. There was no television in the house I grew up in, and there was hardly any such thing as television drama. This was the early Fifties. There was a girl in our village called Jane Grant-Hughes, with a well-off dad, and they had a television. It was as big as a wardrobe with a tiny screen in the middle of it. I remember a bunch of us being invited round to Jane's house to watch a production of *The Merry Wives of Windsor*, and it was very grey and fuzzy and actually excruciatingly boring. The idea of anybody deliberately writing television drama seemed ludicrous to me.

I wanted to be a writer but my father, a teacher, sensibly pointed out that most writers didn't make anywhere near enough money to live on and I should have a job that paid the bills and write in my spare time. Like him, I became a teacher – I was attracted by the short hours and long holidays (time to write) but found that I enjoyed teaching and was quite good at it. I got home at 4.30pm and there were a couple of hours before my wife got home and I wrote in that time: short stories and radio plays mostly. There was a market for short stories in those days, not that I sold any, and there was a market for radio plays by new writers, and there still is (hint hint). I was also writing poetry and articles for *Punch*, sketches and jokes for sketch shows, and a novel, everything, really. Hardly any of it sold, but I was enjoying myself. I always tried to make sure there was at least one thing *out there* with my hopes riding on it. (That's another thing I would recommend to the struggling writer.) When I did sell something, I spent the money immediately, on something specific. I remember I sold a couple of sketches to a radio programme called *Monday Night at Home* and bought a rather fine corduroy jacket with the proceeds.

The late Fifties and early Sixties were a good time for radio plays. There were a lot of poetic and experimental ones on the 'Third Programme' as Radio Three used to be called. Dylan Thomas and Louis MacNeice wrote radio plays; so did Pinter and Stoppard. And my first substantial sale was a radio play. It was based on an extraordinary time I'd spent on teaching practice in a benighted school deep in the Welsh valleys. Hilarious, touching, more than a little obscene, more than a little libellous as it turned out. (I guess another tip is: recognise when you've had a unique experience, and get all the juice you can out of it, but try to avoid getting sued.) The play was later successfully produced after I'd changed the names, physical characteristics and, in some cases, the sex of some of the teachers in the story; but it was a close-run thing, almost the end of my career before I'd even properly got started. That was in 1960.

I continued to write radio plays throughout the Sixties, acquiring an agent in the process. He came to me, not the other way round, and I graciously acceded to his plan to 'exploit me in all media' as he put it. It was the first time I had heard the word 'exploit' used in anything other than a pejorative sense. By 1965 we had a house and a puppy and a baby, and it seemed time to get a television as well. These were the days of the *Wednesday Play*, Dennis Potter, *Cathy Come Home*, and all that. I was entranced. I bought a book of television playscripts – I remember it included a wry little comedy by a guy I'd never heard of called Peter Nichols – and studied the layout and the length of scenes – the whole grammar of television drama. There weren't any creative writing courses or books on how to do it then. But study the best and steal from them has always been a good way to learn.

Early television success

I'm sure there must have been a couple of false starts, but the way I remember it is I sat down and wrote a play about a girl in a knicker factory and sent it off to the *Wednesday Play*, like doing the pools, really, and it was accepted – and produced. And it did very well. I really did think then that I was a made man… but it was FIVE YEARS before I sold another television play. I was still getting the radio plays done, and I could always kid myself I was a teacher really and just a hobby writer, but it was a tough time. And so the next bit of advice is that you have to like writing enough to keep going (that's the most important thing) and have faith in your own ability (also important) and dream the impossible dream (that's complete b******* , actually) and things may eventually get better.

For me they got better when a script editor called Louis Marks took a fancy to a half-hour script I'd written called 'Is That Your Body Boy?' and accepted it for a strand called Thirty-Minute (I keep nagging the BBC to revive the original half-hour play or film, so far with no success.) Anyway, that was done and got great reviews, and Louis Marks became a producer, and for some time his career and mine hung by the same slender thread as he continued to commission me to write single plays, often in 'anthology' series on a common theme. He also recommended me to other producers as fast, clever and cheap. (I am still reasonably fast and clever, I hope, but no longer cheap.) It's still a wonderful and important thing to find a producer who loves your work and will stick his (or nowadays more usually her) neck out for it, but these days producers have very little clout: all depends on the whim (or judgement as they prefer to think of it) of the commissioners.

By the mid-Seventies I was able to think of myself as an established writer, and this was consolidated when I was given the chance to adapt a sprawling Delderfield novel called *To Serve Them All My Days*, about a chap who gets invalided out of the First World War and spends what seems like the next hundred years teaching in a West Country boarding school. This established me as a writer who was capable of the long haul, and led to the commissioning of *A Very Peculiar Practice*, an original serial set in a campus university, which went out in the mid-Eighties, and is probably the television work of which I am most proud.

Becoming a 'proper' writer

It was at this time, 1986 to be precise, that I resigned from the day job at Warwick University and became a 'proper' writer. I celebrated this by suffering my first ever writer's block. Now I *had* to keep my family by writing, the thing seemed quite impossible. But fortunately I didn't have to suffer alone for too long: there were too many people who couldn't start their work until I had done mine, and I was coaxed out of my creative paralysis with the traditional application of bullying and whisky. Writer's block is all about performance anxiety, fear of failure, and there's a bit of it in every project – especially in the early stages. Experience and past successes don't help as much as you would think. In fact I am stuck on a script at the moment, which is why I am writing this article way before its deadline.

And unless inspiration descends like a thunderbolt, I am going to have to take the traditional route: if you can't think of anything good, write something bad and rewrite it later.

Enough of such gloomy thoughts. What are the nice things about being a successful television writer? Money, obviously. Lunch at the Ivy is very nice. Fame can be a bit of a nuisance, though I guess most people would like to try it for a bit to see how it goes. Mostly, for me, the joy comes from working in a collaborative medium, which means that you are being stimulated by the bright ideas of producers and script editors; surprised by the creative flair of directors who do things you wouldn't have thought of with your work, but things that seem utterly right; actors who make your lines sound better than they really are. Just about my favourite part of the process is the 'readthrough'. It's the first time the actors come together, and it's the first time you get a feel for what the final thing will be like. And sometimes, if one of the actors can't make it, I get a chance to 'read in' – and when you're playing a scene with Gillian Anderson, say, life doesn't get much better, even if you're sitting in a draughty church hall, which is where these things always seem to take place.

But if you write for performance, that experience – seeing and hearing your words come alive off the page – is something all dramatists can experience, even if the production is by your local amateur group and never gets any further than that draughty church hall. In fact, that's the last bit of advice I'd give: if you write for performance, try to get it done somehow, even if it's just an informal reading with your friends. It's the best way to learn.

Andrew Davies has been writing for the screen since 1965. His television originals include *A Very Peculiar Practice, Getting Hurt, A Few Short Journeys of the Heart, Filipina Dreamgirls, Boudica (The Warrior Queen), The Chatterley Affair,* and the sitcom *Game On* (with Bernadette Davis.) He has adapted *Middlemarch, Pride and Prejudice, Moll Flanders, Emma, Mother Love, House of Cards* (for which he won an Emmy award) *Vanity Fair, Wives and Daughters* and *Take a Girl Like You* for television. Also *Othello, The Way We Live Now* (for which he won a BAFTA) *Daniel Deronda, Dr Zhivago, Tipping The Velvet, He Knew He Was Right, Bleak House, The Line of Beauty, Northanger Abbey, A Room With a View, Fanny Hill, Affinity, Sense and Sensibility* and *Little Dorrit.* He has big-screen credits for *Circle of Friends, Bridget Jones's Diary, The Tailor of Panama,* and *Bridget Jones: The Edge of Reason.* Andrew was awarded a BAFTA Fellowship in 2002.

Adaptations from books

Although every writer wants to create their own work and find their own voice, adaptation is a good way both to generate income and to learn about how to write for other formats. It can also be a chance for a writer to raise their profile, with a successful adaptation sometimes leading to an original commission. Kate Sinclair explains.

Although every writer wants to create their own work and find their own voice, adaptation is a good way both to generate income and to learn about the disciplines of different media: how to write for other formats.

Writers may be approached to adapt their own work from one medium to another during their career. For example, John Mortimer originally wrote *A Voyage Round My Father* for the radio and later adapted it for stage, film and finally, for television. There are also opportunities for both writers and directors to adapt someone else's work from one performance medium to another or from a novel to any of the above.

Every year classic novels are made into adaptations for all media and it is a growing trend. These may be for the theatre, such as Helen Edmundson's version of *War and Peace* (Shared Experience/RNT), or for radio such as *Rob Roy* (the Classic Serial, Radio 4). Television carries dramatisations like *The Forsyte Saga* (ITV) or *Bleak House* (BBC), and film features screenplays such as Terence Davies' version of Edith Wharton's *The House of Mirth*. Although these are usually costly to produce, involving large casts and – particularly in the visual media – the considerable expense of recreating the period in which they were written, they command loyal audiences and seem to be in steady demand. These classic projects also generate significant income both from DVD/video sales and from sales to overseas companies and networks. Some adapters are as well known as writers who concentrate on their own work. For example, Andrew Davies has become almost a household name for his television dramatisations of *Pride and Prejudice*, *The Way We Live Now* and, more recently, *Sense and Sensibility*.

Producers in radio, television and film are also in regular contact with publishers and literary agents to keep abreast of contemporary novels which may work well in another format. I currently work as a producer and literary consultant and find books, both fiction and non-fiction, for screenwriters, directors or producers for feature films. Both television producers and film companies are also sent potential books by the publicity departments of publishing houses and writers may also make direct approaches to producers and commissioners with material that they feel they can successfully transcribe for that particular medium.

There is clearly a market for adaptations of all types. For example, I found *Slumdog Millionaire* on 50 pages of an unpublished book Q&A by Vikas Swamp for Film4. The added stimulus for the adapter is, as well as having a ready-made story, exploring technically how another writer writes – their use of language, the way they structure a narrative, their characterisation. There is the opportunity to learn from the skill and subtlety of great writers and there is the challenge of finding ways to transport a story from one form to another, with all the creative possibilities that this presents.

What to adapt, and why?

Just because a narrative works in one format doesn't guarantee that it will in another. Form and story are often inextricably bound together. Something works as a radio play precisely because it appeals to a listening audience and is able to exploit the possibilities of sound. A novel may be very literary and concentrate on a character's inner thoughts, and not on external action. While this may be fine for reading quietly alone, it could leave a theatre, television or film audience bored and longing for something to happen.

That said, the key ingredient is story and there are some stories which seem to work in almost any media and which have almost become universal (though different treatments bring out different aspects of the original). For example, Henry James's *The Turn of the Screw* was written as a novella. It subsequently became a much-performed opera, with a libretto by Myfanwy Piper and music by Benjamin Britten; an acclaimed film, retitled *The Innocents* with the screenplay by John Mortimer; and a television adaptation for ITV by Nick Dear. What makes a narrative like this transmute so successfully?

At the most basic level it must be dramatic. Radio, television and film, like the theatre, need drama to hold their audiences. Aristotle's premise that 'all drama is action', and should have protagonists whom we identify with, antagonists who oppose them, and the reversals, climaxes and resolutions which typify a dramatic structure. This is not necessarily the case for a novel; it is easy to be seduced by a tale that has personal resonance or beautiful language and forget the basic template which has, after all, worked for thousands of years. It may seem obvious but reminding yourself of this when considering the suitability of any material for adaptation could spare you a rejection or a great deal of later reworking.

Knowing the media

The other important consideration is a detailed knowledge of the final medium. The adapter needs to understand why that particular story is specifically suited to it. Ideally they will have experience of writing for that form, as well as an awareness of the current market for the project. It is vital to know precisely what is currently being produced and by whom. Staff and policies change very quickly, so the more up-to-date your research is, the better your chance of creating a successful adaptation and being able to get it accepted.

If you are adapting for the theatre, how often do you go and when was the last time you saw a production that wasn't originally written for the stage? As well as observing how successful it was, both artistically and in box office terms, would you know whether that company or theatre regularly programmes adaptations, and if so, what sort? Do they, like Shared Experience, have a reputation primarily for classics, or do they, like the Young Vic, or The Royal Exchange, Manchester, produce versions of contemporary novels? Are you sufficiently aware of the tastes of the current artistic director and the identity of the theatre to know whether to send your project to the West Yorkshire Playhouse or Southwark Playhouse? This is not necessarily just a question of scale or level, but more a reflection of contemporary trends and the specific policy of each of these buildings. Whilst the overall remit of a theatre or company may remain the same – if they are funded to produce only new plays, it is unlikely that this will alter – individual personnel and fashions will change regularly and it is important to keep in touch.

Television and radio

The same holds true for all the other media and, if anything, is even more important in radio and television. All of the broadcast media are now subject to the rigorous demands of ratings, which in turn make for extremely precise scheduling. Channels have strong identities, and conversations with producers and commissioners will inevitably involve a discussion of which slot a project is suited to and what has recently been shown or broadcast. Up-to-the-minute knowledge of the work being produced by a company or broadcaster is therefore essential, and regularly seeing that work and being able to talk about it, even more so.

For example, BBC Radio 3's *Wire* is specifically for new work by contemporary writers and therefore isn't suitable for a classic adaptation of a novel. Radio 4 produces the Classic Serial on Sunday afternoons and *Women's Hour* has a regular serialisation slot that can be contemporary or classic and is often an adapted novel. Biographies or autobiographies are also frequently abridged and read on Radio 4 at 9.45am on weekdays. For a detailed knowledge of this output there can be no substitute for studying the *Radio Times*, seeing what is programmed, and listening to what gets produced in which slots. Being able to envisage the eventual destination for a chosen adaptation helps you to choose the right project and place it successfully.

In television this process of research is more complex. As well as strong competition between the BBC and the larger independent broadcasters (ITV, Channel 4, Carlton, Gra-

Successful collaborations

Here is an entirely subjective list of my personal favourites among successful collaborations, by way of example.

Film

Up in the Air (Walter Kim, screenplay by Jason Reitman and Sheldon Turner)
Slumdog Millionaire (Q&A by Vikas Swamp, screenplay by Simon Beaufoy)
The Diving Bell and the Butterfly (screenplay by Ronald Harwood)
Motorcycle Diaries (Ché Guevara, screenplay Joe Rivera)
Enduring Love (Ian McEwan, screenplay Joe Penhall)
Trainspotting (Irvine Welsh, screenplay John Hodges)
Lord of the Rings (J.R.R. Tolkien, screenplay Fran Walsh)
The House of Mirth (Edith Wharton, screenplay Terence Davies)
Jude (George Eliot, screenplay Hossein Amini)
Persuasion (Jane Austen, screenplay Nick Dear)

Television

Lark Rise to Candleford (Flora Thompson, adaptation Bill Gallagher)
Bleak House (Charles Dickens, adaptation Andrew Davies)
The Way We Live Now (Anthony Trollope, adaptation Andrew Davies)
The Forsyte Saga (John Galsworthy, adaptation Stephen Mallatratt)
Brideshead Revisited (Evelyn Waugh, adaptation John Mortimer)
The Buddha of Suburbia (Hanif Kureshi, adaptation Roger Michell and Hanif Kureshi)
Longitude (Dava Sobel, adaptation Charles Sturridge)

Theatre

Coram Boy (Jamilla Gavin, adaptation Helen Edmundson)
Nana (Emile Zola, adaptation Pam Gems)
The Magic Toyshop (Angela Carter, adaptation Bryony Lavery)

Radio

The Worst Journey in the World (Apsey Cherry-Garrod, adaptation by Stef Penny)
The Old Curiosity Shop (Charles Dickens, adaptation Mike Walker)

nada, etc) to secure an audience, there is also considerable rivalry between the hundreds of independent production companies to receive commissions. The ratings war means that scheduling is paramount and big dramatic adaptations are often programmed at exactly the same time on BBC 2 and ITV. Familiarity with the output of each channel is crucial when suggesting projects for adaptation, either to a commissioner or a production company. Again, watching dramatisations and noting what format they are in, who is producing them, and when they are being broadcast, is all part of the job.

As a general rule it is helpful to know that both adaptations and writing commissioned directly for television, tend to be divided into several basic categories (not including soaps). Single dramas are usually high profile, broadcast at peak times and are about 90 minutes long. Series consist of a number of weekly parts shown over several weeks (3, 4, 6, 8 and ten are all common), each part lasting anywhere between 30 and 60 minutes. Finally there are two-part dramas or event pieces which take place on consecutive nights with each part between one and two hours long. The percentage of adaptations will generally be lower than newly commissioned drama, although this is entirely dependent upon the type of slot and the broadcaster. For example, the BBC has approximately double the budget per hour for drama that Channel 4 has, and produces many more dramatisations of classic novels, particularly recently. Likewise, ITV has currently been producing regular serialisations of classics and single adaptations of both period and contemporary drama. Channel 4, when it commissions adaptations, tends to focus on cutting-edge contemporary novels, such as the *Red Riding* trilogy of novels by David Peace and *White Teeth* by Zadie Smith, adapted by Simon Burke. And there are of course always exceptions to all these trends, which is why it is necessary to be an aware and regular viewer.

If you want to adapt for film, the nature of what will work and when, seems to be more open-ended, though it is of course important to go regularly to the cinema and know what has been produced recently. This may be to do with the nature of distribution – the fact that most films are on in a number of cinemas for several weeks – and the time it takes to make a film – often years between the initial idea and eventual screening. However, you still need to keep up-to-date with who is producing what and when. It is worth noting though that there is a very strong relationship between books and film and remembering that around 50% of all Oscar-winning films are based on books.

The rights

Once you have selected your material and medium, it is vital to establish who has the rights to the original and whether these are available for negotiation. Sometimes this involves a bit of detective work. If the writer is dead, it is necessary to find out whether there is an estate and if the work is still subject to copyright.

Copyright law is extremely complex. In the UK it has altered so some texts that were out of copyright have gone back in again (for further information see *UK copyright law*, page 700). Copyright also varies, however, around the world so it is essential therefore that you seek expert advice concerning the current rules for any potential project, depending on the country of origin.

It is usually possible to begin the search for the copyright holder and source of rights from the imprint page of the novel, play, film script, etc. If this information is not given, try the publisher, the Society of Authors (see page 541) or the Authors' Licensing and Collecting Society (ALCS, page 715).

In the case of a living writer, you will need to establish who their literary agent is – if they have one – and contact them to see if adaptation is possible and how much it will cost. The scale of costs will depend upon the medium. Rights for a stage adaptation are often separate from film or television options. If a book or play has already been optioned, this means that it is probably not available for a period of at least 12–18 months. Should the purchaser of the option choose not to renew, or fail to produce the adaptation within the required timescale, rights may become available again. Many agreements include an extension clause for a further fixed time period, however, and this is particularly common in film as the end-product is rarely produced within 18 months.

Large film companies, particularly in Hollywood, will often buy the rights to a book or script outright, sometimes for a substantial sum. The proposed version may never get made but legally the original will not be available for adaptation by anyone else. If the writer or material is famous enough, or if they have a good agent, a time limit will be part of the original agreement. Complete buy-outs are less common in the UK.

The cost of acquiring rights varies significantly with the scale of the project, the profile of the writer and the intended medium. Usually an initial payment will be needed to secure the rights for a fixed period, followed by the same amount again, should an extension be necessary. In addition, there is nearly always some form of royalty for the original writer or estate in the form of a percentage of the overall profits of the final production, film, or broadcast. This will normally have a 'floor' – a minimum amount or reserve – which must be paid whether or not the final work is financially successful and a 'ceiling' – known as the purchase price. There may also be additional clauses for consultancy. With television, film or radio, there may be a further payment for repeat formats, and in the theatre the rate may well alter if the production transfers. Sometimes, with a low-budget production such as a fringe show or short film, a writer or estate will waive any initial rights fee and only expect a royalty. Whether you use a 'deal memo' to formalise your agreement or a more comprehensive 'long form agreement', it is always worth seeking expert help to make sure you have covered everything you need to.

Legalities aside, time spent forming a relationship with the writer of the original, or whoever manages their estate, has other another much more important function, a creative one, that of getting closer to the source material.

How to adapt

I don't believe it is possible to lay down a set of rules for adapting, any more than one could invent a meaningful template for creative writing. The only observation I can offer, therefore, is personal and a reflection of my own taste.

When I recommend or commission an adaptation, either for film, television or in the theatre, my first requirement is that something in the original story has hooked me and I want to see the original given another life and another audience. I have to be able to imagine that it has the potential to work dramatically in a different format and can often already see or hear fragments of it.

At this stage I ask myself a lot of questions about the material. How strong is the story and how engaging are the characters? Why should it be done in another medium? How is it possible to achieve the narrative, the characters, the tone, the sequences of action, in a way that is different but still truthful, a sort of creative equivalent, like a metaphor. For me, it is all about thinking laterally and being enthused about the new possibilities another form will generate from the original, or vice versa.

This process generally leads me back to the source, be it book, film or play, in order to dig over everything about it and its writer. As well as looking at other adaptations to see what parts of the original have been enhanced or cut, I like to meet and talk to the writer. If they are no longer alive I try to find out about them from books and/or people who knew them. I want to know what interested them; what were they thinking when they were writing; even what they looked at every day. If possible, I like to go and visit the places they have written about or the place in which they wrote. This process of total immersion helps me to get under the skin of the original.

While this is entirely personal, it raises an interesting question which I believe any adapter needs to answer for themselves. How closely do you wish to be faithful to the original material and how much do you intend to depart from it? Choosing not to stick closely to the source may be the most creative decision you make but you must understand why you are doing it and what the effect will be. After all, two different trains of thought, styles and imaginations need to be fused together for this transformation to be complete and it is important that the balance between them works. I once spoke to a writer who was commissioned to adapt a well-known myth for Hollywood. Several drafts later, when he had been asked to alter all the key elements of the story to the point where it was unrecognisable, he decided to quit. It was the right decision and the film was a flop.

While respect for the writer and the source material is fundamental, there are of course lots of examples where enormous lateral and creative changes have been made to make a story work to optimum effect in its new medium. What matters ultimately is the integrity of the final product. At its best, it is like a marriage of two minds, celebrating the talents of both writer and adapter in an equally creative partnership.

Kate Sinclair is the Film Consultant at MBA Literary Agents and the Literary Consultant for Free Range Films. Previously she worked as Books Executive for Film4, where she found *Slumdog Millionaire* for them in an unpublished manuscript and *Brick Lane*. She was the Literary Consultant for the UK Film Council, a consultant for Aardman Animations and See Saw Films and a development producer for Kudos Films. She has also worked as a theatre director and is currently producing, writing and directing her own film projects.

Writing for television

Writing for television can be extremely rewarding. Anji Loman Field says that any writer with the right aptitude and attitude can succeed, and here she gives advice for screenwriters.

The markets

There are various openings for new writers in television, but apart from competitions and special projects these are hardly ever advertised. The BBC's latest information on opportunities for new writers can be found at www.bbc.co.uk/writersroom. The openings fall into five categories:

Single drama

There are fewer slots nowadays for the single play – a 30- or even 60-minute one-off drama is highly unlikely to find a market. Occasionally broadcasters will gather single plays together under a collective banner but it's best to think of individual projects as either standalone television films, two-parters or even four-parters. It's always worth asking television companies for their guidelines on single drama and film. Check broadcasters' websites for current requirements.

Series and serials

Although it has been known for a new writer to sell an original series or serial, it is a relatively rare occurrence – although with new channels popping up all the time it's worth keeping an eye on the market. Nevertheless, writers with a track record of writing for existing strands are far more likely to be taken seriously. Long-running soaps like *EastEnders*, *Doctors* and *Emmerdale* are sometimes in the market for new writers, but check first. If the door is open, a good 'calling card script' is usually the way in. Submit an original piece of work in a similar genre that is at least an hour long and shows your ability to create believable characters, write sparkling dialogue and tell a compelling story. You may be invited to try out for one of these long-running shows.

Dramatisations/adaptations

A new writer is extremely unlikely to be commissioned to adapt or dramatise someone else's work for television. However, if there's something you really want to adapt and you can afford to take out an 'option' on the rights (or already own them, if it is your own novel or play) then write the script on spec. If you have a good script and can show that you own the rights, you could succeed.

Situation comedy

This is the one area where production companies and broadcasters are desperate for new talent to write for existing shows, and there are often competitions open to new writers. If you are a good comedy writer and market your work well, you will undoubtedly succeed (see 'Writing situation comedy' below).

Children's drama/comedy

This is an important market for broadcasters and audiences, and long-running shows always need talented writers.

Aptitude and attitude

The first prerequisite in writing for television is that you enjoy the medium, and actually watch the kinds of shows that you would be interested in writing for. A cynical approach will always show through. And before sitting down to write that first television script, arm yourself with the appropriate skills by examining the medium as a whole.

- **Tape the kind of show you'd like to write for and analyse it**. How many scenes are there? What length are they? How much of the story happens 'off camera'? Knowing the answers to these questions will help you to understand the grammar of screen, and enable you to write a more professional script.
- **Study the structure of story telling**. There are plenty of books on the subject, and although it is never a good idea to follow structural paradigms to the letter, absorb as much information as possible so that the essential 'rules' on character, motivation and plot filter through into your writing.
- **Read scripts**. Some are published in book form, but a huge variety of scripts are also available from specialist bookshops such as Offstage (*tel* 020-7240 3883), the Screenwriter's Store (www.thescreenwritersstore.com) and the internet (e.g. www.bbc.co.uk/writersroom/insight/script_archive.shtml).
- **If you want to write sitcom, see as many live recordings of shows as possible.** This enables you to understand the techniques involved in television production, and particularly the physical constraints imposed by the studio. Free tickets for sitcom recordings are usually available – phone the broadcasters for information.
- **Be realistic.** Don't make your first project too ambitious in terms of screen time, locations or special effects. If you can 'contain the action' and make your first script affordable to shoot, it is far more likely to be taken seriously.

Learning the craft

Even the most successful and experienced screenwriters say they never stop learning. Some have been lucky enough to learn the skill of writing for the screen in a subliminal way. For example, Lynda La Plante (*Prime Suspect*) was an actress with plenty of opportunity for studying scripts and production techniques before she turned her hand to writing; John Sullivan (*Only Fools and Horses*) worked in the props department at the BBC on countless sitcoms, and used to take the scripts home to study. But there are other ways to learn. Script workshops are particularly useful.

There are many courses and workshops available. These range from small self-help groups, where writers give each other feedback on their work, to full- and part-time Screenwriting MA courses at universities (e.g. in London, Sheffield, Leicester, Bournemouth, Manchester, Leeds, Bristol and Edinburgh; see page 691). Evening classes are springing up in local colleges, and there are even script workshops on the internet. Workshops can help in the following ways:

- **Discipline.** The hardest thing most writers ever have to do is sit down and face that blank screen or page. Joining a script workshop – where you *have* to deliver an outline or a treatment, or the next 20 pages of your script by a certain date – provides the push that so many writers need.
- **Feedback**. Reading and giving feedback on other people's work helps you to focus on getting your own script right. It is also good to get used to the idea of showing your own work to others and getting their feedback. Television writing is generally a collaborative process and writers need to be pleasant to work with, and receptive to ideas. Knowing when to argue a point and when to concede are crucial skills which can be developed in good writing workshops.

• **Rewriting**. Learn to Love the Rewrite. It is such a major achievement to get to the end of a first draft that it is all too easy to rush to the post box and send it off to several production companies at once. *Four Weddings and a Funeral*, a Channel 4-funded project, went through 17 rewrites before finally reaching the screen. So before you post your masterpiece:
• Leave it to 'settle' for a few days and do something completely different – allow your head to clear completely. Then re-read the script from beginning to end – from as objective a viewpoint as possible – and make necessary changes.
• Get feedback so that you're sure your script is ready to send. Be warned: knowing how to read and analyse a script properly is a particular skill. Unless they are equipped in this area, *never* ask your friends or relations to read your script. Their comments could either lull you into a false sense of security or destroy your confidence for ever. Feedback from other writers in your workshop group is best. There are some organisations (including Euroscript) which offer a professional script feedback service for a moderate fee.

Writing situation comedy

Situation comedy writing is the most lucrative area of television, and deservedly so. Have you ever tried making an audience laugh several times a minute for 25 minutes for at least six weeks running, and maybe (in the case of *Last of the Summer Wine*) for 20 long years?

Despite its name, sitcom is less about situation and much more about character. It is better to start with funny and engaging characters in mind and then (if it isn't part and parcel of the character) find the perfect situation in which to place them than it is to begin with the premise 'nobody's ever set a sitcom in a nuclear power station before'. It is not the setting that makes the audience laugh, it is the characters.

A good exercise in seeing if you can write funny material is to write an episode of an existing sitcom. If *Fawlty Towers* is your all-time favourite, study a few episodes and then try your own. It will never get made, but you'll learn a lot in the process – and sample scripts like this are often useful as calling card scripts.

Some of the broadcast companies issue guidelines on writing situation comedy – phone their comedy departments for information.

Competitions

Broadcasters occasionally run writing competitions or 'new writing initiatives' (www.bbc.co.uk/writersroom/opportunity). Check their websites – and general screenwriters' websites – for up-to-date information. Also, watch out for annual awards run by organisations such as PAWS (Public Awareness of Science & Engineering, *tel* 020-7483 4545, www.pawsdrama.com) and BBC Talent (www.bbc.co.uk/newtalent). Details can be found in the trade press and via relevant websites and screenwriting organisations. See also *Prizes and awards* on page 588.

Breaking in

Do you need an agent?

Many new writers are keen to get an agent before they attempt to sell anything, but this can be an arduous process and there are few agents prepared to take on a completely untried writer.

The best way to get an agent is to first get an offer of a deal on a project. Most *bona fide* production companies and broadcasters will happily recommend a selection of agents to writers they want to do business with. If you can phone an agent and say 'so-and-so wants to option/commission my project and has recommended you as an agent' he or she is far more likely to be interested. And at that point you can pick and choose the agent who is right for you, rather than going with the first one to say 'yes'.

Selling yourself

Once you are sure you have a good script, where do you send it? If you've done your homework, you will already know which channel is the most likely to be interested. But sometimes it is better to send to an independent production company rather than directly to a broadcaster, so do a bit more research. Check out the companies that are making the kind of show you've written and approach them first.

A preliminary letter or phone call can save you time and money because some smaller companies simply don't have the resources to read unsolicited material. If you feel that a certain production company is absolutely right for your project, write a letter giving a brief synopsis of the project and asking if they will read the script. If they agree, your script will join the 'solicited' pile. And if it fits the bill, they may even pick it up and develop it. But

Useful information

www.emotionaltoolbox.com

A great, inspirational website run by international script consultant/tutor Laurie Hutzler.

www.twelvepoint.com

The online version of *Scriptwriter* magazine (see page 96) which is full of industry information and ideas for writers.

Euroscript

Euroscript Ltd, 64 Hemingford Road, London N1 1DB
tel (07958) 244656
email ask@euroscript.co.uk
website www.euroscript.co.uk

An independent, UK based, script development organisation for film and TV which offers analysis of screenplays from a team of screenwriters, producers and experienced teachers in the field. It also offers day-long training workshops focusing on different aspects of screenwriting and development.

UK Film Council

10 Little Portland Street, London W1W 7JG
tel 020-7861 7861 *fax* 020-7861 7862
email info@ukfilmcouncil.org.uk
website www.ukfilmcouncil.org.uk

Offers funding for short films and features and training for writers.

Pact (Producers' Alliance for Cinema and Television)

3rd Floor, Fitzrovia House, 153–157 Cleveland Street, London W1T 6QW
tel 020-7380 8230
website www.pact.co.uk

Serves the feature film and independent TV production sector. Online fully searchable, password-protected *Directory*. (See also page 573.)

Arts Council England regional offices

Many regional offices offer grants that enable writers, producers and directors to make their projects (see page 548).

The Spotlight

7 Leicester Place, London WC2H 7RJ
tel 020-7437 7631
email questions@spotlight.com
website www.spotlight.com

Publishes an annual handbook, *Contacts*, which contains useful information and contact addresses.

The Writers' Guild of Great Britain

40 Rosebery Avenue, London EC1R 4RX
tel 020-7833 0777 *fax* 020-7833 4777
email erik@writersguild.org.uk
website www.writersguild.org.uk

Trade union-affiliated organisation for professional writers. Negotiates rates for TV drama with the BBC and the ITV Network Centre. (See also page 544.)

don't expect overnight results. It can sometimes take many months before scripts are even read by small and/or busy companies.

Sending your script directly to a broadcaster can lead to a commission, but unless you target a particular producer whose work you admire you will probably have less control over who you work with. However, BBC writersroom remains a dedicated home for all unsolicited drama and comedy submissions (www.bbc.co.uk/writersroom).

Being 'discovered'

If you can get your work 'rehearse-read' by actors in front of an audience it will help your writing, and may even lead to discovery. Many script readings are attended by development executives from television and production companies and there are many stories of individuals being picked up from such projects. TAPS (Training and Performance Showcase; see page 610) and Player–Playwrights (see page 574) both organise rehearsed readings.

Development hell

This is the place between finding someone who wants to produce your script and waiting for the 'suits' at the television companies to give the final go-ahead for the project. In the meantime you will have been paid, perhaps just an option fee, or maybe a commission fee for a script or two. Either way, *never put all your eggs in one development basket.* Aim eventually to have several projects bubbling under for every one that comes to the boil.

A realistic optimism is required for this game. Don't believe anything wonderful will happen until you actually have that signed contract in front of you. In the meantime keep writing, keep marketing and, if you possibly can, keep making contacts in the industry. If you're good at schmoozing, go to as many industry events as possible and make new contacts. If you can send a script to a producer with a covering letter saying 'I heard your talk the other day…' you will immediately arouse interest.

Coping with rejection

The standard rejection letter is the worst part of this business. When it is accompanied by your returned script – looking decidedly unread – it is very easy to become disillusioned. The trick is this: change your mental attitude to the point where if you don't receive at least one rejection letter in the post every day, you feel rejected! So long as you are absolutely sure that your work is good, keep sending it out. Sooner or later you'll get a nicer, more personalised rejection letter, and then eventually perhaps even a cup of tea with the producer.

Selling ideas

Completely new writers do occasionally sell ideas but are much more likely to sell the idea alone, i.e. the 'format rights', and will probably end up not writing the script. If you have a great calling card script or two, or have had a few episodes of something produced, your ideas will be taken much more seriously. At this stage you might well sell a project on the basis of a short outline or synopsis, and be paid to write the script(s).

All scripts must be typed and properly formatted if they are to be taken seriously. If you dread the practical aspects of getting your script onto the page it might be worth investing in a software program for your computer. They take the pain out of screenwriting by auto-formatting and numbering the pages and scenes, thus enabling you to move scenes around and restructure your script with ease. Such facilities allow writers to concentrate wholly on the creative process and can therefore be quite liberating, even for those who type well. Contact the Screenwriters' Store for details and advice.

Summary

Writing for television is not generally something that can be taken up as a hobby. It may look easy but huge amounts of work and commitment are required in order to succeed. If that doesn't put you off, and it is what you really want to do, then go for it. And good luck!

Anji Loman Field worked as researcher/producer of factual programming before switching to writing television, film and radio drama in the early 1990s. She became a regular writer for *EastEnders*, *Holby City* and *Doctors*, and has written several plays for Radio 4 as well as films for the German and Cambodian markets. She now runs an international production company (www.indevelopmentproductions.com) which specialises in producing drama for education and social change in developing countries. She has taught screenwriting at various establishments including the Royal College of Art, London Institute and in Germany, Cambodia and Vietnam.

Further reading

Friedmann, Julian, *How to Make Money Scriptwriting*, Chicago University Press, 2000
Kelsey, Gerald, *Writing for Television*, A&C Black, 3rd edn, 1999
Seger, Linda, *Making a Good Script Great*, Samuel French Inc., 3rd edn, 2010
Vogler, Christopher, *The Writer's Journey*, Pan, 3rd edn, 2007
Wolfe, Ronald, *Writing Comedy*, Robert Hale, 2003

See also ...

• *Dealing with rejection*, page 659

Notes from a successful soap scriptwriter

As the longest serving member of the *Archers'* scriptwriting team, Mary Cutler shares her thoughts about writing for soaps.

A few years ago I was introduced by a friend to someone struggling to establish herself as a playwright. 'I so envy you,' she said, 'writing for the *Archers*. I love soaps.' 'If you love soaps, maybe you should be writing them,' I suggested. I met her again a few years later and she said, 'I want to thank you: I took your advice. I gave it a try, and now I'm writing for *Emmerdale*.' So there you are, dear readers. Ten magic words from me might transform your life. I will try to explore why you might love writing for soaps, or equally helpfully, I hope, why you might not.

I have been writing for the *Archers* for 31 years (the programme was first broadcast on Radio 4 in 1951) and such a long career is by no means unique in soaps. During these years I have had a guaranteed audience for my work, and what's more, an affectionate and engaged audience. I've worked collaboratively with some extremely talented people, while retaining control of my own words. I have had the opportunity to cover almost every dramatic situation – tragic, comic, social, political – I could ever have wanted to, in every possible dramatic form. Yes, you may ask – though I hope not as the question fills me with fury – but what about your own work? This is my own work. Who else wrote all those scripts?

The production process

The process of getting a script ready to be recorded starts with the monthly Monday script conference. This is attended by all the writers (there are nine of us in the team at the moment) and the production team. We each have in front of us the large script pack which would have been emailed to us on the previous Friday. (It helps if you're a quick reader.) We meet to decide on the storyline for the next writing month, for which four of the writers present will each be writing a week's worth of episodes. But we all work on the storyline together – the writers, whether writing or not – and all the production team, at all levels. That is one of the things I like most. I have never felt plotting was a particular strength of mine, but if someone will give me a starting line I can run from it. The delight of a good script conference is when we start with a strong idea which everyone expands and improves on until it's a thing of beauty, and no one can remember whose idea it was first, and it doesn't matter.

To be part of this engrossing process you have to speak. Most soaps have a script conference element where you will be expected to voice, and if necessary, defend your ideas. That doesn't mean you have to shout, or talk all the time – indeed, these would be positive disadvantages. But you need to stand your ground, especially about what a character might or might not do, and also be ready to yield gracefully if you lose the argument. One of our characters was once torn between two lovers, and the team were, too. On the day of the final decision there was a bad hold-up on the motorway, and three writers rooting for one lover didn't arrive until midday, by which time the other had carried the day. Those writers had to find their own ways to make that decision work for them when they wrote their scripts.

After the script conference, the storyline is emailed two days later to all the writers and members of the production team to arrive on Wednesday evening. The writers for that month have until Tuesday to each write their synopsis, which is a scene-by-scene break down of what they intend to write in their six episodes. If it is a well-structured and imaginative synopsis, all that now needs to be written is the dialogue. A script editor speaks with each of the writers for that month on the following Thursday, and they then have ten days to write six scripts – an hour and a quarter's radio. Not everyone can work that fast. One of the best weeks of the *Archers* I ever heard was also that writer's last: he said he could never do it again in the time. It's not a case of locking yourself in your garret and seeing where the muse takes you. The storyline must be covered: while the writer for one week is working on their scripts, the writer for the following week's episodes is writing theirs starting from the point where the storyline is left on the previous week. As all the scripts are written simultaneously each writer needs to let the others know what they're doing. How each writer chooses to dramatise the story is entirely up to them, so there's a lot of scope for individual creative work. There are constraints on the structure of the programme, such as the financial restriction on the number of actors which can be used. Only two of our actors are on a regular contract, so writers may need to tell a story without a character being present because the actor is working elsewhere. Alternatively a writer may swap episodes within their week, or with other writers, to get the actors they need.

Until the script editor sees the writing for all four weeks, she can't tell if stories are going too fast or too slow, have become repetitive, or picked up the wrong tone.There may well be changes to be made following the synopsis discussion. It is only after the synopsis is agreed that the office starts ringing the actors to see if they are still available. Some of them may not be, in which case a writer may have to rethink their beautiful structure and clever stories. But those are just normal run-of-the-mill changes. When we lost the delightful and distinguished actress who played Julia Pargeter (who died suddenly and unexpectedly after a happy day in the recording studio) the whole team had to deal with not only their sorrow and distress, but the fact that this meant rewriting and re-recording scripts that had been completed in the studio, and rewriting those that were about to be recorded, as well as rethinking those that were about to be written. I had two days to turn round my part of this massive undertaking. When the foot-and-mouth crisis hit British farming in 2001 our fictional world was being rewritten practically day by day, so a good soap scriptwriter needs to be fast and flexible. When the Princess of Wales died our redoubtable editor had one day to get something appropriate on air.

My scriptwriting break

So how did scriptwriting for soaps become the job for me? I had always wanted to write, and had been writing since I was quite small. I thought I was going to be a novelist, and wrote several highly autobiographical, very literary quasi novels while at school and university. I should have noticed that the only person prepared to pay me was the editor of *Jackie* magazine to whom I sold three highly autobiographical, although not quite so literary, stories. Then at university I stopped having saleable teenage fantasies, and started having unsaleable literary ones. Real life took over – I decided my ambition to be a writer was a fantasy – I would concentrate on my burgeoning career as a teacher, and stop writing.fjBut I found I couldn't stop. When I realised how I think – rather than seeing images or words, I hear voices (a perpetual radio broadcast!) – I started to write radio plays. To my delight, I found that I could write dialogue till the cows came home(!) though whether it was about anything that would interest even the cows was another matter. I sent my radio plays to the BBC, and sometimes they came back with kind comments (once I was even invited to meet a producer) – and sometimes they just came back. But I persisted.

I am a life-long fan of the *Archers* (I remember Grace Archer dying when I was six and I used to play Phil Archer and his pigs with my little brothers – naturally I was Phil). When an old school friend started writing for the *Archers* I was fascinated to hear her first week on air: it simultaneously sounded like the *Archers* I had known and loved but also very like my friend – her sense of humour, her pre-occupations. I idly wondered what I might find out about my own writing if I tried using these well-loved characters to express myself. So after I heard her Friday episode, I sat down to write the following Monday's, purely as a writing exercise and just for fun, and sent it off.

Some time later I received a letter from the recently appointed editor of the *Archers* saying that although he wasn't looking for new writers my script interested him. He also invited me to meet him. When I went to Pebble Mill the editor offered me a trial week, which I did in the Easter holidays. Following that he offered me a six-month contract. So my big break was a combination of persistence (I had been sending radio plays to the BBC for at least three years, and writing stories since I could hold a pencil) and sheer luck – the new editor *was* looking for new writers, despite what he'd said in his letter. (The *Archers* now has a rather more sophisticated method of finding new writers – see box.) My script also had the necessary ingredients of craft and, dare I say it, talent. I had, without knowing it, written a script of the right length, with the right number of scenes and the right number of characters – all those years of listening had given me a subliminal feel for the form. According to the editor, my first good line was two-thirds of the way down the first page. I can still remember it: 'She can get up a fair lick of speed when she's pushed'. (Maybe you had to be there but I still think it has a certain ring to it!) But it was also a script I wrote for fun for a programme I loved and admired.

Further information

The Archers Office
BBC, The Mailbox, Birmingham B1 1RF
Write to receive a Writer's Pack. NB: If you are asked to write a trial script this will be unpaid. Slots on the writing team do not come up often and at the time of writing there are no spaces.

Mary Cutler has been a scriptwriter for the *Archers* since 1979. She has dramatised five of Lindsey Davis's *Falco* novels for Radio 4, the last one being *Poseidon's Gold*, and three dramatic series – *Live Alone and Like It, Three Women and a Boat* and *Three Women and a Baby* for *Women's Hour*. She has also written for the stage and television, including some scripts for *Crossroads* before she was told that her particular talents did not quite fit its special demands. She'd still like to write a novel.

Writing drama for radio

Writing drama for radio allows a freedom which none of the other performing arts can give. Lee Hall guides the radio drama writer to submit a script which will be well received.

With upwards of 300 hours of radio drama commissioned each year, radio is an insatiable medium and, therefore, one which is constantly seeking new blood. It is no surprise to find that many of our most eminent dramatists, such as Pinter and Stoppard, did important radio work early in their careers.

Although the centrality of radio has been eclipsed somewhat by television and fringe theatre, it continues to launch new writers, and its products often find popular recognition in other media (for example, the film version of Anthony Mingella's *Truly Madly Deeply*). Because radio is often cited as the discoverer and springboard of so many talents, this should not obscure the fact that many writers make a living primarily out of their radio writing and the work itself is massively popular, with plays regularly getting audiences of over 500,000 people.

For the dramatist, the medium offers a variety of work which is difficult to find anywhere else: serials, dramatisations, new commissions of various lengths (from a couple of minutes to several hours), musicals, soap operas, adaptations of the classics, as well as a real enthusiasm to examine new forms.

Because it is no more expensive to be in the Hindu Kush than to be in a laundrette in Deptford, the scope of the world is only limited by the imagination of the writer. However, though radio drama in the Fifties and Sixties was an important conduit for absurdism, there is a perceived notion that radio drama on the BBC is domestic, Home Counties and endlessly trotting out psychological trauma in a rather naturalistic fashion. This is not a fair assessment of the true range of work presented. The BBC itself is anxious to challenge this idea and as the face of broadcasting changes, there is a conscious move to attract new audiences with new kinds of work.

Get to know the form

Listen to as many plays as possible, read plays that are in print, and try to analyse what works, what doesn't and why. This may seem obvious, but it is easy to fall back on your preconceived notions of what radio plays are. The more you hear other people's successes and failures, the more tools you will have to discriminate with when it comes to your own work.

Plays on radio tend to fit into specific time slots: 30, 60, 75, 90 minutes, and each slot will have a different feel – an afternoon play will be targeted at a different audience from one at 10.30pm.

A radio play will be chosen on artistic grounds but nevertheless a writer should be familiar with the market. This should not be seen as an invitation merely to copy forms or to try to make your play 'fit', but an opportunity to gain some sense of what the producers are dealing with. Producers are looking for new and fresh voices, ones which are unique, open new areas or challenge certain preconceptions. This is not to suggest you should be wilfully idiosyncratic but to be aware that it is the individuality of your 'voice' that people will notice.

Write what you feel strongly about, in the way that most attracts you. It should be bold, personal, entertaining, challenging and stimulating. Radio has the scope to explore drama that wouldn't get produced in theatres or on television, so treat it as the most radical forum for new writing. How many times have you listened to the radio with the sense that you've heard it all before? Never feel limited by what exists; instead be aware how your voice can enrich the possibilities of the future.

Who to approach

Opportunities for writing for radio in the UK are dominated by the BBC. Whilst there are increasing opportunities with independent stations, BBC Radio Drama overwhelms the field. Its output is huge. The variety of the work – from soaps to the classics – makes it the true national repertory for drama in its broadest sense. However, the BBC is increasingly commissioning productions from independent producers, so you can:

- Send your unsolicited script to the BBC writersroom (formerly the New Writing Initiative; see page 395) where it will be assessed by a reader. If they find it of interest they will put you in contact with a suitable producer.
- Approach a producer directly. This may be a producer at the BBC or at an independent company (see page 419). Both will give a personal response based on their own taste, rather than an institutional one.

Producers have a broad role: they find new writers, develop projects, edit the script, cast the actors, record and edit the play, and even write up the blurb for the *Radio Times*. Because of this intense involvement, the producer needs to have a strong personal interest in the writer or writing when they take on a project.

The system of commissioning programmes at the BBC is such that staff producers or independent production companies offer projects to commissioning editors to decide upon. Thus, a writer must be linked to a producer in the first instance to either get their play produced or get a commission for a new piece of work. Therefore, going direct to a producer can be a convenient short cut, but it requires more preparation.

Approaching a producer

Discovering and developing the work of new writers is only a small part of a producer's responsibilities, so be selective. Do your homework – there is little point in sending your sci-fi series to a producer who exclusively produces one-off period comedies.

To help decide which producer will be the most receptive to your work, become familiar with the work of each producer you are intersted in and the type of writers they work with. Use the *Radio Times* to help with your research and listen to as many of their plays as possible. It is well worth the effort in order to be sure to send your play to the right person. If you can quote the reasons why you've chosen them in particular, it can only help to get a congenial reception. It will also give you confidence in their response, as the comments – good or bad – will be from someone you respect.

Submitting your work

Don't stuff your manuscript into an envelope as soon as you've written 'The End'. You owe it to yourself to get the script into the best possible state before anyone sees it. First impressions matter and time spent refining will pay dividends in attracting attention.

Ask a person you trust to give you some feedback. Try to edit the work yourself, cutting things that don't work and spending time revising and reinventing anything which you think could be better. Make sure that what you send is the best you can possibly do.

Producers have mountains of scripts to read. The more bulky your tome the less enthusiastically it will be received. (It's better to send a sparkling ten-page sample than your whole 300-page masterpiece.) Try to make the first scene excellent. The more you can surprise, engage or delight in the first few pages, the more chance the rest will be carefully read. The adage that a reader can tell whether a play is any good after the first three pages might be wholly inaccurate but it reflects a cynicism versed by the practice of script reading. The reader will probably approach your script with the expectation that it is unsuitable, and part of getting noticed is jolting them out of their complacency.

Have your script presentably typed. Make sure your letter of introduction is well informed and shows that you haven't just picked a name at random. Do not send it to more than one producer at a time, as this is considered bad etiquette. And don't expect an instantaneous response – it may take a couple of months before you receive a reply. Don't be afraid of calling up if they keep you waiting for an unreasonable length of time, but don't badger people as this will inevitably be counterproductive.

Finally

Don't be discouraged by rejection and *don't* assume that because one person has rejected your script that it is no good. It is all a question of taste. Use the criticism positively to help your work, not as a personal attack.

Lee Hall has written several plays for BBC Radio, including the award-winning *Spoonface Steinberg*, which he has since adapted for television and theatre. His translations of theatre plays include Brecht's *Mr Puntilla and His Man Matti* and *Mother Courage* and Goldoni's *The Servant with Two Masters*. His play *Cooking with Elvis* was nominated for an Olivier Award for Best New Comedy, and his screenplay for *Billy Elliot* was Oscar nominated.

Stories on radio

Getting a story read on BBC Radio 4 is very competitive. Di Speirs outlines how work is selected.

Before they were ever written down, we told stories to each other. And there remains a natural empathy between the written tale and the spoken word. The two make perfect partners in a medium where the imagination has free rein – in other words – radio. And that partnership is particularly effective on the BBC's spoken word station, BBC Radio 4, which plays host to more stories than any other UK network. Stories, of course, can and do appear in many guises there, from original plays to dramatised adaptations, but above all they work on air as themselves, read by some of the finest actors of our day and listened to by upwards of one and a half million listeners at each broadcast.

There are two main fiction slots for stories on Radio 4, as well as the morning non-fiction reading at 9.45am, which is repeated in the late evening. Three afternoons a week (Tuesday to Thursday) at 3.30pm there is a short story that can transport the listener around the globe in 15 minutes. And every weekday evening a *Book at Bedtime* episode can lull you towards (although hopefully not to) sleep, just after *The World Tonight* at 10.45pm.

A number of different producers, both in-house and independent, produce readings for these three slots – finding the books, getting them commissioned by Radio 4 and then producing the final programmes. The process of successfully translating the written work to the airwaves is as intimate as that of any editor within a publishing house. There is nothing like structuring the abridgement of a novel or a short story – which reduces an author's meticulously crafted work down to 2,000 words an episode – to focus the mind on the essential threads and hidden subtleties of a story, be it originally 3,500 perfectly chosen words or an intricately plotted 300-page novel. The author Derek Longman once described the abridging of his *Diana's Story* (one of the most popular readings ever on *Woman's Hour*) as akin to the book 'having gone on a diet'! You aim to retain the essence, but in a trimmer, slimmer version.

Once cut to the bone, finding the right voice to convey and enhance the story is crucial, as performance, in part, compensates for what has been lost. Casting is vital; so is direction in the studio where different stories demand very different approaches: listen to the output and you'll hear everything from a highly characterised monologue to a narrator-driven piece which demands the actor also create a cast of dozens of distinct voices. From the cues that introduce a story, to the music that sets the right mood, a producer works to move a story from the author's original vision into a different but sympathetic medium. As authors mourn what is discarded, it is important to remember what is added by good quality production and top class performance. And of course to remember how effective readings are at taking a book to a whole new audience.

So how do you get your story on air and to all those eager listeners? What is Radio 4 looking for and what works best?

It would be disingenuous to say that it is any easier to get your work read on radio than to get it published. In truth, given the finite number of slots and the volume of submissions it's a tough call. But here are a few hints and guidelines that may help.

Book of the Week

The *Book of the Week* slot is the one that reflects current publishing more than any other. With 52 books a year broadcast on or very close to their original publication date, in five

13-minute episodes, the non-fiction remit is broad and the slot covers everything from biography to humour, politics to travel. Memoir is always an important part of the mix, but so too are good, accessible science books with a narrative thread that can engage the listener, and few subjects are out of bounds if the prose lifts off the page and can catch the attention of what is, by necessity, a largely active and busy audience at that time in the morning.

Submissions come through publishers and agents. The books need to sustain their story over five episodes but also work as individual episodes, for this is an audience that won't necessarily hear all of the book (though the BBC's 'Listen Again' facility is changing this pattern for some). Overly academic prose doesn't work, nor do too many names and facts. The key is a story and, as below, a voice.

Book at Bedtime

Book at Bedtime is a mix of classic and new fiction. The slot is mostly serialised fiction although occasional harder hitting short story collections – for instance by writers like Michel Faber, Julie Orringer and Anne Enright – do find their way in, as do the odd weeks of poetry (*Paradise Lost* and *The Prelude* have been read in the past). The novels divide into, roughly, a third classic fiction; a third established names (e.g. new novels, usually transmitted on publication by popular writers, from William Trevor to Colm Toibin, Tim Winton to Rose Tremain); and a third newer voices, including a high proportion of debut novels (Ross Raisin's *God's Own Country*, Francesca Kay's *An Equal Stillness*, Sadie Jones's *The Outcast*, Amy Sackville's *The Still Point*) and some short stories (e.g. James Lasdun, Clare Keegan). What they all share is a quality of writing that works when you pare it to the core. Abridging a work will show up its literary qualities and its flaws – and there is nowhere to hide. Listen to the slot and you will be aware of both the variety (from classics to crime, domestic dramas to lyrical translations) and the quality of the writing.

There are few other hard-and-fast rules – a linear plot, with sub-plots that can be reduced or lost, is preferable – *The Vanishing Act of Esme Lennox* was a demanding listen in terms of jumps in time and place but the characters were so vivid and the story so powerful it worked; myriad characters are best avoided, but are manageable with a classic (where familiarity helps). Length is also an important issue. The usual run for a book is ten episodes over two weeks; for almost any novel over 350 pages this becomes a cut too far. Exceptions can be made but they are exceptions; *Atonement* by Ian McEwan, *The Colour* by Rose Tremain and *The Interpretation of Murder* by Jed Rubenfeld all ran at 15 episodes, but for new work this is a rarity. (Short novels can run over five episodes.)

New book submissions

New novels are found almost entirely through submissions from agents and publishers to individual producers – the best ones both understand Radio 4 and know the predilections of the main players and play to their tastes. It is extremely rare that an author submits directly, even rarer for them to be successful in what is the most competitive readings slot of all. However, the passion of an individual agent or editor can make a real difference in getting a book read by the producer and that's the first step in the process. Bear in mind that in my office alone we receive upwards of 50 manuscripts and proof sets a week – a lot of work for a team of six. Having a reputable champion who can expand on why your novel really is potentially right for the slot is a genuine plus in getting to the top of the scripts pile.

We usually see work at the manuscript or proof stage, increasingly submitted online though this is far from essential and most producers still prefer to read from paper. New titles are ideally broadcast at or near to the hardback publication date, and so producers need to see them in time to get them commissioned and made – ideally six to nine months in advance. And however passionate a producer is about an individual title, the choice is finally in the hands of the commissioning team at Radio 4 who know what else lies in the complex schedule across the network, and must always weigh individual merits against the broader picture.

What makes a good book to read on Radio 4?

Radio 4 is looking for the quality of the writing, coherence of plot (bear in mind though that complex sub-plots can sometimes be stripped out by skilful abridgers), a comprehensible, identifiable cast and perhaps above all, a sense of engagement with the listener. Although crime is always popular, broadcasting copious amounts of blood and gore at bedtime is unlikely to endear the BBC to the public. Psychological work – like *Engleby* by Sebastian Faulks – works better. Think too, when descriptions are cut, do the clues in the plot stand out like a sore thumb? Consider whether the subject matter is likely to fit with the Radio 4 audience – who are almost certainly much broader-minded and certainly more eclectic than you might imagine – and also highly literate. There is a very real desire to reflect as wide a range of fiction as possible – from a bestseller by Kate Long to a Bangladeshi debut from Tahmima Anan, from a suddenly discovered classic from Irene Nemirovsky to the cutting edge of David Mitchell. It's a broad spectrum but there are of course some issues surrounding language, violence and sexual content; these can be surmountable in many cases – judicious pauses are effective and radio is, after all, a medium that allows the imagination to fill in the blanks as far as you may want to! However there is no point in submitting a novel filled with expletives or subject matter that will simply shock for the sake of it.

Think too about the voice of a novel – this applies, as much does here, to the short story too. It's an aural medium. Does your book have a 'voice' – can you hear it leaping off the page? Would you want to hear it read to you? And will that be easy to do? There are problems with any story or novel that veers from the third to the first person continually. It can be done – Maggie O'Farrell's powerful *The Vanishing Act of Esmé Lennox* was a gift for three narrators, but remember that although every year Radio 4 runs several novels with multiple narrators, they are more expensive to produce and as budgets get ever leaner, slots are even more limited. Be realistic. The competition for this slot is the fiercest of all – and with approximately 26 titles a year, a good number of which are from the ever-popular classic canon, there are really only around 15 opportunities for the year's new titles.

Afternoon Story

Fifty-two weeks of the year, three afternoons a week, Radio 4 broadcasts a short story – about 35 of those weeks, approximately 100 stories annually, are commissioned by producers around the country. The rest comprise of the retelling of old masters and selections from newly published collections, by writers such as Alice Munro, Helen Simpson, Sana Kraskiov and Etgar Kerat. Like novels, these collections are submitted by publishers and agents.

The BBC is arguably the largest single commissioner of short stories in the UK, possibly even the world. It is hugely committed to the short story, that most difficult and often underrated of literary forms, and does provide an unparralelled opportunity for writers who want to explore the genre. However, as with *Book at Bedtime*, the competition here is severe.

Stories are usually grouped in threes across a week and often around a theme. Each year there are weeks broadcast from different literary festivals, such as Edinburgh, Latitude and Hay-on-Wye. Writers for these are often selected from the festival's own programme, either to write original material or to perform something they are already reading.

The majority of other weeks are commissioned by producers around a theme that they've discussed with the commissioning editor. The scope is very wide. There have been stories drawn from the three Benelux countries and others inspired by Tom Waits under the umbrella title 'The Heart of a Saturday Night'. A week of 'Heartbreak' was followed by a week of 'Passion' and later by 'Wedding Feasts', while thornier subjects such as 'Addiction' have allowed writers to explore a surprising variety of subjects from caffeine to love. 'Madame Bovary Speaks' allowed writers to play with various angles from Flaubert's novel while a returning series like 'Curly Tales' plays with the storytelling form and enjoys turning it upside down. These themed weeks offer producers a wonderful opportunity to approach both well-known writers (who usually have a record in short story writing) and to give new writers – perhaps spotted in an anthology or a magazine, or because of a strong debut novel, or through the advocacy of an agent – a chance to get their work on air. Many acclaimed short story writers, like Jackie Kay, Helen Dunmore and Peter Ho Davies, have a long history with Radio 4, and are commissioned regularly because they understand the demands and the possibilities of the slot.

Unsolicited stories

I would love to say that the writers who send in unsolicited material have a good chance of getting their stories read. Some do – for instance the London unit runs a returning series called 'Opening Lines' and accepts submissions at a specific period during the year, and BBC Scotland produces a week of unsolicited 'Scottish Shorts' each year. Others get commissioned to write a story on a theme, rather than having their original idea read. But the short story is a demanding form and skill and practise is perhaps more vital here than anywhere else. Producers have a certain but sadly limited amount of time to work with an author in an editorial capacity. With only 2,000 words there's no room for waste and yet you must, as Alice Munro (the Canadian doyenne of the short story) says, 'create a world in a glance'. The subjects may be wide but the bar is high – the best writers in the country and beyond are writing for this slot and you have to match that standard. You may have a better chance of being considered by aiming your story locally (some local BBC radio stations run short fiction from time to time). Be aware of who works in your geographic area, as the Radio 4 afternoon story slot reflects the regions and nations of the UK.

But above all, as with *Book at Bedtime*, listen to the slot to hear both the range and also what works well. Listen to how writers use the unique qualities of radio – the chance to write a powerful monologue or to use sound or location within a tale – to enhance their story, create a sense of place or person, to flesh out what is in reality a brief moment in time. There are real ways to be experimental in both storytelling and production and producers are always on the lookout for those alongside perfectly pitched and flawless prose.

Finally, for the past five years the BBC has been one of the partners, along with Booktrust, in the BBC National Short Story Award (see page 590), which was established to celebrate and foster the art of the short story, and with an award of £15,000 to the winner is one of the largest in the world for a single story. Over the past five years we have received over 3,600 entries from published writers either from, or resident in, the UK. It is certainly clear that the short story is alive and well across the UK and choosing the winners has been a tremendously hard task each time. If you are a published writer, do consider entering next time around. The BBC NSSA is part of the wider 'Story' campaign which exists to support all short story writers (www.theshortstory.org.uk).

In all the readings slots, Radio 4 is looking for terrific writing, a good story and an ear-catching 'voice'. Despite the fierce competition, producers love to 'discover' new writers for the network and every year sees new talent getting their work on air. Keep listening, get to know the slots, and if you have a story – long or short – that demands to be read aloud, try to find a champion for it. Good luck.

Di Speirs worked in theatre and for the Australian Broadcasting Corporation before joining the BBC in 1991 as a producer for *Woman's Hour*. She edited the *Woman's Hour* serial for three years and produced the first ever *Book of the Week*. She is now Editor of the BBC London Readings Unit, responsible for around a third of the output in *Book of the Week*, a quarter of *Book at Bedtime*, as well as *Afternoon Stories*, Radio 3 readings and *Woman's Hour* dramas, and *Afternoon Plays* adapted from novels and short stories. She has been instrumental in the BBC National Short Story Award since its inception in 2005 and is a regular judge on the panel. She was also a judge of the 2008 Asham Award and was the Chair of the Orange Award for New Writers in 2010.

Inside the BBC

Emma Hurrell has compiled the following information as a guide for writers, artists, agents, publishers and all other media on how to make contact with the BBC. For more detailed information see the BBC website (www.bbc.co.uk).

Introduction

The BBC is the largest broadcasting corporation in the world. Its purpose is to enrich people's lives with programmes that inform, educate and entertain. It is a public service broadcaster, established by a Royal Charter and funded by the licence fee that is paid by UK households.

The BBC uses the income from the licence fee to provide services including 8 national TV channels plus regional programming, 10 national radio stations, 39 local radio stations and an extensive website (bbc.co.uk). BBC World Service broadcasts internationally on radio, on TV and online, providing news and information in 32 languages. It is funded by a government grant, not from the licence fee.

The BBC has a commercial arm, BBC Worldwide, which operates a range of businesses including selling programmes around the world and publishing books, DVDs and merchandise. Its profits are returned to the BBC for investment in new programming and services.

The BBC is governed by the BBC Trust, which represents the interests of licence fee payers and sets the overall strategy. The Trust's Chairman is Sir Michael Lyons. The BBC's Executive Board manages the day-to-day operation of the corporation and is made up of executive directors from within the BBC and 6 non-executive directors from outside:

Director-General Mark Thompson
Deputy Director-General Mark Byford
Director, Audio & Music Tim Davie
Director, Vision Jana Bennett
Director, Marketing, Communications & Audiences Sharon Baylay
Director, Future Media & Technology Erik Huggers
Director, BBC People Lucy Adams
Group Finance Director Zarin Patel
Chief Operating Officer Caroline Thomson

The BBC structure

The BBC has 4 content divisions, 4 support departments and 2 commercial subsidiaries.

Content divisions:
• Vision, including Drama, Knowledge, Entertainment and Children's
• Audio & Music
• Journalism, including News, Sport, Nations, Global News
• Future Media & Technology.

Support departments:
• Operations (strategy, policy, distribution, property, legal affairs & business continuity)
• MC&A (marketing, communication & audiences)
• People (human resources)
• Finance & Business (financial planning & strategy).

Three commercial subsidiaries:
• BBC Worldwide
• BBC Studios and Production
• BBC World News.

How to make contact

Submitting scripts

BBC writersroom

1st Floor, Grafton House, 379 Euston Road, London NW1 3AU
tel 020-7765 2703
website www.bbc.co.uk/writersroom

BBC writersroom is the first point of call at the BBC for unsolicited scripts and new writers. It champions new writing talent in films and TV single drama; TV series, serials and factual drama; TV sitcoms; radio drama; radio sitcoms; and children's drama.

BBC writersroom is on the lookout for writers of any age and experience who show real potential for the BBC. All eligible scripts are logged and assessed primarily for the talent of the writer and suitability of scripts for further development. If the opening 10 pages hooks the attention of the reader, the script will be read fully and the writer will receive feedback. All other scripts are returned without feedback.

BBC writersroom runs schemes to target talent from a range of sources and promote writers across all BBC departments, channels and programmes. It works in partnerships with theatres, writer's organisations, screen agencies and the wider cultural industries. New writers are helped to develop their craft through the website and in open sessions around the country with the UK's best writing talent.

See website for more detailed information about the BBC writersroom. Writers are strongly advised to read the guidelines and checklist on the website before submitting material.

New Talent

website www.bbc.co.uk/newtalent

BBC New Talent exists to find and inspire new talent. Every year it creates and runs a number of schemes offering opportunities in all areas of broadcasting including comedy, drama, film, music, writing, presenting and entertainment. It also runs several schemes aimed specifically for young people aged under 16. A variety of initiatives offer job opportunities within the BBC, provide a platform to showcase new talent, and give individuals the opportunity to network with key industry professionals. The website provides advice and encouragement from experts in the field, and some of the previous winners are profiled. There are also hundreds of useful links, some of which give information about opportunities outside of the BBC.

Jobs and work placements/ experience

Recruitment BBC HR Direct, PO Box 1133, Belfast BT1 9GP
email careers@bbchrdirect.co.uk
website www.bbc.co.uk/jobs

The BBC website provides information and advice about how to get into the BBC and how to apply for BBC jobs, training schemes and work placements. Placements are available in most areas of the BBC across the UK. They are unpaid and can last anything from a few days to 4 weeks. In excess of 20,000 applications are received each year, so applicants must be able to demonstrate a keen interest in the placement.

Submitting programme ideas or formats

If you wish to submit an unsolicited idea to the BBC you need to team up with either a BBC in-house production department or contact an independent production company.

The development and production of a programme is a complex process, needing an in-depth understanding of the production system and involving many people as well as the creator of the original concept. Working with an independent production company or (in some areas) a production department provides this support.

Contacting a BBC production department

Unsolicited proposals (those which are unattached to any industry establishment) can only be accepted in the areas noted below, and should be sent to the relevant address.

Drama and narrative comedy scripts

Paul Ashton, Development Manager, BBC writersroom, 1 Mortimer Street, London W1T 3JA
website writersroom@bbc.co.uk

Note that comedy and drama ideas *must* be in the form of a fully written script; send an sae requesting guidelines.

Entertainment formats (quiz/games shows)

Format Entertainment Development Team, Room 4010, BBC Television Centre, Wood Lane, London W12 7RJ

Factual entertainment treatments

Factual Entertainment Development, Room 4010, BBC Television Centre, Wood Lane, London W12 7RJ
Interested in factual entertainment ideas only; does not accept proposals of a documentary or general factual nature.

Independent production companies

The best way of getting in touch with an independent production company is to do some research about the companies which produce the type of programmes you have an idea for. Many of these companies are members of Pact (Producers' Alliance for Cinema and Television, see page 573), which represents the independent sector. The *Pact Directory*, which can be accessed online for free, contains a whole host of useful information about UK independent producers and digital members, including the programmes they've produced, projects they have in development, distribution catalogues and rights available, key personnel and contact details, and brief company profiles (www.pact.co.uk).

Commissioning

TV including multi-platform

website www.bbc.co.uk/commissioning (select BBC Vision)

Programmes are commissioned by the genre teams. The genres are drama, comedy, entertainment, daytime, knowledge, CBBC, CBeebies, sport and programme acquisition. Each genre handles the entire process – editorial, business, finance and delivery. Contact details can be found on the website under the BBC Vision section. Programme requirements for the genres are updated regularly with development priorities on the website located within each of the genre pages.

Proposals for BBC network content on TV and all other video platforms (e.g. websites, mobile, interactive TV) must be submitted online through the e-Commissioning system and writers must first have teamed up with either an in-house production studio or an independent production company.

e-Commissioning enables the BBC to handle the huge volume of proposals it receives faster and more effectively. When registering for the system, suppliers should supply a short company profile including relevant industry experience of producing TV programmes or multi-platform content for a broadcaster, detailing relevant examples of productions and broadcasters. Approval of the registration is at the BBC's discretion.

Radio

website www.bbc.co.uk/commissioning (select Audio & Music), www.bbc.co.uk/commissioinig/radio/network (Proteus system)

Full information on the detailed commissioning process for each of the networks can be viewed by selecting the relevant network on the website. Before pitching a programme idea first review the website, particularly the Audience Information and the Statement of Programme Policy for the network you propose to approach. New writers or writers without an agent or production company should explore the BBC writersroom (see above).

When a network invites programme proposals it requires them to be submitted in the Proteus system unless otherwise specified. An independent production company must therefore have access to Proteus before it can submit a programme proposal. New suppliers must first talk to the network that they wish to supply. If the network is interested in receiving programme proposals from that supplier, the company can then find out more about registering for the Proteus system via the website.

All contact details can be found under the Audio & Music section on the website.

BBC Vision

BBC Television Centre, Wood Lane,
London W12 7RJ
tel 020-8743 8000
Director, Vision Jana Bennett

BBC Vision is responsible for commissioning, producing, scheduling and broadcasting the content of all the BBC's TV channels. It incorporates the service controllers, genre commissioners, in-house production and operations teams for BBC ONE, TWO, THREE, FOUR, CBBC, Cbeebies, the UKTV channels and BBC America. The service controllers are:

BBC ONE Jay Hunt
BBC TWO Janice Hadlow
BBC THREE Danny Cohen
BBC FOUR Richard Klein
Children's Joe Godwin
Multi-platform & Portfolio Simon Nelson
Daytime Liam Keelan

Genre commissioning

Genre teams now commission all video content on all platforms including www.bbc.co.uk, mobiles and interactive 'red button' services, as well as for TV.

For more detailed information on each genre's commissioning team contacts, priorities for commissioning and how to use the e-Commissioning system go to www.bbc.co.uk/commissioning and select BBC Vision, then select the relevant genre you are interested in.

Fiction

Comprises drama (including films), comedy and programme acquisition.

Head of Drama Commissioning Ben Stephenson
Controller of Comedy Commissioning Cheryl Taylor
Head of Series, Programme Acquisition Sue Deeks
Head of Films, Programme Acquisition Steve Jenkins

Entertainment

Controller, Entertainment Commissioning Mark Linsey

Knowledge

Controller, Knowledge Commissioning George Entwistle
Head of Knowledge Commissioning Emma Swain
Controller, Learning Saul Nassé

Children's

Controller, Children's Joe Godwin

Children's is a self-commissioning, self-scheduling department that manages its own production unit and as such has a different structure to the rest of the BBC.

For more detailed information on CBBC and Cbeebies go to www.bbc.co.uk/commissioning and select BBC Vision, then select either Children's (CBBC) or (CBeebies).

CBBC

Controller Damian Kavanagh

CBBC is for primary school children aged 6–12 years. It offers a distinctive schedule of original drama, animation, comedy, news, factual programming and events on a variety of platforms as well as interactive applications (online, WAP, SMS, enhanced TV) that allow children to get involved, to connect with CBBC and to explore topics further. The CBBC channel runs 7am–7pm and CBBC output runs on BBC ONE and TWO.

Independent suppliers should send in proposals to Damian Kavanagh, and drama, acquisitions and animations enquiries should be made to Steven Andrew, but all submissions must be made via the e-Commissioning system.

CBeebies

Controller Kay Benbow

CBeebies is the BBC's first truly tri-media brand, offering TV, radio and web services on all digital platforms. CBeebies offers a rich portfolio of content on its website, through its TV outlets and most recently via radio on Radio 7. Therefore they are a multi-platform commissioner not just a TV commissioner.

CBeebies is a self-commissioning, self-scheduling department and now operates a rolling commissioning system. Independent suppliers should send all proposals to Kay Benbow (via e-Commissioning).

Enquiries concerning acquisitions and animations should be made to Kay Benbow (but proposals must be submitted via e-Commissioning).

The CBeebies digital TV channel (on satellite, cable and Freeview) is on-air 6am–7pm daily. CBeebies TV may also be found on BBC TWO which runs complementary schedules – sometimes simulcasting CBeebies on weekday mornings.

CBeebies radio is available on Radio 7 (via a DAB radio or digital TV set-top box) 2–5pm daily, and programmes are available on the website for up to 7 days after initial broadcast.

Vision Productions

Vision Productions is responsible for in-house programme making across factual, comedy, drama and entertainment from London, Manchester, Bristol and Birmingham.

Chief Creative Officer, Vision Productions Patrick Younge
Head of Comedy Productions Mark Freeland
Controller, Entertainment Productions Katie Taylor
Controller, Drama Production Nick Brown
Controller, Drama Productions & New Talent John Yorke
Controller, Drama Series & Serials Kate Harwood
Controller of Factual Productions Tom Archer
Head of Multi-Platform Productions Richard Williams
Controller, Production Operations Sally Debonnaire
Head of London Factual Karen O'Connor
Head of Natural History Unit, Bristol Andrew Jackson
Head of Factual, Birmingham and Manchester Nick Patten
Head of Bristol Factual Ben Gale
Head of Development Tessa Finch
Head of Production Talent Ian Critchley

Audio & Music

BBC Broadcasting House, Portland Place, London W1A 1AA
tel 020-7765 4561
Director, Audio & Music Tim Davie

The Audio & Music division is responsible for the 5 national analogue networks (Radio 1, Radio 2, Radio 3, Radio 4 and BBC Radio Five Live) and the 5 digital stations (1Xtra, 6Music, Radio 7, Five Live Sports Extra and the Asian Network). It provides most of the music production for the BBC on national and World Service radio.

The TV Classical Music Unit is responsible for dance, performance and classical music on TV and TV Music Entertainment is responsible for popular music production across the BBC TV channels. Audio & Music Factual producers also provide speech programming covering a wide range of arts, science, features, drama and readings for domestic radio and the World Service. Other programmes are provided by Factual & Learning (Religion and the Natural History Unit), News, Sport and Light Entertainment. All BBC national radio stations are available on DAB radio, digital TV and via the internet.

Controller, Radio 1/1Xtra & Asian Network Andy Parfitt
Controller, Radio 2 & 6Music Bob Shennan
Controller Radio 3, BBC Proms & Performing Groups Roger Wright
Controller, Radio 4 & Radio 7 Mark Damazer
Controller, BBC Radio Five Live, 5 Live Sports Extra Adrian Van-Klaveren
Head of Programmes, 6Music Paul Rodgers
Head of Programmes, Radio 7 Mary Kalemkerian
Head of BBC Asian Network Vijay Sharma

Radio Drama

Head of Radio Drama Alison Hindell
Editor, The Archers/Executive Producer, Radio Drama Vanessa Whitburn

Radio Entertainment

Head, Radio Light Entertainment Jane Berthoud

Audio & Music Factual

Controller of Production for Audio & Music Graham Ellis
Editor, Audio & Music Factual, Bristol Clare McGinn
Executive Editor (Regions), Audio & Music Factual Andrew Thorman
Editor, Audio & Music Factual, Manchester Ian Bent

Radio News

Head of Multimedia Programmes/Radio News Stephen Mitchell
Head of Radio Current Affairs Gwyneth Williams
Director, World Service & Global News Division Richard Sambrook

Radio Sport

Head of Radio Sport Gordon Turnbull
Executive Editor, Radio Sport Graeme Reid-Davies

Journalism Group

Director, Journalism Mark Byford

The Journalism Group comprises BBC News, including the English Regions, BBC Sport, BBC Northern Ireland, BBC Scotland and BBC Wales and BBC Global News divisions. The Group is responsible for the BBC's news, current affairs and sport output on TV, radio and online, at local, national and international levels.

BBC News

BBC Television Centre, Wood Lane, London W12 7RJ
tel 020-8743 8000
website www.bbc.co.uk/news
Director, News Helen Boaden

BBC News is the biggest news organisation in the world with over 2,000 journalists, 45 bureaus worldwide and 15 networks and services across TV, radio and new media, and incorporates the BBC English Regions. It also produces the news for the BBC World Service and BBC World News. These services are funded by commercial income and Foreign Office grants respectively, not by the licence fee.

Deputy Director, BBC News & Head of Multimedia Programmes Stephen Mitchell
Head of Newsroom Mary Hockaday
Head of Newsgathering Fran Unsworth
Controller of BBC News Channel (inc. One O'clock News) Kevin Bakhurst
Controller of Operations & Technology Peter Coles
Head of Political Programmes, Analysis & Research Sue Inglish
Executive Editor & Commissioning Editor for TV Current Affairs Clive Edwards
Executive Editor, Radio Current Affairs Nicola Meyrick
Head of Editorial Development Peter Clifton
Director of MC&A, BBC Journalism Sanjay Nazerali

TV programmes

Editor, Six and Ten O'clock News Craig Oliver
Editor, Newsnight Peter Rippon
Editor, Breakfast Alison Ford
Editor, Panorama Tom Giles

Radio programmes

Editor, Today Ceri Thomas
Editor, PM/Broadcasting House /The World This Weekend/The World at One Joanna Carr
Head of News Five Live Matt Morris
Editor, The World Tonight Alistair Burnett

Online

BBC News Website, Editor Steve Herrmann
BBC Online UK Editor Patrick Heery

BBC English Regions (includes Regional Television, Local Radio and BBC Local Online)

BBC Birmingham, The Mailbox, Royal Mail Street, Birmingham B1 1RF
tel 0121-567 6767
Controller, English Regions David Holdsworth

The BBC's English Regions are responsible for 12 TV regional news operations across England along with related weekly current affairs output, 39 BBC local radio stations and 44 local websites providing news and information for their communities.

BBC Local Radio in England provides a primarily speech-based service of news, information and debate to local communities. Speech output is complemented by music. There is a strong emphasis on interactivity and audience involvement.

Chief Operating Officer Ian Hughes
Business Manager Laura Ellis
Head of Programming TV Craig Henderson
Head of New Media and New Services Laura Ellis
Head of Radio Development Chris Van Schaick
Head of Sport Charles Runcie

BBC East

The Forum, Millennium Plain, Norwich NR2 1BH
tel (01603) 618331
Head of Regional & Local Programmes Tim Bishop

BBC Cambridgeshire

PO Box 96, 104 Hills Road, Cambridge CB2 1LQ
tel (01223) 259696
website cambs@bbc.co.uk

BBC Essex

PO Box 765, 198 New London Road, Chelmsford CM2 9XB
tel (01245) 616000
email essex@bbc.co.uk

BBC Norfolk

The Forum, Millennium Plain, Norwich NR2 1BH
tel (01603) 617411
email radionorfolk@bbc.co.uk

BBC Northampton

Broadcasting House, Abington Street, Northampton NN1 2BH
tel (01604) 239100
email radionorthampton@bbc.co.uk

BBC Suffolk

Broadcasting House, St Matthew's Street, Ipswich IP1 3EP
tel (01473) 250000
email radiosuffolk@bbc.co.uk

BBC Three Counties (BBC Beds., Herts. & Bucks.)

PO Box 3cr, Hastings Street, Luton LU1 5XL
tel (01582) 637400
email 3cr@bbc.co.uk

BBC East Midlands

London Road, Nottingham NG2 4UU
tel 0115-955 0500
Head of Regional & Local Programmes Stuart Thomas

BBC Derby

PO Box 104.5, Derby DE1 3HL
tel (01332) 361111
email radio.derby@bbc.co.uk

BBC Leicester

9 St Nicholas Place, Leicester LE1 5LB
tel 0116-251 6688
email radioleicester@bbc.co.uk

BBC Nottingham

London Road, Nottingham NG2 4UU
tel 0115-955 0500
email radio.nottingham@bbc.co.uk

BBC East Yorkshire and Lincolnshire

Queens Court, Queens Gardens, Hull HU1 3NP
tel (01482) 323232
Head of Regional & Local Programmes David Jennings

BBC Humberside

Queens Court, Queens Gardens, Hull HU1 3RH
tel (01482) 323232
email radio.humberside@bbc.co.uk

BBC Lincolnshire
Radio Buildings, PO Box 219, Newport, Lincoln LN1 3XY
tel (01522) 511411
email radio.lincolnshire@bbc.co.uk

BBC London
35c Marylebone High Street, London W1A 6FL
tel 020-7224 2424
Executive Editor Michael MacFarlane

BBC London 94.9 (BBC London)
PO Box 94.9, Marylebone High Street, London W1A 6FL
tel 020-7224 2424
email yourlondon@bbc.co.uk

BBC North East and Cumbria
Broadcasting Centre, Barrack Road, Newcastle upon Tyne NE99 2NE
tel 0191-232 1313
Head of Regional & Local Programmes Phil Roberts

BBC Tees Broadcasting
House, PO Box 95FM, Newport Road, Middlesbrough TS1 5DG
tel (01642) 225211
email tees@bbc.co.uk

BBC Cumbria
Annetwell Street, Carlisle CA3 8BB
tel (01228) 592444
email radio.cumbria@bbc.co.uk

BBC Newcastle (BBC Tyne/BBC Wear)
Broadcasting Centre, Barrack Road, Newcastle upon Tyne NE99 1RN
tel 0191-232 4141
email radio.newcastle@bbc.co.uk

BBC North West
New Broadcasting House, Oxford Road, Manchester M60 1SJ
tel 0161-200 2000
Head of Regional & Local Programmes Aziz Rashid

BBC Manchester
PO Box 27, Oxford Road, Manchester M60 1SJ
tel 0161-200 2000
email manchester.online@bbc.co.uk

BBC Lancashire
26 Darwen Street, Blackburn, Lancs. BB2 2EA
tel (01254) 262411
email radio.lancashire@bbc.co.uk

BBC Merseyside (BBC Liverpool)
55 Paradise Street, Liverpool L1 3BP
tel 0151-708 5500
email radio.merseyside@bbc.co.uk

BBC South
Broadcasting House, Havelock Road, Southampton SO14 7PU
tel 023-8022 6201
Head of Regional & Local Programmes Jason Horton

BBC Berkshire
Caversham Lodge, Peppard Road, Caversham, Reading RG4 8TZ
tel 0118-946 4200
email radio.berkshire.news@bbc.co.uk

BBC Oxford
269 Banbury Road, Oxford OX2 7DW
tel (08459) 311444
email radio.oxford@bbc.co.uk

BBC Solent (BBC Hampshire/BBC Dorset)
Broadcasting House, Havelock Road, Southampton SO14 7PW
tel 023-8063 1311
email radio.solent@bbc.co.uk

BBC South East
The Great Hall, Mount Pleasant Road, Tunbridge Wells, Kent TN1 1QQ
tel (01892) 670000
Head of Regional & Local Programmes Mick Rawsthorne

BBC Kent
The Great Hall, Mount Pleasant Road, Tunbridge Wells, Kent TN1 1QQ
tel (01892) 670000
email radio.kent@bbc.co.uk

BBC Sussex and BBC Surrey
Broadcasting House, Queens Road, Brighton BN1 3XB
tel (01483) 306306
email southerncounties@bbc.co.uk

BBC South West
Broadcasting House, Seymour Road, Mannamead, Plymouth PL3 5BD
tel (01752) 229201
Head of Regional & Local Programmes Jane McCloskey

BBC Cornwall
Phoenix Wharf, Truro, Cornwall TR1 1UA
tel (01872) 275421
email radio.cornwall@bbc.co.uk

BBC Devon
Broadcasting House, Seymour Road, Mannamead, Plymouth PL3 5BD
tel (01752) 229201
email radio.devon@bbc.co.uk

BBC Guernsey
Bulwer Avenue, St Sampsons, Guernsey GY2 4LA
tel (01481) 200600
email radio.guernsey@bbc.co.uk

BBC Jersey
18–21 Parade Road, St Helier, Jersey JE2 3PL
tel (01534) 870000
email radio.jersey@bbc.co.uk

BBC West
Broadcasting House, Whiteladies Road, Bristol BS8 2LR
tel 0117-973 2211
Head of Regional & Local Programmes Lucio Mesquita

BBC Bristol
PO Box 194, Bristol BS99 7QT
tel 0117-974 1111
email radio.bristol@bbc.co.uk

BBC Gloucestershire
London Road, Gloucester GL1 1SW
tel (01452) 308585
email radio.gloucestershire@bbc.co.uk

BBC Wiltshire
Broadcasting House, 56–58 Prospect Place, Swindon SN1 3RW
tel (01793) 513626
email wiltshire@bbc.co.uk, radio.swindon@bbc.co.uk

BBC Somerset
Broadcasting House, Park Street, Taunton TA1 4DA
tel (01823) 323956
email somerset@bbc.co.uk

BBC West Midlands
The Mailbox, Royal Mail Street, Birmingham B1 1RF
tel 0121-567 6767
Head of Regional & Local Programmes Cath Hearne

BBC Hereford and Worcester
Hylton Road, Worcester WR2 5WW
tel (01905) 748485
email bbchw@bbc.co.uk

BBC Shropshire
2–4 Boscobel Drive, Shrewsbury SY1 3TT
tel (01743) 248484
email radio.shropshire@bbc.co.uk

BBC Stoke (BBC Stoke & Staffordshire)
Cheapside, Hanley, Stoke-on-Trent ST1 1JJ
tel (01782) 208080
email radio.stoke@bbc.co.uk

BBC WM (BBC Birmingham/BBC Black Country)
The Mailbox, Birmingham B1 1RF
tel 0121-567 6000
email radio.wm@bbc.co.uk

BBC Coventry and Warwickshire
Priory Place, Coventry CV1 5SQ
tel (02476) 551000
email coventry@bbc.co.uk, warwickshire@bbc.co.uk

BBC Yorkshire
2 St Peter's Square, Leeds LS9 8AH
tel 0113-244 1188
Head of Regional & Local Programmes Helen Thomas

BBC Leeds (BBC Leeds/BBC Bradford & West Yorkshire)
2 St Peter's Square, Leeds LS9 8AH
tel 0113-244 2131
email radio.leeds@bbc.co.uk

BBC Sheffield (BBC South Yorkshire)
54 Shoreham Street, Sheffield S1 4RS
tel 0114-273 1177
email radio.sheffield@bbc.co.uk, south.yorkshire@bbc.co.uk

BBC York (BBC North Yorkshire)
20 Bootham Row, York YO3 7BR
tel (01904) 641351
email radio.york@bbc.co.uk

BBC Sport
BBC Television Centre, Wood Lane, London W12 7RJ
tel 020-8743 8000
Director, Sport Barbara Slater

BBC Sport produces and, in conjunction with the network TV channels and radio stations, broadcasts a range of live sport and related content to audiences across the country.

BBC Sport produces self-commissioning content across all platforms and invites tenders from independent producers as appropriate. Sports-related content is also created for and broadcast by BBC TV, BBC Radio, bbc.co.uk and local, national and regional services but is commissioned within those specific areas.

Head of TV Sport Philip Bernie
Head of Major Events Dave Gordon
Head of Radio Sport Gordon Turnbull
Head of Sports News Richard Burgess
Head of Interactive and Formula 1 Ben Gallop
Head of Sport Production Jackie Myburgh

BBC Northern Ireland
BBC Broadcasting House, Ormeau Avenue, Belfast BT2 8HQ
tel 028-9033 8000
website www.bbc.co.uk/ni
Director, BBC Northern Ireland Peter Johnston

BBCNI provides programmes and services for both local and network audiences. Its output is broad based and extends across radio, TV and online. A sizeable proportion of non-news programming on local TV is sourced from the independent sector – reflecting BBCNI's role in supporting the creative industries. BBCNI's region-wide remit is supported by a network of news correspondents and studio facilities and BBC Radio Foyle, a dedicated service for audiences in the north-west. Network programming is an important and developing feature of BBCNI's output and includes current affairs, drama, factual entertainment and comedy.

Head of Programmes Ailsa Orr
Head of News & Current Affairs Andrew Colman
Chief Operating Officer Mark Taylor
Head of Public Policy, Corporate and Community Affairs Mark Adair
Head of Drama tba
Head of Marketing, Communications & Audiences Kathy Martin
Head of HR & Development Lawrence Jackson
Head of TV Current Affairs Jeremy Adams
Head of Entertainment & Events Mike Edgar
Head of Factual Paul McGuigan
Head of Radio Ulster Susan Lovell
Editor, Sport Shane Glynn
Head of Multi-platform Commissioning Fergus Keeling
Managing Editor, Learning, Language & Social Action Jane Cassidy
Editor, Radio Foyle tba

BBC Radio Ulster
BBC Broadcasting House, Ormeau Avenue, Belfast BT2 8HQ
tel 028-9033 8000

BBC Radio Foyle
8 Northland Road, Londonderry BT48 7JD
tel 028-7126 2244

BBC Scotland
40 Pacific Quay, Glasgow G51 1DA
tel 0141-422 6000
website www.bbc.co.uk/scotland
Director, Scotland Ken MacQuarrie

BBC Scotland is one of the most varied production centres outside London, providing BBC TV and radio networks with drama, comedy, entertainment, children's, leisure, documentaries, religion, education, arts, music, news, sport, current affairs and political coverage, as well as a wide range of online content, at its new state-of-the-art high definition digital headquarters.

BBC Scotland's TV Drama department produces work for the BBC's TV network and Scotland's only soap opera, *River City*. It collaborates with Scottish Screen and other partners to support a range of schemes nurturing Scottish writing and directing talent for film and TV. BBC Radio Scotland's Drama department also produces distinctive work for the radio networks.

In addition to network contributions, BBC Scotland transmits around 900 hours of TV programming a year for Scottish audiences on BBC One and Two Scotland, covering all of the major genres from a Scottish perspective and including Gaelic programming. BBC ALBA, launched in September 2008, offers a dedicated digital service for the Gaelic audience. It is operated, in partnership, by BBC Scotland and MG ALBA.

BBC Scotland provides the nation's two speech radio networks, Radio Scotland and Radio nan Gaidheal. There are local services for Orkney and Shetland and daily bulletins for listeners in the Highlands, Grampian, Borders, and the South West. Production work takes place at centres across the nation, from Dumfries to Lerwick.

Head of Programmes & Services Donalda MacKinnon
Chief Adviser, Programme & Services Matthew Lee
Chief Operating Officer Bruce Malcolm
Head of Marketing & Communications Mairead Ferguson
Head of Talent Division Donald-Iain Brown
Head of Public Policy & Corporate Affairs Ian Small
Head of HR & Development Wendy Aslett
Head of Strategy Catherine Smith
Head of Drama Anne Mensah
Commissioning Editor, TV & Head of Sport Ewan Angus
Head of Radio Jeff Zycinski
Head of News & Current Affairs Atholl Duncan
Head of Children's Simon Parsons
Head of Factual Andrea Miller
Head of Learning and Executive Editor New Media Nick Simons
Head of Radio Drama Patrick Rayner
Managing Editor, Gaelic Marion MacKinnon
Head of Entertainment & Events Eileen Herlihy
Executive Editor, Comedy Jemma Rodgers
Director, BBC Scottish Symphony Orchestra Gavin Reid
Head of Service, BBC ALBA Margaret Mary Murray

BBC Radio nan Gaidheal
Rosebank, 52 Church Street, Stornoway, Isle of Lewis HS1 2LS
tel (01851) 705000

BBC Inverness
7 Culduthel Road, Inverness IV2 4AD
tel (01463) 720720

BBC Radio Orkney
Castle Street, Kirkwall, Orkney KW15 1DF
tel (01856) 873939

BBC Radio Shetland
Pitt Lane, Lerwick, Shetland ZE1 0DW
tel (01595) 694747

BBC Radio Selkirk
Unit 1, Ettrick Riverside, Dunsdale Road, Selkirk TD7 5EB
tel (01750) 724567

BBC Radio Dumfries
lmbank, Lovers Walk, Dumfries DG1 1NZ
tel (01387) 268008

BBC Cymru/Wales

BBC Broadcasting House, Llandaff, Cardiff CF5 2YQ
tel 029-2032 2000
website www.bbc.co.uk/wales, www.bbc.co.uk/cymru
Director, BBC Wales Menna Richards

BBC Wales provides a wide range of services in Welsh and in English, on radio, TV and online. This includes more than 20 hours a week of programmes on BBC One Wales and BBC Two Wales. Regular output includes the flagship news programme *Wales Today*, the current affairs strand *Week in Week Out*, homegrown and network drama such as *Doctor Who* and *Torchwood*, the comedy *High Hopes*, a range of factual programming and sport, including live rugby on *Scrum V*. Ten hours a week of Welsh-language programmes are shown on S4C, including the news programme *Newyddion* and the nightly soap opera *Pobol y Cwm*, and educational programmes. BBC Radio Wales, in English, and BBC Radio Cymru, in Welsh, each provide 20 hours a day of news, entertainment, music and sports output. Political coverage on all services continues to reflect the increasing importance of the National Assembly for Wales. BBC Wales produces a wide range of programmes for the BBC's network TV channels, and Radios 1, 2, 3 and 4. These include popular documentaries, drama, education and music programmes for audiences throughout the UK, including the biennial BBC Cardiff Singer of the World competition, accompanied by the BBC National Orchestra of Wales.

Head of Programmes (English) Clare Hudson
Head of Programmes (Welsh) Keith Jones
Head of Marketing & Communications Rhodri Talfan Davies
Head of News & Current Affairs Mark O'Callaghan
Head of Broadcast Development Cathryn Allen
Head of Drama Piers Wenger
Acting Head of Sport Geoff Williams
Head of Factual & Music Adrian Davies
Director, BBC National Orchestra of Wales David Murray
Editor, New Media Iain Tweedale
Editor, Radio Cymru (Welsh Language) Sian Gwynedd
Editor, Radio Wales (English Language) tba

BBC Global News

Director, BBC Global News Peter Horrocks

The BBC's international news services including: BBC World Service, BBC World News television and bbc.com/news, the BBC's international-facing online news site. The division also includes BBC Monitoring and the BBC World Service Trust.

BBC World Service

Bush House, PO Box 76, The Strand, London WC2B 4PH
tel 020-7240 3456
website www.bbcworldservice.com

BBC World Service is an international multimedia broadcaster delivering 32 language and regional services. It uses multiple platforms to reach 188 million listeners globally (2009), including shortwave, AM, FM, digital satellite and cable channels. Its news sites, which received 4.7 million weekly visitors in September 2009, include audio and video content and offer opportunities to join the global debate. It has around 2,000 partner radio stations which take BBC content, and numerous partnerships supplying content to mobile phones and other wireless handheld devices. See website for more information.

BBC World News

Media Centre, 201 Wood Lane, London W12 7TQ
tel 020-8433 2419
website www.bbcworldnews.com, *International version* bbc.com/news

Director Sian Kevill
Director of News Content Richard Porter
Head of Programmes Paul Gibbs
Commercial Director Colin Lawrence

BBC World News, the BBC's commercially funded international 24-hour news and information channel, is owned and operated by BBC World News Ltd, a member of the BBC's commercial group of companies. BBC World News attracts 74 million viewers a week, is available in more than 200 countries and territories worldwide, and reaches 295 million households and more than 1.7 million hotel rooms. The channel's content is also available on 81 cruise ships, 46 airlines, 35 mobile phone networks and a number of major online platforms including bbc.com/news. BBC World News broadcasts a diverse mix of authoritative international news, sport, weather, business, current affairs and documentary programming.

BBC Future Media & Technology

Media Centre, 201 Wood Lane, London W12 7TQ
tel 020-8743 8000
website www.bbc.co.uk/commissioning (select Future Media)
Director, FM&T Erik Huggers

BBC Future Media & Technology is responsible for all of the BBC's digital media services. These include BBC Online (the BBC's website), BBC iPlayer, BBC Red Button (interactive TV), BBC Mobile, and new platform developments such as Freesat.

BBC FM&T focuses on the creation and development of services and applications across the site and supports divisional content areas to deliver their products.

Controller BBC Online, bbc.co.uk Seetha Kumar
General Manager, News and Knowledge Phil Fearnley (Responsible for the design and build of

online products in categories including News and Weather, Global/National/Regional/Local, Homepage and Knowledge)
General Manager, On-Demand tba (Responsible for the continuing development of BBC iPlayer and to build online products in categories including Radio Networks, TV Channels, Drama/Comedy/ Entertainment, Archive and Programme Support and Search and Navigation)
General Manager, Children's, Sport and Applications Rahul Chakkara (Responsible for TV platforms and for the design and build of online products in categories including Children's, Sport, Learning, Music, Mobile and Red Button)

Different areas of the BBC commission different types of interactive content and applications:

• **BBC Vision** commissions multi-platform content across genres and TV-related services.
Controller, Vision Multi-platform Commissioning Simon Nelson *email* simon.nelson@bbc.co.uk

• **BBC Audio & Music** commissions multi-platform content and applications that are related to radio and music programming.
Controller, Audio & Music Multi-platform Commissioning Mark Friend
email mark.friend@bbc.co.uk

Commissioning takes place on a rolling basis and when looking to bid for work it is useful to get in touch with the specific commissioning area directly. Contact Rubin Shah, BBC FM&T for guidance on who to contact, or see website.

UKTV and international services

UKTV

160 Great Portland Street, London W1W 5QA
tel 020-7299 6200

Formed in 1997, UKTV is an independent commercial joint venture between BBC Worldwide, the commercial arm of the BBC, and Virgin Media. The network is midway through an ambitious rebrand of its 10 distinctive TV channels – Watch, G.O.L.D., Dave, Alibi, Eden, Blighty, UKTV History (soon to become Yesterday), UKTV Style, UKTV Food, and UKTV Gardens. UKTV currently operates 18 broadcast streams when multiplexes (+1s) and broadband are taken into account, offering a broad range of quality programming across entertainment, lifestyle and factual programming, and 11 complementary websites.
Director of Commissioning, Factual & Factual Entertainment Jane Rogerson
Director of Commissioning, Entertainment Lisa Perrin

For more details on the channels see *Digital, satellite and cable television* on page 414.

BBC America

tel (001) 212-705-9644

BBC America showcases the best of the BBC's drama and entertainment programmes in North America. This digital cable and satellite channel does not directly commission programmes but occasionally invests in UK programmes in production to increase their suitability for the US market.

If you have an idea you would like to discuss or would like more information, contact:
General Manager, BBC America Kathryn Mitchell

BBC Prime

tel 020-8576 9748

BBC Prime, the BBC's international entertainment channel for Europe, the Middle East, Asia and Africa commissions only a very small amount of programming each year.

BBC Japan and a tailor-made Asian version of BBC Prime for Hong Kong launched on 1 December 2004. BBC Prime/Japan are new TV channels for Asia, offering the best British entertainment programmes, from drama to comedy, documentaries to lifestyle. For more information about commissions and acquisitions contact:
Editor, BBC Prime David Weiland

BBC Food

tel 020-8576 9748

BBC Food showcases the best in food and cookery for an international audience. The channel is currently available in South Africa, Scandinavia (Sweden, Norway, Denmark, Finland, Iceland) and the Middle East. For more information about commissions and acquisitions contact:
Editor, BBC Food David Weiland

BBC Worldwide

Woodlands, 80 Wood Lane, London W12 0TT
tel 020-8433 2000
website www.bbcworldwide.com
Chief Executive Officer John Smith

BBC Worldwide is the main commercial arm and a wholly owned subsidiary of the BBC. Its mission is to create, acquire, develop and exploit media content and brands around the world in order to maximise the value of the BBC's assets for the benefit of the UK licence payer.

BBC Worldwide provides a global showcase for the best of British creative talent including actors, journalists, presenters, writers, directors, musicians, designers and technicians. It sells programmes and formats produced by more than 500 different UK independent producers.

The company has 7 core businesses: Channels, Content & Production, Digital Media, Sales & Distribution, Magazines and Children's Licensing, Home Entertainment and Global Brands.

• **Global Brands** *Managing Director* Marcus Arthur
• **Channels** *Managing Director* Darren Childs
• **Content & Production** *Managing Director* Wayne Garvie

- **Magazines & Children's Licensing** *Managing Director* Peter S. Phippen
- **Sales & Distribution** *Managing Director* Steve Macallister
- **Home Entertainment** *Managing Director* Paul Dempsey
- **Digital Media** *Managing Director & Director of Strategy* David Moody

Audiobooks

BBC Audiobooks Ltd, St James House, The Square, Lower Bristol Road, Bath BA2 3BH
tel (01225) 878000
website www.bbcaudiobooks.com

BBC Audiobooks Ltd is part of BBC Worldwide Ltd, the commercial arm of the BBC, and was established in 2003 with the integration of BBC Radio Collection, Cover to Cover and Chivers Audio Books. Since then, it has become a leading trade and library publisher in the UK and publishes a wide range of entertainment digitally and on CD.

Ideas should be pitched with a short synopsis to: *Publishing Director* Jan Paterson

Magazines

website www.bbcmagazines.com

Freelance contributions are regularly used by BBC Worlwide magazines but the use of unsolicited material is rare for some magazines as the editorial links closely follow the BBC programme content.

BBC magazines, London

BBC Worldwide, 80 Wood Lane, London W12 0TT
tel 020-8433 2000

Radio Times

email radio.times@bbc.co.uk
website www.radiotimes.com
Editor Ben Preston

BBC Top Gear

email queries.tgmag@bbc.co.uk
website www.topgear.com
Editor Connor McNichols

BBC Gardeners' World

email gweditorial@bbc.co.uk
website www.gardenersworld.com
Editor Adam Pasco

BBC Good Food

email goodfoodrs@galleon.co.uk
website www.bbcgoodfood.com
Editor Gillian Carter

BBC Olive

email oliveletters@bbc.co.uk
website www.olivemagazine.co.uk
Editor Christine Hayes

BBC Easy Cook

Editor Sara Buenfeld

Lonely Planet

email lpmagazine@bbc.com
website www.lonelyplanet.com/magazine
Editor Peter Grunert

Children's and teenage magazines

All ideas for BBC children's and teenage magazines should be sent to:

Editorial Director Corinn Shaffer

BBC magazines, Bristol

14th Floor, Tower House, Fairfax Street, Bristol BS1 3BN
tel 0117-927 9009

BBC Countryfile

website www.bbccountryfile.com
Editor Fergus Collins

BBC Focus

website www.focusmag.co.uk
Editor Jenny Osman

Before pitching a feature read the guidelines on the website. *BBC Focus* has a limited number of 2-week editorial work experience slots available; see website for more information.

BBC Gardens Illustrated

email gardens@bbcmagazinesbristol.com
website www.gardensillustrated.com
Editor Juliet Roberts

BBC History Magazine

email davemusgrove@bbcmagazinesbristol.com
website www.bbchistorymagazine.com
Editor Dave Musgrove

Email the editor with ideas for contributions plus a brief biography.

BBC Homes & Antiques

email angelalinforth@bbcmagazinesbristol.com
*website*www.homesandantiques.com
Editor Angela Linforth

BBC Knowledge Magazine

website www.bbcknowledgemagazine.com
Editor Sally Palmer

BBC Music Magazine

website www.bbcmusicmagazine.com
Editor Oliver Condy

BBC Sky at Night Magazine

email skyatnight@bbcmagazinesbristol.com
website www.skyatnightmagazine.com
Editor Graham Southorn

BBC Who Do You Think You Are? Magazine

website www.bbcwhodoyouthinkyouare.com
Editor Sarah Williams

Address editorial queries to Dan Cossins.

BBC Wildlife

email ferguscollins@originpublishing.co.uk
website www.bbcwildlifemagazine.com
Editor Sophie Stafford

Interested in stories that are new, topical, relevant, innovative; submit a brief outline (no more than 100 words), preferably by email via the website. Send feature submissions to Fergus Collins.

Emma Hurrell previously worked at the BBC for 14 years as a Business Manager in TV and as a Project Manager, providing key senior management support for the launch of the BBC's digital services. She is currently freelancing.

BBC broadcasting rights and terms

Contributors are advised to check latest details of fees with the BBC.

Rights and terms – television

Specially written material

Fees for submitted material are paid on acceptance. For commissioned material, half the fee is paid on commissioning and half on acceptance as being suitable for television. All fees are subject to negotiation above the minima.

• In November 2002 a new TV script agreement was introduced. It replaced the old BBC/Guild script agreement for dramatic scripts of 15 minutes and over. The terms were agreed with the PMA and the Writers' Guild. The most significant changes are:

On First Day of Principal Photography an advance payment of either 15% or 115% of script fee will be made against:

(a) repeats/commercial exploitation: 100% of script fee plus/or

(b) 5-year licence of Public Service use (excluding BBC1 and BBC2): 15%

(a) only applies to scripts commissioned for BBC1 or BBC2 (but excludes long-running series; (b) applies to BBC1 and BBC2 commissions and also scripts for BBC3 and BBC4 and long-running series on BBC1 and BBC2.

• Rates for one performance of a 60-minute original television play are a minimum of £8,264.64 for a play written by a beginner and a 'going rate' of £10,330.80 for an established writer, or *pro rata* for shorter or longer timings.

• Fees for a 50-minute episode in a series during the same period are a minimum of £6,246.80 for a beginner and a 'going rate' of £7,808.50 for an established writer.

• Fees for a 50-minute dramatisation are a minimum of £4,489.20 for a beginner and a 'going rate' of £5,611.50 for an established writer.

• Fees for a 50-minute adaptation of an existing stage play or other dramatic work are a minimum of £2,732.80 for a beginner and a 'going rate' of £3,416 for an established writer.

Specially written light entertainment sketch material

• The rates for sketch material range from £100 per minute for beginners with a 'going rate' of £120 for established writers.

• The fee for a quickie or news item is half the amount of the writer's per minute rate.

• Fees for submitted material are payable on acceptance and for commissioned material half on signature and half on acceptance.

Published material

• Prose works: £29.44 per minute.

• Poems: £35.32 per half minute.

Stage plays and source material for television

• Fees for stage plays and source novels are negotiable.

Rights and terms – radio

Specially written material

Fees are assessed on the basis of the type of material, its length, the author's status and experience in writing for radio. Fees for submitted material are paid on acceptance. For commissioned material, half the fee is paid on commissioning and half on acceptance as being suitable for broadcasting.

• Rates for specially written radio dramas in English (other than educational programmes) are £56.61 a minute for beginners and a 'going rate' of £86.21 a minute for established writers. This rate covers two broadcasts.

Specially written short stories

• Fees range from £172 for 15 minutes.

Published material

Domestic radio

• Dramatic works: £17.10 per minute.
• Prose works: £17.10 per minute.
• Prose works required for dramatisation: £13.33 per minute.
• Poems: £17.10 per half minute.

World Service Radio (English)

• Dramatic works: £8.55 per minute for broadcasts within a seven-day period.
• Prose works: £8.55 per minute for broadcasts within a seven-day period.
• Prose works required for dramatisation: £6.66 per minute for broadcasts within a seven-day period.
• Poems: £8.55 per half minute for broadcasts within a seven-day period.
• Foreign Language Services are approximately one-fifth of the rate for English Language Services.

Television and radio

Repeats in BBC programmes

• Further proportionate fees are payable for repeats.

Use abroad of recordings of BBC programmes

If the BBC sends abroad recordings of its programmes for use by overseas broadcasting organisations on their own networks or stations, further payments accrue to the author, usually in the form of additional percentages of the basic fee paid for the initial performance or a royalty based on the percentage of the distributors' receipts. This can apply to both sound and television programmes.

Value Added Tax

There is a self-billing system for VAT which covers radio, World Service and television for programmes made in London.

Talks for television

Contributors to talks will be offered the standard television talks contract which provides the BBC certain rights to broadcast the material in a complete, abridged and/or translated manner, and which provides for the payment of further fees for additional usage of the material whether by television, domestic radio or external broadcasting. The contract also covers the assignment of material and limited publication rights. Alternatively, a contract taking in all standard rights may be negotiated. Fees are arranged by the contract authorities in London and the Regions.

Talks for radio

Contributors to talks for domestic radio and World Service broadcasting may be offered either:
• the standard talks contract which takes rights and provides for residual payments, as does the television standard contract; or
• an STC (Short Talks Contract) which takes all rights except print publication rights where the airtime of the contribution does not exceed five minutes and which has set fees or disturbance money payable; or
• an NFC (No Fee Contract) where no payment is made which provides an acknowledgement that a contribution may be used by the BBC.

Independent national television

Channel 4

124 Horseferry Road, London SW1P 2TX
tel 020-7396 4444
website www.channel4.com
Ceo David Abraham, *Director of Television & Content* Kevin Lygo, *Head of Channel 4* Julian Bellamy

Channel 4 transmits across the whole of the UK, except some parts of Wales, which are covered by the Welsh language S4C. It is available on all digital platforms (terrestrial, satellite and cable) as well as through traditional analogue transmission.

Channel 4 also operates a number of other services, including the free-to-air digital TV channels E4, More4 and Film4, and an ever-growing range of online activities at channel4.com, including the broadband service FourDocs and Channel 4's bespoke video-on-demand service 4oD. The Film4 production division produces and co-produces feature films for the UK and global markets.

As a publisher–broadcaster, Channel 4 does not produce its own programmes but commissions them from more than 300 independent production companies across the UK. It works closely with the independent production sector, and invests heavily in training and talent development throughout the industry.

Head of Education & Managing Editor, Commissioning Janey Walker
Head of Cross Platform Louise Brown
Head of Entertainment Justin Gorman
Head of Comedy Shane Allen
Head of T4/Music Neil McCallum
Head of Daytime Helen Warner
Head of Features & Factual Entertainment Sue Murphy
Head of Specialist Factual Ralph Lee
Head of E4 Angela Jain
Head of Documentaries & More4 Hamish Mykura
Head of News & Current Affairs Dorothy Byrne
Controller, Film & Drama Tessa Ross
Head of Acquisitions Gill Hay
Director of Nations & Regions Stuart Cosgrove
Senior Programme Controller News, Current Affairs & Documentaries Chris Shaw
Head of Factual Entertainment & Acting Head of Features Steve Gowans
Head of Factual Andrew O'Connell
Head of Entertainment Donna Taberer
Director of Children's Programming Nick Wilson
Controller of Sport Robert Charles
Managing Director, Acquisitions Jeff Ford

Five

22 Long Acre, London WC2E 9LY
tel 020-7550 5555
website www.five.tv
Channel Controller Five Richard Woolfe

Five is a publisher broadcaster and works with independent companies to produce its programmes. They usually only accept programme proposals from independent production companies.

Five brands include the original channel, Five; digital channels FIVER and Five USA; video-on-demand service Demand Five; and online Five.tv.

GMTV

London Television Centre, Upper Ground, London SE1 9TT
tel 020-7827 7000
website www.gm.tv
Director of Factual, Daytime & GMTV Alison Sharman, *Managing Editor* Neil Thompson

As a franchise holder, GMTV was managed independently until November 2009 when ITV bought the final 25% of shares held by Disney to now wholly own the company. Transmitting daily from 6am to 9.25am, GMTV offers a lively mix of news, views and entertainment. At the weekend the focus moves to children with preschool strand The Fluffy Club followed by Toonattik for older children. GMTV's free-to-air digital channel GMTV Digital, broadcasts a popular mix of children's programming daily from 6am to 9.25am on ITV4, Channel 28 on Freeview and Channel 120 on digital satellite.

ITN (Independent Television News Ltd)

200 Gray's Inn Road, London WC1X 8XZ
tel 020-7833 3000
website www.itn.co.uk
Chairman Maggie Carver, *Ceo* John Hardie

ITN is one of the world's leading news and multimedia content companies creating, packaging and distributing news, entertainment, factual and corporate content on multiple platforms to customers around the globe. As well as providing TV news, ITN operates 3 other divisions:

- ITN News produces high-quality news programming for the country's 2 biggest commercial broadcasters, ITV1 and Channel 4. ITN Source is the footage sales arm of ITN, syndicating on-the-day and archive content to a global customer base which includes the TV, arts, entertainment and education sectors.
- ITN Productions is the central creative hub producing content for major global brands in the broadcast, online, mobile and corporate sectors. As well as creating content, it offers clients award-winning studios and graphics teams for hire.
- ITN Consulting provides strategic and operational advice to businesses operating in the media and communications industries.

ITN is an independent company, owned by 4 shareholders: ITV Plc (40%), Daily Mail and General Trust (20%), Reuters (20%), and United Business Media(20%).

Editor-in-Chief, ITV News David Mannion
Editor, ITV News Deborah Turness
Editor, Channel 4 News Jim Gray
Managing Director, ITN Source Asha Oberoi
Managing Director, ITN Consulting & New Ventures Adam Chadwick
Commercial Director, ITN Productions Mark Browning

ITV Plc

The London Television Centre, Upper Ground, London SE1 9LT
tel 020-7157 3000
website www.itv.com
Chief Executive Adam Crozier, *Director of Television, Channels and Online* Peter Fincham

ITV Plc is the UK's leading advertiser-funded, free-to-air broadcaster and employs 4,000 staff worldwide within its Broadcasting, ITV Studios and Online businesses.

ITV Network is responsible for the commissioning, scheduling and marketing of network programmes on ITV1 and its digital channel portfolio, ITV2, ITV3, ITV4 and CiTV. Programmes from ITV are provided by ITV's in-house production unit and by the independent sector. Network programming covers a full range of genres, including drama, entertainment, news, current affairs, factual, sport and children's programming. Annually, ITV invests around £1 billion in content for its broadcast channels and website.

itv.com is focused on delivering short and long-form video content from ITV programming for viewing in real time or catch-up. The ITV Player allows users to access catch-up and watch clips from the best ITV programmes, all supported by advertising.

ITV Plc's content business, ITV Studios, creates and produces original programming for content buyers worldwide. There are production centres in the UK, USA, Germany, France, Spain, Australia and Scandanavia. The business also generates revenues by distributing ITV and third-party programming internationally and through the sales of associated DVDs and merchandise.

Director of Drama Laura Mackie
Controller of Drama Commissioning Sally Haynes
Director of Entertainment & Comedy Elaine Bedell
Controller of Entertainment John Kaye-Cooper, Layla Smith
Director of Factual, Daytime & GMTV Alison Sharman
Controller, Popular Factual Jo Clinton-Davis
Director of News, Sport & Current Affairs Mike Jermey
Controller of Sport Niall Sloane
Controller of Regions & Current Affairs Ian Squires
Director of Digital Channels & Acquisitions Zai Bennett
Controller of Digital Channels Emma Tennant

Radio Telefís Éireann (RTÉ)

Donnybrook, Dublin 4, Republic of Ireland
tel (01) 208 3111
website www.rte.ie

RTÉ is a Public Service Broadcaster, a non-profit-making organisation owned by the Irish people. RTÉ is Ireland's cross-media leader, providing comprehensive and cost-effective free-to-air TV, radio and online services, which are of the highest quality and are impartial, in accordance with RTÉ's statutory obligations.

RTÉ operates 2 complementary TV channels, RTÉ One and RTÉ Two and 4 radio stations, RTÉ Radio 1, RTÉ 2fm, RTÉ lyric fm and RTÉ Raidió na Gaeltachta. RTÉ also publishes Ireland's bestselling magazine, the *RTÉ Guide*, operates Ireland's leading teletext service, RTÉ Aertel, and provides up-to-date news, current affairs and entertainment information via Ireland's most popular media website, RTÉ.ie. RTÉ is also a major contributor to the arts in Ireland and supports 5 performing groups – the RTÉ National Symphony Orchestra, the RTÉ Concert Orchestra, the RTÉ Vanbrugh Quartet, the RTÉ Philharmonic Choir and RTÉ Cór na nÓg.

Director General Cathal Goan
Managing Director, Television Noel Curran
Managing Director, Radio Clare Duignan

S4C

Parc Ty Glas, Llanishen, Cardiff CF14 5DU
tel 029-20747444
website www.s4c.co.uk
Chief Executive Iona Jones, *Director of Commissioning* Rhian Gibson

Welsh language digital channel S4C is one of the UK's 5 public service broadcasters. A mixed-genre channel, programming includes drama, sport, children's, factual, news, entertainment and culture. Programmes are commissioned from independent production companies with content also produced by BBC Wales and ITV Wales. The channel is available on all digital TV platforms in Wales, plus broadband, and has a video-on-demand service. There are subtitles for non-Welsh speakers and learners, with signing and audio description for the deaf and the hard of hearing.

Independent regional television

The ITV Network is made up of 15 regional licences, providing television to viewers across the UK. Eleven of the licences in England and Wales are owned by ITV Plc, formed in 2004 following the merger of Carlton and Granada, providing local regional news and weather. STV group Plc (formerly SMG) owns the two Scottish licences, STV Central (formerly Scottish Television) and STV North Ltd (formerly Grampian Television); UTV and Channel Television own the licences for Northern Ireland and the Channel Islands respectively.

Channel Television Ltd

Jersey: Television Centre, La Pouquelaye, St Helier, Jersey JE1 3ZD
tel (01534) 816816
Guernsey: Television House, Bulwer Avenue, St Sampson's, Guernsey GY2 4LA
tel (01481) 241888
website www.channeltv.co.uk

ITV Anglia

Anglia Television, Rose Lane, Anglia House, Norwich NR1 3JG
tel 0844 8816000
website www.itv.com/anglia
Head of News Catharine Houlihan

Provides news for the East of England.

ITV Border

ITV Border, The Television Centre, Carlisle CA1 3NT
tel 0844 8815000
website www.itv.com/border
Head of News Lucy West

Provides news for Cumbria, the Borders, South West Scotland and the Isle of Man.

ITV Central

Gas Street, Birmingham B1 2JT
tel 0844 8814000
website www.itv.com/central
Head of News Philip Braund

Provides news for the East, West and South Midlands.

ITV Granada

ITV1 Granada, Quay Street, Manchester M60 9EA
tel 0161-952 1000
website www.itv.com/granada
Head of News Richard Frediani

Provides news for the North West of England.

ITV London

London Television Centre, Upper Ground, London SE1 9LT
tel 020-7261 3300
website www.itv.com/london
Head of News Faye Nicholds

Provides news for Greater London and much of the South East.

ITV Meridian

Forum One, Solent Business Park, Whiteley, Hants PO15 7PA
tel 0844 4422000
website www.itv.com/meridian
Head of News Robin Britton

Provides news for the South and South East.

ITV Tyne Tees

Television House, The Watermark, Gateshead, Tyne & Wear NE11 9SZ
tel 0844 8815069 *fax* 0844 8815010
website www.itv.com/tynetees
Head of News Lucy West

Provides news for North East England and North Yorkshire.

ITV Wales

The Television Centre, Culverhouse Cross, Cardiff CF5 6XJ
tel 029-2059 0590
website www.itv.com/wales
Head of News Phil Henfrey

Provides news for Wales.

ITV Westcountry and ITV West

The Television Centre, 470 Bath Road, Bristol BS4 3HG
tel 0844 8812345
website www.itv.com/westcountry-west, www.itv.com/westcountry-east
Head of News Liz Hannam

Provides news for the South West and the West of England.

ITV Yorkshire

The Television Centre, Kirkstall Road, Leeds LS3 1JS
tel 0113-243 8283
website www.itv.com/yorkshire
Head of News Will Venters

Provides news for the Yorkshire area.

STV (North and Central)

Pacific Quay, Glasgow G51 1PQ
tel 0141-300 3000
website www.stv.tv

Produces dedicated regional programming – STV North (formerly Grampian Television) for North and

North East Scotland and STV Central (formerly Scottish Television) for Central Scotland. News is at the heart of the 2 services but they also produce a varied range of genre programming including drama, special edition programmes and original documentaries.

UTV

Ormeau Road, Belfast BT7 1EB
tel 028-9032 8122
website www.u.tv

Provides regional news (4 hours per week), current affairs (30 mins per week) and non-news (1.5 hours per week) programming for Northern Ireland.

Digital, satellite and cable television

Digital TV offers a far wider choice of TV viewing with lots of extra channels, and uses digital technology to reduce the interference that you may experience on analogue TV (the five channels received via your standard TV aerial). Digital TV also offers other benefits, such as a greater selection of widescreen programming, and onscreen electronic programme guide, interactive services and, in some cases, High Definition and Dolby 5.1 surround sound. By 2012, the UK's TV service will be switched to digital, and you need to be ready for the Digital Switchover. The UK's main digital suppliers and entertainment and factual channels are listed below – for a full list of all sports, news, movies, religion, shopping and music channels visit the digital supplier websites.

DIGITAL, SATELLITE AND CABLE TELEVISION PROVIDERS

British Sky Broadcasting (BSkyB)

Grant Way, Isleworth, Middlesex TW7 5QD
tel 0844 2411542
website www.sky.com
Director of Programmes Sky1, 1 HD, 2 and 3 Stuart Murphy

British Sky Broadcasting (commonly abbreviated to BSkyB, and marketed as Sky) is a British satellite broadcasting company that operates Sky Digital, a subscription TV service in the UK and Ireland. Ninety-eight per cent of the UK is able to receive Sky's satellite signal and it offers the widest number of digital TV channels in the UK. It owns channels Sky1, 2 and 3, Sky Arts, Sky News, Sky Real Lives and Sky Sport News.

Freesat

PO Box 6296, London W1A 3FF
tel (0845) 3130051
website www.freesat.co.uk

A not-for-profit joint venture with the BBC and ITV delivering around 140 free-to-air digital TV and radio channels, BBC iPlayer, 2 HD channels (BBC HD and ITV HD) via a satellite dish.

Freeview

DTV Services Ltd, 27–29 Cursitor Street, London EC4A 1LT
tel (08701) 111270
website www.freeview.co.uk

Free digital service run by 5 shareholders: the BBC, Arqiva, BSkyB, Channel 4 and ITV. Provides free-to-air digital TV channels, radio stations and interactive services via an aerial.

Virgin Media Television

160 Great Portland Street, London W1W 5QA
tel 020-7299 5000
website www.virginmediatv.co.uk
Director of Television Claudia Rosencrantz

Part of Virgin Media, Virgin Media Television provides up to 160 digital TV channels and broadband content to all major digital TV platforms through a fibre optic cable and a set top box. It owns channels Virgin 1,Trouble, Bravo, Bravo 2, Living, Challenge and Challenge Jackpot.

ON-DEMAND PAY TV PROVIDERS

BT Vision

website www.btvision.bt.com

On-demand digital TV for BT Total Broadband customers, with thousands of shows to watch on demand, including sports TV, children's TV, music videos and films, and is free of advertisements and starts by pressing 'play' on the Vision+ box.

Smallworld Cable Ltd

3 Middlegate, White Lund Industrial Estate, Morecambe, Lancs. LA3 3BN
tel 0800 0706150

Cable provider for Scotland and Northern England. Supplies super-fast fibre optic broadband, Digital TV (over 120 channels) and phone services via a set top box to Irvine, Troon, Kilmarnock, Carlisle, Morecambe and Lancaster.

TalkTalk TV

Carphone Warehouse, 1 Portal Way, London W3 6RS
website www.talktalk.co.uk/tv

Users of this digital TV service watch live TV and on-demand content via a broadband-enabled phone line. Delivers over 70 digital TV channels, films on demand, and broadband internet. TalkTalk TV is not available in all parts of the UK. The service was known as Tiscali TV until January 2010 when the Carphone Warehouse took over Tiscali.

Top Up TV Anytime

tel 08444 152030
website www.topuptv.com

A digital TV service that allows you to watch and record live TV, and watch extra content 'on demand'.

The service uses a special set top box with a built-in hard disk that automatically downloads overnight over 120 hours a week of extra TV programmes that can be viewed at your convenience. Launched December 2006.

MULTICHANNEL TELEVISION

Visit the website of the relevant channel to view the programme schedule.

Alibi
UKTV, 160 Great Portland Street, London W1W 5QA
tel 020-7299 6200
website www.uktv.co.uk/alibi

Crime drama.

Animal Planet
Discovery Network Europe, Discovery House, Chiswick Park, Building 2, 566 Chiswick High Road, London W4 5YB
tel 020-8811 3000
website www.yourdiscovery.com/web/animalplanet

Factual.

BBC Four
Television Centre, Wood Lane, London W12 7RJ
tel 020-8743 8000
website www.bbc.co.uk/bbcfour

Entertainment and factual.

BBC News Channel
Television Centre, Wood Lane, London W12 7RJ
tel 020-8743 8000
website www.news.bbc.co.uk

News and weather.

BBC Parliament
4 Millbank, London SW1P 3JA
website www.bbc.co.uk/parliament

Politics.

BBC Three
Television Centre, Wood Lane, London W12 7RJ
tel 020-8743 8000
website www.bbc.co.uk/bbcthree

Entertainment.

BBC World News
Media Centre, 201 Wood Lane, London W12 7TQ
tel 020-8433 2419
website www.bbcworldnews.com

News and information.

Bio
AETN UK, Grant Way, Isleworth, Middlesex TW7 5QD
tel 020-7705 3000
website www.thebiographychannel.co.uk

People's stories.

Blighty
UKTV, 160 Great Portland Street, London W1W 5QA
tel 020-7299 6200
website www.uktv.co.uk/blighty

Programmes about the best in Britain.

Bloomberg
tel 020-7330 7500
website www.bloomberg.co.uk

News.

Bravo
Virgin Media TV, 160 Great Portland Street, London W1W 5QA
tel 020-7299 5000
website www.bravo.co.uk

Entertainment for men and Bravo 2 for a younger audience.

CBS Action
Chello Zone, 105–109 Salusbury Road, London NW6 6RG
tel 020-7328 8808
website www.cbsaction.co.uk

Modern action classics from the USA.

CBS Drama
Chello Zone, 105–109 Salusbury Road, London NW6 6RG
tel 020-7328 8808
website www.cbsadrama.co.uk

Drama classics from the USA.

CBS Reality
Chello Zone, 105–109 Salusbury Road, London NW6 6RG
tel 020-7328 8808
website www.cbsreality.co.uk

Real life drama, crime, the bizarre and unexplained.

Challenge
Virgin Media TV, 160 Great Portland Street, London W1W 5QA
tel 020-7299 5000
website www.challenge.co.uk

Game and quiz shows.

Challenge Jackpot
Virgin Media TV, 160 Great Portland Street, London W1W 5QA
tel 020-7299 5000
website www.challengejackpot.com

Casino-style games.

CNBC

10 Fleet Place, London EC4M 7QS
tel 020-7653 9300
website www.cnbc.com

Business and financial news.

CNN International

Turner Broadcasting System Europe Ltd, Turner House, 16 Great Marlborough Street, London W1F 7HS
tel 020-7693 0939
website www.cnn.com/international

News.

Comedy Central (CC Extra)

MTV, 180 Oxford Street, London W1D 1DS
tel 020-7478 5300
website www.comedycentral.co.uk

Comedy.

Community Channel

2nd Floor, Riverwalk House, 157–161 Millbank, London SW1P 4RR
website www.communitychannel.org

Dedicated to highlighting issues from both local and international communities as well as the voluntary and charitable sectors.

Crime and Investigation (ci)

AETN UK, Grant Way, Iselworth, Middlesex TW7 5QD
website www.crimeandinvestigation.co.uk

True crime stories.

Dave and Dave Ja Vu

UKTV, 160 Great Portland Street, London W1W 5QA
tel 020-7299 6200
website www.uktv.co.uk/dave

Classic and stand-up comedy, and motoring shows.

Discovery Channel

Discovery House, Chiswick Park, Building 2, 566 Chiswick High Road, London W4 5YB
tel 020-8811 3000
website www.yourdiscovery.com

Factual. Also Discovery Max, Discovery Home and Health, Discovery Knowledge, Discovery Realtime, Discovery Science, Discovery Shed, Discovery Travel & Living, Discovery Turbo, Investigation Discovery, and Military Channel.

E4

Channel 4, 124 Horseferry Road, London SW1P 2TX
tel 020-7396 4444
website www.e4.com

Entertainment.

Eden

UKTV, 160 Great Portland Street, London W1W 5QA
tel 020-7299 6200
website www.uktv.co.uk/eden

Wildlife, nature and adventure.

Extreme Sports

Chello Zone, 105–109 Salusbury Road, London NW6 6RG
tel 020-7328 8808
website www.extreme.com

Extreme sports.

Film4

Channel 4, 124 Horseferry Road, London SW1P 2TX
tel 020-7396 4444
website www.film4.com

Feature films.

Five USA

Five, 22 Long Acre, London WC2E 9LY
tel 020-7421 7270
website www.five.tv/channel/five-usa

American drama.

Fiver

Five, 22 Long Acre, London WC2E 9LY
tel 020-7421 7270
website www.five.tv/channel/fiver

Entertainment.

Food Network

Chello Zone, 105–109 Salusbury Road, London NW6 6RG
tel 020-7328 8808
website www.foodnetwork.co.uk

Food.

4 Music

Channel 4, 124 Horseferry Road, London SW1P 2TX
tel 020-7396 4444
website www.4music.com

Music and comedy.

God TV

Angel House, Borough Road, Sunderland SR1 1HW
tel 0191-568 0800
website www.god.tv

Religion.

G.O.L.D.

UKTV, 160 Great Portland Street, London W1W 5QA
tel 020-7299 6200
website www.uktv.co.uk/gold

Classic British comedy.

Good Food
UKTV 160 Great Portland Street, London W1W 5QA
tel 020-7299 6200
website www.uktv.co.uk/food

Food programmes.

Hallmark Channel
234A King's Road, London SW3 5UA
tel 020-7368 9100
website www.hallmarkchannel.co.uk

Entertainment.

History
AETN UK, Grant Way, Isleworth,
Middlesex TW7 5QD
tel 020-7705 3000
website www.history.co.uk

Historical documentaries.

Home
UKTV, 160 Great Portland Street,
London W1W 5QA
tel 020-7299 6200
website www.uktv.co.uk/home

Interior design ideas, home decorating and DIY.

Horror Channel
Chello Zone, 105–109 Salusbury Road,
London NW6 6RG
tel 020-7328 8808
website www.horrorchannel.co.uk

Horror films and supernatural series.

ITV2
The London Television Centre, Upper Ground,
London SE1 9LT
tel 020-7157 3000
website www.itv.com/channels/ITV2

Talent, celebrity gossip and factual.

ITV3
The London Television Centre, Upper Ground,
London SE1 9LT
tel 020-7157 3000
website www.itv.com/channels/ITV3

Classic drama.

ITV4
The London Television Centre, Upper Ground,
London SE1 9LT
tel 020-7157 3000
website www.itv.com/channels/ITV4

Challenging drama, cult films and premium sports.

Living
Virgin Media TV, 160 Great Portland Street,
London W1W 5QA
tel 020-7299 5000
website www.livingtv.co.uk

Entertainment.

More 4
Channel 4, 124 Horseferry Road, London SW1P 2TX
tel 020-7396 4444
website www.channel4.com/more4

Adult dramas and comedies.

MTV
MTV Networks (Europe), 17–29 Hawley Crescent,
London NW1 8TT
tel 020-7284 7777
website www.mtv.co.uk

Music video channels. Plus: MTV Base, MTV Classic, MTV Dance, MTV Hits, MTV Rocks, MTV Shows, TMF, VH1 and Viva.

National Geographic and Nat Geo Wild
National Geographic Television International,
Shepherds Building East – 2nd Floor,
Richmond Way, London W14 0DQ
tel 020-7751 7555
website www.natgeotv-int.com

Really
UKTV, 160 Great Portland Street,
London W1W 5QA
tel 020-7299 6200
website www.uktv.co.uk/really

Women's programmes.

Sky 1
Grant Way, Isleworth, Middlesex TW7 5QD
tel 0870 2403000
website www.sky1.sky.com

Entertainment. Plus: Sky 2, Sky 3, Sky Arts, Sky News, Sky Real Lives, Sky Sports, Sky Sport News and Sky Travel.

Speed Auction TV
Sit-up Ltd, Unit 11 A/B,
Acton Park Industrial Estate, Eastman Road,
London W3 7QE
tel 020-8600 9700
website www.speedauction.tv

TV auctions.

SYFY
NBC Universal Global Networks, Prospect House,
80–110 New Oxford Street, London WC1A 1HB
tel 020-7079 6000
website www.syfy.co.uk

Fantasy, paranormal and horror.

Teachers TV
16–18 Berners Street, London W1T 3LN
tel 020-7182 7430
website www.teachers.tv

Travel Channel
64 Newman Street, London W1T 3EF
tel 020-7636 5401
website www.travelchannel.co.uk

Travel.

Trouble
Virgin Media TV, 160 Great Portland Street, London W1W 5QA
tel 020-7299 5000
website www.trouble.co.uk

Teenage entertainment.

Turner Classic Movies (TCM)
Turner House, 16 Great Marlborough Street, London W1F 7HS
tel 020-7693 1000
website www.tcmuk.tv

Virgin1
Virgin Media TV, 160 Great Portland Street, London W1W 5QA
tel 020-7299 5000
website www.virgin1.co.uk

Watch
UKTV, 160 Great Portland Street, London W1W 5QA
tel 020-7299 6200
website www.uktv.co.uk/watch

Yesterday
UKTV, 160 Great Portland Street, London W1W 5QA
tel 020-7299 6200
website www.uktv.co.uk/yesterday

History.

Television and film producers

Jean McConnell advises on submitting a screenplay for consideration.

The recommended approach for placing material is through a recognised literary agent (see page 473). Most film companies have a story department to which material can be sent for consideration by its editors. If you choose to submit material direct, first check with the company to make sure it is worth your while. Many of the feature films these days are based on already bestselling books. However, there are some companies, particularly those with a television outlet, which will sometimes accept unsolicited material if it seems to be exceptionally original.

When a writer submits material direct to a company, some of the larger ones – usually those based in the United States – may request that a Release Form be signed before they are prepared to read it. This document is ostensibly designed to absolve the company from any charge of plagiarism if they should be working on a similar idea and also to limit their liability in the event of any legal action. Writers must make up their own minds whether they wish to sign this but, in principle, it is not recommended.

There are a number of independent companies making films specifically for television presentation and some of these are included in the list below.

Jean McConnell is a founder member of the Writers' Guild of Great Britain. She has written screenplays, radio and stage plays, and books. She is a Vice President of the Society of Women Writers and Journalists and is a member of the Crime Writers' Association.

Aardman Animations

Gas Ferry Road, Bristol BS1 6UN
tel 0117-984 8485 *fax* 0117-984 8486
email mail@aardman.com
website www.aardman.com

Specialists in model animation. No unsolicited treatments. Founded 1972.

Absolutely Productions

Unit 19, 77 Beak Street, London W1F 9BD
tel 020-7644 5575
website www.absolutely.biz
Director Pete Baikie

Drama and comedy screenplays for cinema and TV, and TV entertainment programmes. Unsolicited scripts are not accepted. Founded 1989.

Acacia Productions Ltd

(not for profit company)
80 Weston Park, London N8 9TB
tel 020-8341 9392
email project@acaciaproductions.co.uk
website www.acaciaproductions.co.uk
Managing Director J. Edward Milner

News, documentaries, current affairs programmes for TV and video for websites. Specialises in environmental issues, human rights, Third World development issues and current affairs. No unsolicited MSS.

All3Media

Berkshire House, 168–173 High Holborne, London WC1V 7AA
tel 020-7845 4377 *fax* 020-7845 4399
email information@all3media.com
website www.all3media.com
Chief Executive Steve Morrison, *Coo* Jules Burns, *Finance Director* John Pfeil, *Creative Director* David Liddiment

Comprised of a group of production companies from across the UK, The Netherlands, New Zealand and the USA. Formed following the acquisition of Chrysalis Group's TV division in 2003.

Angel Eye Media

9 Rudolf Place, Miles Street, London SW8 1RP
tel (0845) 230 0062 *fax* (0845) 230 9562
website www.angeleye.co.uk
Managing Director Richard Osborne

Unsolicited scripts and ideas for TV and film not currently accepted. See website for submission guidelines.

Anglo-Fortunato Films Ltd

170 Popes Lane, London W5 4NJ
tel 020-8932 7676 *fax* 020-8932 7491
email anglofortunato@aol.com
Contact Luciano Celentino (Managing Director)

Action comedy and psychological thriller screenplays for cinema and TV. Will only accept material if submitted through an agent. Founded 1972.

Assembly TV

Berkshire House, 168–173 High Holborn, London WC1V 7AA
website www.allthreemedia.com

Producers of *Black Books* and *Jo Brand's Hot Potatoes.*

Baby Cow Productions Ltd

33 Foley Street, London W1W 7TL
tel 020-7612 3370 *fax* 020-7612 3352
website www.babycow.co.uk

Popular TV entertainment, specialising in cutting edge comedy. Does not invite unsolicited scripts. Send synopsis only. Also Baby Cow Films, Baby Cow Animation.

Bentley Productions

Pinewood Studios, Pinewood Road, Iver, Bucks. SL0 0NH
tel (01753) 656594 *fax* (01753) 652638
website www.bentleyproductions.co.uk

Producers of *Midsomer Murders* and *Ultimate Force.*

Big Heart Media

32 Clerkenwell Green, London EC1R 0DU
tel 020-7608 0352
website www.bigheartmedia.com
Contact Colin Izod

Creates TV drama and documentaries for young people. Founded in 1998.

Big Umbrella Media

BV Innovation Centre, Blythe Valley Park, Solihull, West Midlands B90 8AJ
tel 0121-506 9190
email production@bigumbrellamedia.co.uk
website www.bigumbrellamedia.co.uk

Works with other production companies and individuals to co-develop and umbrella proposals to broadcasters. Interested in ideas for single documentaries, entertainment formats or new long-running factual series. No drama or situation comedy. Ideas welcome via email or post.

Brook Lapping Productions Ltd

6 Anglers Lane, London NW5 3DG
tel 020-7428 3100 *fax* 020-7284 0626
email info@brooklapping.com
website www.brooklapping.com
Directors Brian Lapping, Norma Percy, Andrew McKerlie

TV documentaries, current affairs and radio.

Cactus TV

373 Kennington Road, London SE11 4PS
tel 020-7091 4900 *fax* 020-7091 4901
email touch.us@cactustv.co.uk
website www.cactustv.co.uk
Joint Managing Directors Amanda Ross, Simon Ross, *Head of Entertainment* Charlotte Johnstone

Broad-based entertainment, features and chat shows, including *The TV Book Club, Richard & Judy* and *Saturday Kitchen, Rachel Allen: Bake!, Rachel Allen: Home Cooking, Hairy Bikers Food Tour of Britain* and *Crime Thriller Season and Awards.* Founded 1994.

Carnival Film & Television Ltd

Oxford House, 76 Oxford Street, London W1D 1BS
tel 020-7307 6600 *fax* 020-7307 6666
email info@carnivalfilms.co.uk
website www.carnivalfilms.co.uk
Managing Director Gareth Neame

TV, film productions. No unsolicited material.

Celtic Films

3–4 Portland Mews, London W1F 8JF
tel 020-7494 6886 *fax* 020-7494 9191
email info@celticfilms.co.uk
website www.celticfilms.co.uk
Contact Steven Russell

Feature films and high-end contemporary drama for TV.

Children's Film and Television Foundation Ltd

c/o Simon George, Head of Finance, Ealing Studios, Ealing Green, London W5 5EP
tel (0788) 757 3479
email info@cftf.org.uk
website www.cftf.org.uk
Contact Anna Home

Involved in the development and co-production of films for children and the family, both for the theatric market and for TV. Not currently taking on new projects. Founded 1951.

Cloud Eight Films Ltd

39 Long Acre, London WC2E 9LG
tel 020-7845 6877
Chairman Christian Colson, *Managing Director* Diarmuid McKeown, *Head of Creative Affairs* Ivana MacKinnon

Develops and produces high-quality, commercially viable feature films across all genres. All projects are commissioned and developed in-house. Christian Colson is responsible for the commissioning, development and production of all projects. Unsolicited scripts are not accepted.

Collingwood O'Hare Productions

10–14 Crown Street, London W3 8SB
tel 020-8993 3666 *fax* 020-8993 9595
email info@crownstreet.co.uk
website www.collingwoodohare.com
Contact Helen Stroud, Head of Development

Children's animation series for TV for ages 0–12. Will only consider material submitted via an agent. Founded 1988.

The Comedy Unit

6th Floor, 53 Bothwell Street, Glasgow G2 6TS
tel 0141-220 6400 *fax* 0141-220 6444
email info@comedyunit.co.uk
website www.comedyunit.co.uk
Contact Niall Clark, Script Editor

Develops and produces a wide range of high-quality scripted and broken comedy series, as well as entertainment and factual entertainment programmes. New comedy writing is encouraged, as are entertainment and factual entertainment programme ideas or formats. Submit material by post or email. Response time approx. 3 months. Founded 1996.

Company Pictures

Suffolk House, 1–8 Whitfield Place,
London W1T 5JU
tel 020-7380 3900 *fax* 020-7380 1166
email enquiries@companypictures.co.uk
website www.companypictures.co.uk
Contact Charles Pattinson

Screenplays for TV drama and feature films. All material should be submitted through an agent. Founded 1997.

Cosgrove Hall Films Ltd

ITV Granada, Quay Street, Manchester M60 9EA
tel 0161-952 1382 *fax* 0161-952 1381
email animation@cosgrovehall.com
website www.chf.co.uk
Managing Director Anthony Utley

Screenplays for cinema and TV for animation (drawn, model or CGI) or a 'live action'/animation mix. Series material especially welcome, preschool to adult. Founded 1976.

Crosshands Ltd/ACP Television

Crosshands, Coreley, Ludlow, Shrops. SY8 3AR
tel (01584) 890893 *fax* (01584) 890810
Contact Richard Uridge

Radio and TV documentaries.

Cutting Edge Productions

27 Erpingham Road, London SW15 1BE
tel 020-8780 1476
email juliannorridge@btconnect.com

Documentaries, current affairs. No unsolicited material.

The Walt Disney Company Ltd

3 Queen Caroline Street, London W6 9PE
tel 020-8222 1000
website www.disney.com

Screenplays not accepted by London office. Must be submitted by an agent to The Walt Disney Studios in Burbank, California.

Diverse Production Ltd

6–12 Gorleston Street, London W14 8XS
tel 020-7603 4567 *fax* 020-7603 2148
email info@diverse.tv
website www.diverse.tv

Documentaries, science, history, travel, the arts, music, entertainment, drama.

Eagle and Eagle Production

15 Marlborough Road, London W4 4EU
tel 020-8995 1884 *fax* 020-8995 5648
website www.eagletv.co.uk
Contact Robert Eagle

Documentary, drama and feature films. Currently not accepting unsolicited MSS.

Ecosse Films Ltd

Brigade House, 8 Parsons Green, London SW6 4TN
tel 020-7371 0290 *fax* 020-7736 3436
email info@ecossefilms.com
website www.ecossefilms.com

High-quality films and dramas for cinema and TV. Material is considered only if it is submitted through an agent. Founded 1988.

The Elstree Production Company

Shepperton Studios, Building 20, Room 960,
Studios Road, Shepperton TW17 0QD
tel (01932) 572680 *fax* (01932) 572682
email enquiries@elsprod.com
website www.elsprod.com
Contact Greg Smith

Drama, entertainment and documentaries for TV.

Endemol UK

Shepherd's Studios Central, Charecroft Way,
London W14 0EE
tel (0870) 333 1700
website www.endemoluk.com

Incorporates Brighter Pictures, Cheetah Television, Initial, Zeppotron and Showrunner, which all specialise in a broad range of genres including factual entertainment, reality series, drama series, specialist factual, arts, live events, music entertainment, documentaries, youth shows and comedy.

Eyeworks UK

68 Salusbury Road, London NW6 6NU
tel 020-7644 0000 *fax* 020-7644 0001
website www.eyeworks.tv
Contact Matt Tiffin

Popular entertainment, music, documentary for TV and film. Founded 1997.

Feelgood Fiction Ltd

49 Goldhawk Road, London W12 8QP
tel 020-8746 2535 *fax* 020-8740 6177
email feelgood@feelgoodfiction.co.uk
website www.feelgoodfiction.co.uk

Managing Director Philip Clarke, *Drama Producer* Laurence Bowen

Film and TV drama.

Focus Films Ltd

The Rotunda Studios,
Rear of 116–118 Finchley Road, London NW3 5HT
tel 020-7435 9004 *fax* 020-7431 3562
email focus@focusfilms.co.uk
website www.focusfilms.co.uk
Contact Malcolm Kohll

Screenplays for cinema. Will only consider material submitted through an agent. Founded 1982.

Mark Forstater Productions Ltd

11 Keslake Road, London NW6 6DJ
tel/fax 020-8933 5475

Film production. No unsolicited scripts.

Free@last TV

47 Farringdon Road, London EC1M 3JB
tel 020-7242 4333 *fax* 020-7242 7910
email info@freeatlasttv.co.uk
website www.freeatlasttv.co.uk
Managing and Creative Director Barry Ryan

Music documentaries and performance, entertainment and factual entertainment. Starting drama and DOW-drama development in 2007.

Gaia Communications

20 Pevensey Road, Eastbourne,
East Sussex BN21 3HP
tel (01323) 727183 *tel/fax* (01323) 734809
email production@gaiacommunications.co.uk
website www.gaiacommunications.co.uk
Directors Robert Armstrong, Loni von Grüner

Specialises in Southeast regional documentary programmes, particularly historical and tourist. Founded 1987.

Noel Gay Television

Shepperton Studios, Studios Road, Shepperton,
Middlesex TW17 0QD
tel (01932) 592569 *fax* (01932) 592172
Contact Charles Armitage

Treatments only (no scripts) for TV; entertainment, comedy and drama. Founded 1987.

Ginger Productions

2nd Floor, Garfield House, 86–88 Edgware Road,
London W2 2EA
tel 020-7535 7250 *fax* 020-7535 7285
email productions@ginger.com
website www.ginger.tv/about
Creative Director Ed Stobart

Entertainment, factual entertainment. Part of SMG TV Productions.

The Good Film Company

The Studio, 5–6 Eton Garages, Lambolle Place,
London NW3 4PE
tel 020-7794 6222 *fax* 020-7794 4651
website www.goodfilms.co.uk

Commercials. No unsolicited material.

Green Bay Media

Talbot Studios, 1 Talbot Street, Cardiff CF11 9BW
tel 029-2064 2370 *fax* 029-2023 2210
email post@green-bay.tv
website www.green-bay.tv
Creative Directors John Geraint, Phil George

Film and TV drama, documentary and the arts.

Greenwich Village Productions/The Fiction Factory

14 Greenwich Church Street, London SE10 9BJ
tel 020-8853 5100 *fax* 020-8293 3001
email productions@fictionfactory.co.uk
website www.fictionfactory.co.uk
Creative Director John Taylor

Drama, short films, arts documentaries and features. Unsolicited scripts only via agents.

Happy Films

Collingwood O'Hare, 10–14 Crown Street,
London W3 8SB
tel 020-8752 8307
email info@happyfilms.com
website www.happyfilms.com
Managing Director Lucy Goodman

Produces the preschool live action and animation series, *Bookaboo!*.

Hat Trick Productions Ltd

33 Oval Road, London NW1 7EA
tel 020-7184 7777 *fax* 020-7184 7778
email reception@hattrick.com
website www.hattrick.com
Managing Director Jimmy Mulville

Situation and drama comedy series and light entertainment shows. Founded 1986.

HIT Entertainment Ltd

5th Floor, Maple House,
149 Tottenham Court Road, London W1T 7NF
tel 020-7554 2500
website www.hitentertainment.com

Children's entertainment. Founded 1989.

Icon Films

1–2 Fitzroy Terrace, Bristol BS6 6TF
tel 0117-317 1717 *fax* 0117-973 3890
email info@iconfilms.co.uk
website www.iconfilms.co.uk

TV documentaries. Welcomes new documentary proposals.

Ignition Films Ltd

4 Somerset Street, Bristol BS2 8NB
tel 0117-909 9941

email alison@ignitionfilms.org
website www.ignitionfilms.org
Contact Alison Sterling

Screenplays for cinema and TV. Material only accepted through agents. Founded 1999.

Illuminations Television

19–20 Rheidol Mews, Rheidol Terrace, London N1 8NU
tel 020-7288 8400 *fax* 020-7288 8488
email seb@illuminationsmedia.co.uk
website www.illuminationsmedia.co.uk
Chairman John Wyver, *Managing Director* Linda Zuck

Producing and publishing arts-based media. Founded 1982.

ITN Productions

200 Gray's Inn Road, London WC1X 8XZ
tel 020-7833 3000
website www.itn.co.uk/productions

ITV Studios/Granada

London Television Centre, Upper Ground, London SE1 9LT
tel 020-7491 1441 *fax* 020-7157 6063
Controller of Drama Kate Bartlett

Producers of TV and film. No unsolicited material. Founded 1996.

IWC Media Ltd

Head office St George's Studio, 93–7 St George's Road, Glasgow G3 6JA
tel 0141-353 3222
and The Gloucester Building, Kensington Village, Avonmore Road, London W14 8RF
tel 020-7013 4040 *fax* 020-7013 4041
website www.iwcmedia.co.uk
Managing Director Sue Oriel

Drama, features/factual entertainment, contemporary and specialist factual.

Leopard Films Ltd

1–3 St Peter's Street, London N1 8JD
tel 020-7704 3300 *fax* 020-7704 3301
email enquiry@leopardfilms.com
website www.leopardfilms.com
Managing Director Susie Field

Broad range of TV programmes. Sister companies are Leopard Films USA and Leopardrama, which specialises in drama productions.

Libra Television Ltd

4th Floor, 22 Lever Street, The Northern Quarter, Manchester M1 1EA
tel 0161-236 5599 *fax* 0161-236 6877
email hq@libratelevision.com
website www.libratelevision.com
Contact Louise Lynch

Children's and education TV programmes.

Lion Television

Lion House, 26 Paddenswick Road, London W6 0UB
tel 020-8846 2000 *fax* 020-8846 2001
website www.liontv.co.uk

Light entertainment, documentaries, drama, children's, the arts, news/current affairs, religion.

Little Bird Company Ltd

9 Grafton Mews, London W1T 5HZ
tel 020-7380 3980 *fax* 020-7380 3981
email info@littlebird.co.uk
Contact N. Mirza

Screenplays for cinema and TV. No unsolicited material. Founded 1982.

Little Dancer Films

61 Benthal Road, London N16 7AR
tel 020-8806 7504
email littledancerfilm@aol.com
website www.littledancerfilms.co.uk
Producer Robert Smith

Screenplays for cinema and TV; drama. Founded 1992.

Malone Gill Productions Ltd

27 Camden Hill Road, London W8 7DX
tel 020-7937 0557
Contact Georgina Denison

TV programmes. Founded 1978.

Maya Vision International Ltd

6 Kinghorn Street, London EC1A 7HW
tel 020-7796 4842 *fax* 020-7796 4580
email info@mayavisionint.com
website www.mayavisionint.com
Producer/Director Rebecca Dobbs

Features, TV dramas and documentaries. No unsolicited scripts. Founded 1983.

Mentorn

Elsinore House, 77 Fulham Palace Road, London W6 8JA
tel 020-7258 6700 *fax* 020-7258 6888
website www.mentorn.co.uk

Documentaries, current affairs series, dramas and entertainment.

Mint Productions

205 Lower Rathmines Road, Dublin 6, Republic of Ireland
tel +353 (1) 491 3333 *fax* +353 (1) 491 3334
13 Fitzwilliam Street, Belfast BT9 6AW
tel (28) 90 240555
website www.mint.ie

Documentaries with an emphasis on historical and observational films.

Nexus Productions Ltd

113–114 Shoreditch High Street, London E1 6JN
tel 020-7749 7500 *fax* 020-7749 7501

email info@nexusproductions.com
website www.nexusproductions.com

Animation for TV, commercials, music videos and film. Founded 1997.

North One TV

Mayward House, 46–52 Pentonville Road,
London N1 9HF
tel 020-7502 6000 *fax* 020-7502 5600
website www.northonetv.com

Produces *Speed Sunday* and *Fifth Gear*.

Oxford Scientific (OSF)

Waterside House, 9 Woodfield Road,
London W9 2BA
tel (01844) 262370 *fax* (01844) 262380
website www.osf.co.uk

Natural history and science documentaries. Welcomes new material.

Pathé UK

6 Ramillies Street, London W1F 7TY
tel 020-7323 5151 *fax* 020-7631 3568
website www.pathe.co.uk

Feature film production company. Will consider proposals submitted via an agent or production company.

Pesky Productions

The Brooks, Spring Barn Farm, Kingston Road,
Lewes BN7 3ND
tel/fax (01273) 474026
email claire@pesky.com
website www.pesky.com
Contact Claire Underwood

'One stop shop' for the development and production of original characters for licensing and print, interactive content for the internet and animation for games and TV. Productions include *The Amazing Adrenalini Brothers*, winner of BAFTA 2006 Best Animation. Founded 1997.

Picture Palace Films Ltd

13 Egbert Street, London NW1 8LJ
tel 020-7586 8763 *fax* 020-7586 9048
email info@picturepalace.com
website www.picturepalace.com
Contact Malcolm Craddock

Screenplays for cinema and TV; films; TV drama series. Material only considered if submitted through an agent. Founded 1971.

Portobello Pictures Ltd

12 Addison Avenue, Holland Park,
London W11 4QR
tel 020-7605 1396 *fax* 020-7605 1391
Contact Kristin Irving/Ben Coren

Film, TV and theatre production company. Unsolicited submissions not accepted. Founded 1987.

Pozzitive Television Ltd

5th Floor, Paramount House,
162–170 Wardour Street, London W1F 8AB
tel 020-7734 3258 *fax* 020-7437 3130
email pozzitive@pozzitive.co.uk
website www.pozzitive.co.uk
Contact David Tyler

Comedy and entertainment for TV and radio. Hard copy submissions only. Scripts not returned without sae.

Praxis Films Ltd

Suite 3N, Leroy House, 436 Essex Road,
London N1 3QP
tel 07791 114691
email info@praxisfilms.co.uk
Contact Tony Cook

Documentaries, current affairs, educational, schools programming for TV. New Media, communications consultancy, media training. Founded 1985.

Princess Productions

Whiteley's Centre, 151 Queensway, London W2 4YN
tel 020-7985 1985 *fax* 020-7985 1986
website www.princesstv.com

Popular entertainment.

Prospect Pictures Ltd

Glen House, 22 Glenthorne Road, London W6 0NG
tel 020-7636 1234 *fax* 020-7636 1236
email info@prospect-uk.com
website www.prospect-uk.com

Documentaries, light entertainment, factual television programmes. Part of DCD Media plc.

Ragdoll Productions Ltd

Timothy's Bridge Road,
Stratford-upon-Avon CV37 9NQ
tel (01789) 404100 *fax* (01789) 404136
email stratford@ragdoll.co.uk
website www.ragdoll.co.uk

Children's TV programmes.

Random Entertainment

4 St Ann's Gardens, London NW5 4ER
tel 020-7485 7678
email info@randomentertainment.co.uk
website www.randomentertainment.co.uk
Co-directors Graeme Garden, Jon Naismith

Comedy, drama and entertainment for radio, TV, theatre and film.

RDF Television

The Gloucester Building, Kensington Village,
Avonmore Road, London W14 8RF
tel 020-7013 4000 *fax* 020-7013 4001
email contactus@rdfmedia.com
website www.rdfmedia.com

Light entertainment, documentary, drama, arts, news, current affairs, religion.

September Films Ltd

Glen House, 22 Glenthorne Road, London W6 0NG
tel 020-8563 9393 *fax* 020-8741 7214
email september@septemberfilms.com
website www.septemberfilms.com
Director of Production Elaine Day

Factual entertainment and documentary specialists expanding further into TV drama and film. Founded 1993.

Shine

Primrose Studios, 109 Regent's Park Road, London NW1 8UR
tel 020-7985 7000
email info@shine.tv
website www.shine.tv

Produces *Masterchef*, *Got to Dance*, *Build a New Life* and *Merlin*. Part of Shine Group.

SMG TV Productions

Pacific Quay, Glasgow G51 1PQ
tel 0141-300 3000
email website@smgproductions.tv
website www.smgproductions.tv

Drama, factual, factual/entertainment, entertainment and children's programming. The network TV production arm of SMG plc. Incorporates Ginger Productions.

So Television

18 Hatfields, London SE1 8GN
tel 020-7960 2000 *fax* 020-7960 2095
email info@sotelevision.co.uk
website www.sotelevision.co.uk
Contact Graham Stuart

Entertainment. No unsolicited MSS.

Specific Films

25 Rathbone Street, London W1T 1NQ
tel 020-7580 7476 *fax* 020-7636 6886
Managing Director Michael Hamlyn

Feature-length films.

Spice Factory UK Ltd

14 Regent Hill, Brighton BN1 3ED
tel (01273) 739182 *fax* (01273) 749122
email info@spicefactory.co.uk
website www.spicefactory.co.uk
Contact Michael Cowan, Jason Piette (producers)

Feature film production company. No unsolicited submissions. Founded 1995.

Sunset & Vine

Elsinore House, 77 Fulham Palace Road, London W6 8JA
tel 020-7678 7300 *fax* 020-7478 7407
email enquiries@sunsetvine.co.uk
website www.sunsetvine.co.uk

Documentaries, sports, entertainment.

Talent Television

13–19 Vine Hill, London EC1R 5DW
tel 020-7822 3900
email entertainment@talenttv.com
website www.talenttv.com
Managing Director Tony Humphreys

Current affairs, entertainment, children's.

TalkbackTHAMES

20–21 Newman Street, London W1T 1PG
tel 020-7861 8000 *fax* 020-7861 8001
website www.talkbackthames.tv

TV situation comedies and comedy dramas, features, straight drama. Send material through an agent to Lorraine Heggessey. Founded 1981.

Television Junction

Waterside House, 46 Gas Street, Birmingham B1 2JT
tel 0121-248 4466 *fax* 0121-248 4477
email info@televisionjunction.co.uk
website www.televisionjunction.co.uk

Education programmes for TV.

Tiger Aspect Productions

5 Soho Street, London W1D 3QA
tel 020-7434 6700 *fax* 020-7434 1798
email general@tigeraspect.co.uk
website www.tigeraspect.co.uk
Chairman Peter Bennett-Jones, *Head of Animation & Children's* Claudia Lloyd, *Head of Entertainment* Clive Tulloh, *Head of Drama & Co-Chairman, Tiger Aspect Pictures* Greg Brenman, *Finance Director* John Richards, *Head of Legal & Business Affairs* Emma Cockshutt, *Head of Comedy* Sophie Clarke-Jervoise, *Director of Factual Entertainment* Ricky Kelehar, *HR Director* Helen Matthews

Programme genres include comedy, drama, entertainment, factual, animation, wildlife (Tigress) and feature films (Pictures). Children's programmes include *Star* and *Charlie and Lola*. All material should be submitted through an agent. Founded 1993.

Twentieth Century Fox Productions Ltd

Twentieth Century House, 31–32 Soho Square, London W1V 6AP
tel 020-7437 7766 *fax* 020-7434 2170
website www.fox.co.uk

Will not consider unsolicited material.

Twenty Twenty Television

20 Kentish Town Road, London NW1 9NX
tel 020-7284 2020 *fax* 020-7284 1810
email execs@twentytwenty.tv
website www.twentytwenty.tv

Ceo Tim Carter, *Head of Development* Ana De Moraes, *Head of Factual* Sam Whittaker

Documentaries, factual entertainment, specialist factual, drama and children's programmes. Founded 1982.

Twofour Broadcast Ltd

Twofour Studios, Estover, Plymouth PL6 7RG
tel (01752) 727400 *fax* (01752) 727450
email enq@twofour.co.uk
website www.twofour.co.uk
Contact Melanie Leach (Managing Director)

Factual, factual entertainment, leisure and lifestyle programmes. Founded 1988.

Upfront Television Ltd

39–41 New Oxford Street, London WC1A 1BN
tel 020-7836 7702/3 *fax* 020-7836 7701
email info@upfronttv.com, richard@upfronttv.com
website www.celebritiesworldwide.com
Contact Richard Brecker, Joint Managing Director

Books celebrities for high-profile shows and events around the world. Founded 1991.

Waddell Media Ltd

7–12 St Helen's Business Park, Holywood, Co. Down, Northern Ireland BT18 9HQ
tel 028-9042 7646 *fax* 028-9042 7922
email info@waddellmedia.com
website www.waddellmedia.com

TV documentaries; factual entertainment.

Wall to Wall Television

8–9 Spring Place, London NW5 3ER
tel 020-7485 7424 *fax* 020-7267 5292
email mail@walltowall.co.uk
website www.walltowall.co.uk

Documentaries, drama, the arts.

Warner Bros. Entertainment Ltd

Warner House, 98 Theobald's Road, London WC1X 8WB
tel 020-7984 5000
website www.timewarner.com www.warnerbros.co.uk

Screenplays for cinema. Will only consider material submitted through an agent.

Working Title Films

Oxford House, 76 Oxford Street, London W1N 9FD
tel 020-7307 3000 *fax* 020-7307 3001
website www.workingtitlefilms.com

Screenplays for films; TV drama and comedy; low budget films (WT2).

World Productions Ltd

Lasenby House, 32 Kingly Street, London W1B 5QQ
tel 020-3179 1800 *fax* 020-3179 1801
email helen@world-productions.com
website www.world-productions.com
Contact Helen Saunders

Screenplays for TV; TV drama series and serials; feature films.

Zig Zag Productions

13–14 Great Sutton Street, London EC1V 0BX
tel 020-7017 8755 *fax* 020-7017 8750
email production@zigzag.uk.com
website www.zigzag.uk.com
Head of Production Sophie Ardern, *Head of Entertainment* Ben Paul
Produces *Relentless*, *Superagents* and *Totally Calum Best*.

Independent national radio

UK domestic radio services are broadcast across three wavebands: FM (or VHF), medium wave and long wave (used by BBC Radio 4). A number of national radio stations are now being broadcast in both analogue and digital, as well as a growing number of digital alone (see page 428).

Absolute Radio

1 Golden Square, London W1F 9DJ
tel 020-7434 1215 *fax* 020-7434 1197
website www.absoluteradio.co.uk
Programme Director Clive Dickens

Rock and pop music from the past 40 years.

Classic FM

30 Leicester Square, London WC2H 7LA
tel 020-7343 9000 *fax* 020-7344 2703
email enquiries@classicfm.com
website www.classicfm.com
Managing Director Darren Henley

The UK's only 100% classical music radio station; national and international news. Launched 1992.

Digital One

Digital One Ltd, 30 Leicester Square, London WC2H 7LA
tel 020-7288 4600
website www.ukdigitalradio.com
Acting CEO Glyn Jones, *Operations Executive* Hannah Larkin

National commercial DAB digital radio network reaching more than 90% of the population. Broadcasts Classic FM, Absolute Radio, talkSPORT and Planet Rock. Launched 1999.

The Hits

Castle Quay, Castle Field, Manchester M15 4PR
tel 0161-288 5000 *fax* 0161-288 5004
email studio@thehitsradio.com
website www.thehitsradio.com
Programme Director Anthony Gay

Jazz.

IRN (Independent Radio News)

Mappin House, 4 Winsley Street, London W1W 8HF
tel 020-7182 8591 *fax* 020-7182 8592
email news@irn.co.uk
website www.irn.co.uk
Managing Director Tim Molloy

National news provider to all UK commercial radio stations: live news bulletins, sport and financial news, and coverage of the House of Commons.

Planet Rock

54 Lisson Street, London NW1 5DF
tel 020-7453 1639
email info@planetrock.com
website www.planetrock.com
Station Director Malcolm Bluemel

Classic rock music.

Prime Time Radio

PO Box 5050, London SW1E 6ZR
tel (0870) 9506061 *fax* (0870) 2244844
website www.primetimeradio.org
Programme Director David Atkey

RadioCentre

4th Floor, 5 Golden Square, London W1F 9BS
tel 020-3206 7800 *fax* 020-3206 7801
email info@radiocentre.org
website www.radiocentre.org

Formed in July 2006 from the merger of the Radio Advertising Bureau (RAB) and the Commercial Radio Companies Association (CRCA). Its role is to maintain and build a strong and successful commercial radio industry. It operates in a number of areas, working with government, Ofcom and radio stations themselves.

Smash! Hits Radio

Castle Quay, Castlefield, Manchester M14 4PR
tel 0161-288 5000 *fax* 0161-288 5004
website www.smashhits.net
Programme Manager Anthony Gay

24-hour pop music.

Smooth Radio

26–27 Castlereagh Street, London W1H 5DL
tel 020-7706 4100
website www.smoothradio.com
Station Director Paul Fairburn

Music past and present and lifestyle-orientated talk. Email from website.

talkSPORT

18 Hatfields, London SE1 8DJ
tel 020-7959 7800 *fax* 020-7959 7808
email talksport@tvradio.co.uk
website www.talksport.net
Programme Director Bill Ridley

Live sports, commentary, coverage, updates and features, news and talkback. Launched 1995.

Digital audio broadcasting

DAB (digital audio broadcasting) represents a wider choice of radio listening, less interference, and next-generation radios with features not found on FM and AM receivers. In each area a number of stations are broadcast together in something called a 'multiplex'. The multiplex operators hold a licence and build a transmitter network. This operator then contracts with lots of different radio stations to broadcast on its platform.

There are two national digital radio multiplexes for the UK. There are local multiplexes around the country, each broadcasting an average of seven services, plus the local BBC station. And there are several regional multiplexes covering a wider area and broadcasting up to 11 services each. DAB is reportedly available to over 80% of the UK. As there are so many radio stations available in different areas, it is best to check availablility by using the UK Digital Radio website: www.ukdigitalradio.com/coverage/postcodesearch.

NATIONAL MULTIPLEXES

BBC Radio

Broadcasting House, Portland Place,
London W1A 1AA
tel 020-7580 4468
website www.bbc.co.uk/radio

The BBC's national digital radio multiplex broadcasts on channel 12B. The BBC is gradually increasing its coverage from around 85% to approximately 90% of the UK population — launching a new national DAB transmitter approximately once every fortnight. The BBC broadcasts network services to the UK, Isle of Man and the Channel Islands. There are also national services in Wales, Scotland and Northern Ireland and 39 local radio stations in England and the Channel Islands, all carried on the local commercial DAB multiplexes.

Digital One

(owned by Arqiva)
4th Floor, 2–5 Great Titchfield Street,
London W1D 1NN
website www.ukdigitalradio.com

Digital One is the only national commercial digital radio multiplex and broadcasts on channel 11D in England and Wales and 12A in Scotland but not currently able to broadcast in Northern Ireland. It covers more than 90% of the population and broadcasts Classic FM, Absolute Radio, talkSPORT, Planet Rock, BFBS Radio, Amazing Radio, Premier Christian Radio, UCB UK, Panjab Radio and NME Radio.

OPERATORS AND LOCAL MULTIPLEXES

Arqiva

Crawley Court, Winchester SO21 2QA
tel (01962) 823434
website www.localdigitalradio.co.uk

Operates and controls the following owned multiplexes:

Arqiva Broadcast Ltd: Ayr

Now Digital Ltd: Wolverhampton, Coventry, Peterborough, Cambridge, Essex (Southend & Chelmsford), Norwich, Bournemouth, Berkshire & North Hampshire (Reading & Basingstoke), Swindon, West Wiltshire, Bristol, South East Devon (Exeter & Torbay)

Now Digital (Southern) Ltd: South East Wales (Cardiff & Newposrt), South Hampshire, Sussex Coast, Kent

Now Digital (East Midlands) Ltd: Nottingham, Leicester

South West Digital Radio Ltd: Plymouth, Cornwall

Bauer Digital Radio Ltd

3 South Avenue, Clydebank Business Park,
Glasgow G81 2RX
tel 0141-565 2347
website www.bauermedia.co.uk

Bauer operates 12 wholly owned DAB multiplexes and 6 jointly owned multiplexes with other operators (3 with UTV Radio and 3 with Global Radio).

Bauer wholly owned: Central Lancashire, Dundee & Perth, Edinburgh, Glasgow, Humberside, Inverness, Leeds, Liverpool, Northern Ireland, South Yorkshire, Teesside, Tyne & Wear.

CE Digital Ltd

Joint venture between Bauer and Global Radio: Birmingham, Greater London 1, Manchester.

Digital Radio Group Ltd

30 Leicester Square, London WC2H 7LA
tel 020-7766 6000
website www.thedigitalradiogroup.com

Consortium between Global Radio, UTV, TIML and Carphone Warehouse, operated by Global Radio: Greater London 3.

MXR Digital Radio Ltd

30 Leicester Square, London WC2H 7LA

Consortium between Global Radio, Guardian Media Group Radio, Arqiva and Ford.

North East England: www.mxrnortheast.co.uk
North West England: www.mxrnorthwest.co.uk
South Wales/Severn Estuary: www.mxrwalesandwest.co.uk
West Midlands: www.mxrwestmidlands.co.uk
Yorkshire: www.mxrnorthwest.co.uk

Switch digital (London) Ltd

Joint venture betwen UTV, TIML Radio and Carphone Warehouse: Greater London 2.

Switch digital (Scotland) Ltd

Joint venture between UTV and Carphone Warehouse: Aberdeen, Central Scotland.

UTV-Bauer Digital Ltd

Joint venture between UTV and Bauer: Bradford & Huddersfield, Stoke-on-Trent, Swansea.

UTV Radio

18 Hatfields, London SE1 8DR
tel 020-7959 7813
website www.utvdab.com

Independent radio producers

Many writers approach independent production companies direct and, increasingly, BBC Radio is commissioning independent producers to make programmes.

Above the Title Productions

Level 2, 10–11 St George's Mews, London NW1 8XE
tel 020-7916 1984 *fax* 020-7722 5706
email mail@abovethetitle.com
website www.abovethetitle.com
Chief Executive Simon Clegg, *Creative Director* Adam Bromley

Comedy, factual, drama, documentary, discussion, law, music and arts. Ideas welcome via email from writers with representation or with extensive previous writing credits.

All Out Productions

50 Copperas Street, Manchester M4 1HS
tel 0161-834 9955 *fax* 0161-834 6978
email info@allout.co.uk
website www.allout.co.uk
Contacts Richard McIlroy, Jo Meek

Documentaries and feature programmes. Founded 1994.

Angel Eye Media Ltd

53 Bothwell Street, Suite 7 (4th Floor), Glasgow G2 6TS
tel (0845) 230 0062 *fax* (0845) 230 9562
9 Rudolf Place, Miles Street, London SW8 1RP
tel (0845) 230 0062 *fax* (0845) 230 9562
website www.angeleye.co.uk
Directors James Harding, Richard Osborne, John O'Callaghan

Sitcom and comedy shows. Welcomes new writing talent.

Athena Media

Digital Depot A2.2, Digital Hub, 10–13 Thomas Street, Dublin 8, Republic of Ireland
tel 353 (1) 488 5850
email helen@athenamedia.ie
website www.athenamedia.ie
Managing Director Helen Shaw

Factual programmes, documentaries. Also a specialist consultancy for film, broadcasting and digital media sectors.

Baby Cow Productions Ltd

33 Foley Street, London W1W 7TL
tel 020-7612 3370 *fax* 020-7612 3352
email info@babycow.co.uk
website www.babycow.co.uk

Popular TV entertainment, specialising in cutting edge comedy. No unsolicited scripts. Send synopsis only. Also Baby Cow Films and Baby Cow Animation.

Big Heart Media

Flat 4, 6 Pear Tree Court, London EC1R 0DW
tel 020-7608 0352 *fax* 020-7250 1138
website www.bigheartmedia.com
Contact Colin Izod

Dramas and documentaries. Keen to develop relationships with writers for radio. Interested to receive unsolicited drama scripts or treatments.

Bona Broadcasting

2nd Floor, 9 Gayfield Square, Edinburgh EH1 3NT
tel (0131) 558 1696 *fax* (0131) 558 1694
email enquiries@bonabroadcasting.com
website www.bonabroadcasting.com
Contact Turan Ali

Radio and TV factual drama and comedy producer. No unsolicited MSS. Send a one paragraph summary by email only.

Campbell Davison Media

110 Gloucester Avenue, London NW1 8HX
tel 020-7209 3740 *fax* 020-7483 4541
email clare@campbelldavison.com
website www.campbelldavison.com
Contact Clare Davidson

Daily news programmes, features, live sport, documentaries and entertainment.

Classic Arts Productions Ltd

The Old Rectory, Hampton Lovett, Droitwich, Worcs. WR9 0LY
tel (01299) 851563 *fax* (01299) 851728
email wendy@classicarts.co.uk
St George's House, 15 Hanover Square, London W1S 1HS
tel 020-7495 5881
website www.classicarts.co.uk
Contact Wendy Thompson

Classical music and arts-related programmes. Ideas welcome.

Crosshands Ltd/ACP Television

Crosshands, Coreley, Ludlow, Shrops. SY8 3AR
tel (01584) 890893 *fax* (01584) 890893
email mail@acptv.com
Contact Richard Uridge

Radio and TV documentaries.

CSA Word

6A Archway Mews, London SW15 2PE
tel 020-8871 0220 *fax* 020-8877 0712

email info@csaword.co.uk
website www.csaword.co.uk
Audio Manager Victoria Williams

Produces readings, plays and features/documentaries. Allow approx. 2 months for response to submissions. Founded 1992.

Ruth Evans Productions

4 Offlands Cottages, Moulsford, Oxon OX10 9HP
tel (01491) 651331
email ruthgevans@msn.com
Contact Ruth Evans

Documentaries and feature programmes (not drama) for BBC World Service and Radio 4. Founded 2002.

Festival Productions Ltd

170 North Street, Brighton BN1 1EA
tel (01273) 669595 *fax* (01273) 669596
email info@totallyradio.com
website www.totallyradio.com
Managing Director Steve Stark

Plays, docs, features and programmes. Founded 1989.

Fiction Factory

14 Greenwich Church Street, London SE10 9BJ
tel 020-8853 5100 *fax* 020-8293 3001
email radio@fictionfactory.co.uk
website www.fictionfactory.co.uk
Creative Director John Taylor

Plays, dramatisations, readings, documentaries and features mainly for BBC network radio. Original radio drama scripts considered if targeted at existing BBC slots. Submissions only from established writers or literary agents. Email before submitting MSS. Founded 1993.

First Writes Theatre Co Ltd

Lime Kiln Cottage, High Starlings, Banham, Norwich NR16 2BS
email info@firstwrites.co.uk
website www.firstwrites.co.uk
Producer Ellen Dryden

Drama for BBC Radio 3 and 4: original plays and adaptations. No unsolicited material. Founded 1991.

Flannel

21 Berwick Street, London W1F 0PZ
tel 020-7287 9277 *fax* 020-7287 7785
email mail@flannel.net
Contact Kate Haldane

Drama, comedy and features for BBC Radio. Considers comedy narrative, sketch show and panel game ideas. Will only consider material if submitted via an agent. Founded 2002.

Heavy Entertainment Ltd

111 Wardour Street, London W1F 0UH
tel 020-7494 1000 *fax* 020-7494 1100
email info@heavy-entertainment.com
website www.heavy-entertainment.com
Company Directors David Roper, Davy Nougarède

Audiobooks, radio documentaries and commercials. Showreels and promotional audio and video. Five studios available for hire. Founded 1992.

Loftus Audio Ltd

2A Aldine Street, London W12 8AN
tel 020-8740 4666
email audio@loftusaudio.co.uk
website www.loftusaudio.co.uk
Contact Jo Coombs

Produces features, documentaries, readings and drama for BBC Radio. Produces audioguides and books, and podcasts. Own studio. Founded 1996.

Made in Manchester

Suite 444, Great Northern House, 275 Deansgate, Manchester M3 4EL
tel 0161-834 6446
email ashley@madeinmanchester.tv
website www.madeinmanchester.tv
Directors James Hickman, Ashley Byrne

Documentaries for BBC Radio. Drama and comedy for commercial outlets and broadcasters. Welcomes ideas.

Jane Marshall Productions

The Coach House, Westhill Road, Blackdown, Leamington Spa, Warks. CV32 6RA
tel (01926) 831680
email jane@janemarshallproductions.co.uk
Contact Jane Marshall

Single voice readings for BBC Radio – abridged published fiction and non-fiction. Founded 1994.

Neon

Studio Two, 19 Marine Crescent, Glasgow G51 1HD
tel 0141-429 6366 *fax* 0141-429 6377
email mail@go2neon.com
website www.go2neon.com
Contact Stephanie Pordage

Arts and music, documentary/factual, drama.

Pier Productions

8 St George's Place, Brighton BN1 4GB
tel (01273) 691401 *fax* (01273) 693658
email info@pierproduction.co.uk
website www.pierproductionsltd.co.uk
Contact Peter Hoare

Features, drama and readings for Radio 4.

Promenade Enterprises

71 Endell Street, London WC2H 2AS
tel 020-7240 0944 *fax* 020-7836 4287
email info@promenadeproductions.com
website www.promenadeproductions.com
Contact Nicholas Newton

Drama. Only considers plays if submitted via an agent. Founded 1998.

Random Entertainment

4 St Ann's Gardens, London NW5 4ER
tel 020-7485 7678
email info@randomentertainment.co.uk
website www.randomentertainment.co.uk
Co-directors Graeme Garden, Jon Naismith

Comedy, drama and entertainment for radio, TV, theatre and film.

Short Story Radio

PO Box 1302, Berkhamsted, Herts. HP4 9AE
tel (01442) 862628
email studio@shortstoryradio.com
website www.shortstoryradio.com
Producer Ian Skillicorn

Readings of contemporary short stories. Considers short stories (2500 words max.) and standalone chapters of longer works. Send query email in first instance. Founded 2006.

Smooth Operations

South office PO Box 286, Cambridge CB1 7XW
tel (01223) 244544 *fax* (01223) 244384
email info@smoothoperations.com
Contact Nick Barraclough
North office PO Box 18, Dobcross, Oldham OL3 5FS
tel (01457) 873752 *fax* (01457) 878500
email john@smoothoperations.com
website www.smoothoperations.com
Contact John Leonard
Manchester office Roome 2018, BBC Manchester M60 1SJ
tel/fax 0161-244 4193

Music-based docs and series and online content provision for BBC radio. Founded 1992.

Square Dog Radio LLP

Kilmagadwood Cottage, Scotlandwell, Kinross KY13 9HY
tel (05600) 472247
email mike@squaredogradio.co.uk
website www.squaredogradio.co.uk
Contact Mike Hally

Wide range of features for BBC Radio 3, 4 and World Service, but no book readings, short stories or drama. No unsolicited material – phone, email or write first. Founded 2007.

Lou Stein Associates Ltd

email info@lousteinassociates.com
website www.loustein.co.uk
Contact Lou Stein

Plays for BBC Radio. Founded 2000.

Sweet Talk Productions Ltd

22 Montpelier Street, Brighton BN1 3DJ
tel (01273) 772 913 *fax* (01273) 722 824
email karenrose@btclick.com
Contact Karen Rose

Dramas, comedy, features and readings for radio.

Tintinna Ltd

Summerfield, Bristol Road,Chew Stoke BS40 8UB
tel (01275) 333128 *fax* (01275) 332316
email tintinna@aol.com
Contact Sandy Bell, Ian Bell

Copywriting, business reports and all types of creative consultancy.

Torpedo Ltd

Llantrisant House, Llantrisant CF72 8BS
tel (01443) 231989 *fax* (01443) 231664
email info@torpedoltd.co.uk
website www.torpedoltd.co.uk
Contact Ceri Wyn Richards

Documentaries for radio and TV.

UBC Media Group plc

50 Lisson Street, London NW1 5DF
tel 020-7453 1600 *fax* 020-7723 6132
email info1@ucbmedia.com
website www.ubcmedia.com

Documentaries, entertainment news, comedy, drama, sport, current affairs, music for BBC and digital radio worldwide.

Whistledown Productions Ltd

8A Ayres Street, London SE1 1ES
tel 020-7407 8001
website www.whistledown.net
Contact David Prest, Managing Director

Social, historical and popular culture documentaries as well as authored narratives, biographical features, readings and magazine programmes for BBC network radio. Also syndicated tapes, podcasts and other work for commercial companies. Founded 1998.

Wise Buddah Radio

Wise Budda Creative Ltd, 74 Great Titchfield Street, London W1W 7QP
tel 020-7307 1600 *fax* 020-7307 1600 #
email info@wisebuddah.com
website www.wisebuddah.com
Contact Maria Williams

Music programmes and documentaries for BBC and commercial radio.

Theatre

Writing for the theatre

Writing for the theatre is a competitive market but thoroughly researching this market will improve the chances of your work being accepted. Christopher William Hill offers guidance.

If anybody ever attempts to convince you that writing for the theatre is a soft career option, ignore them and walk away. It is a competitive market and it would be wrong to suggest otherwise. There are many more playwrights than producing theatres. Although the odds are stacked against you, it is still sometimes possible to scrape a living as a playwright. Of course, there are a number of ways in which you can improve the chances of your work being accepted.

Research your market

It is important to try to understand why a theatre company may produce one play and reject another (due to size of theatre, casting limitations, preferences of the artistic management, etc). Go to the theatre as regularly as possible and read as many plays, contemporary and classic, as you can. In addition, theatre reviews in national and regional newspapers can be extremely useful. *Theatre Record* (fortnightly; *tel* 020-8808 3656, *email* editor@theatrerecord.com *website* www.theatrerecord.org, *Editor and Publisher* Ian Shuttleworth) provides comprehensive press cuttings for West End and regional plays. *The Stage* (weekly), gives informed background to current and forthcoming theatre productions.

The Royal National Theatre holds video-taped recordings of its recent productions. It is only possible to view these recordings on site (subject to appointment) but, again, it is a helpful way of expanding your knowledge of contemporary British theatre.

On a more practical level, many theatres offer writing classes. This is an important way of making contact with a theatre and fellow dramatists. Contrary to popular myth, most writers benefit from time away from their draughty garrets.

A number of 'self-help' books on play writing are available, offering advice on every aspect of writing for the theatre. Each author will have a different approach to his or her work, and it is worth spending time finding a book which is suitable for you. As well as providing practical tips on constructing a script, many books also offer reassurance that all the emotions experienced by a playwright (elation, writer's block, despair, etc) are shared by even the most experienced dramatists.

Constructing your script

When writing your play it is worth bearing in mind a number of practical considerations. First and foremost, write the play that you want to write and trust in your own view of the world. Be wary of trying to surf dramatic trends. If you are conscious of a trend developing you have almost certainly missed it.

Be conscious of the cost of mounting a production. It usually follows that the more characters you write into a play, the more actors you need to play them. A script requiring more than six actors may seem prohibitive to a theatre company. From time to time writers will submit plays with casts of 18 plus, and whilst an extremely well-established writer may (occasionally, but rarely) get away with this, an unknown playwright stands little or no chance of having his or her script accepted. Character doubling (with actors playing multiple roles) can be a pragmatic way of negotiating the casting hurdle. This is often a matter for discussion between writer, director and producer, prior to production.

Beware the famous theatrical adage 'you gotta have a gimmick'. Never let anybody convince you that innovation is a bad thing but try not to innovate just for the sake of it. The best way to get noticed is by writing a good play. Be careful of using cynical marketing ploys in order to sell your work. Plays with a strong regional voice are eagerly received by many theatre companies, but do not attempt to 'regionalise' a play that you have already written in order to pitch it at a specific theatre.

It is easy to forget that the primary objective in the theatre is to entertain. Try to grab the audience's attention as quickly as possible. Many scripts suffer from elaborate 'set-up' before the drama of the play can actually begin. A laborious introduction to character and situation is a guaranteed way of losing your audience (metaphorically and physically).

No matter how tightly plotted a play is, it will always be undermined by poor dialogue. Strangely, many writers are apt to forget that dialogue is written to be spoken. It is often useful to read your work aloud, especially if you are new to play writing. If a line is difficult to read, re-write it. Try not to produce 'interchangeable' dialogue. Each character should have their own distinctive voice, tone, rhythm and thought processes (spoken and unspoken). Check back through the play. How easy is it to distinguish between characters?

Do not overload the script with stage directions. Detailed notes about set design and lighting requirements will often be ignored. Ultimately, it is the job of the director to realise your work on stage and, whilst your input will undoubtedly be canvassed, it is not your responsibility to produce the play. It is the director's job to direct and the designer's job to design. Similarly, actors object to detailed notes in the script, indicating how their lines should be delivered.

Reviewing your work

Resist the temptation to start editing your play the moment you have finished writing. Apart from missing glaring errors in the script, you can easily lose sight of the essential qualities of the play, and edit simply for the sake of editing. Allow it to sit for a few weeks before doing anything more. It is very easy to find yourself swept along on a tide of euphoria as you finish writing, but this can be delusional.

Viewing your own work with a truly objective eye is always difficult, but it is an ability that can be cultivated with time. It may be easier to accept constructive criticism from someone whose opinion you value, before entrusting your script to the tender mercies of a theatre's literary department. Make any alterations to your script that you consider appropriate. There will rarely be an opportunity to re-submit a rejected script.

Approaching theatre companies

Once you are satisfied that your script is ready to send out, stop and take stock. Remember, it is not necessary to have an agent in order to send your work to a theatre. Although an agent's relationship with a director or literary manager may result in a faster response to a script, lack of representation should not count against you. Theatre companies are always on the lookout for new talent. However, it is important to bear in mind that a number of opinions about your work will have been formed before the script is even opened.

Many of the initial obstacles you need to overcome are not related to the script itself. Even envelopes and cover letters present problems for the unwary. Never forget that literary managers are sensitive creatures. A script addressed 'dear sir or madam' is an indication that the play is being sent out as a circular, with no specific focus. A bit of research helps avoid this embarrassment. Do not email your script unless a theatre expressly requests that you do this. Even in this technological age, it is still preferable to send a script by post.

Avoid unnecessary script embellishments. A simple cover letter, brief outline of previous work and a clean (white) A4 play text is all that is expected. Fancy binding, photographs, CDs, projected set designs, casting suggestions, etc, will have a strangely dispiriting effect on the script reader. Allow the play to speak for itself. It should go without saying (but unfortunately does not) that all text must be printed in black ink. The use of multi-coloured inks to distinguish between characters will undoubtedly show you up as a novice. Colour blind literary managers will be disinclined to sympathise with you.

You do not need to invest in costly script-formatting software as there is no professionally approved standard for the layout of play texts. A number of software programmes offer script templates; these are also downloadable from the internet. A cursory glance through a handful of contemporary play scripts will reveal the myriad of different page layouts employed by playwrights and publishers. Find the layout that is right for you. Allow wide margins, with space at the head and foot of each page. Secure the script in such a way that pages can be turned easily and make sure that each page is numbered.

Waiting for a response

Once your script has been delivered into the hands of a theatre company, do be prepared to wait. Many theatres will write to acknowledge receipt of the script. Some theatres will also give an indication of how long it will take them to offer a response. If you have heard nothing after six months it might be worth dropping the theatre a line (if only to retrieve your script), but do take into account the sheer volume of scripts they receive.

When the theatre company finally responds, you are unlikely to be offered in-depth analysis of your work, unless they show an interest in producing the play. Again, this is due to the vast quantity of unsolicited material they receive. In certain cases, brief comments may be offered. Companies which focus exclusively on new writing may provide more detailed script reports.

Some theatres offer a script-reading service, providing a comprehensive response to the play for a small fee. This can be one of the most effective ways of gaining objective professional advice about your work. Although charging for this feedback may seem mercenary, it is important to remember that script readers are paid very little for their services. Many readers have considerable knowledge of the theatre and their advice can be invaluable to a new writer.

Even if a script is unsuitable, an artistic director or literary manager may still want to meet with the writer. Although this will not necessarily lead to future production, it is an indication that they see you as a writer of promise. This is a good opportunity to forge a relationship with a theatre, and may result in a speedier response to any work you submit in the future. Unless the theatre requests a rewrite, a play that is rewritten as a result of feedback from the literary department will almost certainly be returned unread.

There is nothing more depressing than the thud of returned play scripts dropping through the letterbox. Choosing a play for production is a subjective process, reflecting the tastes of the literary department and the predilections of the theatre company. Even good plays are rejected. Try not to be disheartened by your first rejection letter. Chances are you will have to endure many more.

Although your play may have been read more than once and discussed at a readers' panel meeting, the literary manager's decision is final. There are stories (sadly not apocryphal) of playwrights attempting to employ strong-arm tactics in order to gain production of their work. This is a risky gambit. There is a subtle distinction between single-minded dedication to your work and psychosis. Be careful not to cross this line. Allow a day of mourning for your rejected script, then move on.

In production

On the other hand, what if a theatre is interested in producing your play? Do not feel pressured into making an immediate decision. It is easy, especially if you have never had your work produced, to succumb to flattery. Bide your time. It is worth considering that many theatres enjoy the kudos of premiering new work, but once your play has had its first production (unless it is a runaway success) other theatres may be reluctant to produce it.

If a theatre expresses an interest in commissioning you or optioning an existing play (offering a fixed term within which to produce your play), it is advisable to seek the professional advice of an agent. However, this can take time, so do not lose heart if an agent is not immediately forthcoming. Most theatres will offer an agreed standard contract, which provides a degree of security for the writer and the theatre. If in doubt, consider taking independent legal advice or contact the Writers' Guild.

Do not despair if you are rejected by an agent. Many agencies are simply too busy with existing clients to take on new writers. An agent may enjoy your work but not feel enthusiastic enough to represent you. It is a question of personal taste. Persevere until you find an agent who is as enthusiastic about your work as you are.

Once a theatre has optioned your work, things can move quickly. Even the largest of theatre companies may discover holes in their programming which need to be filled. Conversely, you may have to wait a considerable period of time before your work can be staged. Either way, in principle you should have the right to agree on a director and designer for your play. In practice this may never happen. Many theatres rely on staff directors, or a pool of tried and tested practitioners. Financial considerations can also be restrictive.

The relationship between the writer and director is, of course, vital to the success of a production. Try not to be precious about your work. Be as objective as possible. Cuts or re-writes will often be suggested, before or during the rehearsal process. This is not an attempt to undermine the writer, but an opportunity to consolidate the script. Of course, if you have any reservations about a script alteration, talk to the director or literary manager about it. Changes to the script cannot be made without your express approval, but do not pull rank just for the sake of it.

Insist on access to the publicity material a theatre produces for your play. It is a contractual obligation and the theatre should honour this. In many cases the marketing department will approach you for blurb (for flyers and press releases). This is the first contact most audience members will have with your play, and you will want to make sure that your work is accurately represented.

Again, if you are unhappy about any aspect of the production, speak to the director. Most problems can be easily rectified if nipped in the bud.

Selling your script

Although you would be hard pressed to find a playwright who took up the profession for financial gain, money is still a consideration. In the case of a non-commissioned play, the majority of the fee will be paid on signature of the contract, with a final sum payable on acceptance of the play. This gives the producing theatre the opportunity to request any revisions to the script before agreeing to production. A proportion of the fee will be a non-returnable advance against royalties. In most cases the royalty will be 8% of the net box office receipts.

If a theatre commissions a play from scratch, the fee should be paid in the following way: roughly half of the total fee on signature of the contract; a further quarter of the fee on completion of the first draft; the final quarter on acceptance of the script for production.

Again, a proportion of the fee will be a non-returnable advance against royalties. As with a non-commissioned play, the royalty will normally be 8% of net box office receipts.

The most difficult thing to predict is when the final sum of the commission fee will arrive. When is a play ready for production? How long is a piece of string? You may well find that you spend anywhere between six and 18 months, even longer, restructuring your play so that it is suitable for production. Only in exceptional cases will the first draft of a script be accepted. Some theatres may never produce the resulting play, although the 'policy' of over-commissioning is perhaps not such a prevalent evil as writers are often led to believe. Of greater concern is the tendency to option a play, then leave the playwright waiting indefinitely for the work to be produced.

A commission does not guarantee production. Once a script has been rejected, all rights revert to the writer, who will then be entitled to offer the script to another company.

Financially, it is important to pace yourself. The commission fee may have to last you a considerable period of time. Tempting though it may be, resist the urge to cash your first cheque and embark on a shopping spree.

Many established writers choose not to write to commission, preferring instead to write a play as and when the muse takes them. For a young or relatively inexperienced writer this may not be the most practical way of keeping body and soul together.

Playing the field

Even if you have managed to secure the services of an agent, this is no guarantee of work. It is in a playwright's best interests to seek employment as actively as possible.

Nowadays, it would be extremely unusual for a writer's first play to be offered a West End run. A play which proves itself in the regions may be offered a transfer, but this would be the exception, not the rule. However, there are a number of fringe venues in London that may provide an opportunity to see your work staged. This will not necessarily result in overnight success, but it can often bring your work to the attention of reviewers and other theatre companies.

There is also a vibrant theatrical community at work outside London. Regional theatres are keen to foster links with local writers, and this can be a very good way of establishing yourself as a playwright. Many subsidised touring companies may also consider commissioning work, although this will usually be tailored to specific considerations, such as the number of performers in the company, suitability for touring, etc.

Although persistence will not always be rewarded, it is certainly an approach worth trying. If all else fails, turn impresario and produce your own work. Many playwrights have established themselves in this way, forming their own companies and producing plays on the fringe circuit. Without a production a play is little more than a blueprint.

Christopher William Hill has worked as a degree lecturer, reader and script editor and has been writer-in-residence at Plymouth Theatre Royal (Pearson Playwrights' Scheme Bursary). His stage plays include *Lam, Song of the Western Men, Multiplex* (Faber and Faber 2003, *Connections* anthology), *Heartbreak Beautiful* (Faber and Faber 2009, *Connections* anthology), *Icons* and *Blood Red, Saffron Yellow. The Jonah Lie, Death to Mr Moody* and *Inglorious Technicolour* are published by Oberon Books in the volume *Inglorious Technicolour and Other Plays.* For BBC Radio 4 he has written two series of the comedy *Tomorrow, Today!* and the plays *Killing Maestros* (winner of a BBC Radio & Music Award and the Peter Tinniswood Award), *Accolades, Suing Mr Spargo, Pundits, Lambeth Palace, Hindenburg, Marmalade For Comrade Philby* and *Love Me, Liberace.*

See also...

• *Theatre producers*, page 438
• *Prizes and awards*, page 588

Theatre producers

This list is divided into London theatres (below), provincial theatres (page 441) and touring companies (page 446). See also *Writing for the theatre* on page 433 and *Literary agents for television, film, radio and theatre* on page 780.

There are various types of theatre companies and it is helpful to know what they include. Metropolitan new writing theatre companies are largely London-based theatres which specialise in new writing (Hampstead Theatre, Royal Court, Bush Theatre, Soho Theatre, etc). Regional repertory theatre companies are theatres based in towns and cities across the country which may do new plays as part of their repertoire. Commercial producing managements are unsubsidised profit-making theatre producers who may occasionally be interested in new plays to take on tour or to present in the West End. Small and/or middle-scale touring companies are companies (mostly touring) which may exist to explore or promote specific themes or are geared towards specific kinds of audiences.

Individuals also have a role. Independent theatre practitioners include, for example, actors who may be looking for interesting plays in which to appear, and independent theatre producers such as young directors or producers who are looking for plays to produce at the onset of their career. There are also drama schools and amateur dramatics companies.

LONDON

Bush Theatre

The Bush Theatre, Shepherds Bush Green, London W12 8QD
tel (admin) 020-8743 3584
email info@bushtheatre.co.uk, tarawilkinson@bushtheatre.co.uk
website www.bushtheatre.co.uk, www.bushgreen.org
Producer Tara Wilkinson

Welcomes unsolicited full-length scripts. Scripts can also be sent online via website www.bushgreen.org. Commissions writers, including those at an early stage in their career. Produces over 8 premieres a year.

Michael Codron Plays Ltd

Aldwych Theatre Offices, Aldwych, London WC2B 4DF
tel 020-7240 8291 *fax* 020-7240 8467

Finborough Theatre

118 Finborough Road, London SW10 9ED
tel 020-7244 7439 *fax* 020-7835 1853
email admin@finboroughtheatre.co.uk
website www.finboroughtheatre.co.uk
Artistic Director Neil McPherson

Presents new writing, revivals of neglected plays from 1800 onwards, music theatre and UK premieres of foreign work, particularly from Ireland, the USA and Canada. Unsolicited scripts are accepted, but see Literary Policy on website before sending. Founded 1980.

Robert Fox Ltd

6 Beauchamp Place, London SW3 1NG
tel 020-7584 6855 *fax* 020-7225 1638
email info@robertfoxltd.com

Independent theatre and film production company. Stages productions mainly in the West End and on Broadway. Currently not accepting any new material. Founded 1980.

Hampstead Theatre

Eton Avenue, London NW3 3EU
tel 020-7449 4200 *fax* 020-7449 4201
email literary@hampsteadtheatre.com
website www.hampsteadtheatre.com
Contact Literary Manager

The company's theatre, built in 2003 was designed with writers in mind, allowing for bold and flexible staging within an intimate auditorium. The artistic policy is the production of the best British and international new plays. All plays are read and discussed, with feedback given to all writers with potential. It usually takes 4 months to respond. Include postage with submissions. No plays accepted by email. See website for details of submission process and new writing initiatives.

Bill Kenwright Ltd

BKL House, 1 Venice Walk, London W2 1RR
tel 020-7446 6200 *fax* 020-7446 6222

email info@kenwright.com
website www.kenwright.com
Managing Director Bill Kenwright

Commercial producing management presenting revivals and new works for the West End and for touring theatres. Recent (or current) productions include: in the West End – *Blood Brothers, Hay Fever, Joseph & The Amazing Technicolor Dreamcoat, Whistle Down the Wind, The Crucible,* and *A Man for All Seasons*; on tour – *Blood Brothers, Festen, The Hollow,* and *This Is Elvis*.

King's Head Theatre

115 Upper Street, London N1 1QN
tel 020-7226 8561 *fax* 020-7226 8507
website www.kingsheadtheatre.org
Contact Adam Spreadbury-Maher, Artistic Director

Off-West End theatre producing premieres of plays and musicals.

Lyric Hammersmith

Lyric Square, King Street, London W6 0QL
tel 0871-221 1722 *fax* 020-8741 5965
email enquiries@lyric.co.uk
website www.lyric.co.uk
Artistic Director Sean Holmes, *Executive Director* Jessica Hepburn

West London's largest producing and receiving theatre. Unsolicited scripts for in-house productions not accepted.

Moral Support

PO Box 52686, London N7 8YL
tel (07958) 418515
Contact Zoe Klinger

The company brings together writers, musicians and other freelance practitioners to create new work with the emphasis on producing new writing and performance styles, to be performed in a variety of locations. Its performance technique has been described as 'an utterly original theatrical language'. Available for commissions of new plays, performance and dance. Do not submit unsolicited scripts. Established 1997.

Neal Street Productions Ltd

1st Floor, 26–28 Neal Street, London WC2H 9QQ
tel 020-7240 8890 *fax* 020-7240 7099
email post@nealstreetproductions.com
website www.nealstreetproductions.com
Contact Milly Leigh

Independent theatre producer of new work and revivals. No unsolicited scripts. Founded 2003.

Off West End Theatres Ltd

27 New End, London NW3 1JD
tel (0870) 033 2733 *fax* 020-7794 4044
email briandaniels@newendtheatre.co.uk
website www.offwestendtheatres.co.uk
Chief Executive/Artistic Director Brian Daniels

Commercial producing management and independent theatre producer of issue-led drama, comedy, musicals, revue, new writing, revivals and cabaret. Stages 25–30 productions a year across several theatres including the New End Theatre, Hampstead and the Shaw Theatre. Occasionally considers scripts from new writers. Founded 2003.

The Old Red Lion Theatre

418 St John Street, London EC1V 4NJ
tel 020-7833 3053 / 020-7837 7816
website www.oldredliontheatre.co.uk
Artistic Director Helen Devine

Interested in contemporary pieces, especially from unproduced writers. No funding: incoming production company pays to rent the theatre. Sae essential with enquiries. Founded 1977.

Orange Tree Theatre

1 Clarence Street, Richmond, Surrey TW9 2SA
tel 020-8940 0141 *fax* 020-8332 0369
email admin@orangetreetheatre.co.uk
website www.orangetreetheatre.co.uk

Producing venue. New works presented generally come from agents or through writers' groups. The theatre asks that writers contact the theatre first by letter and do not send unsolicited scripts.

Polka Theatre

240 The Broadway, London SW19 1SB
tel 020-8543 4888 *fax* 020-8545 8366
email admin@polkatheatre.com
website www.polkatheatre.com
Artistic Director Jonathan Lloyd

Exclusively for children between 0 and 13 years of age, the Main Theatre seats 300 and the Adventure Theatre seats 80. It is programmed 18 months–2 years in advance. Theatre of new work, with targeted commissions. Founded 1967.

The Questors Theatre

Mattock Lane, London W5 5BQ
tel 020-8567 0011 *fax* 020-8567 2275
email enquiries@questors.org.uk
website www.questors.org
Executive Director Christopher Hodgson

Largest independent community theatre in Europe producing around 20 shows a year, specialising in modern and classical world drama. No unsolicited scripts.

The Really Useful Group

22 Tower Street, London WC2H 9TW
tel 020-7240 0880 *fax* 020-7240 1204
email online_team@reallyuseful.co.uk
website www.reallyuseful.com
Chief Executive André Ptaszynski

Owns 7 West End theatres: Adelphi, Cambridge, Her Majesty's, London Palladium, New London, Palace, Theatre Royal Drury Lane. Founded 1978.

Royal Court Theatre

(English Stage Company Ltd)
Sloane Square, London SW1W 8AS
tel 020-7565 5050 *fax* 020-7565 5001
email info@royalcourttheatre.com
website www.royalcourttheatre.com
Literary Manager Ruth Little

New plays.

Royal National Theatre

South Bank, London SE1 9PX
tel 020-7452 3100 *fax* 020-7452 3350
Associate Director (Literary) Sebastian Born

Limited opportunity for the production of unsolicited material, but submissions considered from the UK and Ireland. No synopses, treatments or email submissions. Send to Literary Department, together with an sae with return postage for the script.

Soho Theatre

21 Dean Street, London W1D 3NE
tel 020-7478 0117 *fax* 020-7287 5061
email alix@sohotheatre.com
website www.sohotheatre.com

Aims to discover and develop new playwrights, produce a year-round programme of new plays and attract new audiences. Producing venue (144-seat theatre) of new plays and comedy. The Writers' Centre offers an extensive unsolicited script-reading service and provides a range of development schemes including the Writers' Attachment Programme, Open Access Workshops, the Verity Bargate Award (page 590), the Westminster Prize, a thriving Young Writers' Programme, commissions and seed bursaries and more. There is also a large self-contained studio space with 85-seat capacity plus theatre bar, restaurant, offices, rehearsal, writing and meeting rooms. Founded 1972.

Tabard Theatre

2 Bath Road, London W4 1LW
tel 020-8995 6035 *fax* 020-8994 5985
email info@tabard-theatre.co.uk
website www.tabardtheatre.co.uk

TEG Productions

73 Great Titchfield Street, London W1W 6RD
tel 020-7436 2244
email info@tegproductions.com
website www.tegproductions.com
Contact Jeremy Meadow

Produces new plays and revivals with commercial potential, all with 'star' casting as well as stand-up and other comedy. Send synopses only; no unsolicited MSS. Founded 1997.

Theatre Royal, Stratford East

Gerry Raffles Square, London E15 1BN
tel 020-8534 7374 *fax* 020-8534 8381
website www.stratfordeast.com
Artistic Director Kerry Michael, *Executive Director* Mary Caws

Middle-scale producing theatre. Specialises in new writing: including developing contemporary British musicals. Welcomes new plays that are unproduced, full in length, and which relate to its diverse multicultural, Black and Asian audience.

The Tricycle Theatre Company

Tricycle Theatre, 269 Kilburn High Road, London NW6 7JR
tel 020-7372 6611 *fax* 020-7328 0795
website www.tricycle.co.uk
Artistic Director Nicolas Kent

Metropolitan new writing theatre company with particular focus on Black, Asian, Jewish and Irish writing. Script-reading service but fee charged for unsolicited scripts.

Triumph Proscenium Productions Ltd

First Floor, 18 Exeter Street, London WC2E 7DU
tel 020-7836 0186 *fax* 020-7379 4860

Unicorn Theatre

147 Tooley Street, London SE1 2HZ
tel 020-7645 0500 *fax* 020-7645 0550
email stage.door@unicorntheatre.com
website www.unicorntheatre.com
Artistic Director Tony Graham, *Associate Artistic Director* Rosamunde Hutt, *Associate Director & Literary Manager* Carl Miller, *Associate Artist (Literary)* Charles Way

At the end of 2005 Unicorn moved into its new theatre near Tower Bridge, where it produces a year-round programme of theatre for children and young people (0–19 years). In-house productions of full-length plays with professional casts are staged across 2 auditoriums, alongside visiting companies and education work. Unicorn rarely commissions plays from writers who are new to it, but it is keen to hear from writers who are interested to work with Unicorn in the future. Do not send unsolicited MSS. Send a short statement describing why you would like to write for the Unicorn and a CV or a summary of your relevant experience.

Warehouse Theatre

Dingwall Road, Croydon CR0 2NF
tel 020-8680 4060 (Box Office), 020-8681 1257 (Admin) *fax* 020-8688 6699
email info@warehousetheatre.co.uk
website www.warehousetheatre.co.uk
Artistic Director Ted Craig

South London's new writing theatre. Seats 100. Produces 2–3 in-house plays a year and co-produces with companies who share the commitment to new work. The theatre continues to build upon its tradition of discovering and nurturing new writers:

activities include monthly writers' workshops and the annual International Playwriting Festival (see page 618). Unsolicited scripts are accepted but it is more advisable to submit plays via the Festival. Also hosts a youth theatre workshop, Saturday morning children's theatre and a community outreach programme.

Michael White

13 Duke Street St James's, London SW1Y 6DB

White Bear Theatre Club

138 Kennington Park Road, London SE11 4DJ
tel 020-7793 9193
email info@whitebeartheatre.co.uk
website www.whitebeartheatre.co.uk
Artistic Director Michael Kingsbury

Metropolitan new writing theatre company. Welcomes scripts from new writers. Founded 1988.

Young Vic Theatre Company

66 The Cut, London SE1 8LZ
tel 020-7922 2922
email info@youngvic.org
website www.youngvic.org
Artistic Director David Lan

Metropolitan producing theatre producing great plays of the world repertoire. Founded 1969.

PROVINCIAL

Abbey Theatre Amharclann na Mainistreach

26 Lower Abbey Street, Dublin 1, Republic of Ireland
tel (01) 8872200 *fax* (01) 8729177
email info@abbeytheatre.ie
website www.abbeytheatre.ie
Director Fiach MacConghail

Ireland's national theatre. Produces new plays and contemporary and classic drama from Irish and international writers.

Actual Theatre

25 Hamilton Drive, Glasgow G12 8DN
tel 0141-339 0654 *fax* 0141-339 0654
email susan.triesman@strath.ac.uk
Artistic Director Susan C. Triesman

Produces 'difficult and taboo subjects' as well as experimental theatre. Founded 1980.

Yvonne Arnaud Theatre Management Ltd

Millbrook, Guildford, Surrey GU1 3UX
tel (01483) 440077 *fax* (01483) 564071
email yat@yvonne-arnaud.co.uk
website www.yvonne-arnaud.co.uk
Contact James Barber

Producing theatre which also receives productions.

The Belgrade Theatre

Belgrade Square, Coventry CV1 1GS
tel 024-7625 6431 *fax* 024-7655 0680
email admin@belgrade.co.uk
website www.belgrade.co.uk
Contact Denise Duncombe

Repertory theatre producing drama, comedy and musicals.

Birmingham Repertory Theatre Ltd

Broad Street, Birmingham B1 2EP
tel 0121-245 2000 *fax* 0121-245 2100
email stage.door@birmingham-rep.co.uk
website www.birmingham-rep.co.uk
Artistic Director Rachel Kavanaugh, *Executive Director* Stuart Rogers, *Associate Director (Literary)* Ben Payne

Aims to provide a platform for the best work from new writers from both within and beyond the West Midlands region. The development, commissioning and production of new writing takes place across the full range of the theatre's programme including: the Main House (capacity 830); the Door (capacity 190 max.), a space dedicated to new work; and its annual Community tours. Unsolicited submissions are welcome principally from the point of view of beginning a relationship with a writer. Priority in such development work is given to writers from the region.

The Bootleg Theatre Company

23 Burgess Green, Bishopdown, Salisbury, Wilts. SP1 3EL
tel (01722) 421476
website www.bootlegtheatre.co.uk
Contact Colin Burden

Metropolitan new writing theatre company and independent theatre practitioner. Stages two full length plays a year. Also premieres short new plays at a small music venue, per year. Committed to new writing and welcomes unsolicited scripts. Recent and future productions include: *Girls Allowed* by Trevor Suthers, *Calling Time* by Derek Webb, *A Rainy Night in Soho* by Stephen Giles, and plays by Roger Goldsmith, Alec Taylor and John Foster. Founded 1985.

Bristol Old Vic

King Street, Bristol BS1 4ED
tel 0117-949 3993 *fax* 0117-949 3996
email tom@bristol-old-vic.co.uk
website www.bristol-old-vic.co.uk

Oldest theatre auditorium in UK. Works closely with the Bristol Old Vic Theatre School. See website for more details. Founded 1946.

The Byre Theatre of St Andrews

Abbey Street, St Andrews KY16 9LA
tel (01334) 475000 *fax* (01334) 475370
email enquiries@byretheatre.com
website www.byretheatre.com

Offers an exciting year-round programme of contemporary and classic drama, dance, concerts, comedy and innovative education and community events. Operates a blend of in-house and touring productions. Education programme caters for all ages with Youth workshops and Haydays (for 50+). Offers support for new writing through the Byre Writers, a well-established and successful playwrights group.

Chichester Festival Theatre

Oaklands Park, Chichester, West Sussex PO19 6AP
tel (01243) 784437 *fax* (01243) 787288
email admin@cft.org.uk
website www.cft.org.uk
Artistic Director Jonathan Church
Summer Festival Season April–Sept in Festival and Minerva Theatres together with a year-round education programme, autumn touring programme and youth theatre Christmas show. Unsolicited scripts are not accepted.

Clwyd Theatr Cymru

Mold, Flintshire CH7 1YA
tel (01352) 756331 *fax* (01352) 701558
email william.james@clwyd-theatr-cymru.co.uk
website www.clwyd-theatr-cymru.co.uk
Director Terry Hands, *Literary Manager* William James

Produces a season of plays each year performed by a core ensemble, along with tours throughout Wales (in English and Welsh). Plays are a mix of classics, revivals, contemporary drama and new writing. Considers plays by Welsh writers or with Welsh themes. Also the home of Clwyd Theatr Cymru Theatre for Young People (www.ctctyp.co.uk).

Colchester Mercury Theatre Ltd

Balkerne Gate, Colchester, Essex CO1 1PT
tel (01206) 577006 *fax* (01206) 769607
email info@mercurytheatre.co.uk
website www.mercurytheatre.co.uk
Contact (Playwrights' Group) Tony Casement

Regional repertory theatre presenting works to a wide audience. Produces some new work, mainly commissioned. Runs local Playwrights' Group for adults with a serious commitment to writing plays.

The Coliseum Theatre

Fairbottom Street, Oldham OL1 3SW
tel 0161-624 1731 *fax* 0161-624 5318
Chief Executive Kevin Shaw

Interested in new work, particularly plays set in the North. The Coliseum employs a reader to read all submitted scripts, which should be clearly typed and include a page of casting requirements and a brief synopsis.

Contact Theatre Company

Oxford Road, Manchester M15 6JA
tel 0161-274 0600/0601
website www.contact-theatre.org
Artistic Director Baba Israel

Multidisciplinary arts organisation focused on working with and for young people aged 13–35.

Curve

Rutland Street, Leicester LE1 1SB
tel 0116-242 3560 0116-293 8165
email enquiries@curvetheatre.co.uk
website www.curveonline.co.uk

Regional producing theatre company.

Derby Playhouse Ltd

Theatre Walk, Westfield, Derby DE1 2NF
tel (01332) 361007 *fax* (01332) 547200
email info@derbyplayhouse.co.uk
website www.derbyplayhouse.co.uk
Chief Executive Karen Hebden, *Creative Producer* Stephen Edwards

Regional repertory company. No script submissions. Not able to handle script submissions.

Druid Theatre Company

Druid Theatre, Flood Street, Galway, Ireland
tel (091) 568660 *fax* (091) 563109
email info@druidtheatre.com
website www.druidtheatre.com, www.druidsynge.com
Artistic Director Garry Hynes, *Managing Director* Declan Gibbons

Producing company presenting a wide range of national and international plays. Emphasis on new Irish writing.

The Dukes

Moor Lane, Lancaster LA1 1QE
tel (01524) 598505 *fax* (01524) 598519
email info@dukes-lancaster.org
website www.dukes-lancaster.org
Director Joe Sumsion

Dundee Repertory Theatre

Tay Square, Dundee DD1 1PB
tel (01382) 227684 *fax* (01382) 228609
website www.dundeereptheatre.co.uk
Artistic Director James Brining

Regional repertory theatre company with resident ensemble. Mix of classics, musicals and new commissions.

Everyman Theatre

Regent Street, Cheltenham, Glos. GL50 1HQ
tel (01242) 512515 *fax* (01242) 224305
email admin@everymantheatre.org.uk
website www.everymantheatre.org.uk
Chief Executive Geoffrey Rowe, *Director of ReachOut* Paul Milton

Regional presenting and producing theatre promoting a wide range of plays. Small-scale experimental, youth and educational work encouraged in The Other Space studio theatre. Contact the Director of ReachOut before submitting material.

Exeter Northcott

Stocker Road, Exeter, Devon EX4 4QB
tel (01392) 223999
email info@exeternorthcott.co.uk
website www.exeternorthcott.co.uk
Creative Director Rebecca Manson-Jones

Regional producing theatre company.

Focus Theatre Company (Scotland)

c/o The Ramshorn Theatre, 98 Ingram Street, Glasgow G1 1EX
tel 0141-552 3489 *fax* 0141-553 2036
email susan.triesman@strath.ac.uk
Artistic Director Susan C. Triesman

Produces women's plays and feminist work. Also holds workshops. Founded 1982.

Grand Theatre

Singleton Street, Swansea SA1 3QJ
tel (01792) 475715 *fax* (01792) 475379
email gary.iles@swansea.gov.uk
website www.swanseagrand.co.uk
General Manager Gary Iles

Regional receiving theatre.

Harrogate Theatre

Oxford Street, Harrogate, North Yorkshire HG1 1QF
tel (01423) 502710 *fax* (01423) 563205
email info@harrogatetheatre.co.uk
website www.harrogatetheatre.co.uk
Contact The Administrator

Regional repertory theatre and touring company producing both classic and contemporary plays. Unsolicited scripts not accepted.

Library Theatre Company

St Peter's Square, Manchester M2 5PD
tel 0161-234 1913 *fax* 0161-274 7055
email ltcadmin@manchester.gov.uk
website www.librarytheatre.com
Contact Artistic Director

Contemporary drama, modern classics, plays for children. Aims to produce drama which illuminates the contemporary world. Will consider scripts from new writers. Allow 4 months for response. Founded 1952.

Live Theatre

Broad Chare, Quayside,
Newcastle upon Tyne NE1 3DF
tel 0191-232 1232
email info@live.org.uk
website www.live.org.uk
Enquiries Wendy Barnfather, *Script Submissions* Degna Stone

New writing theatre company and venue. Stages 3–4 productions per year of new writing, comedy, musical comedy, etc.

Liverpool Everyman and Playhouse

Liverpool and Merseyside Theatres Trust Ltd, 13 Hope Street, Liverpool L1 9BH
tel 0151-706 9142 *fax* 0151-708 3701
email development@everymanplayhouse.com
website www.everymanplayhouse.com
Executive Director Deborah Aydon, *Artistic Director* Gemma Bodinetz, *Literary Manager* Suzanne Bell

Produces and presents theatre.

The New Theatre: Dublin

The New Theatre, Temple Bar, 43 East Essex Street, Dublin 2, Republic of Ireland
tel (351-1) 6703361 *fax* (353-1) 6711943
email info@thenewtheatre.com
website www.thenewtheatre.com
Joint Artistic Directors Anthony Fox, Ronan Wilmot

Innovative theatre producing plays by classic as well as Irish writers whose work deals with issues pertaining to contemporary Irish society. Welcomes scripts from new writers. Seats 66 people. Founded 1997.

New Vic Theatre

Etruria Road, Newcastle under Lyme ST5 0JG
tel (01782) 717954 *fax* (01782) 712885
email admin@newvictheatre.org.uk
website www.newvictheatre.org.uk
Artistic Director Theresa Heskins, *Managing Director* Nick Jones

Europe's first purpose built theatre-in-the-round, presenting classics, music theatre, contemporary plays, new plays.

The New Wolsey Theatre

Civic Drive, Ipswich, Suffolk IP1 2AS
tel (01473) 295911 *fax* (01473) 295910
Chief Executive Sarah Holmes, *Artistic Director* Peter Rowe

Mix of producing and co-producing in main house and studio.

Northern Stage (Theatrical Productions) Ltd

Barras Bridge, Newcastle upon Tyne NE1 7RH
tel 0191-232 3366 *fax* 0191-242 7257
email info@northernstage.co.uk
website www.northernstage.co.uk
Chief Executive Erica Whyman

The largest producing theatre company in the north east of England. Presents local, national and international theatre across 3 stages and runs an extensive participation programme.

Nottingham Playhouse

Nottingham Playhouse Trust Ltd, Wellington Circus, Nottingham NG1 5AF

tel 0115-947 4361 *fax* 0115-947 5759
website www.nottinghamplayhouse.co.uk/playhouse
Chief Executive Stephanie Sirr, *Artistic Director* Giles Croft, *Director of Roundabout and Education* Andrew Breakwell

Works closely with communities of Nottingham and Nottinghamshire.

Takes 6 months to read unsolicited MSS.

Nuffield Theatre

University Road, Southampton SO17 1TR
tel 023-8031 5500 *fax* 023-8031 5511
Script Executive John Burgess

Repertory theatre producing straight plays and occasional musicals, and some small-scale fringe work. Interested in new plays.

Octagon Theatre

Howell Croft South, Bolton BL1 1SB
tel (01204) 529407 *fax* (01204) 556502
email info@octagonbolton.co.uk
website www.octagonbolton.co.uk
Executive Director John Blackmore, *Artistic Director* David Thacker, *Head of Administration* Lesley Etherington, *Head of Production* Lesley Chenery

Fully flexible professional theatre. Year round programme of own productions and visiting companies.

Peacock Theatre

Abbey Theatre, 26 Lower Abbey Street, Dublin 1, Republic of Ireland
tel (01) 878 7222 *fax* (01) 872 9177
Director Fiach Mac Conghail

Part of the Abbey Theatre; presents new writing and contemporary classic drama.

Perth Theatre

185 High Street, Perth PH1 5UW
tel (01738) 472700 *fax* (01738) 624576
email info@horsecross.co.uk
website www.horsecross.co.uk
Director of Planning & Resources Paul Hackett

Combination of 3- and 4-weekly repertoire of plays and musicals, incoming tours, one-night variety events and studio productions.

Queen's Theatre, Hornchurch

(Havering Theatre Trust Ltd)
Billet Lane, Hornchurch, Essex RM11 1QT
tel (01708) 462362 *fax* (01708) 462363
email info@queens-theatre.co.uk
website www.queens-theatre.co.uk
Artistic Director Bob Carlton

500-seat producing theatre serving outer East London with permanent company of actors/musicians presenting 8 mainhouse and 4 TIE productions each year. Treatments welcome; unsolicited scripts may be returned unread. Also offers writer's groups at various levels.

The Ramshorn Theatre

University of Strathclyde Drama Centre, 98 Ingram Street, Glasgow G1 1EX
tel 0141-552 3489 *fax* 0141-553 2036
email ramshorn.theatre@strath.ac.uk
Contact Susan C. Triesman (Director of Drama, University of Strathclyde)

Develops new writing (including experimental) through Ramshorn New Playwrights Initiative. Founded 1992.

Royal Exchange Theatre Company Ltd

St Ann's Square, Manchester M2 7DH
tel 0161-833 9333 *fax* 0161-832 0881
website www.royalexchange.co.uk
Executive Director Paul Clay

Varied programme of major classics, new plays, musicals, contemporary British and European drama; also explores the creative work of diverse cultures.

Royal Lyceum Theatre Company

Royal Lyceum Theatre, Grindlay Street, Edinburgh EH3 9AX
tel 0131-248 4800 *fax* 0131-228 3955
email info@lyceum.org.uk
website www.lyceum.org.uk
Artistic Director Mark Thomson

Edinburgh's busiest repertory company, producing an all-year-round programme of classic, contemporary and new drama. Interested in work of Scottish writers.

Royal Shakespeare Company

The Courtyard Theatre, Southern Lane, Stratford-upon-Avon, Warks. CV37 6BB
tel (01789) 403444 *fax* (01789) 272560
website www.rsc.org.uk
Artistic Director Michael Boyd, *Company Dramaturg* Jeanie O'Hare

Based in Stratford-upon-Avon, produces a core repertoire of Shakespeare alongside modern classics and new plays as well as the work of Shakespeare's contemporaries. Commissions adaptations of well-known novels and stories for Christmas shows. Works with contemporary writers, encouraging them to write epic plays. The Literary department seeks out writers it wishes to work with or commission. Does not read unsolicited work, but does monitor the work of emerging writers in production nationally and internationally.

The Company is currently undergoing a four-year rebuilding programme transforming the Royal Shakespeare Theatre and the entire Waterside complex of studios, rehearsal rooms, actors' cottages and workshops. The theatre is being re-modelled to create state-of-the-art facilities for artists.

Salisbury Playhouse

Malthouse Lane, Salisbury, Wilts. SP2 7RA
tel (01722) 320117 *fax* (01722) 421991
box office (01722) 320333
email info@salisburyplayhouse.com
website www.salisburyplayhouse.com
Artistic Director Phillip Wilson, *Executive Director* Michelle Carwardine-Palmer

Regional repertory theatre producing a broad programme of classical and contemporary plays. Unable to accept unsolicited scripts.

Scarborough Theatre Trust Ltd

Stephen Joseph Theatre, Westborough, Scarborough, North Yorkshire YO11 1JW
tel (01723) 370540
email enquiries@sjt.uk.com
website www.sjt.uk.com
Artistic Director Chris Monks

Regional repertory theatre company which produces about 6 plays a year, many of which are premieres. The theatre has an excellent reputation for comedy. Plays should have a strong narrative and a desire to entertain, though nothing too lightweight will be considered. Enclose a sae with all submissions. Send treatments rather than MSS in first instance.

Sheffield Theatres

(Crucible, Crucible Studio & Lyceum)
55 Norfolk Street, Sheffield S1 1DA
tel 0114-249 5999 *fax* 0114-249 6003
website www.sheffieldtheatres.co.uk
Chief Executive Dan Bates

Large-scale producing house with distinctive thrust stage; smallish studio; Victorian proscenium arch theatre used mainly for touring productions.

Sherman Cymru

Senghennydd Road, Cardiff CF24 4YE
tel 029-2064 6901 *fax* 029-2064 6902
email admin@shermancymru.co.uk
website www.shermancymru.co.uk
Director Chris Ricketts, *General Manager* Margaret Jones, *Literary Manager* Siân Summers

Produces new work and revivals, predominantly by Welsh or Wales-based writers, both in English and Welsh. Seeks to stage high quality and innovative drama and dance with a local, national or international perspective. Develops writers through workshops, rehearsed readings and short courses. Participatory work with youth theatres (age 5 to 25), community engagement, and mentorship of new artists. Will accept unsolicited mss, welcomed particularly from Welsh or Wales-based writers (send sae for return of script). Founded 2007.

Show of Strength Theatre Company Ltd

74 Chessel Street, Bedminster, Bristol BS3 3DN
tel 0117-902 0235
email info@showofstrength.org.uk
website www.showofstrength.org.uk
Creative Producer Sheila Hannon

Small-scale company committed to producing new and unperformed work. Founded 1986.

Theatre Royal

32 Thames Street, Windsor, Berks. SL4 1PS
tel (01753) 863444 *fax* (01753) 831673
Executive Producer Bill Kenwright, *Theatre Director* Angela Edwards

Regional producing theatre presenting a wide range of productions from classics to new plays.

Theatre Royal & Drum Theatre Plymouth

Royal Parade, Plymouth PL1 2TR
tel (01752) 668282 *fax* (01752) 230499
website www.theatreroyal.com
Artistic Director Simon Stokes

Stages small, middle and large-scale drama and music theatre. Commissions and produces new plays in the award-winning Drum Theatre. The theatre no longer accepts unsolicited playscripts but will consider plays that come through known channels – theatre practitioners, regional and national scriptwriters groups, and agents. Predominantly a receiving house, the Theatre Royal produces some shows (especially musicals) which transfer to the West End.

Theatre Royal, Bath

Sawclose, Bath BA1 1ET
tel (01225) 448815
website www.theatreroyal.org.uk

The main house presents a wide range of productions from classics to new plays. It is the base for the Peter Hall Company's middle-scale productions. The 140-seat Ustinov Theatre stages an eclectic range of drama, dance and classical music, and is the home of Britain's largest annual international festival of adult puppetry. A new children's theatre, the Egg, opened in 2005.

Traverse Theatre

10 Cambridge Street, Edinburgh EH1 2ED
tel 0131-228 3223 *fax* 0131-229 8443
email jennifer.williams@traverse.co.uk
website www.traverse.co.uk
Literary Manager Katherine Mendelsohn, *Literary Officer* Jennifer Williams

Scotland's new writing theatre with a special interest in writers based in Scotland. Will read unsolicited scripts but an sae must be included for return of script. See website for submission guidelines.

Watford Palace Theatre

20 Clarendon Road, Watford, Herts. WD17 1JZ
tel (01923) 235455 *fax* (01923) 819664

email enquiries@watfordpalacetheatre.co.uk
website www.watfordpalacetheatre.co.uk
Contact Artistic Director, Brigid Larmour

Regional theatre. Produces and co-produces throughout the year, both classic and contemporary drama and new writing. Accepts unsolicited scripts from writers in Hertfordshire.

The West Yorkshire Playhouse

Playhouse Square, Quarry Hill, Leeds LS2 7UP
tel 0113-213 7800 *fax* 0113-213 7250
email mail@wyp.org.uk
website www.wyp.org.uk
Artistic Director Ian Brown, *Associate Director (Literary)* Alex Chisholm

Twin auditoria complex; community theatre. Has a policy of encouraging new writing from Yorkshire and Humberside region. Send script with an sae for its return to the Associate Director (Literary).

York Citizens' Theatre Trust Ltd

Theatre Royal, St Leonard's Place, York YO1 7HD
tel (01904) 658162 *fax* (01904) 550164
website www.yorktheatreroyal.co.uk
Chief Executive Liz Wilson, *Artistic Director* Damian Cruden

Repertory productions, tours.

TOURING COMPANIES

Actors Touring Company

The Tab Centre, 3 Godfrey Place, London E2 7NT
tel 020-7033 7360 *fax* 020-7739 8298
email atc@atctheatre.com
website www.atctheatre.com
Artistic Director Bijan Sheibani

Small to medium-scale company producing international new writing.

Compass Theatre Company

St Jude's Parish Hall, 175 Gibraltar Street, Sheffield S3 8UA
tel 0114-278 6931 *fax* 0114-278 6931
email info@compasstheatrecompany.com
website www.compasstheatrecompany.com
Artistic Director Neil Sissons, *General Manager* Craig Dronfield

Touring classical theatre nationwide. Does not produce new plays.

Eastern Angles

Sir John Mills Theatre, Gatacre Road, Ipswich IP1 2LQ
tel (01473) 218202 *fax* (01473) 384999
email admin@easternangles.co.uk
website www.easternangles.co.uk
Contact Ivan Cutting

Touring company producing new work with a regional theme. Stages 3–4 productions per year. Welcomes scripts from new writers in the East of England region. Founded 1982.

Graeae Theatre Company

Bradbury Studios,
138 Kingsland Road London E2 8DY
tel 020-7613 6900 *fax* 020-7613 6919
email info@graeae.org
website www.graeae.org
Artistic Director Jenny Sealey, *Executive Director* Judith Kilvington, *Building and Facilities Manager* Kevin Walsh, *Literary Manager* Alex Bulmer, *Finance Manager* Ann Lomole, *Access Manager* Michael Achtman

Small-scale touring company. Welcomes scripts from disabled writers. Founded 1980.

Headlong Theatre

34–35 Berwick Street, London W1F 8RP
tel 020-7478 0270 *fax* 020-7434 1749
email info@headlongtheatre.co.uk
website www.headlongtheatre.co.uk
Artistic Director Rupert Goold

A middle-scale touring company presenting 3–4 productions per year: revivals and adaptations of established masterpieces, modern classics, and new work.

The Hiss & Boo Company Ltd

1 Nyes Hill, Wineham Lane, Bolney, West Sussex RH17 5SD
tel (01444) 881707 *fax* (01444) 882057
email ian@hissboo.co.uk
website www.hissboo.co.uk
Managing Director Ian Liston

Not much scope for new plays, but will consider comedy thrillers/chillers and plays/musicals for children. Produces pantomimes. No unsolicited scripts – telephone first. Plays/synopses will be returned only if accompanied by an sae.

Hull Truck Theatre Co. Ltd

50 Ferensway, Hull HU2 8LB
tel (01482) 224800 *fax* (01482) 581182
email admin@hulltruck.co.uk
website www.hulltruck.co.uk
Creative Director John Godber, *Artistic Director* Gareth Tudor Price, *Operations Director* Paul Marshall

Nationally renowned producing and touring company presenting popular and accessible theatre. Commissions up to six new plays each year. Produces plays in-house at Hull Truck Theatre as well as touring throughout the year to large, mid and small scale venues. The venue also hosts Comedy Nights and Jazz Nights and local amateur and student companies. Also presents the world premieres of the plays of John Godber.

The London Bubble

(Bubble Theatre Company)
5 Elephant Lane, London SE16 4JD

tel 020-7237 4434 *fax* 020-7231 2366
email admin@londonbubble.org.uk
website www.londonbubble.org.uk
Creative Director Jonathan Petherbridge

M6 Theatre Company (Studio Theatre)

Hamer C.P. School, Albert Royds Street, Rochdale, Lancs. OL16 2SU
tel (01706) 355898 *fax* (01706) 712601
email info@m6theatre.co.uk
website www.m6theatre.co.uk
Contact Dorothy Wood

Theatre-in-education company providing high-quality theatre for children, young people and community audiences.

New Perspectives Theatre Company

Park Lane Business Centre, Park Lane, Basford, Nottingham NG6 0DW
tel 0115-927 2334 *fax* 0115-927 1612
email info@newperspectives.co.uk
website www.newperspectives.co.uk
Artistic Director Daniel Buckroyd

A new writing company which commisssions 3–4 writers each year and performs small-scale theatre productions to community and arts venues nationally.

NITRO

(formerly Black Theatre Co-operative Ltd)
6 Brewery Road, London N7 9NH
tel 020-7609 1331 *fax* 020-7609 1221
email info@nitro.co.uk
website www.nitro.co.uk
Artistic Director Felix Cross

Commissions and produces new and innovative musical theatre writing by black writers, that expresses the contemporary aspirations, cultures and issues that concern black people.

Northumberland Theatre Company (NTC)

The Playhouse, Bondgate Without, Alnwick, Northumberland NE66 1PQ
tel (01665) 602586 *fax* (01665) 605837
email admin@ntc-touringtheatre.co.uk
website www.ntc-touringtheatre.co.uk
Artistic Director Gillian Hambleton

Performs a wide cross-section of work: new plays, extant scripts, classic and modern. Particularly interested in non-naturalism, physical theatre and plays with direct relevance to rural audiences.

Out of Joint

7 Thane Works, Thane Villas, London N7 7NU
tel 020-7609 0207 *fax* 020-7609 0203
email ojo@outofjoint.co.uk
website www.outofjoint.co.uk
Contact Max Stafford-Clark

Touring company producing new plays and some revivals. Welcomes scripts from writers. Founded 1993.

Paines Plough

4th Floor, 43 Aldwych, London WC2B 4DN
tel 020-7240 4533 *fax* 020-7240 4534
email office@painesplough.com
website www.painesplough.com
Artistic Directors George Perrin, James Grieve, *Executive Producer* Anneliese Davidsen

Commissions and produces new plays by British and international playwrights. Tours 2–4 plays a year nationally and worldwide for small and middle-scale theatres. Also runs a range of projects focused on identifying and launching emerging playwrights – see website for details. Welcomes unsolicited scripts and responds to all submissions. Seeks original plays that engage with the contemporary world and are written in a distinctive voice.

Proteus Theatre Company

Queen Mary's College, Cliddesden Road, Basingstoke, Hants RG21 3HF
tel (01256) 354541 *fax* (01256) 356186
email info@proteustheatre.com
website www.proteustheatre.com
Artistic Director Mary Swan

Small-scale touring company particularly committed to new writing and new work, education and community collaborations. Produces 3 touring shows per year plus several community projects. Founded 1979.

Quicksilver Theatre

The New Diorama Theatre, 15–16 Triton Street, Regents Place, London NW1 3BF
tel 020-7241 2942 *fax* 020-7254 3119
email talktous@quicksilvertheatre.org
website www.quicksilvertheatre.org
Joint Artistic Director/Ceo Guy Holland, *Joint Artistic Director* Carey English

A professional touring theatre company which brings live theatre to theatres and schools all over the country. Delivers good stories, original music, kaleidoscopic design and poignant, often humorous, new writing to entertain and make children and adults think. Two to three new plays a year for 3–5 year-olds, 4–7 year-olds and children 8+ and their families. Mission: to make life-changing theatre to inspire and entertain. Founded 1977.

Real People Theatre Company

37 Curlew Glebe, Dunnington, York YO19 5PQ
tel/fax (01904) 488870
email sueann@curlew.totalserve.co.uk
website www.realpeopletheatre.org.uk
Contact Sue Lister, Artistic Director

Women's theatre company. Welcomes scripts from women writers. Founded 1999.

Red Ladder Theatre Company

3 St Peters Buildings, York Street, Leeds LS9 8AJ
tel 0113-245 5311 *fax* 0113-245 5351
email rod@redladder.co.uk
website www.redladder.co.uk
Artistic Director Rod Dixon

Theatre performances for young people (13–25) in theatre venues and youth clubs. Commissions 1–2 new plays each year. Runs the Red Grit Project, a theatre training programme for young people (18–25) in Yorkshire.

Red Shift Theatre Company

67 Marlborough Road, London SW19 2HF
tel/fax 020-8540 1271
email jonathan@redshifttheatreco.co.uk
website www.redshifttheatreco.co.uk
Artistic Director Jonathan Holloway

Productions include adaptations, classics, new plays.

Shared Experience Theatre

13 Riverside House, 27/29 Vauxhall Grove, London SW8 1SY
tel 020-7587 1596
email admin@sharedexperience.org.uk
website www.sharedexperience.org.uk
Joint Artistic Directors Nancy Meckler, Polly Teale

Middle-scale touring company presenting 2 productions per year: innovative adaptations or translations of classic texts, and some new writing. Tours nationally and internationally. Founded 1975.

Solent Peoples Theatre (SPT)

Bedhampton Arts Centre, Bedhampton Road, Havant, Hants PO9 3ET
tel 023-9242 3399 *fax* 023-9242 3401
email info@solentpeoples.com
website www.solentpeoplestheatre.com
Artistic Director Brendon Burns

SPT has developed its artistic programme through participatory projects, to incorporate a multimedia, cross art form approach to theatre that will offer richer opportunities and experience to both community and company. Works with diverse groups/individuals for whom an integrated approach to the creation/presentation of new work in performance makes that work more exciting, relevant and accessible.

Sphinx Theatre Company

13 Riverside House, 27/29 Vauxhall Grove, London SW8 1SY
tel 020-7587 1596
email info@sphinxtheatre.co.uk
website www.sphinxtheatre.co.uk
Artistic Director Sue Parrish

Specialises in writing by women.

The Steam Industry

c/o Finborough Theatre, 118 Finborough Road, London SW10 9ED
tel 020-7244 7439
email admin@finboroughtheatre.co.uk
website www.steamindustry.co.uk
Artistic Director Phil Willmott

Produces new writing, radical adaptations of classic texts and musicals. Unsolicited scripts are no longer accepted. Founded 1994.

Talawa Theatre Company

Ground Floor, 53–55 East Road, London N1 6AH
tel 020-7251 6644 *fax* 020-7251 5969
email hq@talawa.com
website www.talawa.com
Artistic Director Patricia Cumper

Scripts from new writers considered. Particularly interested in scripts from black writers and plays portraying a black experience.

Theatre Absolute

Institute for Creative Enterprise Technology Park, Puma Way, Coventry CV1 2TT
tel (02476) 158340
email info@theatreabsolute.co.uk
website www.theatreabsolute.co.uk
Contact Julia Negus

Independent theatre producer of contemporary plays. Stages one premiere and tour over 2-year period. Founded 1992.

Theatre Centre

Shoreditch Town Hall, 380 Old Street, London EC1V 9LT
tel 020-7729 3066 *fax* 020-7739 9741
email admin@theatre-centre.co.uk
website www.theatre-centre.co.uk
Artistic Director Natalie Wilson

New writing company producing and touring nationally and internationally. Professional theatre for young people – schools, arts centres, venues. Founded 1953.

Theatre Is...

The Innovation Centre, College Lane, Hatfield AL10 9AB
tel (01707) 281100 *fax* (01707) 281038
email info@theatreis.org
website www.theatreis.org
Contact Michael Corley

Challenging and creating new models of live performance by, with and for young audiences across the East of England.

Theatre Workshop

34 Hamilton Place, Edinburgh EH3 5AX
tel 0131-225 7942 *fax* 0131-220 0112
email eyoung@twe.org.uk
website www.theatre-workshop.com
Contact Edith Young

Cutting edge, professional, inclusive theatre company. Plays include new writing/community/children's/disabled. Scripts from new writers considered.

Literary agents

The role of the literary agent

Depending on their perspective, people have very different ideas as to what literary agents actually do. With over three decades of experience behind him, the late Giles Gordon explains here what the role of the literary agent entails.

It occurs to me (and it really hasn't previously although I've been an agent – don't groan – for more than 30 years) that what writers think of as 'the role' of the literary agent is quite different from the actuality.

Having said that, agents work in more various ways than publishers do. Publishers accept manuscripts from writers, whether 'professional' (meaning having published some books) or 'amateur' (as yet unpublished), and make them available to the world, or at least have them printed and bound. With non-fiction, most books will be commissioned after seeing an outline and a few specimen chapters.

I don't believe an agent has 'a role', in that that makes him or her sound pompous or important. The late publisher Colin Haycraft wrote 'The world is a peculiar place, but it has nothing on the world of books. This is largely a fantasy world in which the pecking order goes as follows: if you can't cope with life, write about it; if you can't write, publish; if you can't get a job in publishing, become a literary agent; if you are a failed literary agent – God help you!'

It's funny and a bit unfair but only a bit. It makes the fundamental point that writers are what count and it is they who keep the book trade in business. No author should ever forget this, or fear and quake when confronted with a literary agent or a publisher. We all live off your talent, such as it is.

Most good agents today (and, of course, there are good agents and bad agents) have been publishers, mostly editors; and thus they have at least a working knowledge of what happens in publishers' offices and how a book gets out into the world.

The dilemma is that agents are interested in books, the written word, yet an agency, large or small, is essentially a business and authors should expect it to be that. Would-be published authors frequently say: it doesn't cost you anything to offer my masterpiece (sorry, manuscript) to publishers. Why don't you take a chance? The answer to that is because time is money, and overheads are inevitably involved in offering each and every manuscript to publishers. Including salaries, postage, paper, packaging, internet costs, office rent, electricity, heating and everything else.

A literary agency most emphatically isn't a finishing school for aspiring authors. Our agency Curtis Brown, probably the biggest in the UK, receives hundreds of unsolicited manuscripts each week. Every one is looked at but time, if nothing else, doesn't permit us to provide detailed responses to manuscripts we don't instantly take to, for whatever reason.

In short, literary agents are professional workers whose primary responsibility is to earn a living for themselves and their dependants. Having said that, they have chosen the world of books which would suggest that they enjoy reading, yet ought to be discriminating about it.

As every second person in the world right now seems to be touting a manuscript, agents are finding it seriously difficult to keep up with the reading demanded of them. Even more so perhaps than publishers because, although they don't always admit it, these days editors and publishing houses very much regard agents as the primary sifters of material, of separating the wheat from the chaff.

The agent's real job is to 'represent' the individual authors he or she has elected to act for. An agent or agency ultimately should be judged by the quality of the writers it represents. Although an agent may choose to act for a particular author, it is essentially the author who has selected the agent, or at least decided to place the fate of his or her writing in the agent's hands.

It is therefore important that the author should be satisfied that he or she is both in reliable hands and has as an agent someone with whom they can get on. Easier said than done perhaps, but I always advocate that new authors who have written anything of the slightest interest should shop around and interview three or four agents and then decide with whom they would get on best. If the manuscript is any good, agents should be in competition to represent it

Every agency is different. PFD and Curtis Brown each employs over 50 staff, and has numerous agents, specialising in different areas: books, journalism, film, television, theatre, talent, even 'horse flesh' – by which I mean actors. There are large accounts departments which have the most fundamental responsibilities in an agency, primarily to check all money for clients that comes in, to ensure that the publisher or other payers have accounted accurately, and to get the money to the client as soon as humanly possible. No agency should sit on clients' money for more than a few days at most.

At the other end of the size scale, there are the very many single person agencies. These are often set up by editors previously employed by publishing conglomerates who persuade authors they have worked with to go with them.

The agent, or agency, makes its income entirely as a result of commission on sales of their clients' work. Increasingly, with office and other business overheads spiralling, agencies are having to charge 15% commission on sales in the UK, and 20% on sales to the USA and in translation: the latter percentage is frequently shared with a sub-agent on the ground in the relevant country.

It is a shock to new agents who have had salaried jobs in publishing to realise how hard it is to earn a living income from 10% or 15% of the average publisher's advance. Whereas the larger agencies have specialised departments, the one-person and other smaller agencies have to become master – or mostly mistresses – of the entire field, although some specialised aspects of the work (e.g. translation and film) are often farmed out. Some writers prefer dealing with an agent who does everything, while others prefer so-called experts who sell different aspects of their work. It depends entirely on the relationship between author and agent, and the temperament of both.

Which takes me really to the heart of the matter. However much I admire an author's work, I wouldn't be an effective agent for him or her unless as human beings we get on. One of my colleagues believes that when an agent undertakes to represent an author, that is a contract for life. The agent has a fiduciary and moral commitment to that writer and his or her financial livelihood. I'm of the view that if the relationship turns sour – either the author has become impossible or the agent has become useless – it is better to part company.

Yet it must never be forgotten that an agent is in the service of the author (Lopakhin in *The Cherry Orchard* comes to mind). The author employs the agent and makes it possible for the agent to earn his or her living thanks to the primary material the author provides. And this is the case even if, paradoxically, the agent, as very occasionally happens, achieves for the author such good contracts that the author becomes a millionaire.

No two authors want the same thing. Some want money, some want security of different kinds, some just want to be published, some want to be bestsellers, some do it as therapy, some do it because they believe they are geniuses, some do it because they believe it will advance their careers in their day jobs. Some want to write part time, some want to write full time. Thus no two authors make the same demands of their agents and thus it is essential that the agent gets to know the author from the beginning of their relationship and tries to find out what the author requires.

From the would-be published writer's point of view, it is useful to know how a literary agent evolves his or her list. It is said, with apparent paradox, that it is easier for a previously unpublished author to acquire a publisher than an agent. This is literally true in that last year over 130,000 different titles were published in the UK, a mind-boggling 2000-plus different books on average every single week of the year. There may be hundreds of individual agents but no agent can adequately represent more than a certain number of authors.

I – and I only use the example of myself because I know my client list better than any other – currently represent 125 authors. Five or six are internationally known, including a Booker Prize winner and a few that have been on the shortlist and haven't yet won. About half my clients write fiction, half non-fiction.

Almost every time I have taken on a writer before having met him or her, the relationship has not in the long term survived. Publishers can get away with never meeting their authors because they publish *books*, whereas agents represent *human beings*. The author has to believe that the agent is doing the best possible job for him or her which probably, but not invariably, means getting the biggest bucks by way of an advance as that way the publisher will strive strenuously in the marketplace to recoup the initial investment.

Not always though, because if the agent is in a position (i.e. it is a first book, and first books these days are more saleable than subsequent books, or one by a *very famous author*) to demand too much money the publisher may, between signature of the agreement and publication of the book, realise that he or she has been blackmailed, made an ass of, and to cut his or her losses not be prepared to spend more money on promoting a lost cause.

Again I will reiterate that the agent works for and is employed by the author. Some inexperienced writers may believe that publishers employ agents and pay them baksheesh to seduce them into offering them their best books. This is not so. If an agent or agency is to survive, or at least become established, there must be an author or two who makes a considerable income to pay for the overtures and beginners who, down the years, will become the future major earners.

And yet the major earners are not subsidising the new authors. I remember years ago John Fowles telling me that he met someone after *The French Lieutenant's Woman* had been on the US bestseller lists for many months who said she couldn't understand why he continued to use a literary agent as obviously he now made more than a respectable living from his writing. Fowles courteously pointed out that it was precisely because there was now money to be made from his books that he needed an agent to make sure he wasn't exploited.

That is the point. No writer needs a literary agent who cannot sell his or her books. In recent years, sadly and depressingly (but I hope not too cynically), I have declined to represent a number of new writers – mostly novelists but sometimes non-fiction writers because of their favoured subject matter. Much as I have admired their talent I haven't believed I would be able to find or persuade a publisher to take on their work. Ultimately failing to find a good publisher for an author means that the agent has failed the writer.

It doesn't really do for the agent to say 'I still think you have written a work of genius; the publishers are idiots for not realising it'. It is the responsibility of the agent to persuade the publisher of the genius or commercial viability of manuscripts submitted.

Saddest of all, any self-respecting agent can usually tell within 20 or 30 seconds of looking at unsolicited submissions, both the letter of submission and the manuscript, whether the book is any good or not. That is the cruellest stroke of all. And no author when submitting a manuscript to an agent should say that his or her family and friends say that it is better than most books published because they would, wouldn't they?

Most books about how to get published tell authors to submit a synopsis and two or three specimen chapters to an agent. Certainly it is in the interests of the agent that the author should do that but if the author believes in his or her book the entire thing should be sent. It is too easy for an agent to decline an author's submission on the strength of a few chapters. If the agent is hooked from the beginning, he or she should want to read on. If he or she isn't, the manuscript is going to go back to the author.

Giles Gordon died on 14 November 2003. He was a very well-respected man, reputed to have single-handedly revolutionised the world of English publishing by being loyal to his clients and placing them in the best publishing houses. His clients included Peter Ackroyd, Sue Townsend, Fay Weldon and Prince Charles. He joined Curtis Brown on 1995; the branch in Scotland where he worked is now closed.

See also...

- *Dos and don'ts of approaching a publisher*, page 126
- *How literary agencies work*, page 455
- *How to get an agent*, page 458

'I think I need an agent'

Mark Le Fanu explains when it is appropriate for an author to have an agent.

If you write fiction, having an agent is becoming almost essential. Publishers are deluged with uncommissioned proposals and rely on agents whose taste they respect to filter the best from the rest. That is why many of the major publishers tell authors they will only accept submissions from agents. But even then, there are very many more novels seeking publishers (and agents) than will ever be accepted or even looked at. This leaves many novelists – however good their work – in a depressingly difficult situation. Having a good website, self-publishing, and other self-promotional activities are ways of trying to stand out from the crowd.

For narrative non-fiction, likely to be stocked by the main booksellers, an agent may well help you to secure improved terms, but is probably not essential. A publisher can tell much about a non-fiction work from a quick glance at a proposal, which is not the case with works of fiction.

Few agents are interested in representing authors of scholarly, professional, reference or highly illustrated works, and generally they don't have the specialist knowledge to do so to great effect. Agents very rarely take on poetry, memoirs or short stories; and they are particularly hesitant about taking on authors writing in their retirement when the chances of building up a lasting full-time career are reduced.

A good agent will be likely to secure better terms (notably the advance) than you can achieve on your own and thereby more than offset their commission. Successful authors say their agent saves them an enormous amount of time looking after the business side of their work. However, an indifferent agent may be of little value; likewise one without good knowledge of rights management and contracts. Be wary of agencies seeking up-front payments, for example joining, reading or editing fees – publishers will pay little attention to recommendations from such an agency, suspecting that its main reason for representing a work is the up-front payment rather than the quality of the material itself.

Details of approximately 150 UK agencies are listed in the *Writers' & Artists' Yearbook*. Very few literary agents take on writers other than of fiction and narrative non-fiction. Within these limitations, agencies represent a variety of authors. Some specialise in children's writers and illustrators; others in film, television and 'talent' (e.g. celebrity writers). Membership of the Association of Authors' Agents is indicative of the literary agency's expertise and professionalism; likewise membership of the Personal Managers' Association for screenwriters' and dramatists' agents. When asked how they came by their agent, many authors suggest that it was as much a matter of luck as anything else. The Society of Authors can give its members confidential advice about particular agencies and look over agency agreements they are offered.

Further information

The Society of Authors
84 Drayton Gardens, London SW10 9SB
tel 020-7373 6642
email info@societyofauthors.org
website www.societyofauthors.org
The Society publishes a *Quick Guide to Literary Agents* (free to members, otherwise £2), which covers the general duties of agents and the terms usually agreed between author and agent. See page 541 for further information about the Society.

If an agency shows interest, arrange a meeting to see if you are compatible and to discuss terms before making up your mind. If you are in the fortunate position of having more than one agent seeking to represent you, or are being courted by an agent even though you are currently happy without one, get the agent to convince you that what they can bring to the party justifies their commission. They should sell themselves to you – after all, the main skill you want from them is the ability to sell.

Most agencies give details on their websites as to how they like to be approached. The harsh reality is that many agents say they will not consider unsolicited typescripts. You will probably need to send just a synopsis and sample chapter (don't telephone) to the agency concerned with a covering letter, retaining a copy of both. Enclose stamps for return postage. Be aware that it can be a matter of weeks before you receive a response to your proposal as agents spend most of their time representing their existing clients.

It may be reassuring to know that many members of the Society of Authors do not have agents; and (whether or not you have an agent) we can help by scrutinising members' publishing and media contracts – without extra charge – and suggesting realistic improvements. Whatever impression publishers may like to give that their contracts, hallowed by years of experience and revered for their fairness, should simply be signed with gratitude, negotiation is invariably in order. Firm but reasonable bargaining, informed by a knowledge of what is achievable, undoubtedly pays off.

Mark Le Fanu is General Secretary of The Society of Authors (see page 541).

See also...

- *The role of the literary agent,* page 449
- *How literary agencies work,* page 455
- *How to get an agent,* page 458
- *How to attract the attention of a literary agent,* page 465
- *Literary agents UK and Ireland,* page 473

How literary agencies work

Catherine Clarke gives an insight into literary agents, both large and small.

When I joined Felicity Bryan as a literary agent in June 2001, I knew I would be making one or two adjustments to my professional mindset. But I didn't fully appreciate how different working for a small agency would be from the publishing job I had left behind – several years as a publishing director for trade books at Oxford University Press, having come up through the editorial route. OUP is a large organisation with a corporate structure and hierarchy, and several divisions which operate effectively as separate companies, not only in the UK but in offices all over the world. I was now joining an agent who had previously been a director at Curtis Brown in London, and had successfully set up her own business in 1988, and who up until this point had operated on her own, with an assistant and a bookkeeper, from a small, pretty office in north Oxford. It was with something of a sigh of relief that I left behind the regular weekly and monthly meetings with colleagues from various publishing departments, which even when they were fun and useful seemed to take up such an inordinate amount of time, and set about learning what the differences were between representing authors and publishing them.

The first eye-opening lesson was that even though the agency itself consisted of just two agents and two staff, it functioned as the hub of a vast, informal network of relationships, not only within the UK but right across the globe. On the day that I started work, an auction was in progress for a new book proposal, a memoir co-written with a ghostwriter. The authors were based in London, but the publishers bidding for it (by phone and email on this occasion) were in Germany. The bids were relayed to Felicity Bryan by our German translation sub-agent at Andrew Nurnberg Associates in London, specialists in translation rights. Felicity called the authors to keep them up to speed with what was happening, and eventually made a recommendation to them for which offer to accept. The deal, once it was done and announced in the trade press, kick-started auctions for the book in many other territories, including the UK and the USA. While all this was happening, Felicity picked up the phone and talked to a London-based agent who deals with film and television rights and agreed that, given the intense interest in the book, it would be a good time to submit it to production companies in London and Los Angeles and get the proposal on track for a film option or sale. The authors were, naturally, over the moon.

Meanwhile I, the novice agent, was learning fast from this on-the-job induction, and was also busy setting up meetings with editors and publishing directors in all the London publishing houses, particularly those who specialised in serious non-fiction – books by historians, literary biographers, and philosophers mostly, as that was my own background as a publisher, and the areas where my earliest clients would be coming from. I wanted to find out what books were selling well for each editor, and what they were looking for. In several cases they were looking for books on particular subjects, and asked if I could help find authors for them.

By the time I attended my first Frankfurt Book Fair in October 2001, I had a small list of my own clients and a few deals already done with UK publishers. In my Filofax I had a miniaturised schedule of 50 or so half-hour meetings with European and US publishers in the International Rights Centre, and several invitations to evening parties. I had already had a number of conversations about 'hot' books and who was buying what with publishers at the check-in at Heathrow airport and again waiting at the baggage claim at Frankfurt. Over the mindbogglingly expensive white wine at the Frankfurterhof bar late at night, thronging with publishers from all over the world, I handed over proposals for books that resulted in deals (which took place later, after the adrenalin rush of the Fair was over and everyone could make a sober decision on what they wanted to buy). During the evening I met the New York-based agent who was to become my first port of call for selling my clients' books on my behalf in the US market (later I added two other US agents who had different tastes and close publishing relationships so I could match each project to a really enthusiastic co-agent). I felt well and truly launched by the time I flew back home. The following spring the London Book Fair was to prove just as intense and influential, and when I went on to develop a list of children's writers, the Bologna Children's Book Fair became another annual fixture in my diary for selling rights, meeting new publishers, checking up on how existing deals were progressing, and for trailing exciting new projects that were still in the offing. Very soon I was factoring in a regular trip to New York to see publishers and co-agents, so I could get a sense of the rather different market patterns and pressures in the USA, and also talk up my clients' books.

That experience is probably not very different for any agent, whatever the size of their business, though some will have less emphasis on the international markets. It undoubtedly helps as an agent starting out to have colleagues or contacts already in the business who can effect introductions and help build the necessary networks.

So what might a prospective writer take into account when looking for an agent to represent them?

There are many literary agencies in the UK – the membership of the Association of Authors' Agents is around 90 – and they vary in size from one person working entirely on their own to very large organisations with many agents and support staff. Most agencies are somewhere in between, with several book agents specialising in fiction or non-fiction, children's and adult, or more usually a mixture, and with support staff or freelance services such as royalty management and accounts. The very large agencies, such as Curtis Brown or United Agents (set up in the wake of a mass exodus from PFD) also have agents who specialise in film and television rights, scriptwriters, directors, presenters, and actors; in other words, they manage a wide range of creative talent. Jonathan Lloyd, Chairman of Curtis Brown, says: 'Compared to almost all publishers, agencies, even the bigger ones, are tiny, but an impressive client list helps us to protect our clients and the "one-stop-shop" ability allows us to exploit clients in the fullest and most effective way.'

At the other end of the spectrum, Rachel Calder at the Sayle Literary Agency, in Cambridge, feels that small is definitely beautiful: 'A small agency can afford to work in the medium and long-term interest of their writers, not just the short term, because they are under less pressure from having to contribute to large overheads ... they can be more flexible in reacting to changing industry circumstances, and still be acting in the writers' best interests.' As Sally Holloway, former publisher and now an associate agent with the Felicity Bryan Agency, says: 'Smaller agents, like smaller publishers, are much more aware of their own bottom line, and therefore will pursue that last little foreign rights deal.'

For the writer, several factors might come into the reckoning if they are thinking about who should represent them. The first is that a relationship with an agent is, ideally, for life, or at least for the longer-term career, and should not be entered into lightly on either part. Whether the agent is part of a small or larger agency is not so great a consideration as whether the writer and agent trust one another's judgement and ability to deliver: whether they can both foresee a happy and fruitful collaboration. For some writers, being part of a list of high-profile writers – or more generally of famous 'talent' – may be the highest comfort factor; they might be less concerned about having the full attention of an agent with a very big list of clients than being part of a particular 'brand' created by that list. For others, that is less of a factor than having a hands-on agent who will work hard with the writer to get a proposal or novel into the best possible shape and then doggedly pursue the best deals in all potential markets – and that would not necessarily mean the highest advances. Of course, most agents can happily combine these qualities.

Because literary agenting is a business based not only on contacts and relationships but also personal tastes, every agency will have a slightly different ethos or feel. As Rachel Calder says, 'A good agent is committed to their author's work and career, has excellent industry contacts at home and abroad, wide publishing experience, confidence about their abilities and good literary judgement ... what matters is how good the deals are that the agent does for those writers.'

Catherine Clarke is a Director at Felicity Bryan Associates.

See also...

- *The role of the literary agent*, page 449
- *How to get an agent*, page 458
- *'I think I need an agent'*, page 453
- *How to attract the attention of a literary agent*, page 465

How to get an agent

Philippa Milnes-Smith demystifies the role of the literary agent.

This article is for all those who are prepared to dedicate themselves to the pursuit of publication. If you are currently experiencing just a vague interest in being a writer or illustrator, stop reading now. You are unlikely to survive the rigorous commercial assessment to which your work will be subjected. If you are a children's writer or illustrator do not think that the process will be any easier. It's just as tough, if not tougher.

So, what is a literary agent and why would I want one?

You will probably already have noticed that contacts for many publishers are provided in the *Writers' & Artists' Yearbook*. This means that there is nothing to prevent you from pursuing publishers directly yourself. Indeed, if you can answer a confident 'yes' to all the questions below, and have the time and resources to devote to this objective, you probably don't need an agent:

1. Do you have a thorough understanding of the publishing market and its dynamics?
2. Do you know who are the best publishers for your book and why? Can you evaluate the pros and cons of each?
3. Are you financially numerate and confident of being able to negotiate the best commercial deal available in current market conditions?
4. Are you confident of being able to understand fully and negotiate a publishing or other media contract?
5. Do you enjoy the process of selling yourself and your work?
6. Do you want to spend your creative time on these activities?

An agent's job is to deal with all of the above on your behalf. A good agent will do all of these well.

So, is that is all an agent does?

Agents aren't all the same. Some will provide more editorial and creative support; some will help on longer term career planning; some will be subject specialists; some will involve themselves more on marketing and promotion. Such extras may well be taken into consideration in the commission rates charged.

I have decided I definitely do want an agent. Where do I begin?

When I left publishing and talked generally to the authors and illustrators I knew, a number of them said it was now more difficult to find an agent than a publisher. Why is this? The answer is a commercial one. An agent will only take someone on if they can see how and why they are going to make money for the client and themselves. To survive, an agent needs to make commission and to do this they need projects they can sell. An agent also knows that if he/she does not sell a client's work, the relationship isn't going to last long.

So the agent just thinks about money?

Well, some agents may just think about money. And it might be all you care about. But good agents do also care about the quality of work and the clients they represent. They are professional people who commit themselves to doing the best job they can. They also know that good personal relationships count – and that they help everyone enjoy business more. This means that, if and when you get as far as talking to a prospective agent, you should ask yourself the questions: 'Do I have a good rapport with this person? Do I think we will get along? Do I understand and trust what they are saying?' Follow your instinct – more often than not it will be right.

So how do I convince an agent that I'm worth taking on?

Start with the basics. Make your approach professional. Make sure you only approach an appropriate agent who deals with the category of book you are writing/illustrating. Check to whom you should send your work and whether there are any specific ways your submission should be made (if it's not clear from the listings in this *Yearbook* or the agency's website). Only submit neat, typed work on single-sided A4 paper. Only make an electronic submission if the agency in question states that it accepts these. Send a short covering letter with your manuscript explaining what it is, why you wrote it, what the intended audience is and providing any other *relevant* context. Always say if and why you are uniquely placed and qualified to write a particular book. Provide your professional credentials, if any. If you are writing an autobiography, justify why it is of public interest and why your experiences set you apart. Also, provide a CV (again, neat, typed, relevant) and a stamped addressed envelope for the return of your manuscript. Think of the whole thing in the same way as you would a job application, for which you would expect to prepare thoroughly in advance. You might only get one go at making your big sales pitch to an agent. Don't mess it up by being anything less than thorough.

And if I get to meet an agent?

Treat it like a job interview (although hopefully it will be more relaxed than this). Be prepared to talk about your work and yourself. An agent knows that a prepossessing personality in an author is a great asset for a publisher in terms of publicity and marketing – they will be looking to see how good your interpersonal skills are.

And if an agent turns my work down? Should I ask them to look again? People say you should not accept rejection.

No means no. Don't pester. It won't make an agent change his/her mind. Instead, move on to the next agency – the agent there might feel more positive. The agents who reject you may be wrong. But the loss is theirs.

Even if an agent turns my work down, isn't it worth asking for help with my creative direction?

No. Agents will often provide editorial advice for clients but will not do so for non-clients. Submissions are usually sorted into two piles of 'yes, worth seeing more' and 'rejections'. There is not another pile of 'promising writer but requires further tutoring'. Creative courses and writers' and artists' groups are better options to pursue for teaching and advice (see *Websites for writers* on page 652, *Taking a writing course* on page 685 and *Creative writing courses* on page 688). It is, however, important to practise and develop your creative skills. You wouldn't expect to be able to play football without working at your ball skills or practise as a lawyer without studying to acquire the relevant knowledge. If you are looking to get your work published, you are going to have to compete with professional writers and artists – and those who have spent years working at their craft.

If I haven't put you off yet, it just remains for me to say good luck – and don't forget to buy plenty of stamps, envelopes and A4 paper. Many agents won't take email submissions.

Philippa Milnes-Smith is a past president of the Association of Authors' Agents and Managing Director of the agency LAW (Lucas Alexander Whitley), and a former publisher of Penguin Children's Books.

See also...

- *Literary agents for children's books*, page 780
- *Literary agents for television, film, radio and theatre*, page 780
- *The role of the literary agent*, page 449
- *How literary agencies work*, page 455

Letter to an unsolicited author

With the benefit of 17 years of experience as a literary agent, Simon Trewin gives valuable advice to unpublished authors on how and when to approach a literary agent with their manuscript.

Dear Author,

Being an agent is not rocket science. There is no agent training school and there is no course that I know of that exclusively trains people to do what I do. All I do, quite simply, is read work, decide if it ticks a number of boxes and then try to seek a publishing home for it. It is as clear and as simple as that – I am not a literary critic, I don't run a creative writing school and I'm not a publisher but I *am* entrepreneurial, I am clear in my mind as to my particular strengths and weaknesses and I am also a nurturer of talent. On top of all of that I continually love the fact that there are thousands and thousands of writers out there looking for book deals. So far so good.

There is an illustrated edition of *Jack and the Beanstalk* that I used to read to my son Jack when he was little and we both loved one particular page – it showed a tiny Jack knocking on the huge wooden door of the giant's castle. The door was reinforced with rivets and there was an intimidating sense of austere formality about it. Jack knocked and knocked on that door but no one came and it felt poignant and it felt uneven. I am absolutely aware that this is how unsolicited and unrepresented authors feel when they are in search of an agent – that they are knocking on a massive door which never seems to open. The reality of course is that on the other side of the publishing door there isn't an ogre or a huge author-eating giant but there are in fact hundreds of busy agents running around doing great work and all faced with a common quest – to find exciting new authors to add to their growing lists. We all want to find the Next Big Thing and any agent who says otherwise is telling porky pies. It is good to remind myself as an agent, and to remind all authors out there at the beginning of their journeys that when I started out as an agent an author called Joanne Rowling was still sitting in a cafe somewhere scribbling the adventures of a young wizard boy at a school called Hogwarts. She wrote to the agent Christopher Little and the rest is history. As the advert for the lottery once said, 'It could be you...'.

We are all looking for our own J.K. Rowling but, unfortunately, many writers put unnecessary barriers in between their work and the potential of an agent picking it up. There is no exact science to breaking into publishing but there are many things you should avoid like the plague....

Agents are a curious bunch (I'm not sure what the collective noun for agents should be – maybe a 'clause of agents'?) and the community I inhabit is made up of not only the mad, the bad and the dangerous to know (as in any profession) but on the whole by a huge number of truly inspiring entrepeneurial people who spend every waking hour as passionate advocates of the powers of prose. If you take a look at various agent websites (and you really should) you will see a diverse list of clients who reflect their agent's idiosyncrasies, their passion and their interests and this should be encouraging to any author in search of representation.

We agents need you – without authors we would be sitting at our desks sucking our pens and looking at empty bookshelves – but we also need you to help us make efficient use of our time and our skills. With 17 years' experience as an agent I can tell you that many prospective authors don't do themselves any favours when they approach the door.

I believe you can judge an agent's soul by their attitude to unsolicited material and, believe me, we at United Agents take it very seriously indeed. My brilliant assistant Ariella Feiner comes into my office every morning with the newly arrived material and we settle down and start reading. Simple as that. A wonderful hush descends over the room, the phone is set to divert, the Blackberry goes on silent mode and we read and read and read. Tea is sipped and occasionally a pencil is produced and a mark made in a margin or on a covering letter. Then we silently swap material that has grabbed our attention and get a silent second opinion. At the end of this zen-like half an hour we have a small collection of 'maybes' and a larger collection of 'no's'.

The no's fall into many categories:

(a) **The Arrogant.** I once received a submission which said, and I quote, 'Dear Mr Terwin (*sic*) I am probably one of the best writers currently working in the English language and, frankly, you are lucky to be seeing this picaresque novel which my tutor at Oxford has already described as "heart-stoppingly wonderful". Personally I don't think I need an agent but someone mentioned your name as being one of the less bad ones so I am giving you an opportunity to persuade me otherwise. If you would like to visit me in Oxford next Wednesday lunchtime that would be convenient.' Sincerely, etc. Frankly I didn't bother reading any more – I knew that we weren't going to get on. I have nothing against writers being confident and passionate and displaying their work to the best of its potential but this crossed the line!

(b) **The Impersonator.** I received a mediocre thriller one day and read about 50 pages and sent it back with a note saying I didn't feel it was going to be a good fit for my list. The next morning a very indignant man called me and told me in no uncertain terms that I was mistaken. 'Oh yes,' said I, 'why is that?' He then proceeded to tell me that he had read the top ten thrillers of the previous year and had decoded each of them onto a graph. When there was a cliffhanger he coloured in the appropriate square on his chart with green crayon, when there was an explosion he whipped out the red crayon, and when there was a sex scene he used blue and so on. He then wrote his own novel based on this equation of what constituted the statistically average 'bestselling novel' and was amazed that I didn't immediately snap it up. What he had done of course was create an impersonation of a thriller rather than a thriller itself, and the book he sent me was very hollow indeed. He hadn't invested anything of himself in it and it really showed. My feeling is that you should write from the inside out and take that storytelling fire in your belly and get it down on paper. Don't analyse the market or the genre – just write.

(c) **The Misguided.** I sing in the bath. I enjoy it and I can just about carry a tune but I don't believe that I am entitled to a record deal and a seven-night residency at the O2. That doesn't bother me because, as I said, I enjoy it. Some of the manuscripts I receive are just not very good but still they come with covering letters reeking of entitlements and that say, 'My friends and family think this is better than most books being published right now'. I would be very apprehensive about suggesting to any author that they use their friends and family's reaction to their work as a selling point. Have you ever told a friend that their ugly baby was anything other than 'beautiful'? Of course not. Go figure! Don't trust anyone's judgement who you share Christmas dinner with.

(d) **The Scattergun.** I am all for authors who have a multiplicity of talents and who write prose, poetry, genre fiction, verse drama and children's books but I would advise them against sending examples of ALL OF THEM AT ONCE to an agent with a note saying, 'I love all this stuff – you decide what I should write next'. I want to hear your undivided passion for one area of your writing because if I become your agent I will need to sell you in a very focused way to a publisher. Variety may be the spice of life but I would suggest you write to an agent about one major project at a time – your publisher will want to launch you as a mini-brand and will want to package you and continue to publish you in a coherent manner that creates a sense of expectation from your growing readership.
(e) **The Misdirected.** Even though I am very open on my website as to what my likes and dislikes are, I still receive material that is in direct opposition to those stated preferences. I don't understand or represent science fiction or fantasy; I don't have an interest in sagas; I don't represent young children's books; I don't represent academic books; I don't represent illustrated books. I'm very clear about this but still, on a daily basis, letters arrive that say things like, 'Dear Simon, I know you say that you don't represent x, y or z, but I hope that once you've read my material you'll make an exception'. The short answer to that is *no* – I know it sounds harsh but it is there to save you time and to make sure that when you send your precious work out it goes to someone who is actively sitting there wanting to read it.
(f) **The Under-developed.** It is virtually impossible to secure a book deal for fiction in the current climate on anything less than the full manuscript, so you shouldn't approach an agent without having completed several drafts of your masterwork. Ideally you will also have put it to one side for a couple of months so you can achieve that all-important 'distance' from your work. This is crucial but it is amazing how many people approach me saying something like, 'I know the second half doesn't work at all and I will probably change the main character entirely but I would love your thoughts now'. My thoughts on this are clear – do not submit your work until you are happy to be judged by it. Again I know this sounds harsh but you wouldn't go into a job interview and say, 'I'm probably completely wrong for this job and sorry I am still wearing my pyjamas and I am half an hour late but let's have a chat … if that's all right with you'. Take the process really seriously and present yourself in a professional way to a professional agent and you will achieve so much more.

Your one aim is to put no barriers between you, your prose and my assessment of it and it really isn't that difficult. The important thing to remember throughout this entire process is that I am sitting at my desk waiting for something wonderful to come into my life. I am looking to find storytellers – non-fiction and fiction – who can make me, for a brief moment or two, forget that I am reading a book. Authors who have a distinctive voice that carries me with it to strange lands of the imagination or simply to a place where I am viewing the mundane from an off-kilter perspective. I am looking, simply, for books that I will feel proud to share with my peers in the publishing world and who will feel the same passion for them that I do.

Last year Brilliant Ariella texted me at home on a Sunday and told me to check my email immediately because she was sending over something amazing that I had to read *at once.* I did and she was right – it was. On the following Tuesday we met the author, Jane Casey, and signed her up. Three weeks later her chilling psychological debut *The Missing* was snapped up by Gillian Green at Ebury Press and I had that wonderful moment as an agent when you ring a client and tell them they are about to become a published author. I live for that moment and it never disappoints.

Jane's novel has now been published to huge acclaim, sold all over the world by my colleague – the amazing Jessica Craig – and the movie rights have been optioned. It all started because Jane finished the novel, did a bit of research about who best to send it to, wrote a confident letter telling me about the authors she enjoyed reading, telling me why she wanted to be a novelist and telling me about *The Missing*. She enclosed the first 10,000 words and sat back patiently while Ariella read it, enthused me and got her in for a meeting. We then suggested some changes which she carried out and then she let us get on with the business of publishing. She played to her strengths and we played to ours and it has worked out like a dream. A year later history is repeating itself with the author Julia Crouch whose debut *Cuckoo* I am sure will take the world by storm in 2011.

If you can avoid transgressing any of the great sins of approaching an agent that I have outlined then you will raise the odds of securing an agent and publication by a factor of at least ten. And if you can avoid doing as one author did when he wrote to me and said, 'I have tried 14 publishers and nine agents and they have all said "no" so I am now approaching you', then even better!

I want to read your work and look forward to the perfect pitch from you.

Simon Trewin is an agent with United Agents.

See also...

- *Dealing with rejection*, page 659
- *How to attract the attention of a literary agent*, page 465
- *How to get an agent*, page 458
- *Literary agents UK and Ireland*, page 473

How to attract the attention of a literary agent

Having a literary agent helps you to get published. When an agent takes on a writer publishers are far more likely to take notice of that writer's work. Alison Baverstock gives advice on how to attract the attention of a literary agent.

Literary agents perform a very valuable sifting function for publishing houses. They are people with lots of publishing experience, who are offered many potential books, in various stages of development. The agents bring those books they favour to the attention of the publishers they think will like them too. Of course that's not to say that all great potential writers have agents, or that all new authors taken on by publishing houses have agents, just that amongst the newly published, there will be more authors with agents than authors without. Stories of what go on to become bestselling books being spotted on a 'slush pile' (the pile of unsolicited manuscripts that all publishing houses accumulate without asking) do occur, but they are memorable precisely because they are rare.

The nature of literary agents

Many agents have been publishers themselves. It follows that they like to specialise (usually in the kind of books they used to publish, or in those they have a strong personal interest in) and that they have an encyclopedic view of the industry.

Agents tend to work a bit like advertising agencies, in that they tend to have just one major client in each field. So just as an advertising agency would not represent two directly competing accounts, it would be unlikely that a literary agent would take on two authors whose books were very similar. This is particularly true in the non-fiction market where having two directly competing authors would be bound to cause difficulties.

Generalising further, literary agents are gregarious, fond of being noticed (they tend to dress quite strikingly), are good talkers (they certainly seem to know everyone), dramatic travellers (fond of hopping on and off planes in a blaze of self-generated publicity), are good negotiators (their livelihood depends on it as well as that of the authors they represent) and are not immune to vanity – so mentioning that you heard them speak, or making it clear you know who they are and particularly want to be represented by *them*, tends to go down well.

What's in it for the agent?

I always think the secret of a good business proposal is to look at it from your would-be collaborator's viewpoint rather than your own. Thus when seeking sponsorship, you get a far better response if you explain what the potential sponsor will get out of a relationship with you than if you tell them how much you need the money. To paraphrase J.F. Kennedy, 'Think not what an agent can do for you, but what you can do for an agent.' Taking the same approach, agents are looking for writers (a) with talent (and can you prove it by providing quotes from satisfied readers/reviewers?); (b) who can sustain their writing beyond one book (and thus will be ongoing earners and repay the initial investment of time they make in you); (c) who are topical (all agents and publishers claim to be looking for the 'next big thing'); (d) who are different, or have a new slant to bring to an existing strand of publishing; and (d) who are *promotable* (a key publishing term meaning interesting or memorable to the media). How you come over (or are likely to come over) in the press/on the air will be a key factor in deciding whether or not to take you on.

The money side of things needs a little more consideration. Whilst most agents are book lovers, and love what they do, their service is not there as a wider service to literature in general but to make a profit. As well as a talent for writing they are looking for financial remuneration. So whilst an agent may be willing to help you shape your novel, provide advice on your style, advise you on how to prepare for an interview, they will be doing these things in the hope that you will reward them with books that sell rather than out of pure altruism.

Whatever advance the author gets, their agent usually gets 15% of it, so it is in the agent's interest to sell the book for the highest amount of money, or to the publishing house that is most likely to make a long-term success of the writer's career. This may lead the cynical to conclude that agents are more likely to be interested in media-friendly (or just media-based) authors than pure literary genius, but it is through success of key names that they are able to take a punt on new writers. An agency that confined itself to literary fiction alone, and ignored the popular market completely, would probably not last long.

Top tips for securing the attention of an agent

1. Do your research. Consult *Literary agents UK and Ireland* starting on page 473 of this *Yearbook* and look at what kind of writers each agent represents and note their specialities. If they say they do not take science fiction, do not assume you are helpfully extending their range by offering it. Send an email outlining what you have in mind and ask who is the right person within their firm to send it to. Don't assume that if the agency is called 'Snodgrass and Wilkins' you must talk only to one of the two key names. The chances are their books will be full already – or they may be long deceased. A more junior member of staff may be hungrier for new authors, and don't forget that their judgement will be backed – because they are a staff member and presumably have been taken on by the partners to widen the range of those they represent. And one day they too may be on the letterhead.

2. Don't necessarily be put off by the request for no unsolicited submissions. If they say 'No unsolicited submissions' you may decide to interpret this as 'No ill-considered submissions'. All agents need some new writers; you have to make the case for their next choice being you.

3. Send in what they ask for, not more or less. Submit your material in exactly the format they ask for – three chapters and a synopsis means just that, it is not code for 'anything over three chapters' or 'as near as you can get to three chapters'. Make the three chapters sequential, not chosen at random.

4. Ensure the book has a really good title. It's tempting to think that writing the book is the really important thing and that the title can grow out of the writing later. Wrong. The title is hugely important. It should catch the agent's attention and stick in the memory. Think how the same thing works for you in bookshops. I recently bought a copy of *Fifty is Not a Four-letter Word* by Linda Kelsey simply because I liked the title. I was looking for a present for a friend and I thought her fancy would be tickled by it too.

Heather Holden-Brown of the hhb agency says: 'The title matters hugely. I want something that excites me, and that will draw a similarly instant reaction from any publisher I mention it to. So go for something that is topical, intriguing or witty and to the point.'

5. Write a synopsis. This should be an outline of what kind of book you are writing, it is not your chance to give a detailed listing of what is in each chapter. It should start by ensuring the agent can grasp in their mind very precisely what kind of writer is on offer – this is important because it may enable them to think what kind of publisher it would appeal to.

If you can, say which section of the bookshop your title would be stocked in (don't just say the table at the front!) and list writers whose books are already in this category. Booksellers are very loathed to stock titles they don't know where to put, and agents may be unwilling to back a title that has no natural home. A friend of a friend wanted to write a book on the menopause and to call it *How Long Before I Can Hang-glide?*. A bookseller friend persuaded her that whilst this would make a very good subtitle, people looking for books on the subject would be in danger of not finding it – unless they were by chance looking in the sports section.

6. Write a book blurb for your work. Think what goes on the back of most books and how important it is in attracting attention to the title inside. A book blurb should be a fair representation of the style of the book, should tempt the reader to want to know more *now*, and should not give away the ending. Writing a book blurb is harder than you think, and is an excellent way of getting yourself noticed by an agent.

7. Send an interesting CV on yourself. This is not the time to rehash your formal one; a literary agent is not interested in how you did at 'O'/GCSE or 'A' level. Rather, what they do need to know is what you have done that makes you an interesting proposition to a publishing house. Remember agents are interested in how 'promotable' any potential new author is.

This could be your job, your family commitments or your past experience. Don't assume that what you consider boring or mundane will be viewed in the same light by those you are approaching. A background working in the City is not the normal path to becoming a novelist and so may be well received by an agent. Similarly your domestic arrangements may be equally ordinary to you but interesting when combined with the fact that you have written a book.

Take an imaginative approach to your past and think creatively. A friend of mine once used a revolving door in an American hotel at the same time as a well-known actor and would proudly boast that she had 'been around in New York with Cary Grant.' I have four children and have always moved house mid-pregnancy, hence the scan and the birth never took place in the same hospital. Whereas this is entirely a function of my husband's peripatetic job, my publishers got quite excited when I told them. What have you done that can be made to sound interesting?

8. Do you have anyone else who can say what you write is good? This does not have to be a celebrity (although they are always useful) but what about other readers, writers and friends with relevant job titles? It's not hard to get testimonials for your work – many people like to be asked; some will oblige out of pure friendship, others for the publicity it may bring them.

9. Can you prove that there is a market for what you write? When an agent approaches a publisher to enthuse about a new author they will have to justify the claims they make on your behalf, and the newer the feel of what you want to write, the harder they will have to work. It's not good enough to say 'everyone will want to read' this new title. So, find out the viewing figures for programmes that relate to the book you want to write, or the sales of magazines that have a strong overlap with your material. Think laterally. For example, I co-wrote a recent book on raising teenagers, and there is very little published in this market. It seemed to me that my subject was really modern morality; how to provide guidance in a fast-changing world. To prove there is a market I took as examples the healthy book sales of popular philosophy titles by A.C. Grayling and the number of people who have taken an Alpha course (over 2 million in the UK and 13 million worldwide so far). The agent I approached told me this widening of the issue really made a difference to how he viewed my proposal.

10. Write a really good letter to accompany the package you send to an agent. This may take you a long time but a good letter of introduction is well worth the trouble. It should outline all of the above: what kind of book you want to publish, how far down the road you have got, what is noteworthy about you as a person, who else thinks so.

Some agents acknowledge what they receive, others do not. You could ask them to email receipt, or enclose a stamped addressed postcard with a reminder to let you know they have received it. This is a further opportunity to remind them you are a human being, so try a witty postcard or add a caption to an image to make the point that you are dying to hear from them! For inspiration, look at the card selection in a local art gallery and think which picture sums up your mood as you wait for them to respond.

Finally, do remember that agents are individuals, and perhaps more individualistic than the key protagonists in many other professions. Just as many are instantly recognisable, they also have very individual taste. It follows that what does not appeal to one may well appeal to another. So if your first choice does not immediately sign you up, there may be others who think you are the next best thing since sliced bread! But they will only find out about you if you have the gumption to keep going. In the long run, getting an agent on your side is invariably worth the effort.

Carole Blake of Blake Friedmann says: 'We receive at least 20 unsolicited manuscripts a day, our books are full and to be honest we are looking for reasons to say no – but I still get such excitement from a really new voice writing something that grabs my attention. I have known the world stand still as I ignore the rest of the post and just read on until I have finished. When that happens it's really special – and I will fight to get that author published. Sometimes it takes years, but if I believe in an author I will keep going.'

Alison Baverstock is a former publisher who has written 18 books. *Marketing Your Book: An Author's Guide* (A&C Black, 2nd edn 2008) gives writers guidance on how to present their work to agents, publishers and readers. *Is There a Book in You?* (A&C Black 2006) outlines the resources needed by writers and offers advice on how to achieve publication. She teaches marketing – to authors, publishers and others – at Kingston University and is represented by Jenny Brown of Jenny Brown Associates. Her website is www.alisonbaverstock.com.

Notes from a literary scout

Suzy Lucas gives an insight into the role of the literary scout.

If you ask those in the know how long literary scouts have been around, the answer is 'forever'. Yet not many people outside the industry know what the scouts do, despite them performing an essential role in international publishing – a small business that still thrives on spreading the word about interesting books.

I worked with one of the best scouts in the business, Anne-Louise Fisher, who comes in a long line of formidable women (and they are almost all women) who have shaped the business of scouting and played a crucial role in the development of the lists of the publishers they work with.

Of course, the business has changed significantly over the years. In pre-war and postwar publishing, long before faxes and email and the ease of worldwide travel, publishers relied heavily on their scouts for news of books from abroad. Around this time in London for instance, East End born scout Gwenda David and Swedish-born Lena Wickman both functioned in salon-like atmospheres, hosting glittering dinner parties, nurturing friendships with some of the great writers of the time and bringing those writers to the publishers that they worked for. Weekly letters from London would be despatched, carrying news of books read and general industry gossip.

Now with information so readily available, either through the use of email or the internet, you might think that the scouts are becoming obsolete. But, no, they are as valuable as ever simply because of the increased competition in an IT-dominant culture. What hasn't changed is the value of their speed and editorial input – these are the two vital things that a publisher will look for in a scout.

Publishers worldwide employ literary scouts in other markets to help them find the best books for their lists in foreign territories. The scout's primary aim is to determine whether a book might be successful in other markets and to help publishers in those markets to acquire the rights to promising titles. So a British scout will be working for a select list of clients in Europe, the USA, Canada, Asia and the rest of the world to find forthcomingUK titles for their lists: in effect, to act as the eyes and ears of foreign publishers who want completely current news about UK publishing.

There are currently around 20 scouts operating in London. Some have two or three clients, others up to 12 or more. Most of them will be operating in the critical European territories of Germany and Italy – critical simply because they are the biggest buyers of English language books. America is of course an important market too, though few UK scouts work there. This is perhaps because of the readiness these days of US publishers to keep in touch with the UK publishers – travelling here themselves to explore a market that is relatively small compared to their own.

What can a scout do for the writer?

As a rule neither you, the writer, nor your book will cross paths with a scout until you are well on your way to finding a publisher – this is simply because without a UK sale, or the strong prospect of one, your book will not be of interest to foreign publishers who will rely on the success of the original edition before publishing in their home territory.

In this respect the word 'scout' is rather misleading. I often found over the years that when I met people and told them I was a scout, an eager look would enter their eyes and they would ask if I wouldn't mind having a quick peek at their novel. This isn't surprising, since outside the world of good deeds and woodcraft 'scout' conjures up images of talentspotters plucking people out of obscurity and putting them on the path to stardom. This may be so for footballers and models, but in publishing a scout is really only looking out for authors who have already been discovered by agents or publishers.

So, once books are well and truly in the system, it's a scout's job to see material or at least know about its existence and prospects as quickly as possible. Scouts are constantly talking to agents and publishers about what new books there are floating around, and their ears will prick up at the sound of any first offers coming in from publishers for new material out on offer; even if money has not been mentioned, but an editor or agent is particularly excited about something, that's when the scout becomes interested too.

The scout will quickly pass this information on to those clients that she thinks will be interested, usually in the shape of a weekly report. If a publisher in the USA or Italy or Germany is keen, they register their interest with the rightsholder – be it the agent or the publisher – thereby making sure that they are in the front of the queue when that book is offered for sale abroad. It is the job of the scout to ensure that the client gets the material as early as possible: what you don't want is another publisher in your client's territory receiving that material first and making a pre-emptive offer – indeed, you want to be the one pre-empting.

At this stage in the process the material in question can sometimes be quite raw. For non-fiction, decisions regarding whether to publish a book are usually made on the strength of a proposal alone. First novels and new novels by published authors are frequently sold on a partial script or on a draft which is still in need of work. At such an early stage agents and publishers can be protective of an author's work, feeling, understandably, that there is no sense in firing off material around the world before the book has reached its full potential. So trust between the rightsholder and the scout is essential – they should be working hand-in-hand and always with the shared interest of the author at heart.

Email has meant that it has become much harder to control material. Gone are the days when a scout would have to think carefully before standing over a photocopier for several hours copying that hot, new, usually epic novel for 12 different foreign clients; now it can be done at the touch of a button. But good scouts will never just broadcast material willynilly to their clients. They will prefer to read the material and make a qualitative decision about whether each client would benefit from reading it: perhaps it would be better to wait for an edited copy; perhaps there is a certain foreign editor who will definitely see the book's potential, or indeed love it as it stands; perhaps it's a brilliant book but too distinctively British to be suitable for any foreign clients at all. It should be said that a large proportion of scouts' time is spent helping clients to filter out books that will simply not work in their lists. But if a client does express interest in a book, the scout's primary concern is then to get a copy into the hands of the publisher client, ideally via the rightsholder.

No one should underestimate the positive effect of scouts and their clients showing interest in a book early on. If an author is in the lucky position of having their book at auction, with one or several UK publishers offering, news of foreign interest may make the British publishers just that little bit more eager and more confident that they want the book for themselves. And if the author's agent or publisher can catch the wave of the UK interest, then they are more likely to get deals abroad: it's a truth in every territory that nothing beats the thrill of scooping up that latest book early on in its life.

So including the scouts in the process can certainly pay off, often throughout a book's journey from early manuscript to its appearance in the bookshops. A good example of this at Anne-Louise Fisher Associates was Diane Setterfield's first novel *The Thirteenth Tale.* Anne-Louise Fisher received material just as the UK editors were beginning to show an interest, read it quickly and sent it immediately to her Canadian client, Doubleday, who loved it and offered within 48 hours, before the UK sale was even finalised. The manuscript was then requested by Anne-Louise Fisher's clients in France, Germany, Italy, Sweden, Norway, Holland and by Heyday Films in London. All made offers and acquired rights over the next few weeks.

The book has been a huge success in the USA and all its publishers have benefited from a successful campaign that shared marketing material and as a result lifted the book's potential in all territories. Of course, it doesn't always work like this, and in fact it is rare for one agency to have such a clean sweep amongst its clients, not least because it's rare that all their clients are excited by the same book. What's more, it is unusual for one book to sell well in every territory in which it has been bought, though there are exceptions to the rule – Dan Brown's *The Da Vinci Code* being the most obvious.

Every territory is different

The example of Diane Setterfield's novel raises important issues surrounding the different needs of individual territories. It's not insignificant that Doubleday Canada made an offer for the book before the UK deal was finalised, since UK publishers frequently acquire UK and Commonwealth rights that include Canada, thereby taking it out of circulation for dedicated Canadian publishers like Doubleday. (Be aware that there are huge advantages to having a book published properly in Canada rather than just being distributed there by a UK publisher.)

This brings us to the thorny issue of royalties on export editions, a subject that authors should be keenly aware of. UK publishers print export editions for Canada, Australia and New Zealand. They also produce 'airside editions', which are cheaper paperback copies that are sold at airports and into Europe and for which the author gets a lower royalty (percentage of cover price) than they would on the local editions. This is a particular problem in Holland and Germany thanks to the number of English language readers who are buying early UK export editions instead of waiting for the Dutch or German versions to appear. The loss to the author in royalties is significant. Of course the damage to the foreign publishers which have bought rights to the book is huge too, and this is where the scouts play a vital role in helping their Dutch and German clients to get material quickly and their editions into the shops before being flooded out by the export editions.

The scout's year

There are two critical events in the scout's publishing diary: the London Book Fair in April and the Frankfurt Book Fair in October. At these two fairs, publishers and agents from around the world meet with editors to discuss what new books they are either about to publish or have just published. Rights to these books may be bought during the fair, but perhaps more frequently after it, once editors have returned home and read material. But it is the scouts' job to be one step ahead of the game and to help their clients to snap up the most important new UK titles, ideally even before the fair has begun.

Rightsholders will often hold back material that they think might be particularly successful in other territories to the weeks just before the fairs begin. A publisher or agent may ask an author to deliver their book, or at least some of it, in time for these fairs. There is no doubt that the spirit of 'all the fun of the fair' can fan vigorously even the smallest spark of enthusiasm; this is a time when the scouts are asked on an hourly basis what the 'hot book' of the fair is. Memorably, in Frankfurt 1997 the Wylie Agency took just 80 pages of Zadie Smith's first novel *White Teeth* to the fair and I remember vividly the moment we got our hands on those pages, the excitement of reading a clear new talent and the subsequent thrill of helping to secure rights for our Italian publisher Mondadori before the UK sale had been concluded.

It can be tempting to talk about the sensational moments in the business of scouting, but it tends only rarely to be about 'hot books'. Most scouts have an eclectic mix of clients ranging from the commercial to the literary, each having big lists to fill with a multitude of different titles in a variety of markets that all have their own peculiarities.

So when your book is out there and you hear the words 'the scouts are interested' fingers crossed that it just may result in helping towards a few foreign deals for you.

Suzy Lucas has worked in publishing since she joined Bloomsbury Publishing in 1987. She worked as a literary scout with Anne-Louise Fisher from 1997 to 2005 and is now Literary Consultant to the UK Film Council's Film Fund.

Literary agents UK and Ireland

The *Writers' & Artists' Yearbook*, along with the Association of Authors Agents and the Society of Authors, takes a dim view of any literary agent who asks potential clients for a fee prior to a manuscript being placed with a publisher. We advise you to treat any such request with caution and to let us know if that agent appears in the listings below. However, agents may charge additional costs later in the process but these should only arise once a book has been accepted by a publisher and the author is earning an income. We urge authors to make the distinction between upfront and additional charges.

*Full member of the Association of Authors' Agents

A & B Personal Management Ltd

Suite 330, Linen Hall, 162-168 Regent Street, London W1B 5TD
tel 020-7434 4262 *fax* 020-7038 3699
email billellis@aandb.co.uk
Directors RW Ellis, R Ellis

Full-length MSS. Scripts for TV, theatre, cinema; also novels, fiction and non-fiction (home 12.5%, overseas 15%), performance rights (12.5%). No unsolicited material: write first before submitting synopsis. No reading fee for synopsis, plays or screenplays, but fee charged for full-length MSS. Return postage required. Founded 1982.

Sheila Ableman Literary Agency*

48–56 Bayham Place, London NW1 0EU
tel 020-7388 7222
email sheila@sheilaableman.co.uk
website www.sheilaableman.com
Contact Sheila Ableman

Non-fiction including history, science, cookery, biography, autobiography (home 15%, USA/translation 20%). Specialises in TV tie-ins and celebrity ghostwriting. No poetry, children's, gardening or sport. Unsolicited MSS welcome. Approach in writing with publishing history, CV, synopsis, 3 chapters and sae for return. No reading fee. Founded 1999.

The Agency (London) Ltd*

24 Pottery Lane, London W11 4LZ
tel 020-7727 1346 *fax* 020-7727 9037
email info@theagency.co.uk
website www.theagency.co.uk

Represents writers for films, TV, radio and theatre (10%). Adult novels represented only for existing clients. For Film/TV/Theatre Executives please contact info@theagency.co.uk separately.

Children's Books Executive Hilary Delamere. Represents children's book writers and illustrators (15% unless sub agents are employed for overseas). Works in conjunction with agents in the USA and overseas. Strictly no unsolicited material. Founded 1995.

Aitken Alexander Associates Ltd*

18–21 Cavaye Place, London SW10 9PT
tel 020-7373 8672 *fax* 020-7373 6002
email reception@aitkenalexander.co.uk
website www.aitkenalexander.co.uk
Contacts Gillon Aitken, Clare Alexander, Andrew Kidd, Sally Riley (Directors), Matthew Hamilton, Ayesha Karim, Charlotte Robertson, Lesley Thorne (also handles film/TV), *Associated Agents* Anthony Sheil, Mary Pachnos, Lucy Luck

Fiction and non-fiction (home 15%, USA 20%, translation 20%, film/TV 10%). No plays or scripts. Send preliminary letter with half-page synopsis and first 30pp of sample material and adequate return postage in first instance. No reading fee.

Clients include Clare Allan, Lisa Appignanesi, Pat Barker, Jung Chang, Clare Clark, John Cornwell, Sarah Dunant, Susan Elderkin, Diana Evans, Roopa Farooki, Sebastian Faulks, Helen Fielding, Germaine Greer, Mark Haddon, Mohammed Hanif, Susan Howatch, Liz Jensen, John Keegan, Holly McQueen, Pankaj Mishra, Caroline Moorehead, Jonathan Raban, Anna Ralph, Louise Rennison, Michèle Roberts, Jennie Rooney, James Scudamore, Nicholas Shakespeare, Gillian Slovo, Rory Stewart, Nick Stone, Colin Thubron, Robert Twigger, Amanda Vickery, Penny Vincenzi, Willy Vlautin, AN Wilson, Andrew Wilson, Robert Wilson. UK only – Harper Lee, J.D. Salinger.

Estates – John Betjeman, Bruce Chatwin, Paul Gallico, Ian Hamilton, Ngaio Marsh, Shiva Naipaul, Mary Norton, Slavomir Rawicz. Founded 1977.

Jacintha Alexander Associates – see LAW (Lucas Alexander Whitley Ltd)

The Ampersand Agency Ltd*

Ryman's Cottages, Little Tew, Oxon OX7 4JJ
tel (01608) 683677 *fax* (01608) 683449
email info@theampersandagency.co.uk
website www.theampersandagency.co.uk
Contact Peter Buckman, Anne-Marie Doulton

Literary and commercial fiction and non-fiction (home 15%, USA 15–20%, translation 20%). No reading fee. Will suggest revision.

Clients include the Georgette Heyer Estate, Helen Black, S.J. Bolton, Druin Burch, Vanessa Curtis, Will Davis, Cora Harrison, Ivo Stourton, Vikas Swarup, Michael Walters. Founded 2003.

Darley Anderson Literary, TV and Film Agency*

Estelle House, 11 Eustace Road, London SW6 1JB
tel 020-7386 2674 *fax* 020-7386 5571
email enquiries@darleyanderson.com
website www.darleyanderson.com, www.darleyandersonchildrens.com
Contacts Darley Anderson (thrillers, women's fiction), Zoe King (non-fiction), Camilla Bolton (crime & mystery), Becky Stradwick (children's), Madeleine Buston (Head of Rights & women's fiction; children's), Kasia Behnke (Rights Manager), Rosanna Bellingham (financial controller)

Commercial fiction and non-fiction; children's fiction, non-fiction and picture books (home 15%, USA/translation 20%, film/TV/radio 20%). No poetry or academic books. Send preliminary letter, synopsis and first 3 chapters. Return postage/sae essential for reply. *Overseas associates* APA Talent & Literary Agency (LA/Hollywood) and leading foreign agents worldwide.

Special interests (fiction): all types of thrillers, crime/mystery and young male fiction. All types of American and Irish novels. All types of women's fiction. Sagas, chick lit, romantic comedy; contemporary and literary. Also comic fiction. Children's fiction, all ages, and picture books.

Special interests (non-fiction): celebrity autobiographies, biographies, sports books, 'true-life' women in jeopardy, revelatory history and science, popular psychology, self improvement, diet, beauty, health, fashion, animals, humour/cartoon, cookery, gardening, inspirational, religious.

Clients include Anne Baker, Alex Barclay, Constance Briscoe, Jenna Burtenshaw, Paul Carson, Chris Carter, Cathy Cassidy, Lee Child, Martina Cole, John Connolly, Jane Costello, Margaret Dickinson, Clare Dowling, Phil Earle, Tana French, Helen Grant, Pea Horsley, Tara Hyland, Carolyn Jess-Cooke, Milly Johnson, Patrick Lennon, Rani Manicka, Chris Mooney, Annie Murray, Lesley Pearse, Lynda Page, Adrian Plass, Carmen Reid, Rebecca Shaw, Peter Sheridan, Graeme Sims, Sean Slater, Cally Taylor, Elizabeth Waite, Tim Weaver, Ahmet Zappa.

Anubis Literary Agency

7 Birdhaven Close, Lighthorne, Warwick CV35 0BE
tel (01926) 642588 *fax* (01926) 642588
Contacts Steve Calcutt

Genre fiction: science fiction, fantasy and horror (home 15%, USA/translation 20%). No other material considered. Send 50pp with a one-page synopsis (sae essential). No reading fee. No telephone calls. Works with the Marsh Agency Ltd on translation rights. Founded 1994.

Author Literary Agents

53 Talbot Road, London N6 4QX
tel 020-8341 0442 *mobile* (07767) 022659
Contact John Havergal

Novels, thrillers, faction, non-fiction, graphic novels, and children's books, and graphic and illustrated media edutainment concepts (home 15%, overseas/translations 20%, advertising/sales promotion one-third). Pitches to publishers and producers. Send first chapter, scene or section, and graphics samples (if any), plus a half to one page plot or topic outline together with sae. No reading fee. Founded 1997.

Diane Banks Associates Ltd*

email submissions@dianebanks.co.uk
website www.dianebanks.co.uk
Contact Diane Banks

Commercial fiction and non-fiction (home 15%, overseas 20%). Fiction: women's, crime, thrillers, Irish, literary fiction with a strong storyline, young adult. Non-fiction: memoir, real-life stories, celebrity, autobiography, biography, business, popular history, popular science, self-help, popular psychology, fashion, health & beauty. No poetry, children's, academic books, plays, scripts or short stories. Send brief CV, synopsis and sample chapters as Word attachments. Aim to give initial response within 2 weeks. No reading fee. Will suggest revision.

Authors include Sasha Wagstaff, Tara Moore, Polly Courtney, David Kessler, Alex Higgins, Andy Taylor (Duran Duran), Miss S, Shelina Janmohamed and Merisa Merico. Founded 2006.

The Bell Lomax Moreton Agency

James House, 1 Babmaes Street, London SW1Y 6HF
tel 020-7930 4447 *fax* 020-7925 0118
email info@bell-lomax.co.uk
website www.bell-lomax.co.uk
Executives Eddie Bell, Pat Lomax, Paul Moreton, June Bell

Quality fiction and non-fiction, biography, children's, business and sport. No unsolicited MSS without preliminary letter. No scripts. No reading fee. Founded 2000.

Michael Berenti Literary Management

46 Warwick Way, Suite 16, London SW1 1RY
email admin@michaelberenti.com
website www.michaelberenti.com
Director Michael Berenti

Fiction: literary, general commercial, thrillers, crime, suspense, drama, fantasy, sci-fi. Non-fiction: politics, social sciences, current affairs, history, military. Also film and TV scripts. Accepts published authors only but may provide evaluations for unpublished authors, for which a reading fee is charged. Founded 2008.

Blake Friedmann Literary, TV & Film Agency Ltd*

122 Arlington Road, London NW1 7HP
tel 020-7284 0408 *fax* 020-7284 0442

email firstname@blakefriedmann.co.uk
website www.blakefriedmann.co.uk
Directors Carole Blake, Julian Friedmann, Isobel Dixon *Agents* Oliver Munson, Conrad Williams, Katie Williams

Full-length MSS. Fiction: thrillers, women's novels and literary fiction; non-fiction: investigative books, biography, travel; no poetry or plays (home 15%, overseas 20%). Specialises in film and TV rights; place journalism and short stories for existing clients only. Represented worldwide in 26 markets. Preliminary letter, synopsis and first 2 chapters preferred. No reading fee.

Authors include Gilbert Adair, Sandy Balfour, Edward Carey, Elizabeth Chadwick, Anna Davis, Barbara Erskine, Garen Ewing, David Gillman, Ann Granger, David Hewson, Ken Hom, Peter James, Deon Meyer, Lawrence Norfolk, Gregory Norminton, Joseph O'Connor, Sheila O'Flanagan, Mario Reading, Michael Ridpath, Craig Russell, Julian Stockwin, Michael White. Founded 1977.

Luigi Bonomi Associates Ltd*

91 Great Russell Street, London WC1B 3PS
tel 020-7637 1234 *fax* 020-7637 2111
email info@bonomiassociates.co.uk
website www.bonomiassociates.co.uk
Directors Luigi Bonomi, Amanda Preston

Fiction and non-fiction (home 15%, overseas 20%). Fiction: commercial and literary fiction, thrillers, crime, young adult, women's fiction. Non-fiction: history, science, parenting, lifestyle, diet, health, TV tie-ins. No poetry. Keen to find new authors and help them develop their careers. Send preliminary letter, synopsis and first 3 chapters. No reading fee. Works with foreign agencies and has links with TV presenters' agencies and production companies.

Authors include Will Adams, James Barrington, James Becker, Sean Black, Jason Bradbury, Fern Britten, Toby Buckland, Kay Burley, Jo Carnegie, Gennaro Contaldo, Josephine Cox, David Gibbins, Richard Hammond, Jane Hill, Matt Hilton, John Humphrys, Graham Joyce, Simon Kernick, Colin McDowell, Gillian McKeith, James May, Mike Morley, Sue Palmer, Andrew Pepper, Melanie Phillips, Gervase Phinn, Esther Rantzen, John Rickards, Alice Roberts, Mike Rossiter, Catherine Samson, Karen Swan, Prof. Bryan Sykes, Alan Titchmarsh, Martin Townsend, Phil Vickery, Sir Terry Wogan. Founded 2005.

The Book Bureau Literary Agency

7 Duncairn Avenue, Bray, Co. Wicklow, Republic of Ireland
tel/fax (01) 276 4996
email thebookbureau@oceanfree.net
Managing Director Geraldine Nichol

Full-length MSS (home 10%, USA/translation 20%). Fiction preferred – thrillers, crime, Irish novels, literary fiction, women's commercial novels and general fiction. No horror, science fiction, children's or poetry. Strong editorial support. No reading fee. Preliminary letter, synopsis and 3 sample chapters (single line spacing). Return postage essential, IRCs from UK and abroad. Works with agents overseas.

BookBlast Ltd

PO Box 20184, London W10 5AU
tel 020-8968 3089
email gen@bookblast.com
website www.bookblast.com
Contact Address material to the Company

Full-length MSS (home 12%, overseas 20%), TV and radio (15%), film (20%). Fiction and non-fiction. Literary and general adult fiction and non-fiction (memoir, travel, popular culture, multicultural writing only). Radio, TV and film rights sold mainly in works by existing clients. No unsolicited approaches at present. No reading fee. Editorial advice given to own authors. Initiates in-house projects. Also offers translation consultancy and literary PR services. Currently not taking on new clients. Founded 1997.

Brandon & Associates Literary Agency

1 Wellis Gardens, St Leonard's on Sea, East Sussex TN38 0UX
tel (01424) 714150
email brandon-associates@hotmail.co.uk
website www.brandon-associates.co.uk
Directors Jenni Stace, John A. King

Commercial fiction and non-fiction, autobiography, real-life stories, history, military (home 15%, overseas 20%). No poetry, short stories or sci-fi. No reading fee. Will suggest revision. See website for full submission guidelines.

Alan Brodie Representation Ltd

Paddock Suite, The Courtyard, 55 Charterhouse Street, London EC1M 6HA
tel 020-7253 6226 *fax* 020-7183 7999
email info@alanbrodie.com
website www.alanbrodie.com
Contacts Lisa Foster, Sarah McNair, Harriet Pennington Legh

Specialises in stage plays, radio, TV, film (home 10%, overseas 15%); no prose fiction or general MSS. Represented in all major countries. No unsolicited scripts; recommendation from known professional required.

Jenny Brown Associates*

33 Argyle Place, Edinburgh EH9 1JT
tel 0131-229 5334
email info@jennybrownassociates.com
website www.jennybrownassociates.com
Contact Jenny Brown, Mark Stanton, Lucy Juckes, Allan Guthrie

Literary fiction, crime writing and writing for children; non-fiction: biography, history, sport, music popular culture (home 12.5%, overseas/translation 20%). No poetry, science fiction, fantasy or academic. No reading fee. See website for submission guidelines.

Clients include Lin Anderson, Alex Gray, Keith Gray, Doug Jackson, Sara Maitland, Richard Moore, Tom Pow, Suhayl Saadi, Natasha Solomons, Paul Torday, Esther Woolfson. Founded 2002.

Felicity Bryan Associates*

2A North Parade, Banbury Road, Oxford OX2 6LX
tel (01865) 513816 *fax* (01865) 310055
email agency@felicitybryan.com
website www.felicitybryan.com

Fiction and general non-fiction with emphasis on history, biography, science and current affairs (home 15%, overseas 20%). No scripts for TV, radio or theatre, no crafts, how-to, science fiction, light romance or poetry. No email submissions.

Clients include Carlos Acosta, Karen Armstrong, Simon Blackburn, Archie Brown, Sarah Chellis, Isla Dewar, John Dickie, Tim Harford, A.C. Grayling, Sadie Jones, Simon Lelic, Diarmaid MacCulloch, Martin Meredith, James Naughtie, John Julius Norwich, Gemma O'Connor, Iain Pears, Robin Pilcher, Rosamunde Pilcher, Matt Ridley, Miriam Stoppard, Roy Strong, Adrian Tinniswood and the Estates of Robertson Davies and Humphrey Carpenter.

Campbell Thomson & McLaughlin Ltd

50 Albemarle Street, London W1S 4BD
tel 020-7493 4361 *fax* 020-7495 8961
website www.ctmcl.co.uk
Contact Charlotte Bruton

Full-length book MSS (home 15%, overseas up to 20% including commission to foreign agent). No poetry, plays or TV/film scripts, short stories or children's books. Submissions via website. Preliminary enquiry essential. No unsolicited synopses or MSS. No reading fee. USA agents represented: Raines & Raines, the Fox Chase Agency, Inc. Translation rights handled by The Marsh Agency.

Capel & Land Ltd*

29 Wardour Street, London W1D 6PS
tel 020-7734 2414 *fax* 020-7734 8101
email rosie@capelland.co.uk
website www.capelland.com
Agents Georgina Capel (literary), Anita Land (TV)

Literary and commercial fiction, history, biography; film and TV (home/overseas 15%). No reading fee; will suggest revision.

Clients include Simon Barnes, Nicky Campbell, Flora Fraser, John Gimlette, Adrian Goldsworthy, K.M. Grant, Andrew Greig, Tristram Hunt, Tobias Jones, Leanda de Lisle, Colleen McCullough, Marion McGilvary, Jonathan Meades, Adam Nicolson, Jeremy Paxman, Andrew Roberts, Ian Sansom, Simon Sebag Montefiore, Diana Souhami, Stella Rimington, Louis Theroux, Giles Tremlett, Fay Weldon. Founded 1999.

CardenWright Literary Agency

27 Khyber Road, London SW11 2PZ
mobile 07789 000608
email gen@cardenwright.com
website www.cardenwright.com
Contact Genevieve Carden (Managing Partner, book/theatre agent), Philippe Carden (Partner, theatre agent), Rachel Wright (TV/film consultant)

Commercial and literary fiction and non-fiction (home 15%, overseas 20%), scripts for theatre (15%), film and TV (10%). No reading fee. Will suggest revision. Submit by email a covering letter, one-page synopsis and CV plus the first 50pp (novel), chapter outline and sample chapter (non-fiction), or play script.

Authors include Robert Dinsdale, R.J. Morgan, Nedim Gursel, Margaret Moore, Daniela Norris, Shireen Anabtawi, Samuel Kerr. Founded 2009.

Casarotto Ramsay & Associates Ltd

(formerly Margaret Ramsay Ltd and Casarotto Company Ltd)
Waverley House, 7–12 Noel Street,
London W1F 8GQ
tel 020-7287 4450 *fax* 020-7287 9128
email info@casarotto.co.uk
website www.casarotto.co.uk
Directors Jenne Casarotto, Giorgio Casarotto, Tom Erhardt, Mel Kenyon, Jodi Shields, Rachel Holroyd

MSS – theatre, films, TV, sound broadcasting only (10%). Works in conjunction with agents in USA and other foreign countries. Preliminary letter essential.

Authors include Alan Ayckbourn, J.G. Ballard, Edward Bond, Howard Brenton, Caryl Churchill, Tony Grisoni, Christopher Hampton, David Hare, Nick Hornby, Amy Jenkins, Laura Jones, Neil Jordan, Frank McGuiness, Phyllis Nagy, Neal Purvis, Mark Ravenhill, Willy Russell, Martin Sherman, Shawn Slovo, Robert Wade, Timberlake Wertenbaker, David Wood. For full client list see website. Founded 1989.

Celia Catchpole

56 Gilpin Avenue, London SW14 8QY
tel 0208 -8255 4835
email celiacatchpole@yahoo.co.uk, (submissions) catchpolesubmissions@googlemail.com
website www.celiacatchpole.co.uk
Director Celia Catchpole, *Agent* James Catchpole

Agent for authors and illustrators of children's books for all ages. Send complete stories if under 5000 words or the first three chapters if longer. Founded 1996.

Chambers Literary Agency

The Clovers, Dinedor Hill, Herefordshire HR2 6PD
tel (01432) 870584 *fax* (01432) 870639

email lychamberssolicitors@hotmail
Ceo Leina Yadev

General fiction, science fiction, fantasy, children's fiction (home 15%, overseas 20%). Send preliminary letter, synopsis of whole work, first 3 chapters and brief author biography. Return postage/sae essential for reply. Disk and email submissions cannot be considered. No reading fee. Will suggest revision. Works in conjunction with Associated Practice and is a branch of Chambers Solicitors. Founded 2006.

Chapman & Vincent*

7 Dilke Street, London SW3 4JE
tel/fax 020-7352 5582
email chapmanvincent@hotmail.co.uk
Directors Jennifer Chapman, Gilly Vincent

Handles illustrated non-fiction work only. Not actively seeking new clients but will consider original work – not travel, domestic tragedies or academic books. Submissions require synopsis, 2 sample chapters and sae. Also considers email enquiries without attachments. Do not telephone. No reading fee. Works with The Elaine Markson Agency. Commission: home 15%; US and Europe 20%.

Clients include George Carter, Leslie Geddes-Brown, Lucinda Lambton, Rowley Leigh and Eve Pollard. Founded 1992.

Mic Cheetham Associates Ltd

50 Albemarle Street, London W1S 4BD
tel 020-7495 2002 *fax* 020-7399 2801
website www.miccheetham.com
Director Mic Cheetham, *Contact* Mic Cheetham, Simon Kavanagh

General and literary fiction, science fiction, some non-fiction (home/overseas 15–20%); film, TV and radio rights (10–20%); will suggest revision. Works with the Marsh Agency Ltd for foreign rights. No unsolicited MSS. No reading fee. Founded 1994.

Judith Chilcote Agency*

8 Wentworth Mansions, Keats Grove, London NW3 2RL
tel 020-7794 3717
email judybks@aol.com
Director Judith Chilcote

Commercial fiction, non-fiction – memoirs, current affairs, TV tie-ins (home 15%, overseas 20–25%). No short stories, science fiction, poetry. Works in conjunction with overseas agents and New York affiliate. No reading fee but preliminary letter with 3 chapters only, CV and sae essential. Founded 1990.

Teresa Chris Literary Agency Ltd*

43 Musard Road, London W6 8NR
tel 020-7386 0633
Director Teresa Chris

All fiction, especially crime, women's commercial, general and literary fiction. No science fiction, horror, fantasy, short stories, poetry, academic books (home 10%, overseas 20%). No reading fee. Send introductory letter describing work, first 3 chapters and sae. Representation in all overseas territories. Founded 1988.

Mary Clemmey Literary Agency*

6 Dunollie Road, London NW5 2XP
tel 020-7267 1290 *fax* 020-7813 9757
email mcwords@googlemail.com

High-quality fiction and non-fiction with an international market (home 15%, overseas 20%, performance rights 15%). No children's books or science fiction. TV, film, radio and theatre scripts from existing clients only. Works in conjunction with US agent. No reading fee. No unsolicited MSS and no email submissions. Approach first by letter (including sae).

US clients include Frederick Hill, Bonnie Nadell Inc., Lynn C. Franklin Associates Ltd, The Miller Agency, Roslyn Targ, Weingel-Fidel Agency Inc. and Betsy Amster Literary Enterprises. Founded 1992.

Jonathan Clowes Ltd*

10 Iron Bridge House, Bridge Approach, London NW1 8BD
tel 020-7722 7674 *fax* 020-7722 7677
email admin@jonathanclowes.co.uk
website www.jonathanclowes.co.uk
Directors Jonathan Clowes, Ann Evans

Literary and commercial fiction and non-fiction, film, TV, theatre and radio (home 15%, overseas 20%). No reading fee. No unsolicited MSS. Email for general enquiries. Works in association with agents overseas. Founded 1960.

Clients include Sir Kingsley Amis Estate, Dr David Bellamy, Len Deighton, Elizabeth Jane Howard, Doris Lessing, David Nobbs, Gillian White.

Elspeth Cochrane Personal Management

16 Trinity Close, The Pavement, London SW4 0JD
tel 020-7622 3566
email elspethcochrane@talktalk.net
website www.elspethcochrane.com
Contacts Elspeth Cochrane, Tony Barlow

Fiction, non-fiction, biographies, screenplays and plays (12.5%). No children's fiction. No unsolicited MSS. Send preliminary letter, synopsis and sae in first instance. No reading fee.

Clients include Royce Ryton, Robert Tanitch. Founded 1960.

Rosica Colin Ltd

1 Clareville Grove Mews, London SW7 5AH
tel 020-7370 1080 *fax* 020-7244 6441
Directors Sylvie Marston, Joanna Marston

All full-length MSS (excluding science fiction and poetry); also theatre, film and sound broadcasting (home 10%, overseas 10–20%). No reading fee, but may take 3–4 months to consider full MSS. Send synopsis only in first instance, with letter outlining writing credits and whether MS has been previously submitted, plus return postage.

Authors include Richard Aldington, Simone de Beauvoir (in UK), Samuel Beckett (publication rights), Steven Berkoff, Alan Brownjohn, Sandy Brownjohn, Donald Campbell, Nick Dear, Neil Donnelly, J.T. Edson, Bernard Farrell, Rainer Werner Fassbinder (in UK), Jean Genet, Franz Xaver Kroetz, Don McCamphill, Heiner Müller (in UK), Graham Reid, Alan Sillitoe, Botho Strauss (in UK), Rina Vergano, Anthony Vivis, Wim Wenders (in UK). Founded 1949.

Conville & Walsh Ltd*

2 Ganton Street, London W1F 7QL
tel 020-7287 3030 *fax* 020-7287 4545
email (firstname)@convilleandwalsh.com
website www.convilleandwalsh.com
Directors Clare Conville, Patrick Walsh

All genres of fiction and non-fiction (generally upmarket to mass market), children's books. No poetry, screenplays or short stories. No reading fee.

Clients Literary and commercial fiction across a spectrum from the Booker Prize winner D.B.C. Pierre to recent shortlist nominees such as Sarah Hall, and the Orwell Prize winner Delia Jarrett-Macauley; and commercial novelists such as Isabel Wolff, Matt Dunn and Michael Cordy. Non-fiction authors include historians such as Tom Holland and Helen Castor, science writers such as Simon Singh and Richard Wiseman, the poet Ruth Padel and prize-winning journalists such as Misha Glenny, Clive Stafford Smith and Michael Bywater. Also handles the Estate of the artist Francis Bacon. Children's and young adult list ranges from John Burningham to Steve Voake and the Estate of Astrid Lindgren (Pippi Longstocking). Founded 2000.

Jane Conway-Gordon Ltd*

213 Westbourne Grove, London W11 2SE
tel 020-7792 3718
email jane@conway-gordon.co.uk

Full length MSS (home 15%, overseas 20%). No poetry, sci-fi or children's. Represented in all foreign countries. No reading fee but preliminary letter and return postage essential. Founded 1982.

Coombs Moylett Literary Agency

3 Askew Road Road, London W12 9AA
tel 020-8740 0454 *fax* 020-8354 3065
email lisamoylett@dial.pipex.com
Contacts Lisa Moylett, Victoria Ross

Commercial and literary fiction and non-fiction (home 15%, overseas 20%, film/TV 20%). Fiction: thrillers, crime/mystery; women's literary and contemporary. Non-fiction: biography; history and current affairs. Send synopsis, first 3 chapters and sae (essential). No disk or email submissions. No reading fee. Works with foreign agents.

Creative Authors Ltd

11A Woodlawn Street, Whitstable, Kent CT5 1HQ
tel (01227) 770947
email write@creativeauthors.co.uk
website www.creativeauthors.co.uk
Director Isabel Atherton

Fiction, women's fiction, literary fiction, non-fiction, humour, history, autobiography, memoir, Mind, Body & Spirit, health, cookery, arts and crafts, crime, children's fiction (home 15%, overseas 20%). Prefers email submissions.

Authors include Mark Beaumont, Lee Bullman, Janine Bullman, E.A. Hanks, Amanda Hallay, Sarah Herman, Adele Nozedar, Feargus O'Sullivan. Established 2008.

Rupert Crew Ltd*

1A King's Mews, London WC1N 2JA
tel 020-7242 8586 *fax* 020-7831 7914
email info@rupertcrew.co.uk
website www.rupertcrew.co.uk
Directors Doreen Montgomery, Caroline Montgomery

International representation, handling volume and subsidiary rights in fiction and non-fiction properties (home 15%, elsewhere 20%); no plays, screenplays, poetry, journalism, science fiction, horror, fantasy or short stories. No reading fee, but preliminary letter and return postage essential. Also acts independently as publishers' consultants. Founded 1927 by F. Rupert Crew.

Curtis Brown Group Ltd*

Haymarket House, 28–29 Haymarket, London SW1Y 4SP
tel 020-7393 4400 *fax* 020-7393 4401
email cb@curtisbrown.co.uk
website www.curtisbrown.co.uk
Ceo Jonathan Lloyd, *Director of Operations* Ben Hall, *Directors* Jacquie Drewe, Jonny Geller, Nick Marston, Sarah Spear
Books Jonny Geller (Managing Director, Books Division), Camilla Hornby, Jonathan Lloyd, Vivienne Schuster, Elizabeth Sheinkman, Karolina Sutton, Stephanie Thwaites, Gordon Wise, *Foreign Rights (books)* Kate Cooper (joint Head of Foreign Rights), Betsy Robbins (joint Head of Foreign Rights), Carol Jackson, Katie McGowan, Elizabeth Iveson, Daisy Meyrick
Film/TV/Theatre Nick Marston (Managing Director, Media Division), Amanda Davis, Tally Garner, Ben Hall, Joe Phillips
Actors Sarah Spear (Head of Acting Dept), Grace Clissold, Mary FitzGerald, Maxine Hoffman, Lucy Johnson, Sarah MacCormick, Kate Staddon, Olivia Woodward

Presenters Jacquie Drewe
Commercials and personal appearances Claire Cosgrove

Novels, general non-fiction, children's books and associated rights (including multimedia), as well as film, theatre, TV and radio scripts. Send outline for non-fiction and short synopsis for fiction with 2–3 sample chapters and autobiographical note. No reading fee. Return postage essential. No submissions by email. See website for further submission guidelines. Also represents playwrights, film and TV writers and directors, theatre directors and designers, TV and radio presenters and actors. Overseas associates in Australia and the US. Founded 1899.

Judy Daish Associates Ltd

2 St Charles Place, London W10 6EG
tel 020-8964 8811 *fax* 020-8964 8966
email judy@judydaish.com
website www.judydaish.com
Agents Judy Daish, Howard Gooding, Tracey Elliston

Theatre, film, TV, radio (rates by negotiation). No unsolicited MSS. No reading fee. Founded 1978.

Caroline Davidson Literary Agency*

5 Queen Anne's Gardens, London W4 1TU
tel 020-8995 5768 *fax* 020-8994 2770
email caroline@cdla.co.uk
website www.cdla.co.uk

Handles novels and non-fiction of high quality, including reference works (12.5%). Send preliminary letter with CV and detailed, well thought-out book proposal/synopsis and/or first 50pp of novel. No email submissions. Large sae with return postage essential. No reading fee. Quick response.

Authors include Peter Barham, Nigel Barlow, Andrew Beatty, Andrew Dalby, Emma Donoghue, Chris Greenhalgh, Tom Jaine, Huon Mallalieu, Simon Unwin, Caroline Williams. Founded 1988.

Merric Davidson Literary Agency – see MBA Literary Agents Ltd

Felix de Wolfe

Kingsway House, 103 Kingsway, London WC2B 6QX
tel 020-7242 5066 *fax* 020-7242 8119

Theatre, films, TV, sound broadcasting, fiction (home 10–15%, overseas 20%). No reading fee. Works in conjunction with many foreign agencies.

DGA Ltd

55 Monmouth Street, London WC2H 9DG
tel 020-7240 9992 *fax* 020-7395 6110
email assistant@davidgodwinassociates.co.uk
website www.davidgodwinassociates.co.uk
Directors David Godwin, Heather Godwin

Literary fiction and general non-fiction (home 15%, overseas 20%, film 15%). No reading fee; send sae for return of MSS. Founded 1995.

Dorian Literary Agency (DLA)*

Upper Thornehill, 27 Church Road, St Marychurch, Torquay, Devon TQ1 4QY
tel (01803) 312095
Contact Dorothy Lumley (proprietor)

General fiction, and specialising in popular fiction (home 12.5%, USA 15%, translation 20%). For adults: women's fiction, romance, historicals; crime and thrillers; science fiction, fantasy, dark fantasy and horror. Reading only very selectively. No short stories, young adult or children's fiction, non-fiction, comic material, poetry or drama. No reading fee. Contact initially by post with the first 3 chapters and brief outline plus return postage/sae. No telephone calls, faxes or emails.

Authors include Gillian Bradshaw, Kate Charles, Kate Hardy, Glenda Larke, Brian Lumley, Stephen Jones, Andy Remic, Rosemary Rowe, Lyndon Stacey, Julia Williams. Founded 1986.

Bryan Drew Ltd

Quadrant House, 80-82 Regent Street, London W1B 5AU
tel 020-7437 2293 *fax* 020-7437 0561
email bryan@bryandrewltd.com
website www.bryandrew.com
Literary Manager Bryan Drew

Scripts for TV, films and theatre (home 12.5%, overseas 15%). General fiction, thrillers, biographies. No reading fee. Enclose sae. Founded 1962.

Robert Dudley Agency

50 Rannoch Road, London W6 9SR
mobile (07879) 426574
email info@robertdudleyagency.co.uk
website www.robertdudleyagency.co.uk
Proprietor Robert Dudley

Fiction and non-fiction. Specialises in history, biography, sport, management, politics, military history, current affairs (home 15%, overseas 20%; film/TV/radio 20%). No reading fee. Will suggest revision. All material sent at owner's risk. No MSS returned without sae.

Authors include Steve Biko, Simon Caulkin, Chris Green, Terry Macalister, Mungo Melvin, Brian Holden Reid, Tim Phillips, Chris Sidwells, James Taylor, Rosy Thornton, Dan Wilson. Founded 2000.

Toby Eady Associates Ltd

3rd Floor, 9 Orme Court, London W2 4RL
tel 020-7792 0092 *fax* 020-7792 0879
email toby@tobyeady.demon.co.uk
website www.tobyeadyassociates.co.uk
Contacts Toby Eady, Jamie Coleman, Samar Hammam

Fiction and non-fiction (home 15%, overseas/ film/ TV 20%). Special interests: China, Middle East, Africa, India. No film/TV scripts or poetry. Approach by personal recommendation. *Overseas associates* La

Nouvelle Agence (France), Jan Michael (Holland), Joanne Wang (China), ICM (USA). Film & TV: ICM.

Submission details Send to Pamela Hunt (pamela@tobyeady.demon.co.uk)

Clients include Nada Awar Jarrar, Mark Burnell, John Carey, Bernard Cornwell, Gavin Elser, Fadia Faqir, Sophie Gee, Ching-He Huang, Susan Lewis, Diane Wei Liang, Julia Lovell, Francesca Marciano, Patrick Marnham, Richard Lloyd Parry, Deborah Scroggins, Samia Serageldin, Rachel Seiffert, John Stubbs, Robert Winder, Zhu Wen, Alison Wong, Fan Wu, Xinran Xue. Estates of Peter Cheyney, Ted Lewis, Mary Wesley. Founded 1968.

Eddison Pearson Ltd*

West Hill House, 6 Swains Lane, London N6 6QS
tel 020-7700 7763 *fax* 020-7700 7866
email info@eddisonpearson.com
website www.eddisonpearson.com
Contact Clare Pearson

Children's and young adult books, fiction and non-fiction, poetry (home 10%, overseas 15–20%). Small personally run agency. Enquiries and submissions by email only; please email for up-to-date submission guidelines by return. No reading fee. May suggest revision where appropriate.

Authors include Valerie Bloom, Sue Heap, Caroline Lawrence, Robert Muchamore.

Edwards Fuglewicz*

49 Great Ormond Street, London WC1N 3HZ
tel 020-7405 6725 *fax* 020-7405 6726
Partners Ros Edwards, Helenka Fuglewicz

Literary and commercial fiction (but no children's fiction, science fiction, horror or fantasy); non-fiction: biography, history, popular culture (home 15%, USA/translation 20%). No unsolicited MSS or email submissions. No reading fee. Founded 1996.

Faith Evans Associates*

27 Park Avenue North, London N8 7RU
tel 020-8340 9920
email faith@faith-evans.co.uk

Small agency (home 15%, overseas 20%). Co-agents in most countries. No phone calls or submissions.

Authors include Melissa Benn, Eleanor Bron, Midge Gillies, Ed Glinert, Vesna Goldsworthy, Cate Haste, Jim Kelly, Helena Kennedy, Tom Paulin, Sheila Rowbotham, Rebecca Stott, Harriet Walter, Elizabeth Wilson, and the estates of Madeleine Bourdouxhe and Lorna Sage. Founded 1987.

Janet Fillingham Associates

52 Lowther Road, London SW13 9NU
tel 020-8748 5594 *fax* 020-8748 7374
email info@jfillassoc.co.uk
website www.janetfillingham.com
Agents Janet Fillingham, Kate Weston

Film and TV only (home 15%, overseas 15–20%). Strictly no unsolicited MSS; professional recommendation required. Founded 1992.

Film Rights Ltd

Suite 306, Belsize Business Centre, 258 Belsize Road, London NW6 4BT
tel 020-7316 1837 *fax* 020-7624 3629
email information@filmrights.ltd.uk
website www.filmrights.ltd.uk
Directors Brendan Davis, Joan Potts

Theatre, films, TV and sound broadcasting (home 10%, overseas 15%). No reading fee. Represented in USA and abroad. Founded 1932.

Laurence Fitch Ltd

(incorporating The London Play Company 1922)
Suite 306, Belsize Business Centre, 258 Belsize Road, London NW6 4BT
tel 020-7316 1837 *fax* 020-7624 3629
email information@laurencefitch.com
website www.laurencefitch.com
Directors F.H.L. Fitch, Joan Potts, Brendan Davis

Commission: home 10%, overseas 15%.

Authors include Carlo Ardito, John Chapman, Peter Coke, Ray Cooney OBE, Dave Freeman, John Graham, Robin Hawdon, Jeremy Lloyd (plays) Dawn Lowe-Watson, Glyn Robbins, Edward Taylor and the Estate of the late Dodie Smith.

Font Literary Agency

Hollyville House, Hollybrook Road, Clontarf, Dublin 3, Republic of Ireland
tel 353 1 8532356
email info@fontlitagency.com
website www.fontlitagency.com
Agent Ita O'Driscoll

Fiction and non-fiction (home 15%, overseas 20%). No drama, sci-fi, erotic, technical, children's or poetry. No reading fee. Will suggest revision. Contact by email in first instance.

Authors include Amanda Brunker, Evelyn Cosgrave, Garbhan Downey, Paul Kilduff, Susanne O'Leary, Dearbhail McDonald, Orna Ross. Established 2003.

Jill Foster Ltd (JFL)

9 Barb Mews, Brook Green, London W6 7PA
tel 020-7602 1263 *fax* 020-7602 9336
email agents@jflagency.com
website www.jflagency.com
Agents Alison Finch, Simon Williamson, Dominic Lord, Gary Wild, Jill Foster

Theatre, films, TV and sound broadcasting (12.5%). Particularly interested in film and TV comedy and drama. No novels or short stories. No reading fee. Preliminary letter essential. No submissions by email. Do not send material in the first instance. Founded 1978.

Fox & Howard Literary Agency*

4 Bramerton Street, London SW3 5JX
tel 020-7352 8691 *fax* 020-7352 8691

Partners Chelsey Fox, Charlotte Howard

General non-fiction: biography, history and popular culture, reference, business, mind, body & spirit, health and personal development, popular psychology (home 15%, overseas 20%). No reading fee, but preliminary letter and synopsis with sae essential for response. Founded 1992.

Fraser Ross Associates

6 Wellington Place, Edinburgh EH6 7EQ
tel 0131-553 2759, 0131-657 4412
email lindsey.fraser@tiscali.co.uk, kjross@tiscali.co.uk
website www.fraserross.co.uk
Partners Lindsey Fraser, Kathryn Ross

Futerman, Rose & Associates*

91 St Leonards Road, London SW14 7BL
tel 020-8255 7755
email enquiries@futermanrose.co.uk
website www.futermanrose.co.uk
Contact Guy Rose

Fiction, biography, show business, current affairs, teen fiction and scripts for TV and film (15–20%). No children's, science fiction or fantasy. No unsolicited MSS. Send preliminary letter with brief résumé, synopsis, first 30pp and sae.

Clients include Larry Barker, Christian Piers Betley, David Bret, Tom Conti, Richard Digance, Iain Duncan Smith, Sir Martin Ewans, Susan George, Mandasve Heller, Paul Hendy, Keith R Lindsay, Eric MacInnes, Paul Marx, Vartan Melkonian, Max Morgan-Witts, Judge Chris Nicholson, Ciaran O'Keeffe, Antonia Owen, Liz Rettig, Peter Sallis, Paul Stinchcombe, Jim Sullivan, Gordon Thomas, Bill Tidy, Toyah Willcox, Simon Woodham, Allen Zeleski. Founded 1984.

Jüri Gabriel

35 Camberwell Grove, London SE5 8JA
tel 020-7703 6186

Quality fiction and non-fiction (i.e. anything that shows wit and intelligence); radio, TV and film, but selling these rights only in existing works by existing clients. Full-length MSS (home 10%, overseas 20%); performance rights (10%). Will suggest revision where appropriate. No short stories, articles, verse or books for children. No reading fee; return postage essential. Jüri Gabriel is the chairman of Dedalus (publishers).

Authors include Maurice Caldera, Diana Constance, Miriam Dunne, Matt Fox, Paul Genney, Pat Gray, Mikka Haugaard, Robert Irwin, Andrew Killeen, John Lucas, 'David Madsen', Richard Mankiewicz, David Miller, Andy Oakes, John Outram, Philip Roberts, Stefan Szymanski, Adisakdi Tantimedh, Jeremy Weingard, Dr Terence White.

Eric Glass Ltd

25 Ladbroke Crescent, London W11 1PS
tel 020-7229 9500 *fax* 020-7229 6220
email eglassltd@aol.com
Director Janet Glass

Full-length MSS only; also theatre, films, and TV. No unsolicited MSS. Founded 1932.

David Godwin Associates – see DGA Ltd

Graham Maw Christie

19 Thornhill Crescent, London N1 1BJ
tel 020-7737 4766
email enquiries@grahammawchristie.com
website www.grahammawchristie.com, twitter.com/gmclitagency
Contacts Jane Graham Maw, Jennifer Christie

General non-fiction: autobiography/memoir, business, web-to-book, humour and gift, food and drink, health, lifestyle, parenting, self-help/how to, popular science/history/culture/reference, TV tie-in. No fiction, children's or poetry. No reading fee. Will suggest revisions. Also represents ghostwriters. See website for submission guidelines.

Authors include Lindsey Agness, Sacha Baveystock, Dr Patrick Bowler, Jane Brocket, Sheila Chandra, Simon Dawson, Kasey Edwards, Michael Foley, Alan & Jackie Gear, Becky Jones, Mosey Jones, Dr Philippa Kaye, Dr Penny Kendall-Reed, Rosie Millard, Dr Stephen Reed, Clare Lewis, Gael Lindenfield, Nick Moran, James Ramsden, Corinne Sweet, Dale Vince, Richard Wilson. Founded 2005.

Annette Green Authors' Agency*

1 East Cliff Road, Tunbridge Wells, Kent TN4 9AD
tel (01892) 514275
email enquiries@annettegreenagency.co.uk
website www.annettegreenagency.co.uk
Partners Annette Green, David Smith

Full-length MSS (home 15%, overseas 20%). Literary and general fiction and non-fiction, popular culture, history, science, teenage fiction. No dramatic scripts, poetry, science fiction or fantasy. No reading fee. Preliminary letter, synopsis, sample chapter and sae essential.

Authors include Andrew Baker, Tim Bradford, Bill Broady, Meg Cabot, Simon Conway, Maria McCann, Adam MacQueen, Ian Marchant, Lembit Opik MP, Prof Charles Pasternak, Imogen Robertson, Kirsty Scott, Peter Shapiro, Bernadette Strachan, Elizabeth Woodcraft. Founded 1998.

Christine Green Authors' Agent*

6 Whitehorse Mews, Westminster Bridge Road, London SE1 7QD
tel 020-7401 8844 *fax* 020-7401 8860
website www.christinegreen.co.uk

Literary and commercial fiction, general non-fiction. Crime and historical fiction welcome. No science fiction, travelogues, self-help or children's fiction; no plays. Full-length MSS (home 10%, overseas 20%). Works in conjunction with agencies in Europe and

Scandinavia. No reading fee, but preliminary letter required. No submissions by email. Return postage essential; alternatively a request for an email response must be clearly stated on covering letter. See website for further guidelines. Founded 1984.

Louise Greenberg Books Ltd*

The End House, Church Crescent, London N3 1BG
tel 020-8349 1179 *fax* 020-8343 4559
email louisegreenberg@msn.com

Full-length MSS (home 15%, overseas 20–25%). Literary fiction and non-fiction. No reading fee. Return postage and sae essential. No telephone enquiries. Founded 1997.

Greene & Heaton Ltd*

37 Goldhawk Road, London W12 8QQ
tel 020-8749 0315 *fax* 020-8749 0318
email info@greeneheaton.co.uk
website www.greeneheaton.co.uk
Contacts Carol Heaton, Judith Murray, Antony Topping, Linda Davis (children's)

All types of fiction and non-fiction (home 15%, USA/translation 20%). No poetry or original scripts for theatre, film or TV. Send a covering letter, synopsis and first 3 chapters with sae and/or return postage. Email submissions considered at discretion. Overseas associates worldwide.

Clients include Poppy Adams, Bill Bryson, Jane Dalley, Suzannah Dunn, Marcus du Sautoy, Hugh Fearnley-Whittingstall, Michael Frayn, Andrea Gillies, Maeve Haran, P.D. James, William Leith, James McGee, Shona MacLean, Thomasina Miers, C.J. Sansom, William Shawcross, Sarah Waters, Jackie Wullschlager. *Children's authors* include Helen Craig, Josh Lacey, Lucy Christopher, Pat Walsh. Founded 1963.

The Greenhouse Literary Agency

Stanley House, St Chad's Place, London WC1X 9HH
tel 020-7841 3959 *fax* 020-7841 3940
email submissions@greenhouseliterary.com
website www.greenhouseliterary.com
Director Sarah Davies, *Agent* Julia Churchill

Children's fiction from age 5 through to teen/young adult (USA/UK 15%, elsewhere 25%). Represents both US and UK authors. No picture books or non-fiction. No reading fee. Will suggest revision. Queries by email only, see website for details.

Authors include Sarwat Chadda, Lindsey Leavitt, Jon Mayhew, Brenna Yovanoff. Founded 2008.

Gregory & Company Authors' Agents*

3 Barb Mews, London W6 7PA
tel 020-7610 4676 *fax* 020-7610 4686
email info@gregoryandcompany.co.uk (general enquiries), maryjones@gregoryandcompany.co.uk (submissions)
website www.gregoryandcompany.co.uk
Contacts Jane Gregory, Stephanie Glencross (editorial), Claire Morris and Jemma McDonagh (rights)

Fiction and general non-fiction (home 15%, USA/translation/radio/film/TV 20%). Special interests (fiction): literary, commercial, women's fiction, crime, suspense and thrillers. Particularly interested in books which will also sell to publishers abroad. No original plays, film or TV scripts (only published books are sold to film and TV), science fiction, fantasy, poetry, academic or children's books. No reading fee. Editorial advice given to own authors. No unsolicited MSS: send preliminary letter with CV, synopsis, first 10 pages and future writing plans plus return postage. Submissions can also be sent by email to maryjones@gregoryandcompany.co.uk. Due to volume not all email submissions will be replied to. Represented throughout Europe, Asia and USA. Founded 1987.

David Grossman Literary Agency Ltd

118B Holland Park Avenue, London W11 4UA
tel 020-7221 2770 *fax* 020-7221 1445

Full-length MSS (home 10–15%, overseas 20% including foreign agent's commission, performance rights 15%). Works in conjunction with agents in New York, Los Angeles, Europe, Japan. No reading fee but preliminary letter required. No submissions by fax or email. Founded 1976.

Gunn Media

50 Albemarle Street, London W1S 4BD
tel 020-7351 5141
email ali@gunnmedia.co.uk
Directors Ali Gunn (managing), Doug Kean, Georgie Bean

Commercial fiction and non-fiction including literary, thrillers and celebrity autobiographies (home 15%, overseas 20%).

Authors include Jenny Colgan, Brian Freeman, Carole Malone, Mil Millington, Carol Thatcher.

Marianne Gunn O'Connor Literary Agency

Morrison Chambers, Suite 17, 32 Nassau Street, Dublin 2, Republic of Ireland
email mgoclitagency@eircom.net
Contact Marianne Gunn O' Connor

Commercial and literary fiction, non-fiction, biography, children's fiction (home 15%, overseas 20%, film/TV 20%). No unsolicited MSS. Translation rights handled by Vicki Satlow Literary Agency, Milan.

Clients include Cecilia Ahern, Chris Binchy, Claudia Carroll, Brinda Charry, Julie Dam, Louise Douglas, Thrity Engineer, Helen Falconer, Carla Glynn, Noelle Harrison, John Lynch, Mike McCormack, Caroline McFarlane-Watts, Paddy McMahon, Peter Murphy, Anita Notaro, Morag Prunty, Gisele Scanlon (Goddess Guide). Founded 1996.

The Rod Hall Agency Ltd

Suite 5.4B, The Old Fire Station,
140 Tabernacle Street, London EC2A 4SD
tel 020-7300 7266 *fax* 020-7079 7988
email office@rodhallagency.com
website www.rodhallagency.com
Director Charlotte Knight, Martin Knight, *Contacts* Tanya Tillett, Emily Hayward

Specialises in writers for stage, screen and radio but also deals in TV and film rights in novels and non-fiction (home 10%, overseas 15%). No reading fee.

Clients include Simon Beaufoy, Jeremy Brock, Liz Lochhead, Tim Lott, Martin McDonagh, Simon Nye, Ol Parker, Lucy Prebble, Philip Ridley, Laura Wade. Founded 1997.

The Hanbury Agency*

28 Moreton Street, London SW1V 2PE
tel 020-7630 6768
email enquiries@hanburyagency.com
website www.hanburyagency.com

Fiction and non-fiction (home 15%, overseas 20%). See website for submission details.

Authors include George Alagiah, Simon Callow, Rebecca Farnworth, Jane Glover, Judith Lennox, Katie Price. Founded 1983.

Antony Harwood Ltd*

103 Walton Street, Oxford OX2 6EB
tel (01865) 559615 *fax* (01865) 310660
email mail@antonyharwood.com
website www.antonyharwood.com
Contacts Antony Harwood, James Macdonald Lockhart, Jo Williamson (children's)

General and genre fiction; general non-fiction (home 15%, overseas 20%). Will suggest revision. No reading fee.

Clients include Amanda Craig, Louise Doughty, Peter F. Hamilton, Alan Hollinghurst, A.L. Kennedy, Douglas Kennedy, Dorothy Koomson, Chris Manby, George Monbiot, Garth Nix, Tim Parks. Founded 2000.

A.M. Heath & Co. Ltd

6 Warwick Court, London WC1R 5DJ
tel 020-7242 2811 *fax* 020-7242 2711
website www.amheath.com
Contacts Bill Hamilton, Victoria Hobbs, Euan Thorneycroft

Full-length MSS. Literary and commercial fiction and non-fiction, children's (home 15%, USA/translation 20%), film/TV (20%). No science fiction, screenplays, poetry or short stories except for established clients. No reading fee. Agents in USA and all European countries and Japan.

Clients include Prof. Christopher Andrew, Nadeem Aslam, Anita Brookner, Prof. Kathleen Burk, Stevie Davies, John Dougherty, Geoff Dyer, R.J. Ellory, Katie Fforde, Graham Hancock, Tobias Hill, Conn Iggulden, Marina Lewycka, Lucy Mangan, Hilary Mantel, Maggie O'Farrell, Ben Richards, Barbara Trapido. Founded 1919.

hhb agency ltd*

6 Warwick Court, London WC1R 5DJ
tel 020-7405 5525
email heather@hhbagency.com, elly@hhbagency.com
website www.hhbagency.com
Contacts Heather Holden-Brown, Elly James

Non-fiction: journalism, history and politics, travel and adventure, contemporary autobiography and biography, books about words, popular culture, entertainment and TV, business, family memoir, food and cookery a speciality. 15%. No reading fee. Founded 2005.

David Higham Associates Ltd*

(incorporating Murray Pollinger)
5–8 Lower John Street, Golden Square, London W1F 9HA
tel 020-7434 5900 *fax* 020-7437 1072
email dha@davidhigham.co.uk
website www.davidhigham.co.uk
Managing Director Anthony Goff, *Books* Veronique Baxter, Georgia Glover, Anthony Goff, Andrew Gordon, Bruce Hunter, Lizzy Kremer, Caroline Walsh, *Foreign Rights* Ania Corless, Tine Nielsen, *Film/TV/Theatre* Nicky Lund, Georgina Ruffhead

Agents for the negotiation of all rights in fiction, general non-fiction, children's fiction and picture books, plays, film and TV scripts (home 15%, USA/translation 20%, scripts 10%). Represented in all foreign markets. See website for submissions policy. No reading fee. Founded 1935.

Vanessa Holt Ltd*

59 Crescent Road, Leigh-on-Sea, Essex SS9 2PF
tel/fax (01702) 473787

General fiction and non-fiction (home 15%, overseas 20%, TV/film/radio 15%). Works in conjunction with foreign agencies in all markets. No reading fee. No unsolicited MSS and submissions preferred by arrangement. No overseas submissions. Founded 1989.

Valerie Hoskins Associates Ltd

20 Charlotte Street, London W1T 2NA
tel 020-7637 4490 *fax* 020-7637 4493
email vha@vhassociates.co.uk
Proprietor Valerie Hoskins, *Agent* Rebecca Watson

Film, TV and radio; specialises in animation (home 12.5%, overseas max. 20%). No unsolicited MSS; preliminary letter essential. No reading fee, but sae essential. Works in conjunction with US agents.

Tanja Howarth Literary Agency*

19 New Row, London WC2N 4LA
tel 020-7240 5553

email tanja.howarth@btinternet.com

General fiction and non-fiction, thrillers, contemporary and historical novels (home 15%, USA/translation 20%). No unsolicited MSS, and no submissions by email. No reading fee. Specialists in handling German translation rights. Represented in the USA by various agents.

Clients include Frank Schätzing, Andrea Maria Schenkel, Patrick Süskind and the Estates of Joseph Roth and Heinrich Böll. Founded 1970.

IMG UK Ltd

McCormack House, Burlington Lane, London W4 2TH
tel 020-8233 5000 *fax* 020-8233 5268
Consultant Sarah Wooldridge

Celebrity books, sports-related books, non-fiction and how-to business books (home 15%, USA 20%, elsewhere 25%). No theatre, fiction, children's, academic or poetry. No emails. No reading fee.

Independent Talent Group Ltd

Oxford House, 76 Oxford Street, London W1D 1BS
tel 020-7636 6565 *fax* 020-7323 0101
email writers@icmlondon.co.uk
Directors Duncan Heath, Susan Rodgers, Lyndsey Posner, Sally Long-Innes, Paul Lyon-Maris, *Literary Agents* Susan Rodgers, Jessica Sykes, Catherine King, Greg Hunt, Hugo Young, Michael McCoy, Duncan Heath, Paul Lyon-Maris, Laura Rourke, Josh Varney

Specialises in scripts for film, theatre, TV, radio (home 10%, overseas 10%).

Intercontinental Literary Agency*

Centric House, 390–391 Strand, London WC2R 0LT
tel 020-7379 6611 *fax* 020-7240 4724
email ila@ila-agency.co.uk
website www.ila-agency.co.uk
Contacts Nicki Kennedy, Sam Edenborough, Mary Esdaile, Tessa Girvan, Katherine West, Jenny Robson

Represents translation rights only. Founded 1965.

Barrie James Literary Agency

(including New Authors Showcase)
Rivendell, Kingsgate Close, Torquay, Devon TQ2 8QA
tel (01803) 326617
email mail@newauthors.org.uk
website www.newauthors.org.uk
Contact Barrie James

Internet site for new writers and poets to display their work to publishers. No unsolicited MSS. First contact: send sae or email. Founded 1997.

Janklow & Nesbit (UK) Ltd*

33 Drayson Mews, London W8 4LY
tel 020-7376 2733 *fax* 020-7376 2915
email queries@janklow.co.uk
website www.janklowandnesbit.co.uk
Agents Tif Loehnis, Claire Paterson, Will Francis, *Translation rights* Rebecca Folland

Commercial and literary fiction and non-fiction. No poetry, plays, film/TV scripts. No reading fee. Send informative covering letter and return postage with full outline (non-fiction), synopsis and first 3 sample chapters (fiction). US rights handled by Janklow & Nesbit Associates in New York. Founded 2000.

Johnson & Alcock Ltd*

Clerkenwell House, 45–47 Clerkenwell Green, London EC1R 0HT
tel 020-7251 0125 *fax* 020-7251 2172
email info@johnsonandalcock.co.uk
website www.johnsonandalcock.co.uk
Contacts Michael Alcock, Andrew Hewson, Anna Power, Ed Wilson

All types of commercial and literary fiction, and general non-fiction (home 15%, USA/translation/film 20%). YA and children's fiction (ages 8+). No poetry, screenplays or board-/picture-books.

For fiction and non-fiction, send first 3 chapters (or 50pp), full synopsis and brief covering letter with details of writing experience. No email submissions. No reading fee but return postage essential. Founded 1956.

Robin Jones Literary Agency

6B Marmora Road, London SE22 0RX
tel 020-8693 6062
email robijones@gmail.com
Director Robin Jones

Fiction and non-fiction: literary and commercial (home 15%, overseas 20%). No reading fee. Founded 2007.

Tibor Jones & Associates

Unit 12B, Piano House, 9 Brighton Terrace, London SW9 8DJ
tel 020-7733 0555
email enquiries@tiborjones.com
website www.tiborjones.com
Director Kevin Conroy Scott

Literary fiction and non-fiction, music autobiographies and biographies. Send first 5pp, synopsis and covering letter via email.

Authors include V.W. Adams, Sulaiman Smy Addonia, Sarah Bilston, Brian Chikwava, Jason Cowley, Lewis Crofts, Peter Culshaw, Colin Grant, Matthew Green, Denise Meredith, Hisham Matar, Hans Ulrich Obrist, Kevin Cummins, Sophia Al-Maria, Tod Wodicka, Hala Jaber, Tali Sharot, Brian Schofield, Richard T. Kelly, Salena Godden, Oscar Guardiola-Rivera, Alice de Smith, Gary Barker. Founded 2007.

Jane Judd Literary Agency*

18 Belitha Villas, London N1 1PD
tel 020-7607 0273 *fax* 020-7607 0623

website www.janejudd.com

General non-fiction and fiction (home 10%, overseas 20%). Special interests: women's fiction, crime, thrillers, narrative non-fiction. No short stories, film/TV scripts, poetry or plays. No reading fee, but preliminary letter with synopsis, first chapter and sae essential. Works with agents in USA and most foreign countries. Founded 1986.

Michelle Kass Associates*

85 Charing Cross Road, London WC2H 0AA
tel 020-7439 1624 *fax* 020-7734 3394
Proprietor Michelle Kass

Full-length MSS. Literary fiction (home 10%, overseas 15–20%) and scripts for film and TV. Works with agents around the world. No reading fee. No email submissions. No unsolicited material, phone in first instance. Founded 1991.

Frances Kelly Agency*

111 Clifton Road, Kingston-upon-Thames, Surrey KT2 6PL
tel 020-8549 7830 *fax* 020-8547 0051

Full-length MSS. Non-fiction: general and academic, reference and professional books, all subjects (home 10%, overseas 20%, TV/radio 10%). No reading fee, but no unsolicited MSS; preliminary letter with synopsis, CV and return postage essential. Founded 1978.

Peter Knight Agency

20 Crescent Grove, London SW4 7AH
tel 020-7622 1467 *fax* 020-7622 1522
website www.knightfeatures.com
Director Peter Knight, *Associates* Gaby Martin, Andrew Knight, Samantha Ferris

Motor sports, cartoon books, business, history and factual and biographical material. No poetry, science fiction or cookery. No unsolicited MSS. Send letter accompanied by CV and sae with synopsis of proposed work. No email submissions. *Overseas associates* United Media (USA), Auspac Media (Australia), Puzzle Company (NZ).

Clients include Ralph Barker, David Bodycombe, Frank Dickens, John Dodd, Gray Jolliffe, Angus McGill, Barbara Minto, Lisa Wild. Founded 1985.

LAW (Lucas Alexander Whitley Ltd)*

14 Vernon Street, London W14 0RJ
tel 020-7471 7900 *fax* 020-7471 7910
website www.lawagency.co.uk
Contacts Adult: Mark Lucas, Julian Alexander, Araminta Whitley, Alice Saunders, Peta Nightingale, Ben Clarke, Lucy Foley, Harry Man; Children's: Philippa Milnes-Smith, Holly Vitow

Full-length commercial and literary fiction, non-fiction and children's books (home 15%, USA/translation 20%). No fantasy (except children's), plays, poetry or textbooks. Film and TV scripts handled for established clients only. Unsolicited MSS considered; send brief covering letter, short synopsis and 2 sample chapters. Sae essential. No emailed or disk submissions. Overseas associates worldwide. Founded 1996.

LBLA (Lorella Belli Literary Agency)*

54 Hartford House, 35 Tavistock Crescent, London W11 1AY
tel 020-7727 8547 *fax* (0870) 7874194
email info@lorellabelliagency.com
website www.lorellabelliagency.com
Proprietor Lorella Belli

Fiction and general non-fiction (home 15%, overseas/dramatic 20%). Particularly interested in first-time writers, journalists, international and multicultural writing and books on Italy. No children's, science fiction, fantasy, academic, poetry, original scripts. No reading fee. May suggest revision. Send an enquiry letter or email before submitting work. Do not send attachments by email unless asked; submissions should be sent in hard copy to the office address. Do not return materials unless the correct sae postage is provided. Enclose a stamped acknowledgement card with submission if receipt acknowledgment is required. Works with dramatic and overseas associates; represents American, Canadian and Australian agencies in the UK.

Authors include Sean Bidder, Susan Brackney, Zoë Brân, Gesine Bullock-Prado, Sally Corner, Emily Giffin, Linda Kavanagh, Ed Kritzler, William Little, Nisha Minhas, Alanna Mitchell, Rick Mofina, Sandro Monetti, Angela Murrills, Ingrid Newkirk, Annalisa Coppolaro-Nowell, Judy Nunn, Jennifer Ouellette, Robert J. Ray, Anneli Rufus, Grace Saunders, Dave Singleton, Rupert Steiner, Justine Trueman, Diana Winston, Carol Wright. Founded 2002.

Susanna Lea Associates Ltd

34 Lexington Street, London W1F 0LH
tel 020-7287 7757 *fax* 020-7287 7775
email kglencorse@susannalea.com
website www.susannalea.com
Directors Susanna Lea, Kerry Glencorse

General fiction and non-fiction with international appeal. No plays, screenplays or poetry. Send query letter, brief synopsis, the first 3 chapters and/or proposal via website. Established in Paris 2000; New York 2004; London 2008.

Barbara Levy Literary Agency*

64 Greenhill, Hampstead High Street, London NW3 5TZ
tel 020-7435 9046 *fax* 020-7431 2063
Director Barbara Levy, *Associate* John Selby (solicitor)

Full-length MSS. Fiction and general non-fiction (home 15%, overseas by arrangement). Film and TV rights for existing clients only. No reading fee, but preliminary letter with synopsis and sae essential.

Translation rights handled by the Buckman Agency; works in conjunction with US agents. Founded 1986.

Limelight Management*

33 Newman Street, London W1T 1PY
tel 020-7637 2529 *fax* 020-7637 2538
email limelight.management@virgin.net
website www.limelightmanagement.com
Contacts Fiona Lindsay, Mary Bekhait

Full-length and short MSS. Food, wine, health, crafts, gardening, interior design, literary fiction, biography, travel, history, women's fiction, crime, children's fiction, art, fashion, humour, business, politics (home 15%, overseas 20%), TV and radio rights (10–20%); will suggest revision where appropriate. No reading fee. Founded 1991.

Lindsay Literary Agency

East Worldham House, Alton, Hants GU34 3AT
tel (01420) 83143
email info@lindsayliteraryagency.co.uk
website www.lindsayliteraryagency.co.uk
Directors Becky Bagnell, Kate Holroyd Smith

Literary fiction, serious non-fiction, children's (10–15%). No reading fee. Will suggest revision. Founded 2005.

Authors include Mike Lancaster, Sue Lloyd-Roberts, Stella Wiseman.

Christopher Little Literary Agency*

10 Eel Brook Studios, 125 Moore Park Road, London SW6 4PS
tel 020-7736 4455 *fax* 020-7736 4490
email info@christopherlittle.net
website www.christopherlittle.net
Contact Christopher Little

Commercial and literary full-length fiction and non-fiction (home 15%; USA, Canada, translation, audio, motion picture 20%). No poetry, plays, science fiction, fantasy, textbooks, illustrated children's or short stories. Film scripts for established clients only. No reading fee. First contact – send detailed preliminary letter in the first instance with synopsis, first 2–3 chapters and sae. Founded 1979.

Authors include Steve Barlow and Steve Skidmore, Paul Bajoria, Janet Gleeson, Gorillaz, Carol Hughes, General Mike Jackson (Sir), Alastair MacNeil, Robert Mawson, Haydn Middleton, Shiromi Pinto, A.J. Quinnell, Robert Radcliffe, J.K. Rowling, Darren Shan, Wladyslaw Szpilman, Shane Ward, John Watson, Angela Woolfe, Anne Zouroudi.

London Independent Books

26 Chalcot Crescent, London NW1 8YD
tel 020-7706 0486 *fax* 020-7724 3122
Proprietor Carolyn Whitaker

Specialises in commercial, fantasy and teenage fiction, travel. Full-length MSS (home 15%, overseas 20%). Will suggest revision of promising MSS. No reading fee.

Authors include Alex Bell, Joseph Delaney, Elizabeth Kay, Tim Mackintosh-Smith, Glenn Mitchell, Connie Monk, Richard Morgan, Steve Mosby, Chris Wooding. Founded 1971.

Andrew Lownie Literary Agency*

36 Great Smith Street, London SW1P 3BU
tel 020-7222 7574 *fax* 020-7222 7576
email lownie@globalnet.co.uk
website www.andrewlownie.co.uk
Director Andrew Lownie

Full-length MSS. Biography, history, reference, current affairs, and packaging journalists and celebrities for the book market (worldwide 15%). No reading fee; will suggest a revision.

Authors include Juliet Barker, the Joyce Cary Estate, Roger Crowley, Tom Devine, Duncan Falconer, Jonathan Fryer, Laurence Gardner, Cathy Glass, Timothy Good, David Hasselhoff, Lawrence James, Christopher Lloyd, Julian Maclaren-Ross Estate, Norma Major, Nick Pope, Martin Pugh, Sian Rees, Desmond Seward, David Stafford, Daniel Tammet, Christian Wolmar; *The Oxford Classical Dictionary*, *The Cambridge Guide to Literature in English*. Founded 1988.

Lucas Alexander Whitley – see LAW (Lucas Alexander Whitley Ltd)

Lucy Luck Associates (in association with Aitken Alexander Associates Ltd)

18-21 Cavaye Place, London SW10 9PT
tel 020-7373 8672
email lucy@lucyluck.com
website www.lucyluck.com
Contact Lucy Luck

Adult quality fiction and non-fiction (home 15%, overseas 20%, films/TV 15%). No reading fee.

Authors include Adam Thorpe, Catherine O'Flynn, Ewan Morrison, Ron Butlin, Philip Óceallaigh, Jon Hotten, Rupert Wright, Rebbecca Ray, Kevin Barry. Founded 2006.

Jennifer Luithlen Agency

88 Holmfield Road, Leicester LE2 1SB
tel 0116-273 8863 and 0116-273 5697
website www.luithlenagency.com
Agents Jennifer Luithlen, Penny Luithlen

Client list full. Children's fiction (home 15%, overseas 20%), performance rights (15%). Founded 1986.

Lutyens & Rubinstein*

21 Kensington Park Road, London W11 2EV
tel 020-7792 4855
email submissions@lutyensrubinstein.co.uk
Directors Sarah Lutyens, Felicity Rubinstein
Submissions Susannah Godman

Fiction and non-fiction, commercial and literary (home 15%, overseas 20%). Send outline/2 sample chapters, preferably by email, or by post including sae. No reading fee. Founded 1993.

Luxton Harris Ltd*

104a Park Street, London W1K 6NG
tel 020-7318 1247
email rebecca.winfield@btopenworld.com
website www.luxtonharris.co.uk
Contacts Jonathan Harris, David Luxton, Rebecca Winfield

Non-fiction and fiction, especially sport, history, music and biography (home 15%, overseas 20%, film 15%). No unsolicited MSS without prior consultation. No scripts, plays, poetry, science fiction, fantasy or children's books. No reading fee. Strong overseas representation. Founded 2003.

Duncan McAra

28 Beresford Gardens, Edinburgh EH5 3ES
tel 0131-552 1558
email duncanmcara@mac.com

Literary fiction; non-fiction: art, architecture, archaeology, biography, military, Scottish, travel (home 15%, USA/translation 20%). Preliminary letter with sae essential. No reading fee. Founded 1988.

The McKernan Literary Agency & Consultancy

5 Gayfield Square, Edinburgh EH1 3NW
tel 0131-557 1771
email maggie@mckernanagency.co.uk
website www.mckernanagency.co.uk
Contact Maggie McKernan

Literary and commercial fiction and non-fiction: Scottish, biography, history, current affairs, memoirs (home 15%, overseas 15%). No reading fee.

Authors include Michael Collins, Alan Taylor, Belinda Seaward, Michael Fry, Michael Schmidt. Founded 2005.

Eunice McMullen Ltd

Low Ibbotsholme Cottage, Off Bridge Lane, Troutbeck Bridge, Windermere, Cumbria LA23 1HU
tel (01539) 448551
email eunicemcmullen@totalise.co.uk
website www.eunicemcmullen.co.uk
Director Eunice McMullen

All types of children's fiction, particularly picture books and older fiction (home 10%, overseas 15%). No unsolicited scripts. Telephone or email enquiries only. Founded 1992.

Authors include Wayne Anderson, Sam Childs, Caroline Jayne Church, Jason Cockcroft, Ross Collins, Charles Fuge, Maggie Kneen, David Melling, Angela McAllister, Angie Sage, Gillian Shields. Founded 1992.

Andrew Mann Ltd*

1 Old Compton Street, London W1D 5JA
tel 020-7734 4751 *fax* 020-7287 9264
email info@andrewmann.co.uk
website www.andrewmann.co.uk
Contacts Anne Dewe, Tina Betts, Louise Burns

Full-length MSS. Scripts for TV, cinema, radio and theatre (home 15%, USA/Europe 20%). Associated with agents worldwide. No reading fee. Unsolicited MSS with preliminary letter, first 3 chapters and sae. Email synopses submissions only; no attachments. Founded 1968.

Sarah Manson Literary Agent

6 Totnes Walk, London N2 0AD
tel 020-8442 0396
email info@sarahmanson.com
website www.sarahmanson.com
Proprietor Sarah Manson

Specialises exclusively in fiction for children and young adults (home 10%, overseas 20%).Consult website for submission guidelines. Founded 2002.

Marjacq Scripts

34 Devonshire Place, London W1G 6JW
tel 020-7935 9499 *fax* 020-7935 9115
email enquiries@marjacq.com
website www.marjacq.com
Contact Philip Patterson (books), Isabella Floris (books), Luke Speed (film/TV)

All full-length MSS (home 10%, overseas 20%), including commercial and literary fiction and non-fiction, crime, thrillers, commercial, women's fiction, children's, science fiction, history, biography, sport, travel, health. No poetry. Send first 3 chapters with synopsis. May suggest revision. Film and TV rights, screenplays, radio plays, documentaries, screenplays/radio plays: send full script with 1–2pp synopsis/outline. Interested in documentary concepts and will accept proposals from writer/directors: send show reel with script. Sae essential for return of submissions.

Clients include: Victoria Arch, Richard Asplin, Sean Bates, Bert & Bertie, Catrin Collier, JJ Connolly, John Connor, Ross Cramer, Katie Ellwood, James Follett, Christopher Goffard, Stephen Graham, Tom Hinshelwood, Rebecca Hobbs, Ros Jay, Katherine John, Jessica Kedward, Stuart MacBride, Jane McLoughlin, John Meyers, Pat Mills, Graham Oakley, Kirsty Peart, Connor Potts, Greg Read, Alex Reynolds, Stanley Reynolds, Jack Sheffield, Brian Sibley, Michael Taylor, Kevin Wignall, Estate of R.D. Wingfield and the Estate of George Markstein. Founded 1974.

The Marsh Agency Ltd*

50 Albemarle Street, London W1S 4BD
tel 020-7493 4311 *fax* 020-7495 8961
email submissions@marsh-agency.co.uk
website www.marsh-agency.co.uk
Managing Director Paul Marsh, *Rights Director* Camilla Ferrier, *Agents* Geraldine Cooke, Jessica

Woollard, Leyla Moghadam, Caroline Hardman (junior agent)

Founded as international rights specialists for British, American and Canadian agencies. Expanded to act as agents handling fiction and non-fiction, specialising in authors with international potential. See website for futher information on individual agents' areas of interest. No reading fee. Unsolicited submissions considered: send a brief email enquiry with outline (non-fiction) or synopsis and 2 chapters (fiction). See also Paterson Marsh Ltd. Founded 1994.

Blanche Marvin

21A St John's Wood High Street, London NW8 7NG
tel 020-7722 2313 *fax* 020-7722 2313

Full-length MSS (15%), performance rights. No reading fee but return postage essential.

Authors include Christopher Bond.

MayerBenham Ltd

55 Athenlay Road, London SE15 3EN
tel 07801 627903
email simon@mayerbenham.co.uk
website www.mayerbenham.com
Directors Simon Benham, Jo Mayer

Non-fiction. Specialises in popular culture, humour, music, history, business (home 10%). No reading fee. No unsolicited MS; email in first instance.

Authors include Mathew Clayton, Edwin Collins, Peter Fisk, Sadie Frost, Heavenly Records, Will Hodgkinson, Michael Holding, The Idler, Gary Kemp, Dan Kieran, London Business Forum, Ian McCulloch, Paul Moody, Ben Myeis, Danielle Proud, Robin Turner, Ian Vince, Chris Yates. Founded 2002.

MBA Literary Agents Ltd*

(incorporating Merric Davidson Literary Agency)
62 Grafton Way, London W1T 5DW
tel 020-7387 2076 *fax* 020-7387 2042
email firstname@mbalit.co.uk
website www.mbalit.co.uk
Contacts Diana Tyler, Meg Davis, Laura Longrigg, David Riding, Susan Smith, Sophie Gorell Barnes

Fiction and non-fiction, children's books, and TV, film, radio and theatre scripts (home 15%, overseas 20%; theatre, TV, radio 10%; films 10–20%). See website for submission guidelines. Works in conjunction with agents in most countries. UK representative for the Donald Maass Agency, the Martha Millard Agency and the Frances Collin Agency. Founded 1971.

Authors include Catherine Webb, Brian Keaney, Mibi Thebo, Rebecca Promitzer, Sita Brahmachari, Christopher and Christine Russell.

William Morris Endeavor Entertainment*

(William Morris Agency (UK) Ltd)
Centre Point, 103 New Oxford Street, London WC1A 1DD
tel 020-7534 6800 *fax* 020-7534 6900
website www.wma.com
Books Eugenie Furniss, Cathryn Summerhayes; *TV* Isabella Zoltowski, Coz Jackson

Literary and commercial fiction, memoir, history, popular culture, TV formats, TV scripts (film/TV 10%, UK books 15%, USA books/translation 20%). No sci-fi, fantasy, poetry, self-help or children's picture books. Accepts submissions by post only. Send a synopsis and 3 sample chapters (50pp or fewer). No reading fee. Worldwide talent and literary agency with offices in New York, Beverly Hills, Nashville and Miami.

Judith Murdoch Literary Agency*

19 Chalcot Square, London NW1 8YA
tel 020-7722 4197
Contact Judith Murdoch

Full-length fiction only, especially accessible literary and commercial women's fiction (home 15%, overseas 20%). No science fiction/fantasy, poetry, short stories or children's. Approach by letter, *not* telephone, sending the first 2 chapters and synopsis. Submissions by email cannot be considered. Return postage/sae essential. Editorial advice given; no reading fee. Translation rights handled by the Marsh Agency Ltd. Founded 1993.

Clients include Trisha Ashley, Anne Berry, Tony Black, Alison Bond, Anne Bennett, Leah Fleming, Meg Hutchinson, Lola Jaye, Pamela Jooste, Jessie Keane, Catherine King, Eve Makis, Kitty Neale.

Maggie Noach Literary Agency

7 Peacock Yard, Iliffe Street, London SE17 3LH
tel (07506) 717726
email info@mnla.co.uk
website www.mnla.co.uk
Contacts Jill Hughes, Josie Stapleton

No unsolicited manuscripts – submission by arrangement only. Fiction and general non-fiction for adults, plus full length fiction for older children. No illustrated books or specialist non-fiction. Home 15%, USA and translation 20%. Founded 1982.

Andrew Nurnberg Associates Ltd*

Clerkenwell House, 45–47 Clerkenwell Green, London EC1R 0QX
tel 020-3327 0400 *fax* 020-7253 4851
email contact@andrewnurnberg.com
website www.andrewnurnberg.com

Sells rights internationally on behalf of UK/US agencies and publishers. Agent for UK and international authors, including children's writers. See website for full information and submission guidelines.

Alexandra Nye, Writers & Agents

Craigower, 6 Kinnoull Avenue, Dunblane, Perthshire FK15 9JG

tel (01786) 825114
Director Alexandra Nye

Literary fiction, Scottish history, biographies; no poetry or plays (home 10%, overseas 20%, translation 15%). No phone calls. Preliminary letter with synopsis preferred; sae essential for return. Reading fee for supply of detailed report on MSS. Founded 1991.

Deborah Owen Ltd*

78 Narrow Street, Limehouse, London E14 8BP
tel 020-7987 5119/5441 *fax* 020-7538 4004
Contact Deborah Owen

Small agency specialising in only three authors: Delia Smith, Amos Oz and David Owen. No new authors. Founded 1971.

Paterson Marsh Ltd

50 Albemarle Street, London W1S 4BD
tel 020-7297 4311 *fax* 020-7495 8961
website www.patersonmarsh.co.uk
Contact Stephanie Ebdon

General and academic non-fiction, particularly with international appeal. Also specialises in psychoanalysis and related fields. (20% worldwide including sub-agent's commission). No fiction, articles, short stories, screenplays or scripts. No children's books. See website for information about our specific interests and electronic submission details. Postal submissions accepted – preliminary letter with synopsis, sample material and return postage essential. No reading fee.

Authors include Anne Alvarez, Patrick Casement, Peter Moss, Robert Rowland Smith, John Seely. Estates include Wilfred Bion, Sir Arthur Evans, Sigmund Freud, Anna Freud, Dorothy Richardson, D.W. Winnicott. Founded 1955, merged with the Marsh Agency Ltd in 2001.

John Pawsey

8 Snowshill Court, Giffard Park,
Milton Keynes MK14 5QG
tel (01908) 217179

General non-fiction only, particularly biography, popular culture and sport. Preliminary letter and return postage with all correspondence essential. No submissions by email. Works in association with agencies in the USA, Europe and the Far East. Will suggest revision if MS sufficiently promising. No reading fee.

Authors include William Fotheringham, Don Hale, Patricia Hall, Gary Imlach, Gavin Newsham, Matt Rendell, Kathryn Spink. Founded 1981.

PBJ Management

5 Soho Square, London W1D 3QA
tel 020-7287 1112 *fax* 020-7787 1191
email suzanne@pbjmgt.co.uk
website www.pbjmgt.co.uk
Chairman Peter Bennett-Jones, *Managing Director* Caroline Chignell, *Agent* Suzanne Milligan

Represents writers (no novels or short stories), performers, presenters, composers, directors, producers and DJs (theatre 15%, film/TV/radio 12.5%). No reading fee.

Authors include Armando Iannucci, Barry Humphries, Chris Morris, Drew Pearce, Dylan Moran, Eddie Izzard, Harry Enfield, Jon Canter, Lenny Henry, the Mighty Boosh, Rowan Atkinson, Sean Hughes. Founded 1987.

Maggie Pearlstine Associates Ltd**

31 Ashley Gardens, Ambrosden Avenue,
London SW1P 1QE
tel 020-7828 4212 *fax* 020-7834 5546
email maggie@pearlstine.co.uk

Small agency representing a select few authors. No new authors. Translation rights handled by Aitken Alexander Associates Ltd.

Authors include Matthew Baylis, Roy Hattersley, Charles Kennedy, Quentin Letts, Claire Macdonald, Dr Raj Persaud, Prof. Lesley Regan, Malcolm Rifkind, Henrietta Spencer-Churchill, Prof. Robert Winston, Winifred Robinson and Prof. Kathy Sykes . Founded 1989.

PFD (The Peters Fraser & Dunlop Group Ltd)*

(A literary division of The Rights House, formed through the merger of PFD (The Peters Fraser & Dunlop Group) and Michael Foster MF Management in 2010)
Drury House, 34–43 Russell Street,
London WC2B 5HA
tel 020-7344 1000 *fax* 020-7836 9543
email info@pfd.co.uk
website www.pfd.co.uk
Ceo Caroline Michel, *Books* Caroline Michel, Michael Sissons, Annabel Merullo, Rowan Lawton, *Books & Journalism* Robert Caskie, *Foreign Rights* Annabel Merullo, Claire Daniel, *Head of Factual TV & Digital* Alexandra Henderson, *TV & Film* Michael Foster MF Management, *Estates* Camilla Shestopal
Represents authors of fiction and non-fiction, documentary makers, presenters, and public speakers throughout the world. No children's. Has 85 years of international experience in all media and also provides new digital services, e.g. software Apps.

Outline sample chapters and author biographies should be addressed to the books department. Material should be submitted on an exclusive basis; or in any event disclose if material is being submitted to other agencies or publishers. Return postage essential. No reading fee. Email submissions will not be answered. See website for submission guidelines.

Pollinger Limited

(formerly Laurence Pollinger Ltd, successor of Pearn, Pollinger and Higham)

9 Staple Inn, Holborn, London WC1V 7QH
tel 020-7404 0342 *fax* 020-7242 5737
email info@pollingerltd.com
website www.pollingerltd.com
Managing Director Lesley Pollinger, *Agents* Joanna Devereux, Tim Bates, Leigh Pollinger, Hayley Yeeles

All types of general trade adult and children's fiction and non-fiction books; intellectual property developments, illustrators/photographers (home 15%, translation 20%). Overseas, media and theatrical associates. For submission guidelines see website.

Clients include Kimberley Chambers, Michael Coleman, Catherine Fisher, Philip Gross, Hayley Long, Kelly McKain, Jeremy Poolman, Nicholas Rhea and Robert Sellers. Also the estates of H.E. Bates, Erskine Caldwell, Rachel Carson, D.H. Lawrence, Carson McCullers, John Masters, W.H. Robinson, Eric Frank Russell, Clifford D. Simak and other notables. Founded 1935.

Shelley Power Literary Agency Ltd*

13 rue du Pre Saint Gervais, 75019 Paris, France
tel 0142 38 36 49 *fax* 0140 40 70 08
email shelley.power@wanadoo.fr

General fiction and non-fiction. Full-length MSS (home 10%, USA/translation 19%, new clients: home 12.5%, USA/translation 20%). No children's books, poetry or plays. Works in conjunction with agents abroad. No reading fee, but preliminary letter with return postage as from UK or France essential. No submissions by email. Also based in the UK. Founded 1976.

Puttick Agency

46 Brookfield, Highgate West Hill, London N6 6AT
tel 020-8340 6383 *fax* 0870 751 8098
email enquiries@puttick.com
website www.puttick.com
Director Elizabeth Puttick

Full-length MSS (home 15%, overseas 20%). General and narrative non-fiction including health and personal development, biography and memoir, current affairs, business, history, philosophy, science. No fiction, poetry, screenplays, drama, children's books. Currently not accepting new proposals. Founded 1995.

PVA Management Ltd

County House, St Mary's Street,
Worcester WR1 1HB
tel (01905) 616100 *fax* (01905) 610709
email clients@pva.co.uk
website www.pva.co.uk
Managing Director Paul Vaughan

Full-length MSS. Non-fiction only (home 15%, overseas 20%, performance rights 15%). Send synopsis and sample chapters together with return postage.

Redhammer Management Ltd*

186 Bickenhall Mansions, Bickenhall Street,
London W1U 6BX
tel 020-7486 3465 *fax* 020-7000 1249
website www.redhammer.info
Vice President Peter Cox

Specialises in works with international potential (home 17.5%, overseas 20%). Unpublished authors must be professional in their approach and have major international potential, ideally book, film and/or TV. Submissions must follow the guidelines given on the website. Do not send unsolicited MSS by post. No radio or theatre scripts. No reading fee.

Clients include Donna Ballman, Martin Bell, Peggy Brusseau, Brian Clegg, Maria (M.G.) Harris, Lucy Johnson, Amanda Lees, Sarah Mussi, Michelle Paver, David Yelland. Founded 1993.

The Lisa Richards Agency

108 Upper Leeson Street, Dublin 4,
Republic of Ireland
tel (01) 637 5000 *fax* (01) 667 1256
email faith@lisarichards.ie
website www.lisarichards.ie
Contact Faith O'Grady

Handles fiction and general non-fiction (home 10%, UK 15%, USA/translation 20%, film/TV 15%). Approach with proposal and sample chapter for non-fiction and 3–4 chapters and synopsis for fiction (sae essential). No reading fee. *Overseas associate* The Marsh Agency for translation rights.

Clients include Laura Cassidy, Helena Close, Susan Connolly, June Considine (aka Laura Elliot), Matt Cooper, Damian Corless, Christine Dwyer Hickey, Robert Fannin, Karen Gillece, Tara Heavey, Paul Howard (aka Ross O'Carroll-Kelly), Amy Huberman, Arlene Hunt, Roisin Ingle, Alison Jameson, Declan Lynch, David Maybury, Roisin Meaney, Dearbhail McDonald, Pauline McLynn, Anna McPartlin, David O'Doherty, Mary O'Donoghue, Damien Owens, Kevin Rafter, Orla Tinsley, Sheena Wilkinson. Founded 1998.

Robinson Literary Agency Ltd – see Rogers, Coleridge & White Ltd

Rogers, Coleridge & White Ltd*

20 Powis Mews, London W11 1JN
tel 020-7221 3717 *fax* 020-7229 9084
email info@rcwlitagency.com
website www.rcwlitagency.com
Chairman Deborah Rogers, *Directors* Peter Straus (managing), Gill Coleridge, Patricia White (children's), David Miller, Laurence Laluyaux, Zoe Waldie, *Agents* Hannah Westland, Catherine Pellegrino (children's)

Full-length book MSS, including children's books (home 15%, USA 20%, translation 20%). No unsolicited MSS, and no submissions by fax or email. Founded 1967.

Elizabeth Roy Literary Agency

White Cottage, Greatford, Nr Stamford, Lincs. PE9 4PR
tel (01778) 560672 *fax* (01778) 560672
website www.elizabethroyliteraryagency.co.uk

Children's fiction and non-fiction – writers and illustrators (home 15%, overseas 20%). Send preliminary letter, synopsis and sample chapters with names of publishers and agents previously contacted. Return postage essential. No reading fee. Founded 1990.

Uli Rushby-Smith Literary Agency

72 Plimsoll Road, London N4 2EE
tel 020-7354 2718 *fax* 020-7354 2718
Director Uli Rushby-Smith

Fiction and non-fiction, literary and commercial (home 15%, USA/foreign 20%). No poetry, picture books, plays or film scripts. Send outline, sample chapters (no disks) and return postage. No reading fee. Founded 1993.

Rosemary Sandberg Ltd

6 Bayley Street, London WC1B 3HE
tel 020-7304 4110 *fax* 020-7304 4109
email rosemary@sandberg.demon.co.uk
Directors Rosemary Sandberg, Ed Victor

Children's writers and illustrators, general fiction and non-fiction. Absolutely no unsolicited MSS: client list is full. Founded 1991.

The Sayle Literary Agency*

1 Petersfield, Cambridge CB1 1BB
tel (01223) 303035 *fax* (01223) 301638
email info@sayleliteraryagency.com
website www.sayleliteraryagency.com
Proprietor and Agent Rachel Calder

Fiction: general, literary and crime. Non-fiction: current affairs, social issues, travel, biographies, history (home 15%, USA/translation 20%). No plays, poetry, textbooks, children's, technical, legal or medical books. No reading fee. See website for submission guidelines. Translation rights handled by the Marsh Agency Ltd. Film and TV rights handled by Sayle Screen Ltd. *Overseas associates* Dunow & Carlson Agency, Darhansoff, Verrill and Feldman, New England Publishing Associates, USA.

Sayle Screen Ltd

11 Jubilee Place, London SW3 3TD
tel 020-7823 3883 *fax* 020-7823 3363
email info@saylescreen.com
website www.saylescreen.com
Agents Jane Villiers, Matthew Bates, Toby Moorcroft

Specialises in scripts for film, TV, theatre and radio (home 10%, overseas 15–20%). No reading fee. Preliminary letter and return postage essential. No email submissions. Represents film and TV rights in fiction and non-fiction for the Sayle Literary Agency, Greene and Heaton Ltd and Peter Robinson Ltd. Works in conjunction with agents in New York and Los Angeles.

The Science Factory Ltd

Scheideweg 34C, 20253 Hamburg, Germany
tel 020-7193 7296
email info@sciencefactory.co.uk
website www.sciencefactory.co.uk
Director Peter Tallack

Serious popular non-fiction, particularly science, history and current affairs, by academics and journalists (home 15%, overseas 20%). No fiction. In first instance send proposal with chapter summaries and sample chapter (not the first). Email submissions encouraged and given priority over hard-copy submissions (sae required). No reading fee. Will suggest revision.

Authors include Anjana Ahuja, Anil Ananthaswamy, Jim Baggott, David Bainbridge, Jesse Bering, Piers Bizony, Daniel Bor, Dennis Bray, Dean Buonomano, Rita Carter, Stuart Clark, Matthew Cobb, Michael Corballis, Donna Dickenson, Clare Dudman, Nicholas Dunbar, John Duncan, Richard Elwes, Georgina Ferry, Lone Frank, Christine Garwood, Simon Ings, Stephen Joseph, Manjit Kumar, Peter Lamont, Jo Marchant, Arthur I. Miller, Ted Nield, Michael Nielsen, Paul Parsons, Aarathi Prasad, Ian Sample, Nicholas J. Saunders, P.D. Smith, Tom Stafford, Ian Stewart, Frank Swain, Brian Switek, Mark Van Vugt, Geerat J. Vermeij, Adam Zeman. Established 2008.

Scott Ferris Associates

Brynfield, Reynoldston, Swansea SA3 1AE
tel (01792) 390009
email scottferris@macunlimited.net
Partners Gloria Ferris and Rivers Scott

General fiction and non-fiction (home 15%, overseas/TV/radio 20%). No unsolicited MSS or submissions by email. Preliminary letter and postage essential. Reading fee by arrangement. Founded 1981.

The Sharland Organisation Ltd

The Manor House, Manor Street, Raunds, Northants NN9 6JW
tel (01933) 626600
email tso@btconnect.com
website www.sharlandorganisation.co.uk
Directors Mike Sharland, Alice Sharland

Specialises in film, TV, stage and radio rights throughout the world (home 15%, overseas 20%). Preliminary letter and return postage is essential. No reading fee. Works in conjunction with overseas agents. Founded 1988.

Anthony Sheil in association with Aitken Alexander Associates

18–21 Cavaye Place, London SW10 9PT
tel 020-7373 8672 *fax* 020-7373 6002

website www.aitkenalexander.co.uk
Proprietor Anthony Sheil

Quality fiction and non-fiction (home 10%, overseas 20%). No plays, film/TV scripts, poetry, short stories or children's fiction. Send preliminary letter with half-page synopsis and first consecutive 30pp of sample material. Include return postage. No reading fee.

Authors include Caroline Alexander, John Fowles, John Keegan, Robert Wilson.

Sheil Land Associates Ltd*

(incorporating Richard Scott Simon Ltd 1971 and Christy & Moore Ltd 1912)
52 Doughty Street, London WC1N 2LS
tel 020-7405 9351 *fax* 020-7831 2127
email info@sheilland.co.uk
Agents UK & US Sonia Land, Vivien Green, Piers Blofeld, Ian Drury *Film/theatre/TV* Sophie Janson, Lucy Fawcett, *Foreign* Gaia Banks, Emily Dyson

Quality literary and commercial fiction and non-fiction, including: politics, history, military history, gardening, thrillers, crime, romance, drama, science fiction, fantasy, biography, travel, cookery, humour, UK and foreign estates (home 15%, USA/translation 20%). Also theatre, film, radio and TV scripts. Welcomes approaches from new clients to start or to develop their careers. Preliminary letter with sae essential. No reading fee. *Overseas associates* Georges Borchardt, Inc. (Richard Scott Simon). *US film and TV representation* CAA, APA and others.

Clients include Peter Ackroyd, Benedict Allen, Charles Allen, Pam Ayres, Hugh Bicheno, Melvyn Bragg, Steven Carroll, Mark Chadbourn, Lana Citron, David Cohen, Anna del Conte, Elspeth Cooper, Elizabeth Corley, Seamus Deane, Mia Dolan, Angus Donald, Alex Dryden, Greg Dyke, Chris Ewan, Robert Fabbri, Alan Gilbey, Rosie Goodwin, Jean Goodhind, Robert Green, Susan Hill, Richard Holmes, Ian Johnstone, Richard Mabey, The Brothers McLeod, Graham Rice, Anthony Seldon, Diane Setterfield, Tom Sharpe, Louise Soraya Black, Laura Summers, Martin Stephen, Jeffrey Tayler, Andrew Taylor, Rose Tremain, Barry Unsworth, Prof. Stanley Wells, Neil White and the Estates of Catherine Cookson, Patrick O'Brian, Penelope Mortimer, Jean Rhys, F.A. Wesley and Stephen Gately. Founded 1962.

Caroline Sheldon Literary Agency Ltd*

71 Hillgate Place, London W8 7SS
tel 0207-727 9102
email carolinesheldon@carolinesheldon.co.uk, pennyholroyde@carolinesheldon.co.uk
website www.carolinesheldon.co.uk
Contacts Caroline Sheldon, Penny Holroyde

Fiction and non-fiction and children's books (home 15%, USA/translation 20%, film/TV 15%). Special interests: fiction – all fiction for women, sagas, suspense, contemporary, chick lit, historical fiction, fantasy and humour; non-fiction – true life stories, animal stories, memoirs and humour; children's – fiction for all age groups, contemporary, comic, fantasy and ; illustration – all quality illustrations for children's books.

Send submissions by email only with Submissions/ Title of work/Name of author in subject line. Include full introductory information about yourself and your writing and the first 3 chapters only or equivalent length of work.

Does not represent TV or film scripts except for existing book writing clients. No reading fee. Gives editorial advice on work of exceptional promise. Founded 1985.

Jeffrey Simmons

15 Penn House, Mallory Street, London NW8 8SX
tel 020-7224 8917
email jasimmons@unicombox.co.uk

Specialises in fiction (no science fiction, horror or fantasy), biography, autobiography, show business, personality books, law, crime, politics, world affairs. Full-length MSS (home from 10%, overseas from 15%). Will suggest revision. No reading fee, but preliminary letter essential.

Sinclair-Stevenson

3 South Terrace, London SW7 2TB
tel 020-7581 2550 *fax* 020-7581 2550
Directors Christopher Sinclair-Stevenson, Deborah Sinclair-Stevenson

Full-length MSS (home 10%, USA/translation 20%). General – no children's books. No reading fee; will suggest a revision. Founded 1995.

Robert Smith Literary Agency Ltd*

12 Bridge Wharf, 156 Caledonian Road, London N1 9UU
tel 020-7278 2444 *fax* 020-7833 5680
email robertsmith.literaryagency@virgin.net
Directors Robert Smith, Anne Smith

Non-fiction only: autobiography and biography, topical subjects, history, lifestyle, popular culture, entertainment, sport, true crime, health and nutrition, illustrated books (home 15%, overseas 20%). No unsolicited MSS. No reading fee. Will suggest revision.

Authors include Kate Adie (serialisations), Martin Allen, Peta Bee, Kevin Booth, Martyn and Michelle Compton, Judy Cook, Stewart Evans, Neil and Christine Hamilton, Bob Harris, James Haspiel, Albert Jack, Lois Jenkins, Heidi Kingstone, Roberta Kray, Angela Levin, Ann Ming, Michelle Morgan, Theo Paphitis, Howard Raymond, Frances Reilly, Keith Skinner, Jayne Sterne. Founded 1997.

The Standen Literary Agency

53 Hardwicke Road, London N13 4SL
tel/fax 020-8889 1167

website www.standenliteraryagency.com
Director Yasmin Standen

Literary and commercial fiction and children's fiction and picture books (home 15%, overseas 20%). Interested in new writers. Send first 3 chapters, a synopsis (one side of A4) and a covering letter by post only in first instance (no submissions via email; submit the entire MS of children's stories (500 words and under). Include postage for return of MSS. No reading fee. See website for further information.

Authors include Zara Kane, Zoe Marriott, Andrew Murray. Founded 2004.

Abner Stein*

10 Roland Gardens, London SW7 3PH
tel 020-7373 0456 *fax* 020-7370 6316
Contact Caspian Dennis, Arabella Stein

Fiction, general non-fiction and children's (home 10%, overseas 20%). Not taking on any new clients at present.

Micheline Steinberg Associates

104 Great Portland Street, London W1W 6PE
tel 020-7631 1310
email info@steinplays.com
website www.steinplays.com
Agents Micheline Steinberg, Helen MacAuley

Represents writers for theatre, TV, film, radio and animation. Film and TV rights in fiction and non-fiction on behalf of book agents (home 10%, overseas 15–20%). Works in association with agents in USA and overseas. No unsolicited submissions. Industry recommendation preferred. Founded 1987.

Rochelle Stevens & Co

2 Terretts Place, Upper Street, London N1 1QZ
tel 020-7359 3900 *fax* 020-7354 5729
email info@rochellestevens.com
website www.rochellestevens.com
Directors Rochelle Stevens, Frances Arnold

Drama scripts for film, TV, theatre and radio. Preliminary letter, CV and sae essential. Founded 1984.

Shirley Stewart Literary Agency*

3rd Floor, 4A Nelson Road, London SE10 9JB
tel 020-8293 3000
Director Shirley Stewart

Specialises in literary fiction and general non-fiction (home 10–15%, overseas 20%). No poetry, plays, film scripts, science fiction, fantasy or children's books. No reading fee. Send preliminary letter, synopsis and first 3 chapters plus return postage. Founded 1993.

Sarah Such Literary Agency

81 Arabella Drive, London SW15 5LL
tel 020-8876 4228 *fax* 020-8878 8705
email info@sarahsuch.com
website www.sarahsuch.com
Proprietor Sarah Such

High-quality literary and commercial non-fiction and fiction for adults and children (home 15%, TV/film 20%, overseas 20%). No reading fee. Will suggest revision. Submit synopsis and a sample chapter (as a Word attachment if sending by email) plus author biography. Sae essential for postal submissions. No unsolicited MSS or telephone enquiries. TV/film scripts for established clients only. No radio or theatre scripts, poetry, fantasy, self-help or short stories. Film/TV representation: Aitken Alexander Associates Ltd. Established 2006.

The Susijn Agency Ltd

3rd Floor, 64 Great Titchfield Street, London W1W 7QH
tel 020-7580 6341 *fax* 020-7580 8626
email info@thesusijnagency.com
website www.thesusijnagency.com
Agents Laura Susijn, Nicola Barr

Specialises in world rights in English- and non-English-language literature: literary fiction and general non-fiction (home 15%, overseas 20%, theatre/film/TV/ radio 15%). Send synopsis and 2 sample chapters. No reading fee.

Authors include Peter Ackroyd, Bidisha, Jon Butler and Bruno Vincent, Uzma Aslam Khan, Robin Baker, Abdelkader Benali, Robert Craig, Tessa De Loo, Gwynne Dyer, Travis Elborough, Radhika Jha, Kolton Lee, Karen Mcleod, Jeffrey Moore, Karl Shaw, Paul Sussman, Dubravka Ugrešić, Alex Wheatle, Adam Zameenzad. Founded 1998.

The Tennyson Agency

10 Cleveland Avenue, London SW20 9EW
tel 020-8543 5939
email submissions@tenagy.co.uk
website www.tenagy.co.uk
Theatre, TV & Film Scripts Christopher Oxford, *Arts/Humanities* Adam Sheldon

Scripts and related material for theatre, film and TV (home 15%, overseas 20%). No reading fee.

Clients include Tony Bagley, Kristina Bedford, Alice D. Cooper, Alastair Cording, Caroline Coxon, Iain Grant, Jonathan Holloway, Philip Hurd-Wood, Joanna Leigh, Steve Macgregor, Antony Mann, Elizabeth Moynihan, Ken Ross, John Ryan, Matthew Salkeld, Walter Saunders, Graeme Scarfe, Diane Speakman, Diana Ward and the Estate of Julian Howell. Founded 2002.

JM Thurley Management

Archery House, 33 Archery Square, Walmer, Deal, Kent CT14 7JA
tel (01304) 371721
email JMThurley@aol.com
website www.thecuttingedge.biz
Contact Jon Thurley

Specialises in commercial and literary full-length fiction and commercial work for film and TV. No plays, poetry, short stories, articles or fantasy. No reading fee but preliminary letter and sae essential. Editorial/creative advice provided to clients (home 15%, overseas 20%). Links with leading US and European agents. Founded 1976.

Jane Turnbull*

Mailing address Barn Cottage, Veryan Churchtown, Truro TR2 5QA
tel (01872) 501317
email jane@janeturnbull.co.uk
London Office 58 Elgin Crescent, London W11 2JJ
tel 020-7727 9409
website www.janeturnbull.co.uk

High quality non-fiction; biography, history, natural history, lifestyle, humour; TV tie-ins, some literary fiction (home 15%, USA/translation 20%), performance rights (15%). No science fiction or children's. Works in conjunction with Aitken Alexander Associates Ltd for sale of translation rights. No reading fee. Preliminary letter (NOT email) essential; no unsolicited MSS. Founded 1986.

United Agents*

12–26 Lexington Street, London W1F 0LE
tel 020-3214 0800
email info@unitedagents.co.uk
website www.unitedagents.co.uk
Agents Sarah Ballard, Rosemary Canter, Jessica Craig (adult foreign rights), Caroline Dawnay, James Gill, Robert Kirby, Jodie Marsh, Rosemary Scoular, Simon Trewin, Charles Walker, Anna Webber, Jane Willis (children's foreign rights)

Fiction and non-fiction (home 15%, USA/translation 20%). No reading fee. Founded 2008.

Ed Victor Ltd*

6 Bayley Street, Bedford Square, London WC1B 3HE
tel 020-7304 4100 *fax* 020-7304 4111
Executive Chairman Ed Victor, *Joint Managing Directors* Sophie Hicks, Margaret Phillips, *Directors* Carol Ryan, Graham C. Greene CBE, Leon Morgan, Hitesh Shah, *Editorial Director* Philippa Harrison

Fiction, non-fiction and children's books (home 15%, USA 15%, children's 10%, translation 20%). No short stories, poetry or film/TV scripts or plays. No reading fee. No unsolicited MSS. No response to submissions by email. Represented in all foreign markets.

Authors include John Banville, Herbie Brennan, Eoin Colfer, Sir Ranulph Fiennes, Frederick Forsyth, A.A. Gill, Josephine Hart, Jack Higgins, Nigella Lawson, Kathy Lette, Allan Mallinson, Andrew Marr, Frederic Raphael, Danny Scheinmann and the Estates of Douglas Adams, Raymond Chandler, Dame Iris Murdoch, Sir Stephen Spender, Irving Wallace. Founded 1976.

Wade and Doherty Literary Agency Ltd

33 Cormorant Lodge, Thomas More Street, London E1W 1AU
tel 020-7488 4171 *fax* 020-7488 4172
email rw@rwla.com, bd@rwla.com
website www.rwla.com
Directors Robin Wade, Broo Doherty

General fiction and non-fiction, children's books (home 10%, overseas 20%). No poetry, plays, picture books or short stories. See website for submission guidelines. Email submissions preferred. New authors welcome. No reading fee. Founded 2001.

Watson, Little Ltd*

48–56 Bayham Place, London NW1 0EU
tel 020-7388 7529 *fax* 020-7388 8501
email office@watsonlittle.com
website www.watsonlittle.com
Contact Mandy Little, James Wills, Sallyanne Sweeney

Fiction, commercial women's fiction, crime and literary fiction. Non-fiction special interests include history, science, popular psychology, self-help and general leisure books. Also children's fiction and non-fiction (home 15%, USA/translation 20%). No short stories, poetry, TV, play or film scripts. Not interested in purely academic writers. Send informative preliminary letter and synopsis with return postage. *Overseas associates* The Marsh Agency Ltd; *Film and TV associates* The Sharland Organisation Ltd and MBA Literary Agents Ltd; *USA associates* Howard Morhaim Literary Agency (adult) and the Chudney Agency (children's).

AP Watt Ltd*

20 John Street, London WC1N 2DR
tel 020-7405 6774
fax 020-7831 2154 (books), 020-7430 1952 (drama)
email apw@apwatt.co.uk
website www.apwatt.co.uk
Directors Caradoc King, Linda Shaughnessy, Derek Johns, Georgia Garrett, Natasha Fairweather, Rob Kraitt (associate)

Full-length MSS; dramatic works for all media (home 15%, overseas 20% including commission to foreign agent). No poetry. No reading fee. Does not accept unsolicited MSS or any other material. Send a query letter in first instance. Founded 1875.

Authors include Monica Ali, Trezza Azzopardi, David Baddiel, Lynn Barber, Sebastian Barry, Quentin Blake, Marika Cobbold, Helen Dunmore, Nicholas Evans, Giles Foden, Esther Freud, Janice Galloway, Martin Gilbert, Nadine Gordimer, Linda Grant, Reginald Hill, Michael Holroyd, Michael Ignatieff, Mick Jackson, Philip Kerr, Dick King-Smith, India Knight, John Lanchester, Alison Lurie, Jan Morris, Andrew O'Hagan, Susie Orbach, Caryl Phillips, Philip Pullman, James Robertson, Jancis Robinson, Jon Ronson, Elaine Showalter, Zadie Smith, Graham Swift, Salley Vickers, and the estates of Graves and Maugham.

Josef Weinberger Plays Ltd

(formerly Warner/Chappell Plays Ltd)
12–14 Mortimer Street, London W1T 3JJ

tel 020-7580 2827 *fax* 020-7436 9616

Specialises in stage plays. Works in conjunction with overseas agents. No unsolicited MSS; preliminary letter essential. Founded 1938.

Whispering Buffalo Literary Agency Ltd

97 Chesson Road, London W14 9QS
tel 020-7565 4737
email info@whisperingbuffalo.com
website www.whisperingbuffalo.com
Director Mariam Keen

Commercial/literary fiction and non-fiction, children's and young adult fiction (home 12.5%, overseas 20%). No reading fee. Will suggest revision. Founded 2008.

Eve White*

54 Gloucester Street, London SW1V 4EG
tel 020-7630 1155
email eve@evewhite.co.uk
website www.evewhite.co.uk
Contact Eve White

Commercial and literary fiction and non-fiction, children's fiction (home 15%, overseas 20%). No reading fee. Will suggest revision where appropriate. See website for up-to-date submission requirements.

Authors include Susanna Corbett, Tracey Corderoy, Jimmy Docherty, Rae Earl, Abie Longstaff, Kate Maryon, Vijay Medtia, Rachael Mortimer, Ciaran Murtagh, Chris Pascoe, Gillian Rogerson, Ruth Saberton, Alexander Stobbs, Tabitha Suzuma, Andy Stanton. Founded 2003.

Isabel White Literary Agent

1–2 Universal House, 88–94 Wentworth Street, London E1 7SA
tel 020-3070 1602 *fax* 020-3006 8791
email isabel@isabelwhite.co.uk (trade), query.isabelwhite@googlemail.com (submissions)
website www.isabelwhite.co.uk
Proprietor Isabel White

Fiction and non-fiction (home 15%, overseas 20%). Books only – no film, TV or stage plays, poetry, short stories or academic monographs. Email submissions only. See website for submission guidelines. No reading fee.

Authors include The Bourbon Kid, Suzi Brent, Iain Clark, Lynne Connolly, Graeme Kent, Ivy Ngeow. Founded 2008.

Dinah Wiener Ltd*

12 Cornwall Grove, London W4 2LB
tel 020-8994 6011 *fax* 020-8994 6044
Director Dinah Wiener

Fiction and general non-fiction (home 15%, overseas 20%), film and TV in association (15%). No plays, scripts, poetry, short stories or children's books. No reading fee, but preliminary letter and return postage essential.

Jonathan Williams Literary Agency

Rosney Mews, Upper Glenageary Road, Glenageary, Co. Dublin, Republic of Ireland
tel (01) 2803482 *fax* (01) 2803482
Director Jonathan Williams

General fiction and non-fiction, preferably by Irish authors (home 10%). Will suggest revision; no reading fee unless a very fast decision is required. Return postage appreciated (no British stamps – use IRCs). Sub-agents in Holland, Germany, Italy, Spain, Portugal, Japan. Founded 1981.

Elisabeth Wilson

24 Thornhill Square, London N1 1BQ

Rights agent and consultant; illustrated books, non-fiction (no children's). No reading fee. Founded 1979.

The Wylie Agency (UK) Ltd

17 Bedford Square, London WC1B 3JA
tel 020-7908 5900 *fax* 020-7908 5901
email mail@wylieagency.co.uk
website www.wylieagency.co.uk
President Andrew Wylie

Literary fiction and non-fiction (home 10%, overseas 20%, USA 15%). No unsolicited MSS; send preliminary letter with 2 sample chapters and sae in first instance. Founded 1996.

Susan Yearwood Literary Agency

2 Knebworth House, Londesborough Road, London N16 8RL
tel 020-7503 0954
email susan@susanyearwood.com
website www.susanyearwood.com
Contact Susan Yearwood

Literary and commercial fiction (home 15%, overseas 20%), including thrillers, women's and young adult. Send 3 chapters and a synopsis via email. No reading fee. Established 2007.

Literary agents overseas

Before submitting material, writers are advised to send a preliminary letter with a sae or IRC (International Reply Coupon) and to ascertain terms.

ARGENTINA

International Editors Co.

Avenida Cabildo 1156, 1426 Buenos Aires
tel 54-11-4788-2992 *fax* 54-11-4786-0888
email costa@iecobaires.com.ar

The Nancy H. Smith Literary Agency

(formerly The Lawrence Smith Agency)
Ayacucho 1867, 2B, Buenos Aires 1112
tel (54 11) 4804 5508 *fax* (54 11) 4804 5508
email memurray@ciudad.com.ar
London 30 Acton Lane, London W4 5ED
tel 020-8995 4769 *fax* 020-8747 4012
email distobart@aol.com
Contact Margaret Murray, Diana Stobart

No unsolicited MSS. No response to submissions by email. Founded 1938.

AUSTRALIA

Bryson Agency Australia Pty Ltd

PO Box 13327, Law Courts PO, Melbourne 8010
tel (613) 9329 2517 *fax* (613) 9600 9131
email fran@bryson.com.au
website www.bryson.com.au
Contact Fran Bryson

Represents writers operating in all media: print, film, TV, radio, the stage and electronic derivatives; specialises in representation of book writers. Query first before sending unsolicited MSS. Not accepting until further notice.

Curtis Brown (Australia) Pty Ltd

PO Box 19, Paddington, NSW 2021
tel (02) 9331 5301 *fax* (02) 9360 3935
email info@curtisbrown.com.au
website www.curtisbrown.com.au
Contact Fiona Inglis

No reading fee.

Diversity Management

PO Box 1449, Darlinghurst, Sydney, NSW 1300
tel (02) 9130 4305
email bill@diversitym.com.au
Director Bill Tikos

All genres of non-fiction, illustrated books (home/overseas 20%). No reading fee. Founded 2001.

BRAZIL

Agencia Riff

Av. Calógeras, no.6/sala 1007,
20030–070 Rio de Janeiro, RJ
tel (55-21) 2287-6299 *fax* (55-21) 2287-6393
email lucia@agenciariff.com.br
website www.agenciariff.com.br
Contacts Lucia Riff, Laura Riff, João Paulo Riff

Home 10%, overseas 20%. No reading fee. Founded 1991.

Tassy Barham Associates

23 Elgin Crescent, London W11 2JD
tel/fax 020-7229 8667
email tassy@tassybarham.com
Proprietor Tassy Barham

Specialises in representing European and American authors, agents and publishers in Brazil. Founded 1999.

Karin Schindler and Suely Pedro dos Santos Rights Representatives

Caixa Postal 19051, 04505–970 São Paulo, SP
tel 55-11-5041-9177 *fax* 55-11-5041-9077
email kschind@terr.com.br,
suelypedrosantos@uol.com.br

CANADA

Acacia House Publishing Services Ltd

62 Chestnut Avenue, Brantford, Ontario N3T 4C2
tel 519-752-8349
email fhanna.acacia@rogers.com
Managing Director Mrs Frances A. Hanna, *Vice President* Bill Hanna

Literary fiction/non-fiction, quality commercial fiction, most non-fiction, except business books (15% English worldwide, 25% translation, performance 20%). No science fiction, horror or occult. Works with overseas agents. Query first with sample of 50pp max. Include return postage. No reading fee. Founded 1985.

Authors' Marketing Services Ltd

683 Annette Street, Toronto M6S 2C9
tel 416-763-8797 *fax* 416-763-1504
email authorslhoffman@cs.com
website www.hoffmanagency.ca
Directors Larry Hoffman, Antonia Hoffman, Sharon DeWynter

Adult fiction, biography and autobiography (home 15%, overseas 20%). Reading fee charged for unpublished writers; will suggest a revision. Founded 1978.

The Cooke Agency

278 Bloor Street East, Suite 305, Toronto,
Ontario M4W 3M4

tel 416-406-3390 *fax* 416-406-3389
email agents@cookeagency.ca
website www.cookeagency.ca
Agents Dean Cooke, Sally Harding, Suzanne Brandreth, Mary Hu

Literary fiction, commercial fiction (science fiction, fantasy and romance), non-fiction (specifically narrative-driven works in the areas of popular culture, science, history, politics and natural history), and middle-grade and young adult books. No children's picture books, poetry or screenplays. Either submit query only by email (no attachments) or complete submission by post FAO Elizabeth Griffin. Represesnts more than 100 writers. Co-agents: Curtis Brown Canada, Greene & Heaton, The Turnbull Agency. Founded 1992.

Anne McDermid & Associates Ltd

83 Willcocks Street, Toronto, Ontario M5S 1C9
tel 416-324-8845 *fax* 416-324-8870
email info@mcdermidagency.com
website www.mcdermidagency.com
Director Anne McDermid, *West Coast Associate* Lise Henderson

Literary fiction and non-fiction, and quality commercial fiction.

West Coast office Literary fiction, children's and young adult literature (home 15%, USA 15%, overseas 20%). No reading fee. Founded 1996.

Bella Pomer Agency Inc.

355 St Clair Avenue West, Suite 801, Toronto, Ontario M5P 1N5
tel 416-920-4949
President Bella Pomer

Not considering new clients. Founded 1978.

Carolyn Swayze Literary Agency Ltd

W.R.P.O. Box 39588, White Rock, British Columbia V4B 5L6
email reception@swayzeagency.com
website www.swayzeagency.com
Proprietor Carolyn Swayze

Literary fiction, a limited list of commercial fiction and non-fiction. No romance, science fiction, poetry, screenplays or children's picture books. Eager to discover lively, thought-provoking narrative non-fiction, especially in the fields of science, history, travel, politics and memoir.

Submission details No telephone calls: make contact by email or post. Send query including synopsis and short sample. Provide resume, publication credits, writing awards, education and experience relevant to the book project. If querying by post include email or sase for return of materials. No original artwork or photographs. Allow 6 weeks for a reply. Founded 1994.

EASTERN EUROPE

Aura-Pont, Theatrical and Literary Agency Ltd

Veslařský Ostrov 62, 147 00, Prague 4, Czech Republic
tel (420) 2 51 55 49 38 *fax* (420) 2 51 55 02 07
email aura-pont@aura-pont.cz
website www.aura-pont.cz
Director Petra Marková

Handles authors' rights in theatre, film, TV, radio, software – both Czech and foreign (home 10%, overseas 15%). Founded 1990.

DILIA

Krátkého 1, 190 03 Prague 9, Czech Republic
tel (420) 283 891 598 *fax* (420) 2 83 89 35 99
email info@dilia.cz
website www.dilia.cz
Managing Director Ladislav Simon

Theatrical and literary agency.

Lex Copyright

Szemere utca 21, 1054 Budapest, Hungary
tel (36) 1 332 9340 *fax* (36) 1 331 6181
email lexcopy.bp@mail.datanet.hu
website www.lexcopyright.hu
Director Dr Gyorgy Tibor Szanto

Specialises in representing American and British authors in Hungary. Founded 1991.

Andrew Nurnberg Associates Prague, s.r.o.

Jugoslávských partyzánů 17, 160 00 Prague 6, Czech Republic
tel (420) 222 782 041
email anaprague@nurnberg.cz
Contacts Petra Tobišková (tobiskova@nurnberg.cz), Jitka Němečková (nemeckova@nurnberg.cz), Jana Borouanova

Prava I Prevodi Literary Agency Permissions & Rights Ltd

Yu-Business Centre, Blvd Mihaila Pupina 10B/I, 5th Floor, Suite 4, 11070 Belgrade, Serbia and Montenegro
tel (381) 11 3119880 *fax* (381) 11 3119879
email office@pravaiprevodi.org
website www.pravaiprevodi.org
Director Predraq Milenkovic, *Foreign Rights* Ana Milenkovic

Specialises in representing American and British authors in former Eastern Europe (15 languages). Founded 1983.

FRANCE

Agence Hoffman

77 Boulevard Saint-Michel, 75005 Paris
tel (1) 43 26 56 94 *fax* (1) 43 26 34 07
email info@agence-hoffman.com
Contact Georges Hoffman, Christine Scholz

Agence Michelle Lapautre

6 rue Jean Carriès, 75007 Paris
tel (1) 47 34 82 41 *fax* (1) 47 34 00 90
email agence@lapautre.com

Bureau Littéraire International
24 rue Saint Denis, F–92100 Boulogne Billancourt
tel (1) 46 05 39 11
Contact Geneviéve Ulmann

La Nouvelle Agence
7 rue Corneille, 75006 Paris
tel (1) 43 25 85 60 *fax* (1) 43 25 47 98
email ind@lanouvelleagence.fr
Contacts Mary Kling

Susanna Lea Associates
28 rue Bonaparte, 75006 Paris
tel (01) 53 10 28 40 *fax* (01) 53 10 28 49
email postmaster@susannalea.com
website www.susannaleaassociates.com

Fiction and non-fiction with international potential. No poetry, plays, screenplays, science fiction, educational text books, short stories or illustrated works. No unsolicited email or fax queries. Submit by mail a query letter, brief synopsis, the first 3 chapters and/or proposal. Founded 2000.

Promotion Littéraire
12 rue Pergolèse, 75116 Paris
tel (1) 45 00 42 10 *fax* (01) 45 00 10 18
email promolit@free.fr
Director Mariella Giannetti

Fiction, essays. Founded 1977.

GERMANY (SEE ALSO SWITZERLAND)

Michael Meller Literary Agency
Sandstrasse 33, 80335 Munich
tel (089) 366371 *fax* (089) 366372
email info@melleragency.com
website www.melleragency.com

Fiction and non-fiction (home 15%, overseas 20%). Send outline and first 50pp. No reading fee. Founded 1988.

Thomas Schlück GmbH
Literary Agency, Hinter der Worth 12, 30827 Garbsen
tel 05131-497560 *fax* 05131-497589
email mail@schlueckagent.com
website www.schlueckagent.com

No reading fee.

INDIA

Ajanta Books International
1 U.B. Jawahar Nagar, Bungalow Road, Delhi 110007
tel 91-11-23926182 *fax* 91-11-27415016
email ajantabi@vsnf.com
Proprietor S. Balwant

Full-length MSS in social sciences and humanities (commission varies according to market – Indian books in Indian and foreign languages, foreign books into Indian languages). Will suggest revision; charges made if agency undertakes revision; reading fee. Founded 1975.

ITALY

Agenzia Letteraria Internazionale SRL
Via Valpetrosa 1, 20123 Milano
tel (02) 865445, 861572 *fax* (02) 876222
email barbieri@aglettinternazionale.it, info@agenzialetterariainternazionale.com
Manager Director Donatella Barbieri

Eulama SRL
Via Guido de Ruggiero 28, 00142 Rome
tel/fax (06) 540 7309
email eulama@fastwebnet.it
website www.eulama.com
President Karin von Prellwitz, *Directors* Norbert von Prellwitz, Pina Ocello von Prellwitz

International licensing agency representing publishing houses, agents and authors of adult and children's books worldwide. General and literary fiction, non-fiction, humanities. Promoting authors and publishers worldwide. Reading fee. Founded 1962.

Grandi & Associati SRL
Via Degli Olivetani 12, 20123 Milan
tel (02) 469 55 41/481 89 62 *fax* (02) 481 95108
email agenzia@grandieassociati.it
website www.grandieassociati.it
Directors Laura Grandi, Stefano Tettamanti

Provides publicity and foreign rights consultation for publishers and authors as well as sub-agent services; will suggest revision where appropriate. Reading fee. Founded 1988.

New Blitz Literary & TV Agency
Via di Panico 67, 00186 Rome
postal address CP 30047–00193, Rome 47
tel (06) 686 4859 *fax* (06) 686 4859
email blitzgacs@inwind.it
Literary Department Giovanni A.S. Congiu

No reading fee.

Piergiorgio Nicolazzini Literary Agency
Via GB Moroni 22, Milano 20146
tel/fax (02) 487 13365
email info@pnla.it
website www.pnla.it
Director Piergiorgio Nicolazzini

Literary and commerical fiction and non-fiction (home 10%, overseas 15–20%). No reading fee. Will suggest revision. Founded 1998.

JAPAN

The English Agency (Japan) Ltd
Sakuragi Building 4F, 6–7–3 Minami Aoyama, Minato-ku, Tokyo 107–0062

tel 03-3406 5385 *fax* 03-3406 5387
email info@eaj.co.jp
website www.eajco.jp
Managing Director Hamish Macaskill

Handles work by English-language writers living in Japan; arranges Japanese translations for internationally established publishers, agents and authors; arranges Japanese contracts for Japanese versions of all media. Standard commission: 10%. Own representatives in New York and London. No reading fee. Founded 1979.

THE NETHERLANDS

Internationaal Literatuur Bureau B.V.

Nieuwezÿds Voorburgwal 292 IV,
1012 RT Amsterdam, The Netherlands
tel (020) 330 6658
email lkohn@planet.nl
website www.ilb.nu
Contacts Linda Kohn

NEW ZEALAND

Glenys Bean Writer's Agent

PO Box 639, Warkworth
email info@glenysbean.com
website www.glenysbean.com
Directors Fay Weldon, Glenys Bean

Adult and children's fiction, educational, non-fiction, film, TV, radio (10–20%). Send preliminary letter, synopsis and sae. No reading fee. Represented by Sanford Greenburger Associates Ltd (USA). *Translation/foreign rights* the Marsh Agency Ltd. Founded 1989.

Michael Gifkins & Associates

PO Box 6496, Wellesley Street PO, Auckland 1141
tel (09) 523-5032 *fax* (09) 523-5033
email michael.gifkins@xtra.co.nz
Director Michael Gifkins

Literary and popular fiction, fine arts, children's and young adult fiction, substantial non-fiction (non-academic) co-publications (home 15%, overseas 20%). No reading fee. Will suggest revision. Founded 1985.

Playmarket

Level 2, 16 Cambridge Terrace, Te Aro, Wellington, PO Box 9767, Wellington
tel (04) 3828462 *fax* (04) 3828461
email info@playmarket.org.nz
website www.playmarket.org.nz
Director Mark Amery

Playwrights' agency and script advisory service. Its focus is the development and representation of New Zealand playwrights and their plays and it currently licences around 250 productions of New Zealand plays each year, both in New Zealand and around the world. Founded 1973.

Richards Literary Agency

postal address PO Box 31–240, Milford, North Shore City 0620
tel/fax (649) 410-0209
email rla.richards@clear.net.nz
Staff Ray Richards, Elaine Blake, Judy Bartlam, Frances Plumpton

Full-length MSS, fiction, non-fiction, adult, juvenile, educational, academic books; films, TV, radio (home 15%, overseas 20%). Preliminary letter, synopsis with sae required. No reading fee. Co-agents in London and New York. 100 clients. Founded 1977.

Total Fiction Services

PO Box 46-031, Park Avenue, Lower Hutt 5044
tel (04) 565 4429
email tfs@elseware.co.nz
website www.elseware.co.nz

General fiction, non-fiction, children's books. No poetry, or individual short stories or articles. Enquiries from New Zealand authors only. Email queries but no attachments. Hard copy preferred. No reading fee. Also offers assessment reports, mentoring and courses.

PORTUGAL

Ilidio da Fonseca Matos, Agente Literário Lda

Avenida Gomes Pereira, 105-3°–B, 1500–328 Lisbon
tel (21) 716 2988 *fax* (21) 715 4445
email ilidio.matos@oniduo.pt

No reading fee.

SCANDINAVIA, INC. FINLAND AND ICELAND

Bookman Literary Agency

Bastager 3, DK–2950 Vedbaek, Denmark
tel (45) 45 89 25 20 *fax* (45) 45 89 25 01
email ihl@bookman.dk
website www.bookman.dk
Contact Mr Ib H. Lauritzen

Handles rights in Denmark, Sweden, Norway, Finland and Iceland for foreign authors.

Leonhardt & Høier Literary Agency A/S

Studiestraede 35, DK–1455 Copenhagen K, Denmark
tel (45) 3313 2523 *fax* (45) 3313 4992
email anneli@leonhardt-hoier.dk, monica@leonhardt-hoier.dk
website www.leonhardt-hoier.dk

No reading fee.

Lennart Sane Agency AB

Holländareplan 9, S–374 34 Karlshamm, Sweden
tel (+46) 454 123 56 *fax* 0454 149 20

email lennart.sane@lennartsaneagency.com
website www.lennartsaneagency.com
Directors Lennart Sane, Elisabeth Sane, Philip Sane

Fiction, non-fiction, children's books. Founded 1969.

Sane Töregård Agency AB

Holländareplan 9, S–374 34 Karlshamn, Sweden
tel (46) 454 12356 *fax* (46) 454 14920
email toregard@algonet.se
Directors Lennart Sane, Ulf Töregård

Represents authors, agents and publishers in Scandinavia and Holland for rights in fiction, non-fiction and children's books. Founded 1995.

SOUTH AFRICA

Bond Literary Agents & Specialized Services

PO Box 164, Umhlanga Rocks 4320, South Africa
tel/fax (031) 584 8888
email jeangaiser@telkomsa.net
Chief Executives Jean Davidson, Jean Gaiser, *Chief Editor* Eileen Molver, *Poetry Advisor* Irene Aarons

Full length MSS. Fiction and non-fiction; juvenile and children's literature. Consultancy service on contracts and copyright. Preliminary phone call or letter and sase required. Reading fee; terms on application. Founded 1985.

Cherokee Literary Agency

3 Blythwood Road, Rondebosch, Cape 7700
tel (021) 671 4508
email dklee@mweb.co.za
Director D.K. Lee

Children's picture books in translation (home 10%). Founded 1988.

SPAIN

Carmen Balcells Agencia Literaria S.A.

Diagonal 580, 08021 Barcelona
tel 93-200-89-33 *fax* 93-200-70-41
email ag-balcells@ag-balcells.com
Contact Gloria Gutiérrez

International Editors Co., S.L.

Provenza 276, Barcelona 08008
tel 93-215-88-12 *fax* 93-487-35-83
email ieco@internationaleditors.com
Contact Isabel Monteagudo

RDC Agencia Literaria SL

C Fernando VI, No 13–15, Madrid 28004
tel 91-308-55-85 *fax* 91-308-56-00
email rdc@idecnet.com
Director Raquel de la Concha

Representing foreign fiction, non-fiction, children's books and Spanish authors. No reading fee.

Lennart Sane Agency AB

C/ Infanta Mercedes 90. ES-28020 Madrid
tel 91-579-80-46 *fax* 91-579-89-84
email lennart.sane@lennartsaneagency.com
website www.lennartsaneagency.com
President Lennart Sane

Fiction, non-fiction, children's books, film and TV scripts. Founded 1965.

Julio F. Yañez Agencia Literaria S.L.

Via Augusta 139, 6–2A, 08021 Barcelona
tel 93-200-71-07 *fax* 93-200-76-56
email montse@yanezag.com
Director Montse F-Yañez

SWITZERLAND

Paul & Peter Fritz AG Literary Agency

Jupiterstrasse 1, CH–8032 Zürich
tel 41 44 388 41 40 *fax* 41 44 388 41 30
email info@fritzagency.com
website www.fritzagency.com

Represents authors, agents and publishers in German-language areas. No reading fee.

Liepman AG

Englischviertelstrasse 59, CH-8032 Zürich
tel (043) 268 23 80 *fax* (043) 268 23 81
email info@liepmanagency.com
website www.liepmanagency.com
Contacts Eva Koralnik, Ruth Weibel

Represents authors, agents and publishers from all over the world for German translation rights, and selected international authors for world rights. No reading fee.

Mohrbooks AG, Literary Agency

Klosbachstrasse 110, CH–8032 Zürich
tel (043) 244 8626 *fax* (043) 244 8627
email info@mohrbooks.com
website www.mohrbooks.de
Contacts Sabine Ibach, Sebastian Ritscher

No reading fee.

NPA (Neue Presse Agentur)

Haldenstrasse 5, Haus am Herterberg, 8500 Frauenfeld-Herten
tel (052) 721 43 74
Director René Marti

Looking for occasional contributors to write for German/Swiss papers and magazines in the German language. Founded 1950.

USA

**Member of the Association of Authors' Representatives*

AMG/Renaissance – see The Firm

The Axelrod Agency*

55 Main Street, PO Box 357, Chatham, NY 12037
tel 518-392-2100

email steve@axelrodagency.com
President Steven Axelrod

Full-length MSS. Fiction (home 15%, overseas 20%), film and TV rights (15%); will suggest revision where appropriate. Works with overseas agents. No reading fee. Founded 1983.

The Balkin Agency Inc.*

PO Box 222, Amherst, MA 01004
tel/fax 413-322 8697
email rick62838@crocker.com
Director Richard Balkin

Full-length MSS – adult non-fiction only (home 15%, overseas 20%). Query first. May suggest revision. No reading fee. European and British Representative: Chandler Crawford Agency USA.

Berman, Boals & Flynn

208 West 30th Street, Room 401, New York, NY 10001
tel 212-500-1424 *fax* 212-500 1426
email judybbf@earthlink.net

Dramatic writing only, and only by recommendation.

BigScore Productions Inc.

PO Box 4575, Lancaster, PA 17604
tel 717-293-0247 *fax* 717-293-1945
email bigscore@bigscoreproductions.com
website www.bigscoreproductions.com
Contact David A. Robie

Fiction and non-fiction (home 15%). No poetry or TV/film scripts. Contact by email only. Founded 1995.

Georges Borchardt Inc.*

136 East 57th Street, New York, NY 10022
tel 212-753-5785 *fax* 212-838-6518
Directors Georges Borchardt, Anne Borchardt, Valerie Brochardt

Full-length and short MSS (home/ British/ performance 15%, translations 20%). Agents in most foreign countries. No unsolicited MSS. No reading fee. Founded 1967.

Brandt & Hochman Literary Agents Inc.*

1501 Broadway, Suite 2310, New York, NY 10036
tel 212-840-5760 *fax* 212-840-5776
Contact Gail Hochman, *UK Representative* A.M. Heath & Co. Ltd

Full-length and short MSS (home 15%, overseas 20%), performance rights (15%). No reading fee.

The Helen Brann Agency Inc.*

94 Curtis Road, Bridgewater, CT 06752
tel 860-354-9580 *fax* 860-355-2572
email helenbrannagency@earthlink.net
President Helen Brann

Pema Browne Ltd

11 Tena Place, Valley Cottage, NY 10989
email ppbltd@optonline.net
website www.pemabrowneltd.com
President Pema Browne, *Vice President* Perry J. Browne

Fiction, non-fiction and juvenile books (home/ overseas 20%). Only published children's book authors will be accepted for review. Will only review MSS if never sent out to publishers; no simultaneous submissions to other agents. Send query with sase; no phone, fax or email queries with attachments. Founded 1966.

Browne & Miller Literary Associates

(formerly Multimedia Product Development Inc.)
410 South Michigan Avenue, Suite 460, Chicago, IL 60605
tel 312-922-3063 *fax* 312-922-1905
email mail@browneandmiller.com
website www.browneandmiller.com
Contact Danielle Egan-Miller

General fiction and non-fiction (home 15%, overseas 20%). Select young adult projects. Works in conjunction with foreign agents. Will suggest revision; no reading fee. Founded 1971.

Maria Carvainis Agency Inc.*

1270 Avenue of the Americas, Suite 2320, New York, NY 10020
tel 212-245-6365 *fax* 212-245-7196
email mca@mariacarvainis.com
President & Literary Agent Maria Carvainis

Adult fiction and non-fiction (home 15%, overseas 20%). Fiction: all categories except science fiction and fantasy, especially literary and mainstream; mystery, thrillers and suspense; historical, Regency, young adult. Non-fiction: biography and memoir, health and women's issues, business, finance, psychology, popular science, popular culture. No reading fee. Query first; no unsolicited MSS. No queries by fax or email. Works in conjunction with foreign, TV and movie agents.

Frances Collin Literary Agent*

PO Box 33, Wayne, PA 19087-0033
tel 610-254-0555 *fax* 610-254-5029
Owner Frances Collin, *Associate Agent* Sarah Yake

Home 15%, overseas 20%, performance rights 20%. Specialisations of interest to UK writers: mysteries, women's fiction, history, biography, science fiction, fantasy. No screenplays. No reading fee. No unsolicited MSS. Letter queries must include sufficient IRCs (*email* queries@francescollin.com – no attachments). Works in conjunction with agents worldwide. Founded 1948; successor to Marie Rodell-Frances Collin Literary Agency.

Don Congdon Associates Inc.*

156 Fifth Avenue, Suite 625, New York, NY 10010
tel 212-645-1229 *fax* 212-727-2688
email dca@doncongdon.com
Agents Michael Congdon, Susan Ramer, Cristina Concepcion, Maura Kye-Casella, Katie Grimm, Katie Kotchman

Full-length and short MSS. General fiction and non-fiction (home 15%, overseas 19%, performance rights 15%). Works with co-agents overseas. No reading fee but no unsolicited MSS – query first with sase (no IRCs) or email for reply. Does not accept phone calls from querying authors. Founded 1983.

Richard Curtis Associates Inc.

171 East 74th Street, Floor 2, New York, NY 10021
tel 212-772-7363 *fax* 212-772-7393
website www.curtisagency.com
President Richard Curtis

All types of commercial non-fiction (home 15%, overseas 25%, film/TV 15%). See guidelines on website before submitting. Foreign rights handled by Baror International. Founded 1970.

Curtis Brown Ltd*

10 Astor Place, New York, NY 10003
tel 212-473-5400
Branch office 1750 Montgomery Street, San Francisco, CA 94111
tel 415-954 8566
President Peter Ginsberg (at CA branch office), *Ceo* Timothy Knowlton, *Contact* Query Dept (NY office), *Book* Katherine Fausset, Laura Blake Peterson

Fiction and non-fiction, juvenile, film and TV rights. No unsolicited MSS; query first with sase. No reading fee; no handling fees.

DeFiore and Company*

47 East 19th Street, 3rd Floor, New York, NY 10003
email info@defioreandco.com, submissions@defioreandco.com
website www.defioreandco.com
Contact Brian DeFiore, Laurie Abkemeier, Kate Garrick, Melissa Moy

Fiction and non-fiction (home 15%, overseas 20%). No poetry, science fiction, fantasy or romance. Send query with sase or send an email. Founded 1999.

Sandra Dijkstra Literary Agency*

PMB 515, 1155 Camino Del Mar, Del Mar, CA 92104–2605
tel 858-755-3115
website www.dijkstraagency.com
President Sandra Dijkstra, *Sub-agents* Elise Capron, Taryn Fagerness, Kevan Lyon, Jill Marsal, Kelly Sonnack

Fiction and non-fiction: narrative, history, business, psychology, self-help, science, memoir/biography, contemporary, women's, suspense, thrillers, romance, children's literature and young adults (home 15%, overseas 20%). Works in conjunction with foreign and film agents. All submissions must include synopsis and sase or IRC. No reading fee. Founded 1981.

Donadio & Olson Inc.*

121 West 27th Street, Suite 704, New York, NY 10001
tel 212-691-8077 *fax* 212-633-2837
email mail@donadio.com
Associates Edward Hibbert, Neil Olson, Carrie Howland

Literary fiction and non-fiction.

Dunham Literary, Inc.*

156 Fifth Avenue, Suite 625, New York, NY 10010–7002
website www.dunhamlit.com
Contact Jennie Dunham

Literary fiction and non-fiction, children's books (home 15%, overseas 20%). No reading fee. Founded 2000.

Dystel & Goderich Literary Management*

1 Union Square West, New York, NY 10003
tel 212-627-9100 *fax* 212-627-9313
website www.dystel.com
Contact Jane D. Dystel, Miriam Goderich, Michael Bourret, Jim McCarthy, Lauren Abramo, Stacey Glick, Jessica Papin

General fiction and non-fiction (home 15%, overseas 19%, film/TV/radio 15%): literary and commercial fiction, narrative non-fiction, self-help, cookbooks, parenting, science fiction/fantasy, children's and young adults. Send a query letter with a synopsis and up to 50pp of sample MS. Will accept email queries. No reading fee. Will suggest revision. Founded 1994.

The Ethan Ellenberg Literary Agency*

548 Broadway, Suite 5E, New York, NY 10012
tel 212-431-4554 *fax* 212-941-4652
email agent@ethanellenberg.com
website www.ethanellenberg.com
President & Agent Ethan Ellenberg

Fiction and non-fiction (home 15%, overseas 20%). Commercial fiction: thrillers, mysteries, children's, romance, women's, ethnic, science fiction, fantasy and general fiction; also literary fiction with a strong narrative. Non-fiction: current affairs, health, science, psychology, cookbooks, new age, spirituality, pop-culture, adventure, true crime, biography and memoir. No scholarly works, poetry, short stories or screenplays.

Will accept unsolicited MSS and seriously consider all submissions, including first-time writers. For fiction submit synopsis and first 3 chapters. For non-fiction send a proposal (outline, sample material, author CV, etc). For children's works send complete MS. Illustrators should send a representative selection of colour copies (no orginal artwork). Unable to return any material from overseas. For response include a sase with correct US postage. Submissions without a sase will receive only an email response if interested. Founded 1983.

Ann Elmo Agency Inc.*

60 East 42nd Street, New York, NY 10165
tel 212-661-2880 *fax* 212-661-2883

email elmolit@aol.com
Director Lettie Lee

Full-length fiction and non-fiction MSS (home 15%, overseas 20%), theatre (15%). Works with foreign agencies. No reading fee. Send query letter only with sase or IRC. New clients only by referral.

Diana Finch Literary Agency*

116 West 23rd Street, Suite 500, New York, NY 10011
tel 646-375-2081
email diana.finch@verizon.net
Owner Diana Finch

Memoirs, narrative non-fiction, literary fiction (home 15%, overseas 20%). No reading fee. Queries by email or letter only. No phone or fax. Previously agent with Ellen Levine Literary Agency since 1984. Founded 2003.

The Firm

9465 Wilshire Boulevard, Beverly Hills, CA 90212
tel 310-860-8000 *fax* 310-860-8132
email query@thefirmbooks.com
Contacts Alan Nevins

Full-length MSS. Fiction and non-fiction, plays, film and TV rights, performance rights. No unsolicited MSS; query first, submit outline. No reading fee.

Fletcher & Company*

78 Fifth Avenue, 3rd Floor, New York, NY 10011
email info@fletcherandco.com
website www.fletcherandco.com
Director Christy D. Fletcher

Narrative non-fiction, science, history, biography, literary and commercial fiction (home 15%, overseas 20%). Founded 2002.

The Fox Chase Agency Inc.*

701 Lee Road, Suite 102, Chesterbrook, PA 19087
tel 610-640-7560 *fax* 610-640-7562
Contact A.L. Hart

No unsolicited MSS. No reading fee. Founded 1972.

Jeanne Fredericks Literary Agency Inc.*

221 Benedict Hill Road, New Canaan, CT 06840
tel 203-972-3011 *fax* 203-972-3011
email jeanne.fredericks@gmail.com
website www.jeannefredericks.com

Quality non-fiction, especially health, science, women's issues, gardening, antiques and decorative arts, biography, cookbooks, popular reference, business, natural history (home 15%, overseas 20%). No reading fee. Query first, enclosing sase. Member of AAR and Authors Guild. Founded 1997.

Robert A. Freedman Dramatic Agency Inc.*

(formerly Harold Freedman Brandt & Brandt Dramatic Dept. Inc.)
1501 Broadway, Suite 2310, New York, NY 10036
tel 212-840-5760

Plays, motion picture and TV scripts. Send letter of enquiry first, with sase. No reading fee.

Samuel French Inc.*

45 West 25th Street, New York, NY 10010
tel 212-206-8990 *fax* 212-206-1429
email info@samuelfrench.com
President & Ceo Leon Embry

Play publishers; authors' representatives. No reading fee.

Sarah Jane Freymann Literary Agency

59 West 71st Street, Suite 9B, New York, NY 10023
tel 212-362-9277 *fax* 212-501-8240
email sarah@sarahjanefreymann.com
website www.sarahjanefreymann.com
President Sarah Jane Freymann

Book-length fiction and general non-fiction. Special interest in serious non-fiction, mainstream commercial fiction, contemporary women's fiction, Latino American, Asian American, African American fiction and non-fiction. Non-fiction: women's issues, biography, health/fitness, psychology, self-help, spiritual, natural science, cookbooks, pop culture. Works in conjunction with Abner Stein in London. No reading fee. Query with sase. Founded 1974.

Gelfman Schneider Literary Agents Inc.*

250 West 57th Street, Suite 2122, New York, NY 10107
tel 212-245-1993 *fax* 212-245-8678
email mail@gelfmanschneider.com
Directors Jane Gelfman, Deborah Schneider

General adult fiction and non-fiction (home 15%, overseas 20%). Will suggest revision. No reading fee. Send sase for return of material. Query by post only. Works in conjunction with Curtis Brown, London.

Frances Goldin Literary Agency*

57 East 11th Street, Suite 5B, New York, NY 10003
tel 212-777-0047
email agency@goldinlit.com
website www.goldinlit.com
Agents Frances Goldin, Ellen Geiger, Matt McGowan, Sam Stoloff, Sarah Bridgins, Phyllis Jenkins

Fiction (literary and high-quality commercial) and non-fiction, particularly books with a progressive political orientation. Send query with sase. No unsolicited MSS. Founded 1977.

Goodman Associates, Literary Agents*

500 West End Avenue, New York, NY 10024
tel 212-873-4806
Partners Arnold P. Goodman, Elise Simon Goodman

Adult book length fiction and non-fiction (home 15%, overseas 20%). No reading fee. Accept new clients by referral only. Founded 1976.

Sanford J. Greenburger Associates Inc.*

55 Fifth Avenue, New York, NY 10003
tel 212-206-5600 *fax* 212-463-8718
website www.greenburger.com
Contacts Heide Lange, Faith Hamlin, Daniel Mandel, Matt Bialer, Brenda Bowen, Lisa Fallagher, Courtney Miller-Callihan, Michael Harriot

Fiction and non-fiction, film and TV rights. No unsolicited MSS; query first. No reading fee.

The Joy Harris Literary Agency Inc.*

381 Park Avenue South, Suite 428, New York 10016
tel 212-924-6269 *fax* 212-725 5275
email joyharris@jhlitagent.com, adamreed@jhlitagent.com
website www.joyharrisliterary.com
President Joy Harris

John Hawkins & Associates Inc.*

(formerly Paul R. Reynolds Inc.)
71 West 23rd Street, Suite 1600, New York, NY 10010
tel 212-807-7040 *fax* 212-807-9555
website www.jhalit.com
President John Hawkins, *Vice-President* William Reiss, *Foreign Rights* Moses Cardona, *Other Agents* Warren Frazier, Anne Hawkins

Fiction, non-fiction, young adult. No reading fee. Founded 1893.

The Jeff Herman Agency LLC

PO Box 1522, Stockblidge, MA 01262
tel 413-298-0077 *fax* 413-298-8188
email jeff@jeffherman.com
website www.jeffherman.com

Business, reference, popular psychology, technology, health, spirituality, general non-fiction (home/overseas 15%); will suggest revision where appropriate. Works with overseas agents. No reading fee. Founded 1986.

Frederick Hill/Bonnie Nadell Inc.

8899 Beverly Bdvd, Suite 805, Los Angeles, CA 90048
tel 310-860-9605 *fax* 310-860-9672
website www.hillnadell.com

Full-length fiction and non-fiction (home 15%, overseas 20%). Send query letter initially. Works in conjunction with agents in Scandinavia, France, Germany, Holland, Japan, Spain and more. No reading fee. Founded 1979.

InkWell Management

521 Fifth Avenue, 26th Floor, New York, NY 10175
tel 212-922-8500 *fax* 212-922 0535
email info@inkwellmanagement.com
website www.inkwellmanagement.com
Contact Kimberly Witherspoon, Michael V. Carlisle, Richard Pine, Larry Ashmead, Ethan Bassoff, Catherine Drayton, David Forrer, Susan Hobson, Alexis Hurley, Nathaniel Jacks, George Lucas, Elisa Petrini, Julie Schilder, Jenny Witherell, Charlie Olsen, Mairead Duffy, Rose Marie Morse

Fiction and non-fiction (home/overseas 15%). Send query with sase or by email. Obtains most clients through recommendations from others. Founded 2004.

International Creative Management Inc.*

825 Eighth Avenue, New York, NY 10019
tel 212-556-5600 *fax* 212-556-5665
London office 66 Charlotte Street, London W1T 4QE
tel 020-7851 4853
website www.icmtalent.com

No unsolicited MSS; send query letter.

Janklow & Nesbit Associates

445 Park Avenue, New York, NY 10022
tel 212-421-1700 *fax* 212-980-3671
email postmaster@janklow.com
Partners Morton L. Janklow, Lynn Nesbit, *Agents* Anne Sibbald, Tina Bennett, Luke Janklow, Richard Morris, Cullen Stanley

Commercial and literary fiction and non-fiction. No unsolicited MSS. Works in conjunction with Janklow & Nesbit (UK) Ltd. Founded 1989.

JCA Literary Agency Inc.*

174 Sullivan Street, New York, NY 10012
email tom@jcalit.com, tony@jcalit.com
website www.jcalit.com
Contacts Tom Cushman, Tony Outhwait

Adult fiction, non-fiction and young adult. No unsolicited MSS; query first.

Keller Media Inc.

23852 West Pacific Coast Highway, Suite 701, Malibu, CA 90265
email query@kellermedia.com
website www.kellermedia.com, www.famefinders.com, www.bookpunchpublicity.com
Ceo/Senior Agent Wendy Keller, *Associate Agent* Megan Collins

Non-fiction for adults: business (all types); self-improvement; parenting; relationships; wellness; health and non-traditional health; science; nature; history; politics; psychology; personal finance; ecology/green movement; autobiographies (considered only by well-known people). No children's books, poetry, screenplays or illustrated books. Founded 1989.

Virginia Kidd Agency Inc.

PO Box 278, 538 East Hartford Street, Milford, PA 18337
tel 570-296-6205 *fax* 570-296-7266
website www.vk-agency.com
Contact Christine Cohen, Vaughne Hansen

Fiction, specialising in science fiction and fantasy (home 15%, overseas 20–25%). Send synopsis (1–3 pages), cover letter and sase. Founded 1965.

Harvey Klinger Inc.*
300 West 55th Street, Suite 11V, New York, NY 10019
email queries@harveyklinger.com
website www.harveyklinger.com
Agents Harvey Klinger, David Dunton, Sara Crowe, Andrea Somberg

Commercial and literary fiction, and non-fiction – serious narrative through to self-help psychology books (home 15%, overseas 25%). Send query with sase or by email. Exclusive submissions are preferred and given priority. Do not phone or fax. Founded 1977.

Barbara S. Kouts, Literary Agent*
PO Box 560, Bellport, NY 11713
tel 516-286-1278 *fax* 516-286-1538
email bkouts@aol.com
Owner Barbara S. Kouts

Fiction and non-fiction, children's (home 15%, overseas 20%). Works with overseas agents. No reading fee. No phone calls. Send query letter first. Founded 1980.

kt literary
9249 S. Broadway 200–543, Highlands Ranch, CO 80129
tel 720-344-4728
email contact@ktliterary.com
website www.ktliterary.com
Contact Kate Schafer Testerman

Primarily middle-grade and young adult fiction but no picture books; also adult commercial fiction and narrative non-fiction. Seeking 'brilliant, funny, original middle-grade and young adult fiction, both literary and commercial; witty women's fiction; pop-culture narrative non-fiction'. Email a query letter and the first 3pp of MS in the body of the email (no attachments). No snail mail.

Clients include Maureen Johnson, Ellen Booraem, S. Terrell French, Stephanie Perkins, Josie Bloss, Matthew Cody. Founded 2008.

The Lazear Agency Inc.
431 2nd Street, Ste 300, Hudson, WI 54016
tel 715-531-0012 *fax* 715-531-0016
email admin@lazear.com
website www.lazear.com
Contacts Jonathon Lazear, Christi Cardenas, Julie Mayo, Anne Blackstone

Fiction: full-length MSS; non-fiction: proposals. Adult fiction and non-fiction; film and TV rights; foreign language rights; audio, video and electronic rights (home 15%, overseas 20%). No reading fee. No unsolicited MSS; 2–3pp query first with sase for response. No faxed queries. Founded 1984.

The Lescher Agency Inc.*
7 Peter Cooper Road, Suite 11-F, New York, NY 10010
tel 212-673-5748 *fax* 212-396-1991
email susanlescher@aol.com
Director Susan Lescher

Fiction and non-fiction (home 15%, overseas 20%). No unsolicited MSS; query first with sase, or email. No reading fee.

Lescher & Lescher Ltd*
346 East 84th Street (ground floor), New York, NY 10028
tel 212-396-1999 *fax* 212-396-1991
Director Robert Lescher

Full-length MSS (home 15%, overseas 20%). No unsolicited MSS; query first with sase. No reading fee. Founded 1966.

Donald Maass Literary Agency*
Suite 801, 121 West 27th Street, New York, NY 10001
tel 212-727-8383 *fax* 212-727-3271
email info@maassagency.com
website www.maassagency.com
Agents Donald Maass, Jennifer Jackson, Cameron McClure, J. L. Stermer

Specialises in fiction, all genres (home 15%, overseas 20%). No poetry or picture books. Query with first 5pp of MS and a one-page synopsis with sase, or by email with 'query' in the subject line. Founded 1980.

Margret McBride Literary Agency*
7744 Fay Avenue, Suite 200, La Jolla, CA 92037
tel 858-454-1550 *fax* 858-454-2156
email staff@mcbridelit.com
website www.mcbrideliterary.com
President Michael Daley

Business, mainstream fiction and non-fiction (home 15%, overseas 25%). No poetry or children's books. No reading fee. Submit query letter with sase to Margret McBride. Founded 1981.

Anita D. McClellan Associates*
464 Common Street, Suite 142, Belmont, MA 02478
website www.anitamcclellan.com
Director Anita D. McClellan

General fiction and non-fiction. Full-length MSS (USA 15%, overseas 20%). Will suggest revision for agency clients. No unsolicited MSS. Send preliminary letter and sase bearing US postage or IRC. No email submissions.

McIntosh & Otis Inc.*
353 Lexington Avenue, New York, NY 10016
tel 212-687-7400 *fax* 212-687-6894
email info@mcintoshandotis.com
website www.mcintoshandotis.com
Adult Eugene H. Winick, Elizabeth Winick, *Juvenile* Edward Necarsulmer IV

Adult and juvenile literary fiction and non-fiction, film and TV rights. No unsolicited MSS; query first with outline, sample chapters and sase. No reading fee. Founded 1928.

Carol Mann Agency*

55 Fifth Avenue, New York, NY 10003
tel 212-206-5635 *fax* 212-675-4809
website http://carolmannagency.wordpress.com
Associates Carol Mann, Laura Yorke, Gareth Esersky

Psychology, popular history, biography, pop culture, general non-fiction; fiction (home 15%, overseas 20%). Works in conjunction with foreign agents. No reading fee. Founded 1977.

The Evan Marshall Agency*

Six Tristam Place, Pine Brook, NJ 07058–9445
tel 973-882-1122 *fax* 973-882-3099
email evanmarshall@thenovelist.com
President Evan Marshall

General fiction (home 15%, overseas 20%). Works in conjunction with overseas agents. Will suggest revision; no reading fee. Accepting new clients by professional referral only. Founded 1987.

The Marton Agency Inc.*

1 Union Square West, Suite 815, New York, NY 10003–3303
tel 212-255-1908 *fax* 212-691-9061
email info@martonagency.com
Owner Tonda Marton

Stage plays and musicals. Principally foreign language licensing.

William Morris Agency Inc.*

(incorporating the Writers Shop, formerly Virginia Barber Literary Agency)
1325 Avenue of the Americas, New York, NY 10019
tel 310-285-9000 *fax* 212-246-3583
website www.wma.com
Executive VP Owen Laster, *Senior VPs* Jennifer Rudolph Walsh, Suzanne Gluck, Joni Evans, Mel Berger, Jay Mandel, Tracy Fisher

General fiction and non-fiction (home 15%, overseas 20%, performance rights 15%). Will suggest revision. No reading fee.

Muse Literary Management

189 Waverly Place, Suite 4, New York, NY 10014–3135
tel 212-925-3721
email MuseLiteraryMgmt@aol.com
website www.museliterary.com
Agent Deborah Carter

Fiction and non-fiction (home 15%, overseas 20%). Special interests: literary novels and short stories with popular appeal, mysteries/thrillers, espionage fiction/non-fiction, literary narrative non-fiction and children's fiction/non-fiction. Particularly interested in multicultural fiction for adults and children. Special call for first novels with characters in their 20s and 30s. No romance, chick lit, sci-fi, fantasy, vampire stories, horror, religion, spirituality, stories of victimhood or illness. Prefers queries by email with no attachments.

Jean V. Naggar Literary Agency Inc.*

216 East 75th Street, Suite 1E, New York, NY 10021
tel 212-794-1082
President Jean V. Naggar, *Vice President* Jennifer Weltz, *Agents* Alice Tasman, Jessica Regel, Elizabeth Evans

Mainstream commercial and literary fiction; non-fiction: psychology, science, biography (home 15%, overseas 20%), performance rights (15%). Works in conjunction with foreign agents. No reading fee. Founded 1978.

Harold Ober Associates Inc.*

425 Madison Avenue, New York, NY 10017
tel 212-759-8600 *fax* 212-759-9428
website www.haroldober.com
Directors Phyllis Westberg, Pamela Malpas, Jake Elwell, Craig Tenney

Full-length MSS (home 15%, UK/overseas 20%), performance rights (15%). No screenplays or playscripts. No email or fax queries; see website for submission instructions. No reading fee. Founded 1929.

Fifi Oscard Agency Inc.

110 West 40th Street, New York, NY 10018
tel 212-764-1100 *fax* 212-840-5019
email agency@fifioscard.com
website www.fifioscard.com
Agents Peter Sawyer, Carolyn French, Carmen La Via, Kevin McShane

Full-length MSS (home 15%, overseas 20%), theatrical performance rights (10%). Will suggest revision. Works in conjunction with many foreign agencies. No reading fee, but no unsolicited submissions.

James Peter Associates Inc.

PO Box 358, New Canaan, CT 06840
tel 203-972-1070
email gene_brissie@msm.com
Contact Gene Brissie

Non-fiction, especially history, politics, popular culture, health, psychology, reference, biography (home 15%, overseas 20%). Will suggest revision. No reading fee. Foreign rights handled by JPA. Founded 1971.

The Pimlico Agency Inc.

PO Box 20447, Cherokee Station, New York, NY 10021
Contacts Christopher Shepard, Catherine Brooks, *Directors* Kay McCauley, Kirby McCauley

Adult non-fiction and fiction. No unsolicited MSS.

PMA Literary and Film Management Inc.

PO Box 1817, Old Chelsea Station, New York, NY 10113

tel 212-929-1222 *fax* 212-206-0238
email queries@pmalitfilm.com
website www.pmalitfilm.com
President Peter Miller, *Associates* Kelly Skillen, Adrienne Rosado

Full-length MSS. Specialises in commercial fiction (especially thrillers), true crime, non-fiction (all types), and all books with global publishing and film/TV potential (home 15%, overseas 25%), films, TV (10–20%). Works in conjunction with agents worldwide. Preliminary enquiry with career goals, synopsis and résumé essential. Founded 1976.

Rees Literary Agency*

14 Beacon Street, #710, Boston, MA 02108
email reesagency@reesagency.com
website www.reesagency.com
Contact Helen Rees, *Associates* Ann Collette, Lorin Rees

Business books, self-help, biography, autobiography, political, literary fiction, memoirs, history, current affairs (home 15%). No reading fee. Submit query letter with sase. Founded 1982.

The Angela Rinaldi Literary Agency*

PO Box 7877, Beverly Hills, CA 90212–7877
tel 310-842-7665
email amr@rinaldiliterary.com
President Angela Rinaldi

Mainstream and literary adult fiction; non-fiction (home 15%, overseas 25%). No reading fee. Founded 1994.

Russell & Volkening Inc.*

50 West 29th Street, Suite 7E, New York, NY 10001
tel 212-684-6050 *fax* 212-889-3026
website www.randvinc.com
Contact Timothy Seldes (President), Jesseca Salky (agent, women's fiction), Carrie Hannigan (agent, children's and young adult), Joy Azmitia (junior agent, fiction and non-fiction)

General fiction and non-fiction, film and TV rights. No screenplays. No unsolicited MSS; query first with letter and sase. No reading fee.

Schiavone Literary Agency, Inc.

Corporate offices 236 Trails End, West Palm Beach, FL 33413–2135
tel/fax 516-966-9294
email profschia@aol.com
3671 Hudson Manor Terrace No 11H, Bronx, NY 10463–1139
tel/fax 718-548-5332
email jendu77@aol.com
400 East 11th Street, Suite 7, New York, NY 10009
email kvn.mcadams@yahoo.com
website www.publishersmarketplace.com/members/profschia
Ceo James Schiavone, *President* Jennifer DuVall, *Executive V.P.* Kevin McAdams

Fiction and non-fiction, specialising in celebrity biography and memoirs (home 15%, overseas 20%). No reading fee. Send query letter only with return envelope and IRCs or US postage. Accepts email queries (no attachments). Founded 1996.

Susan Schulman Literary & Dramatic Agents Inc.*

454 West 44th Street, New York, NY 10036
tel 212-713-1633 *fax* 212-581-8830
email schulman@aol.com

Agents for negotiation in all markets (with co-agents) of fiction, general non-fiction, children's books, academic and professional works, and associated subsidiary rights including plays and film (home 15%, UK 7.5%, overseas 20%). No reading fee. Return postage required.

Scott Meredith Literary Agency LP

200 West 57th Street, Suite 904, New York, NY 10019
tel 646-274-1970 *fax* 212-977-5997
website www.scottmeredith.com
President Arthur Klebanoff

General fiction and non-fiction. Founded 1946.

The Shukat Company Ltd

340 West 55th Street, Suite 1A, New York, NY 10019
tel 212-582-7614
email staff@shukat.com
President Scott Shukat, *Contacts* Maribel Rivas, Lysna Scriven-Marzani

Theatre, films, TV, radio (15%). No reading fee. No unsolicited material accepted.

The Spieler Agency

27 West 20th Street, Room 305, New York, NY 10011
tel 212-757-4439
email spieleragency@spieleragency.com
Directors F. Joseph Spieler, Eric Myers

History, politics, ecology, business, consumer reference, biography, spirituality, serious non-fiction; some fiction (home 15%, overseas 20%). No reading fee. Query first with sample and sase. Founded 1982.

Philip G. Spitzer Literary Agency, Inc.*

50 Talmage Farm Lane, East Hampton, NY 11937
tel 631-329-3650 *fax* 631-329-3651
email lukas.ortiz@spitzeragency.com
website www.spitzeragency.com
Literary Manager L. Lukas Ortiz

General fiction and non-fiction; specialises in mystery/suspense, sports, politics, biography, social issues.

Rebecca Strong International Literary Agency

235 West 108th Street, Suite 35, New York, NY 10025
tel 212-865-1569
email info@rsila.com
website www.rsila.com
Owner/Agent Rebecca Strong

Literary and commercial fiction, narrative non-fiction, memoir and biography, self-improvement/how-to (home 15%, overseas 20%). No reading fee. Founded 2003.

Submission details only accepts email submissions. See website for further details.

Trident Media Group

41 Madison Avenue, New York, NY 10010
tel 212-262-4810 *fax* 212-262-4849
website www.tridentmediagroup.com
Executive Vice President Ellen Levine

Full-length MSS: biography, contemporary affairs, women's issues, history, science, literary and commercial fiction (home 15%, overseas 20%); in conjunction with co-agents, theatre, films, TV (15%). Will suggest revision. Works direct in UK, France, Germany, Italy, Spain and Holland; co-agents in other territories. No reading fee; preliminary letter and sase and US postage essential.

Ralph M. Vicinanza Ltd*

303 West 18th Street, New York, NY 10011-4440
tel 212-924-7090 *fax* 212-691-9644
Contacts Ralph Vicinanza, Christopher Lotts, Christopher Schelling, Adam Lefton

Fiction: literary, popular (especially science fiction, fantasy, thrillers), children's. Non-fiction: history, business, science, biography, popular culture. Foreign rights specialists. New clients by professional recommendation only. No unsolicited MSS.

Austin Wahl Agency Inc.

1820 North 76th Court, Elmwood Park, IL 60707–3631
tel 708-456-2301
President Thomas Wahl

Full-length and short MSS (home 15%, overseas 20%), theatre, films, TV (10%). No reading fee; professional writers only. Founded 1935.

Wallace Literary Agency Inc.

301 East 79th Street, No 14–J, New York, NY 10075
tel 212-570-9090 *fax* 212-772-8979
email walliter@aol.com
Director Lois Wallace

No cookery, humour, how-to, children's or young adult; film, TV, theatre for agency clients. Will suggest revision. No unsolicited MSS; no faxed queries. Will only answer queries with return postage. Founded 1988.

Watkins/Loomis Agency Inc.

PO Box 20925, Park West Finance Station, New York, NY 10025
tel 212-532-0080 *fax* 212-889-0506
email assistant@watkinsloomis.com
website www.watkinsloomis.com
President Gloria Loomis

Fiction and non-fiction. No unsolicited MSS. *Representatives* Abner Stein (UK), the Marsh Agency Ltd (foreign).

Rhoda Weyr Agency – see Dunham Literary, Inc.

Writers House LLC*

21 West 26th Street, New York, NY 10010
tel 212-685-2400 *fax* 212-685-1781
London agent: Ground Floor Flat, 24 Harvist Road, London NW6 6SH
020-8960 2966, 7534 494814
website www.writershouse.com
Chairman Albert Zuckerman, *President* Amy Berkower, *Agents* Simon Lipskar, Merrilee Heifetz, Robin Rue, Susan Ginsburg, Dan Conaway, Dan Lazar, Angharad Kowal (London)

Fiction and non-fiction, including all rights; film and TV rights. No screenplays or software. Send a one-page letter in the first instance, saying what's wonderful about your book, what it is about and why you are the best person to write it. No reading fee. Founded 1974.

Wylie-Merrick Literary Agency*

1138 South Webster Street, Kokomo, IN 46902
tel 765-459-8258
email robertbrown@wylie-merrick.com, sharenembrown@wylie-merrick.com
website www.wylie-merrick.com
Partners Robert Brown, Sharene Martin

Adult and juvenile fiction and non-fiction (home 15%, overseas 20%). Interested in romance, sci-fi and fantasy, women's, gay/lesbian, suspense/thrillers. No picture books or graphic novels. Query by email only; no unsolicited MSS. See website for full submission guidelines. Founded 1999.

The Wylie Agency Inc.

250 West 57th Street, Suite 2114, New York, NY 10107
tel 212-246-0069 *fax* 212-586-8953
email mail@wylieagency.com
website www.wylieagency.com
President Andrew Wylie, *Contact* Sarah Chalfant, Scott Moyers

Literary fiction/non-fiction. No unsolicited MSS accepted. London office: the Wylie Agency UK Ltd.

Art and illustration
Freelancing for beginners

Fig Taylor describes the opportunities open to freelance illustrators and discusses types of fee and how to negotiate one to your best advantage.

Full-time posts for illustrators are extremely rare. Because commissioners' needs tend to change on a regular basis, most artists have little choice but to freelance – offering their skills to a variety of clients in order to make a living.

Illustration is highly competitive and a professional attitude towards targeting, presenting, promoting and delivering your work will be vital to your success. Likewise, a realistic understanding of how the industry works and of your place within it will be key. Without adequate research into your chosen field(s) of interest, you may find yourself approaching inappropriate clients – a frustrating and disheartening experience for both parties and a waste of your time and money.

Who commissions illustration?

Magazines and newspapers

Whatever your illustrative ambitions, you are most likely to receive your first commissions from editorial clients. The comparatively modest fees involved allow art editors the freedom to take risks, so many are keen to commission newcomers. Briefs are generally fairly loose though deadlines can be short, particularly where daily and weekly publications are concerned. However, fast turnover also ensures a swift appearance in print, thus reassuring clients in other, more lucrative, spheres of your professional status. Given then that it is possible to use magazines as a springboard, it is essential to research them thoroughly when seeking to identify your own individual market. Collectively, editorial clients accommodate an infinite variety of illustrative styles and techniques. Don't limit your horizons by approaching only the most obvious titles and/or those you would read yourself. Consider also trade and professional journals, customer magazines (such as inflight magazines and those produced for supermarkets) and those available on subscription from membership organisations or charities. Seeking out as many potential clients as possible will benefit you in the long term. In addition to the titles listed in this *Yearbook*, the Association of Illustrators (AOI) publishes an *Editorial Directory* which gives specific client contact details, and is updated annually.

Book publishing

With the exception of children's picture books, where illustration is unlikely to fall out of fashion, many publishers are using significantly less illustration than they once did. While publishers of traditional mass market genres, such as science fiction and fantasy, still favour strong, representational, full-colour work on their covers, photography has begun to predominate in others, such as the family saga and historical romance. However, the recent fashion illustration renaissance has strongly influenced packaging of contemporary women's fiction, where quirky, humorous and graphic styles are also popular. A broader range of styles can be accommodated by those smaller publishers specialising in literary, upmarket fiction, though many opt to use stock imagery in order to operate within a limited budget. Meanwhile, although specialist and technical illustrators still have a vital part to play in non-fiction publishing, there is less decorative work being commissioned for lifestyle-related subjects as photography currently predominates.

Children's publishers use a wide variety of styles, covering the gamut from baby books, activity and early learning, through to full-colour picture books, covers for young adults and black and white line illustrations for the 8–11 year-old age group (particularly for boys, who tend to be more reluctant readers than girls). Author/illustrators are particularly welcomed by picture book publishers – though, whatever your style, you must be able to develop believable characters and sustain them throughout a narrative. See *Illustrating for children's books* on page 516. Some children's book illustrators initially find their feet in educational publishing. However, all ages are catered for within this area, including adults with learning difficulties, those learning languages for business purposes and teachers working right across the educational spectrum. Consequently, a wide variety of illustrators can be accommodated. With the exception of educational publishing, which tends to have a faster turnover, most publishing deadlines are civilised and mass market covers particularly well paid. There are numerous publishing clients listed elsewhere in this *Yearbook* and visiting individual websites is a good way to get a flavour of the kind of illustration they may favour. In addition, the Association of Illustrators publishes a *Publishing Directory*, which is updated yearly and gives specific client contact details.

Greeting cards

Many illustrators are interested in providing designs for cards and giftwrap. Illustrative styles favoured include decorative, graphic, humorous, children's and cute. For specific information on the gift industry which, unlike the areas covered here, works on a speculative basis, see *Winning the greeting card game* on page 527.

Design companies

Both designers and their clients (who are largely uncreative and will, ultimately, be footing the bill) will be impressed and reassured by relevant, published work so wait until you're in print before approaching them. Although fees are significantly higher than those in editorial and publishing, this third-party involvement generally results in a more restrictive brief. Deadlines may vary and styles favoured range from conceptual through to realistic, decorative, humorous and technical – with those involved in multimedia and web design favouring illustrators with character development and flash animation skills.

Magazines such as *Design Week*, *Creative Review* (both published by Centaur Media Plc) and *Grafik* will keep you abreast of developments in the design world and help you identify clients' individual areas of expertise. Meanwhile, *The Creative Handbook* (also published by Centaur), carries many listings, which can also be found on its website. Individual contact names are also available at a price from database specialists File FX, who can provide creative suppliers with up-to-date information on commissioners in all spheres. A similar service is provided by Bikini Lists, an online subscription-based resource that specialises in providing categorised mailing lists for single or multiple usage.

Advertising agencies

As with design, you should ideally be in print before seeking advertising commissions. Fees can be high, deadlines short and clients extremely demanding. A wide range of styles are used and commissions might be incorporated into direct mail or press advertising, featured on websites, hoardings or animated for television. There is also a growing interest in advertising on the internet. Fees will vary, depending on whether a campaign is local, national or even global.

Most agencies employ an art buyer to look at portfolios. A good one will know what each creative team is currently working on and may refer you to specific art directors. These days many art buyers are open to being approached by freelance illustrators. Agency listings and client details may be found in *ALF* (Account List File, published by BRAD Insight and sometimes stocked in the reference section of art school libraries), while *Creative Review* and the weekly *Campaign* (published by Haymarket Business Publications) carry agency news. The Association of Illustrators also publish an *Advertising Directory*, updated yearly.

Useful addresses

Association of Illustrators (AOI)
2nd Floor, Back Building, 150 Curtain Road, London EC2A 3AR
tel 020-7613 4328 *fax* 020-7613 4417
email info@theaoi.com
website www.theaoi.com, www.aoiportfolios.com
Publishes *Images*, *The Illustrator's Guide to Law and Business Practice* and various client directories. See also page 550.

Bikini Lists
Unit 1/18 Govanhill Workspace, 69 Dixon Road, Glasgow G42 8AT
tel 0141-636 3901
email ross@bikinilists.com
website www.bikinilists.com
Contact Ann-Kirsten Neeson

Boomerang Media Ltd
Manor House, Manor Park, Church Hill, Aldershot, Hants GU11 4JU
tel (01252) 368368
email sales@boomerangmedia.co.uk
website www.boomerangmedia.co.uk

BRAD Insight
Greater London House, Hampstead Road, London NW1 7TZ
tel 020-7728 8431
website www.bradinsight.com
Publishes *ALF* (Account List File).

Centaur Media Plc
50 Poland Street, London W1V 4AX
tel 020-7970 4000
website www.creativereview.co.uk, www.designweek.co.uk, www.chb.com
Publishes *Design Week*, *Creative Review* and *The Creative Handbook*.

Contact Creative UK LLP
Surrey House, 31 Church Street, Leatherhead, Surrey KT22 8EF
tel (01372) 220330 *fax* (01372) 220340
email mail@contactacreative.com
website www.contactacreative.com
Publishes *Contact Illustration*.

File FX
Unit 7, 83–93 Shepperton Road, London N1 3DF
tel 020-7226 6646
email info@filefx.co.uk
website www.filefx.com
Specialises in providing creative suppliers with up-to-date information on commissioning clients in all spheres.

Grafik Ltd
3rd Floor, 104 Great Portland Street, London W1W 6PE
tel 020-7637 5900
email hello@grafikmagazine.co.uk
website www.grafikmagazine.co.uk
Publishes *Grafik*.

Haymarket Media Group
174 Hammersmith Road, London W6 7JP
tel 020-8267 5000
email campaign@haymarket.com
website www.campaignlive.com
Publishes *Campaign*.

Portfolio presentation

In general, UK commissioners prefer to see someone with a strong, consistent, recognisable style rather than an unfocused jack-of-all-trades type. Thus, when assembling your professional portfolio – whether print or digital – try to exclude samples which are, in your own eyes, weak, irrelevant, uncharacteristic or simply unenjoyable to do and focus on your strengths instead. Should you be one of those rare, multi-talented individuals who finds it hard to limit themselves stylistically, try splitting conflicting work into separate portfolios geared towards different kinds of clients.

A lack of formal training need not be a handicap providing your portfolio accurately reflects the needs of the clients you target. Some illustrators find it useful to assemble 'mock-ups' using existing magazine layouts. By responding to the copy and replacing original images with your own illustrations, it is easier to see how your work will look in context. Eventually, as you become established you'll be able to augment these with published pieces.

If you are presenting a print portfolio, ideally it should be of the zip-up, ring-bound variety and never exceed A2 in size (A3 or A4 is best) as clients usually have little desk space; portfolio boxes are also acceptable, though you could run the risk of samples going astray. Alternatively, you may choose to give a laptop presentation, in which case strive to keep it simple and well organised. Always ensure that you bring your own laptop or borrow one with which you are familiar. (Also make sure it is fully charged and that you have emergency back-up such as a power brick, memory sticks, DVDs, etc. If your presentation involves talking a client through your website rather than files on your hard disk, check you will have wireless internet access.) Complexity of style and diversity of subject matter will dictate how many samples to include but if you are opting for a traditional portfolio presentation, all should be neatly mounted on lightweight paper or card and placed inside protective plastic sleeves. High-quality photographs, computer printouts and laser copies are acceptable to clients but tacky out-of-focus snapshots are not. Also avoid including multiple sketchbooks and life drawings, which are anathema to clients. It will be taken for granted that you know how to draw from observation.

Interviews and beyond

Making appointments can be hard work but clients take a dim view of spontaneous visits from passing illustrators. Having established the contact name (either from a written source or by asking the company directly), clients are still best approached by letter or telephone call. Emails can be overlooked, ignored or simply end up in the company spam filter. Many publishing houses are happy to see freelances, though portfolio 'drop-offs' are also quite common. Some clients will automatically take photocopies of your work for reference. However, it's advisable to have some kind of promotional material to leave behind such as a CD, postcard, broadsheet or advertising tearsheet. Always ask an enthusiastic client if they know of others who might be interested in your work. Personal recommendation almost always guarantees an interview.

Cleanliness, punctuality and enthusiasm are more important to clients than how you dress – as is a professional attitude to taking and fulfilling a brief. A thorough understanding of each commission is paramount from the outset. You will need to know your client's requirements regarding roughs; format and – if relevant – size and flexibility of artwork; preferred medium; and whether the artwork is needed in colour or black and white. You will also need to know when the deadline is. Never, under any circumstances agree to undertake a commission unless you are certain you can deliver on time and always work within your limitations. Talent is nothing without reliability.

Self-promotion

There are many ways an illustrator can ensure their work stays uppermost in the industry's consciousness, some more expensive than others. Images can be emailed in a variety of formats, put onto CD, posted in a blog, or showcased on a personal or hosting website. Advertising in prestigious hardback annuals such as Contact Creative UK's *Contact Illustration* and the AOI's *Images* – which are distributed free to commissioners – can be effective but doesn't come cheap and, in the case of *Images*, only those professionally selected are permitted to buy pages for their winning entries. However, these publications have a long shelf life and are well respected by industry professionals.

As commissioners increasingly turn to the internet for inspiration, websites are becoming an essential and affordable method of self-promotion (see *Setting up a website*, page 641). Make sure your website loads quickly, is simple and straightforward to negotiate and displays decent-sized images. Advertisers in *Contact Illustration* automatically qualify for a web portfolio of 20 images with links back to individual websites. It is also possible for illustrators to promote their work on the *Contact* website without appearing in the annual (www.contactacreative.com). Currently, both AOI members and non-members can promote their work online at www.aoiportfolios.com, though members can do so at a reduced rate.

Free publicity can be had courtesy of Boomerang Media Ltd, who will print appropriate images to go in postcard advertising racks. Distribution includes cafés, bars, cinemas, health clubs, universities and schools.

Be organised

Once you are up and running, it is imperative to keep organised records of all your commissions. Contracts can be verbal as well as written, though details – both financial and otherwise – should always be confirmed in writing (an email fulfils this purpose) and duplicated for your files. Likewise, keep corresponding client faxes, letters, emails and order forms. The AOI publication *The Illustrator's Guide to Law and Business Practice* offers a wealth of practical, legal and ethical information. Subjects covered include contracts, fee negotiation, agents, licences, royalties and copyright issues.

Money matters

The type of client, the purpose for which you are being commissioned and the usage of your work can all affect the fee you can expect to receive, as can your own professional attitude. Given that it is *extremely* inadvisable to undertake a commission without first agreeing on a fee, you will have to learn to be upfront about funds.

Licence *v.* copyright

Put simply, according to current EU legislation, copyright is the right to reproduce a piece of work anywhere, *ad infinitum*, for any purpose, for a period ending 70 years after the death of the person who created it. This makes it an extremely valuable commodity.

By law, copyright automatically belongs to you, the creator of your artwork, unless you agree to sell it to another party. In most cases, clients have no need to purchase it, and the recommended alternative is for you to grant them a licence instead, governing the precise usage of the artwork. This is far cheaper from the client's perspective and, should they subsequently decide to use your work for some purpose other than those outlined in your initial agreement, will benefit you too as a separate fee will have to be negotiated. It's also worth noting that even if you were ill-advised enough to sell the copyright, the artwork would still belong to you unless you had also agreed to sell that.

Rejection and cancellation fees

Most commissioners will not expect you to work for nothing unless you are involved in a speculative pitch, in which case it will be up to you to weigh up the pros and cons of your possible involvement. Assuming you have given a job your best shot – i.e. carried out the client's instructions to the letter – it's customary to receive a rejection fee even if the client doesn't care for the outcome: 25% is customary at developmental/rough stage and 50% at finished artwork stage. (Clear this with the client before you start, as there are exceptions to the rule.) Cancellation fees are paid when a job is terminated through no fault of the artist or, on occasion, even the client. Customary rates in this instance are 25% before rough stage, 33% on delivery of roughs and 100% on delivery of artwork.

Fixed *v.* negotiable fees

Editorial and publishing fees are almost always fixed with little, if any, room for haggling and are generally considerably lower than advertising and design fees, which tend to be negotiable. A national full-colour 48-sheet poster advertising Marks & Spencer is likely to pay more than a local black and white press ad plugging a poodle parlour. If, having paid your editorial dues, you find yourself hankering after commissions from the big boys, fee negotiation – confusing and complicated as it can sometimes be – will become a fact of life. However you choose to go about the business of cutting a deal, it will help if you disabuse yourself of the notion that the client is doing you a whopping favour by considering you for the job. Believe it or not, the client *needs* your skills to bring his/her ideas to life. In short, you are worth the money and the client knows it.

Pricing a commission

Before you can quote on a job, you'll need to know exactly what it entails. For what purpose is the work to be used? Will it be used several times and/or for more than one purpose? Will its use be local or national? For how long is the client intending to use it? Who is the client and how soon do they want the work? Are you up against anyone else (who could possibly undercut you)?

Next, ask the client what the budget is. Believe it or not there's a fair chance they might tell you. Whether they are forthcoming or not, don't feel you have to pluck a figure out of thin air or agree to their offer immediately. Play for time. Tell them you need to review your current workload and that you'll get back to them within a brief, specified period of time. If nothing else, haggling over the phone is less daunting than doing it face to face. If you've had no comparable commissions to date and are an AOI member, check out the going rate by calling them for pricing advice (or check out their report on illustration fees and standards of pricing on the AOI website, which is only available to members). Failing that, try speaking to a friendly client or a fellow illustrator who's worked on similar jobs.

When you begin negotiating, have in mind a bottom-line price you're prepared to do the job for and always ask for slightly more than your ideal fee as the client will invariably try to beat you down. You may find it useful to break down your asking price in order to explain exactly what it is the client is paying for. How you do this is up to you. Some people find it helpful to work out a daily rate incorporating overheads such as rent, heating, materials, travel and telephone charges, while others prefer to negotiate on a flat fee basis.

There are also illustrators who charge extra for something needed yesterday, time spent researching, model hire if applicable and so on. It pays to be flexible, so if your initial quote exceeds the client's budget and you really want the job, tell them you are open to negotiation. If, on the other hand, the job looks suspiciously thankless, stick to your guns. If the client agrees to your exorbitant demands, the job might start to look more appetising.

Getting paid

Once you've traded terms and conditions, done the job and invoiced the client, you'll then have the unenviable task of getting your hands on your fee. It is customary to send your invoice to the accounts department stating payment within 30 days. It is also customary for them to ignore this entreaty, regardless of the wolf at your door, and pay you when it suits them. Magazines pay promptly, usually within 4–6 weeks; everyone else takes 60–90 days – no matter what.

Be methodical when chasing up your invoice. Send out a statement the moment your 30 days has elapsed and call the accounts department as soon as you like. Take names, note dates and the gist of their feeble excuses. ('It's in the post', 'He's in a meeting', 'She's on holiday and forgot to sign the cheque before she went'), and keep on chasing. Don't worry about your incessant nagging scuppering your plans of further commissions as these decisions are solely down to the art department, and they think you're a gem. Should payment still not be forthcoming three months down the line, it might be advisable to ask your commissioner to follow things up on your behalf. Chances are they'll be horrified you haven't been paid yet and things will be speedily resolved. In the meantime, you'll have had a good deal of practice talking money, which can only make things easier next time around.

And finally...

Basic book-keeping – making a simple, legible record of all your financial transactions, both incoming and outgoing – will be crucial to your sanity once the tax inspector starts to loom. It will also make your accountant's job easier, thereby saving you money. If your annual turnover is less than £30,000, it is unnecessary to provide the Inland Revenue with detailed accounts of your earnings. Information regarding your turnover, allowable expenses and net profit may simply be entered on your tax return. Although an accountant is not necessary to this process, many find it advantageous to employ one. The tax system is complicated and dealing with the Inland Revenue can be stressful, intimidating and time consuming. Accountants offer invaluable advice on tax allowances, National Insurance and tax assessments, as well as dealing expertly with the Inland Revenue on your behalf – thereby enabling you to attend to the business of illustrating. See *Income tax* on page 731, *Social security contributions* on page 741 and *Social security benefits* on page 749.

Fig Taylor initially began her career as an illustrators' agent in 1983. For 25 years she has been the resident 'portfolio surgeon' at the Association of Illustrators and also operates as a private consultant to non-AOI member artists. In addition, she lectures extensively in Professional Practice to illustration students throughout the UK.

See also...

- *Websites for artists,* page 656
- *Art agents and commercial studios,* page 519
- *Winning the greeting card game,* page 527
- *Card and stationery publishers that accept illustrations and verses,* page 531
- *Setting up a website,* page 641
- *Design and Artists Copyright Society, page 717*

Illustrating for children's books

The world of children's publishing is big business. The huge range of books published each year all carry artwork – lots of it. Maggie Mundy offers guidance for people who are at the start of their career in illustrating for children's books.

The portfolio

Your portfolio should reflect the best of you and your work, and should speak for itself. Keep its content simple – if too many styles are included, for instance, your work will not leave a lasting impression.

Include some artwork other than those carried out for college projects, for example an illustration from a timeless classic to show your abilities, and something modern which reflects your own taste and the area in which you wish to work.

If your strength is for black and white illustration, include pieces with and without tone and with or without a wash. Some publishers want line and tone and some want only line. As cross hatching and stippling can add a lot of extra time to an illustration deadline, it might be advisable to leave out these samples. If you can, include a selection of humour as it can be used effectively in educational books and elsewhere. It is best not to sign and date your work: some artworks can stand the test of time and still look good after a year or two, but if it looks dated … so is the illustrator!

An A3 portfolio is probably the ideal size. Place your best piece of artwork on the opening page and your next best piece on the last page. See *Freelancing for beginners* on page 509 for further information on portfolio presentation.

Looking at the market

Start by looking thoroughly at what is being published today for children. Take your studies to branches of big retail chains, some independent bookshops, as well as your local library (a helpful librarian should be able to tell you which are the most borrowed books). Absorb the picture books, explore the novelty books, look at the variety of colour covers, and note the range of black line illustrations inside books for children and teenagers. Make a list of the publishers you think may be able to use your particular style.

By making these investigations you will gain an insight into not only the current trends and styles but also the much favoured, oft-published classic children's literature. Most importantly, it will help you identify your market.

In books for a young age range every picture must tell the story – some books have no text and the illustrations say it all. Artwork should be uncluttered, shapes clear, and colour bright. If this does not appeal to you, go up a year or two and note the extra details that are added to the artwork (which still tells the story). Children now need to see more than just clear shapes: they need extra details added to the scene – for example a quirky spider hanging around, or a mouse under the bed.

Children are your most critical audience: never think that you can get away with 'any old thing'. Indeed, at the Bologna Book Fair it is a panel of children which judges what they consider to be the best picture book.

Current trends

Innovative publishers are always on the lookout for something new in illustration styles: something completely different from the tried and tested. More and more they are turning to European and overseas illustrators, often sourced from the Bologna Book Fair exhibitions and illustrators catalogue.

Always strive to improve on your work. Don't be afraid to try out something different and to work it up into acceptable examples. Above all, don't get left behind.

Making approaches for work

With your portfolio arranged and your target audience in mind, compile a list of publishing houses, packagers and magazines which you think may be suitable for your work.

An agent should know exactly where to place your work, and this may be the easier option (see below). However, you may wish to market yourself by making and going to appointments until you crack your first job.

Alternatively, you could make up a simple broadsheet comprising a black and white and two or three colour illustrations, together with your contact details, and have it colour photocopied or printed. Another inexpensive option is to have your own CDs made up and to send them instead. Send a copy to either the Art Director, the Creative Director or the Senior Commissioning Editor (for picture books) of each potential client on your list. Try to find out the name of the person you would like to see your work. Wait at least a week and then follow up your mailing with a phone call to ask if someone would like to see your portfolio.

Also consider investing in your own website which you can easily update yourself.

Know your capabilities

Know your strengths, but be even more aware of your weaknesses. You will gain far more respect if you admit to not being able to draw something particularly well than by going ahead and producing an embarrassing piece of artwork and having it rejected. You will be remembered for your professional honesty and that client may well try to give you a job where you can use your expertise.

Publishers need to know that you can turn out imaginative, creative artwork while closely following a text or brief, and be able to meet their deadline. It may take an illustrator three weeks to prepare roughs for 32 pages, three weeks to finish the artwork, plus a week to make any corrections. In addition, time has to be allowed for the roughs to be returned. On this basis, how many books can an illustrator realistically take on? Scheduling is of paramount importance (see below).

You will need to become familiar with 'publishing speak' – terms such as gutters, full bleed, holding line, overlays, vignettes, tps, etc. If you don't know the meaning of a term, ask – after all, if you have only recently left college you will not be expected to know all the jargon.

In the course of your work you will have to deal with such issues as contracts, copyright, royalties, Public Lending Right, rejection fees, etc. The Association of Illustrators, which exists to give help to illustrators in all areas, is well worth joining.

Organising your workload

When you have reached the stage when you have jobs coming through on a fairly regular basis, organise a comprehensive schedule for yourself so you do not overburden yourself with work. Include on it when roughs have to be submitted, how much work you can fit in while waiting for their approval, the deadline for the artwork, and so on. A wall chart can be helpful for this but another system may work better for you. It is totally unacceptable to deliver artwork late. If you think that you might run over time with your work, let your client know in advance as it may be possible to reach a new agreement for delivery.

Payment

There are two ways in which an illustrator may be paid for a commission for a book: a flat fee on receipt and acceptance of the artwork, or by an advance against a royalty of future sales. The advance offered could be less than a flat fee but it may result in higher earnings overall. If the book sells well, the illustrator will receive royalty payments twice a year for as long the book is in print.

You need to know from the outset how you are going to be paid. If it is by a flat fee, you may be given an artwork order with a number to be quoted when you invoice. Always read through orders to make sure you understand the terms and conditions. If you haven't been paid within 30 days, send a statement to remind the client, or make a quick phone call to ask when you can expect to receive payment.

With a royalty offer, a contract will be drawn up and this must be checked carefully. One of the clauses will state the breakdown of how and when you will be paid.

Once you have illustrated your first book you should register with the Public Lending Right Office (see page 338) so that you can receive a yearly payment on all UK library borrowings. You will need to cooperate with the author regarding percentages before submitting your own form. The PLR office will give you a reference number, and you then submit details to them of each book you illustrate. It mounts up and is a nice little earner!

Agents

The role of the agent is to represent the illustrator to the best of their ability and to the illustrator's best advantage. A good agent knows the marketplace and will promote illustrators' work where it will count. An agent may ask you to do one or two sample pieces to strengthen your portfolio, giving them a better chance of securing work for you.

Generally speaking, agents will look after you, your work schedules, payments, contracts, royalties, copyright issues, and try to ensure you have a regular flow of work which you not only enjoy but will stretch your talents to taking on bigger and better jobs. Without exposing your weaknesses, check that you have adequate time in which to do a job and that you are paid a fair rate for the work.

Some illustrators manage well without an agent, and having one is not necessarily a pathway to fame and fortune. Choose carefully: you need to both like and trust the agent and vice versa.

Agents' charges range from 25% to 30%. Find out from the outset how much a prospective agent will charge.

Finally

Do not be downhearted if progress is at first slow. Everyone starts by serving an apprenticeship, and it is a great opportunity to learn, absorb and soak up as much of the business as possible. Ask questions, get all the advice you can, and use what you learn to improve your craft and thereby your chances of landing a job. Publishers are always on the lookout for fresh talent and new ideas, and one day your talent will be the one they want.

Maggie Mundy represented illustrators for children's books from 1983 until she retired at the end of 2009.

Art agents and commercial art studios

Before submitting work, artists are advised to make preliminary enquiries and to ascertain terms of work. Commission varies but averages 25–30%. The Association of Illustrators (see page 550) provides a valuable service for illustrators, agents and clients.

*Member of the Society of Artists Agents
†Member of the Association of Illustrators

Advocate

39 Church Road, Wimbledon Village, London SW19 5DQ
tel 020-8879 1166 *fax* 020-8879 3303
email mail@advocate-art.com
website www.advocate-art.com
Director Edward Burns

Has 5 agents representing 110 artists and illustrators. Supplies work to book and magazine publishers, design and advertising agencies, greeting card and fine art publishers, and gift and ceramic manufacturers. Also has an original art gallery, stock library and website in German, Spanish and French. Founded as a co-operative in 1996.

Allied Artists/Artistic License

mobile (07971) 111256
email info@allied-artists.net
website www.allied-artists.net
Contacts Gary Mills, Mary Burtenshaw

Represents over 40 artists specialising in highly finished realistic figure illustrations, stylised juvenile illustrations for children's books, and cartoons for magazines, books, plates, prints, cards and advertising. Extensive library of stock illustrations. Commission: 33%. Founded 1983.

Arena*†

Quantum Artists Ltd, 31 Eleanor Road, London E15 4AB
tel (0845) 050 7600
email info@arenaworks.com
website www.arenaworks.com
Contact Tamlyn Francis

Represents 30 artists working mostly for book covers, children's books and design groups. Average commission 25%. Founded 1970.

The Art Agency (Wildlife Art Ltd)

The Lodge, Cargate Lane, Saxlingham Thorpe, Norwich NR15 1TU
tel (01508) 471500 *fax* (01508) 470391
email info@the-art-agency.co.uk
website www.the-art-agency.co.uk

Represents more than 40 artists producing top-quality, highly accurate and imaginative illustrations across a wide variety of subjects and for all age groups, both digitally and traditionally. Clients are children's fiction and non-fiction publishers. Include sae with submissions. Do not email portfolios. Commission: 30%. Founded 1992.

The Art Market*†

51 Oxford Drive, London SE1 2FB
tel 020-7407 8111
email info@artmarketillustration.com
website www.artmarketillustration.com
Director Philip Reed

Represents 40 artists creating illustrations for publishing, design and advertising. Founded 1989.

Artist Partners Ltd*†

2E The Chandlery, 50 Westminster Bridge Road, London SE1 7QY
tel 020-7401 7904 *fax* 020-7401 3378
email chris@artistpartners.demon.co.uk
website www.artistpartners.com
Managing Director Christine Isteed

Represents artists, including specialists in their field, producing artwork in every genre for advertising campaigns, storyboards, children's and adult book covers, newspaper and magazine features and album covers. New artists are only considered if their work is of an exceptionally high standard, in which case submission should be by post only and include an sae. Commission: 30%. Founded 1951.

The Artworks*†

40 Frith Street, London W1D 5LN
tel 020-7734 3333 *fax* 020-7734 3484
email info@theartworksinc.com, steph@theartworksinc.com
website www.theartworksinc.com
Contact Lucy Scherer, Stephanie Alexander, Alex Gardner

Represents 20 artists for illustrated gift books and children's books. Commission: 25% advances, 15% royalties.

Beehive Illustration

42A Cricklade Street, Cirencester, Glos. GL7 1JH
tel (01285) 885149 *fax* (01285) 641291

email info@beehiveillustration.co.uk
website www.beehiveillustration.co.uk
Contact Paul Beebee

Represents over 70 artists specialising in education and general children's publishing illustration. Commission: 25%. Founded 1989.

Central Illustration Agency

29 Heddon Street, 1st Floor, London W1B 4BL
tel 020-7734 7187 *fax* 020-7434 0974
email info@centralillustration.com
website www.centralillustration.com
Contact Benjamin Cox

Represents 70 artists producing illustrations for design, publishing, animation and advertising. Commission: 30%. Founded 1983.

Début Art & The Coningsby Gallery*†

30 Tottenham Street, London W1T 4RJ
tel 020-7636 1064
email info@debutart.com
website www.debutart.com, www.coningsbygallery.com
Directors Andrew Coningsby, Samuel Summerskill, Jonathan Hedley

Represents 120 of the world's leading and contemporary illustrators. Commission: 20%. Worldwide commissioning clientele and artist base. Submissions from new illustrators always welcome via email. Founded 1985.

Eastwing*†

99 Chase Side, Enfield EN2 6NL
tel 020-8367 6760 *fax* 020-8367 6730
email representation@inkshed.co.uk
website www.inkshed.co.uk
Partners Andrea Plummer, Gordon Allen, *Contact* Abby Glassfield

Represents 31 artists who work across the board – advertising, design, publishing, editorial. Commission: 25–30%. Founded 1985.

Eye Candy Illustration

Pepperpot Corner, Manor Yard, Blithbury Road, Hamstall, Ridware, Staffs. WS15 3RS
tel 020-8291 0729
email info@eyecandy.co.uk
website www.eyecandy.co.uk
Managing Director Mark Wilson

Represents 40 artists producing work for advertising campaigns, packaging, publishing, editorials, greetings cards, merchandising, and a huge variety of design projects. Submit printed samples with sae or email low-res jpeg files via website. Founded 2002.

Ian Fleming Associates – see Phosphor Art Ltd

Folio Illustrators' & Designers' Agents

10 Gate Street, Lincoln's Inn Fields, London WC2A 3HP
tel 020-7242 9562 *fax* 020-7242 1816
email info@folioart.co.uk
website www.folioart.co.uk, www.folioboutique.com

All areas of illustration. Send sae with samples. Founded 1976.

Good Illustration Ltd

11–15 Betterton Street, London WC2H 9BP
tel 020-8123 0243 , (US) 347-627-0243
email draw@goodillustration.com
website www.goodillustration.com
Directors Doreen Thorogood, Stephen Thorogood

Represents 30 artists for advertising, design, publishing and animation work. Send return postage with samples. Commission: 30%. Founded 1977.

Graham-Cameron Illustration

The Studio, 23 Holt Road, Sheringham, Norfolk NR26 8NB
tel (01263) 821333 *fax* (01263) 821334
email enquiry@graham-cameron-illustration.com
and Duncan Graham-Cameron, Graham-Cameron Illustration, 59 Hertford Road, Brighton BN1 7GG
tel (01273) 385890
website www.gciforillustration.com
Partners Mike Graham-Cameron, Helen Graham-Cameron, Duncan Graham-Cameron

Represents 37 artists. Undertakes all forms of illustration for publishing and communications. Specialises in educational, children's and information books. Telephone before sending A4 sample illustrations with sae. Do not send MSS. Founded 1985.

The Guild of Aviation Artists

Trenchard House, 85 Farnborough Road, Farnborough, Hants GU14 6TF
tel (01252) 513123 *fax* (01252) 510505
email admin@gava.org.uk
website www.gava.org.uk
President Michael Turner FGAvA, *Secretary/ Administrator* Susan Gardner

Specialises in aviation art in all mediums and comprising 450 members, the Guild sells, commissions and exhibits members' work. Founded 1971.

John Hodgson Agency

38 Westminster Palace Gardens, Artillery Row, London SW1P 1RR
tel 0171-580 3773 *fax* 0171-222-4468

Publishing (children's picture books). Essential to send sae with samples. Commission: 25%. Founded 1965.

Illustration Ltd

2 Brooks Court, Cringle Street, London SW8 5BX
tel 020-7720 5202 *fax* 020-7720 5920
email hello@illustrationweb.com
website www.illustrationweb.com

Contact Harry Lyon-Smith, Juliette Lott, Victoria Pearce, Mike Cowley, Vanessa Dell

Represents 150 artists producing illustrations and animation for international advertisers, designers, publishers and editorial clients. Artists should send submissions via the website. Commission: 33.3% or 25%. Founded 1929.

Image by Design Licensing

The Cottage, Pryor House, Preston, Hitchin, Herts. SG4 7UD
tel (01462) 422244
email enquiries@ibd-licensing.co.uk
website www.ibd-licensing.co.uk
Contact Lucy Brenham

Quality artwork, design and photography for a range of applications including greeting cards, fine art prints, stationery, calendars, ceramics, book illustration, table top, jigsaws, giftware and needlecraft. New artists always considered. Founded 1987.

Libba Jones Associates

Hopton Manor, Hopton, Nr Wirksworth, Derbyshire DE4 4DF
tel (01629) 540353 *fax* (01629) 540577
website http://gallery.mac.com/LJassociates
Contacts Libba Jones, Ieuan Jones

High-quality artwork and design for china, greetings cards and giftwrap, jigsaw puzzles, calendars, prints, posters, stationery, book illustration, fabric design. Submission of samples required for consideration. Founded 1983.

Lemonade Illustration Agency

Hill House, Suite 231, 210 Upper Richmond Road, London SW15 6NP
tel (07891) 390750
email info@lemonadeillustration.com
website www.lemonadeillustration.com
Contact Studio Manager

Represents 45 artists who create illustrations for a variety of applications. Its new division, Fizzy Illustration Agency, specialises in creating for the children's market and represents 16 artists. Email a website link (no attachments) or post hard copies of samples with sae.

David Lewis Illustration Agency

Worlds End Studios, 134 Lots Road, London SW10 0RJ
tel 020-7435 7762 *mobile* (07931) 824674
fax 020-7351 5044
email davidlewis34@hotmail.com
website www.davidlewisillustration.com
Director David Lewis, *Associate Director* Ramon Johns

Considers all types of illustration for a variety of applications but mostly suitable for book and magazine publishers, design groups, recording companies and corporate institutions. Also offers a comprehensive selection of images suitable for subsidiary rights purposes. Send return postage with samples. Commission: 30%. Founded 1974.

Frances McKay Illustration

18 Lammas Green, Sydenham Hill, London SE26 6LT
tel 020-8693 7006 *mobile* (07703) 344334
email frances@francesmckay.com
website www.francesmckay.com
Proprietor Frances McKay

Represents 20+ artists for illustration mainly for children's books, magazines and products, greetings cards and stationery. Submit colour copies of recent work or email low-res scans; sae essential for return of all unsolicited samples. Commission: 25–35%. Founded 1999.

Meiklejohn Illustration*†

5 Risborough Street, London SE1 0HF
tel 020-7593 0500 *fax* 020-7593 0501
email info@meiklejohn.co.uk
website www.meiklejohn.co.uk
Contact Claire Meiklejohn

All types of illustration.

N.E. Middleton Artists' Agency

email kathy.bishop@btinternet.com
website www.nemiddleton.co.uk

Designs for greetings cards, stationery, prints, calendars, china and jigsaws etc. Submissions may be emailed only, following link from website.

The Monkey Feet Illustration Agency

Oakwood Cottage, 107 Grove Lane, Cheadle Hulme, Cheshire SK8 7NE
tel 0808 1200 996
email enquiries@monkeyfeetillustration.co.uk
website www.monkeyfeetillustration.co.uk
Director Adam Rushton

Represents 48 artists creating work for children's book publishers, design agencies, greeting card companies and toy manufacturers. Commission: 15–30%. Founded 2002.

NB Illustration

40 Bowling Green Lane, London EC1R 0NE
tel 020-7278 9131 *fax* 020-7278 9121
email info@nbillustration.co.uk
website www.nbillustration.co.uk
Directors Joe Najman, Charlotte Berens, Paul Najman

Represents 50+ artists and will consider all material for the commercial illustration market. Sae essential. Commission: 30%. Founded 2000.

The Organisation*†

The Basement, 69 Caledonian Road, London N1 9BT
tel 0845-054 8033 *fax* 020-7833 8269
email lorraine@organisart.co.uk
website www.organisart.co.uk
Contact Lorraine Owen

Represents over 60 international illustrators. Contemporary and traditional styles for all areas of publishing. Stock illustration also available. See website for submission guidelines. Founded 1987.

Oxford Designers & Illustrators Ltd

Aristotle Lane, Oxford OX2 6TR
tel (01865) 512331 *fax* (01865) 512408
email richardcorfield@odi-illustration.co.uk
website www.o-d-i.com
Directors Peter Lawrence (managing), Richard Corfield, Andrew King

Studio of 20 staff working for educational publishers and businesses. Design for print and the web. All types of artwork including scientific, technical, medical, natural history, figures, 3-D, cartoons, animation, maps and diagrams – computer generated and hand drawn. Not an agency. Founded 1968.

Phosphor Art Ltd*

41 The Pump House, Pump House Close, London SE16 7HS
tel 020-7064 4666 *fax* 020-7064 4660
email info@phosphorart.com
website www.phosphorart.com
Directors Jon Rogers, Catriona Wydmanski

Represents 46 artists and specialises in innovative graphic digital illustration with artists working in watercolour, oil and gouche methods as well as pen and ink, scraper, charcoal and engraving styles. Also animation. Incorporates Ian Fleming Associates and The Black and White Line. Commission: 33.3%.

Plum Pudding Illustration

9 Lydden Road, London SW18 4LT
tel 020-3004 7135 *fax* 020-3004 7136
email info@plumpuddingillustration.com
website www.plumpuddingillustration.com
Contact Mark Mills

Children's publishing (all genres), advertising, editorial, greetings cards and packaging. See website for submission procedure. Represents 30+ artists. Commission: 30%. Founded 2006.

Sylvie Poggio Artists Agency

36 Haslemere Road, London N8 9RB
tel 020-8341 2722 *fax* 020-8374 1725
email sylviepoggio@blueyonder.co.uk
website www.sylviepoggio.com
Directors Slyvie Poggio, Bruno Caurat

Represents 40 artists producing illustrations for publishing and advertising. Commission: 25%. Founded 1992.

Linda Rogers Associates

163 Half Moon Lane, London SE24 9JG
tel 020-7501 9106
email lr@lindarogers.net
website www.lindarogers.net
Partners Linda Rogers, Peter Sims, Jess Sims

Represents 65 illustrators and author/illustrators in all fields of illustration. Specialises in children's books, educational, information books; adult leisure books and magazines. Reply only with sae. Artwork samples only viewed via post, *not* by email. Commission: 25%. Founded 1973.

Specs Art

93 London Road, Cheltenham, Glos. GL52 6HL
tel (01242) 515951
email roland@specsart.com
website www.specsart.com
Partners Roland Berry, Stephanie Prosser

High-quality illustration for advertisers, publishers and all other forms of visual communication. Specialises in licensed character illustration.

Vicki Thomas Associates

195 Tollgate Road, London E6 5JY
tel 020-7511 5767 *fax* 020-7473 5177
email vickithomasassociates@yahoo.co.uk
website www.vickithomasassociates.com
Consultant Vicki Thomas

Considers the work of illustrators and designers working in greetings and gift industries, and promotes such work to gift, toy, publishing and related industries. Written application and b&w photocopies required. Commission: 30%. Founded 1985.

How to get ahead in cartooning

Earning a living from creating cartoons is highly competitive. But if you feel that you were born to be a cartoonist, Martin Rowson offers some advice on how to get your work published.

I can't say precisely when I first realised I wanted to be a cartoonist. I personally believe that cartoonists are born and not made so perhaps I should be talking about when I realised I *was* a cartoonist. I do know that, aged ten, I nicked my sister's 1950s British history textbook, which was illustrated throughout by cartoons (from Gillray via Tenniel to Low) and somewhere inside me stirred an unquantifiable yearning to draw – to express myself in the unique style that is the equally unique talent of the 'cartoonist'. So, shortly afterwards I started copying the way Wally Fawkes (better known by his *nom de plume* 'Trog') drew the then Prime Minister Edward Heath.

I've spent most of my life drawing. I drew cartoons for school magazines, designed posters for school societies which invariably turned into political cartoons displayed, in the good old-fashioned way, on walls. I also developed a useful party trick of caricaturing teachers on blackboards. I did Art 'O' and 'A' levels (only a grade B in the latter) but that didn't have much to do with cartoons, and I certainly never contemplated for a moment going to art school. Instead I went to Pembroke College, Cambridge, to read English Literature, and as things turned out I hated it and I spent most of my time doing cartoons for two-bit student magazines, which partly explains how I ended up with a truly terrible degree. More on this later.

At the same time I was half-heartedly putting together a portfolio of work, in the hope that what I'd always done for fun (despite the fact that it was also a compulsion) might just end up being what I did for a living. I'd occasionally send off the portfolio to magazines, never to hear anything back. Then, shortly after graduating I had an idea for a series which I hoped would appeal to a particular demographic at the time (1982). It was called 'Scenes from the Lives of the Great Socialists' and consisted of a number of stylised depictions of leading socialist thinkers and politicians from history, with the added value of an appallingly bad pun thrown into the mixture. One example is 'Proudhon and Bakunin have tea in Tunbridge Wells', which showed the 19th century French and Russian anarchists sitting round a tea table, with Bakunin spitting out his cup of tea and exclaiming 'Proudhon! This tea is disgusting! This isn't proper tea at all!', to which Proudhon replied 'Ah, my dear Bakunin, but Property is Theft!'

I sent about half a dozen of these drawings to the *New Statesman* (then going through one of its periodic lefty phases) and, as usual, heard nothing for months. Then, just before Christmas 1982, in bed suffering from chickenpox, I received a phone call from the art director who said they were going to publish four of the cartoons in their Christmas issue, and would like me to do a series. (I was paid £40 a cartoon, which throughout 1983 meant I was earning £40 a month, which also meant I still had to sign on in order to stay alive.) Thus began my career as a cartoonist.

My three-year deadline

Now living in London, I found myself an agent and *She* magazine was the first offer to come in. They proposed to pay their standard fee of £6 for anything they published. I instructed my agent to inform them that this barely covered my expenses for materials and postage and they could forget it (although I used two other words, one of them also beginning with 'f') – I don't know if he passed on the message. Then someone wanted to do a book of the *New Statesman* cartoons, with the offer of an advance of £750. This took my earned income for that year to somewhere perilously close to a thousand pounds.

At around this time I went to a College reunion and remember skulking around in my Oxfam suit listening with growing irritation to my contemporaries outlining how they'd got into computing/merchant banking/ systems analysis or whatever at just the right time, and were earning fifty times more than I was. But I knew I was in for the long haul. As a slight nod to my father's ceaseless injunctions that it was time I got a proper job, I'd set myself a limit of three years, sort of promising that, if I wasn't making a fist of it by then I'd give up (although I doubt I actually meant it).

Luckily, a year into my putative career other contemporaries from university were starting out in journalism, and found they could earn important brownie points from their editors by bringing in a cartoonist to liven up the dull magazines they worked for. That's how I found myself working for *Satellite and Cable TV News* and *One Two Testing*... The fact that I neither knew nor cared about what I was illustrating and lampooning didn't matter. It was work, and also an essential lesson in how to master a brief, however obscure.

However, the true catalyst for my career came when another university acquaintance started working on *Financial Weekly* and, for the usual self-aggrandising reasons, suggested to the editor that they might use me. Again, this was something I knew and cared nothing about but it offered plenty of scope to lampoon truly awful people and of course frequently crossed over into political satire, where my real interest lay. More significantly, the editor himself was so nice, kind and amenable that he consequently drove his staff mad with frustration to the point that they would leave for better things. And when they went, they often took me with them.

Part of the *Financial Weekly* diaspora fled to Eddie Shah's infant *Today* newspaper, and so, just inside my self-imposed three-year time limit, I was producing a daily pocket cartoon for the business pages as well as drawing editorial cartoons for both *Today* and its short-lived sister paper *Sunday Today*. From there, another university friend brought me onto the books pages of the *Sunday Correspondent* and, in doing so, to broadsheet respectability. After that I never really had to solicit for work again. I'd reached cartooning critical mass; the people commissioning knew who I was and, more importantly, knew my work so the hard part was over. And, rather nicely, when I went to another College reunion, I discovered that all the smart boys in computing and banking had been sacked in the recession of the early 1990s.

How can other people get ahead in cartooning?

At one level you could say, between gritted teeth, that all that I've written above proves is that it's just about the old boy network – not what you know but who you know. To an extent that's true, but I'd like to think that none of the publications I'd worked for would have given me a second glance if I couldn't cut the mustard and delivered the goods. So, what do you need to get ahead in cartooning?

First of all, and most importantly, you need to recognise whether or not you truly are a cartoonist, and to do that you need to know what cartoons are. It won't do just to be able to draw; nor is it enough to have a sense of humour. You need to combine the two, and understand that in so doing you are creating something that can't be expressed in any other way. This requires a mindset which, I believe, is innate. Moreover, I don't believe you can teach people how to be cartoonists – they have to teach themselves, and from an early age at that. If you copy other cartoonists to find out how it's done, then slowly but surely you'll develop a style of your own which you feel comfortable with.

Once you recognise what you are, and that you're determined to embark on a career that, like poetry or acting, offers a dream of glamour out of all proportion to its guaranteed financial reward, you then need to create a frame of mind which combines, in equal measure, arrogance and sloth. In other words, you *know* that you're good, and actually better than anyone else who's ever lived, but you're also, crucially, too lazy to do anything else, like accountancy.

Then comes the hard part, which is not for the faint-hearted. You have to work very very hard, to make sure what you're producing is really good, and is the best you can do (of which you will always, ultimately, be the best judge). If you're a caricaturist, practice your caricature (and by all means steal other, more established cartoonists' tricks in order to develop your own; after all, they do). If you're a gag cartoonist, hone the gag and work on the drawing so it's clear what's going on (cartooning is the last bastion of realism in the visual arts – abstract cartoons don't work). If you're a political cartoonist, immerse yourself in current affairs and, most importantly, either develop or clearly express your point of view, which can be either right or left wing (a fair, unopinionated cartoonist is as useless and boring as a newspaper columnist with no opinions and nothing to say). A good editorial cartoon is a newspaper column by other means, and is best described as visual journalism, using tricks – like irony, humour, violence and vile imagery – that the big boys in newspaper punditry are too dumb to understand. But remember – while you go through this stage you'll be papering your bedroom wall with rejection slips.

Practical advice

Always try to make your artwork look professional. This means using good paper drawn on in indelible ink, centrally placed. This might sound obvious, but I've seen many cartoons by aspiring cartoonists drawn in crayon on lined file paper going right up to the edge of the sheet. This won't even get halfway out of the envelope before any editor bins it.

Second, always remember that, although you are a genius you have to start somewhere, and some work is always better than no work. If you want to get into newspapers or magazines (which is all there really is if you want to earn some money and not just feel complacent about your beautiful website), identify parts of the press that would benefit from your input.

Journalists producing gardening or travel or, most of all, personal finance sections are crying out for something to liven their pages, something other than a photo which will mark them out as different. In other words, be arrogant enough to be sufficiently humble to illustrate copy you'd never in a million years personally read. Many famous and established cartoonists still knock out stuff for trade papers of crashing obscurity and dullness, this being as good a way as any other of paying the mortgage.

Once you've identified a potential gap in the market, *always* submit your idea or portfolio to the editor of that section, and *never* send it to the art director (despite my experience with the *New Statesman*). There are several reasons for this. First, art directors are inundated with unsolicited work, and so the odds are immediately pitched against you. Second, there's the danger that, in the endless little territorial feuds that pertain in journalism, you will become the exclusive property of the art director who, because he or she hates the gardening editor, will never pass your work on. Third, the section editor will be flattered and delighted to receive something different from the usual dross of press releases and letters of pedantic complaint. If your work tickles their fancy, then you're in, and a section editor always pulls rank over an art director, whatever anyone may imagine.

From these first steps, you will have the beginnings of a portfolio of published work which will stand you in excellent stead on your way to reaching that critical mass of recognition I mentioned earlier.

Finally, never forget that cartoons are something different from anything else. While they combine text journalism and illustration, they end up as something greater than their component parts. In a way, a cartoon is a kind of voodoo, doing harm to someone (whether a politician or a castaway on a desert island) at a distance with a sharp object, which in this case is a pen. It's hard to get established, the number of successful cartoonists earning a decent wedge is tiny and there will always be a generational logjam as the clapped-out old has-beens whose work enrages and disgusts you cling tenaciously to the precious few slots. But – if you're determined and tough enough, stick with it and you, too, could become one of those clapped-out has-beens. Until then, just bear in mind that it's a small and crowded profession, and despite everything I've said, the last thing I need is anyone good coming along and muscling in on my territory. In my heart of hearts, I should really advise all aspiring young cartoonists to give up now. Such churlishness apart, however, I'll stick with wishing you good luck.

Martin Rowson is a freelance cartoonist and his work appears regularly in the *Guardian*, *The Times*, the *Independent on Sunday*, the *Daily Mirror*, the *Scotsman* and many other publications. In 2002 Ken Livingstone appointed him as the first Cartoonist Laureate for London, and he was named Political Cartoonist of the Year in 2000 and 2003. His books include comic book versions of *The Waste Land* and *Tristram Shandy*, and until 2005 he was vice-president of the Zoological Society of London.

See also...

- *Design and Artists Copyright Society, page 717*

Winning the greeting card game

The UK population spends more than £1.3 billion a year on greeting cards. Jakki Brown helps to guide artists to success in this fiercely competitive industry.

The UK greeting card industry leads the world on two counts – design and innovation and per capita send. On average people in the UK send 55 cards a year, 85% of which are bought by women.

But just how do you, as an artist, go about satisfying this voracious appetite of the card-sending public? There are two main options: either to become a greeting card publisher yourself or to supply existing greeting card publishers with your artwork and be paid a fee for doing so.

The idea of setting up your own greeting card publishing company may sound exciting, but this decision should not be taken lightly. Going down this route will involve taking on all the set up and running costs of a publishing company as well as the production, selling and administrative responsibilities. This often leaves little time for you to do what you do best – creating the artwork.

Some greeting card language

Own brand/bespoke publishers. These design specific to a retailer's needs.

Spring Seasons. The industry term to describe greeting cards for Valentine's Day, Mother's Day, Easter and Father's Day. Publishers generally launch these ranges all together in June/July.

Greeting card types. Traditional; cute or whimsical; contemporary/quirky art; juvenile; handmade or hand-finished; fine art; photographic, humorous.

Finishes and treatments. Artists will not be expected to know the production techniques and finishes, but a working knowledge is often an advantage. Some of the most commonly used finishes and treatments include: embossing (raised portion of a design), die-cutting (where the card is cut into a shape or includes an aperture), foiling (metallic film) and flitter (a glitter-like substance).

There are estimated to be around 800 greeting card publishers in the UK, ranging in size from one-person operations to multinational corporations, roughly 200 of which are regarded as 'serious' publishers (see page 531).

Finding the right publishers

While some publishers concentrate on producing a certain type of greeting card (e.g. humorous, fine art or juvenile), the majority publish a variety of greeting card ranges. Unfortunately, this makes it more difficult for you as an artist to target the most appropriate potential publishers for your work. There are various ways in which you can research the market, quickly improve your publisher knowledge and, therefore, reduce the amount of wasted correspondence:

• **Go shopping.** Browse the displays in card shops and other high street shops, department stores, supermarkets, garden centres and gift shops. This will not only give you an insight into what is already available but also which publishers may be interested in your work. Most publishers include their contact details on the backs of the cards.

• **Trade fairs.** There are a number of trade exhibitions held during the year at which publishers exhibit their greeting card ranges to retailers and overseas distributors. By visiting these exhibitions, you will gain a broad overview of the design trends in the industry, as well as the current ranges of individual publishers. Some publishers are willing to meet bnartists and look through their portfolios on the stand but others are not. Never interrupt a sale. If you believe your work could be relevant for them, when they are free, ask for a contact name and follow it up afterwards. Have a supply of business cards handy, perhaps illustrated with some of your work, to leave with publishers.

• **The Greeting Card Association website** (www.greetingcardassociation.org.uk). This resource provides advice about submitting designs and a list of publishers looking for freelance designers.

Further information

The Greeting Card Association
United House, North Road, London N7 9DP
tel 020-7619 0396
email gca@max-publishing.co.uk
website www.greetingcardassociation.org.uk

The UK trade association for greeting card publishers. Its online information resource contains pages on freelance designing and writing for greeting cards complete with lists of publishers which accept freelance work. The Ladder Club is an annual one-day seminar for would-be/fledgling publishers, many of whom are artists or photographers looking to publish their own work. The seminar covers all aspects of publishing and costs approx. £35 (*tel* (01702) 480180, *email* waiteandtaitbakery@hotmail.com).

TRADE FAIRS

Top Drawer Spring, Earls Court 1
website www.topdrawerspring.co.uk
Contact Clarion Events *tel* 020-7370 8051
Takes place 18–20 Jan 2011

Spring Fair Birmingham, NEC
website www.springfair.com
Contact TPS/Emap *tel* 020-7728 5000
Takes place Feb 2011

Progressive Greetings Live
website www.progressivegreetingslive.co.uk
Contact Max Exhibitions *tel* (01635) 297070
Takes place May 2011

Pulse, Earls Court 1
website www.pulse-london.com
Contact Clarion Events *tel* 020-7370 8207
Takes place June 2011

Home and Gift, Harrogate
website homeandgift.co.uk
Contact Clarion Events *tel* 020-7370 8043
Takes place 18–21 July 2010

Autumn Fair Birmingham, NEC
website www.autumnfair.com
Contact TPS/Emap *tel* 020-7728 5000
Takes place 5–8 Sept 2010

Top Drawer Autumn, Olympia
website www.topdrawerautumn.com
Contact Clarion Events *tel* 020-7370 8051
Takes place 12–14 Sept 2010

TRADE MAGAZINES

Greetings Today
Lema Publishing, Unit 1, Queen Mary's Avenue, Watford, Herts. WD18 7JR
tel (01923) 250909 *fax* (01923) 250995
Publisher-in-Chief Malcolm Naish, *Editor* Lewis Eckett
Monthly £45 p.a. (other rates on application)

Articles, features and news related to the greetings card industry. Includes Artists Directory for aspiring artists wishing to attract the eye of publishers. Runs seminars for small publishers and artists.

Progressive Greetings Worldwide
Max Publishing, United House, North Road, London N7 9DP
tel 020-7700 6740 *fax* 020-7607 6411
12 p.a. (£50 p.a.)
Editor and co-owner Jakki Brown

The official magazine of the Greeting Card Association and the only greeting card trade magazine in the world. Provides an insight to the industry, including news and features, an up-to-date list of publishers, a new product section and a free showcase for artists, illustrators and verses. Special supplements include *Focus on Art Cards, Focus on Humorous Cards, Focus on Words & Sentiments, Focus on Kids* and *Focus on Giftwrap.*

Progressive Greetings hosts The Henries, the greeting card industry awards. The September edition includes details of the finalists in the 14 different product categories and the November issue features the winners.

Types of publishers

There are two broad categories of publisher – wholesale and direct-to-retail – each employing a different method of distribution to reach the retailer.

Wholesale publishers distribute their products to the retailer via greeting card wholesalers or cash-and-carry outlets. They work on volume sales and have a rapid turnover of designs, many being used with a variety of different captions. For example, the same floral design may be used for cards for mothers, grandmothers, aunts and sisters. It is therefore usual for the artist to leave a blank space on the design to accommodate the caption. Until recently, wholesale publishers were generally only interested in traditional, cute and juvenile designs, but they now publish across the board, including contemporary and humorous ranges.

Direct-to-retail (DTR) publishers supply retailers via sales agents or reps. Most greeting cards sold through specialist card shops and gift shops are supplied by DTR publishers, which range from multinational corporations down to small, trendy niche publishing companies. These publishers market series of ranges based on distinctive design themes or characters. Categories of DTR cards include contemporary art/fun, fine art, humour, words and sentiment, children's, photographic, traditional and handmade/hand-finished and, of course, Christmas cards.

Approaching a publisher

Unfortunately, there is no standard way of approaching and submitting work to a card publisher. The first step is to establish that the publisher you wish to approach accepts work from freelance artists; then find out their requirements for submission and to whom it should be addressed.

It is always better to send several examples of your work to show the breadth of your artistic skills. Some publishers prefer to see finished designs while others are happy with well-presented sketches. Never send originals: instead supply your images on disk, or as photocopies, laser copies or photographs, and include at least one design in colour. You can initially send your designs to as many publishers as you like, but never be tempted to sell similar designs to two publishers – a bad reputation will follow you around.

Some publishers will be looking to purchase individual designs for specific sending occasions (e.g. new baby, new home, sympathy) while others will be more intent on looking for designs which could be developed to make up a range. Bear in mind that publishers work a long way in advance, for example Christmas ranges are launched to the retailers the previous January. Development of a range may take up to six months prior to launching.

Also remember that cards in retail outlets are rarely displayed in their entirety with many of the racking display systems obscuring part of the design. Therefore, when designing a card make sure that some of the 'action' appears in the top half.

When interest is shown

Some publishers respond to submissions from artists immediately while others prefer to deal with them on a monthly basis. A publisher's response may be in the form of a request for more submissions of a specific design style or of a specific character. This speculative development work is usually carried out free of charge. Always meet your deadline (news travels fast in the industry).

A publisher interested in buying your artwork will probably then issue you with a contract. This may cover aspects such as the terms of payment; rights of usage of the design (e.g. is it just for greeting cards or will it include giftwrap and/or stationery?); territory of usage (most publishers want worldwide rights); and ownership of copyright or license period.

There is no set industry standard rate of pay for greeting card artists. Publishers pay artists either on a per design or per range basis in one of the following ways:

• **Flat fee.** A one-off payment is made to the artist for ownership of a design for an unlimited period. The industry standard is around £200–£250 for a single design, and payment on a sliding scale for more than one design.

• **Licensing fee.** The publisher is granted the right to use a piece of artwork for a specified number of years, after which the full rights revert to the artist. Payment to the artist is approximately £150 upwards per design.

• **Licensing fee plus royalty.** As above plus a royalty payment on each card sold. Artists would generally receive a minimum of £100 for the licensing fee plus 3–7% of the trade price of each card sold.

• **Advance royalty deal.** A goodwill advance on royalties is paid to the artist. In the case of a range, the artist would receive a goodwill advance of say £500–£1,000 plus 5–8% additional royalty payment once the threshold is reached.

• **Royalty only.** The artist receives regular royalty payments, generally paid quarterly, based on the number of cards sold. Artists should expect to receive a 5–8% royalty, sales reports and royalty statements.

The fees stated above should only be regarded as a rough guideline. Fees and advances are generally paid on completion of artwork. Publishers which have worldwide rights pay royalties for sales overseas to artists, although these will be on a pro rata basis to the export trade price.

Jakki Brown is editor of *Progressive Greetings Worldwide* and general secretary of the Greeting Card Association.

See also...

- *Websites for artists*, page 656
- *Art agents and commercial studios*, page 519
- *Card and stationery publishers that accept illustrations and verses*, page 531
- *Design and Artists Copyright Society, page 717*

Card and stationery publishers that accept illustrations and photographs

Before submitting work, artists and photographers are advised to ascertain requirements of the company they are approaching, including terms and conditions. Only top quality material should be submitted; inferior work is never accepted.

*Member of the Greeting Card Association

Card Connection Ltd*

Park House, South Street, Farnham, Surrey GU9 7QQ
tel (01252) 892300 *fax* (01252) 892363
email ho@card-connection.co.uk
website www.card-connection.co.uk
Managing Director Michael Johnson

Everyday and seasonal designs. Styles include cute, fun, traditional, contemporary, humour and photographic. Humorous copy and jokes plus sentimental verse. Founded 1992.

Carlton Cards Ltd

Mill Street East, Dewsbury, West Yorkshire WF12 9AW
tel (01924) 465200 *fax* (01924) 453908
website www.carltoncards.co.uk
Group Marketing Director Keith Auty, *Product Development Director* Josephine Loughran

All types of artwork, any size; submit as colour roughs, colour copies or transparencies. Especially interested in humorous artwork and ideas.

Caspari Ltd*

1st Floor, Crown Chambers, 34–36 High Street, Saffron Walden, Essex CB10 1EP
tel (01799) 513010 *fax* (01799) 513101
website www.casparionline.com
Managing Director Keith Entwisle

Traditional fine art/classic images; 5 x 4in transparencies. No verses. Founded 1990.

Chapter and Verse

Granta House, 94/96 High Street, Linton, Cambs. CB21 4JT
tel (01223) 891951 *fax* (01223) 894137
website www.chapter-and-verse-stationery.co.uk

Buildings, animals, flowers, scenic, or domestic subjects in series, suitable for greetings cards and postcards. All sizes of transparency or on disk. No verses.

Colneis Marketing Ltd*

York House, 2–4 York Road, Felixstowe IP11 7QQ
tel (01394) 271668 *fax* (01394) 275114
email colneiscards@btconnect.com
website www.colneisgreetingcards.com
Proprietor John Botting

Photographs (preferably medium format) and colour artwork of nature and cute images. Founded 1994.

Colour House Graphics Ltd*

York House, 2–4 York Road, Felixstowe IP11 7QQ
tel (01394) 271668 *fax* (01394) 275114
email colourhousegraphics@hotmail.com
website www.colourhousegraphics.co.uk
Contact John Batting

Contemporary styles of painting of subjects relating to people's everyday lives. Particularly interested in sophisticated, loose, graphic styles. No verses. Founded 1990.

Simon Elvin Ltd*

Wooburn Industrial Park, Wooburn Green, Bucks HP10 0PE
tel (01628) 526711 *fax* (01628) 531483
email studioadmin@simonelvin.com
website www.simonelvin.com
Art Director Fiona Buszard, *Studio Manager* Rachel Bradley

Female/male traditional and contemporary designs, female/male cute, wedding/anniversary, birth congratulations, fine art, photographic animals, flowers and male imagery, traditional sympathy, juvenile ages, special occasions and gift wrap.

Looking for submissions that show flair, imagination and an understanding of greeting card design. Artists should familiarise themselves with the ranges, style and content. Submit a small collection of either colour copies or prints (no original artwork) and include an sae for return of work. Alternatively email jpegs.

4C–Charity Christmas Card Council

Cards World Ltd, 49 Cross Street, London N1 2BB
tel (0845) 230 0046 *fax* (0845) 230 0048
email 4c@charitycards.org
website www.charitycards.org

Traditional and contemporary Christmas cards for the corporate market. Submit artwork on CD-Rom or 5 x 4in transparencies. No verses. Works for 70+ charities. Founded 1966.

Gallery Five Ltd*

The Old Bakery, 1 Bellingham Road, London SE6 2PN
tel 020-8697 1629 *fax* 020-8461 5015
website www.galleryfive.co.uk

Send samples of work FAO 'Gallery Five Art Studio'. Colour photocopies, Mac-formatted zip/CD acceptable, plus sae. No verses.

Gemma International Ltd*

Linmar House, 6 East Portway, Andover, Hants SP10 3LU
tel (01264) 388400 *fax* (01264) 366243
email sales@gemma-international.co.uk
website www.gemma-international.co.uk
Directors L. Rudd-Clarke, A. Parkin, T. Rudd-Clarke, W. O'Loughlin, K. Bishop

Cute, contemporary, leading-edge designs for children, teens and young adults. Founded 1984.

Gibson Greetings International Ltd

Gibson House, Hortonwood 30, Telford, Shrops. TF1 7YF
tel (01952) 608333 *fax* (01952) 605259
email helen-tomkins@gibson-greetings.co.uk
Product Director Helen Tomkins

All everyday and seasonal illustrations: cute, humorous, juvenile, traditional and contemporary designs, as well as surface pattern. Greeting card traditional and humorous verse. Founded 1991.

Graphic Humour Ltd

PO Box 717, North Shields, Tyne & Wear NE30 4WR
tel 0191-215 5006 *fax* (01207) 566842
email enquiries@graphichumour.com
website www.graphichumour.com

Risqué and everyday artwork ideas for greetings cards; short, humorous copy. Founded 1984.

The Greetings Factory Ltd

PO Box 264, Hampton, Middlesex TW12 2ZT
tel 020-8783 0303 *fax* 020-8941 9929
email art@hotchpotchcards.com
website www.thegreetingsfactory.com
Design Manager Kelly Courtenay

Colour artwork for greetings cards, giftwrap and social stationery. Considers verses. Founded 1997.

Hallmark Cards Plc*

Hallmark House, Bingley Road, Heaton, Bradford BD9 6SD
tel (01274) 252523
email creativesubmissions@hallmark-uk.com
website www.hallmarkuk.com

See website for freelance opportunities and submission details.

Hanson White – UK Greetings

2nd Floor, AMP House, Dingwall Road, Croydon CR0 2LX
tel 020-8260 1200 *fax* 020-8260 1213
email hannah.turpin@ukgreetings.co.uk, sally.hipkins@ukgreetings.co.uk
Submissions Editors Hannah Turpin, Sally Hipkins

Humorous artwork and cartoons/photographs for greeting cards, including Christmas, Valentine's Day, Mother's Day, Father's Day, general birthday and everyday occasions. Humorous copy lines and punchline jokes, funny poems and rhymes - guidelines available on request. Founded 1958.

Jodds*

PO Box 353, Bicester, Oxon OX27 0GS
tel (01869) 278550 *fax* (01869) 278551
email joddscard@hotmail.co.uk
website www.joddscards.com
Partners M. Payne and J.S. Payne

Children's and contemporary art style greetings cards. Submit colour photocopies with sae, or email low resolution jpegs. No photographic. Established 1988.

Leeds Postcards

4 Granby Road, Leeds LS6 3AS
email xtine@leedspostcards.com
website www.poptel.org.uk/leedspostcards
Contact Christine Hankinson

Publisher and distributor of satirical radical postcards for the wall and post.

Lima Design*

1 Lordship Lane, London SE22 8EW
tel 020-8693 4257 *fax* 020-8693 8723
email info@limadesign.co.uk
website www.limadesign.co.uk
Proprietor Lisa Breakwell

Produces contemporary, design-conscious cards which are all hand applied using resisters and capacitors, ribbon, indoor sparklers, animal-shaped rubber bands, metallic thread and beads. Founded 2002.

Ling Design Ltd*

Westmoreland House, Westmoreland Street, Bath BA2 3HE
tel (01225) 489760 *fax* (01225) 448190
email info@lingdesign.co.uk
website www.lingdesign.co.uk
Creative Director Isabel Scott Evans

Artwork for greetings cards, stationery and giftwrap.

Medici Cards Limited

Waterwells Drive, Gloucester, Glos. GL2 2PH
tel (01452) 888999 *fax* (01452) 888912
email sales@medicicards.co.uk
website www.medicicards.co.uk

Specialises in market leading art and photographic cards.

Paperlink Ltd*

356 Kennington Road, London SE11 4LD
tel 020-7582 8244 *fax* 020-7587 5212
email info@paperlink.co.uk
website www.paperlink.co.uk
Directors Louise Tighe, Tim Porte, Tim Purcell

Publishers of ranges of humorous and contemporary art greetings cards. Produce products under licence for charities. Founded 1986.

Pineapple Park*

Unit 9, Henlow Trading Estate, Henlow Camp, Beds. SG16 6DS
tel (01462) 814817 *fax* (01462) 819443
email info@pineapplepark.co.uk
website www.pineapplepark.co.uk
Directors Peter M. Cockerline, Sarah M. Parker

Illustrations and photographs for publication as greetings cards. Contemporary, cute, humour: submit artwork or laser copies with sae. Photographic florals always needed. Humour copy/jokes accepted without artwork. Also concepts for ranges. Founded 1993.

Powell Publishing*

Millyard House, Millyard Way, Eythorne, Dover, Kent CT17 4NL
tel (01304) 833550 *fax* (01304) 833555
email fiona@powellpublishing.co.uk
website www.powellpublishing.co.uk
Directors B.W. Powell (chairman), T.J. Paulett (managing), *Art & Design Manager* Fiona Bale

Greetings card publishers. Interested in Christmas designs for the charity card market. Division of Powell Print Ltd.

The Publishing House

PO Box 81, Banbury, Oxon OX16 3YL
tel (01295) 271144 *fax* (01295) 277403
email naval@thepublishinghouse.co.uk
Contact Naval Phandey

General and multicultural cards across all faiths. No verses.

Nigel Quiney Publications Ltd*

Cloudesley House, Shire Hill, Saffron Walden, Essex CB11 3FB
tel (01799) 520200 *fax* (01799) 520100
website www.nigelquiney.com
Contact Alison Butterworth, Creative Director

Everyday and seasonal greetings cards including fine art, photographic, humour, contemporary and cute. Submit colour copies, photographs, transparencies or disk: no original artwork.

Rainbow Cards Ltd*

Kingswood Business Park, Holyhead Road, Albrighton, Wolverhampton, West Midlands WV7 3AU
tel (01902) 376000 *fax* (01902) 376001
email sales@rainbowcards.co.uk
website www.rainbowcards.co.uk

Artwork for humorous and traditional greetings cards. Founded 1976.

Really Good*

The Old Mast House, The Square, Abingdon, Oxon OX14 5AR
tel (01235) 537888 *fax* (01235) 537779
email potatoes@reallygood.uk.com
website www.reallygood.uk.com
Director David Hicks

Always looking for fun and funny artwork in a quirky or modern way to publish on cards, stationery or gifts. Send samples on paper rather than on disk, or email website link or small files to view. Allow plenty of time for review. Founded 1987.

Felix Rosenstiel's Widow & Son Ltd

Fine Art Publishers, 33–35 Markham Street, London SW3 3NR
tel 020-7352 3551 *fax* 020-7351 5300
email sales@felixr.com
website www.felixr.com

Invites offers of artwork of a professional standard for reproduction as picture prints for the picture framing trade. Any type of subject considered. See our website for submission details.

Royle Publications Ltd – see Medici Cards Limited

J. Salmon Ltd

100 London Road, Sevenoaks, Kent TN13 1BB
tel (01732) 452381 *fax* (01732) 450951
email enquiries@jsalmon.co.uk
website www.jsalmon.co.uk

Picture postcards, calendars, greeting cards and local view booklets.

Santoro Graphics Ltd

Rotunda Point, 11 Hartfield Crescent, London SW19 3RL
tel 020-8781 1100 *fax* 020-8781 1101
email submissions@santorographics.com
website www.santorographics.com
Directors Lucio Santoro, Meera Santoro (art)

Publishers of innovative and award-winning designs for greetings cards, giftwrap and gift stationery. Bold, contemporary images with an international appeal. Subjects covered: contemporary, pop-up, cute, quirky, fashion, fine art, retro. Submit samples as colour photocopies, transparencies, CD-Roms or via email as jpeg or PDF files. Founded 1985.

Second Nature Ltd*

10 Malton Road, London W10 5UP
tel 020-8960 0212 *fax* 020-8960 8700

email rods@secondnature.co.uk
website www.secondnature.co.uk
Publishing Director Rod Schragger

Contemporary artwork for greetings cards and handmade cards; jokes for humorous range; short modern sentiment; verses. Founded 1981.

Solomon & Whitehead Ltd

Lynn Lane, Shenstone, Staffs. WS14 0DX
tel (01543) 483000 *fax* (01543) 481619
email sales@fineartgroup.co.uk
website www.fineartgroup.co.uk

Fine art prints, limited editions and originals, framed and unframed.

Soul*

Old Mast House, The Square, Abingdon, Oxon OX14 5AR
tel (01235) 537816 *fax* (01235) 537817
email smile@souluk.com
website www.souluk.com
Director David Hicks

Publishers of contemporary, fine and quirky art. Email website link or small files to view. Allow time for review. Do not send originals. Sister company of Really Good.

Noel Tatt Group/Impress Publishing*

Appledown House, Barton Business Park, Appledown Way, New Dover Road, Canterbury, Kent CT1 3TE
tel (01227) 811600 *fax* (01227) 811601
email mail@noeltatt.co.uk
website www.noeltatt.co.uk
Directors Jarle Tatt, Diane Tatt, Richard Parsons, Ian Hylands

General everyday cards – broad mix; Christmas. Will consider verses. Founded 1964.

The Webb Group

Queen Street, Burton-on-Trent, Staffs. DE14 3LP
tel (0845) 218 4530 *fax* (01283) 506306
website www.thewebbgroup.co.uk

High-quality Christmas cards and paper products.

Wishing Well Studios Ltd*

Kellet Close, Martland Park, Wigan, Lancs. WN5 0LP
tel (01942) 218888 *fax* (01942) 218899
email nickyh@wishingwell.co.uk
website www.wishingwell.co.uk
Contact Nicky Harrison

Rhyming and prose verse 4–24 lines long; also jokes. All artwork styles considered but do not send originals.

Woodmansterne Publications Ltd*

1 The Boulevard, Blackmoor Lane, Watford, Herts. WD18 8UW
tel (01923) 200600 *fax* (01923) 200601
website www.woodmansterne.co.uk

Publisher of greeting cards and social stationery featuring fine and contemporary art and photography (colour and b&w). Submit colour copies, photographs or jpegs by email.

The freelance photographer

Becoming a successful freelance photographer is as much about marketing as photographic talent. Professional photographer Ian Thraves highlights possibilities for the freelancer.

Having an outstanding portfolio is one thing, but to receive regular commissions takes a good business head and sound market knowledge. Although working as a professional photographer can be tough, it is undoubtedly one of the most interesting and rewarding ways of earning a living.

Entering professional photography

A good starting point is to embark on one of the many college courses available, which range from GCSE to degree level, and higher. These form a good foundation, though most teach only the technical aspects of photography and very few cover the basics of running a business. But a good college course will provide students with the opportunity to become familiar with photographic equipment and develop skills without the restrictions and pressures found in the workplace.

In certain fields, such as commercial photography, it is possible to learn the trade as an assistant to an established photographer. A photographer's assistant will undertake many varied tasks, including preparing camera equipment and lighting, building sets, obtaining props and organising locations, as well as general mundane chores. It usually takes only a year or two for an assistant to become a fully competent photographer, having during that time learnt many technical aspects of a particular field of photography and the fundamentals of running a successful business. There is, however, the danger of a long-standing assistant becoming a clone of the photographer worked for, and it is for this reason that some assistants prefer to gain experience with other photographers rather than working for just one for a long period of time. The Association of Photographers (AOP) can help place an assistant.

However, in other fields of photography, such as photojournalism or wildlife photography, an assistant is not generally required, and photographers in these fields have to learn for themselves as they work.

Identifying your market

From the outset, identify which markets are most suitable for the kind of subjects you photograph. Study each market carefully and only offer images which suit the client's requirements.

Usually photographers who specialise in a particular field do better than those who generalise. By concentrating on one or two subject areas they become expert at what they do. Those who make a name for themselves are invariably specialists, and it is far easier for the images of, for example, an exceptional fashion photographer or an award-winning wildlife photographer to be remembered than the work of someone who covers a broad range of subjects.

In addition, photographers who produce work with individual style (e.g. by experimenting with camera angles or manipulating images to create unusual and distinctive effects) are far more likely to make an impact. Alternative images which attract attention and can help sell a product or service are always sought after. This is especially true of advertising photography, but applies also to other markets such as book and magazine publishers, who are always seeking eye-catching images to use on front covers.

Promoting yourself

Effective self-promotion tells the market who you are and what service you offer. A first step should be to create an outstanding portfolio of images, tailored to appeal to the targeted market. Photographers targeting a few different markets should create an individual portfolio for each rather than presenting a single general one, including only a few relevant images. A portfolio should only contain a photographer's most outstanding work. Including substandard images will show inconsistent quality, leaving a potential client in doubt about the photographer's ability.

Images should be presented in a format which the client is used to handling. Usually, a high-quality printed portfolio, backed up by a well-designed website is adequate. Many photographers also produce an additional portfolio in the form of a DVD slideshow or movie. These can be very cheap to create and duplicate and can be handed or posted out to potential and existing clients. Any published material (often referred to as 'tearsheets') should also be added to a portfolio. Tearsheets are often presented mounted and laminated in plastic.

Business cards and letterheads should be designed to reflect style and professionalism. Consider using a good graphic designer to design a logo for use on cards, letterheads and any other promotional literature. Many photographers produce postcard-size business cards and include an image as well as their name and logo.

Other than word of mouth, advertising is probably the best way of making your services known to potential clients. For a local market, a business directory such as *Yellow Pages* is a good start. Specialist directories in which photographers can advertise include *The Creative Handbook* and *Contact Photography* (see page 538).

Cold calling by telephone is probably the most cost-effective and productive way of making contacts, and these should be followed up by an appointment for a personal visit

Professional organisations

The Association of Photographers (AOP)
Co-Secretary Gwen Thomas, 81 Leonard Street, London EC2A 4QS
tel 020-7739 6669 *fax* 020-7739 8707
email general@aophoto.co.uk
website www.the-aop.org
See page 550.

British Institute of Professional Photography (BIPP)
1 Prebendal Court, Oxford Road, Aylesbury, Bucks. HP19 8EY
tel (01296) 718530
email info@bipp.com
website www.bipp.com
See page 555.

Master Photographers Association
Jubilee House, 1 Chancery Lane, Darlington, Co. Durham DL1 5QP
tel (01325) 356555 *fax* (01325) 357813
email info@mpauk.com
website www.thempa.com
See page 570.

The Royal Photographic Society
Fenton House, 122 Wells Road, Bath BA2 3AH
tel (01225) 325733 *fax* (01225) 448688
email rps@rps.org
website www.rps.org
See page 577.

BAPLA (British Association of Picture Libraries and Agencies)
See page 552.

(if possible) in order to show a portfolio of images. This helps to ensure you will not be forgotten.

Photographers should also use the internet as a primary medium to promote themselves. A cleverly designed website is essential and is a stylish and cost-effective way to expose a photographer's portfolio to a global market, as well as being a convenient way for a potential client to view a photographer's work. A personal website address should be added to business stationery and to other forms of advertising together with the usual address and telephone number information.

Creating a website can be much cheaper than advertising using conventional published print media. However, its design should be carefully composed and is probably best left to a professional website designer (see *Setting up a website*, page 641). Although many images and details about your business can be placed on a website, one limiting factor is the time it can take to navigate an over-complicated site. Unless this is a relatively quick process the viewer may lose patience and cancel access to the site.

In addition to a traditional website, many photographers have taken to 'blogging' as another form of web-based marketing. The beauty of a blog is the ease at which the owner can update the content. Updatable items may include your latest images, news articles and equipment reviews, plus any other interesting posts that relate to the industry. Blogs and other types of social media, such as Twitter, Facebook and LinkedIn, can all work hand-in-hand to increase a photographer's 'fan-base' or 'following', all serving to strengthen a photographer's market presence on a global basis.

A well-organised exhibition of images is a very effective way of bringing your work to the attention of current and potential new clients. Throw a preview party with refreshments for friends, colleagues and specially invited guests from the industry. A show which is well reviewed by critics who write for newspapers and magazines can generate additional interest.

As a photographer's career develops, the budget for self-promotion should increase. Many established photographers will go as far as producing full-colour mailers, posters, and even calendars, which all contain examples of their work.

Digital photography

Digital photography and image-enhancement and manipulation using computer technology are widely used in the photographic industry. Since the cost of digital cameras and other hardware can be considerably cheaper than using large quantities of film, most photographers now use this technology.

There are various levels of quality produced by digital cameras and photographers should consider the requirements of their market prior to investing in expensive hardware which is prone to rapid change and improvement. At the cheaper level, 35mm-style digital cameras manufactured by companies such as Nikon and Canon can produce outstanding quality images suitable for many end uses. Cameras like these are now used predominantly for press, PR and general commercial work.

At a higher level, many commercial studio photographers have invested in a 'digital capture back', which is a high-quality chip which can be adapted to fit many of the conventional studio cameras. This system is far more expensive, but is capable of producing file sizes which closely compare in quality to a high-resolution scan from large format film. Thus the images are suitable for any end use, such as top-quality advertisements. Photographers thinking of supplying stock libraries with digital images should consider the quality of the camera they use. Stock libraries often supply a diverse range of clients, including advertising, and will therefore only accept the highest standard in order to meet the demands of the market.

Image-enhancement and manipulation using a computer program such as Adobe Photoshop provides photographers with an onscreen darkroom where the possibilities for creating imaginative images are endless. As well as being useful for retouching purposes and creating photo compositions, it provides the photographer with an opportunity to create more unusual images. It is therefore especially useful for targeting the advertising market, where fantasy images are more important than reality.

Using a stock library

As well as undertaking commissions, photographers have the option of selling their images through a photographic stock library or agency. There are many stock libraries in the UK, some specialising in specific subject areas, such as wildlife photography, and others covering general subjects (see *Picture agencies and libraries* on this *Yearbook's* website, www.writersandartists.co.uk).

Stock libraries are fiercely competitive, all fighting for a share of the market, and it is therefore best to aim to place images with an established name, although competition amongst photographers will be strong. Each stock library has different specific requirements and established markets, so contact them first before making a submission. Some libraries will ask to see a large number of images from a photographer in order to judge for consistency of quality and saleability. Stock libraries selling images through catalogues or over the internet will often consider an initial submission of just a few images, knowing that it is possible to accumulate significant fees from a small number of outstanding individual images marketed this way.

Images placed with a library usually remain the property of the photographer and libraries do not normally sell images outright to clients, but lease them for a specific use for a fee, from which commission is deducted. This means that a single image can accumulate many sales over a period of time. The commission rate can be up to 50% of every sale generated by the library. This may sound high, but it should be borne in mind that

Useful information

Bureau of Freelance Photographers
Focus House, 497 Green Lanes, London N13 4BP
tel 020-8882 3315 *fax* 020-8886 5174
email info@thebfp.com
website www.thebfp.com
Chief Executive John Tracy
Membership £54 p.a.
Helps the freelance photographer by providing information on markets and a free advisory service. Publishes *Market Newsletter* (monthly).

Directories

Centaur Communications
50 Poland Street, London W1F 7AX
tel 020-7970 4000
website www.creativereview.co.uk
Publishes *The Creative Handbook*.

Contact Creative UK LLP
Surrey House, 31 Church Street, Leatherhead, Surrey KT22 8EF
tel (01372) 220330 *fax* (01372) 220340
email mail@contactacreative.com
website www.contactacreative.com
Publishes *Contact Photography*.

the library takes on all overheads, marketing costs and other responsibilities involved in the smooth running of a business, allowing the photographer the freedom to spend more time taking pictures.

Photographers should realise, however, that stock photography is a long-term investment and it can take some time for sales to build up to a significant income. Clearly, photographers who supply the right images for the market, and are prolific, are those who do well, and there are a good number of photographers who make their entire living as full-time stock photographers, never having to undertake commissioned work.

Royalty-free CD companies

Many stock libraries are now marketing royalty-free images on CD-Rom. These companies usually obtain images by purchasing them from photographers for a flat fee or pay royalties to the photographer based on CD sales. Once a CD has been purchased by a client they, in effect, own the images on the CD and are therefore able to reproduce them as many times as they wish, paying no further fees. A typical CD may contain one hundred high-resolution reproduction-quality images in a variety of subject areas, including most specialist subjects.

Although photographers may be tempted to sell images to these companies in order to gain an instant fee, they should be aware that placing images with a traditional stock library can be far more fruitful financially in the long term, since a good image can accumulate very high fees over a period of time and go on selling for many years to come. Furthermore, the photographer always retains the rights to his or her own images.

Running your own library

Photographers choosing to market their own images or start up their own library have the advantage of retaining a full fee for every picture sale they make. But it is unlikely that an individual photographer could ever match the rates of an established library, or make the same volume of sales per image. However, the internet has opened a new marketing avenue for photographers, who now have the opportunity to sell their images worldwide. Previously, only an established stock library would have been able to do this. Before embarking on establishing a 'home' library, photographers should be aware that the business of marketing images is essentially a desk job which involves a considerable amount of paperwork and time, which could be spent taking pictures.

When setting up a picture library, your first consideration should be whether to build up a library of your own images, or to take on other contributing photographers. Many photographers running their own libraries submit additional images to bigger libraries to increase the odds of making a good income. Often, a photographer's personal library is made up of work rejected by the larger libraries, which are usually only interested in images that will regularly sell and generate a high turnover. However, occasional sales can generate a significant amount of income for the individual. Furthermore, a photographer with a library of specialised subjects stands a good chance of gaining recognition with niche markets, which can be very lucrative if the competition for those particular subjects is low.

If you take on contributing photographers, the responsibility for another's work becomes yours, so it is important to draw up a contract with terms of business for both your contributing photographers and your clients. Since images are now predominantly distributed in digital formats, via CD/DVD or broadband, there is no real problem with loss or damage, which used to be a big problem in the days of film-based originals. However, another issue has emerged since the advent of digital technology in the form of copyright abuse, which is now rife in the industry. Therefore, if representing another's work, it will be the library or agent's responsibility to protect image copyright on behalf of the photographer and also take any necessary legal steps in cases where copyright has been abused.

Reproduction fees should also be established on a strict basis, bearing in mind that you owe it to your contributing photographers to command fees which are as high as possible when selling the rights to their images. It is also essential that you control how pictures will be used and the amount of exposure they will receive. The fees should be established according to the type of client using the image and how the image itself will be reproduced. Important factors to consider are where the image will appear, to what size it will be reproduced, the size of the print run, and the territorial rights required by the client.

Working in any field of professional photography is fiercely competitive and successful businesses commonly spend a great deal of time researching their client's needs and marketing accordingly – the ultimate goal to ensure their name is always ahead of the ever-increasing competition.

Ian Thraves is a self-employed photographer and former picture editor at Bruce Coleman The Natural World Photo Agency (www.thravesphoto.co.uk).

See also...

• *Design and Artists Copyright Society*, page 717

Societies, prizes and festivals

The Society of Authors

The Society of Authors is an independent trade union, representing writers' interests in all aspects of the writing profession, particularly publishing, but also broadcasting, television and film, theatre and translation.

Founded over 100 years ago, the Society now has more than 8500 members. It has a professional staff, responsible to a Management Committee of 12 authors, and a Council (an advisory body meeting twice a year) consisting of 60 eminent writers. There are specialist groups within the Society to serve particular needs: the Broadcasting Group, the Children's Writers and Illustrators Group, the Educational Writers Group and the Translators Association (see page 584). There are also groups representing Scotland and the North of England.

Membership

The Society of Authors
84 Drayton Gardens, London SW10 9SB
tel 020-7373 6642
email info@societyofauthors.org
website www.societyofauthors.org
General Secretary Mark Le Fanu

Membership is open to authors who have had a full-length work published, broadcast or performed commercially in the UK and to those who have had a full-length work accepted for publication, but not yet published; and those who have had occasional items broadcast or performed, or translations, articles, illustrations or short stories published. The owner or administrator of a deceased author's copyrights can become a member on behalf of the author's estate. Writers who have been offered a contract seeking a contribution towards publication costs may apply for associate membership and have the contract vetted.

The annual subscription (which is tax deductible) is £90 (£85 by direct debit after the first year). There is a special rate for partners living at the same address. Authors under 35 not yet earning a significant income from writing, may pay a lower subscription of £64. Authors over 65 may pay at the reduced rate after their first year of membership.

Contact the Society for a membership booklet or visit the website for an application form.

What the Society does for members

Through its permanent staff (including a solicitor), the Society is able to give its members a comprehensive personal and professional service covering the business aspects of authorship, including:

• providing information about agents, publishers, and others concerned with the book trade, journalism, broadcasting and the performing arts;
• advising on negotiations, including the individual vetting of contracts, clause by clause, and assessing their terms both financial and otherwise;
• helping with members' queries, major or minor, over any aspect of the business of writing;
• taking up complaints on behalf of members on any issue concerned with the business of authorship;
• pursuing legal actions for breach of contract, copyright infringement, and the non-payment of royalties and fees, when the risk and cost preclude individual action by a member and issues of general concern to the profession are at stake;

• holding conferences, seminars, meetings and social occasions;
• producing a comprehensive range of publications, free of charge to members, including the Society's quarterly journal, *The Author*. *Quick Guides* cover many aspects of the profession such as: copyright, publishing contracts, libel, income tax, VAT, authors' agents, permissions, indexing and self-publishing. The Society also publishes occasional papers on subjects such as film agreements and packaged books.

The Society frequently secures improved conditions and better returns for members. It is common for members to report that, through the help and facilities offered, they have saved more, and sometimes substantially more, than their annual subscriptions (which are an allowable expense against income tax).

Further membership benefits

Members have access to:
• books, hotels and other products and services at special rates;
• free membership of the Authors' Licensing and Collecting Society (ALCS);
• a group Medical Insurance Scheme with BUPA;
• the Contingency Fund (which provides financial relief for authors or their dependents in sudden financial difficulties);
• the Pension Fund (which offers discretionary pensions to a number of members);
• membership of the Royal Over-Seas League at a discount.

> 'It does no harm to repeat, as often as you can, "Without me the literary industry would not exist: the publishers, the agents, the sub-agents, the accountants, the libel lawyers, the departments of literature, the professors, the theses, the books of criticism, the reviewers, the book pages – all this vast and proliferating edifice is because of this small, patronised, put-down and underpaid person."' – *Doris Lessing*

What the Society does for authors

The Society lobbies Members of Parliament, Ministers and Government Departments on all issues of concern to writers, litigates in matters of importance to authors and campaigns for better terms for writers.

The Society is recognised by the BBC for the purpose of negotiating rates for writers' contributions to radio drama, as well as for the broadcasting of published material. It was instrumental in setting up the ALCS (see page 715), which collects and distributes fees from reprography and other methods whereby copyright material is exploited without direct payment to the originators.

The Society keeps in close touch with the Association of Authors' Agents, the Booksellers Association and Publishers Association, the British Council, the Department for Culture, Media and Sport, the National Union of Journalists and the Writers' Guild of Great Britain. It is a member of the European Writers Council and the British Copyright Council.

Awards

The Society of Authors administers:
• the Authors' Foundation and Kathleen Blundell Trust, which give grants to assist authors working on their next book;
• the Francis Head Bequest for assisting authors who, through physical mishap, are temporarily unable to maintain themselves or their families;
• Travelling Scholarships which give honorary awards;
• three prizes for novels: the Betty Trask Awards, the Encore Award and the McKitterick Prize;

• two prizes for a full-length published work: the Somerset Maugham Awards and the *Sunday Times* Young Writer of the Year Award;
• two poetry awards: the Eric Gregory Awards and the Cholmondeley Awards;
• the Tom-Gallon and Olive Cook Awards for short story writers;
• two radio drama prizes: the Richard Imison Award for a writer new to radio drama and the Peter Tinniswood Award;
• awards for translations from Arabic, Dutch/Flemish, French, German, Greek, Italian, Portuguese, Spanish and Swedish into English;
• educational book awards;
• medical book awards.

The Writers' Guild of Great Britain

The Writers' Guild of Great Britain is the TUC-affiliated trade union for writers.

The Writers' Guild of Great Britain is a trade union, affiliated to the TUC, and represents writers' interests in film, television, radio, theatre, books and video games. Formed in 1959 as the Screenwriters' Guild, the union gradually extended into all areas of freelance writing activity and copyright protection. In 1974, when book authors and stage dramatists became eligible for membership, substantial numbers joined. In June 1997 the Theatre Writers' Union membership unified with that of the Writers' Guild to create a larger, more powerful writers' union.

Apart from necessary dealings with Government and policies on legislative matters affecting writers, the Guild is, by constitution, non-political, has no involvement with any political party, and members pay no political levy.

The Guild employs a permanent general secretary and other permanent staff and is administered by an Executive Council of 20 members. The Guild comprises professional writers in all media, united in common concern for one another and regulating the conditions under which they work.

Membership

The Writers' Guild of Great Britain
40 Rosebery Avenue, London EC1R 4RX
tel 020-7833 0777 *fax* 020-7833 4777
email admin@writersguild.org.uk
website www.writersguild.org.uk
General Secretary Bernie Corbett
Full Membership: 1.2% of earnings from professional writing (min. £180, max. £1,800 p.a.)
Candidate Membership: £100 p.a. (restricted to writers who have not had work published or produced at Guild-approved rates)
Student Membership: £20 p.a. (open to anyone on an accredited writing course or on attachment with a theatre)
Affiliate Membership: £275 p.a. (for people who work professionally with writers, e.g. agents, technical advisers)

Members receive the Guild's quarterly *UK Writer* magazine, which carries articles, letters and reports written by members, plus a weekly email newsletter every Friday afternoon. Other benefits include: legal advice and contract vetting; free entry to the British Library reading rooms.

The Writers' Guild and agreements

The Guild's basic function is to negotiate minimum terms in those areas in which its members work. Those agreements form the basis of the individual contracts signed by members. Further details are given below. The Guild also gives individual advice to its members on contracts and other matters which the writer encounters in his or her professional life. It also organises informative and social events for members, and maintains a benevolent fund to help writers in financial trouble.

Television

The Guild negotiates minimum terms agreements with the BBC, ITV, Pact (Producers' Alliance for Cinema and Television) and has also talked to Channel 4 and Five about various new internet services.

The Guild also has a minimum terms agreement in place with TAC (representing Welsh-language television producers), which has been reviewed because of the early analogue/digital switchover in Wales.

These agreements regulate minimum fees, residuals and royalties, copyright, credits, and general conditions for television plays, series and serials, dramatisations and adaptations, soaps and sitcoms. One of the Guild's most important achievements has been the establishment of pension rights for members. The BBC, ITV and independent producers pay a pension contribution on top of the standard writer's fee on the understanding that the Guild member also pays a contribution.

The advent of digital and cable television channels, video-on-demand and download-to-own services, mobile phone technology and the expansion of the BBC's commercial arm have seen the Guild in constant negotiation over the past ten years. The Guild now has agreements for all of the BBC's digital channels and for its joint venture channels.

Film

In 1985 an important agreement was signed with the two producer organisations: the British Film and Television Producers' Association and the Independent Programme Producers' Association (now known as Pact). Since then there has been an industrial agreement covering UK film productions. Pension fund contributions have been negotiated for Guild members in the same way as for the BBC and ITV. The Agreement was renegotiated in February 1992 and consultations on an updated arrangement, led by the Guild's Film Committee, are in progress. The Guild now has a presence at the Cannes Film Festival each year. The Guild has recently published updated guidelines for film writers.

Radio

The Guild has a standard agreement for Radio Drama with the BBC, establishing a fee structure that is reviewed annually. This agreement was comprehensively renegotiated in 2005, with input from the Guild's Radio Committee, resulting in an agreement covering various new developments such as digital radio. In 1985 the BBC agreed to extend the pension scheme already established for television writers to include radio writers. The Guild has special agreements for Radio 4's *The Archers* and for the online streaming of BBC Radio services ('Listen Again'). A separate agreement covers the reuse of old comedy and drama material on digital BBC7. The Guild has opened discussions with the Radio Independents Group to establish a minimum terms agreement covering its members' ouptut.

Books

The Guild fought long, hard and successfully for the loans-based Public Lending Right to reimburse authors for books lent in libraries. This is now law and the Guild is frequently in touch with the Registrar of the scheme.

The Guild has an active Books Committee, which works on behalf of book writers and poets. Recently, the committee has been discussing and advising members about new trends in self-publishing, print-on-demand services and ebooks. It has also announced a new co-operative self-publishing venture: www.writersguildbookscoop.co.uk.

Theatre

In 1979 the Guild, together with the Theatre Writers' Union, negotiated the first industrial agreement for theatre writers. The Theatres National Committee Agreement (TNC) covers the Royal Shakespeare Company, the National Theatre Company and the English Stage Company. When their agreement was renegotiated in 2007 the Guild achieved a long-standing ambition of a minimum fee of £10,000 for a new play.

In June 1986, a new agreement was signed with the Theatrical Management Association (TMA), which covers 95 provincial theatres. In 1993, this agreement was comprehensively revised and included a provision for a year-on-year increase in fees in line with the Retail Price Index. The TMA agreement is now being renegotiated.

After many years of negotiation, an agreement was concluded in 1991 between the Guild and the Independent Theatre Council, which represents 200 of the smaller and fringe theatres as well as educational and touring companies. This agreement was revised in 2002 and the minimum fees are reviewed annually. The Guild is currently talking to the ITC about updating the agreement again and making it more user-friendly.

The Guild's Theatre Committee holds an annual forum for Literary Managers, runs a Theatre Encouragement Award and has regular meetings with Arts Council England to inform its theatre policy.

Other activities

The Guild is in touch with Government and national institutions wherever and whenever the interests of writers are in question or are being discussed. It holds cross-party Parliamentary lobbies with Equity and the Musicians' Union to ensure that the various artforms they represent are properly cared for.

Working with the Federation of Entertainment Unions, the Guild makes its views known to Government bodies on a broader basis. It keeps in touch with Arts Council England, the BBC Trust, Ofcom and other national bodies.

The Guild is an active affiliate of the British Copyright Council, Creators' Rights Alliance, Save Kids' TV, Voice of the Listener and Viewer, and other organisations whose activities are relevant to professional writers. It has an Anti-Censorship Committee, which has intervened strongly to protect freedom of speech.

Internationally, the Guild plays a leading role in the International Affiliation of Writers Guilds, which includes the American Guilds East and West, the Canadian Guilds (French and English), and the Irish, Australian and New Zealand Guilds. When it is possible to make common cause, the Guilds act accordingly. The Guild takes a leading role in the European Writers' Council and the Fédération des Scénaristes d'Europe. The Guild is becoming more involved with matters at European level where the harmonisation of copyright law and the regulation of a converged audiovisual/telecommunications industry are of immediate interest.

Membership activities

The Guild in its day-to-day work helps with problems on behalf of individual members, gives advice on contracts, and takes up issues that affect the lives of its members as professional writers. Members have access to free legal advice and professional contract vetting. Regular committee meetings are held by the Guild's various specialist Craft Committees.

In conclusion

The writer is an isolated individual in a world in which individual voices are not always heard. The Guild brings together those writers to make common cause on many vitally important matters, making full use of its collective strength.

Societies, associations and clubs

The societies, associations and clubs listed here will be of interest to both writers and artists. They include appreciation societies devoted to specific authors, professional bodies and national institutions. Some also offer prizes and awards (see page 588).

Academi (Welsh Academy)

Main Office 3rd Floor, Mount Stuart House, Mount Stuart Square, Cardiff CF10 5FQ
tel 029-2047 2266 *fax* 029-2049 2930
email post@academi.org
and Academi Glyn Jones Centre, Wales Millennium Centre, Cardiff Bay, Cardiff CF10 5AL
tel 029-2047 2266 *fax* 029-2047 0691
email post@academi.org
North West Wales Office Tŷ Newydd, Llanystumdwy, Cricieth, Gwynedd LL52 0LW
tel (01766) 522817 *fax* (01766) 523095
email post@tynewydd.org
South West Wales Office Dylan Thomas Centre, Somerset Place, Swansea SA1 1RR
tel (01792) 463980 *fax* (01792) 463993
website www.academi.org
Chief Executive Peter Finch
Membership Associate: £15 p.a. (waged), £7.50 (unwaged)

Academi is the trading name of Yr Academi Gymreig, the Welsh National Literature Promotion Agency and Society of Writers. With funds mostly provided from public sources, it has been constitutionally independent since 1978. It runs courses, competitions (including the Cardiff International Poetry and Wales Book of the Year Competition), conferences, tours by authors, festivals and represents the interests of Welsh writers and Welsh writing both inside Wales and beyond. Its publications include *Taliesin* (3 p.a.), a literary journal in the Welsh language; *A470* (quarterly), a literature information magazine; *The Oxford Companion to the Literature of Wales*, *The Welsh Academy English–Welsh Dictionary*, *Welsh Academy Encyclopaedia of Wales* and a variety of translated works.

Academi administers a range of schemes including Writers on Tour, Writers Residencies and Writing Squads for young people. Academi also runs services for writers in Wales such as bursaries, critical advice and mentoring. Founded 1959.

Academic Writers Group – see The Society of Authors

All Party Parliamentary Writers Group

tel 020-7264 5709 *fax* 020-7264 5755
email barbara.hayes@alcs.co.uk
website www.allpartywritersgroup.co.uk
Chair Janet Anderson MP, *Administrator* Barbara Hayes

The Group has some 27 Members from both Houses and seeks 'to represent the interests of all writers; to safeguard their intellectual property rights and ensure they receive a fair level of recognition and reward for their contribution to the economy and society as a whole.' Founded 2007.

Alliance of Literary Societies

Chair Linda J. Curry, 59 Bryony Road, Birmingham B29 4BY
tel 0121-475 1805
email L.j.curry@bham.ac.uk
website www.allianceofliterarysocieties.org.uk
Membership Charge depends on size of society

Membership comprises 100+ affiliated literary societies. Aims to act as a valuable liaison body between member societies as a means of sharing knowledge, skills and expertise, and may also act as a pressure group when necessary. The Alliance can assist in the preservation of buildings, places and objects which have literary associations. Produces 2 newsletters a year, plus a literary magazine.

American Literary Translators Association (ALTA)

c/o University of Texas at Dallas, 800 W. Campbell Road, J051 Richardson, TX 75080–3021, USA
tel 972-883-2093 *fax* 972-883-6303
email lindy.jolly@atdallas.edu
website www.literarytranslators.org
Administrative Assistant Lindy Jolly

A broad-based organisation dedicated to the promotion of literary translation through services to literary translators, forums on the theory and practice of translation, collaboration with the international literary community, and advocacy on behalf of the library translator. Founded 1978.

American Society for Indexing (ASI)

(formerly American Society of Indexers)
10200 West 44th Avenue, Suite 304, Wheat Ridge, CO 80033, USA
tel 303-463-2887 *fax* 303-422-8894
email info@asindexing.org
website www.asindexing.org
Executive Director Francine Butler

Aims to increase awareness of the value of high-quality indexes and indexing; offer members access to educational resources that enable them to strengthen their indexing performance; keep members up to date on indexing technology; defend and safeguard the professional interests of indexers.

American Society of Composers, Authors and Publishers

One Lincoln Plaza, New York, NY 10023, USA
tel 212-621-6000 *fax* 212-621-8453
London contact: 8 Cork Street, London W1S 3LT
website www.ascap.com
President & Chairman Paul Williams

Arts Club

40 Dover Street, London W1S 4NP
tel 020-7499 8581 *fax* 020-7409 0913
email bc@theartsclub.co.uk
website www.theartsclub.co.uk
Club Secretary Brian Clivaz

For all those connected with or interested in the arts, literature and science. A social arts club, bar open until 2am.

Arts Council England

14 Great Peter Street, London SW1P 3NQ
tel (0845) 300 6200 *fax* (0161) 934 4426
email enquiries@artscouncil.org.uk
website www.artscouncil.org.uk
Chief Executive Alan Davey

The national development agency for the arts in England, distributing public money from Government and the National Lottery. Arts Council England's main funding programme is Grants for the Arts, which is open to individuals, arts organisations, national touring companies and other people who use the arts in their work.

Arts Council England has one national and 9 regional offices. It has a single contact telephone and email address for general enquiries (see above). Founded 1946.

East
Eden House, 48–49 Bateman Street, Cambridge CB2 1LR
tel (0845) 300 6200 *textphone* (01223) 306893
fax (0870) 242 1271

East Midlands
St Nicholas Court, 25–27 Castle Gate, Nottingham NG1 7AR
tel (0845) 300 6200 *fax* 0115-950 2467

London
2 Pear Tree Court, London EC1R 0DS
tel (0845) 300 6200 *textphone* 020-7973 6564
fax 020-7608 4100

North East
Central Square, Forth Street, Newcastle upon Tyne NE1 3PJ
tel (0845) 300 6200 *textphone* 0191-255 8585
fax 0191-230 1020

North West
The Hive, 49 Lever Street, Manchester M1 1FN
tel (0845) 300 6200 *textphone* 0161-834 9131
fax 0161-834 6969

South East
Sovereign House, Church Street, Brighton BN1 1RA
tel (0845) 300 6200 *textphone* (01273) 710659
fax (0870) 2421257

South West
Senate Court, Southernhay Gardens, Exeter EX1 1UG
tel (0845) 300 6200 *textphone* (01392) 433503
fax (01392) 433503

West Midlands
82 Granville Street, Birmingham B1 2LH
tel (0845) 300 6200 *textphone* 0121-643 2815
fax 0121-643 7239

Yorkshire
21 Bond Street, Dewsbury, West Yorkshire WF13 1AX
tel (0845) 300 6200 *textphone* (01924) 438585
fax (01924) 466522

Arts Council/An Chomhairle Ealaíon

70 Merrion Square, Dublin 2, Republic of Ireland
tel (01) 618 0200 *fax* (01) 6761302
email stephanie.ocallaghan@artscouncil.ie
website www.artscouncil.ie
Arts Programme Director John O'Kane

The national development agency for the arts in Ireland. Founded 1951.

Arts Council of Northern Ireland

77 Malone Road, Belfast BT9 6AQ
tel 028-9038 5200 *fax* 028-90661715
email info@artscouncil-ni.org
website www.artscouncil-ni.org
Chief Executive Roisín McDonough, *Literature Officer* Damian Smyth, *Visual Arts Officer* Suzanne Lyle

Promotes and encourages the arts throughout Northern Ireland. Artists in drama, dance, music and jazz, literature, the visual arts, traditional arts and community arts can apply for support for specific schemes and projects. The value of the grant will be set according to the aims of the application. Applicants must have contributed regularly to the artistic activities of the community, and been resident for at least 1 year in Northern Ireland.

Arts Council of Wales

Bute Place, Cardiff CF10 5AL
tel 0845-873 4900 *fax* 029-2044 1400
email info@artswales.org.uk
website www.artswales.org.uk
Chairman Prof. Dai Smith, *Arts Director* David Alston, *Head of Communications* Betsan Moses, *Wales Arts International Director* Eluned Haf

National organisation with specific responsibility for the funding and development of the arts in Wales. Arts Council of Wales receives funding from the National Assembly for Wales and also distributes National Lottery funds for the arts in Wales. From these resources, Arts Council of Wales makes grants to support arts activities and facilities. Some of the funds are allocated in the form of annual revenue grants to full-time arts organisations such as the Academi. It also operates schemes which provide financial and other forms of support for individual artists or projects. Arts Council of Wales undertakes this work in both the English and Welsh languages. Wales Arts International is the unique partnership between the Arts Council of Wales and British Council Wales, which works to promote knowledge about contemporary arts and culture from Wales and encourages international exchange and collaboration.

North Wales Regional Office
36 Princes Drive, Colwyn Bay LL29 8LA
tel (01492) 533440 *minicom* (01492) 532288
fax (01492) 533677

Mid and West Wales Regional Office
6 Gardd Llydaw, Jackson Lane, Carmarthen SA31 1QD
tel (01267) 234248 *minicom* (01267) 223496
fax (01267) 233084

South Wales Office
Bute Place, Cardiff CF10 5AL
tel 0845-873 4900 *fax* 029-2044 1400

Aslib (The Association for Information Management)

207 Davina House, 137–149 Goswell Road, London EC1V 7ET
tel 020-7253 3349 *fax* 020-7490 0577
email furtherinformation@aslib.com
website www.aslib.com
Ceo Roger Bowes

Actively promotes best practice in the management of information resources. It represents its members and lobbies on all aspects of the management of and legislation concerning information at local, national and international levels. Aslib provides consultancy and information services, professional development training, conferences, specialist recruitment, internet products, and publishes primary and secondary journals, conference proceedings, directories and monographs. Founded 1924.

Association for Scottish Literary Studies (ASLS)

c/o Dept of Scottish Literature, 7 University Gardens, University of Glasgow G12 8QH
tel 0141-330 5309
email office@asls.org.uk
website www.asls.org.uk
Hon. President Alan Riach, *Hon. Secretary* Lorna Borrowman Smith, *Publishing Manager* Duncan Jones
Membership £40 p.a. individuals, £10 UK students, £67 corporate

Promotes the study, teaching and writing of Scottish literature and furthers the study of the languages of Scotland. Publishes annually an edited text of Scottish literature, an anthology of new Scottish writing, a series of academic journals and a Newsletter (2 p.a.). Also publishes *Scotnotes* (comprehensive study guides to major Scottish writers), literary texts and commentary CDs designed to assist the classroom teacher, and a series of occasional papers. Organises 3 conferences a year. Founded 1970.

Association of American Correspondents in London (AACL)

AACL, PO Box 645, Pinner HA5 9JJ
email secretary@theaacl.co.uk
website www.theaacl.co.uk
Contact Monique Jessen

Association of American Publishers Inc.

71 Fifth Avenue, New York, NY 10003, USA
tel 212-255-0200 *fax* 212-255-7007
email jplatt@publishers.org
website www.publishers.org
President & Ceo Tom Allen

Founded 1970.

Association of Art Historians (AAH)

70 Cowcross Street, London EC1M 6EJ
tel 020-7490 3211 *fax* 020-7490 3277
email admin@aah.org.uk
website www.aah.org.uk
Administrator Claire Davies (Senior Programme Co-ordinator), Matt Lodder (Senior Administrator)
Membership Various options for personal membership; institutional membership available

Formed to promote the study of art history and ensure wider public recognition of the field. Publishes *Art History* journal, *The Art Book* magazine, *Bulletin* newsletter. Manages the Artists' Papers Register (APR). Annual conference and book fair in March/April. Founded 1974.

Association of Assistant Librarians – see Career Development Group

The Association of Authors' Agents

c/o 14 Vernon Street, London W14 0RJ
tel 020-7471 7900
website www.agentsassoc.co.uk
President Anthony Goff, *Treasurer* Anna Davis, *Secretary* James Wills

Maintains a code of professional practice to which all members commit themselves; holds regular meetings to discuss matters of common professional interest; provides a vehicle for representing the view of authors' agents in discussion of matters of common interest with other professional bodies. Founded 1974.

Association of Authors' Representatives Inc.

676A, Suite 312 9th Avenue, New York, NY 10036, USA

tel 212-840-5770
email aarinc@mindspring.com
website www.aar-online.org
Founded 1991.

Association of British Science Writers (ABSW)

Wellcome Wolfson Building, 165 Queen's Gate, London SW7 5HD
tel (0870) 7703361 *fax* (0870) 7707102
email absw@absw.org.uk
website www.absw.org.uk
Chair Dr Natasha Loder

Association of science writers, editors, and radio, film and TV producers concerned with the presentation and communication of science, technology and medicine. Aims to improve the standard of science writing and to assist its members in their work.

Association of Canadian Publishers

174 Spadina Avenue, Suite 306, Toronto, Ontario M5T 2C2, Canada
tel 416-487-6116 *fax* 416-487-8815
email admin@canbook.org
website www.publishers.ca
Executive Director Carolyn Wood

Founded 1976; formerly Independent Publishers Association, 1971.

Association of Christian Writers

Administrator Rev. Simon Baynes, 23 Moorend Lane, Thame, Oxon OX9 3BQ
tel (01844) 213673
email baynes@clearmail.net, admin@christianwriters.org.uk
website www.christianwriters.org.uk
Membership £22 p.a. (£18.50 DD)

Resigtered charity that aims to see the quality of writing in every area of the media, either overtly Christian or shaped by a Christian perspective, reaching the widest range of people across the UK and beyond. To inspire and equip people to use their talents and skills with integrity to devise, write and market excellent material which comes from a Christian world view. Founded 1971.

Association of Freelance Editors, Proofreaders and Indexers

Contact 1 Brenda O'Hanlon, 11 Clonard Road, Sandyford, Dublin 16, Republic of Ireland
tel (+353 1) 295 2194
email brenda@ohanlonmedia.com
Contact 2 Winifred Power, 28 Parklane Avenue, Abbeyside, Dungarvan, Co. Waterford, Republic of Ireland
tel (+353 58) 48458 *fax* (+353 58) 48458
email powerediting@eircom.net
website www.afepi.ie

Provides information to publishers on freelances through a list of members and their qualifications. Also protects the interests of freelances, and provides social contact for isolated workers.

The Association of Illustrators

2nd Floor, Back Building, 150 Curtain Road, London EC2A 3AT
tel 020-7613 4328 *fax* 020-7613 4417
email info@theaoi.com
website www.theaoi.com
Contact Membership Coordinator

Exists to support illustrators, promote illustration and encourage professional standards in the industry. Publishes *Varoom* magazine (3 p.a.); presents an annual programme of events; annual competition, exhibition and tour of Images – the Best of British Contemporary Illustration (call for entries: July/August). Founded 1973.

The Association of Learned and Professional Society Publishers

Chief Executive Ian Russell, 1–3 Ship Street, Shoreham-by-Sea, West Sussex BN43 5DH
tel (01235) 847776 *fax* 0870-706 0332
email ian.russell@alpsp.org
website www.alpsp.org
Membership Open to not-for-profit publishers and allied organisations

The International trade association for non-profit publishers. Founded 1972.

The Association of Photographers (AOP)

Co-Secretary Gwen Thomas, 81 Leonard Street, London EC2A 4QS
tel 020-7739 6669 *fax* 020-7739 8707
email general@aophoto.co.uk
website www.the-aop.org
Membership £280 p.a.

Managing Director Kingsley Marten

Exists to protect and promote the interests of fashion advertising and editorial photographers. Founded 1968.

The Jane Austen Society

Secretary Maureen Stiller, 9 Nicola Close, South Croydon, Surrey CR2 6NA
email HQ@jasoc.co.uk
website www.janeaustensoci.freeuk.com
Membership £20 p.a., student for 3 years £10, UK; £20 overseas; £300 life

Aims to promote interest in, and enjoyment of, the novels and letters of Jane Austen (1775–1817). Regular publications, meetings and conferences. Eleven branches in UK. Founded 1940.

Australia Council

PO Box 788, Strawberry Hills, NSW 2012, Australia
located at 372 Elizabeth Street, Surry Hills, NSW 2010, Australia

tel (02) 9215 9000 *fax* (02) 9215 9111
email mail@australiacouncil.gov.au
website www.australiacouncil.gov.au
Ceo Kathy Keele

Provides a broad range of support for the arts in Australia, embracing music, theatre, literature, visual arts, crafts, Aboriginal arts, community and new media arts. It has 7 Boards: Literature, Visual Arts, Music, Theatre, Dance, Major Performing Arts, as well as the Aboriginal and Torres Strait Islander Arts Board.

The Literature Board's chief objective is to support the writing of all forms of creative literature – novels, short stories, poetry, plays and literary non-fiction. It also assists with the publication of literary magazines, has a book publishing subsidies programme, and initiates and supports projects of many kinds designed to promote Australian literature both within Australia and abroad.

Australian Copyright Council

PO Box 1986, Strawberry Hills, NSW 2012, Australia
tel (02) 8815 9777 *fax* (02) 8815 9799
email info@copyright.org.au
website www.copyright.org.au

An independent non-profit organisation which aims to assist creators and other copyright owners to exercise their rights effectively; raise awareness in the community generally about the importance of copyright; research and identify areas of copyright law which are inadequate or unfair; seek changes to law and practice to enhance the effectiveness and fairness of copyright; foster cooperation amongst bodies representing creators and owners of copyright.

The Council comprises 23 organisations or associations of owners and creators of copyright material, including the Australian Society of Authors, the Australian Writers Guild and the Australian Book Publishers Association. Founded 1968.

Australian Library and Information Association

PO Box 6335, Kingston, ACT 2604, Australia
tel (02) 6215 8222 *fax* (02) 6282 2249
email enquiry@alia.org.au, sue.huntley@alia.org.au
website www.alia.org.au
Executive Director Sue Hutley

Aims to promote and improve the services of libraries and other information agencies; to improve the standard of library and information personnel and foster their professional interests; to represent the interests of members to governments, other organisations and the community; and to encourage people to contribute to the improvement of library and information services by supporting the association.

Australian Publishers Association (APA)

60–89 Jones Street, Ultimo, NSW 2007, Australia
tel (02) 9281 9788 *fax* (02) 9281 1073
email apa@publishers.asn.au
website www.publishers.asn.au
Ceo Maree McCaskill

The Australian Society of Authors

PO Box 1566, Strawberry Hills NSW 2012, Australia
tel (02) 9318 0877 *fax* (02) 9318 0530
email asa@asauthors.org
located at 98 Pitt Street, Redfern NSW 2016, Australia
website www.asauthors.org
Executive Director Angelo Loukakis

Australian Writers' Guild (AWG)

5 Blackfriars Street, Chippendale, NSW 2008
tel (02) 9319 0339 *fax* (02) 9319 0141
email admin@awg.com.au
website www.awg.com.au
Executive Director Jacqueline Woodman

The professional association for all performance writers, i.e. writers for film, TV, radio, theatre, video and new media. The AWG is recognised throughout the industry in Australia as being the voice of performance writers. Established 1962.

Authors' Club (at The Arts Club)

40 Dover Street, London W1S 4NP
tel 020-7499 8581 *fax* 020-7409 0913
email stella@theartsclub.co.uk
website www.theartsclub.co.uk
Chairman Chris Schuler, *Secretary* Stella Kane
Membership Apply to Secretary

Founded by Sir Walter Besant, the Authors' Club welcomes as members writers, publishers, critics, journalists, academics and anyone involved with literature. Administers the Authors' Club Best First Novel Award, the Sir Banister Fletcher Award and the Dolman Best Travel Book Award. Founded 1891.

Authors' Licensing and Collecting Society Ltd – see page 715

Axis – the online resource for contemporary art

Studio 17/18, Leeds Design Innovation Centre, 46 The Calls, Leeds LS2 7EY
tel (0113) 242 9830 *fax* (0113) 217 9665
email info@axisweb.org
website www.axisweb.org
Membership From £27 p.a.

The leading online resource for information about contemporary art. The website features profiles of professional artists and curators, interviews, discussions, art news and debates, and showcases the artists to watch.

Artist and curator members can profile their work online and are a part of the Axis art community. Axis also commissions interviews, essays and articles by leading and emerging writers inspired by the artists on the website. Axis is a charity funded by Arts

Council England, and the Arts Council of Wales. Established 1991.

BAFTA (The British Academy of Film and Television Arts)

195 Piccadilly, London W1J 9LN
tel 020-7734 0022 *fax* 020-7734 1792
email info@bafta.org
website www.bafta.org
Chief Executive Amanda Berry

The pre-eminent organisation in the UK for the film, TV and video games arts, recognising and promoting the achievement and endeavour of industry practitioners. BAFTA Awards are awarded annually by members to their peers in recognition of their skills and expertise. The Academy's premises provide club facilities with a 200-seat cinema and 40-seat preview theatre. Provides a full and varied programme of industry-related events, masterclasses, seminars and panel discussions, which are open to both members and non-members. Founded 1947.

BANA (Bath Area Network for Artists)

The Old Malthouse, Comfortable Place, Upper Bristol Road, Bath BA1 3AJ
tel 01225 471714
email enquiries@bana-arts.co.uk
website www.bana-arts.co.uk
Membership from €20 p.a.

An artist-led network that aims to raise the profile of arts activity in the Bath area, to establish and strengthen links between artists, artists' groups and art promoters, and advocate for increased investment in local arts activities. BANA was established by artists, for artists, and works through artists to achieve its aims. It is a non-selective network and its membership is made up of artists committed to professional practice. Core activities and services include its website and artists' database, a newsletter, artist networking events, and yearly exhibitions for members, and the provision of public liability insurance for artists. Founded 1998.

BAPLA (British Association of Picture Libraries and Agencies)

18 Vine Hill, London EC1R 5DZ
tel 020-7713 1780 *fax* 020-7713 1211
email enquiries@bapla.org.uk
website www.bapla.org.uk
Membership and Communications Manager Susanne Kittlinger

The British Association of Picture Libraries and Agencies, or BAPLA, is the trade association for picture libraries in the UK and the largest organisation of its kind in the world. With over 380 member companies, it represents the vast majority of commercial picture libraries and agencies in the UK. See website for details.

The Beckford Society

The Timber Cottage, Crockerton, Warminster BA12 8AX
tel (01985) 213195
email Sidney.Blackmore@btinternet.com
Membership £20 p.a. minimum

Aims to promote an interest in the life and works of William Beckford of Fonthill (1760–1844) and his circle. Encourages Beckford studies and scholarship through exhibitions, lectures and publications, including *The Beckford Journal* (annual) and occasional newsletters. Founded 1995.

Thomas Lovell Beddoes Society

9 Amber Court, Belper, Derbyshire DE56 1HG
tel (01773) 828066
email john@beddoes.demon.co.uk
website www.phantomwooer.org

Aims to promote an interest in the life and works of Thomas Lovell Beddoes (1803–49). The Society promotes and undertakes Beddoes studies, and disseminates and publishes useful research. Founded 1994.

The Arnold Bennett Society

Secretary Carol Gorton, 4 Field End Close, Trentham, Stoke-on-Trent ST4 8DA
email arnoldbennettscty@btinternet.com
website www.arnoldbennettsociety.org.uk
Membership £12 p.a. individuals, £14 p.a. family plus £2 if living outside Europe

Aims to promote the study and appreciation of the life, works and times not only of Arnold Bennett (1867–1931) himself, but also of other provincial writers with particular relationship to North Staffordshire.

The E.F. Benson Society

The Old Coach House, High Street, Rye, East Sussex TN31 7JF
tel (01797) 223114
website www.efbensonsociety.org
Secretary Allan Downend
Membership £7.50 p.a. single, £8.50 2 people at same address, £12.50 overseas

Aims to promote interest in the author E.F. Benson (1867–1940) and the Benson family. Arranges annual literary evening, annual outing to Rye (July) and other places of Benson interest, talks on the Bensons and exhibitions. Archive includes the Austin Seckersen Collection, transcriptions of the Benson diaries and letters. Publishes postcards, anthologies of Benson's works, a Benson biography, books on Benson and an annual journal, *The Dodo*. Also sells out-of-print Bensons to members. Founded 1984.

Bibliographical Society

c/o Institute of English Studies, University of London, Senate House, Malet Street, London WC1E 7HU
tel 020-7782 3279
email secretary@bibsoc.org.uk
website www.bibsoc.org.uk
President John Barnard, *Secretary* Meg Ford

Acquisition and dissemination of information on subjects connected with historical bibliography. Publishes the journal The Library. Founded 1892.

The Blackpool Art Society

email sec@blackpoolartsociety.co.uk
website www.blackpoolartsociety.co.uk
President Mr Ray Swift
Hon. Secretary Margaret Barston, 66 Alexandra Road, Thornton Cleveleys FY5 5DA

Autumn exhibition (members' work only). Studio meetings, practicals, lectures, etc, out-of-door sketching, workshops. Founded 1884.

Book Aid International

39–41 Coldharbour Lane, London SE5 9NR
tel 020-7733 3577 *fax* 020-7978 8006
email info@bookaid.org
website www.bookaid.org
Director Clive Nettleton

Works in 12 countries in sub-Saharan Africa, Palestine and Sri Lanka, providing over half a million books and journals each year to libraries, hospitals, refugee camps and schools. Also supports the provision of good basic education and the development of community libraries.

The Booksellers Association of the United Kingdom & Ireland Ltd

272 Vauxhall Bridge Road, London SW1V 1BA
tel 020-7802 0802 *fax* 020-7802 0803
email mail@booksellers.org.uk
website www.booksellers.org.uk
Chief Executive T.E. Godfray

Founded 1895.

Booktrust

(formerly the National Book League, founded 1925)
Book House, 45 East Hill, London SW18 2QZ
tel 020-8516 2977 *fax* 020-8516 2978
email query@booktrust.org.uk
website www.booktrust.org.uk
Director Viv Bird, *Chairman* Sue Horner (acting)

An independent charity dedicated to encouraging people of all ages and cultures to engage with books. It is responsible for a number of successful national reading promotions, sponsored book prizes and creative reading projects aimed at encouraging readers to discover and enjoy books. These include the Orange Prize for Fiction, the Children's Laureate, the Get London Reading campaign, the Booktrust Teenage Prize and Bookstart, the national programme that works through locally based organisations to give a free pack of books to young children, with guidance materials for parents and carers. Booktrust has developed 2 further free book programmes in the UK: Booktime, run in association with Pearson, gives a free book to every Year 1 pupil, and Booked Up, which gives a free book, from a choice of 12, to every Year 7 pupil.

The George Borrow Society

Membership Secretary Michael Skillman, 60 Upper Marsh Road, Warminster, Wilts. BA12 9PN
website www.clough5.fsnet.co.uk/gb.html
Membership £15 p.a., £22.50 joint members at same address, £10 students

Promotes knowledge of the life and works of George Borrow (1803–81), traveller and author. Publishes *Bulletin* (bi-annual). Founded 1991.

British Academy

10 Carlton House Terrace, London SW1Y 5AH
tel 020-7969 5200 *fax* 020-7969 5300
email chiefexec@britac.ac.uk
website www.britac.ac.uk
President Sir Adam Roberts, *Vice-President (Humanities)* Prof. Karin Barber, *Vice-President (Social Sciences)* Prof. Susan Mendus, *Treasurer* Prof. Roger Kain, *Foreign Secretary* Prof. Duncan Gallie, *Publications Secretary* Prof. Christopher Wickham, *Research Chair Professor* Albert Weale, *Communications Chair* Dame Hazel Genn, *Chief Executive & Secretary* Dr Robin Jackson

The national Academy for the humanities and social sciences: an independent and self-governing fellowship of scholars, elected for distinction and achievement in one or more branches of the academic disciplines that make up the humanities and social sciences. Its primary purpose is to promote research and scholarship in those areas: through research grants and other awards, the sponsorship of a number of research projects and of research institutes overseas; the award of prizes and medals (including the Crawshay prizes for critical literary studies by a female scholar); and the publication both of sponsored lectures and seminar papers and of fundamental texts and research aids prepared under the direction of Academy committees. It also acts as a forum for the discussion of issues of interest and concern to scholars in the humanities and the social sciences, and it provides advice to the Government and other public bodies. Founded 1901.

British Academy of Composers and Songwriters

British Music House, 26 Berners Street, London W1T 3LR
tel 020-7636 2929 *fax* 020-7636 2212
email info@britishacademy.com
website www.britishacademy.com
Contact Vicky Hunt, Head of Membership

The Academy represents the interests of composers and songwriters across all genres, providing advice on professional and artistic matters. It administers a number of major events, including the annual Ivor Novello Awards and British Composer Awards.

The British Association of Communicators in Business

Suite GA 2, Oak House, Woodlands Business Park, Breckland, Linford Wood West, Milton Keynes MK14 6EY

tel (01908) 313755 *fax* (01908) 313661
email enquiries@cib.uk.com
website www.cib.uk.com

The market leader in internal communications for those involved in corporate media management and practice by providing professional, authoritative, dynamic, supportive and innovative services. Founded 1949.

British Association of Journalists

General Secretary Steve Turner, 89 Fleet Street, London EC4Y 1DH
tel 020-7353 3003 *fax* 020-7353 2310
email office@bajunion.org.uk
website www.bajunion.org.uk
Membership £17.50 per month national newspaper staff, national broadcasting staff and national news agency staff; £10 p.m. other seniors including magazine journalists, PRs, freelances; £7.50 p.m. under age 24

Aims to protect and promote the industrial and professional interests of journalists. Founded 1992.

British Association of Picture Libraries and Agencies – see BAPLA (British Association of Picture Libraries and Agencies)

British Centre for Literary Translation (BCLT)

University of East Anglia, Norwich NR4 7TJ
tel (01603) 592785 *fax* (01603) 592737
email bclt@uea.ac.uk
website www.bclt.org.uk

Jointly funded by Arts Council England and the University of East Anglia, BCLT raises the profile of literary translation in the UK through events, publications, activities and research aimed at professional translators, students and the general reader. Activities include the Sebald Lecture in London, Summer School and public talks and events. BCLT coordinates a PhD programme in literary translation and offers units at undergraduate and postgraduate level. It is joint sponsor of the John Dryden Translation Prize and publishes the journals *In Other Words* and *New Books in German*. Member of the international RECIT literary translation network. Founded 1989 by the author and UEA Professor W.G. Sebald.

British Copyright Council

Copyright House, 29–33 Berners Street, London W1T 3AB
tel (01986) 788 122
email secretary@britishcopyright.org
website www.britishcopyright.org
Vice-Presidents Prof. Adrian Sterling, Geoffrey Adams, *President of Honour* Maureen Duffy, *Chairman* Paul Mitchell, *Directors* Bernie Corbett, John Smith, Andrew Yeates, Derek Brazell, Peter Leatham, Richard Combes, *Ceo* Janet Ibbotson, *Treasurer* Hugh Jones

Aims to defend and foster the true principles of copyright and its acceptance throughout the world, to bring together bodies representing all who are interested in the protection of such copyright, and to keep watch on any legal or other changes which may require an amendment of the law.

The British Council

London office 10 Spring Gardens, London SW1A 2BN
tel 020-7930 8466 *fax* 020-7839 6347
email general.enquiries@britishcouncil.org
Headquarters Bridgewater House, 58 Whitworth Street, Manchester M1 6BB
tel 0161-957 7000
website www.britishcouncil.org, www.britishcouncil.org/arts, www.contemporarywriters.com, www.encompassculture.com, www.literarytranslation.com
Chair The Rt Hon. Lord Kinnock, *Chief Executive* Martin Davidson, *Director of Arts* Venu Dhupa

The British Council connects people worldwide with learning opportunities and creative ideas from the UK, and builds lasting relationships between the UK and other countries. It has 7400 staff in offices, teaching centres, libraries, and information and resource centres in the UK and 110 countries and territories worldwide.

Working in close collaboration with book trade associations, British Council offices participate in major international book fairs.

The British Council is an authority on teaching English as a second or foreign language. It also gives advice and information on curriculum, methodology, materials and testing.

The British Council promotes British literature overseas through writers' tours, academic visits, workshops, conferences, seminars and exhibitions. It publishes *New Writing*, an annual anthology of unpublished short stories, poems and extracts from works in progress and essays; and a series of literary bibliographies, including *Tbooks: UK Teenage Literature, Crime Literature* and *Reading in the City*. Through its Literature Department, the British Council provides an overview of UK literature and a range of online resources (see above). This includes a literary portal, information about UK and Commonwealth authors, translation workshops and a worldwide online book club and reading group for adults, teenagers and children with over 10,000 books plus reading group advice.

The Visual Arts Department, part of the British Council's Arts Group, develops and enlarges overseas knowledge and appreciation of British achievement in the fields of painting, sculpture, printmaking, design, photography, the crafts and architecture, working closely with the British Council's overseas offices and with professional colleagues in the UK and abroad.

Further information about the work of the British Council is available from Arts Press at the above address, or from British Council offices overseas by emailing arts@britishcouncil.org.

The British Fantasy Society

email secretary@britishfantasysociety.org
website www.britishfantasysociety.org
Membership £30 p.a. single; £45 joint; £40 Europe; £55 rest of world

For devotees of fantasy, horror and related fields, in literature, art and the cinema. Publications include *Prism* (quarterly) featuring news and reviews, and *Dark Horizons* or a new third magazine which alternate every quarter. There is a small-press library and an annual convention, FantasyCon, and fantasy awards sponsored by the Society. Founded 1971.

BFI (British Film Institute)

21 Stephen Street, London W1T 1LN
tel 020-7255 1444
BFI events line (0870) 240 4050 *fax* 020-7436 0439
website www.bfi.org.uk
Chair Greg Dyke *Director* Amanda Nevill

Provides a wide range of services: BFI Southbank (formerly NFT); BFI London IMAX Cinema (Britain's largest screen); BFI National Library (the world's leading specialist film and TV library); BFI National Archive (one of the world's oldest and largest culturally significant film and TV archives); BFI London Film Festival; BFI London Lesbian & Gay Film Festival; BFI Distribution (making world cinema available for screening in the UK); the BFI DVD and Video catalogue of world and historic cinema; a wide range of award-winning publications and education materials, guides and resources; film footage; film stills; research services for the commercial media industry; and *Sight & Sound* magazine. Founded 1933.

British Guild of Beer Writers

Secretary Adrian Tierney-Jones, Woodcote, 2 Jury Road, Dulverton, Somerset TA22 9DU
tel (01398) 324314
email tierneyjones@btinternet.com
website www.beerwriters.co.uk
Membership £40 p.a

Aims to improve standards in beer writing and at the same time extend public knowledge of beers and brewing. The Gold and Silver Tankard Awards are given annually to writers and broadcasters judged to have made the most valuable contribution to this end. Publishes a directory of members with details of their publications and their particular areas of interest, which is circulated to the media. Founded 1988.

The British Guild of Travel Writers

335 Lordship Road, London N16 5HG
tel 020-8144 8713
email secretariat@bgtw.org
website www.bgtw.org

Arranges meetings, discussions and visits for its 220 members (who are all professional travel journalists) to promote and encourage the public's interest in travel. Publishes a monthly newsletter (for members only), website and annual *Yearbook*, which contain details of members and lists travel industry PRs and contacts. Annual awards for journalism (members only) and the travel trade.

The British Haiku Society

Flat 4, 2 Clifton Lawns, Ramsgate, Kent CT11 9PB
website www.britishhaikusociety.org
General Secretary Jon Baldwin

Promotes the appreciation and writing of haiku and related forms; welcomes overseas members. Provides tutorials, workshops, readings, critical comment and information. Specialist advisers are available. Runs a library, and administers a contest. The journal, *Blithe Spirit*, is produced quarterly. The Society has active local groups and it issues a regular newsletter. Current membership details can be obtained from the website. Founded 1990.

British Institute of Professional Photography

1 Prebendal Court, Oxford Road, Aylesbury, Bucks HP19 8EY
tel (01296) 718530 *fax* (01296) 336367
email info@bipp.com
website www.bipp.com

Represents all who practise photography as a profession in any field; to improve the quality of photography; establish recognised qualifications and a high standard of conduct; to safeguard the interests of the public and the profession. Admission can be obtained by submission of work and other information to the appropriate examining board. Fellows, Associates and Licentiates are entitled to the designation FBIPP, ABIPP or LBIPP in accordance with the qualification awarded. Organises numerous meetings and conferences in various parts of the country throughout the year; publishes *The Photographer* magazine (bi-monthly), plus various pamphlets and leaflets on professional photography. Founded 1901; incorporated 1921.

British Interactive Media Association (BIMA)

The Lightwell, 12-16 Laystall Street, London EC1R 4PF
email info@bima.co.uk
website www.bima.co.uk
Office Administrator Sharlene Gerus
Membership Open to any organisation or individual with an interest in multimedia. £690 p.a. commercial, £320 institutional, £40 individual plus VAT

Established to promote a wider understanding of the benefits of interactive multimedia to industry, government and education and to provide a regular forum for the exchange of views amongst members. Founded 1984.

The British Science Fiction Association Ltd

Membership Secretary Peter Wilkinson,
39 Glyn Avenue, New Barnet EN4 9PJ
email bsfamemberships@yahoo.co.uk
website www.bsfa.co.uk
Chair Tony Cullen

For authors, publishers, booksellers and readers of science fiction, fantasy and allied genres. Publishes *Matrix*, an informal magazine of news and information; *Focus*, an amateur writers' magazine; *Vector*, a critical magazine and the Orbiter Service, a network of postal writers workshops. Trophies are awarded annually to the winner in each category of the BSFA Awards: best UK-published novel, best short story, best artwork. Founded 1958.

British Society of Comedy Writers

President Kenneth Rock, 61 Parry Road,
Ashmore Park, Wolverhampton,
West Midlands WV11 2PS
tel (01902) 722729 *fax* (01902) 722729
email info@bscw.co.uk
website www.bscw.co.uk
Membership £75 p.a. full, £40 p.a. subscriber

Aims to bring together writers and industry representatives in order to develop new projects and ideas. Holds an annual international comedy conference, networking days and workshops to train new writers to professional standards. Founded 1999.

British Society of Magazine Editors

137 Hale Lane, Edgware, Middlesex HA8 9QP
tel 020-8906 4664
email admin@bsme.com
website www.bsme.com

British Society of Miniaturists

13 Manor Orchards, Knaresborough,
North Yorkshire HG5 0BW
tel (01423) 540603
email info@britpaint.com
website www.britpaint.com
Membership By selection

'The world's oldest miniature society.' Holds 2 open exhibitions a year. Founded 1895.

British Society of Painters

13 Manor Orchards, Knaresborough,
North Yorkshire HG5 0BW
tel (01423) 540603
email info@britpaint.com
website www.britpaint.com
Director Leslie Simpson
Membership By selection

Promotes interest and encourages high quality in the work of painters in these media. Holds 2 open exhibitions a year. Founded 1988.

British Watercolour Society

13 Manor Orchards, Knaresborough,
North Yorkshire HG5 0BW
tel (01423) 540603
email info@britpaint.com
website www.britpaint.com

Promotes the best in traditional watercolour painting. Holds 2 open exhibitions a year. Founded 1830.

Broadcasting Entertainment Cinematograph and Theatre Union (BECTU), Writers Section

373–377 Clapham Road, London SW9 9BT
tel 020-7346 0900 *fax* 020-7346 0901
email info@bectu.org.uk
website www.bectu.org.uk
General Secretary G. Morrissey

Aims to defend the interests of writers in film, TV and radio. By virtue of its industrial strength, the Union is able to help its writer members to secure favourable terms and conditions. In cases of disputes with employers, the Union can intervene in order to ensure an equitable settlement. Its production agreement with PACT lays down minimum terms for writers working in the documentary area. Founded 1991.

Broadcasting Group – see The Society of Authors, page 541

The Brontë Society

Membership Officer The Brontë Parsonage Museum,
Haworth, Keighley, West Yorkshire BD22 8DR
tel (01535) 642323 *fax* (01535) 647131
email info@bronte.org.uk
website www.bronte.info

Acquisition, preservation, promotion of the memoirs and literary remains of the Brontë family; exhibitions of MSS and other subjects. Publishes *Brontë Studies* (3 p.a.) and *The Brontë Gazette* (tri-annual). Its Museum is open throughout the year, except for the month of January.

The Browning Society

Hon. Secretary Department of English Literature,
5 University Gardens, University of Glasgow,
Glasgow G12 8QQ
tel 0141-330 1897
email r.williams@englit.arts.gla.ac.uk
website www.browningsociety.org
Contact Dr Rhian Williams, Hon. Secretary
Membership £15 p.a.

Aims to widen the appreciation and understanding of the lives and poetry of Robert Browning (1812–89) and Elizabeth Barrett Browning (1806–61), as well as other Victorian writers and poets. Founded 1881; refounded 1969.

The John Buchan Society

Membership Secretary Mrs Diana Durden, Barnack, Goring Road, Steyning, West Sussex BN44 3GF
tel (01903) 813603
email durdens@tiscali.co.uk
website www.johnbuchansociety.co.uk
Membership £15 p.a. – full; overseas and other rates on application

Promotes a wider understanding and appreciation of the life and works of John Buchan (1875–1940). Encourages publication of a complete annotated edition of Buchan's works, and supports the John Buchan Centre and Museum at Broughton, Borders. Holds regular meetings and social gatherings; produces a Newsletter and a Journal. Founded 1979.

Bureau of Freelance Photographers

Focus House, 497 Green Lanes, London N13 4BP
tel 020-8882 3315
email mail@thebfp.com
website www.thebfp.com
Chief Executive John Tracy
Membership £54 p.a. UK; £70 p.a. overseas

Exists to help the freelance photographer by providing information on markets, and free advisory service. Publishes *Market Newsletter* (monthly). Founded 1965.

Byron Society (International)

Acushla, Halam Road, Southwell, Notts. NG25 0AD
website www.internationalbyronsociety.org
Chairman P.K. Purslow
Membership £30 p.a.

Aims to promote research into the life and works of Lord Byron (1788–1824) by seminars, discussions, lectures and readings. Publishes *The Byron Journal* (annual, £6.50 plus postage). Founded 1971.

Randolph Caldecott Society

Secretary Kenn Oultram, Blue Grass Cottage, Clatterwick Lane, Little Leigh, Northwich, Cheshire CW8 4RJ
tel (01606) 891303 (office), 781731 (evening)
website www.randolphcaldecott.org.uk
Membership £12.50 p.a. individual, £17.50 p.a. families/corporate

Aims to encourage an interest in the life and works of Randolph Caldecott (1846–86), the Victorian artist, illustrator and sculptor. Meetings held in Chester. Liaises with the American Caldecott Society. Founded 1983.

Cambridge Bibliographical Society

University Library, West Road, Cambridge CB3 9DR
tel (01223) 333123 *fax* (01223) 333160
email nas1000@cam.ac.uk
website www.lib.cam.ac.uk/cambibsoc
Secretary Nicholas Smith

To encourage the study of bibliography, including book and MS production, book collecting and the history of libraries. It publishes *Transactions* (annual) and a series of monographs, and arranges a programme of lectures and visits. Founded 1949.

Campaign for Freedom of Information

Suite 102, 16 Baldwins Gardens, London EC1N 7RJ
tel 020-7831 7477 *fax* 020-7831 7461
email admin@cfoi.demon.co.uk
website ww.cfoi.org.uk

A non-profit organisation working to improve public access to official information and to ensure that the Freedom of Information Act is implemented effectively.

Campaign for Press and Broadcasting Freedom

2nd Floor, Vi & Garner Smith House, 23 Orford Road, London E17 9NL
tel 020-8521 5932
email freepress@cpbf.org.uk
website www.cpbf.org.uk

Canadian Authors Association

PO Box 851, Stn Main Orillia, ON L3V 6KS
tel 705-653-0323, 866-216-6222 (toll free)
email admin@canauthors.org
website www.canauthors.org
President Anthony Dalton, *Executive Director* Anita Purcell

Canadian Magazine Publishers Association

425 Adelaide Street West, Suite 700, Toronto, Ontario M5V 3C1, Canada
tel 416-504-0274 *fax* 416-504-0437
email friends@magazinescanada.ca
website www.magazinescanada.ca
Chief Executive Mark Jamison

Canadian Publishers' Council

250 Merton Street, Suite 203, Toronto, Ontario M4S 1B1, Canada
tel 416-322-7011 *fax* 416-322-6999
website www.pubcouncil.ca
Executive Director Jacqueline Hushion

CANSCAIP (Canadian Society of Children's Authors, Illustrators & Performers)

40 Orchard View Boulevard, Suite 104, Toronto, Ontario M4R 1B9, Canada
tel 416-515-1559
email office@canscaip.org
website www.canscaip.org

Administrative Director Lena Coakley
Membership $85 p.a. Full member (published authors and illustrators), $45 Friend

A non-profit support network for children's artists. Promotes children's literature and performances through Canada and internationally. Founded 1977.

Career Development Group

(formerly Association of Assistant Librarians)
c/o CILIP, 7 Ridgmount Street, London WC1E 7AE
website www.cilip.org.uk/cdg
President John Scown, *Secretary* Stella Wisdom

Publishes the journal *Impact* and represents the development needs of new and existing library and information workers. Founded 1895.

Careers Writers' Association

Membership Secretary Ann Goodman,
16 Caewal Road, Llandaff, Cardiff CF5 2BT
tel 029-2056 3444 *fax* 029-2065 8190
email helen.scott@btinternet.com
website www.careerswriting.co.uk
Membership £40 p.a.

Society for established writers on the inter-related topics of education, training and careers. Holds occasional meetings on subjects of interest to members, and circulates details of members to information providers. Founded 1979.

The Lewis Carroll Society

Secretary Mark Richards, 50 Lauderdale Mansions, Lauderdale Road, London W9 1NE
email markrichards@aznet.co.uk
website www.lewiscarrollsociety.org.uk
Membership £20 p.a. UK, £23 Europe, £26 elsewhere; special rates for institutions

Aims to promote interest in the life and works of Lewis Carroll (Revd Charles Lutwidge Dodgson) (1832–98) and to encourage research. Activities include regular meetings, exhibitions, and a publishing programme that includes the first annotated, unexpurgated edition of his diaries in 9 volumes, the Society's journal *The Carrollian* (2 p.a.), a newsletter, *Bandersnatch* (quarterly) and the *Lewis Carroll Review* (occasional). Founded 1969.

Lewis Carroll Society (Daresbury)

Secretary Kenn Oultram, Blue Grass Cottage, Clatterwick Lane, Little Leigh, Northwich, Cheshire CW8 4RJ
tel (01606) 891303 (office), 781731 (evening)
Membership £7 p.a.

Aims to encourage an interest in the life and works of Lewis Carroll (1832–98), author of *Alice's Adventures*. Meetings take place at Carroll's birth village (Daresbury, Cheshire). Founded 1970.

Cartoonists Club of Great Britain

Secretary Jed Stone, 75 Jacobs Wells Road, Clifton, Bristol BS8 1DJ
tel (01173) 169277
email secretary@thecartoonistsclub.com
website www.ccgb.org.uk
Membership Fee on joining £50; thereafter £35 p.a.

Aims to encourage social contact between members and endeavours to promote the professional standing and prestige of cartoonists.

The Chartered Institute of Journalists

General Secretary Dominic Cooper, 2 Dock Offices, Surrey Quays Road, London SE16 2XU
tel 020-7252 1187 *fax* 020-7232 2302
email memberservices@cioj.co.uk
website www.cioj.co.uk
Membership £195 p.a. maximum, £97.50 trainees, £133 affiliate

The senior organisation of the profession, the Chartered Institute has accumulated funds for the assistance of members. A Freelance Division links editors and publishers with freelances and a Directory is published of freelance writers, with their specialisations. There are special sections for broadcasters, motoring correspondents, public relations practitioners and overseas members. Occasional contributors to the media may qualify for election as Affiliates. Founded in 1884; incorporated by Royal Charter in 1890.

Chartered Institute of Linguists (IoL)

Saxon House, 48 Southwark Street, London SE1 1UN
tel 020-7940 3100 *fax* 020-7940 3101
email info@iol.org.uk
website www.iol.org.uk

An international professional membership organisation. It promotes proficiency in modern languages worldwide amongst professional linguists, including translators, interpreters and educationalists, as well as those in the public and private sectors for whom languages are an important skill. Through its wholly owned subsidiary IoL Language Services Ltd (LSL) it offers translation, production and recruitment services, validation of language qualifications and assessments as well as training courses. The IoL Educational Trust, an associated charity, is an accredited awarding body offering high level exams. The Institute helps to ensure equal access for all to the public services (law, health, local government) by providing interpreting qualifications in most of the languages spoken in the UK and running the National Register of Public Service Interpreters (NRPSI Ltd).

The Chartered Society of Designers

1 Cedar Court, Royal Oak Yard, Bermondsey Street, London SE1 3GA
tel 020-7357 8088 *fax* 020-7407 9878
email csd@csd.org.uk
website www.csd.org.uk
Chief Executive Frank Peters

Works to promote and regulate standards of competence, professional conduct and integrity, including representation on government and official bodies, design education and awards. The services to members include general information, publications, guidance on copyright and other professional issues, access to professional indemnity insurance, as well as the membership magazine *The Designer*. Activities in the regions are included in an extensive annual programme of events and training courses.

The Chesterton Society

Hon. Secretary Rev. Robert Hughes KCHS,
11 Lawrence Leys, Bloxham, Nr Banbury,
Oxon OX15 4NU
tel/fax (01295) 720869
mobile 077667 11984
email roberthughesII@talktalk.com
Membership £12.50 p.a.

Aims to promote interest in the life and work of G.K. Chesterton (1874–1936) and those associated with him or influenced by his writings. Two lectures a year. Publishes the *Chesterton Quarterly Review* (4 p.a.). Founded 1974.

The Children's Book Circle

67A Holly Street, Hackney, London E8 3HS
email childrensbookcircle@hotmail.co.uk
website www.childrensbookcircle.org.uk
Membership £20 p.a. if working inside M25; £15 outside

Provides a discussion forum for anybody involved with children's books. Meetings are addressed by a panel of invited speakers and topics focus on current and controversial issues. Holds the annual Patrick Hardy lecture and administers the Eleanor Farjeon Award. Founded 1962.

Children's Books Ireland

17 North Great Georges Street, Dublin 1,
Republic of Ireland
tel (01) 872 7475 *fax* (01) 872 7476
email info@childrensbooksireland.ie
website www.childrensbooksireland.ie
Director Mags Walsh, *Administrator* Jenny Murray
Membership €30/£20 p.a. individual, €50/£35 p.a. institutions, €45/£30/$55 p.a. overseas individual, €60/£40/$70 p.a. overseas institutions, €20/£15 p.a. student

Dedicated to ensuring that books are at the centre of young people's lives, through advocacy, resource and innovative programming and outreach. Formed in 1996.

Children's Writers and Illustrators Group – see The Society of Authors, page 541

CILIP (Chartered Institute of Library and Information Professionals)

7 Ridgmount Street, London WC1E 7AE
tel 020-7255 0500 *fax* 020-7255 0501
email info@cilip.org.uk
website www.cilip.org.uk
Chief Executive Bob McKee PhD, FRSA, MCLIP
Membership Varies according to income

The leading body for librarians, information specialists and knowledge managers. Forms a community of around 36,000 people engaged in library and information work, of whom around 21,000 are CILIP members and around 15,000 are regular customers of CILIP Enterprises.

Circle of Wine Writers

Administrator Andrea Warren, Scots Firs,
70 Joiners Lane, Chalfont St Peter, Bucks. SL9 0AU
tel/fax (01753) 882320
email administrator@winewriters.org
website www.winewriters.org
Membership By election, £50 p.a.

An association for those engaged in communicating about wines and spirits. Produces *Circle Update* newsletter (5 p.a.), organises tasting sessions as well as a programme of meetings and talks. Founded 1960.

The John Clare Society

Hon. Secretary 9 The Chase, Ely, Cambs. CB6 3DR
tel (01353) 668438
email l.j.curry@bham.ac.uk,
sue.holgate@hotmail.com
website www.johnclare.org.uk
Membership £12 p.a. UK individual; other rates on application

Promotes a wider appreciation of the life and works of the poet John Clare (1793–1864). Founded 1981.

Classical Association

Secretary Claire Davenport, Senate House,
Malet Street, London WC1E 7HU
tel 020-7862 8706 *fax* 020-7862 8729
email office@classicalassociation.org
website www.classicalassociation.org

Exists to promote and sustain interest in classical studies, to maintain their rightful position in universities and schools, and to give scholars and teachers opportunities for meeting and discussing their problems.

The William Cobbett Society

Chairman Barbara Biddell, 3 Park Terrace,
Tillington, Petworth GU28 9AE
website www.williamcobbett.org.uk
Membership £8 p.a.

Aims to make the life and work of William Cobbett (1763–1835) better known. Founded 1976.

The Wilkie Collins Society

Membership Secretary Paul Lewis, 4 Ernest Gardens,
London W4 3QU
email paul@paullewis.co.uk
website www.wilkiecollins.org

Chairman Andrew Gasson
Membership £10 p.a. EU, £18 international

Aims to promote interest in the life and works of Wilkie Collins (1824–89). Publishes a newsletter, an annual scholarly journal and reprints of Collins's lesser known works. Founded 1981.

Comhairle nan Leabhraichean/The Gaelic Books Council

22 Mansfield Street, Glasgow G11 5QP
tel 0141-337 6211 *fax* 0141-353 0515
email brath@gaelicbooks.net
website www.gaelicbooks.org
Chair Prof. Roibeard Ó Maolalaigh

Stimulates Scottish Gaelic publishing by awarding publication grants for new books, commissioning authors and providing editorial services and general assistance to writers and readers. Has its own bookshop of all Gaelic and Gaelic-related books in print and runs a book club. All the stock is listed on the website and a paper catalogue is also available. Founded 1968.

The Joseph Conrad Society (UK)

The Secretary c/o The Polish Social and Cultural Association, 238–246 King Street, London W6 0RF
email theconradian@aol.com
website www.josephconradsociety.org
Chairman Keith Carabine, *Secretary* Hugh Epstein, *Editor* Allan Simmons

Activities include an annual international conference; publication of *The Conradian* and a series of pamphlets; and maintenance of a substantial reference library as part of the Polish Library at the Polish Cultural Centre, 238–246 King Street, London W6 0RF. Administers the Juliet McLauchlan Prize, £200 annual award for the winner of an essay competition, and travel grants for scholars wishing to attend Conrad conferences. Founded 1973.

Copyright Clearance Center Inc.

222 Rosewood Drive, Danvers, MA 01923, USA
tel 978-750-8400 *fax* 978-646-8600
email info@copyright.com
website www.copyright.com

Copyright Council of New Zealand Inc.

PO Box 331488, Takapuna 0740, North Shore City, New Zealand
tel (09) 486-6250 *fax* (09) 486-6260
email ksheat@copyright.co.nz
website www.copyright.org.nz
Chairman Anthony Healey, *Secretary* Kathy Sheat

The Copyright Licensing Agency Ltd – see page 713

Crime Writers' Association

email secretary@thecwa.co.uk
website www.thecwa.co.uk
Membership Associate membership open to publishers, journalists, booksellers specialising in crime literature and literary agents

Full membership open to professional writers of crime novels, short stories, plays for stage, TV and radio, or of other serious works on crime. Publishes *Red Herrings* (monthly), available to members only. Founded 1953.

The Critics' Circle

Contact William Russell, c/o 50 Finland Road, Brockley, London SE4 2JH
tel 020-7732 9636
email williamfinland@gmail.com
website www.criticscircle.org.uk
President Charles Spencer, *Hon. General Secretary* William Russell
Membership By invitation of the Council

Aims to promote the art of criticism, to uphold its integrity in practice, to foster and safeguard the professional interests of its members, to provide opportunities for social intercourse among them, and to support the advancement of the arts. Such invitations are issued only to persons engaged professionally, regularly and substantially in the writing or broadcasting of criticism of drama, music, films, dance and the visual arts. Founded 1913.

Cwlwm Cyhoeddwyr Cymru

c/o Bethan Mair, Gellimanwydd, 54 Stryd Fawr, Rhydaman SA18 2NB
tel (01269) 592050
email geiriau@googlemail.com
website www.bedwenlyfrau.com (Welsh language only)

Represents and promotes Welsh-language publishers. Founded 2002.

Cyngor Llyfrau Cymru – see Welsh Books Council/Cyngor Llyfrau Cymru

Data Publishers Association (DPA)

Queen's House, 28 Kingsway, London WC2B 6JR
tel 020-7405 0836 *fax* 020-7404 4167
email info@dpa.org.uk
website www.dpa.org.uk
Membership £480–£2500 p.a.

Maintains a code of professional practice; aims to raise the standard and professional status of UK directory and data publishing and to protect (and promote) the legal, statutory and common interests of directory and data publishers. Annual Conference and Awards. Founded 1970.

Walter de la Mare Society

PO Box 25351, London NW5 1ZT
tel 020-8886 1771
Membership £15 p.a.

To promote the study and deepen the appreciation of the works of Walter de la Mare (1873–1956) through

Societies, prizes and festivals

a magazine, talks, discussions and other activities. Founded 1997.

Design and Artists Copyright Society – see page 717

Dickens Fellowship

The Charles Dickens Museum, 48 Doughty Street, London WC1N 2LX
tel 020-7405 2127 *fax* 020-7831 5175
Joint Hon. Secretaries Mrs Lee Ault, Mrs Joan Dicks
Membership On application

Based in house occupied by Charles Dickens (1812–75) during the period 1837–9. Publishes *The Dickensian* (3 p.a.). Founded 1902.

Directory of Writers' Circles, Courses and Workshops

39 Lincoln Way, Harlington, Beds. LU5 6NG
tel (01525) 873197
email diana@writers-circles.com
website www.writers-circles.com
Publisher & Editor Diana Hayden

Directory of writers' circles, courses and workshops published annually.

'Sean Dorman' Manuscript Society

3 High Road, Britford, Salisbury SP5 4DS
tel (01722) 332821
Director Jan Smith

Provides mutual help among writers and aspiring writers in the UK. By means of circulating MSS parcels, members receive constructive comments on their own work and read and comment on the work of others. Each 'Circulator' has up to 7 participants and members' contributions may be in any medium: short stories, chapters of a novel, poetry, magazine articles, etc. Send sae for full details and application form. Founded 1957.

The Arthur Conan Doyle Society

Organisers Christopher and Barbara Roden, PO Box 1360, Ashcroft, B.C., Canada V0K 1A0
tel 250-453-2045 *fax* 250-453-2075
email sirhenry@telus.net
website www.ash-tree.bc.ca/acdsocy.html

Promotes the study of the life and works of Sir Arthur Conan Doyle (1859–1930). Publishes *ACD* journal (bi-annual) and occasional reprints of Conan Doyle material. Occasional conventions. Founded 1989.

Early English Text Society

Lady Margaret Hall, Oxford OX2 6QA
website www.eets.org.uk
Hon. Director Prof. Anne Hudson *Executive Secretary* Prof. V. Gillespie
Membership £20 p.a.

Aims to bring unprinted early English literature within the reach of students in sound texts. Founded 1864.

Edinburgh Bibliographical Society

Rare Books Collections,
National Library of Scotland, George IV Bridge, Edinburgh EH1 9EW
tel 0131-650 6864
email h.vincent@nls.uk
website http://mcs.qmuc.ac.uk/EBS/
Secretary Dr W. McDougall, *Treasurer* J. Marshall
Membership £15 p.a., £20 institutions; £10 full-time students

Encourages bibliographical activity through organising talks for members, particularly on bibliographical topics relating to Scotland, and visits to libraries. Publishes *Journal* (annual, free to members) and other occasional publications. Founded 1890.

Educational Writers Group – see The Society of Authors, page 541

The George Eliot Fellowship

Secretary Elizabeth Mellor, 12 Fair Isle Drive, Nuneaton CV10 7LJ
tel (024) 7634 1200
email blueyorkshirecat@yahoo.co.uk
website www.george-eliot-fellowship.com
President Jonathan G. Ouvry
Membership £10 p.a.

Promotes an interest in the life and work of George Eliot (1819–80) and helps to extend her influence; arranges meetings; produces an annual journal and newsletters and other publications. Awards the annual George Eliot Fellowship Prize (£500) for an essay on Eliot's life or work, which must be previously unpublished and not exceed 4000 words. Founded 1930.

English Association

University of Leicester, University Road, Leicester LE1 7RH
tel 0116-252 3982 *fax* 0116-252 2301
email engassoc@leicester.ac.uk
website www.le.ac.uk/engassoc/
Chair Maureen Moran, *Chief Executive* Helen Lucas

Aims to further knowledge, understanding and enjoyment of English literature and the English language, by working towards a fuller recognition of English as an essential element in education and in the community at large; by encouraging the study of English literature and language by means of conferences, lectures and publications; and by fostering the discussion of methods of teaching English of all kinds.

English Speaking Board (International) Ltd

9 Hattersley Court, Burscough Road, Ormskirk LG39 2AY

tel (01704) 501730 *fax* (01704) 539637
email admin@esbuk.org
website www.esbuk.org
Ceo Lesley Cook
Membership £37.50 p.a. individuals, £75 p.a. corporate, £20 for new individual members

Aims to foster all activities concerned with oral communication. Offers assessment qualifications in practical speaking and listening skills for candidates at all levels in schools, vocational and business contexts; also for those with learning difficulties and those for whom English is an acquired language. Also provides training courses in teaching and delivery of oral communication. Offers membership to all those concerned with the development and expression of the English language. Members receive *Speaking English* (2 p.a.); articles are invited on any special aspect of spoken English.

The English-Speaking Union

Dartmouth House, 37 Charles Street, London W1J 5ED
tel 020-7529 1550
email esu@esu.org
website www.esu.org
Membership Various categories

Aims to promote international understanding and human achievement through the widening use of the English language throughout the world. The ESU is an educational charity which sponsors scholarships and exchanges, educational programmes promoting the effective use of English, and a wide range of international and cultural events. Members contribute to its work across the world. Administers several awards, including the Marsh Biography Award and the Marsh Award for Children's Literature in Translation (see page 603). Founded 1918.

European Broadcasting Union

General Headquarters, Ancienne Route 17A, CH–1218 Grand Saconnex (Geneva), Switzerland
tel 41 22 717 2111 *fax* 41 22 747 4000
email ebu@ebu.ch
website www.ebu.ch
Secretary-General Ingrid Deltenre

The largest professional association of national broadcasters. Working on behalf of its members in the European area, the EBU negotiates broadcasting rights for major sports events; operates the Eurovision and Euroradio networks; organises programme exchanges; stimulates and coordinates co-productions; and provides a full range of other operational, commercial, technical, legal and strategic services. Founded 1950.

Fabian Society

11 Dartmouth Street, London SW1H 9BN
tel 020-7227 4900 *fax* 020-7976 7153
email info@fabian-society.org.uk
website www.fabians.org.uk
General Secretary Mr Sunder Katwala

Current affairs, political thought, economics, education, environment, foreign affairs, social policy. Also controls NCLC Publishing Society Ltd. Founded 1884.

Federation Against Copyright Theft Ltd (FACT)

Europa House, Church Street, Old Isleworth, Middlesex TW7 6DA
tel 020-8568 6646 *fax* 020-8560 6364
email contact@fact-uk.org.uk
website www.fact-uk.org.uk
Contact Kieron Sharp, Director General

Aims to protect the interests of its members and others against infringement in the UK of copyright in cinematograph films, TV programmes and all forms of audiovisual recording. Founded 1982.

The Copyright Hotline offers advice and information to anyone who wants to use film, music or software copyrights. It is part of a collective initiative by FACT, Federation Against Software Theft (FAST), Music Publishers Association (MPA), Mechanical-Copyright Protection Society (MCPS), Performing Right Society (PRS) and British Music Rights (BMR).

Federation of British Artists

17 Carlton House Terrace, London SW1Y 5BD
tel 020-7930 6844 *fax* 020-7839 7830
email info@mallgalleries.com
website www.mallgalleries.org.uk

Administers 9 major National Art Societies, as well as Originals: The Contemporary Printmaking Show, and the Threadneedle Prize at the Mall Galleries, The Mall, London SW1.

Federation of European Publishers

Rue Montoyer 31 Bte 8, B–1000 Brussels, Belgium
tel (0032 2) 770 11 10 *fax* (0032 2) 771 20 71
email info@fep-fee.eu
website www.fep-fee.eu
President Federico Motta, *Director* Anne Bergman-Tahon

Represents the interests of European publishers on EU affairs; informs members on the development of EU policies which could affect the publishing industry. Founded 1967.

The Federation of Indian Publishers

18/1C Institutional Area,
Aruna Asaf Ali Marg (near JNU), New Delhi 110067, India
tel 26852263, 26964847 *fax* 26864054
email fip1@satyam.net.in
website www.fipindia.org
President Shri R.C. Govil

Federation of Spanish Publishers' Association

(Federación de Gremios de Editores de España)
Cea Bermúdez, 44–2 Dcha. 28003 Madrid, Spain
tel (91) 534 51 95 *fax* (91) 535 26 25
email fgee@fge.es
website www.federacioneditores.org
President Sr D. Pedro de Andrés

The Federation of Worker Writers and Community Publishers

Burslem School of Art, Queen Street,
Stoke-on-Trent ST6 3EJ
tel (01782) 822327
email thefwwcp@tiscali.co.uk
website www.fedonline.org.uk
Membership £40 p.a. funded groups; £20 unfunded

A network of writers groups and community publishers which promotes working-class writing and publishing. Founded 1976.

The Fine Art Trade Guild

16–18 Empress Place, London SW6 1TT
tel 020-7381 6616 *fax* 020-7381 2596
email info@fineart.co.uk
website www.fineart.co.uk
Managing Director Rosie Sumner

Promotes the sale of fine art prints and picture framing in the UK and overseas markets; establishes and raises standards amongst members and communicates these to the buying public. The Guild publishes *The Directory* and *Art Business Today*, the trade's longest established magazine, and various specialist books. Founded 1910.

FOCAL International Ltd (Federation of Commercial AudioVisual Libraries International Ltd)

79 College Road, Harrow, Middlesex HA1 1BD
tel 020-3178 3535
email info@focalint.org
website www.focalint.org
Commerical Manager Anne Johnson, *General Manager* Julie Lewis

Founded 1985.

The Folklore Society

c/o The Warburg Institute, Woburn Square,
London WC1H 0AB
tel 020-7862 8564
email enquiries@folklore-society.com
website www.folklore-society.com
Hon. Secretary Prof James H. Grayson
Membership £45 p.a.

Collection, recording and study of folklore. Founded 1878.

Foreign Press Association in London

Registered Office 25 Northumberland Avenue,
London WC2N 5AP
tel 020-7930 0445
email briefings@foreign-press.org.uk
website www.foreign-press.org.uk
Director Christopher Wyld
Membership Subcription £200 p.a. Full membership open to those working for news media organisations with headquarters overseas. Associate membership £265 p.a.

Aims to promote access for journalists from overseas. Founded 1888.

Free Painters & Sculptors

Registered office 14 John Street, London WC1N 2EB
Hon. Secretary Owen Legg, 152 Hadlow Road,
Tonbridge, Kent TN9 1PB
Membership Secretary Keith Stanfield, 18 Quantock Gardens, Golders Green Estate, London NW2 1PH

Promotes group shows 4 times a year in prestigious galleries in London. Sponsors all that is exciting in contemporary art.

French Publishers' Association

(Syndicat National de l'Edition)
115 Blvd St Germain, 75006 Paris, France
tel (1) 44 41 40 50 *fax* (1) 44 41 40 77
website www.sne.fr

The Gaelic Books Council – see Comhairle nan Leabhraichean/The Gaelic Books Council

The Garden Media Guild

(Formerly the Garden Writers' Guild)
Katepwa House, Ashfield Park Avenue,
Ross-on-Wye, Herefordshire HR9 5AX
tel (01989) 567393 *fax* (01989) 567676
email admin@gardenmediaguild.co.uk
website www.gardenmediaguild.co.uk
Membership £60 p.a.

Aims are to raise the quality of garden writing, photography and broadcasting, to help members operate efficiently and profitably, to improve communication between members and to promote liaison between members and the broader horticultural industry. The Guild administers annual awards to encourage excellence in garden writing, photography, trade and consumer press journalism, TV and radio broadcasting. Founded 1991.

The Gaskell Society

Far Yew Tree House, Chester Road, Tabley,
Knutsford, Cheshire WA16 0HN
tel (01565) 634668
email joanleach@aol.com
website www.gaskellsociety.co.uk
Hon. Secretary Mrs Joan Leach
Membership £17 p.a., £22 corporate/overseas

Promotes and encourages the study and appreciation of the work and life of Elizabeth Cleghorn Gaskell (1810–65). Holds regular meetings in Knutsford,

London, Manchester, Bath and York, visits and residential conferences; produces an annual Journal and bi-annual Newsletters. Founded 1985.

Gay Authors Workshop

Kathryn Byrd, BM Box 5700, London WC1N 3XX
email eandk2@btinternet.com
Membership £7 p.a., £3 unwaged

Exists to encourage writers who are lesbian, gay or bisexual. Quarterly newsletter. Founded 1978.

German Publishers' and Booksellers' Association

(Börsenverein des Deutschen Buchhandels e.V.)
Postfach 100442, 60004 Frankfurt am Main, Germany
tel (069) 13060 *fax* (069) 1306201
email info@boev.de
website www.boersenverein.de
General Manager Alexander Skipis, *President* Gottfried Honnefelder

The Ghost Story Society

PO Box 1360, Ashcroft, British Columbia V0K 1A0, Canada
tel 250-453-2045 *fax* 250-453-2075
email nebuly@telus.net
website www.ash-tree.bc.ca/GSS.html
Secretary Barbara Roden
Membership £25/US$45/Can.$45 p.a.

Provides enthusiasts of the classic ghost story with a forum to discuss and appreciate the genre. Publishes *All Hallows* (3 p.a.) journal which contains news, articles, reviews and approx. 100pp of new fiction. Founded 1989.

Graham Greene Birthplace Trust

Colin Garrett, 17 North Road, Berkhamsted, Herts. HP4 3DX
tel (01442) 866694
email secretary@grahamgreenebt.org
website www.grahamgreenebt.org
Membership £10 p.a., £25 3 years

Exists to study the works of Graham Greene (1904–91). The Trust promotes the Annual Graham Greene Festival and Graham Greene trails. It publishes a quarterly newsletter, occasional papers, videos and CDs, and maintains a small library. It administers the Graham Greene Memorial Awards. Founded 1997.

The Greeting Card Association

United House, North Road, London N7 9DP
tel 020-7619 0396
website www.greetingcardassociation.org.uk
Chief Executive Sharon Little

The trade association for greeting card publishers. See website for information on freelance designing and writing for greeting cards. Official magazine: *Progressive Greetings Worldwide* (see page 528).

Guernsey Arts Council

St James's Street, St James's Concert Hall, St Peter Port, Guernsey GY1 2NZ
tel (01481) 721902
Chairman Michael Rivett-Carnac

Guild of Agricultural Journalists

Hon. General Secretary Don Gomery, Isfield Cottage, Church Road, Crowsborough, East Sussex TN6 1BN
tel (01892) 610628 *mobile* (07786) 168324
email don.gomery@btinternet.com
website www.gaj.org.uk
President Countess of Mar, *Chairman* Nick Bond

Established to promote a high standard among journalists who specialise in agricultural matters and to assist them to increase their sources of information and technical knowledge.

The Guild of Aviation Artists

(incorporating the Society of Aviation Artists)
Trenchard House, 85 Farnborough Road, Farnborough, Hants GU14 6TF
tel (01252) 513123 *fax* (01252) 510505
email admin@gava.org.uk
website www.gava.org.uk
President Michael Turner FGAvA, *Secretary/Administrator* Susan Gardner
Membership £60 p.a. Full (by invitation), £45 Associates (by selection), £25 Friends

Formed to promote aviation art through the organisation of exhibitions and meetings. Holds annual open exhibition in July in London; £1000 prize for 'Aviation Painting of the Year'. Quarterly members' newsletter. Founded 1971.

Guild of Food Writers

Administrator Jonathan Woods,
255 Kent House Road, Beckenham, Kent BR3 1JQ
tel 020-8659 0422
email guild@gfw.co.uk
website www.gfw.co.uk
Membership £85 p.a.

Aims to bring together professional food writers including journalists, broadcasters and authors, to print and issue an annual list of members, to extend the range of members' knowledge and experience by arranging discussions, tastings and visits, and to encourage the development of new writers by every means, including competitions and awards. There are 12 awards and entry is not restricted to members of the Guild. Founded 1984.

Guild of Health Writers

Administrator Jatinder Dua, Dale Lodge, 88 Wensleydale Road, Hampton, Middlesex TW12 2LX
tel 020-8941 2977
email admin@healthwriters.com
website www.healthwriters.com
Membership £45 p.a., Student £12 p.a.

Brings together professional journalists dedicated to providing accurate, broad-based information about health and related subjects to the public. Publishes a directory of members. Founded 1995.

The Guild of International Songwriters & Composers

Sovereign House, 12 Trewartha Road, Praa Sands, Penzance, Cornwall TR20 9ST
tel (01736) 762826 *fax* (01736) 763328
email songmag@aol.com
website www.songwriters-guild.co.uk
Secretary Carole Ann Jones
Membership £50

Gives advice to members on contractual and copyright matters; assists with protection of members rights; assists with analysis of members' works; international collaboration register free to members; outlines requirements to record companies, publishers, artists. Publishes *Songwriting & Composing* (quarterly).

The Guild of Motoring Writers

Contact The Guild of Motoring Writers' Secretariat, 40 Baring Road, Bournemouth BH6 4DT
tel (01202) 422424
email generalsec@gomw.co.uk
website www.guildofmotoringwriters.co.uk

International organisation for automotive journalists. Aims to raise the standard of motoring journalism, to encourage motoring, motorsport and road safety, to provide a link between fellow members around the world and to safeguard the interests of members in relation to the aims of the Guild.

Guild of Railway Artists

Chief Executive Officer F.P. Hodges, Hon. GRA, 45 Dickins Road, Warwick CV34 5NS
tel (01926) 499246
email frank.hodges@virgin.net
website www.railart.co.uk

Aims to forge a link between artists depicting railway subjects and to give members a corporate identity; also stages railway art exhibitions and members' meetings and produces books of members' works. Founded 1979.

Hakluyt Society

c/o The Map Library, The British Library, 96 Euston Road, London NW1 2DB
tel (01428) 641850 *fax* (01428) 641933
email office@hakluyt.com
website www.hakluyt.com
President Prof. W.F. Ryan, *Administrator* Mr R.M. Bateman

Publication of original narratives of voyages, travels, naval expeditions, and other geographical records. Founded 1846.

The Thomas Hardy Society

c/o Dorset County Museum, High West Street, Dorchester, Dorset DT1 1XA
tel (01305) 251501 *fax* (01305) 251501
email info@hardysociety.org
website www.hardysociety.org
Membership £18 p.a., £22.50 overseas

Aims to promote and celebrate the work of Thomas Hardy (1840–1928). Publishes *The Thomas Hardy Journal* (annual) and *The Hardy Society Journal* (2 p.a.). Biennial conference in Dorchester takes place in July/Aug 2010. Founded 1967.

Harleian Society

College of Arms, Queen Victoria Street, London EC4V 4BT
tel 020-7236 7728 *fax* 020-7248 6448
website http://harleian.org.uk
Chairman T. Woodcock LVO, DL, FSA, Norroy & Ulster King of Arms, *Hon. Secretary* T.H.S. Duke, Chester Herald of Arms

Instituted for transcribing, printing and publishing the heraldic visitations of Counties, Parish Registers and any manuscripts relating to genealogy, family history and heraldry. Founded 1869.

Hesketh Hubbard Art Society

17 Carlton House Terrace, London SW1Y 5BD
tel 020-7930 6844 *fax* 020-7839 7830
email info@mallgalleries.com
website www.mallgalleries.org.uk
President Simon Whittle

Weekly life drawing classes.

The Hilliard Society of Miniaturists

The Executive Officer Priory Lodge, 7 Priory Road, Wells, Somerset BA5 1SR
tel (01749) 674472
website www.art-in-miniature.org
President Paddy Davison
Membership From £40 p.a.

Aims to increase knowledge and promote the art of miniature painting. Annual exhibition held in June at Wells; produces a newsletter. Member of the World Federation of Miniaturists. Founded 1982.

The James Hilton Society

Hon. Secretary Dr J.R. Hammond, 49 Beckingthorpe Drive, Bottesford, Nottingham NG13 0DN
website www.jameshiltonsociety.co.uk
Membership £13 p.a. (£10 concessions)

Aims to promote interest in the life and work of novelist and scriptwriter James Hilton (1900–54). Publishes quarterly newsletter and an annual scholarly journal, and organises conferences. Founded 2000.

Historical Novel Society

Secretary Richard Lee, Marine Cottage, The Strand, Starcross, Devon EX6 8NY
tel (01626) 891962

email richard@historicalnovelsociety.org
website www.historicalnovelsociety.org
Membership £25 p.a.

Promotes the historical novel via short story competitions, conferences, a society magazine *Solander* (2 p.a.) and reviews (*Historical Novels Review*, quarterly). Membership is open to all and includes eminent novelists. Founded 1997.

The Sherlock Holmes Society of London

General enquiries Roger Johnson, 41 Sandford Road, Chelmsford CM2 6DE
tel (01245) 284006
Membership David Jones, The North Wing, Groton Place, Groton Street, Groton, Sudbury, Suffolk CO10 5EE
tel (01787) 211104
email shsl221b@aol.com
website www.sherlock-holmes.org.uk
President Guy Marriott, *Chairman* Jonathan McCafferty
Membership £20 p.a. UK; £23 EU; £27/US$54 N & S America, Africa, Asia (except China, Japan, Korea); £28/$56 China, Japan, Korea, Australasia, Pacific Islands

The Society is open to anyone with an interest in Sherlock Holmes, Dr John H. Watson and their world. A literary and social society, publishing a biannual scholarly journal and occasional papers, and holding meetings, dinners and excursions. Founded 1951.

Horror Writers Association (HWA)

244 5th Avenue, Suite 2767, New York, NY 10001
email hwa@horror.org
UK Jo Fletcher, 24 Pearl Road, London E17 4QZ
email fletcherove@hotmail.com
website www.horror.org
Membership $65 p.a. (individual), $110 (corporate), $85 (family)

A worldwide organisation of writers and publishing professionals dedicated to promoting the interests of writers of horror and dark fantasy. There are 3 levels of membership: for new writers, established writers and non-writing horror professionals. Founded 1987.

Housman Society

80 New Road, Bromsgrove, Worcs. B60 2LA
tel (01527) 874136
email info@housman-society.co.uk
website www.housman-society.co.uk
Chairman Jim Page
Membership £10 p.a.

Aims to foster interest in and promote knowledge of A.E. Housman (1859–1936) and his family. Sponsors a lecture at the Guardian Hay Festival. Publishes an annual journal and bi-annual newsletter. Founded 1973.

Incorporated Society of Musicians

10 Stratford Place, London W1C 1AA
tel 020-7629 4413 *fax* 020-7408 1538
email membership@ism.org
website www.ism.org
President Kenneth Ian Hÿtch, *Chief Executive* Deborah Annetts
Membership £140 p.a., £50 students

Professional body for musicians. Aims to promote the art of music; protect the interests and raise the standards of the musical profession; provide services, support and advice for its members. Publishes *Music Journal* (12 p.a.), a yearbook and Registers of Specialists annually.

Independent Publishers Guild

PO Box 12, Llain, Whitland SA34 0WU
tel (01437) 563335 *fax* (01437) 562071
website www.ipg.uk.com
Membership £165 + VAT p.a. min. Open to new and established publishers and book packagers; supplier membership is available to specialists in fields allied to publishing. Ask for details.

Provides an information and contact network for independent publishers. Also voices concerns of member companies within the book trade. Founded 1962.

Independent Theatre Council (ITC)

12 The Leather Market, Weston Street, London SE1 3ER
tel 020-7403 1727 *fax* 020-7403 1745
email admin@itc-arts.org
website www.itc-arts.org
Chief Executive Charlotte Jones
Membership Prices vary according to type of membership

ITC represents a wide range of performing arts organisations, venues and individuals in the fields of drama, dance, opera, music theatre, puppetry, mixed media, mime, physical theatre and circus. These organisations predominantly work on the middle and small scale around the UK. It has around 700 members across the performing arts who are united by their commitment to producing innovative, contemporary work (24% of the membership work specifically in the educational field reaching over 2 million children and young people). Founded 1974.

Institute of Designers in Ireland

The Digital Hub, Roe Lane, Thomas Street, Dublin 8, Republic of Ireland
tel (01) 4893650 *fax* (01) 4885801
email idi@indigo.ie
website www.idi-design.ie
Membership €225 p.a. full, €85 associate

Irish design profession's representative body, covering every field of design. Founded 1972.

The Institute of Translation & Interpreting (ITI)

Contact The Secretary, Fortuna House, South Fifth Street, Milton Keynes MK9 2PQ

tel (01908) 325250 *fax* (01908) 325259
email info@iti.org.uk
website www.iti.org.uk

A professional association of translators and interpreters which aims to promote the highest standards in translating and interpreting. It has a strong corporate membership and runs professional development courses and conferences, sometimes in conjunction with its language, regional and subject networks. Membership is open to those with a genuine and proven involvement in translation and interpreting of all kinds, but particularly technical and commercial translation. As a full and active member of the International Federation of Translators, it maintains good contacts with translators and interpreters worldwide. ITI's directory of members (online) and its bi-monthly bulletin are available from the Secretariat.

International Amateur Theatre Association (IATA)

Maison de la Bellone, 46 Rue de Flandre, B-1000 Brussels, Belgium
tel 372-6418 405 *fax* 372-6418 406
email secretariat@aitaiata.org
website www.aitaiata.org
Secretariat Ene Jürna

Aims to encourage, foster and promote exchanges of community and non-professional theatre; student, educational, adult, theatre activities at international level. To organise international seminars, workshops, courses and conferences, and to collect and collate information of all types for national and international dissemination. UK centre of IATA.

International PEN

Brownlow House, 50–51 High Holborn, London WC1V 6ER
tel 020-7405 0338 *fax* 020-7405 0339
email cerian.eiles@internationalpen.org.uk
website www.internationalpen.org.uk
Executive Director Caroline McCormick
Membership Apply to Centres

A world association of writers. PEN was founded in 1921 by C.A. Dawson Scott under the presidency of John Galsworthy, to promote friendship and understanding between writers and to defend freedom of expression within and between all nations. The initials PEN stand for Poets, Playwrights, Editors, Essayists, Novelists – but membership is open to all writers of standing (including translators), whether men or women, without distinction of creed or race, who subscribe to these fundamental principles. PEN takes no part in state or party politics. The International PEN Writers in Prison Committee works on behalf of writers imprisoned for exercising their right to freedom of expression, a right implicit in the PEN Charter to which all members subscribe. The International PEN Translations and Linguistic Rights Committee strives to promote the translations of works by writers in the lesser-known languages and to defend those languages. The Writers for Peace Committee exists to find ways in which writers can work for peaceful co-existence in the world. The Women Writers' Committee works to promote women's writing and publishing in developing countries. The Writers in Exile Network helps exiled writers. International Congresses are held annually.

Membership of any one Centre implies membership of all Centres; at present 145 autonomous Centres exist throughout the world. Associate membership is available for writers not yet eligible for full membership and for persons connected with literature. The English Centre has a programme of literary lectures, discussion, dinners and parties.

English PEN Centre

Administrative Director Jonathan Heawood, Free Word Centre, 60 Farringdon Road, London EC1R 3GA
tel 020-7324 2535
email enquiries@englishpen.org
website www.englishpen.org
President Lisa Appignanesi

Scottish PEN Centre

President Jenni Calder OBE, The Writers' Museum, Lady Stair's House, Lady Stair's Close, Lawnmarket, Edinburgh EH1 2PE
email office@scottishpen.org
website www.scottishpen.org

Irish PEN Centre

email irishpen@ireland.com
President Brian Friel
Secretary Christine Dwyer Hickey, Irish Pen Cente, Dunoon, Old Lucan Road, Palmerstown, Dublin 20, Republic of Ireland
tel (353) 1 623 9133

International Publishers Association

3 avenue de Miremont, CH–1206 Geneva, Switzerland
tel (022) 704 18 20 *fax* (022) 704 18 21
email secretariat@internationalpublishers.org
website www.internationalpublishers.org
President Herman P. Spruijt, *Secretary-General* Mr Jens Bammel

Founded 1896.

International Society of Typographic Designers

PO Box 725, Taunton, Somerset TA2 8WE
tel 020-7436 0984 *fax* 020-7637 7352
email mail@istd.org.uk
Chair Jonathan Doney FISTD, *President* Freda Sack

Establishes and maintains typographic standards within the professional design and education communities through the forum of debate and design practice, and aims to foster a symbiotic relationship between education and industry by publishing and promoting quality contemporary design practice amongst its international membership. It publishes a journal, *Typographic*. Students of typography and graphic design are encouraged to gain membership of the Society by entering the annual student assessment scheme. Founded 1928.

International Visual Communication Association (IVCA)

19 Pepper Street, Glengall Bridge, London E14 9RP
tel 020-7512 0571 *fax* 020-7512 0591
email info@ivca.org
website www.ivca.org
Membership & Events Manager Marco Forgione
Membership From £175 p.a.

For those who work in business communication. Aims to promote the industry and provide a collective voice; provides a range of services, publications and events to help existing and potential users to make the most of what video, film, multimedia and live events can offer their business. Founded 1987.

The Irish Book Publishers' Association – see Publishing Ireland - Foilsiú Éireann

The Irish Copyright Licensing Agency

25 Denzille Lane, Dublin 2, Republic of Ireland
tel (01) 6624211 *fax* (01) 6624213
email info@icla.ie
website www.icla.ie
Executive Director Samantha Holman

Licences schools and other users of copyright material to photocopy extracts of such material, and distributes the monies collected to the authors and publishers whose works have been copied. Founded 1992.

Irish Playwrights and Screenwriters Guild

(formerly the Society of Irish Playwrights)
Art House, Curved Street, Temple Bar, Dublin 2, Republic of Ireland
tel (01) 670 9970
email info@script.ie
website www.script.ie
Chairperson Audrey O'Reilly, *Executive Officer* David Kavanagh

Represents writers' interests in theatre, radio and screen. Founded 1969.

Irish Translators' and Interpreters' Association

Irish Writers' Centre, 19 Parnell Square, Dublin 1, Republic of Ireland
tel (01) 6738386 *fax* (01) 8726282
website www.translatorsassociation.ie
Hon. Secretary Mary Phelan
Membership p.a. €100 professional, €50 ordinary, €25 student, €250 corporate

Promotes translation in Ireland, the translation of Irish authors abroad and the practical training of translators, and promotes the interests of translators. Maintains a detailed register of translators and interpreters. Founded 1986.

Irish Writers' Centre

19 Parnell Square, Dublin 1, Republic of Ireland
tel (01) 8721302 *fax* (01) 8726282
email info@writerscentre.ie
website www.writerscentre.ie
Contact Chairperson, Jack Harte

National organisation for the promotion of writers, writing and literature in Ireland. Provides a wide range of services and facilities to individual writers. Runs an extensive programme of events at its headquarters, including readings and book launches, seminars and discussions. Offers an education programme of workshops and masterclasses in writing and provides a venue for visiting international writers. See website for further details. Founded 1987.

Irish Writers' Union/Comhar na Scríbhneoirí

Irish Writers' Centre, 19 Parnell Square, Dublin 1, Republic of Ireland
tel (01) 8721302 *fax* (01) 8726282
email iwu@ireland-writers.com
website www.ireland-writers.com
Chairperson Helen Dwyer, *Secretary* Bríd Quinn

The Union aims to advance the cause of writing as a profession, to achieve better remuneration and more favourable conditions for writers and to provide a means for the expression of the collective opinion of writers on matters affecting their profession. Founded 1986.

The Richard Jefferies Society

Hon. Secretary Jean Saunders, Pear Tree Cottage, Longcot, Faringdon, Oxon SN7 7SS
tel (01793) 783040
email info@richardjefferiessociety.co.uk
website www.richardjefferiessociety.co.uk
Membership £7 p.a. Worldwide membership

Promotes interest in the life, works and associations of the naturalist and novelist, Richard Jefferies (1848–87); helps to preserve buildings and memorials, and cooperates in the development of a Museum in his birthplace. Arranges regular meetings in Swindon, and occasionally elsewhere; organises outings and displays; publishes a Journal and a Newsletter in the spring and an Annual Report in September. Founded 1950.

The Johnson Society

Johnson Birthplace Museum, Breadmarket Street, Lichfield, Staffs. WS13 6LG
tel (01543) 264972
email info@thejohnsonsociety.org.uk
website www.thejohnsonsociety.org.uk
Hon. General Secretary Norma Hooper

Aims to encourage the study of the life and works of Dr Samuel Johnson (1709–84); to preserve the memorials, associations, books, manuscripts and letters of Dr Johnson and his contemporaries; and to work with the local council in the preservation of his birthplace.

Johnson Society of London

Secretary Mrs Zandra O'Donnell MA, 255 Baring Road, London SE12 0BQ
email allanzandy@btinternet.com
website http://www.johnstonsocietyoflondon.org
President Lord Harmsworth

Aims to study the life and works of Dr Johnson (1709–84), and to perpetuate his memory in the city of his adoption. Founded 1928.

Journalists' Charity

Dickens House, 35 Wathen Road, Dorking, Surrey RH4 1JY
tel (01306) 887511 *fax* (01306) 888212
email enquiries@journalistscharity.org.uk
website www.journalistscharity.org.uk
Director David Ilott

For the relief of hardship amongst journalists, their widows and dependants. Financial assistance and retirement housing are provided.

The Sheila Kaye-Smith Society

Secretary Christine Hayward, 22 The Cloisters, St John's Road, St Leonards-on-Sea, East Sussex TN37 6JT
tel (01424) 422139
Membership £6 p.a. single, £9 joint

Aims to stimulate and widen interest in the work of the Sussex writer and novelist, Sheila Kaye-Smith (1887–1956). Produces *The Gleam* (annual) and occasional papers, and organises talks. Founded 1987.

Keats-Shelley Memorial Association

Bedford House, 76A Bedford Street, Leamington Spa CV32 5DT
tel (01926) 427400 *fax* (01926) 335133
Chairman Hon. Mrs H. Cullen, *Hon. Secretary* David Leigh-Hunt
Membership £15 p.a. minimum

Owns and supports house in Rome where John Keats died, as a museum open to the public; celebrates the poets Keats (1795–1821), Shelley (1792–1822) and Leigh Hunt (1784–1859). Regular meetings; poetry competitions; annual *Review;* 2 literary awards; and progress reports. Founded 1903.

Kent and Sussex Poetry Society

Contact John Arnold, 39 Rockington Way, Crowborough, East Sussex TN6 2NJ
tel (01892) 662781
email keith@kentandsussexpoetrysociety.org
website www.kentandsussexpoetrysociety.org
Secretary Keith Francis
President Laurence Lerner, *Chairman* Clive Eastwood
Membership £15 p.a. full, £10 country members/concessions

Based in Tunbridge Wells, the Society was formed to create a greater interest in poetry. Well-known poets address the Society, a Folio of members' work is produced and a full programme of recitals, discussions, competitions (see page 600) and readings is provided. Founded 1946.

The Kipling Society

Hon. Secretary Jane Keskar, 6 Clifton Road, London W9 1SS
tel 020-7286 0194
email jmkeskar@btinternet.com
website www.kipling.org.uk
Membership £24 p.a. (£22 p.a. standing orders; £12 under age 23)

Aims to honour and extend the influence of Rudyard Kipling (1865–1936), to assist in the study of his writings, to hold discussion meetings, to publish a quarterly journal, and to maintain a Kipling Library in London and a Kipling Room in The Grange, Rottingdean, near Brighton.

The Charles Lamb Society

BM Elia, London WC1N 3XX
Chairman Nicholas Powell, *Membership Secretary* Cecilia Powell
Membership Personal: £18/$35 p.a. (single), £24 (double); Corporate: £24/$48 p.a.

Publishes the academic journal *The Charles Lamb Bulletin* (quarterly). The Society's extensive library of books and MSS by and about Charles Lamb (1775–1834) is housed at the Guildhall Library, Aldermanbury, London EC2P 2EJ. Founded 1935.

The Lancashire Authors' Association

General Secretary Michael Finney, 53 Loch Street, Orrell, Wigan, Lancs. WN5 0AN
tel (01942) 216748
Membership £10 p.a. single, £13 p.a. joint

'For writers and lovers of Lancashire literature and history.' Publishes *The Record* (quarterly). Founded 1909.

The D.H. Lawrence Society

Secretary Brenda Sumner, 1 Church Street, Swepstone, Leics. LE67 2SA
tel 01530 207367
Membership £14 UK, £16 Europe, £19 rest of world, UK retired persons and students £12

Aims to bring together people interested in D.H. Lawrence (1885–1930), to encourage study of his work, and to provide information and guides for people visiting Eastwood. Founded 1974.

The T.E. Lawrence Society

PO Box 728, Oxford OX2 9ZJ
email memsec@telsociety.org.uk
website www.telstudies.info
Membership £18 p.a., £23 overseas
Contact Jeremy Wilson

Promotes the memory of T.E. Lawrence (1888–1935) and furthers knowledge by research into his life; publishes *Journal* (bi-annual) and *Newsletter* (quarterly). Founded 1985.

League of Canadian Poets

312–192 Spadina Avenue, Toronto, Ontario M5T 2C2, Canada
tel 416-504-1657 *fax* 416-504 0096
email joanna@poets.ca
website www.poets.ca
Executive Director Joanna Poblocka
Membership $175 p.a.

Aims to promote the interests of poets and to advance Canadian poetry in Canada and abroad. Administers 3 annual awards; runs National Poetry Month; publishes a newsletter and *Poetry Markets for Canadians, Who's Who in The League of Canadian Poets*, and *Poets in the Classroom* (teaching guide). Founded 1966.

Little Theatre Guild of Great Britain

National Secretary, Barbara Watson, 181 Brampton Road, Carlisle CA3 9AX
tel (01228) 522649
email ltgcontact@btinternet.com
website www.littletheatreguild.org

Aims to promote closer cooperation amongst the little theatres constituting its membership; to act as coordinating and representative body on behalf of the little theatres; to maintain and advance the highest standards in the art of theatre; and to assist in encouraging the establishment of other little theatres. Its yearbook is available to non-members for £6.

The Marlowe Society

Honorary Secretary Valerie Colin-Russ, 27 Melbourne Court, Little Venice, London W9 1BJ
tel 020-7289 2535
email val.cr@zen.co.uk
Newsletter Editor Roger Hards, Parkhyde, 70 Park Road, Congresbury, North Somerset BS49 5HH
tel (01934) 834780
email rogerhards@parkhyde.go-plus.net
website www.marlowe-society.org
Membership £15 p.a., £10 concessions, £20 joint (couple), £300 life; non-UK postage supplement: Europe £3, elsewhere £6, airmail £10.

Registered charity that aims to extend appreciation and widen recognition of Christopher Marlowe (1564–93) as the foremost poet and dramatist preceding Shakespeare, whose development he influenced. Holds meetings and cultural visits, and issues a bi-annual magazine and an occasional research journal. Founded 1955.

The John Masefield Society

Chairman Peter J.R. Carter, The Frith, Ledbury, Herefordshire HR8 1LW
tel (01531) 633800
email carter-p@btconnect.com
website www.ies.sas.ac.uk/cmps/Projects/Masefield/Society/jmsws.htm
Membership £5 p.a., £10 overseas, £8 family/institution

Aims to stimulate interest in, and public awareness and enjoyment of, the life and works of the poet John Masefield (1878–1967). Holds an annual lecture and other, less formal, readings and gatherings; publishes an annual journal and frequent newsletters. Founded 1992.

Master Photographers Association

Jubilee House, 1 Chancery Lane, Darlington, Co. Durham DL1 5QP
tel (01325) 356555 *fax* (01325) 357813
email general@mpauk.com
website www.thempa.com
Membership £150 p.a.

Exists to promote and protect professional photographers. Members qualify for awards of Licentiate, Associate and Fellowship.

Mechanical-Copyright Protection Society Ltd (MCPS)

Copyright House, 29–33 Berners Street, London W1T 3AB
tel 020-7580 5544 *fax* 020-7306 4455
website www.mcps.co.uk

The Media Society

66 Lincoln's Inn Fields, London WC2A 3LH
tel 020-7223 5631 *fax* 020-7223 5631
website www.themediasociety.com
President Geraldine Sharpe-Newton
Membership £35 p.a.

Exists to promote and encourage collective and independent research into the standards, performance, organisation and economics of the media and hold regular discussions, debates, etc on subjects of topical or special interest and concern to print and broadcast journalists and others working in or with the media. Founded 1973.

Mediawatch-UK

(formerly National Viewers' and Listeners' Association)

Director Vivienne Pattison, 3 Willow House, Kennington Road, Ashford, Kent TN24 0NR
tel (01233) 633936 *fax* (01233) 633836
email info@mediawatchuk.org
website www.mediawatchuk.org
Membership £15 p.a.

Aims to encourage viewers and listeners to react effectively to programme content; to initiate and stimulate public discussion and parliamentary debate concerning the effects of broadcasting, and other mass media, on the individual, the family and society; to secure, then uphold, effective legislation to control obscenity and pornography in the media. Founded 1965.

Medical Writers Group – see The Society of Authors, page 541

The Memoir Writing Club

Kinvara, Co. Galway, Republic of Ireland
tel (353 86) 2523428
email office@thememoirwritingclub.com
website www.thememoirwritingclub.com
Secretary Irene Graham

Provides a platform for memoir writers to initiate memoir writing clubs throughout the world. Each club member receives *The Memoir Writing Workbook*, based on 36 right-brain/left-brain exercises, to write their memoir in. Approx. 1,000 members. Founded 2008.

William Morris Society

Kelmscott House, 26 Upper Mall, London W6 9TA
tel 020-8741 3735 *fax* 020-8748 5207
email uk@morrissociety.org
website www.morrissociety.org
Secretary Mark Samuels Losner

Aims to spread knowledge of the life, work and ideas of William Morris (1834–96); publishes *Newsletter* (quarterly) and *Journal* (2 p.a.). Library and collections open to the public Thurs and Sat, 2–5pm. Founded 1955.

Music Publishers Association Ltd

6th Floor, British Music House, 26 Berners Street, London W1T 3LR
tel 020-7580 0126 *fax* 020-7637 3929
email info@mpaonline.org.uk
website www.mpaonline.org.uk
Chief Executive Stephen Navin
Membership Details on request

Trade organisation representing over 200 UK music publisher members: promotes and safeguards its members' interests in copyright, trade and related matters. Sub-committees and groups deal with particular interests. Founded 1881.

National Acrylic Painters' Association (NAPA)

134 Rake Lane, Wallasey, Wirral, Merseyside CH45 1JW
tel 0151-639 2980 *fax* 0151-639 2980
Membership The Executive Council, c/o Alan Edwards, 6 Berwyn Boulevard, Bebington, Wirral CH63 5LR
tel 0151-645 8433
email alan.edwards420@ntlworld.com, kjnaga@hotmail.com
website www.napauk.org, www.isap-usa.com
President Alwyn Crawshaw, *Director/Founder* Kenneth J. Hodgson

Promotes interest in, and encourages excellence and innovation in, the work of painters in acrylic. Holds an annual exhibition and regional shows: awards are made. Worldwide membership. Publishes a newsletter known as the *International NAPA Newspages*. Founded 1985; American Division established 1995, now known as International Society of Acrylic Painters (ISAP).

National Association of Press Agencies (NAPA)

c/o Mercury Press Agency, Unit 218, Century Buildings, Tower Street, Liverpool L3 4BJ
tel (0870) 609 1935
email enquiries@napa.org.uk
website www.napa.org.uk
Directors Denis Cassidy, Chris Johnson, Matt Bell, Mark Solomons
Membership £250 p.a.

A network of independent, established and experienced press agencies serving newspapers, magazines, TV and radio networks. Founded 1983.

National Association of Writers' Groups

PO Box 3266, Stoke-on-Trent ST10 9BD
tel (01262) 609228
email secretary@nawg.co.uk
website www.nawg.co.uk
Membership £35 p.a. plus £5 registration per group; £16 Associate individuals

Aims 'to advance the education of the general public throughout the UK, including the Channel Islands, by promoting the study and art of writing in all its aspects'. Publishes *Link* bimonthly magazine. Annual Festival of Writing held in Durham in September. Annual Creative Writing Competition. Founded 1995.

National Campaign for the Arts (NCA)

1 Kingly Street, London W1B 5PA
tel 020-7287 3777 *fax* 020-7287 4777
email nca@artscampaign.org.uk
website www.artscampaign.org.uk
Director Louise de Winter

The UK's only independent lobbying organisation representing all the arts. It provides a voice for the arts world in all its diversity and seeks to safeguard, promote and develop the arts and win public and political recognition for their importance as a key element in our national culture. The NCA is a membership organisation. See website for information.

National Council for the Training of Journalists (NCTJ)

The New Granary, Station Road, Newport, Essex CB11 3PL
tel (01799) 544014 *fax* (01799) 544015
email info@nctj.com
website www.nctj.com

A registered charity which aims to advance the education and training of trainee journalists, including press photographers. Full-time courses run at 40 colleges/universities in the UK. Distance learning courses also available in newspaper and magazine journalism and sub-editing. Founded 1952.

National Literacy Trust

68 South Lambeth Road, London SW8 1RL
tel 020-7587 1842
email contact@literacytrust.org.uk
website www.literacytrust.org.uk

An independent charity that aims to help change lives through literacy. It campaigns to improve public understanding of the importance of literacy, as well as delivering projects and working in partnership to reach those most in need of support.

National Society for Education in Art and Design

3 Mason's Wharf, Potley Lane, Corsham, Wilts. SN13 9FY
tel (01225) 810134 *fax* (01225) 812730
website www.nsead.org
General Secretary Dr John Steers NDD, ATC, PhD

The leading national authority concerned with art, craft and design across all phases of education in the UK. Offers the benefits of membership of a professional association, a learned society and a trade union. Has representatives on National and Regional Committees concerned with Art and Design Education. Publishes *International Journal of Art and Design Education* (3 p.a.; Blackwells) and *Start* magazine for primary schools. Founded 1888.

National Society of Painters, Sculptors and Printmakers

Hon. Secretary Gwen Spencer, 122 Copse Hill, London SW20 0NL
tel 020-8946 7878
website www.nationalsociety.org

An annual exhibition at the Menier Gallery, Southwark Street, London SE1. Not an open exhibition but artists are welcome to apply for membership. Newsletter (2 p.a.) for members. Founded 1930.

National Union of Journalists

Head Office Headland House, 308–312 Gray's Inn Road, London WC1X 8DP
tel 020-7278 7916 *fax* 020-7837 8143
email info@nuj.org.uk
website www.nuj.org.uk

Trade union for working journalists with 38,000 members and 140 branches throughout the UK and the Republic of Ireland, and in Paris, Brussels, and the Netherlands. It covers the newspaper press, news agencies and broadcasting, the major part of periodical and book publishing, and a number of public relations departments and consultancies, information services and Prestel-Viewdata services. Administers disputes, unemployment, benevolent and provident benefits. Official publications: *The Journalist* (bi-monthly), *Freelance Directory*, *Freelance Fees Guide* and policy pamphlets.

National Viewers' and Listeners' Association – see Mediawatch-UK

NCTJ – see National Council for the Training of Journalists (NCTJ)

The Edith Nesbit Society

21 Churchfields, West Malling, Kent ME19 6RJ
email mccarthy804@aol.com
website www.edithnesbit.co.uk
Membership £7 p.a., £14 organisations/overseas

Aims to promote an interest in the life and works of Edith Nesbit (1858–1924) by means of talks, a regular newsletter and and other publications, and visits to relevant places. Founded 1996.

New English Art Club

17 Carlton House Terrace, London SW1Y 5BD
tel 020-7930 6844 *fax* 020-7839 7830
email info@mallgalleries.com
website www.mallgalleries.org.uk
President Jason Bowyer

For all those interested in the art of painting, and the promotion of fine arts. Open Annual Exhibition at the Mall Galleries, The Mall, London SW1, open to all working in painting, drawing, pastels and prints.

New Writing North

Holy Jesus Hospital, City Road, Newcastle upon Tyne NE1 2AS
tel 0191-233 3850 *fax* 0191-447 7686
email office@newwritingnorth.com
website www.newwritingnorth.com
Director Claire Malcolm

The literature development agency for the North East. Offers advice and support to writers of poetry, prose and plays. See website. Founded 1996.

New Writing South

9 Jew Street, Brighton, East Sussex BN1 1UT
tel (01273) 735353

email admin@newwritingsouth.com
website www.newwritingsouth.com
Director Chris Taylor
Membership £40/£25 concs. p.a.

Aims to support and encourage writers and their writing in all its forms. Activities include a script-reading service, workshops from visiting professionals, and a monthly newsletter. New Writing South is a registered charity supported by the Arts Council and is open to all creative writers in South East England. Founded 1990.

New Zealand Writers Guild

PO Box 47 886, Ponsonby, Auckland 1144, New Zealand
tel (09) 360-1408 *fax* (09) 360-1409
email info@nzwritersguild.org.nz
website www.nzwritersguild.org.nz
Membership $175–$400 p.a. full, $125 associate

Aims to represent the interests of New Zealand writers (TV, film, radio and theatre); to establish and improve minimum conditions of work and rates of compensation for writers; to provide professional services for members. Founded 1975.

The Newspaper Publishers Association Ltd

8th Floor, St Andrew's House,
18–20 St Andrew Street, London EC4A 3AY
tel 020-7632 7430 *fax* 020-7632 7431

Newspaper Society

8th Floor, St Andrew's House,
18–20 St Andrew Street, London EC4A 3AY
tel 020-7632 7400 *fax* 020-7632 7401
email ns@newspapersoc.org.uk
website www.newspapersoc.org.uk
Director David Newell

Outdoor Writers and Photographers Guild

1 Waterside Close, Garstang, Preston PR3 1HJ
tel (01995) 605340 *fax* (0871) 266 8621
email secretary@owg.org.uk
website www.owpg.org.uk
Membership £70 p.a.

Association of the leading practitioners in outdoor media; represents members' interests to representative bodies in the outdoor industry; circulates members with news of media opportunities; provides a forum for members to meet colleagues and others in the outdoor industry. Presents annual literary and photographic awards. Members include writers, journalists, broadcasters, illustrators, photographers, editors and publishers. Founded 1980.

Wilfred Owen Association

29 Arthur Road, London SW19 7DN
website www.wilfredowen.org.uk
Membership £10 p.a. individual; £15 p.a. couple; £8 concessions (children, students, pensioners); £13 couple concession; £15 overseas; £20 overseas couple; Joint membership of The Wilfred Owen Association and the Siegfried Sassoon Fellowship: £18 individual; £15 concessions; £27 couples; £25 couple concessions; £25 overseas; £30 overseas couple.

Aims to commemorate the life and work of Wilfred Owen (1893–1918), and to encourage and enhance appreciation of his work through visits, public events and a bi-annual journal. Founded 1989.

Oxford Bibliographical Society

Bodleian Library, Broad Street, Oxford OX1 3BG
email membership@oxbibsoc.org.uk
Secretary Dr Christina Neagu, Christ Church, Oxford
website www.oxbibsoc.org.uk
Membership £20 p.a.

Exists to encourage bibliographical research. Founded 1922.

Pact (Producers' Alliance for Cinema and Television)

3rd Floor, Fitzrovia House,
153–157 Cleveland Street, London W1T 6QW
tel 020-7380 8230
email info@pact.co.uk
website www.pact.co.uk
Online Resources Manager David Alan Mills

The UK trade association that represents and promotes the commercial interests of independent feature film, television, animation and interactive media companies. Headquartered in London, it has regional representation throughout the UK, in order to support its members. An effective lobbying organisation, it has regular and constructive dialogues with government, regulators, public agencies and opinion formers on all issues affecting its members and contributes to key public policy debates on the media industry, both in the UK and in Europe. It negotiates terms of trade with all public service broadcasters in the UK and supports members in their business dealings with cable and satellite channels. It also lobbies for a properly structured and funded UK film industry and maintains close contact with the UK Film Council and other relevant film organisations and government departments.

The Pastel Society

17 Carlton House Terrace, London SW1Y 5BD
tel 020-7930 6844 *fax* 020-7839 7830
email info@mallgalleries.com
website www.mallgalleries.org.uk
President John Ivor Stewart

Pastel and drawings in pencil or chalk. Annual Exhibition open to all artists working in dry media held at the Mall Galleries, The Mall, London SW1. Members elected from approved candidates' list. Founded 1899.

Performing Right Society Ltd (PRS)

Copyright House, 29–33 Berners Street,
London W1T 3AB

tel 020-7580 5544 *fax* 020-7306 4455
website www.prs.co.uk

Periodical Publishers Association

Queens House, 28 Kingsway, Holborn,
London WC2B 6JR
tel 020-7404 4166
email info1@ppa.co.uk
website www.ppa.co.uk
Chief Executive Jonathan Shephard

The Personal Managers' Association Ltd

Liaison Secretary PO Box 63819, London N1P 1HL
tel 0845-602 7191
email info@thepma.com
website www.thepma.com

Association of theatrical agents in the theatre, film and entertainment world generally.

The Picture Research Association

Box 105 Hampstead House, 176 Finchley Road,
London NW3
mobile 07771 982308
email chair@picture-research.org.uk
website www.picture-research.org.uk

Professional organisation of picture researchers and picture editors. Its aims are:

• to promote the recognition of picture research, management, editing, picture buying and supplying as a profession requiring particular skills and knowledge;
• to bring together all those involved in the picture profession and provide a forum for information exchange and interaction;
• to encourage publishers, TV and video production organisations, internet companies, and any other users of images to use the PRA freelance register and engage a member of PRA to obtain them, thus ensuring that professional standards are maintained;
• to advise those specifically wishing to embark on a profession in the research and supply of pictures for all types of visual media information, providing guidelines and standards in so doing.

Player–Playwrights

Secretary Peter Thompson, 9 Hillfield Park,
Muswell Hill, London N10 3QT
email publicity@playerplaywrights.co.uk
website www.playerplaywrights.co.uk
Membership £12 in first year and £8 thereafter (plus £2.50 per attendance)

Meets on Monday evenings downstairs in the Porter's Bar at The Green Man Pub, 383 Euston Road, London NW1 3AU. The society reads, performs and discusses plays and scripts submitted by members, with a view to assisting the writers in improving and marketing their work. Newcomers and new acting members are always welcome. Founded 1948.

The Poetry Book Society – see page 361

The Poetry Library – see page 363

The Poetry Society – see page 362

The Beatrix Potter Society

c/o The Lodge, Salisbury Avenue, Harpenden,
Herts. AL5 2PS
tel (01582) 769755
email beatrixpottersociety@tiscali.co.uk
website www.beatrixpottersociety.org.uk
Membership £20 p.a. UK (£25 overseas), £25/£30 commercial/institutional

Promotes the study and appreciation of the life and works of Beatrix Potter (1866–1943) as author, artist, diarist, farmer and conservationist. Regular lecture meetings, conferences and events in the UK and USA. Quarterly newsletter. Small publishing programme. Founded 1980.

The Powys Society

Hon. Secretary Chris Thomas, Flat D,
87 Ledbury Road, London W11 2AG
tel 020-7243 0168
email chris.thomas@defra.gsi.gov.uk
website www.powys-society.org
Membership £18.50 p.a. UK (£22 overseas)

Aims to promote the greater public recognition and enjoyment of the writings, thought and contribution to the arts of the Powys family, particularly John Cowper (1872–1963), Theodore (1875–1953) and Llewelyn (1884–1939) Powys, and the many other family members and their close friends. Publishes an annual scholarly journal (*The Powys Journal*) and 3 newsletters per year, and holds an annual weekend conference in August, as well as other activities. Founded 1967.

The Press Complaints Commission

Director Stephen Abell, Halton House,
20–23 Holborn, London EC1N 2JD
tel 020-7831 0022, (0845) 600 2757 (helpline)
fax 020-7831 0025
email complaints@pcc.org.uk
website www.pcc.org.uk

Independent body founded to oversee self-regulation of the Press. Deals with complaints by the public about the contents and conduct of British newspapers and magazines and advises editors on journalistic ethics. Complaints must be about the failure of newspapers or magazines to follow the letter or spirit of a Code of Practice, drafted by newspaper and magazine editors, adopted by the industry and supervised by the Commission. Founded 1991.

The J.B. Priestley Society

Secretary Rod Slater, 24 St Lawrence Quay,
Salford Quays, Manchester M50 3XT

tel 0161-872 0332
email rodslater@btinternet.com
Membership £12 p.a. single, £18 family, £7 concessions

Aims to widen the knowledge, understanding and appreciation of the published works of J.B. Priestley (1894–1984) and to promote the study of his life and career. Holds lectures and discussions and shows films. Publishes a newsletter and journal. Organises walks to areas with Priestley connections, Annual Priestley Night and other social events. Founded 1997.

Printmakers Council

Ground Floor Unit, 23 Blue Anchor Lane, London SE16 3UL
tel/fax 020-7237 6789
email printpmc@googlemail.com
website www.printmakerscouncil.com
President Stanley Jones, *Chair* Sheila Sloss
Membership £60 p.a., £30 students

Artist-led group which aims to promote the use of both traditional and innovative printmaking techniques by:
• holding exhibitions of prints;
• providing information on prints and printmaking to both its membership and the public;
• encouraging cooperation and exchanges between members, other associations and interested individuals. Founded 1965.

Private Libraries Association

Leader House, Carfraemill, nr Oxton, Lauderdale TD2 6RA
website www.plabooks.org
President Keith Fletcher, *Hon. Editors* David Chambers, David Butcher, *Hon. Secretary* Stan Brett
Membership £30 p.a.

International society of book collectors and private libraries. Publications include *The Private Library* (quarterly), annual *Private Press Books*, and other books on book collecting. Founded 1956.

Professional Cartoonists' Organisation

65 Victoria Road, Cambridge CB4 3BW
tel (01223) 517737 *fax* 020-7900 1677
email info@procartoonists.org
website www.procartoonists.org, www.thebloghorn.org
Secretary Clive Goddard, 25 Paget Road, Oxford OX4 2TB
Membership £80 p.a.

An organisation dedicated to the promotion of UK cartoon art in new media and old. Cartoons provide much-needed humour and satire to society and are a universally appreciated, effective method of communication for business. The organisation showcases UK cartoonists via its magazine, *Foghorn*, cartoon news blog (*Bloghorn*), and public events such as the annual Big Draw and cartoon festivals.

The Publishers Association

29B Montague Street, London WC1B 5BW
tel 020-7691 9191 *fax* 020-7691 9199
email mail@publishers.org.uk
website www.publishers.org.uk
Chief Executive tba, *Director of International and Trade Services* Emma House, *Director of Educational, Academic & Professional Publishing* Graham Taylor, *Operations Director* Mark Wharton

Founded 1896.

Publishers Association of New Zealand (PANZ)

PO Box 102006, North Shore 0745, Auckland, New Zealand
tel (09) 477-5589 *fax* (09) 477-5570
email admin@publishers.org.nz
website www.publishers.org.nz
Association Director Anne de Lautour

Publishers' Association of South Africa (PASA)

PO Box 106, Green Point, 8051, South Africa
tel (021) 425-2721 *fax* (021) 421-3270
email pasa@publishsa.co.za
website www.publishsa.co.za

Publishers Licensing Society Ltd (PLS)

37–41 Gower Street, London WC1E 6HH
tel 020-7299 7730 *fax* 020-7299 7780
email pls@pls.org.uk
website www.pls.org.uk
Chairman Graham Taylor, *Chief Executive* Alicia Wise

PLS serves the UK publishing industry by working to protect publishers' rights, and leads on industry-wide initiatives involving rights management and collective licensing. It is a not-for-profit organisation and has mandates from over 2700 publishers. PLS is dedicated to protecting and strengthening the copyright framework by motivating good practice in rights management. One of the most important ways it does this is by facilitating licence solutions that protect rights and provide revenue for publishers through collective licensing. PLS strives to ensure a high level of service that works on behalf of publishers and readers to uphold copyright legislation. Founded 1981.

Publishers Publicity Circle

Secretary/Treasurer Heather White, 65 Airedale Avenue, London W4 2NN
tel 020-8994 1881
email ppc-@lineone.net
website www.publisherspublicitycircle.co.uk

Enables all book publicists to meet and share information regularly. Monthly meetings provide a forum for press journalists, TV and radio researchers and producers to meet publicists collectively. Awards are presented for the best PR campaigns. Monthly newsletter includes recruitment advertising. Founded 1955.

Publishing Ireland - Foilsiú Éireann

Guinness Enterprise Centre, Taylor's Lane, Dublin 8, Republic or Ireland
tel (01) 415 1210
email info@publishingireland.com
website www.publishingireland.com
President Alan Hayes

Publishing Scotland

(formerly Scottish Publishers Association)
Scottish Book Centre, 137 Dundee Street, Edinburgh EH11 1BG
tel 0131-228 6866 *fax* 0131-228 3220
email enquiries@publishingscotland.org
website www.publishingscotland.co.uk
Chairman Dr Keith Whittles, *Treasurer* Christian MacLean, *Chief Executive* Marion Sinclair, *Information & Training Administrator* Joan Lyle

Founded 1973.

The Radio Academy

5 Market Place, London W1W 8AE
tel 020-7927 9920
email info@radioacademy.org
website www.radioacademy.org
Ceo Trevor Dann

The professional association for those engaged in the UK radio industry with over 2000 individual members and 30 corporate patrons. Organises conferences, seminars, debates, the annual UK Radio Festival and social events for members in all regions of the UK; publishes *Off Air* (quarterly) newsletter and an annual *Yearbook*. Provides administrative support for the Student Radio Association and the Radio Studies Network and organises a series of regional training events for those interested in getting into radio.

Regional Arts Offices – see Arts Council England

Ridley Art Society

50 Crowborough Road, London SW17 9QQ
tel 020-8682 1212
email info@ridleyart.com
President Ken Howard RA, *Chairman* dickon

Represents a wide variety of attitudes towards the making of art. In recent years has sought to encourage younger artists. At least one Central London Members' exhibition a year. Founded 1889.

The Romantic Novelists' Association

Chairman Katie Fforde
Hon. Secretary Evelyn Ryle
email RNAHonSec@emryle.waitrose.com
website www.rna-uk.org

Aims to raise the prestige of Romantic Authorship. Open to romantic and historical novelists. See also page 607.

Royal Academy of Arts

Piccadilly, London W1J 0BD
tel 020-7300 8000 *fax* 020-7300 8001
website www.royalacademy.org.uk
President Sir Nicholas Grimshaw, *Keeper* Maurice Cockrill RA

Royal Academicians are elected from the most distinguished artists in the UK. Holds major loan exhibitions throughout the year including the Annual Summer Exhibition (June–Aug). Also runs Royal Academy Schools for 60 postgraduate students in painting and sculpture.

Royal Birmingham Society of Artists

4 Brook Street, St Paul's, Birmingham B3 1SA
tel 0121-236 4353 *fax* 0121-236 4555
website www.rbsa.org.uk
Membership Friends £25 p.a.

The Society has 2 floors of exhibition space and a craft gallery in the city centre. Members (RBSA) and Associates (ARBSA) are elected annually. Holds a number of Open Exhibitions: send sae or visit website for schedules, available 6 weeks prior to Exhibition. A further Open £1000 First Prize Exhibition is held (June/July) for works in any media. Other substantial money prizes can be won with no preference given to Members and Associates. Also a varying programme of exhibitions throughout the year, including the Autumn Exhibition, open to Members and Associates, and 2 Friends Exhibitions (February and Sept). Friends of the RBSA are entitled to attend various functions and to submit work for the Annual Exhibitions.

Royal Institute of Oil Painters

17 Carlton House Terrace, London SW1Y 5BD
tel 020-7930 6844 *fax* 020-7839 7830
email info@mallgalleries.com
website www.mallgalleries.org.uk
President Peter Wileman

Promotes and encourages the art of painting in oils. Open Annual Exhibition at the Mall Galleries, The Mall, London SW1.

Royal Institute of Painters in Water Colours

17 Carlton House Terrace, London SW1Y 5BD
tel 020-7930 6844 *fax* 020-7839 7830
email info@mallgalleries.com
website www.mallgalleries.org.uk
President Ronald Maddox Hon. RWS
Membership Elected from approved candidates' list

Promotes the appreciation of watercolour painting in its traditional and contemporary forms, primarily by means of an annual exhibition at the Mall Galleries,

The Mall, London SW1 of members' and non-members' work and also by members' exhibitions at selected venues in Britain and abroad. Founded 1831.

The Royal Literary Fund

3 Johnson's Court, off Fleet Street,
London EC4A 3EA
tel 020-7353 7150 *fax* 020-7353 1350
email egunnrlf@globalnet.co.uk
website www.rlf.org.uk
President Ronald Harwood CBE, *General Secretary* Eileen Gunn

Founded in 1790, the Fund is the oldest charity serving literature, set up to help writers and their families who face hardship. It does not offer grants to writers who can earn their living in other ways, nor does it provide financial support for writing projects. But it sustains authors who have for one reason or another fallen on hard times – illness, family misfortune, or sheer loss of writing form. Applicants must have published work of approved literary merit. The literary claim of every new applicant must be accepted by the General Committee before the question of need can be considered.

The Royal Musical Association

Secretary Dr Jeffrey Dean, 4 Chandos Road, Chorlton-cum-Hardy, Manchester M21 0ST
tel 0161-861 7542 *fax* 0161-861 7543
email jeffrey.dean@stingrayoffice.com
website www.rma.ac.uk

The Royal Photographic Society

Fenton House, 122 Wells Road, Bath BA2 3AH
tel (01225) 325733
email reception@rps.org
website www.rps.org

Open membership organisation which promotes the art and science of photography and electronic imagery. Publishes *The RPS Journal* (monthly) and *Imaging Science Journal* (quarterly). Founded 1853.

The Royal Scottish Academy of Art and Architecture

The Mound, Edinburgh EH2 2EL
tel 0131-225 6671 *fax* 0131-220 6016
email info@royalscottishacademy.org
website www.royalscottishacademy.org

Founded in 1826 the RSA maintains a unique position in Scotland as an independent, privately funded institution led by eminent artists and architects whose purpose is to promote and support the visual arts through an ongoing programme of exhibitions and related educational events. Also administers a number of scholarships, awards and residencies and has an historic collection of Scottish artworks and archive available for consultation by appointment. For open submission exhibitions and artist scholarships and residencies, contact the RSA office or see website.

The Royal Society

6–9 Carlton House Terrace, London SW1Y 5AG
tel 020-7451 2500 *fax* 020-7930 2170
email press@royalsociety.org
website royalsociety.org
President Prof. Martin Rees, Lord Rees of Ludlow Kt, PRS, *Treasurer* Sir Peter Williams CBE, FRS, *Biological Secretary* Dame Jean Thomas DBE FRS, *Physical Secretary* Prof. John Pethica FRS, *Foreign Secretary* Prof. Lorna Casselton FRS, *Executive Secretary* Mr S. Cox CVO

The Royal Society for Asian Affairs

2 Belgrave Square, London SW1X 8PJ
tel 020-7235 5122 *fax* 020-7259 6771
email info@rsaa.org.uk
website www.rsaa.org.uk
President The Lord Denman CBE, MC TD, *Chairman of Council* Sir David John KCMG, *Secretary* Colonel Neil Porter
Membership £55 p.a. London, £45 more than 60 miles from London and overseas, £10 up to age 25

For the study of all Asia present and recent past; fortnightly lectures, etc; library. Publishes *Asian Affairs* (3 p.a.), free to members. Founded 1901.

Royal Society for the encouragement of Arts, Manufactures and Commerce (RSA)

8 John Adam Street, London WC2N 6EZ
tel 020-7930 5115
email general@rsa.org.uk
website www.thersa.org

Works to remove the barriers to social progress, driving ideas, innovation and social change through an ambitious programme of projects, events and lectures. Supported by over 27,000 Fellows, an international network of influencers and innovators from every field and background across the UK and overseas. Welcomes women and men of any nationality and background who will support the organisation's aims. Its activities are detailed in the *RSA Journal*. Founded 1754.

Royal Society of British Artists

17 Carlton House Terrace, London SW1Y 5BD
tel 020-7930 6844 *fax* 020-7839 7830
email info@mallgalleries.com
website www.mallgalleries.org.uk
President James Horton

Incorporated by Royal Charter for the purpose of encouraging the study and practice of the arts of painting, sculpture and architectural designs. Annual Open Exhibition at the Mall Galleries, The Mall, London SW1, open to artists working in any 2- or 3-dimensional medium.

Royal Society of Literature

Somerset House, Strand, London WC2R 1LA
tel 020-7845 4676 *fax* 020-7845 4679

email info@rslit.org
website www.rslit.org
Chair of Council Anne Chisholm, FRSL, *Secretary* Maggie Fergusson, FRSL
Membership £50 p.a.

For the promotion of literature and encouragement of writers by way of lectures, discussions, readings, and by publications. Administers the VS Pritchett Memorial Prize, the Royal Society of Literature Ondaatje Prize, and the Royal Society of Literature/Jerwood Awards. Founded 1820.

Royal Society of Marine Artists

17 Carlton House Terrace, London SW1Y 5BD
tel 020-7930 6844 *fax* 020-7839 7830
email info@mallgalleries.com
website www.mallgalleries.org.uk
President David Howell

Aims to promote and encourage marine painting. Open Annual Exhibition at the Mall Galleries, The Mall, London SW1 for any artists whose main interest is the sea, or tidal waters, or some object essentially connected therewith.

The Royal Society of Miniature Painters, Sculptors and Gravers

Executive Secretary Phyllis Rennell, 3 Briar Walk, London SW15 6UD
tel 020-8785 2338
email info@royal-miniature-society.org.uk
website www.royal-miniature-society.org.uk
President Elisabeth R. Meek, PRMS, PPSWA, HS, FRSA, *Hon. Secretary* Helen White RMS, HS
Membership By selection and standard of work over a period of years (ARMS associate, RMS full member)

Annual Open Exhibition in October at the Mall Galleries, The Mall, London SW1. Hand in August; schedules available in July (send sae). Applications and enquiries to the Executive Secretary. Founded 1895.

Royal Society of Painter-Printmakers

Bankside Gallery, 48 Hopton Street, London SE1 9JH
tel 020-7928 7521
email info@banksidegallery.com
website www.banksidegallery.com
President Hilary Paynter PRE
Membership Open to British and overseas artists. An election of Associates is held annually; for particulars apply to the Secretary. Friends membership is open to all those interested in artists' original printmaking

Organises workshops and lectures on original printmaking and holds one members' exhibition per year. Founded 1880.

Royal Society of Portrait Painters

17 Carlton House Terrace, London SW1Y 5BD
tel 020-7930 6844 *fax* 020-7839 7830
email enquiries@therp.co.uk
website www.therp.co.uk
President Alastair Adams

Annual Exhibition at the Mall Galleries, The Mall, London SW1, of members' work and that of selected non-members. Five high-profile artists' awards are made: the Ondaatje Prize for Portraiture (£10,000), the De Laszlo Prize (£3000), the Prince of Wales's Award for Portrait Drawing (£2000), the Changing Faces Prize (£2000). Also commissions consultancy service. Founded 1891.

Royal Television Society

5th Floor, Kildare House, 3 Dorset Rise, London EC4Y 8EN
tel 020-7822-2810 020-7822 2811
email info@rts.org.uk
website www.rts.org.uk

The leading forum for discussion and debate on all aspects of the TV community. In a fast changing sector, it reflects the full range of perspectives and views. Holds awards, conferences, dinners, lectures and workshops. Founded 1927.

Royal Watercolour Society

Bankside Gallery, 48 Hopton Street, London SE1 9JH
tel 020-7928 7521
email info@banksidegallery.com
website www.banksidegallery.com
President David Paskett, PRWS, Hon RE
Membership Open to British and overseas artists; election of Associates held annually. Friends membership is open to all those interested in watercolour painting

Arranges lectures and courses on watercolour paintings; holds an annual open exhibition in February. Exhibitions in the spring and autumn. Founded 1804.

Royal West of England Academy

Queens Road, Clifton, Bristol BS8 1PX
tel 0117-973 5129 *fax* 0117-923 7874
email info@rwa.org.uk
website www.rwa.org.uk
President Derek Balmer

An art academy/gallery/museum whose objectives are to advance the education of the public in the fine arts and in particular to promote the appreciation and practice of the fine arts and to encourage and develop talent in the fine arts. Founded 1844.

The Ruskin Society

Hon. Secretary Dr C.J. Gamble, 49 Hallam Street, London W1W 6JP
tel: 020-7580 1894
website www.theruskinsociety.com
Membership £10 p.a.

Aims to encourage a wider understanding of John Ruskin (1819–1900) and his contemporaries. Organises lectures and events which seek to explain to the public the nature of Ruskin's theories and to place these in a modern context. Affiliated to the Ruskin Foundation. Founded 1997.

SAA (Society for All Artists)

PO Box 50, Newark, Notts. NG23 5GY
tel (01949) 844050 *fax* (01949) 844051
email info@saa.co.uk
website www.saa.co.uk
Membership from £25 p.a.

Aims to encourage and inspire all artists. Members range from complete beginners to leisure painters. SAA is the largest art society with over 45,000 members, and welcomes new members. Membership includes paintings insurance for exhibitions and third party public liability, discounted art materials from the society's *Home Shop* catalogue and the *Paint* newsletter (bi-monthly). Founded 1992.

The Malcolm Saville Society

6 Redcliffe Street, London SW10 9DS
email mystery@witchend.com
website www.witchend.com
Membership £10 p.a. (£12.50 Europe, £16 elsewhere)

Aims to remember and promote interest in the work of Malcolm Saville (1901–82), children's author. Regular social activities, library, contact directory and magazine (4 p.a.). Founded 1994.

The Dorothy L. Sayers Society

Chairman Christopher J. Dean, Rose Cottage, Malthouse Lane, Hurstpierpoint, West Sussex BN6 9JY
tel (01273) 833444 *fax* (01273) 835988
website www.sayers.org.uk
Secretaries Lenelle Davis, Jasmine Simeone
Membership £15 p.a. UK, £17.50 Europe, $36 USA, £20 rest of world

Aims to promote and encourage the study of the works of Dorothy L. Sayers (1893–1957); to collect archive materials and reminiscences about her and make them available to students and biographers; to hold an annual conference and other meetings; to publish proceedings, pamphlets and a bi-monthly bulletin; to make grants and awards. Founded 1976.

Scattered Authors Society

Secretary Damian Harvey, 9 Maxwell Grove, Bispham, Blackpool, Lancs FY2 0QG
email author@damianharvey.co.uk
website www.scatteredauthors.org

Aims to provide a forum for informal discussion, contact and support for professional writers in children's fiction. Founded 1998.

Scottish Arts Club

24 Rutland Square, Edinburgh EH1 2BW
tel 0131-229 8157
email scottishartsclub@btconnect.com
website www.scottishartsclub.co.uk
Hon. Secretary tel 0131-229 8157
Membership £396 p.a. full; reductions available

Art, literature, music.

Scottish Arts Council

12 Manor Place, Edinburgh EH3 7DD
tel 0131-226 6051, (0845) 603 6000 (help desk; local rate) *fax* 0131-225 9833
email help.desk@scottisharts.org.uk
website www.scottisharts.org.uk
Chairman Dr Richard Holloway, *Head of Literature* Dr Gavin Wallace, *Head of Visual Arts* Amanda Catto

The lead body for the funding, development and advocacy of the arts in Scotland. Offers a unique national perspective on the provision and management of the arts which seeks to balance the needs of all arts sectors and all parts of Scotland. The expertise and experience of Scottish Arts Council in developing sound policy and good practice includes the ability to make links between the intrinsic value of the arts and their instrumental value in delivering social and economic benefits at a national level. Also offers a focus on research, information provision and international working.

The Council is an executive non-departmental public body (NDPB), which is one of the main channels for government funding for the arts in Scotland. Funding mostly comes from the Scottish Executive but it also distributes National Lottery funds.

Creative Scotland is the name of the proposed new strategic body which will lead the development of the arts, creative and screen industries across Scotland. It is due to be launched in the summer of 2010. The new organisation will take over the functions and resources of the Scottish Arts Council and Scottish Screen, as well as having a wider set of responsibilities for developing the sector.

Scottish Book Trust (SBT)

Sandeman House, 55 High Street, Edinburgh EH1 1SR
tel 0131-524 0160 *fax* 0131-524 0161
email info@scottishbooktrust.com
website www.scottishbooktrust.com

With a responsibility towards Scottish writing, SBT exists to inspire readers and writers, and through the promotion of reading, to reach and create a wider reading public. Programmes include: management of Live Literature funding, a national initiative enabling Scottish citizens to engage with authors, playwrights, poets, storytellers and illustrators; Writer Development, offering mentoring and professional development for emerging and established writers; an ambitious children's programme including national tours, a children's festival and the Royal Mail Scottish Children's Book Awards; and an international programme showcasing Scottish writing abroad. An information service for readers, writers and occasional exhibitions and publications all contribute to SBT's mission to bring readers and writers together.

Scottish Fellowship of Christian Writers

c/o Diana Lynch, 56 Oak Drive, Kirkintilloch G66 4BU

email info@sfcw.info
website www.sfcw.info
Membership Secretary Diana Lynch
£10 p.a.

To encourage Christians living in Scotland to make use of their creative writing talents. Over 140 members. Founded 1980.

Scottish Newspaper Publishers Association

108 Holyrood Road, Edinburgh EH8 8AS
tel 0131-220 4353 *fax* 0131-220 4344
email info@snpa.org.uk
website www.snpa.org.uk
President Michael Johnston

Scottish Newspaper Society

21 Lansdowne Crescent, Edinburgh EH12 5EH
tel 0131-535 1064
email info@scotns.org.uk
Director J.B. Raeburn OBE, FCIS

Scottish Screen

2nd Floor, 249 West George Street, Glasgow G2 4QE
tel 0845-300 7300
email info@scottishscreen.com
website www.scottishscreen.com

Develops, encourages and promotes every aspect of film, TV and new media in Scotland through script development, short film production, distribution of National Lottery film production finance, training, education, exhibition funding and Film Commission Locations support.

Seven Stories – the Centre for Children's Books

30 Lime Street, Ouseburn Valley, Newcastle upon Tyne NE1 2PQ
tel (0845) 271 0777
email info@sevenstories.org.uk
website www.sevenstories.org.uk

Centre to celebrate children's books with interactive galleries, a bookshop, creative activities and author/illustrator events.

The Shaw Society

1 Buckland Court, 37 Belsize Park, London NW3 4EB
tel 020-7226 4266
email contact@shawsociety.org.uk
website www.shawsociety.org.uk
Hon. Secretary Alan Knight
Membership £15/$30 p.a.

Works towards the improvement and diffusion of knowledge of the life and works of Bernard Shaw (1856–1950) and his circle. Publishes *The Shavian*.

Society for Editors and Proofreaders (SfEP)

Office Erico House, 93–99 Upper Richmond Road, London SW15 2TG
tel 020-8785 5617
email admin@sfep.org.uk
website www.sfep.org.uk

Works to promote high editorial standards and achieve recognition of its members' professional status, through local and national meetings, an annual conference, email discussion groups, a regular magazine and a programme of reasonably priced workshops/training sessions. These sessions help newcomers to acquire basic skills, enable experienced editors to update their skills or broaden their competence, and also cover aspects of professional practice or business for the self-employed. An online Directory of editorial services is available. The Society supports moves towards recognised standards of training and accreditation for editors and proofreaders and has developed its own Accreditation in Proofreading qualification. It has close links with the Publishing Training Centre and the Society of Indexers, is represented on the BSI Technical Committee dealing with copy preparation and proof correction (BS 5261), and works to foster good relations with all relevant bodies and organisations in the UK and worldwide. Founded 1988.

The Society for Theatre Research

c/o PO Box 53971, London SW15 6UL
email contact@str.org.uk
website www.str.org.uk
Hon. Secretaries Eileen Cottis, Valerie Kaneko-Lucas

Publishes journal *Theatre Notebook* (3 p.a.) and at least one major book per annum, holds lectures and makes annual research grants (current annual total sum approx. £5000). Also awards an annual prize of up to £500 for best book published in English on the historical or current practice of the British Theatre.

Society of Artists Agents

website www.saahub.com

Formed to promote professionalism in the illustration industry and to forge closer links between clients and artists through an agreed set of guidelines. The Society believes in an ethical approach through proper terms and conditions, thereby protecting the interests of the artists and clients. Founded 1992.

The Society of Authors – see page 541

The Society of Botanical Artists

Executive Secretary Mrs Pam Henderson, 1 Knapp Cottages, Wyke, Gillingham, Dorset SP8 4NQ
tel (01747) 825718
email pam@soc-botanical-artists.org
website www.soc-botanical-artists.org
President Margaret Stevens
Membership Through selection. £140 p.a.; £20 friend members

Aims to encourage the art of botanical painting. Annual Open Exhibition held in April at

Westminster Central Hall, London SW1. Hand in February. Entry schedules available from the Executive Secretary from December on receipt of sae. Founded 1985.

Society of Children's Book Writers and Illustrators (SCBWI)

36 Mackenzie Road, Beckenham, Kent BR3 4RU
email ra@britishscbwi.org
website www.britishscbwi.org
Regional Adviser, SCBWI–British Isles Natascha Biebow
Membership £50 p.a.

An international network for the exchange of knowledge between professional writers, illustrators, editors, publishers, agents, librarians, educators, booksellers and others involved with literature for young people. Sponsors conferences on writing and illustrating children's books and multimedia – in New York (February, annual), Los Angeles (August, annual) and Bologna (spring, bi-annual) – as well as dozens of regional conferences and events throughout the world. Publishes a bi-monthly newsletter, *The Bulletin*, and information publications, and awards grants for works in progress. The SCBWI also presents the annual Golden Kite Award for the best fiction and non-fiction books, which is open both to published and unpublished writers and illustrators.

The SCBWI British Isles region meets regularly for speaker or professional development workshop events. Also sponsors local critique groups and publishes *Words and Pictures* quarterly newsletter, which includes up-to-date events and marketing information, interviews and articles on the craft of children's writing and illustrating in the British Isles. The yearly two-day Writers' and Illustrators' Conference includes workshops and the opportunity to meet publishing professionals. Founded 1971.

The Society of Civil and Public Service Writers

Secretary Mrs J.M. Lewis, 17 The Green, Corby Glen, Grantham, Lincs. NG33 4NP
email joan@lewis5634.fsnet.co.uk
website www.scpsw.co.uk
Membership £15 p.a.; Poetry Workshop add £5

Welcomes serving and retired members of the Civil Service, Armed Forces, Post Office and BT, the nursing profession, and other public servants. Members can be aspiring or published writers. Holds annual competitions for short stories, articles and poetry, plus occasional for longer works. Offers postal folios for short stories and articles; holds an AGM and occasional meetings; publishes *The Civil Service Author* (quarterly) magazine. Poetry Workshop offers magazine, postal folio, anthology and weekend. Send sae for details. Founded 1935.

Society of Editors

Director Bob Satchwell, University Centre, Granta Place, Mill Lane, Cambridge CB2 1RU
tel (01223) 304080 *fax* (01223) 304090
email info@societyofeditors.org
website www.societyofeditors.org
Membership £230 p.a.

Formed from the merger of the Guild of Editors and the Association of British Editors, the Society has more than 400 members in national, regional and local newspapers, magazines, broadcasting, new media, journalism education and media law, campaigning for media freedom. Founded 1999.

Society of Graphic Fine Art

The Drawing Society, 27 Lorne Avenue, Croydon, Surrey CR0 7RQ
website www.sgfa.org.uk
President Roger Lewis PSGFA, UKCPS
Membership by election

Exists to promote fine art drawing skills. Welcomes artists working in modern or traditional styles in any wet or dry medium (except oils) plus all forms of original printmaking. Holds an annual open exhibition. Founded 1919.

Society of Heraldic Arts

10–12 Ridgeway, Ottery St Mary, Devon EX11 1DT
email sha.hon-sec@tiscali.co.uk
website www.heraldic-arts.com
Secretary Kevin Arkinstall HSDAD SHA, *Membership Secretary* David Hopkinson SHA (*email* chris-david.hopkinson3@ntlworld.com)
Membership Craft £25 p.a., Associate £17

Aims to serve the interests of heraldic artists, craftsmen, designers and writers, to provide a 'shop window' for their work, to obtain commissions on their behalf and to act as a forum for the exchange of information and ideas. Also offers an information service to the public. Candidates for admission as craft members should be artists or craftsmen whose work comprises a substantial element of heraldry and is of a sufficiently high standard to satisfy the requirements of the Society's advisory council. Founded 1987.

Society of Indexers – see page 669

The Society of Limners

Contact Richard East, 16 Tudor Close, Hove, East Sussex BN3 7NR
tel (01273) 770628
email rgeast.limners@ntlworld.com
website www.societyoflimners.co.uk
Membership £35 p.a., £15 Friends (open to non-exhibitors); £40/£18 overseas

The Society's aims are to promote an interest in miniature painting (in any medium), calligraphy and heraldry and encourage their development to a high standard. New members are elected after the submission of 4 works of acceptable standard and guidelines are provided for new artists. Members receive up to 3 newsletters a year and an annual exhibition is arranged. Seminars and painting weekends are held at least every two years. Founded 1986.

The Society of Medical Writers

Dr R. Cutler, 30 Dollis Hill Lane, London NW2 6JE
website www.somw.org.uk

Aims to recruit members from all branches of the medical profession, together with all professions allied to medicine, to foster interest in literature and in writing – not solely about medicine but also about art, history, music, theatre, etc. Members are encouraged to write fiction, poetry, plays, book reviews, non-fiction articles. Poetry, short story and biography (Roger Bacon Award) prizes, for best non-fiction and best written clinical paper. Publishes *The Writer* (2 p.a.) and a register of members and their writing interests. Holds a bi-annual conference in which various aspects of literature and writing are explored in a relaxed and informal atmosphere. Founded 2001 as successor to the General Practitioner Writers Association.

Society of Scribes and Illuminators (SSI)

Hon. Secretary 6 Queen Square, London WC1N 3AR
email scribe@calligraphyonline.org
website www.calligraphyonline.org
Membership £28 Lay members; £23 Friends

Aims to advance the crafts of writing and illumination. Holds regular exhibitions, provides opportunities for discussion, demonstration and sharing of research. Founded 1921.

The Society of Sussex Authors

Secretary David Arscott, Dolphin House, 51 St Nicholas Lane, Lewes, East Sussex BN7 2JZ
tel (01273) 470100 *fax* (01273) 470100
email sussexbooks@aol.com
Membership £10 p.a.

Aims to encourage social contact between members, and to promote interest in literature and authors. Membership is open to writers living in Sussex who have had at least one book commercially published or who have worked extensively in journalism, radio, TV or the theatre. Founded 1969.

Society of Wildlife Artists

17 Carlton House Terrace, London SW1Y 5BD
tel 020-7930 6844 *fax* 020-7839 7830
website www.mallgalleries.org.uk
President Harriet Mead

Aims to promote and encourage the art of wildlife painting and sculpture. Open Annual Exhibition at the Mall Galleries, The Mall, London SW1, for any artist whose work depicts wildlife subjects (botanical and domestic animals are not admissable).

The Society of Women Artists

Executive Secretary 1 Knapp Cottages, Wyke, Gillingham, Dorset SP8 4NQ
tel (01747) 825718 *fax* (01747) 826835
email pamhenderson@dsl.pipex.com
website www.society-women-artists.org.uk
President Barbara Penketh Simpson RMS, FRSA
Membership Election by invitation, based on work submitted to the exhibition

Founded in 1855 when women were not considered as serious contributors to art and could not compete for professional honours, the Society continues to promote art by women. Receiving day in April for annual open exhibition held in May at Mall Galleries, The Mall, London SW1.

Society of Women Writers & Journalists (SWWJ)

Membership Secretary Wendy Hughes, 14 Laburnum Walk, Rustington, Littlehampton, West Sussex BN16 3QW
tel (01903) 785771
email wendy@stickler.org
website www.swwj.co.uk
Membership Secretary W.L. Hughes
Membership £40 p.a. Full, £30 Male Associates, £25 probationary/student, £30 overseas, £15 joining fee. Friends of the SWWJ £15 (no joining fee)

For women writers: the SWWJ upholds professional standards and literary achievements through regular workshops for all genre of writing where work-in-progress can be evaluated. Regional group meetings; residential weekends; postal critique service; competitions and outings. For Full members, membership card doubles as a press card. Publishes *The Woman Writer* (5 p.a.). Men writers are accepted as Associate members. Founded 1894.

Society of Young Publishers

Contact The Secretary, c/o The Publishers Association, 29B Montague Street, London WC1B 5BW
email info@thesyp.org.uk
website www.thesyp.org.uk
Membership Open to anyone employed in publishing or hoping to be soon; standard membership £30, student/unwaged £24; associate membership available to those over the age of 35

Organises monthly speaker meetings at which senior figures talk on topics of key importance to the industry today, and social and other events. Runs a job database which matches candidates with potential employers. Meetings are held in Central London, usually on the last Wednesday of the month at 6.30pm. Also a branch in Oxford. Founded 1949.

South African Writers' Circle

Postnet, Suite 522, Post Bag X4, Kloof 3640, South Africa
email sawriter@webmail.co.za
website www.sawc.sos.co.za
Membership R160 p.a. local, R210 p.a. overseas

Aims to help and encourage all writers, new and experienced, in the art of writing. Publishes a monthly *Newsletter*, and runs competitions with prizes for the winners. Founded 1960.

Southwest Scriptwriters

email info@southwest-scriptwriters.co.uk
website www.southwest-scriptwriters.co.uk
Membership £6 p.a.

Artistic Director Tim Massey

Workshops members' drama scripts for stage, screen, radio and TV with the aim of improving their chances of professional production, meeting at the Famous Royal Naval Volunteer pub, Bristol. Also hosts talks by professional dramatists. Projects to present members' work to a wider audience have included theatre and short film productions, as well as public rehearsed readings. Bi-monthly e-newsletter. Founded 1994.

Sports Journalists' Association of Great Britain (SJA)

c/o Start2Finish Event Management, Unit 92, Capital Business Centre, 22 Carlton Road, Surrey CR2 0BS
tel 020-8916 2234 *fax* 020-8916 2235
website www.sportsjournalists.co.uk
President Michael Parkinson CBE
Membership £30 p.a., £20 regional

Represents sports journalists across the country and is Britain's voice in international sporting affairs. Offers advice to members covering major events, acts as a consultant to organisers of major sporting events on media requirements. Member of the BOA Press Advisory Committee. Founded 1948.

The Robert Louis Stevenson Club

Secretary John W.S. Macfie, 17 Heriot Row, Edinburgh EH3 6HP
tel/fax 0131-556 1896
email mail@stevenson-house.co.uk
Membership £20 p.a., £150 10 years

Aims to foster interest in Robert Louis Stevenson's life (1850–94) and works through various events and its newsletter. Founded 1920.

Sussex Playwrights' Club

Hon. Secretary, 2 Brunswick Mews, Hove, East Sussex BN3 1HD
website www.sussexplaywrights.com

Swedish Publishers' Association

(Svenska Förläggareföreningen)
Drottninggaten 97, 15 tr., 113 60 Stockholm, Sweden
tel 46-8-736-1940 *fax* 46-8-736-1944
email info@forlaggare.se
website www.forlaggare.se
Director Kristina Ahlinder

Founded 1843.

The Tennyson Society

Central Library, Free School lane, Lincoln LN2 1EZ
tel (01522) 552851 *fax* (01522) 552858
email kathleen.jefferson@lincolnshire.gov.uk
website www.tennysonsociety.org.uk
Membership £10 p.a., £12 family, £15 institutions

Promotes the study and understanding of the life and work of the poet Alfred, Lord Tennyson (1809–92) and supports the Tennyson Research Centre in Lincoln. Holds lectures, visits and seminars; publishes the *Tennyson Research Bulletin* (annual), Monographs and Occasional Papers; tapes/recordings available. Founded 1960.

The English-Speaking Union

The English-Speaking Union of the Commonwealth, Dartmouth House, 37 Charles Street, London W1J 5ED
tel 020-7529 1550 *fax* 020-7495 6108
email esu@esu.org
The English Speaking Union of the United States, 144 East 39th Street, New York, NY 10016, USA
tel 212-818-1200 *fax* 212-867-4177
email info@esu.org
website www.esu.org

World voluntary organisation devoted to the promotion of international understanding and friendship. Runs the biennial Marsh Biography Award, the annual HRH Duke of Edinburgh's English Language Book Award and the President's Award for non-book resources on the English language.

Theatre Writers' Union – see page 544

Angela Thirkell Society

Chairman Mrs I.J. Cox, 32 Murvagh Close, Cheltenham, Glos. GL53 7QY
tel (01242) 251604
email penny.aldred@ntlworld.com
Secretary Mrs P. Aldred, 54 Belmont Park, London SE13 5BN
tel 020-8244 9339
website www.angelathirkellsociety.com
Membership £10 p.a.

Aims 'to honour the memory of Angela Thirkell (1890–1960) as a writer, and to make her works available to new generations'. Publishes an *Annual Journal*, and encourages Thirkell studies. Founded 1980.

The Edward Thomas Fellowship

1 Carfax, Undercliff Drive, St Lawrence, Isle of Wight PO38 1XG
tel (01983) 853366
email colingthornton@btopenworld.com
Hon. Secretary Colin G. Thornton
Membership single £10 p.a., joint £15 p.a.

Aims to perpetuate the memory of Edward Thomas (1878–1917), poet and writer, foster an interest in his life and work, to assist in the preservation of places associated with him and to arrange events which extend fellowship amongst his admirers. Founded 1980.

Dylan Thomas Society of Great Britain

4 Bishops Grove, Sketty, Swansea SA2 8BE
website thedylanthomassocietyofgb.co.uk
Chair Mr John Rhys Thomas
Membership £5 p.a. single, £8 p.a. double

Aims to promote an interest in the works of Dylan Thomas (1914–53) and other Anglo–Welsh writers. Founded 1977.

The Tolkien Society

Membership Secretary Marion Kershaw, 655 Rochdale Road, Walsden, Todmorden, Lancashire OL14 6SX
email membership@tolkiensociety.org
website www.tolkiensociety.org
Membership £21 p.a. (Full), £10.50 p.a. (Associate), £2 p.a. (Entings)

The Translators Association

84 Drayton Gardens, London SW10 9SB
tel 020-7373 6642
email info@societyofauthors.org
website www.societyofauthors.org

Specialist unit within the membership of the Society of Authors (see page 541), exclusively concerned with the interests and special problems of translators into English whose work is published or performed commercially in Great Britain. Members are entitled to general and legal advice on all questions connected with their work, including remuneration and contractual arrangements with publishers, editors, broadcasting organisations. Founded 1958.

The Trollope Society

Maritime House, Clapham Old Town, London SW4 0JW
tel 020-7720 6789 *fax* 020-7627 2965
email info@trollopesociety.org
website www.trollopesociety.org
Chairman Michael Williamson JP DL
Membership £26 p.a.

Has produced the first ever complete edition of the novels of Anthony Trollope (1815–82). Founded 1987.

The Turner Society

BCM Box Turner, London WC1N 3XX
website www.turnersociety.org.uk
Chairman Andrew Wilton
Membership £25 p.a. individuals, £25 p.a. overseas surface mail, £37.50 p.a. overseas airmail, Life Member £500

Aims to foster a wider appreciation of all facets of the work of J.M.W. Turner RA (1775–1851); to encourage exhibitions of his paintings, drawings and engravings. Publishes *Turner Society News* (3 p.a.). Founded 1975.

Ver Poets

Secretary Daphne Schiller
email daphneschiller@ntlworld.com
website www.verpoets.org.uk
Contact Daphne Schiller (tel: 01727-864898)
Membership £18 p.a. UK, £24 overseas, £12 students

Encourages the writing and study of poetry. Holds evening meetings and daytime workshops in the St Albans area. Holds members' competitions and the annual Open Competition. Founded 1966.

Visiting Arts

4.01 and 4.02 Enterprise House, 1–2 Hatfields, London SE1 9PG
tel 020-7960 9631 *fax* 020-7960 9643
email information@visitingarts.org.uk
website www.visitingarts.org.uk
Director Yvette Vaughan Jones

Aims to strengthen intercultural understanding through the arts. It provides information and intelligence in order to strengthen intercultural dialogue, and creates opportunities to experience intercultural exploration. This is done through mediated performances, exhibitions, and by initiating and promoting collaborations. Visiting Arts seeks to expand the skills and knowledge of existing cultural players and develop new talent to ensure a wide, diverse and sustainable group of players.

Visiting Arts creates, produces and distributes authoritative directories and help-sheets, targeted briefings and the latest advice through print, web and word of mouth. It organises seminars, conferences and networking events to deepen intercultural understanding; establishes and fosters opportunities for ground-breaking artist exchanges; promotes cutting edge exhibitions; and contributes to some of the world's biggest and most innovative festivals. It works with the most exciting next generation of artists and cultural players, inviting them to the UK, expanding knowledge and horizons and championing intercultural working.

Visiting Arts is an independent registered charity. It is funded by the British Council, Arts Council England, the Scottish Arts Council, the Arts Council of Wales, the Arts Council of Northern Ireland and the Department of Culture, Media and Sport. Founded 1977.

Voice of the Listener & Viewer Ltd (VLV)

PO Box 401, Gravesend, Kent DA12 9FY
tel (01474) 352835 *fax* (01474) 351112
email info@vlv.org.uk
website www.vlv.org.uk
Deputy Chairman John Clark, *Administrative Secretary* Sue Washbrook

Represents the citizen and consumer interests in broadcasting: it is an independent, non-profit-making society working to ensure independence, quality and diversity in broadcasting. VLV is funded by its members and is free from sectarian, commercial and political affiliations. It holds public lectures, seminars and conferences, and has frequent contact with MPs and other relevant parties. It provides an independent forum where all with an interest in broadcasting can speak on equal terms. It produces a quarterly news bulletin and holds its own archive and those of the former Broadcasting Research Unit (1980–90) and BACTV (British Action for Children's Television). It maintains a panel of speakers, the VLV Forum for Children's Broadcasting, the VLV Forum for Educational Broadcasting, and acts as a secretariat for the European Alliance of Listeners' and Viewers' Associations (EURALVA). VLV does not handle complaints. Founded 1984.

The Walmsley Society

Secretary Fred Lane, April Cottage, 1 Brand Road, Hampden Park, Eastbourne, East Sussex BN22 9PX
website www.walmsleysoc.org
Membership Secretary Mrs Elizabeth Buckley, 21 The Crescent, Hipperholm, Halifax, West Yorkshire HX3 8NQ

Aims to promote and encourage an appreciation of the literary and artistic heritage left to us by Leo Walmsley (1892–1966) and J. Ulric Walmsley (1860–1954). Founded 1985.

Mary Webb Society

Secretary Sue Higginbotham, 8 The Knowe, Willaston, Neston, Cheshire CH64 1TA
tel 0151-327 5843
email suehigginbotham@yahoo.co.uk
website www.marywebbsociety.co.uk

For devotees of the literature and works of Mary Webb (1881–1927) and of the beautiful Shropshire countryside of her novels. Publishes a bi-annual Journal, organises summer schools and other events in various locations related to Webb's life and works. Archives, lectures; tours arranged for individuals and groups. Founded 1972.

The H.G. Wells Society

Hon. General Secretary Mark Egerton, Flat 3, 27B Church Road, London NW4 4EB
email secretaryhgwellssociety@hotmail.com
website www.hgwellsusa.50megs.com
Membership £18 p.a. UK/Eu, £21 p.a. rest of world

Promotes an active interest in and an appreciation of the life, work and thought of H.G. Wells (1866–1946). Publishes *The Wellsian* (annual) and *The Newsletter* (bi-annual). Founded 1960.

Welsh Academy – see Academi (Welsh Academy)

Welsh Books Council/Cyngor Llyfrau Cymru

Castell Brychan, Aberystwyth, Ceredigion SY23 2JB
tel (01970) 624151 *fax* (01970) 625385
email castellbrychan@cllc.org.uk
website www.cllc.org.uk, www.gwales.com
Director Elwyn Jones

A national body funded directly by the Welsh Assembly Government which provides a focus for the publishing industry in Wales. Awards grants for publishing in Welsh and English. Provides services to the trade in the fields of editing, design, marketing and distribution. The Council is a key enabling institution in the world of books and provides services and information in this field to all who are associated with it. Founded 1961.

The West Country Writers' Association

Fiona McAughey, Trevean, Yeolmbridge, Launceston PL15 8NJ
tel (01566) 773615
website www.westcountrywriters.com
President Lady Rachel Billington, *Chair* Rosemary Aitken
Membership Open to published authors, joining fee plus first year membership £20 – thereafter £10 p.a.

Aims to foster love of literature in the West Country and to give authors an opportunity of meeting to exchange news and views. Holds Annual Weekend Congress and Regional Meetings. Plus newsletters.

The Oscar Wilde Society

Kambah, Harcourt Hill, Oxford OX2 9AS
email cressida.battersby@virgin.net
website www.oscarwildesociety.co.uk
Membership Secretary Cressida Battersby

Aims to promote knowledge, appreciation and study of the life, personality and works of the writer and wit Oscar Wilde (1854–1900). Activities include meetings, lectures, readings and exhibitions, and visits to associated locations. Members receive a journal, *The Wildean* (2 p.a.), and a newsletter, *Intentions* (6 p.a.). Founded 1990.

Charles Williams Society

Secretary Richard Sturch, 35 Broomfield, Stacey Bushes, Milton Keynes MK12 6HA
email charles_wms_soc@yahoo.co.uk
website www.charleswilliamssociety.org.uk

Aims to promote interest in the life and work of Charles Walter Stansby Williams (1886–1945) and to make his writings more easily available. Founded 1975.

The Henry Williamson Society

General Secretary Sue Cumming, 7 Monmouth Road, Dorchester, Dorset DT1 2DE
tel (01305) 264092
email zseagull@aol.com
Membership Secretary Margaret Murphy, 16 Doran Drive, Redhill, Surrey RH1 6AX
tel (01737) 763228
email mm@misterman.freeserve.co.uk
website www.henrywilliamson.co.uk

Chairman Tony Boakes
Membership £15 p.a. from Sept. 2010

Aims to encourage a wider readership and greater understanding of the literary heritage left by Henry Williamson (1895–1977). Two meetings annually; also weekend activities. Publishes an annual journal. Founded 1980.

The P.G. Wodehouse Society (UK)

Details Tony Ring, 34 Longfield, Great Missenden, Bucks. HP16 0EG
tel (01494) 864848
website www.pgwodehousesociety.org.uk
Membership £15 p.a.

Aims to promote enjoyment of P.G. Wodehouse (1881–1975). Publishes *Wooster Sauce* (quarterly) and *By The Way* papers (4 p.a.) which cover diverse subjects of Wodehousean interest. Holds events, entertainments and meetings throughout Britain. Founded 1997.

Women in Publishing (WiP)

c/o Kathryn King,
Multilingual Matters/Channel View Publications, Frankfurt Lodge, Clevedon Hall, Victoria Road, Clevedon BS21 7HH
email info@wipub.org.uk
website www.wipub.org.uk
Membership £27.50 p.a.

Promotes the status of women within publishing; encourages networking and mutual support among women; provides a forum for the discussion of ideas, trends and subjects to women in the trade; offers advice on publishing careers; supports and publicises women's achievements and successes. Each year WiP presents 2 awards: the Pandora Award is given in recognition of significant personal contributions to women in publishing, and the New Venture Award is presented to a recent venture which reflects the interests and concerns of women or minority groups in the 21st century. Founded 1979.

Virginia Woolf Society of Great Britain

Details Stuart N. Clarke, Fairhaven, Charnleys Lane, Banks, Southport PR9 8HJ
tel (01903) 764655 *fax* (01903) 764655
email stuart.n.clarke@btinternet.com
website www.virginiawoolfsociety.co.uk
Membership £16 p.a., £21 overseas

Acts as a forum for British admirers of Virginia Woolf (1882–1941) to meet, correspond and share their enjoyment of her work. Publishes the *Virginia Woolf Bulletin*. Founded 1998.

The Wordsworth Trust

Dove Cottage, Grasmere, Cumbria LA22 9SH
tel (015394) 35544 *fax* (015394) 35748
email enquiries@wordsworth.org.uk
website www.wordsworth.org.uk
Membership Officer Sally Robinson
Membership £20 p.a. (individual)

To preserve and enhance Dove Cottage, the Collection and the historic environment of Town End for future generations; to give people of all ages the chance to fulfill their creative potential; to develop the education and lifelong learning programmes for the benefit of the widest possible audience. Founded 1891.

Worshipful Company of Stationers and Newspaper Makers

Stationers' Hall, London EC4M 7DD
tel 020-7248 2934 *fax* 020-7489 1975
Master Christopher H. McKane, *Clerk* William J. Alden MBE DL

One of the Livery Companies of the City of London. Connected with the printing, publishing, bookselling, newspaper and allied trades. Founded 1403.

Writers Advice Centre for Children's Books

16 Smith's Yard, London SW18 4HR
tel 07979 905353
email info@writersadvice.co.uk
website www.writersadvice.co.uk
Managing Editor Louise Jordan

Dedicated to helping new and published children's writers by offering both editorial advice and tips on how to get published. The Centre also runs an online children's writing correspondence course plus a mentoring scheme for both ideas and manuscripts. Founded 1994.

Writers Guild of America, East Inc. (WGAE)

555 West 57 Street, Suite 1230, New York, NY 10019, USA
tel 212-767-7800
President Michael Winship
Membership 1.5% of covered earnings

Represents writers in screen, TV and new media for collective bargaining. It provides member services including pension and health, as well as educational and professional activities. Founded 1954.

Writers Guild of America, West Inc. (WGA)

7000 West 3rd Street, Los Angeles, CA 90048, USA
tel 323-951-4000 *fax* 323-782-4800
website www.wga.org
Membership $2500 initiation, $25 quarterly, 1.5% of income annually

Union representing and servicing 9000 writers in film, broadcast, cable and multimedia industries for purposes of collective bargaining, contract administration and other services, and functions to protect and advance the economic, professional and creative interests of writers. Monthly publication, *Written By*, available by subscription. Founded 1933.

Writers Guild of Canada

366 Adelaide Street West, Suite 401, Toronto, Ontario M5V 1R9, Canada
tel 416-979-7907
toll free 1-800-567-9974 *fax* 416-979-9273
email info@wgc.ca
website www.wgc.ca
Executive Director Maureen Parker
Membership One-off initiation fee of $350 + $150 p.a. + 2% of fees earned in the Guild's jurisdiction

Represents over 1800 professional writers of film, TV, animation, radio, documentary and digital media. Negotiates and administers collective agreements with independent producers and broadcasters. The Guild also publishes *Canadian Screenwriter* magazine.

The Writers' Guild of Great Britain – see page 544

Writers in Oxford

email wio_membership@yahoo.co.uk
website www.writersinoxford.org
Chair Frank Egerton
Membership £25 p.a.

Promotes discussion and social meetings among published writers in and around Oxfordshire. Activities include: topical lunches and dinners, where subjects important to the writer are discussed; outings and parties. Publishes a regular newsletter, *The Oxford Writer*. Founded 1992.

The Writers' Union of Canada

90 Richmond Street East, Suite 200, Toronto, Ontario M5C 1P1
tel 416-703-8982 *fax* 416-504-9090
email info@writersunion.ca
website www.writersunion.ca

Yachting Journalists' Association

36 Church Lane, Lymington, Hants SO41 3RB
tel (01590) 673894
email secretary@yja.co.uk
website www.yja.co.uk
Membership £40 p.a.

Aims to further the interests of yachting, sail and power, and yachting journalism. Members vote annually for the Yachtsman of the Year and the Young Sailor of the Year Award. Founded 1969.

The Yorkshire Dialect Society

Publicity & Information Officer 19 Prospect Close, Swinefleet, East Yorkshire DN14 8FB
website www.yorkshiredialectsociety.org.uk
Membership £10 p.a.

Aims to encourage interest in: dialect speech, the writing of dialect verse, prose and drama; the publication and circulation of dialect literature; the study of the origins and the history of dialect and kindred subjects. Organises meetings; publishes *Transactions* (annual) and *The Summer Bulletin* free to members; list of other publications on request. Founded 1897.

Francis Brett Young Society

Secretary Mrs J. Hadley, 92 Gower Road, Halesowen, West Midlands B62 9BT
tel 0121-422 8969
website www.fbysociety.co.uk
Membership £7 p.a., £70 p.a. life

Aims to provide opportunities for members to meet, correspond, and to share the enjoyment of the works of Francis Brett Young (1884–1954). Publishes a journal (2 p.a.). Founded 1979.

Prizes and awards

This list provides details of many British prizes, competitions and awards for writers and artists, including grants, bursaries and fellowships, as well as details of major international prizes. See page 782 for a quick reference to its contents.

Academi Cardiff International Poetry Competition

Details/entry form Academi, Mount Stuart House, Mount Stuart Square, Cardiff, Wales CF10 5FQ
tel 029-2047 2266
email post@academi.org
website www.academi.org
Chief Executive Peter Finch

Eight prizes awarded annually for unpublished poetry written in English and not a translation of another author's work (1st £5000; 2nd £500; 3rd £250; plus 5 prizes of £50). For submission details, contact Academi or send sae. Closing date: January.

J.R. Ackerley Prize for Autobiography

English PEN, 60 Farringdon Road, London EC1R 3GA
tel 020-7324 2535
email enquiries@englishpen.org
website www.englishpen.org

An annual prize of £1000 is given for an outstanding work of literary autobiography written in English and published during the previous year by an author of British nationality or an author who has been a long-term resident in the UK. No submissions: books are nominated by the judges only. Founded 1982.

The Aeon Award

8 Bachelor's Walk, Dublin 1, Republic of Ireland
email fraslaw@yahoo.co.uk
website www.albedo1.com

An annual contest for short fiction (up to 8000 words) in genres of fantasy, science fiction, horror or anything in between. A grand prize of €1000 will be awarded to the winner (2nd prize €200, 3rd €100) plus publication in Albedo One. The contest runs for 4 rounds throughout the year; deadlines are 31 March (1st round), 30 June (2nd round), 30 September (3rd round) and 30 November (final round). At the end of each round the best story submissions will be shortlisted for the award. Online and postal submissions accepted. Entry fee: €7.

The Hans Christian Andersen Awards

Details International Board on Books for Young People, Nonnenweg 12, Postfach, CH–4003 Basel, Switzerland
tel (61) 272 29 17 *fax* (61) 272 27 57
email ibby@ibby.org, liz.page@ibby.org
website www.ibby.org

The Medals are awarded every 2 years to a living author and an illustrator who by the outstanding value of their work are judged to have made a lasting contribution to literature for children and young people.

Arts Council England

Details The Literature Dept, Arts Council England, 14 Great Peter Street, London SW1P 3NQ
tel 0845-300 6200 *textphone* 020-7973 6564
fax (0161) 934 4426
email enquiries@artscouncil.org.uk
website www.artscouncil.org.uk

Arts Council England presents national prizes rewarding creative talent in literature. These are awarded through the Council's flexible funds and are not necessarily open to application: the David Cohen Prize for Literature, and the Independent Foreign Fiction Prize.

Arts Council England, London

Details Literature Administrator, Arts Council England, London, 2 Pear Tree Court, London EC1R 0DS
tel 0845-300 6200 *fax* 020-7973 6590
website www.artscouncil.org.uk
Contact Gemma Seltzer

Arts Council England, London, is the regional office for the Capital, covering 33 boroughs and the City of London. Grants are available through the 'Grants for the arts' scheme throughout the year to support a variety of literature projects, concentrating particularly on:

- original works of poetry and literary fiction and professional development for individual writers, including writers of children's books;
- touring and live literature;
- small independent literary publishers; and
- literary translation into English.

Contact the Literature Unit for more information, or see website for an application form.

The Arts Council/An Chomhairle Ealaíon

Details 70 Merrion Square, Dublin 2, Republic of Ireland
tel (01) 618 0200 *fax* (01) 676 1302
email artistsservices@artscouncil.ie
website www.artscouncil.ie

Publishes a guide for individuals and organisations to Arts Council bursaries, awards and schemes. It is also available online. This guide is called *Supports for Artists.*

Arts Council YouWriteOn.com Book Awards

tel (07948) 392634
email edward@youwriteon.com
website www.youwriteon.com

Arts Council-funded publishing awards for new fiction writers with editors for Random House and Orion giving free professional critiques for the highest rated new writers' opening chapters and short stories on the YouWriteOn books charts each month. The highest rated writers of the year are published, 3 in each of the adult and children's categories, through YouWriteOn's free publishing service for writers. The novel publishing awards total £1000. Writers can enter at any time throughout the year by joining the website. Closing date: 31 December each year. Founded 2005.

Arvon Foundation International Poetry Competition

Details Arvon Foundation Poetry Competition, Free Word Centre, 60 Farringdon Road, London EC1R 3GA
tel 020-7324 2554
email london@arvonfoundation.org
website www.arvonfoundation.org

A biennial competition for previously unpublished poems written in English. First prize £5,000, plus at least £5,000 in other cash prizes. Next competition: spring 2012. Founded 1980.

The Asham Award

Details The Administrator, Asham Literary Endowment Trust, c/o Town Hall, High Street, Lewes, East Sussex BN7 2QS
website www.ashamaward.com

A biennial national short story competition for women writers over the age of 18 and currently resident in the UK, who have not previously had a novel or anthology of their work published. Twelve winning writers will receive cash prizes (sponsored by Much Ado Books of Alfriston, East Sussex) and their stories will be published in an anthology alongside specially commissioned established writers. The next Award is scheduled to be launched in early summer 2012. The results of the 2010 Award will be announced in the summer of 2011. See website or send sae for details. Founded 1996.

The Australian/Vogel Literary Award

PO Box 8500, St Leonards, NSW 1590, Australia
website www.allenandunwin.com

An annual award of $20,000 for a chosen unpublished work of fiction, Australian history or biography. Entrants must be under 35 years of age on the closing date and must normally be residents of Australia. The MS must be between 30,000 and 100,000 words and must be an original work entirely by the entrant written in English. It cannot be under consideration to any publisher or award. See website for details. Closing date: 31 May. Founded 1980.

Authors' Club Awards

Details Stella Kane, Secretary, Authors' Club, The Arts Club, 40 Dover Street, London W1S 4NP
tel 020-7499 8581 *fax* 020-7409 0913
email stella@theartsclub.co.uk
website www.theartsclub.co.uk

Best First Novel Award

An award of £1000 is presented at a dinner held in the Club, to the author of the most promising first novel published in the UK during each year. Entries are accepted during August and must be full-length novels – short stories are not eligible. Instituted by Lawrence Meynell in 1954.

Sir Banister Fletcher Award for Authors' Club

The late Sir Banister Fletcher, a former President of both the Authors' Club and the Royal Institute of British Architects instituted an annual prize 'for the book on architecture or the arts most deserving'. Books eligible are those written by British authors or those resident in the UK and published under a British imprint and should be submitted by the end of May of the year after publication. The prize of £1000 is awarded by the Authors' Club during October. First awarded in 1954.

Dolman Best Travel Book Award

An award of £2500 is presented annually for the best literary travel book (no guidebooks accepted). Instituted by William Dolman in 2005.

The Authors' Contingency Fund

Details Sarah Baxter, The Society of Authors, 84 Drayton Gardens, London SW10 9SB
tel 020-7373 6642 *fax* 020-7373 5768
email info@societyofauthors.org
website www.societyofauthors.org

This fund makes modest grants to established, published authors who find themselves in sudden financial difficulty. Apply for guidelines and application form.

The Authors' Foundation

The Society of Authors, 84 Drayton Gardens, London SW10 9SB
tel 020-7373 6642
email info@societyofauthors.org
website www.societyofauthors.org

Grants are available to novelists, poets and writers of non-fiction who are published authors working on their next book. The aim is to provide funding (in addition to a proper advance) for research, travel or other necessary expenditure. Closing dates: 30 April and 30 September. Download or send sae for an information sheet. Founded in 1984 to mark the centenary of the Society of Authors.

BAFTA (British Academy of Film and Television Arts)

Chief Executive Amanda Berry, 195 Piccadilly, London W1J 9LN
tel 020-7734 0022 *fax* 020-7292 5868
email info@bafta.org
website www.bafta.org

The pre-eminent organisation in the UK for film, TV and video games, recognising and promoting the achievement and endeavour of industry practitioners. BAFTA Awards are awarded annually by members to their peers in recognition of their skills and expertise. Founded 1947.

Bardd Plant Cymru (Children's Poet Laureate)

Welsh Books Council, Castell Brychan, Aberystwyth, Ceredigion SY23 2JB
tel (01970) 624151 *fax* (01970) 625385
email castellbrychan@wbc.org.uk
website www.cllc.org.uk

The main aim is to raise the profile of poetry amongst children and to encourage them to compose and enjoy poetry. Twm Morys is Bardd Plant Cymru 2009–10. During his term of office he will visit schools as well as helping children to create poetry through electronic workshops. Established by S4C, the Welsh Books Council, Urdd Gobaith Cymru, and the Academi.

Verity Bargate Award

Details Writers' Centre Assistant, Soho Theatre, 21 Dean Street, London W1D 3NE
email writers@sohotheatre.com
website www.sohotheatre.com

This biennial award is made to the writer of a new and previously unperformed full-length play. It is the only award in the UK designed specifically for emerging writers and is only eligible to playwrights with less than 3 professional credits. The winner receives: a prize of £5000, a residency at the Soho Theatre, and the prize-winning play may be professionally produced by the Soho Theatre Company. Next award: 2011 (tbc). See website for information on workshops and events associated with the award. Established 1982.

BBC FOUR Samuel Johnson Prize for Non-Fiction

Colman Getty Consultancy, 28 Windmill Street, London W1T 2JJ
tel 020-7631 2666 *fax* 020-7631 2699
email hannah@colmangetty.co.uk
website www.samueljohnsonprize.co.uk
Contact Hannah Blake

This annual prize is the biggest non-fiction prize in the UK and is worth £20,000. Closing date: mid January. The winner is announced in June. Sponsored by BBC FOUR. Founded 1999.

BBC National Short Story Award

Booktrust, Book House, 45 East Hill, London SW18 2QZ
tel 020-8516 2973
email claire.shanahan@booktrust.org.uk
website www.theshortstory.org.uk
Contact Claire Shanahan

Part of the Booktrust campaign to celebrate short stories, a prize of £15,000 is awarded for the winning story, plus £3000 for the runner-up and £500 for the 3 other shortlisted stories. One of the most prestigious prizes for a single short story, the BBC NSSA, run in partnership with Booktrust, is celebrating its fifth year. Closing date: June. Winner announced: end November. Founded 2005.

The David Berry Prize

Administrative Secretary of the Royal Historical Society, University College London, Gower Street, London WC1E 6BT
tel 020-7387 7532 *fax* 020-7387 7532
email royalhistsoc@ucl.ac.uk
website www.royalhistoricalsociety.org

Candidates may select any subject dealing with Scottish history. Value of prize: £250. Closing date: 31 December each year.

Besterman/McColvin Medals – see The ISG (CILIP)/BookData Reference Awards

The Bisto Book of the Year Awards – see The CBI Bisto Book of the Year Awards

The K. Blundell Trust

K. Blundell Trust, The Society of Authors, 84 Drayton Gardens, London SW10 9SB
tel 020-7373 6642
email info@societyofauthors.org
website www.societyofauthors.org

Awards are given to published writers under the age of 40 to assist them with their next book. The author's work must 'contribute to the greater understanding of existing social and economic organisation', but fiction is not excluded. Closing dates: 30 April and 30 September. Download from the website or send sae for an information sheet.

The Boardman Tasker Prize

Details Maggie Body, Pound House, Llangennith, Swansea SA3 1JQ
email margaretbody@lineone.net
website www.boardmantasker.co.uk

This annual prize of £3000 is given for a work of fiction, non-fiction or poetry, the central theme of which is concerned with the mountain environment. Authors of any nationality are eligible but the work must be published or distributed in the UK. Entries from publishers only. Founded 1983.

The Bollinger Everyman Wodehouse Prize for Comic Fiction

Submissions Katy MacMillan-Scott,
Colman Getty Consultancy, 28 Windmill Street,
London W1T 2JJ
tel 020-7631 2666 *fax* 020-7631 2699
email katy@colmangetty.co.uk

UK's only prize for comic fiction. Awarded to the most original comic novel of the previous 12 months. The winner receives a case of Bollinger Special Cuvée, a jeroboam of Bollinger, a complete set of the Everyman Wodehouse collection and a rare breed pig named after the winning novel. Eligible novels are published in the UK between 1 May and 30 April. The winner is announced at the Guardian Hay Festival in late May/early June. Closing date: late February; shortlist announced in mid-April. Launched in 2000 on the 25th anniversary of the death of P.G. Wodehouse.

The Book to Talk About

email worldbookday@blueyonder.co.uk
website www.worldbookday.com,
www.spread-the-word.org.uk

Online voting determines the winning title, which is announced on World Book Day. The winning author will receive a £5000 prize. See World Book Day (page 623).

The *Bookseller* Retail Awards

The Bookseller, 5th Floor, Endeavour House,
189 Shaftesbury Avenue, London WC2H 8TJ
tel 020-7420 6120 *fax* 020-7420 6103
website www.thebookseller.com
Contact Louise Lenzi, Events Manager

Awards to celebrate the fine art of selling books, open to retailers in the UK and the Republic of Ireland. Closing date: May.

Booktrust Early Years Awards

Booktrust, Book House, 45 East Hill,
London SW18 2QZ
tel 020-8516 2973
email prizes@booktrust.org.uk
website www.booktrust.org.uk
Contact Claire Shanahan

The winners of each of 3 categories, Baby Book Award, Pre-School Award and Best Emerging Illustrator, each receive a cheque for £2000 and a crystal award. The winner of the Best Emerging Illustrator also receives a specially commissioned piece of artwork from a well-known children's illustrator. The winning publishers receive a commemorative award. Closing date: end April. Established 1999 (formerly the Sainsbury's Baby Book Award).

The Booktrust Teenage Prize

Booktrust, Book House, 45 East Hill,
London SW18 2QZ
tel 020-8516 2973
email prizes@booktrust.org.uk
website www.booktrust.org.uk
Contact Claire Shanahan

The first annual national book prize to recognise and celebrate the best in young adult fiction. The author of the best book for teenagers receives £2500 and is chosen from a shortlist of 6–8. The prize is open to works of fiction and non-fiction (including short story collections, graphic novels, poetry and reference books), aimed at teenagers aged 13–16 and written in English by a citizen of the UK, or an author resident in the UK. The work must be published between 1 July and the following 30 June by a UK publisher. Closing date: early March. Established 2003.

Alfred Bradley Bursary Award

Details BBC Writersroom, 379–381 Euston Road,
London NW1 3AU
tel 0161-244 4253
website www.bbc.co.uk/writersroom

This biennial development opportunity is awarded to a writer or writers resident now or in the past in the North of England. The scheme also allows for a group of finalists to receive small bursaries and develop ideas for radio drama commissions. Next closing date: February 2011 (tbc). Founded 1992.

The Branford Boase Award

Library and Information HQ, 5–6 Moorside Place,
Moorside Road, Winchester SO23 7FZ
tel (01962) 826658
email anne.marley@tiscali.co.uk
website www.branfordboaseaward.org.uk

An annual award of £1000 is made to a first-time writer of a full-length children's novel (age 7+) published in the preceding year; the editor is also recognised. Its aim is to encourage new writers for children and to recognise the role of perceptive editors in developing new talent. The Award was set up in memory of the outstanding children's writer Henrietta Branford and the gifted editor and publisher Wendy Boase who both died in 1999. Closing date for nominations: end of December each year. Founded 2000.

The Bridport Prize

Details The Bridport Prize, PO Box 6910,
Dorset DT6 9BQ
tel (01308) 428333
email frances@bridportprize.org.uk
website www.bridportprize.org.uk

Annual prizes are awarded for poetry and short stories (1st £5000, 2nd £1000, 3rd £500) in both categories, and £1000 for short short stories (under 250 words). Entries should be in English, original work, typed or clearly written, and never published, read on radio/TV/stage. Winning stories are read by a leading London literary agent, without obligation, and an anthology of winning entries is published each autumn. Top 4 poems are submitted to the Forward Poetry Prizes and top 13 eligible stories are submitted to the National Short Story Award and *The Sunday Times* Short Story Prize. Send sae for entry form or enter online. Closing date: 30 June each year.

Bristol Festival of Ideas Book Prize

Details Bristol Festival of Ideas,
Bristol Cultural Development Partnership,
Leigh Court, Abbots Leigh, Bristol BS8 3RA
email ideas@gwebusinesswest.co.uk
website www.ideasfestival.co.uk

A prize of £10,000 is awarded to the book which is judged to present new, important and challenging ideas, which is rigorously argued, and which is engaging and accessible. A book of ideas may be a work of fiction or non-fiction, poetry or prose. Submission deadline: October. Awarded in association with Arts & Business and Blackwell bookshops. Founded 2008.

British Academy Medals and Prizes

The British Academy, 10 Carlton House Terrace,
London SW1Y 5AH
tel 020-7969 5200 *fax* 020-7969 5300
email secretary@britac.ac.uk
website www.britac.ac.uk

A number of medals and prizes are awarded for outstanding work in various fields of the humanities on the recommendation of specialist committees: Burkitt Medal for Biblical Studies; Derek Allen Prize (made annually in turn for musicology, numismatics and Celtic studies); Sir Israel Gollancz Prize (for English studies); Grahame Clark Medal for Prehistoric Archaeology; Kenyon Medal for Classical Studies; Rose Mary Crawshay Prize (for English literature); Serena Medal for Italian Studies; Leverhulme Medal and Prize; The John Coles Medal for Landscape Archaeology, The Wiley Prize in Psychology.

British Book Awards – see Galaxy British Book Awards

British Czech & Slovak Association Writing Competition

24 Ferndale, Tunbridge Wells, Kent TN2 3NS
tel (01892) 543206
email prize@bcsa.co.uk
website www.bcsa.co.uk
Contact BCSA Prize Administrator

Annual competition (1st prize: £300; 2nd prize: £100) for fiction or non-fiction on the theme of the links between Britain and the Czech and Slovak Republics, at any time in their history, or society in transition in those republics since the Velvet Revolution in 1989. Winning entries published in 'British Czech & Slovak Review'. Length: 2000 words max. Closing date: 30 June each year. Established 2002.

British Press Awards

Press Gazette, Brunel House,
55–57 North Wharf Road, London W2 1AL
tel 020-7936 6433
email pged@pressgazette.co.uk
website www.britishpressawards.com,
www.pressgazette.co.uk

Annual awards for British journalism judged by more than 80 respected, influential judges as well as representatives from all the national newspaper groups. Closing date: mid January.

The Caine Prize for African Writing

Details Nick Elam, Administrator,
The Menier Gallery, Menier Chocolate Factory,
51 Southwark Street, London SE5 1RU
tel 020-7378 6234 *fax* 020-7378 6235
email info@caineprize.com
website www.caineprize.com

An annual award of £10,000 for a short story published in English (may be a translation into English) by an African writer in the 5 years before the closing date, and not previously submitted. Indicative length 3000–10,000 words. Submissions only by publishers. Closing date: 31 January each year. Founded 1999.

Carnegie Medal – see The CILIP Carnegie and Kate Greenaway Awards

The CBI Bisto Book of the Year Awards

Details The Administrator, Children's Books Ireland,
17 North Great Georges Street, Dublin 1,
Republic of Ireland
tel (01) 8727475 *fax* (01) 8727476
email info@childrensbooksireland.ie
website www.childrensbooksireland.ie

Awards made annually to authors and illustrators born or resident in Ireland, open to books written in Irish or English. Closing date: December 2011 for work published between 1 January and 31 December 2010. Winners announced in May. Sponsored by Bisto (Premier Foods). Founded 1990.

The CBI Bisto Book of the Year Award

An award of €10,000 is presented to the overall winner (text and/or illustration).

The CBI Bisto Honour Awards

An award of €2000 each is given for fiction and illustration.

The CBI Bisto Eilís Dillon Award

An award of €3000 is presented to an author for a first children's book.

Cheltenham Illustration Awards

The CIA, University of Gloucestershire,
Pittville Studios, Cheltenham, Glos. GL52 3JG
tel (01242) 714953
email cheltillustrationawards@glos.ac.uk
website www.cheltenham-illustration-awards.com

Awards for student and new illustrators. The winning entries together with a selection of runners up will have their work exhibited and also published as a full colour annual. The Emerging Talent First Prize is £1500 and the runner up will receive £750, and both will have their work showcased. Artwork must be supplied as jpegs on CD-Rom; up to 5 entries per person. Entry fee: £10 per entry. See website for details.

The Children's Laureate

Booktrust, Book House, 45 East Hill,
London SW18 2QZ
tel 020-8516 2977
email childrenslaureate@booktrust.org.uk
website www.childrenslaureate.org.uk

The role of Children's Laureate, which has a bursary of £15,000, is awarded once every 2 years to honour a writer or illustrator of children's books to celebrate outstanding achievement. It highlights the importance of exceptional children's book creators in developing the readers of tomorrow. Children's Laureates: Anthony Browne (2009–11), Michael Rosen (2007–9), Jacqueline Wilson (2005–7), Michael Morpurgo (2003–5), Anne Fine (2001–3), Quentin Blake (1999–2001). Founded 1998.

Cholmondeley Awards

Awards Secretary, The Society of Authors,
84 Drayton Gardens, London SW10 9SB
tel 020-7373 6642
email info@societyofauthors.org
website www.societyofauthors.org

These honorary awards are to recognise the achievement and distinction of individual poets. Submissions are not accepted. Total value of awards about £8000. Established by the then Dowager Marchioness of Cholmondeley in 1965.

The CILIP Carnegie and Kate Greenaway Awards

CILIP, 7 Ridgmount Street, London WC1E 7AE
tel 020-7255 0650 *fax* 020-7255 0651
email ckg@cilip.org.uk
website www.carnegiegreenaway.org.uk

Recommendations for the following 2 awards are invited from members of CILIP (the Chartered Institute of Library and Information Professionals), who are asked to submit a preliminary list of not more than 2 titles for each award, accompanied by a 50-word appraisal justifying the recommendation of each book. The awards are selected by the Youth Libraries Group of CILIP.

Carnegie Medal

Awarded annually for an outstanding book for children (fiction or non-fiction) written in English and first published in the UK during the preceding year or co-published elsewhere within a 3-month time lapse.

Kate Greenaway Medal

Awarded annually for an outstanding illustrated book for children first published in the UK during the preceding year or co-published elsewhere within a 3-month time lapse. Books intended for older as well as younger children are included, and reproduction will be taken into account. The Colin Mears Award (£5000) is awarded annually to the winner of the Kate Greenaway Medal.

Arthur C. Clarke Award

website www.clarkeaward.com

An annual award of £2010 plus engraved bookend is given for the best science fiction novel with first UK publication during the previous calendar year. Titles are submitted by publishers. Founded 1985.

The David Cohen Prize for Literature

Details The Literature Dept, Arts Council England,
14 Great Peter Street, London SW1P 3NQ
tel (0845) 300 6200
website www.artscouncil.org.uk

This biennial prize marks a lifetime's literary achievement. The winner receives £40,000 plus an additional £12,500 to support a young writer.

Commonwealth Writers Prize

Details Commonwealth Foundation,
Marlborough House, Pall Mall, London SW1Y 5HY
tel 020-7930 3783 *fax* 020-7839 8157
website www.commonwealthfoundation.com

This annual award is for the best work of fiction in English by a citizen of the Commonwealth published in the year prior to the award. Prizes are given for the Best Book and Best First Book, valued at £1000, in each of the 4 Commonwealth Regions: Africa, Canada and the Caribbean, Europe and South Asia, South East Asia and the South Pacific. From these regions, the overall winner for the Best Book and Best First Book prizes are chosen. A prize of £10,000 is awarded for overall best book and £5000 is awarded to the overall best first published book. Organised and funded by the Commonwealth Foundation with the support of the Macquarie Foundation in 2 of the 4 regions. Established 1987.

The Duff Cooper Prize

Details Artemis Cooper, 54 St Maur Road,
London SW6 4DP
tel 020-7736 3729
website www.theduffcooperprize.org

An annual prize for a literary work in the field of biography, history, politics or poetry published in

English or French and submitted by a recognised publisher during the previous 12 months. The prize of £4000 comes from a Trust Fund established by the friends and admirers of Duff Cooper, 1st Viscount Norwich (1890–1954) after his death.

Cordon d'Or – Gold Ribbon Culinary Academy Awards

PO Box 40868, St Petersburg, FL 33743–0868, USA
website www.goldribboncookery.com
Contact Noreen Kinney, President

Awards for authors, writers, journalists, photographers, newsletters, websites, cookbooks and culinary literature. Overall winner receives $1000. See website for details. Founded 2003.

Costa Book Awards

(formerly the Whitbread Book Awards)
Details The Booksellers Association, Minster House, 272 Vauxhall Bridge Road, London SW1V 1BA
tel 020-7802 0802 *fax* 020-7802 0803
email info@costabookawards.com
website www.costabookawards.co.uk
Contact Naomi Gane

The awards celebrate and promote the most enjoyable contemporary British writing. Judged in 2 stages and offering a total of £50,000 prize money, there are 5 categories: Novel, First Novel, Biography, Poetry and Children's. They are judged by a panel of 3 judges and the winner in each category receives £5000. Nine final judges then choose the Costa Book of the Year from the 5 category winners. The overall winner receives £25,000. Writers must be resident in Great Britain or Ireland for 3 or more years. Submissions must be received from publishers. Closing date: end of June.

The Rose Mary Crawshay Prizes

The British Academy, 10 Carlton House Terrace, London SW1Y 5AH
tel 020-7969 5200 *fax* 020-7969 5300
email secretary@britac.ac.uk
website www.britac.ac.uk

One or more prizes are awarded each year to women of any nationality who, in the judgement of the Council of the British Academy, have written or published within the 3 calendar years immediately preceding the date of the award an historical or critical work of sufficient value on any subject connected with English literature, preference being given to a work regarding Byron, Shelley or Keats. Founded 1888.

The John D. Criticos Prize

Coordinator Michael Moschos, The London Hellenic Society, The Hellenic Centre, 16–18 Paddington Street, London W1U 5AS
tel (+30) 210-729-8494
email msmoschos@yahoo.com
website www.criticosprize.org

A prize of £10,000 will be awarded to an artist, writer or researcher for an original work on Hellenic culture. Areas of particular interest are archaeology, art, art history, history and literature. No application necessary: send 2 copies of book plus covering letter. Closing date: 31 January. Founded 1996.

CWA Awards

email secretary@thecwa.co.uk
website www.thecwa.co.uk

Awards for crime writing: the Cartier Diamond Dagger; the New Blood Dagger; the CWA International Dagger; the CWA Gold Dagger for Fiction; the Gold Dagger for Non-Fiction; the CWA Ellis Peters Historical Award; the CWA Short Story Award; the Debut Dagger; the Ian Fleming Steel Dagger, the Dagger in the Library. See website for details.

The Rhys Davies Trust

Details Prof Meic Stephens, The Secretary, The Rhys Davies Trust, 10 Heol Don, Whitchurch, Cardiff CF14 2AU
tel 029-2062 3359

The Trust aims to foster Welsh writing in English and offers financial assistance to English-language literary projects in Wales, directly or in association with other bodies.

Deutsche Börse Photography Prize

The Photographers' Gallery, 16–18 Ramillies Street, London W1F 7LW
tel 0845-262 1618
email info@photonet.org.uk
website www.photonet.org.uk

Aims to reward a living photographer, of any nationality, who has made the most significant contribution to the medium of photography during the past year (1st prize £30,000; 3 runners up will each receive £3000). Photographers will be nominated for a significant exhibition that took place or publication that was published in Europe during that time, and 4 shortlisted photographers will be selected and invited to present their work in an exhibition at the Gallery. Founded in 1996 by the Photographers' Gallery.

The Dundee International Book Prize

Details 5th Floor, Tower Building, Perth Road, Dundee DD1 4HN
tel (01382) 384413 *fax* (01382) 434650
email book.prize@dundeecity.gov.uk
website www.dundeebookprize.com

A biennial prize (£10,000 and the chance of publication by Polygon) awarded for an unpublished novel. Next award: 2011. Founded 1996.

Edge Hill Short Story Prize

Edge Hill University, St Helens Road, Ormskirk, Lancs. L39 4QP

tel (01695) 584121
email ailsa.cox@edgehill.ac.uk
website www.edgehill.ac.uk/shortstory
Contact Ailsa Cox

This prize is awarded annually by Edge Hill University for excellence in a published single author short story collection. The winner will receive £5000 and a Readers' Choice prize of £1000 is awarded to a writer from the shortlist. Publishers are entitled to submit 2 collections published during the preceding year. Authors must be born or normally resident in the British Isles (including Ireland). Deadline: 1 March. Sponsored by Blackwell.

The T.S. Eliot Prize

Applications Poetry Book Society, 4th Floor, 2 Tavistock Place, London WC1H 9RA
tel 020-7833 9247
email info@poetrybooks.co.uk
website www.poetrybooks.co.uk, www.poetrybookshoponline.com

An annual prize of £15,000, with £1,000 for each of the ten shortlisted poets, is awarded by the Poetry Book Society to the best collection of new poetry published in the UK or the Republic of Ireland during the year. Submissions are invited from publishers in the summer. The prize money is provided by Valerie Eliot. The prize is accompanied by a Shadowing Scheme for schools, which enables students to read the best new poetry and shadow the judges. Founded 1993.

The Desmond Elliott Prize

Emma Manderson, Administrator, The Desmond Elliott Charitable Trust, 84 Godolphin Road, London W12 8JW
tel 020-8222 6580
email ema.manderson@googlemail.com
website www.desmondelliottprize.org

An annual prize for a first novel written in English and published in the UK. Worth £10,000 to the winner, the prize is named after the literary agent and publisher, Desmond Elliott, who died in 2003. Qualities the judges will be looking for are: a debut novel of depth and breadth with a compelling narrative, original and arresting characters, vividly written and confidently realised. Founded 2007.

Encore Award

Details Awards Secretary, The Society of Authors, 84 Drayton Gardens, London SW10 9SB
tel 020-7373 6642
email info@societyofauthors.org
website www.societyofauthors.org

This biennial award of £10,000 is for the best second novel of the previous two years. The work submitted must be: a novel by one author who has had one (and only one) novel published previously, and in the English language, first published in the UK. Entries should be submitted by the publisher. Closing date: 30 November.

The European Publishers Award

Details Dewi Lewis Publishing, 8 Broomfield Road, Heaton Moor, Stockport SK4 4ND
tel 0161-442 9450 *fax* 0161-442 9450
email mail@dewilewispublishing.com
website www.dewilewispublishing.com

Annual competition for the best set of photographs suitable for publication as a book. All photographic material must be completed and unpublished in book form and be original. Projects conceived as anthologies are not acceptable. Copyright must belong to the photographer. See website for details. Founded 1994.

The Geoffrey Faber Memorial Prize

An annual prize of £1000 is awarded in alternate years for a volume of verse and for a volume of prose fiction, first published originally in the UK during the 2 years preceding the year in which the award is given which is, in the opinion of the judges, of the greatest literary merit. Eligible writers must be not more than 40 years old at the date of publication of the book and a citizen of the UK and Colonies, of any other Commonwealth state or of the Republic of Ireland. The 3 judges are reviewers of poetry or fiction who are nominated each year by the literary editors of newspapers and magazines which regularly publish such reviews. Faber and Faber invite nominations from reviewers and literary editors. No submissions for the prize are to be made. Established in 1963 by Faber and Faber Ltd, as a memorial to the founder and first Chairman of the firm.

The Alfred Fagon Award

The Alfred Fagon Award, c/o Talawa Theatre Company, 53–55 East Road, London N1 6AH
email info@alfredfagonaward.co.uk
website www.alfredfagonaward.co.uk

An annual award of £5000 for the best new play (which need not have been produced) for the theatre in English. TV and radio plays and film scripts will not be considered. Only writers from the Caribbean or with Caribbean antecedence and who are resident in the UK are eligible. Applicants should submit 2 copies of their play plus sae for return of their script and a CV which includes details of the writer's Caribbean connection. Closing date: end August. Founded 1997.

The Eleanor Farjeon Award

website www.childrensbookcircle.org.uk

An annual award may be given to an individual or an organisation. Librarians, authors, publishers, teachers, reviewers and others who have given exceptional service to the children's book industry are eligible for nomination. It was instituted in 1965 by the Children's Book Circle (page 559) for distinguished services to children's books and named after the much-loved children's writer Eleanor Farjeon.

Financial Times and Goldman Sachs Business Book of the Year Award

email bookaward@ft.com
website www.ft.com/bookaward

To identify the book that provides the most compelling and enjoyable insight into modern business issues, including management, finance and economics. Books that have appeared for the first time in English between 31 October and 1 November of the following year are eligible. Submissions should come via the publisher. The winner will receive £30,000 and 5 other shortlisted authors will win £5000 each. Closing date: end of June.

Fish Short Story Prize, One Page Prize, and Poetry Prize

Contact Clem Cairns, Fish Publishing, Durrus, Bantry, Bantry, Co. Cork, Republic of Ireland
email info@fishpublishing.com
website www.fishpublishing.com

International literary prizes set up to publish and encourage new writers. The best ten or more from each competition are published in the annual Fish Anthology in July.

• Fish Short Story Prize: €3000 first, second €300 and a week at Anam Cara Writers and Artists' Retreat in West Cork. Entry €20 for 5000 words or less. Closing date 30 November. Results 17 March. *Hon. Patrons* Roddy Doyle, Colum McCann, Dermot Healy. Established 1994.
• Fish One Page Prize: €1000. Closing date 20 March. Results 30 April. €12 entry for stories up to 300 words.
• Fish Poetry Prize: €1000. Closing date 30 March. Results 30 April. €12 entry for poems up to 200 words.
• The Fish Critique service is available all year for help with short fiction and poetry, while the Editorial Consultancy is for writers requiring help with longer work. See website for details.

The Paul Foot Award

tel 020-7590 8909
email margot.weale@midaspr.co.uk
website www.private-eye.co.uk
Contact Margot Weale

An award to honour campaigning journalism in the UK, in memory of revered investigative journalist Paul Foot. Submissions will be accepted for material that has been published in a newspaper, magazine or online between 1 September and 31 August each year. No broadcast material is eligible. Individual journalists, teams of journalists or entire publications may enter and entries will be considered for anything from single pieces to entire campaigns. The overall winner will be awarded £5000, with the 5 runners up each receiving £1000. See website for downloadable application form. Closing date: September. Sponsored by *Private Eye* and the *Guardian*.

E.M. Forster Award

American Academy of Arts and Letters, 633 West 155th Street, New York, NY 10032, USA
tel 212-368-5900
website www.artsandletters.org

The distinguished English author, E.M. Forster, bequeathed the American publication rights and royalties of his posthumous novel *Maurice* to Christopher Isherwood, who transferred them to the American Academy of Arts and Letters, for the establishment of an E.M. Forster Award, currently $20,000, to be given annually to a British or Irish writer for a stay in the USA. Applications for this award are not accepted.

Forward Prizes for Poetry

Details Forward Poetry Prize Administrator, Colman Getty Consultancy, 28 Windmill Street, London W1T 2JJ
tel 020-7631 2666 *fax* 020-7631 2699
email pr@colmangetty.co.uk

3 prizes are awarded annually:

• The Forward Prize for best collection published between 1 October and 30 September (£10,000);
• The Felix Dennis Prize for best first collection published between 1 October and 30 September (£5000); and
• The Forward Prize for best single poem in memory of Michael Donaghy, published but not as part of a collection between 1 May and 30 April (£1000).

All poems entered are also considered for inclusion in the *Forward Book of Poetry*, an annual anthology. Entries must be submitted by book publishers and editors of newspapers, periodicals and magazines in the UK and Eire. Entries from individual poets of their unpublished or self-published work will not be accepted. Established 1992.

Miles Franklin Literary Award

Details Cauz Group Pty Ltd, PO Box 229, Pymble BC, NSW 2073, Australia
tel (02) 9928 1552
email trustawards@cauzgroup.com.au
website www.trust.com.au

This annual award of $42,000 is for a novel or play first published in the preceding year, which presents Australian life in any of its phases. More than one entry may be submitted by each author. Biographies, collections of short stories or children's books are not eligible. Closing date: 2nd Friday in December. Founded 1954.

Galaxy British Book Awards

Details Merric Davidson, PO Box 60, Cranbrook, Kent TN17 2ZR

tel (01580) 212041
email nibbies@mdla.co.uk
website www.britishbookawards.com

Referred to as the 'Nibbies' and presented annually, major categories include: Author of the Year (biography, crime thriller, popular fiction, non-fiction, etc), Children's Book of the Year. Sponsored by Galaxy. Founded 1989.

The Lionel Gelber Prize

Details Prize Manager, The Lionel Gelber Prize, c/o Munk Centre for International Studies, University of Toronto, 1 Devonshire Place, Toronto, Ontario M5S 3K7, Canada
tel 416-946 8901 *fax* 416-946 8915
email gelberprize.munk@utoronto.ca
website www.utoronto.ca/mcis/gelber

This international prize is awarded annually in Canada to the author of the year's most outstanding work of non-fiction in the field of international relations. Submissions must be published in English or in English translation. Books must be submitted by the publisher. Full eligibility details are on website. Established 1989.

Gladstone History Book Prize

Submissions Administrative Secretary, Royal Historical Society, University College London, Gower Street, London WC1E 6BT
tel 020-7387 7532
email royalhistsoc@ucl.ac.uk
website www.royalhistsoc.org/grants.htm

An annual award (value £1000) for a history book. The book must:
• be on any historical subject which is not primarily related to British history;
• be its author's first solely written history book;
• have been published in English during the calendar year of 2010 by a scholar normally resident in the UK;
• be an original and scholarly work of historical research.

One non-returnable copy of an eligible book should be submitted before 31 December. Should the book be shortlisted, 2 further copies will be required.

Kate Greenaway Medal – see The CILIP Carnegie and Kate Greenaway Awards

The Eric Gregory Trust Fund

Awards Secretary, The Society of Authors, 84 Drayton Gardens, London SW10 9SB
tel 020-7373 6642
email info@societyofauthors.org
website www.societyofauthors.org

A number of substantial awards are made annually for the encouragement of young poets who can show that they are likely to benefit from an opportunity to give more time to writing. An eligible candidate must:
• be a British subject by birth, but not a national of Eire or any of the British dominions or colonies, and be ordinarily resident in the UK or Northern Ireland;
• be under the age of 30 on 31 March in the year of the Award (i.e. the year following submission).
Download or send sae for entry form. Closing date, 31 October.

Griffin Poetry Prize

The Griffin Trust for Excellence in Poetry, 363 Parkridge Crescent, Oakville, Ontario L6M 1A8
tel 905-618 0420
email info@griffinpoetryprize.com
website www.griffinpoetryprize.com

Two annual prizes of Can.$50,000 will be awarded for collections of poetry published in English during the preceding year. One prize will go to a living Canadian poet, the other to a living poet from any country. Collections of poetry translated into English from other languages are also eligible and will be assessed for their literary quality in English. Submissions only from publishers. Closing date: 31 December. Founded 2000.

The Guardian Children's Fiction Prize

tel 020-3353 2000
email books@guardian.co.uk

The *Guardian's* annual prize of £1500 is for a work of fiction for children over 8 (no picture books) published by a British or Commonwealth writer. The winning book is chosen by the Children's Book Editor together with a team of 3–4 authors of children's books.

The Guardian First Book Award

Contact Claire Armitstead
tel 020-3353 2000
email books@guardian.co.uk
Submissions Literary Editor, The Guardian, Kings Place, 90 York Way, London N1 9GU

Open to first-time authors published in English in the UK across all genres of writing, the award will recognise and reward new writing by honouring an author's first book. The winner will receive £10,000 plus an advertising package within the *Guardian* and the *Observer*. Publishers may submit up to 3 titles per imprint with publication dates between January and December each year. Closing date: late July.

The Guardian Research Fellowship

Details Academic Administrator, The Guardian Research Fellowship, Nuffield College, Oxford OX1 1NF
tel (01865) 278542 *fax* (01865) 278666
email academic.administrator@nuffield.oxford.ac.uk

A biennial Fellowship to be held for one year at Nuffield College, Oxford, to research or study any project related to the experience of working in the media. It is hoped that the Fellow will produce a book or substantial piece of written work. The Fellow will be asked to give the *Guardian* lecture following the end of their Fellowship. The Fellowship is open to people working in newspapers, TV, the internet or other media. Advertised: October 2011. Founded 1987.

Hawthornden Fellowships

The Director, International Retreat for Writers, Hawthornden Castle, Lasswade, Midlothian EH18 1EG
tel 0131-440 2180 *fax* 0131-440 1989

Applications are invited from novelists, poets, dramatists and other creative writers whose work has already been published by reputable or recognised presses. Four-week fellowships are offered to those working on a current project. Translators may also apply. Application forms are available from January for Fellowships awarded in the following year. Deadline for applications 30 June.

The Hawthornden Prize

c/o Director, Hawthornden Retreat for Writers, Hawthornden Castle, Lasswade, Midlothian, Scotland EH18 1EG

This prize of £10,000 is awarded annually to the author of what, in the opinion of the Committee, is the best work of imaginative literature published during the preceding calendar year by a British author. Books do not have to be specially submitted.

Francis Head Bequest

Details Sarah Baxter, The Society of Authors, 84 Drayton Gardens, London SW10 9SB
tel 020-7373 6642 *fax* 020-7373 5768
email info@societyofauthors.org
website www.societyofauthors.org

This fund provides grants to published British authors over the age of 35 who need financial help during a period of illness, disablement or temporary financial crisis. Apply for guidelines and application form.

The Felicia Hemans Prize for Lyrical Poetry

Submissions Ms Karen Banks, Faculty Manager, The Felicia Hemans Prize for Lyrical Poetry, Faculty of Arts, The University of Liverpool, 3rd Floor, The Foundation Building, Brownlow Hill, Liverpool L69 7ZX
tel 0151-795 0424
email Karen.Banks@liverpool.ac.uk

This annual prize of books or money, open to past and present members and students of the University of Liverpool only, is awarded for a lyrical poem, the subject of which may be chosen by the competitor. Only one poem, either published or unpublished, may be submitted. The prize shall not be awarded more than once to the same competitor. Poems, endorsed 'Hemans Prize', must be submitted by 1 May.

Hessell-Tiltman Prize

English PEN, 60 Farringdon Road, London EC1R 3GA
tel 020-7324 2535
email enquiries@englishpen.org
website www.englishpen.org

An annual prize made possible by a bequest to the PEN Literary Foundation of £100,000 from PEN member Marjorie Hessell-Tiltman. Each year the prize is awarded to a non-fiction work of high literary merit covering any historical period until the end of the Second World War. Submissions are not accepted. Founded 2002.

William Hill Sports Book of the Year Award

Details Graham Sharpe, William Hill Organisation, Greenside House, 50 Station Road, London N22 4TP
tel 07899 798885
website www.williamhillmedia.com

This award is given annually in November for a book with a sporting theme (record books and listings excluded). The title must be in the English language, and published for the first time in the UK during the relevant calendar year. Total value of prize is £23,000, including £20,000 in cash. An award for the best cover design has total value of £1000. Founded 1989.

The Calvin and Rose G. Hoffman Memorial Prize for Distinguished Publication on Christopher Marlowe

Applications The Bursar, The King's School, Canterbury, Kent CT1 2ES
tel (01227) 595544 *fax* (01227) 595589

This annual prize of around £7000 is awarded to the best unpublished work that examines the life and works of Christopher Marlowe and the relationship between the works of Marlowe and Shakespeare. Closing date: 1 September.

L. Ron Hubbard's Writers and Illustrators of the Future Contests

Administrator Andrea Grant-Webb, PO Box 218, East Grinstead, West Sussex RH19 4GH

Aims to encourage new and aspiring writers and illustrators of science fiction and fantasy. In addition to the quarterly prizes there is an annual prize of £2500 for each contest. All 24 winners are invited to the annual L. Ron Hubbard Achievement Awards, which include a series of writers' and illustrators' workshops, and their work is published in an anthology. Write for an entry form.

Writers of the Future Contest

Entrants should submit a short story of up to 10,000 words or a novelette of less than 17,000 words. Prizes of £600 (1st), £450 (2nd) and £300 (3rd) are awarded each quarter. Founded 1984.

Illustrators of the Future Contest

Entrants should submit 3 b&w illustrations on different themes. Three prizes of £300 are awarded each quarter. Founded 1988.

The Ted Hughes Award for New Work in Poetry

Competition Organiser, The Poetry Society, 22 Betterton Street, London WC2H 9BX
tel 020-7420 9880 *fax* 020-7240 4818
email info@poetrysociety.org.uk
website www.poetrysociety.org.uk

An annual award of £5000 for a living UK poet, working in any form, who has made the most exciting contribution to poetry over the year. Funded by Carol Ann Duffy with the honorarium which the Poet Laureate traditionally receives from H.M. the Queen.

Images – The Best of British Contemporary Illustration

Details Association of Illustrators, 2nd Floor, Back Building, 150 Curtain Road, London EC2A 3AT
tel 020-7613 4328 *fax* 020-7613 4417
email info@theaoi.com
website www.theaoi.com, www.aoiimages.com
Contact Images Co-ordinator

Illustrators are invited to submit work for possible inclusion in the *Images* annual, a jury-selected showcase of the best of contemporary British illustration, which is distributed to 4000 commissioners. Selected work forms the Images exhibition, which tours the UK. UK illustrators or illustrators working for UK clients are all eligible. See website for entry details in the Spring. Founded 1975.

The Imison Award

Details/entry form The Secretary, The Broadcasting Committee, The Society of Authors, 84 Drayton Gardens, London SW10 9SB
tel 020-7373 6642 *fax* 020-7373 5768
email info@societyofauthors.org
website www.societyofauthors.org

This annual prize of £1500 is awarded to any new writer of radio drama first transmitted within the UK during the previous year by a writer new to radio. Founded 1995.

Independent Foreign Fiction Prize

Details Arts Council England, 14 Great Peter Street, London SW1P 3NQ
website www.artscouncil.org.uk/iffp

In collaboration with the *Independent* newspaper and Champagne Taittinger, Arts Council England awards the £10,000 prize to honour a great work of fiction by a living author which has been translated into English from any other language and published in the UK. The prize is shared equally between the author and the translator.

Insight Guides Travel Photography Prize

Details APA Publications (UK) Ltd, 58 Borough High Street, London SE1 1XF
tel 020-7403 0284 *fax* 020-7403 0290
website www.insightguides.com

An annual competition open to amateur and professional photographers resident in the UK (theme to be announced). First prize is a commission to photograph for an *Insight Guide* worth £3000. Closing date: September. Founded 2000.

International IMPAC Dublin Literary Award

Details Ms Cathy McKenna, The International IMPAC Dublin Literary Award, Dublin City Library & Archive, 138–144 Pearse Street, Dublin 2, Republic of Ireland
tel 353 1 674 4802 *fax* 353 1 674 4879
email literaryaward@dublincity.ie
website www.impacdublinaward.ie

This award is the largest and most international prize of its kind. Administered by Dublin City Public Libraries, nominations are made by libraries in capital and major cities throughout the world. Titles are nominated solely on the basis of 'high literary merit' and books may be written in any language.

The prize is €100,000 which is awarded to the author if the book is written in English. If the winning book is in English translation, the author receives €75,000 and the translator €25,000. The Award, an initiative of Dublin City Council, is a partnership between Dublin City Council, the Municipal Government of Dublin City, and IMPAC. Established 1996.

International Playwriting Festival

Details/entry form Festival Administrator, Warehouse Theatre, Dingwall Road, Croydon CR0 2NF
tel 020-8681 1257 *fax* 020-8688 6699
email info@warehousetheatre.co.uk
website www.warehousetheatre.co.uk

An annual competition for full-length unperformed plays. Selected plays are showcased during the festival weekend in November. Plays are also presented in Italy at the leading Italian playwriting festival Premio Candoni Arta Terme. Entries are welcome from all parts of the world. Send sae for further details or visit the website. Deadline for entries: 30 June. See also page 618. Founded 1985.

The ISG (CILIP)/BookData Reference Awards

7 Ridgemount Street, London WC1E 7AE
tel 020-7255 0500 *fax* 020-7255 0501

email ISGRefAwards@cilip.org.uk
website www.cilip.org.uk

The Besterman/McColvin Medals

Awarded annually for outstanding works of reference published in the UK during the preceding year. There are 2 categories, one for electronic formats and one for printed works. Recommendations are invited from Members of CILIP (the Chartered Institute of Library and Information Professionals), publishers and others, who are asked to submit a preliminary list of not more than 3 titles via the website. Winners receive a cash prize, a certificate and a prestigious golden medal.

The Walford Award

Awarded annually to an individual who has made a sustained and continued contribution to the science and art of British bibliography over a period of years. The bibliographer's work can encompass effort in the history, classification and description of printed, written, audiovisual and machine-readable materials. Recommendations may be made for the work of a living person or persons, or for an organisation. The award can be made to a British bibliographer or to a person or organisation working in the UK. The winner receives a cash prize.

Jewish Quarterly – Wingate Literary Prizes

Details Marion Cohen, Haskell House,
152 West End Lane, London NW6 1SD
tel 020-8444 0253
email editorial@jewishquarterly.org
website www.jewishquarterly.org

Annual prize of £4000 awarded for a work of fiction or non-fiction which best stimulate an interest in and awareness of themes of Jewish concern among a wider reading public. Founded 1977.

Samuel Johnson Prize for Non-Fiction – see BBC FOUR Samuel Johnson Prize for Non-Fiction

Kent and Sussex Poetry Society Open Poetry Competition

Submissions The Organiser, 13 Ruscombe Close, Southborough, Tunbridge Wells, Kent TN4 0SG

This competition is open to all unpublished poems, no longer than 40 lines in length. Prizes: 1st £800, 2nd £300, 3rd £150, 4th 4 at £75. Closing date: 31 January. Entries should include an entry fee of £4 per poem, the author's name and address and a list of poems submitted. Founded 1985.

Kerry Group Irish Fiction Award

Details Writers' Week, 24 The Square, Listowel, Co. Kerry, Republic of Ireland
tel (353) 6821074 *fax* (353) 6822893
email info@writersweek.ie
website www.writersweek.ie

An annual award of €15,000 for a published work of fiction by an Irish author. No entry fee. Submit 8 copies. Closing date: February.

Kraszna-Krausz Awards

Details Jenny Boyce, Administrator,
Kraszna-Krausz Foundation, 37 Eton Avenue,
London N12 0BD
tel 020-7100 2523
email awards@kraszna-krausz.org.uk
website www.kraszna-krausz.org.uk

Awards totalling over £10,000 are made each year for the best photography book and best moving image book published in English. Entries to be submitted by publishers only. The Foundation is also open to applications for grants (UK only) concerned with the literature of photography and the moving image. Instituted in 1985.

Leverhulme Research Fellowships

The Leverhulme Trust, 1 Pemberton Row,
London EC4A 3BG
tel 020-7042 9862
email jcater@leverhulme.ac.uk
website www.leverhulme.ac.uk

The Leverhulme Trustees offer annually approximately 90 fellowships to individuals in aid of original research – not for study of any sort. These awards are not available as replacement for past support from other sources. Applications will be considered in all subject areas. Total monies for one 2010 fellowship was £45,000. Completed application forms must be received by mid November 2010 for 2011 awards. Founded 1933.

Literary Review Grand Poetry Prize

44 Lexington Street, London W1F 0LW
tel 020-7437 9392
email editorial@literaryreview.co.uk
website www.literaryreview.co.uk

Runs a competition each month for poems on a given subject which rhyme, scan and make sense and are no more than 24 lines. Monthly prizes of £300 and £150 are awarded. The Grand Prize of £5000 is awarded to the best of these each year. Closing date: September. Founded 1990.

John Llewellyn Rhys Prize

Booktrust, Book House, 45 East Hill,
London SW18 2QZ
tel 020-8516 2973
email query@booktrust.org.uk
website www.booktrust.org.uk
Contact Claire Shanahan

This annual prize of £5000 (plus £500 to each shortlisted author) is made to an author aged 35 or under for a work of literature (fiction, poetry, drama, non-fiction, etc) which has been published in the UK during the calendar year of the prize. The author must be a UK or Commonwealth national. The prize was inaugurated in memory of the writer John Llewellyn Rhys who died in World War II, by his widow Jane Oliver. Established 1942.

London Press Club Awards

Details London Press Club, St Bride Institute, 14 Bride Lane, Fleet Street, London EC4Y 8EQ
tel 020-7353 7086 *fax* 020-7353 7087
email info@londonpressclub.co.uk
website www.londonpressclub.co.uk

Business Journalist of the Year, Consumer Affairs Journalist of the Year, Daily Newspaper of the Year, Sunday Newspaper of the Year and Broadcasting Journalist of the Year.

Scoop of the Year Award

Chosen by a panel of senior editors, this annual award of a bronze statuette is given for the reporting scoop of the year, appearing in a newspaper. Founded 1990.

Edgar Wallace Award

Chosen by a panel of senior editors, this annual award of a silver inkstand is given for outstanding writing or reporting by a journalist. Founded 1990.

The Elizabeth Longford Grants

Details Awards Secretary, The Society of Authors, 84 Drayton Gardens, London SW10 9SB
tel 020-7373 6642 *fax* 020-7373 5768
email info@societyofauthors.org
website www.societyofauthors.org

Grants of £2500 are made payable to 2 historical biographers each year whose publisher's advance is insufficient to cover the costs of research involved. Send sae for information. Sponsored by Flora Fraser and Peter Soros. Entry dates: 30 April and 30 September.

The Elizabeth Longford Prize for Historical Biography

Details Awards Secretary, The Society of Authors, 84 Drayton Gardens, London SW10 9SB
tel 020-7373 6642 *fax* 020-7373 5768
email info@societyofauthors.org
website www.societyofauthors.org

A prize of £5000 is awarded annually for a historical biography published in the year preceding the prize. No unsolicited submissions. Established in 2003 in affectionate memory of Elizabeth Longford, the acclaimed biographer, and sponsored by Flora Fraser and Peter Soros.

The Sir William Lyons Award

Details The Guild of Motoring Writers' Secretariat, 40 Baring Road, Bournemouth BH6 4DT
tel (01202) 422424
email generalsec@gomw.co.uk
website www.guildofmotoringwriters.co.uk

Sponsored by Jaguar Cars in memory of Sir William Lyons, founder and president of Jaguar Cars, this annual award – trophy, £2000 and two years' probationary membership of The Guild of Motoring Writers – was set up to encourage young people to foster interest in motoring and the motor industry through automotive journalism. Open to any person of British nationality resident in the UK aged 17–23 years, the entry consists of writing two essays and an interview with the Award Committee.

The McKitterick Prize

Details Awards Secretary, The Society of Authors, 84 Drayton Gardens, London SW10 9SB
tel 020-7373 6642
email info@societyofauthors.org
website www.societyofauthors.org

This annual award of £4000 is open to first published novels (excluding works for children) and unpublished typescripts by authors over the age of 40. Closing date: 31 October. Endowed by the late Tom McKitterick. Download or send sae for entry form.

The Franco-British Society's Enid McLeod Literary Prize

Details Executive Secretary, Franco–British Society, 2 Dovedale Studios, 465 Battersea Park Road, London SW11 4LR
tel 020-7924 3511
email francobritish@googlemail.com
website www.francobritishsociety.org.uk

This annual prize of £500 is given for a full-length work of literature which contributes most to Franco–British understanding. It must be first published in the UK between 1 January and 31 December, and written in English by a citizen of the UK, British Commonwealth or the Republic of Ireland. Closing date: 31 December.

Bryan MacMahon Short Story Award

Writers' Week, 24 The Square, Listowel, Co. Kerry, Republic of Ireland
tel (353) 6821074 *fax* (353) 6822893
email info@writersweek.ie
website www.writersweek.ie

An annual award for the best short story (up to 3000 words) on any subject. Prize: €2000. Entry fee: €10. No entry form required. Closing date: February. Founded 1971.

The Macmillan Prize for Children's Picture Book Illustration

Applications Macmillan Children's Books, 20 New Wharf Road, London N1 9RR

tel 020-7014 6124
email children@macmillan.co.uk

Three prizes are awarded annually for unpublished children's book illustrations by art students in higher education establishments in the UK. Prizes: £1000 (1st), £500 (2nd) and £250 (3rd).

Man Asian Literary Prize

email info@manasianliteraryprize.org
website www.manasianliteraryprize.org
Contact Prize Manager, Marina Ma

An annual award (US$10,000) for an unpublished Asian novel in English. Submissions accepted online between December and March. See website for details. Supported financially by the Man Group plc. Founded 2007.

The Man Booker International Prize

Colman Getty Consultancy, 28 Windmill Street, London W1T 2JJ
tel 020-7631 2666
email info@colmangetty.co.uk
website www.themanbookerprize.com

A prize of £60,000 to complement the annual Man Booker Prize by recognising one writer's achievement in continued creativity, development and overall contribution to world fiction. It will be awarded once every 2 years to a living author who has published fiction either originally in English, or generally available in translation in the English language.

The Man Booker International Prize will echo and reinforce the annual Man Booker Prize for Fiction in that literary excellence will be its sole focus. The winner will be announced in early summer. Sponsored by Man Group plc.

The Man Booker Prize

Colman Getty Consultancy, 28 Windmill Street, London W1T 2JJ
tel 020-7631 2666
email info@colmangetty.co.uk
website www.themanbookerprize.com

This annual prize for fiction of £50,000, including £2500 to each of 6 shortlisted authors, is awarded to the best novel published each year. It is open to novels written in English by citizens of the British Commonwealth and Republic of Ireland and published for the first time in the UK by a British publisher, although previous publication of a book outside the UK does not disqualify it. Entries only from UK publishers who may each submit not more than 2 novels with scheduled publication dates between 1 October of the previous year and 30 September of the current year, but the judges may also ask for other eligible novels to be submitted to them. In addition, publishers may submit eligible titles by authors who have been shortlisted in the past 10 years or won the Man Booker Prize previously. Sponsored by Man Group plc.

The Manchester Fiction Prize 2011

Contact James Draper, Project Manager, The Manchester Writing School, Dept of English, Manchester Metropolitan University (MMU), All Saints Building, All Saints, Manchester M15 6BH
tel 0161-247 1787
email j.draper@mmu.ac.uk
website www.manchesterwritingcompetition.co.uk

This competition is designed to celebrate the best new writing from around the world. An award of £10,000 will be made to the overall winner, or winners, as well as a bursary for study at MMU to an entrant aged 18–25 as part of the Manchester Young Writer of the Year Award. Alternates between poetry and fiction on an annual basis. See website for further information.

The Manchester Poetry Prize 2012

Contact James Draper, Project Manager, The Manchester Writing School, Dept of English, Manchester Metropolitan University, All Saints Building, All Saints, Manchester M15 6BH
tel 0161-247 1787
email j.draper@mmu.ac.uk
website www.manchesterwritingcompetition.co.uk

The Manchester Writing School, the home of creative writing within the Department of English at Manchester Metropolitan University (MMU), hosts this competition which is designed to attract and celebrate the best new writing from around the world. An award of £10,000 will be made to the overall winner, or winners, as well as a bursary for study at MMU to an entrant aged 18–25 as part of the Manchester Young Writer of the Year Award. The competition will alternate between poetry and fiction on an annual basis. See website for further information.

The Michael Marks Awards for Poetry Pamphlets

Details Hilary Davidson, Awards Administrator, The Michael Marks Awards for Poetry Pamphlets, Poetry Book Society, 4th Floor, 2 Tavistock Place, London WC1H 9RA
tel 020-7833 9247
email pamphlets@poetrybooks.co.uk
website www.bl.uk/poetrypamphlets

The Poetry Book Society and the British Library inaugurated these awards in 2009 to raise the profile of poetry pamphlets and also recognise and reward the enormous contribution that poets and their pamphlet publishers make to the poetry world in the UK. There are 2 awards worth £5000 each:

- The Michael Marks Poetry Award will recognise a single outstanding work of poetry published in pamphlet form in the UK during 2010. This award is open to self-published work.
- The Michael Marks Publishers' Award will recognise an outstanding UK publisher of poetry in pamphlet form, based on their 2010 publishing programme.

See website for full details and submission guidelines. Supported by the Michael Marks Charitable Trust. Deadline: March.

Marsh Award for Children's Literature in Translation

Administered by The English-Speaking Union, Dartmouth House, 37 Charles Street, London W1J 5ED
tel 020-7529 1550
email esu@esu.org
website www.esu.org
Contact Katharine Plummer

This biennial award of £2000 is given to the translator of a book for children (aged 4–16) from a foreign language into English and published in the UK by a British publisher. Electronic books, and encyclopedias and other reference books, are not eligible. Next award: January 2011.

Marsh Biography Award

Administered by The English-Speaking Union, Dartmouth House, 37 Charles Street, London W1J 5ED
tel 020-7529 1550 *fax* 020-7495 6108
email gillian_parker@esu.org

This major national biography prize of £5000 plus a trophy is presented every 2 years. Entries must be serious biographies written by British authors and published in the UK. Next awards: October 2011. Founded 1985–6.

The John Masefield Memorial Trust

Details Sarah Baxter, The Society of Authors, 84 Drayton Gardens, London SW10 9SB
tel 020-7373 6642 *fax* 020-7373 5768
email info@societyofauthors.org
website www.societyofauthors.org

This trust makes occasional grants to professional poets who find themselves with sudden financial problems. Apply for guidelines and application form.

The Somerset Maugham Awards

Details Awards Secretary, The Society of Authors, 84 Drayton Gardens, London SW10 9SB
tel 020-7373 6642
email info@societyofauthors.org
website www.societyofauthors.org

These annual awards, totalling about £10,000, are for writers under the age of 35. Candidates must be British subjects by birth, and ordinarily resident in the UK or Northern Ireland. Poetry, fiction, non-fiction, belles-lettres or philosophy, but not dramatic works, are eligible. Entries should be submitted by the publisher. Closing date: 30 November.

Mind Book of the Year

Details Anny Brackx, Information Department, Granta House, 15–19 Broadway, London E15 4BQ
tel 020-8519 2122 *fax* 020-8522 1725

This £1500 award is given to the author of any book (fiction or non-fiction) published in the UK in the current year which outstandingly furthers public understanding of the prevention, causes, treatment or experience of mental health problems. Entries by 30 November. Administered by Mind, the National Association for Mental Health. Inaugurated in memory of Sir Allen Lane in 1981.

Kathleen Mitchell Award

Clare Stanford, Level 4, 35 Clarence Street, Sydney, NSW 2000, Australia
tel (02) 8295 8596
email awards@trust.com.au
website www.trust.com.au

A biennial literary award ($7500) for authors 30 years of age, or under, for the advancement and improvement of Australian literature. Eligible authors must be born in Australia or the UK and must have been resident in Australia for the 12 months preceeding close of entries, or be a naturalised Australian. Founded 1996.

Montana New Zealand Book Awards

Details c/o Booksellers New Zealand, PO Box 25033, Panama Street, Wellington 6146, New Zealand
tel (04) 472 1908 *fax* (04) 472 1912
email info@booksellers.co.nz
website www.montananzbookawards.co.nz

Annual awards to celebrate excellence in, and provide recognition for, the best books written and illustrated by New Zealanders each year. Awards are presented in 8 categories. The winner of each category wins $5000. Category winners are considered for the Montana Medal for Non-Fiction or the Montana Medal for Fiction or Poetry. Medal winners each receive an additional $10,000. Eligible authors' and illustrators' books must have been published in New Zealand in the calendar year preceding the awards year. Closing date: December. Founded 1996.

Sheridan Morley Prize for the Best Theatre Biography

Administered by Oberon Books Ltd, 521 Caledonian Road, London N7 9RH
tel 020-7607 3637 *fax* 020-7607 3629
email info@oberonbooks.com
Contact The Administrator

In memory of the late critic Sheridan Morley, a cash prize of £2000 will be awarded to the winner chosen by the panel of judges chaired by critic, broadcaster and biographaer Ruth Leon. Awarded in the spring of each year for biographies published in English in the preceding calendar year. Launched 2008.

The Melissa Nathan Award for Comedy Romance

Melissa Nathan Foundation & Award, PO Box 56923, London N10 3YU

email information@melissanathan.com
website www.melissanathan.com

Set up in memory of Melissa Nathan, who died in 2006, this award of £5000 honours the criteria that Melissa drew up herself: she wanted to encourage and reward writers who can combine in a novel the magical, life-enhancing elements of humour and love. Books published between January and December each year are eligible.

National Poetry Competition

Competition Organiser, The Poetry Society, 22 Betterton Street, London WC2H 9BX
tel 020-7420 9880 *fax* 020-7240 4818
email info@poetrysociety.org.uk
website www.poetrysociety.org.uk

One of the UK's major annual open poetry competitions. Accepts poems up to 40 lines long on any theme (previously unpublished and written in English). Prizes: 1st £5000, 2nd £2000, 3rd £1000, plus 7 commendations of £100. Judged by a panel of 3 leading poets. For rules and an entry form send an sae or visit website. Closing date: 31 October each year. Founded 1978.

The New Writer Prose and Poetry Prizes

Details PO Box 60, Cranbrook, Kent TN17 2ZR
tel (01580) 212626
email admin@thenewwriter.com
website www.thenewwriter.com

Short stories up to 4000 words, novellas, essays and articles; poets may submit either one or a collection of 6–10 previously unpublished poems. Total prize money £2000 as well as publication for the prize-winners in the *New Writer* magazine. Entry fees: £4 per poem; £12 for a collection of 6–10 poems. Send for an entry form or visit the website for information about the short fiction and non-fiction sections. Closing date: 30 November each year. Founded 1997.

New Zealand Post Book Awards for Children and Young Adults

Details c/o Booksellers New Zealand, PO Box 25033, Panama Street, Wellington 6146, New Zealand
tel (04) 472 1908 *fax* (04) 472 1912
email info@booksellers.co.nz
website www.bookseller.co.uk/awards

Annual awards to celebrate excellence in, and provide recognition for, the best books for children and young adults published annually in New Zealand. Awards are presented in 4 categories: non-fiction, picture book, junior fiction and young adult fiction. The winner of each category wins $7500. One category winner is chosen as the *New Zealand Post* Book of the Year and receives an additional $7500. Eligible authors' and illustrators' books must have been published in New Zealand in the calendar year preceding the awards year. Closing date: December. Founded 1990.

Nielsen Gold and Platinum Book Awards

tel (01483) 712200 *fax* (01483) 712201
email marketing.book@nielsen.com

The awards are a recognition of sales purchases of a book by the general public. Eligible books are those that reach 500,000 unit sales (Gold) or 1,000,000 unit sales (Platinum) as measured by Nielsen BookScan within a 5-year period. All qualifying titles may receive an award funded for the author by their publisher. Founded 2000.

The Nobel Prize in Literature

Awarding authority Swedish Academy, Box 2118, S–10313 Stockholm, Sweden
tel (08) 555 12554 *fax* (08) 555 12549
email sekretariat@svenskaakademien.se
website www.svenskaakademien.se

This is one of the awards stipulated in the will of the late Alfred Nobel, the Swedish scientist who invented dynamite. No direct application for a prize will be taken into consideration. For authors writing in English it was bestowed upon Rudyard Kipling in 1907, W.B. Yeats in 1923, George Bernard Shaw in 1925, Sinclair Lewis in 1930, John Galsworthy in 1932, Eugene O'Neill in 1936, Pearl Buck in 1938, T.S. Eliot in 1948, William Faulkner in 1949, Bertrand Russell in 1950, Sir Winston Churchill in 1953, Ernest Hemingway in 1954, John Steinbeck in 1962, Samuel Beckett in 1969, Patrick White in 1973, Saul Bellow in 1976, William Golding in 1983, Wole Soyinka in 1986, Nadine Gordimer in 1991, Derek Walcott in 1992, Toni Morrison in 1993, Seamus Heaney in 1995, V.S. Naipaul in 2001, Harold Pinter in 2005 and Doris Lessing in 2007.

Northern Writers' Awards

Administered by New Writing North, Holy Jesus Hospital, City Road, Newcastle upon Tyne NE1 2AS
tel 0191-233 3850
email office@newwritingnorth.com
website www.newwritingnorth.com
Contact Olivia Mantle

Awards (from £1000 to £5000) are aimed at developing writers at different stages in their careers. A panel of professional writers shortlists and makes awards once a year. Applicants must be resident in the Arts Council England North East region (Northumberland, Tyne & Wear, Durham, Tees Valley). See website for details. Deadline for applications: end January.

The Observer/Jonathan Cape/Comica Graphic Short Story Prize

website www.comicafestival.com

An annual graphic short story competition offering a £1000 cash prize and the chance to see your story printed in the Observer. Founded 2007.

Orange Award for New Writers

Booktrust, Book House, 45 East Hill,
London SW18 2QZ
tel 020-8516 2973
email prizes@booktrust.org.uk
website www.orangeprize.co.uk
Contact Claire Shanahan

This award of £10,000 is awarded annually to recognise emerging female fiction-writing talent published in the UK. The prize will be awarded to a woman for her first work of fiction – a novel, novella or collection of short stories. Women of any age or nationality may be entered providing their first work of fiction is published in the UK between 1 April and the following 31 March. The emphasis of the award is on emerging talent and the evidence of future potential. Established 2005.

Orange Prize for Fiction

Details Booktrust, Book House, 45 East Hill,
London SW18 2QZ
tel 020-8516 2973
email prizes@booktrust.org.uk
website www.orangeprize.co.uk
Contact Claire Shanahan

This award of £30,000, and a statuette known as 'The Bessie', is for a full-length novel written in English by a woman of any nationality and first published in the UK between 1 April and 31 March the following year. Sponsored by Orange PCS. Established 1996.

George Orwell Memorial Prize

5/7 Vernon Yard, Portobello Road,
London W11 2DX
tel (020) 7229 5722
website www.theorwellprize.co.uk

Two prizes of £1000 each are awarded in April each year – one for the best political book, and one for best political journalism, either fiction or non-fiction – of the previous year, giving equal merit to content and good style accessible to the general public. Founded 1993.

Penguin Prize for African Writing

website www.penguinbooks.co.za/african-winners/index.php

A new literary award for writers from the African continent with 2 categories: one each for a previously unpublished full-length work of adult fiction and non-fiction. The prize in each category will be R50,000 and a publishing contract with Penguin Books South Africa, with worldwide distribution via Penguin Group companies. Submissions deadline: end January. See website for further details. Founded 2009.

The Samuel Pepys Award

Details Paul Gray, Haremoor House, Faringdon,
Oxon SN7 8PN
website www.pepys-club.org.uk

A biennial prize is given to a book published in English making the greatest contribution to the understanding of Samuel Pepys, his times, or his contemporaries. The winner receives £2000 and the Robert Latham Medal. Founded by the Samuel Pepys Award Trust in 2003 on the tercentenary of the death of Pepys. Closing date: May 2011.

Charles Pick Fellowship

School of Literature and Creative Writing,
University of East Anglia, Norwich NR4 7TJ
tel (01603) 592286 *fax* (01603) 507728
email charlespickfellowship@uea.ac.uk
website www.uea.ac.uk/lit/awards/pick

An annual fellowship to assist and support the work of a new and unpublished writer of fiction or non-fiction, dedicated to the memory of the distinguished publisher and literary agent, Charles Pick. Writers of any age or nationality are eligible to apply. The award is £10,000 plus free accommodation on UEA campus. Residential: 1 Sept–end Feb. Closing date for applications: 31 January each year. Founded 2002.

The Plough Prize

The Plough Arts Centre, 9–11 Fore Street,
Great Torrington, Devon EX38 8HQ
tel (01805) 624624
website www.theploughprize.co.uk

Entries are invited in 2 categories: Open Poem (up to 40 lines) and Short Poem (up to 10 lines). Both postal and online entry are eligible. See website for rules. Entry fee: £4, 4 poems £14, £3.50 thereafter. Closing date: 30 November; free tick-box critiques will be available to entries that arrive before 30 October.

The Poetry Business Book & Pamphlet Competition

Competition Administrator The Poetry Business,
Bank Street Arts, 32–40 Bank Street, Sheffield S1 2DS
tel 0114-346 3037
email office@poetrybusiness.co.uk
website www.poetrybusiness.co.uk
Directors Peter Sansom, Ann Sansom

An annual award is made for a poetry collection. The judges select up to 5 short collections for publication as pamphlets; on further submission of more poems, one of these will be selected for a full-length collection. To be published under the Poetry Business's Smith/Doorstop imprint. All winners share a cash prize of £1000. Poets over the age of 18 writing in English from anywhere in the world are eligible. Entry fee £20/£25. Founded 1986.

The Corneliu M. Popescu Prize for Poetry in Translation

Competition Organiser, The Poetry Society,
22 Betterton Street, London WC2H 9BX

tel 020-7420 9880 *fax* 020-7240 4818
email info@poetrysociety.org.uk
website www.poetrysociety.org.uk

Awarded biennially by the Poetry Society and the Ratiu Family Charitable Foundation, this award of £1500 rewards a published collection of poetry translated from a European language into English. Founded 2003.

The Portico Prize

Details Miss Emma Marigliano, Librarian, Portico Library, 57 Mosley Street, Manchester M2 3HY
tel 0161-236 6785 *fax* 0161-236 6803
email librarian@theportico.org.uk
website www.theportico.org.uk

This biennial prize is awarded for a published work of fiction or non-fiction, of general interest and literary merit set wholly or mainly in the North of England with prizes for fiction and non-fiction totaling £8000. Next award: 2012. Founded 1985.

Prequel to Cannes Short Film Script Competition

Creative Thoughts Productions Ltd, The Office, 67 Dunyeats Road, Broadstone, Dorset BH18 8AE
tel (01202) 691994
email rosiecreativethoughts@btinternet.com
website www.prequeltocannes.biz, www.prequel.biz, www.sequeltocannes.biz
Contact Rosie Jones

Competition for film scripts. Prizes of £350, £50 and £25 will be awarded to writers of the top 3 scripts by a prestigious film industry judging panel. Scripts will be read by a professional script reader and selected production companies and a one-page script summary on the strengths and opportunities of the script will be supplied. See website for details. Entry fee: £25. Deadline: 30 November. Founded 2009.

Le Prince Maurice Prize

Colman Getty Consultancy, 28 Windmill Street, London W1T 2JJ
tel 020-7631 2666 *fax* 020-7631 2699
email info@colmangetty.co.uk
website www.colmangetty.co.uk
Contact Ruth Cairns

A prize for the best novel that takes as its theme the love between people in any of its myriad forms. It aims to reward not just the highest literary merit but emotional intelligence – writing which comes from the heart as well as the head. The winner receives the Prince Maurice Prize Trophy and an all-expenses paid 2-week writer's retreat at Le Prince Maurice (worth £12,500), a hotel in Mauritius, and the 3 shortlisted authors will be invited to spend a week as guest of the hotel while the judging process takes place. The prize is awarded to an English-speaking writer every second year, alternating with a French-speaking winner. Next English language prize: 2012. Founded 2002.

The V.S. Pritchett Memorial Prize

Details The Royal Society of Literature, Somerset House, Strand, London WC2R 1LA
tel 020-7845 4676 *fax* 020-7845 4679
email info@rslit.org
website www.rslit.org

An annual prize of £1000 is awarded for a previously unpublished short story of up to 5000 words. Entry fee: £5 per story. For entry forms contact the Secretary from mid-November. The writer must be a citizen of the UK or Ireland. Founded 1999.

Prize for New Media Writing

14 Dover Road, Poole BH13 6DZ
email prize@poolelitfest.com
website www.poolelitfest.com
Editor Contact Sue Luminati

In partnership with The Media School at Bournemouth University, the Poole Literary Festival will establish this prize for storytelling (fiction or non-fiction) written specifically for delivery and reading/viewing on a PC or Mac, on the web, or via mobile phone. Deadline for entries: 15 September 2010. See website for details. Founded 2010.

The Peggy Ramsay Foundation

G. Laurence Harbottle, Hanover House, 14 Hanover Square, London W1S 1HP
tel 020-7667 5000 *fax* 020-7667 5100
email laurence.harbottle@harbottle.com
website www.peggyramsayfoundation.org

Grants are made to established writers of stage plays and to theatrical organisations to facilitate new writing for the stage. Awards are made at intervals during each year. A total of approx. £200,000 is expended annually. Founded 1992.

The Red House Children's Book Award

Details Sinead Kromer, 2 Bridge Wood View, Horsforth, Leeds, West Yorkshire LS18 5PE
tel (0113) 258 8910
email info@fcbg.org.uk
website www.redhousechildrensbookaward.co.uk

This award is given annually to authors of works of fiction for children published in the UK. Children participate in the judging of the award. 'Pick of the Year' book list is published in conjunction with the award. Founded in 1980 by the Federation of Children's Book Groups.

Trevor Reese Memorial Prize

Details Institute of Commonwealth Studies, School of Advanced Study, University of London, South Block, Senate House, Malet Street, London WC1E 7HU

tel 020-7862 8844 *fax* 020-7862 8820
email ics@sas.ac.uk
website www.commonwealth.sas.ac.uk/reese.htm

This prize of £1000 is awarded every 2 years to the author of a work which has made a wide-ranging, innovative and scholarly contribution in the broadly defined field of Imperial and Commonwealth History. Next award (for a work published in 2006, 2007 or 2008): December 2012.

Romantic Novel of the Year Award

Details Elizabeth Harris, 6 St Leonard's Close, Watlington OX49 5PQ
tel (01491) 612492
email rnaawardorganiser@hotmail.com
website www.rna-uk.org

This annual award for the best romantic novel of the year is open to both members and non-members of the Romantic Novelists' Association (see page 576. Novels must be published first in the UK between 1 January and 31 December of the year of entry. Four copies of the novel are required. Send sae for entry form and details or visit website.

Joan Hessayon Award

Details Melanie Hilton
email melaniehilton@tiscali.co.uk

For writers previously unpublished in the adult novel field and who are members of the Romantic Novelists' Association's New Writers' Scheme. MSS can be submitted, by members only, until the end of August. All receive a critique. Any MSS subsequently accepted for publication become eligible for the Award.

Romance Prize

See website for details.

Royal Mail Awards for Scottish Children's Books

Scottish Book Trust, Sandeman House, Trunk's Close, 55 High Street, Edinburgh EH1 1SR
tel 0131-524 0160 *fax* 0131-524 0161
email jasmine.fassl@scottishbooktrust.com
website www.scottishbooktrust.com/royalmailawards
Contact Jasmine Fassl, Children's Programme Manager

Awards totalling £14,000 are given to new and established authors of published books in recognition of high standards of writing for children in 3 age group categories: younger children (0–7 years), younger readers (8–11 years) and older readers (12–16 years). A shortlist is drawn up by a panel of children's book experts and then a winner in each category is decided by children and young people by voting for their favourites in book groups in schools and libraries across Scotland. An award of £3000 is made for the winner in each category and £500 for runners-up. Books published in the preceding calendar year are eligible. Authors should be Scottish or resident in Scotland. Guidelines available on request. Closing date: 31 March. Award presented: February. Administered by Scottish Book Trust, in partnership with the Scottish Arts Council.

The Royal Society of Literature Ondaatje Prize

Submissions Paula Johnson, The Royal Society of Literature, Somerset House, Strand, London WC2R 1LA
tel 020-7845 4676 *fax* 020-7845 4679
email paulaj@rsl.org
website www.rslit.org

This annual £10,000 award, administered by the Royal Society of Literature and endowed by Sir Christopher Ondaatje, is awarded to a book of literary merit, fiction, poetry or non-fiction, best evoking the spirit of a place. All entries must be published within the calendar year and should be submitted between 1 September and 1 December. The writer must be a citizen of the UK, Commonwealth or Ireland. See website for further details.

The Royal Society of Literature Jerwood Awards

Submissions Paula Johnson, The Royal Society of Literature, Somerset House, Strand, London WC2R 1LA
tel 020-7845 4676 *fax* 020-7845 4679
email paulaj@rslit.org
website www.rslit.org

Awards offering financial assistance to authors engaged in writing their first major commissioned works of non-fiction. Three awards – one of £10,000 and 2 of £5,000 – will be offered annually to writers working on substantial non-fiction projects. The awards are open to UK and Irish writers and writers who have been resident in the UK for at least 3 years. See website for further details.

The Royal Society Prizes for Science Books

Details The Royal Society, 6–9 Carlton House Terrace, London SW1Y 5AG
tel 020-7451 2500 *fax* 020-7930 2170
email events@royalsociety.org
website www.royalsoc.org/sciencebooks

These annual prizes reward books that make science more accessible to readers of all ages and backgrounds. Prizes of up to a total of £15,000 are awarded in 1 category: General (£10,000) for a book with a general readership. Up to 5 shortlisted authors in each category receive £1000.

Eligible books should be written in English and their first publication in the UK must have been between 1 January and 31 December each year. Seven copies of each entry should be supplied with a fully completed entry form. Publishers may submit any number of books for each prize. Entries may cover any aspect of science and technology but educational textbooks published for professional or specialist audiences are not eligible. Founded 1988.

RSPCA Young Photographer Awards (YPA)

Details Publications Department, RSPCA, Wilberforce Way, Southwater, Horsham, West Sussex RH13 9RS
tel (0300) 123 0455 *fax* (0303) 123 0455
email publications@rspca.org.uk
website www.rspca.org.uk/ypa

Annual awards are made for animal photographs taken by young people in categories: under 12; 12–18 year-olds; Portfolio (5 pictures); Pets Personalities. Prizes: overall winner (photography break, £1,000-worth of Olympus vouchers), age group winners (cameras, photoshoots). Four runners-up in each age group receive a camera. Closing date for entries: September. Sponsored by Warners and Olympus Cameras. Founded 1990.

RTÉ P.J. O'Connor Radio Drama Awards

RTÉ Radio Drama, Dublin 4, Republic of Ireland
tel (01) 2083111 *fax* (01) 2083304
email radiodrama@rte.ie
website www.rte.ie/radio1/drama
Contact Fionnuala Hayes

An annual competition for a 55-minute play open to writers with a maximum of one hour of professionally produced radio drama who are born or living in Ireland. See website for details.

RTÉ Radio 1 Francis MacManus Awards

RTÉ Radio 1 Short Story Competition, RTÉ Radio Centre, Features & Drama Dept, Dublin 4, Republic of Ireland.
tel (01) 2083111
website www.rte.ie/radio1/francismacmanus/
Producer Seamus Hosey

An annual competition for short stories of 1800–2000 words, open to writers born or living in Ireland. First prize €3000. Entries, in Irish or English, should not have been previously published or broadcast. See website for details. Winning entries are broadcast on RTÉ Radio 1.

Runciman Award

Details The Administrator, The Anglo-Hellenic League, 16–18 Paddington Street, London W1U 5AS
tel 020-7486 9410
fax 020-7486 4254 (mark FAO The Anglo-Hellenic League)
email info@anglohellenicleague.org
website www.anglohellenicleague.org

An annual award of £9000 to promote Anglo–Greek understanding and friendship. Works must be wholly or mainly about some aspect of Greece or the world of Hellenism, which has been published in English in any country in its first edition during the previous year. Shortlisted books must be available for purchase to readers in the UK at the time of the award ceremony. No category of writing will be excluded from consideration, e.g. history, literary studies, biography, travel and topography, the arts, architecture, archaeology, the environment, social and political sciences or current affairs; fiction, poetry or drama. Works in translation, with the exception of translations from Greek literature, will not be considered. Final entries: late January; award presented in May/June. Sponsored by the National Bank of Greece and named after Sir Steven Runciman, former Chairman of the Anglo-Hellenic League. Established 1985.

Sainsbury's Baby Book Award – see Booktrust Early Years Awards

The David St John Thomas Charitable Trust Competitions & Awards

The David St John Thomas Charitable Trust, PO Box 6055, Nairn IV12 4YB
tel (01667) 453351 *fax* (01667) 452365
email dsjtcharitynairn@fsmail.net
website www.dstjtcharitabletrust.co.uk
Contact Anne Hill

Two Annual Competitions – The Self-Publishing Awards are open to anyone who has self-published a book during the preceding 18 months with a total award of £2,250 and the Anthology Trophy, an annual award to writers' groups for Anthologies published in the last 18 months. For details of either send a large sae or see the website for details.

The Saltire Society Awards

Details The Saltire Society, 9 Fountain Close, 22 High Street, Edinburgh EH1 1TF
tel 0131-556 1836 *fax* 0131-557 1675
email saltire@saltiresociety.org.uk
website www.saltiresociety.org.uk

Books published between 1 September and 31 August are eligible for the following awards:

Scottish Book of the Year

An annual award of £5000 open to authors of Scottish descent or living in Scotland, or for a book by anyone which deals with a Scottish topic. Established 1982.

Scottish First Book of the Year

An annual award of £1500 open to any author who has not previously published a book. Authors of Scottish descent or living in Scotland, or for any book which deals with the work or life of a Scot or with a Scottish problem, event or situation are eligible. Established 1988.

Scottish Research Book Award

An annual award of £1500 is open to the authors of books which represent a significant body of research; offer new insight or dimension to the subject; and add knowledge and understanding of Scotland and the Scots. Established 1998.

Scottish History Book of the Year

An annual award of £1500 for a work of Scottish historical research. Editions of texts are not eligible. Nominations are invited from professors of Scottish History and editors of historical reviews.

The Kim Scott Walwyn Prize

Booktrust, Book House, 45 East Hill,
London SW18 2QZ
tel 020-8516 2960 *fax* 020-8516 2978
email claire.shanahan@booktrust.org.uk
website www.booktrust.org.uk
Contact Claire Shanahan

This award of £3000 is given to a woman who has made an outstanding contribution in any area of UK book publishing. It commemorates the life and career of Kim Scott Walwyn, publishing director at Oxford University Press until her death in 2002. Applications are made by nominating a woman of any age in any area of book publishing in the UK. Nominations should include a written description of a particular achievement for which they wish the nominee to be recognised, or an aspect of their publishing career which merits recognition. The prize is funded by donations from Kim's family, colleagues, authors and friends. The award will not be awarded in 2010 but will return soon.

Scottish Arts Council

Scottish Arts Council, 12 Manor Place,
Edinburgh EH3 7DD
tel 0131-226 6051
email gavin.wallace@scottisharts.org.uk
website www.scottisharts.org.uk
Contact Dr Gavin Wallace, Head of Literature

A limited number of writers' bursaries – up to £15,000 each – are offered to enable professional writers based in Scotland, including writers for children, to devote more time to writing. Priority is given to writers of fiction and verse and playwrights, but writers of literary non-fiction are also considered. Applications may be discussed with Gavin Wallace. See also Royal Mail Awards for Scottish Children's Books (page 607).

Scottish Mortgage Investment Trust Book Awards

email aly.barr@scottisharts.org.uk
Contact Aly Barr, Literature Officer

Scotland's largest literary prize, which recognises and rewards literary excellence and merit. There are 4 awards, each worth £5000, selected by a distinguished panel of judges at the end of February. They are: Fiction, First Book, Non-fiction, and Poetry. The 4 category winning titles will be considered for the Book of the Year award and the winning title will secure an overall prize of £30,000.

Eligible books are those published for the first time between January and December and should be submitted by 31 December each year. While preference is given to literary fiction and poetry, many other types of books are eligible, in particular literary non-fiction such as biography, history, essays, etc. Reprints, technical or scientific books, and books that are highly specialised will not be considered. Authors of submitted books should be Scottish or resident in Scotland but books of particular Scottish interest by other authors are eligible for consideration. Posthumous awards cannot be made. Publishers are invited to enter suitable books on behalf of their authors by submitting 6 copies of each title, together with biographical information on the author. Publishers of books selected for the shortlist will be requested to submit additional copies. Writers may not submit entries.

Scottish Book of the Year – see The Saltire Society Awards

Scottish First Book of the Year – see The Saltire Society Awards

Scottish Research Book Award – see The Saltire Society Awards

The André Simon Memorial Fund Book Awards

Details Katie Lander, 1 Westbourne Gardens,
Glasgow G12 9XE
tel 07801 310973
email katie@andresimon.co.uk

Celebrating excellent new writing in the fields of food and drink. Two awards of £2000 are given annually, one each for the best new books on food and on drink. There is also a Special Commendation of £1000 in either category. All works first published in the calendar year of the award are eligible (publisher entry only). Closing date: November each year. Awards are given in the spring of the following year. Founded 1978.

The Jill Smythies Award

The Linnean Society of London, Burlington House,
Piccadilly, London W1J 0BF
tel 020-7434 4479 *fax* 020-7287 9364
email info@linnean.org
website www.linnean.org

Established in honour of Jill Smythies whose career as a botanical artist was cut short by an accident to her right hand. The rubic states that 'the Award, to be made by Council usually annually consisting of a silver medal and a purse … is for published illustrations, such as drawings and paintings, in aid of plant identification, with the emphasis on botanical accuracy and the accurate portrayal of diagnostic characteristics. Illustrations of cultivars of garden origin are not eligible.' Closing date for nominations: 15 October. Founded 1988.

The Society of Authors Medical Book Awards

Details The Secretary, Medical Book Awards, The Society of Authors, 84 Drayton Gardens, London SW10 9SB
tel 020-7373 6642
email info@societyofauthors.org
website www.societyofauthors.org

Please contact The Society of Authors and see the website for up-to-date information.

Sony Radio Academy Awards

Details Sony Radio Academy Awards Secretariat, Zafer Associates, 47–48 Chagford Street, London NW1 6EB
tel 020-7723 0106 *fax* 020-7724 6163
email info@radioawards.org
website www.radioawards.org

The Sony Radio Academy Awards celebrate excellence in UK radio broadcasting. The Awards offer an opportunity to enter work in a range of categories which reflect today's local, regional and national radio. The Awards are for everyone regardless of resources – for stations big and small, for a team or for one person with a microphone. See website for further information. Founded 1982.

The Sunday Times EFG Private Bank Short Story Award

Booktrust, Book House, 45 East Hill, London SW18 2QZ
tel 020-8516 2973
email prizes@booktrust.org.uk
website www.booktrust.org.uk
Contact Claire Shanahan

A new annual literary prize which builds on the success of the weekly short story slot in *The Sunday Times Magazine*. Judges shortlist 6 authors from a longlist of 20 and the winner is announced in March. Authors will, in 2011, compete for a prize of £30,000, the largest short story prize in the world, and their story is published in the magazine. Established 2010.

The Sunday Times Young Writer of the Year Award

Details The Society of Authors, 84 Drayton Gardens, London SW10 9SB
tel 020-7373 6642
email info@societyofauthors.org
website www.societyofauthors.org

Annual award to published fiction and non-fiction writers under the age of 35. The panel consists of *Sunday Times* journalists and critics. Entry by publishers. Closing date: 31 October. Established 1991.

The James Tait Black Memorial Prizes

Submissions Department of English Literature, David Hume Tower, George Square, Edinburgh EH8 9JX
tel 0131-650 3619 *fax* 0131-650 6898
website www.englit.ed.ac.uk/jtbinf.htm

Two prizes of £10,000 are awarded annually: one for the best biography or work of that nature, the other for the best work of fiction, published during the calendar year 1 January to 31 December. The adjudicators are Professors of English Literature at the University of Edinburgh, with the assistance of teams of postgraduate readers. Eligible novels and biographies are those written in English and first published or co-published in Britain in the year of the award. Both prizes may go to the same author, but neither to the same author a second time.

Publishers should submit a copy of any appropriate biography, or work of fiction, as early as possible with a note of the date of publication, marked 'James Tait Black Prize'. Closing date for submissions: 1 December. Founded in memory of a partner in the publishing house of A&C Black, these prizes were instituted in 1918.

TAPS (Training and Performance Showcase)

Details Shepperton Studios, Studios Road, Shepperton, Middlesex TW17 0QD
tel (01932) 592151 *fax* (01932) 592233
email admin@tapsnet.org
website www.tapsnet.org

A national scheme to train and promote new writers for film and TV. TAPS workshop training courses are open to all British scriptwriters. Full-length drama (min. 60 mins), comedy (30 mins) or shorts (10 mins) will be accepted as qualifying script submissions for the appropriate courses. Scripts selected from each course are showcased by professional actors, taped and screened to industry executives.

Reginald Taylor and Lord Fletcher Essay Competition

Submissions John McNeill, Hon. Secretary, British Archaeological Association, 18 Stanley Road, Oxford OX4 1QZ
email jsmcneill@btinternet.com

A prize of a medal and £300 is awarded biennially for the best unpublished essay of high scholarly standard, which shows original research on a subject of archaeological, art-historical or antiquarian interest within the period from the Roman era to AD1830. The successful competitor will be invited to read the essay before the Association and the essay may be published in the Association's *Journal*. Competitors should notify the Hon. Editor in advance of the intended subject of their work. Next award: Autumn 2012. The essay should be submitted not later than 30 April 2012, enclosing an sae. Founded in memory of E. Reginald Taylor FSA and Lord Fletcher FSA.

The Times/Chicken House Children's Fiction Competition

Details Chicken House, 2 Palmer Street, Frome, Somerset BA11 IDS
tel (01373) 454488
email claire@doublecluck.com
website www.doublecluck.com
Contact Claire Skuse

This annual competition is open to first-time writers of a full-length children's novel (age 9–16). Entrants must be over 18 and novels must not exceed 80,000 words in length. The winner will be announced in *The Times* and receives a worldwide publishing contract with Chicken House with a royalty advance of £10,000. The winner is selected by a panel of judges which includes children's authors, journalists, publishers, librarians and others involved in children's literature. Submissions are invited between August and the end of October, with a shortlist announced the following February and the winner chosen at Easter. See website for further details. Previous winners: *Reavers' Ransom* by Emily Diamand (2007); *Threads* by Sophia Bennett (2008); *Muncle Trogg* by Janet Foxley (2009).

Dylan Thomas Literary Prize

The Dylan Thomas Centre, Ty Llen, Somerset Place, Swansea SA1 1RR
tel (01792) 474051
email sian@dylanthomasprize.com
website www.dylanthomasprize.com

An award of £60,000 is given to the winner of this prize, which was established to encourage, promote and reward exciting new writing in the English-speaking world and to celebrate the poetry and prose of Dylan Thomas. Entrants should be the author of a published book (in English), under the age of 30, writing within one of the following categories: poetry, novel, collection of short stories by one author, play that has been professionally performed, a broadcast radio play, a professionally produced screenplay that has resulted in a feature-length film. Authors need to be nominated by their publishers, or producers in the case of performance art. Closing date: May. Established 2005.

Tir na n-Og Awards

Details Welsh Books Council, Castell Brychan, Aberystwyth, Ceredigion SY23 2JB
tel (01970) 624151 *fax* (01970) 625385
email menna.lloydwilliams@cllc.org.uk
website www.cllc.org.uk

Established with the intention of raising the standard of children's and young people's books published during the year, and to encourage the buying and reading of good books. Three awards are presented annually:

• The best English language book of the year with an authentic Welsh background. Fiction and factual books originally in English are eligible; translations from Welsh or any other language are not eligible. Prize: £1000.
• Welsh language books aimed at the primary sector. Prize: £1000.
• Welsh language books aimed at the secondary sector. Prize: £1000.

Sponsored by the Chartered Institute of Library and Information Professional and the Welsh Books Council. Founded 1976.

The Tom-Gallon Trust Award and the Olive Cook Prize

Details Awards Secretary, The Society of Authors, 84 Drayton Gardens, London SW10 9SB
tel 020-7373 6642
email info@societyofauthors.org
website www.societyofauthors.org

An award of £1000 is made on the basis of a submitted short story to fiction writers of limited means who have had at least one short story accepted for publication. Both awards are biennial and are awarded in alternate years. Send sae or download entry forms. Closing date: 31 October each year.

The Translation Prizes

Details The Awards Secretary, The Society of Authors, 84 Drayton Gardens, London SW10 9SB
tel 020-7373 6642
email info@societyofauthors.org
website www.societyofauthors.org

The Society of Authors administers a number of prizes for published translations into English. There are prizes for translations of Arabic, Dutch and Flemish, French, German, Greek, Italian, Portuguese, Spanish and Swedish works. Closing date 31 January. Entries should be submitted by the publisher.

The Betty Trask Awards

Details Awards Secretary, The Society of Authors, 84 Drayton Gardens, London SW10 9SB
tel 020-7373 6642
email info@societyofauthors.org
website www.societyofauthors.org

These awards are for the benefit of young authors under the age of 35 and are given on the strength of a first novel (published or unpublished) of a traditional or romantic nature. It is expected that prizes totalling £25,000 will be presented each year. The winners are required to use the money for a period or periods of foreign travel. Send sae or download from the website for entry form. Closing date: 30 November. Made possible through a generous bequest from the novelist Betty Trask.

The Travelling Scholarships

Administered by The Society of Authors, 84 Drayton Gardens, London SW10 9SB
tel 020-7373 6642
email info@societyofauthors.org
website www.societyofauthors.org

These are honorary awards established in 1944 by an anonymous benefactor. Submissions are not accepted.

John Tripp Award for Spoken Poetry

Academi, Mount Stuart House, Mount Stuart Square, Cardiff CF10 5FQ
tel 029-2047 2266 *fax* 029-2049 2930
email post@academi.org
website www.academi.org
Contact Peter Finch, Chief Executive

A competition for any form of spoken poetry in the English language. There are 5 regional heats around Wales, with the winners from each heat going forward to a Grand Final. Performers have 5 minutes to read their work at each stage of the competition and are judged on the content of their poetry and their performance skills. Anyone either born or currently living in Wales is eligible to enter, and all works must be unpublished. Founded 1990.

The V&A Illustration Awards

Enquiries The Word & Image Dept, Victoria & Albert Museum, London SW7 2RL
tel/fax 020-7942 2000
email vanda@vam.ac.uk
website www.vam.ac.uk/illustrationawards
Contact Martin Flynn

These annual awards are given to practising book and magazine illustrators, for work first published in the UK during the 12 months preceding the closing date of the awards. Cash prizes will be awarded for best book cover, illustrated book and newspaper, magazine and comic illustration. Also student illustrator of the year category. Closing date: December.

Ver Poets Open Competition

Competition Secretary Gill Knibbs, 181 Sandridge Road, St Albans, Herts. AL1 4AH
tel (01727) 762601
email gillknibbs@yahoo.co.uk
website www.verpoets.org.uk

A competition open to all for poems of up to 30 lines of any genre or subject matter, which must be unpublished work in English. Prizes: £500 (1st), £300 (2nd), £100 (3rd), and £100 for Young Writers (age 16–21). Send 2 copies of each poem with no name or address; either put address on separate sheet or send sae or email for entry form. Closing date: 30 April. Anthology of winning and selected poems with Adjudicator's Report usually available from mid-June, free to those included. See website for details.

The Walford Award – see The ISG (CILIP)/BookData Reference Awards

Warwick Prize for Writing

Contact Helen May, Warwick Prize for Writing, Communications Office, University House, University of Warwick CV4 8UW
tel (0247) 615 0708
email prizeforwriting@warwick.ac.uk
website www.warwick.ac.uk/go/prizeforwriting/

An international cross-disciplinary biennial prize worth £50,000 awarded for an excellent and substantial piece of writing in the English language, in any genre or form, on a theme that changes with every award. The theme for 2009 was 'Complexity' and for 2011 'Colour'. Nominations are invited from Warwick staff, students, honorary and emeritus professors, and honorary graduates. See website for full details.

The Wellcome Trust Book Prize

tel 020-7611 8540
email bookprize@wellcome.ac.uk, k.nevin-ridley@wellcome.ac.uk
website www.wellcomebookprize.org
Contact Katrina Nevin-Ridley

Celebrates the best of medicine in literature by awarding £25,000 each year for the finest fiction or non-fiction book centred around medicine. With this prize, the Wellcome Trust aims to stimulate interest, excitement and debate about medicine and literature, reaching audiences not normally engaged with medical science. Closing date for submission forms: 31 March. See website for further details. Founded 2009.

Whitbread Book Awards – see Costa Book Awards

The Whitfield Prize

Administrative Secretary, Royal Historical Society, University College London, Gower Street, London WC1E 6BT
tel 020-7387 7532 *fax* 020-7387 7532
email royalhistsoc@ucl.ac.uk
website www.royalhistoricalsociety.org

The Prize (value £1000) is announced in July each year for the best work on a subject within a field of British or Irish history. It must be its author's first solely written history book, an original and scholarly work of historical research and have been published in the UK or Republic of Ireland in the preceding calendar year. One non-returnable copy of an eligible book should be submitted before 31 December to the

Administrative Secretary. Should the book be shortlisted, 2 further copies will be required.

Wildlife Photographer of the Year

Details The Natural History Museum, Cromwell Road, London SW7 5BD
tel 020-7942 5015
website www.nhm.ac.uk/wildphoto

An annual award given to the photographer whose individual image or portfolio is judged to be the most striking and memorable. The overall adult winner receives £10,000. The Young Wildlife Photographer of the Year receives £500, plus a day out with a photographer. Open to all ages. Closing date: March.

Winchester Writers' Conference Competitions

Contact Barbara Large, Faculty of Arts, University of Winchester, Winchester, Hants SO22 4NR
tel (01962) 827238
email barbara.large@winchester.ac.uk
website www.writersconference.co.uk
Honorary Patrons Dame Beryl Bainbridge, Jacqueline Wilson OBE, Maureen Lipman, Baroness James OBE, Colin Dexter OBE

Seventeen writing competitions are attached to this major international Festival of Writing, which takes place at the end of June/early July (see page 691). Each entry is adjudicated and 70 sponsored prizes are presented at the Writers' Awards Dinner. Categories are the First Three Pages of the Novel, Short Stories, Shorter Short Stories, Writing for Children, A Page of Prose, Lifewriting, Slim Volume, Small Edition, Poetry, Retirement, Writing Can be Murder, Local History, Young Writers' Poetry Competition and Sustainability of our Climate. Deadline for entries: 3 June 2011.

The Wolfson Foundation

Details The Prize Administrator, The Wolfson Foundation, 8 Queen Anne Street, London W1G 9LD
tel 020-7323 5730 ext. 202 *fax* 020-7323 3241
website www.wolfson.org.uk

Annual awards are made to encourage and recognise books by British historians that can be enjoyed by a general readership and will stimulate public interest in history. The awards total up to £40,000. Authors must be British citizens and normally resident in the UK. The book must be published in the calendar year of the prize. Closing date: January following the prize year. Founded 1972.

David T.K. Wong Fellowship

Details School of Literature and Creative Writing, University of East Anglia, Norwich NR4 7TJ
tel (01603) 592286 *fax* (01603) 507728
email davidtkwongfellowship@uea.ac.uk
website www.uea.ac.uk/lit/awards/wong

This annual fellowship (award £26,000) at the University of East Anglia will give a writer of exceptional talent the chance to produce a work of fiction in English which deals seriously with some aspect of life in the Far East. Applications will be considered from established published as well as unpublished writers of any age and any nationality. Residential: 1 academic year. Closing date for applications: 31 January each year. Founded in 1997 by Mr David T.K. Wong, retired senior civil servant, journalist and businessman.

Write A Story for Children Competition

Entry forms The Academy of Children's Writers, PO Box 95, Huntingdon, Cambs. PE28 5RL
tel (01487) 832752
website www.childrens-writers.co.uk

Three prizes (1st £2000, 2nd £300, 3rd £200) are awarded annually for a short story for children, maximum 1500 words, by an unpublished writer of children's fiction. Send sae for details or see website. Founded 1984.

Writers' & Artists' Yearbook 2011 Short Story Competition

website www.writersandartists.co.uk

See website for details.

Writers' Week Poetry Competition

Details Writers' Week, 24 The Square, Listowel, Co. Kerry, Republic of Ireland
tel (353) 6821074 *fax* (353) 6822893
email info@writersweek.ie
website www.writersweek.ie

Holds 3 poetry competitions, with various prizes. Contact as above for full details, and submission guidelines. No entry form required. Closing date: February 2011.

Yorkshire Post Book of the Year

Submissions & Correspondence Duncan Hamilton, Deputy Editor, Yorkshire Post Newspapers Ltd, PO Box 168, Wellington Street, Leeds LS1 1RF
tel (01132) 432701

There are 3 awards: *Yorkshire Post* Non-fiction Award (£1200), *Yorkshire Post* Fiction Award (£1200) and *Yorkshire Post* Award for Best Book with a Yorkshire Theme (£500).

Young Writers' Programme

Details Young Writers' Programme, Royal Court Young Writers' Programme, Sloane Square, London SW1W 8AS
tel 020-7565 5050 *fax* 020-7565 5001
email info@royalcourttheatre.com
website www.royalcourttheatre.com

Competition open to 18–25 year olds. See website for further information for how to submit plays and the progression for the winners.

YoungMinds Book Award

48–50 St John Street, London EC1M 4DG
email hannah.smith@youngminds.org.uk
website www.youngminds.org.uk
Contact Hannah Smith

This annual book award of £2000 seeks to raise awareness and create understanding of mental health needs of children and young people. Eligible books must have been published between 1 June and 31 May and may be works of fiction or biography for young people aged 12+ which helps them to cope with the stresses and challenges of growing up. Founded 2003.

YouWriteOn.com – see Arts Council YouWriteOn.com Book Awards

Literature festivals

There are hundreds of arts festivals held in the UK each year – too many to mention in this *Yearbook* and many of which are not applicable specifically to writers. We give here a selection of literature festivals and general arts festivals which include literature events. Space constraints and the nature of an annual publication together determine that only brief details are given; contact festival organisers for a full programme of events. The British Council will supply a list of forthcoming literature festivals on receipt of a large sae.

Aldeburgh Poetry Festival

The Poetry Trust, 9 New Cut, Halesworth, Suffolk IP19 8BY
tel (01986) 835950
email info@thepoetrytrust.org
website www.thepoetrytrust.org
Director Naomi Jaffa
Takes place annually on the first weekend in November

Annual festival of contemporary poetry with readings, workshops, talks, discussions, public masterclass, children's event. Features leading international and national poets, including the winner of the Aldeburgh First Collection Prize.

Appledore Book Festival

Festival Office, Appledore Library, The Quay, Appledore, Bideford, Devon EX39 1QS
website www. appledorebookfestival.co.uk
Takes place 25 Sept–3 Oct 2010

Public and school events with visiting authors. Founded 2007.

Asia House Festival of Asian Literature

Asia House, 63 New Cavendish Street, London W1G 7LP
tel 020-7307 5454 *fax* 020-7307 5459
email enquiries@asiahouse.co.uk
website www.asiahouse.co.uk, www.festivalofasianliterature.com
Takes place May

The only festival in the UK dedicated to writing about Asia and Asians. It covers Asia in the broadest context, from the Persian Gulf in the West to Indonesia in the East. Tickets go on sale in March.

Contact: Adrienne Loftus Parkins (Festival Director) at adrienne.parkins@asiahouse.co.uk

Aspects Irish Literature Festival

Town Hall, The Castle, Bangor, Co. Down BT20 4BT
tel (028) 91 278032, 91 271200 (box office)
fax (028) 91 271370
website www.northdown.gov.uk
Contact Gail Prentice, Arts Officer/Festival Director
Takes place 22–26 Sept 2010

An annual celebration of contemporary Irish writing with novelists, poets and playwrights. Includes readings, discussions, workshops and an Aspects showcase day for young writers.

Autumn International Literary Festival

University of East Anglia, Norwich NR4 7TJ
tel (01603) 592286 *fax* (01603) 507728
email n.orr@uea.ac.uk
website www.uea.ac.uk/litfest
Contact Festival Administrator
Takes place Late Sept–early Dec

An annual festival of events to bring well-established international writers of fiction, biography, poetry, etc to a public audience in the Eastern region.

Ballymena Arts Festival

The Braid Ballymena Town Hall, Museums & Arts Centre, 1-29 Bridge Street, Ballymena, Co. Antrim BT43 5EJ
tel (028) 25 657161, (028) 25 635988
email rosalind.lowry@ballymena.gov.uk
website www.ballymena.gov.uk
Festival Director Rosalind Lowry
Takes place March–April

Bath Literature Festival

Bath Festivals, Abbey Chambers, Kingston Buildings, Bath BA1 1NT
tel (01225) 462231 *fax* (01225) 445551
Box Office *tel* (01225) 463362
email info@bathfestivals.org.uk
website www.bathlitfest.org.uk
Artistic Director James Runcie
Takes place February–March

An annual 9-day festival with leading guest writers. Includes readings, debates, discussions and workshops, and events for children and young people. Programme available from box office in December.

Bay Lit

Academi, Mount Stuart House, Mount Stuart Square, Cardiff CF10 5FQ
tel 029-2047 2266 *fax* 029-2049 2930
email post@academi.org
website www.academi.org
Contact Peter Finch, Chief Executive
Takes place varies (contact Academi)

A bilingual (Welsh and English) literature festival,

held in Cardiff Bay. It is organised by Academi, the Welsh National Literature Promotion Agency and Society for Authors, and features an array of writers from Wales and beyond.

Beverley Literature Festival

Wordquake, Council Offices, Skirlaugh, East Riding of Yorkshire HU11 5HN
tel (01482) 392745
email john@bevlit.org
website www.beverley-literature-festival.org
Festival Director John Clarke
Takes place 1–10 Oct 2010

This festival offers author readings, readers' group sessions, writers' workshops and masterclasses. It involves all kinds of good writing but a special emphasis is placed on poetry.

Birmingham Book Festival

Unit 116, The Custard Factory, Gibb Street, Birmingham B9 4AA
tel 0121-246 2770 *fax* 0121-246 2771
email sara@birminghambookfestival.org
website www.birminghambookfestival.org
Programmer Sara Beadle, *Artistic Director* Jonathan Davidson
Takes place 5–21 Oct 2010

An annual festival which presents a range of events with all types of writers of both fiction and non-fiction, workshops and seminars.

Book Now! Literature Festival, Arts Service

Orleans House Gallery, Riverside, Twickenham TW1 3DJ
tel 020-8831 6000 *fax* 020-8744 0501
email artsinfo@richmond.gov.uk
website www.richmond.gov.uk
Takes place November

An annual literature festival covering a broad range of subjects. Leading contemporary authors hold discussions, talks, debates and readings. There are also exhibitions and storytelling sessions for children and adults.

Brighton Festival

29 New Road, Brighton BN1 1NG
tel (01273) 700747 *fax* (01273) 707505
email info@brightonfestival.org.uk
website www.brightonfestival.org.uk
Takes place May

An annual arts festival with an extensive national and international programme featuring theatre, dance, music, opera, literature, outdoor and family events. Programme published end of February.

Bristol Poetry Festival

Poetry Can, 12 Great George Street, Bristol BS1 5RH
tel 0117-933 0900
email admin@poetrycan.co.uk
website www.poetrycan.co.uk
Festival Director Colin Brown
Takes place April–May and Sept at Bristol Old Vic, Arnolfini, and other venues in Bristol

An annual celebration of language. Features award-winning poets and performers from all over the UK and abroad.

Buxton Festival

3 The Square, Buxton SK17 6AZ
tel (01298) 70395
email info@buxtonfestival.co.uk
website www.buxtonfestival.co.uk
Artistic Director Andrew Greenwood, *Chief Executive* Glyn Foley
Takes place 7–25 July 2010, 6–24 July 2011

The incredible opera and music programme is complemented by a much envied Literary Series, featuring distinguished authors, which takes place every morning.

Canterbury Festival

Festival Office, Christ Church Gate, The Precincts, Canterbury, Kent CT1 2EE
tel (01227) 452853 *fax* (01227) 781830
email info@canterburyfestival.co.uk
website www.canterburyfestival.co.uk
Takes place 16–30 October 2010

An annual general arts festival with a literature programme. Programme published in July.

Charleston Festival

The Charleston Trust, Charleston, Firle, Lewes, East Sussex BN8 6LL
tel (01323) 811265 (information), 811626 (administration) *fax* (01323) 811628
email info@charleston.org.uk
website www.charleston.org.uk
Contact Diana Reich
Takes place May

Charleston, country home of Bloomsbury artists Duncan Grant and Vanessa Bell hosts an annual literary festival.

The Times Cheltenham Literature Festival

109–111 Bath Road, Cheltenham, Glos. GL53 7LS
tel (01242) 774400
email clair.greenaway@cheltenhamfestivals.com
website www.cheltenhamfestivals.com
Artistic Director Sarah Smyth
Takes place October

This annual festival is the largest of its kind in Europe. Events include talks and lectures, poetry readings, novelists in conversation, exhibitions, discussions, workshops and a large bookshop. *Book It!* is a festival for children within the main festival with an extensive programme of events. Brochures are available in August.

Chester Literature Festival

Chester Railway Station, 1st Floor,
West Wing Offices, Chester CH1 3NT
tel (01244) 405605
email info@chesterfestivals.org
website www.chesterfestivals.co.uk
Programme Manager Katherine Seddon
Takes place October

An annual festival commencing the first weekend in October. Events featuring international, national and local writers and poets are part of the programme, as well as a literary lunch and festival dinner. There is a poetry competition for school children, events for children and workshops for adults. A Cheshire Prize for Literature is awarded each year; only residents of Cheshire are eligible.

Chichester Festivities

Canon Gate House, South Street, Chichester,
West Sussex PO19 1PU
tel (01243) 785718 *fax* (01243) 528356
email info@chifest.org.uk
website www.chifest.org.uk
Takes place June/July

City of London Festival

Fitz Eylwin House, 25 Holborn Viaduct,
London EC1A 2BP
tel 020-7583 3585 *fax* 020-7353 0455
email admin@colf.org
website www.colf.org
Director Ian Ritchie
Takes place Last week of June and first 2 weeks of July

An annual multi-arts festival with a programme predominantly of music. Programme published in April.

The Cúirt International Festival of Literature

Galway Arts Centre, 47 Dominick Street, Galway,
Republic of Ireland
tel (091) 565886 *fax* (091) 568642
email info@galwayartscentre.ie
website www.galwayartscentre.cuirt
Progamme Director Maureen Kennelly
Takes place April

An annual week-long festival to celebrate writing, bringing together national and international writers to promote literary discussion. Events include readings, performances, workshops, seminars, lectures, poetry slams and talks. The festival is renowned for its convivial atmosphere ('cúirt' means a 'bardic court or gathering').

Dublin Book Festival

Publishing Ireland, Guinness Enterprise Centre,
Taylor's Lane, Dublin 8
tel 01 4151210, 01 4151203
email info@dublinbookfestival.com
website www.dublinbookfestival.com
Takes place March each year

Held in Dublin's City Hall, the festival's events include an *In conversation with* series.

Dublin Writers' Festival

c/o Dublin City Council, Arts Office, The Lab,
Foley Street, Dublin 1, Republic of Ireland
tel (01) 222 5455
email info@dublinwritersfestival.com
website www.dublinwritersfestival.com
Takes place June

An annual festival with readings by major Irish and international poets and writers to celebrate the best in contemporary literature.

Durham Book Festival

c/o Durham City Arts Ltd, 2 The Cottages,
Fowlers Yard, Back Silver Street, Durham DH1 3RA
tel 0191-375 0763
email enquiries@durhamcityarts.org.uk
website www.bookfestival.org.uk
Takes place October

Festival managed by DCA.

Edinburgh International Book Festival

5A Charlotte Square, Edinburgh EH2 4DR
tel 0131-718 5666 *fax* 0131-226 5335
email admin@edbookfest.co.uk
website www.edbookfest.co.uk
Director Nick Barley
Takes place August

Now established as Europe's largest book event for the public. In addition to a unique independent bookselling operation, more than 800 writers contribute to the programme of events. Programme details available in June.

Ennis Book Club Festival

c/o Clare Library HQ, Mill Road, Ennis, Co. Care,
Republic of Ireland
tel (87) 226 2259
email info@ennisbookclubfestival.com
website www.ennisbookclubfestival.com
Chairperson Frances O'Gorman
Takes place First weekend in March

An annual literary weekend which brings together book club members, book lovers and writers. Includes lectures, readings, discussions, workshops and exhibitions.

Essex Poetry Festival

2 The Drive, Hullbridge, Essex SS5 6LN
tel (01702) 230596
email derek@essex-poetry-festival.co.uk
website www.essex-poetry-festival.co.uk
Contact Derek Adams

Takes place October

A poetry festival across Essex. Also includes the Young Essex Poet of the Year Competition.

Exeter Festival

Festival Office, Civic Centre, Exeter EX1 1JJ
tel (01392) 265200 *fax* (01392) 265265
website www.exeter.gov.uk
Festival Manager Val Wilson
Takes place June/July and October–November

An annual general arts festival which includes a programme of literary activities. Programme of events available in May.

Festival at the Edge

The Morgan Library, Aston Street, Wem, Shrops. SY4 5AU
tel (01939) 236626
email info@festivalattheedge.org
website www.festivalattheedge.org
Contact Sue Chand
Takes place July

A storytelling festival with a mix of stories, music and performance, held in Much Wenlock, Shropshire.

Folkestone Book Festival

Creative Foundation Offices, The Block, 65–69 Tontine Street, Folkestone, Kent CT20 1SE
tel (01303) 245799
email info@creativefoundation.org.uk (FAO Folkestone Book Festival)
website www.quarterhouse.co.uk
Takes place November

An annual festival with over 40 events, including a Children's Day.

Free the Word!

International PEN, Brownlow House, 50–51 High Holborn, London WC1V 6ER
tel 020-7405 0338 *fax* 020-7405 0339
email info@internationalpen.org.uk
website www.internationalpen.org.uk/go/literary-events/free-the-word-
Takes place April

'Free the Word! is International PEN in spirit and action – a festival for authors and readers to make sparks across the divide between national literatures' – Sir Tom Stoppard. Presents writers from countries worldwide at events in London.

The Guardian Hay Festival

Festival Office, The Drill Hall, 25 Lion Street, Hay-on-Wye HR3 5AD
tel (01497) 822620 (admin)
email admin@hayfestival.com
website www.hayfestival.com
Takes place May/June

This annual festival aims to celebrate the best in writing and performance from around the world, to commission new work, and to promote and encourage young writers of excellence and potential. More than 500 events over 10 days, with leading guest writers. Programme published April.

Guildford Book Festival

c/o Tourist Information Office, 14 Tunsgate, Guildford GU1 3QT
tel (01483) 444334
email deputy@guildfordbookfestival.co.uk
website www.guildfordbookfestival.co.uk
Festival Director Glenis Pycraft
Takes place Last 2 weeks in October

An annual festival. Diverse, provocative and entertaining, held throughout the historic town. Author events, poetry, workshops for all age groups from 6 months onwards. Its aim is to further an interest and love of literature by involvement and entertainment. Founded 1989.

Hay Festival – see The Guardian Hay Festival

Huddersfield Literature Festival

School of Humanities, Music and Media, University of Huddersfield HD1 3DH
tel (01484) 430528
email litfest@hud.ac.uk
website www.litfest.org.uk
Festival Director Michael Stewart

The festival programmes events to support and showcase new, emerging and established writers/artists, offering a platform to promote new work as well as the opportunity to attend intensive writing workshops and masterclasses. Founded 2006.

Ilkley Literature Festival

The Manor House, 2 Castle Hill, Ilkley LS29 9DT
tel (01943) 601210 *fax* (01943) 817079
email admin@ilkleyliteraturefestival.org.uk
website www.ilkleyliteraturefestival.org.uk
Festival Director Rachel Feldberg
Takes place First two weeks in October

The north of England's most prestigious literature festival with over 180 events, from author's discussions to workshops, readings, literary walks, children's events and a festival fringe.

International Playwriting Festival

Warehouse Theatre, Dingwall Road, Croydon CR0 2NF
tel 020-8681 1257
email info@warehousetheatre.co.uk
website www.warehousetheatre.co.uk
Contact Rose Marie Vernon
Takes place March

It starts with the competition, which has entries accepted from all over the world and is judged by a panel of distinguished theatre practitioners. Closing date for entries is the end of June each year. The festival itself forms second part, which features a showcase of the best work from the IPF competition, and selected plays from the festival's international partners – the leading Italian playwriting festival, Extra Candoni, and Theatro Ena, Cyprus.

Jewish Book Week

Jewish Book Council, ORT House, 126 Albert Street, London NW1 7NE
tel 020-7446 8771 *fax* 020-7446 8777
email info@jewishbookweek.com
website www.jewishbookweek.com
Administrator Pam Lewis
Takes place Feb/March

A festival of Jewish writing, with contributors from around the world and sessions in London and nationwide. Includes events for children and teenagers.

King's Lynn Festival

5 Thoresby College, Queen Street, King's Lynn, Norfolk PE30 1HX
tel (01553) 767557 *fax* (01553) 767688
website www.kingslynnfestival.org.uk
Administrator Joanne Mawson
Takes place 18–31 July 2010, 17–30 July 2011

An annual general arts festival with literature events featuring leading guest writers.

King's Lynn Literature Festivals

19 Tuesday Market Place, King's Lynn, Norfolk PE30 1JW
tel (01553) 691661 *fax* (01553) 691779
Chairman Tony Ellis
Takes place Sept/March

26th Poetry Festival (24–26 Sept 2010): An annual festival which brings 12 published poets to King's Lynn for the weekend for readings and discussions.

23rd Fiction Festival (12–15 March 2011): An annual festival which brings 12 published novelists to King's Lynn for the weekend for readings and discussions.

Kingston Readers' Festival

Kingston University, River House, 53–57 High Street, Kingston upon Thames KT1 1LQ
tel 020-8417 9000
email events@kingston.ac.uk
website www.kingston.ac.uk/krf
Festival Director Sandy Williams
Takes place April/May

A small non-profit-making limited company with charitable and educational aims to:

- Foster and celebrate a love of reading
- Promote a broad range of events for all ages, including short story, poetry and writing for performance competitions
- Develop an outreach programme comprising workshops and authors' talks
- Promote the work of Kingston University and the Rose Theatre, Kingston
- Raise money for local good causes and other reading-related charities. Established 2002.

Knutsford Literature Festival

37 Manor Park South, Knutsford, Cheshire WA16 8AG
tel (01565) 640750
email julia.jary@ntlworld.com
website www.knutsfordlitfest.blogspot.com
Contact Julia Jary
Takes place First 3 weeks of Oct

An annual festival to celebrate writing and performance, with distinguished national, international and local authors. Events include readings and discussions, a literary lunch and theatrical performances.

Ledbury Poetry Festival

Town Council Offices, Church Street, Ledbury HR8 1DH
tel (0845) 458 1743
email admin@poetry-festival.com
website www.poetry-festival.com
Festival Director Chloe Garner
Takes place July

An annual festival featuring top poets from around the world, together with a poet-in-residence programme, competitions (send sae for entry form), workshops and exhibitions. Full programme available in May.

Lewes Live Literature

PO Box 2766, Lewes, East Sussex BN7 2WF
tel (07972) 037612
email info@leweslivelit.co.uk
website www.leweslivelit.co.uk
Artistic Director Mark Hewitt
Takes place see website

A live literature production company developing performances and projects with writers for presentation as part of a season or festival of new work.

Lincoln Book Festival

Freeschool Lane, Lincoln, Lincs. LN2 1EY
tel (01522) 545458 *fax* (01522) 842718
email Sara.Bullimore@lincoln.gov.uk, info@lincolnbookfestival.co.uk
website www.lincolnbookfestival.co.uk
Contact Sara Bullimore (Arts & Cultural Sector Officer)
Takes place May

A festival that celebrates books but also includes other art forms that books initiate and inspire – comedy, film, performance, conversation. It aims to celebrate local, national and international writers and artists, historical and contemporary works of art as well as offering the public a chance to see both emerging and well-known writers and artists. Includes a programme of children's events.

Lit.com

Arts Development, Origin One, One Origin Way, Europarc, Grimsby DN37 9TZ
tel (01472) 323382
email charlotte.bowen@nelincs.gov.uk
website www.nelincs.gov.uk/leisure/arts
Contact Arts Development Unit
Takes place Oct

Reflecting the heritage and culture of the area, this combined literature and comedy festival aims to be accessible to all ages and abilities through a varied and unusual programme.

Litfest

The Storey Creative Industries Centre, Meeting House Lane, Lancaster LA1 1TH
tel (01524) 62166
email all@litfest.org
website www.litfest.org
Artistic Director Andrew Darby
Takes place October

Annual literature festival featuring prose and poetry from local, national and international writers. Litfest is the literature development agency for the Northwest. Year round programme of seasonal readings and workshops. Publisher of new writing from Lancashire and Cumbria via Flax imprint.

London Literature Festival

Southbank Centre, Belvedere Road, London SE1 8XX
tel (0871) 633 2501
email customer@southbankcentre.co.uk
website www.southbankcentre.co.uk, www.londonlitfest.com
Takes place July

A 2-week festival featuring international and prize-winning authors, historians, poets, performers and artists, children's events, specially commissioned work, debate and discussion, interactive and improvised writing and performance. Established 2007.

Lowdham Book Festival

c/o The Bookcase, 50 Main Street, Lowdham NG14 7BE
tel 0115-966 4143
email info@fiveleaves.co.uk
website www.lowdhambookfestival.co.uk
Contact Jane Streeter, Ross Bradshaw
Takes place June

An annual 10-day festival of literature events for adults and children, with a daily programme of high-profile national writers. The last day always features dozens of free events and a large book fair.

Manchester Children's Book Festival

The Manchester Writing School, Dept of English, Manchester Metropolitan University (MMU), All Saints Building, All Saints, Manchester M15 6BH
tel 0161-247 1787
email mcbf@mmu.ac.uk
website www.manchesterchildrensbookfestival.co.uk
Festival Director Carol Ann Duffy, *Contact* James Draper, Project Manager, The Manchester Writing School
Takes place 1–4 July 2010

A new festival featuring some of today's favourite children's writers and artists for children (aged 0–15) and anyone who loves children's books.

Manchester Literature Festival

Beehive Mill, Jersey Street, Manchester M4 6JG
tel 0161-236 5555
email admin@manchesterliteraturefestival.co.uk
website www.manchesterliteraturefestival.co.uk
Director Cathy Bolton
Takes place 14–24 Oct 2010

An annual festival celebrating new literature, new technology and the original modern city of Manchester.

National Eisteddfod of Wales

40 Parc Ty Glas, Llanisien, Cardiff CF14 5DU
tel 029-2076 3777 *fax* 029-2076 3737
email elfed@eisteddfod.org.uk
website www.eisteddfod.org.uk
Chief Executive Elfed Roberts
Takes place August

Wales's largest cultural festival, based on 800 years of tradition. Activities include competitions in all aspects of the arts, fringe performances and majestic ceremonies. In addition to activities held in the main pavilion, it houses over 300 trade stands along with a literary pavilion, a music studio, a movement and dance theatre, outdoor performance stages and a purpose-built theatre. The event is set in a different location each year, and will take place in Ebbw Vale in 2010 and in Wrexham in 2011.

Norfolk & Norwich Festival

Augustine Steward House, 14 Tombland, Norwich NR3 1HF
tel (01603) 877750 *fax* (01603) 877766
email info@nnfestival.org.uk
website www.nnfestival.org.uk
Artistic Director Jonathan Holloway
Takes place annually in May

Northern Children's Book Festival

22 Highbury, Jesmond, Newcastle upon Tyne NE2 3DY
tel 0191-2813289
website www.ncbf.org.uk
Chairperson Ann Key

Takes place November

An annual festival to bring authors, illustrators, poets and performers to children in schools, libraries and community centres across the North East of England. About 36 authors visit the North East over the 2-week period for 2–8 days, organised by the 12 local authorities. The climax of the festival is a huge public event in a different part of the North East each year when over 4000 children and their families visit to take part in author seminars, drama workshops, and to enjoy a variety of book-related activities.

Off the Shelf Literature Festival

Central Library, Surrey Street, Sheffield S1 1XZ
tel 0114-273 4716
email offtheshelf@sheffield.gov.uk
website www.offtheshelf.org.uk
Contact Maria de Souza, Su Walker, Lesley Webster
Takes place October

The festival comprises a wide range of events for adults and children, including author visits, writing workshops, storytelling, competitions and exhibitions. Programme available in September.

Oundle Festival of Literature

2 New Road, Oundle, Peterborough, Northants PE8 4LA
tel (01832) 273050
email enquiries@oundlelitfest.org.uk
website www.oundlelitfest.org.uk
Contact Liz Dillarstone (Publicity)
Takes place March (festival fortnight) plus all-year-round programme

Featuring a full programme of author events, poetry, philosophy, politics, story-telling, biography, illustrators and novelists for young and old. Includes events for children.

Oxford Literary Festival – see The Sunday Times Oxford Literary Festival

Poetry International

Literature Department, Southbank Centre, Belvedere Road, London SE1 8XX
tel (0207) 921 0904
website www.southbankcentre.co.uk
Contact Martin Colthorpe
Takes place October 2012 (biennial)

The biggest poetry festival in the British Isles, bringing together a wide range of poets from around the world. Includes readings, workshops and discussions. The Literature + Spoken Word department also runs a year-round programme of readings, talks and debates.

Quite Literary

The Plough Arts Centre, 9–11 Fore Street, Torrington, Devon EX38 8HQ
tel (01805) 622552
email richard@theploughartscentre.org.uk
website www.theploughartscentre.co.uk
Contact Richard Wolfenden-Brown
Takes place Throughout the year

An occasional literature programme including workshops, readings, performances and exhibitions, as part of a larger programme of arts work, including community and educational workshops, projects, residencies and performances.

Redbridge Book and Media Festival

London Borough of Redbridge, Arts & Events Team, 3rd Floor, Central Library, Clements Road, Ilford IG1 1EA
tel 020-8708 2855
website www.redbridge.gov.uk
Contact Arts & Events Team
Takes place April and May

Features author talks, performances, panel debates, Urdu poetry events, an exhibition, workshops, children's activities and events, and a schools outreach programme.

Royal Court Young Writers' Festival

The Royal Court Theatre, Sloane Square, London SW1W 8AS
tel 020-7565 5050
email studio@royalcourttheatre.com
website www.royalcourttheatre.com
Contact Nina Lyndon, Administrator
Takes place Biennially (2011)

A national festival which anyone aged 18–25 can enter. Promising plays which arise from the workshops are then developed and performed at the Royal Court's Theatre Upstairs (see page 440).

Rye Festival

Literary Events Director, Court Lodge Oast, Udimore, Rye, East Sussex TN31 7YB
tel (0179) 722 4442
website www.ryefestival.co.uk
Literary Director Catherine Bingham
Takes place middle two weeks of Sept (15 days)

Annual festival of literary events featuring biographers, novelists, political and environmental writers with book signings and discussions. Runs concurrently with festival of music and visual arts.

Salisbury International Arts Festival

87 Crane Street, Salisbury, Wilts. SP1 2PU
tel (01722) 332977
email info@salisburyfestival.co.uk
website www.salisburyfestival.co.uk
Takes place May–June

An annual multi-arts festival that includes a thriving literature programme. Programme published in March.

Spring International Literary Festival

University of East Anglia, Norwich NR4 7TJ
tel (01603) 592286 *fax* (01603) 507728

email n.orr@uea.ac.uk
website www.uea.ac.uk/litfest
Contact Festival Administrator
Takes place Late Jan–mid May

An annual festival of events to bring well-established international writers of fiction, biography, poetry, etc to a public audience in the Eastern region.

St Ives Literature Festival

St Ives Arts Club, The Warren, St Ives, Cornwall TR26 2DY
email info@stiveslitfest.co.uk
website www.stiveslitfest.co.uk
Contact Bob Devereux
Takes place First week in May

Organised in association with a number of Cornwall and West Country publishers, the festival consists of readings, talks, workshops and performance events.

StAnza: Scotland's International Poetry Festival

tel (05600) 433847 (administration), (01334) 475000 (box office), (01334) 474610 (programmes)
email info@stanzapoetry.org
website www.stanzapoetry.org
Festival Director Brian Johnstone
Takes place March

The festival engages with all forms of poetry: read and spoken verse, poetry in exhibition, performance poetry, cross-media collaboration, schools work, book launches and poetry workshops, with numerous UK and international guests and weekend children's events.

Stratford-upon-Avon Poetry Festival

Shakespeare Centre, Henley Street, Stratford-upon-Avon CV37 6QW
tel (01789) 204016 *fax* (01789) 296083
email info@shakespeare.org.uk
website www.shakespeare.org.uk
Takes place April/May

Now in its 57th year, this festival celebrates poetry past and present with special reference to the works of Shakespeare. Events include: evenings of children's verse, a Poetry Mass and a local poets' evening. Full details available on the website from March. Sponsored by the Shakespeare Birthplace Trust.

The Sunday Times Oxford Literary Festival

Christ Church, Oxford OX1 1DP
tel (01865) 276152
email info@oxfordliteraryfestival.co.uk
website www.oxfordliteraryfestival.com
Festival Chief Executive Sally Dunsmore
Takes place March

An annual 6-day festival for both adults and children. Presents topical debates, fiction and non-fiction discussion panels, and adult and children's authors who have recently published books. Topics range from contemporary fiction to discussions on politics, history, science, gardening, food, poetry, philosophy, art and crime fiction. An additional 2 days of events for schools.

Swindon Festival of Literature

Lower Shaw Farm, Shaw, Swindon, Wilts. SN5 5PJ
tel (01793) 771080
email swindonlitfest@lowershawfarm.co.uk
website www.swindonfestivalofliterature.co.uk
Festival Director Matt Holland
Takes place May

An annual celebration of live literature through prose, poetry, drama and storytelling, with readings, discussions, performances and talks in theatres, arts centres, parks and pubs. A festival of ideas with leading authors, speakers and performers.

Theakstons Old Peculier Crime Writing Festival

Raglan House, Raglan Street, Harrogate, North Yorkshire HG1 1LE
tel (01423) 562303 *fax* (01423) 521264
email box@harrogate-festival.org.uk
crime@harrogate-festival.org.uk
website www.harrogate-festival.org.uk/crime
Takes place July

Four days of events featuring the best of British and American crime writers.

The Dylan Thomas Festival

The Dylan Thomas Centre, Somerset Place, Swansea SA1 1RR
tel (01792) 463980 *fax* (01792) 463993
email dylanthomas.lit@swansea.gov.uk
website www.dylanthomas.com
Events Manager David Woolley
Takes place 27 Oct–9 Nov 2010

An annual festival celebrating the life and work of Swansea's most famous son: performances, lectures, debates, poetry, music and film. Also, regular events throughout the year and talks and tours by arrangement.

Tŷ Newydd Festival

Tŷ Newydd, Llanystumdwy, Gwynedd LL52 0LW
tel (01766) 522811 *fax* (01766) 523095
email post@tynewydd.org
website www.tynewydd.org
Contact Sally Baker, Executive Director
Takes place April

Events are centred on the writing centre at Llanystumdwy in Gwynedd, and feature a mix of Welsh and English events including Poetry Stomps and guest readers. The Academi, the Welsh National Literature Promotion Agency, supports Ty Newydd to create this festival.

Ulster Bank Belfast Festival at Queen's
Culture & Arts Unit, Queen's University,
8 Fitzwilliam Street, Belfast BT9 6AW
tel 028-9097 1034
email festival.operations@qub.ac.uk
website www.belfastfestival.com
Director Graeme Farrow
Takes place from 15 Oct 2010 for 16 days

The largest annual arts event in Ireland. Includes literature events. Programme available end August.

Warwick International Festival
Pageant House, 2 Jury Street, Warwick CV34 4EW
tel (01926) 410018
email wmladmin@armonico.org.uk
website www.warwickinternationalfestival.com
Festival Director James Adam
Takes place June/July

A multi-arts festival which includes some literature and poetry events: readings, performances and workshops.

Warwick Words – Festival of Literature and Spoken Word
The Court House, Jury Street, Warwick CV34 4EW
tel (07944) 768607
email info@warwickwords.co.uk
website www.warwickwords.co.uk
Takes place beginning of October

Founded 1999.

Ways With Words Literature Festival
Droridge Farm, Dartington, Totnes, Devon TQ9 6JG
tel (01803) 867373 *fax* (01803) 863688
email admin@wayswithwords.co.uk
website www.wayswithwords.co.uk
Contact Kay Dunbar
Takes place 10 days in middle of July each year

200 speakers give readings, talks, interviews, discussions, seminars, workshops with leading guest writers. Also organises Words by the Water: a Cumbrian literature festival (March) and Southwold (Nov), and writing and painting holidays in Italy and France.

Wells Festival of Literature
Gable House, Parbrook, Glastonbury BA6 8PB
tel (01749) 670929
website www.wellsfest.co.uk
Takes place Mid-October

An annual week-long festival featuring leading writers and poets. It includes theatre and cinema events, writing workshops and short story and poetry competitions. Events take place in the historic Bishop's Palace and other venues around the historic city of Wells.

Wigtown Book Festival
County Buildings, Wigtown,
Dumfries & Galloway DG8 9JH
tel (01988) 402036
email mail@wigtownbookfestival.com
website www.wigtownbookfestival.com
Festival Director Adrian Turpin
Takes place 24 Sept–3 Oct 2010

An annual celebration of literature and the arts in Scotland's National Book Town. Over 150 events including author events, theatre, music, film and a full children's programme. Venues include the Festival Marquee, County Buildings, bookshops and Bladnoch Distillery.

Word – University of Aberdeen Writers Festival
University of Aberdeen, Office of External Affairs,
University of Aberdeen, King's College,
Aberdeen AB24 3FX
tel (01224) 273874 *fax* (01224) 272086
email word@abdn.ac.uk
website www.abdn.ac.uk/word
Artistic Director Alan Spence
Takes place May

Over 70 of the world's finest writers and artists take part in a packed weekend of readings, music, art exhibitions and film screenings. The festival hosts some of the UK's best-loved children's writers and some of the richest talents in Gaelic literature.

World Book Day
c/o The Booksellers Association,
272 Vauxhall Bridge Road, London SW1V 1BA
tel (01634) 729810
email wbd@education.co.uk
website www.worldbookday.com
Takes place March

An annual celebration of books and reading aimed at promoting their value and creating the readers of the future. Every schoolchild in full-time education receives a £1 book token. Events take place all over the UK in schools, bookshops, libraries and arts centres. World Book Day was designated by UNESCO as a worldwide celebration of books and reading, and is marked in over 30 countries. It is a partnership of publishers, booksellers and interested parties who work together to promote books and reading for the personal enrichment and enjoyment of all.

See also the Book to Talk About (page 591).

Writers' Week
24 The Square, Listowel, Co. Kerry,
Republic of Ireland
tel (068) 21074 *fax* (068) 22893
email info@writersweek.ie
website www.writersweek.ie
Administrators Eilish Wren, Máire Logue
Takes place June

Aims to promote the work of Irish writers in both the English and Irish language, and to provide a platform for new and established writers to discuss their works. Events include readings, seminars, lectures and book launches.

Young Readers Birmingham

Children's Office, Central Library,
Chamberlain Square, Birmingham B3 3HQ
tel 0121-303 3368 *fax* 0121-464 1004
email patsy.heap@birmingham.gov.uk
website www.birmingham.gov.uk/youngreaders
Contact Patsy Heap
Takes place May/June 2011

An annual festival targeted at children, young people and families. It aims to promote the enjoyment of reading; to provide imaginative access to books, writers, performers and storytellers; to encourage families to use libraries and to share reading for pleasure; to provide a focus for the celebration of books and reading for children and young people and help raise the media profile of children's books and writing. Approximately 150 events take place.

Writers and artists online

Marketing yourself online

Mathew F. Riley and Simon Appleby outline how writers can use the internet to get noticed.

Make some noise!

Some basic things have not changed in the 12 months since the 2010 edition of this *Yearbook* was published. Writers are writing. Readers are reading. This is good, but whether you're a published writer with an ongoing deal, or an aspiring writer with a whole load of ideas, and even a finished manuscript, the challenge will always be the same: how do you get your name known, your words read, your manuscripts taken on, your book bought, and then sell *more* books to justify a second book?

Important aspects of the literary environment are unquestionably changing: more people are reading and writing *online*. This trend will continue. Another change: readers have *become* writers. The ceaseless development of the internet enables anyone to say anything at anytime to anyone who's reading. Whether fiction, news, opinion or reviews, everybody's having their say, shouting the loudest to lure readers to their writing; readers and critics wanting to attract writers and publishers to their reviews. One more change: risk-averse publishers (and agents) look to the internet for inspiration (see *Books published from blogs* on page 281), and will do so increasingly to gauge marketability, because books as hold-in-the-hand, textured entertainment will *always* be published. Much of your activity should be geared towards demonstrating to a publisher that people like your work and would pay to read more of it. Hence an author (budding or otherwise) who is entrepreneurial, has developed a loyal fan-base, and a positive vibe about their work, has a chance of standing out from the crowd, with more to put on their CV (and in their covering letter to a publisher) and evidence that they really have put in the effort to try to achieve publication.

By the time this article is published some of the technologies, publishing platforms and communities referenced will have evolved, but the concepts behind developing a manageable approach to promoting you and your writing on the internet, *to get you closer to your readers and them closer to you*, will absolutely hold true. This article won't give you detailed DIY instructions (see *Setting up a website* on page 641 and *Writing a blog* on page 647, and look on the internet), but it will hopefully provide you with a focus from which to develop your presence on the internet in a structured and achievable fashion.

There's a lot of noise out there, and to be heard you will have to make some of your own. So, how do you do it?

The technical side of things is not rocket science – the numerous (and free) solutions available out there do most of it for you, but it does take persistence and require an idea of where you want to be, and who you want to talk to. At the risk of teaching an old dog new tricks this means setting aside an amount of time to plan your approach. Just like writing. Once you've put the building blocks in place, it *is* writing. And (you already know this) when you start writing, you won't be able to stop!

Set up your own blog

Chances are you're already doing this: check out the authors who are selling themselves well (and badly). Look at professional authors with well-designed websites, as well as lesser-known authors who are simply utilising the blogging platforms available to all of us. Note what blogging platform these authors are using. You don't need to have an all-singing, all-dancing, beautifully designed website and blog from day one.

A blog is *your* website. It can be whatever you want it to be. Publish your work to find out what people think about it, discuss other authors' work, the writing market, and the places on the internet where they hang out. Give readers extra content they cannot get anywhere else. Study the statistics (try to avoid becoming addicted!) that your blog automatically provides and follow the links. Make yourself accessible. When someone sends you a message or leaves you a comment it's an opportunity to enter into a discussion about your writing. Get back to them while they're still interested. Make your blog the centre of your online universe, and explore the threads that will grow from this centre. To aid this you must exploit and be a willing participant of the social internet.

> *'At my publisher's behest, and very reluctantly, I began my online marketing with a MySpace profile. Facebook and Twitter swiftly followed. More recently, with fellow Bloody Books author Bill Hussey, we set up www.horrorreanimated.com. The blog promotes the resurgence in horror, our publisher and our books. Awareness and sales of my novels have spread globally and it has cost me almost nothing.'* – Joseph D'Lacey

Social networking and communities

There are innumerable communities on the internet – each one an island floating on an ocean of 'noise'. Navigating your way to these oases of context is vital and you'll find them just as you find a good book – by searching according to your tastes, and listening to the recommendations of your friends. At Bookgeeks (www.bookgeeks.co.uk) we do all that follows, and slowly but surely it works: your friends and visitors increase, your words are read and your name and reputation spreads.

Here are the main categories to think about:

- **Writing communities**, where you can get your work evaluated and rate the work of others – these are both a source of useful feedback and encouragement, and a place to get noticed by publishers (even leading to book deals for the best).
- **General book communities** – where book owners, librarians, collectors and authors come together, an instant source of like-minded people.
- **Forums** – these can be wide ranging or frighteningly focused on one subject, but if you find one you like, hang around and join in. You should not expect to drop in, plug your work and have other users be grateful for your contribution if you don't stick around.
- **Social networking** – this is the broadest category, encompassing thousands of sites large and small. Find the one that's right for you.

'Friends'

Set up Facebook and Twitter profiles. *Eww*, we hear you say! Well we say, just do it! Thousands of writers have already done so, and they're talking to each other and their fans. Facebook and Twitter are *all* about talking. Use these platforms to promote your wares – friendships may even develop too. It's an excuse to talk to complete strangers and you'll soon find things in common. Search for the topics that interest you, the areas you write about and the markets you work in. It's no exaggeration to say that you'll be sure to find people and groups who like what you do. As well as your profile you can set up pages for your books and invite people to be fans. You can import your content from your blog and send people updates as your content changes. All this can be done automatically. Ten minutes a day is all you'll need after the initial set-up.

A tool for every job

As in life, so online, there is a tool for every possible situation. We can't tell you everything a good toolkit should contain, but we can suggest some general principles and a few key tools, all of which are totally free and easy to use.

• **Stay on 'brand'** – keep handy a standard biography and a decent photo of yourself when setting up user profiles. It helps to represent yourself consistently wherever people encounter you. Try to always use the same username as well.

• **Social conversation** – use social networking sites, micro-blogging services (like Twitter) and your own site to get engaged with your current and potential readers and your fellow authors.

• **Share and enjoy** – for any type of content you create, there's a platform to share it on, whether it's video (YouTube), photos (Flickr or Photobucket), audio/podcasts and, of course, writing of all kinds. When you share content, consider whether it needs to be under copyright or whether Creative Commons licensing might help it be more widely seen.

• **Listening tools** – make sure you know when people are talking about you and your work, or linking to your website – then you can drop in and make a contribution, or link to the content in question. For this, *Google Alerts* is your friend. More broadly, use Really Simple Syndication (RSS) to follow the blogs that interest you and keep track of new writers, industry trends and more – we suggest Google Reader, but there are numerous feed readers available.

• **Keep current** – wherever there is information about you, make sure it's current and as detailed as possible. Keep your Wikipedia entry up to date (taking care to stay factual); update information about yourself on sites like LibraryThing (www.librarything.com); make sure your publisher knows about your online activities so they can link to them.

Engagement

As a writer spending time online, you are inevitably going to come in contact with criticism of your work at some point, perhaps even abuse. Keep your cool and when deciding how to react to something, one of these four responses will usually be appropriate:

• **Endorse** – if something's really positive (a good review, or creativity inspired by your work) link to it, shout about it, tell your publisher, encourage the creator.

• **Engage** – enter in to discussion with fans and critics alike on their forum of choice; respond to constructive criticism professionally and never take it personally.

• **Ignore** – if you can't say anything nice...

• **Enforce** – if anyone is getting abusive, infringing your rights or going too far, take measured steps to do something about it (like contacting their forum moderator or ISP), but never descend to their level.

One other thing – *never* pretend to be someone you're not, anywhere, for any reason. Always represent yourself honestly as 'the author in question'.

Online PR

This is a glorified way of saying 'Talk to people about your work in order to get them to write about it'. If you are willing to put in the time to contact bloggers and offer review copies, interviews, competition prizes or other content they can use, some of them are likely to respond positively. Understand their pressures – they want to find things to write about, and that's where you come in.

Use some of the same organisational skills that you use researching and talking to agents and publishers – much as you do when you look through the *Writers' & Artists' Yearbook* for suitable publishers and agents, do your homework on blogs too. Read a blog thoroughly before you approach the blogger to make sure your work is right for that blog, and read any submission guidelines the site may have. Keep a record of who you contact and when, to make sure you don't repeat yourself. Follow up after a suitable time any sites that offer to look at your work. Present yourself professionally: it's all good common sense, but in our experience that doesn't mean everyone does it right!

> *I went down the independent publishing route and got my book out in the USA and UK with BookSurge, a branch of Amazon. The pivotal moment for me was reading an article in the Guardian, 'Is it curtains for critics?', describing the eclipse of professional critics by bloggers, and mentioning an influential book blogger, dovegreyreader. I emailed her and most of the other bloggers listed on her page, asking if they would review an independently published book. Most said they would, and most of those read and reviewed my book. This led to enquiries by publishers. The result: 'War on the Margins: A Novel' was released by Duckworth Publishers in the UK in July 2009.* – Libby Cone

Getting creative on a budget

You can get creative and get noticed even if you have little or no money to spend: write a blog or an article 'in character'. Set up a Twitter feed in your character's name, or write micro-fiction. Enlist the services of friends and family, and their cameras, video cameras, computers and, most importantly, skills to create images or videos that you can promote yourself with. We know you're creative, or you wouldn't be reading this, so we bet you can think of something imaginative (and don't get hung up on being wholly original, or you might never get started).

What does the future look like?

You don't need us to tell you this is a hard question to answer – especially for anything relating to the online world. What we do know is that the internet is rapidly eroding the barriers between writers, readers and publishers, posing new challenges for all three groups. This is an opportunity for you as a writer: it's a chance to get feedback earlier, from more people than ever before; a chance to hone your own marketing and presentational skills not just to literary agents, but to a much broader base of enthusiastic bloggers and fans; and most importantly, a chance to take your destiny into your own hands in a way that writers would not have imagined possible only a few years ago.

So let us hear you make some noise!

Mathew F. Riley and **Simon Appleby** have a combined total of 20 years' experience working with digital media, including setting up many publisher and author websites. They co-run www.bookhugger.co.uk and www.bookdagger.com, online literary and crime magazines. They also co-run the book review blog www.bookgeeks.co.uk.

E-publishing

E-publishers offer a variety of services to authors and have no set standards of quality or provision. Jane Dorner looks at the electronic minefield facing authors.

In recent years we've seen launched the Sony Reader, the Amazon Kindle, the Apple iPad, and the Barnes & Noble Nook. Agents and publishers love them because they can load dozens of scripts to browse through on their train journey home, and people who travel a lot may like to have hundreds of Classics (which are free) at their fingertips. But all are still expensive and haven't captured the British public. Authors such as J.K. Rowling say they will never allow their books to be made available as ebooks, but for niche markets there is money to be made. Research into a type of screen that would roll up or fold (known as e-paper) has not produced results yet. The story of e-publishing is in slight limbo until a ready device as popular as the mobile phone is brought to market.

All major UK publishers have websites on which they promote their books. Some are publishing electronic versions downloadable directly from the web and some are sharing the revenue from e-titles 50–50 with their authors. This is still basically traditional publishing and all the brand name expectations apply.

There's another set of e-publishers who do not have an established track record or brand identity (high standards, quality provision, peer review, integrity). Some are genuine publishers operating in the new environment and some come perilously close to vanity publishers eager to make money out of the unwary. Others offer useful services to self-publishers. And some call themselves publishers, but are effectively book showrooms. The boundaries can sometimes be so vague that it is difficult to be dogmatic about what value they provide. Above all, be wary of sites that do not declare what the costs are and who pays them.

Until reputations form, writers will have to look closely at the e-publisher's websites, read carefully through submission statements, look for an online contract or terms and conditions and judge for themselves. Enter into an email dialogue and get as much information as you can before you send in anything. Look at authors who are already publishing with the e-publisher – the chances are you won't have heard of any of them. Might that be a warning sign? Try not to license your rights for more than a year or two at a time – so if they ask for *exclusive* rights, pass on to the next publisher.

The most obvious appeal is to writers who have unpublished works, out-of-print works where rights have reverted to them, previously published material that could have a renewed life in a new format, or memoires for the family.

Ebooks

An e-publisher will convert your word-processed document into one, or more, of the three basic software formats for making ebooks readable on notebook PCs, personal digital organisers (PDAs), mobile phones and desktop computers. They are not interchangeable:
- Adobe Portable Document Format (PDF) which is a universal standard for preserving the original appearance – fonts, formatting, colours, and graphics – of any source document, regardless of the application and platform used to create it;
- Dedicated reader formats – similar electronic reading software designed for easy onscreen reading, e.g. Microsoft and Sony;

• Mobipocket Reader for new generation mobile phones – another format like the two above;
• ePub – the current favourite industry standard which incorporates encryption and digital rights management programming.

All content can be downloaded into the reading devices from a website and can be paid for at that time. These formats are relatively cheap for a publisher to produce – but only assuming they do nothing to add to the editorial value. None of the electronic formats are secure from plagiarists, though some make a better attempt at security than others. At present, PDF files are the most secure (though hackable), with options ranging from preventing text selection (so users cannot cut and paste), disabling reading onscreen (so only one print copy can be made), or, conversely, disabling printing, to password-protection. However, accessibility to those with disabilities is also important and may mean compromising on full security. The question here is whether yours is the sort of book that people will want to read from screens – small or large.

Print on demand

Some printers offer Print-on-demand (POD) services for good quality paper copies in runs of 1 to 1000. This has a double appeal to authors: for self-publishing and for bringing an out-of-print book back into circulation. You don't have to grant any licence of rights and you don't need to let anyone else have control over production matters.

The self-publishing route is attractive. There's a set-up cost and a per title cost, but they're generally lower than the self-publishing options that have been available up to now. This option may well be of interest to authors who don't mind doing their own promotion. POD offers a potentially viable digital production model to the publishing industry as a whole. If the technology settles and origination costs come down a little lower than they are now, we could see certain types of book being ordered on the internet for collection an hour later at the local bookshop where it is bound and printed. Authors in some genres may be able to bypass publishers.

The author is expected to supply a completely finished, edited file and this is poured into a standard template. Some e-publishers take anything they are offered (within the bounds of censorship) and others have strict filtering systems. Not many provide editing, design or quality control. Prices are hugely variable, but expect to pay about £300 for 50 copies of a 150-page book without any pictures and from fully formatted files. Individual or quality-vetted services can raise costs into the £1,000+ bracket – typically: cover design, £350; proofreading, £1.50 per 1,000 words; assigning an ISBN, £50; marketing package, £200; adding pictures, £30 an hour; and other dubious add-ons. Some e-publishers offer a single price for the whole service – for example £450 is the lowest I have found, but it can be unclear what exact book length and print run this includes. You may also be tempted by being offered registration with Amazon, or free distribution to a given number of bookshops in the UK, or a variety of other seeming benefits. Read the offers with circumspection and do comparative research. For example, you can register ten ISBNs with the ISBN Agency for £111.80. As for Amazon, they get their information from Nielsen BookData and registration with them is free (see listing). Get a quote for your book from a few sources. A detailed quote setting down exactly what the specifications are is probably more reliable than opting for a preset package. The Society of Authors has a *Quick Guide* (No 17, see page 541) which will answer more detailed questions.

Out-of-print publishing is more complex. It is unlikely that the author will have a digital copy of a former work. Corrections, design and late changes to the latest version of either the author's or the editor's file is not the final version. This means a published copy must be scanned in and converted. To do this at reasonable cost and with acceptable accuracy requires a sophisticated scanner and two copies of the book with cut spines, merged and assembled in book order. There are two problems. With older books, the author may only have one precious copy and may not be willing to cut it up. With newer books, the chances are the rights have reverted, but the typographical right still belongs to the publisher for 25 years after publication. It's arguable that scanning violates that right. See also *Print on demand* on page 332.

Showcasing

The listing below is a cross-section of services to authors who would like to sell or resell their works in one of the formats described. Some market in the same way as traditional publishers. Some are printers. Many e-publishers double as online booksellers, so they are not publishers in the sense we have been used to – although they also promote their bestselling authors more aggressively than the ones no one has heard of. The difference is that they can offer showcase capacity to any author, well known or not. Most guarantee visitors against pornography and real rubbish, but it's fairly rudimentary quality control. Showcasing is generally just that – a space on the bookshelf. And in this environment bookshelving is infinitely expandable. Most are sited in the US, but that doesn't matter since this is global exposure anyway.

Blogging

One increasingly popular form of personal e-publishing is the blog, which means 'web log' or 'online diary' (see *Writing a blog* on page 647). Sites for authors to self-promote through blogs have been increasing. There are even cult sites of people who are widely read online as well as in a print version. You can also use the blog format as a news page linked to a static website hosted elsewhere so that news announcements are in your own control.

In addition to blog sites are social networking 'clubs', of which the most famous are Facebook, Twitter, MySpace, and YouTube where users share words, pictures, music and video. The word 'vlog' applies to people who share video diaries – a tradition that goes back to the 1980s and is now very popular, especially for news stories that more traditional outlets do not cover. Television channels are increasingly drawing on these resources.

The content and purposes of blogs varies greatly – from news about a family, person or idea, to diaries, photos, poetry, mini-essays and fiction. It was on 11 September 2001, when New York's twin towers so catastrophically fell, that blogging really came of age as thousands of individuals gave their own perspectives and thoughts on the tragedies of that day. This was personal journalism at an emotional peak and ever since the media have been drawing on individual accounts. Be wary of linking to videos on YouTube as content isn't necessarily copyright-cleared and technically speaking a link even from a blog is an infringement.

Sites where you can get started are listed below and they are very easy to use, but give yourself time if you are new to blogging because the technical people who design the software don't know what authors and artists want. It's easy, but not necessarily intuitive. It's instant electronic publishing and limited only by your own imagination.

Some web aficionados claim that the future of web publishing is in blogs. Not only is it a testament to the state of the world, but people enjoy cataloguing their lives, interests or random musings and other people like reading them and linking to them. Literary agents now regularly trawl blogs for new talent and many new authors have been 'discovered' in this way. Some have even sold film rights as a result of blogging – the film *Julie & Julia* being a popular example. This shows, perhaps, that paper publishing still rules. There is probably an art form tucked away in blogging – if it can overcome its unfortunate nomenclature. Even the *Writers' & Artists' Yearbook* website (www.writersandartists.co.uk) has a blog – with guest writers offering advice to new writers.

Websites

Note, this is a fast-moving area and more online publishers will spring up and some of these will disappear. In all cases, authors should check all details of the contracts.

The *Writers' & Artists' Yearbook* cannot be held responsible for any content on any of these sites. It came to our attention that in a previous edition one site led to a pornography page. This was because the original owner of the domain had not yet paid for a renewal and another party had instantly acquired it. They posted an offensive page and they effectively blackmailed the e-publisher to pay a large sum to get it back. Be aware that this can happen.

Print on demand

Antony Rowe
www.antonyrowe.co.uk

An established printer offering short runs. There is a quote calculator on the site.

Author House
www.authorhouse.com

US-based self-publishing site. Packages from $599.

Authors Online
www.authorsonline.co.uk

A Bedfordshire-based POD self-publishing venue. Their full standard service costs £725 and there are a lot of extras.

Fast Print
www.fast-print.net

About £146 for 25 copies of a 128pp book – nice calculator online.

iUniverse
www.iuniverse.com

A service for redeploying out-of-print books; check the author contract carefully. Packages range from $599 to $4,200.

Lightning Source
www.lightningsource.com

Established POD and ebook supplier. No prices given but there is an exhaustive list of FAQs.

Lulu
www.lulu.com/uk

A showcase for services supplied by people in the book trade, with reliability ratings. A certain amount of free advice but you have to register (free).

Pro Print
www.proprintpublishers.co.uk

Cambridgeshire printer which offers a short-run POD service. Has a useful online calculator to help work out costs, e.g. £209 for 25 copies of a 64pp book.

Unlimited Publishing
www.unlimitedpublishing.com

A POD system for new and out-of-print titles; will cost new authors about $1,000 as long as they use Word or similar. Non-fiction only.

Virtual Bookworm
www.virtualbookworm.com

POD and ebook supplier; packages range from $360 to $1,950.

Writers World
www.writersworld.co.uk

A self-publishing resource for writers to publish their books by POD or ebooks. Quotation given on request. Free newsletter and chatroom.

Xlibris
www.xlibris.com

POD packages ranging from $399 to $13,999 (for picture books) plus marketing packages. Has been in the market for 10 years.

E-publishing resources

Axis
www.axisweb.org

Opportunities site for practising artists. Free to register – quality control in operation. You can advertise your work on a free web page.

eBooks.com
www.ebooks.com

Internet Digital Bookstore. Invites authors to let their publisher or agent know about it; authors should check rights deals with their publisher.

fotoLIBRA
www.fotolibra.com

Picture library – photographers can upload and sell pictures for a monthly subscription. Terms: 50%.

Nielsen's BookData Services
www.nielsenbookdata.co.uk

ISBN, SAN and DOI agents. Bibliographic records of books in print.

International Digital Publishing Forum
www.idpf.org

Format specifications, sponsored by the National Institute of Standards and Technology (formerly the Open Book Forum).

UK Children's Books
www.ukchildrensbooks.co.uk

Listings of authors, illustrators and publishers.

Writers Co-operative
www.rabbitbooks.com

Mixed collection of UK self-publishing writers' work and its authors publishing venue.

Writing.com
www.writing.com

Online community for writers offering advice and publishing suggestions.

Blogging

Bebo
www.bebo.com

The name means 'Blog early, blog often' and is an online social media network.

Blogger
http://blogger.com

One of the first, and easiest to use, sites for starting a blog.

Bookarazzi
www.bookarazzi.com

For bloggers who are interested in book deals.

Facebook
www.facebook.com

Social networking area with profile pages and password access.

MySpace
www.myspace.com

Cult social networking site that offers email, a forum, communities, videos and blog space.

Twitter
http://twitter.com

Sharing what you are doing with anyone who cares. Well-known writers use it.

Writers' & Artists' Yearbook
www.writersandartists.co.uk

Established writers offer advice to new writers.

Windows Live Writer
www.windowslivewriter.spaces.live.com

Blog environment designed with writers in mind.

Wordpress
http://wordpress.org

A 'personal publishing platform': in other words a free home for your blog.

YouTube
www.youtube.com

A video sharing website where users can upload, view and share video clips.

e-Reading devices

Apple iPad
www.apple.com/uk/ipad

The latest 'must have' piece of kit for internet surfers. It is also very acceptable for reading books on, if publishers provide for it. At £429, it is still pitched at early adopters.

Kindle
www.amazon.co.uk

UK-compatible Kindle Wireless Reading Device. Enter 'kindle' in the search box.

Microsoft Reader
www.microsoft.com/reader

Free downloadable software for reading ebooks on Windows-based devices.

Nook
www.barnesandnoble.com/nook

Recently launched contender to the Kindle; not yet UK-compatible.

Que proReader

www.que.com

The Barnes & Noble luxury on-the-move e-reader suitable for books, newspapers and magazines, but not available for the UK market yet.

Sony Reader

www.Sony.co.uk/Reader

Book exchange sites

www.bookcrossing.com
www.bookhopper.co.uk
www.bookmooch.com
www.paperbackswap.com

The above sites all offer book swapping facilities. You offer your books and recommendations and collect points for sending the book to someone who wants it. In return you exchange points for a book you want. The benefits to writers are as yet unclear.

Jane Dorner is the author of 22 books and formerly represented authors' interests on the boards of the Authors' Licensing and Collecting Society and the Copyright Licensing Agency.

See also...

- *Setting up a website*, page 641
- *Writing a blog*, page 647
- *Ebooks*, page 635
- *Marketing yourself online*, page 625
- *Print on demand*, page 332

Ebooks

Thousands of new ebook titles are launched every month. Stephen Cole assesses how ebooks are impacting the publishing world and identifies who is reading them.

What is an ebook?

The term 'ebook' is commonly used to mean one of two things: either a literary work that is published, stored and used in digital form, or an electronic device that displays books in digital form. In this article, I will refer to the first meaning simply as 'ebook' and the second as 'ebook device'. All stats and figures refer to the English language market.

A note on spelling: When consumers and industry insiders write about ebooks, they spell it thus: 'ebooks'. Journalists, academics and librarians often spell it 'e-books'. In the early days, the 'b' was often capitalised, 'eBooks', although that is becoming less common as the term enters mainstream usage.

Origins of ebooks

Ebook devices first appeared as reading gadgets in science fiction novels and television series, like *Star Trek*, in the 1970s. But it was not until the late 1990s that dedicated ebook devices were marketed commercially. The first successful effort to assemble a body of downloadable ebooks was started by Michael Hart at the University of Illinois in 1971, under the name 'Project Gutenberg'. The aim of the project was to aggregate over 10,000 public domain works and make them freely available to all.

The rapid adoption of the internet in the late 1990s saw the launch of a plethora of ebook initiatives from established companies and start-ups, mostly in the USA. But a stock market correction in 2000, combined with the generally poor adoption of downloadable books, sapped all available investment capital away from internet technology companies, leaving a wasteland of broken dreams in its wake. Over the next two years, over a billion dollars was written off the value of ebook companies, large and small.

In subsequent years, the market for downloadable books kept growing from its small initial user base, such that the total market for ebooks is now substantial. This continuous growth is due to three unique features of the digital medium: immediacy, searchability, and portability.

Ebooks today

Today, every major book publisher releases ebook versions of their frontlist titles. Thousands of new ebook titles are launched every month. The total number of ebooks now available from mainstream publishers is close to 250,000. Amazon, Borders, Sony, Adobe, Google, Apple, Barnes & Noble and other market participants are investing heavily in their visions of the digital future of book distribution. And specialist ebook companies are reporting exceptional growth and profits.

Who is reading ebooks?

One surprising statistic to emerge from ebook adoption data is the number of people who just seem to like reading books on a computer screen. Of the ebooks sold by eBooks.com, 74.6% are read on computers, while the remainder is read on a vast

Who is reading ebooks?	
Travellers	8%
Students and researchers	31%
Impaired readers	4%
Business and professionals	21%
Leisure reading	36%

variety of hand-held devices, including personal digital organisers (PDAs), mobile phones and ebook devices.

As expected, students, researchers and professionals have adopted ebooks much faster than the larger consumer market. This is most likely due to the instant accessibility of ebooks, and the fact that you can search the entire contents of a book in a second.

Ebooks are very popular with travellers because of their portability: you can carry 500 books in your smart phone, and download more while you're on the road.

Where are ebooks being read?

North America accounts for 71% of global consumer ebook sales, compared with 7% for the UK and 6% for Australia. If you take the USA as the benchmark, Australia is hitting above its weight, considering its population and the size of its economy. But, market-for-market the UK is far behind: at this stage in the cycle it should account for over 13% of the global ebook market but instead it's sitting at just under 7%. This underperformance is largely attributable to the fact that UK trade publishers have simply not embraced the model. The results are in the figures.

Where are ebooks selling today?

This data refers to trade sales (consumer), not academic or scholarly sales.

USA	67%
UK	7%
Europe	7%
Australia	6%
Canada	4%
Others	9%

In contrast to their colleagues in the consumer book business, UK scholarly publisher Taylor & Francis (T&F), has been the absolute leader of the pack in driving the digital revolution. A division of Informa, T&F adopted an aggressive digital strategy from as early as 1999, when Christoph Chesher announced their extraordinary plan to digitise 19,000 backlist and frontlist titles. Because of their early entry to the digital space, T&F had all the bugs ironed out years ago, and are now running a very successful ebook programme.

In 2008 there was a shift in UK trade publishers' stance towards ebooks. By March, every major UK trade publisher was planning or had announced an ebook publishing programme that would parallel their print book publishing activities. So far, 2010 has seen a rapid increase in the number of ebooks published by UK trade publishers.

Will ebooks affect book sales?

There are innumerable ways in which ebooks create incremental (additional) sales for authors. Ebooks reach parts of markets that printed books cannot. An expatriate geologist in Azerbaijan was never going to get those thrillers she downloaded via satellite in the steppes, except as ebooks. Busy travellers are clearly buying and reading ebooks on the fly now, where otherwise they would be reading in-flight magazines or watching movies. Students preparing at 3am for an exam the next day are buying ebooks and accessing them immediately.

The immediacy of the medium encourages a growing number of net-savvy readers to opt for digital access instead of the printed version; so, in addition to creating new sales, ebooks are also replacing some print book sales.

Because most major publishers only release ebooks in copy-protected formats, it is unlikely that unauthorised redistribution (i.e. piracy) will affect sales to the same extent that recorded music sales have been affected.

Will it be easier to get published?

When ebooks first appeared, many new writers saw it as a way to get their work out there on the internet. This is true today: at the very least, authors can post their work on their website and charge fees for access. But that's quite a different thing from being published. If you want a respected publisher to take your book, then the internet hasn't made things any easier. Whether a book is published in paper or digitally, the editorial policies and practices of major publishers are unlikely to shift in the near future.

Market size

The International Digital Publishing Foundation (IDPF), a US-based industry group, has estimated that the 2009 ebook market was about US$330 million. The IDPF's figures are drawn from data provided by US trade (consumer) publishers. If library, educational and professional electronic sales are included, that figure will be closer to US$600 million. With the success of Amazon's Kindle and Sony's Reader, Apple's iPad and Google Editions, market analysts expect that ebook sales will more than double in 2010.

The overall English language book market is over US$50 billion, which makes the ebook segment 0.66% of the total world book market. There's a long way to go. The printed book will be with us for a long time to come.

Ebook market sectors

The ebook market has coalesced into three general segments: Consumer ('Trade' books), Scientific, Technical and Medical (STM), and Business and Professional. Each segment is characterised by different pricing, access policies and business models, and is served by different providers.

What is being read on ebooks?

The reading tastes of ebook users are very similar to those of mainstream book buyers.

Top ebook subjects (by volume)	%
Fiction	65.2
Business	8.2
Computers	2.6
Family and relationships	2.4
Body, Mind & Spirit	1.6
History	1.6
Children's and young adult fiction	1.5
Religion	1.4
Language arts and disciplines	1.2
Health and fitness	1.2
Other	13.1

Trade ebooks

If you're a writer of fiction or another category that aims for a wide, popular audience – the kind of books sold in your local bookshop – you'll want to have your book listed on the major consumer ebook services. This is not something that you can do yourself; it's the publisher's job to supply these vendors with your ebook files. There are hundreds of sites selling ebooks today, but only a handful of 'aggregators' which provide fulfilment services for those retailers. Your publisher will need to supply files to these aggregators (OverDrive, Lightning Source, Ebooks Corporation, Kobo, MobiPocket, Amazon, Google, Apple, Sony).

2010 has seen a raging battle in the USA over the pricing of ebooks. Amazon caused consternation amongst publishers and delight to its customers by aggressively fixing a maximum price for popular trade ebooks sold through its Kindle store: $9.99. Even books that were priced by publishers at $30 were for sale on Amazon.com for less than $10. This meant that Amazon was actually losing money on thousands of sales, but winning the hearts of its customers. Publishers were horrified that Amazon's actions would set unrealistic expectations on the part of ebook buyers, and lead ultimately to a reduction of their own revenues. The response of publishers was to try and take control of retail pricing by renaming retailers like Amazon and eBooks.com 'agents'. Authorised agents are required by contract to adhere to published prices and may not discount ebooks. Ebook pricing is still an unfolding story. Publishers in the UK, Australia and other English language markets have yet to decide whether to follow the US agency model, or to continue pricing ebooks much as they price printed books.

When a consumer buys an ebook, they generally do so by presenting their credit card at the retailer's website and downloading the complete book as a file which can be read on a computer and/or hand-held device. Some retailers, like eBooks.com and Dymocks.com, also provide the end user with lifetime online access, via a web-based 'reader' called eb20.

Scientific, technical and medical ebooks

The market for STM ebooks is centred around academic and research libraries, and is dominated by a small number of gigantic international publishers. These publishers sell ebook collections direct to libraries, and also sell ebooks through wholesale booksellers, including netLibrary, ebrary, EBL: The Ebook Library and MyILibrary.

The pricing of STM ebooks varies according to the business model that applies. If a library subscribes to a collection of ebooks, they will pay an annual fee which is anything from a few hundred pounds to tens of thousands of pounds, depending on the size and nature of the collection and the number of potential users of the library itself.

If a library selects ebooks one at a time to add to their collection in perpetuity, then the library typically pays separately for each ebook title. The price is usually the same as that of the printed version of the book, although some publishers add a 'digital premium'.

When a library buys an ebook, it is typically granted the right to enable its patrons access to the work, subject to certain constraints. These constraints are imposed by book publishers in an effort to (a) protect them against the risk of digital piracy, and (b) ensure that, where a book is used by a large number of patrons, the library is required to pay more for the access.

Business and professional ebooks

A large number of business and professional ebooks are sold through trade ebookstores and to libraries. But there is also a very specialised business and professional ebook distribution channel wherein specialist aggregators provide ebooks direct to corporates and other organisations. The three leading aggregators in this field are Books24x7, Safari and Knovel.

Books24x7's strength has traditionally been in business books, while Safari's roots are in computing titles. Knovel targets applied scientists and practising engineers. Each company offers organisations the ability to provide their members or personnel with access to a wide selection of current works in their fields.

The pricing model for business and professional ebooks is similar to that of STM ebooks; the customer organisation subscribes to a collection of relevant material that is updated periodically by the aggregator.

Self-publishing

Authors often find that, although their book has considerable merit, they are unable to find a publisher to take it on. For centuries, one way around this bind has been for authors to publish their works themselves. Things are no different in the digital realm. A number of services have sprung up in recent years serving the needs of authors who want to bypass the traditional publishing route, for example www.scribd.com, www.lulu.com and wwww.lightningsource.com.

DRM: protecting your assets

Digital rights management (DRM) refers to the technical and legal measures that publishers use to control how ebooks are used and distributed.

DRM has provoked controversy since concerns about digital piracy first emerged in the 1990s. On one side are those who argue that 'knowledge wants to be free', and on the other are the writers and publishers who believe that their hard work and investment ought to be rewarded. This sounds like an ideological debate, but it has enormous ramifications for the shape of the book industry in the coming years. For ten years book publishers watched aghast as the music industry was decimated by the advent of digital distribution.

In practice, publishers apply DRM by authorising their ebooks to be stored, distributed and used in a few recognised encryption formats, the most common being Adobe, Mobipocket, eReader, Microsoft Reader, Sony (only used by Sony Connect and Borders) and Kindle (only used by Amazon) iPhone applications and Apple's DRM. Ebooks are sold in the first four formats listed above by a large number of online retailers.

Recent developments

Sony, the global media giant, launched the Sony Reader in 2006, which was marketed directly from its content website, Sony Connect (http://ebookstore.sony.com), and in Borders (although the 45 bookstores in the UK closed in 2009). By all accounts, the device has been a success and in 2007 Sony enabled Borders.com to sell ebooks alongside printed books.

In 2007 there emerged what many believe was the tipping point for ebooks: Amazon.com launched a dedicated ebook reading device called the Kindle. Its relatively low price and innovative wireless delivery system, combined with Amazon's massive brand suggest that they may be on a winner. The device sold out within days of its launch, and publishers are reported to be pleasantly surprised by the strength of initial ebook sales. The Kindle is designed to display copy-protected ebooks that have been bought from Amazon's own online ebookstore.

In the last two years, a plethora of dedicated ebook devices have hit the market in the USA, Europe and elsewhere. However, the two early leaders, Sony and Amazon, still dominate this nascent market.

The launch of Apple's iPhone delivered a whole new digital platform for books, and retailers, including Amazon, were quick to launch iPhone applications that enable users to buy and read books on the road. The successful launch of Apple's iPad and its own ebook sales channel added momentum to an already rapidly growing segment.

The future

Many industry watchers believe that the ebook market will take off once there is a groundbreaking device available on which to read ebooks. The next few years will show how that plays out. My own view is that the digital future of books is more complex. Devices are an important part of the picture, but there will be more to it.

The success of an ebook device depends on many factors including price, distribution and content availability; but the most important determinant is usability. The simplicity of the user experience will be paramount in determining the adoption of an ebook device.

In addition to targeting those people who might want to carry a portable ebook device around with them (who today number in the hundreds of thousands) we should not overlook another installed user base: the billion of us that use computers and mobile phones every day. The sales of ebooks for use on computers and phones have, to date, been constrained by the complexity of the user experience. With each step forward in simplicity more and more mainstream readers are adopting digital books.

If the future of books is a hybrid, made up of paper, digital files, websites, mobile phones, computers and devices, it is also a global future. In this article I've spoken as if the ebook market is an English language, US-centric phenomenon. Until now, that is mostly what it has been but, as the axis of economic activity shifts, so will the consumption of ebooks. In Japan, Taiwan and Korea, for example, there is a growing audience for fiction that is delivered in snippets via SMS to mobile phones. Inevitably, authors are writing for a global audience, and that audience will increasingly discover, acquire and read their work on some kind of screen.

Stephen Cole is the founder and Ceo of Ebooks Corporation, an Australian public company that operates two of the world's leading ebook businesses, eBooks.com and EBL: The Ebook Library.

See also...

- *A year in view of the publishing industry*, page 328
- *Doing it on your own*, page 310
- *E-publishing*, page 629
- *Writing a blog*, page 647

Setting up a website

Computer users who have email almost certainly have web space available to them. Jane Dorner explains the points for writers and artists to consider when setting up a personal website and how to best make it work for them.

To set up your own website the main investment you need to make is in time, perhaps more than you initially think. The process may have its frustrating moments, but it is ultimately creative.

Personal websites

A website can be a useful self-publicity medium for writers. It can be especially useful if you self-publish, but equally worthwhile for showing the world a portfolio of your artistic achievements and accomplishments. Many writers and artists are polymaths and the web shows up such diversity to advantage.

A personal website can be set up to demonstrate your writing or illustration style(s) and areas of interest with examples of work so that commissioning editors can see if they are choosing the right writer or artist for the job. You can include an outline of your skills and achievements, and list your publications – or you could even offer a personal syndication service for stories, articles, photographs or illustrations (if first or resale rights are yours).

You need to let people know that your website exists – there is no point having a wonderful site if no one visits it – for which old-fashioned marketing techniques are necessary. Posting your site on the web and registering hopefully with a few (or even a hundred) search engines is no substitute for careful targeting. You will probably be easily found on Google, but only if people know about you, and you need to register with Google. Refer potential clients to your website, and make sure it attracts them sufficiently to explore it. Asking other sites to link to yours improves your chances of coming up near the top of a Google search.

Skills required

In order to create the website yourself, you will need to have: a capacity for logical thinking; secure language expertise; some technical understanding; good visual sense; patience; and familiarity with applicable law.

If you don't have (or can't acquire) these skills then it is worth thinking about asking someone else to build the site for you. Expect to pay for at least one day of a professional designer's time (between £300 and £500) to create a modest suite of individually tailored pages with some attention to what you want and need. Bear in mind that the less you pay, the more likely it is that your material is simply being poured into a standard template, as is the case with sites that offer five pages for £250. The alternative is to use a managed environment for a monthly fee of about £6. You choose and organise the content yourself, working online with templates and 'widgets' that they provide. This gives you a lot of clever things you would find it hard to do yourself, and it is easy to change and to mix and match features.

Planning a website

Whether you get involved with the technological side or not, you will still have to plan and write the copy yourself. Writing for the web is a new art form that uses writerly skills: it is genuinely creative; requires writers, not programmers; and needs editors with an understanding of traditional editorial values.

Writing the text for a website is like any other writing project. The more effort that goes into the planning stage, the better the result. You need to identify whom you are targeting and be clear about the purpose of the website. For instance, is it your calling card; a PR brochure; a sales outlet; an information resource; a literary club or part of a network; a designer's showcase; or a medium of self-expression? The website needs to be planned and created accordingly. For example, if you just want a simple calling card, then a single screen – called a splash page – might suffice. It would have your name, perhaps a photograph of you, a few lines about your specialist skills and interests, possibly some work you have had published, and your contact details. You can then be found by anyone who uses the internet; your personal front cover is on the world bookshelf.

Writing for screen reading

If you write for radio, you will have an advantage over other writers. Writing for the web is a bit like writing for broadcasting: the style has to compensate for the loss of the visual impact of words. It's a mistake to cut and paste from documents created for print because the text will not read as well on a website.

The average adult spends eight hours a week reading as opposed to 27 hours watching television. And that's reading from paper – reading from a screen has so far proved less efficient than paper.

When writing the introductory text for a website, aim for the reluctant reader with a less than three-minute attention span and use easy words and short sentences. As readers delve deeper into a site, their acceptance of more discursive reading matter increases. Once they are committed to the subject material, you can write in your normal style and assume they will print out the text and read from paper. Take writing for radio or television as the paradigm and then make it even simpler. Here are a few pointers:

- **Use the tadpole or pyramid structure**. Present the main points at the top of the page (people are reluctant to scroll) and use interior pages to unfold details.
- **Be concise**. The overall length of a radio or television piece is about a third of a print article; a web page should be even shorter. Cut every word that doesn't contribute. A good web page length is under 200 words – it is better to divide anything longer than that into sub-topics.
- **Write short paragraphs**. Paragraph breaks refresh the eye: between two and five sentences is enough.
- **Write simple sentences**. Ideas are easier to digest in a simple subject-verb-object progression. Make subclauses into separate sentences. Use one idea per sentence. Make them under the 17-word print average.
- **Use the present or present perfect tense**. The web is here and now. Keep passives away.
- **Be consistent**. Use the same font, type size, alignment and background colour throughout your site. Or use different colour bands to denote different 'areas' (novels, poetry, teaching and so on). Remember that capital letters onscreen look like SHOUTING.
- **Consider navigation**. If a visitor makes Choice A here, what are the ramifications for Choice B there? Web writing is not static, but writing dynamically is something that most writers have not learned. It is, perhaps, something we will all have to discover as we progress into the web publishing age.
- **Links**. Don't link every prompt phrase that leads somewhere else. If you want readers to stay with you to absorb your point, put the link outside the main text area. Don't link just because you can.

• **Define the main areas of your site**. Consider synonyms for your top level labels (the four to six main areas of your site). How often have you got lost in a website simply because the way in which your mind works isn't the same as the mindset of the person who created it? Try to second guess what visitors to your site will want to see when they come to each page then find a single word that most unambiguously describes it.

Designing for screens

The first thing to remember about designing for screens is that you cannot control how the screen page will look as there are so many variables, such as screen resolution and type of web browser. You should therefore test your design on several different types of computer. Design depends on purpose, but here are a few good practice points:

• **Colour**. Have a white or pale cream background and black or very dark type (studies show that sharp contrasts aid readability). There are 216 'web-safe' colours based on RGB, which simply stands for Red, Green, Blue – nature's three primary colours. Monitors and television sets transmit RGB – after all colour is light. Many designers now feel it is unnecessary to limit the palette to 'web-safe' colours (see box).

• **Fonts**. How typefaces appear onscreen depends on which ones are on that particular system, not what you specify on yours. The ones you can rely on to look good on screens – and are universally available – are known as 'web-safe' fonts (see box).

• **Line length**. Put the text in invisible tables so that the line length is limited to about ten words in standard browsers – this is an optimum reading line length. If you do not set a limit, the chances are that at high screen resolutions readers might get a line length of 25 words on the default reading typeface. This leads to what is known as 'regression pauses' while the reader struggles to make sense of the text.

• **Page size**. In the days of dial-up, we had to remember that pages might load very slowly, but this is no longer the case as broadband becomes more common (and faster). It is still wise to keep your pictures small and to size them down to 72 pixels per inch. Simplicity is also coming back into vogue as more and more people view websites on their mobile phones, so a page that needs a lot of scrolling is difficult to read on a mobile screen.

• **Graphics**. Every graphic must speak: make sure its iconography is clear and unambiguous. Remember that when you insert a picture you must give an explanatory note in the ALT (Alternative) command so that software that reads to the partially sighted or blind can tell the user what the pictures are. It also pops up as a little yellow box hovering over the image area and presents an opportunity to preview in words what the picture illustrates.

• **Artist's portfolio**. A gallery of small thumbnail illustrations is useful for showcasing an artist's range of work, with a click-link to larger pictures. Take care not to offer high-quality graphics that could be plagiarised: most internet graphics are in jpeg format, which is 72 ppi and not suitable for print reproduction. It's advisable to watermark all artwork.

• **Animation**. Bullet points or graphic elements help pick out key words but animations should be avoided. Studies show that the message is lost when television images fail to reinforce spoken words. The same is true of the web.

• **Frames**. Using frames used to be an elegant solution to navigation problems but for the user it's not ideal, especially for anyone with accessibility problems. Because the page name on the URL never varies, the visitor never knows where they are. They cannot bookmark a particular page, or find it again on a second visit and that can be very frustrating.

Going online

Once you have the planning, writing and graphics of your website organised, you need a little basic technical understanding to get it online. Your service provider will have a starter kit of instructions – although whether they make sense is another matter. Fortunately, the internet is chock-a-block with instructional material. Try 1st Site Free (see *Useful websites* box), which outlines and expands on seven easy steps – plan, design, code, upload, test, promote and maintain – or Google sites.

An alternative is to use software that 'talks you through' setting up a small site with what are called 'wizards'. Wizards come in software programs such as FrontPage (a stand-

Useful websites

Amazon Bookshop Associates Scheme
http://affiliate-program.amazon.co.uk
For linking to sales of your own (or recommended) books. Small source of income.

Alert Box
www.useit.com/alertbox
Web usability and readability analysis. Opinionated but pertinent and kept up to date.

The CGI Resource Index
www.cgi-resources.com
Scripts that you can buy (some are free), e.g. automatic forms, page counters and pop-up boxes.

1st Site Free
www.1stsitefree.com
Create a website in 7 easy steps. A good starting point; links to useful tools.

Google sites
www.google.com/sites
A free and easy way to create a website without learning code. Limited design.

Joomla
www.joomla.com
An open source content management system for those who want to use database systems. Free, complex but well supported.

Namesco
www.names.co.uk
Cheap and easy registration of domain names. They'll even talk to you on the phone.

Pedalo
www.pedalo.co.uk
Website design and promotion services for writers. Used by Ian Rankin, Jeannette Winterson, Philip Pullman, the Arvon Foundation and many others.

Square Space
www.squarespace.com
A managed environment for creating a website without learning any code. From $8–$50 a month.

Validator
http://validator.w3.org
Free online validation of HTML code.

Vimeo
http://vimeo.com
Allows you to add large video clips to your website.

Virtual Internet
www.vti.net
Full range of internet hosting and domain registration facilities.

Web Style Guide
www.webstyleguide.com
Excellent guide to aspects of web writing. Used to be the Yale Style Manual.

WinSCP
http://winscp.net/eng
Free transfer file software for PCs.

YouSendIt
www.yousendit.com
Send very large files that are too big for ordinary email. There's a free version that will suit most authors.

YouTube
www.youtube.com
Also good for embedding a code in your website to link to a video, but smaller clips than Vimeo.

Zone Alarm
www.zonealarm.com
Firewall (free and pro versions) to protect you against intrusions, spam and pop-ups. It is worth investing in the security suite.

alone addition to Microsoft Office). It resembles word processors and keeps the coding hidden from view. Hard core web designers will sneer at these programs, because programmers like to control the way the code works themselves. What they do not realise is that writers want to concentrate on the words, not the coding, and as long as it functions, the refinements of the underlying structure are of less importance. For artists who are more concerned with design, the best package is Dreamweaver (which is expensive and not easy to learn).

Once the pages are ready, the next step is to transmit them to the service provider's machines. The mechanics of this are frequently opaque even when you are offered a handy button that says 'Publish'. The chances are that your service provider will not have the extensions that make the 'Publish' button work and you will have to acquire a (free) File Transfer Protocol (ftp) program. If you are technophobe, this may seem frightening at first. However, it is really very simple and once you have successfully transferred (or uploaded) the pages from your computer to the web space on the remote server, you will wonder what the problem was. For this transfer process you will need to know the host name, your user ID and your password, information available from your provider. Even simpler for those who have WiFi or Bluetooth is automatic synchronisation (particularly on the Mac).

HTML

If you want to learn HTML (HyperText Markup Language) – the code that tags elements such as text, links and graphics so that browser software will know how to display a document – then you need only a plain text program, like Notepad, and an HTML primer (there are plenty online as well as in printed form). Find some website pages which you like and look at their source code to see how they have been constructed (click the subsidiary button of the mouse, usually the right button, and select View Source).

Websites for design

Art and the Zen of Web Sites
www.tlc-systems.com/webtips.shtml
Why the web is not a place to show off artistic skills.

Craft & Design Selected
www.craftmaker.co.uk
Free online gallery for makers and designers.

Lightbox
www.huddletogether.com/projects/lightbox2
A very nice downloadable code that allows you to have thumbnails of pictures onscreen which enlarge as you hover over them.

Mini Gallery
www.minigallery.co.uk
A platform for British artists to promote themselves on the internet.

UK Web Design Association
www.ukwda.org
Promotes industry standards.

VisiBone
www.visibone.com
Web-safe colours, style sheets and other resources

Web-safe fonts
www.microsoft.com/typography/web/fonts

Websites for Artists
www.beyondthenorthwind.co.uk
Artscape package designed for artists to add pictures to their own site. Affordable.

Going a step further

You may wish to have a web address or URL that is short or memorable so that it is easier for people to find your website. You can choose this domain name yourself, and is now relatively cheap (see box on page 644).

It is probably best to leave e-commerce (having a secure site that can handle credit card sales) till later. In the meantime, however, a simple way to boost your income is to become an Amazon Associate. If your book titles are linked to Amazon, you'll make a percentage on a direct sale made from your site.

Jane Dorner is the author of 22 books and formerly represented authors' interests on the boards of the Authors' Licensing and Collecting Society and the Copyright Licensing Agency.

See also...

- *E-publishing*, page 629
- *Writing a blog*, page 647
- *Ebooks*, page 635
- *Websites for writers*, page 652
- *Marketing yourself online*, page 625

Writing a blog

A blog is a way to publish your ideas instantaneously for an online audience. It allows for readers to comment just as swiftly on what you have to say. Isabella Pereira introduces the world of blogging and describes how to set up a blog of your own.

Whether you're finishing a feature or crafting a novel, writing can be a lonely life. And while some might argue that seclusion is the only way to produce half decent work, unless you're an Emily Dickinson type, staring at a blank screen waiting for the 'flow' is probably going to send you potty. So, should the four walls of your 'room of one's own' be closing in, writing a blog could be the perfect tonic: both a steam vent for your inspirations and a gateway to the real world and real readers. All you'll need are a little time, energy and – if you're lucky enough to attract lots of readers – a thick skin.

What is a blog?

A blog (short for 'weblog') is a personal website to which you can make regular updates ('posts') – an online platform for your thoughts, laced with links to other websites, pictures and even sound or video clips. The latest material appears at the top, where readers can comment on it, link to it, or (worst of all) ignore it. Your posts are tagged by date and category, and stored chronologically in an archive which you can access through links on your site. You can use a blog to publish journalism, opinion, creative writing or technical expertise. It's completely free because the 'hosting' of your site (in other words, your webspace) is paid for by advertising revenue generated by the website you use to create the blog. And, in the finest spirit of the web, it's a living thing, part of a global community of the sophisticated, the sympathetic, the opinionated and the downright rude.

The glory of blogging lies not just in its immediacy but in its lack of rules, its openness and in the sheer diversity of the 'blogosphere'. The best bloggers can open a window into private worlds and passions, or provide a blast of fresh air in an era when corporate giants control most of our media. From new mums to teachers to Whitehall wonks, bloggers will tell you the unadulterated truth, often artfully veiled in the anonymity of cyberspace. Indeed anonymity has been the key to the success of many blogs, liberating the voices of writers who have taken politics and journalism by the scruff of the neck, demystified the web and quite simply made people laugh and look at the world differently.

What are writers blogging about?

Bloggers are a far from homogenous bunch and, unlike the competitive, sometimes forbidding, world of getting between hard covers, there is absolutely nothing to stop you joining them. Unsurprisingly, more than a handful of established writers are among their number.

Some have put blogging firmly at the centre of their universe, happily dedicating the weekly stints it takes to make a site take off. Adult and children's writer Neil Gaiman's site (see box) is one of the best. A blogger since 2001, Gaiman continues to make the most of blogging's potential with a rich, regularly updated and very personal site which has his thousands of fans addicted. His daily posts tell fans about new enthusiasms: music, books, tour news and work-in-progress. Novelist and columnist Will Self is a newcomer to blogging but the medium suits his pithy, observational style perfectly. Poet George Szirtes's blog is home to elegant daily disquisitions on politics, art and, sometimes, domesticity – an example of how wonderful writing can make the most mundane of life's occurrences well worth getting Broadband for. And short story writer, novelist and poet Sarah Salway uses her blog for 'regular writing prompts and inspiration, but mostly random notes of things that take my fancy' – reassuring reading for her fellow writers.

And what about the others?

You don't have to be an established wordsmith to write a cracking blog. Some of the best online opinions about books, publishing and writing can be found on the blogs of 'amateur' writers, whose work is often anything but. The artful Fiction Bitch uses her blog to comment on 'bookworld' debate, opinion and news. And publishers haven't wanted to miss the boat: on the Penguin blog you'll find details of the travails of writing a blurb, creating a jacket and the pleasures and pains of being a commissioning editor.

Why should I write a blog?

Blogs are a great place to test out new material, get some feedback from the like-minded and enjoy the gratifying experience of actually seeing yourself in print. If you've already got a website, you should take heed of how blogs are used by writers to keep fans coming back, with juicy new material that is updated regularly. This is as true for writers with a profile as for those without. A blog is also a fine way to control your public image. Many writers use their sites as their 'official mouthpiece' to dispel rumours and give their opinion from the horse's mouth. A blog can help you construct and manage what you present to the public. Whether you prefer a greater openness or less speculation, blogging means that you can have the final word rather than leaving it to the press.

But what if no one's heard of me?

That's the point! With or without the public profile, a blog can be the perfect place to cut your teeth or test new material – with the additional kick of seeing yourself published straight away. If you're having trouble motivating yourself to write 2000 words a day, the regular deadline of a blog update can be an excellent way of accumulating material. Blogs can be fertile ground for fiction: Jeremy Blachman, author of the recent blog-turned-novel *Anonymous Lawyer,* wrote such a convincing character that readers were certain that the writer was a monstrous L.A. lawyer rather than a humble student. Bestselling author of *Labyrinth*, Kate Mosse, generated her novel through a blog, sharing characters, scenarios and her motivation for writing the book with her audience and drawing directly on their responses. Some of book industry's most successful recent finds have been blogs first of all, notably those of self-professed London call girl Belle de Jour and Salam Pax, the famous 'Baghdad Blogger'. For these writers, the success of their blogs brought their writing to the attention of agents and publishers – in the same way that what Helen Fielding's long-running column in the *Independent* did for *Bridget Jones' Diary*. The only difference these days is that you don't have to be an established writer to try it. Which takes us to the next pressing question about blogs.

How do I get started?

A blogging 'portal' (a website for creating and hosting blogs) will lead you through all the steps to setting up a personal blog – see box for some of the best ones. You simply need to register on the site, choose a name under which to write, select a layout for the page from the templates on offer and you're practically ready to go. All you'll need now is something to say…

What should I write?

The best blogs have a distinctive voice – they're warm, witty, acerbic, opinionated, emotional or all of the above. Most of all, they're honest. Blogs work best when they have an unusual viewpoint. They aren't usually high art – they're timely and bitesized. To capture the notoriously short attention span of the internet audience you'll need to be short, sharp and, ideally, have an unusual angle for your blog. You don't have to be trapped in a war zone (though it definitely helps). If you're short of ideas, think about an aspect of your life that you could write about in a distinctive way: your job, your family, an organisation you're involved with. You can keep an account of an event you're taking part in, a hobby or art form you're passionate about and, of course, if you're writing fiction you could try your characters for size.

Guidelines

Strictly speaking, there are no rules in cyberspace. But if you want your blog to have regular readers, and even better, to have people linking to you, it may help if you:

- keep your posts short – the average internet reader doesn't dawdle;
- write in the first person and use declarative sentences;
- keep your writing uncomplicated and avoid jargon at all costs;
- use short paragraphs – web readers need white space, because it is difficult to read a solid block of text on a computer screen;

Useful websites

Setting up a site

http://blogger.com
A blogging portal.

http://typepad.com
A blogging portal.

http://wordpress.org
A blogging portal.

http://flickr.com
A photo storage website.

http://photobucket.com
A photo storage website.

http://twitter.com
The home of twittering.

Some writers' blogs

http://neilgaiman.com
Neil Gaiman's website.

http://georgeszirtes.co.uk
George Szirtes's website.

http://will-self.com
Will Self's website.

http://sarahsalway.blogspot.com
Novelist Sarah Salway's blog.

Also worth a visit

http://thepenguinblog.typepad.com
Penguin's publishing blog.

http://fictionbitch.blogspot.com
Fiction Bitch's books and publishing blog.

http://anonymouslawyer.blogspot.com
Jeremy Blachman's blog.

http://mosselabyrinth.co.uk
Kate and Greg Mosse's *Labyrinth* site.

www.dynamicobjects.com/d2r/planb
Diego Doval's 'blognovel', *Plan B.*

http://commentisfree.guardian.co.uk/jackie_ashley/2006/05/in_defence_of_professional_col.html
Jackie Ashley on the perils of being a high-profile blogger (the *Guardian*).

http://guardian.co.uk/g2/story/0,,2051394,00.html
Jessica Valenti on blogging (the *Guardian*, 6 April 2007).

- use subheadings, and bold and italicised text liberally;
- if you can't be brief, be very, very interesting and make sure you entertain your readers. This goes for all kinds of writing but never more so than when trying to fix the attention of ruthlessly surf-happy web-readers;
- be conversational, funny and opinionated — the internet is not a formal place and a sense of humour is essential, not just in your content but in readiness for animated feedback on your work;
- use your headlines and tell as much of the story as possible in them – the headline should not only hook the reader but express the content explicitly. Many people use 'news feeders' which scan headlines for keywords, so keep this in mind when writing if you're looking to get picked up in searches;
- use lots of links – links uniquely enrich writing for the web and readers expect them. Make sure you link to all the blogs, articles, biographies and sites you mention and use links wherever they can help clarify or add depth to your post. It pays to be as original with links as your writing – seek out some of the more offbeat material on the web, and offer a full opinion on sites you link to;
- express yourself – blogging is an opportunity to be published with complete artistic freedom, so make sure you make the most of it;
- be thick-skinned – opinions online are untrammelled, so be ready for unwelcome 'flamings' from fellow bloggers who might not like your style. What's more, irony is rife and taking yourself too seriously can be asking for trouble.

How often should I write?

Blogs do die if they're not updated but blogger burnout is an equally likely cause of death. If you try to update every day but don't have the time or the energy, your site will be the next burnout casualty, so it's important to decide upon a realistic schedule for posting. Updating daily makes perfect sense if you're doing something newsworthy each day but if not, save your thoughts for the next post. It's fine not to post for a few days or even weeks but don't go completely silent. A blog is a living thing and it needs feeding.

What about pictures?

You can get away without them but it would be a shame not to use photos to make the most of the web's all-singing, all-dancing capacities. Good writing is vital but visual layout is also important on the web. Pictures break up blocks of text and can bring your blog to life. All custom blogging websites allow you to add simple pictures and, for a larger catalogue of images, you can link through to a photo-sharing site (see box for some links). Use some judgement in which pictures you post up, though – even your die-hard fans won't want to plough through every holiday snap. On the web this makes for very tedious 'scrolling through' time.

How will people find me?

Keywords in the headlines of your blog posts will ensure that you're picked up by searches made through blogging portals and search engines. Be aware people can sign up for email updates from blog aggregators and through RSS feeds (RSS stands for 'Rich Site Summary' and is a digested version of the new content on a website) to keep them updated with new posts they are interested in. Your blogging portal will give you the option to add RSS feeds to your own site. Finally, start exploring your community: make friends with other like-minded bloggers and swap links on your sites.

Vlog and twitter

When you've got the pictures licked, you might want to graduate to adding 'podcasts' (regular digital audio clips) or a 'vlog' (a 'video log', i.e. regularly updated digital video clips) to your site. As digital video is becoming increasingly simple to use, vlogs are becoming more common on sites. If you can beg or borrow a digital video camera, it's worth considering adding this extra dimension.

Brevity being the soul of the blog, if you haven't the energy to write an entire post you can now 'twitter' instead (see box). Twitter is blogging-lite – you simply update your site with what you're doing right at that moment and all those signed up in your online social circle are instantly updated on your activities.

A final word

Writing a blog means you can see yourself published in minutes, test out material and ensure you're writing regularly. Yet without the time-honoured authority of the printed page behind you, you're vulnerable to the many sharpened wits of cyberspace – or even their indifference. Jackie Ashley, writing in the *Guardian* and Jessica Valenti (www.feministing.com) have written about the occasional perils of a blogging profile (see box) so you need to be aware that the web community is enormous, diverse and deeply opinionated. As much of a marketplace as any bookshop but many millions of times bigger, browsers on the web are disinclined to linger. But good writing and engaging with the blogging community can compel readers to come back and ensure your blog develops a life of its own. Most of all, blogging is simple, free and has huge creative potential – don't be afraid to try it.

Isabella Pereira is an editor and intermittent blogger who has worked in book publishing.

See also...

- *Books published from blogs*, page 281
- *Setting up a website*, page 641
- *E-publishing*, page 629
- *Websites for writers*, page 652
- *Ebooks*, page 635
- *Marketing yourself online*, page 625

Websites for writers

Jane Dorner lists some online resources for writers.

New to the internet

BBC Web Wise
www.bbc.co.uk/education/webwise/course

How to get started on the internet.

FAQ
www.faqs.org

Frequently Asked Questions on just about anything to do with the internet.

Google
www.google.co.uk

The current favourite amongst search engines.

How Stuff Works
www.howstuffworks.com

Fairly technical explanations about how the internet works, and much more.

Fact finding online

Ananova (UK Press Association)
www.ananova.com

Latest stories from the UK's top news and information websites; useful free daily round-up of news, sport and information by email.

Ask Oxford
www.askoxford.com

Various bits from the language dictionaries; changing word news and word-based interest.

Bartlett's Familiar Quotations
www.bartleby.com

Bibliomania
www.bibliomania.com

Excellent full text with a good word or phrase retrieval; includes the wonderful Brewer's *Dictionary of Phrase & Fable* (which no author can do without).

British Library
http://portico.bl.uk

Free search for material held in the major Reference and Document Supply collections of the British Library.

CIA World Factbook
www.cia.gov/cia/publications/factbook

Statistical data about countries and other useful data.

Crossref
www.crossref.org

A collaborative reference linking service for publishers and researchers.

Encyclopaedia Britannica
www.britannica.com

Full text and searching, together with a huge resource of information, grammar and reference links. Some free; premium subscription £9.95 p.a.

Free Pint
www.freepint.com

Free bi-monthly email newsletter with tips and articles on finding reliable sites and searching more effectively. Written by information professionals.

Internet Public Library
www.ipl.org

Reference section containing subject overviews, biography, etc. Now part of a larger consortium.

Response Source
http://sourcewire.com

UK journalists can request business information in a single step from over 300 organisations.

Roget's Thesaurus
www.bartleby.com/62

Third edition (1995).

WATCH – Writers, Artists and their Copyright Holders
http://tyler.hrc.utexas.edu

Database of information on whom to contact for permission to publish in copyright text and images. Not fully comprehensive. A joint project of the University of Texas and the University of Reading.

Wikipedia
http://en.wikipedia.org

Free encyclopedia based on the 1960 edition of *Encyclopaedia Britannica*. Can't always be relied upon as individuals can edit it and occasionally do so maliciously.

Writing communities

Agent Research
www.agentresearch.com

For professional writers and agents in the UK, USA and Canada.

Apples and Snakes
www.applesandsnakes.org

For poets.

ArtScape
www.artscape.org.uk

National directory for arts in education.

Ask About Writing
www.askaboutwriting.net

Reviews writing websites from a writer's point of view. Also shows Swanwick news.

Authonomy
www.authonomy.com

Book community supported by HarperCollins.

BBC writersroom
www.bbc.co.uk/writersroom
www.bbc.co.uk/commissioning

How to submit ideas and scripts to the BBC.

Contact an Author
www.contactanauthor.co.uk

The Word Pool, run by a writer for writers.

Children's Discovery
www.childrensdiscovery.org.uk

Writers in schools.

E-Writers
http://e-writers.net

Sponsored links for goods, services, competitions and advice.

Expert Sources
www.expertsources.co.uk

Journalist resource.

Freelancers in the UK
www.freelancersintheuk.co.uk

Well authenticated resource for and about journalists.

HackWriters
www.hackwriters.com

UK-based free internet magazine devoted to good writing on any subject. No fees; forum of exchange.

LibraryThing
www.librarything.com

You can have your own profile page and share book passions.

Literature North East
www.literaturenortheast.co.uk

Events taking place in North East England.

New Writing South
www.newwritingsouth.com

Organisation for the encouragement of dramatic writing in the UK.

Nibweb
www.nibweb.co.uk

Network for UK non-fiction educational writers.

Second Life
http://secondlife.com

A virtual community for people who enjoy imaginary lives.

SunOasis
www.sunoasis.com

A site for writers, editors and copywriters with some international job opportunities. US-based.

You Write On
www.youwriteon.com

Arts Council England-sponsored free website to help new writers.

Worthy of Publishing
www.worthyofpublishing.com

Community of writers.

Writers Net
www.writers.net

US-based forum for writers, editors, agents and publishers. Participants exchange ideas about the writing life and the business of writing.

Writelink
www.writelink.co.uk

Resource site linking to paying markets, competitions, reference sites, software and so on. Well maintained. Free registration.

WritersServices.com
www.writersservices.com

Offers editorial services and advice from well-known writers; pitched largely at unpublished authors.

New media writing prizes

Eppie Awards for E-books
www.epicauthors.com

Fiction and non-fiction categories as well as book design.

Java Museum Online Awards
www.javamuseum.org/start1.htm

For innovative art and new media installations and computer-based art.

Nesta Awards for Art and Science
www.nesta.org.uk

Up to £75,000 to spend a year developing a new creative idea; very competitive.

Miscellany

Note: Some of these are archive sites and most have a US bias.

Dying Words
www.corsinet.com/braincandy/dying.html

For the historical novelist.

EasyBib.com
www.easybib.com

Works out for you how to do citations for books, maps, photographs, etc. in different accepted styles.

Famous Birthdays
www.famousbirthdays.com

Month-by-month and day-by-day listing of birth dates, historical and in the media.

Famous Firsts
www.corsinet.com/trivia/1-triv.html

People-who-did-something-first arranged in ascending date order.

First Writer
www.firstwriter.com

Listing of prizes, publishers, agents, for first-time writers.

Flickr
www.flickr.com

A site where you can show your photographs either to the general public or to targeted groups of people.

Google Reader
www.google.com/reader

An aid to help you keep up with new content on favourite websites.

Ideas for writers
www.ideas4writers.com

A miscellany containing anniversaries and genre ideas – membership gained by buying a self-help book for £5.99.

iTools
www.itools.com/research-it

Little battery of dictionaries and acronym converters. Significant literary events.

Perpetual Virtual Calendars
www.vpcalendar.net

A historical or science fiction novelist's dream: verify any date or day of the week in the 20th and 21st centuries.

Photobucket
http://photobucket.com

A site where you can show your photographs either to the general public or to targeted groups of people.

Picasa
http://picasa.google.com

A site where you can show your photographs either to the general public or to targeted groups of people.

Proceedings of the Old Bailey
www.oldbaileyonline.org

Useful resource for crime writers containing a searchable database of 197,745 criminal trials held at London's central criminal court from 1674 to 1913.

Rhyming Dictionary
www.rhymezone.com

Time Zone Converter
www.timezoneconverter.com

What time it is or will be anywhere in the world.

What's on When
www.whatsonwhen.com

Useful for newspaper and magazine writers (or for planning holidays).

Who is or Was
www.biography.com

Good for checking people's dates; incorporates the *Cambridge Dictionary of American Biography.*

Writer Pictures
www.writerpictures.com

A global resource for images of authors.

Texts online

Bible Gateway
http://bible.gospelcom.net/bible

Electronic Text Center
http://etext.lib.virginia.edu/english.html

Collection of online English language texts; links to other texts online by subject or by author.

The English Server
http://eserver.org

Large publishing co-operative of interesting resources. Holds 35,000 free works.

Internet Archive
www.archive.org

Texts, audio, video and music archive. The Wayback Machine archives previous websites.

Oxford Text Archive
www.ota.ahds.ac.uk

Distributes more than 2500 resources in over 25 different languages for study purposes only. Maintenance erratic.

Project Gutenberg
www.gutenberg.net

The official sites (many mirrors all over the world); vast library of e-texts, mostly public domain; all in plain text format.

Shakespeare Resources
www.shakespeare.com

Links to many other sites.

Writing tools

Check compatibility with all the following software as some do not work under Windows Vista and Windows 7.

Screenwriting

Dramatica
www.dramatica.com

Screenplay software; not free – compare it with ScreenForge (below).

Final Draft
www.finaldraft.com

Apparently the bees knees of scripting software – expensive (about $250), high functionality and cross-platform compatibility.

ScreenForge
www.apotheosispictures.com

Almost free Hollywood scriptwriting format bolt-on for Word. No maintenance.

Storyware

Creativity Unleashed
www.cul.co.uk

Software to stimulate creative thinking, originally intended for business.

New Novelist
www.newnovelist.com

Software to help you write a novel – it doesn't do it *for* you, of course.

StoryBoard Quick
www.powerproduction.com

Storyboard software for films, animation, games, etc.

Story Wizard
www.storywizard.co.uk

Software that helps 9–16 year-olds to write stories.

Web Store for Writers and Creative Pros
www.masterfreelancer.com

Plots Unlimited, Writer's Software Companion and other software aids.

Word processing aids

Scrivener
www.literatureandlatte.com/scrivener.html

A word processor and project management tool for writers of long texts. For Mac only.

WordTips
www.vitalnews.com/wordtips

How to get the best out of Microsoft Word; useful tips, many a real boon for writers. Opening page greets the viewer with 'It's not your fault'.

Jane Dorner is the author of 22 books and formerly represented authors' interests on the boards of the Authors' Licensing and Collecting Society and the Copyright Licensing Agency. She edits *Glass Circle News*.

See also...

- *Setting up a website*, page 641
- *E-publishing*, page 629
- *Writing a blog*, page 647
- *Ebooks*, page 635
- *Marketing yourself online*, page 625

Websites for artists

Several of the regional arts offices sites provide useful information for artists, as do some of the government sites, and many artist organisation sites provide links to other sites. Alison Baverstock introduces some web addresses which will be useful as a starting point.

Information for artists

a-n The Artists Information Company

www.a-n.co.uk

Comprehensive knowledge bank with sections covering self-employment, markets for art, employment options, professional practice, the art world and artists' strategies complemented by daily-updated jobs and opportunities, interactive toolkits for calculating fees, contracts and professional development and related resources. Archive since 2001 of *a-n Magazine*, *a-n Collections* and *Research papers*. Some free access material including *Code of practice for the visual arts*.

www.a-n.co.uk/interface

Platform for visual art exhibitions and events and critical writing, with continuously updated what's on, reviews (unedited) and venue and reviewer index. Free access.

www.a-n.co.uk/artists_talking

Exposing the practices of contemporary visual artists through projects' unedited artists' blogs, commissioned portfolio of artists' stories and the UK's largest editorially selected image bank with over 8000 works by some 3000 artists. Free access.

AN publishes *a-n Magazine*; see page 34.

APD Network

www.apd-network.info

Lists over 40 UK organisations concerned with supporting artists' professional development through information, advice and training programmes.

Arena

www.arenaworks.com

Represents a diverse group of illustrators with a range of distinctive styles.

Artquest

www.artquest.org.uk

Advice and information service for visual artists and craftspeople in London. Information and advice on creating new work, exhibiting and selling work, managing your career, and working internationally. Includes Artel.i.ier and Artroute sections.

The Art Net Directory

www.artnetdirectory.co.uk

A wide range of information for professional and amateur artists.

Arts Access UK

www.artsaccessuk.org

An access guide to the arts in the UK.

Artscape

www.artscape.org.uk

A national directory for organisations and individuals who undertake educational work.

Arts Council England

www.artscouncil.org.uk

The national development agency for the arts in England, distributing public money to fund a range of activities. The website offers useful information on public policy towards the arts and current funding (such as which areas of the arts each organisation handles). The 'press and news' section offers useful statistics on the arts in England as well as links to other sites.

The Arts Council of Northern Ireland

www.artscouncil-ni.org

Information on arts policy, funding schemes and contacts in Northern Ireland.

The Arts Council of Wales

www.artswales.org.uk

Information on arts policy, funding schemes and contacts in Wales.

Axis – the online resource for contemporary art

www.axisweb.org

The leading online resource for information about contemporary art. Features profiles of professional artists and curators, interviews, discussions, art news and debates, and showcases the artists to watch. You can join as an artist or curator member to profile your work online and become a part of the Axis art community from as little as £22.50 p.a. Axis also commissions interviews, essays and articles by leading and emerging writers inspired by the artists on the website. Axis is a non-for-profit charity funded by Arts Council England, the Arts Council of Wales and the Scottish Arts Council. Established 1991.

Birkbeck College, University of London

www.bbk.ac.uk/lib/subguides/artshum/historyofart

Offers details of art history libraries in London.

The Crafts Council
www.craftscouncil.org.uk

Offers services for both makers and members of the public interested in craft practice and purchase.

Creative Entrepreneurs Club
www.creativeentrepreneurs.com

The network for creative industries in Scotland.

Cultural Enterprise – Menter Diwylliannol
www.cultural-enterprise.com

Information on business support for creative industries in Wales.

Cultural Enterprise Office
www.culturalenterpriseoffice.co.uk

Scotland's specialist creative and cultural industry service, assisting individuals with the development of their business, arts practice and continued professional development through information and advice.

Cywaith Cymru – Artworks Wales
www.cywaithcymru.org

Listings of public art and residency projects in Wales.

Department for Culture, Media and Sport
www.culture.gov.uk

Holds the latest research reports on the creative industries.

Design and Artists Copyright Society (DACS)
www.dacs.co.uk

Information for members on copyright and intellectual property. UK collection agency for Artist's Resale Right. See also page 717.

HM Revenue & Customs
www.hmrc.gov.uk

Useful information on tax, national insurance and self-assessment – particularly helpful if you are new to being self employed.

Institute of International Visual Arts (inIVA)
www.iniva.org

A contemporary visual arts organisation with a special interest in new technologies, commissioning site-specific artworks and international collaborations.

Intellectual Property
www.ipo.gov.uk

The Government's information site on copyright and other intellectual property rights.

International Association of Residential Arts Centres
www.resartis.org

An online directory of residency centres worldwide.

The London Schools Arts Service
www.lonsas.org.uk

Promotes contact between artists and schools; includes a database of artist-in-residence opportunities.

National Statistics: the official UK statistics site
www.statistics.gov.uk

Publishes a range of general and specific statistics on the arts.

The New York Foundation for the Arts
www.nyfa.org

A campaigning organisation seeking to link artists and arts organisations with funding.

Public Art South West
www.publicartonline.org.uk

Offers information on contacts, opportunities and practical advice on public art.

The Scottish Arts Council
www.sac.org.uk

Information on arts policy, funding schemes and contacts in Scotland.

Trans Artists
www.transartists.nl

Netherlands-based site providing information on international artists-in-residence and exchange programmes, finances, cultural institutes (with links to their websites).

UK Trade and Investment
www.uktradeinvest.gov.uk

UK Trade and Investment assistance with helping a business grow internationally.

Your Creative Future
www.yourcreativefuture.org

A career-planning site for those involved in the arts.

Selling art online

Selling art online is becoming big business and is a popular and convenient method for viewing, commissioning and buying works of art. For the artist, online galleries are a very cost-effective, and occasionally free, method of trying out new pieces of work or bringing new custom to your own linked web pages. Some of the larger sites allow you to exhibit for nothing; on the other hand, payment for inclusion may mean there is less competition to distract potential buyers from your work.

www.artshole.co.uk

A website dedicated to promoting and selling the work of new contemporary artists, as well as providing information on exhibitions throughout the UK. No charge for artists to register.

www.bigart.co.uk

Specialises in original contemporary art, currently offering the work of 10 artists to the public.

www.britart.com

Eyestorm: a leading online gallery of limited edition contemporary art.

www.larts.co.uk

Displays the work of over 100 contemporary artists. No charge to have a page (subject to the work being approved).

www.minigallery.co.uk

Artists pay an all-inclusive annual membership subscription for personal mini website and a mini gallery. All sales are commission free with purchases made direct from the artist.

www.newbloodart.com

Specialises in early and mid-career artists. As well as showing work online, it also holds exhibitions and participates in fairs and shows (prices £50–£5000). No charge to have a page (subject to the work being approved); charges 35% commission.

www.numasters.com

Exhibits professional work free of charge but takes a commission when works are sold/loaned/made copyright. Also includes information on maintaining and developing an art collection for work or home.

www.saa.co.uk

The Society for All Artists allows artists to compete to show work in the Members' Gallery. Themes vary and artists can link to their own sites. Various membership packages and associated benefits.

www.ukartstore.com

A venue for artists to showcase their work and offer opportunities for commissioning. Now a sister website (www.theplaceforart.com) allows artists to apply for and subscribe to a user account and – if accepted – offer their work for sale via the site. For prints, artists will have the option of using the 'buy here' button to allow customers to order prints online via Paypal. For all original works and prints over £500 in value, artists are asked to deal directly with the customer. Artist's subscription: £5 per month to display up to 24 images plus 10% commission; no subscription fee for full-time art students.

www.wwar.com

US-based site where artists can exhibit through 3 levels of online portfolio to promote their work. Huge with supporting chat room, opportunities for advertising, etc.

Alison Baverstock is a former publisher who has written 18 books. The most recent are *Marketing Your Book: An Author's Guide* (A&C Black, 2nd edn 2008), which gives writers guidance on how to present their work to agents, publishers and readers, and *Is There a Book in You?* (A&C Black, 2006) outlines the resources needed by writers and offers advice on how to achieve publication. She teaches marketing – to authors and others – at Kingston University. Her website is www.alisonbaverstock.com.

See also...

- *Freelancing for beginners*, page 509
- *Winning the greeting card game*, page 527
- *Art agents and commercial art studios*, page 519

Resources for writers

Dealing with rejection

Alison Straw discusses how to deal with rejection by building resilience.

When you look back over the careers of the most successful writers and artists you will see that they've managed to navigate their way through rejection and failure. Perhaps one of the most quoted examples is that of the first Harry Potter book, which is reported to have been rejected by 14 publishers.

It's almost inevitable that at some point in your literary career your work will be rejected too. So how you manage rejection and build resilience is essential to your success. In fact the only way to avoid your work being rejected is to keep it to yourself.

It's not about you

What sets resilient people apart from others is the fact that they don't take rejection personally. Rejection hurts. It can be like a body blow but it's not about you or your value as a person. It's about your work and in the world of publishing rejection comes with the territory. In building your resilience, you need to make sure that this hurt doesn't translate into a loss of faith in yourself or in your work.

Ray Bradbury said that the secret of being a good writer was knowing when to reject success and when to accept rejection. I've heard others say that a 'no thank you' is not a rejection but rather an acknowledgement that you are trying: you are getting your work out there; you are a real writer and you believe in your work. You merely need to find the right person who shares your belief; and the publisher, agent or editor who has decided not to take your work is simply not that person.

There are many reasons for your work being rejected – it could be that it's just not good enough yet, that the typescript is too long, too short, too good, too similar to a story recently published, or it is simply not right for the reader at that moment in time. Remember it's about your work, not you.

Also remember that when you experience a setback it is temporary. So avoid blowing it out of proportion, otherwise you may predict the future negatively without considering other, more positive outcomes. Setbacks are difficult, but they are experiences which give you the opportunity to create a different and more positive future.

Pause

Even though you know that the bad news of rejection is not about you personally, it is important to take time out and recognise its impact. There is some truth to the old adage of dusting yourself off, but first let the dust settle. Everyone reacts differently, so create a natural pause by doing something that you find recuperative such as a going for a walk, having a nice meal, or talk it through with friends – whatever helps to lift your spirits and get a balanced perspective on the situation.

Reflect

One of the best ways to deal with rejection is to reflect. We make sense of things retrospectively, gathering valuable wisdom from reflecting on our experiences. Those that don't reflect on their experience and learn from their rejection can become stuck. For some this could lead to becoming bitter, helpless, frozen in a negative place or blaming others for not recognising the quality or importance of the work. In contrast, the traits of resilience, creativity, growth and optimism – all demand that you look forward.

Once you have recovered from your initial reaction to a rejection, take the time and effort to work things out for yourself. Often the quality of feedback you receive doesn't provide the information you need so you may need to make the connections yourself. Keep writing as most people write better if they practice. One of the best methods of reflecting on your work is to think of it in the context of others. So read widely and this may help you adapt, alter or simply inspire you.

Creating a book is a difficult and exacting process. If you look back over your work, you may feel that some of the text you've submitted to a publisher or literary agent is the best you can do. But other work, even though you thought it was good at the time you wrote it, may make you cringe when you reread it now. Reflect and hone your work – making sure that you are presenting your best work in the best possible way.

Move on

Building your resilience is all about managing strong feelings, emotions and impulses and channelling these emotions into positive activity. People who are not resilient stay in a place where their thoughts feed their insecurities and lack of belief. If you believe that you have just not reached the right person at the right time, then moving on is critical to your success.

So plan your action. You may need to ask yourself questions about what change is necessary to achieve success. Have I contacted the right people? Have I approached them in the right way? Who has been successful and what are they doing, that I could learn from? Used well, this *Yearbook* can give you many ideas. Or maybe it's time to do something completely different, and new technology offers new and creative ways of both publishing and promoting your work which are not too costly.

Ask for advice

When you receive a rejection for a typescript, you may get a standard response like 'we can see no market for that' or 'this doesn't fit with our current list', both of which don't give you much to work on. Ask for advice from people whose opinion you respect. It's always refreshing to experience how genuinely helpful people can be if approached in the right way. A starting point could be questions such as: Who else should I be talking to? What could I do differently? Are there examples of a successful proposal? If you feel awkward about this approach, perhaps you should seek out someone who can give professional editorial advice, appraisal and mentoring (see www.writersandartists.co.uk for listings of such services). Whilst this kind of feedback will come at a cost, it may result in receiving valuable advice or making the right contact which could generate the desired result. Alternatively, join a writing group, either in person or on the internet. Just being with like-minded people immediately removes the sense of isolation that writers sometimes experience and can also short-cut your learning by understanding what others have done, what has been successful and why.

Also, get out and meet people in the publishing world – go to writing group meetings; one of the many literary festivals such as the Crime Writing Festival or The Guardian Hay

Festival (see *Literature festivals* on page 615); book launches; anywhere you think is relevant. In time you may meet someone who provides another contact or whose experience makes you think again about your approach. Again, simple questions work best, such as: What advice would you give to a new author? If you were starting again what would you do differently? What's the best advice you've been given? Also explore opportunities on the internet; see *Websites for writers* on page 652.

Focus on success

It's important to understand what success looks and feels like and to make it part of your daily life. When do you feel successful? What leads to a sense of achievement? A solid and firm foundation builds resilience and will counterbalance the affect of receiving a rejection. All effective techniques for developing skills at feeling good will help you to understand about achievement.

Set realistic goals

Focusing on success means keeping the end goal in mind. By keeping your focus and expressing it repeatedly, whatever you are aiming for will become real. In resilient people their goal remains constant; however, their journey may take a variety of twists and turns.

Develop some realistic goals for yourself and do something regularly which moves you towards them, even if it seems like a small accomplishment at the time. Instead of focusing on tasks that seem unachievable, ask yourself, 'What's the one thing I know I can accomplish today or this week that helps me move in the direction I want to go?'

Become a problem solver

It's likely that in working towards a goal you will experience an impasse, but don't let this knock you. Think laterally and apply all your problem-solving skills to the situation. Reflect on an experience when you have faced a similar challenge and how you managed the problem or navigated the obstacle. Alternatively, think about the approaches you've used to problem solve in the past and apply them. These may be to walk away from the problem, share it, view it from another angle and hopefully something creative may develop, which could be just the right approach.

Try again

The more risks you take, the more successes you'll celebrate! Don't give up, bounce back, persevere, try something new – as a successful golfer once said, 'the more I practise the luckier I get'.

Sir Winston Churchill said: 'Success is the ability to go from one failure to another with no loss of enthusiasm.' I may replace the word 'failure' with 'rejection' or 'setback', but the sentiment remains the same. So keep trying, keep talking to others about your work and your aspirations and success will follow.

Alison Straw is a coach and trainer. She works with individuals and organisations on developing their capability to deal with challenges and change.

The writer's ultimate workspace

Arranging for a space to write in a domestic environment can be a mammoth challenge for some people. Rib Davis gives the benefit of his experience of writing from home.

This is a work of fiction. It is based on fact – as much of the best fiction is – but there is certainly more of the wish than the accomplishment in what follows. I have been asked to write an article giving advice to the prospective writer about some of the day-to-day material conditions and habits of mind that one should attempt to establish in order to be able to work happily and efficiently. I assume that I was chosen on the basis that I have, over 25 years, failed to do these so spectacularly that I am now considered an expert in the field. I may not have learned much from my mistakes but at least I can list some of them, and let the reader do the learning.

Finding the ideal workspace

Where should the workspace be located? When we have to, we can write anywhere. At my most desperate I have written parts of scripts on trains, in crowded offices, in pubs and even leaning on a car steering wheel while waiting for the AA to rescue me. Such is the power of the deadline. Sometimes, strangely, I have produced some rather good work while battling with the distractions and other limitations of the immediate environment; I would hesitate, however, to recommend the practice too highly.

So what would be the ideal workspace location? It seems to be generally agreed that a writer (or writers, if you are working collaboratively) should work in a place where distractions are minimal. Some highly successful writers have taken this to the extreme of working in a shed or a caravan at the bottom of the garden, with only elves for company. I have never owned a caravan, and unless I learn to write seated on a bicycle I will always have trouble squashing into our slowly rotting shed, so that has never been an option. But where possible a degree of isolation – and particularly isolation from family activities and domestic duties – does seem desirable. Sustained concentration is extremely important for any sort of creative work, and such a location helps to facilitate it. In my own case, when I am actually scripting (as opposed to researching or planning) I usually find that I have to read my notes and then the latest part of the script for about an hour before I can even begin to put new words onto the page, so anything that breaks the concentration is unwelcome.

At the same time, though, we are only as strong as our will-power. Many of us could stick ourselves in an arctic igloo to write and yet still manage to find distractions (examining snowflakes can be so fascinating). For about a year I did my writing in a room at the back of a bookshop in Milton Keynes, well away from my home. It seemed to offer the ideal combination of relative isolation along with a congenial, supportive and vaguely arty environment. But the lure of the books and the customers ultimately proved too much; I soon found myself helping out at the till rather then tapping away at my *magnum opus*.

Perhaps my need to write was not sufficiently urgent. Certainly it is true that in those days I was driven by blind hope rather than deadlines, but I don't think that was the problem. The problem was (and is) fear: fear of writing badly, of not living up to one's own – and others' – expectations. For me, at least, it is this fear above all that gets in the way of creativity. First I fear the blank page (of course), then the writing, and then the finishing. This is why those awful distractions can seem, in fact, very welcome indeed. And it is part of the reason why we should try to avoid them as far as possible.

For a few years, remarkably, I did work in a suitable location. Quite simply, this was a room in the house that I was able to turn into my study. It was not totally cut off from the rest of Life, but it was sufficiently separate to allow generally uninterrupted concentration. My small son had difficulty understanding why, if I was behind the door, I refused to open it, but apart from that it worked well. I am shortly to return to that blissful state of having a personal study, but for years now I have done most of my writing on the living room table. My laptop and notes are moved away at meal times; people traipse through the living room to get to the kitchen (why didn't we think of this when we bought the house?); the television is in the same room. In short, my workplace is set in the teeming hub of the house. Big mistake. Even with a family that has been whipped into acknowledging the needs of a writer, it is still a big mistake.

Cordial domestic relations

A word on educating one's family. A writer's partner and/or children will generally recognise and respect the writer's need to focus on the work in hand, but there is at least one point which needs clarifying. When I write, I take breaks. These breaks can occur for a variety of reasons. Perhaps I have reached an interim target, or I have become stuck, or I am thirsty, or just tired. So I might stop and play the piano, or make a cup of coffee, or – exceptionally – even do some washing up, and then return to the writing with a clearer head. No problem, except that this might be observed, and the observing partner/child may think, 'Ah, so he doesn't mind his concentration being broken after all.' This can be a problem. You have to be selfish. You have to make clear that you can break your own concentration as and when you feel the need – you can wrong-note your way through a whole Beethoven sonata if you feel like it – but that does not give others the green light to break your concentration as and when they feel the need. Be unreasonable.

So much for location. Now, what should the workspace look like? My answer would simply be: pleasant. It should be a welcoming place, where you will feel comfortable and not oppressed. For me, this means well decorated in soft colours, with the desk facing out to a window, preferably with a view, and a temperature that's warm but not sleep-inducing. For others, windows may present yet another distraction, colours should be severe, the radiator should be off and the whole place should be tatty. The point is that you should feel comfortable in it – it should feel like *your* space.

Where I have been able to, I have turned my space into an almost self-sufficient world. This requires at the very least coffee (stimulation), Scotch (counter the extreme effects of coffee) and a variety of non-laxative snacks (counter the other effects of coffee). Ideally I suppose an en-suite bathroom would be a good idea, but we should keep to the feasible. When I am really rich and famous I will also have an extra piano in my study, but for now I make do with a stereo. I find music (at least, some music) can create a less intense atmosphere when I am researching or planning, but when I am actually scripting I tend to turn it off, as otherwise I find the writing being influenced moment-to-moment by every passing mood of the music, which does not tend to improve the quality of my literary product at all.

Working efficiently

Writing is of course more than simply tapping words onto a page. It is also thinking, researching, planning and finally doing all the administrative work connected to the sale and then either publication or production of the work, whether through an agent or otherwise. So your workspace must be able to accommodate all this too. Give yourself as much work surface as possible, so that you can refer to as many materials as you need simultaneously, and you can even have materials left out for more than one project at a time. And set up an efficient filing system from the start. Or if, as in my case, this is certainly not the start, do it now anyway. Do not simply put every new publisher's letter, piece of research and pizza takeaway leaflet together in an in-tray. The in-tray eventually overflows; you get a second one; that overflows too. You will eventually be surrounded by in-trays. File everything as it comes along, and don't hesitate to open a new file for even the germ of a new project.

This filing particularly applies to emails. One can make the mistake of thinking that because something is there on the computer it has been filed. It hasn't. Electronic documents – and emails most of all – can be just as much of a mess as a physical desktop. When you receive an email, save it in the relevant project file elsewhere in the computer. If you are feeling super-efficient, you could also print it off and keep it in that same project's hard-copy file.

Mention of emails leads me on to phones. Both can take over your whole existence if you allow them to; they will certainly try. Deal with emails when you are at your least productive as a writer. If you think of yourself as a 'morning person' then that is when you should be writing; do the emails in the evening. Or if mornings tend to be barren periods of grogginess and haze, those are the times for doing emails. And try to deal with all the day's emails in one sitting; certainly don't let them interrupt you whenever they feel like it. Set up your computer in such a way that it does not let you know when emails have arrived; instead, just check them once or twice per day.

Similarly, don't simply answer the phone whenever it rings. The phone can of course be very useful for your writing, particularly for research, but in general – put the answerphone on. Better still, put it on and set it to silent. If the caller doesn't leave a message, it can't be very important.

A great deal of research is now done on the web, but I still like having books around. One of them is Jane Dorner's *The Internet: A Writer's Guide* (A&C Black 2000). Obviously a writer should have a really good dictionary (some of the larger ones give a date for each word usage, which is particularly helpful for period writing), and I also find a large thesaurus very useful (the original format, not the alphabetical kind; the latter is simpler to use but as it is necessarily so repetitive it contains far fewer options). Then there are always the books needed for the particular project in hand, alongside Ann Hoffmann's excellent *Research for Writers.*

Most writers actually fit their research and other writing activities in with other work, whether writing-related or not. This means that time becomes a very precious commodity. I have always worked best when I have been able to arrange my writing time in large chunks, preferably whole days. An hour here or there really is hardly any use. And whenever possible I have tried to establish routines. The truth is that I have been particularly bad at this, perhaps because I have often had too many projects at different stages simultaneously, but I would still recommend adopting a daily routine as far as possible. It means there is just one less decision to have to make: your writing times have been decided and that's it.

Writer's block

So now you are all set. You have bought yourself Final Draft software (or something similar) and you have the workspace, the materials, the books, the filing – the lot. You write and write. You pin the best rejection slips onto the wall (we've all had them). You write and write. And then you don't. You get writer's block. I have had this. It is a particularly nasty affliction as in almost everyone else's eyes 'writer's block' translates as 'laziness'. This is not the place for a full discussion, but I can pass on a couple of pieces of advice I received, which worked for me. Firstly, don't always try to see the whole piece of work, as that may be overwhelming to you. Try to focus on a particular section of it and nothing more. Secondly, when you have writer's block a whole day of writing ahead of you looks interminable. So don't do it. Strictly limit yourself to writing for two hours and no more. You may well find yourself writing with real urgency, trying to cram all that you can into those two allotted hours. Only much later can you gradually increase the limit back to a normal day.

Well, it worked for me. But then there are all sorts of writers. My old friend Jack Trevor Story had a writer's solution for insomnia: he wrote right through the night. Every night. It worked for him.

Now, as usual, I am going to try to learn from what I've written.

Rib Davis has been writing professionally for 28 years. He has over 60 credits, including scripts for radio, television and stage, as well as two books on the art of writing scripts. He is close to sorting out his domestic writing arrangements.

Writers' retreats

Some writers find that spending some time at a writers' retreat proves bountiful. An author who has twice benefited from this experience is Maggie Gee.

Writers' retreats are not for everyone. They aren't, for example, for the poet who once said to me, *a propos* of Hawthornden Castle International Writers' Retreat, 'But it's so quiet. And Edinburgh is *half an hour away* by bus.' For him, to be half an hour from the metropolis was a penance.

Retreats overseas

Creative Cauldron
website www.creativecauldron.com/retreats
A useful encyclopedic web page of retreats in the USA.

Before going into the desert, think long and hard. Are you quarrelsome, or oversensitive, or both? The other writers will, for the most part, be busy and quiet, but mealtimes are generally communal. People are more vulnerable when they are off their own territory and away from loved ones. Do not always eat the last piece of cake (food gains an emotional significance when other props are missing) or be competitive about how much you have written, or how much you get paid. Actual numbers of words and pounds should never be quoted. Do not give a reading from your new work unless asked.

Ask yourself hard questions before you go. Do you mind very much being away from your loved ones, your cat, your garden? Will you be wracked by guilt? Are you addicted to television? Do you feel anxious if you can't pick up emails or vary the monotony of your work with half-hourly binges on Google or Facebook? Most retreats have no televisions and some still have no internet connection.

But if you are a writer who can never get enough time uninterrupted by phone calls, plumbers, pets, children, and the washing-machine, writers' retreats are absolute heaven. For me personally, two widely spaced four-week stays at Hawthornden Castle produced the first drafts of two novels, *Where are the Snows* (1991) and my ninth novel, *The Flood*. When I am away from all the things I ought to do at home, 200–300 words a day swells into 2,000–3,000.

Prose writers have to come to terms with the leaden truth that you cannot write a book without hours of immobility. I personally prefer concentrating those hours into a smaller number of weeks and months. I speak as one whose eighth novel (*The White Family*), took seven years to write and rewrite (no retreats), whereas *The Flood*, after 18 months of mulling over, took just a month to dream up and write (at a retreat) and six months to rewrite. Poets like retreats too. I was at Hawthornden Castle last time with, among others, the poet Jean Sprackland, and while she was there she wrote most of her book *Hard Water*, since shortlisted for the T.S. Eliot Prize.

In the USA there is a wider choice of retreats. Google will present you with a bewildering variety of American retreats, many of them luxurious and long established. But although most of them are free, you have to find the air fare. In the UK there are fewer choices and only one retreat is free, Hawthornden Castle in Scotland, but unfortunately writers can only go there once every five years. You must make a formal application to the trustees and if you are accepted you can look forward to a stay in a beautiful castle in dramatic wooded grounds. The rooms are warm and attractive, the food is good, the staff are kind and the five or six writers who are in residence at any one time pay only for their pre-prandial sherry. The Arvon Foundation, which specialises in tutored retreats, also offers one week for plain untutored retreats at each of its four centres. Ireland has scenic, remote, beautiful Anam Cara, on the coast of Western Cork.

There are alternatives. When I struck a complete log jam in my work a few years ago, I tried a few days at St Cuthman's in Coolham, near Billingshurst in Sussex. A former Anglican retreat of long standing, this beautiful, peaceful place has been completely revivified by the Catholics who have now taken it over. As before, it is open to those of any or no faith who need rest. The rooms are simple, comfortable and elegant, with views over a lake and swans, fresh vegetables and home baking. There are prayers night and morning but you don't have to attend, though they seemed to work wonders for my novel.

There again, there are bargain weekly deals at out-of-season seaside hotels, or if you once went to a college or university, you could try ringing up to see if they let former *alumni* stay there cheaply in empty rooms. Many do, and they should have decent desks and chairs. As a last resort, send yourself on 'day retreats' to the local library or park, and don't go home until the pages are done. Once the washing machine, the telephone and the pets have fallen silent, the dream of the book will begin.

Maggie Gee has written one book of short stories and 11 acclaimed novels, including *The White Family*, shortlisted for the Orange Prize, *The Ice People* (revised edn 2008), and most recently two comedies about the UK and Uganda, *My Cleaner* and *My Driver* (Telegram, 2009). She was the first female Chair of the Royal Society of Literature (2004–8), is a Visiting Professor at Sheffield Hallam University and has been translated into 13 languages.

Anam Cara

website www.ugr.com/anamcararetreat

The Arvon Foundation

Free Word, 60 Farringdon Road, London EC1R 3GA
tel 020-7324 2554
website www.arvonfoundation.org
National Director Ruth Borthwick

See individual entries for the Foundation's 4 centres: The Hurst – The John Osborne Arvon Centre, Lumb Bank – The Ted Hughes Arvon Centre, Moniack Mhor and Totleigh Barton. As well as facilitating writers' retreats, the centres run many creative writing courses.

Hawthornden Castle

International Retreat for Writers, Lasswade, Midlothian EH18 1EG
tel 0131-440 2180 *fax* 0131-440 1989
Contact The Director

Exists to provide a peaceful setting where published writers can work without disturbance. The Retreat houses up to 6 writers at a time, who are known as Hawthornden Fellows. Writers from any part of the world may apply for the fellowships. No monetary assistance is given, nor any contribution to travelling expenses, but once arrived at Hawthornden, the writer is the guest of the Retreat. Application forms are available from January for the following calendar year. Deadline for applications 30 June. Previous occupants include Les Murray, Alasdair Gray, Helen Vendler, Olive Senior, Hilary Spurling and Maggie Gee.

The Hurst – The John Osborne Arvon Centre

The Arvon Foundation, The Hurst, Clunton, Craven Arms, Shrops. SY7 0JA
tel (01588) 640658
email thehurst@arvonfoundation.org
website www.arvonfoundation.org
Centre Directors Kerry Watson, Peter Salmon

Offers residential writing courses April–December. The Hurst is situated in the beautiful Clun Valley in South Shropshire, 12 miles from Ludlow, and is set in 30 acres of woodland, with gardens and a lake.

Irish Writers' Centre

19 Parnell Square, Dublin 1, Republic of Ireland
tel (01) 8721302 *fax* (01) 8726282
email info@writerscentre.ie
website www.writerscentre.ie
Contact Chairperson, Jack Harte

Residencies at the Irish Writers' Centre awarded on an occasional basis to enable writers to work on specific projects, for a period up to 3 monthsMost recent Writer-in Residence was Catherine Morris, who completed her biography of the poet Alice Milligan at the Irish Writers' Centre, in collaboration with University College Dublin and the National Library of Ireland. See website for further details.

Lumb Bank – The Ted Hughes Arvon Centre

The Arvon Foundation, Lumb Bank, Heptonstall, Hebden Bridge, West Yorkshire HX7 6DF
tel (01422) 843714 *fax* (01422) 843714
email lumbbank@arvonfoundation.org
website www.arvonfoundation.org
Centre Directors Liz Flanagan, Ben Jancovich, *Administrator* Ilona Jones

Offers one-week writing retreats. Lumb Bank is an 18th-century former mill-owner's house set in 20 acres of steep pasture land.

Moniack Mhor

The Arvon Foundation, Moniack Mhor, Teavarran, Kiltarlity, Beauly, Inverness-shire IV4 7HT
tel (01463) 741675
email m-mhor@arvonfoundation.org
website www.arvonfoundation.org, www.moniackmhor.org.uk
Centre Directors Cynthia Rogerson, Hamish MacDonald

Moniack Mhor is a traditional croft house commanding panoramic views over Highland landscapes with forest walks nearby. Courses run from April to November and are mainly tutored. Centre available at other times for schools, writing groups, etc.

St Cuthman's

Cowfold Road, Coolham, West Sussex RH13 8QL
tel (01403) 741220 *fax* (01403) 741026
email stcuthmans@dabnet.org
website www.stcuthmans.com
Contact The bookings secretary

Retreat house run by the RC Diocese of Arundel and Brighton offering peace, comfort and tranquillity in a wonderful setting. The Garden Room day facility for groups of up to 22 people.

Totleigh Barton

The Arvon Foundation, Totleigh Barton, Sheepwash, Beaworthy, Devon EX21 5NS
tel (01409) 231338 *fax* (01409) 231144
email t-barton@arvonfoundation.org
website www.arvonfoundation.org
Centre Directors Claire Berliner, Oliver Meek

Offers a writing retreat in August. Totleigh Barton is a thatched, pre-Domesday manor house, surrounded by farmland in Devon, 2 miles from the village of Sheepwash.

Tŷ Newydd

Tŷ Newydd Writers' Centre, Llanystumdwy, Cricieth, Gwynedd LL52 0LW
tel (01766) 522811 *fax* (01766) 523095
email post@tynewydd.org
website www.tynewydd.org

Writers' retreats are organised at different times during the year to give writers the opportunity to find a week's peace and quiet in Ty Newydd's stimulating environment. Everyone has a single room and stays on a self-catering basis with a shared meal in the evening.

Indexing

A good index is a joy to the user of a non-fiction book; a bad index will downgrade an otherwise good book. The function of indexes, and the skills needed to compile them, are examined here.

An index is a detailed key to the contents of a document, in contrast to a contents list, which gives only the titles of the parts into which the document is divided (e.g. chapters). Precisely, an index is 'A systematic arrangement of entries designed to enable users to locate information in a document'. The document may be a book, a series of books, an issue of a periodical, a run of several volumes of a periodical, an audiotape, a map, a film, a picture, a CD-Rom, a website, a database, an object, or any other information source in print or non-print form.

The objective of an index is to guide enquirers to information on given subjects in a document by providing the terms of their choice (single words, phrases, abbreviations, acronyms, dates, names, and so on) in an appropriately organised list which refers them to specific locations using page, column, section, frame, figure, table, paragraph, line or other appropriate numbers or hyperlinks.

An index differs from a catalogue, which is a record of the documents held in a particular collection, such as a library; though a catalogue may require an index, for example to guide searchers from subject words to class numbers.

A document may have separate indexes for different classes of heading, so that personal names are distinguished from subjects, for example, or a single index in which all classes of heading are interfiled.

The Society of Indexers

The Society of Indexers was founded in 1957 and is the only autonomous professional body for indexers in the UK. It is affiliated with the American Society for Indexing, the Australian and New Zealand Society of Indexers, the China Society of Indexers, the Indexing Society of Canada, and the Association of Southern African Indexers and Bibliographers, and has close ties with the Chartered Institute of Library and Information Professionals (CILIP) and the Society for Editors and Proofreaders (SfEP).

> **Further information**
>
> **Society of Indexers**
> Woodbourn Business Centre, 10 Jessell Street, Sheffield S9 3HY
> *tel* 0114-244 9561 *fax* 0114-244 9563
> *email* admin@indexers.org.uk
> *website* www.indexers.org.uk
> *Administrator* Wendy Burrow
> *Membership (2010)* £95.50 p.a. UK/Europe, £120 overseas; £185 corporate
>
> Publishers and authors seeking to commission an indexer should consult *Indexers Available* on the website.

The main objectives of the Society are to promote high standards in all types of indexing and highlight the role of indexers in the organisation of knowledge; to provide, promote and recognise facilities for both the initial and the further training of indexers; to establish criteria for assessing conformity to indexing standards; and to conduct research and publish guidance, ideas and information about indexing. It seeks to establish good relationships between indexers, librarians, publishers and authors, both to advance good indexing and to ensure that the contribution of indexers to the organisation and retrieval of knowledge is properly recognised.

Services to indexers

The Society publishes a learned journal *The Indexer* (quarterly), a newsletter and *Occasional Papers on Indexing*. Additional resources for members are published in electronic form on the Society's website (www.indexers.org.uk). Local and special interest groups provide the chance for members to meet to discuss common interests, while email discussion lists have encouraged the development of a virtual community of indexers. A two-day conference is held every year. All levels of training are supported by regular workshops held at various different venues throughout the country, plus online tutorials.

Professional competence is recognised in three stages by the Society. Professional Members (MSocInd) have successfully completed initial training (usually the Society's open-learning course – see below) or have many years' continuous experience. Advanced Professional Members (MSocInd(Adv)) have demonstrated skills and experience gained since their initial training, while Fellows of the Society of Indexers (FSI) have been through a rigorous assessment procedure to demonstrate the quality of their work. All trained and experienced members have the opportunity to take an annual entry in *Indexers Available*, a directory available on the Society's website to help publishers find an indexer.

The Society recommends minimum rates for indexing (£20.50 per hour; approx. £2.30 per page; £5.25 per 1,000 words in 2010) and provides advice on the business side of indexing to its members.

Services to publishers and authors

Anyone who commissions indexes needs to be certain of engaging a professional indexer working to the highest standards and able to meet deadlines. *Indexers Available*, now regularly updated on the Society's website, lists qualified and experienced members of the Society and gives basic contact details, subject specialisms and professional grade. The website also includes much useful advice on commissioning indexes, including a sample contract.

The Society awards the Wheatley Medal for an outstanding index.

Training in indexing

The Society's training course has received the CILIP Seal of Recognition and is based on the principle of open learning, so that individuals can learn in their own way and at their own pace. A web-based platform offers seamless access to study materials, practice exercises and quizzes, and links to a wide range of useful resources. Online tutorials are undertaken at various stages during the course. After completing the four assessed modules, which cover the core indexing skills, trainees undertake a practical indexing assignment to prepare them for work in the commercial world. The course is open to members of the Society and to members of the affiliated societies in Australia/New Zealand, Canada and Southern Africa. Successful completion of the course leads to Accreditation, designation as a Professional Indexer (MSocInd), and entry in the Society's online directory, *Indexers Available* (members of other indexing societies receive a certificate).

Further reading

Booth, P.F., *Indexing: the manual of good practice*, K.G. Saur, 2001

British Standards Institution, *British Standard recommendations for examining documents, determining their subjects and selecting indexing terms*, (BS6529:1984)

International Standards Organisation, *Information and documentation – guidelines for the content, organization and presentation of indexes* (ISO 999:1996)

Correcting proofs

Proofreading is a vital part of the publishing process and even the most trivial of errors can result in embarrassment, delay or unexpected costs. In this article Lauren Simpson identifies the skills and knowledge required to produce perfect proofs.

Writing is only one part of the journey to producing publishable material. In addition to transforming thoughts into elegant or cogent words and phrases, there are a number of other processes involved – chiefly, copy editing and proofreading.

What happens when?

While processes differ from publisher to publisher, or printer to printer, the chain of events from draft copy to printed copy can be *broadly* summarised as follows:

- Author delivers completed manuscript to publisher
- Publisher copy edits manuscript
- Copy edited material is typeset or put through an electronic 'page layout' process
- Typeset page proofs are proofread
- Corrections are incorporated and revised page proofs are produced
- Revised page proofs are corrected and signed off for printing.

Copy editing versus proofreading

Copy editing and proofreading are crucial final stages of the publishing process and, while the two can often be confused, there are important differences. The copy editing function normally takes place when the writing of an article, document, book, etc. is completed, and involves checking that the content is accurate, clearly and logically expressed, conveys the appropriate message or tone, and comes together to form a coherent and cohesive whole. Copy editors must be analytical in their approach and able to weed out factual errors, as well as annotate diagrams, cross check references and impose a publisher's house style on a text. They may also be required to have general or specialist knowledge of the written subject matter, particularly in the case of science and maths. Proofreading, on the other hand, involves scrutinising the content in very fine detail after copy editing (and, usually, typesetting) has taken place, to ensure that errors relating to syntax, grammar, punctuation, design and format are eliminated. Proofreaders, therefore, must have good technical language skills and an excellent eye for detail. Attention to detail is especially important in order to effectively deal with errors in technical or complex text, or when applying a style guide.

The importance of exemplary proofreading is highlighted by the fact that in addition to publishers, typesetters and reproduction teams often employ people whose job it is to ensure that the finished article is as finely polished and technically accurate as possible.

Proofreading symbols

Despite occupying very distinct roles, both copy editors (to a lesser extent due to onscreen editing) and proofreaders require knowledge of the 'shorthand' for correcting written material. Typesetters, designers and printers require this knowledge as part of correcting page layout, style and format.

Correcting proofs or 'marking up' copy effectively relies on the use of proofreading symbols (or 'marks') which instruct the typesetter, printer, or whoever, what changes need

Marks/symbols for general instructions

INSTRUCTIONS	MARGIN	TEXT
Leave the text in its original state and ignore any marks that have been made, commonly referred to as 'stet'		under the characters to be left as they were
Query for the author/typesetter/ printer/publisher.		A circle should be placed around text to be queried
Remove non-textual marks		A circle should be placed around marks to be removed
End of change		None

Marks/symbols for inserting, deleting and changing text

INSTRUCTIONS	MARGIN	TEXT
Text to be inserted	New text, followed by	
Additional text supplied separately	followed by a letter in a diamond which identifies additional text	
Delete a character		through the character
Delete text		through text
Delete character and close space		through the character
Delete text and close space		through text
Character to replace marked character	New character, followed by	through the character
Text to replace marked text	New text, followed by	through text

Marks/symbols for grammar and punctuation

INSTRUCTIONS	MARGIN	TEXT
Full stop		at insertion point or through character
Comma		As above
Semi-colon		As above
Colon		As above
Hyphen		As above
Single quote marks	or	As above
Double quote marks	or	As above
Apostrophe		As above
Ellipses or leader dots		As above
Insert/replace dash	1en Size of dash to be stated between uprights	As above

Marks/symbols for altering the look/style/layout of text

INSTRUCTIONS	MARGIN	TEXT
Put text in italics		under text to be changed
Remove italics, replace with roman text		Circle text to be changed
Put text in bold		under text to be changed
Remove bold		Circle text to be changed
Put text in capitals		under text to be changed
Put text in small capitals		under text to be changed
Put text in lower case	or	Circle text to be changed
Change character to superscript	under character	through character to be changed
Insert a superscript character	under character	at point of insertion
Change character to subscript	above character	through character to be changed
Insert a subscript character	above character	at point of insertion
Remove bold and italics		Circle text to be changed
Paragraph break		
Remove paragraph break, run on text		
Indent text		
Remove indent		
Insert or replace space between characters or words		at relevant point of insertion or through character
Reduce space between characters or words		
Insert space between lines or paragraphs	Mark extends into margin	or
Reduce space between lines or paragraphs	Mark extends into margin	or
Transpose lines		
Transpose characters or words		
Close space between characters		character character
Underline words	underline	circle words
Take over character(s) or word(s) to next line/column/page	Mark extends into margin	
Take back character(s) or word(s) to previous line/column/page	Mark extends into margin	

Marked proof of text

One hundred years of the *Writers& Artists Year book*
a century of *success*

The *Writers' & Artists' Yearbook* celebrated its 100th anniversary in 2006. For a century it's provided a bredth of factual, unbiased information and practical advice, an insight into the people and processes involved in the publishing industry and boundless encouragement and motivational tips from trusted authors and experts.

It has continuously attracted correspondence from aspiring, disgruntled and successful writers, as well as playing a part in reminding publishers of the ethics of the trade and their obligation to their contributors. The *Writers' & Artists' Yearbook* has grown into a compendious source of information selling over two million sales worldwide and placing itself in the Number One best seller spot of books of it's kind.

The *Yearbook* had humble beginnings back in 1906. It began as a small 80 page red booklet, containing a mere seven literary agents and 89 publishers and costing a modest one/shilling. It even existed in pamphlet form prior to its first book edition. A&C Black added many more lists of markets for the work of illustrators as well as writers and later for **photographers**. A 1910 press quote from *The Standard* states:

In 1914 the first articles by the experts of the day were added. The content and the language of each edition are indications of the changing face of publishing and the media – from silent movies and hot metal presses to e-books and ipods. The *Yearbook*, like another of A&C Black's famous reference works Who's Who, even put in a new, thoroughly revised edition during the two World Wars. The 1940 edit/ ion contained a special war supplement, outlining emergency and evacuation contact details

(A) 'Professional and amateur dabblers in ink no longer have any excuse for sending the offspring of their brains on the wrong road to public admiration and emolument'.

Revised proof of text incorporating corrections

One hundred years of the *Writers' & Artists' Yearbook*
A century of success

The *Writers' & Artists' Yearbook* celebrated its 100th anniversary in 2006. For a century it has provided a breadth of factual, unbiased information and practical advice, an insight into the people and processes involved in the publishing industry and boundless encouragement and motivational tips from trusted authors and experts. It has continuously attracted correspondence from aspiring, disgruntled and successful writers, as well as playing a part in reminding publishers of the ethics of the trade and their obligation to their contributors.

The *Writers' & Artists' Yearbook* has grown into a compendious source of information selling over two million copies worldwide and placing itself in the number one bestseller spot of books of its kind.

The *Yearbook* had humble beginnings back in 1906. It began as a small 80-page red booklet, containing a mere seven literary agents and 89 publishers and costing a modest one shilling. It even existed in pamphlet form prior to its first book edition. A&C Black added many more lists of markets for the work of illustrators as well as writers and later for photographers. A 1910 quote from *The Standard* states: 'Professional and amateur dabblers in ink no longer have any excuse for sending the offspring of their brains on the wrong road to public admiration and emolument'.

In 1914 the first articles by the experts of the day were added. The content and the language of each edition are indications of the changing face of publishing and the media – from silent movies and hot metal presses to e-books and iPods. The *Yearbook*, like another of A&C Black's famous reference works, *Who's Who*, even put in a new, thoroughly revised edition during the two World Wars. The 1940 edition contained a special war supplement, outlining emergency and evacuation contact details.

to be made, in a uniform and concise way. The full set of proofreading marks is defined by the British Standards Institute (BS 5261); however, most proofreading can be carried out using only the most common proofreading symbols. Proofreading marks fall into separate categories:

- Marks/symbols for general instructions
- Marks/symbols for inserting, deleting and changing text
- Marks/symbols for grammar and punctuation
- Marks/symbols for altering the look/style/layout of text.

Depending on the nature of the changes needed, proofreading marks are typically positioned in the margin of the document undergoing correction, with some changes requiring a mark within the text or some additional instruction.

The most commonly used proofreading marks are shown on the following pages.

Marked proofs

Anyone who has ever seen a marked-up proof will probably acknowledge the fact that proof corrections are not always executed perfectly. Pressured schedules, last minute changes and familiarity between, e.g. proofreaders and typesetters, often result in shortcuts to the way corrections are applied. That said, proof corrections should, in accordance with BS 5261, be made in the following way:

- Alterations and instructions made by the publisher and/or his agents should be marked up using dark blue or black ink.
- Errors made by the typesetter/printer should be marked up by the publisher and/or his agents using red ink.
- Errors made by the typesetter/printer should be marked up by the typesetter/printer using green ink.

Looking at a page covered in proofreading marks can look rather daunting to the untrained eye but with experience, the application and deciphering of proof corrections becomes second nature.

Mistakes to look out for

Clearly, no two sets of page proofs will have exactly the same problems. However, there are a number of mistakes that commonly crop up:

- Similar words used incorrectly, e.g. effect/affect
- Phrases used inappropriately, e.g. 'should of' instead of 'should have'
- Apostrophe misuse, especially in respect of its/it's
- Words with similar spelling or pronunciation but different meanings used incorrectly, e.g. their/they're/there
- References in the text that do not correspond to footnotes
- Inaccurate or inadequate cross-referencing
- Index listings which cannot be found on the page given in the index
- Text inadvertently reordered or cut during the typesetting process
- Headings formatted as ordinary text
- Running heads that do not always correspond to chapter headings
- Fonts and font sizes that may have been used incorrectly
- Inconsistent use of abbreviations and acronyms
- Format inconsistencies such as poorly aligned margins or uneven columns

- Captions/headings omitted from illustrations, photographs or diagrams
- Illustrations/photographs/diagrams without appropriate copyright references
- Missing bullet points or numbers in a sequenced list
- Word processing errors, e.g. '3' instead of '£'
- Incorrect layout of names, addresses, telephone numbers and email/web addresses.
- Incorrect use of trademarks, e.g. blackberry instead of BlackBerry™
- Abbreviations that have not been defined in full
- Widows and orphans, e.g. text which runs over page breaks and leaves a word or line stranded
- Past and present tenses mixed within a piece of text
- Use of plural verb conjugations with single subjects, e.g. 'one in five children are…' instead of 'one in five children is…'

Tips for perfect proofreading

Effective and accurate proofreading takes time and practice. These tips will help ensure that proof corrections result in a top-notch finished product, every time.

- Set aside adequate time for proofreading. It is a job that requires concentration and should not be rushed.
- Before starting on a proofreading task, make sure you have easy access to a dictionary and thesaurus, and ensure that you have appropriate style guides for language style and format/design.
- If possible, proofread a document several times concentrating on different aspects each time, e.g. sense/tone, format, grammar/punctuation/use of language.
- Try not to proofread copy that you wrote yourself to avoid repeating mistakes.
- When proofreading scientific or mathematical material, ensure you are confident with the subject matter. If not, seek an expert opinion.
- Spot typos by reading the text backwards – that way you will not be distracted by the meaning of the text.
- Always double check scientific, mathematical or medical symbols – they can often be corrupted during the typesetting process.
- If possible, have a version of the marked-up copy-edited text alongside you while you proofread – it might help solve minor inaccuracies or inconsistencies, or at least help you flag up whether text needs to be referred back to the author for clarification.

Lauren Simpson is a freelance editor and publisher who has worked in reference publishing for 16 years. She has contributed to and developed a wide range of print and electronic publications covering subjects as diverse as agriculture, banking, marketing, English language teaching and boating. In addition, she has been editor of a number of prestigious reference works including *The Municipal Year Book* (Hemming Group) and *Whitaker's Almanack* (A&C Black).

See also...

- *Dos and don'ts of approaching a publisher,* page 126
- *Understanding the publishing process,* page 230

Libraries

Listed below are specialist, reference and general libraries. Contact individual libraries to find out about accessibility and opening hours.

University of Aberdeen

Queen Mother Library, Meston Walk, Aberdeen AB24 3UE
tel (01224) 273600 *fax* (01224) 273956
email library@abdn.ac.uk
website www.abdn.ac.uk/library

Aberdeen City Libraries, Central Library

Rosemount Viaduct, Aberdeen AB25 1GW
tel (01224) 652500 *fax* (01224) 641985
email centrallibrary@aberdeencity.gov.uk
website www.aberdeencity.gov.uk/libraries

Barbican Library

Barbican Centre, London EC2Y 8DS
tel 020-7638 0569, 020-7628 9447 (Children's Library), 020-7638 0672 (Music Library)
website www.cityoflondon.gov.uk/barbicanlibrary

The largest of the City of London's lending libraries with a strong arts and music section, a London collection, literature events programme and reading groups.

Bath Central Library

19 The Podium, Northgate Street, Bath BA1 5AN
tel (01225) 394041
email councilconnect@bathnes.gov.uk
website www.bathnes.gov.uk/libraries

BBC Written Archives Centre

Caversham Park, Reading RG4 8TZ
tel 0118-948 6281 *fax* 0118-946 1145
email heritage@bbc.co.uk
website www.bbc.co.uk/historyofthebbc/contacts/wac.shtml

Home of the BBC's written records. Holds thousands of files, scripts and working papers from the BBC's formation in 1922 to c. 2000 together with information about past programmes and the history of broadcasting. Does not have recordings or information about current programmes.

Bedford Central Library

Harpur Street, Bedford MK40 1PG
tel (01234) 718178 *fax* (01234) 342163

Belfast Central Library

Royal Avenue, Belfast BT1 1EA
tel 028-9050 9117 *fax* 028-9033 2819
email infobelb@librariesni.org.uk
website www.ni-libraries.net

BFI National Library

BFI, 21 Stephen Street, London W1T 1LN
tel 020-7255 1444 *fax* 020-7436 2338
email library@bfi.org.uk
website www.bfi.org.uk/filmtvinfo/library

A major national research collection. Provides coverage of British film and television primarily but is also international in scope. Includes over 60,000 books, 5,000 periodical titles and over 25,000 scripts.

Birmingham Central Library

Chamberlain Square, Birmingham B3 3HQ
tel 0121-303 4511 *minicom* 0121-303 4547
fax 0121-233 4458
email central.library@birmingham.gov.uk
website www.birmingham.gov.uk

The Henry Bloom Noble Library

10 Victoria Street, Douglas, Isle of Man IM1 2LH
tel (01624) 696461 *fax* (01624) 696400
email enquiries@douglas.gov.im

Bodleian Library

Broad Street, Oxford OX1 3BG
tel (01865) 277162 *fax* (01865) 277182
email reader.services@bodleian.ox.ac.uk
website www.bodley.ox.ac.uk

The main research library of the University of Oxford. It is also a legal deposit library.

The Booktrust Collection – see Newcastle University Library

Bristol Central Library

College Green, Bristol BS1 5TL
tel 0117-903 7200 (switchboard), 0117-903 7202 (Reference Library & art enquiries), 0117-903 7215 (Children's Library), 0117-903 7250 (Lending enquiries) *fax* 0117-922 1081
email bristol.library.service@bristol.gov.uk
website www.bristol.gov.uk

The British Library

96 Euston Road, London NW1 2DB
tel 0843-208 1144
(Switchboard), 020-7412 7676 (Advance Reservations, St Pancras Reading Rooms and Humanities enquiries), 020-7412 7702 (Maps), 020-7412 7513 (Manuscripts), 020-7412 7772 (Music), 020-7412 7873 (Asia, Pacific & Africa Collections)
website www.bl.uk

The national library of the UK and a legal deposit library. The collection includes in excess of 150 million items, in most known languages. Online catalogues. See also other British Library listings below.

British Library Business and Intellectual Property Service (BIS)
96 Euston Road, London NW1 2DB
tel 020-7412 7333 *fax* 020-7412 7168
email developmentc@bl.uk
website www.bl.uk

Holds the most comprehensive collection of business information literature in the UK.

British Library Document Supply Centre
Boston Spa, Wetherby, West Yorkshire LS23 7BQ
tel (01937) 546060 *fax* (01937) 546333

British Library for Development Studies (BLDS)
Institute of Development Studies at the University of Sussex, Brighton BN1 9RE, East Sussex
tel (01273) 915659 *fax* (01273) 621202
email blds@ids.ac.uk
website www.blds.ids.ac.uk

Europe's largest research collection on economic and social change in developing countries.

British Library Newspapers
Colindale Avenue, London NW9 5HE
tel 020-7412 7353 *fax* 020-7412 7379
email newspaper@bl.uk
website www.bl.uk

National archive collections in the UK of British and overseas newspapers, made available in hard copy, in microform, and on CD-Rom in the Newspaper Reading Rooms. Online catalogue.

The British Library Sound Archive
The British Library, 96 Euston Road, London NW1 2DB
tel 020-7412 7676 *fax* 020-7412 7441
email sound-archive@bl.uk
website www.bl.uk/soundarchive

The collections come from all over the world and cover the entire range of recorded sound from music, drama and literature to oral history and wildlife sounds. Holds over a million discs. The online catalogue holds over 3 million recordings, the biggest archive of its kind in the world.

Reference & Information Service (Buckinghamshire)
Walton Street, Aylesbury, Bucks. HP20 1UU
tel (0845) 230 3132 *fax* (01296) 382405
email lib-ref@buckscc.gov.uk
website www.buckscc.gov.uk/lis

Camberwell College of Arts Library
Peckham Road, London SE5 8UF
tel 020-7514 6349
website www.arts.ac.uk/library

Ceramics, conservation, fine art, graphics, illustration, metalwork, photography, printmaking, silversmithing and product design.

Cambridge University Library
West Road, Cambridge CB3 9DR
tel (01223) 333000 *fax* (01223) 333160
email library@lib.cam.ac.uk
website www.lib.cam.ac.uk

Collections are housed in the University Library and its 4 dependent libraries. It is also a legal deposit library.

Cardiff Central Library
Mill Lane, Cardiff CF10 1FL
tel 029-2038 2116
email centrallibrary@cardiff.gov.uk
website www.cardiff.gov.uk/centrallibrary

The largest public library in Wales.

Catholic National Library
St Michael's Abbey, Farnborough Road, Farnborough, Hants GU14 7NQ
tel (01252) 543818
email library@catholic-library.org.uk
website www.catholic-library.org.uk

Holds 65,000 books and periodicals on theology, spirituality and related subjects, biography and history.

Central St Martins College of Art & Design Library
Southampton Row, London WC1B 4AP
Charing Cross Road Library, 107 Charing Cross Road, London WC2H 8DU
tel 020-7514 7023
website www.arts.ac.uk/library

Chawton House Library
Chawton, Alton, Hants GU34 1SJ
tel (01420) 541010 *fax* (01420) 595900
email library@chawton.net
website www.chawtonhouse.org

A collection of over 8000 volumes focusing on women's writing in English from 1600 to 1830 including some manuscripts. The library also houses the Knight Collection.

Chelsea College of Art & Design Library
16 John Islip Street, London SW1P 4JU
tel 020-7514 7751
email enquiries@chelsea.arts.ac.uk
website www.arts.ac.uk/library

Modern and contemporary art (including women's art), Afro–American art, Afro–Carribean British art and Asian British art.

City Business Library
Aldermanbury, London EC2V 7HH
tel 020-7332 1812

website www.cityofLondon.gov.uk/citybusinesslibrary

One of the leading business information sources in the UK.

City of London Libraries – see City Business Library, Guildhall Library, St Bride Printing Library and Barbican Library

Civil Aviation Authority Library and Information Centre (CAA)

Aviation House, Gatwick Airport South, West Sussex RH6 0YR
tel (01293) 567171 *fax* (01293) 573181
email infoservices@caa.co.uk
website www.caa.co.uk

Holds books, reports, directories, statistics, videos and periodicals on most aspects of civil aviation and related subjects.

College of Psychic Studies Library

16 Queensberry Place, London SW7 2EB
tel 020-7589 3293
email admin@collegeofpsychicstudies.co.uk
website www.collegeofpsychicstudies.co.uk

The Library of the Commonwealth Secretariat

Commonwealth Secretariat, Marlborough House, Pall Mall, London SW1Y 5HX
tel 020-7747 6500 *fax* 020-7930 0827
email library@commonwealth.int
Librarian Catherine Hume

Collection covers politics and international relations, economics, education, health, gender, environment and management. Holds a comprehensive collection of Commonwealth Secretariat publications and its archives.

Cornwall Library Service

Reference and Information Library, Union Place, Truro, Cornwall TR1 1EP
tel (0300) 123 4111
email reference.library@cornwall.gov.uk
Enquiry and Information Serivce, Unit 17, Threemilestone Industrial Estate, Truro, Cornwall TR4 9LD
tel (01872) 272702
email reference.library@cornwall.gov.uk
website www.cornwall.gov.uk/library

Crafts Council Research Library

Crafts Council, 44A Pentonville Road, London N1 9BY
tel 020-7806 2501
email reference@craftscouncil.org.uk
website www.craftscouncil.org.uk

A unique collection of materials mapping the development of contemporary craft since the mid-20th century. Holdings include over 7000 books and catalogues, and 100 journals and magazines. Online acces to Photostore, the national register of makers, and funding resources also provided. Open every Weds and Thurs 10am–5pm by appointment.

Cranfield Library and Information Service

Cranfield University, Cranfield, Beds. MK43 0AL
tel (01234) 754444 *fax* (01234) 752391
email library@cranfield.ac.uk
website www.cranfield.ac.uk/library/cranfield

Croydon Central Library

Croydon Clocktower, Katharine Street, Croydon CR9 1ET
tel 020-8726 6900 *fax* 020-8253 1004
email libraries@croydon.gov.uk
website www.croydon.gov.uk

Derby Central Library

The Wardwick, Derby DE1 1HS
tel (01332) 641702 *fax* (01332) 369570
email central.library@derby.gov.uk
website www.derby.gov.uk/libraries

Durham University Library

Stockton Road, Durham DH1 3LY
tel 0191-334 3042 *fax* 0191-334 2971
website www.dur.ac.uk/library

Edinburgh University Library

30 George Square, Edinburgh EH8 9LJ
tel 0131-650 3409 *fax* 0131-651 5041
email IS.Helpdesk@ed.ac.uk
website www.lib.ed.ac.uk

University of Exeter Library

Stocker Road, Exeter EX4 4PT
tel (01392) 263867 *fax* (01392) 263871
email library@exeter.ac.uk
website www.ex.ac.uk/library

The website lists sites on the internet which are especially useful resources maintained by libraries, museums and centres of research, as well as publishers.

University of Glasgow Library

Hillhead Street, Glasgow G12 8QE
tel 0141-330 6704 *fax* 0141-330 4952
email library@lib.gla.ac.uk
website www.lib.gla.ac.uk

Glasgow Women's Library

81 Parnie Street, Glasgow G1 5RH
tel 0141-552 8345
email info@womenslibrary.org.uk
website www.womenslibrary.org.uk

Reference and lending library of information for and about women.

Goethe-Institut London Library

50 Princes Gate, Exhibition Road, London SW7 2PH
tel 020-7596 4044 *fax* 020-7594 0230

email infoservice@london.goethe.org
website www.goethe.de/london

Specialises in German literature, especially contemporary fiction and drama and books/audiovisual material on German culture and recent history.

Guildhall Library

Aldermanbury, London EC2V 7HH
tel 020-7332 1868/1870 (printed books), 020-7332 1862 (manuscripts) *fax* 020-7600 3384
email manuscripts.guildhall@cityoflondon.gov.uk, printedbooks.guildhall@cityoflondon.gov.uk
website www.cityoflondon.gov.uk/guildhalllibrary

Specialises in the history of London, especially the City, as well as holding other significant collections including business history, maritime history, clock and watchmaking, food and wine.

High Wycombe Library

5 Eden Place, High Wycombe, Bucks. HP11 2OH
tel (0845) 230 3232 (general enquiries), (01494) 475900 (local studies) *fax* (01494) 533086
email lib-hiw@buckscc.gov.uk
website www.buckscc.gov.uk/sites/bcc/libraries/libraries.page

Jersey Library

Halkett Place, St Helier, Jersey JE2 4WH, Channel Islands
tel (01534) 448700 *fax* (01534) 448730
email je.library@gov.je
website www.gov.je/library

Lambeth Palace Library

London SE1 7JU
tel 020-7898 1400 *fax* 020-7928 7932
website www.lambethpalacelibrary.org

The historic library of the archbishops of Canterbury and the principal library and record office for the Church of England.

Leeds Central Library

Calverley Street, Leeds LS1 3AB
tel 0113-247 6016 *fax* 0113-247 4222
email enquiry.express@leeds.gov.uk
website www.leeds.gov.uk/libraries

Lending library with specialist art, music, local and family history and information departments, and Europe Direct Leeds.

Leeds University Library

University of Leeds, Leeds LS2 9JT
tel 0113-343 5663 *fax* 0113-343 5561
email libraryenquiries@leeds.ac.uk
website www.leeds.ac.uk/library

Learning and Information Library (Leicester)

Bishop Street, Leicester LE1 6AA
tel 0116-299 5401 *fax* 0116-299 5444
email central.reference@leicester.gov.uk
website www.leicester.gov.uk/libraries

University of Leicester Library

University Road, Leicester LE1 9QD
tel 0116-252 2043 *fax* 0116-252 2066
email library@le.ac.uk
Mailing address PO Box 248, Leicester LE1 9QD
website www.le.ac.uk/library

The Linen Hall Library

17 Donegall Square North, Belfast BT1 5GB
tel 028-9032 1707 *fax* 028-9043 8586
email info@linenhall.com
website www.linenhall.com
Acting Librarian John Killen, *Irish & Local Studies Librarian* Gerry Healey

Renowned for its Irish and Local Studies Collection ranging from early Belfast and Ulster printed books to the 300,000 items in the internationally acclaimed Northern Ireland Political Collection (NIPC). Also expansive General Lending Collection. Open free to the public.

Liverpool Central Library

William Brown Street, Liverpool L3 8EW
tel 0151-233 5829 *fax* 0151-233 5886
email refbt.central.library@liverpool.gov.uk
website www.liverpool.gov.uk

London College of Communication / Library and Learning Resources

Elephant & Castle, London SE1 6SB
tel 020-7514 6527
website www.lcc.arts.ac.uk

London College of Fashion Library

20 John Princes Street, London W1G 0BJ
tel 020-7514 7552, 020-7514 7455
email library@fashion.arts.ac.uk
website www.arts.ac.uk/library

London Institute Libraries – see

Camberwell College of Arts Library, Central St Martins College of Art & Design, Chelsea College of Art & Design Library, London College of Fashion Library and London College of Printing Libraries

The London Library

14 St James's Square, London SW1Y 4LG
tel 020-7930 7705 *fax* 020-7766 4766
email membership@londonlibrary.co.uk
website www.londonlibrary.co.uk

Subscription lending library holding approximately one million books in all European languages and a subject range across the humanities, with particular emphasis on literature, history and related subjects. Membership is open to all.

Library of the London School of Economics and Political Science

10 Portugal Street, London WC2A 2HD
tel 020-7955 7229 *fax* 020-7955 7454
website www.lse.ac.uk/library

Manchester Central Library
St Peter's Square, Manchester M2 5PD
tel 0161-234 1900 *fax* 0161-274 7053
email libraries@manchester.gov.uk
website www.manchester.gov.uk/libraries

The Mitchell Library
North Street, Glasgow G3 7DN
tel 0141-287 2999 *fax* 0141-287 2815
email LIL@csglasgow.org
website www.csglasgow.org/services

One of Europe's largest public reference libraries with almost 2 million volumes. Holds an unrivalled collection of material relating to the City of Glasgow.

National Art Library
Victoria & Albert Museum, South Kensington, London SW7 2RL
tel 020-7942 2000
email nal.enquiries@vam.ac.uk
website www.vam.ac.uk/nal

A major reference library and the Victoria and Albert Museum's curatorial department for the art, craft and design of the book.

National Library of Ireland
Kildare Street, Dublin 2, Republic of Ireland
tel (353) 1 603 02 00 *fax* (353) 1 676 66 90
email info@nli.ie
website www.nli.ie

The world's largest collection of Irish documentary material.

The National Library of Scotland
George IV Bridge, Edinburgh EH1 1EW
tel 0131-623 3700 (switchboard), 0131-623 3876 (manuscripts and archives enquiries), 0131-623 3899 (Rare Books Collections)
email enquiries@scotbis.com (Scottish Business Information Service), manuscripts@nls.uk (manuscripts and archives enquiries), rarebooks@nls.uk (Rare Books Collections)
website www.nls.uk

A legal deposit library and Scotland's largest reference library.

The National Library of Wales
Aberystwyth, Ceredigion SY23 3BU
tel (01970) 632800 *fax* (01970) 615709
email holi@llgc.org.uk
website www.llgc.org.uk

A legal deposit library. Holds large collection of works about Wales and other Celtic countries, including manuscripts, maps, portraits and paintings, screen and sound archives.

National Maritime Museum
Greenwich, London SE10 9NF
tel 020-8858 4422 *fax* 020-8312 6632
website www.nmm.ac.uk, www.rog.nmm.ac.uk (astronomy information)

Specialist maritime research library.

Natural History Museum Library and Information Services
Cromwell Road, London SW7 5BD
tel 020-7942 5507/5873 (archives), 020-7942 5685 (Botany Library), 020-7942 5476 (Earth Sciences Library), 020-7942 5751 (Entomology Library), 020-7942 5460 (General Library and Zoology Library), 020-7942 6156 (Ornithology Library)
website www.nhm.ac.uk

Online catalogue contains all library material acquired since 1989 and about 80% of earlier items. The collections are of international importance with extensive holdings of early works, periodicals and current literature, including over 800,000 books, 20,000 periodical titles (about half of them current) and original watercolour drawings, as well as maps, manuscripts and archives of the Museum.

Newcastle University Library
Robinson Library, Newcastle University, Newcastle upon Tyne NE1 7RU
tel 0191-222 7662 *fax* 0191-222 6235
email lib-readersservices@ncl.ac.uk
website www.ncl.ac.uk/library

Newcastle upon Tyne City Library
City Library, Charles Avison Building, 33 Newbridge Street West, Newcastle upon Tyne NE1 8AX
tel (0191) 277 4100 *fax* (0191) 277 4137
website www.newcastle.gov.uk/libraries

Norfolk and Norwich Millennium Library
The Forum, Millennium Plain, Norwich NR2 1AW
tel (01603) 77740 *fax* (01603) 774775
email millennium.lib@norfolk.gov.uk
website www.library.norfolk.gov.uk

The Northern Poetry Library
– see page 362

Nottingham Central Library
Angel Row, Nottingham NG1 6HP
tel 0115-915 2828 *fax* 0115-915 2850
email enquiryline@nottinghamcity.gov.uk
website www.nottinghamcity.gov.uk

Open Library
Open University, Walton Hall, Milton Keynes, MK7 6AA
tel 0845-300 6090
email lib-help@open.ac.uk
website http://library.open.ac.uk

The Open University's electronic library service.

School of Oriental & African Studies (SOAS) Library

University of London, Thornhough Street, Russell Square, London WC1H 0XG
tel 020-7637 2388 *fax* 020-7898 4159
email libsuggestions@soas.ac.uk
website www.soas.ac.uk/library

Oxford Central Library

Westgate, Oxford OX1 1DJ
tel (01865) 815509 (general enquiries), (01865) 815549 (information desk), (01865) 815373 (children's library), (01865) 815388 (music library), (01865) 815409 (periodicals room)
fax (01865) 721694
email oxfordcentral.library@oxfordshire.gov.uk
website www.oxfordshire.gov.uk

PA News Library

Central Park, New Lane, Leeds LS11 5DZ
tel (0870) 830 6824
email palibrary@pressassociation.co.uk
website www.pressassociation.co.uk

Holds electronically over ten years of Press Association articles.

The Poetry Library – see page 363

The Portico Library & Gallery

57 Mosley Street, Manchester M2 3HY
tel 0161-236 6785
email librarian@theportico.org.uk
website www.theportico.org.uk

Independent library which stocks mainly 19th century literature available to subscribers and researchers.

University of Reading Library

Whiteknights, PO Box 223, Reading RG6 6AE
tel 0118-378 8770 *fax* 0118-378 6636
email library@reading.ac.uk
website www.reading.ac.uk/library

RNIB National Library Service

Far Cromwell Road, Bredbury, Stockport SK6 2SG
tel 0303-123 9999 *fax* 0161-355 2098
email library@rnib.org.uk
website www.rnib.org.uk/reading

The largest specialist library for readers with sight loss in the UK. Offers a comprehensive range of books and accessible information for children and adults in a range of formats including braille, large print and unabridged audio. Also provides free access to online reference material, braille sheet music, themed book lists and a quarterly reader magazine.

The John Rylands University Library, The University of Manchester

Oxford Road, Manchester M13 9PP
tel 0161-275 3751 *fax* 0161-273 7488
website www.manchester.ac.uk/library

St Albans Central Library

The Maltings, St Albans, Herts. AL1 3JQ
tel (0300) 123 4049 *minicom* (01438) 737599
website www.hertsdirect.org/libsleisure/libraries

St Bride Library

Bride Lane, Fleet Street, London EC4Y 8EE
tel 020-7353 4660 *fax* 020-7583 7073
email library@stbridefoundation.org
website www.stbride.org

Collections cover printing and allied subjects including paper and binding, graphic design and typography, typefaces and calligraphy, illustration and printmaking, publishing and bookselling, and the social and economic aspects of the printing, book, newspaper and magazine trades generally.

Salisbury Library

Market Place, Salisbury, Wilts. SP1 1BL
tel (01722) 324145
website www.wiltshire.gov.uk/libraries

Science Museum Library

Imperial College Road, London SW7 5NH
tel 020-7942 4242 *fax* 020-7942 4243
email SMLinfo@sciencemuseum.org.uk
website www.sciencemuseum.org.uk/about_us/about_the_museum/science_library.aspx

In recent years the Library has specialised in the history of science and technology as its key role as part of the National Museum of Science & Industry.

The Scottish Poetry Library – see page 362

Senate House Library, University of London

Senate House, Malet Street, London WC1E 7HU
tel 020-7862 8500
email enquiries@shl.lon.ac.uk
website www.shl.lon.ac.uk

One of the major academic libraries of the UK.

Sheffield Central Library

Surrey Street, Sheffield S1 1XZ
tel 0114-273 4727
email centrallending.library@sheffield.gov.uk
website www.sheffield.gov.uk/libraries

University of Southampton Libraries

University Road, Highfield, Southampton SO17 1BJ
tel 023-8059 2180
email libengs@soton.ac.uk
website www.library.soton.ac.uk

The Society for Storytelling Library

St Margarets House, 12 Belle Avenue, Reading RG6 7BL
tel 0118-935 1381

email admin@sfs.org.uk
website www.sfs.org.uk, www.mythstories.com/sfslibrary.html

Folktale and folklore books, storytelling magazines from the UK and abroad, an archive of press cuttings and flyers for storytellers and events; tapes of conference proceedings, achive tellings and performances.

Tate Library & Archive

Hyman Kreitman Reading Rooms, Tate Britain, Millbank, London SW1P 4RG
tel 020-7887 8838
email reading.rooms@tate.org.uk
website www.tate.org.uk/research/researchservices/readingrooms

Broadly covers those areas in which the Tate collects. Library collects British art from the Renaissance to the present day and international modern art from 1900. Archive covers British art from 1900 and contains a wealth of unpublished material on artists, art world figures and organisations.

Trinity College Library

Cambridge CB2 1TQ
tel (01223) 338488 *fax* (01223) 338532
email college.library@trin.cam.ac.uk
website www.trin.cam.ac.uk

Trinity College Library Dublin

College Street, Dublin 2, Republic of Ireland
tel (01) 896 1661 *fax* (01) 896 3774
website www.tcd.ie/library

Wellcome Library

183 Euston Road, London NW1 2BE
tel 020-7611 8722 *fax* 020-7611 8369
email library@wellcome.ac.uk
website http://library.wellcome.ac.uk

Wellcome Images

tel 020-7611 8348 *fax* 020-7611 8577
email images@wellcome.ac.uk
website http://images.wellcome.ac.uk

Moving Image and Sound Collections

tel 020-7611 8766 *fax* 020-7611 8765
email misc@wellcome.ac.uk
website http://library.wellcome.ac.uk/misc.html

Westminster Music Library

Victoria Library, 160 Buckingham Palace Road, London SW1W 9UD
tel 020-7641 1300 *fax* 020-7641 4281
email victorialibrary@westminster.gov.uk, musiclibrary@westminster.gov.uk
website www.westminster.gov.uk/libraries/victoria

Housed by Victoria Library, the Westminster Music Library holds a wide range of scores, orchestral sets, books on music and the GLASS collection of Mozart sound recordings.

Westminster Reference Library

35 St Martin's Street, London WC2H 7HP
tel 020-7641 1300 (Contact Centre: ask for Westminster Reference Library) *fax* 020-7641 5232
email referencelibrarywc2@westminster.gov.uk
website www.westminster.gov.uk/libraries/findalibrary/westref.cfm
General reference library with special collections in Performing Arts and Art & Design. Also has a range of business resources including market research, company and legal databases. The library is open to all 10am–8pm weekdays and 10am–5pm Saturdays. See website for further information.

Winchester Discovery Centre

Jewry Street, Winchester, Hants SO23 8SB
tel 0845-603 5631
email winchester.dc.enquiries@hants.gov.uk
website www.hants.gov.uk

The Women's Library

25 Old Castle Street, London E1 7NT
tel 020-7320 2222 *fax* 020-7320 2333
email moreinfo@the womenslibrary.ac.uk
website www.thewomenslibrary.ac.uk

Houses the most extensive collection of women's history in the UK. Part of the London Metropolitan University.

Working Class Movement Library

51 The Crescent, Salford M5 4WX
tel 0161-736 3601
email enquiries@wcml.org.uk
website www.wcml.org.uk
Librarian Lynette Cawthra

Records over 200 years of organising and campaigning by ordinary men and women. The collection provides an insight into working people's daily lives. Collection contains: books, pamphlets, archives, photographs, plays, poetry, songs, banners, posters, badges, cartoons, journals, biographies, reports.

Explore York Library Learning Centre

Museum Street, York YO1 7DS
tel (01904) 552824, 552828 *fax* (01904) 552835
email reference.library@york.gov.uk
website www.york.gov.uk/libraries

The Zoological Society of London Library

Regent's Park, London NW1 4RY
tel 020-7449 6293
email library@zsl.org
website www.zsl.org

Taking a writing course

Alison Baverstock discusses whether a writing course might be right for you.

Most writers can remember a turning point when they decided they really did want to take themselves seriously. Maybe it took place during a conversation with a near stranger when an ambition was confessed, and having been heard out loud, seemed significant. Others have reported the realisation of a sudden surge of competitive adrenaline on hearing that a former colleague had made it into print, and that their own determination felt super-charged. As an impoverished student I can remember my first encounter with the *Writers' & Artists' Yearbook* and thinking, 'As someone who plans to be published, I need to buy this...'. This article is about the merits or otherwise of spending time and money on what is claimed to be the second most common New Year's resolution – to publish a book – and supporting that ambition, through enrolling on a formal course in creative writing.

Be warned. The very subject of taking courses in creative writing attracts negativity. The legacy of *La Boheme* and the legend of the struggling artist in the garret cast a long shadow – shouldn't writing just be got on with, in painful isolation, rather than studied through courses? Of course the writing bit has to be done on your own, but its development can benefit enormously from the input/feedback/support of others. And why writing should be singled out as a necessarily completely solitary pursuit is baffling, when we accept that most of us can't learn a musical instrument without assistance, and that classes can help establish whether a long-held passing interest, whether in ballroom dancing or flower arranging, has the potential for deeper passion.

> *'Exposure to authors on Faculty, as well as visiting writers, agents and publishers, helps draw emergent writers into the literary scene and gives them the confidence needed to take their own work seriously. An MA may not make a writer of you, but it will challenge you to become one!'* – Siobhan Campbell and Adam Baron,Course Leaders, MA in Creative Writing, Kingston University

The first tip when thinking about such courses is to match the level of commitment required to the time and motivation you have available. There are courses on offer at different levels. At the top of the pile there are MAs in Creative Writing (see page 688), often set up within a university English Department although increasingly gaining departmental independence as more students enrol. The key thing to note here is that such courses are structured towards the award of a formal degree, either at undergraduate or postgraduate level, and so will require a great deal of involvement on your part. Don't think either that writing is all you will do. Writing will be put in the context of reading (on writing, around your chosen area of specialisation, and in general) and there will be workshops and specialist seminars to attend. A university with an effective course in creative writing will be a lively place with lots of opportunities for discussion and experimentation – but the costs will be correspondingly high. You should expect to pay course fees of around £5,000–£6,000 for an MA, whether you spread it over one or two years. And if you find the world congenial you can go on to study for a Master of Fine Arts or a PhD.

On a less formal level many local authorities run daytime/evening courses in creative writing, in the same way that they offer pottery and IT skills, and you can find out what is available in your local area from the local newspaper or websites (google 'creative writing' and see how many opportunities emerge). Often these classes have been running for a long time with experienced tutors, and simply getting to the class each week and responding to the writing exercises set, can help improve your discipline as a writer. But there may be frustrations – long-term attendees (in your opinion of assorted levels of talent) may be resistant to the arrival of new class members, punctuality can be a problem, and those who see the occasion as social rather than developmental can be frustrating to the writer who really wants to progress. Enrolment times are usually in September and January and you have to be quick as these classes tend to fill up rapidly.

If you decide you would rather go for a short burst rather than a weekly drip feed, then there are a number of other options available. Many universities offer short courses, and others are run through bookshops and private initiatives – so watch the notice-board in your local library, bookshop or community centre. Literature festivals often provide the genesis for accompanying events on the craft of writing, and several have scheduled relevant talks/weekend courses. For example, the Edinburgh International Book Festival (see page 617) has a programme on writing (*The Writing Business*), as does the Cheltenham Literary Festival (*Write Away*, see page 616), and Winchester (the Winchester Writers' Conference and Bookfair, see page 691) has a whole festival devoted to writing, with a variety of options from 15 minute one-to-one appointments to day-long seminars (see page 613).

So if any of this tempts you, here are some things to think about:

- **Enrolling for a course in creative writing means you will be required to confess your ambition to write.** Your writing may up to now have been carried out in private, on your own, with not even your closest friends or family aware. Applying for a place on a creative writing course means both your ambition and your work will be opened up for the examination of others. For university level courses you will have to submit samples of your work and justify your desire for a place, with a rationale you may never have thought through before. This can give some writers the spur they need to take themselves seriously, but after years of nurturing a private desire, don't underestimate how odd it may feel.
- **The teaching method may feel similarly invasive.** At the heart of most creative writing courses are weekly workshops when the writing of one or two individuals is discussed. This means you have to circulate your work before the class and then have it discussed in front of you. The discussion should be moderated – a good tutor will ensure that feedback is delivered in a constructive context and that the act of writing itself is always seen as a positive rather than a negative – but the process can feel challenging, as well as highly revealing. By the way, sometimes you learn as much from listening to the work of others being critiqued as you do when your own is in the hot seat – because being the centre of attention can make it difficult to truly *hear* what is being said.
- **Match the level of commitment required to the time you have available.** A weekly class can be an excellent way of sparking your motivation but will lead to frustration if your personal/work commitments do not allow you to benefit from all the add-ons available. For example, most universities offer students access to a range of other stimulating events, which you often only hear of late in the day, and trying to fit these around child care and work can produce stress. Maybe you would be better waiting to enrol until you have slightly more time available.

• **It's still you who has to write**. Sometimes enrolling in a class, and in particular if large amounts of money have changed hands, can make you feel you have delegated the responsibility of drawing out the inner writer to those you have paid. A tempting path, but one to be resisted. As Stephen King wrote in his wonderful memoir, *On Writing: A Memoir of the Craft* (New English Library, 2001): 'It is, after all, the dab of grit that seeps into an oyster's shell that makes the pearl, not the pearl making seminars with other oysters.'

• **Paying for a course does not guarantee publication**. Most courses advertise themselves on the basis of those who have passed through their hands on their way to writing fame, and in the case of the better known courses a variety of publishers and agents may visit and talk to tutors about talent they have spotted so far. But taking such a course does not guarantee you a publishing deal – or of course that you will complete either what you started out writing, or the course as a whole. Nor can you predict (or reasonably feel annoyed – although it's very tempting) when other members of the course get snapped up by those bearing publishing contracts before you do.

• **You may end up taking classes in genres you do not think are suited to you or what you want to write**. And of course this can be liberating. Experimenting with poetry or writing a screenplay can be exciting for those who have never tried it before, and can really stretch you. But if you have a very clear idea of what you want to produce, and just need advice on how to do so more effectively, then a general course may not be a wise choice.

• **The most valuable thing about the course may be not on the syllabus**. One of the real values of a formal creative writing class tends to take place outside teaching time. The act of writing is solitary and can be lonely, and the chance to meet other people who are serious about their work offers you the opportunity to set up a writers' group and motivate each other. At Kingston I have seen some of these groups operate long after the course has finished, as a supportive and regular mechanism for encouragement. One in particular involves four women writing different kinds of work, who encourage each other – and even recently mounted a lunchtime event for the Kingston Readers' Festival.

A word of warning before I end this article. Any burgeoning market attracts the offer of services, and writing courses are not the only way in which the writer can invest money and time in their future. For example, you can pay for advice on your manuscript (companies such as The Literary Consultancy (TLC) offer this service; see this *Yearbook's* website, www.writersandartists.co.uk); seek professional help on your mental resources (there is psychotherapy and counselling aimed at writers); take part in online writing groups or engage a professional tutor to work with you on a one-to-one basis. The small ads in any writing magazine will show you the range of services on offer. Or you could, as I heard literary agent Heather Holden-Brown recommend recently, just take a trip to your local bookshop, buy all the books in the genre in which you wish your writing to be published, read them – and then try to think why these titles have been successful. A total spend of about £50.

If you do decide on a course, bear in mind that your attitude as you approach it will matter as much as your incipient writing talent. It should be viewed as a partnership not a purchase.

Alison Baverstock teaches marketing to creative writers at Kingston University. Her seminal *Is there a book in you?* (A&C Black 2006) is required reading for most writing courses. For information on short courses at Kingston see http://fass.kingston.ac.uk/activities/conferences.

Creative writing courses

Anyone wishing to participate in a writing course should first satisfy themselves as to its content and quality. For day and evening courses consult your local Adult Education Centre. Details of postgraduate writing courses follow on page 691.

Alston Hall College

Alston Lane, Longridge, Preston PR3 3BP
tel (01772) 784661 *fax* (01772) 785835
email alston.hall@ed.lancscc.gov.uk
website www.alstonhall.com

The Arvon Foundation

Lumb Bank, The Ted Hughes Arvon Centre, Heptonstall, Hebden Bridge, West Yorkshire HX7 6DF
tel (01422) 843714 *fax* (01422) 843714
email london@arvonfoundation.org
website www.arvonfoundation.org
Contact Ilona Jones
Moniack Mhor, Teavarran, Kiltarlity, Beauly, Inverness-shire IV4 7HT
tel (01463) 741675 *fax* (01463) 741733
email moniackmhor@arvonfoundation.org
Contact Lyndy Batty
The Arvon Foundation, Totleigh Barton, Sheepwash, Beaworthy, Devon EX21 5NS
tel (01409) 231338 *fax* (01409) 231144
email totleighbarton@arvonfoundation.org
Contact Julia Wheadon
The Hurst – The John Osborne Arvon Centre Clunton, Craven Arms, Shrops. SY7 0JA
tel (01588) 640658 *fax* (01588) 640509
email thehurst@arvonfoundation.org
Contact Dan Pavitt

Burton Manor

Burton, Neston, Cheshire CH64 5SJ
tel 0151-336 5172 *fax* 0151-336 6586
email enquiry@burtonmanor.com
website www.burtonmanor.com
Principal Keith Chandler

College offering a wide range of residential courses.

Caboodle Writing Retreats

69 Southwold Road, Wrentham, Beccles, Suffolk NR34 7JE
tel/fax (01502) 676101
Director Ruby C. Ormerod

Creative writing courses in Halesworth, Suffolk. Manuscript reading service. Mentor of Nicky Hodgkinson, winner of the 2009 Alan Titchmarsh 'People's Author' prize.

University of Cambridge

Institute of Continuing Education, Madingley Hall, Madingley, Cambridge CB23 8AQ
tel (01223) 746262 *fax* (01954) 280200
email registration@cont-ed.cam.ac.uk
website www.cont-ed.cam.ac.uk
Contact The Registration Team

A wide range of courses on literature and creative writing. See website for details.

Centerprise Trust

136 Kingsland High Street, London E8 2NS
tel 020-7249 6572 *fax* 020-7923 1951
website www.centerprisetrust.org.uk

Central St Martins College of Art & Design, Short Course Office

10 Back Hill, London EC1 5EN
tel 020-7514 7015 *fax* 020-7514 7016
email shortcourse@csm.arts.ac.uk
website http://courses.csm.arts.ac.uk
Contact The Short Course Office

Evening and day-time courses for beginners and intermediate levels.

Community Creative Writing and Publishing

Sea Winds, 2 St Helens Terr, Spittal, Berwick-upon-Tweed, Northumberland TD15 1RJ
tel/fax (01289) 305213
email mavismaureen@btinternet.com
Contact Maureen Raper MBE, (member of Society of Authors) author/tutor/moderator

Classes for beginners and intermediates in Writing for Children, Writing Romantic Fiction, Writing Crime and Mystery, Writing Comedy, Writing for Radio and Television. Distance learning available. Writing groups fortnightly, reading groups monthly at Berwick Library.

Dingle Writing Courses

Ballintlea, Ventry, Co Kerry, Republic of Ireland
tel 00 353 66 9159815
email info@dinglewritingcourses.ie
website www.dinglewritingcourses.ie
Directors Abigail Joffe, Nicholas McLachlan

The Earnley Concourse

Earnley Trust Ltd, Earnley, Chichester, West Sussex PO20 7JN
tel (01243) 670392 *fax* (01243) 670832
email info@earnley.co.uk
website www.earnley.co.uk

Emerson College

Emerson College, Forest Row, East Sussex RH18 5JX
tel (01342) 822238 *fax* (01342) 826055
email info@emerson.org.uk
website www.emerson.org.uk
Contact Patricia Tippett
Takes place August

Poetry OtherWise: a week of writing workshops, readings by established poets, space for paticipants to share their poetry, together with music, dancing, conversation, talks and social events.

The Faber Academy

Faber and Faber Ltd, Bloomsbury House, 74–77 Great Russell Street, London WC1B 3DA
tel 020-7927 3800 *fax* 020-7927 3801
email patrickk@faber.co.uk
website www.faber.co.uk/academy
Contact Patrick Keogh

Committed to innovation, with both an international and UK focus, the Faber Academy delivers high-quality events, from one-day workshops to 6-month mentoring schemes, devised by the foremost practitioners in their fields. Launched October 2008.

Far West

23 Chapel Street, Penzance, Cornwall TR18 4AP
tel (01736) 363146
email angela@farwest.co.uk
website www.farwest.co.uk
Contact Angela Stoner

Offers a range of creative writing courses and workshops.

Federation of Worker Writers and Community Publishers Festival of Writing – see page 563

Fire in the Head

PO Box 17, Yelverton, Devon PL20 6YF
tel (01822) 841081
email roselle.angwin@internet-today.co.uk
website www.fire-in-the-head.co.uk
Contact Roselle Angwin

Poetry and prose; journaling and personal development; retreats and short courses; correspondence courses, mentoring.

Indian King Arts

Garmoe Cottage, 2 Trefrew Road, Camelford, Cornwall PL32 9TP
tel (01840) 212161
email indianking@btconnect.com

Weekly poetry morning group, occasional all day poetry workshop, and bi-monthly novel workshop led by Karen Hayes. Also the home of the Poetry Society's Camelford Stanza.

Inkwell Writers Workshops

The Old Post Office, Kilmacanogue, Co. Wicklow, Republic of Ireland
tel (01) 2765921 / (087) 2835382
website www.inkwellwriters.ie
Contact Vanessa O'Loughlin

One-day intensive fiction-writing workshops facilitated by bestselling authors. Full manuscript critiquing service. Online workshops. Writers Weekends. Inkwell 4 Kids Summer Camps. Inkwell are scouts for leading Irish and UK agents and publishers. Founded 2006.

Irish Writers' Centre

19 Parnell Square, Dublin 1, Republic of Ireland
tel (01) 8721302 *fax* (01) 8726282
email courses@writerscentre.ie
website www.writerscentre.ie
Contact Chairperson, Jack Harte

National organisation for the promotion of writers, writing and literature in Ireland. Runs an extensive education programme offering courses, workshops, masterclasses and seminars, calibrated to assist new and emerging writers at every stage in their development. All course are facilitated by published authors and poets. See website for further details.

Kilkenny Campus NUI Maynooth

College Road, Kilkenny, Republic of Ireland
tel (56) 7775910 *fax* (56) 7761369
email kilkenny.campus@nuim.ie
website http://kilkenny.nuim.ie

NUI Certificate in Creative Writing for Publication held over 10 weekends.

Knuston Hall

Irchester, Wellingborough, Northants. NN29 7EU
tel (01933) 312104 *fax* (01933) 357596
email enquiries@knustonhall.org.uk
website www.knustonhall.org.uk

University of Leeds

Lifelong Learning Centre, Leeds LS2 9JT
tel 0113-343 3212
email part-time@leeds.ac.uk
website www.leeds.ac.uk/lifelonglearningcentre

Various part-time creative writing courses.

Liberato

16 Middle King, Braintree, Essex CM7 3XY
tel (01376) 551379 *mobile* (07718) 339636
email liberato@talktalk.net
website www.liberato.co.uk
Contact Maureen Blundell, Tutor and novelist

Weekend fiction courses and MS critiques. Editing of fiction MS via post or email. Mentoring offered for dedicated novelists.

Marlborough College Summer School

Marlborough, Wilts. SN8 1PA
tel (01672) 892388 *fax* (01672) 892476
email admin@mcsummerschool.org.uk
website www.mcsummerschool.org.uk
Contact Jon Copp

A 3-week summer school where participants can attend for 1, 2 or 3 weeks. There are a large variety of courses, including 5 creative writing courses, with each course being 5 half days Monday-Friday. Accomodation available.

Middlesex University Summer School

Summer School Office, Middlesex University, Trent Park, Bramley Road, London N14 4YZ
tel 020-8411 5782 *fax* 020-8411 2297
email sschool@mdx.ac.uk
website www.mdx.ac.uk/study/summer

Offers a number of creative writing courses.

Missenden Abbey

Great Missenden, Bucks HP16 0BD
tel (01296) 383582 *fax* (01753) 783756
email dcevreham@buckscc.gov.uk
website www.arca.uk.net/missendenabbey

Weekend and summer-school writing courses.

Morley College

61 Westminster Bridge, London SE1 7HT
tel 020-7450 1889 *fax* 020-7928 4074
email enquiries@morleycollege.ac.uk
website www.morleycollege.ac.uk

Offers a number of creative writing courses – one day, one week and part-time day and evening throughout the year.

Newcastle University

School of English, Percy Building, Newcastle upon Tyne NE1 7RU
tel 0191-222 7619 *fax* 0191-222 8708
email melanie.birch@ncl.ac.uk
website www.ncl.ac.uk/elll/creative
Contact Melanie Birch

Short courses, spring and summer schools, a postgraduate certificate (available via distance learning) and degrees at MA and PhD level.

North West Kent College

Oakfield Lane, Dartford DA1 2JT
tel (0800) 0741447 *fax* (01322) 629468
email enquiries@nwkcollege.ac.uk
website www.courses.nwkent.ac.uk
Contact Neil Nixon, Pathway Leader, Professional Writing

Offers full-time, part-time and one-off courses in professional writing.

Open College of the Arts

The Michael Young Arts Centre, Redbrook Business Park, Wilthorpe Road, Barnsley S75 1JN
tel 0800-731 2116
email enquiries@oca-uk.com
website www.oca-uk.com

Distance learning writing courses to develop skills or gain credits towards a degree.

Open Studies – Part-time Courses for Adults: Office of Lifelong Learning

University of Edinburgh, 11 Buccleuch Place, Edinburgh EH8 9LW
tel 0131-650 4400 *fax* 0131-667 6097
email oll@ed.ac.uk
website www.lifelong.ed.ac.uk

Offers a large number of creative writing courses.

Oxford University Summer School for Adults

Dept for Continuing Education, Rewley House, 1 Wellington Square, Oxford OX1 2JA
tel (01865) 270396 *fax* (01865) 280761
email oussa@conted.ox.ac.uk
website http://summerschool.conted.ox.ac.uk
Contact Programme Administrator

A 4-week summer school with a variety of courses on offer, including creative writing. Students choose one course and follow it for a week.

Pitstop Refuelling Writers' Weekend Workshops – see The Winchester Writers' Conference Festival and Bookfair, Centre for Research and Knowledge Exchange

Scottish Universities', International Summer School

21 Buccleuch Place, Edinburgh EH8 9LN
tel 0131-650 4369 *fax* 0161-662 0275
email suiss@ed.ac.uk
website www.summer-school.hss.ed.ac.uk/suiss
Directors Dr Stella Bolaki, Julia Boll

A 3-week creative writing course for undergraduates, postgraduates and teachers, as well as published writers keen to widen their skills.

Southern Writers' Conference

Stable House, Home Farm, Coldharbour Lane, Dorking, Surrey RH4 3JG
Contact Lucia White
Venue The Earnley Concourse, Chichester

Caters for published and serious writers.

Swanwick, The Writers' Summer School

Contact Fiona McFadzean, The Secretary
website www.wss.org.uk

Has been in existence for 60 years, teaching new skills to (and honing old ones for) poets, playwrights, journalists and songwriters.

Travellers' Tales

92 Hillfield Road, London NW6 1QA
email info@travellerstales.org
website www.travellerstales.org
Director Jonathan Lorie, Contributing Editor of *Traveller* magazine

UK's leading training agency for travel writers and photographers. Offers vocational courses with the UK's top travel photographers and writers in London, Marrakech, Istanbul and Andalucia including beginners' weekends, masterclasses and creative retreats. Hosts the annual Travellers' Tales Festival of the world's leading travel writers and photographers.

Tŷ Newydd

Tŷ Newydd, National Writers' Centre for Wales, Llanystumdwy, Cricieth, Gwynedd LL52 0LW
tel (01766) 522811 *fax* (01766) 523095
email post@tynewydd.org
website www.tynewydd.org

Week and weekend courses on all aspects of creative writing. Full programme available.

Urchfont Manor College

Urchfont, Devizes, Wilts. SN10 4RG
tel (01380) 840495 *fax* (01380) 840005
email urchfontmanor@wiltshire.gov.uk
website www.urchfontmanor.co.uk

Wedgwood Memorial College

Station Road, Barlaston, Stoke-on-Trent ST12 9DG
tel (01782) 372105
email wedgewood.memorial@stoke.gov.uk
website www.stoke.gov.uk

The Winchester Writers' Conference Festival and Bookfair, Centre for Research and Knowledge Exchange

University of Winchester, Winchester, Hants SO22 4NR
tel (01962) 827238
email barbara.large@winchester.ac.uk
website www.writersconference.co.uk
Conference Director Barbara Large MBE, FRSA, HFUW,
Honorary Patrons Jacqueline Wilson OBE, Maureen Lipman, Colin Dexter OBE, Dame Beryl Bainbridge, Baroness James OBE
Takes place University of Winchester, 1–3 July 2011; Workshops 27 June–1 July

This Festival of Writing, celebrating its 31st year in 2011, attracts 65 internationally renowned authors, poets, playwrights, agents and commissioning editors who give 12 mini-courses, 22 workshops, 60 talks, seminars and 500 one-to-one appointments to help writers harness their creativity and develop their writing, editing and marketing skills. Seventeen writing competitions, including Writing for Children, are adjudicated and 70 prizes are awarded at the Writers' Awards Reception. All first place winners are published annually in *The Best of* series with the Plenary Address given by Sir Terry Pratchett (2010).

The Bookfair offers delegates a wide choice of exhibits including authors' and internet services, publishers, booksellers, printers and trade associations.

Pitstop Refuelling Writers' Weekend Workshops are planned for 23–25 October 2010, 25–27 March and 28–30 October 2011, including Writing Marketable Children's Fiction and Non-fiction; Editing and Marketing your Novel; and How to Self-Publish Your Book day workshops on 17 September 2010 and 11 February, 6 May, 16 September and 16 November 2011 at a major book production company, CPI Antony Rowe, Chippenham.

A retreat in Mallorca, the Great Fiction Workshop, is planned for 24–30 October 2011 (www.centromallorca.com) to cover creating, writing, editing and marketing fiction.

Writers' Holiday at Caerleon

School Bungalow, Church Road, Pontnewydd, Cwmbran, South Wales NP44 1AT
tel (01633) 489438
email gerry@writersholiday.net
website www.writersholiday.net
Contact Gerry Hobbs

A 6-day annual conference for writers of all standards from absolute beginner to bestselling author. The event includes 14 courses. Also weekend workshops.

The Writing College

The Glebe House, Whitestone, Exeter EX4 2LF
tel (01392) 811642
email enquiries@writingcollege.com
website www.writingcollege.com
Director Richard Littler

'The Complete Writer' correspondence course: 28 modules divided into the practice and art of writing, writing genres and the business of writing. An MS appraisal service is also available. Founded 2000.

Written Words

5 Queen Elizabeth Close, London N16 0HL
tel 020-8809 4725
email henrietta@writtenwords.net
website www.WrittenWords.net
Contact Henrietta Soames

Workshops, tutorials and mentoring offered to all writers by experienced author, lively discussion and clear constructive feedback.

Wye Valley Arts Centre

Hephzibah Gallery, Llandogo, Monmouthshire NP25 4TW
tel (01594) 530214, (01291) 689463
email info@wyearts.co.uk
website www.wyearts.co.uk

Writing workshop.

POSTGRADUATE COURSES

Aberystwyth University

Department of English and Creative Writing, Hugh Owen Building, Aberystwyth University, Penglais Campus, Aberystwyth, Ceredigion SY23 3DY

tel (01970) 621946
email www.aber.ac.uk/english
Contact The Administrator

MA in Creative Writing. PhD in Creative Writing.

Bath Spa University

School of Humanities and Cultural Industries, Bath Spa University, Newton Park, Newton St Loe, Bath BA2 9BN
tel (01225) 875875 *fax* (01225) 875503
email enquiries@bathspa.ac.uk
website www.bathspa.ac.uk

MA in Creative Writing. MA in Writing for Young People. MA in Scriptwriting. PhD in Creative Writing.

Birkbeck College, University of London

Malet Street, London WC1E 7HX
tel 020-7631 6000
email info@bbk.ac.uk
website www.bbk.ac.uk
Contact Anne-Marie Taylor

MA in Creative Writing. Full- and part-time evening course.

University of Bolton

School of Arts, Media and Education, University of Bolton, Dean Campus, Bolton BL3 5AB
tel (01204) 900600 *fax* (01204) 903232
email j.glover@bolton.ac.uk
website www.bolton.ac.uk
Contact John Glover, Programme Leader, Creative Writing

MA in Creative Writing.

Brunel University

School of Arts, Brunel University, Uxbridge, Middlesex UB8 3PH
tel (01895) 274000 *fax* (01895) 232806
email pg-arts-admissions@brunel.ac.uk
website www.brunel.ac.uk

MA in Creative and Professional Writing. MA Creative Writing: The Novel with Celia Brayfield and Fay Weldon (visiting Professor).

Cardiff University

Cardiff University, Cardiff School of English and Philosophy, Humanities Building, Colum Drive, Cardiff CF10 3EU
tel 029-2087 5624 *fax* 029-2087 4647
email creativewriting@cardiff.ac.uk
website www.cf.ac.uk/encap
Contact Nicola Bassett

MA in the Teaching and Practice of Creative Writing.

The Central School of Speech and Drama

Embassy Theatre, Eton Avenue, London NW3 3HY
tel 020-7722 8183
website www.cssd.ac.uk

MA in Advanced Theatre Practice: Playwriting. MA in Writing for Stage and Broadcast Media.

University of Chichester

Bishop Otter Campus, College Lane, Chichester, West Sussex PO19 6PE
tel (01243) 816000
email s.norgate@chi.ac.uk
website www.chi.ac.uk
Contact Stephanie Norgate, MA in Creative Writing Programme Coordinator

MA in Creative Writing.

City University

Dept of Journalism and Publishing, City University, Northampton Square, London EC1V 0HB
tel 020-7040 5060 *fax* 020-7040 8887
email journalism@city.ac.uk
website www.city.ac.uk
Contact The Course Officer (Journalism and Publishing)

MA in Creative Writing (Plays and Scripts) and MA in Creative Writing (Novels).

The Creative Writer's Workshop

Kinvara, Co. Galway, Republic of Ireland
tel (353 086) 2523428
email creativewriting@ireland.com
website www.thecreativewritersworkshop.com
Contact Irene Graham

Writing retreat for new and established writers and an online writing workshop. Founded 1991.

University of Cumbria

Bowerham Road, Lancaster LA1 3JD
tel (01524) 384328
website www.cumbria.ac.uk

MA in Scriptwriting.

De Montfort University

Dept of Media, Film and Journalism, De Montfort University, The Gateway, Leicester LE1 9BH
tel 0116-250 6470 *fax* 0116-257 7199
email pghums@dmu.ac.uk
website www.dmu.ac.uk/humanities
Contact Promotion and Recruitment Centre

MA in TV Scriptwriting.

University of East Anglia

Admissions Office, School of Literature and Creative Writing, Faculty of Arts and Humanities, University of East Anglia, Norwich NR4 7TJ
tel (01603) 592154
email pgt.hum.admiss@uea.ac.uk
website www.uea.ac.uk/creativewriting/
Contact Admissions Office

MA in Creative Writing: Prose Fiction. MA in Creative Writing: Poetry. MA in Creative Writing: Scriptwriting. MA in Life Writing.

Edge Hill University

Department of English and History, St Helens Road, Ormskirk L39 4QP
tel (01695) 584274 *fax* (01695) 579997
email shepparr@edgehill.ac.uk
website www.edgehill.ac.uk
Contact Prof Robert Sheppard (Shepparr@edgehill.ac.uk)

MA in Creative Writing (full time and part time). PhD programmes in creative writing. Contact Mr Daniele Pantano (pantanod@edgehill.ac.uk) for BA in Creative Writing.

University of Edinburgh

Graduate School of Literatures, Languages & Cultures, 19 George Square, Edinburgh EH8 9JX
tel 0131-650 3620
website www.ed.ac.uk/englit/
Contact The Graduate Secretary

MSc in Creative Writing.

University of Essex

Wivenhoe Park, Colchester CO4 3SQ
tel (01206) 873333
email thorj@essex.ac.uk
website www.essex.ac.uk
Contact Dept of Literature, Film & Theatre Studies

MA in Literature with option to specialise in creative writing.

University of Exeter

School of Arts, Languages and Literatures, Department of Drama, Thornlea, New North Road, Exeter EX4 4LA
tel (01392) 724580 *fax* (01392) 264594
email drama@ex.ac.uk
website www.exeter.ac.uk/drama

MA in Playwriting and Script Development: playwriting for stage and radio, performance writing.

University College Falmouth — incorporating Dartington College of Arts

Falmouth, Cornwall TR11 4RH
tel (01326) 211077
email admissions@falmouth.ac.uk
website www.falmouth.ac.uk
Contact Admissions Office

MA Professional Writing, MA Professional Writing (Distance Learning).

The French House Party

The Jaylands, Abberley, Worcs. WR6 6BN
tel (01299) 896819
email enquiries@frenchhouseparty.eu
website www.frenchhouseparty.eu
Director Moira Martingale

Learning retreat in South of France which includes creative writing and songwriting courses.

University of Glamorgan

Faculty of Humanities and Social Sciences, University of Glamorgan, Treforest, Pontypridd CF37 1DL
tel (01443) 654450 , 482501 *fax* (01443) 654050
email tcurtis@glam.ac.uk
website www.glam.ac.uk
Contacts Prof. T. Curtis, Director of Studies

M.Phil in Writing.

University of Glasgow

Dept of English Literature, University of Glasgow, 6 University Gardens, Glasgow G12 8QQ
tel 0141-330 8538
email m.schmidt@englit.arts.gla.ac.uk
website www.glasgow.ac.uk/creativewriting
Head of Creative Writing Programmes Prof. Michael Schmidt

MLitt, MFA and PhD in Creative Writing.

University of Greenwich

School of Humanities and Social Sciences, University of Greenwich, Old Royal Naval College, 30 Park Row, Greenwich, London SE10 9LS
tel/fax 020-8331 8800
email s.a.rowland@gre.ac.uk
website www.greenwich.ac.uk
Contact Prof. Susan Rowland

MA by Research (Creative Writing).

University of Hull

Faculty of Arts, Dept of English, University of Hull, Cottingham Road, Hull HU6 7RX
tel (01482) 465623
email m.j.goodman@hull.ac.uk
website www.hull.ac.uk
Contact Prof. Martin Goodman

MA/PhD in Creative Writing.

Kingston University

River House , 53–57 High Street, Kingston upon Thames, Surrey KT1 1LQ
tel 020-8417 9000
website www.kingston.ac.uk
Contact Postgraduate Admissions Administrator

MAs in Creative Writing, Travel Writing, Writing Fiction and Writing Children's Literature.

Lancaster University

Dept of English & Creative Writing, County College, Lancaster University, Lancaster LA1 4YT
tel (01524) 594169

email l.kellett@lancaster.ac.uk
website www.lancs.ac.uk/fass/english
Contact The Secretary

MA in Creative Writing. MA in Creative Writing by Distance Learning.

University of Leeds

School of Performance and Cultural Industries, Leeds LS2 9JT
tel 0113-343 8710 *fax* 0113-343 8711
email enquiries-pci@leeds.ac.uk
website www.leeds.ac.uk
Contact Postgraduate Secretary

MA in Writing for Performance and Publication.

Leeds Metropolitan University

School of Film, Television and Performing Arts, Electric Press Building, 1 Millennium Square, Leeds LS2 3AD
tel 0113-812 3860
email filmenquiries@leedsmet.ac.uk
website www.leedsmet.ac.uk
Contact Chris Pugh, Course Administrator

MA in Filmmaking.

Liverpool John Moores University

School of Media, Critical and Creative Arts, Liverpool John Moores University, Dean Walters Building, Upper Duke Street, Liverpool L1 7BT
tel 0151-231 5196 *fax* 0151-231 5049
website www.ljmu.ac.uk
Contact Programme Administrator

MA in Screenwriting and MA in Writing.

Goldsmiths, University of London

Dept of English and Comparative Literature, Goldsmiths, University of London, London SE14 6NW
tel 020-7919 7752 *fax* 020-7919 7453
email r.bolley@gold.ac.uk
website www.goldsmiths.ac.uk
Contact Richard Bolley, Departmental Administrator

MA in Creative and Life Writing, MPhil/PhD Creative Writing.

University of London, Goldsmiths College

Dept of Drama, Goldsmiths College, University of London, London SE14 6NW
tel 020-7919 7171 *fax* 020-7919 7413
email submissions@gold.ac.uk
website www.gold.ac.uk
Contact Drama Secretary

MA in Writing for Performance.

University of London, King's College

School of Humanities, University of London, King's College, Strand, London WC2R 2LS
tel 020-7836 5454 *fax* 020-7848 2257
email englishdept@kcl.ac.uk
website www.kcl.ac.uk
Contact Helene Hokland (course administrator)

MA in Text and Performance Studies; scriptwriting option supervised at RADA.

University of London, Royal Holloway

Dept of English, Royal Holloway, University of London, Egham, Surrey TW20 0EX
tel (01784) 434455/437520
email k.kingsley@rhul.ac.uk
website www.rhul.ac.uk/English
Contacts Prof. Andrew Motion (Creative Writing), Prof. Redell Olsen (Poetic Practice)

MA in Creative Writing. MA in Poetic Practice.

University of London, Royal Holloway

Dept of Media Arts, Royal Holloway, University of London, Egham, Surrey TW20 0EX
tel (01784) 443214
email mediaarts@rhul.ac.uk
website www.rhul.ac.uk/media-arts
Contact Susan Rogers, Sue Clayton (Retreat Programme)

MA in Film Screenwriting and MA in Screenwriting for Film and TV (Retreat Programme).

London College of Communication

LCC School of Media, Elephant & Castle, London SE1 6SB
tel 020-7514 6569
email info@lcc.arts.ac.uk
website www.lcc.arts.ac.uk
Contact S. Paskell, Postgraduate Administrator

MA in Screenwriting (2 year part-time degree).

The London Film School

London Film School, 24 Shelton Street, London WC2H 9UB
tel 020-7836 9642 *fax* 020-7497 3718
email screenwriting@lfs.org.uk
website www.lfs.org.uk
Contact Brian Dunnigan

MA in Screenwriting.

University of Manchester

Centre for New Writing, Mansfield Cooper Building, University of Manchester, Oxford Road, Manchester M13 9PL
tel 0161-306 1240 *fax* 0161-306 1241
email info-cnw@manchester.ac.uk
website www.manchester.ac.uk/arts/newwriting

MA and PhD in Creative Writing. MA and PhD in Contemporary Literature.

The Manchester Writing School at Manchester Metropolitan University

Dept of English, Rosamond Street West, Off Oxford Road, Manchester M15 6LL

tel 0161-247 1787 *fax* 0161-247 6345
email j.draper@mmu.ac.uk
website www.mmu.ac.uk/english/writingschool
Contact James Draper, Project Manager: The Manager Writing School

MA in Creative Writing: Novel Writing, Poetry and Writing for Children (campus-based and online).

Middlesex University

Oakleigh Road South, London N11 1QS
tel 020-8411 5555
email admissions@mdx.ac.uk
website www.mdx.ac.uk
Contact Admissions Office

MA/Postgraduate Diploma/Postgraduate Certificate in Writing (Prose Fiction) and MPhil/PhD in Creative Writing.

National Film and Television School

National Film and Television School, Beaconsfield Studios, Station Road, Beaconsfield, Bucks. HP9 1LG
tel (01494) 671234 *fax* (01494) 674042
email info@nfts.co.uk
website www.nfts.co.uk

MA in Screenwriting and Diploma in Script Development. See website for application information.

Newcastle University

School of English Literature, Language and Linguistics, Newcastle University, Newcastle upon Tyne NE1 7RU
tel 0191-222 7625 *fax* 0191-222 8708
website www.ncl.ac.uk/elll
Contact Postgraduate Admission Secretary

MA in Creative Writing. Postgraduate Certificate in Creative Writing. Phd in Creative Writing.

Northumbria University

School of Arts and Social Sciences, University of Northumbria at Newcastle, Room 126, Lipman Building, Sandyford Road, Newcastle upon Tyne NE1 8ST
tel 0191-227 4473
email admissions@northumbria.ac.uk
website www.northumbria.ac.uk
Contact The Admissions Tutor

MA in Creative Writing, combining prose and script.

Nottingham Trent University

Dept of English and Media Studies, Nottingham Trent University, Clifton Lane, Nottingham NG11 8NS
tel 0115-848 8977
email hum.postgrad@ntu.ac.uk
website www.ntu.ac.uk/creativewriting
Contact David Belbin

MA in Creative Writing.

Oxford University

Dept for Continuing Education, 1 Wellington Square, Oxford OX1 2JA
tel (01865) 270369 *fax* (01865) 270309
email ppaward@conted.ox.ac.uk
website www.conted.ox.ac.uk/mstcw
Contact M.St. Administrator

Master of Studies (M.St.) in Creative Writing from Oxford University: a 2-year part-time course covering prose fiction, radio and TV drama, poetry, stage drama and screenwriting. A 2-year part-time Diploma and Summer Schools in creative writing are also offered.

University of Plymouth

Faculty of Arts, University of Plymouth, Drake Circus, Plymouth PL4 8AA
tel (01752) 585100
email anthony.caleshu@plymouth.ac.uk, artspostgrad@plymouth.ac.uk
website www.plymouth.ac.uk
Contact Dr Anthony Caleshu, Senior Lecturer in English and Creative Writing

MA/Postgraduate Diploma in Creative Writing. PhD in Creative Writing.

The Poet's House – see The Poet's House/ Teach na hÉigse

Queen's University, Belfast

School of English, Queen's University, Belfast, Belfast BT7 1NN
tel 028-9024 5133 ext. 5103 *fax* 028-9031 4615
website www.qub.ac.uk
Contact Linda Drain (Postgraduate Secretary)

MA/Postgraduate Diploma in Creative Writing. PhD in Creative Writing.

University of St Andrews

School of English, University of St Andrews, St Andrews, Fife KY16 9AJ
tel (01334) 462666 *fax* (01334) 462655
email english@st-andrews.ac.uk
website www.st-andrews.ac.uk
Contact Postgraduate Director

M.Litt/Graduate Diploma in Creative Writing.

University of Salford

University of Salford, Adelphi Building, Peru Street, Salford, Greater Manchester M3 6EQ
tel 0161-295 6026 *fax* 0161-295 6027
email course-enquiries@salford.ac.uk
website www.salford.ac.uk
Contact Admission Tutor

MA/Postgraduate Diploma in Television and Radio Scriptwriting.

Sheffield Hallam University

Admissions Office, Faculty of Development and Society, Sheffield Hallam University, Sheffield S1 1WB

tel 0114-225 5555 *fax* 0114-225 4449
website www.shu.ac.uk/humanities

MA/Postgraduate Diploma/Postgraduate Certificate in Creative Writing.

University of Sussex

Centre for Community Engagement,
Mantell Building, University of Sussex,
Brighton BN1 7RF
tel (01273) 873211
email cce@sussex.ac.uk
website www.sussex.ac.uk
Contact Dr. Sue Roe

MA in Creative Writing and Authorship.

Trinity College, Carmarthen

School of Creative Arts & Humanities,
Trinity College, Carmarthen, Dyfed SA31 3EP
tel (01267) 676767 *fax* (01267) 676766
email p.wright@trinity-cm.ac.uk
website www.trinity-cm.ac.uk
Contact Dr Paul Wright

MA in Creative Writing.

University of Warwick

Dept of English and Comparative Literary Studies,
Humanities Building, University of Warwick,
Coventry CV4 7AL
tel 024-7652 3665
email cheryl.cave@warwick.ac.uk
website www.warwick.ac.uk
Contact Cheryl Cave, Programme Secretary

MA in Writing.

University of Winchester

Winchester SO22 4NR
tel (01962) 827234 *fax* (01962) 827406
email course.enquiries@winchester.ac.uk
website www.winchester.ac.uk
Contact Course Enquiries & Admissions

MA Writing for Children and MA Creative and Critical Writing.

Copyright and libel

Copyright questions

Copyright is a vital part of any writer's assets, and should never be assigned or sold without due consideration and the advice of a competent authority, such as the Society of Authors, the Writers' Guild of Great Britain, or the National Union of Journalists. Michael Legat answers some of the most commonly asked questions about copyright.

Is there a period of time after which the copyright expires?

Copyright in the European Union lasts for the lifetime of the author and for a further 70 years from the end of the year of death, or, if the work is first published posthumously, for 70 years from the end of the year of publication. In most other countries of the world copyright exists similarly for the lifetime and for either 50 years or 70 years after death or posthumous publication.

If I want to include an extract from a book, poem or article, do I have to seek copyright? How much may be used without permission? What happens if I apply for copyright permission but do not get a reply?

It is essential to seek permission to quote from another author's work, unless that author has been dead for 70 years or more, or 70 years or more has passed from the date of publication of a work published posthumously. Only if you are quoting for purposes of criticism or review are you allowed to do so without obtaining permission, and even then the Copyright, Designs and Patents Act of 1988 restricts you to 400 words of prose in a single extract from a copyright work, or a series of extracts of up to 300 words each, totalling no more than 800 words, or up to 40 lines of poetry, which must not be more than 25% of the poem. However, a quotation of no more than, say, half a dozen words may usually be used without permission since it will probably not extend beyond a brief and familiar reference, as, for example, Rider Haggard's well-known phrase, 'she who must be obeyed'. If in doubt, always check. If you do not get a reply when you ask for permission to quote, insert a notice in your work saying that you have tried without success to contact the copyright owner, and would be pleased to hear from him or her so that the matter could be cleared up – and keep a copy of all the relevant correspondence, in order to back up your claim of having tried to get in touch.

If a newspaper pays for an article and I then want to sell the story to a magazine, am I free under the copyright law to do so?

Yes, provided that you have not granted copyright or exclusive use to the newspaper. When selling your work to newspapers or magazines make it clear, in writing, that you are selling only First or Second Serial Rights, not your copyright.

If I agree to have an article published for no payment do I retain any rights over how it appears?

Whether or not you are paid for the work has no bearing on the legal situation. However, the Moral Rights which apply to books, plays, television and radio scripts, do not cover you against a failure to acknowledge you as the author of an article, nor against the mutilation of your text, when it is published in a newspaper or magazine.

I want to publish a photograph that was taken in 1950. I am not sure how to contact the photographer or even if he is still alive. Am I allowed to go ahead and publish it?

The Copyright, Designs and Patents Act of 1988 works retrospectively, so a photograph taken in 1950 is bound to be in copyright until at least 2020, and the copyright will be owned by the photographer, even though, when it was taken, the copyright would have belonged to the person who commissioned it, according to the laws then in place. You should therefore make every effort to contact the photographer, keeping copies of any relevant correspondence, and in case of failure take the same course of action as described above in relation to a textual extract the copyright owner of which you have been unable to trace.

I recently read an article on the same subject as one I have written. It contained many identical facts. Did this writer breach my copyright? What if I send ideas for an article to a magazine editor and those ideas are used despite the fact that I was not commissioned? May I sue the magazine?

Facts are normally in the public domain and may be used by anyone. However, if your article contains a fact which you have discovered and no one else has published, there could be an infringement of copyright if the author who uses it fails to attribute it to you. There is no copyright in ideas, so you cannot sue a writer or a journal for using ideas that you have put forward; in any case you would find it very difficult to prove that the idea belonged to you and to no one else. There is also no copyright in titles.

Does being paid a kill fee affect my copyright in a given piece?

No, provided that you have not sold the magazine or newspaper your copyright.

Do I need to copyright a piece of writing physically – whether an essay or a novel – or is it copyrighted automatically? Does it have to carry the © symbol?

Anything that you write is your copyright, assuming that it is not copied from the work of someone else, as soon as you have written it on paper or recorded it on the disk of a computer or on tape, or broadcast it, or posted it on the internet. It is not essential for the work to carry the © symbol, although its inclusion may act as a warning and help to stop another writer from plagiarising it.

Am I legally required to inform an interviewee that our conversation is being recorded?

The interviewee owns the copyright of any words that he or she speaks as soon as they are recorded on your tape. Unless you have received permission to use those words in direct quotation, you could be liable to an action for infringement of copyright. You should therefore certainly inform the interviewee that the conversation is being recorded and seek permission to quote what is said directly.

More and more newspapers and magazines have versions both in print and on the internet. How can I ensure that my work is not published on the internet without my permission?

Make sure that any clause granting electronic rights to anyone in any agreement that you sign in respect of your work specifies not only the proportion of any fees received which you will get, but that your agreement must be sought before the rights are sold. Copyright extends to electronic rights, and therefore to publication on the internet, in just the same way as to other uses of the material.

I commissioned a designer to design a business card for me, and I paid her well. Does the design belong to me or to her?

Copyright would belong to the designer, and not to the person who commissioned it (as is also true in the case of a photograph, copyright in which belongs to the photographer). However, copyright in the business card might be transferred to you if a court considered you to have gained beneficially from the card.

Michael Legat became a full-time writer after a long and successful publishing career. He is the author of a number of highly regarded books on publishing and writing.

See also...

- *UK copyright law*, page 700
- *The Society of Authors*, page 541
- *The Writers' Guild of Great Britain*, page 544
- *Authors' Licensing and Collecting Society*, page 715
- *Design and Artists Copyright Society*, page 717
- *The Copyright Licensing Agency Ltd*, page 713

UK copyright law

Amanda Michaels describes the main types of work which may qualify for copyright protection, or related protection as a design, together with some of the problems which may be faced by readers of this *Yearbook* in terms of protecting their own works or avoiding infringement of existing works in the UK. This is a technical area of the law, and one which is constantly developing; in an article of this length, it is not possible to deal fully with all the complexities of the law. It must also be emphasised that copyright is national in scope, so whilst works of UK authors will be protected in many other countries of the world, and works of foreign authors will generally be protected in the UK, foreign laws may deal differently with questions of subsistence, ownership and infringement.

Copyright is a creation of statute, now shaped and influenced significantly by EU harmonisation measures. On 1 August 1989, the Copyright, Designs & Patents Act 1988 ('the Act') replaced the Copyright Act 1956, which in turn replaced the Copyright Act 1911. All three Acts are still relevant to copyright today. Whilst the Act to a large degree restated the existing law, it was also innovative, in particular in the creation of a new 'design right' offering protection (generally speaking in lieu of copyright) for many industrial or commercial designs, and in the wider protection of moral rights.

Useful websites

www.ipo.gov.uk

Useful information, guidance notes and legislation are available on the website of the UK Intellectual Property Office (previously the Patent Office).

www.wipo.int

Website of the World Intellectual Property Organisation.

www.bailii.org

Provides free and broadly comprehensive access to UK case-law and legislation, with links to equivalent foreign websites. Legislation on the site may be in an unamended form.

There have been almost continual amendments of the law since 1989, largely due to EU directives. An important change occurred on 1 January 1996, when the duration of copyright protection in respect of most works (see below) was extended from 'life of the author' plus 50 years to life plus 70 years. New rights have been created, such as the database right which came into existence on 1 January 1998, and the important Community registered and unregistered design rights which came into effect in 2003. Numerous other changes have been made, for instance, to the rules on fair dealing with copyright works by the Copyright and Related Rights Regulations 2003 (see below) and changes to remedies required by the Enforcement Directive, 2004/48 and by the Digital Economy Act 2010.

These continuing changes do mean that it is important to check that you are using the current version of the Act. The website of the UK Intellectual Property Office (see box) is a useful resource.

Continuing relevance of old law

In this article, I discuss the law as it currently stands, but where a work was made before 1 August 1989 one needs to consider the law in force at the time of creation (or, possibly, first publication) in order to assess the existence or scope of any rights. Particular difficulties arise with foreign works, which may qualify for protection in the UK as a matter of international obligation. Each Act has contained transitional provisions and these, as well as the substantive provisions of any relevant earlier Act, need to be considered where, for instance, you wish to use an earlier work and need to decide whether permission is needed and, if so, who may grant it. In addition, publishing or licence agreements designed for use under older Acts and prior to the development of modern technologies may be unsuitable for current use.

Copyright protection of works

The overall policy justifying copyright protection is 'to prevent the unauthorised copying of material forms of expression (literary, dramatic, artistic and musical, for example) resulting from intellectual exertions of the human mind.... The important point is that copyright can be used to prevent copying of a substantial part of the relevant form of expression, but it does not prevent use of the information, thoughts or emotions expressed in the copyright work. It does not prevent another person from coincidentally creating a similar work by his own independent efforts' (see Mummery LJ in *Sawkins* v. *Hyperion Records* [2005] 1 WLR 3281).

Copyright does not subsist in ideas – that is the province of patents and the law of confidence. Copyright protects the expression of ideas, the particular form in which the author's idea has been expressed, not the idea itself. This distinction was examined in *Baigent & Leigh* v. *The Random House Group* [2007] FSR 24: Dan Brown was alleged to have copied the 'Central Theme', consisting of a series of historical facts, conjectures or theories, from the Claimants' book, *The Holy Blood and the Holy Grail*, in writing his bestselling novel *The Da Vinci Code*. Whilst the judge found evidence of copying, the Court of Appeal held that what Dan Brown took from HBHG "amounted to generalised propositions, at too high a level of abstraction to qualify for copyright protection, because it was not the product of the application of skill and labour by the authors of HBHG in the creation of their literary work. It lay on the wrong side of the line between ideas and their expression." (Lloyd LJ at para. 99). Copyright does not "extend to clothing information, facts, ideas, theories and themes with exclusive property rights, so as to enable the Claimants to monopolise historical research or knowledge and prevent the legitimate use of historical and biographical material, theories ... arguments ...general hypotheses ... or general themes" (Mummery LJ at para. 156).

The difficulty in seeking to apply this guidance to other cases is that the Court of Appeal emphasised that case-law cannot lay down any clear principle from which one may tell whether what is sought to be protected in any particular case is on the 'ideas' side of the dividing line, or on the 'expression' side. What can be said is that in cases of artistic copyright at least, "...the more abstract and simple the copied idea, the less likely it is to constitute a substantial part. Originality, in the sense of the contribution of the author's skill and labour, tends to lie in the detail with which the basic idea is presented." (Lord Hoffman in *Designers Guild* v. *Russell Williams (Textiles) Ltd* [2000] 1 WLR 2416).

Of course, if someone has written an outline, script or screenplay for a television show, film, etc and that idea is confidential, then dual protection may arise in the confidential idea embodied in the documents and in the literary (and sometimes artistic) works in which the idea is recorded. If the idea is used, but not the form, this might give rise to an action for breach of confidence, but not for infringement of copyright. Copyright prevents the copying of the *material form* in which the idea has been presented, or of a substantial part of it, measured in terms of quality, not quantity. One result is that so-called 'format right' cases rarely succeed.

Section 1 of the Act sets out a number of different categories of works which can be the subject of copyright protection. These are:

- original literary, dramatic, musical or artistic works,
- sound recordings, films or broadcasts, and
- typographical arrangements of published editions.

These works are further defined in ss.3–8 (see box for examples).

However, no work of any description enjoys copyright protection until it has been recorded in a tangible form, as s.3(2) provides that no copyright shall subsist in a literary, musical or artistic work until it has been recorded in writing or otherwise.

On the other hand, all that is required to achieve copyright protection is to record the original work in an appropriate medium. Once that has been done, copyright will subsist in the work in the UK (assuming that the qualifying features set out below are present) without any formality of registration or otherwise. There is, for instance, no need to publish a work to protect it.

Nonetheless, there can be a real benefit in keeping a proper record of the creation of a work. Drafts or preliminary sketches should be kept and dated, as should source or research material, so as to be able to show the development of your work. It is also a wise precaution (especially where works are to be submitted to potential publishers or purchasers) to take a complete copy of the documents and send them to oneself or lodge them with a responsible third party, sealed and dated, so as to be able to provide cogent evidence of the form or content of the work at that date. Such evidence may help the author, whether as claimant or defendant, to prove the independence of the creation of his work, and its originality in a copyright infringement or breach of confidence action.

Originality

Literary, dramatic, artistic and musical works must all be 'original' to gain copyright protection, but this does not impose any concept of objective novelty. Just as the law protects the form, rather than the idea, originality relates to the 'expression of the thought', rather than to the thought itself. The policy of copyright protection and its limited scope (set out above) explain why the threshold requirement of originality does not impose 'any objective standard of novelty, usefulness, inventiveness, aesthetic merit, quality or value'; so, a work may be 'complete rubbish', yet have copyright protection (see again Mummery LJ in *Sawkins*). A work need only be original in the sense of being the product of skill and labour on the part of the author. This can be seen for instance in the definition of certain artistic works, for copyright protects works like directories, tables (including mathematical tables) and databases, which may be protected as copyright works, or under the specific Copyright and Rights in Databases Regulations, 1997, see for example *Football Dataco* v. *Brittens Pools* [2010] EWHC 841.

There may be considerable difficulty, at times, in deciding whether a work is of sufficient originality, or has original features, particularly where there is a series of similar designs or amendments of existing works. *Sawkins* was just such a case: the question was whether or not the editorial work done by Dr Sawkins on works by the baroque composer, Lalande, had created new musical works. The result turned partly on the definition of 'music', but the nature of Dr Sawkins' input was such that he was found to have created an original musical work with its own copyright. See also *L.A. Gear Inc.* [1993] FSR 121, *Biotrading* [1998] FSR 109. So an adaptation of an existing work may have its own copyright protection (see *Cala Homes* [1995] FSR 818) but making a '*slavish* copy' of a work will not create an original work: (*Interlego AG* [1989] AC 217) but this is a matter of degree – some copying may take skill (Jacob LJ in *Sawkins*). If the work gives particular expression to a commonplace idea or an old tale, copyright may subsist in it, for example *Christoffer* v. *Poseidon Film Distributors Limited* (6/10/99) in which it was held that a script for an animated film of a story from Homer's *Odyssey* was an original literary work. But, as the *Da Vinci* case showed, whilst copyright may subsist in the work, the unlicensed use only of facts or ideas contained in it may not infringe that copyright. Copyright protection will be limited to the original features of the work, or those features created or chosen by the author's input of skill and labour.

Sound recordings or films which are copies of pre-existing sound recordings or films, and broadcasts which infringe rights in another broadcast are not protected by copyright.

'Works' such as the titles of books or periodicals, or advertising slogans, which may have required a good deal of original thought, generally are not accorded copyright protection, because they are too short to be deemed literary works. Computer 'languages', and the ideas or logic underlying them, are not protected as copyright works; such protection extends only to the computer programs: see *Navitaire* v. *Easyjet* [2004] EWHC 1725. So it is legitimate to emulate a program for a computer game so as to produce a game with similar characteristics, as long as the program code and the graphics are not copied (*Nova Productions Limited* v. *Mazooma Games Limited* [2007] RPC 25).

Qualification

The Act is limited in its effects to the UK (and to colonies to which it may be extended by Order). It is aimed primarily at protecting the works of British citizens, or works first published here. However, in line with various international conventions, copyright protection in the UK is also accorded to the works of nationals of many foreign states, as well as to works first published in those states, on a reciprocal basis.

As for works of nationals of other member states of the European Union, there is a principle of equal treatment, so that protection must be offered to such works here: see *Phil Collins* [1993] 3 CMLR 773.

The importance of these rules mainly arises when one is trying to find out whether a foreign work is protected by copyright here, for instance, to make a film based upon a foreign novel.

Ownership

The general rule is that the copyright in a work will first be owned by its author, the creator of the work. In most cases this is self-explanatory, but the definition of 'author' in relation

Definitions under the Act

Literary work is defined as: 'any work, other than a dramatic or musical work, which is written, spoken or sung, and accordingly includes: (a) a table or compilation other than a database, (b) a computer program, (c) preparatory design material for a computer program and (d) a database.'

A musical work means: 'a work consisting of music, exclusive of any words or action intended to be sung, spoken or performed with the music.'

An artistic work means: '(a) a graphic work, photograph, sculpture or collage, irrespective of artistic quality, (b) a work of architecture being a building or model for a building, or (c) a work of artistic craftsmanship.' What constitutes a sculpture or work of artistic craftsmanship was discussed in relation to *Star Wars* stormtrooper helmets in *Lucasfilm* v. *Ainsworth* [2009] FSR 2.

These categories of work are not mutually exclusive, e.g. a film may be protected both as a film and as a dramatic work. See *Norowzian* v. *Arks* [2000] FSR 363.

to films and sound recordings has changed over the years; currently, the author of a sound recording is its producer, and the authors of a film are the producer and principal director.

One important exception to the general rule is that the copyright in a work made by an employee in the course of his or her employment will belong to their employer, subject to any agreement to the contrary. However, this rule does not apply to freelance designers, journalists, etc, and not even to self-employed company directors. This obviously may lead to problems if the question of copyright ownership is not dealt with when an agreement is made to create, purchase or use a work. In the absence of an appropriate agreement, the legal title may simply not be owned by the apparent owner, who will need it if he wishes to sue for infringement, and it is often difficult to formalise the position long after creation of the work. More importantly, perhaps, there have been numerous cases in which the extent of the rights obtained in a 'commissioned' work has been disputed, simply because of the lack of any clear agreement at the outset between the author and the 'commissioner'. See for example *Griggs* v. *Evans* (below). It is very important for writers and artists of all kinds to agree about ownership/terms of use at the outset and record them in writing. It is equally important to understand the difference between an assignment and a licence (again, see below).

Where a work is produced by several people who collaborate so that each one's contribution is not distinct from that of the other(s), then they will be joint authors of the work, for example where two people write a play, each rewriting what the other produces, there will be a joint work. But where two people collaborate to write a song, one producing the lyrics and the other the music, there will be two separate copyright works, the copyright of which will be owned by each of the authors separately. The importance of knowing whether the copyright is joint or not arises:

- in working out the duration of the copyright, and
- from the fact that joint works can only be exploited with the agreement of all the joint authors, so that all of them have to join in any licence, although each of them can sue for infringement without joining the other(s) as a claimant in the proceedings. This issue was illustrated recently by the claim brought by Matthew Fisher that he had been a joint author of the music of Procol Harum's hit record *Whiter Shade of Pale*. He was found to be a joint author, having added the distinctive organ solo to the song, and the House of Lords held that in the circumstances even his 40-year delay in making his claim did not bar it: *Fisher* v. *Brooker* [2009] UKHL 41.

Duration of copyright

With effect from 1 January 1996, copyright in literary, dramatic, musical or artistic works expires at the end of the period of 70 years from the end of the calendar year in which the author dies (s.12(1)). Where there are joint authors, then the 70 years runs from the death of the last of them to die. If the author is unknown, there will be 70 years protection from the date the work was made or (where applicable) first made available to the public. Previously, the protection was for 'life plus 50'. (NB See 'Infringement' below for important limits on copyright protection of artistic works.)

The extended 70-year term also applies to films, and runs from the end of the calendar year in which the death occurs of the last to die of the principal director, the author of the screenplay or the dialogue, or the composer of any music created for the film (s.13B). This obviously may be a nightmare to establish, and there are certain presumptions in s.66A which may help someone wishing to use material from an old film.

However, sound recordings are still protected by copyright only for 50 years from the year of making or release (s.13A). This affects many 'classic' recordings of pop music, and (after much international negotiation) it is possible, though not certain, that the term may be extended to 70 or even 95 years. Broadcasts and computer-generated works still get only 50 years protection.

The new longer term applies without difficulty to works created after 1 January 1996 and to works in copyright on 31 December 1995. The owner of the extended copyright will be the person who owned it on 31 December 1995, unless he had only a limited term of ownership, in which case the extra 20 years will be added on to the reversionary term.

Where copyright had expired here, but the author died between 50 and 70 years ago, the position is more complicated. EC Directive 93/98 provided that if a work was protected by copyright anywhere in the EU on 1 July 1995, copyright would revive for it in the other EU states until the end of the same 70-year period. This may make it necessary to look at the position in the states offering a longer term of protection, namely Germany, France and Spain.

Ownership of the *revived* term of copyright will belong to the person who was the owner of the copyright when the initial term expired, though if that person died (or a company, etc, ceased to exist) before 1 January 1996, then the revived term will vest in his personal representatives.

Any licence affecting a copyright work which was in force on 31 December 1995 and was for the full term of the copyright continues to have effect during any extended term of copyright, subject to any agreement to the contrary.

The increased term offered to works of other EU nationals as a result of the Term Directive is not offered automatically to the nationals of other states, but will only apply where an equally long term is offered in their state of origin.

Where acts are carried out in relation to such revived copyright works as a result of things done whilst they were in the public domain, protection from infringement is available. A licence as of right may also be available, on giving notice to the copyright owner and paying a royalty.

Dealing with copyright works

Ownership of the copyright in a work gives the exclusive right to deal with the work in a number of ways, and essentially stops all unauthorised exploitation of the work. Ownership of the copyright is capable of being separated from ownership of the material form in which the work is embodied, depending upon the terms of any agreement or the circumstances. So, buying an original piece of artwork will not in general carry with it the legal title to the copyright, as an effective assignment must be in writing signed by the assignor (although beneficial ownership might pass: see below).

Copyright works can be exploited by their owners in two ways:

- **Assignment**. In an assignment, rights in the work are sold, with the owner retaining no interest in it (except, possibly, for a claim to royalties). An assignment must be in writing, signed by or on behalf of the assignor, but no other formality is required. One can make an assignment of future copyright under s.91. Where the author of a work not yet made agrees in writing that he will assign the rights in the future work to another, copyright vests in the assignee immediately upon the creation of the work, without further formalities.

These rules do not affect the common law as to beneficial interests in copyright. The Court may, in the right circumstances, find or infer an agreement to assign the copyright in a work. For example where a sole trader who had title to the copyright used in his business later incorporated the business and allowed the company to exploit the software as if it were its own, an agreement to assign was inferred (see *Lakeview Computers plc* 26/11/99). Alternatively, if the court finds that a work was commissioned to be made, and that there was a common intention that the purchaser should own the copyright, the Court may order the author to assign the copyright to him. Where a freelance designer produced a logo for an advertising agency, a term was implied in the contract that the client (Doc Martens) for which the logo was designed was to be the owner of the worldwide copyrights in the logo: see *R. Griggs Group* v. *Ross Evans* [2005] FSR 31. 'Commission' in this context means only to order a particular piece of work to be done: see *Apple Corps Ltd* v. *Cooper* [1993] FSR 286 (a 1956 Act case).

• **Licensing**. A licence arises where permission is granted to another to exploit the right whilst the licensor retains overall ownership. Licences do not need to take any particular form, and may indeed be granted orally. However, an exclusive licence (i.e. one which excludes even the copyright owner himself from exploiting the work) must be in writing if the licensee is to enjoy rights in respect of infringements concurrent with those of the copyright owner. Non-exclusive licensees get more limited rights. See ss.101 and 101A of the Act.

Agreements dealing with copyright should make it clear whether an assignment or a licence is being granted. There may be significant advantages for an author in granting only a licence, for a third party who acquires the assignee's rights will not necessarily be subject to the assignee's obligations, for example to pay royalties (see *Barker* v. *Stickney* [1919] 1 KB 121). However, an assignment may expressly provide for the rights to revert to the author if the assignee breaches the agreement (see *Crosstown Music* v. *Rive Droite Music* [2009] EWHC 600). If the agreement is unclear, the Court is likely to find that the grantee took the minimum rights necessary for his intended use of the work, quite probably an exclusive licence rather than an assignment (*Ray* v. *Classic FM plc* [1998] FSR 622), unless the work was 'commissioned' from the author. This case, *Griggs* (see above), and many other similar disputes, show how very important it is, if you make an agreement to create a work for someone else, or ask someone to make a work for you or your business, to discuss who is to own the copyright, or what is to be the extent of any licence, and to record the agreed position in writing. The question of moral rights (see below) should also be considered by the parties.

Assignments and licences often split up the various rights contained within the copyright. So, for instance, a licence might be granted to one person to publish a novel in book form, another person might be granted the film, television and video rights, and yet another the right to translate the novel into other languages. Obviously, the author should seek to grant the narrowest possible rights on each occasion, so retaining other rights for future exploitation; this means scrutinising draft publishing agreements carefully and negotiating as best one can.

Assignments and licences may also confer rights according to territory, dividing the USA from the EU or different EU countries one from the other. Any such agreement should take into account divergences between different national copyright laws. Furthermore, when seeking to divide rights between different territories of the EU there is a danger of infringing the competition rules of the EU. Professional advice should be taken, as breach of these rules may attract a fine and can render the agreement void in whole or in part.

Licences can, of course, be of varying lengths. There is no need for a licence to be granted for the whole term of copyright. Well-drafted licences will provide for termination on breach, including the failure of the licensee to exploit the work, and on the insolvency of the licensee and will specify whether the rights may be assigned or sub-licensed.

Copyright may be assigned by will. A bequest of an original document, etc embodying an unpublished copyright work will carry the copyright.

Infringement

The main type of infringement is what is commonly thought of as plagiarism, that is, copying the work. In fact, copyright confers on the owner the exclusive right to do a number of specified acts, so that anyone doing those acts without his permission will normally infringe. It is important to note that it is not necessary to copy a work exactly or use all of it; it is sufficient if a substantial part is used. That question is to be judged on a qualitative not a quantitative basis, bearing in mind that it is the skill and labour of the author which is to be protected (see *Ravenscroft* v. *Herbert* [1980] RPC 193 and *Designers Guild*). The ECJ has recently held that an extract just 11 words long might be protected, if it reproduced 'the expression of the intellectual creation of their author' – see Case C-5/08, *Infopaq* v. *Danske Dagblades* (16 July 2009). It is also important that primary infringement, such as copying, can be committed innocently of any intention to infringe.

The form of infringement common to all forms of copyright works is that of copying. This means reproducing the work in any material form. Infringement may occur where an existing work provides the inspiration for a later one, for example by including edited extracts from a history book in a novel (*Ravenscroft*), using a photograph as the inspiration for a painting (*Baumann* v. *Fussell* [1978] RPC 485), or words from a verse of one song in another (*Ludlow Music* v. *Williams* [2001] FSR 271). Infringement will not necessarily be prevented merely by the application of significant new skill and labour by the infringer, nor by a change of medium.

In the case of a two-dimensional artistic work, reproduction can mean making a copy in three dimensions, and vice versa. However, s.51 of the Act provides that in the case of a 'design document or model' (for definition, see 'Design right' below) for something which is not *itself* an artistic work, it is no infringement to make an article to that design. This means that whilst it would be an infringement of copyright to make an article from a design drawing for, say, a sculpture, it will not be an infringement of copyright to make a handbag from a copy of the design drawing for it, or from a handbag which one has purchased. In *Lucasfilm* v. *Ainsworth* [2009] EWCA 1328, a Star Wars helmet was found not to be protected as a 'sculpture'. The defendant (who had made the original model and was selling replicas) had a defence under s.51. Instead, such designs are generally protected by design right or as registered designs (for both see below). Some cases fall into a gap between the two rights. UK design right does not protect 'surface decoration', but nor (because of s.51) does copyright protect elements of surface decoration if they are dictated by the shape of the article on which the decoration appears. Hence, the design of stripes on a T-shirt was not protected either by copyright or by UK design right. However, such designs may well now be protected as Community designs. See *Lambretta* v. *Teddy Smith* [2005] RPC 6. Contrast *Flashing Badge* v. *Groves* [2007] FSR 36 which found no s.51 defence to infringement of the artistic works designed to decorate badges.

Copying a film, broadcast or cable programme can include making a copy of the whole or a substantial part of any image from it (see s.17(4)). This means that copying one frame of the film will be an infringement. It is not an infringement of copyright in a film to reshoot the film (*Norowzian*) (though there would doubtless be an infringement of the copyright in underlying works such as the literary copyright in the screenplay).

Copying is generally proved by showing substantial similarities between the original and the alleged copy, plus an opportunity to copy. Surprisingly often, minor errors in the original are reproduced by an infringer.

Copying need not be direct, so that, for instance, where the copyright is in a fabric design, copying the material without ever having seen the original drawing will still be an infringement, as will 'reverse engineering' of industrial designs, for example to make unlicensed spare parts (*British Leyland* [1986] AC 577; *Mars* v. *Teknowledge* [2000] FSR 138).

Issuing copies of a work to the public (e.g. by putting them on sale) when they have not previously been put into circulation in the UK is also a primary infringement of all types of work.

Other acts which may amount to an infringement depend upon the nature of the work. It will be an infringement of the copyright in a literary, dramatic or musical work to perform it in public, whether by live performance or by playing recordings. Similarly, it is an infringement of the copyright in a sound recording, film, broadcast or cable programme to play or show it in public. Many copyright works will also be infringed by the rental or lending of copies of the work.

It is also an infringement to 'communicate' a work to the public, especially by making it available electronically, such as on the internet (s.20). See, for example, *Twentieth Century Fox* v. *Newzbin* [2010] EWHC 608 (infringement by facilitating illegal downloading). In addition, the Digital Economy Act 2010 is designed to control online infringement of copyright (especially in music, films and games) by imposing duties on ISPs, with an industry code to be approved or made by Ofcom. It is also possible to infringe by making an adaptation of a literary, dramatic or musical work. An adaptation includes, in the case of a literary work, a translation, in the case of a non-dramatic work, making a dramatic work of it, and vice versa. A transcription or arrangement of a musical work is an adaptation of it.

There are also a number of 'secondary' (but nonetheless very common and commercially important) infringements – see box.

Exceptions to infringement

The Act provides a large number of exceptions to the rules on infringement. They are far too numerous to be dealt with here in full, but they include:

'Secondary' infringements

Secondary infringements consist not of making infringing copies, but of dealing with existing infringing copies in some way. It is an infringement to import an infringing copy into the UK, and to possess in the course of business, or to sell, hire, offer for sale or hire, or distribute in the course of trade an infringing copy. However, none of these acts will be an infringement unless the alleged infringer knew or had reason to believe that the articles were infringing copies. What is sufficient knowledge will depend upon the facts of each case (see *LA Gear Inc.* [1992] FSR 121, *ZYX Records* v. *King* [1997] 2 All ER 132 and *Pensher Security* [2000] RPC 249). Merely putting someone on notice of a dispute as to ownership of copyright may not suffice to give him or her reason to believe in infringement for this purpose. But someone who is informed that he is infringing 'yet carries out no sensible enquiries, and does nothing in the face of continued assertions of the copyright' may become someone with 'reason to believe' the claim: *Nouveau Fabrics* v. *Voyage Decoration* [2004] EWHC 895; *Hutchison* [1995] FSR 365.

Other secondary infringements consist of permitting a place to be used for a public performance in which copyright is infringed and supplying apparatus to be used for infringing public performance, again, in each case, with safeguards for innocent acts.

• fair dealing with literary, dramatic, musical or artistic works for the purpose of non-commercial research or private study (s.29). See e.g. *HMSO* v. *Green Amps Limited* [2007] EWHC 2755;
• fair dealing for the purpose of criticism or review or reporting current events, as to which see e.g. *Pro Sieben Media* [1999] FSR 610; *Hyde Park* v. *Yelland* [2001] Ch. 143; *NLA* v. *Marks & Spencer Plc* [2002] RPC 4) (s.30);
• incidental inclusion of a work in an artistic work, sound recording, film, broadcast or cable programme (s.31);
• educational exceptions (ss.32–36A);
• exceptions for libraries (ss.37–44A) and public administration (ss.45–50);
• making transient copies as part of a technological process (s.28A) and backing-up, or converting a computer program or accessing a licensed database (s.50A–D);
• dealing with a work where the author cannot be identified and the work seems likely to be out of copyright (s.57).

The effect of the Human Rights Act on copyright in relation to the right to free speech seems likely to be limited, as sufficient protection is to be found in the fair dealing provisions: *Ashdown* v. *Telegraph Group Limited* [2002] Ch. 149.

There is no defence of parody.

Remedies for infringements

The copyright owner will usually want to prevent the repetition or continuation of the infringement and will want compensation.

In almost all cases an injunction will be sought to stop the infringement. The Courts have useful powers to grant an injunction at an early stage, even before any infringement takes place, if a real threat of damage can be shown. Such an interim injunction can be applied for on three days' notice (or without notice in appropriate cases), but will not be granted unless the claimant has a reasonably good case and can show that he would suffer 'unquantifiable' damage if the defendant's activities continued pending trial. Delay in bringing an interim application may be fatal to its success. An injunction may not be granted where the claimant clearly only wants financial compensation (*Ludlow Music*).

Financial compensation may be sought in one of two forms. Firstly, damages. These will usually be calculated upon evidence of the loss caused to the claimant, sometimes based upon loss of business, or upon the basis of what would have been a proper licence fee for the defendant's acts. Additional damages may be awarded in rare cases for flagrant infringements, and can be substantial. See for example *Notts. Healthcare* v. *News Group Newspapers* [2002] RPC 49.

Damages will not be awarded for infringement where the infringer did not know, and had no reason to believe, that copyright subsisted in the work. This exception is of limited use to a defendant, though, in the usual situation where the work was of such a nature that he should have known that copyright would subsist in it.

The alternative to damages is an account of profits, that is, the net profits made by the infringer by virtue of his illicit exploitation of the copyright. Where an account of profits is sought, no award of flagrant damages can be made; see *Redrow Homes Limited* [1999] 1 AC 197. But there may now be an overlap between damages and profits, by reason of Article 13 of the Enforcement Directive, 2004/48.

A copyright owner may also apply for delivery up of infringing copies.

Finally, there are various criminal offences relating to the making, importation, possession, sale, hire, distribution, etc of infringing copies.

UK design right

Many designs are excluded from copyright protection by s.51 (see above). Section 52 of the Act may also limit the term of copyright protection given to certain types of artistic works, if they are applied industrially, to 25 years from first industrial application. Such artistic works may instead be protected by the UK unregistered 'design right' created by ss.213–64 or by Community design right. Like copyright, design right depends upon the creation of a suitable design by a 'qualifying person'.

UK unregistered design right is granted to original designs consisting of the shape or configuration (internal or external) of the whole or part of an article, not being merely 'surface decoration'. Even very simple designs may be protected. However, a design is not original if it was commonplace in the design field in question at the time of its creation. In *Farmers Build* [1999] RPC 461, 'commonplace' was defined as meaning a design of a type which would excite no 'peculiar attention' amongst those in the trade, or one which amounts to a run-of-the-mill combination of well-known features. Designs are not protected if they consist of a method or principle of construction, or are dictated by the shape, etc of an article to which the new article is to be connected or of which it is to form part, the so-called 'must-fit' and 'must-match' exclusions. In *Ocular Sciences* [1997] RPC 289, these exclusions had a devastating effect upon design rights claimed for contact lens designs. See also *Dyson* v. *Qualtex* [2006] RPC 31 in which these exclusions were applied to spare parts for Dyson vacuum cleaners.

UK design right subsists in designs made by or for qualifying persons (see, broadly, 'Qualification', above) or first marketed in the UK or EU or any other country to which the provision may be extended by Order.

UK design right lasts only 15 years from the end of the year in which it was first recorded or an article made to the design, or (if shorter) ten years from the end of the year in which articles made according to the design were first sold or hired out. During the last five years of the term of protection, a licence to use the design can be obtained 'as of right' on payment of a proper licence fee. Hence, design right may give only five years 'absolute' protection, as opposed to the 'life plus 70' of copyright.

The designer will be the owner of the right, unless it was commissioned, in which case the commissioner will be the first owner. An employee's designs made in the course of employment will belong to the employer. The right given to the owner of a design right is the exclusive right to reproduce the design for commercial purposes. The rules as to assignments, licensing and infringement, both primary and secondary, are substantially similar to those described above in relation to copyright, as are the remedies available.

The law on UK registered designs coexists with the right given by the unregistered UK design right discussed above. The Registered Design Act 1949 has been amended (and expanded) in line with EU legislation, and permits the registration of designs consisting of the appearance of the whole or any part of a product resulting from features of the product itself, such as shape, materials, etc or from the ornamentation of the product. It covers industrial or handicraft items, their packaging or get-up, etc. Designs must be novel and not solely dictated by function. The range of designs which may be registered is wider than under the old law, and designs need not necessarily have 'eye appeal'. Such designs provide a monopoly right renewable for up to 25 years. For further explanation see the guidance on the Patent Office website.

Community designs

In addition to UK design right and registered designs, EU Regulation 6/2002 created two Community design regimes, one for registered and one for unregistered designs. It is increasingly common for designers to rely on Community design right, especially where there are problems in relying on UK design right, for example where a pattern or colouring is central to the design. Artists and industrial designers may wish to consider registering their designs, whilst infringements should now generally be considered under both the UK and Community design right regimes.

It is not possible in the space available here to describe these new regimes in detail but the Regulation is available online (www.europa.ue.int/eur-lex). In brief, Community designs are *very* broadly defined in Article 3 and can include the outward appearance of a product or part of it, shape, texture, materials and/or its ornamentation. 'Products' include any industrial or handicraft item, packaging, graphic symbols and typographic typefaces but not computer programs. Huge numbers of designs have been registered, especially for furniture and for packaging; see *Procter & Gamble* v. *Reckitt Benckiser* [2008] FSR 8 about the design of an air-freshener spray can. However, the designs must be 'new' and have 'individual character'. This means that the 'overall impression' the design has on an 'informed user' (someone who is familiar with the existing designs in the field) is different from that of prior designs. The registered right lasts up to 25 years in five-year tranches, but an unregistered Community design right lasts only three years. The unregistered right protects the design from copying, but the registered right gives 'absolute' exclusivity, in that it may be infringed without copying. This benefit, when the registration process is relatively cheap and quick, doubtless explains why some quarter of a million Community designs have already been registered.

Moral rights

The Act also provides for the protection of certain 'moral rights'.

The right of 'paternity' is for the author of a copyright literary, dramatic, musical or artistic work, or the director of a copyright film, to be identified as the author/director, largely whenever the work is commercially exploited (s.77). See *Sawkins*.

However, the right does not arise unless it has been 'asserted' by appropriate words in writing (see end), or in the case of an artistic work by ensuring that the artist's name appears on the frame, etc. There are exceptions to the right, in particular where first ownership of the copyright vested in the author's or director's employer.

The right of 'integrity' protects work from 'derogatory treatment', meaning an addition to, deletion from, alteration or adaptation of a work which amounts to distortion or mutilation of the work or is otherwise prejudicial to the honour or reputation of the author/director. Again, infringement of the right takes place when the maltreated work is published commercially or performed or exhibited in public. There are various exceptions set out in s.81 of the Act, in particular where the publication is in a newspaper, etc, and the work was made for inclusion in it or made available with the author's consent.

Where the copyright in the work vested first in the author's or director's employer, he or she has no right to 'integrity' unless identified at the time of the relevant act or on published copies of the work.

These rights subsist for as long as the copyright in the work subsists.

A third moral right conferred by the Act is not to have a literary, dramatic, musical or artistic work falsely attributed to one as author, or to have a film falsely attributed to one as director, again where the work in question is published, etc. This right subsists until 20 years after a person's death.

None of these rights can be assigned during the person's lifetime, but all of them either pass on the person's death as directed by his or her will or fall into his residuary estate.

A fourth but rather different moral right is conferred by s.85. It gives a person who has commissioned the taking of photographs for private purposes a right to prevent copies of the work being issued to the public, etc.

The remedies for breach of these moral rights again include damages and an injunction, although s.103(2) specifically foresees the granting of an injunction qualified by a right to the defendant to do the acts complained of, if subject to a suitable disclaimer.

Moral rights are exercisable in relation to works in which the copyright has revived subject to any waiver or assertion of the right made before 1 January 1996 (see details as to who may exercise rights in paragraph 22 of the Regulations).

NOTICE
AMANDA LOUISE MICHAELS hereby asserts and gives notice of her right under s.77 of the Copyright, Designs & Patents Act 1988 to be identified as the author of the foregoing article.
AMANDA MICHAELS

Amanda L. Michaels is a barrister in private practice in London, and specialises in copyright, designs, trade marks, and similar intellectual property and 'media' work. She is author of *A Practical Guide to Trade Mark Law* (Sweet & Maxwell, 3rd edn 2002) and is an Appointed Person under the Trade Marks Act 1994, hearing appeals from decisions of the UK Registrar of Trade Marks.

Further reading

Adams, John, *Merchandising Intellectual Property*,Tottel Publishing, 3rd edn, 2007
Bently, Lionel and Sherman, Brad, *Intellectual Property Law*, Cambridge, 2008
Garnett, Rayner James and Davies, *Copinger and Skone James on Copyright*, Sweet & Maxwell, 16th edn, 2010

Copyright Acts

Copyright, Designs and Patents Act 1998 (but it is vital to use an up-to-date amended version). See www.ipo.gov.uk
The Duration of Copyright and Rights in Performances Regulations 1995 (SI 1995 No 3297)
The Copyright and Rights in Databases Regulations 1997 (SI 1997/3032) amended by the Copyright and Rights in Databases (Amendment) Regulations 2003 (SI 2003/2501)
The Copyright and Related Rights Regulations 2003 (SI 2003 No 2498)
The Intellectual Property (Enforcement, etc) Regulations 2006 (SI 2006 No 1028)
The Performances (Moral Rights, etc) Regulations 2006 (SI 2006 No 18)
see also Numerous Orders in Council
Council Regulation 6/2002
Directive 2006/116/EC (codifying provisions)

See also...

- *Publishing agreements*, page 303
- *Copyright questions*, page 697
- *Design and Artists Copyright Society*, page 717

The Copyright Licensing Agency Ltd

The Copyright Licensing Agency (CLA) licenses organisations to copy extracts from copyright publications on behalf of the authors, publishers and visual creators it represents. CLA's licences permit photocopying, scanning and emailing of articles and extracts from books, journals and magazines, as well as digital and online publications. CLA issues licences to schools, further and higher education, businesses and government bodies. The money collected is distributed to rights owners to ensure that they are properly rewarded for the use of their intellectual property.

Further information

The Copyright Licensing Agency Ltd
Saffron House, 6–10 Kirby Street,
London EC1N 8TS
tel 020-7400 3100 *fax* 020-7400 3101
email cla@cla.co.uk
website www.cla.co.uk

Why was CLA established?

CLA was set up by its owners, the Authors' Licensing and Collecting Society (ALCS) and the Publishers Licensing Society (PLS) and has an agency agreement with the Design and Artists Copyright Society (DACS), which represents visual artists, such as photographers, illustrators and painters.

CLA exists to represent creators and publishers by licensing the copying of their work and promoting the value of copyright generally. This way CLA helps to protect the value of creativity.

How CLA helps artists and writers

CLA allows licensed users access to millions of titles worldwide. In return, CLA ensures that artists and writers, along with publishers, are fairly recompensed through the payment of royalties derived from the licence fees which CLA collects and distributes.

Through this collective licensing system CLA is able to provide users with the simplest and most cost-effective means of obtaining authorisation for photocopying and scanning of published works, albeit under strict copy limits.

CLA has licences which enable digitisation of existing print material, enabling users to scan and electronically send extracts from printed copyright works.

CLA has recently also launched a series of new licences for business and government which allow users to re-use and copy from born digital electronic and online publications. Writers and publishers can benefit further from the increased income generated from these licences which operate under the same copy limits as the established photocopying licences.

Who is licensed?

CLA's licences are available to three principal sectors:

- education (schools, further and higher education);
- government (central, local authorities, public bodies); and
- business (businesses, industry and the professions).

CLA offers licences to meet the specific needs of each sector and user groups within each sector. Depending on the requirement, there are both blanket and transactional licences available. Every licence allows the photocopying of most books, journals, magazines and periodicals published in the UK.

International dimension

Many countries have established equivalents to CLA and the number of such agencies is set to grow. Nearly all these agencies, including CLA, are members of the International Federation of Reproduction Rights Organisations (IFRRO).

Through reciprocal arrangements covering more than 30 overseas territories including the USA, Canada and most EU countries, CLA's licences allow copying from an expanding list of international publications. CLA receives monies from these territories for the copying of UK material abroad and passes it on to UK rights holders.

Distribution of licence fees

The fees collected from licensees are forwarded to publishers, authors and visual artists via PLS, ALCS and DACS respectively, and the allocation of fees is based on subscriptions, library holdings and detailed surveys of copying activity. To date, CLA has collected and distributed over £460 million to rights holders since its establishment. For the year 2008/9 over £52 million was paid to creators and publishers.

Enabling access, protecting creativity

CLA believes it is important to raise awareness of copyright and the need to protect the creativity of artists, authors and publishers. To this end, it organises a range of activities such as copyright workshops in schools, seminars for businesses and institutions and an extensive programme of exhibitions and other events.

CLA believes in working positively together with representative bodies in each sector, meaning legal action is rare. However, organisations – especially in the business sector – are made aware that copyright is a legally enforceable right and not a voluntary option. CLA's compliance arm, Copywatch, is active in these sectors to educate users and seek out illegal copying.

By supporting rights holders in this way, CLA plays an important role in maintaining the value of their work, thereby sustaining creativity and its benefit to all. Through protection of this sort the creative industries in the UK have been able to grow to support millions of jobs and to produce over 8% of UK GDP.

See also...

- *Authors' Licensing and Collecting Society*, page 715
- *Design and Artists Copyright Society*, page 717
- *UK copyright law*, page 700

Authors' Licensing and Collecting Society

The Authors' Licensing and Collecting Society is the rights management society for UK writers.

> **Membership**
>
> **Authors' Licensing and Collecting Society Ltd**
> The Writers' House, 13 Haydon Street,
> London EC3N 1DB
> *tel* 020-7264 5700 *fax* 020-7264 5755
> *email* alcs@alcs.co.uk
> *website* www.alcs.co.uk
> *Chief Executive* Owen Atkinson
>
> Membership is open to all writers and successors to their estates at a one-off fee of £25 for Ordinary membership. Members of the Society of Authors and the Writers' Guild of Great Britain have free Ordinary membership of ALCS. Operations are primarily funded through a commission levied on distributions and membership fees. The commission on funds generated for Ordinary members is currently 9.5%. Most writers will find that this, together with a number of other membership benefits, provides good value.

The Authors' Licensing and Collecting Society (ALCS) is the UK collective rights management society for writers. Established in 1977, it represents the interests of all UK writers and aims to ensure that they are fairly compensated for any works that are copied, broadcast or recorded.

A non-profit company, ALCS was set up in the wake of the campaign to establish a Public Lending Right to help writers protect and exploit their collective rights. Today, it is the largest writers' organisation in the UK with a membership of approximately 70,000. In the financial year of 2009/10, £25.4 million in royalties were paid out to writers.

The Society is committed to ensuring that the rights of writers, both intellectual property and moral, are fully respected and fairly rewarded. It represents all types of writers and includes educational, research and academic authors drawn from the professions: scriptwriters, adaptors, playwrights, poets, editors and freelance journalists, across the print and broadcast media.

Internationally recognised as a leading authority on copyright matters and authors' interests, ALCS is committed to fostering an awareness of intellectual property issues among the writing community. It maintains a close watching brief on all matters affecting copyright both in the UK and internationally and makes regular representations to the UK government and the European Union.

The Society collects fees that are difficult, time-consuming or legally impossible for writers and their representatives to claim on an individual basis, money that is nonetheless due to them. To date, it has distributed over £230 million in secondary royalties to writers.

Over the years, ALCS has developed highly specialised knowledge and sophisticated systems that can track writers and their works against any secondary use for which they are due payment. A network of international contacts and reciprocal agreements with foreign collecting societies also ensures that British writers are compensated for any similar use overseas.

The primary sources of fees due to writers are secondary royalties from the following:

Photocopying

The single largest source of income, this is administered by the Copyright Licensing Agency (CLA – see page 713). Created in 1982 by ALCS and the Publishers Licensing Society (PLS), the CLA grants licences to users for the copying of books and serials. This includes schools, colleges, universities, central and local government departments as well as the British Library, businesses and other institutions. Licence fees are based on the number of people who benefit and the number of copies made. The revenue from this is then split between the rightsholders: authors, publishers and artists. Money due to authors is transferred to ALCS for distribution. ALCS also receives photocopying payments from foreign sources.

Digitisation

In 1999, the CLA launched its licensing scheme for the digitisation of printed texts. It offers licences to organisations for storing and using digital versions of authors' printed works, which have been scanned into a computer. Again, the fees are split between authors and publishers.

Foreign Public Lending Right

The Public Lending Right (PLR) system pays authors whose books are borrowed from public libraries. Through reciprocal agreements with VG Wort (the German collecting society), Stichting Leenrecht (the Dutch collecting society) and Literar Mechana (the Austrian collecting society) ALCS members receive payment whenever their books are borrowed from German, Dutch, French, Austrian and Spanish libraries. (Please note that ALCS does not administer the UK Public Lending Right, this is managed directly by the UK PLR Office; see page 338.)

ALCS also receives other payments from Germany. These cover the loan of academic, scientific and technical titles from academic libraries; extracts of authors' works in textbooks and the press, together with other one-off fees.

Simultaneous cable retransmission

This involves the simultaneous showing of one country's television signals in another country, via a cable network. Cable companies pay a central collecting organisation a percentage of their subscription fees, which must be collectively administered. This sum is then divided by the rightsholders. ALCS receives the writers' share for British programmes containing literary and dramatic material and distributes it to them.

Educational recording

ALCS, together with the main broadcasters and rightsholders, set up the Educational Recording Agency (ERA) in 1989 to offer licences to educational establishments. ERA collects fees from the licensees and pays ALCS the amount due to writers for their literary works.

Other sources of income include a blank tape levy and small, miscellaneous literary rights.

Tracing authors

ALCS is dedicated to protecting and promoting authors' rights and enabling writers to maximise their income. It is committed to ensuring that royalties due to writers are efficiently collected and speedily distributed to them. One of its greatest challenges is finding some of the writers for whom it holds funds and ensuring that they claim their money.

Any published author or broadcast writer could have some funds held by ALCS for them. It may be a nominal sum or it could run in to several thousand pounds. Either call or visit the ALCS website – see box for contact details.

Design and Artists Copyright Society

DACS (the Design and Artists Copyright Society) is the UK's leading copyright licensing and collecting society for artists and visual creators.

About DACS

DACS helps artists and visual creators receive recognition and reward for their work. They provide three rights management services for artists: Payback, Artist's Resale Right and Copyright Licensing. It represents over 36,000 international fine artists, as well as 16,000 commercial photographers, illustrators, craftspeople, cartoonists, architects, animators and designers.

Contact details

Design and Artists Copyright Society (DACS)
33 Great Sutton Street, London EC1V 0DX
tel 020-7336 8811 *fax* 020-7336 8822
email info@dacs.org.uk
website www.dacs.org.uk

DACS is a not-for-profit organisation. DACS offers three services for artists and visual creators: Payback, Artist's Resale Right and Copyright Licensing. It makes an administrative charge on the revenue it receives on behalf of artists and visual creators in order to cover operating costs.

Payback

DACS' annual Payback service pays thousands of artists, photographers, illustrators and many other visual creators a share of revenue generated through collective licensing. Collective licensing is used in situations where it would be difficult or near impossible for artists and visual creators to license their rights on an individual basis. For example, when a university wishes to photocopy pages of a book which features their work.

DACS' Payback service exists for all visual creators and not just those who are members of DACS. Any visual creator whose work has been reproduced in a UK book, magazine or included in a programme broadcast on terrestrial UK television can make a claim for their share of Payback royalties.

Artist's Resale Right

The Artist's Resale Right entitles living artists to receive a royalty each time their work is resold by an art market professional such as an auction house, art dealer or gallery (subject to certain conditions). DACS manages the Right on behalf of over 2,500 artists who have registered with them and also those artists who do not join another collecting society. Painters, bookbinders, photographers, sculptors, furniture designers and ceramicists are just some of the many thousands of artists and visual creators who have been paid Artist's Resale Right royalties by DACS.

The Artist's Resale Right was introduced in the UK on 14 February 2006 and currently only applies to living artists. It will not apply to the beneficiaries of deceased artists until 2012.

Copyright licensing

DACS has been successfully selling copyright licences on behalf of its members for 25 years. Artists who appoint DACS to manage their copyright licensing needs can be assured that their work is legally licensed, fairly paid for and its integrity respected.

DACS now represents over 36,000 UK and international artists for this service. Each month DACS receives over 100 licence applications from publishers, museums, television companies and many other organisations looking to license works of art. Uses range from greetings cards to film sets and websites to silk scarves and much more.

Copyright advice

DACS has a number of free copyright fact sheets available for download from its website. Artists and visual creators who join DACS for Artist's Resale Right and Copyright Licensing are also entitled to free telephone copyright advice.

Copyright facts

• Copyright is a right granted to creators under law.

• Copyright in all artistic works is established from the moment of creation – the only qualification is that the work must be original.

• There is no registration system in the UK; copyright comes into operation automatically and lasts the lifetime of the visual creator plus a period of 70 years after their death.

• After death, copyright is usually transferred to the visual creator's heirs or beneficiaries. When the 70-year period has expired, the work then enters the public domain and no longer benefits from copyright protection.

• The copyright owner has the exclusive right to authorise the reproduction (or copy) of a work in any medium by any other party.

• Any reproduction can only take place with the copyright owner's consent.

• Permission is usually granted in return for a fee, which enables the visual creator to derive some income from other people using his or her work.

• If a visual creator is commissioned to produce a work, he or she will usually retain the copyright unless an agreement is signed which specifically assigns the copyright. When visual creators are employees and create work during the course of their employment, the employer retains the copyright in those works.

See also...

- *Copyright questions*, page 697
- *Freelancing for beginners*, page 509
- *UK copyright law*, page 700
- *The Copyright Licensing Agency Ltd*, page 713

Libel

Any writer should be aware of the law of libel. Antony Whitaker gives an outline of the main principles, concentrating on points which are most frequently misunderstood. However, specific legal advice should be taken when practical problems arise.

The law discussed is the law of England and Wales. Scotland has its own, albeit somewhat similar, rules. A summary of the main differences between the two systems appears in the box (below). The Defamation Act 1996 is now fully in force, being designed mainly to streamline and simplify libel litigation.

Libel: liability to pay damages

English law draws a distinction between defamation published in permanent form and that which is not. The former is libel, the latter slander. 'Permanent form' includes writing, printing, drawings and photographs and radio and television broadcasts. It also includes, for as long as it remains there, dissemination on the internet. It follows that it is the law of libel rather than slander which most concerns writers and artists professionally, and the slightly differing rules applicable to slander will not be mentioned in this article.

Publication of a libel can result in a civil action for damages, an injunction to prevent repetition and/or in certain cases a criminal prosecution against those responsible, who include the author (or artist or photographer), the publishers and the editor, if any, of the publication in which the libel appeared. 'Innocent disseminators', such as printers, distributors, broadcasters, internet service providers and retailers, who can show they took reasonable care and had no reason to believe what they were handling contained a libel, are protected under the 1996 Act. Prosecutions are rare. Certain special rules apply to them and these will be explained below after a discussion of the question of civil liability, which in practice arises much more frequently.

Libel claims have never qualified for legal aid, unless the Legal Services Commission considers a case incapable of being fairly tried without it. But the closely analagous remedy of malicious falsehood does so qualify. Most libel cases are usually heard by a judge and jury, and it is the jury which decides the amount of any award, which is tax-free. It is not necessary for the plaintiff to prove that he or she has actually suffered any loss, because the law presumes damage. While the main purpose of a libel claim is to compensate the plaintiff for the injury to his or her reputation, a jury may give additional sums either as 'aggravated' damages, if it appears a defendant has behaved malevolently or spitefully, or as 'exemplary' or 'punitive', damages where a defendant hopes the economic advantages of publication will outweigh any sum awarded. Damages can also be 'nominal' if the libel complained of is trivial. It is generally very difficult to forecast the amounts juries are likely to award, though awards against newspapers disclose a tendency towards considerable generosity. The Court of Appeal has power to reduce excessive awards of damages. Proposals have recently been advanced for a 'single publication' rule to ensure that only one action can be launched against a defamatory article. There is also a proposal to give articles that have been online for more than a year an automatic archive defence of qualified privilege (see below).

In an action for damages for libel, it is for the plaintiff to establish that the matter he or she complains of has been published by the defendant; refers to the plaintiff; and is defamatory. If this is done, the plaintiff establishes a *prima facie* case. However, the defendant will escape liability if he or she can show he has a good defence. There are five defences to a libel action. They are: Justification; Fair Comment; Privilege; Offer of Amends: ss.2–4 of the Defamation Act, 1996; Apology, etc, under the Libel Acts, 1843 and 1845. A libel claim can also become barred under the Limitation Acts, as explained below. These matters must now be examined in detail.

The plaintiff's case

The meaning of 'published'

'Published' in the legal sense means communicated to a person other than the plaintiff. Thus the legal sense is wider than the lay sense but includes it. It follows that the content of a book is published in the legal sense when the manuscript is first sent to the publishing firm just as much as it is when the book is later placed on sale to the public. Subject to the 'innocent dissemination' defence referred to above, both types of publication are sufficient for the purpose of establishing liability for libel, but the law differentiates between them, since the scope of publication can properly be taken into account by the jury in considering the actual amount of damages to award. Material placed on the internet is unquestionably 'published' there, with a potential audience of millions worldwide. The extent of publication can be judged by the number of visits made to the relevant website. If challenged as defamatory, it is generally wise to remove such material, in order to block potential claims of continuing publication. It should be noted that Internet Service Providers can compel website operators to identify the authors of defamatory material anonymously posted to their discussion boards.

Establishing identity

The plaintiff must also establish that the matter complained of refers to him or her. It is of course by no means necessary to mention a person's name before it is clear that he or she is referred to. Nicknames by which he or she is known or corruptions of his name are just two ways in which his or her identity can be indicated. There are more subtle methods. The sole question is whether the plaintiff is indicated to those who read the matter complained of. In some cases he or she will not be unless it is read in the light of facts known to the reader from other sources, but this is sufficient for the plaintiff's purpose. The test is purely objective and does not depend at all on whether the writer intended to refer to the plaintiff.

> **English and Scottish law**
>
> Much of the terminology of the Scots law of defamation differs from that of English law, and in certain minor respects the law itself is different. North of the border, libel and slander are virtually indistinguishable, both as to the nature of the wrongs and their consequences; and Scots law does not recognise the offence of criminal libel. Where individual English litigants enjoy absolute privilege for what they say in court, their Scottish counterparts have only qualified privilege. 'Exemplary', or 'punitive', damages are not awarded by the Scottish courts. Until recently, libel cases in Scotland were for the most part heard by judges sitting alone, but there is now a marked trend towards trial by jury, which has been accompanied by a significant increase in the levels of damages awarded.

It is because it is impossible to establish reference to any individual that generalisations, broadly speaking, are not successfully actionable. To say boldly 'All lawyers are crooks' does not give any single lawyer a cause of action, because the statement does not point a finger at any individual. However, if anyone is named in conjunction with a generalisation, then it may lose its general character and become particular from the context. Again, if one says 'One of the X Committee has been convicted of murder' and the X Committee consists of, say, four persons, it cannot be said that the statement is not actionable because no individual is indicated and it could be referring to any of the committee. This is precisely why it is actionable at the suit of each of them as suspicion has been cast on all. Subject to the same proviso that individuals are in no way identified, it has been a rule of public policy since 1993 that government departments, whether national or local, cannot sue for libel.

Determining what is defamatory

It is for the plaintiff to show that the matter complained of is defamatory. What is defamatory is decided by the jury except in the extreme cases where the judge rules that the words cannot bear a defamatory meaning. Various tests have been laid down for determining this. It is sufficient that any one test is satisfied. The basic tests are:

- Does the matter complained of tend to lower the plaintiff in the estimation of society?
- Does it tend to bring him or her into hatred, ridicule, contempt, dislike or disesteem with society?
- Does it tend to make him shunned or avoided or cut off from society? The mere fact that what is published is inaccurate is not enough to involve liability; it is the adverse impact on the plaintiff's reputation that matters. For example, merely to overstate a person's income is not defamatory; but it will be if the context implies he has not fully declared it to the tax authorities.

'Society' means right-thinking members of society generally. It is by reference to such people that the above tests must be applied. A libel action against a newspaper which had stated that the police had taken a statement from the plaintiff failed, notwithstanding that the plaintiff gave evidence that his apparent assistance to the police (which he denied) had brought him into grave disrepute with the underworld. It was not by their wrongheaded standards that the matter fell to be judged.

Further, it is not necessary to imply that the plaintiff is at fault in some way in order to defame him. To say of a woman that she has been raped or of someone that he is insane imputes to them no degree of blame, but nonetheless both statements are defamatory. Lawyers disagree over whether the claim that an individual is 'ugly' is, or could be, defamatory.

Sometimes a defamatory meaning is conveyed by words which on the face of them have no such meaning. 'But Brutus is an honourable man' is an example. If a jury finds that words are meant ironically they will consider this ironical sense when determining whether the words are defamatory. In deciding, therefore, whether or not the words are defamatory, the jury seeks to discover what, without straining the words or putting a perverse construction on them, they will be understood to mean. In some cases this may differ substantially from their literal meaning.

Matter may also be defamatory by innuendo. Strictly so called, an innuendo is a meaning that words acquire by virtue of facts known to the reader but not stated in the passage complained of. Words, quite innocent on the face of them, may acquire a defamatory meaning when read in the light of these facts. For example, where a newspaper published a photograph of a man and a woman, with the caption that they had just announced their engagement, it was held to be defamatory of the man's wife since those who knew that she had cohabited with him were led to the belief that she had done so only as his mistress.

The newspaper was unaware that the man was already married, but some of its readers were not. In general, however, imputations of unchastity against members of either sex would today be regarded as far less defamatory than they were in 1929 when this case was decided.

Defences to a libel action

Quite apart from the provisions concerning statutory apologies mentioned below, a swift and well publicised apology will always go some way towards assuaging injured feelings and help reduce an award of damages.

Justification

English law does not protect the reputation that a person either does not or should not possess. Stating the truth therefore does not incur liability, and the plea of justification – namely, that what is complained of is true in substance and in fact – is a complete answer to an action for damages. However, this defence is by no means to be undertaken lightly. For instance, to prove one instance of using bad language will be insufficient to justify the allegation that a person is 'foulmouthed'. It would be necessary to prove several instances, and the defendant is obliged in most cases to particularise in his pleadings giving details, dates and places. However, the requirement that the truth of every allegation must be proved is not absolute, and is qualified by the 'multiple charge – no worse off' defence. This applies where two or more distinct charges are levelled against a plaintiff, and some of what is said turns out to be inaccurate. If his or her reputation in the light of what is shown to be true is made no worse by the unprovable defamatory allegations – for example, mistaken accusations that a convicted pickpocket and car thief is also a shoplifter – the publisher will be safe. This is the extent of the law's recognition that some individuals are so disreputable as to be beyond redemption by awards of damages regardless of what is said about them. Subject to this, however, it is for the defendant to prove that what he or she has published is true, not for the plaintiff to disprove it, though if he can do so, so much the better for him.

A 2006 House of Lords decision has, however, relaxed the hitherto rigid nature of this defence. For the protection of serious journalism on matters of public concern, the Lords held that editorial decisions reached under the pressure of newsroom deadlines are to be judged more according to whether the material challenged was gathered fairly and responsibly than on the basis of its strict accuracy. The Lords ruled that 'Where the information is of public importance, the fact that it contains relevant but (unproved or unprovable) defamatory allegations against prominent people will not permit them to recover damages.'

One point requires special mention. It is insufficient for the defendant to prove that he or she has accurately repeated what a third person has written or said or that such statements have gone uncontradicted when made on occasions in the past. If X writes 'Y told me that Z is a liar', it is no defence to an action against X merely to prove that Y did say that. X has given currency to a defamatory statement concerning Z and has so made it his own. His only defence is to prove that Z is a liar by establishing a number of instances of Z's untruthfulness. Nor does it help a defence of justification to prove that the defendant genuinely believed what he or she published to be true. This may, however, form part of a qualified privilege defence (see below), and might well be a complete answer in an action, other than a libel action, based on a false but non-defamatory statement. For such statements do not incur liability in the absence of fraud or malice which, in this context, means a dishonest or otherwise improper motive. Bona fide belief, however, may be relevant to the assessment of damages, even in a libel action.

Special care should be taken in relation to references to a person's convictions, however accurately described. Since the Rehabilitation of Offenders Act, 1974, a person's less serious convictions may become 'spent' and thereafter it may involve liability to refer to them. Reference to the Act and orders thereunder must be made in order to determine the position in any particular case.

Fair comment

It is a defence to prove that what is complained of is fair comment made in good faith and without malice on a matter of public interest. 'Fair' in this context means 'honest'. 'Fair comment' means therefore the expression of the writer's genuinely held opinion. It does not necessarily mean opinion with which the jury agree. Comment may therefore be quite extreme and still be 'fair' in the legal sense. However, if it is utterly perverse the jury may be led to think that no one could have genuinely held such views. In such a case the defence would fail, for the comment could not be honest. 'Malice' here covers any dishonest or improper motive but, in contrast to its application in the context of qualified privilege (see below), it does not include actuation by spite or animosity, even if this is the dominant or sole motive. Care should, however, be taken since evidence of such motivation could also be seen as a lack of genuine belief in the view expressed.

The defence only applies when what is complained of is comment as distinct from a statement of fact. The line between comment and fact is notoriously difficult to draw in some cases. Comment means a statement of opinion. The facts on which comment is made must be stated together with the comment or be sufficiently indicated with it. This is merely another way of saying that it must be clear that the defamatory statement is one of opinion and not of fact, for which the only defence would be the onerous one of justification. The exact extent to which the facts commented on must be stated or referred to is a difficult question, but some help may be derived in answering it by considering the purpose of the rule, which is to enable the reader to exercise his own judgement and to agree or disagree with the comment. It is quite plain that it is not necessary to state every single detail of the facts. In one case it was sufficient merely to mention the name of one of the Press lords in an article about a newspaper though not one owned by him. He was so well known that to mention his name indicated the substratum of fact commented upon, namely his control of his group of newspapers. No universal rule can be laid down, except that, in general, the fuller the facts set out or referred to with the comment, the better. All these facts must be proved to be true subject, however, to the flexibility of the 'proportionate truth' rule. This means that the defence remains available even if, for example, only three out of five factual claims can be proved true, provided that these three are by themselves sufficient to sustain, and are proportionate to, the fairness of the comment. The impact of the two unproven claims would probably fall to be assessed in accordance with the 'multiple charge – no worse off' rule in justification, set out above.

The defence only applies where the matters commented on are of public interest, i.e. of legitimate concern to the public or a substantial section of it. Thus the conduct of national and local government, international affairs, the administration of justice, etc, are all matters of public interest, whereas other people's private affairs may very well not be, although they undoubtedly interest the public, or provoke curiosity.

In addition, matters of which criticism has been expressly or impliedly invited, such as publicly performed plays and published books, are a legitimate subject of comment. Criticism need not be confined merely to their artistic merit but equally may deal with the attitudes to life and the opinions therein expressed.

Privilege

Privilege in the law of libel is either 'absolute' or 'qualified', and denotes the two levels of protection from liability afforded, in the public interest, to defamatory statements made on certain occasions. Absolute privilege – where the individual defamed has no remedy whatever – has applied to Parliamentary papers published by the direction of either House, or full republications thereof, since early in the 19th century. Following the implementation of section 14 of the 1996 Defamation Act, this privilege also applies to fair, accurate and contemporaneous reports of public judicial proceedings in the United Kingdom, the European Courts of Justice and Human Rights, and any international criminal tribunal established by the Security Council.

Qualified privilege confers protection provided the subject matter of the article is in the public interest. This is for the court alone to decide; and where it decides that it is, it assumes there is both a duty to communicate the information as well as an interest by the public in receiving it. It is then for the court to decide whether such an article containing defamatory material is justifiable – in the sense that it is relevant and important to the story – having regard to the editor's judgement. If it decides that the material, thus presented, is in the public interest, the question then arises whether the steps taken to gather and publish it have been responsible and fair, and journalists must show they did their best to uncover the truth, by acting responsibly in checking their sources and, where appropriate, seeking comment from potential plaintiffs, who must be given adequate opportunity to respond. Whether this test is satisfied has to be assessed in a practical, realistic and flexible manner.

A case in which such a defence was raised – and was held to be valid, but only for as long as it was reasonable to accept it as well founded – occurred in 2009. The court held that as soon as the newspaper in question discovered the falsity of its original account, it should have then and there published a withdrawal. The failure to take adequate steps to achieve this was not, in the eyes of the court, responsible journalism.

The defence also applies, under section 15 of the Act, to fair and accurate reports of public proceedings before a legislature, a court, a government inquiry and an international organisation or conference anywhere in the world, and of certain documents, or extracts from such documents, issued by those bodies. While there is no requirement to correct or publish explanations concerning these reports, such an obligation does arise under section 15 in respect of a separate category of reports of notices issued by various bodies within the European Community and of proceedings of certain bodies or organisations within the United Kingdom. Apart from the Act, such privilege also attaches to extracts from Parliamentary papers and fair and accurate reports of Parliamentary proceedings.

This list of privileged occasions is by no means exhaustive, and the second category may now be expanded by an order of the Lord Chancellor. The privilege defence is extended to the media generally, rather than being restricted, as it was hitherto, simply to newspapers.

Offers of Amends under the 1996 Act

Sections 2, 3 and 4 of the 1996 Act offer a flexible method of nipping in the bud potential libel actions by those who have been unintentionally defamed. The range of libel meanings for which this defence caters is much wider than that previously available. It envisages the payment of damages as well as costs, together with the offer of a correction and apology, and the damages figure will be fixed by a judge if the parties cannot agree. He or she will do this bearing in mind the generosity of the correction and apology, and the extent of its publication. While recourse to this defence excludes reliance on the defences of justification, privilege and fair comment, it offers a considerable incentive to settle complaints and will save substantially on costs.

Apology under 1843 and 1845 Acts

This defence is rarely utilised, since if any condition of it is not fulfilled, the plaintiff must succeed and the only question is the actual amount of damages. It only applies to actions in respect of libels in newspapers and periodicals. The defendant pleads that the libel was inserted without actual malice and without gross negligence and that before the action commenced or as soon afterwards as possible he inserted a full apology in the same newspaper, etc, or had offered to publish it in a newspaper, etc, of the plaintiff's choice, where the original newspaper is published at intervals greater than a week. Further a sum must be paid into court with this defence to compensate the plaintiff.

'Fast-track disposal' procedure

In its recognition of the generally cumbersome nature of libel litigation, the 1996 Act provides a simplified mechanism for dealing with less serious complaints. Sections 8, 9 and 10 enable a judge alone to dismiss unrealistic claims at the outset; and he will also be able to dispose 'summarily' of relatively minor, but well-founded, claims, on the basis of an award of up to £10,000, a declaration that the publication was libellous, an order for an apology and an order forbidding repetition.

Limitation and death

The 1996 Act has reduced from three years to one the period within which a libel action must generally be started if it is not to become 'statute-barred' through lapse of time. But successive and subsequent publications, such as the issue of later editions of the same book, or the sale of surplus copies of an old newspaper, or the failure to remove libellous material from the internet, can give rise to fresh claims.

Civil claims for libel cannot be brought on behalf of the dead. If an individual living plaintiff or defendant in a libel case dies before the jury gives their verdict, the action 'abates', i.e. comes to an end, so far as their involvement is concerned, and no rights arising out of it survive either for or against their personal representatives.

Insurance

For an author, the importance of at least an awareness of this branch of law lies first, in the fact that most book contracts contain a clause enabling the publisher to look to him should any libel claims result; and second, in the unpredictable awards of damages. It is therefore advisable to check what libel insurance a publisher carries, and whether it also covers the author who, if he or she is to have the benefit of it, should always alert the publisher to any potential risk. This insurance for authors can now only be obtained through an insurance broker or company registered with the Financial Services Authority, and one such company is Royal Sun Alliance, Professional and Financial Risks, 4th Floor, Leadenhall Court, Leadenhall Street, London EC3V 1PP (*tel* 020-7283 9000). Premiums start at £1000, and can be substantially higher if the book is tendentious or likely to be controversial. The company generally insists on the author obtaining, and paying for, a legal opinion first. Indemnity limits vary between £250,000 and £1 million, and the author is generally required to bear at least the first £5,000 of any loss. It is worth remembering that 'losses' include legal costs as well as damages, which they can often exceed.

Criminal liability in libel

Whereas the object of a civil action is to obtain compensation for the wrong done or to prevent repetition, the object of criminal proceedings is to punish the wrongdoer by fine or imprisonment or both. There are four main types of writing which may provoke a prosecution: defamatory libel; obscene publications; sedition and incitement to racial hatred; until July 2008, blasphemous libel.

Defamatory libel

The publication of defamatory matter is in certain circumstances a crime as well as a civil wrong. But whereas the principal object of civil proceedings will normally be to obtain compensation, the principal object of a criminal prosecution will be to secure punishment of the accused, for example by way of a fine. Prosecutions are rare. There are important differences between the rules applicable to criminal libel and its civil counterpart. For example, a criminal libel may be 'published' even though only communicated to the person defamed and may be found to have occurred even where the person defamed is dead, or where only a group of persons but no particular individual has been maligned. During election campaigns, it is an 'illegal practice' to publish false statements about the personal character or conduct of a candidate irrespective of whether they are also defamatory.

Obscene publications

It is an offence to publish obscene matter. By the Obscene Publications Act, 1959, matter is obscene if its effect is such as to tend to deprave and corrupt persons who are likely, having regard to all relevant circumstances, to read, see or hear it. 'To deprave and corrupt' is to be distinguished from 'to shock and disgust'. It is a defence to a prosecution to prove that publication of the matter in question is justified as being for the public good, on the ground that it is in the interests of science, literature, art or learning, or of other objects of general concern. Expert evidence may be given as to its literary, artistic, scientific or other merits. Playwrights, directors and producers should note that the Theatres Act, 1968, though designed to afford similar protection to stage productions, does not necessarily prevent prosecutions for indecency under other statutes.

Sedition/incitement to racial hatred

Writings which tend to destroy the peace of the realm may be prosecuted as being seditious or as amounting to incitement to racial hatred. Seditious writings include those which advocate reform by unconstitutional or violent means or incite contempt or hatred for the monarch or Parliament. These institutions may be criticised stringently, but not in a manner which is likely to lead to insurrection or civil commotion or indeed any physical force. Prosecutions are a rarity, but it should be remembered that writers of matter contemptuous of the House of Commons, though not prosecuted for seditious libel are, from time to time, punished by that House for breach of its privileges, although, if a full apology is made, it is often an end of the matter. The Public Order Act 1986 makes it an offence, irrespective of the author's or publisher's intention, to publish, or put on plays containing, threatening, abusive or insulting matter if hatred is likely to be stirred up against any racial group in Great Britain or elsewhere. The Racial and Religious Hatred Act, 2006, brought into force on 1 October 2007 and extending to England and Wales, penalises the publication of material likely to incite or stir up such hatred.

Blasphemous libel

This common law offence consisted of the vilification of the Christian religion or its ceremonies, specifically within the tenets of the Church of England. Generally, it embargoed discussion defined as 'so scurrilous and offensive as to pass the limits of decent controversy and outrage any Christian feeling.' The law did not apply to Scotland or Northern Ireland.

The last conviction for the offence was in 1977, and the last successful public prosecution was in 1922. There have been no cases since the Human Rights Act 1998. After several attempts, Parliament finally abolished the offence in England and Wales by s.79 of the Criminal Justice and Immigration Act 2008, as from 14 July 2008.

The privacy dimension

While the purpose of the law of libel is to protect – and when damaged, to restore – an individual's reputation, a developing law of privacy has emerged over the past four or five years. This poses an additional risk for authors and writers. Damages have been awarded for material the truth of which is not challenged, but the publication of which may be to an individual's discredit.

Recent cases show that the revelation of people's sexual activities, adulterous or otherwise, their drug habits or, generally speaking, personal and/or medical matters they do not want disclosed can very easily result in awards of damages. One recent case concerned the publication of a model's drug problems, and another the attendance of individuals at a sex party. Public approval or censure of such activities is generally not a factor the court takes into account in making an award – it is the breach of privacy alone which is relevant.

The examples outlined above arose primarily out of the context of Articles 8 and 10 of the European Convention of Human Rights. Article 8 protects an individual's privacy – of his family life, home and correspondence – and Article 10 protects freedom of expression. These two Articles are inherently likely to, and often do, conflict, as recent case law has shown. In the case brought by the model, Naomi Campbell, against the *Daily Mirror*, in which the House of Lords finally held she was entitled to damages for the revelation of her attendance at a drug clinic, her award of damages by the High Court – reversed by the Court of Appeal – was restored by the Lords on the ground that her treatment was private and confidential. Likewise, the decision in July 2008 of Mr Justice Eady awarding damages of £60,000 to Max Mosley against the *News of the World* confirmed Mosley's right to privacy for a sex party.

A separate, but growing, problem has been the recent emergence of what are known as 'super-injunctions'. These are highly secret injunctions where the press cannot even refer to the fact that an injunction has been issued. It has been suggested that around 3,000 have been granted since 2004.

Whether such injunctions will proliferate is an open question. Two High Court judges have already expressed conflicting views on the issue, which in turn reflects a conflict between articles 8 and 10 of the Convention. For the time being, the future legal development in this area is unpredictable. Either there will be a curtailment of press freedom, or the merits of disclosing sportsmen's secrets (footballers have displayed a marked anxiety to cover up details of their private lives) will prevail.

Which route the law will follow remains to be seen. The most that can be said at present is that the question badly needs a Court of Appeal or House of Lords pronouncement of principle to afford future guidance.

It seems likely that the law of privacy will continue to develop on a case by case basis, and that Parliament will probably refrain from interfering, for the time being at least.

Antony Whitaker OBE is a barrister, an independent media legal adviser and author of *The Regicide's Widow – Lady Alice Lisle and the Bloody Assize* (Sutton Publishing 2006), the analysis of a treason trial. His email address is blairwhitaker@btinternet.com.

Finance for writers and artists

FAQs for writers

Peter Vaines, a chartered accountant and barrister, addresses some frequently asked questions.

What can a working writer claim against tax?

A working writer is carrying on a business and can therefore claim all the expenses which are incurred wholly and exclusively for the purposes of that business. A list showing most of the usual expenses can be found in the article on *Income tax*, starting on page 731 of this *Yearbook*, but there will be other expenses that can be allowed in special circumstances.

Strictly, only expenses which are incurred for the sole purpose of the business can be claimed; there must be no 'duality of purpose' so an item of expenditure cannot be divided into private and business parts. However, HM Revenue & Customs (formerly the Inland Revenue) is usually quite flexible and is prepared to allow all reasonable expenses (including apportioned sums) where the amounts can be commercially justified.

Allowances can also be claimed for the cost of business assets such as a motor car, personal computers, fax, copying machines and all other equipment (including books) which may be used by the writer. An allowance of 100% of the cost can now be claimed for most assets except cars, for which a lower allowance can be claimed. See the article on *Income tax* (page 731) for further details of the deductions available in respect of capital expenditure.

Can I request interest on fees owed to me beyond 30 days of my invoice?

Yes. A writer is like any other person carrying on a business and is entitled to charge interest at a rate of 8% over bank base rate on any debt outstanding for more than 30 days – although the period of credit can be varied by agreement between the parties. It is not compulsory to claim the interest; it is up to you to decide whether to enforce the right.

What can I do about bad debts?

A writer is in exactly the same position as anybody else carrying on a business over the payment of his or her invoices. It is generally not commercially sensible to insist on payment in advance but where the work involved is substantial (e.g. a book), it is usual to receive one third of the fee on signature, one third of the fee on delivery of the manuscript and the remaining one third on publication. On other assignments, perhaps not as substantial as a book, it could be worthwhile seeking 50% of the fee on signature and the other 50% on delivery. This would provide a degree of protection in case of cancellation of the assignment because of changes of policy or personnel at the publisher.

What financial disputes can I take to the Small Claims Court?

If somebody owes you money you can take them to the Small Claims Section of your local County Court, which deals with financial disputes up to £5,000. The procedure is much less formal than normal court proceedings and involves little expense. It is not necessary to have a solicitor. You fill in a number of forms, turn up on the day and explain the background to why you are owed the money (see www.courtservice.gov.uk).

If I receive an advance, can I divide it between two tax years?

Yes. There used to be a system known as 'spreading' but in 2001 a new system called 'averaging' was introduced. This enables writers (and others engaged in the creation of literary, dramatic works or designs) to average the profits of two or more consecutive years if the profits for one year are less than 75% of the profits for the highest year. This relief can apply even if the work takes less than 12 months to create and it allows the writer to avoid the higher rates of tax which might arise if the income in respect of a number of years' work were all to be concentrated in a single year.

How do I make sure I am taxed as a self-employed person so that tax and National Insurance contributions are not deducted at source?

To be taxed as a self-employed person you have to make sure that the contract for the writing cannot be regarded as a contract of employment. This is unlikely to be the case with a professional author. The subject is highly complex but one of the most important features is that the publisher must not be in a position to direct or control the author's work. Where any doubt exists, the author might find the publisher deducting tax and National Insurance contributions as a precaution and that would clearly be highly disadvantageous. The author would be well advised to discuss the position with the publisher before the contract is signed to agree that he or she should be treated as self-employed and that no tax or National Insurance contributions will be deducted from any payments. If such agreement cannot be reached, professional advice should immediately be sought so that the detailed technical position can be explained to the publisher.

Is it a good idea to operate through a limited company?

It can be a good idea for a self-employed writer to operate through a company but generally only where the income is quite large. The costs of operating a company can outweigh any benefit if the writer is paying tax only at the basic rate. Where the writer is paying tax at the higher rate of 40% (or 50%), being able to retain some of the income in a company at a tax rate of only 21% is obviously attractive. However, this will be entirely ineffective if the writer's contract with the publisher would otherwise be an employment. The whole subject of operating through a company is complex and professional advice is essential.

When does it become necessary to register for VAT?

Where the writer's self-employed income (from all sources, not only writing) exceeds £70,000 in the previous 12 months or is expected to do so in the next 30 days, he or she must register for VAT and add VAT to all his/her fees. The publisher will pay the VAT to the writer, who must pay the VAT over to the Customs and Excise each quarter. Any VAT the writer has paid on business expenses and on the purchase of business assets can be deducted. It is possible for some authors to take advantage of the simplified system for VAT payments which applies to small businesses. This involves a flat rate payment of VAT without any need to keep records of VAT on expenses.

If I make a loss from my writing can I get any tax back?

Where a writer makes a loss, HM Revenue & Customs may suggest that the writing is only a hobby and not a professional activity thereby denying any relief or tax deduction for the loss. However, providing the writing is carried out on a sensible commercial basis with an expectation of profits, any resulting loss can be offset against any other income the writer may have for the same or the previous year.

Income tax

Despite attempts by successive Governments to simplify our taxation system, the subject has become increasingly complicated. Peter Vaines, a chartered accountant and barrister, gives a broad outline of taxation from the point of view of writers and other creative professionals. The proposals in the April 2010 Budget are broadly reflected in this article.

How income is taxed

Generally

Authors are usually treated for tax purposes as carrying on a profession and are taxed in a similar fashion to other self-employed professionals. This article is directed to self-employed persons only, because if a writer is employed he or she will be subject to the much less advantageous rules which apply to employment income.

Attempts are often made by employed persons to shake off the status of 'employee' and to attain 'freelance' status so as to qualify for the tax advantages, such attempts meeting with varying degrees of success. The problems involved in making this transition are considerable and space does not permit a detailed explanation to be made here – individual advice is necessary if difficulties are to be avoided.

Particular attention has been paid by HM Revenue & Customs to journalists and to those engaged in the entertainment industry with a view to reclassifying them as employees so that PAYE is deducted from their earnings. This blanket treatment has been extended to other areas and, although it is obviously open to challenge by individual taxpayers, it is always difficult to persuade HM Revenue & Customs to change its views.

There is no reason why employed people cannot carry on a freelance business in their spare time. Indeed, aspiring authors, painters, musicians, etc, often derive so little income from their craft that the financial security of an employment, perhaps in a different sphere of activity, is necessary. The existence of the employment is irrelevant to the taxation of the freelance earnings although it is most important not to confuse the income or expenditure of the employment with the income or expenditure of the self-employed activity. HM Revenue & Customs is aware of the advantages which can be derived by an individual having 'freelance' income from an organisation of which he or she is also an employee, and where such circumstances are contrived, it can be extremely difficult to convince an Inspector of Taxes that a genuine freelance activity is being carried on. Where the individual operates through a company or partnership providing services personally to a particular client, and would be regarded as an employee if the services were supplied directly by the individual, additional problems arise from the notorious IR35 legislation and professional advice is essential.

For those starting in business or commencing work on a freelance basis HM Revenue & Customs produces a very useful booklet, *Starting in Business (IR28)*, which is available from any tax office.

Income

For income to be taxable it need not be substantial, nor even the author's only source of income; earnings from casual writing are also taxable but this can be an advantage, because occasional writers do not often make a profit from their writing. The expenses incurred in connection with writing may well exceed any income receivable and the resultant loss may then be used to reclaim tax paid on other income. There may be deducted from the income certain allowable expenses and capital allowances which are set out in more detail below. The possibility of a loss being used as a basis for a tax repayment is fully appreciated by HM Revenue & Customs, which sometimes attempts to treat casual writing as a hobby so that any losses incurred cannot be used to reclaim tax; of course by the same token any income receivable would not be chargeable to tax. This treatment may sound attractive but it should be resisted vigorously because HM Revenue & Customs does not hesitate to change its mind when profits begin to arise. In the case of exceptional or non-recurring writing, such as the autobiography of a sports personality or the memoirs of a politician, it could be better to be treated as pursuing a hobby and not as a professional author. Sales of copyright cannot be charged to income tax unless the recipient is a professional author. However, the proceeds of sale of copyright may be charged to capital gains tax, even by an individual who is not a professional author.

Royalties

Where the recipient is a professional author, a series of cases has laid down a clear principle that sales of copyright are taxable as income and not as capital receipts. Similarly, lump sums on account of, or in advance of royalties are also taxable as income in the year of receipt, subject to a claim for averaging relief (see below).

Copyright royalties are generally paid without deduction of income tax. However, if royalties are paid to a person who normally lives abroad, tax must be deducted by the

Arts Council awards

Arts Council category A awards

- Direct or indirect musical, design or choreographic commissions and direct or indirect commission of sculpture and paintings for public sites.
- The Royalty Supplement Guarantee Scheme.
- The contract writers' scheme.
- Jazz bursaries.
- Translators' grants.
- Photographic awards and bursaries.
- Film and video awards and bursaries.
- Performance Art Awards.
- Art Publishing Grants.
- Grants to assist with a specific project or projects (such as the writing of a book) or to meet specific professional expenses such as a contribution towards copying expenses made to a composer or to an artist's studio expenses.

Arts Council category B awards

- Bursaries to trainee directors.
- Bursaries for associate directors.
- Bursaries to people attending full-time courses in arts administration (the practical training course).
- In-service bursaries to theatre designers and bursaries to trainees on the theatre designers' scheme.
- In-service bursaries for administrators.
- Bursaries for actors and actresses.
- Bursaries for technicians and stage managers.
- Bursaries made to students attending the City University Arts Administration courses.
- Awards, known as the Buying Time Awards, made not to assist with a specific project or professional expenses but to maintain the recipient to enable him or her to take time off to develop his personal talents. These at present include the awards and bursaries known as the Theatre Writing Bursaries, awards and bursaries to composers, awards and bursaries to painters, sculptures and print makers, literature awards and bursaries.

payer or his agent at the time the payment is made unless arrangements are made with HM Revenue & Customs for payments to be made gross under the terms of a Double Taxation Agreement with the other country.

Arts Council grants

Persons in receipt of grants from the Arts Council or similar bodies will be concerned whether or not such grants are liable to income tax. HM Revenue & Customs has issued a Statement of Practice after detailed discussions with the Arts Council regarding the tax treatment of the awards. Grants and other receipts of a similar nature have now been divided into two categories (see box) – those which are to be treated by HM Revenue & Customs as chargeable to tax and those which are not. Category A awards are considered to be taxable; awards made under category B are not chargeable to tax.

This Statement of Practice has no legal force and is used merely to ease the administration of the tax system. It is open to anyone in receipt of a grant or award to disregard the agreed statement and challenge HM Revenue & Customs view on the merits of their particular case. However, it must be recognised that HM Revenue & Customs does not issue such statements lightly and any challenge to their view would almost certainly involve a lengthy and expensive action through the Courts.

The tax position of persons in receipt of literary prizes will generally follow a decision by the Special Commissioners in connection with the Whitbread Book Awards (now called the Costa Book Awards). In that case it was decided that the prize was not part of the author's professional income and accordingly not chargeable to tax. The precise details are not available because decisions of the Special Commissioners were not, at that time, reported unless an appeal was made to the High Court; HM Revenue & Customs chose not to appeal against this decision. Details of the many literary awards that are given each year start on page 588, and this decision is of considerable significance to the winners of each of these prizes. It would be unwise to assume that all such awards will be free of tax as the precise facts which were present in the case of the Whitbread awards may not be repeated in another case; however it is clear that an author winning a prize has some very powerful arguments in his or her favour, should HM Revenue & Customs seek to charge tax on the award.

Allowable expenses

To qualify as an allowable business expense, expenditure has to be laid out wholly and exclusively for business purposes. Strictly there must be no 'duality of purpose', which means that expenditure cannot be apportioned to reflect the private and business usage, e.g. food, clothing, telephone, travelling expenses, etc. However, HM Revenue & Customs does not usually interpret this principle strictly and is prepared to allow all reasonable expenses (including apportioned sums) where the amounts can be commercially justified.

It should be noted carefully that the expenditure does not have to be 'necessary', it merely has to be incurred 'wholly and exclusively' for business purposes. Naturally, however, expenditure of an outrageous and wholly unnecessary character might well give rise to a presumption that it was not really for business purposes. As with all things, some expenses are unquestionably allowable and some expenses are equally unquestionably not allowable – it is the grey area in between which gives rise to all the difficulties and the outcome invariably depends on negotiation with HM Revenue & Customs.

Great care should be taken when claiming a deduction for items where there may be a 'duality of purpose' and negotiations should be conducted with more than usual care and courtesy – if provoked the Inspector of Taxes may well choose to allow nothing. An appeal is always possible although unlikely to succeed as a string of cases in the Courts has clearly demonstrated. An example is the case of *Caillebotte* v. *Quinn* where the taxpayer (who normally had lunch at home) sought to claim the excess cost of meals incurred because he was working a long way from his home. The taxpayer's arguments failed because he did not eat only in order to work, one of the reasons for his eating was in order to sustain his life; a duality of purpose therefore existed and no tax relief was due.

Other cases have shown that expenditure on clothing can also be disallowed if it is the kind of clothing which is in everyday use, because clothing is worn not only to assist the pursuit of one's profession but also to accord with public decency. This duality of purpose may be sufficient to deny relief – even where the particular type of clothing is of a kind not otherwise worn by the taxpayer. In the case of *Mallalieu* v. *Drummond* a barrister failed to obtain a tax deduction for items of sombre clothing that she purchased specifically for wearing in Court. The House of Lords decided that a duality of purpose existed because clothing represented part of her needs as a human being.

Allowances

Despite the above, Inspectors of Taxes are not usually inflexible and the following list of expenses are among those generally allowed.

(a) Cost of all materials used up in the course of preparation of the work.

(b) Cost of typewriting and secretarial assistance, etc; if this or other help is obtained from one's spouse then it is entirely proper for a deduction to be claimed for the amounts paid for the work. The amounts claimed must actually be paid to the spouse and should be at the market rate although some uplift can be made for unsocial hours, etc. Payments to a wife (or husband) are of course taxable in her (or his) hands and should therefore be most carefully considered. The wife's earnings may also be liable for National Insurance contributions and it is important to take care because otherwise you may find that these contributions outweigh the tax savings. The impact of the National Minimum Wage should also be considered.

(c) All expenditure on normal business items such as postage, stationery, telephone, email, fax and answering machines, agent's fees, accountancy charges, photography, subscriptions, periodicals, magazines, etc, may be claimed. The cost of daily papers should not be overlooked if these form part of research material. Visits to theatres, cinemas, etc, for research purposes may also be permissible (but not the cost relating to guests). Unfortunately, expenditure on all types of business entertaining is specifically denied tax relief.

(d) If work is conducted at home, a deduction for 'use of home' is usually allowed providing the amount claimed is reasonable. If the claim is based on an appropriate proportion of the total costs of rent, light and heat, cleaning and maintenance, insurance, etc (but not the Council Tax), care should be taken to ensure that no single room is used 'exclusively' for business purposes, because this may result in the Capital Gains Tax exemption on the house as the only or main residence being partially forfeited. However, it would be a strange household where one room was in fact used exclusively for business purposes and for no other purpose whatsoever (e.g. storing personal bank statements and other private papers); the usual formula is to claim a deduction on the basis that most or all of the rooms in the house are used at one time or another for business purposes, thereby avoiding any suggestion that any part was used exclusively for business purposes.

(e) The appropriate business proportion of motor running expenses may also be claimed although what is the appropriate proportion will naturally depend on the particular circumstances of each case; it should be appreciated that the well-known scale of benefits, whereby employees were taxed according to the size and cost of the car (and are now taxed on the basis of their CO^2 emissions), do not apply to self-employed persons.

(f) It has been long established that the cost of travelling from home to work (whether employed or self-employed) is not an allowable expense. However, if home is one's place of work then no expenditure under this heading is likely to be incurred and difficulties are unlikely to arise.

(g) Travelling and hotel expenses incurred for business purposes will normally be allowed but if any part could be construed as disguised holiday or pleasure expenditure, considerable thought would need to be given to the commercial reasons for the journey in order to justify the claim. The principle of 'duality of purpose' will always be a difficult hurdle in this connection – although not insurmountable.

(h) If a separate business bank account is maintained, any overdraft interest thereon will be an allowable expense. This is the only circumstance in which overdraft interest is allowed for tax purposes and care should be taken to avoid overdrafts in all other circumstances.

(i) Where capital allowances (see below) are claimed for a personal computer, fax, modem, television, video, CD or tape player, etc, used for business purposes the costs of maintenance and repair of the equipment may also be claimed.

Clearly many other allowable items may be claimed in addition to those listed. Wherever there is any reasonable business motive for some expenditure it should be claimed as a deduction although it is necessary to preserve all records relating to the expense. It is sensible to avoid an excess of imagination as this would naturally cause the Inspector of Taxes to doubt the genuineness of other expenses claimed.

The question is often raised whether the whole amount of an expense may be deducted or whether the VAT content must be excluded. Where VAT is reclaimed from the Customs and Excise by someone who is registered for VAT, the VAT element of the expense cannot be treated as an allowable deduction. Where the VAT is not reclaimed, the whole expense (inclusive of VAT) is allowable for income tax purposes.

Capital allowances

Allowances

Where expenditure of a capital nature is incurred, it cannot be deducted from income as an expense – a separate and sometimes more valuable capital allowance being available instead. Capital allowances are given for many different types of expenditure, but authors and similar professional people are likely to claim only for 'plant and machinery'; this is a very wide expression which may include motor cars, personal computers, fax and photocopying machines, modems, televisions, CD, video and cassette players used for business purposes. Plant and machinery generally qualifies for an allowance of 100% (reduced to 40% for expenditure over £100,000). Where the useful life of an asset is expected to be short, it is possible to claim special treatment as a 'short life asset' enabling the allowances to be accelerated.

The reason these allowances can be more valuable than allowable expenses is that they may be wholly or partly disclaimed in any year that full benefit cannot be obtained – ordinary business expenses cannot be similarly disclaimed. Where, for example, the income of an author does not exceed his personal allowances, he would not be liable to tax and a claim for capital allowances would be wasted. If the capital allowances were to be disclaimed their benefit would be carried forward for use in subsequent years. This would also be advantageous where the income is likely to be taxable at the higher rate of 40% (or even the new 50% rate) in a subsequent year. Careful planning with claims for capital allowances is therefore essential if maximum benefit is to be obtained.

As an alternative to capital allowances, claims can be made on the 'renewals' basis whereby all renewals are treated as allowable deductions in the year; no allowance is obtained for the initial purchase, but the cost of replacement (excluding any improvement element) is allowed in full. This basis is no longer widely used, as it is considerably less advantageous than claiming capital allowances as described above.

Leasing is a popular method of acquiring fixed assets, and where cash is not available to enable an outright purchase to be made, assets may be leased over a period of time. Whilst leasing may have financial benefits in certain circumstances, in normal cases there is likely to be no tax advantage in leasing an asset where the alternative of outright purchase is available.

Books

The question of whether the cost of books is eligible for tax relief has long been a source of difficulty. The annual cost of replacing books used for the purposes of one's professional activities (e.g. the cost of a new *Writers' & Artists' Yearbook* each year) has always been an allowable expense; the difficulty arose because the initial cost of reference books, etc (e.g. when commencing one's profession) was treated as capital expenditure but no allowances were due as the books were not considered to be 'plant'. However, the matter was clarified by the case of *Munby* v. *Furlong* in which the Court of Appeal decided that the initial cost of law books purchased by a barrister was expenditure on 'plant' and eligible for capital allowances. This is clearly a most important decision, particularly relevant to any person who uses expensive books in the course of exercising his or her profession.

Pension contributions

Where a self-employed person makes contributions to a pension scheme, those contributions are usually deductible.

These arrangements are generally advantageous in providing for a pension as contributions are usually paid when the income is high (and the tax relief is also high) and the pension (taxed as earned income when received) usually arises when the income is low and little tax is payable. There is also the opportunity to take part of the pension entitlement as a tax-free lump sum. It is necessary to take into account the possibility that the tax advantages could go into reverse. When the pension is paid it could, if rates rise again, be taxed at a higher rate than the rate of tax relief at the moment. From 6 April 2006 a whole new regime for pensions was introduced to create a much simpler system. Each individual has a lifetime allowance (set at £1.8 million for 2010/11 and rising annually). When benefits crystallise, which will generally be when a pension begins to be paid, this is measured against the individual's lifetime allowance; any excess will be taxed at 25%, or at 55% if the excess is taken as a lump sum.

Each individual also has an annual allowance for contributions to the pension fund which is set at £255,000 for 2010/11 but will increase in later years. If the annual increase in an individual's rights under all registered schemes of which he is a member exceeds the annual allowance, the excess is chargeable to tax.

For those whose income exceeds £130,000, the tax relief on pension contributions will be reduced to the basic rate of 20% from 6 April 2011. Special rules prevent advantages being obtained by paying large contributions early.

For most writers and artists this means that they can effectively contribute the whole of their earnings to a pension scheme (if they can afford to do so) without any of the previous complications. It is still necessary to be careful where there is other income giving rise to a pension because the whole of the pension entitlement has to be taken into account.

Flexible retirement is possible allowing members of occupational pension schemes to continue working while also drawing retirement benefits. As part of this reform, however, the normal minimum pension age was raised from 50 to 55 on 6 April 2010.

Class 4 National Insurance contributions

Allied to pensions is the payment of Class 4 National Insurance contributions, although no pension or other benefit is obtained by the contributions; the Class 4 contributions are designed solely to extract additional amounts from self-employed persons and are payable in addition to the normal Class 2 (self-employed) contributions. The rates are changed each year and for 2009/10 self-employed persons will be obliged to contribute 8% of their profits between the range £5,715–£43,875 per annum plus 1% on earnings above £43,875. This amount is collected in conjunction with the annual income tax liability.

Averaging relief

Relief for copyright payments

For many years special provisions enabled authors and similar persons engaged on a literary, dramatic, musical or artistic work for a period of more than 12 months, to spread certain amounts received over two or three years depending on the time spent in preparing the work.

Since 2001 there has been a simpler system of averaging. Under these rules, professional authors and artists engaged in the creation of literary, dramatic works or designs may claim to average the profits of two or more consecutive years if the profits for one year are less than 75% of the profits for the highest year. This new relief can apply even if the work took less than 12 months to create and is available to people who create works in partnership with others.

The purpose of the relief is to enable the creative artist to utilise his allowances fully and to avoid the higher rates of tax which might apply if all the income were to arise in a single year.

Collection of tax

Self-assessment

In 1997, the system of sending in a tax return showing all your income and HM Revenue & Customs raising an assessment to collect the tax was abolished. So was the idea that you pay tax on your profits for the preceding year. Now, when you send in your tax return you have to work out your own tax liability and send a cheque; this is called 'self-assessment'. If you get it wrong, or if you are late with your tax return or the payment of tax, interest and penalties will be charged.

Under this system, HM Revenue & Customs rarely issue assessments; they are no longer necessary because the idea is that you assess yourself. A colour-coded tax return was created, designed to help individuals meet their tax obligations. This is a daunting task but the term 'self-assessment' is not intended to imply that individuals have to do it themselves; they can (and often will) engage professional help. The term is only intended to convey that it is the taxpayer, and not HM Revenue & Customs, who is responsible for getting the tax liability right and for it to be paid on time.

The deadline for sending in the tax return is 31 October following the end of the tax year. This is the deadline for paper tax returns. You can file online, in which case you have until 31 January following the end of the tax year. If for some reason you are unwilling or unable to calculate the tax payable, you can ask HM Revenue & Customs to do it for you on your paper tax return.

Income tax on self-employed earnings remains payable in two instalments on 31 January and 31 July each year. Because the accurate figures may not necessarily be known, these payments in January and July will therefore be only payments on account based on the previous year's liability. The final balancing figure will be paid the following 31 January together with the first instalment of the liability for the following year.

When HM Revenue & Customs receives the self-assessment tax return, it is checked to see if there is anything obviously wrong; if there is, a letter will be sent to you immediately. Otherwise, HM Revenue & Customs has 12 months from the filing date in which to make further enquiries; if it doesn't, it will have no further opportunity to do so and your tax liabilities are final – unless there is something seriously wrong such as the omission of income or capital gains. In that event, HM Revenue & Customs will raise an assessment later to collect any extra tax together with appropriate penalties. It is essential for the operation of the new system that all records relevant to your tax returns are retained for at least 12 months in case they are needed by HM Revenue & Customs. For the self-employed, the record-keeping requirement is much more onerous because the records need to be kept for nearly six years. One important change in the rules is that if you claim a tax deduction for an expense, it will be necessary to have a receipt or other document proving that the expenditure has been made. Because the existence of the underlying records is so important to the operation of self-assessment, HM Revenue & Customs will treat them very seriously and there is a penalty of £3,000 for any failure to keep adequate records.

Interest

Interest is chargeable on overdue tax at a variable rate, which at the time of writing is 3% per annum. It does not rank for any tax relief, which can make HM Revenue & Customs an expensive source of credit.

However, HM Revenue & Customs can also be obliged to pay interest (known as repayment supplement) tax-free where repayments are delayed. The rules relating to repayment supplement are less beneficial and even more complicated than the rules for interest payable but they do exist and can be very welcome if a large repayment has been delayed for a long time. Unfortunately, the rate of repayment supplement is only 0.5% and is always less than the rate charged by HMRC on overdue tax.

Value added tax

The activities of writers, painters, composers, etc are all 'taxable supplies' within the scope of VAT and chargeable at the standard rate. (Zero rating which applies to publishers, booksellers, etc on the supply of books does not extend to the work performed by writers.) Accordingly, authors are obliged to register for VAT if their income for the past 12 months exceeds £68,000 or if their income for the coming month will exceed that figure.

Delay in registering can be a most serious matter because if registration is not effected at the proper time, the Customs and Excise can (and invariably do) claim VAT from all the income received since the date on which registration should have been made. As no

VAT would have been included in the amounts received during this period the amount claimed by the Customs and Excise must inevitably come straight from the pocket of the author.

The author may be entitled to seek reimbursement of the VAT from those whom he or she ought to have charged VAT but this is obviously a matter of some difficulty and may indeed damage his commercial relationships. Apart from these disadvantages there is also a penalty for late registration. The rules are extremely harsh and are imposed automatically even in cases of innocent error. It is therefore extremely important to monitor the income very carefully because if in any period of 12 months the income exceeds the £70,000 limit, the Customs and Excise must be notified within 30 days of the end of the period. Failure to do so will give rise to an automatic penalty. It should be emphasised that this is a penalty for failing to submit a form and has nothing to do with any real or potential loss of tax. Furthermore, whether the failure was innocent or deliberate will not matter. Only the existence of a 'reasonable excuse' will be a defence to the penalty. However, a reasonable excuse does not include ignorance, error, a lack of funds or reliance on any third party.

However, it is possible to regard VAT registration as a privilege and not a penalty, because only VAT registered persons can reclaim VAT paid on their expenses such as stationery, telephone, professional fees, etc, and even computers and other plant and machinery (excluding cars). However, many find that the administrative inconvenience – the cost of maintaining the necessary records and completing the necessary forms – more than outweighs the benefits to be gained from registration and prefer to stay outside the scope of VAT for as long as possible.

Overseas matters

The general observation may be made that self-employed persons resident and domiciled in the UK are not well treated with regard to their overseas work, being taxable on their worldwide income. It is important to emphasise that if fees are earned abroad, no tax saving can be achieved merely by keeping the money outside the country. Although exchange control regulations no longer exist to require repatriation of foreign earnings, such income remains taxable in the UK and must be disclosed to HM Revenue & Customs; the same applies to interest or other income arising on any investment of these earnings overseas. Accordingly, whenever foreign earnings are likely to become substantial, prompt and effective action is required to limit the impact of UK and foreign taxation. In the case of non-resident authors it is important that arrangements concerning writing for publication in the UK, e.g. in newspapers, are undertaken with great care. A case concerning the wife of one of the great train robbers who provided detailed information for a series of articles in a Sunday newspaper is most instructive. Although she was acknowledged to be resident in Canada for all the relevant years, the income from the articles was treated as arising in this country and fully chargeable to UK tax.

The UK has double taxation agreements with many other countries and these agreements are designed to ensure that income arising in a foreign country is taxed either in that country or in the UK. Where a withholding tax is deducted from payments received from another country (or where tax is paid in full in the absence of a double taxation agreement), the amount of foreign tax paid can usually be set off against the related UK tax liability. Many successful authors can be found living in Eire because of the complete exemption from tax which attaches to works of cultural or artistic merit by persons who are resident there. However, such a step should only be contemplated having careful regard to all the other domestic and commercial considerations and specialist advice is essential if the exemption is to be obtained and kept; a careless breach of the conditions could cause the exemption to be withdrawn with catastrophic consequences.

Further information concerning the precise conditions to be satisfied for exemption from tax in Eire can be obtained from the Revenue Commissioners in Dublin or from their website (www.revenue.ie).

Companies

When an author becomes successful the prospect of paying tax at the higher rate may drive them to take hasty action such as the formation of companies, etc, which may not always be to their advantage. Indeed some authors seeing the exodus into tax exile of their more successful colleagues even form companies in low tax areas in the naive expectation of saving large amounts of tax. HM Revenue & Customs is fully aware of these possibilities and have extensive powers to charge tax and combat avoidance. Accordingly, such action is just as likely to increase tax liabilities and generate other costs and should never be contemplated without expert advice; some very expensive mistakes are often made in this area which are not always able to be remedied.

To conduct one's business through the medium of a company can be a most effective method of mitigating tax liabilities, and providing it is done at the right time and under the right circumstances very substantial advantages can be derived. However, if done without due care and attention the intended advantages will simply evaporate. At the very least it is essential to ensure that the company's business is genuine and conducted properly with regard to the realities of the situation. If the author continues his or her activities unchanged, simply paying all the receipts from his work into a company's bank account, he cannot expect to persuade HM Revenue & Customs that it is the company and not himself who is entitled to, and should be assessed to tax on, that income.

It must be strongly emphasised that many pitfalls exist which can easily eliminate all the tax benefits expected to arise by the formation of the company. For example, company directors are employees of the company and will be liable to pay much higher National Insurance contributions; the company must also pay the employer's proportion of the contribution and a total liability of over 23% of gross salary may arise. This compares most unfavourably with the position of a self-employed person. Moreover, on the commencement of the company's business the individual's profession will cease and the possibility of revisions being made by HM Revenue & Customs to earlier tax liabilities means that the timing of a change has to be considered very carefully.

The tax return

No mention has been made above of personal reliefs and allowances; this is because these allowances and the rates of tax are subject to constant change and are always set out in detail in the explanatory notes which accompany the Tax Return. The annual Tax Return is an important document and should be completed promptly with extreme care, particularly since the introduction of self-assessment. If filling in the Return is a source of difficulty or anxiety, comfort may be found in the Consumer Association's publication *Money Which? – Tax Saving Guide*, which is published in March of each year and includes much which is likely to be of interest and assistance.

Peter Vaines FCA, CTA, barrister, is a partner in the international law firm of Squire Sanders & Dempsey LLP and writes and speaks widely on tax matters. He is on the Editorial Boards of *Taxation* and *Personal Tax Planning Review*, tax columnist of the *New Law Journal* and author of a number of books on taxation.

Social security contributions

In general, every individual who works in Great Britain either as an employee or as a self-employed person is liable to pay social security contributions. The law governing this subject is complex and Peter Arrowsmith FCA gives here a summary of the position. This article should be regarded as a general guide only.

All contributions are payable in respect of years ending on 5 April. See box (below) for the classes of contributions.

Employed or self-employed?

The question as to whether a person is employed under a contract *of* service and is thereby an employee liable to Class 1 contributions, or performs services (either solely or in partnership) under a contract *for* service and is thereby self-employed liable to Class 2 and Class 4 contributions, often has to be decided in practice. One of the best guides can be found in the case of *Market Investigations Ltd* v. *Minister of Social Security* (1969 2 WLR 1) when Cooke J. remarked:

'… the fundamental test to be applied is this: "Is the person who has engaged himself to perform these services performing them as a person in business on his own account?" If the answer to that question is 'yes', then the contract is a contract for services. If the answer is 'no', then the contract is a contract of service. No exhaustive list has been compiled and perhaps no exhaustive list can be compiled of the considerations which are relevant in determining that question, nor can strict rules be laid down as to the relative weight which the various considerations should carry in particular cases. The most that can be said is that control will no doubt always have to be considered, although it can no longer be regarded as the sole determining factor; and that factors which may be of importance are such matters as:

- whether the man performing the services provides his own equipment,
- whether he hires his own helpers,
- what degree of financial risk he takes,
- what degree of responsibility for investment and management he has, and
- whether and how far he has an opportunity of profiting from sound management in the performance of his task.'

The above case has often been considered subsequently – notably in November 1993 by the Court of Appeal in the case of *Hall* v. *Lorimer*. In this case a vision mixer with around 20 clients and undertaking around 120–150 separate engagements per annum was held to be self-employed. This follows the, perhaps surprising, contention of the former Inland Revenue that the taxpayer was an employee.

Classes of contributions

Class 1 These are payable by employees (primary contributions) and their employers (secondary contributions) and are based on earnings.

Class 1A Payable only by employers in respect of all taxable benefits in kind (cars and fuel only prior to 6 April 2000).

Class 1B Payable only by employers in respect of PAYE Settlement Agreements entered into by them.

Class 2 These are weekly flat rate contributions, payable by the self-employed.

Class 3 These are weekly flat rate contributions, payable on a voluntary basis in order to provide, or make up entitlement to, certain social security benefits.

Class 4 These are payable by the self-employed in respect of their trading or professional income and are based on earnings.

Exceptions

There are certain exceptions to the above rules, those most relevant to artists and writers being:

• The employment of a wife by her husband, or vice versa, is disregarded for social security purposes unless it is for the purposes of a trade or profession (e.g. the employment of his wife by an author would not be disregarded and would result in a liability for contributions if her salary reached the minimum levels). The same provisions also apply to civil partners from 5 December 2005.

• The employment of certain relatives in a private dwelling house in which both employee and employer reside is disregarded for social security purposes provided the employment is not for the purposes of a trade or business carried on at those premises by the employer. This would cover the employment of a relative (as defined) as a housekeeper in a private residence.

In general, lecturers, teachers and instructors engaged by an educational establishment to teach on at least four days in three consecutive months are regarded as employees for social security purposes, although this rule does not apply to fees received by persons giving public lectures.

Freelance film workers

There is a list of grades in the film industry in respect of which PAYE need not be deducted and who are regarded as self-employed for tax purposes.

Further information can be obtained from the guidance notes on the application of PAYE to casual and freelance staff in the film industry issued by the former Inland Revenue. In view of the Inland Revenue announcement that the same status will apply for PAYE and National Insurance contributions purposes, no liability for employee's and employer's contributions should arise in the case of any of the grades mentioned above.

However, in the film and television industry this general rule was not always followed in practice. In December 1992, after a long review, the DSS agreed that individuals working behind the camera and who have jobs on the Inland Revenue Schedule D list are self-employed for social security purposes.

There are special rules for, *inter alia*, personnel appearing before the camera, short engagements, payments to limited companies and payments to overseas personalities.

Artistes, performers/non-performers

The status of artistes and performers for tax purposes will depend on the individual circumstances but for social security purposes new regulations which took effect on 17 July 1998 require most actors, musicians or similar performers to be treated as employees, whether or not this status applies under general and/or tax law. It also applies whether or not the individual is supplied through an agency.

Personal service companies

From 6 April 2000, those who have control of their own 'one-man service companies' are subject to special rules. If the work that the owner of the company does for the company's customers would – but for the one-man company – be considered as an employment of that individual (i.e. rather than self-employment), a deemed salary may arise. If it does, then some or all of the income of the company will be treated as salary liable to PAYE and National Insurance contributions. This will be the case whether or not such salary is actually paid by the company. The same situation may arise where the worker owns as little as 5% of a company's share capital.

The calculations required by HM Revenue & Customs are complicated and have to be done very quickly at the end of each tax year (even if the company's year-end is different). It is essential that affected businesses seek detailed professional advice about these rules which may also, in certain circumstances, apply to partnerships.

In order to escape the application of these rules, a number of workers have arranged their engagements through 'managed service companies', etc. where the promoter is heavily involved in all the company management to the exclusion of the workers themselves. Such companies are now subjected to similar, but different, rules from 6 April 2007 for tax and 6 August 2007 for NIC.

Pension age

The current pensionable age for men is 65. In the case of women the previous age of 60 no longer applies as from 6 April 2010 to 5 April 2020 the female pensionable age is now rising evenly to 65. This means that NICs will be payable by women up to the extended pension age. In 2010 and 2011 women will reach state pension age on the following dates dependent on date of birth:

Date of birth	Pension age
6 April 1950 to 5 May 1950	6 May 2010
6 May 1950 to 5 June 1950	6 July 2010
6 June 1950 to 5 July 1950	6 September 2010
6 July 1950 to 5 August 1950	6 November 2010
6 August 1950 to 5 September 1950	6 January 2011
6 September 1950 to 5 October 1950	6 March 2011
6 October 1950 to 5 November 1950	6 May 2011
6 November 1950 to 5 December 1950	6 July 2011
6 December 1950 to 5 January 1951	6 September 2011
6 January 1951 to 5 February 1951	6 November 2011

From 6 April 2024 (as currently legislated, though this may change after the 2010 General Election) the pensionable age for both men and women will rise to 66 (gradually over a two-year period), and likewise to 67 from 2034–6 and then to 68 from 2044–6.

Class 1 contributions

As mentioned above, these are related to earnings, the amount payable depending upon whether the employer has applied for his employees to be 'contracted-out' of the State earnings-related pension scheme; such application can be made where the employer's own pension scheme provides a requisite level of benefits for his or her employees and their dependants or, in the case of a money purchase scheme (COMPS) certain minimum safeguards are covered. Employers with employees contributing to 'stakeholder pension plans' continue to pay the full not contracted-out rate. Such employees have their contracting out arrangements handled separately by government authorities.

Contributions are payable by employees and employers on earnings that exceed the earnings threshold. Contributions are normally collected via the PAYE tax deduction machinery, and there are penalties for late submission of returns and for errors therein. From 19 April 1993, interest is charged automatically on PAYE and social security contributions paid late.

Employees liable to pay

Contributions are payable by any employee who is aged 16 years and over (even though they may still be at school) and who is paid an amount equal to, or exceeding, the earnings threshold. Nationality is irrelevant for contribution purposes and, subject to special rules covering employees not normally resident in Great Britain, Northern Ireland or the Isle of Man, or resident in EEA countries or those with which there are reciprocal agreements, contributions must be paid whether the employee concerned is a British subject or not provided he is gainfully employed in Great Britain.

Employees exempt from liability to pay

Persons over pensionable age are exempt from liability to pay primary contributions, even if they have not retired. However, the fact that an employee may be exempt from liability does not relieve an employer from liability to pay secondary contributions in respect of that employee.

Employees' (primary) contributions

From 6 April 2010, the rate of employees' contributions on earnings from the earnings threshold to the upper earnings limit is 11% (for contracted-out employment 9.4% up to the upper accrual point, then 11% to the upper earnings limit). Certain married women who made appropriate elections before 12 May 1977 may be entitled to pay a reduced rate of 4.85%. However, they will have no entitlement to benefits in respect of these contributions.

From April 2003, earnings above the upper earnings limit attract an employee contribution liability of 1% – previously, there was no such liability.

Employers' (secondary) contributions

All employers are liable to pay contributions on the gross earnings of employees. As mentioned above, an employer's liability is not reduced as a result of employees being exempted from contributions, or being liable to pay only the reduced rate (4.85%) of contributions.

For earnings paid on or after 6 April 2010 employers are liable at a rate of 12.8% on earnings paid above the earnings threshold (without any upper earnings limit), 9.1% where the employment is contracted out (salary related) or 11.4% contracted out (money purchase). In addition, special rebates apply in respect of earnings falling between the lower earnings limit and the earnings threshold. This provides, effectively, a negative rate of contribution in that small band of earnings. It should be noted that the contracted-out rates of 9.1% and 11.4% now apply only up to the upper accrual point. Thereafter, the not contracted-out rate of 12.8% is applicable. Prior to 6 April 2009 the contracted-out rates applied up to the upper earnings limit.

Whilst the Chancellor of the Exchequer announced on 13 May 2008 an additional increase to the personal tax allowance for 2008–9, this was not matched for social security.

The employer is responsible for the payment of both employees' and employer's contributions, but is entitled to deduct the employees' contributions from the earnings on which they are calculated. Effectively, therefore, the employee suffers a deduction in respect of his or her social security contributions in arriving at his weekly or monthly wage or salary. Special rules apply to company directors and persons employed through agencies.

Items included in, or excluded from, earnings

Contributions are calculated on the basis of a person's gross earnings from their employment. This will normally be the figure shown on the deduction working sheet, except where the employee pays superannuation contributions and, from 6 April 1987, charitable gifts under payroll giving – these must be added back for the purposes of calculating Class 1 liability.

Earnings include salary, wages, overtime pay, commissions, bonuses, holiday pay, payments made while the employee is sick or absent from work, payments to cover travel between home and office, and payments under the statutory sick pay, statutory maternity pay, statutory paternity pay and statutory adoption pay schemes.

However, certain payments, some of which may be regarded as taxable income for income tax purposes, are ignored for Class 1 purposes. These include:

- certain gratuities paid other than by the employer;
- redundancy payments and some payments in lieu of notice;
- certain payments in kind;
- reimbursement of specific expenses incurred in the carrying out of the employment;
- benefits given on an individual basis for personal reasons (e.g. wedding and birthday presents);
- compensation for loss of office.

Booklet CWG 2 (2010 edition) gives a list of items to include in or exclude from earnings for Class 1 contribution purposes. Some such items may, however, be liable to Class 1A (employer only) contributions.

Miscellaneous rules

There are detailed rules covering a person with two or more employments; where a person receives a bonus or commission in addition to a regular wage or salary; and where a person is in receipt of holiday pay. From 6 April 1991 employers' social security contributions arise under Class 1A in respect of the private use of a company car, and of fuel provided for private use therein. From 6 April 2000, this charge was extended to cover most taxable benefits in kind. The rate is now 12.8%. From 6 April 1999, Class 1B contributions are payable by employers using PAYE Settlement Agreements in respect of small and/or irregular expense payments and benefits, etc. This rate is also currently 12.8%.

Upper accrual point

From 6 April 2009 there was introduced a new upper accrual point (UAP) from which entitlement to benefit (principally earnings-related state pension) ceases, even though main

Rates of Class 1 contributions and earnings limits from 6 April 2010

Earnings per week	*Rates payable on earnings in each band*			
	Not contracted out		*Contracted out*	
	Employee	*Employer*	*Employee*	*Employer*
£	*%*	*%*	*%*	*%*
Below 97.00	–	–	–	–
97.00–109.99	–	–	– (*)	– (*)
110.00–769.99	11	12.8	9.4	9.1 or 11.4
770.00–844.00	11	12.8	11	12.8
Over 844.00	1	12.8	1	12.8

* Special rebates deductible in respect of this band of earnings.

rate Class 1 contributions continue to be due. This impacts on contracted-out employees in particular. The UAP is fixed at a constant cash amount of £770 per week and will eliminate any earnings-related element of the state pension by around 2031.

Class 2 contributions

Class 2 contributions are payable at the weekly rate of £2.40 as from 6 April 2010 (unchanged from the previous year). Exemptions from Class 2 liability are:

- A person over pensionable age.
- A person who has not attained the age of 16.
- A married woman or, in certain cases, a widow either of whom elected prior to 12 May 1977 not to pay Class 2 contributions.
- Persons with small earnings (see below).
- Persons not ordinarily self-employed (see below).

Small earnings

Application for a certificate of exception from Class 2 contributions may be made by any person who can show that his or her net self-employed earnings per his profit and loss account (as opposed to taxable profits):

- for the year of application are expected to be less than a specified limit (£5,075 in the 2010/11 tax year); or
- for the year preceding the application were less than the limit specified for that year (£5,075 for 2009/10) and there has been no material change of circumstances.

Certificates of exception must be renewed in accordance with the instructions stated thereon. At HM Revenue & Customs' discretion the certificate may commence up to 13 weeks before the date on which the application is made. Despite a certificate of exception being in force, a person who is self-employed is still entitled to pay Class 2 contributions if they wish, in order to maintain entitlement to social security benefits.

Persons not ordinarily self-employed

Part-time self-employed activities (including as a writer or artist) are disregarded for contribution purposes if the person concerned is not ordinarily employed in such activities and has a full-time job as an employee. There is no definition of 'ordinarily employed' for this purpose but a person who has a regular job and whose earnings from spare-time occupation are not expected to be more than £1,300 per annum may fall within this category. Persons qualifying for this relief do not require certificates of exception but may be well advised to apply for one nonetheless.

Method of payment

From April 1993, Class 2 contributions may be paid by monthly direct debit in arrears or, alternatively, by cheque, bank giro, etc. following receipt of a quarterly (in arrears) bill.

Overpaid contributions

If, following the payment of Class 2 contributions, it is found that the earnings are below the exception limit (e.g. the relevant accounts are prepared late), the Class 2 contributions that have been overpaid can be reclaimed, provided a claim is made between 6 April and 31 January immediately following the end of the tax year. Such a refund may, however, prejudice entitlement to contributory benefits.

Class 3 contributions

Class 3 contributions are payable voluntarily, at the weekly rate of £12.05 per week from 6 April 2010 (unchanged from the previous year), by persons aged 16 or over with a view to enabling them to qualify for a limited range of benefits if their contribution record is not otherwise sufficient. In general, Class 3 contributions can be paid by employees, the self-employed and the non employed.

Broadly speaking, no more than 52 Class 3 contributions are payable for any one tax year, and contributions cannot be paid in respect of tax years after the one in which the individual concerned reaches state pension age. Class 3 contributions may be paid in the same manner as Class 2 (see above) or by annual cheque in arrears.

Class 4 contributions

In addition to Class 2 contributions, self-employed persons are liable to pay Class 4 contributions. These are calculated at the rate of 8% on the amount of profits or gains chargeable to income tax which exceed £5,715 per annum but which do not exceed £43,875 per annum for 2010/11 (unchanged from the previous year). Profits above the upper limit of £43,875 attract a Class 4 charge at the rate of 1%. The income tax profit on which Class 4 contributions are calculated is after deducting capital allowances and losses, but before deducting personal tax allowances or retirement annuity or personal pension or stakeholder pension plan premiums.

Class 4 contributions produce no additional benefits, but were introduced to ensure that self-employed persons as a whole pay a fair share of the cost of pensions and other social security benefits, yet without those who make only small profits having to pay excessively high flat rate contributions.

Payment of contributions

In general, Class 4 contributions are now self-assessed and paid to HM Revenue & Customs together with the income tax as a result of the self-assessment income tax return, and accordingly the contributions are due and payable at the same time as the income tax liability on the relevant profits. Under self-assessment, interim payments of Class 4 contributions are payable at the same time as interim payments of tax.

Further information

Further information can be obtained from the many booklets published by HM Revenue & Customs, available from local Enquiry Centres and on their website (www.hmrc.gov.uk).

National Insurance Contributions Office, Charities, Assets & Residency
Newcastle upon Tyne NE98 1ZZ
tel (08459) 154811 (local call rates apply)
Address for enquiries for individuals resident abroad.

Class 4 exemptions

The following persons are exempt from Class 4 contributions:

- Persons over state pension age at the commencement of the year of assessment (i.e. on 6 April).
- An individual not resident in the United Kingdom for income tax purposes in the year of assessment.
- Persons whose earnings are not 'immediately derived' from carrying on a trade, profession or vocation (e.g. sleeping partners).
- A child under 16 on 6 April of the year of assessment.
- Persons not ordinarily self-employed.

Married persons and partnerships

Under independent taxation of husband and wife from 1990/1 onwards, each spouse is responsible for his or her own Class 4 liability.

In partnerships, each partner's liability is calculated separately. If a partner also carries on another trade or profession, the profits of all such businesses are aggregated for the purposes of calculating their Class 4 liability.

When an assessment has become final and conclusive for the purposes of income tax, it is also final and conclusive for the purposes of calculating Class 4 liability.

Maximum contributions

There is a form of limit to the total liability for social security contributions payable by a person who is employed in more than one employment, or is also self-employed or a partner.

Where only not contracted-out Class 1 contributions, or not contracted-out Class 1 and Class 2 contributions, are payable, the maximum contribution payable at the main rates (11%, 9.4% or 4.85% as the case may be) is limited to 53 primary Class 1 contributions at the maximum weekly not contracted-out standard rate. For 2010/11 this 'maximum' will thus be £4,279.22 (amounts paid at only 1% are to be excluded in making this comparison).

However, where contracted-out Class 1 contributions are payable, the maximum primary Class 1 contributions payable for 2010/11 where all employments are contracted out are £3,708.52 (again excluding amounts paid at only 1%).

Where Class 4 contributions are payable in addition to Class 1 and/or Class 2 contributions, the Class 4 contributions payable at the full 8% rate are restricted for 2010/11 so that they shall not exceed the excess of £3,180.00 (i.e. 53 Class 2 contributions plus maximum Class 4 contributions) over the aggregate of the Class 1 and Class 2 contributions paid at the full (i.e. other than 1%) rates.

Transfer of government departmental functions

The administrative functions of the former Contributions Agency transferred to the Inland Revenue from 1 April 1999. Responsibility for National Insurance contribution policy matters was also transferred from DSS Ministers to the Inland Revenue and Treasury Ministers on the same date. The DSS is now known as the Department for Work and Pensions (DWP). From 18 April 2005, the functions of the former Inland Revenue and former HM Customs and Excise were merged to become HM Revenue & Customs.

Peter Arrowsmith FCA is a sole practitioner specialising in National Insurance matters. He is a member and former chairman of the Employment Taxes and National Insurance Committee of the Institute of Chartered Accountants in England and Wales, and Consulting Editor to *Tolley's National Insurance Contributions 2010/11*.

Social security benefits

Peter Arrowsmith FCA summarises some of the more usual benefits that are available.

The social security benefits regime has undertaken major changes over the past decade and further changes continue.

The Pensions Act 1995 incorporated the provision for an equal state pension age of 65 for men and women to be phased in over a ten-year period beginning 6 April 2010. Certain benefits which were formerly available to men from the age of 60 are, from 6 April 2010, only available – to either sex – from the female state pension age. A table showing female state pension ages in 2010 and 2011 is given in *Socal security contributions* starting on page 741.

There are now four types of State Benefits:

• Pension age benefits (for those over female state pension age) are administered by the Pensions Service.

• Tax credits for families with children and people in work are administered by HM Revenue & Customs (formerly the Inland Revenue).

• Disability and carer benefits are administered by the Disability and Carer Benefits Scheme.

• Working age benefits (for those under female state pension age) are administered by Jobcentre Plus.

All benefit rates stated in this article are weekly amounts, except where stated otherwise.

Family benefits

Child Benefit is payable for all children who are either under 16 or under 19 and receiving full-time education at a recognised educational establishment. The rate is £20.30 for the first or eldest child and £13.40 for each subsequent child. It is payable to the person who is responsible for the child but excludes foster parents or people exempt from UK tax.

Those with little money may apply for a maternity loan or grant from the Social Fund. Those claiming Working Families Tax Credit or Disabled Person's Tax Credit can apply for a Sure Start Maternity Grant of £500 for each baby expected, born, adopted or subject to a parental order. Any savings over £500 are taken into account. This grant will only be paid on the provision of a relevant certificate from a doctor, midwife or health visitor.

A Guardian's Allowance is paid at the rate of £14.30 to people who have taken orphans into their own family. Usually both of the child's parents must be dead and at least one of them must have satisfied a residence condition. The allowance can only be paid to the person who is entitled to Child Benefit for the child (or to that person's spouse). It is not necessary to be the legal guardian. The claim should be made within three months of the date of entitlement.

Pensions

The state pension is divided into two parts – the basic pension, presently £97.65 for a single person or £156.15 for a married couple, together with any increments and/or earnings-related pension earned – and Pension Credit. The former can be claimed by men from the age of 65.

Women paying standard rate contributions into the scheme are eligible for the same amount of pension as men but until 5 April 2020 from an earlier age – rising gradually from 60 to 65. If a woman stays at home to bring up her children or to look after a person receiving Attendance Allowance she can have her basic pension rights protected without paying contributions.

Pension Credit is a separate entitlement for people of female state pension age or over. It guarantees everyone of that age an income of at least £132.60 for a single person; or £202.40 for those with a partner. ('Partner' means a spouse or a person with whom one lives as if married to them.)

People aged 65 and over will be rewarded for some of their savings and income they have for their retirement. In the past, those who had saved a little money were no better off than those who had not saved at all. Pension Credit has changed this by giving new money to those who have saved – up to £20.52 for a single person, or £27.09 for those with a partner. The person who applies for Pension Credit must be at least state pension age but their partner can be under that age.

Child Tax Credits

Child Tax Credits were introduced on 6 April 2003. To obtain them, a claim form has to be submitted (Tax Credits Form TC600 is available by telephoning 0845 366 7820).

Child Tax Credit has replaced the Children's Tax Credit previously claimed through tax paid. It is paid directly to the person who is mainly responsible for caring for the child or children.

Child Tax Credits are especially complicated for those on variable income and for the self-employed.

Working Tax Credit

Working Tax Credit is paid to support people in work and is administered by HM Revenue & Customs. It is not necessary to have paid National Insurance contributions (NICs) to qualify. People over 16 who are responsible for a child or young person and work at least 16 hours a week qualify. People without children can claim if:

- They are over 25 and work at least 30 hours a week;
- They are aged 16 or over and work at least 16 hours a week and have a disability that puts them at a disadvantage in obtaining a job;
- A person or their partner are aged 50 or more and work at least 16 hours a week and are returning to work after time spent on obtaining a qualification.

Working Tax Credit is paid as well as any Child Tax Credit entitlement. The calculations for how much a person receives are complicated and depend on how many hours he/she works and his/her income or the joint income.

Payment is now made direct by HMRC, but until 31 March 2006 employed persons generally received payment via their employer. To check eligibility to receive Working Tax Credit, telephone 0845 764 6646.

Benefits for the ill

Employees who meet certain conditions (including having average earnings of at least £97 per week) will be paid Statutory Sick Pay (SSP) by their employer. The rate is £79.15 and this can be paid for up to 28 weeks in a single or linked spells of sickness.

Employment and Support Allowance (ESA) replaced Incapacity Benefit on 27 October 2008. The contribution conditions haven't changed but a new medical test has been brought in which includes a comprehensive questionnaire. There is in addition a means-tested element to replace Income Support for the sick and disabled. ESA can be claimed by the self-employed, employees who do not qualify for SSP and those employees whose entitlement to SSP is exhausted. Incapacity benefits for existing claimants as at 27 October 2008 will be gradually replaced by ESA over forthcoming years. The rates from April 2010 are:

	£
Statutory Sick Pay	£79.15
Employment and Support Allowance	
Singe, basic allowance	
– under 25	£51.85
– 25 or over	£65.45
Components	
– suppport	£31.40
– work-related activity	£25.95
Long-term Incapacity Benefit	91.40
Short-term Incapacity Benefit	68.95
Increase of long-term Incapacity Benefit for age:	
Higher rate	15.00
Lower rate	5.80

Carer's Allowance, formerly Invalid Care Allowance, is a taxable benefit paid to people of working age who cannot take a job because they have to stay at home to look after a severely disabled person. The basic allowance is £53.90. An extra £8.10 is paid for the first dependent child and £11.35 for each subsequent child.

Disability Living Allowance

Disability Living Allowance (DLA) replaced Attendance Allowance for disabled people before they reach the age of 65, and also replaced Mobility Allowance. Those who are disabled after reaching 65 may be able to claim Attendance Allowance. The Attendance Allowance Board decide whether, and for how long, a person is eligible.

DLA is paid at different rates depending on how the disability affects the claimant. DLA is in two parts – the care component and the mobility component. It is possible to receive just one component or both.

Individual circumstances will affect how much a person can receive.

Care component	£
Highest rate	71.40
Middle rate	47.80
Lowest rate	18.95
Mobility component	
Higher rate	49.85
Lower rate	18.95

Widowed Parent's Allowance

This is a system of bereavement benefits for men and women introduced in April 2001. Women who were receiving benefits under the previous scheme are unaffected as long as they still qualify under the rules. A Widowed Parent's Allowance is a regular payment based on the late husband's or wife's contributions, and is for widows or widowers bringing up children. The main conditions for receiving this benefit are:

- You must have a dependent child or children;

• If you were over the state pension age when you were widowed you may receive Retirement Pension based on the husband's or wife's NICs;
• If the spouse died as a result of their job, it is possible to receive bereavement benefits even if they did not pay sufficient NICs;
• You cannot receive bereavement benefits if you remarry or if you live with a partner as if you are married to them.

Bereavement benefits are not affected if you work. The allowance is £97.65. There are increases for dependent children of £8.10 for the oldest child who qualifies for Child Benefit and £11.35 for each other child who qualifies.

Bereavement Payment and benefits

From 9 April 2001 bereavement benefits are payable to both widows and widowers but the weekly benefits are only paid to those aged 45 and over. Benefits are based on the NICs of the deceased. No benefit is payable if the couple were divorced at the date of death or if either of the survivors remarries or cohabits.

The widow's/widower's pension, payable for only 12 months, is £97.65 for those aged over 55 at the time of death with lesser rates applying between the ages of 45 and 55.

Widows and widowers bereaved on or after 9 April 2001 are also entitled to a tax-free Bereavement Payment of £2,000 (a one-off lump sum).

The death grant to cover funeral expenses was abolished from 6 April 1987. It has been replaced by a funeral payment from the Social Fund where the claimant is in receipt of Income Support, income-based Jobseeker's Allowance, income-based ESA, Disabled Person's Tax Credit, Working Families' Tax Credit or Housing Benefit. The full cost of a reasonable funeral is paid up to a maximum of £700.

Jobseeker's Allowance

People of working age but unemployed and actively seeking work may be able to obtain Jobseeker's Allowance (JSA). To be eligible a person must be out of work or working less than 16 hours a week on average. He/she must also be capable of working, available for work, actively seeking work and below retirement age.

Jobseeker's Allowance is not paid to people under the age of 18 or full-time students. There are exceptions – particularly if a person looks after children – so it's worth checking with the local Jobcentre Plus.

Contribution-based JSA may be received by those who have paid, or are treated as having paid, enough NICs. A flat weekly rate is paid according to the recipient's age: £51.85 for people aged 18–24 and £65.45 for those aged 25 or over. Payments may be reduced if the recipient is receiving a pension, or delayed if he/she is getting final payments from their last job.

Income-based JSA may be paid to those who haven't paid enough NICs (or have only paid contributions for self-employment), are on a low income and have little capital. The maximum weekly rates are:

Status	£
Single people aged 18–24	50.95
Single people aged 25 or over	65.45
Couples and civil partnerships (both aged 18 or over)	102.75
Lone parents	51.85 or 65.45

Those with savings of over £6,000 will receive less; and applicants with savings of over £16,000 probably won't qualify. If the applicant's partner or civil partner works 24 hours or more a week on average, income-based JSA is usually not allowed (contribution-based JSA isn't affected). If they work less than 24 hours, it may affect the amount received.

Unemployed 16- or 17-year-olds may be able to receive income-based JSA for a short period if, for example, they are forced to live away from their parents; will suffer severe hardship if they don't get JSA; or are part of a couple responsible for a child.

Statutory Maternity Pay

To help women to take time off work when they have a baby, Statutory Maternity Pay (SMP), a weekly payment from employers, may be paid. To qualify for SMP the woman must have been:

• employed by the same employer without a break for at least 26 weeks into the 15th week before the week the baby is due;

• earning an average of at least £97 a week (before tax).

Women not eligible for SMP may be able to get Maternity Allowance instead (see below). Those who do not qualify for either SMP or Maternity Allowance may be able to get some ESA or a Sure Start Maternity Grant instead if the woman or her partner or civil partner are claiming benefits or tax credits.

• SMP is 90% of the woman's average weekly earnings with no upper limit for the first six weeks of her maternity leave, and for the remaining 33 weeks either £124.88 or 90% of her average earnings, if this 90% rate is less than £124.88.

Maternity Allowance

If a woman is pregnant or has a new baby but doesn't qualify for SMP, she may be able to claim Maternity Allowance (MA). There were changes to MA that apply to women with babies due on or after 1 April 2007. A woman may be eligible for MA if:

• She is employed, but not eligible for SMP, or is registered self-employed and paying Class 2 NICs, or holds a Small Earnings Exception certificate;

• She has been at work for at least 26 weeks of the 'test period' (66 weeks prior to and including the week before her baby is due) – part weeks count as full weeks;

• She earned an average of £30 in any 13 of the weeks in the test period.

A woman who is entitled to SMP will not be eligible for MA.

MA pays a standard rate of £124.88 or 90% of the woman's average weekly earnings (before tax), whichever is the smaller. Extra money for her husband, civil partner or someone else who looks after her children may be obtained, if that person is on a very low income.

Statutory Adoption Pay

From April 2003, a person may be able to obtain Statutory Adoption Pay (SAP), which is paid by their employer to help them take time off work when adopting a child either within the UK or, in some circumstances, from overseas. The payment and its requirements are broadly equivalent to those applying to SMP, including the rate and maximum period of payment.

Statutory Paternity Pay

When a wife, partner or civil partner gives birth or adopts a child, a man may be able to obtain Statutory Paternity Pay (SPP), which is paid by his employer to help him take time off work. To qualify for SPP, all of the following must apply:

• The man must be the biological father or adopter of the child or be the mother's husband, partner or civil partner or have or expect to have responsibility for the child's upbringing;
• He must have continued to work for the same employer without a break for at least 26 weeks by the 15th week before the baby is due, or employed up to and including the week his wife, partner or civil partner was matched with a child;
• He must continue to work for that employer without a break up to the date the child is born or placed for adoption;
• He must be earning an average of at least £97 a week (before tax).

SPP is due for one or two consecutive weeks at £124.88 or 90% of his average weekly earnings if this is less.

Peter Arrowsmith FCA is a sole practitioner specialising in National Insurance matters. He is a member and former Chairman of the Employment Taxes and National Insurance Committee of the Institute of Chartered Accountants in England and Wales, and Consulting Editor to *Tolley's National Insurance Contributions 2010/11*.

Magazines by subject area

These lists can be only a broad classification. They should be regarded as a pointer to possible markets and be used with discrimination. Addresses for magazines start on page 33.

Fiction

Aesthetica Magazine
Ambit
Aquila
The Australian Women's Weekly
Best
The Black Static
Chapman
Chat
Climb Magazine
Critical Quarterly
Cyphers
The Dalhousie Review
Descant
Diva
The Dublin Review
The Edge
The Erotic Review
The Fiddlehead
Fly-Fishing & Fly-Tying
Granta
Ideas
Interzone: Science Fiction and Fantasy
Ireland's Own
Irish Pages: A Journal of Contemporary Writing
The Jewish Quarterly
Junior
Kent Life
The Lady
The London Magazine: A Review of Literature and the Arts
Lothian Life
The Malahat Review
Mayfair
More!
Mslexia
My Weekly
My Weekly Pocket Novel
Neo-opsis Science Fiction Magazine
The New Writer
New Zealand Woman's Day
The Newspaper
Overland
People's Friend
People's Friend Story CollectionPocket Novel
Planet
Pride
Prospect Magazine
Quadrant
Queen's Quarterly
Sarasvati
The Scots Magazine
Springboard
Stand Magazine
Staple
Takahe
Take a Break
that's life!
Time Out
TLS (The Times Literary Supplement)
walk
The Weekly News
Woman and Home
Woman's Day
Woman's Own
Woman's Weekly
Woman's Weekly Fiction Special
Young Writer Magazine
Your Cat Magazine
Yours

Letters to the Editor

Architecture Today
The Australian Women's Weekly
Bella
Best
The Big Issue
Bizarre
Caravan Magazine
Chat
Classics Monthly
Dolly
The Economist
Executive PA
Fairlady
Femina Magazine
FHM (For Him Magazine)
Flora International
The Furrow
H&E Naturist
Ideas
Moneywise
Mother & Baby
My Weekly
New Law Journal
New Zealand Woman's Day
Now
Nursery Education Plus
NW Magazine
People's Friend
PN Review
Practical Parenting
The Practising Midwife
Prima
Racing Post
Retail Week
Saga Magazine
Ski and Board
Television
that's life!
Third Way
TV Quick
The Weekly News
What's on TV
Woman's Day
Woman's Way
Woman's Weekly
Yours

Gossip paragraphs

The Big Issue
Bookseller & Publisher
Broadcast
Buses
Campaign
Church of England Newspaper
Classical Music
Country Life
Fairlady
Femina Magazine
FHM (For Him Magazine)
Flora International
Garden News
Geographical
Golf World
Hampshire – The County Magazine
Irish Medical Times
Irish Printer
Junior
The Lawyer
Marketing Week
Men Only
Minor Monthly
Mojo
Motor Cycle News
Music Week
My Weekly
New Welsh Review

Nursing Times
Opera Now
The Pink Paper
Pride
Radio Times
Retail Week
Rugby World
Runner's World
Running Fitness
Time Out
The Voice
World Soccer
Your Dog Magazine

Brief filler paragraphs

The Architects' Journal
The Big Issue
Bookseller & Publisher
Broadcast
Country Life
The Countryman
Decanter
Fairlady
Flight International
Flora International
The Furrow
Garden News
Geographical
Gibbons Stamp Monthly
Golf World
Greetings Today
H&E Naturist
Hampshire – The County Magazine
Insurance Age
Inuit Art Quarterly
Ireland's Own
Irish Medical Times
Irish Printer
Jane's Defence Weekly
The Lawyer
Marketing Week
Men Only
Motor Cycle News
My Weekly
New Welsh Review
Nursing Times
Opera Now
Overland
Picture Postcard Monthly
The Pink Paper
Post Magazine & Insurance Week
Pride
Radio Times
Reader's Digest
Reader's Digest (Australia)
Retail Week
Runner's World
Running Fitness
Snooker Scene
Southern Cross
Technology Ireland
The TES
Trucking
Weight Watchers Magazine
The Woodworker
World Airnews
World Fishing
World Soccer
Your Dog Magazine

Puzzles and quizzes

The following take puzzles and/or quizzes on an occasional or, in some cases, regular basis. Ideas must be tailored to suit each publication: approach in writing in the first instance.

The Australian Women's Weekly
Best of British
The Big Issue in the North
Bird Watching
Bona
The Catholic Herald
(Christchurch) The Press
Climb Magazine
Country Life
The Dandy
Executive PA
Fairlady
Farmer's Weekly
Femina Magazine
FIRE
Flora International
France
Garden and Home
Irish Medical Times
Kids Alive! (The Young Soldier)
Living and Loving
(Melbourne) Herald Sun
More!
The Newspaper
Nursing Times
Opera Now
Picture Postcard Monthly
Runner's World
Running Fitness
Scottish Home and Country
Snooker Scene
Southern Cross
The Spectator
Take a Break
Take a Break's Take a Puzzle
TLS (The Times Literary Supplement)
TV Quick
The Universe
The War Cry
Woman's Way
The Woodworker
World Soccer
Your Dog Magazine
Your Family

UK ethnic weekly newspapers

The Voice

Women's interest magazines

The Australian Women's Weekly
Bella
Best
Black Beauty & Hair
Bliss
Bona
Candis
Chat
Chatelaine
Company
Cosmopolitan
Dare
Diva
ELLE (UK)
Essentials
Executive PA
Fairlady
Femina Magazine
Full House
Glamour
Good Housekeeping
Hairflair & Beauty
Harper's Bazaar
Harper's Bazaar
Heat
Hello!
Ideas
In Style
Inside Soap
Irish Tatler
Junior
The Lady
Living and Loving
Marie Claire
More!
Mother & Baby
Mslexia
My Weekly
My Weekly Pocket Novel
New Zealand Woman's Day
Now
Nursery World
OK!
OS Magazine
People's Friend

Pick Me Up
The Pink Paper
Pride
Prima
Prima Baby
Psychologies
Real People
Red
She
Take a Break
Tatler
that's life!
U magazine
Vanity Fair
Vogue
Vogue Australia
Wedding Magazine
WI Life
Woman
Woman Alive
Woman and Home
Woman's Day
Woman's Own
Woman's Way
Woman's Weekly
Woman's Weekly Fiction Special
You & Your Wedding
Your Family

Men's interest magazines

Attitude
Country
Esquire
FHM (For Him Magazine)
Gay Times – GT
GQ
Loaded
Maxim
Mayfair
Men Only
Men's Health
The Pink Paper

Children's and young adult magazines

Aquila
The Beano
Commando
The Dandy
Dolly
Hot Press
Mizz
The Newspaper
PONY Magazine
Shout
Young Writer Magazine

Subject articles

Advertising, design, printing and publishing

Bookseller & Publisher
British Journalism Review
Campaign
Canadian Bookseller
Freelance Market News
Greetings Today
Irish Printer
Media Week
New Media Age
PR Week
Press Gazette
Slightly Foxed
Waterstone's Books Quarterly

Agriculture, farming and horticulture

Country Life
Country Smallholding
The Countryman
Dairy Farmer
Farmers Weekly
Farmer's Weekly
The Field
Irish Farmers Journal
Old Tractor
Poultry World
The Scottish Farmer
Smallholder
Vintage Tractor & Countryside Heritage

Architecture and building

The Architects' Journal
Architectural Design
The Architectural Review
Architecture Today
Blueprint
Building
Building Design
Country Homes and Interiors
Country Life
Education Journal
Homes and Gardens
Housebuilder
SelfBuild & Design

Art and collecting

AN Magazine
Apollo
Art Business Today
Art Monthly
Art Monthly Australia
The Art Newspaper
Art Quarterly
Art Review
The Artist
Artists and& Illustrators
Artlink
The Book Collector
Book and Magazine Collector
The Burlington Magazine
Ceramic Review
Coin News
Contemporary
Country Life
Craftsman craft&design Magazine
Eastern Art Report
Embroidery
Galleries
Gibbons Stamp Monthly
Green Pebble
Inuit Art Quarterly
Irish Arts Review
Leisure Painter
Medal News
RA Magazine
Stamp Magazine
TATE ETC

Aviation

Aeroplane Monthly
AIR International
Australian Flying
Aviation Business
Aviation News
Flight International
Today's Pilot
World Airnews

Business, industry and management

Business Life
Chartered Secretary
Director
Executive PA
FIRE
Fishing News
ICIS Chemical Business
Management Magazine
Management Today
OS Magazine
People Management
Restaurant Magazine
Spear's Wealth Management Survey (WMS)
Spectator Business
Ulster Business
The Woodworker

Cinema and films

Campaign
The Edge
Empire
Film Ireland
Acting Editor Nerea Aymerich
Film Review

Screen International
Sight and Sound
Total Film
TwelvePoint.com

Computers

Computer Arts
Computer Weekly
Computeractive
Custom PC
GamesMaster
MacUser
Macworld
.net
PC Advisor
PC Answers
PC Plus
PC Pro
Personal Computer World
Scientific Computing World
Smartphone & PDA Essentials
What Laptop
Windows Vista: The Official Magazine

Economics, accountancy and finance

Accountancy
Accountancy Age
Accounting & Business
Africa-Asia Confidential
Africa Confidential
African Business
The Australian Financial Review
The Banker
Contemporary Review
Economica
The Economist
Financial Adviser
Insurance Age
Insurance Brokers' Monthly
Investors Chronicle
Moneywise
Pensions World
Post Magazine & Insurance Week
Spear's Wealth Management Survey (WMS)
Taxation

Education

Aquila
Carousel – The Guide to Children's Books
Child Education PLUS
Education Journal
The Linguist
Modern Language Review
Music Teacher
Nursery Education Plus
Nursery World
Practical Parenting
Reality
Report
Right Start
Safety Education Journal
The School Librarian
The Teacher
The TES
The TESS
Times Higher Education
Under 5

Engineering and mechanics

Car Mechanics
EA Books
Electrical Review
Energy Engineering
The Engineer
Engineering in Miniature
Everyday Practical Electronics
FIRE
Model Engineer
Practical Woodworking
Rail
Railway Gazette International
Railway Magazine

Gardening

Country
Country Life
The Field
Garden and Home
Garden News
House & Garden
NZ House & Garden

Health and home

Australian Home Beautiful
Australian House and Garden
Black Beauty & Hair
British Deaf News
Candis
Classic Stitches
Country Homes and Interiors
Country Living
Garden and Home
H&E Naturist
Homes and Gardens
House & Garden
House Beautiful
Ideal Home
Ideas
Junior
Living France Magazine
Natural Health and Vegetarian Life
NZ House & Garden
Period Living
Practical Parenting
Prediction
Prima Baby
Running Fitness
Safety Education Journal
Saga Magazine
Sainsbury's Magazine
Scottish Home and Country
Slim at Home
The Vegan
Weight Watchers Magazine
The World of Interiors
Your Family
Your Home and Garden
Yours
Zest

History and archaeology

Best of British
Coin News
Geographical
History Today
The National Trust Magazine
Picture Postcard Monthly
Scottish Memories

Hotel, catering and leisure

Caterer & Hotelkeeper
Health Club Management
Inform

Humour and satire

Private Eye
Viz

Inflight magazines

Business Life
High Life

Legal and police

Criminal Law & Justice Weekly (incorporating Justice of the Peace)
Family Law Journal
The Lawyer
Legal Week
New Law Journal
Police Journal
Police Review
Solicitors' Journal

Leisure interests, pets

Astronomy Now
Bird Watching

Birdwatch
British Philatelic Bulletin
British Woodworking
Canals & Rivers
Caravan Magazine
Classic Stitches
Classics Monthly
Climber
Country Walking
Decanter
Dogs Today
Family Tree
The Field
Flora International
Folio
Gibbons Stamp Monthly
Green Pebble
Guiding Magazine
Koi
The List
Military Modelling
Mixmag
Model Boats
Motor Caravan Magazine
Motorcaravan Motorhome Monthly (MMM)
Our Dogs
Park Home & Holiday Caravan
Practical Caravan
Practical Fishkeeping
Radio Control Models and Electronics
Scottish Field
Sewing World
The Spark Magazine
Stamp Magazine
Swimming Times Magazine
TGO (The Great Outdoors) Magazine
Time Out
Venue
The Woodworker
Workbox
Your Cat Magazine
Your Dog Magazine
Your Horse

Literary (see also Poetry)

Aesthetica Magazine
The Author
The Black Static
The Book Collector
Books Ireland
Bookseller & Publisher
The Bookseller
British Journalism Review
Canadian Literature
Canadian Writer's Journal
Carousel – The Guide to Children's Books
Chapman
Contemporary Review
Critical Quarterly
The Dalhousie Review
Descant
The Dickensian
The Dublin Review
The Edge
Edinburgh Review
The Fiddlehead
Freelance
Granta
Index on Censorship
International Affairs
International Journal of Canadian Studies
Irish Pages: A Journal of Contemporary Writing
The Literary Review
LOGOS
The London Magazine: A Review of Literature and the Arts
London Review of Books
The Malahat Review
Market Newsletter
Meanjin
Modern Language Review
Mslexia
Neo-opsis Science Fiction Magazine
New Welsh Review
The New Writer
The Oldie
Orbis
Overland
Planet
Prospect Magazine
Quadrant
Queen's Quarterly
Quill & Quire
Reality
Slightly Foxed
The Spectator
Springboard
Stand Magazine
Studies, An Irish quarterly review
Takahe
TLS (The Times Literary Supplement)
Tribune
Writers' News
Writing Magazine
Young Writer Magazine

Local government and civil service

Community Care
Criminal Law & Justice Weekly (incorporating Justice of the Peace)
LGC (Local Government Chronicle)

Marketing and retailing

Accountancy
Drapers
Greetings Today
The Grocer
Marketing Week
Retail Week
Ulster Grocer

Medicine and nursing

Accountancy
Balance
BMA News
British Medical Journal
Caring Business
Disability Now
Irish Journal of Medical Science
Irish Medical Times
Journal of Alternative and Complementary Medicine
Lancet
Nursery World
Nursing Times
The Practising Midwife
The Practitioner
Pulse

Military

Jane's Defence Weekly
RUSI Journal

Motor transport and cycling

Auto Express
Autocar
Back Street Heroes
Bike
Buses
Car
Car
Car Mechanics
Classic Cars
Classics Monthly
Commercial Motor
Custom Car
Cycling Weekly
Minor Monthly
Motor Cycle News
Truck & Driver
Trucking
Vintage Tractor & Countryside Heritage
What Car?

Music and recording

Brass Band World Magazine
Classic Rock
Classical Music
Early Music
Hi-Fi News
Kerrang!
Mojo
Music Teacher
Music Week
Musical Opinion
Musical Times
New Musical Express (NME)
Opera
Opera Now
Q Magazine
Record Collector
The Songwriter
Songwriting and Composing
The Strad
Tempo

Natural history

Australian Heritage
Bird Watching
Birding World
Birdwatch
British Birds
Cat World
The Ecologist
Geographical
The National Trust Magazine
Natural World
Naturalist
Nature
Our Dogs

Nautical and marine

Australian Powerboat
Canals & Rivers
Classic Boat Magazine
Diver
Motor Boat and Yachting
Motor Boats Monthly
Nautical Magazine
Practical Boat Owner
Sea Breezes
Ships Monthly
Waterways World
Yachting Monthly
Yachting World
Yachts and Yachting

Photography

Amateur Photographer
Australian Photography
The British Journal of Photography
Camera
Digital Camera Buyer
Market Newsletter
Photo Life
Practical Photography
Professional Photographer

Poetry

Some magazines only take the occasional poem. Check with the Editor before submitting.

Acumen Literary Journal
Aesthetica Magazine
Agenda
Ambit
Assent
Chapman
Cordite Poetry Review
Critical Quarterly
Cumbria Magazine
Cyphers
The Dalhousie Review
The Dawntreader
Descant
Edinburgh Review
Envoi
The Fiddlehead
HQ Poetry Magazine
Irish Pages: A Journal of Contemporary Writing
The Literary Review
The London Magazine: A Review of Literature and the Arts
London Review of Books
The Malahat Review
Meanjin
New Welsh Review
Orbis
Other Poetry
Overland
Planet
PN Review
Poetry Ireland Review/Éigse Éireann
Poetry London
Poetry Review
Poetry Wales
Pride
Quadrant
Queen's Quarterly
Reach Poetry
The Rialto
Sarasvati
The Shop: A Magazine of Poetry
Springboard
Stand Magazine
Staple
Takahe
Young Writer Magazine

Politics

Africa-Asia Confidential
Africa Confidential
Australian Journal of Politics and History
Contemporary Review
Criminal Law & Justice Weekly (incorporating Justice of the Peace)
Fortnight – An Independent Review of Politics and the Arts
Green Futures
Inspire Magazine, CPO
International Affairs
New Internationalist
New Statesman
Peace News
The Political Quarterly
Prospect Magazine
Red Pepper
Studies, An Irish quarterly review
Tribune
The Week
The World Today

Radio, TV and DVD

Broadcast
Campaign
Empire
Film Review
GamesMaster
Hi-Fi News
InterMedia
Opera Now
Practical Wireless
Radio Times
The Stage
Television
TV Quick
TVTimes Magazine
What's on TV

Religion, philosophy and New Age

Africa: St Patrick's Missions
Baptist Times
The Catholic Herald
Catholic Pictorial
Catholic Times
Church of England Newspaper
Church Times
Contemporary Review
The Dawntreader
Families First
Fortean Times
The Friend
The Furrow

Home Words
Inspire Magazine, CPO
Jewish Chronicle
The Jewish Quarterly
Jewish Telegraph
Kids Alive! (The Young Soldier)
Life & Work: Editorially Independent Magazine of the Church of Scotland
Methodist Recorder
New Humanist
Reality
Reform
The Sign
Southern Cross
Studies, An Irish quarterly review
The Tablet
Third Way
The Universe
The War Cry
Woman Alive

Rural life and country

Cambridgeshire Journal
Country
Country Life
The Countryman
Cumbria Magazine
Dalesman
Derbyshire Life and Countryside
Dorset Life – The Dorset Magazine
East Lothian Life
Essex Life
Evergreen
The Field
Hampshire – The County Magazine
Hertfordshire Countryside
Kent Life
Lancashire Magazine
Lincolnshire Life
Lothian Life
The National Trust Magazine
The Scots Magazine
Scottish Field
Scottish Home and Country
Shooting Times and Country Magazine
The Shropshire Magazine
Staffordshire Life Magazine
This England
Yorkshire Ridings Magazine

Sciences

Geological Magazine
Nature
New Scientist
Scientific Computing World
Technology Ireland

Sports and games

Angler's Mail
Angling Times
Athletics Weekly
Australian Powerboat
Bowls International
Climb Magazine
Cycle Sport
Darts World
Descent
Eventing
The Field
Fly-Fishing & Fly-Tying
FourFourTwo
GamesMaster
Golf Monthly
Golf World
Horse & Hound
Horse and Rider
MBUK (Mountain Biking UK)
Our Dogs
Outdoor Canada
Racing Post
Rock
Rugby World
Runner's World
Running Fitness
Sea Angler
Shooting Times and Country Magazine
Ski and Board
The Skier and Snowboarder Magazine
Snooker Scene
The Squash Player
Swimming Times Magazine
TGO (The Great Outdoors) Magazine
Today's Golfer
Total Off-Road
Trail
Trout and Salmon
The Wisden Cricketer
World Fishing
World Soccer

Theatre, drama and dancing (see also Cinema and films, Music and recording)

AS Magazine
Canadian Screenwriter
Dance Australia
Dance Today
Dancing Times
New Theatre Quarterly
Radio Times
The Stage
Tribune
TVTimes Magazine

Travel and geography

Australian Geographic
Australian Heritage
Caravan Magazine
Condé Nast Traveller
France
Geographical
Geographical Journal
Living France Magazine
Traveller
Traveltalk
Wanderlust
Wild
The Witness

Publishers of fiction

Addresses for *Book publishers UK and Ireland* start on page 136.

Adventure/thrillers

Bantam
Bantam Press
Black Ace Books
Black Swan
Blackstaff Press Ltd
Bloomsbury Publishing Plc
Chatto & Windus (imprint)
Constable & Robinson Ltd
Faber and Faber Ltd
Fourth Estate (imprint)
Hachette UK
Robert Hale Ltd
Harlequin Mills & Boon Ltd
Headline Publishing Group
Honno Ltd (Welsh Women's Press)
Hutchinson (imprint)
Little, Brown Book Group
Macmillan Publishers Ltd
Mentor Books
John Murray (Publishers)
The Orion Publishing Group Ltd
Penguin Group (UK)
Piatkus (division)
The Random House Group Ltd
Seafarer Books Ltd
Time Warner
Transworld Publishers
Vintage
Virago
The X Press

Crime/mystery/suspense

Allison & Busby Ltd
Arcadia Books Ltd
Arrow Books Ltd
Bantam
Bantam Press
Black Ace Books
Black Swan
Blackstaff Press Ltd
Bloomsbury Publishing Plc
Constable & Robinson Ltd
Corgi
Creme de la Crime
Euro Crime (imprint)
Everyman's Library
Faber and Faber Ltd
Flambard Press
Fourth Estate (imprint)
Hachette UK
Robert Hale Ltd
Hamish Hamilton
HarperCollins Publishers
William Heinemann
Honno Ltd (Welsh Women's Press)
Hutchinson
Hutchinson (imprint)
Michael Joseph
Little, Brown Book Group
Macmillan (imprint)
Macmillan Publishers Ltd
Mentor Books
Michael Joseph (commercial division)
No Exit Press (imprint)
Michael O'Mara Books Ltd
The Orion Publishing Group Ltd
Pan (imprint)
Penguin Group (UK)
Piatkus (division)
Polygon
The Random House Group Ltd
Sceptre
Seren
Serpent's Tail (imprint)
Severn House Publishers
Time Warner
Transworld Publishers
Viking
Vintage
Virago
The Women's Press
The X Press

Erotic

Black Lace
Honno Ltd (Welsh Women's Press)
Nexus
The Women's Press

Ethnic

Allison & Busby Ltd
Arcadia Books Ltd
BlackAmber (imprint)
Chapman Publishing
Honno Ltd (Welsh Women's Press)
Mango Publishing
The Women's Press
The X Press

Gay/lesbian

Arcadia Books Ltd
Bantam
Black Swan
Marion Boyars Publishers Ltd
Chapman Publishing
Corgi
Fourth Estate (imprint)
Hamish Hamilton
HarperCollins Publishers
Hodder & Stoughton
Little, Brown Book Group
Macmillan Publishers Ltd
Michael O'Mara Books Ltd
Onlywomen Press Ltd
Penguin Group (UK)
Polygon
Sceptre
Serpent's Tail (imprint)
Time Warner
Vintage
Virago
The Women's Press

General

Abacus
Allison & Busby Ltd
Arcadia Books Ltd
Authentic Media Ltd
Bantam
Bantam Press
Black Ace Books
Black Swan
Blackstaff Press Ltd
Bliss Books (imprint)
Bloomsbury Publishing Plc
Marion Boyars Publishers Ltd
Canongate Books Ltd
Jonathan Cape (imprint)
Century
Chapman Publishing
Cló Iar-Chonnachta Teo.
Corgi
Crescent Moon Publishing
Doubleday (UK)
11:9 (imprint)
Faber and Faber Ltd
Fourth Estate (imprint)
The Gallery Press
Garnet Publishing Ltd
Halban Publishers
Robert Hale Ltd

Hamish Hamilton
Harlequin Mills & Boon Ltd
HarperCollins Publishers
William Heinemann
Hodder & Stoughton
Honno Ltd (Welsh Women's Press)
Hothouse Fiction Ltd
Hutchinson
Michael Joseph
Little, Brown Book Group
Macmillan (imprint)
Macmillan Publishers Ltd
The Maia Press Ltd
Mentor Books
Methuen Publishing Ltd
Michael Joseph (commercial division)
NB Publishers (Pty) Ltd
New Island Books
The Oleander Press
Michael O'Mara Books Ltd
Oneworld Classics/Calder Publications
The Orion Publishing Group Ltd
Pan (imprint)
Paperbooks Publishing Ltd
Piatkus (division)
Pipers' Ash Ltd
Pocket Books
Pocket Books (imprint)
Pomona Books
Poolbeg Press Ltd
Preface Publishing (imprint)
The Random House Group Ltd
Route
Sceptre
SCP Publishers Ltd
Seren
Serpent's Tail (imprint)
Severn House Publishers
Simon & Schuster UK Ltd
Time Warner
Transworld Publishers
Troubador Publishing Ltd
Viking
Vintage
Virago
The Women's Press
Y Lolfa Cyf.

Graphic

Jonathan Cape (imprint)
Classical Comics
Titan Books

Historical

Allison & Busby Ltd
Bantam
Bantam Press
Birlinn Ltd
Black Ace Books
Blackstaff Press Ltd
Chapman Publishing
Constable & Robinson Ltd
Doubleday (UK)
Everyman's Library
Flambard Press
Fourth Estate (imprint)
Robert Hale Ltd
Harlequin Mills & Boon Ltd
HarperCollins Publishers
William Heinemann
Honno Ltd (Welsh Women's Press)
Hutchinson
Imperial War Museum
Michael Joseph
The Lilliput Press Ltd
Little, Brown Book Group
Macmillan Publishers Ltd
Mentor Books
Michael Joseph (commercial division)
O-Books Publishing Ltd
The Oleander Press
Penguin Group (UK)
Piatkus (division)
Sceptre
SCP Publishers Ltd
Severn House Publishers
Time Warner
Transworld Publishers
Vintage
Virago
The Women's Press

Horror

Black Ace Books
Gold Eagle Books (imprint)
Mentor Books
Snowbooks Ltd
Titan Books

Humour

Allison & Busby Ltd
Authentic Media Ltd
Black Swan
Corgi
Everyman's Library
Little, Brown Book Group
Methuen Publishing Ltd
The Oleander Press
Michael O'Mara Books Ltd
The Orion Publishing Group Ltd
Piccadilly Press
Transworld Publishers
The Women's Press

Literary

Abacus
Allison & Busby Ltd
Alma Books
Arcadia Books Ltd
Atlantic Books
Authentic Media Ltd
Bantam
Bantam Press
Black Ace Books
Black Swan
Blackstaff Press Ltd
Bloomsbury Publishing Plc
Marion Boyars Publishers Ltd
Canongate Books Ltd
Jonathan Cape (imprint)
Cassell Reference
Chapman Publishing
Chatto & Windus (imprint)
Constable & Robinson Ltd
Corgi
Crescent Moon Publishing
Dedalus Ltd
Doubleday (UK)
Enitharmon Press/Enitharmon Editions
Everyman's Library
Faber and Faber Ltd
Flambard Press
Fourth Estate (imprint)
Gomer Press
Granta Publications
Halban Publishers
Robert Hale Ltd
Hamish Hamilton
HarperCollins Publishers
Harvill Secker
Headline Publishing Group
William Heinemann
Hodder & Stoughton
Honno Ltd (Welsh Women's Press)
Hutchinson
The Lilliput Press Ltd
Little, Brown Book Group
Macmillan Publishers Ltd
Mentor Books
The Mercier Press
Methuen Publishing Ltd
John Murray (Publishers)
Myriad Editions
New Beacon Books
The Oleander Press
Oneworld Classics/Calder Publications
Peter Owen Publishers
Penguin Group (UK)
Piatkus (division)
Picador (imprint)
Polygon

Portobello Books Ltd
Quercus Publishing Plc
The Random House Group Ltd
Sceptre
SCP Publishers Ltd
Seren
Serpent's Tail (imprint)
Simon & Schuster UK Ltd
Time Warner
Transworld Publishers
Viking
Vintage
Virago
Wordsworth Editions Ltd
The X Press

New/experimental

Canongate Books Ltd
Chapman Publishing
Crescent Moon Publishing
Faber and Faber Ltd
Flambard Press
Honno Ltd (Welsh Women's Press)
Oneworld Classics/Calder Publications
Paperbooks Publishing Ltd
Polygon
Seren
Serpent's Tail (imprint)

Romantic

Avon
Bantam
Bantam Press
Black Swan
Blackstaff Press Ltd
Corgi
Doubleday (UK)
Gill & Macmillan Ltd
Hachette UK
Harlequin Mills & Boon Ltd
William Heinemann
Historical™ (imprint)
Honno Ltd (Welsh Women's Press)
Little, Brown Book Group
Macmillan (imprint)
Macmillan Publishers Ltd
Medical™ (imprint)
Mentor Books
Michael Joseph (commercial division)
Pan (imprint)
Piatkus (division)
The Random House Group Ltd
Severn House Publishers
Silhouette®
Transworld Publishers

Science fiction

Angry Robot (imprint)
Arrow Books Ltd
Bantam
Bantam Press
Black Swan
Corgi
Gollancz
Gollancz (imprint)
Hachette UK
HarperCollins Publishers
Honno Ltd (Welsh Women's Press)
Little, Brown Book Group
Macmillan Publishers Ltd
Orbit
The Orion Publishing Group Ltd
Penguin Group (UK)
Pipers' Ash Ltd
The Random House Group Ltd
Simon & Schuster UK Ltd
Snowbooks Ltd
Tor (imprint)
Transworld Publishers
Voyager (imprint)
The Women's Press

Short stories

Chapman Publishing
Cló Iar-Chonnachta Teo.
Everyman's Library
Faber and Faber Ltd
Flambard Press
Fourth Estate (imprint)
Granta Publications
Hamish Hamilton
William Heinemann
Honno Ltd (Welsh Women's Press)
The Lilliput Press Ltd
Macmillan Publishers Ltd
Methuen Publishing Ltd
The Octagon Press Ltd
Penguin Group (UK)
Pipers' Ash Ltd
Polygon
The Random House Group Ltd
Route
SCP Publishers Ltd
Seren
Transworld Publishers
The Women's Press
Y Lolfa Cyf.

Teenage/young adult

Andersen Press Ltd
The Chicken House
Dref Wen
Egmont Books
Faber and Faber Ltd
David Fickling Books (imprint)
Floris Books
Hachette Children's Books
HarperCollins Children's Books
Livewire (imprint)
Mantra Lingua
Mentor Books
Orion Children's Books (division)
Piccadilly Press
Poolbeg Press Ltd
Razorbill (imprint)
Scholastic Children's Books (division)
Walker Books Ltd
Young Picador (imprint)

Translations

Alma Books
Arcadia Books Ltd
Canongate Books Ltd
Chapman Publishing
Cló Iar-Chonnachta Teo.
Dedalus Ltd
Enitharmon Press/Enitharmon Editions
Everyman's Library
Faber and Faber Ltd
Flambard Press
Gomer Press
Halban Publishers
Harvill Secker
Honno Ltd (Welsh Women's Press)
NB Publishers (Pty) Ltd
The Oleander Press
Oneworld Classics/Calder Publications
The Orion Publishing Group Ltd
Pipers' Ash Ltd
Portobello Books Ltd
Pushkin Press
Seren
Serpent's Tail (imprint)
The Women's Press

War

Little, Brown Book Group
Oneworld Classics/Calder Publications
The Orion Publishing Group Ltd
Severn House Publishers
Transworld Publishers
Ulric Publishing

Westerns

Robert Hale Ltd

Publishers of non-fiction

Addresses for *Book publishers UK and Ireland* start on page 136.

Academic and professional

Addison-Wesley (imprint)
Allyn & Bacon (imprint)
Ashgate Publishing Ltd
BIOS Scientific Publishers
Bloomsbury Academic (imprint of A&C Black)
Brilliant Publications
Cambridge University Press
Paul Chapman Publishing (imprint)
Chartered Institute of Personnel and Development
James Clarke & Co. Ltd
The Continuum International Publishing Group Ltd
Cork University Press
Council for British Archaeology
CRC Press (imprint)
John Donald (imprint)
University College Dublin Press
Gerald Duckworth & Co. Ltd
Dunedin Academic Press
Earthscan
Edinburgh University Press
Éditions Aubrey Walter/Gay Men's Press
The Educational Company of Ireland
Elsevier Ltd
Elsevier Ltd (Butterworth Heinemann)
Elsevier Ltd (Health Sciences)
University of Exeter Press
Four Courts Press
FT Prentice Hall (imprint)
Garland Science (imprint)
Harcourt (imprint)
ICSA Information & Training Ltd
Institute of Public Administration
Irish Academic Press Ltd
Ithaca Press (imprint)
Jane's Information Group
Peter Lang Ltd
Liverpool University Press
McGraw-Hill Education
Management Books 2000 Ltd
Manchester University Press
Manson Publishing Ltd
NCVO Publications
New Rider (imprint)
Oxford University Press
Palgrave Macmillan (division)
Policy Studies Institute (PSI)
Polity Press
Portland Press Ltd
Prentice Hall (imprint)
Princeton University Press – Europe
Psychology Press
RBI Search
William Reed Directories
Routledge (imprint)
SAGE Publications Ltd
SAMS Publishing (imprint)
Scholastic Educational Resources (division)
SCM Press (imprint)
Sussex Academic Press
Tauris Academic Studies (imprint)
Taylor & Francis (imprint)
Taylor and Francis Group
Trentham Books Ltd
TSO (The Stationery Office)
V&A Publishing
Veritas Publications
Virtue Books Ltd
University of Wales Press
Welsh Academic Press
John Wiley & Sons Ltd
Wiley-Blackwell
WLR Media & Entertainment
Yale University Press London

Agriculture, farming and horticulture

Think Books
Whittet Books Ltd

Animals and birds

J.A. Allen
Arris Publishing Ltd
A&C Black Publishers Ltd
The Crowood Press
David & Charles Ltd
Christopher Helm (imprint)
Kenilworth Press (imprint)
New Holland Publishers (UK) Ltd
Open Gate Press
Pica Press (imprint)
T & AD Poyser (imprint)
Think Books
Whittet Books Ltd

Archaeology

Ashmolean Museum Publications
Birlinn Ltd
Boydell & Brewer Ltd
British Museum Company Ltd
Cambridge University Press
Council for British Archaeology
University of Exeter Press
Logaston Press
Routledge (imprint)
Shire Publications
Souvenir Press Ltd
I.B.Tauris & Co. Ltd
Thames & Hudson Ltd
Weidenfeld & Nicolson Illustrated

Architecture and building

Antique Collectors' Club Ltd
Ashgate Publishing Ltd
Black Dog Publishing London UK
Giles de la Mare Publishers Ltd
The Dovecote Press Ltd
Garnet Publishing Ltd
Laurence King Publishing Ltd
Frances Lincoln Ltd
Lund Humphries (imprint)
Manchester University Press
Merrell Publishers Ltd
Oxford University Press
Prestel Publishing Ltd
Quiller Press (imprint)
Reaktion Books
River Books (associate imprint)
Scala Publishers
Sheldrake Press
Spon (imprint)
Taschen UK Ltd
Tauris Parke Books (imprint)
Thames & Hudson Ltd
V&A Publishing
Weidenfeld & Nicolson Illustrated
Yale University Press London

Art and craft

a-n The Artists Information Company
Anness Publishing
Aquamarine (hardback imprint)
Ashgate Publishing Ltd
Aurum Press Ltd

Batsford (imprint)
A&C Black Publishers Ltd
Black Dog Publishing London UK
Booth-Clibborn Editions
Cico Books (imprint)
Collins & Brown (imprint)
Collins Reference (division and imprint)
The Crowood Press
David & Charles Ltd
Floris Books
Guild of Master Craftsman Publications Ltd
Halsgrove Publishing
The Herbert Press (imprint)
Frances Lincoln Ltd
Lorenz Books (hardback imprint)
Mitchell Beazley (imprint)
Murdoch Books UK Ltd
New Holland Publishers (UK) Ltd
Pavilion (imprint)
Quadrille Publishing
The Quarto Group, Inc.
Salamander (imprint)
Search Press Ltd
Weidenfeld & Nicolson Illustrated

Astronomy

Canopus Publishing Ltd
National Maritime Museum Publishing
Philip's (imprint)

Aviation

Ian Allan Publishing Ltd
Arcadia Books Ltd
Classic Publications (imprint)
Conway (inc. Brasseys Military, Putnam Aeronautical)
The Crowood Press
Grub Street Publishing
Jane's Information Group
Midland Publishing (imprint)
Osprey Publishing Ltd
Pen & Sword Books Ltd

Bibliography

Bowker
The British Library (Publications)
CBD Research Ltd

Biography, autobiography and memoir

Anvil Books/The Children's Press
Arcadia Books Ltd
Atlantic Books
Attic Press and Atrium (imprints)
Aureus Publishing Ltd
Aurum Press Ltd
Bantam Press (imprint)
Black & White Publishing Ltd
Blackstaff Press Ltd
John Blake Publishing Ltd
Bloomsbury Publishing UK (imprint)
The Bodley Head (imprint)
Marion Boyars Publishers Ltd
Brandon/Mount Eagle Publications
Canongate Books Ltd
Jonathan Cape (imprint)
Century (imprint)
Chatto & Windus (imprint)
James Clarke & Co. Ltd
Constable (imprint)
Giles de la Mare Publishers Ltd
André Deutsch (division)
Ebury Press (imprint)
Fourth Estate (imprint)
Free Press (imprint)
Gibson Square
Gill & Macmillan Ltd
Granta Publications
Halban Publishers
Hamish Hamilton (imprint)
HarperCollins (imprint)
HarperTrue (imprint)
Haus Publishing Ltd
Headline Publishing Group
Hodder & Stoughton
Hutchinson (imprint)
Independent Music Press
William Heinemann (imprint)
The Lilliput Press Ltd
Little, Brown (division)
Lutterworth Press (subsidiary)
Mainstream Publishing Co. (Edinburgh) Ltd
Mandrake of Oxford
Mentor Books
Methuen Publishing Ltd
Michael Joseph (commercial division)
Milo Books Ltd
Monarch Books
Morrigan Book Company
Murdoch Books UK Ltd
John Murray (Publishers)
New Island Books
Nonsuch (imprint)
The O'Brien Press Ltd
Michael O'Mara Books Ltd
Omnibus Press/Music Sales Ltd
Oneworld Classics/Calder Publications
Peter Owen Publishers
Oxford University Press
Pan Macmillan (division)
Pimlico (imprint)
Pipers' Ash Ltd
Plexus Publishing Ltd
Pomona Books
Politico's Publishing (imprint)
Profile Books Ltd
Quiller Press (imprint)
Rider (imprint)
Robson Books (imprint)
Salt Publishing
Serpent's Tail (imprint)
Shepheard-Walwyn (Publishers) Ltd
Sigma Press
Souvenir Press Ltd
Square Peg (imprint)
I.B.Tauris & Co. Ltd
Tauris Parke Paperbacks (imprint)
Veritas Publications
Virgin (imprint)
Weidenfeld & Nicolson
Welsh Academic Press
The Women's Press
Yale University Press London

Business, industry and management

Ashgate Publishing Ltd
Bantam Press (imprint)
Nicholas Brealey Publishing
CBD Research Ltd
Crown House Publishing Ltd
Edward Elgar Publishing Ltd
ELM Publications and Training
Euromonitor International plc
FT Prentice Hall (imprint)
Gower (imprint)
Jordan Publishing Ltd
Kogan Page Ltd
McGraw-Hill Education
Management Books 2000 Ltd
NCVO Publications
Oak Tree Press
Pan Macmillan (division)
Portfolio (imprint)
Profile Books Ltd
Random House Books (imprint)
William Reed Directories
Routledge (imprint)
Spon (imprint)
TSO (The Stationery Office)
Wharton (imprint)
Wiley-Blackwell
WLR Media & Entertainment
Wolters Kluwer (UK) Ltd
Woodhead Publishing Ltd

Cartography/maps

AA Publishing
Bodleian Library Publishing

The British Library (Publications)
Collins Geo (division and imprint)
Collins Reference (division and imprint)
Thomas Cook Publishing
Discovery Walking Guides Ltd
Everyman's Library
HarperCollins Publishers
Michelin Maps and Guides
Myriad Editions
Philip's (imprint)

Computers and computing

Brady (division)
McGraw-Hill Education
Osborne (imprint)
Peachpit Press (imprint)
QUE Publishing (imprint)
The Reader's Digest Association Ltd
SAMS Publishing (imprint)
Springer-Verlag London Ltd

Cookery, food and drink

Absolute Press
The Angels' Share (imprint)
Anness Publishing
Aquamarine (hardback imprint)
Attic Press and Atrium (imprints)
Duncan Baird Publishers
Bantam Press (imprint)
Berg Publishers
Black & White Publishing Ltd
Blackstaff Press Ltd
John Blake Publishing Ltd
Marion Boyars Publishers Ltd
Kyle Cathie Ltd
Collins & Brown (imprint)
Collins Reference (division and imprint)
Conran Octopus (imprint)
André Deutsch (division)
Dorling Kindersley (division)
Ebury Press (imprint)
Elliott & Thompson
Flame Tree Publishing
W. Foulsham & Co. Ltd
Gill & Macmillan Ltd
Grub Street Publishing
Hamlyn (imprint)
Headline Publishing Group
Hodder & Stoughton
Igloo Books Ltd
Lorenz Books (hardback imprint)
Michael Joseph (commercial division)
Mitchell Beazley (imprint)
Murdoch Books UK Ltd
National Trust (imprint)
New Holland Publishers (UK) Ltd
On Stream Publications Ltd
Pan Macmillan (division)
Pavilion (imprint)
Prion Books (division)
Quadrille Publishing
The Quarto Group, Inc.
Quiller Press (imprint)
The Reader's Digest Association Ltd
Right Way (imprint)
Ryland Peters & Small
Salamander (imprint)
Sheldrake Press
Square Peg (imprint)
Telegraph Books
Transworld Sport & Entertainment (imprint)
Weidenfeld & Nicolson Illustrated
Which? Books (imprint)

Crime

Bantam Press (imprint)
Black & White Publishing Ltd
John Blake Publishing Ltd
Century (imprint)
Mainstream Publishing Co. (Edinburgh) Ltd
Mandrake of Oxford
Mentor Books
Milo Books Ltd
NWP (imprint)
The O'Brien Press Ltd
The Policy Press
Routledge-Cavendish (imprint)
Routledge (imprint)
Virgin (imprint)

Cultural studies

Attic Press and Atrium (imprints)
Berg Publishers
Marion Boyars Publishers Ltd
Nicholas Brealey Publishing
British Museum Company Ltd
Crescent Moon Publishing
Edinburgh University Press
Free Association Books
Gibson Square
Lawrence & Wishart Ltd
Manchester University Press
Phaidon Press Ltd
Pluto Press
Polity Press
Prestel Publishing Ltd
Random House Books (imprint)
Reaktion Books
Rivers Oram Press
I.B.Tauris & Co. Ltd
Tauris Parke Books (imprint)
Tauris Parke Paperbacks (imprint)
Thames & Hudson Ltd
Verso Ltd

Current affairs

Atlantic Books
The Bodley Head (imprint)
Brandon/Mount Eagle Publications
Jonathan Cape (imprint)
Chatto & Windus (imprint)
Constable (imprint)
André Deutsch (division)
Fabian Society
Fourth Estate (imprint)
Free Press (imprint)
Gibson Square
Gill & Macmillan Ltd
Hamish Hamilton (imprint)
Harvill Secker (imprint)
Hutchinson (imprint)
Lawrence & Wishart Ltd
Mainstream Publishing Co. (Edinburgh) Ltd
The Mercier Press
Milo Books Ltd
New Island Books
Oneworld Publications
Oxford University Press
Poolbeg Press Ltd
Politico's Publishing (imprint)
Portobello Books Ltd
Profile Books Ltd
Random House Books (imprint)
Rider (imprint)
Rivers Oram Press
Serpent's Tail (imprint)
South Street Press (imprint)
I.B.Tauris & Co. Ltd
TSO (The Stationery Office)
Verso Ltd
Weidenfeld & Nicolson
Yale University Press London

Design

Antique Collectors' Club Ltd
Berg Publishers
Black Dog Publishing London UK
Booth-Clibborn Editions
Kyle Cathie Ltd
Flame Tree Publishing
The Ilex Press Ltd
Laurence King Publishing Ltd
Frances Lincoln Ltd
Manchester University Press
Merrell Publishers Ltd
New Rider (imprint)

Prestel Publishing Ltd
Reaktion Books
RotoVision
Taschen UK Ltd
Tauris Parke Books (imprint)
Thames & Hudson Ltd
V&A Publishing
Weidenfeld & Nicolson Illustrated

Economics, accountancy and finance

The Bodley Head (imprint)
Nicholas Brealey Publishing
Butterworths (imprint)
Edward Elgar Publishing Ltd
Fabian Society
W.H. Freeman (imprint)
Institute of Public Administration
Kogan Page Ltd
LexisNexis
McGraw-Hill Education
W.W. Norton & Company
Oxford University Press
Pluto Press
Princeton University Press – Europe
Routledge (imprint)
Tolley (imprint)
Verso Ltd
Yale University Press London

Education

BBC Active (imprint)
Brilliant Publications
Cambridge University Press
Paul Chapman Publishing (imprint)
Colourpoint Books
Crown House Publishing Ltd
Benjamin Cummings (imprint)
Dref Wen
The Educational Company of Ireland
Educational Explorers (Publishers)
Evans Publishing Group
Fabian Society
CJ Fallon
First and Best in Education
Flame Tree Publishing
Folens Publishers
Folens Publishers
David Fulton (imprint)
Gill & Macmillan Ltd
GL Assessment
Harcourt (imprint)
Hodder Education Group
Hodder Gibson
Hopscotch Educational Publishing Ltd
Kingscourt (imprint)
Jessica Kingsley Publishers
Kogan Page Ltd
Letts and Lonsdale
Longman (imprint)
Lutterworth Press (subsidiary)
McGraw-Hill Education
Macmillan Education Ltd (division)
Mentor Books
Nelson Thornes Ltd
Northcote House Publishers Ltd
Oxford University Press
Pearson UK
Prentice Hall (imprint)
Scholastic Educational Resources (division)
Souvenir Press Ltd
Step Forward Publishing Ltd
Trentham Books Ltd
Welsh Academic Press
Wolters Kluwer (UK) Ltd
ZigZag Education

Engineering and mechanics

Bernard Babani (publishing) Ltd
Cambridge University Press
CRC Press (imprint)
Osborne (imprint)
Spon (imprint)
Springer-Verlag London Ltd
Woodhead Publishing Ltd

Environment and development

Earthscan
Eden (imprint)
Green Books
Green Print (imprint)
Frances Lincoln Ltd
Oneworld Publications
Open Gate Press
Pluto Press
Routledge (imprint)
Alastair Sawday Publishing Ltd
Virgin (imprint)
Zed Books Ltd

Fashion

Antique Collectors' Club Ltd
Aurum Press Ltd
Batsford (imprint)
Berg Publishers
Laurence King Publishing Ltd
Thames & Hudson Ltd
V&A Publishing
Weidenfeld & Nicolson Illustrated

Film and cinema

Arrow Books Ltd (imprint)
Aurum Press Ltd
Batsford (imprint)
Berg Publishers
BFI Publishing
Marion Boyars Publishers Ltd
The Continuum International Publishing Group Ltd
Crescent Moon Publishing
Dorling Kindersley (division)
University of Exeter Press
Faber and Faber Ltd
Kamera (imprint)
Methuen Publishing Ltd
Pan Macmillan (division)
Plexus Publishing Ltd
Reaktion Books
Reynolds & Hearn Ltd
Roundhouse Group
Taschen UK Ltd
I.B.Tauris & Co. Ltd
Tauris Parke Paperbacks (imprint)
Time Out (imprint, in partnership with Time Out Group)
Titan Books
Virgin (imprint)
Wallflower Press

Fine art and antiques

Antique Collectors' Club Ltd
Ashmolean Museum Publications
Bodleian Library Publishing
Boydell & Brewer Ltd
British Museum Company Ltd
Cambridge University Press
Co & Bear Productions
Giles de la Mare Publishers Ltd
Richard Dennis Publications
André Deutsch (division)
Éditions Aubrey Walter/Gay Men's Press
Flame Tree Publishing
Four Courts Press
Garnet Publishing Ltd
Gibson Square
The Goldsmith Press Ltd
Goss & Crested China Club
Hilmarton Manor Press
Laurence King Publishing Ltd
Frances Lincoln Ltd
Liverpool University Press
Lund Humphries (imprint)
Lutterworth Press (subsidiary)
Manchester University Press
Mandrake of Oxford
Merrell Publishers Ltd
Miller's (imprint)

Mitchell Beazley (imprint)
New Cavendish Books
Oneworld Classics/Calder Publications
Peter Owen Publishers
Phaidon Press Ltd
Prestel Publishing Ltd
Reaktion Books
River Books (associate imprint)
Royal Collection Publications
Scala Publishers
Stacey International
Taschen UK Ltd
Tate Publishing
I.B.Tauris & Co. Ltd
Tauris Parke Paperbacks (imprint)
Thames & Hudson Ltd
Unicorn Press
V&A Publishing
Philip Wilson Publishers Ltd
Yale University Press London

Gardening

Anness Publishing
Antique Collectors' Club Ltd
Aquamarine (hardback imprint)
Batsford (imprint)
Cassell Illustrated (imprint)
Kyle Cathie Ltd
Collins & Brown (imprint)
Collins Reference (division and imprint)
Conran Octopus (imprint)
The Crowood Press
David & Charles Ltd
Dorling Kindersley (division)
Expert Books (imprint)
W. Foulsham & Co. Ltd
Hamlyn (imprint)
Headline Publishing Group
Frances Lincoln Ltd
Lorenz Books (hardback imprint)
Mitchell Beazley (imprint)
Murdoch Books UK Ltd
National Trust (imprint)
New Holland Publishers (UK) Ltd
Pan Macmillan (division)
Pavilion (imprint)
Quadrille Publishing
Quiller Press (imprint)
The Reader's Digest Association Ltd
Right Way (imprint)
Ryland Peters & Small
Salamander (imprint)
Telegraph Books
Thames & Hudson Ltd
Think Books
Weidenfeld & Nicolson Illustrated

Gender studies and gay and lesbian

Arcadia Books Ltd
Attic Press and Atrium (imprints)
Crescent Moon Publishing
Éditions Aubrey Walter/Gay Men's Press
Onlywomen Press Ltd
Pandora Press (imprint)
Polity Press
Rivers Oram Press
Routledge (imprint)
Serpent's Tail (imprint)
Trentham Books Ltd
Virago (division)
The Women's Press
Zed Books Ltd

General non-fiction

Allison & Busby Ltd
Alma Books
Arrow Books Ltd (imprint)
Aurora Metro
Bantam (imprint)
Beautiful Books
Birlinn Ltd
Black Ace Books
Black & White Publishing Ltd
Blackwater Press (imprint)
Bliss Books (imprint)
Bloomsbury Publishing UK (imprint)
Canongate Books Ltd
Century (imprint)
Chancery House Press (imprint)
Colourpoint Books
Corgi (imprint)
Cressrelles Publishing Co. Ltd
Terence Dalton Ltd
Doubleday (UK) (imprint)
Faber and Faber Ltd
Fig Tree (imprint)
Halban Publishers
Robert Hale Ltd
HarperCollins Publishers
Haus Publishing Ltd
Headline Publishing Group
Hodder & Stoughton
Little, Brown Book Group
Michael Joseph (commercial division)
Myriad Editions
New Beacon Books
Octopus Publishing Group
Orion Paperbacks (division)
The Orion Publishing Group Ltd
Peter Owen Publishers
Particular Books (imprint)
Penguin Group (UK)
Penguin Ireland (imprint)
Penguin Press (division)
Piatkus (division)
Picador (imprint)
Pipers' Ash Ltd
Pocket Books (imprint)
Poolbeg Press Ltd
Preface Publishing (imprint)
Quercus Publishing Plc
The Random House Group Ltd
Robson Books (imprint)
Royal National Institute of Blind People (RNIB)
Short Books Ltd
Simon & Schuster UK Ltd
Snowbooks Ltd
Souvenir Press Ltd
Sphere (division)
Telegraph Books
Transworld Ireland (imprint)
Transworld Publishers
Troubador Publishing Ltd
Ulverscroft Group Ltd
Viking (imprint)
Vintage (imprint)
Windmill Books (imprint)

Gift books

Appletree Press Ltd
Connections Book Publishing Ltd
Crombie Jardine Publishing Ltd
Helen Exley®
Igloo Books Ltd
Frances Lincoln Ltd
New Holland Publishers (UK) Ltd
Nightingale Press
Pan Macmillan (division)
Pavilion (imprint)
Quadrille Publishing
Ryland Peters & Small
Shepheard-Walwyn (Publishers) Ltd
Square Peg (imprint)
Summersdale Publishers Ltd

Health

Age UK
Anness Publishing
Duncan Baird Publishers
Bantam Press (imprint)
John Blake Publishing Ltd
BMJ Books (imprint)
Cassell Illustrated (imprint)
Kyle Cathie Ltd
Collins & Brown (imprint)
Connections Book Publishing Ltd
Dorling Kindersley (division)
W. Foulsham & Co. Ltd
Gaia Books (imprint)
Hamlyn (imprint)

Mainstream Publishing Co. (Edinburgh) Ltd
Kenneth Mason Publications Ltd
The Mercier Press
New Holland Publishers (UK) Ltd
Nightingale Press
Pan Macmillan (division)
Pavilion Publishing (Brighton) Ltd
Quadrille Publishing
Radcliffe Publishing Ltd
Routledge (imprint)
Sheldon Press (imprint)
Telegraph Books
Vermilion (imprint)
Virgin (imprint)
Weidenfeld & Nicolson Illustrated
Wolters Kluwer (UK) Ltd
The Women's Press

Heritage

Cassell Illustrated (imprint)
Country Books
Countryside Books
The Derby Books Publishing Company Ltd
Irish Academic Press Ltd
National Trust (imprint)
Pitkin (imprint)
Sigma Press
Weidenfeld & Nicolson Illustrated

History

Ian Allan Publishing Ltd
The Alpha Press (imprint)
Amberley Publishing
Amgueddfa Cymru – National Museum Wales
Anvil Books/The Children's Press
Appletree Press Ltd
Arris Publishing Ltd
Ashmolean Museum Publications
Atlantic Books
Bantam Press (imprint)
Birlinn Ltd
Blackstaff Press Ltd
Bodleian Library Publishing
The Bodley Head (imprint)
Boydell & Brewer Ltd
The British Library (Publications)
British Museum Company Ltd
Cambridge University Press
Canongate Books Ltd
Jonathan Cape (imprint)
Cassell Illustrated (imprint)
Chatto & Windus (imprint)
James Clarke & Co. Ltd
Cló Iar-Chonnachta Teo.
Collins & Brown (imprint)
Constable (imprint)
The Continuum International Publishing Group Ltd
Conway (inc. Brasseys Military, Putnam Aeronautical)
Cork University Press
Country Books
Giles de la Mare Publishers Ltd
André Deutsch (division)
Dorling Kindersley (division)
The Dovecote Press Ltd
University College Dublin Press
Ebury Press (imprint)
Edinburgh University Press
University of Exeter Press
Four Courts Press
Free Press (imprint)
Frontline (imprint)
Gibson Square
Gill & Macmillan Ltd
Halban Publishers
Hamish Hamilton (imprint)
Harvill Secker (imprint)
Headline Publishing Group
Hodder & Stoughton
Hutchinson (imprint)
Imperial War Museum
Irish Academic Press Ltd
William Heinemann (imprint)
Lawrence & Wishart Ltd
The Lilliput Press Ltd
Liverpool University Press
Logaston Press
Mainstream Publishing Co. (Edinburgh) Ltd
Manchester University Press
Mentor Books
The Mercier Press
Merlin Press Ltd
Methuen Publishing Ltd
Morrigan Book Company
Murdoch Books UK Ltd
John Murray (Publishers)
Nonsuch (imprint)
NWP (imprint)
The O'Brien Press Ltd
The Oleander Press
Michael O'Mara Books Ltd
Oneworld Publications
Peter Owen Publishers
Oxford University Press
Pan Macmillan (division)
Pavilion (imprint)
Pen & Sword Books Ltd
Phillimore (imprint)
Pimlico (imprint)
Pitkin (imprint)
Pluto Press
Polity Press
Profile Books Ltd
Random House Books (imprint)
Reaktion Books
Rider (imprint)
Robinson (imprint: paperbacks)
Routledge (imprint)
Sheldrake Press
Shepheard-Walwyn (Publishers) Ltd
Shire Publications
Society of Genealogists Enterprises Ltd
Sussex Academic Press
Sutton Publishing (imprint)
I.B.Tauris & Co. Ltd
Tauris Academic Studies (imprint)
Tauris Parke Paperbacks (imprint)
Telegraph Books
Vallentine Mitchell
Variorum (imprint)
Verso Ltd
Warburg Institute
Weidenfeld & Nicolson
Weidenfeld & Nicolson Illustrated
Welsh Academic Press
Wharncliffe (imprint)

Hotel, catering and leisure

Virtue Books Ltd

Humour

Arrow Books Ltd (imprint)
Bantam Press (imprint)
Birlinn Ltd
Black & White Publishing Ltd
Blackstaff Press Ltd
Canongate Books Ltd
Cassell Illustrated (imprint)
Century (imprint)
Crombie Jardine Publishing Ltd
André Deutsch (division)
Ebury Press (imprint)
Fourth Estate (imprint)
Hodder & Stoughton
Kudos Books (imprint)
Mainstream Publishing Co. (Edinburgh) Ltd
Mentor Books
The Mercier Press
Methuen Publishing Ltd
New Holland Publishers (UK) Ltd
New Island Books
Nightingale Press
The O'Brien Press Ltd
Michael O'Mara Books Ltd

Pan Macmillan (division)
Portico (imprint)
Prion Books (division)
Profile Books Ltd
Quadrille Publishing
Quiller Press (imprint)
Robson Books (imprint)
Souvenir Press Ltd
Square Peg (imprint)
Summersdale Publishers Ltd
Telegraph Books
Virgin (imprint)
The Vital Spark (imprint)

Illustrated books

Bloomsbury Publishing UK (imprint)
Cassell Illustrated (imprint)
Conran Octopus (imprint)
Dorling Kindersley (division)
Gaia Books (imprint)
Godsfield Press (imprint)
Haldane Mason Ltd
Hamlyn (imprint)
Laurence King Publishing Ltd
Frances Lincoln Ltd
Merrell Publishers Ltd
Miller's (imprint)
Mitchell Beazley (imprint)
New Holland Publishers (UK) Ltd
Osprey Publishing Ltd
Quadrille Publishing
The Quarto Group, Inc.
Ryland Peters & Small
Simon & Schuster (imprint)
Square Peg (imprint)
Stacey International
Weidenfeld & Nicolson Illustrated

International issues

Earthscan
Edinburgh University Press
Europa (imprint)
Fabian Society
Pan Macmillan (division)
Pluto Press
Rider (imprint)
Stacey International
I.B.Tauris & Co. Ltd
University of Wales Press
Zed Books Ltd

Irish interest

Anvil Books/The Children's Press
Appletree Press Ltd
Attic Press and Atrium (imprints)
Blackwater Press (imprint)
Cló Iar-Chonnachta Teo.
Colourpoint Books
Cork University Press
University College Dublin Press
The Educational Company of Ireland
Flyleaf Press
Folens Publishers
Four Courts Press
Gill & Macmillan Ltd
The Goldsmith Press Ltd
The Lilliput Press Ltd
The Mercier Press
Morrigan Book Company
On Stream Publications Ltd
Pluto Press
Colin Smythe Ltd

Languages and ELT

Cambridge University Press
Chambers Harrap Publishers Ltd
The Continuum International Publishing Group Ltd
Longman (imprint)
Macmillan Education Ltd (division)
Marshall Cavendish
Nightingale Press
The Oleander Press
Oxford University Press
Penguin Longman (imprint)

Law

Butterworths (imprint)
Cambridge University Press
Edinburgh University Press
Edward Elgar Publishing Ltd
Institute of Public Administration
Jordan Publishing Ltd
Jessica Kingsley Publishers
Kluwer Law International
Charles Knight (imprint)
LexisNexis
Manchester University Press
Oxford University Press
The Reader's Digest Association Ltd
Routledge-Cavendish (imprint)
Sweet & Maxwell
Thomson Round Hall
Tolley (imprint)
Which? Books (imprint)

Leisure interests and hobbies

Batsford (imprint)
Collins & Brown (imprint)
Collins Reference (division and imprint)
Countryside Books
David & Charles Ltd
W. Foulsham & Co. Ltd
Guild of Master Craftsman Publications Ltd
Right Way (imprint)
Search Press Ltd

Lifestyle, home and DIY

Age UK
Anness Publishing
Aquamarine (hardback imprint)
Aurum Press Ltd
Cico Books (imprint)
Co & Bear Productions
Collins & Brown (imprint)
Collins Geo (division and imprint)
Collins Reference (division and imprint)
Conran Octopus (imprint)
The Crowood Press
David & Charles Ltd
Elliott & Thompson
Expert Books (imprint)
W. Foulsham & Co. Ltd
Hamlyn (imprint)
Haynes Publishing
Kudos Books (imprint)
Lorenz Books (hardback imprint)
Mitchell Beazley (imprint)
Murdoch Books UK Ltd
New Holland Publishers (UK) Ltd
Nightingale Press
Quadrille Publishing
Quiller Press (imprint)
The Reader's Digest Association Ltd

Literary criticism and essays

Bodleian Library Publishing
Boydell & Brewer Ltd
The British Library (Publications)
James Clarke & Co. Ltd
The Continuum International Publishing Group Ltd
University College Dublin Press
Edinburgh University Press
Enitharmon Press/Enitharmon Editions
Hamish Hamilton (imprint)
Harvill Secker (imprint)
The Lilliput Press Ltd
Liverpool University Press
Lutterworth Press (subsidiary)
Manchester University Press
Northcote House Publishers Ltd
Oneworld Classics/Calder Publications

Pimlico (imprint)
Polity Press
Routledge (imprint)
Salt Publishing
Colin Smythe Ltd
University of Wales Press
The Women's Press
York Notes (imprint)

Local government and civil service

Edward Elgar Publishing Ltd
Government Supplies Agency
Institute of Public Administration

Local interest

Fineleaf Publishing
Halsgrove Publishing
Logaston Press
Lonely Planet
S.B. Publications
Stenlake Publishing Ltd

The media

The Continuum International Publishing Group Ltd
HarperCollins (imprint)
Pluto Press

Medicine and nursing

BMJ Books (imprint)
Cambridge University Press
Dorling Kindersley (division)
Elsevier Ltd
Elsevier Ltd (Health Sciences)
W.H. Freeman (imprint)
Hodder Education Group
McGraw-Hill Education
Manson Publishing Ltd
Oxford University Press
Quay Books
Radcliffe Publishing Ltd
Routledge (imprint)
SAGE Publications Ltd
Science Navigation Group
Springer-Verlag London Ltd
John Wiley & Sons Ltd
Wiley-Blackwell

Military

Ian Allan Publishing Ltd
Aurum Press Ltd
Bantam Press (imprint)
Birlinn Ltd
Classic Publications (imprint)
Collins Reference (division and imprint)
Conway (inc. Brasseys Military, Putnam Aeronautical)
The Crowood Press
David & Charles Ltd
Frontline (imprint)
Grub Street Publishing
Imperial War Museum
Jane's Information Group
Michael Joseph (commercial division)
Midland Publishing (imprint)
Nonsuch (imprint)
Osprey Publishing Ltd
Pen & Sword Books Ltd
Salamander (imprint)
Spellmount (imprint)
Ulric Publishing
Weidenfeld & Nicolson

Mind, Body & Spirit

Duncan Baird Publishers
Bantam (imprint)
Kyle Cathie Ltd
Cico Books (imprint)
Connections Book Publishing Ltd
Crown House Publishing Ltd
Findhorn Press Ltd
Floris Books
Gaia Books (imprint)
Godsfield Press (imprint)
Hay House Publishers
Hodder & Stoughton
The Mercier Press
O-Books Publishing Ltd
Piatkus (division)
Quadrille Publishing
Quantum (imprint)

Music

Aureus Publishing Ltd
Bantam Press (imprint)
Marion Boyars Publishers Ltd
Boydell & Brewer Ltd
The British Library (Publications)
Cambridge University Press
The Continuum International Publishing Group Ltd
Cork University Press
Giles de la Mare Publishers Ltd
Ebury Press (imprint)
Elliott & Thompson
Faber and Faber Ltd
Flame Tree Publishing
Harvill Secker (imprint)
Independent Music Press
W.W. Norton & Company
Omnibus Press/Music Sales Ltd
Oneworld Classics/Calder Publications
Oxford University Press
Plexus Publishing Ltd
Reynolds & Hearn Ltd
Robson Books (imprint)
Salamander (imprint)
Serpent's Tail (imprint)
Sheldrake Press
Stainer & Bell Ltd
Yale University Press London

Natural history

Blackstaff Press Ltd
Bodleian Library Publishing
Co & Bear Productions
Collins & Brown (imprint)
Collins Geo (division and imprint)
Collins Reference (division and imprint)
The Crowood Press
David & Charles Ltd
Dorling Kindersley (division)
The Dovecote Press Ltd
Little Toller Books (imprint)
Natural History Museum Publishing
New Holland Publishers (UK) Ltd
Pan Macmillan (division)
Salamander (imprint)
Square Peg (imprint)
Think Books
Weidenfeld & Nicolson Illustrated
Whittet Books Ltd

Nautical and marine

Adlard Coles Nautical (imprint)
Ian Allan Publishing Ltd
Boydell & Brewer Ltd
Brown, Son & Ferguson, Ltd
Conway (inc. Brasseys Military, Putnam Aeronautical)
University of Exeter Press
Jane's Information Group
Kenneth Mason Publications Ltd
National Maritime Museum Publishing
Nautical Data Ltd
Pen & Sword Books Ltd
Thomas Reed (imprint)
Reeds Nautical Almanac (imprint)
Seafarer Books Ltd

Parenting, relationships and self-help

Bantam (imprint)
Bantam Press (imprint)
Nicholas Brealey Publishing
The Columba Press
Connections Book Publishing Ltd

Free Association Books
Hamlyn (imprint)
Right Way (imprint)
Robinson (imprint: paperbacks)
Ryland Peters & Small
Sheldon Press (imprint)
Square Peg (imprint)
Vermilion (imprint)

Performing arts

A&C Black Publishers Ltd
The Crowood Press
University of Exeter Press
Faber and Faber Ltd
J. Garnet Miller (imprint)
Kenyon-Deane (imprint)
Methuen Drama (imprint)
Methuen Publishing Ltd
National Trust (imprint)
Northcote House Publishers Ltd
Oberon Books
Peter Owen Publishers
Oxford University Press
Pan Macmillan (division)
RotoVision
Roundhouse Group
Routledge (imprint)

Photography

Appletree Press Ltd
Black Dog Publishing London UK
Booth-Clibborn Editions
Jonathan Cape (imprint)
Co & Bear Productions
Collins & Brown (imprint)
Constable (imprint)
David & Charles Ltd
Dorling Kindersley (division)
The Ilex Press Ltd
Merrell Publishers Ltd
Pavilion (imprint)
Prestel Publishing Ltd
Reaktion Books
Reynolds & Hearn Ltd
RotoVision
Taschen UK Ltd
Tauris Parke Books (imprint)
Thames & Hudson Ltd
V&A Publishing

Politics

Arris Publishing Ltd
Atlantic Books
Blackstaff Press Ltd
The Bodley Head (imprint)
Cambridge University Press
Jonathan Cape (imprint)
Chatto & Windus (imprint)
The Continuum International Publishing Group Ltd
University College Dublin Press
Edinburgh University Press
Gibson Square
Granta Publications
Green Print (imprint)
Hamish Hamilton (imprint)
Hutchinson (imprint)
Imprint Academic
Institute of Public Administration
Lawrence & Wishart Ltd
Little, Brown (division)
Mainstream Publishing Co. (Edinburgh) Ltd
Manchester University Press
Mentor Books
The Mercier Press
The O'Brien Press Ltd
Oneworld Publications
Pan Macmillan (division)
Pluto Press
Polity Press
Politico's Publishing (imprint)
Princeton University Press – Europe
Profile Books Ltd
Rivers Oram Press
Routledge (imprint)
Serpent's Tail (imprint)
Shepheard-Walwyn (Publishers) Ltd
Tauris Academic Studies (imprint)
Verso Ltd
Welsh Academic Press
The Women's Press
Zed Books Ltd

Popular culture

Ian Allan Publishing Ltd
Booth-Clibborn Editions
Boxtree (imprint)
Canongate Books Ltd
Lawrence & Wishart Ltd
Michael Joseph (commercial division)
Pavilion (imprint)
Penguin Group (UK)
Plexus Publishing Ltd
Portico (imprint)
Random House Books (imprint)
Serpent's Tail (imprint)
Sidgwick & Jackson (imprint)
Taschen UK Ltd
Virgin (imprint)
Weidenfeld & Nicolson Illustrated

Popular reference

Collins Reference (division and imprint)
The Crowood Press
Ebury Press (imprint)
W. Foulsham & Co. Ltd
Gaia Books (imprint)
Geddes & Grosset
Hamlyn (imprint)
HarperCollins Publishers
Headline Publishing Group
How To Books Ltd
Icon Books Ltd
Infinite Ideas
Lorenz Books (hardback imprint)
Pan Macmillan (division)
Pocket Essentials (imprint)
The Quarto Group, Inc.
Quiller Press (imprint)
The Reader's Digest Association Ltd
Right Way (imprint)
Salamander (imprint)
Shire Publications
Southwater (paperback imprint)
Thames & Hudson Ltd
Time Out (imprint, in partnership with Time Out Group)
Virgin (imprint)
Which? Books (imprint)

Puzzles and crosswords

Chambers Harrap Publishers Ltd
Igloo Books Ltd

Reference

Anness Publishing
Atlantic Books
A&C Black Publishers Ltd
Bloomsbury Information (imprint)
The British Library (Publications)
Cambridge University Press
Kyle Cathie Ltd
CBD Research Ltd
Chambers Harrap Publishers Ltd
James Clarke & Co. Ltd
Collins Language (division and imprint)
The Continuum International Publishing Group Ltd
Dorling Kindersley (division)
Elsevier Ltd
Encyclopaedia Britannica (UK) Ltd
Euromonitor International plc
Europa (imprint)
Facet Publishing
Flame Tree Publishing
Guinness World Records
HarperCollins Publishers
Hobsons Publishing plc

Hodder Education Group
John Murray (Publishers)
NWP (imprint)
The O'Brien Press Ltd
The Oleander Press
Oxford University Press
Penguin Press (division)
Philip's (imprint)
Prentice Hall (imprint)
Random House Books (imprint)
RBI Search
William Reed Directories
Routledge (imprint)
Scala Publishers
Stacey International
Taylor and Francis Group
Tempus (imprint)
Unicorn Press
V&A Publishing
WLR Media & Entertainment
Wordsworth Editions Ltd

Religion, philosophy and New Age

The Alpha Press (imprint)
Authentic Media Ltd
Bryntirion Press
Cambridge University Press
Canterbury Press (imprint)
Catholic Truth Society
Chatto & Windus (imprint)
Christian Education
James Clarke & Co. Ltd
The Columba Press
The Continuum International Publishing Group Ltd
Darton, Longman & Todd Ltd
Edinburgh University Press
Floris Books
W. Foulsham & Co. Ltd
Four Courts Press
Garnet Publishing Ltd
Gresham Books Ltd
Hodder Faith
Imprint Academic
Inter-Varsity Press
Jessica Kingsley Publishers
Kube Publishing Ltd
Lion Hudson plc
Lion (imprint)
Lutterworth Press (subsidiary)
Mandrake of Oxford
Kevin Mayhew Ltd
Methodist Publishing House
Monarch Books
O-Books Publishing Ltd
The Octagon Press Ltd
Oneworld Publications
Open Gate Press
Oxford University Press
Pan Macmillan (division)
Religious and Moral Education Press (RMEP)
Rider (imprint)
George Ronald
Routledge (imprint)
St Pauls
SCM Canterbury Press Ltd
SCM Press (imprint)
Scripture Union
SPCK (imprint)
Stainer & Bell Ltd
Sussex Academic Press
I.B.Tauris & Co. Ltd
Thames & Hudson Ltd
Vallentine Mitchell
Veritas Publications
Verso Ltd
Wooden Books

Rural life and country

The Crowood Press
In Pinn (imprint)
Quiller Press (imprint)
Merlin Unwin Books Ltd
Whittet Books Ltd

Sciences

Bantam Press (imprint)
BIOS Scientific Publishers (imprint)
The Bodley Head (imprint)
Canopus Publishing Ltd
CRC Press (imprint)
Benjamin Cummings (imprint)
Dunedin Academic Press
Ebury Press (imprint)
Elsevier Ltd
Elsevier Ltd (Butterworth Heinemann)
Floris Books
Free Press (imprint)
W.H. Freeman (imprint)
Garland Science (imprint)
William Heinemann (imprint)
Frances Lincoln Ltd
McGraw-Hill Education
Manson Publishing Ltd
Natural History Museum Publishing
W.W. Norton & Company
Oneworld Publications
Osborne (imprint)
Oxford University Press
Portland Press Ltd
Profile Books Ltd
Routledge (imprint)
SAGE Publications Ltd
Science Museum
Science Navigation Group
Spon (imprint)
Springer-Verlag London Ltd
Taylor & Francis (imprint)
John Wiley & Sons Ltd
Wiley-Blackwell
Woodhead Publishing Ltd
Yale University Press London

Scottish interest

Appletree Press Ltd
Birlinn Ltd
Black Ace Books
John Donald (imprint)
Edinburgh University Press
Floris Books
House of Lochar
NWP (imprint)
SCP Publishers Ltd
Shepheard-Walwyn (Publishers) Ltd
The Vital Spark (imprint)

Social sciences

Allyn & Bacon (imprint)
Ashgate Publishing Ltd
Cambridge University Press
University College Dublin Press
Free Association Books
W.H. Freeman (imprint)
Jessica Kingsley Publishers
Peter Lang Ltd
Liverpool University Press
McGraw-Hill Education
W.W. Norton & Company
Oneworld Classics/Calder Publications
Open Gate Press
Open University Press (imprint)
Pavilion Publishing (Brighton) Ltd
The Policy Press
Policy Studies Institute (PSI)
Polity Press
Psychology Press
Rivers Oram Press
Routledge (imprint)
SAGE Publications Ltd
Souvenir Press Ltd
Tauris Academic Studies (imprint)
University of Wales Press
Wiley-Blackwell
Zed Books Ltd

Sports and games

Ian Allan Publishing Ltd
J.A. Allen
The Alpha Press (imprint)
Appletree Press Ltd
Aureus Publishing Ltd

Aurum Press Ltd
Bantam Press (imprint)
Batsford (imprint)
Birlinn Ltd
A&C Black Publishers Ltd
Black & White Publishing Ltd
Blackstaff Press Ltd
The Crowood Press
The Derby Books Publishing Company Ltd
Ebury Press (imprint)
Elliott & Thompson
W. Foulsham & Co. Ltd
Hamlyn (imprint)
HarperSport (imprint)
High Stakes (imprint)
In Pinn (imprint)
Mainstream Publishing Co. (Edinburgh) Ltd
Methuen Publishing Ltd
Milo Books Ltd
New Holland Publishers (UK) Ltd
The O'Brien Press Ltd
Pavilion (imprint)
Portico (imprint)
Quiller Press (imprint)
Robson Books (imprint)
Salamander (imprint)
Sigma Press
Souvenir Press Ltd
Spon (imprint)
Sportsbooks Ltd
The Sportsman's Press (imprint)
Swan Hill Press (imprint)
Telegraph Books
Virgin (imprint)
Weidenfeld & Nicolson Illustrated
John Wisden and Co. Ltd (imprint)
Yellow Jersey Press (imprint)

Transport, including cycling

AA Publishing
Ian Allan Publishing Ltd
Classic Publications (imprint)
The Crowood Press
Haynes Publishing
Midland Publishing (imprint)
Oxford Publishing Company (imprint)
Salamander (imprint)
Stenlake Publishing Ltd
Ulric Publishing

Travel and geography

AA Publishing
Appletree Press Ltd
Arcadia Books Ltd
Arris Publishing Ltd
Aurum Press Ltd
Bantam (imprint)
Bantam Press (imprint)
Blackstaff Press Ltd
Bloomsbury Publishing UK (imprint)
Blue Guides Ltd
Bradt Travel Guides Ltd
Nicholas Brealey Publishing
Cadogan Guides (imprint)
Canongate Books Ltd
Jonathan Cape (imprint)
Chatto & Windus (imprint)
Cicerone Press
Constable (imprint)
Thomas Cook Publishing
Countryside Books
Giles de la Mare Publishers Ltd
Discovery Walking Guides Ltd
Dorling Kindersley (division)
Ebury Press (imprint)
Eland Publishing Ltd
Footprint Handbooks
W. Foulsham & Co. Ltd
Fourth Estate (imprint)
Garnet Publishing Ltd
Gibson Square
Granta Publications
Hamish Hamilton (imprint)
Hodder & Stoughton
Insight Guides/Berlitz Publishing
Lonely Planet
Methuen Publishing Ltd
Michelin Maps and Guides
Murdoch Books UK Ltd
John Murray (Publishers)
New Cavendish Books
New Holland Publishers (UK) Ltd
Nonsuch (imprint)
The Octagon Press Ltd
The Oleander Press
On Stream Publications Ltd
Pavilion (imprint)
Penguin Group (UK)
Pitkin (imprint)
Prestel Publishing Ltd
Quiller Press (imprint)
Reaktion Books
Rider (imprint)
Alastair Sawday Publishing Ltd
Sheldrake Press
Souvenir Press Ltd
Square Peg (imprint)
Stacey International
Summersdale Publishers Ltd
Sunflower Books
I.B.Tauris & Co. Ltd
Tauris Parke Books (imprint)
Tauris Parke Paperbacks (imprint)
Time Out (imprint, in partnership with Time Out Group)
Virgin (imprint)
Weidenfeld & Nicolson

TV, TV tie-ins and radio

BBC Books (imprint)
BFI Publishing
Boxtree (imprint)
Dorling Kindersley (division)
Ebury Press (imprint)
HarperCollins (imprint)
Reynolds & Hearn Ltd
Titan Books
Virgin (imprint)
Wallflower Press

Welsh interest

Amgueddfa Cymru – National Museum Wales
Dref Wen
Gomer Press
Honno Ltd (Welsh Women's Press)
Seren
University of Wales Press
Welsh Academic Press
Y Lolfa Cyf.

Writers' guides

A&C Black Publishers Ltd
Chambers Harrap Publishers Ltd
Country Books
David & Charles Ltd

Children's book publishers and packagers

Listings for *Book publishers UK and Ireland* start on page 136 and listings for *Book packagers* start on page 224.

Children's fiction

Book publishers

Andersen Press Ltd
Anvil Books/The Children's Press
Barefoot Books Ltd
A&C Black Publishers Ltd
Bloomsbury Publishing Plc
Bodley Head Children's Books
Jonathan Cape Children's Books
Child's Play (International) Ltd
Cló Iar-Chonnachta Teo.
Dref Wen
Egmont Books
Evans Publishing Group
Everyman's Library
Faber and Faber Ltd
Floris Books
Gomer Press
Hachette Children's Books
HarperCollins Publishers
Honno Ltd (Welsh Women's Press)
House of Lochar
Indepenpress Publishing Ltd
Ladybird
Lion Hudson plc
Macmillan Children's Books Ltd
Magi Publications
Mantra Lingua
Kevin Mayhew Ltd
Meadowside Children's Books
Mentor Books
The Mercier Press
The O'Brien Press Ltd
Orchard Books
The Orion Publishing Group Ltd
Oxford University Press
Phoenix Yard Books
Piccadilly Press
Pipers' Ash Ltd
Point
Puffin
Ransom Publishing Ltd
Red Fox Children's Books
Scripture Union
Simon & Schuster UK Ltd
D.C. Thomson & Co. Ltd – Publications
Usborne Publishing Ltd
Walker Books Ltd
The Women's Press
Wordsworth Editions Ltd
Y Lolfa Cyf.
Zero to Ten Ltd

Book packagers

Graham-Cameron Publishing & Illustration
Hothouse Fiction Ltd
Working Partners Ltd

Children's non-fiction

Book publishers

Anness Publishing
Atlantic Europe Publishing Co. Ltd
Authentic Media Ltd
Award Publications Ltd
A&C Black Publishers Ltd
Boxtree
British Museum Company Ltd
Child's Play (International) Ltd
Dref Wen
Egmont Books
Encyclopaedia Britannica (UK) Ltd
Evans Publishing Group
Faber and Faber Ltd
First and Best in Education
Folens Publishers
Geddes & Grosset
GL Assessment
Gomer Press
Hachette Children's Books
Haldane Mason Ltd
HarperCollins Publishers
Hodder Wayland
Igloo Books Ltd
Imperial War Museum
Ladybird
Lion Hudson plc
Macmillan Children's Books Ltd
Mantra Lingua
Mentor Books
Neate Publishing
The O'Brien Press Ltd
Michael O'Mara Books Ltd
The Orion Publishing Group Ltd
Oxford University Press
Pavilion Children's Books
Piccadilly Press
Pipers' Ash Ltd
Portland Press Ltd
Puffin
Ransom Publishing Ltd
Salariya Book Company Ltd
Schofield & Sims Ltd
Science Museum
Scripture Union
Simon & Schuster UK Ltd
Ulric Publishing
Usborne Publishing Ltd
Walker Books Ltd
Warne
The Women's Press
Y Lolfa Cyf.
Zero to Ten Ltd
ZigZag Education

Book packagers

Aladdin Books Ltd
Amber Books Ltd
Bender Richardson White
BLA Publishing Ltd
Breslich & Foss Ltd
John Brown Group – Children's Division
The Brown Reference Group Ltd
Brown Wells & Jacobs Ltd
Cambridge Publishing Management Ltd
Design Eye Ltd
Graham-Cameron Publishing & Illustration
Hart McLeod Ltd
Marshall Editions Ltd
Monkey Puzzle Media Ltd
Orpheus Books Ltd
Toucan Books Ltd
Tucker Slingsby Ltd

Picture books

Book publishers

Andersen Press Ltd
Authentic Media Ltd

Award Publications Ltd
Barefoot Books Ltd
Bloomsbury Publishing Plc
Bodley Head Children's Books
Jonathan Cape Children's Books
Child's Play (International) Ltd
Cló Iar-Chonnachta Teo.
Dref Wen
Egmont Books
Evans Publishing Group
Everyman's Library
Faber and Faber Ltd
Floris Books
Gomer Press
Gullane Children's Books
Hachette Children's Books
HarperCollins Publishers
Igloo Books Ltd
Ladybird
Frances Lincoln Ltd
Lion Hudson plc
Macmillan Children's Books Ltd
Magi Publications
Mantra Lingua
Meadowside Children's Books
The O'Brien Press Ltd
Michael O'Mara Books Ltd
Orchard Books
The Orion Publishing Group Ltd
Oxford University Press
Pavilion Children's Books
Phoenix Yard Books
Piccadilly Press
Puffin
Ragged Bears Publishing Ltd
Red Fox Children's Books
Scripture Union
The Templar Company Ltd
Usborne Publishing Ltd
Walker Books Ltd
Warne
Zero to Ten Ltd

Book packagers

Aladdin Books Ltd
The Albion Press Ltd
Breslich & Foss Ltd
John Brown Group – Children's Division
Brown Wells & Jacobs Ltd
Graham-Cameron Publishing & Illustration
Marshall Editions Ltd
Tangerine Designs Ltd
The Templar Company Ltd
Tucker Slingsby Ltd

Other

Activity and novelty

Book publishers

Alligator Books Ltd
Award Publications Ltd
A&C Black Publishers Ltd
Bloomsbury Publishing Plc
Child's Play (International) Ltd
Dref Wen
Egmont Books
First and Best in Education
Flame Tree Publishing
Floris Books
Hachette Children's Books
Igloo Books Ltd
Ladybird
Frances Lincoln Ltd
Lion Hudson plc
Macmillan Children's Books Ltd
Magi Publications
Kevin Mayhew Ltd
Mentor Books
Michael O'Mara Books Ltd
Orchard Books
Oxford University Press
Pavilion Children's Books
Puffin
Ransom Publishing Ltd
Robinson
Scripture Union
Tango Books Ltd
Tarquin Publications
The Templar Company Ltd
Usborne Publishing Ltd
Walker Books Ltd
Warne

Book packagers

Aladdin Books Ltd
Breslich & Foss Ltd
John Brown Group – Children's Division
Brown Wells & Jacobs Ltd
Cowley Robinson Publishing Ltd
Design Eye Ltd
Playne Books Ltd
Tangerine Designs Ltd
The Templar Company Ltd
Emma Treehouse Ltd
Tucker Slingsby Ltd

Audiobooks

Book publishers

Barefoot Books Ltd
BBC Audiobooks Ltd
Child's Play (International) Ltd
Dref Wen
HarperCollins Publishers
Ladybird
Mantra Lingua
The Orion Publishing Group Ltd
The Random House Group Ltd
St Pauls
Scripture Union

Multimedia

Book publishers

Atlantic Europe Publishing Co. Ltd
Authentic Media Ltd
Ginn
GL Assessment
HarperCollins Publishers
Heinemann
Macmillan Children's Books Ltd
Mantra Lingua
Nelson Thornes Ltd
Oxford University Press
Puffin
The Random House Group Ltd
Ransom Publishing Ltd
St Pauls
Warne

Book packagers

John Brown Group – Children's Division

Poetry

Book publishers

Anvil Press Poetry
Authentic Media Ltd
A&C Black Publishers Ltd
Bloomsbury Publishing Plc
Bodley Head Children's Books
Jonathan Cape Children's Books
Cló Iar-Chonnachta Teo.
Dref Wen
Evans Publishing Group
Everyman's Library
Faber and Faber Ltd
Gomer Press
HarperCollins Publishers
Honno Ltd (Welsh Women's Press)
Frances Lincoln Ltd
Macmillan Children's Books Ltd
Orchard Books
Oxford University Press
Phoenix Yard Books
Pipers' Ash Ltd
Puffin
The Random House Group Ltd
Red Fox Children's Books
Walker Books Ltd
Wordsworth Editions Ltd

Book packagers

The Albion Press Ltd

Religion

Book publishers

Atlantic Europe Publishing Co. Ltd
Authentic Media Ltd
A&C Black Publishers Ltd
Catholic Truth Society
Christian Education
Dref Wen
Gresham Books Ltd
HarperCollins Publishers
Kube Publishing Ltd
Frances Lincoln Ltd
Lion Hudson plc
Mantra Lingua
Kevin Mayhew Ltd
Oxford University Press
George Ronald
St Pauls
Scripture Union
Society for Promoting Christian Knowledge
Stacey International
Usborne Publishing Ltd
Veritas Publications

Book packagers

The Albion Press Ltd
Tucker Slingsby Ltd

Publishers of plays

Playwrights are reminded that it is unusual for a publisher of trade editions of plays to publish plays which have not had at least reasonably successful, usually professional, productions on stage first. See listings beginning on page 136 for addresses.

A&C Black Publishers Ltd
Brown, Son & Ferguson, Ltd
Chapman Publishing
Cló Iar-Chonnachta Teo.
Cressrelles Publishing Co. Ltd
Everyman's Library
Faber and Faber Ltd
Samuel French Ltd
The Gallery Press
J. Garnet Miller
Nick Hern Books Ltd
Kenyon-Deane
The Lilliput Press Ltd
Kevin Mayhew Ltd
New Playwrights' Network
New Theatre Publications/The Playwrights' Co-operative
Oberon Books
The Oleander Press
Oneworld Classics/Calder Publications
Pipers' Ash Ltd
The Playwrights Publishing Company
SCP Publishers Ltd
Seren
Colin Smythe Ltd
Ward Lock Educational Co. Ltd
Josef Weinberger Plays Ltd

Publishers of poetry

Addresses for *Book publishers UK and Ireland* start on page 136.

Anvil Press Poetry
Arc Publications
Blackstaff Press Ltd
Bloodaxe Books Ltd
Jonathan Cape (imprint)
Carcanet Press Ltd
Chapman Publishing
Chatto & Windus (imprint)
Cló Iar-Chonnachta Teo.
Crescent Moon Publishing
diehard
Enitharmon Press/Enitharmon Editions
Everyman's Library
Faber and Faber Ltd
Flambard Press
The Gallery Press
The Goldsmith Press Ltd
Gomer Press
Headland Publications
Hippopotamus Press
Honno Ltd (Welsh Women's Press)
The Lilliput Press Ltd
Liverpool University Press
Luath Press Ltd
Mango Publishing
New Beacon Books
New Island Books
The Oleander Press
Oneworld Classics/Calder Publications
Oversteps Books Ltd
Penguin Group (UK)
Picador (imprint)
Pipers' Ash Ltd
Polygon
The Random House Group Ltd
Route
SCP Publishers Ltd
Seren
Wordsworth Editions Ltd

Literary agents for children's books

The following literary agents will consider work suitable for children's books, from both authors and illustrators. Listings start on page 473. See also *Writing and the children's book market* on page 291 and *Art agents and commercial art studios* on page 519.

The Agency (London) Ltd
Darley Anderson Literary, TV and Film Agency
The Bell Lomax Moreton Agency
Celia Catchpole
Curtis Brown Group Ltd
Eddison Pearson Ltd
The Ethan Ellenberg Literary Agency
Fraser Ross Associates
Marianne Gunn O'Connor Literary Agency
A.M. Heath & Co. Ltd
David Higham Associates Ltd
LAW (Lucas Alexander Whitley Ltd)
Christopher Little Literary Agency
Eunice McMullen Ltd
Andrew Mann Ltd
Sarah Manson Literary Agent
Maggie Noach Literary Agency
Pollinger Limited
The Lisa Richards Agency
Rogers, Coleridge & White Ltd
Elizabeth Roy Literary Agency
Rosemary Sandberg Ltd
Caroline Sheldon Literary Agency Ltd
Ed Victor Ltd
AP Watt Ltd
Eve White

Literary agents for television, film, radio and theatre

Listings for these and other literary agents start on page 473.

A & B Personal Management Ltd
The Agency (London) Ltd
Aitken Alexander Associates Ltd
Berman, Boals & Flynn
Blake Friedmann Literary, TV & Film Agency Ltd
Alan Brodie Representation Ltd
Browne & Miller Literary Associates
Capel & Land Ltd
CardenWright Literary Agency
Casarotto Ramsay & Associates Ltd
Mic Cheetham Associates Ltd
Jonathan Clowes Ltd
Elspeth Cochrane Personal Management
Rosica Colin Ltd
Jane Conway-Gordon Ltd
Richard Curtis Associates Inc.
Curtis Brown Group Ltd
Curtis Brown Ltd
Judy Daish Associates Ltd
Felix Dde Wolfe
Bryan Drew Ltd
Robert Dudley Agency
Ann Elmo Agency Inc.
Janet Fillingham Associates
Film Rights Ltd
The Firm
Laurence Fitch Ltd
Jill Foster Ltd (JFL)
Robert A. Freedman Dramatic Agency Inc.
Samuel French Inc.
Futerman, Rose & Associates
Jüri Gabriel
Eric Glass Ltd
The Rod Hall Agency Ltd
David Higham Associates Ltd
Valerie Hoskins Associates Ltd
Independent Talent Group Ltd
Michelle Kass Associates
Frances Kelly Agency
The Lazear Agency Inc.
LBLA (Lorella Belli Literary Agency)
Limelight Management
Andrew Mann Ltd
Marjacq Scripts
The Marton Agency Inc.
Blanche Marvin
MBA Literary Agents Ltd
William Morris Agency Inc.
William Morris Endeavor Entertainment
Fifi Oscard Agency Inc.
PFD (The Peters Fraser & Dunlop Group Ltd)
Playmarket
PMA Literary and Film Management Inc.
PVA Management Ltd
The Lisa Richards Agency
Sayle Screen Ltd
Susan Schulman Literary & Dramatic Agents Inc.
The Sharland Organisation Ltd
Sheil Land Associates Ltd
The Shukat Company Ltd
Micheline Steinberg Associates
Rochelle Stevens & Co
The Tennyson Agency
JM Thurley Management
Trident Media Group
Watkins/Loomis Agency Inc.
AP Watt Ltd
Josef Weinberger Plays Ltd

Newspapers and magazines that accept cartoons

Listed below are newspapers and magazines which take cartoons – either occasionally, or on a regular basis. Approach in writing in the first instance (for addresses see listings starting on page 11 for newspapers and page 33 for magazines) to ascertain the Editor's requirements.

Newspapers and colour supplements

(Adelaide) Advertiser
(Brisbane) The Sunday Mail
(Christchurch) The Press
Daily Dispatch
Independent Newspapers Gauteng
Independent Newspapers Kwa-Zulu Natal Ltd
Independent Newspapers (South Africa) Ltd
(Invercargill) The Southland Times
(Melbourne) Herald Sun
(Sydney) The Sunday Telegraph
Taranaki Daily News
(Wellington) The Dominion Post

Consumer and special interest magazines

Aeroplane Monthly
African Business
Art Business Today
The Author
Back Street Heroes
Bella
Best of British
Bowls International
British Philatelic Bulletin
Canals & Rivers
Car
Chapman
Church of England Newspaper
Classic Cars
Computer Weekly
The Countryman
Cycle Sport
Cycling Weekly
Dance Australia
The Dandy
Disability Now
Dogs Today
Dolly
East Lothian Life
The Erotic Review
Flora International
Fortean Times
The Friend
Garden News
Gay Times – GT
Golf Monthly
Golf World
GQ
H&E Naturist
Index on Censorship
Inspire Magazine, CPO
Ireland's Own
Jewish Telegraph
Kids Alive! (The Young Soldier)
Lothian Life
Mayfair
Men Only
More!
Motor Caravan Magazine
Mslexia
New Internationalist
New Musical Express (NME)
New Scientist
New Statesman
The Oldie
Opera Now
Overland
Park Home & Holiday Caravan
Picture Postcard Monthly
Planet
Poetry Review
PONY Magazine
Pride
Private Eye
Red Pepper
Reform
Rugby World
Running Fitness
Scottish Home and Country
Sight and Sound
Ski and Board
The Spectator
The Squash Player
Staple
The Strad
Suffolk Norfolk Life
The Tablet
that's life!
Time Out
Tribune
Trout and Salmon
The Universe
The Vegan
Viz
The Voice
The War Cry
The Weekly News
Weight Watchers Magazine
WI Life
Yachting Monthly
Yachting World
Young Writer Magazine
Yours

Business and professional magazines

Accountancy
BMA News
Broadcast
Education Journal
Electrical Review
Housebuilder
Irish Medical Times
LGC (Local Government Chronicle)
Police Review
Post Magazine & Insurance Week
Truck & Driver

Prizes and awards by subject area

This index gives the major subject area(s) only of each entry in the main listing which begins on page 588, and should be used with discrimination.

Biography

J.R. Ackerley Prize for Autobiography
The Australian/Vogel Literary Award
The Duff Cooper Prize
Costa Book Awards
The Elizabeth Longford Prize for Historical Biography
Marsh Award for Children's Literature in Translation
Sheridan Morley Prize for the Best Theatre Biography
The Samuel Pepys Award
Runciman Award
Scottish Mortgage Investment Trust Book Awards
The James Tait Black Memorial Prizes

Children

The Hans Christian Andersen Awards
Arts Council YouWriteOn.com Book Awards
Booktrust Early Years Awards
The Booktrust Teenage Prize
The CBI Bisto Book of the Year Awards
Cheltenham Illustration Awards
The Children's Laureate
The CILIP Carnegie and Kate Greenaway Awards
The Eleanor Farjeon Award
The Guardian Children's Fiction Prize
The Macmillan Prize for Children's Picture Book Illustration
New Zealand Post Book Awards for Children and Young Adults
The Red House Children's Book Award
Royal Mail Awards for Scottish Children's Books
The Times/Chicken House Children's Fiction Competition
Tir na n-Og Awards
Wildlife Photographer of the Year
Winchester Writers' Conference Competitions
Write A Story for Children Competition
YoungMinds Book Award

Drama – theatre, TV and radio

BAFTA (British Academy of Film and Television Arts)
Verity Bargate Award
The David Cohen Prize for Literature
Miles Franklin Literary Award
The Imison Award
Prequel to Cannes Short Film Script Competition
The Peggy Ramsay Foundation
RTÉ P.J. O'Connor Radio Drama Awards
RTÉ Radio 1 Francis MacManus Awards
Sony Radio Academy Awards
TAPS (Training and Performance Showcase)
Dylan Thomas Literary Prize
Young Writers' Programme

Essays

The David Cohen Prize for Literature
Scottish Mortgage Investment Trust Book Awards
Reginald Taylor and Lord Fletcher Essay Competition

Fiction

The Aeon Award
Arts Council England, London
Arts Council YouWriteOn.com Book Awards
The Australian/Vogel Literary Award
Authors' Club Awards
The Book to Talk About
The Booktrust Teenage Prize
Bristol Festival of Ideas Book Prize
Arthur C. Clarke Award
The David Cohen Prize for Literature
Commonwealth Writers Prize
Costa Book Awards
CWA Awards
The Dundee International Book Prize
The Desmond Elliott Prize
Encore Award
The Geoffrey Faber Memorial Prize
Miles Franklin Literary Award
The Guardian First Book Award
The Hawthornden Prize
International IMPAC Dublin Literary Award
Jewish Quarterly – Wingate Literary Prizes
Kerry Group Irish Fiction Award
John Llewellyn Rhys Prize
The McKitterick Prize
The Franco-British Society's Enid McLeod Literary Prize
Man Asian Literary Prize
The Man Booker International Prize
The Man Booker Prize
The Manchester Fiction Prize 2011
The Somerset Maugham Awards
Mind Book of the Year
Kathleen Mitchell Award
Montana New Zealand Book Awards
The Melissa Nathan Award for Comedy Romance
Orange Award for New Writers
Orange Prize for Fiction
Penguin Prize for African Writing
The Portico Prize
Le Prince Maurice Prize
Romantic Novel of the Year Award
The Royal Society of Literature Ondaatje Prize
Runciman Award
Scottish Arts Council
Scottish Mortgage Investment Trust Book Awards
The Sunday Times Young Writer of the Year Award
The James Tait Black Memorial Prizes
Dylan Thomas Literary Prize

The Betty Trask Awards
Warwick Prize for Writing
The Wellcome Trust Book Prize
Winchester Writers' Conference Competitions
David T.K. Wong Fellowship
Yorkshire Post Book of the Year

Grants, bursaries and fellowships

Arts Council England
Arts Council England, London
The Arts Council/An Chomhairle Ealaíon
The Authors' Contingency Fund
The Authors' Foundation
The K. Blundell Trust
Alfred Bradley Bursary Award
The Rhys Davies Trust
E.M. Forster Award
The Eric Gregory Trust Fund
Hawthornden Fellowships
Francis Head Bequest
Leverhulme Research Fellowships
The Elizabeth Longford Grants
The John Masefield Memorial Trust
Northern Writers' Awards
Charles Pick Fellowship
The Peggy Ramsay Foundation
Scottish Arts Council
The Travelling Scholarships
David T.K. Wong Fellowship

Illustration

The Hans Christian Andersen Awards
Booktrust Early Years Awards
The CBI Bisto Book of the Year Awards
Cheltenham Illustration Awards
The John D. Criticos Prize
The Eleanor Farjeon Award
L. Ron Hubbard's Writers and Illustrators of the Future Contests
Images – The Best of British Contemporary Illustration
The Macmillan Prize for Children's Picture Book Illustration
The Jill Smythies Award
Tir na n-Og Awards
The V&A Illustration Awards

Journalism

British Press Awards
The Paul Foot Award
London Press Club Awards
George Orwell Memorial Prize

Non-fiction

The Australian/Vogel Literary Award
Authors' Club Awards
BBC FOUR Samuel Johnson Prize for Non-Fiction
The David Berry Prize
Bristol Festival of Ideas Book Prize
British Academy Medals and Prizes
The Duff Cooper Prize
The Rose Mary Crawshay Prizes
CWA Awards
Financial Times and Goldman Sachs Business Book of the Year Award
Gladstone History Book Prize
The Calvin and Rose G. Hoffman Memorial Prize for Distinguished Publication on Christopher Marlowe
The ISG (CILIP)/BookData Reference Awards
Jewish Quarterly – Wingate Literary Prizes
Kraszna-Krausz Awards
John Llewellyn Rhys Prize
The Franco-British Society's Enid McLeod Literary Prize
The Somerset Maugham Awards
Mind Book of the Year
Montana New Zealand Book Awards
Penguin Prize for African Writing
The Portico Prize
Trevor Reese Memorial Prize
The Royal Society of Literature Ondaatje Prize
The Royal Society of Literature Jerwood Awards
The Royal Society Prizes for Science Books
Runciman Award
The Saltire Society Awards
Scottish Arts Council
Scottish Mortgage Investment Trust Book Awards
The André Simon Memorial Fund Book Awards
The Society of Authors Medical Book Awards
The Sunday Times Young Writer of the Year Award
Warwick Prize for Writing
The Wellcome Trust Book Prize
The Whitfield Prize
Winchester Writers' Conference Competitions
The Wolfson Foundation
Yorkshire Post Book of the Year

Photography

Deutsche Börse Photography Prize
RSPCA Young Photographer Awards (YPA)
Wildlife Photographer of the Year

Poetry

Academi Cardiff International Poetry Competition
Arts Council England
Arts Council England, London
The Arts Council/An Chomhairle Ealaíon
Arts Council YouWriteOn.com Book Awards
Arvon Foundation International Poetry Competition
The Bridport Prize
Bristol Festival of Ideas Book Prize
Cholmondeley Awards
The David Cohen Prize for Literature
Costa Book Awards
The T.S. Eliot Prize
The Geoffrey Faber Memorial Prize
Forward Prizes for Poetry
The Felicia Hemans Prize for Lyrical Poetry
The Ted Hughes Award for New Work in Poetry
Kent and Sussex Poetry Society Open Poetry Competition
The Manchester Poetry Prize 2012
The Michael Marks Awards for Poetry Pamphlets
The Somerset Maugham Awards
National Poetry Competition
The New Writer Prose and Poetry Prizes
The Plough Prize
The Poetry Business Book & Pamphlet Competition
The Corneliu M. Popescu Prize for Poetry in Translation
Runciman Award
The David St John Thomas Charitable Trust Competitions & Awards

Scottish Arts Council
Dylan Thomas Literary Prize
John Tripp Award for Spoken Poetry
Ver Poets Open Competition
Winchester Writers' Conference Competitions
Writers' Week Poetry Competition

Short stories

Arts Council YouWriteOn.com Book Awards
BBC National Short Story Award
The Bridport Prize
The David Cohen Prize for Literature
CWA Awards
Edge Hill Short Story Prize
Fish Short Story Prize, One Page Prize, and Poetry Prize
L. Ron Hubbard's Writers and Illustrators of the Future Contests
Bryan MacMahon Short Story Award
The Observer/Jonathan Cape/ Comica Graphic Short Story Prize
RTÉ Radio 1 Francis MacManus Awards
The David St John Thomas Charitable Trust Competitions & Awards
The Sunday Times EFG Private Bank Short Story Award
Dylan Thomas Literary Prize
The Tom-Gallon Trust Award and the Olive Cook Prize
Winchester Writers' Conference Competitions
Write A Story for Children Competition
Writers' & Artists' Yearbook 2011 Short Story Competition

Translation

Marsh Award for Children's Literature in Translation
The Translation Prizes

Specialist

The Boardman Tasker Prize
The Bollinger Everyman Wodehouse Prize for Comic Fiction
British Academy Medals and Prizes
British Czech & Slovak Association Writing Competition
Cordon d'Or – Gold Ribbon Culinary Academy Awards
The John D. Criticos Prize
Financial Times and Goldman Sachs Business Book of the Year Award
Galaxy British Book Awards
The Lionel Gelber Prize
The Guardian Research Fellowship
William Hill Sports Book of the Year Award
The ISG (CILIP)/BookData Reference Awards
The Franco-British Society's Enid McLeod Literary Prize
The Somerset Maugham Awards
Nielsen Gold and Platinum Book Awards
The Nobel Prize in Literature
The Observer/Jonathan Cape/ Comica Graphic Short Story Prize
The Portico Prize
Prequel to Cannes Short Film Script Competition
Prize for New Media Writing
Runciman Award
The David St John Thomas Charitable Trust Competitions & Awards
The Saltire Society Awards
The Kim Scott Walwyn Prize
Scottish Arts Council
Sony Radio Academy Awards
The Wellcome Trust Book Prize
YoungMinds Book Award

Index

A & B Personal Management Ltd 473
AA 268
AA Publishing 136
Aardman Animations 419
Abacus 136
Abbeville Press, Inc. 206
Abbey Home Media plc 221
Abbey Theatre Amharclann na Mainistreach 441
ABC-Clio 206
Aberdeen City Libraries, Central Library 678
University of Aberdeen 678
Aberystwyth University 691
Abingdon Press 206
Sheila Ableman Literary Agency 473
Above the Title Productions 430
Harry N. Abrams Inc. 206
abridgements, for radio 390
Absolute Classics 136
Absolute Press 136
Absolute Radio 427
Absolutely Productions 419
Acacia House Publishing Services Ltd 496
Acacia Productions Ltd 419
Academi Cardiff International Poetry Competition 588
Academi (Welsh Academy) 361, 547
Academic File Information Services 118
Academic Press 136
Academic Writers Group 547
Access Press 196
Accountancy 33
Accountancy Age 33
Accounting & Business 33
accounting procedures 9, 304, 515, 234
Ace 206
ACER Press 196
J.R. Ackerley Prize for Autobiography 588
Acorn Editions 136
act-two ltd 224
Actors Touring Company 446
Actual Theatre 441
Acumen Literary Journal 33
Ad Donker 204
adaptation from books 372
adaptations
  dramatised 390
  for film 375
  of classic novels 732
  television 378
Addison-Wesley 136
(Adelaide) Advertiser 104
(Adelaide) Sunday Mail 104
Adichie, Chimamanda Ngozi 243
Adlard Coles Nautical 136
Adobe 635, 639
Advance Features 118
advances (against royalties) 234, 300, 453, 466, 518, 530, 730, 732
advertising 233, 236, 536
advertising agencies 465, 510
Advertising Standards Authority 343
Advocate 519
Aeon Award, The 588
Aeroplane Monthly 33
Aesthetica Magazine 33
AFP (Agence France-Presse) 118
Africa Confidential 33
Africa: St Patrick's Missions 34
Africa Wild 113
Africa-Asia Confidential 33
African Business 34
Afternoon Story 392
Age UK 136
Agence Hoffman 497
Agence Michelle Lapautre 497
Carmen Balcells Agencia Literaria S.A. 500
Agencia Riff 496
Agency (London) Ltd, The 473
Agenda 34
Agenzia Letteraria Internazionale SRL 498
AIR International 34
Airlife Publishing 136
airside editions 471
Aitken Alexander Associates Ltd 473
Ajanta Books International 498
University of Alabama Press, The 206
Aladdin Books Ltd 224
Albion Press Ltd, The 224
Aldeburgh Poetry Festival 615
Alderman, Naomi 391
Jacintha Alexander Associates 473
Alibi 415
All Out Cricket 34
All Out Productions 430
All Party Parliamentary Writers Group 547
All3Media 419
Philip Allan 136
Ian Allan Publishing Ltd 136
Allen & Unwin Pty Ltd 196
George Allen & Unwin Publishers 136
J.A. Allen 136
Allen Lane 136
Alliance of Literary Societies 547
Allied Artists/Artistic License 519
Alligator Books Ltd 136
Allison & Busby Ltd 137

Allyn & Bacon 137
Alma Books 137
Alpha 206
Alpha course 468
Alpha Press, The 137
Alston Hall College 688
Amateur Gardening 34
Amateur Photographer 34
Amazon 299, 319, 325, 328, 345, 635, 639
Amazon Associates 646
Amber Books Ltd 224
Amberley Publishing 137
Ambit 34
American Literary Translators Association (ALTA) 547
American Markets Newsletter 116
American Society for Indexing (ASI) 547
American Society of Composers, Authors and Publishers 548
AMG/Renaissance 500
Amgueddfa Cymru – National Museum Wales 137
Amistad 206
Ampersand Agency Ltd, The 473
AN Magazine 34
a-n Artists Information Company, The 137
Anam Cara 667
Hans Christian Andersen Awards, The 588
Andersen Press Ltd 137
Darley Anderson Literary, TV and Film Agency 474
Michelle Anderson Publishing Pty Ltd 196
Andriod 330
Angel Eye Media Ltd 419, 430
Angels' Share, The 137
Angler's Mail 35
Angling Times 35
Anglo-Fortunato Films Ltd 419
Angry Robot 137
Animal Planet 415
Anne-Louise Fisher Associates 471
Anness Publishing 137
Annick Press Ltd 199
Anova Books 138
Anova Children's Books 138
Antiquarian Booksellers Association 266
Antique Collectors' Club Ltd 138
Anubis Literary Agency 474
Anvil Books/Children's Press, The 138
Anvil Press Poetry 138
Apollo 35
Applause Theatre and Cinema Book Publishers 206
Apple 331
Appledore Book Festival 615
Apples & Snakes Performance Poetry 364
Appletree Press Ltd 138
apps 330
AQ – Australian Quarterly 104
Aquamarine 138
Aquila 35
Arabia Books 138
Arc Publications 138
Arcade Publishing 206
Arcadia Books Ltd 138
Arche Books Publishing Inc. 206
Archers 384
Architects' Journal, The 35
Architectural Design 35
Architectural Press 139
Architectural Review, The 35
Architecture Today 35
Arcturus 139
Arden Shakespeare 139
Arena 519
Argus, The 23
University of Arkansas Press, The 206
Armitstead, Claire 284
Yvonne Arnaud Theatre Management Ltd 441
Arqiva 428
Arris Publishing Ltd 139
Arrow Books Ltd 139
Arrowsmith, Peter 741
Art Agency (Wildlife Art Ltd), The 519
Art & Australia 104
Art Business Today 35
art buyers 511
Art Market, The 519
Art Monthly 36
Art Monthly Australia 104
Art Newspaper, The 36
Art Quarterly 36
Art Review 36
Artist, The 36
Artist Partners Ltd 519
Artists & Illustrators 36
Artists' Choice 346
Artlink 104
Arts Club 548
Arts Council England 361, 363, 548, 588
  grants 733
Arts Council England, London 588
Arts Council/An Chomhairle Ealaíon 548, 588
Arts Council of Northern Ireland 548
Arts Council of Wales 548
Arts Council YouWriteOn.com Book Awards 589
Artworks, The 519
Arvon Foundation 359, 364, 667, 688
  International Poetry Competition 364, 589
AS Magazine 36
Asham Award, The 589
Ashgate Publishing Ltd 139
Ashley, Jackie 651
Ashmolean Museum Publications 139
Asia House Festival of Asian Literature 615
Aslib (Association for Information Management), The 139, 549
Aspects Irish Literature Festival 615
Assembly TV 420
Assent 36
Association for Scottish Literary Studies (ASLS) 549
Association of American Correspondents in London (AACL) 549
Association of American Publishers Inc. 549
Association of Art Historians (AAH) 549
Association of Assistant Librarians 549

Index

Association of Authors' Agents 306, 549
Association of Authors' Representatives Inc. 549
Association of British Science Writers (ABSW) 550
Association of Canadian Publishers 550
Association of Christian Writers 550
Association of Freelance Editors, Proofreaders and Indexers 550
Association of Illustrators (AOI) 341, 514, 550
Association of Learned and Professional Society Publishers, The 550
Association of Photographers 535, 550
Association of Authors' Agents 453, 456
Astronomy Now 36
Athena Media 430
Athletics Weekly 36
Atlantic Books 139
Atlantic Europe Publishing Co. Ltd 139
Atlantic Monthly Press 207
Atom 140
Atrium 140
Attendance Allowance 750–751
Attic Press 140
Attitude 37
(Auckland) New Zealand Herald 111
(Auckland) Sunday News 111
Auckland University Press 202
Aura-Pont, Theatrical and Literary Agency Ltd 497
Aureus Publishing Ltd 140
Aurora Metro 140
Aurum Press Ltd 140
Jane Austen Society, The 550
Austin Clarke Library 362
Australia Council 550
Australian Associated Press 118
Australian Copyright Council 551
Australian Financial Review, The 104
Australian Flying 104
Australian Geographic 104
Australian Heritage 105
Australian Home Beautiful 105
Australian House and Garden 105
Australian Journal of Politics and History 105
Australian Library and Information Association 551
Australian Photography 105
Australian Powerboat 105
Australian Publishers Association (APA) 551
Australian Society of Authors, The 551
Australian Women's Weekly, The 105
Australian Writers' Guild (AWG) 551
Australian/Vogel Literary Award, The 589
Authentic Media Ltd 140
Author, The 37, 542
Author Literary Agents 474
authors 235, 339
  crossover 287
  events 319, 326
  interviews with 233
  photographs 317
  self-publicity 318, 324
  tracing 716
  websites 312, 325
Authors' Club (at Arts Club), The 551
Authors' Club Awards 589
Authors' Contingency Fund, The 589
Authors' Foundation, The 589
Authors' Licensing and Collecting Society (ALCS) 342, 542, 551, 713, 715
Authors' Marketing Services Ltd 496
Auto Express 37
autobiographies 278
  abridged for radio 374
Autocar 37
Autumn International Literary Festival 615
averaging relief 730, 737
Avery 207
Aviation Business 105
Aviation News 37
Avon 140, 207, 287
Award Publications Ltd 140
Axelrod Agency, The 500
Axis – the online resource for contemporary art 551

Bernard Babani (publishing) Ltd 140
babies, books for 291
Baby Cow Productions Ltd 420, 430
Back Bay Books 207
Back Street Heroes 37
Backtrack 37
Baedeker, Karl 266
BAFTA (British Academy of Film and Television Arts), The 552, 590
Baggins Book Bazaar 363
Bailliere Tindall 140
Duncan Baird Publishers 140
Baker Books 346
Baker's Plays 207
Balance 37
Balkin Agency Inc., The 501
Jonathan Ball Publishers (Pty) Ltd 204
Ballantine Books 207
Ballymena Arts Festival 615
BANA (Bath Area Network for Artists) 552
Banker, The 37
Diane Banks Associates Ltd 474
Bantam Books 207
Bantam Press 140
Bantam Press (children's) 140
BAPLA (British Association of Picture Libraries and Agencies) 552
Baptist Times 38
Barbican Library 678
barcoding 315
Bardd Plant Cymru (Children's Poet Laureate) 590
Barefoot Books Ltd 140, 221
Verity Bargate Award 590
Tassy Barham Associates 496
Barrie, J. M 236
Barrington Stoke 140, 221
Barron's Educational Series Inc. 207
David Bateman Ltd 202

Bath Central Library 678
Bath Literature Festival 615
Bath Spa University 692
Batsford 141
Bauer Digital Radio Ltd 428
Baverstock, Alison 134, 295, 320, 465, 656, 685
Nicola Baxter Ltd 224
Bay Lit 615
BBC 545
  and Society of Authors 542
  broadcasting rights and terms 407
  Radio 4 384
  radio drama 387
  use abroad of recordings 408
  WritersRoom 388
BBC Audiobooks Ltd 141, 221
BBC Books 141
BBC Children's Books 141
BBC Four 415
BBC FOUR Samuel Johnson Prize for Non-Fiction 590
BBC magazines 38
BBC National Short Story Award 590
BBC News Channel 415
BBC Parliament 415
BBC Radio 428
BBC Radio 4 390
BBC Scotland 393
BBC Three 415
BBC World News 415
BBC Worldwide Ltd 141
BBC Written Archives Centre 678
BCA 346
BCS Publishing Ltd 224
Beacon Press 207
Glenys Bean Writer's Agent 499
Beano, The 38
Beautiful Books 141
Beautiful Sounds 221
Beaver: Canada's History Magazine, The 109
Beckford Society, The 552
Thomas Lovell Beddoes Society 552
Bedford Central Library 678
Beehive Illustration 519
Belair 141
Belfast Central Library 678
Belfast Telegraph 19
Belgrade Theatre, The 441
Bell & Hyman Ltd 141
Bell Lomax Moreton Agency, The 474
Bella 38
Bella Books 207
Belle de Jour 282, 648
Bender Richardson White 224
Arnold Bennett Society, The 552
E.F. Benson Society, The 552
Bentley Productions 420
bereavement benefits 751
Michael Berenti Literary Management 474
Berg Publishers 141
Berkley Books 207
Berlin Verlag 141
Berlitz 268
Berlitz Publishing 141
Berman, Boals & Flynn 501
David Berry Prize, The 590
Best 38
Best of British 38
Besterman/McColvin Medals 590
bestsellers 235, 245, 299, 302
  charts 302
  fiction 237
Beverley Literature Festival 616
BFI National Library 678
BFI Publishing 141
Bibliographical Society 552
Bibliophile 346
Big Heart Media 420, 430
Big Issue, The 38
Big Issue Australia, The 105
Big Issue Cymru, The 39
Big Issue in the North, The 39
Big Issue in Scotland, The 39
Big Issue South West, The 39
Big Umbrella Media 420
Big Score Productions Inc. 501
Bike 39
Billingham, Mark 251
Clive Bingley Ltd 141
Bio 415
biographical note 133
biographies, abridged for radio 374
biography 259, 284
  historical and literary 259
BIOS Scientific Publishers 141
Bird Watching 39
Birding World 39
Birdwatch 39
Birkbeck College, University of London 692
Birlinn Ltd 141
Birmingham Book Festival 616
Birmingham Central Library 678
Birmingham Mail 26
Birmingham Post, The 26
Birmingham Repertory Theatre Ltd 441
Birnbaum 141
Bisto Book of the Year Awards, The 590
Bizarre 40
BLA Publishing Ltd 224
Blachman, Jeremy 648
A&C Black Publishers Ltd 141
Black Ace Books 142
Black & White Publishing Ltd 142
Black Beauty & Hair 40
Black Dagger Crime 142
Black Dog Publishing London UK 142
Black Lace 142
Black Static 40
Black Swan 142
Black Amber 142
Blackberry 330
Blackpool Art Society, The 553
Blackpool Gazette, The 22
Blackstaff Press Ltd 142

Index

Blackstone Press Ltd 142
Blackwater Press 142
Blake, Carole 468
Blake Friedmann Literary, TV & Film Agency Ltd 468, 474
John Blake Publishing Ltd 142
blasphemous libel 727
Blighty 415
Bliss 40
Bliss Books 142
blogs 3, 301, 647
  and pictures 650
  books published from 281
  platforms 626
  portals 649
  profile 651
  setting up 625
Bloodaxe Books Ltd 142
blooks (blogs turned into books) 282
Henry Bloom Noble Library, The 678
Bloom, William 272
Bloomberg 415
Bloomsbury Publishing Plc 142, 221, 287-288
Bloomsbury USA 207
Blue Door 143
Blue Guides Ltd 143
Blueprint 40
K. Blundell Trust, The 590
blurb 131, 322
BMA News 40
BMJ Books 143
board books 291
Boardman Tasker Prize, The 590
Boardwalk Books 199
Boatswain Press Ltd 143
Bodleian Library 678
Bodleian Library Publishing 143
Bodley Head, The 143
Bodley Head Children's Books 143
Bollinger Everyman Wodehouse Prize for Comic Fiction, The 591
Bologna Book Fair 516
Bologna Children's Book Fair 456
University of Bolton 692
Bolton News, The 22
Bona 113
Bona Broadcasting 430
Bond, Katie 316
Bond Literary Agents & Specialized Services 500
Luigi Bonomi Associates Ltd 475
Book Aid International 553
Book at Bedtime 390
Book Bureau Literary Agency, The 475
book clubs 232, 326
Book Collector, The 40
book fairs 233, 471
Book Guild Ltd, The 224
Book Industry Communication website 315
book launches 286
Book and Magazine Collector 40
Book Now! Literature Festival, Arts Service 616
Book People Ltd, The 346
The Book to Talk About 591
BookBlast Ltd 475
Booker Prize 310
Bookman Literary Agency 499
Books & Writers Network Pty Ltd 196
Books Ireland 41
books24x7 638
BookScan 300
Bookseller, The 41
Bookseller & Publisher 106
Bookseller Retail Awards, The 591
booksellers 467
  wholesale 638
Booksellers Association of the United Kingdom & Ireland Ltd, The 553
bookshops, authors and 326
Booktrust 553
  Collection, The 678
  Early Years Awards 591
  Teenage Prize, The 591
Bookworld 41
Booth-Clibborn Editions 143
Bootleg Theatre Company, The 441
Georges Borchardt Inc. 501
Borders 300, 328, 635
George Borrow Society, The 553
Bound Originals 225
Bounty 143
Bowker 143
R.R. Bowker 207
Bowls International 41
Boxtree 143
Marion Boyars Publishers Ltd 143
Boyd, William 316
Boydell & Brewer Ltd 143
Boyds Mills Press 207
Alfred Bradley Bursary Award 591
Neil Bradley Puzzles 118
Bradt Travel Guides Ltd 143, 269
Brainwarp 118
Brandon & Associates Literary Agency 475
Brandon/Mount Eagle Publications 143
Brandt & Hochman Literary Agents Inc. 501
Branford Boase Award, The 591
Helen Brann Agency Inc., The 501
Brass Band World Magazine 41
Brasseys Military 144
Bravo 415
Nicholas Brealey Publishing 144
Breedon Books Publishing Co. Ltd 144
Breslich & Foss Ltd 225
Bridget Jones' Diary. 648
Bridport Prize, The 591
Brighton Festival 616
Brilliant Publications 144
(Brisbane) Courier-Mail, The 106
(Brisbane) Sunday Mail, The 106
Bristol Central Library 678
Bristol Evening Post 24
Bristol Festival of Ideas Book Prize 592
Bristol Old Vic 441
Bristol Poetry Festival 616

British Academy 553
British Academy Medals and Prizes 592
British Academy of Composers and Songwriters 553
British Association of Communicators in Business, The 553
British Association of Journalists 554
British Association of Picture Libraries and Agencies 554
British Birds 41
British Book Awards 592
British Centre for Literary Translation (BCLT) 554
British Chess Magazine 41
British Copyright Council 554
British Council, The 364, 554
British Czech & Slovak Association Writing Competition 592
British Deaf News 41
British Fantasy Society, The 555
British Film and Television Producers' Association 545
BFI (British Film Institute) 555
British Guild of Beer Writers 555
British Guild of Travel Writers, The 555
British Haiku Society, The 361, 555
British Institute of Professional Photography 555
British Interactive Media Association (BIMA) 555
British Journal of Photography, The 41
British Journalism Review 42
British Library 260, 312, 678
  Business and Intellectual Property Service (BIS) 679
  Document Supply Centre 679
  for Development Studies (BLDS) 679
  Newspapers 679
  Publications, The 144
  Sound Archive, The 679
British Medical Journal 42
British Museum Company Ltd 144
British Philatelic Bulletin 42
British Press Awards 592
British Science Fiction Association Ltd, The 556
British Sky Broadcasting (BSkyB) 414
British Society of Comedy Writers 556
British Society of Magazine Editors 556
British Society of Miniaturists 556
British Society of Painters 556
British Watercolour Society 556
British Woodworking 42
British Standards Institute 676
Broadcast 42
Broadcasting Entertainment Cinematograph and Theatre Union (BECTU), Writers Section 556
Broadcasting Group 556
Brockhampton Press 144
Andrew Brodie 144
Alan Brodie Representation Ltd 475
Brontë Society, The 556
Brook Lapping Productions Ltd 420
Jenny Brown Associates 475
Brown, Dan 329, 471
John Brown Group – Children's Division 225
Brown Reference Group Ltd, The 225
Brown, Son & Ferguson, Ltd 144
Brown Wells & Jacobs Ltd 225
Pema Browne Ltd 501
Browne & Miller Literary Associates 501
Browning Society, The 556
Brunel University 692
Felicity Bryan Associates 476
Bryntirion Press 144
Bryson Agency Australia Pty Ltd 496
BT Vision 414
John Buchan Society, The 557
Reference & Information Service (Buckinghamshire) 679
Building 42
Building Design 42
Bulls Presstjänst AB 118
Bureau Littéraire International 498
Bureau of Freelance Photographers 557
Burford Books 207
Burlington Magazine, The 42
Burns & Oates 144
Burton Mail 20
Burton Manor 688
Buses 42
Bush Press Communications Ltd 202
Bush Theatre 438
business cards and letterheads 536
Business Life 43
Business Plus 144
business proposals 465
Business Traveller 43
Buster Books 144
Butterworth-Heinemann 144
Butterworths 144
Butterworths Canada Ltd 199
Buxton Festival 616
Byre Theatre of St Andrews, The 441
Byron, Lord 266
Byron Society (International) 557

cable retransmission, simultaneous 716
Caboodle Writing Retreats 688
Cactus TV 420
Cadogan Guides 144, 268
Caine Prize for African Writing, The 592
Randolph Caldecott Society 557
Calmann & King Ltd 144
Camberwell College of Arts Library 679
Cambridge Bibliographical Society 557
Cambridge Evening News 20
Cambridge Publishing Management Ltd 225
Cambridge University Library 679
University of Cambridge 688
Cambridge University Press 144, 196, 204, 207
Cambridgeshire Journal 43
Camden Poetry Group 365
Camera 106
Campaign 43
Campaign for Freedom of Information 557

Campaign for Press and Broadcasting Freedom 557
Campbell Books 145
Campbell Davison Media 430
Campbell Thomson & McLaughlin Ltd 476
Canadian Authors Association 557
Canadian Bookseller 109
Canadian Literature 109
Canadian Magazine Publishers Association 557
Canadian Publishers' Council 557
Canadian Screenwriter 109
Canadian Writer's Journal 109
Canals & Rivers 43
cancellation fees 514
Candis 43
Candlewick Press 207
Cannongate US 208
Canongate Books Ltd 145
Canopus Publishing Ltd 145, 225
CANSCAIP (Canadian Society of Children's Authors, Illustrators & Performers) 557
Canterbury Festival 616
Canterbury Press 145
Jonathan Cape Children's Books 145
(Cape Town) Cape Times 113
Capel & Land Ltd 476
capital allowances 735
Capra, Fritjof 275
Car 43, 113
Car Mechanics 43
Caravan Magazine 44
Carcanet Press Ltd 145
Card Connection Ltd 531
Carden Wright Literary Agency 476
Cardiff Central Library 679
Cardiff University 692
Career Development Group 558
Careers Writers' Association 558
Carer's Allowance 751
Caring Business 44
Carlisle News and Star 21
Carlton Cards Ltd 531
Carlton Poets 364
Carlton Publishing Group 145
Carnegie Medal 592
Carnival Film & Television Ltd 420
Carousel – Guide to Children's Books, The 44
Carroll & Brown Ltd 225
Lewis Carroll Society (Daresbury) 558
Lewis Carroll Society, The 558
Cartoonists Club of Great Britain 558
cartoons, getting published 523–524
Cartoons & Wordgames 119
Maria Carvainis Agency Inc. 501
Casarotto Ramsay & Associates Ltd 476
Caspari Ltd 531
Cassell Illustrated 145
Cassell Reference 145
Castle Street Mysteries 199
Cat World 44
Celia Catchpole 476
Caterer & Hotelkeeper 44
Caterpillar Books 145
Kyle Cathie Ltd 145
Catholic Herald, The 44
Catholic National Library 679
Catholic Pictorial 44
Catholic Times 44
Catholic Truth Society 145
Caxton Press, The 202
Caxton Publishing Group 145
CB1 Poetry 364
CBD Research Ltd 145
CBI Bisto Book of the Year Awards, The 592
CBS Action 415
CBS Drama 415
CBS Reality 415
CD companies, royalty-free 539
CE Digital Ltd 428
Celebritext 119
celebrity books 299, 330, 453
Celtic Films 420
Cengage Learning 146
Cengage Learning Australia 196
Cengage Learning New Zealand 202
Center Street 208
Centerprise Literature Development Project 365
Centerprise Trust 688
Central Illustration Agency 520
Central St Martins College of Art & Design, Short Course Office 688
Central School of Speech and Drama, The 692
Central St Martins College of Art & Design Library 679
Century 146
Ceramic Review 44
Chalford Press, The 146
Challenge 415
Challenge Jackpot 415
Chambers Harrap Publishers Ltd 146
Chambers Literary Agency 476
Chancery House Press 146
Channel 4 295, 410
  Independent Film & Video department 378
Channel 4 Books 146
Channel Television Ltd 412
Chapman 45
Chapman & Vincent 477
Chapman Publishing 146
Paul Chapman Publishing 146
Chapter and Verse 531
Charleston Festival 616
Charlton Press, The 199
Chartered Institute of Journalists, The 558
Chartered Institute of Linguists (IoL) 558
Chartered Institute of Personnel and Development 146
Chartered Secretary 45
Chartered Society of Designers, The 558
Chat 45
Chatelaine 109
Chatwin, Bruce 262
Chawton House Library 679
Mic Cheetham Associates Ltd 477
Chelsea College of Art & Design Library 679

Cheltenham Illustration Awards 593
Times Cheltenham Literature Festival, The 616
Cheltenham Literary Festival 686
Cherokee Literary Agency 500
Cherrytree Books 146
Chesher, Christoph 636
Chester Literature Festival 617
Chesterton Society, The 559
University of Chicago Press 208
Chichester Festival Theatre 442
Chichester Festivities 617
University of Chichester 692
chick lit 253
Chicken House, The 146
Judith Chilcote Agency 477
Child Benefit 749
Child Education PLUS 45
Child Tax Credits 750
Children's Book Circle, The 559
children's books 123, 287, 292, 296
  illustrating for 510
Children's Books Ireland 559
Children's Film and Television Foundation Ltd 420
Children's Laureate, The 593
Children's Tax Credit 750
Children's Writers and Illustrators Group 559
Child's Play (International) Ltd 146
Chivers Press 146
Cholmondeley Awards 593
Chopra, Deepak 272, 274
Teresa Chris Literary Agency Ltd 477
(Christchurch)Press, The 111
Christian Education 146
Chrome Dreams 221
Chronicle & Echo, Northampton 20
Chronicle Books 208
Chrysalis Books Group 146
Church of England Newspaper 45
Church Times 45
Churchill Livingstone 146
Churchwarden Publications Ltd 146
Cicerone Press 146
CILIP Carnegie and Kate Greenaway Awards, The 593
CILIP (Chartered Institute of Library and Information Professionals) 559
Cima Books 147
CIRCA 45
Circle of Wine Writers 559
Cisco Press 147
Citizen, The 24
City Business Library 679
City Lit 365
City of London Festival 617
City of London Libraries 680
City University 692
  Creative Writing and Poetry Courses 365
Civil Aviation Authority Library and Information Centre (CAA) 680
John Clare Society, The 559
T&T Clark International 147
James Clarke & Co. Ltd 147
Arthur C. Clarke Award 593
Clarke, Catherine 455
Classic Arts Productions Ltd 430
Classic Boat Magazine 45
Classic Cars 45
Classic FM 427
classic novels 372, 391
Classic Rock 46
Classic Stitches 46
Classical Association 559
Classical Comics 147
Classical Music 46
Classics Monthly 46
Clee, Nicholas 299
Mary Clemmey Literary Agency 477
Clever Books Pty Ltd 204
Clifford, Johnathon 343
Climb Magazine 46
Climber 46
Clitheroe Books Open Floor Readings 364
Cló Iar-Chonnachta Teo. 147, 221
Closer 46
Cloud Eight Films Ltd 420
Jonathan Clowes Ltd 477
Clwyd Theatr Cymru 442
CNBC 416
CNN International 416
Co & Bear Productions 147
co-authors, dead or untraceable 340
Cobb, Richard 260
William Cobbett Society, The 559
Elspeth Cochrane Personal Management 477
Michael Codron Plays Ltd 438
Coffee House Poetry 364
Coffee House Press 208
David Cohen Prize for Literature, The 593
Coin News 46
Colchester Mercury Theatre Ltd 442
Cole, Stephen 635
Coleman, Bruce 535
Rosica Colin Ltd 477
Coliseum Theatre, The 442
College of Psychic Studies Library 680
Frances Collin Literary Agent 501
Collingwood O'Hare Productions 420
Collins 208
Collins & Brown 147
Collins Languages/COBUILD 147
Collins Gem 147
Collins Geo 147
Wilkie Collins Society, The 559
Colneis Marketing Ltd 531
Colour House Graphics Ltd 531
Colourpoint Books 147
Columba Press, The 147
Columbia University Press 208
Comedy Central (CC Extra) 416
Comedy Unit, The 421
comedy, writing 369
Comhairle nan Leabhraichean/Gaelic Books Council, The 560
comic author 245

comics 287
Commando 46
Commercial Motor 47
commissioning policies 299
commissions, pricing 514
Library of the Commonwealth Secretariat, The 680
Commonwealth Writers Prize 593
Commonword 361
Community Care 47
Community Channel 416
Community Creative Writing and Publishing 688
Company 47
company, operating as 730, 740
Company Pictures 421
Compass Theatre Company 446
competitions
  poetry 356, 359–360
  screenwriting 380
compilers 340
Computer Arts 47
computer technology 537, 639
Computer Weekly 47
Computeractive 47
computing ebooks 638
Concordia Publishing House 208
Condé Nast Traveller 47
Don Congdon Associates Inc. 501
Connections Book Publishing Ltd 147
Joseph Conrad Society (UK), The 560
Conran Octopus 147
Constable & Robinson Ltd 147
Consumers' Association 148
Contact Theatre Company 442
Contemporary 47
Contemporary Books 208
Contemporary Review 47
Continuum International Publishing Group Ltd, The 148
Continuum International Publishing Group Inc., The 208
contracts 287, 303, 305, 334, 453–454, 513, 530
  BBC 409
  newspapers 7
  photographer's 539
Conville & Walsh Ltd 478
Conway 148
Jane Conway-Gordon Ltd 478
Cook, John Mason 267
Thomas Cook Publishing 148
Cook, Thomas 267
Cooke Agency, The 496
Coombs Moylett Literary Agency 478
Duff Cooper Prize, The 593
Cooper Square Publishing 208
copyediting 230, 671
copying 707, 713, 716
Copyline Scotland 119
copyright 32, 129, 304, 331, 339, 353, 375, 513, 697
  and libel 713
  assignment of 697, 705
  duration of 697, 704
  in photographs 698
  infringement of 698, 707
  law 700
  licences 706
  outright sale of 306
  ownership 703
  protection 701
  royalties 732
  use of symbol 698
  works, dealing with 705
Copyright Acts 312
Copyright and Related Rights Regulations 2003 700
Copyright Clearance Center Inc. 560
Copyright Council of New Zealand Inc. 560
Copyright, Designs and Patents Act (1988) 697, 700
Copyright Licensing Agency (CLA) 560, 713, 715
Cordite Poetry Review 106
Cordon d'Or – Gold Ribbon Culinary Academy Awards 594
Corgi 148
Corgi Children's Books 148
Cork University Press 148
Corneliu M. Popescu Prize for European Poetry in Translation 362
Cornell University Press 209
Cornwall Library Service 680
Cornwell, Bernard 256
Cosgrove Hall Films Ltd 421
Cosmopolitan 48
Costa Book Awards 329, 594
Cotswold Life 48
Council for British Archaeology 148
Country 48
Country Books 148
Country Homes and Interiors 48
Country Life 48
Country Living 48
Country Smallholding 48
Country Walking 48
Countryman, The 48
Countryman Press, The 209
Countryside Books 148
Courier and Advertiser, The 23
courses
  creative writing 459
  for screenwriters 379
  photography 535
  writing 257
  Coventry Telegraph 26
Cover to Cover 148
cover letter 133
Cowley Robinson Publishing Ltd 225
Crafts Council Research Library 680
Craftsman craft & design Magazine 49
Cranfield Library and Information Service 680
Rose Mary Crawshay Prizes, The 594
CRC Press 148
Creative Arts East 361
Creative Authors Ltd 478
Creative Content Ltd 221
Creative Plus Publishing Ltd 225
Creative Review 510
Creative Writer's Workshop, The 692

Index

creative writing 685
Creme de la Crime 148
Crescent Moon Publishing 149
Cressrelles Publishing Co. Ltd 149
Rupert Crew Ltd 478
Crime and Investigation (ci) 416
Crime Writers' Association 560
crime writing 237, 251
Criminal Law & Justice Weekly (incorporating Justice of the Peace) 49
Critical Quarterly 49
John D. Criticos Prize, The 594
critics 247
Critics' Circle, The 560
Crofts, Andrew 276
Crombie Jardine Publishing Ltd 149
Crosshands Ltd/ACP Television 421, 430
crossover authors 287
Crown House Publishing Ltd 149
Crown Publishing Group 209
Crowood Press, The 149
Croydon Central Library 680
CSA Word 221, 430
Cúirt International Festival of Literature, The 617
Cumbria Magazine 49
University of Cumbria 692
Benjamin Cummings 149
James Currey 149
Richard Curtis Associates Inc. 502
Curtis Brown (Australia) Pty Ltd 496
Curtis Brown Group Ltd 478, 502
Curve 442
Curzon Press Ltd 149
Custom Car 49
Custom PC 49
Cutler, Mary 384
Cutting Edge Productions 421
CVs 467
CWA Awards 594
Cwlwm Cyhoeddwyr Cymru 560
Cycle Sport 49
Cycling Weekly 49
Cygnus Book Club 346
Cyngor Llyfrau Cymru 560
Cyphers 50

Daily & Sunday Telegraph Syndication, The 119
Daily Dispatch 113
Daily Echo 24
Daily Express 11
Daily Mail 11
Daily Mirror 11
Daily Record 11
Daily Sport 11
Daily Star 12
Daily Star Sunday 12
Daily Telegraph, The 12
Dairy Farmer 50
Judy Daish Associates Ltd 479
Dalesman 50
Dalhousie Review, The 109
Dalrymple, William 262
Terence Dalton Ltd 149
damages, liability to pay 719
Dance Australia 106
Dance Today 50
Dancing Times 50
Dandy, The 50
Dare 50
Darton, Longman & Todd Ltd 149
Darts World 50
Data Publishers Association (DPA) 560
Dave and Dave Ja Vu 416
David & Charles Ltd 149
David, Gwenda 469
Caroline Davidson Literary Agency 479
Merric Davidson Literary Agency 479
Davies, Andrew 369
Rhys Davies Trust, The 594
Davis, Rib 662
DAW Books Inc. 209
Dawntreader, The 50
Giles de la Mare Publishers Ltd 149
Walter de la Mare Society 560
De Montfort University 692
Felix de Wolfe 479
Dead Good Poets Society 364
deadlines 5
Dean 149
death grant 752
debts, bad 729
Début Art & Coningsby Gallery, The 520
Decanter 50
Dedalus Ltd 149
defamation 719
Defamation Act 1996 719
DeFiore and Company 502
Delacorte 209
delicious. 51
Delta Books 204
Richard Dennis Publications 150
Department for Work and Pensions (DWP) 748
Derby Books Publishing Company Ltd, The 150
Derby Central Library 680
Derby Evening Telegraph 20
Derby Playhouse Ltd 442
Derbyshire Life and Countryside 51
Descant 109
Descent 51
design 231
- companies 510
- design right 699
- of websites 643
- right 710
- theatre 436

Design and Artists Copyright Society (DACS) 561, 713
Design Eye Ltd 226
Design Week 510
Destiny 113
detective fiction 237
André Deutsch 150

Deutsche Börse Photography Prize 594
Devon Life 51
DGA Ltd 479
Diagram Visual Information Ltd 226
Dial Books for Young Readers 209
dialogue, writing 264
Diana, Princess of Wales 385
Dickens Fellowship 561
Dickensian, The 51
diehard 150
Digital Camera 51
Digital Camera Buyer 51
Digital One 427–428
digital 716
  photography 537
  piracy 639
  printing 332
  publishing 330
  rights management (DRM) 638
  video 651
Digital Press 150
Digital Radio Group Ltd 428
Sandra Dijkstra Literary Agency 502
DILIA 497
Dingle Writing Courses 688
Director 51
directories 536
directors, theatre 436
Directory of Writers' Circles, Courses and Workshops 561
Disability Allowance (DLA) 751
Disability and Carer Benefits Scheme 749
Disability Now 51
Disabled Person's Tax Credit 749, 752
Discovery Channel 416
Discovery Walking Guides Ltd 150
Walt Disney Company Ltd, The 421
distribution 312
Diva 52
Diver 52
Diverse Production Ltd 421
Diversity Management 496
DIY Week 52
DNA Press 209
Dogs Today 52
Tom Doherty Associates, LLC 209
Dolls' House Magazine, The 52
Dolly 106
Dominie Pty Ltd 196
Donadio & Olson Inc. 502
John Donald 150
Dorian Literary Agency (DLA) 479
Dorling & Kindersley 268
Dorling Kindersley 150
'Sean Dorman' Manuscript Society 561
Dorner, Jane 629, 641
Dorset Echo 24
Dorset Life – Dorset Magazine, The 52
double taxation agreements 733, 739
Doubleday 471
Doubleday Canada 199
Doubleday Children's Books 150
Doubleday (UK) 150
Douglas & McIntyre Ltd 199
Dovecote Press Ltd, The 150
Dover Publications Inc. 209
downloadable books 635
Arthur Conan Doyle Society, The 561
dramatisations
  radio 387
  television 372, 378
Drapers 52
Dref Wen 150
Bryan Drew Ltd 479
Druid Theatre Company 442
Drum 113
Dublin Book Festival 617
University College Dublin Press 150
Dublin Review, The 52
Dublin Writers' Festival 617
Gerald Duckworth & Co. Ltd 150
Robert Dudley Agency 479
Dukes, The 442
Dundee Evening Telegraph and Post 23
Dundee International Book Prize, The 594
Dundee Repertory Theatre 442
Dundurn Press 199
Dunedin Academic Press 150
(Dunedin) Otago Daily Times 112
Dunham Literary, Inc. 502
Dunmore Press Ltd 202
(Durban)Mercury, The 114
Durham Book Festival 617
Durham University Library 680
Dutton 209
Dutton Children's Books 209
Dymocks.com 638
Dystel & Goderich Literary Management 502

e-formats 629
e-publishing 313, 629
e-readers 330
E4 416
EA Books 196
Toby Eady Associates Ltd 479
Eagle and Eagle Production 421
Early English Text Society 561
Early Music 52
Earnley Concourse, The 688
Earthscan 151
University of East Anglia 692
East Anglian Daily Times 20
East Lothian Life 53
Eastern Angles 446
Eastern Art Report 53
Eastern Daily Press 20
Eastwing 520
Easy Living 53
eb20 (reader) 638
EBL: Ebook Library, The 638

ebooks 124, 234, 300, 330, 635
business and professional 638
computing 639
devices 635, 630
services 637
stores 638
self publishing 638
eBooks.com 638
ebrary 638
Ebury Press 151
Echo 23
Ecologist, The 53
Economica 53
Economist, The 53
Ecosse Films Ltd 421
ECW Press Ltd 199
Eddison Pearson Ltd 480
Eddison Sadd Editions Ltd 226
Eden 151, 416
Edge, The 53
Edge Hill Short Story Prize 594
Edge Hill University 693
Edinburgh Bibliographical Society 561
Edinburgh Festival 393
Edinburgh International Book Festival 617, 686
Edinburgh Review 53
Edinburgh University Library 680
University of Edinburgh 693
Edinburgh University Press 151
editing consultation 305
Edition 226
Éditions Aubrey Walter/Gay Men's Press 151
Editor and Publisher 433
editorial department 230
editors 230, 235, 340
commissioning 230
freelance 255
literary 284
Education Journal 53
Educational Company of Ireland, The 151
Educational Explorers (Publishers) 151
Educational Recording Agency (ERA) 716
Educational Writers Group 561
Edwards Fuglewicz 480
Egmont Books 151
Eland Books 262
Eland Publishing Ltd 151
Electrical Review 54
electronic books *see* ebooks
Element 151
11:9 151
Edward Elgar Publishing Ltd 151
George Eliot Fellowship, The 561
T.S. Eliot Prize, The 595
ELLE (UK) 54
Ethan Ellenberg Literary Agency, The 502
Ellingham, Mark 267
Elliot Right Way Books 152
Elliott & Thompson 152
Desmond Elliott Prize, The 595
Elm Grove Books Ltd 226
ELM Publications and Training 152
Ann Elmo Agency Inc. 502
Elsevier Australia 196
Elsevier Ltd 152
Elsevier Ltd (Butterworth Heinemann) 152
Elsevier Ltd (Health Sciences) 152
Elstree Production Company, The 421
Simon Elvin Ltd 531
email 1, 9, 230, 469
Embroidery 54
Emerson College 689
Emmerdale 384
Empire 54
Encore Award 595
encryption 639
Encyclopaedia Britannica (UK) Ltd 152
Endemol UK 421
Energy Engineering 54
Engineer, The 54
Engineering in Miniature 54
English Agency (Japan) Ltd, The 498
English Association 561
English Garden, The 54
English Speaking Board (International) Ltd 561
English-Speaking Union, The 562
Enitharmon Press/Enitharmon Editions 152
Ennis Book Club Festival 617
Envoi 54
Epsom Writers' Workshop 365
eReader 639
Eric Gregory Awards 359
Lawrence Erlbaum Associates 152
Erotic Review, The 55
Esquire 55
Essentials 55
Essex Life 55
Essex Poetry Festival 617
University of Essex 693
ethical/political dilemmas 7, 30
Eulama SRL 498
Euro Crime 152
Euromonitor International plc 152
Europa Publications Ltd 152
Europa-Press 119
European Broadcasting Union 562
European market 469
European Publishers Award, The 595
European Rail Timetable 267
Europress Features (UK) 119
Evangelical Press of Wales 152
Faith Evans Associates 480
Ruth Evans Productions 431
Evans Publishing Group 152
Evans, Richard 287
Evening Chronicle 21
Evening Courier 26
Evening Echo (Cork) 19
Evening Express (Aberdeen) 23
Evening Gazette 21
Evening Herald 19
Evening News 27
Evening News (Edinburgh) 23
Evening Standard 21
Evening Star 20
Eventing 55

Evergreen 55
Everyday Practical Electronics 55
Everyman 153, 268
Everyman Theatre 442
Everyman's Library 153
Executive PA 55
Exeter Festival 618
University of Exeter Library 680
Exeter Northcott 443
University of Exeter Press 153
University of Exeter 693
exhibitions, photographic 537
Helen Exley® 153
expenses, claimed against tax 9, 729, 733
Expert Books 153
export editions 471
export sales 232
Express & Echo 24
Express & Star 26
Express Excess 364
Extreme Sports 416
Eye Candy Illustration 520
Eyeworks UK 421

Faber Academy, The 689
Faber and Faber, Inc. 209
Faber and Faber Ltd 153
Geoffrey Faber Memorial Prize, The 595
Faber, Michel 391
Fabian Society 153, 562
Facebook 301, 626
Facet Publishing 153
Facts On File Inc. 209
Alfred Fagon Award, The 595
Fairlady 114
fairs, trade, greeting-card 527
CJ Fallon 153
Falmer Press 153
University College Falmouth 693
Families First 55
Family History Monthly 55
Family Law Journal 56
Family Tree 56, 209
FAMOUS 119
fantasy genre, writing in 249
Far West 689
Eleanor Farjeon Award, The 595
Farmers Weekly 56, 114
Farrar, Straus and Giroux, LLC 209
fastsellers 240
Faulks, Sebastian 392
features, writing 28, 30
Federation Against Copyright Theft Ltd (FACT) 562
Federation of British Artists 562
Federation of European Publishers 562
Federation of Indian Publishers, The 562
Federation of Spanish Publishers' Association 563
Federation of Worker Writers and Community Publishers, The 563
Festival of Writing 689
Feelgood Fiction Ltd 421
fees 513
chasing 515
editing 305
fixed v. negotiable 514
kill 698
photographers' 539
play script 436
rejection 514
repeat 408
reproduction 540
television 407
Femina Magazine 114
Feminist Review, The 56
Fernwood Press CC 204
Festival at the Edge 618
Festival Productions Ltd 431
festivals, literary 393
FHM (For Him Magazine) 56
David Fickling Books 153
fiction 123, 241, 287, 292, 296
bestselling 237
children's 292
classic 391
crime 237
for radio 390
historical 256
online 282
romantic 253
teenage 123
Fiction Bitch 648
Fiction Factory 431
Fiddlehead, The 110
Field, The 56
Field, Anji Loman 378
Fielding, Helen 648
57 Productions 222
Fig Tree 153
Janet Fillingham Associates 480
film, producers 372
Film Ireland 56
Film Review 56
Film Rights Ltd 480
Film4 416
finance 729
Financial Adviser 57
Financial Times 12
Financial Times and Goldman Sachs Business Book of the Year Award 596
Finborough Theatre 438
Diana Finch Literary Agency 503
Finch, Peter 310
Findhorn Press Ltd 153
Fine Art Trade Guild, The 563
Fineleaf Publishing 154
FIRE 57
Fire in the Head 689
Firebird 210
Firm, The 503
First and Best in Education 154
First Writes Theatre Co Ltd 431

Fish Short Story Prize, One Page Prize, and Poetry Prize 596
Fisher, Anne-Louise 469
Fishing News 57
Fishlock, Trevor 266
Laurence Fitch Ltd 480
Fitzhenry & Whiteside Ltd 199
Fitzrovia Press Ltd 154
Five 410
Five Star 154
Five USA 416
Fiver 416
Flambard Press 154
Flame Tree Publishing 154
Flannel 431
Ian Fleming Associates 520
Fletcher & Company 503
Flight International 57
Flora International 57
Floris Books 154
Fly-Fishing & Fly-Tying 57
Flyleaf Press 154
FOCAL International Ltd (Federation of Commercial AudioVisual Libraries International Ltd) 563
Focal Press 154
Focus Films Ltd 422
Focus Publishing 226
Focus Theatre Company (Scotland) 443
Fodor's Travel Publications 210
Folens Publishers 154 154
Folio 57
Folio Illustrators' & Designers' Agents 520
Folio Society, The 346
Folkestone Book Festival 618
Folklore Society, The 563
Font Literary Agency 480
Food Network 416
Paul Foot Award, The 596
Footprint 269
Footprint Handbooks 154
Foreign Press Association in London 563
Foresight News 119
Mark Forstater Productions Ltd 422
E.M. Forster Award 596
Fortean Times 57
Fortnight – An Independent Review of Politics and the Arts 57
Forward Prizes for Poetry 596
Jill Foster Ltd (JFL) 480
W. Foulsham & Co. Ltd 155
4C–Charity Christmas Card Council 531
Four Courts Press 155
4 Music 416
FourFourTwo 58
Fourth Estate 155
Fox & Howard Literary Agency 480
Fox Chase Agency Inc., The 503
Robert Fox Ltd 438
Foyle Young Poets of the Year Award 362, 367
France 58
Frankfurt Book Fair 233, 455, 471
Miles Franklin Literary Award 596
Fraser Ross Associates 481
Jeanne Fredericks Literary Agency Inc. 503
Free Association Books 155
Free Painters & Sculptors 563
Free Press 155
Free the Word! 618
Free@last TV 422
Robert A. Freedman Dramatic Agency Inc. 503
Freelance 112
Freelance Market News 58
freelance rates, minimum 32, 731
W.H. Freeman 155
Freesat 414
Freeview 414
French House Party, The 693
Samuel French Inc 210, 503
Samuel French Ltd 155
French Publishers' Association 563
Sarah Jane Freymann Literary Agency 503
Friday Project, The 155
Friend, The 58
Frieze 58
Paul & Peter Fritz AG Literary Agency 500
Frommer, Arthur 268
front-of-store promotions 317
Frontline 155
FT Prentice Hall 155
Full House 58
David Fulton 155
funeral payment 752
Furrow, The 58
Futerman, Rose & Associates 481

Jüri Gabriel 481
Gaelic Books Council, The 563
Gaia Books 155
Gaia Communications 422
Gaiman, Neil 287, 647
Galago Publishing (Pty) Ltd 204
Galaxy British Book Awards 596
Galaxy Children's Large Print 155
Galleries 58
Gallery Five Ltd 532
Gallery Press, The 155
Gallic Books 155
Gallimard Presse 268
Games Master 58
Garden, The 59
Garden and Home 114
Garden Answers 59
Garden Media Guild, The 563
Garden News 59
Garland Science 155
Garner, Alan 250
J. Garnet Miller 155
Garnet Publishing Ltd 155
Gaskell Society, The 563
Gay Authors Workshop 564

Index

Noel Gay Television 422
Gay Times – GT 59
Geddes & Grosset 155
Gee, Maggie 666
Lionel Gelber Prize, The 597
Gelfman Schneider Literary Agents Inc. 503
Gemma International Ltd 532
General Insurance Standards Council 726
Geographical 59
Geographical Journal 59
Geological Magazine 59
German Publishers' and Booksellers' Association 564
Getty Publications 210
Ghost Story Society, The 564
ghostwriting 276
Gibbons Stamp Monthly 59
Gibson Greetings International Ltd 532
Gibson Square 156
Michael Gifkins & Associates 499
Gill & Macmillan Ltd 156
Ginger Productions 422
Ginn 156
GL Assessment 156
Gladstone History Book Prize 597
University of Glamorgan 693
Glamour 59
Glasgow Evening Times 23
University of Glasgow Library 680
University of Glasgow 693
Glasgow Women's Library 680
Eric Glass Ltd 481
Gloucestershire Echo 25
GMTV 410
Go Girl Magazine 60
Go! 114
God TV 416
David R. Godine, Publisher Inc. 210
Godsfield Press 156
David Godwin Associates 481
Godwin, Tony 260
Goethe-Institut London Library 680
G.O.L.D. 416
Gold Eagle Books 199
Frances Goldin Literary Agency 503
Goldsmith Press Ltd, The 156
Goleman, Daniel 275
Golf Monthly 60
Golf World 60
Gollancz 156, 287
Gomer Press 156
Good Book Guide, The 60
Good Film Company, The 422
Good Food 417
Good Housekeeping 60
Good Illustration Ltd 520
Goodman Associates, Literary Agents 503
Google Books Settlement 331
Gordon, Giles 449
Goss & Crested China Club 156
Gotham 210
Government News Network (GNN) 119
Government Supplies Agency 156
Gower 156
GQ 60
Graeae Theatre Company 446
Grafik 510
Graham Maw Christie 481
Graham-Cameron Publishing & Illustration 226, 520
Grand Central Publishing 210
Grand Theatre 443
Grandi & Associati SRL 498
Granta 60
Granta Publications 156
Graphic Humour Ltd 532
Graphic Syndication 119
Grayling, A.C. 468
Grazia 60
Annette Green Authors' Agency 481
Christine Green Authors' Agent 481
Green Bay Media 422
Green Books 156
Green Futures 60
Green, Jane 253
Green Pebble 61
Green Print 156
Kate Greenaway Medal 597
Louise Greenberg Books Ltd 482
Sanford J. Greenburger Associates Inc. 504
Greene & Heaton Ltd 482
Graham Greene Birthplace Trust 564
Greenhouse Literary Agency, The 482
University of Greenwich 693
Greenwich Village Productions/Fiction Factory, The 422
Greeting Card Association, The 564
greeting cards 510, 527
Greetings Factory Ltd, The 532
Greetings Today 61
Gregory & Company Authors' Agents 482
Eric Gregory Trust Fund, The 597
Gresham Books Ltd 156
Grey, John 274
Griffin Poetry Prize 597
Grimsby Telegraph 27
Grocer, The 61
Grosset & Dunlap 210
David Grossman Literary Agency Ltd 482
Grove/Atlantic Inc. 210
Grow Your Own 61
Grub Street Publishing 157
Guardian, The 12, 651
  Children's Fiction Prize, The 597
  First Book Award, The 597
  Hay Festival, The 393, 618
  Research Fellowship, The 597
Guardian Review 284
Guardian Unlimited 284
Guardian/Observer Syndication 120
Guardian's Allowance 749
Guernsey Arts Council 564

Guernsey Press and Star 19
Guiding Magazine 61
Guild of Agricultural Journalists 564
Guild of Aviation Artists, The 520, 564
Guild of British Travel Writers 269
Guild of Food Writers 564
Guild of Health Writers 564
Guild of International Songwriters & Composers, The 565
Guild of Master Craftsman Publications Ltd 157
Guild of Motoring Writers, The 565
Guild of Railway Artists 565
Guildford Book Festival 618
Guildhall Library 681
Guinness World Records 157
Guitarist 61
Gulf Professional Press 157
Gullane Children's Books 157
Gunn Media 482
Marianne Gunn O'Connor Literary Agency 482

Hachette Australia Pty Ltd 197
Hachette Book Group USA 210
Hachette Children's Books 157
Hachette Digital 222
Hachette New Zealand Ltd 203
Hachette UK 157, 328
Hairflair & Beauty 61
Hakluyt Society 565
Halban Publishers 157
Halcyon Publishing Ltd 203
Haldane Mason Ltd 157
Robert Hale Ltd 158
Rod Hall Agency Ltd, The 483
Hall, Lee 387
Hallmark Cards Plc 532
Hallmark Channel 417
Halsgrove Publishing 158
Hamilton, Alex 237, 266
(Hamilton)Spectator, The 110
Hamish Hamilton 158
Hamlyn 158
Hammer and Tongue 364
Hampshire – County Magazine, The 61
Hampstead Theatre 438
Hanbury Agency, The 483
H&E Naturist 61
Hanson White – UK Greetings 532
Happy Films 422
Harcourt Trade Publishers 210
hardbacks 331
Patrick Hardy Books 158
Thomas Hardy Society, The 565
Harleian Society 565
Harlequin Enterprises Ltd 199
Harlequin Mills & Boon Ltd 158
Harper NonFiction 222
HarperCollins Audio Books 222
HarperCollins Children's 287
HarperCollins Entertainment 158
HarperCollins Publishers (Australia) Pty Ltd Group 197
HarperCollins Publishers Ltd 158, 200, 210, 287, 328
HarperCollins Publishers (New Zealand) Ltd 203
Harper's Bazaar 62, 106
HarperTrue 159
Harrap Columbus 267
Joy Harris Literary Agency Inc., The 504
Harris, Robert 391
Harrogate Theatre 443
Hart McLeod Ltd 226
Hart, Michael 635
Hartlepool Mail 21
Harvard University Press 211
Harvill Secker 159
Antony Harwood Ltd 483
Hastings House/Daytrips Publishers 211
Hat Trick Productions Ltd 422
Haus Publishing Ltd 159
Hawke's Bay Today 112
John Hawkins & Associates Inc. 504
Hawthorn Press 159
Hawthornden Castle 666–667
Hawthornden Fellowships 598
Hawthornden Prize, The 598
Hay Festival 393, 618
Hay House Publishers 159
Hay, Louise 272
Haynes Publishing 159
Hayters Teamwork 120
Francis Head Bequest 598
Headland Publications 160
Headline Publishing Group 160
Headliners 120
Headlong Theatre 446
Health Club Management 62
Healthy 62
Heat 62
A.M. Heath & Co. Ltd 483
Heavy Entertainment Ltd 431
Heinemann 160
William Heinemann 160
Hello! 62
Christopher Helm 160
Felicia Hemans Prize for Lyrical Poetry, The 598
Herald, The 13, 25
Herald Express 25
Herbert Press, The 160
Jeff Herman Agency LLC, The 504
Hermes House 160
Nick Hern Books Ltd 160
Hershey, Jennifer 287
Hertfordshire Countryside 62
Hesketh Hubbard Art Society 565
Hesperus Press Ltd 160
Hessell-Tiltman Prize 598
Heyday Films 471
hhb agency ltd 466, 483
Hi-Fi News 62

Index

High Life 62
High Wycombe Library 681
David Higham Associates Ltd 483
Hill and Wang 211
Frederick Hill/Bonnie Nadell Inc. 504
Hill, Christopher William 433
William Hill Sports Book of the Year Award 598
Hilliard Society of Miniaturists, The 565
Hilmarton Manor Press 160
James Hilton Society, The 565
Hippo 160
Hippocrene Books Inc. 211
Hippopotamus Press 160
Hiss & Boo Company Ltd, The 446
Historical™ 160
Historical Novel Society 565
historical romances 238, 256
History 417
History Press Ltd, The 160
History Today 62
HIT Entertainment Ltd 422
Hits, The 427
HL Studios Ltd 226
HM Revenue & Customs 749
Ho Davies, Peter 393
Hobsons Publishing plc 161
Hodder & Stoughton 161
Hodder & Stoughton Audiobooks 222
Hodder Children's Books 161
Hodder Education Group 161
Hodder Faith 161
Hodder Gibson 161
Hodder Headline Ltd 161
Hodder Wayland 161
John Hodgson Agency 520
Hoffer, Hans 268
Calvin and Rose G. Hoffman Memorial Prize for Distinguished Publication on Christopher Marlowe, The 598
Holden-Brown, Heather 466
Holiday House Inc. 211
Sherlock Holmes Society of London, The 566
Henry Holt and Company LLC 211
Vanessa Holt Ltd 483
Home 417
Home Words 63
Homes and Gardens 63
Honno Ltd (Welsh Women's Press) 161
Johns Hopkins University Press, The 211
Hopscotch Educational Publishing Ltd 161
Horror Channel 417
Horror Writers Association (HWA) 566
Horse & Hound 63
Horse & Pony Magazine 63
Horse and Rider 63
Hortus 63
Valerie Hoskins Associates Ltd 483
Hot Press 63
Hothouse Fiction Ltd 226
Houghton Mifflin 211
Hounslow Press 200
House & Garden 63
House Beautiful 63
House of Lochar 162
house style 9, 671
Housebuilder 64
Housing Benefit 752
Housman Society 566
How To Books Ltd 162
Tanja Howarth Literary Agency 483
HP Books 211
HQ Poetry Magazine 64
HQN Books 200
L. Ron Hubbard's Writers and Illustrators of the Future Contests 598
Huddersfield Daily Examiner, The 27
Huddersfield Literature Festival 618
Hudson Street Press 211
Ted Hughes Award for New Work in Poetry, The 599
Hull Daily Mail 27
Hull Truck Theatre Co. Ltd 446
University of Hull 693
humour 246
Hurst – The John Osborne Arvon Centre, The 667
Hutchinson 162
Hutchinson Children's Books 162
Hyperion 211

I'm Pregnant! 64
ICIS Chemical Business 64
Icon Books Ltd 162
Icon Films 422
Icon Magazine 64
ICSA Information & Training Ltd 162
Ideal Home 64
Ideas 114
ideas, pitching 31
Igloo Books Ltd 162
Ignition Films Ltd 422
Ilex Press Ltd, The 162
Ilidio da Fonseca Matos, Agente Literário Lda 499
Ilkley Literature Festival 618
University of Illinois Press 211, 635
Illuminations Television 423
Illustration Ltd 520
illustrations, illustrators 291, 340, 509, 516
Image by Design Licensing 521
Images – Best of British Contemporary Illustration, The 599
IMG UK Ltd 484
Imison Award, The 599
Imperial War Museum 162
Imprint Academic 162
Improve Your Coarse Fishing 64
In Pinn 162
In Style 64
Incapacity Benefit 750, 753
Income Support 752
income tax 729, 731

interest on overdue 738
self-assessment 737
tax return 737
Incorporated Society of Musicians 566
Independent, The 13, 648
Independent Foreign Fiction Prize 599
Independent Music Press 162
Independent Newspapers Gauteng 114
Independent Newspapers Kwa-Zulu Natal Ltd 114
Independent Newspapers (South Africa) Ltd 115
Independent on Sunday 13
Independent Publishers Guild 566
Independent Radio News (IRN) 120
Independent Talent Group Ltd 484
Independent Theatre Council (ITC) 566
Indepenpress Publishing Ltd 162
Index on Censorship 64
Indexers Available 670
indexing 231, 304, 669–670
Indian King Arts 689
Indiana University Press 212
Infinite Ideas 163
Inform 64
Informa 636
InkWell Management 504
Inkwell Writers Workshops 689
INS (International News Service) and Irish News Service 120
Inside Soap 65
Insight Guides 268
Insight Guides Travel Photography Prize 599
Insight Guides/Berlitz Publishing 163
Inspire Magazine, CPO 65
Institute of Designers in Ireland 566
Institute of Public Administration 163
Institute of Translation & Interpreting (ITI), The 566
insurance, libel 725
Insurance Age 65
Insurance Brokers' Monthly 65
Inter-Varsity Press 163
Intercontinental Literary Agency 484
InterMedia 65
Internationaal Literatuur Bureau B.V. 499
International Affairs 65
International Amateur Theatre Association (IATA) 567
International Creative Management Inc. 504
International Digital Publishing Foundation (IDPF) 637
International Editors Co., S.L. 496, 500
International Fashion Press Agency 120
International Federation of Reproduction Rights Organisations (IFRRO) 714
International IMPAC Dublin Literary Award 599
International Journal of Canadian Studies 110
International Marine Publishing 212
International PEN 567
International Playwriting Festival 599, 618
International Press Agency (Pty) Ltd 120
International Publishers Association 567
International Reply Coupons (IRCs) 116, 124
International Society of Typographic Designers 567
International Visual Communication Association (IVCA) 568
internet 254, 349, 469, 635–636
access to 9
and copyright 698
and self-publishing 312
book sales on 232
poetry groups on 366
interviews 7, 29
author 233, 325
copyright in 698
with potential clients 512
Interzone 65
Inuit Art Quarterly 110
Invalid Care Allowance 751
(Invercargill)Southland Times, The 112
Inverness Courier 23
Investors Chronicle 65
iPad 234, 330
iPhone 330
Ireland's Own 65
Irish Academic Press Ltd 163
Irish Arts Review 66
Irish Book Publishers' Association, The 568
Irish Copyright Licensing Agency, The 568
Irish Daily Star 14
Irish Examiner 14
Irish Farmers Journal 66
Irish Independent 14
Irish Journal of Medical Science 66
Irish Medical Times 66
Irish News 19
Irish Pages: A Journal of Contemporary Writing 66
Irish Playwrights and Screenwriters Guild 568
Irish Post, The 66
Irish Printer 66
Irish Tatler 66
Irish Times, The 14
Irish Translators' and Interpreters' Association 568
Irish Writers' Centre 568, 667, 689
Irish Writers' Union/Comhar na Scríbhneoirí 568
IRN (Independent Radio News) 427
ISBN Agency 345
ISBNs 310, 339, 341, 345
FAQs about 314
ISG (CILIP)/BookData Reference Awards, The 599
Isis/Soundings 222
Island 106
ISSNs 315
Ithaca Press 163
ITN (Independent Television News Ltd) 410
ITN Productions 423
ITV Anglia 412
ITV Border 412
ITV Central 412
ITV Granada 412
ITV London 412
ITV Meridian 412
ITV Plc 411
ITV Studios/Granada 423
ITV Tyne Tees 412

ITV Wales 412
ITV Westcountry and ITV West 412
ITV Yorkshire 412
ITV2 417
ITV3 417
ITV4 417
Ivy Contract 227
Ivy Press Ltd, The 227
IWC Media Ltd 423

jacket, book 317
Jackie 385
Jacklin Enterprises (Pty) Ltd 204
JAI 163
Barrie James Literary Agency 484
James W. Hackett International Haiku Award 361
Jane's 163
Jane's Defence Weekly 66
Jane's Information Group 163
Janklow & Nesbit Associates 504
Janklow & Nesbit (UK) Ltd 484
Jarrold Publishing 163
JCA Literary Agency Inc. 504
Richard Jefferies Society, The 568
Jersey Evening Post 19
Jersey Library 681
Jewish Book Week 619
Jewish Chronicle 67
Jewish Quarterly, The 67
  Wingate Literary Prizes 600
Jewish Telegraph 67
Jobcentre Plus 749
Jobseeker's Allowance 752
Jodds 532
(Johannesburg) Sunday Times 115
John Kinsella's 366
Johnson & Alcock Ltd 484
Samuel Johnson Prize for Non-Fiction 600
Johnson Society, The 569
Johnson Society of London 569
joint authorship 306
joint works 704
Joker Feature Service (JFS) 120
Libba Jones Associates 521
Robin Jones Literary Agency 484
Tibor Jones & Associates 484
Jordan Publishing Ltd 163
Michael Joseph 163
Journal, The 21
Journal of Alternative and Complementary Medicine 67
journalism 3, 28
Journalists' Charity 569
Jove 212
Jane Judd Literary Agency 484
Junior 67
Juta & Company Ltd 205

Kangaroo Press 197
University Press of Kansas 212
Michelle Kass Associates 485
Kay, Jackie 393
Sheila Kaye-Smith Society, The 569
Keats-Shelley Memorial Association 569
Keeble, Richard 28
Keller Media Inc. 504
Frances Kelly Agency 485
Kelsey, Linda 466
Kenilworth Press 163
Kent & Sussex Poetry Society 365, 569
Kent and Sussex Poetry Society Open Poetry Competition 600
Kent Life 67
Bill Kenwright Ltd 438
Kenyon-Deane 163
Kerrang! 67
Kerry Group Irish Fiction Award 600
Key Porter Books Ltd 200
Virginia Kidd Agency Inc. 504
Kids Alive! (Young Soldier), The 67
Kids Can Press Ltd 200
Kilkenny Campus NUI Maynooth 689
kill fees 698
Kimani Press 200
Kindle 234, 330, 639
Laurence King Publishing Ltd 163
Kingfisher 164
King's Head Theatre 439
King's Lynn Literature Festivals 619
Kingscourt 164
Jessica Kingsley Publishers 164
Kingston Readers' Festival 619, 687
Kingston University 693
Kipling Society, The 569
Kitchen Garden 68
Harvey Klinger Inc. 505
Kloet, Chris 291
Kluwer Law International 164
Peter Knight Agency 485
Charles Knight 164
Knight Features 120
Knight Paperbacks 164
Knopf Canada 200
Knopf Doubleday Publishing Group 212
Knovel 638
Knuston Hall 689
Knutsford Literature Festival 619
Kogan Page Ltd 164
Koi 68
Barbara S. Kouts, Literary Agent 505
Kraszna-Krausz Awards 600
Krause Publications 212
kt literary 505
Kube Publishing Ltd 164
Kudos Books 164
University of KwaZulu-Natal Press 205

La Nouvelle Agence 498
Lady, The 68

Ladybird 164
Charles Lamb Society, The 569
Lambeth Palace Library 681
Lancashire Authors' Association, The 569
Lancashire Evening Post 22
Lancashire Magazine 68
Lancashire Telegraph 22
Lancaster University 365, 693
Lancet 68
Peter Lang Ltd 164
Lantern 197
(Launceston) Examiner 106
launches, book 286
LAW (Lucas Alexander Whitley Ltd) 485
Lawbook Co. 197
Lawrence & Wishart Ltd 164
D.H. Lawrence Society, The 569
T.E. Lawrence Society, The 570
Lawyer, The 68
Lazear Agency Inc., The 505
LBLA (Lorella Belli Literary Agency) 485
Le Fanu, Mark 453
Susanna Lea Associates Ltd 485, 498
Leader, The 25
League of Canadian Poets 570
Learning Media Ltd 203
Ledbury Poetry Festival 619
Leeds Central Library 681
Leeds Metropolitan University 694
Leeds Postcards 532
Leeds University Library 681
University of Leeds 689, 694
Legal Week 68
Legat, Michael 303, 697
Learning and Information Library (Leicester) 681
University of Leicester Library 681
Leicester Mercury, The 20
Leigh Fermor, Patrick 262, 266
Leisure Painter 68
Lemonade Illustration Agency 521
Lemony Snicket books 288
Leonhardt & Høier Literary Agency A/S 499
Leopard Films Ltd 423
Lescher & Lescher Ltd 505
Lette, Kathy 245
Letterbox Library 346
letters of introduction 468
Letts and Lonsdale 164
Leverhulme Research Fellowships 600
Levi, Peter 266
Barbara Levy Literary Agency 485
Lewes Live Literature 619
David Lewis Illustration Agency 521
Lewis Mason 164
Lex Copyright 497
LexisNexis Canada Inc. 200
LexisNexis 164
LexisNexis Butterworths Australia 197
LexisNexis NZ Ltd 203
Lexus Ltd 227
LGC (Local Government Chronicle) 68
libel
  blasphemous 727
  insurance 725
  law of 719
  priviledge 724
Liberato 689
Libra Television Ltd 423
libraries 638
Library Association Publishing 164
Library Magna Books Ltd 222
Library Theatre Company 443
licence to copy 713
licensing 530
Liepman AG 500
Life & Work: Editorially Independent Magazine of the Church of Scotland 69
Lightning Source 333
Lilliput Press Ltd, The 164
Lima Design 532
Limelight Management 486
Lincoln Book Festival 619
Frances Lincoln Ltd 165
Lincolnshire Echo 27
Lincolnshire Life 69
Lindsay Literary Agency 486
Linen Hall Library, The 681
Ling Design Ltd 532
Linguist, The 69
Lion Hudson plc 165
Lion Television 423
List, The 69
Lit.com 620
literary agents 123, 131, 230, 252, 254, 265, 277, 290–291, 295, 298, 372, 376, 380, 391, 419, 436, 449, 455, 461, 465, 471
  how to get 458
  when needed 453
literary critics 286
literary editors 284
Literary Review, The 69
Literary Review Grand Poetry Prize 600
literary scouts 230, 469
Literary Consultancy, (TLC), The 687
Litfest 620
Little Bird Company Ltd 423
Little Black Dress 165
Little, Brown & Company 212
Little, Brown Book Group 165
Little Dancer Films 423
Christopher Little Literary Agency 486
Little People Books 227
Little Theatre Guild of Great Britain 570
Little Tiger Press 165
Live Theatre 443
Liverpool Central Library 681
Liverpool Daily Post 22
Liverpool Echo 22
Liverpool Everyman and Playhouse 443
Liverpool John Moores University 694
Liverpool University Press 165
Livewire 166

Index

Living 417
Living and Loving 115
Living France Magazine 69
John Llewellyn Rhys Prize 600
Llewellyn Worldwide 212
Loaded 69
Loftus Audio Ltd 431
Logaston Press 166
LOGOS 69, 536
London at Large Ltd 120
London Book Fair 233, 268, 312, 471
London Bubble, The 446
London College of Communication 694
Library and Learning Resources 681
London College of Fashion Library 681
London Film School, The 694
University of London, Goldsmiths College 694
London Independent Books 486
London Institute Libraries 681
University of London, King's College 694
London Library, The 681
London Literature Festival 620
London Magazine: A Review of Literature and the Arts, The 70
London Press Club Awards 601
London Press Service 121
London Review of Books 70
University of London, Royal Holloway 694
Library of the London School of Economics and Political Science 681
London Writers' Circle 365
London Book Fair 456
Lone Pine Publishing 200
Lonely Planet 166, 197, 267
Long, Kate 392
Elizabeth Longford Grants, The 601
Elizabeth Longford Prize for Historical Biography, The 601
Longman 166
Longman, Derek 390
Lorenz Books 166
Losada, Isabel 324
Lothian Life 70
Lowdham Book Festival 620
Andrew Lownie Literary Agency 486
Luath Press Ltd 166
Lucas Alexander Whitley 486
Lucas, Suzy 469
Lucy Luck Associates 486
Jennifer Luithlen Agency 486
Lumb Bank –Ted Hughes Arvon Centre, The 668
Lumsden, Roddy 357
Luna Books 200
Lund Humphries 166
Lutterworth Press 166
Lutyens & Rubinstein 486
Luxton Harris Ltd 487
Sir William Lyons Award, The 601
Lyons Press, The 212
Lyric Hammersmith 439

M6 Theatre Company (Studio Theatre) 447
Donald Maass Literary Agency 505
Duncan McAra 487
Margret McBride Literary Agency 505
Anita D. McClellan Associates 505
McClelland & Stewart Ltd 200
Anne McDermid & Associates Ltd 497
McGill-Queen's University Press 200
McGraw-Hill Book Company New Zealand Ltd 203
McGraw-Hill Education 166, 197
McGraw-Hill Professional 212
McGraw-Hill Ryerson Ltd 201
McIntosh & Otis Inc. 505
Frances McKay Illustration 521
McKernan Literary Agency & Consultancy, The 487
McKitterick Prize, The 601
Franco-British Society's Enid McLeod Literary Prize, The 601
Bryan MacMahon Short Story Award 601
Macmillan Children's Books Ltd 166
Macmillan Digital Audio 222
Macmillan Education Australia Pty Ltd 197
Macmillan Heinemann English Language Teaching 166
Macmillan Prize for Children's Picture Book Illustration, The 601
Macmillan Publishers Ltd 166, 213
Eunice McMullen Ltd 487
McPherson & Company 213
MacUser 70
Macworld 70
Made in Manchester 431
Made Simple Books 167
magazines
illustrations 509
poetry 353, 358
sales 468
writing for 30, 296
Magi Publications 167
Maharaja Features Pvt. Ltd (1969) 121
Maia Press Ltd, The 168
Mail on Sunday 14
Mainstream Publishing Co. (Edinburgh) Ltd 168
Malahat Review, The 110
Malone Gill Productions Ltd 423
Man Asian Literary Prize 602
Man Booker International Prize, The 318, 329, 602
Management Books 2000 Ltd 168
Management Magazine 112
Management Today 70
Manchester Central Library 682
Manchester Children's Book Festival 620
Manchester Evening News 22
Manchester Fiction Prize 2011, The 602
Manchester Literature Festival 620
Manchester Poetry Prize 2012, The 602
University of Manchester 694
Manchester University Press 168
Manchester Writing School at Manchester Metropolitan University, The 694
Mandrake of Oxford 168

Mango Publishing 168
Carol Mann Agency 506
Andrew Mann Ltd 487
Sarah Manson Literary Agent 487
Manson Publishing Ltd 168
Mantra Lingua 168
manuscripts 131, 255, 453, 625, 660, 671, 687
unsolicited 230, 255, 291, 308, 453
Marchand, Pierre 268
Marie Claire 70
Marino Books 168
Marjacq Scripts 487
Market House Books Ltd 227
Market News International 121
Market Newsletter 70
market research 354
marketing 231–232, 236, 291, 316, 320, 631
after publication 322
Marketing Week 70
Michael Marks Awards for Poetry Pamphlets, The 602
Marks, Louis 370
Marlborough College Summer School 689
Marlowe Society, The 570
Marsh Agency Ltd, The 487
Marsh Award for Children's Literature in Translation 603
Marsh Biography Award 603
Evan Marshall Agency, The 506
Marshall Cavendish 168
Marshall Editions Ltd 227
Jane Marshall Productions 431
Marton Agency Inc., The 506
Blanche Marvin 488
John Masefield Memorial Trust, The 603
John Masefield Society, The 570
Maskew Miller Longman (Pty) Ltd 205
Kenneth Mason Publications Ltd 168
University of Massachusetts Press, The 213
Master Photographers Association 570
Maternity Allowance 753
maternity loans and grants 749
Somerset Maugham Awards, The 603
Maxim 70
Maya Vision International Ltd 423
MayerBenham Ltd 488
Mayfair 71
Kevin Mayhew Ltd 168
MBA Literary Agents Ltd 488
MBUK (Mountain Biking UK) 71
McConnell, Jean 419
McEwan, Ian 391
McKean, Dave 288
Meadowside Children's Books 169
Meanjin 107
Mechanical-Copyright Protection Society Ltd (MCPS) 570
Medal News 71
Media Society, The 570
Media Week 71
Mediawatch-UK 570
Medical™ 169
Medical Writers Group 571
Medici Cards Limited 532
Medway Messenger 24
Meiklejohn Illustration 521
(Melbourne)Age, The 107
(Melbourne) Herald Sun 107
(Melbourne) Sunday Herald Sun 107
Melbourne University Publishing 197
Michael Meller Literary Agency 498
Memoir Writing Club, The 571
Men Only 71
Men's Health 71, 115
Mentor Books 169
Mentorn 423
Mercat Press 169
Mercier Press, The 169
Merlin Press Ltd 169
Merrell Publishers Ltd 169
Methodist Publishing House 169
Methodist Recorder 71
Methuen Drama 169
Methuen Publishing Ltd 169
Metro 21
Metro Books 169
Meyer, Stephanie 329
Michaels, Amanda 700
Michelin Maps and Guides 169
University of Michigan Press, The 213
Microsoft Press 213
Microsoft Reader 639
Middlesex University 695
Summer School 690
N.E. Middleton Artists' Agency 521
Midland Publishing 169
Military Modelling 71
Milkweed Editions 213
Millennium 268
Miller's 169
Mills & Boon Romance™ 169, 253
Mills, Merope 5
Milo Books Ltd 169
Mind, Body & Spirit (MBS) 272
Mind Book of the Year 603
Minimum Terms Agreement (MTA) 303
Minor Monthly 71
Mint Productions 423
Mira Books® 170, 201
Missenden Abbey 690
University of Missouri Press 213
MIT Press, The 213
Kathleen Mitchell Award 603
Mitchell Beazley 170
Mitchell, David 392
Mitchell Library, The 682
Mixmag 72
Mizz 72
mobile phones 636, 639
Mobility Allowance 751
Mobipocket 639
Mobius 170

Index

Model Boats 72
Model Engineer 72
Modern Extra™ 170
Modern Language Review 72
Modern Romance™ 170
Mohrbooks AG, Literary Agency 500
Mojo 72
Monacelli Press, The 213
Monarch Books 170
Mondadori 472
Moneywise 72
Moniack Mhor 668
Monkey Feet Illustration Agency, The 521
Monkey Puzzle Media Ltd 227
Montana New Zealand Book Awards 603
Moral Support 439
More! 72
More 4 417
Morehouse Publishing Co. 213
Morgan Kauffman 170
Morley College 690
Sheridan Morley Prize for the Best Theatre Biography 603
Morning Star 15
Morrigan Book Company 170
William Morris Agency Inc. 506
William Morris Endeavor Entertainment 488
William Morris Society 571
William Morrow 213
Mosby 170
Mosse, Kate 301, 648
Mother & Baby 72
Motor Boat and Yachting 72
Motor Boats Monthly 73
Motor Caravan Magazine 73
Motor Cycle News 73
Motorcaravan Motorhome Monthly (MMM) 73
Mount Eagle Publications Ltd 170
Move! 115
MPC Guides 268
Mslexia 73
MSS *see* manuscripts
MTV 417
Mundy, Maggie 516
Munro, Alice 393
Murdoch Books UK Ltd 170
Judith Murdoch Literary Agency 488
Murray, John 266
John Murray (Publishers) 170
Muscle & Fitness 73
Muse Literary Management 506
Music Publishers Association Ltd 571
Music Teacher 73
Music Week 73
Musical Opinion 74
Musical Times 74
MXR Digital Radio Ltd 429
My Weekly 74
My Weekly Pocket Novel 74
MyILibrary 638
Myriad Editions 170
Myss, Caroline 274
Jean V. Naggar Literary Agency Inc. 506
NAL 213
Napoleon & Company 201
narrators 390
Melissa Nathan Award for Comedy Romance, The 603
National Acrylic Painters' Association (NAPA) 571
National Archives of Australia 197
National Art Library 682
National Association of Press Agencies (NAPA) 121, 571
National Association of Writers' Groups 571
National Association of Writers in Education (NAWE) 366
National Campaign for the Arts (NCA) 571
National Council for the Training of Journalists (NCTJ) 572
National Eisteddfod of Wales 620
National Film and Television School 695
National Geographic and Nat Geo Wild 417
National Insurance Contributions 730, 734, 737, 740, 742
  exemptions 747
  maximum 748
National Library of Ireland 682
National Library of Scotland, The 682
National Library of Wales, The 682
National Literacy Trust 572
National Maritime Museum 682
National Maritime Museum Publishing 170
National Poetry competition 359, 362, 364, 604
National Poetry Day 362
National Poetry Foundation 343
National Society for Education in Art and Design 572
National Society of Painters, Sculptors and Printmakers 572
National Trust 170
National Trust Magazine, The 74
National Union of Journalists (NUJ) 5, 9, 32, 572, 697
National Viewers' and Listeners' Association 572
Natural Health and Vegetarian Life 107
Natural History Museum Library and Information Services 682
Natural History Museum Publishing 170
Natural World 74
Naturalist 74
Nature 74
Nautical Data Ltd 170
Nautical Magazine 74
Naxos AudioBooks 222
NB Illustration 521
NB Magazine 74
NB Publishers (Pty) Ltd 205
NCTJ 572
NCVO Publications 170
Neal Street Productions Ltd 439
Neate Publishing 170
Nelson Education 201
Nelson Mail, The 112

Thomas Nelson Publisher 213
Nelson Thornes Ltd 171
Nemirovsky, Irene 392
Neo-opsis Science Fiction Magazine 110
Neon 431
Edith Nesbit Society, The 572
.net 75
Net Book Agreement 299
netLibrary 638
networking 125
New Africa Books (Pty) Ltd 205
New Age 272
New Beacon Books 171
New Blitz Literary & TV Agency 121, 498
New Cavendish Books 171
New English Art Club 572
New Holland Publishers (UK) Ltd 171
New Humanist 75
New Internationalist 75
New Island Books 171
New Law Journal 75
New Media Age 75
University of New Mexico Press 214
New Musical Express (NME) 75
New Perspectives Theatre Company 447
New Playwrights' Network 171
New Rider 171
New Scientist 75
New Statesman 75
New Theatre: Dublin, The 443
New Theatre Publications/Playwrights' Co-operative, The 171
New Theatre Quarterly 75
New Vic Theatre 443
New Welsh Review 76
New Wolsey Theatre, The 443
New Writer, The 76
New Writer Prose and Poetry Prizes, The 604
New Writing North 572
New Writing South 572
New Zealand Council for Educational Research 203
New Zealand Post Book Awards for Children and Young Adults 604
(New Zealand) Sunday Star-Times 112
New Zealand Woman's Day 112
New Zealand Writers Guild 573
newbooks magazine 76
Newcastle University 690
Newcastle University Library 682
Newcastle University 695
Newcastle upon Tyne City Library 682
NeWest Press 201
Newnes 171
News Letter 19
News of the World 15
News, Portsmouth, The 24
Newspaper, The 76
Newspaper Publishers Association Ltd, The 573
Newspaper Society 573
Nexus 171
Nexus Productions Ltd 423
Nia 171
Piergiorgio Nicolazzini Literary Agency 498
Nielsen Gold and Platinum Book Awards 604
Nightingale Press 171
NITRO 447
Maggie Noach Literary Agency 488
Nobel Prize in Literature, The 604
Nobuyuki Yuasa Annual International Award for Haibun 361
non-fiction 123, 470
  children's 293
  for radio 390
  reviews 284
  writing 270
non-publication 305
Nonsuch Publishing Ltd 171
Norfolk & Norwich Festival 620
Norfolk and Norwich Millennium Library 682
University of North Carolina Press, The 214
North Light Books 214
North One TV 424
North Point Press 214
North West Kent College 690
North-Holland 171
North-West Evening Mail 21
Northcote House Publishers Ltd 171
Northern and Southern Arts Councils of Ireland 362
Northern Children's Book Festival 620
Northern Echo, The 21
Northern Poetry Library, The 363, 682
Northern Stage (Theatrical Productions) Ltd 443
Northern Writers' Awards 604
Northland Publishing 214
Northumberland Theatre Company (NTC) 447
Northumbria University 695
NorthWord Books for Young Readers 214
W.W. Norton & Company 172
W.W. Norton & Company Inc. 214
Norwich Evening News 20
Nottingham Central Library 682
Nottingham Evening Post 20
Nottingham Playhouse 443
Nottingham Trent University 695
novels 244
novelty books 516
Now 76
NPA (Neue Presse Agentur) 500
Nuffield Theatre 444
Andrew Nurnberg Associates Ltd 488
Andrew Nurnberg Associates Prague, s.r.o. 497
Nursery Education Plus 76
Nursery World 76
Nursing Times 76
Nuts 77
NW Magazine 107
NWP 172
Alexandra Nye, Writers & Agents 488
NZ House & Garden 112

O:Oprah Magazine, The 115
Oak Tree Press 172

Harold Ober Associates Inc. 506
Oberon Books 172
Oberon Press 201
O-Books Publishing Ltd 172
O'Brien, Martin 266
O'Brien Press Ltd, The 172
Obscene Publications Act, 1959 726
Observer, The 15
Observer/Jonathan Cape/Comica Graphic Short Story Prize, The 604
Octagon Press Ltd, The 172
Octagon Theatre 444
Octopus Publishing Group 172
Off the Shelf Literature Festival 621
Off West End Theatres Ltd 439
Official UK Playstation 2 Magazine 77
OK! 77, 107
University of Oklahoma Press 214
Old Red Lion Theatre, The 439
Old Tractor 77
Oldham Evening Chronicle 23
Oldie, The 77
Oleander Press, The 173
Michael O'Mara Books Ltd 173
Omnibus Press/Music Sales Ltd 173
On Stream Publications Ltd 173
Oneworld Classics/Calder Publications 173
Oneworld Publications 173
online
- fiction 282
- marketing 627
- writing 625
- writing communities 626
- writing groups 687

Onlywomen Press Ltd 173
Open College of the Arts 690
Open Gate Press 173
Open Library 682
Open Studies – Part-time Courses for Adults: Office of Lifelong Learning 690
Open University Press 174
Opera 77
Opera Now 77
option clause 305
options 378
oral traditions 349
Orange Award for New Writers 605
Orange Prize for Fiction 605
Orange prize 253
Orange Tree Theatre 439
Orbis 77
Orbit 174, 214
Orchard Books 174
Organisation, The 521
School of Oriental & African Studies (SOAS) Library 683
originality 702
Orion Publishing Group Ltd, The 174, 222
Orpheus Books Ltd 227
George Orwell Memorial Prize 605
OS Magazine 77
Osborne 174
Fifi Oscard Agency Inc. 506
Oshun 174
Osprey Publishing Ltd 174
Otago University Press 203
Other Poetry 78
Oundle Festival of Literature 621
Our Dogs 78
Out of Joint 447
out-of-print publishing 630
Outdoor Canada 110
Outdoor Writers and Photographers Guild 573
Overland 107
Overlook Press, The 214
overseas, earnings from 739
Oversteps Books Ltd 174
Wilfred Owen Association 573
Deborah Owen Ltd 489
Peter Owen Publishers 174
Oxford Bibliographical Society 573
Oxford Central Library 683
Oxford Designers & Illustrators Ltd 522
Oxford Literary Festival 621
Oxford Mail 24
Oxford Publishing Company 174
Oxford Scientific (OSF) 424
Oxford University 695
Oxford University Press 174, 214
Oxford University Press, Canada 201
Oxford University Press Southern Africa 205
Oxford University Summer School for Adults 690

PA News Library 683
PA Puzzles 121
Pack, Scott 281
Pact (Producers' Alliance for Cinema and Television) 573
Paines Plough 447
Paisley Daily Express 23
Palgrave Macmillan 175
Pan 175
Pan Macmillan 175
Pan Macmillan Australia Pty Ltd 197
Pan Macmillan South Africa 205
Pandora Press 175
Paper Tiger 175
paperbacks 233, 285, 300, 322, 331
Paperbooks Publishing Ltd 175
Paperlink Ltd 533
Paragon House Publishers 214
Paragon Publishing 227
Park Home & Holiday Caravan 78
Particular Books 175
Pastel Society, The 573
Paterson Marsh Ltd 489
Pathé UK 424
Pausanias 266
Pavilion 175
Pavilion Children's Books 175

Pavilion Publishing (Brighton) Ltd 175
PAWS (People's Awareness of Science) 380
John Pawsey 489
Pax, Salam 648
payments, rates of 2, 265, 278
Payne-Gallway 175
PBJ Management 489
PC Advisor 78
PC Answers 78
PC Plus 78
PC Pro 78
Peace News 78
Peachpit Press 175
Peachtree Publishers 214
Peacock Theatre 444
Maggie Pearlstine Associates Ltd 489
Pearson Canada 201
Pearson Education New Zealand Ltd 203
Pearson UK 175
Peck, M. Scott 274
Pelican Publishing Company 214
Pen & Sword Books Ltd 175
Pen Press 176
Penguin Audiobooks 222
Penguin Group (Australia) 198
Penguin Group (Canada) 201
Penguin Group (NZ) 203
Penguin Group (UK) 176, 268, 328, 648
Penguin Group (USA), Inc. 214
Penguin Longman 177
Penguin Prize for African Writing 605
University of Pennsylvania Press 215
Pennsylvania State University Press 216
Pension Credit 749
pensions 9, 736, 749
Pensions Service 749
Pensions World 78
People, The 15, 115
People Magazine 107
People Management 79
People's Friend 79
People's Friend Pocket Novel 79
Samuel Pepys Award, The 605
Pereira, Isabella 647
performance poets 350
Performing Right Society Ltd (PRS) 573
Pergamon 177
Perigee 216
Period Living 79
Periodical Publishers Association 574
Permanent Press, The 216
permissions 304, 697
Persephone Books 177
Personal Computer World 79
personal digital organisers (PDAs) 636
Personal Managers' Association Ltd, The 453, 574
personal service companies 742
(Perth)Sunday Times, The 107
Perth Theatre 444
(Perth)West Australian, The 107
Pesky Productions 424
James Peter Associates Inc. 506
Peterborough Evening Telegraph 21
PFD (Peters Fraser & Dunlop Group Ltd), The 489
Phaidon Press Ltd 177
Philip's 177
Phillimore & Co. Ltd 177
Philomel 216
Phoenix 177
Phoenix Yard Books 177
Phosphor Art Ltd 522
Photo Life 110
photo-sharing sites 650
Photographer, The 79
photographers, freelance 535
photographs
  commercial 535
  copyright in 698
Photoshot 121
Piatkus 177
Pica Press 177
Picador 177
Piccadilly Press 177
Charles Pick Fellowship 605
Pick Me Up 79
picture agencies 538, 539
picture books 291
Picture Palace Films Ltd 424
Picture Postcard Monthly 79
picture research 260
Picture Research Association, The 574
Pier Productions 431
Pimlico 177
Pimlico Agency Inc., The 506
Pineapple Park 533
Pink Paper, The 79
Pink Press 177
Pinwheel Children's Books 177
Pipers' Ash Ltd 177
Pippin Publishing Corporation 201
piracy 331
pitch 4, 464
Pitkin Publishing Ltd 177
Pitstop Refuelling Writers' Weekend Workshops 690
Pixfeatures 121
Planet 79
Planet Rock 427
Player–Playwrights 574
Playmarket 499
Playne Books Ltd 227
Playwrights Publishing Company, The 177
Plexus Publishing Ltd 177
plots 391
Plough Prize, The 605
Plum Pudding Illustration 522
Plume 216
Pluto Press 178
University of Plymouth 695
PMA Literary and Film Management Inc. 506
PN Review 80
Pocket Books 178

POD 332–334
podcasts 651
poetry 369
for adults 123
for children 123
getting published 349, 351, 357
performance 349
Poetry Book Society, The 346, 355, 360–361, 574
Poetry Bookshop, The 363
Poetry Business, The 361
Poetry Business Book & Pamphlet Competition, The 605
Poetry Café 364
Poetry Can, The 361
Poetry International 621
Poetry Ireland 362
Poetry Ireland Review/Éigse Éireann 80
Poetry Kit 363, 366
Poetry Landmarks of Britain 362
Poetry Library, The 363–364, 366, 574, 683
Poetry London 80
Poetry on Loan 362
Poetry Prescription 362
Poetry Review 80
Poetry Round 365
Poetry School, The 365
Poetry Society 360, 362, 574
Poetry Society Education 367
Poetry Society of America 363
Poetry Wales 80
Poets Anonymous 365
Poet's House, The 695
Poet's House/Teach na hÉigse, The 365
Sylvie Poggio Artists Agency 522
Point 178
Police Journal 80
Police Review 80
Policy Press, The 178
Policy Studies Institute (PSI) 178
Political Quarterly, The 80
Politico's Publishing 178
Polity Press 178
Polka Theatre 439
Pollinger Limited 489
Polygon 178
Bella Pomer Agency Inc. 497
Pomona Books 178
Pont Books 178
PONY Magazine 80
Poolbeg Press Ltd 178
Corneliu M. Popescu Prize for Poetry in Translation, The 605
Popular Woodworking 216
portal, blogging 649
Portfolio 178, 216, 516, 523, 527
portfolio
photographer's 535–536
presentation 512
Portico 178
Portico Library & Gallery, The 683
Portico Prize, The 606
Portland Press Ltd 178
Portobello Books Ltd 178
Portobello Pictures Ltd 424
Positive Words 108
Post Magazine & Insurance Week 81
Potomac Books Inc. 216
Beatrix Potter Society, The 574
Tony Potter Publishing Ltd 228
Poultry World 81
Powell Publishing 533
Shelley Power Literary Agency Ltd 490
Powys Society, The 574
T & AD Poyser 178
Pozzitive Television Ltd 424
PR Week 81
Practical Boat Owner 81
Practical Caravan 81
Practical Fishkeeping 81
Practical Parenting 81
Practical Photography 81
Practical Wireless 81
Practical Woodworking 82
Practising Midwife, The 82
Practitioner, The 82
Pratchett, Terry 249, 287, 330
Prava I Prevodi Literary Agency Permissions & Rights Ltd 497
Praxis Films Ltd 424
Prediction 82
Preface Publishing 178
Prentice Hall Press 216
Prequel to Cannes Short Film Script Competition 606
presentation 124, 126
Press, The 27
Press and Journal, The 23
Press Association, The 121
Press Complaints Commission 8, 574
press cuttings 325
Press Gazette 82
press release 321
Prestel Publishing Ltd 178
Mathew Price Ltd 216
Price Stern Sloan 216
Pride 82
J.B. Priestley Society, The 574
Prima 82
Prima Baby 82
Prime Time Radio 427
Le Prince Maurice Prize 606
Princess Productions 424
Princeton University Press 216
Princeton University Press – Europe 179
Pringle, Alexandra 235, 299
print run 232, 317
print-on-demand (POD) 311, 332, 344
printers 232
Printmakers Council 575
Prion Books 179
V.S. Pritchett Memorial Prize, The 606
Private Eye 82

Private Libraries Association 575
privilege (in law of libel) 724
Prize for New Media Writing 606
prizes and awards, book and illustration, tax position 733
producers
  radio 388, 390
  television and film 419
production 231
production companies, independent 381, 388
Professional Cartoonists' Organisation 575
Professional Photographer 83
Profile Books Ltd 179
profiles 29
Project Gutenberg 635
Promenade Enterprises 431
Promotion Littéraire 498
promotional literature 312, 536
proof correction marks/symbols 671
proofreading 231, 671
proposals 300
Prospect Magazine 83
Prospect Pictures Ltd 424
Proteus Theatre Company 447
Psychologies 83
Psychology Press 179
public domain 635
Public Lending Right Act 1979 338
Public Lending Right Office 518
Public Lending Right (PLR) 338, 342, 715
  books eligible for 341
  foreign 716
  reciprocal arrangements 342
  sampling arrangements 341
Public Order Act 198 727
publication dates 304
publicity 233, 316, 321, 324
publicity material, theatre 436
'published', meaning of 720
publishers 123, 295, 298
  agreements (contracts) 265
  and ISBNs 315
  approaching 124, 291, 527, 529
  direct-to-retail 529
  finding 126
  poetry 355
  poetry, approaching 357
  sole 305
Publishers Association, The 575
Publishers Association of New Zealand (PANZ) 575
Publishers' Association of South Africa (PASA) 575
Publishers Licensing Society Ltd (PLS) 575, 713, 715
Publishers Publicity Circle 575
publishing agreements 303
  termination 305
  rights and terms 530
Publishing House, The 533
Publishing Ireland - Foilsiú Éireann 576
Publishing Scotland 576
Puffin 179
Puffin Books 216
Pullman, Philip 288
Pulp Press 179
Pulse 83
Pushkin Press 179
G.P. Putnam's Sons 216
Putnam Aeronautical 179
Puttick Agency 490
Puzzle House, The 121
PVA Management Ltd 490

Q Magazine 83
Quadrant 108
Quadrille Publishing 179
Quantum 179
Quantum Publishing 228
Quarto Group, Inc., The 179, 228
QUE Publishing 180
Queen's Quarterly 110
Queen's Theatre, Hornchurch 444
Queen's University, Belfast 695
University of Queensland Press 198
Quercus Publishing Plc 180
Quest 180
Questors Theatre, The 439
Quicksilver Theatre 447
Quill & Quire 111
Quiller Publishing Ltd 180
Nigel Quiney Publications Ltd 533
Quite Literary 621

RA Magazine 83
racial hatred, incitement to 726
Racing Post 83
Radcliffe Publishing Ltd 180
radio
  plays 386
  poetry on 353
  producers 372
  rights and terms 408
  stories for 390
  writing drama for 369, 387
Radio Academy, The 576
Radio Control Models and Electronics 83
Radio Telefís Éireann (RTÉ) 411
Radio Times 83
Radio Centre 427
Ragdoll Productions Ltd 424
Ragged Bears Publishing Ltd 180
Rail 84
Railway Gazette International 84
Railway Magazine 84
Rainbow Cards Ltd 533
Raintree 180
Peggy Ramsay Foundation, The 606
Ramshorn Theatre, The 444
Rand McNally 216

Index

Random Entertainment 424, 432
Random House Audio Books 223
Random House Australia Pty Ltd 198
Random House Group Ltd, The 180, 328
Random House Inc. 216
Random House New Zealand Ltd 203
Random House of Canada Ltd 201
Random House Struik (Pty) Ltd 205
Rankin, Ian 302
Rann Communication 122
Ransom Publishing Ltd 182
ratings, media 373
Rayo 217
Razorbill 217
RBI Search 182
RDC Agencia Literaria SL 500
RDF Television 424
Reach Poetry 84
Reader's Digest 84
Reader's Digest Association Ltd, The 182
Reader's Digest (Australia) 108
Reader's Digest (Canada) 111
Reading Evening Post 24
University of Reading Library 683
reading fees 453
readings 325
Reaktion Books 182
Real People 84
Real People Theatre Company 447
Reality 84
Really 417
Really Good 533
Really Useful Group, The 439
reciprocal arrangements, PLR 342
Record Collector 84
Red 85
Red Audio 223
Red Dress Ink™ 183, 201
Red Fox Children's Books 183
Red House 346
Red House Children's Book Award, The 606
Red Ladder Theatre Company 448
Red Pepper 85
Red Shift Theatre Company 448
Redbridge Book and Media Festival 621
Redhammer Management Ltd 490
Reed Books 183
William Reed Directories 183
Reed Educational and Professional Publishing Ltd 183
Thomas Reed 183
Reeds Nautical Almanac 183
Rees Literary Agency 507
Trevor Reese Memorial Prize 606
Reform 85
Regional Arts Offices 576
Rehabilitation of Offenders Act, 1974 723
rehearsed readings 382
rejections 243, 254, 297, 349, 382, 514, 659
Release Forms 419
Religious and Moral Education Press (RMEP) 183
repeats, fees for 408
Report 85
reproduction fees 540
research 241, 257, 259, 263
Restaurant Magazine 85
Retail Week 85
Retirement Pension 752
retreats, writers' 666
Reuters News 122
reviews 8, 29, 284, 325
  of first editions 285
  on Amazon 325
Reynolds & Hearn Ltd 183
Rialto, The 85
Richard & Judy 295
Lisa Richards Agency, The 490
Richards Literary Agency 499
Riddell, Pau 288
Rider 183
Ridley Art Society 576
Rigby 183
Right of Paternity 304
Right Start 85
rights 233, 375, 453
  assigning of 305
  authors' 716
  electronic, digital and other multimedia 305, 698
  foreign 233, 470
  licensed to publisher 304
  moral 697, 711
  serial 233, 697
  subsidiary 304, 356
  translation 455
Peter Riley 363
Angela Rinaldi Literary Agency, The 507
Rising Moon 217
Rising Stars 183
River Books 183
Riverhead Books 217
Rivers Oram Press 183
Rizzoli International Publications Inc. 217
RNIB National Library Service 683
Roar Publishing 183
Robinson 183
Robinson Literary Agency Ltd 490
Robson Books 183
Rock 108
Rodale Book Group 217
Linda Rogers Associates 522
Rogers, Coleridge & White Ltd 490
romantic fiction 253
Romantic Novel of the Year Award 607
Romantic Novelists' Association, The 576
George Ronald 183
Ronsdale Press 201
Felix Rosenstiel's Widow & Son Ltd 533
RotoVision 183
Rough Guides 183, 267
Roundhouse Group 183
Route 184
Routledge 184, 217

Routledge & Kegan Paul 267
Routledge-Cavendish 184
Rowling, J.K. 290, 299, 329, 461
Rowson, Martin 523
Elizabeth Roy Literary Agency 491
Royal Academy of Arts 576
Royal Birmingham Society of Artists 576
Royal Collection Publications 184
Royal Court Theatre 440
Royal Court Young Writers' Festival 621
Royal Exchange Theatre Company Ltd 444
Royal Institute of Oil Painters 576
Royal Institute of Painters in Water Colours 576
Royal Literary Fund, The 577
Royal Lyceum Theatre Company 444
Royal Mail Awards for Scottish Children's Books 607
Royal Musical Association, The 577
Royal National Institute of Blind People (RNIB) 85, 184
Royal National Theatre 433, 440
Royal Photographic Society, The 577
Royal Scottish Academy of Art and Architecture, The 577
Royal Shakespeare Company 444
Royal Society, The 577
Royal Society for Asian Affairs, The 577
Royal Society for the encouragement of Arts, Manufactures and Commerce (RSA) 577
Royal Society of British Artists 577
Royal Society of Literature 577
  Ondaatje Prize, The 607
  Jerwood Awards, The 607
Royal Society of Marine Artists 578
Royal Society of Miniature Painters, Sculptors and Gravers, The 578
Royal Society of Painter-Printmakers 578
Royal Society of Portrait Painters 578
Royal Society Prizes for Science Books, The 607
Royal Television Society 578
Royal Watercolour Society 578
Royal West of England Academy 578
royalties 234, 299, 303, 471
  on export editions 471
  rates 305
Royle Publications Ltd 533
RSPCA Young Photographer Awards (YPA) 608
RSS feeds 650
RSVP Publishing Company 203
RTÉ P.J. O'Connor Radio Drama Awards 608
RTÉ Radio 1 Francis MacManus Awards 608
Rugby World 86
Runciman Award 608
Runner's World 86
Running Fitness 86
Running Press Book Publishers 217
Uli Rushby-Smith Literary Agency 491
RUSI Journal 86
Ruskin Society, The 578
Russell & Volkening Inc. 507
Rutgers University Press 217
Rye Festival 621
Ryland Peters & Small 184
John Rylands University Library, The University of Manchester, The 683

S4C 411
SAA (Society for All Artists) 579
Safari 638
Safety Education Journal 86
Saga Magazine 86
SAGE Publications Ltd 184
Sailing 115
Sainsbury's Baby Book Award 608
Sainsbury's Magazine 86
St Albans Central Library 683
University of St Andrews 695
St Bride Library 683
St Cuthman's 668
David St John Thomas Charitable Trust Competitions & Awards, The 608
St Martin's Press Inc. 217
St Pauls 184
Salamander 184, 228
Salariya Book Company Ltd 184
sales material 231, 232, 317, 320
University of Salford 695
Salisbury International Arts Festival 621
Salisbury Library 683
Salisbury Playhouse 445
J. Salmon Ltd 533
Salt Publishing 184
Saltire Society Awards, The 608
Salway, Sara 648
sampling arrangements, PLR 341
SAMS Publishing 184
Rosemary Sandberg Ltd 491
Sandcastle Books 202
Lennart Sane Agency AB 499–500
Sane Töregård Agency AB 500
Santoro Graphics Ltd 533
Sarasvati 86
Sasakawa Prize 361
satire 245
Saunders 184
Malcolm Saville Society, The 579
Savitri Books Ltd 228
Alastair Sawday Publishing Ltd 184
Dorothy L. Sayers Society, The 579
Sayle Literary Agency, The 491
Sayle Screen Ltd 491
S.B. Publications 185
Scala Publishers 185
Scarborough Theatre Trust Ltd 445
Scattered Authors Society 579
Sceptre 185
Schiavone Literary Agency, Inc. 507
Karin Schindler and Suely Pedro dos Santos Rights Representatives 496
Thomas Schlück GmbH 498

Schmidt, Michael 351
Schofield & Sims Ltd 185
Scholastic Australia Pty Ltd 198
Scholastic Book Clubs and Fairs 346
Scholastic Book Fairs 347
Scholastic Inc. 217
Scholastic Ltd 185
Scholastic New Zealand Ltd 204
School Librarian, The 87
schools, marketing to 292
Susan Schulman Literary & Dramatic Agents Inc. 507
Science Factory Ltd, The 491
science fiction 635
Science Museum 185
Science Museum Library 683
Science Navigation Group 185
Scientific Computing World 87
SCM Canterbury Press Ltd 185
SCM Press 185
Scotland on Sunday 16
Scots Magazine, The 87
Scotsman, The 16
Scott Ferris Associates 491
Scott Meredith Literary Agency LP 507
Kim Scott Walwyn Prize, The 609
Scottish Arts Club 579
Scottish Arts Council 579, 609
Scottish Book of the Year 609
Scottish Book Trust (SBT) 579
Scottish Farmer, The 87
Scottish Fellowship of Christian Writers 579
Scottish Field 87
Scottish First Book of the Year 609
Scottish Home and Country 87
Scottish Memories 87
Scottish Newspaper Publishers Association 580
Scottish Newspaper Society 580
Scottish Poetry Library, The 363, 683
Scottish Research Book Award 609
Scottish Screen 580
Scottish Sun, The 16
Scottish Universities', International Summer School 690
scouts, literary 230
SCP Publishers Ltd 185
Screen International 87
screenplays, submitting 419
Screenwriters' Store 383
screenwriting, software programs 382
script agreements, television 407
script conference 384
script editors 385
Scripture Union 186
scriptwriting, for soaps 384
Sea Angler 87
Sea Breezes 88
Seafarer Books Ltd 186
Seamus Heaney Centre for Poetry, The 362
Search Press Ltd 186
Second Nature Ltd 533
sedition 726
Self, Will 647
self-employed status 730, 741
self-promotion 326, 513, 536, 641
self-publishing 124, 299, 308, 310, 334, 453, 630, 641
  definition 345
  ebooks 638
SelfBuild & Design 88
sell-in 317
sell-out 317
Senate House Library, University of London 683
Sentinel, The 26, 218
September Films Ltd 425
Seren 186
series and serials, television and radio 374, 378
Setterfield, Diane 471
Seven Stories – the Centre for Children's Books 580
Severn House Publishers 186
Sewing World 88
SFX Magazine 88
Shapero, Bernard 266
Shared Experience Theatre 448
Sharland Organisation Ltd, The 491
Shaw Society, The 580
She 88
Shearsman Books 186
Sheffield Central Library 683
Sheffield Hallam University 695
Sheffield Star 27
Sheffield Theatres 445
Anthony Sheil in association with Aitken Alexander Associates 491
Sheil Land Associates Ltd 492
Caroline Sheldon Literary Agency Ltd 492
Sheldon Press 186
Sheldrake Press 186
Shepheard-Walwyn (Publishers) Ltd 186
Sheridan House Inc. 218
Sherman Cymru 445
Shields Gazette, The 22
Shine 425
Ships Monthly 88
Shire Publications 186
Shooting Times and Country Magazine 88
Shop: A Magazine of Poetry, The 88
Short Books Ltd 186
short stories 243
Short Story Radio 432
Shortfuse 364
shorthand 7
Shortlands Poetry Circle 366
Shout 88
Show of Strength Theatre Company Ltd 445
Shropshire Magazine, The 89
Shropshire Star 26
Shukat Company Ltd, The 507
Shuter and Shooter Publishers (Pty) Ltd 205
Sidgwick & Jackson 187
Sight and Sound 89
Sigma Press 187

Sign, The 89
Silhouette® 187
Silhouette Books 202
Jeffrey Simmons 492
Simon & Pierre Publishing 202
Simon & Schuster Adult Publishing Group 218
Simon & Schuster Audio 223
Simon & Schuster (Australia) Pty Ltd 198
Simon & Schuster Children's Publishing Division 218
Simon & Schuster UK Ltd 187
André Simon Memorial Fund Book Awards, The 609
Simpson, Lauren 671
Sinclair, Kate 372
Sinclair-Stevenson 492
Sirius Media Services 122
situation comedy 378
Ski and Board 89
Skier and Snowboarder Magazine, The 89
Sky 1 417
Slightly Foxed 89
Slim at Home 89
Slimming World magazine 89
slush pile 465
Small Claims 729
Smallholder 89
Smallworld Cable Ltd 414
SmartPass Ltd 223
Smartphone Essentials 90
Smash! Hits Radio 427
SMG TV Productions 425
Smith Gryphon Ltd 187
Robert Smith Literary Agency Ltd 492
Nancy H. Smith Literary Agency, The 496
Smith, Zadie 472
Smooth Operations 432
Smooth Radio 427
Colin Smythe Ltd 187
Jill Smythies Award, The 609
Snooker Scene 90
Snowbooks Ltd 187
So Television 425
soaps, writing for 384
Social Fund 749
social security benefits 749
social security contributions 741
social networking sites 626
Society for Editors and Proofreaders (SfEP) 580
Society for Promoting Christian Knowledge 187
Society for Theatre Research, The 580
Society of Artists Agents 580
Society of Authors 303, 305–306, 308, 359, 375, 541, 580, 697
Society of Authors Medical Book Awards, The 610
Society of Botanical Artists, The 580
Society of Children's Book Writers and Illustrators (SCBWI) 581
Society of Civil and Public Service Writers, The 581
Society of Editors 581
Society of Genealogists Enterprises Ltd 187
Society of Graphic Fine Art 581
Society of Heraldic Arts 581
Society of Indexers 581, 669
Society of Limners, The 581
Society of Medical Writers, The 582
Society of Scribes and Illuminators (SSI) 582
Society of Sussex Authors, The 582
Society of Wildlife Artists 582
Society of Women Artists, The 582
Society of Women Writers & Journalists (SWWJ) 582
Society of Young Publishers 582
Soho Press Inc. 218
Soho Theatre 440
Solent Peoples Theatre (SPT) 448
Solicitors' Journal 90
Solo Syndication Ltd 122
Solomon & Whitehead Ltd 534
Songwriter, The 90
Songwriting and Composing 90
Sony 635, 639
Sony Connect 639
Sony Radio Academy Awards 610
Sony Reader 234, 639
Soul 115, 534
South African Writers' Circle 582
South Norwood Writers' Workshop 366
South Street Press 187
South Wales Argus 25
South Wales Echo 25
South Wales Evening Post 25
University of Southampton Libraries 683
Southern Cross 115
Southern Daily Echo, The 24
Southern News Service 122
Southern Writers' Conference 690
Southwater 187
Southwest Scriptwriters 583
Souvenir Press Ltd 187
Spark Magazine, The 90
SPCK 187
Speak 218
Spear's Wealth Management Survey (WMS) 90
Specific Films 425
Specs Art 522
Spectator, The 90
Spectator Business 90
Speed Auction TV 417
Speirs, Di 390
Spellmount Ltd 187
Sphere 187
Sphinx Theatre Company 448
Spice 202
Spice Factory UK Ltd 425
Spieler Agency, The 507
Spinifex Press 198
Spirit & Destiny 91
Philip G. Spitzer Literary Agency, Inc. 507
Spon 187
Sports Journalists' Association of Great Britain (SJA) 583

Sportsbooks Ltd 187
Sportsman's Press, The 188
Spread the Word 366
Spring International Literary Festival 621
Springboard 91
Springer-Verlag London Ltd 188
Square Dog Radio LLP 432
Squash Player, The 91
St Cuthman's 667
St Ives Literature Festival 622
Stacey International 188
Stackpole Books 218
Staffordshire Life Magazine 91
Stage, The 91, 433
Stainer & Bell Ltd 188
Stamp Magazine 91
Stand Magazine 91
Standard Book Numbering Agency 310
Standen Literary Agency, The 492
Stanford University Press 218
StAnza: Scotland's International Poetry Festival 622
Staple 91
Star Sunday 16
Star Trek Magazine 91
Starke, Mariana 266
state benefits 749
state pension 749
Statutory Maternity Pay (SMP) 753
Statutory Paternity Pay (SPP) 753
Steam Industry, The 448
Steeple Hill 202
Abner Stein 493
Lou Stein Associates Ltd 432
Micheline Steinberg Associates 493
Stenlake Publishing Ltd 188
Rochelle Stevens & Co 493
Robert Louis Stevenson Club, The 583
Shirley Stewart Literary Agency 493
Stichting Leenrecht 716
STM (scientific, technical and medical) ebooks 638
stock libraries 538
stories for radio 390
stories, short 369
'Story' campaign 394
storylines, for soaps 384
Society for Storytelling Library, The 683
Strad, The 91
Stratford-upon-Avon Poetry Festival 622
Straw, Alison 659
Stripes 188
Rebecca Strong International Literary Agency 507
structural edit 230
Studies, An Irish quarterly review 92
Studio Cactus Ltd 228
Stuff 92
STV (North and Central) 412
stylebook 9
submissions *see also* manuscripts 1, 124, 126, 255, 296, 453
  for radio 391
  unsolicited 466
subsidies 306
subventions 344
success, dealing with 355
Sarah Such Literary Agency 493
Suffolk Norfolk Life 92
Sugar 92
Summersdale Publishers Ltd 188
Sun, The 16
Sun-Herald, The 108
Sunbird Publishers 205
Sunday Business Post, The 16
Sunday Express 16
Sunday Herald 17
Sunday Independent 17 25
Sunday Life 19
Sunday Mail 17
Sunday Mercury 26
Sunday Mirror 17
Sunday Post 17
Sunday Sun, The 22
Sunday Telegraph 17
Sunday Times, The 18
Sunday Times EFG Private Bank Short Story Award, The 610
Sunday Times Oxford Literary Festival, The 622
Sunday Times Scotland, The 18
Sunday Times Young Writer of the Year Award, The 610
Sunday Tribune, The 19
Sunderland Echo 22
Sunflower Books 188
Sunset & Vine 425
Sure Start Maternity Grant 749, 753
Surrey Life 92
Surrey Poetry Circle 366
Survivors Poetry 362
Susijn Agency Ltd, The 493
Sussex Academic Press 188
Sussex Playwrights' Club 583
University of Sussex 696
Sutton Publishing 188
Swainson, Bill 230
Swan Hill Press 188
Swanwick,Writers' Summer School, The 690
Carolyn Swayze Literary Agency Ltd 497
Swedish Publishers' Association 583
Sweet & Maxwell 188
Sweet Talk Productions Ltd 432
Sweetens of Bolton 363
Swimming Times Magazine 92
Swindon Advertiser 24
Swindon Festival of Literature 622
Switch digital (London) Ltd 429
Switch digital (Scotland) Ltd 429
(Sydney)Daily Telegraph, The 108
Sydney Morning Herald, The 108
(Sydney)Sunday Telegraph, The 108
SYFY 417
syndicates 2
synopsis 131, 133, 255, 277, 293, 381, 452–454, 467
  for TV script 385
Szirtes, George 647

Index

Tŷ Newydd 668
Tabard Theatre 440
Tablet, The 92
James Tait Black Memorial Prizes, The 610
Takahe 112
Take a Break 92
Take a Break's Take a Puzzle 93
Talawa Theatre Company 448
Talent Television 425
TalkbackTHAMES 425
talks
 for radio 409
 for television 409
talkSPORT 427
TalkTalk TV 414
Tamarind Books 188
Tangerine Designs Ltd 228
Tango Books Ltd 188
TAPS (Television Arts Performance Showcase) 382, 610
Taranaki Daily News 112
Tarquin Publications 189
Taschen UK Ltd 189
TATE ETC 93
Tate Library & Archive 684
Tate Publishing 189
Tatler 93
Noel Tatt Group/Impress Publishing 534
I.B.Tauris & Co. Ltd 189
taxation 9, 93
 Children's, Tax Credit 750
 credits 749
 expenses, claimed 9, 729, 733
 Income 729, 731, 737, 738
 prizes and awards 733
 relief on books purchased 736
 return 740
 Value Added (VAT) 9, 408, 730, 738
Taylor and Francis Group 189
Taylor & Francis (T&F) 636
Reginald Taylor and Lord Fletcher Essay Competition 610
Taylor, Fig 509
Taylor, G.P. 308
Taylor, David 332
Teach Yourself 189
Teacher, The 93
Teachers TV 417
Technology Ireland 93
teenage fiction 123, 293
TEG Productions 440
Telegraph & Argus 27
Telegraph Books 189
Television 93
television
 film and radio 544
 producers 372
 rights and terms 407
 viewing figures 468
 writing for 296, 369, 378
Television Junction 425
Templar Company Ltd, The 189, 229
Tempo 93
Tempus 190
Ten Speed Press 218
University of Tennessee Press 218
Tennyson Agency, The 493
Tennyson Society, The 583
TES, The 93
TES Cymru, The 94
TESS, The 94
University of Texas Press 218
TGO (Great Outdoors) Magazine, The 94
Thames & Hudson Ltd 190
that's life! 94
English-Speaking Union, The 583
Times, The 18
Times/Chicken House Children's Fiction Competition, The 611
Theakstons Old Peculier Crime Writing Festival 622
theatre 433, 437
 adaptations for 372
Theatre Absolute 448
Theatre Centre 448
theatre companies, approaching 434
theatre for children 545
Theatre Is... 448
Theatre Record 433
Theatre Royal 445
Theatre Royal & Drum Theatre Plymouth 445
Theatre Royal, Bath 445
Theatre Royal, Stratford East 440
Theatre Workshop 448
Theatre Writers' Union 545, 583
Theatres Act, 1968 726
Theroux, Paul 262
Think Books 190
Third Way 94
Angela Thirkell Society 583
This England 94
Thoemmes Press 190
Vicki Thomas Associates 522
Thomas Cook Travel Writing Award, The 262
Dylan Thomas Festival, The 622
Edward Thomas Fellowship, The 583
Dylan Thomas Literary Prize 611
Dylan Thomas Society of Great Britain 584
Thompson Educational Publishing 202
D.C. Thomson & Co. Ltd – Publications 190
Thomson Financial News 122
Thomson Round Hall 190
Stanley Thornes (Publishers) Ltd 190
thrillers 238
JM Thurley Management 493
Tide Mill Press 190
Tiger Aspect Productions 425
Timaru Herald, The 113
Time Out 94, 190
Time Warner 190
Times Books 190
Times Educational Supplement, The 94

Index

Times Educational Supplement Scotland, The 94
Times Higher Education 94
Tintinna Ltd 432
Tir na n-Og Awards 611
Titan Books 190
title, book 466
Tivnan, Tom 328
TLC 131
TLS (Times Literary Supplement), The 95
Today's Golfer 95
Today's Pilot 95
toddlers, books for 291
Tolkien Society, The 584
Tolle, Eckhart 274
Tolley 190
Tom-Gallon Trust Award and the Olive Cook Prize, The 611
Tomalin, Claire 259
Tongues and Grooves 364
Top Santé Health & Beauty 95
Top That! Publishing plc 190
Top Up TV Anytime 414
Tor 191
Tor Books 218
(Toronto) Globe and Mail, The 111
Toronto Life 111
University of Toronto Press Inc. 202
Toronto Star 111
Torpedo Ltd 432
Torque 191
Total Fiction Services 499
Total Film 95
Total Off-Road 95
Totleigh Barton 668
Toucan Books Ltd 229
Christopher Tower Poetry Prize 367
Trail 95
Translation Prizes, The 611
translations 340, 455
Translators Association 541, 584
Transworld Publishers 191
Betty Trask Awards, The 611
Travel Channel 418
travel guides 266
travel writers 269
travel writing 262
Traveller 95
Travellers' Tales 690
Travelling Scholarships, The 612
Traveltalk 108
Traverse Theatre 445
Emma Treehouse Ltd 229
Tremain, Rose 391
trends in publishing 285, 328
Trentham Books Ltd 191
Trevor, William 392
Trewin, Simon 461
Tribune 95
Tricycle Theatre Company, The 440
Trident Media Group 508
Trinity College, Carmarthen 696
Trinity College Library 684
Trinity College Library Dublin 684
John Tripp Award for Spoken Poetry 612
Triumph Proscenium Productions Ltd 440
Trollope, Joanna 241, 319
Trollope Society, The 584
Trotman 191
Troubador Publishing Ltd 191
Trouble 418
Trout and Salmon 96
Truck & Driver 96
Trucking 96
True Love 116
Trumpet, The 96
T.S. Eliot Prize 361
TSO (Stationery Office), The 191
Tucker Slingsby Ltd 229
Tundra Books Inc. 202
Jane Turnbull 494
Turner Classic Movies (TCM) 418
Turner Society, The 584
Tuttle Publishing/Periplus Editions 218
TV Quick 96
TVTimes Magazine 96
TwelvePoint.com 96
Twentieth Century Fox Productions Ltd 425
Twenty Twenty Television 425
Twitter 301, 626, 628, 651
Two-Can 219
Twofour Broadcast Ltd 426
Tŷ Newydd 366, 691
Tŷ Newydd Festival 622
typesetting 232, 671

U magazine 96
UBC Media Group plc 432
Ulric Publishing 191
Ulster Bank Belfast Festival at Queen's 623
Ulster Business 96
Ulster Grocer 97
Ulverscroft Group Ltd 191, 223
Under 5 97
Unicorn Press 192
Unicorn Theatre 440
Unisa Press 205
United Agents 494
Universe, The 97
unsolicited manuscripts 230, 291, 308, 462
UNSW Press 198
Merlin Unwin Books Ltd 192
Upfront Television Ltd 426
Urchfont Manor College 691
US market 469
Usborne Publishing Ltd 192
UTV 413
UTV Radio 429
UTV-Bauer Digital Ltd 429
UWA Publishing 198

V&A Publishing 192
Vaines, Peter 729, 731
Valenti, Jessica 651
Vallentine Mitchell 192
Value Added Tax (VAT) 9, 408, 730, 738
Van Schaik Publishers 206
(Vancouver) Province, The 111
Vancouver Sun 111
V&A Illustration Awards, The 612
Vanity Fair 97
vanity publishing 124, 306, 308, 310, 343, 352
Variorum 192
Vegan, The 97
Venue 97
Ver Poets 584
Ver Poets Open Competition 612
Veritas Publications 192
Vermilion 192
Verso Ltd 192
VG Wort 716
Ralph M. Vicinanza Ltd 508
Ed Victor Ltd 494
Victoria University Press 204
video logs 651
Viking 192, 198
Viking Children's Books 219
Viking Press 219
Viking Sevenseas NZ Ltd 204
Vintage 192
Vintage Tractor & Countryside Heritage 97
Virago 192
Virgin Books 192
Virgin Media Television 414
Virgin1 418
Virtue Books Ltd 192
Visiting Arts 584
Visual Humour 122
Vital Spark, The 192
Viz 97
vlogs 651
Vogue 97
Vogue Australia 108
Voice, The 98
Voice of the Listener & Viewer Ltd (VLV) 584
Vonnegut, Kurt 257
vox pop 30
Voyager 192

Waddell Media Ltd 426
Wade and Doherty Literary Agency Ltd 494
Austin Wahl Agency Inc. 508
Wales on Sunday 18
University of Wales Press 192
Walford Award, The 612
walk 98
Walker & Co. 219
Walker Books Ltd 192, 223
Wall to Wall Television 426
Wallace Literary Agency Inc. 508
Wallflower Press 193
Wallpaper 98
Walmsley Society, The 585
Walsh, Neil Donald 274
Wanderlust 98
War Cry, The 98
Warburg Institute 193
Ward Lock Educational Co. Ltd 193
Warehouse Theatre 440
Warne 193
Warner Bros. Entertainment Ltd 426
Warner/Chappell Plays Ltd 193
Warwick International Festival 623
Warwick Prize for Writing 612
University of Warwick 696
Warwick Words – Festival of Literature and Spoken Word 623
University of Washington Press 219
Watch 418
WaterBrook Press 219
Waterstone's 299, 329
Waterstone's Books Quarterly 98
Waterways World 98
Watford Palace Theatre 445
Watkins/Loomis Agency Inc. 508
Watson, Little Ltd 494
Watson-Guptill Publications 219
AP Watt Ltd 494
Franklin Watts 193
Watts Publishing Group Ltd, The 193
Wayland 193
Ways With Words Literature Festival 623
web publication 353
Webb Group, The 534
Mary Webb Society 585
website designers 537, 641
websites 513, 537, 543, 625, 647
  authors' 325–326, 637
  defamation on 720
  for artists 656
  personal 517
  personal, setting up 641
  poetry 352
  publishers' 232, 319
  writing for 641
Wedding Magazine 98
Wedgwood Memorial College 691
Week, The 98
Weekly News, The 99
Weidenfeld & Nicolson 193
Weight Watchers Magazine 99
Josef Weinberger Plays Ltd 193, 494
Wellcome Library 684
Wellcome Library of Medical History 259
Wellcome Trust Book Prize, The 612
(Wellington)Dominion Post, The 113
Wells Festival of Literature 623
H.G. Wells Society, The 585
Welsh Academic Press 193
Welsh Academy 585
Welsh Books Council/Cygnor Llyfrau Cymru 585
Wessex News, Features and Photos Agency 122
West Country Writers' Association, The 585

Index

West Yorkshire Playhouse, The 446
Western Daily Press 25
Western Mail 26
Western Morning News, The 25
Westminster John Knox Press 219
Westminster Music Library 684
Westminster Reference Library 684
Rhoda Weyr Agency 508
Wharncliffe 193
What Car? 99
What Laptop 99
What's on TV 99
Wheatley Medal 670
Which? Ltd 193
Whispering Buffalo Literary Agency Ltd 495
Whistledown Productions Ltd 432
Whitaker, Antony 719
Whitbread Book Awards 612
Whitbread Literary Award 733
White Bear Theatre Club 441
Eve White 495
Isabel White Literary Agent 495
Michael White 441
Whitfield Prize, The 612
Whittet Books Ltd 193
WI Life 99
Wickman, Lena 469
Widowed Parent's Allowance 751
Dinah Wiener Ltd 495
Wigtown Book Festival 623
Wild 109
Oscar Wilde Society, The 585
Wildlife Photographer of the Year 613
John Wiley & Sons Ltd 193
John Wiley & Sons Australia, Ltd 198
John Wiley & Sons Inc. 219
Wiley-Blackwell Publishing 194, 199
Jonathan Williams Literary Agency 495
Charles Williams Society 585
Henry Williamson Society, The 585
Willings Press Guide 1, 116
Elisabeth Wilson 495
Neil Wilson Publishing Ltd 194
Philip Wilson Publishers Ltd 194
Wimbledon and Merton Poetry Group 366
University of Winchester 696
Winchester Discovery Centre 684
Winchester, Simon 270
Winchester Writers' Conference Competitions 613
Winchester Writers' Conference Festival and Bookfair 686, 691
Windmill Books 194
Windows Vista:Official Magazine, The 99
Windsor Large Print 194
Winnipeg Free Press 111
John Wisden and Co. Ltd 194
Wisden Cricketer, The 99
Wise Buddah Radio 432
Wishing Well Studios Ltd 534
Witness, The 116
Wits University Press 206
Wizard 194
WLR Media & Entertainment 194
P.G. Wodehouse Society (UK), The 586
Wolfe, Peter 256
Wolters Kluwer (UK) Ltd 194
Wolfson Foundation, The 613
Woman 99
Woman Alive 100
Woman and Home 100
Woman's Day 109
Woman's Hour 390
Woman's Own 100
Woman's Way 100
Woman's Weekly 100
Woman's Weekly Fiction Special 100
women, as crime writers 237
Women in Publishing (WiP) 586
Women's Library, The 684
Women's Press, The 194, 202
David T.K. Wong Fellowship 613
Wooden Books 194
Woodhead Publishing Ltd 195
Woodmansterne Publications Ltd 534
Woodworker, The 100
Virginia Woolf Society of Great Britain 586
Worcester News 26
Word, The 100
Word – University of Aberdeen Writers Festival 623
word-of-mouth sales 316
Wordsworth Editions Ltd 195
Wordsworth Trust, The 586
Workbox 101
working age benefits 749
Working Class Movement Library 684
Working Families Tax Credit 749, 752
Working Partners Ltd 229
Working Tax Credit 750
Working Title Films 426
Workman Publishing Company 219
workshops 686
workspace, writer's 662
World Airnews 116
World Book Day 623
World Entertainment News Network (WENN) 122
World Fishing 101
World of Interiors, The 101
World Productions Ltd 426
World Soccer 101
World Today, The 101
Worldwide Mystery 202
Worshipful Company of Stationers and Newspaper Makers 586
Write A Story for Children Competition 613
Writer, The 116
Writers Advice Centre for Children's Books 586
writers' and artists' groups 257, 459
Writers' & Artists' Yearbook 2011 Short Story Competition 613
writer's block 254, 370, 664
Writers' Bookshelf 347
Writer's Digest 116
Writer's Digest Books 117, 219

Writers' Guild 375
Writers Guild of America, East Inc. (WGAE) 586
Writers Guild of America, West Inc. (WGA) 586
Writers Guild of Canada 587
Writers' Guild of Great Britain, The 303, 305, 436, 544, 587, 697
Writers' Holiday at Caerleon 691
Writers House LLC 508
Writers in Oxford 587
Writers' News 101
Writers' Union of Canada, The 587
Writers' Week 623
Writers' Week Poetry Competition 613
Writing College, The 691
Writing Magazine 101
Written Words 691
Wye Valley Arts Centre 691
Wylie Agency 472
Wylie Agency Inc., The 508
Wylie Agency (UK) Ltd, The 495
Wylie-Merrick Literary Agency 508

X Press, The 195

Y Lolfa Cyf. 195
Yachting Journalists' Association 587
Yachting Monthly 101
Yachting World 101
Yachts and Yachting 102
Yale University Press 220
Yale University Press London 195
Julio F. Yañez Agencia Literaria S.L. 500
Susan Yearwood Literary Agency 495
Yellow Jersey Press 195
Yen Press 220
Yesterday 418
Yoga & Health 102
York Citizens' Theatre Trust Ltd 446
Explore York Library Learning Centre 684
York Notes 195
Yorkshire Dialect Society, The 587
Yorkshire Evening Post 27
Yorkshire Life 102
Yorkshire Post 27
Yorkshire Post Book of the Year 613
Yorkshire Ridings Magazine 102
You & Your Wedding 102
Young Adult Library Services awards (USA) 288
Young Picador 195
Young Readers Birmingham 624
Francis Brett Young Society 587
Young Vic Theatre Company 441
Young Writer Magazine 102
Young Writers' Programme 613
younger readers, books for 292, 516
Young Minds Book Award 614
Your Cat Magazine 102
Your Dog Magazine 102
Your Family 116
Your Home and Garden 113
Your Horse 102
Yours 103
YouTube 4
YouWriteOn.com 614

Zambezi Publishing Ltd 195
Zebra Press 206
Zed Books Ltd 195
Zephaniah, Benjamin 349
Zero to Ten Ltd 195
Zest 103
Zig Zag Productions 426
ZigZag Education 195
Zoo 103
Zoological Society of London Library, The 684

Index